A History of Historical Writing

THE MACMILLAN COMPANY
NEW YORK · BOSTON · CHICAGO · DALLAS
ATLANTA · SAN FRANCISCO

MACMILLAN AND CO., Limited
LONDON · BOMBAY · CALCUTTA · MADRAS
MELBOURNE

THE MACMILLAN COMPANY
OF CANADA, Limited
TORONTO

A HISTORY OF HISTORICAL WRITING

VOLUME II

The Eighteenth and Nineteenth Centuries

by *James Westfall Thompson,* SIDNEY HELLMAN EHRMAN
PROFESSOR OF EUROPEAN HISTORY (EMERITUS), THE UNIVERSITY OF CALIFORNIA

with the collaboration of Bernard J. Holm, ASSISTANT PROFESSOR OF
HISTORY, THE UNIVERSITY OF MARYLAND. FORMER RESEARCH ASSOCIATE IN HISTORY,
THE UNIVERSITY OF CALIFORNIA

THE MACMILLAN COMPANY · NEW YORK

1942

TABLE OF CONTENTS

BOOK VI

THE RISE OF MODERN HISTORICAL SCHOLARSHIP

BOOK VII

THE FOUNDING OF MODERN GERMAN HISTORICAL SCHOLARSHIP

BOOK VIII

FRENCH AND ENGLISH HISTORIANS OF THE NINETEENTH CENTURY

BOOK IX

HISTORIANS OF INSTITUTIONS

v

LIST OF ABBREVIATIONS

Note: In order to conserve space in the extensive footnotes the following system of abbreviations has been adopted. Certain books frequently mentioned are cited by the surname of the author or editor in small capitals. The titles of periodicals and sets are reduced to their chief initial letters.

ASHLEY
W. J. Ashley, *Surveys, Historic and Economic* (London and New York, 1900).

BERNHEIM
Ernst Bernheim, *Lehrbuch der historischen Methode und der Geschichtsphilosophie* (5th and 6th rev. ed., Leipzig, 1908).

BIEDERMANN
Karl Biedermann, *Deutschland im achtzehnten Jahrhundert* (Leipzig, 1858–67, 2 v.).

BLACK
J. B. Black, *The Art of History; A Study of Four Great Historians of the Eighteenth Century* (London, 1926).

DAHLMANN-WAITZ
Dahlmann-Waitz, *Quellenkunde der deutschen Geschichte*, 9th ed. edited by Hermann Haering (Leipzig, 1931).

FUETER
Eduard Fueter, *Histoire de l'historiographie moderne*, tr. by Émile Jeanmaire, with revisions and additions by the author (Paris, 1914). All references are to the French edition, but the original German edition can easily be used by consulting the index (*Geschichte der neueren Historiographie*, Munich and Berlin, 1911).

GIBBON
Edward Gibbon, *The History of the Decline and Fall of the Roman Empire*, ed. by J. B. Bury (London, 1897–1900, 7 v.).

GOOCH
G. P. Gooch, *History and Historians in the Nineteenth Century* (London and New York, 1913; 2nd ed. [new impression], London, 1935).

GUILDAY
Peter K. Guilday, ed., *Church Historians* (New York, 1926).

GUILLAND
Antoine Guilland, *Modern Germany and Her Historians*, tr. from the French (London and New York, 1915).

HALPHEN
Louis Halphen, *L'Histoire en France depuis cent ans* (Paris, 1914).

vii

HISTOIRE ET   *Histoire et historiens depuis cinquante ans; méthodes,*
  HISTORIENS   *organisation et résultats du travail historique de 1876 à
                 1926*, a survey by more than two score scholars for
                 the fiftieth anniversary of the *Revue Historique* (Paris,
                 1927, 2 v.: Bibliothèque de la Revue Historique).

PATTISON   *Essays by the Late Mark Pattison*, collected and ar-
                 ranged by Henry Nettleship (Oxford, 1889, 2 v.).

SANDYS   J. E. Sandys, *A History of Classical Scholarship* (Cam-
                 bridge, vols. II–III in first ed., 1908; vol. I in 2nd
                 ed., 1906).

SCHAUMKELL   Ernst Schaumkell, *Geschichte der deutschen Kultur-
                 geschichtschreibung von der Mitte des 18. Jahrhunderts
                 bis zur Romantik* (Leipzig, 1905).

SMITH   Preserved Smith, *History of Modern Culture* (New
                 York, 1930–34, 2 v.).

WARD   A. W. Ward and A. R. Waller, eds., *Cambridge History of
                 English Literature* (Cambridge, 1907–16, 1927, 15 v.
                 with index).

WEGELE   Franz X. v. Wegele, *Geschichte der deutschen Histo-
                 riographie seit dem Auftreten des Humanismus* (Mu-
                 nich and Leipzig, 1885).

WOLF   Gustav Wolf, *Einführung in das Studium der neueren
                 Geschichte* (Berlin, 1910).

AHR   *American Historical Review* (New York, 1895–   ).
ASI   *Archivio Storico Italiano* (Florence, 1842–   ).
ASMP   *Séances et Travaux de l'Académie des Sciences Morales
                 et Politiques* (Paris, 1842–   ).
BEC   *Bibliothèque de l'École des Chartes* (Paris, 1839–   ).
BQR   *British Quarterly Review* (London, 1845–   ).
CR   *Contemporary Review* (London, 1866–   ).
CQR   *Church Quarterly Review* (London, 1875–   ).
DNB   *Dictionary of National Biography*, ed. by L. Stephen
                 and S. Lee (London, 1885–1901, 66 v.; several sup-
                 plements have been published).
DR   *Dublin Review* (London, 1836–   ).
EHR   *English Historical Review* (London, 1886–   ).
ER   *Edinburgh Review* (Edinburgh, 1802–   ).

ESS   *Encyclopaedia of the Social Sciences*, ed. by E. R. A. Seligman and Alvin Johnson (New York, 1930–35, 15 v.).

FDG   *Forschungen zur deutschen Geschichte* (Göttingen, 1862–86, 26 v.).

FM   *Fraser's Magazine* (London, 1830–82, 106 v.).

FQR   *Foreign Quarterly Review* (London, 1827–47, 38 v.).

HZ   *Historische Zeitschrift* (Munich, 1859–).

JS   *Journal des Savants* (Paris, 1816–).

LTLS   [London] *Times Literary Supplement* (London, 1902– **).**

LQR   *London Quarterly Review* (London, 1853–).

NA   *Neues Archiv der Gesellschaft für ältere deutsche Geschichtskunde* (Hanover, 1876–1935, 50 v.).

NAR   *North American Review* (Boston, 1815–77, New York, 1878–).

NBR   *North British Review* (Edinburgh, 1844–69; London, 1870–71, 53 v.).

PJ   *Preussische Jahrbücher* (Berlin, 1858–).

QR   *Quarterly Review* (London, 1809–).

RCC   *Revue des Cours et Conférences* (Paris, 1893–).

RDM   *Revue des Deux Mondes* (Paris, 1829–).

RH   *Revue Historique* (Paris, 1876–).

RQH   *Revue des Questions Historiques* (Paris, 1866–).

RSH   *Revue de Synthèse Historique* (Paris, 1900– **).**

BOOK VI

THE RISE OF MODERN HISTORICAL SCHOLARSHIP

CHAPTER XXXVII

THE AGE OF ERUDITION (*Ca.* 1600–1750) [1]

MODERN historical scholarship had its inception in the Reformation and Counter-Reformation. Lutheranism and Calvinism alike were attacks upon the historical foundations and historical claims of the Roman Church. What Lorenzo Valla had done with the forged donation of Constantine might be done with many other traditions and documents upon which the Church rested its authority. Historical criticism became a Protestant weapon and documents were made missiles in the hands of the Magdeburg Centuriators. The Roman Church was slow to take alarm over the Protestant appeal to history. It vainly endeavored to confine the dispute to questions of theology. But the historical attack finally became so effective that Rome was compelled to fight history with history. Since the Reformation was an appeal to history, the Counter-Reformation was forced to use the same instrument, with incalculable importance for the development of historical scholarship. [2] The responsibility of replying to the *Magdeburg Centuries* and the Protestant historical school was entrusted by the papacy to Cardinal Baronius (1538–1605), the first volume of whose *Annales ecclesiastici* was issued from the Vatican press in 1588— a significant year!

The politics and wars of the Reformation era curiously promoted and facilitated this new interest in history by throwing into the light thousands of documents and other manuscript materials hitherto inaccessible and unknown. The dissolution of the monasteries in England under Henry VIII, the Peasants' War and the War of the Schmalkaldic League in Germany, the Huguenot wars in France, which were accompanied by the pillage of monastic and cathedral libraries, had thrown upon the market vast quantities of manuscripts and other documents which often could be bought for a song. Scholars and book-collectors

[1] There is no comprehensive account of this important period in historical scholarship in any language. The literature is almost wholly of a monographic or periodical character. The best brief accounts are found in FUETER, 381–410, with excellent bibliographies, cp. also his introduction, pp. iii–vii; Auguste Molinier, *Les sources de l'histoire de France des origines aux guerres d'Italie, 1494* (Paris, 1901–06, 6 v.), V, pp. clix–clxx; in English see G. N. Clark, *The Seventeenth Century* (Oxford, 1929), ch. xvi; and SMITH, I, ch. vi. The intellectual atmosphere of the new age is analyzed and interpreted in the admirable work of Paul Hazard, *La crise de la conscience européenne, 1680–1715* (Paris, 1935, 3 v.).

[2] Gabriel Monod, "La réforme catholique," *RH*, CXXI (1916), 281–315.

soon awakened to the opportunity and began to salvage these treasures. The libraries of the new Protestant universities in Germany in the sixteenth century were almost wholly formed out of the loot of the monasteries.[3] Manuscripts from Corbie and Fleury found their way into the libraries of De Thou, Pithou, Duchesne, and other French scholars of the sixteenth century. This condition was continued into the seventeenth century. Mazarin's first great collection was scattered when the mob sacked his palace during the Fronde. The civil war in England saw the pillage of many an ecclesiastical library, and of the collections in the great country-houses of royalist nobles. Even Oxford and Cambridge suffered. In Germany in the Thirty Years' War Gustavus Adolphus swept libraries into his grasp as a reaper binds the sheaves. Prague was almost stripped of books and manuscripts.[4] And who has not heard of Tilly's seizure of the rich library of Heidelberg University?

New times, new interests, new conditions of scholarship, new scholars. France was the pioneer in this new research. The initiative was taken by Pierre Pithou (1539–96), of a distinguished family of French legists, a friend of the historian De Thou, who with him shared the glory of historical scholarship in the reign of Henry IV. He edited and published the works of Salvian, Paul the Deacon, and Otto of Freising, and the Capitularies of Charlemagne, Louis the Pious, and Charles the Bald. At the time of his death he was preparing the historical fragments of Hilary of Poitiers. His friend Nicholas Le Fèvre brought out the book and prefixed a dedicatory letter to De Thou in which he described the manuscripts and Pithou's proposed edition of them. Pithou's dream of collecting and editing the sources of the history of France in the Middle Ages was later realized by the Benedictines of St. Maur.[5]

Pithou, however, was not alone in cherishing this idea. He divides the honor with André Duchesne (1584–1640), who was an indefatigable collector of manuscripts in a time when the French monasteries, as the English ones earlier, had suffered sack of their treasures and books by the ravages of the Huguenot Wars. Part of his enormous collection of manuscripts, of which it has been said that it formed "une véritable bibliothèque de l'histoire de France depuis les origines jusqu'au XVIᵉ siècle," afterwards passed into the hands of Colbert; part of it is pre-

[3] Gustav Bogeng, Die grossen Bibliophilen. Geschichte der Büchersammler und ihrer Sammlungen (Leipzig, 1922, 3 v.), III, 113–19.

[4] See Otto Walde, Storhetstiden litterära krigsbyten, en kulturhistorisk-bibliografisk studie (Upsala and Stockholm, 1916–20, 2 v.); R. Ehwald, "Geschichte der Gothaer Bibliothek," Zentralblatt für Bibliothekswesen, XVIII (1901), 434–63; C. P. Cooper, An Account of the Most Important Public Records of Great Britain, etc. (London: Record Commission, 1832, 2 v.), I, 51. Isak Collijn's Katalog der Inkunabeln der kgl. Universitäts-Bibliothek zu Uppsala (Upsala, 1907) reveals that almost every book among 500 was part of the "Swedish loot."

[5] For a complete list of his works see La Grande Encyclopédie, XXVI, 992. He wrote a great number of legal works, of which the most notable was his edition of the Leges Visigothorum.

served as the Collection Duchesne, in fifty-nine huge bound volumes, at the Bibliothèque Nationale.. Duchesne published a mere tithe of his enormous accumulations. He projected a gigantic work on the history of France, in twenty-four folio volumes. The first fourteen were to contain the writings of all the great historians of France from Gregory of Tours to the end of the fifteenth century. Ten additional tomes were to be devoted to the history of the provinces of France. The only part of the first series ever issued was the *Historiae Francorum scriptores ad Pipinum usque regem*, which was completed in five volumes by his son after his father's death in a carriage accident in 1640. The only part of the provincial series accomplished was the *Historiae Normannorum scriptores antiqui* (1619, 5 v.), which forms Duchesne's first and greatest historical work. The volumes were published without prolegomena or notes. As texts these have been indispensable to all students of Norman history until the late nineteenth century, when new and critical editions of the Norman chroniclers began to supplant them. Duchesne enjoyed the favor of Richelieu, by whom he was appointed historiographer and geographer to the king. He may truly be called the founder of French historical scholarship.[6]

In methodology French scholarship also led the way in Jean Bodin's *Methodus ad facilem historiarum cognitionem* (Paris, 1566), the earliest manual of the kind.[7] Chronology for the first time was put upon a scientific basis by J. J. Scaliger (1540–1609), whose *Thesaurus temporum* (first ed. 1583) was inspired by his examination and reconstruction of the *Eusebian Chronicle*. "Scaliger's great works in historical criticism," says Mark Pattison,[8] "outstripped any power of appreciation which the succeeding age possessed. . . . Only a scholar of comprehensive knowledge, here and there one, . . . was capable of measuring the stride of Scaliger. . . . [He was] the founder of historical criticism. . . . The Jesuit onslaught on Scaliger . . . is an important feature of his life." His correspondence was as wide as Protestant Europe. Camden sent him a copy of his *Britannia* in 1594. In England, which had few Roman inscriptions, Scaliger was chiefly interested in libraries and disappointed to find so few Greek collections. But he was no dry-as-dust

---

[6] The principal works of André Duchesne are *Les Antiquités et Recherches de la Grandeur et Majesté des Rois de France* (Paris, 1609); *Les Antiquités et Recherches des Villes, Châteaux, . . . de toute la France*, etc. (Paris, 1608, 2 v.); *Histoire d'Angleterre, d'Ecosse, et d'Irelande* (Paris, 1614); *Histoire des Papes jusqu'à Paul V* (Paris, 1616); and *Histoire des Rois, Ducs, et Comtes de Bourgogne, 408–1350* (Paris, 1619–28, quarto; 1634, 2 v. folio). Besides these Duchesne published a great number of genealogical histories of illustrious French families, of which the best is said to be that of the house of Montmorency. His *Lives of the French Cardinals and of the Saints of France* have been published by the Bollandists, Mabillon, and others. He published a translation of the *Satires* of Juvenal, and editions of the works of Abelard, Alain Chartier, and Etienne Pasquier. See *La Grande Encyclopédie*, XIV, 1185–86.

[7] BERNHEIM, 217–20. [8] PATTISON, I, 132–34, for Scaliger see 132–243.

pedant. He was struck with the absence in England of seignorial jurisdiction; the literary charm of the Border Ballads; the beauty of Mary
Stuart; the use of coal instead of wood in the north; the laziness of the
fellows of Oxford and Cambridge.[9]

French legists and antiquarians also had their share in promoting the
new learning. The great Cujacius' *Commentaries on Roman Law* was
published in 1578. Denis Gothofredus, or Godefroy l'Ancien (1549–
1621) edited an imposing array of works or collections of laws—Roman,
feudal, ecclesiastical—a labor which his son Jacques Godefroy (1580–
1652) continued. His magnum opus is his edition of the *Codex Theodosi-
anus* in six volumes, on which he labored for thirty years. The 'para-
titla' of this work have commanded the admiration of every student of
Roman history from that time to the present. Gibbon, Mommsen, and
Dill have used it without stint.[10]

Etienne Pasquier (1529–1615), one of the glories of the French bar,
pertains to this goodly company of historical scholars. In 1560 he
published the first book of his great work, *Recherches de la France*, a
series of antiquarian and historical studies, the most remarkable of
which deal with the history of the Grands Jours, an institution which
fell into decay in the next century. In 1585 Pasquier was made advo-
cate-general of the Chambre des Escomptes. He was present at the
States General of Blois in 1588, where the Duke of Guise was assassinated, and where he met Montaigne.

Such is the historical and bibliographical background of the Age of
Erudition in the seventeenth century. It was an honorable heritage.
But before entering a particular consideration, it is worth pausing to
reflect that there are sequences or phases in historical writing and historical scholarship like the phases and transitions in other forms of
literature. The seventeenth century may be regarded as the second

----

[9] Scaliger's removal to Leyden in 1590 to succeed Lipsius, who had turned Catholic, is a landmark in sixteenth-century scholarship. See the *Autobiography of Joseph Scaliger*, translated
into English by G. W. Robinson, with selections from Scaliger's letters, his testament, and the
funeral orations by Daniel Heinsius and Dominicus Baudius (Cambridge, Mass., 1927:
Harvard Translations). For further information see Jacob Bernays, *Joseph Justus Scaliger*
(Berlin, 1855), reviewed at length in QR, CVIII (1860), 34–81; PATTISON, I, essays vi–vii, and
consult the index of the same author's *Isaac Casaubon, 1559–1614* (2nd ed., Oxford, 1892);
SANDYS, II, 199–204; and Eugène and Em. Haag, *La France protestante, ou Vies des protestants
français qui se sont fait un nom dans l'histoire*, etc. (Paris and Geneva, 1846–59, 10 v.), VII,
1–26.

[10] The Godefroys, father and son, were Huguenots. The former was professor of law in
Heidelberg University from 1600 to 1621, when he was driven out by Tilly's sack of Heidel-
berg, in which he lost his library. Jacques Godefroy was born at Geneva, and spent his life
there. His brother Theodore Godefroy (1580–1649) forsook Protestantism and became a
Catholic and resided in France, where he was appointed royal historiographer in 1617 and
employed in an ambassadorial capacity on several occasions. He died at Münster in 1649.
He was a copious historian. For complete lists of the works of all three Godefroys see *La
Grande Encyclopédie*, XVIII, 1145–47.

Alexandrian period of scholarship. The difference between the Age of Erudition and the Renaissance, or between it and the Reformation, was far greater than the mere lapse of years between these epochs would superficially indicate. The difference was one of change in mental texture, in intellectual interest, in spirit. It has been admirably described in an essay by the late Professor J. Franklin Jameson.

From such an age we see the world deriving humanistic and historical fruits of a peculiar type. Prodigies of learning are much more abundant than prodigies of genius. Sober and orderly accumulation of material is the mode. The presentation of texts and of historical documents in the completest abundance is more esteemed than the production of narrative histories, or brilliant discourses on antiquity. Folios are more in favor than octavos or duodecimos, Latin more than the vernacular. The chief reviewer of Mascou's *Teutsche Geschichte* [11] declared with enthusiasm that it was so good that it was a pity that it had not been written in Latin. . . . No qualitative description can give an adequate conception of the work of that age, for one of its most salient traits is the prodigious quantity of its published achievement. Within the hundred years (1650–1750) . . . and making no account of any books but those filled with original documents for early ecclesiastical and medieval history, it may be computed that France alone produced more than four hundred folio volumes of such material alone. . . . It would be a mistake to suppose that this wonderful mass of scholarly achievement was the mere fruit of laborious industry, purblind or indifferent as to relative values, and as to the higher uses of learning. That this was not the case, that a conscious purpose ran through these gigantic labors of accumulation, is plain from the intelligence and methodical skill with which the sciences auxiliary to history and to the study of the classics were then developed, and with which monumental books of reference were prepared.

In pure classical erudition the men of the sixteenth century, the Scaligers and Casaubons and Lipsiuses, might claim a higher distinction than Bentley or Gronovius. But the science of inscriptions was given a new advancement by Fabretti and Muratori. The Sieur Du Cange brought out his encyclopaedic dictionaries of late and medieval Greek and Latin. Mabillon by his classical treatise, *De re diplomaticâ*, laid securely and for all time the foundation of the science of diplomatics. Others gave systematic and scientific form to chronology and palaeography, to bibliography and numismatics. Such folio dissertations on the auxiliary sciences, or such encyclopaedias of learning as Bayle's *Dictionary*, showed that the age, myopic though it might be, was at least partly aware that, beside accumulation, the proper development of European learning demanded order, scientific method, critical attention and careful thought as to what was worth while, and what was not.

The result is that, while the scholarship of our time would often desire texts more critically executed, few of the mighty folios of that age are by reason of their subjects deemed useless by the modern student. Its great series of medieval chronicles, or saintly biographies, of letters and documents of kings and popes and prelates and monasteries and ecclesiastical councils, its volumes of patristic literature or of provincial and local materials, are still the inexhaustible quarry of the historian. There is no large subject in the history of the Church or of the Middle Ages which can be thoroughly studied

---

[11] *Geschichte der Teutschen bis zu Anfang der fränkischen Monarchie*, in ten books (Leipzig, 1726). It was translated into English by Thomas Lediard as *History of the Ancient Germans* (London, 1737–38, 2 v.). This version was one of Gibbon's main authorities—fortunately for him, for he could not read German.

without recourse to some of the collections prepared for us by the dauntless industry of the Age of Erudition.[12]

The intense devotion, the tireless application, the prodigiously productive capacity of the historical scholars of the Age of Erudition astonish the modern student even when it is remembered that there were then no newspapers, no periodicals, no fiction to dissipate the scholar's time and attention; that the common subjects of education were much less than now; that public lectures and the telephone did not distract the scholar's mind; that he required only one language, Latin—or Greek in addition, if he was a classicist or a theologian—in order to keep abreast of the world's scholarship. Moreover, this wonderful scholarship was without knowledge of the governments for the most part, and entirely independent of government direction. The scholar was free from politics and the influence of political control. Even the world of letters and science was hardly tangent to the world of historical research.

A striking fact to observe in this new era of scholarship is the co-operative nature of much of the labor. While individual and independent workers of eminence are to be found, group organization was widely prevalent. This in itself stamps the age as one widely different from the Renaissance in which individualism was so dominant a characteristic.

The earliest example of such co-operative historical scholarship is the association of the Bollandist Fathers, a society of Jesuit scholars.[13] In

---

[12] J. Franklin Jameson, "The Age of Erudition," being the Annual Phi Beta Kappa Address delivered at the University of Chicago on June 12, 1905, and printed in the [Chicago] *University Record*, X (1905), 19–28. I feel justified in making this long quotation because this remarkable essay has not been reprinted and is practically inaccessible.

[13] The literature on the Bollandists and the *Acta Sanctorum* is very large. See the article by Ch. De Smedt in the *Catholic Encyclopaedia*, II, 630–39, with copious bibliography; GUILDAY, 190–211, on "Bollandus," with bibliography; the article on Bollandus in the *Biographie nationale de Belgique*, I, 630–41; Hippolyte Delehaye, *A travers trois siècles: L'oeuvre des Bollandistes, 1615–1915* (Brussels, 1921), tr. into English as *The Work of the Bollandists Through Three Centuries, 1615–1915* (Princeton University Press, 1922); the same, *Les légendes hagiographiques* (3rd rev. ed., Brussels, 1927), tr. from the 2nd ed. by Mrs. V. M. Crawford as *The Legends of the Saints, An Introduction to Hagiography* (London and New York, 1907); F. Baix, "Le centenaire de la restauration du Bollandisme," *Revue d'histoire ecclésiastique*, XXXIV (1938), 270–96; De Smedt's essay on the founders of the Bollandists in the [Mélanges] *A Godefroid Kurth*, etc. (Liege, 1899), I, 297 ff.; "The Bollandist *Acta Sanctorum*," *Catholic World*, XXVII (1878), 756–65 and XXVIII (1878–79), 81–87; Aurelio Palmieri, "The Bollandists," *Catholic Historical Review*, n.s., III (1923), 341–67 and 517–29; Robert Lechat, "Les Acta Sanctorum des Bollandists," *ibid.*, VI (1920–21), 334–42; Sabine Baring-Gould, *The Lives of the Saints* (new rev. ed., Edinburgh, 1914, 16 v.), I, introduction; Thurston, in *The Tablet*, April 8, 1922; B. Aubé, "Les travaux des Bollandistes," *RDM*, LXXIII (1885), 169–99; Dom Cardinal Jean Baptiste Pitra, *Études sur la collection des Actes des Saints par les RR. PP. Jesuites Bollandistes* (Paris, 1850); Charles Dejob, *De l'influence du Concile de Trente sur la littérature et les beaux-arts chez les peuples catholiques: essai d'introduction à l'histoire littéraire du siècle de Louis XIV* (Paris, 1884), ch. iii; Ernest Renan, *Études d'histoire religieuse* (7th ed., Paris, 1864), 301–15; Hippolyte Delehaye, *La méthode hagiographique* (Brussels, 1934); G. F. Stokes, "The Bollandists," *CR*, XLIII (1883), 69–84; F. C. Burkitt and others, *Franciscan Essays, II* (Manchester, 1932).

the first period of its history (1540–90) the Society of Jesus had conquered the hearts of men by sentimentalizing and idealizing the religious
life. "It had almost monopolized the reputation of sanctity, of the
skill to handle the tender conscience. . . . It had gained for the Church
a complete triumph upon the purely religious and devotional ground." [14]
In its second period (1590–1715) it made a strenuous effort to capture
the field of scholarship. Until the seventeenth century no attempt had
been made to apply the canons of criticism to that vast body of medieval
literature known as the *Acta Sanctorum*, or *Lives of the Saints*. Previous
workers in this field, Mombritius, Lipomanus, and Surius, had been industrious compilers and pious commentators, but devoid of critical
spirit or critical method. In the course of past centuries the lives of
the saints had become embellished with legendary matter and encrusted
with apocryphal anecdotes, and often silly fables which had provoked
the derision of humanists and Protestants. To rescue the lives of the
saints from contempt and to establish their true nature and value as a
great body of religious and historical literature was the purpose of the
Bollandists.

This stupendous project was begun by Herbert Rosweyde, of the
Society of Jesus, who was born at Utrecht in 1569 and died in 1629
before much more than the outlines of the design had been accomplished.
Both in his student days and later as a teacher in the College of Douai,
Rosweyde had spent all his spare time in browsing in monastic and cathedral libraries in the Low Countries, and had discovered an enormous
amount of hagiographical material which was practically unknown.
He planned to produce a great work in eighteen folio volumes. Volume
I was to be devoted to the life of Jesus and the feasts in His honor;
volume II was to be devoted similarly to the Virgin; volume III was to
deal with the solemn festivals of the Saints. These initial three volumes
were to be followed by other volumes on the lives of the saints, one
volume for each calendar month. These fifteen volumes were to be
supplemented by three concluding volumes of critical and explanatory
notes and an index to the series. The annotations were intended to
deal with authorship, images, ecclesiastical rites, chronology, topography, etc., concluding with a glossary of technical and obscure words.

Father Rosweyde followed time-honored precedent by planning to
arrange the lives of the saints according to Saints' Days instead of in
historical sequence. Thus, regardless of when a saint had lived, whether
in the third or the sixth or the ninth century, etc., all those saints whose
festival days were celebrated in January were to be incorporated in the
first volume. For in the calendar of the Church of Rome, every day has

[14] PATTISON, I, 187.

its saint or saints, and every saint has his or her day. This custom dated as far back as the Early Church.[15] It is apparent that Rosweyde had slight perception of the magnitude of his design. When Cardinal Bellarmine heard of the project he exclaimed: "Does this man expect to live to be two hundred years old?"

When Rosweyde died in 1629 he left his collected materials and the continuance of the design to John Bollandus (1596–1665), another Jesuit, not a Hollander but a Belgian whose scholarship and prolonged labors gave the organization its name, the "Bollandists." Bollandus soon perceived that the work was of so gigantic a nature that it would be impossible for him to execute it alone, and accordingly he associated others with him, men of immense learning and indefatigable application. The two most eminent of these were Geoffrey Henschen (1600–81) and Daniel Papebroche (1628–1714). The latter devoted his ample fortune to the undertaking and lived to a great age.

Bollandus brought organization to bear upon the enterprise. The collection of sources was far from complete. Accordingly he set to work to get in touch with representatives of the Order of the Jesuits throughout Europe. Letters were dispatched into Spain and Portugal, into Italy, Germany, Poland, and Bohemia, and into France and England, seeking the co-operation of fellow-scholars everywhere in exploring all possible repositories for lives of the saints in manuscript form. The volume of collections made under Rosweyde was quadrupled under Bollandus.

Henschen, who was a former pupil of Bollandus, began his work on the *Acta Sanctorum* in 1635. The January volume was still unfinished. Bollandus took the biographies of the saints of Spain, England, and Germany, and Henschen those of France, Italy, the Greek church, and the Orient. In 1643 the first two volumes of the *Acta* appeared. They cover the saints whose feast days fall in January. In 1658 three more volumes, dealing with February, were issued. This was seven years before the death of Bollandus, who had the satisfaction of seeing his great work well under way. Henschen had the leading part in the production of the three volumes for April which appeared in 1675, the seven volumes for May which were brought out at intervals between 1680 and 1688, and those for June also, although the latter were not actually published till long after his death in 1681. He was succeeded in the direction by Daniel Papebroche, in some respects the greatest of the Bollandist Fathers, who had joined the group in 1660.

---

[15] In consequence of this peculiar arrangement, citation from the *Acta Sanctorum* (abridged *AA.SS.*) differs from any other sort of citation, being specified first *by day*, then by volume and page.

The Prolegomena or *Propylaea*, as they are denominated, which are prefixed to many of the volumes of the *Acta Sanctorum*, especially the early volumes, are landmarks in the literature of historical method and criticism, and the first of their kind. The preface of Bollandus to the first volume "must always have a place in the history of historical method."[16] The most notable prefaces are those written by Papebroche. In addition the volume for March 1 contains a life of Bollandus by Henschen; that for May 7 a life of Henschen by Papebroche; and that for June 6 a life of Papebroche by Pinius.

In one of these *propylaea*, however, Papebroche's scholarship slipped, for he ventured into the field of diplomatics, of which he was not a master. He had been impressed with the help which medieval charters and title-deeds might afford, and when in Luxembourg discovered an old charter attributed to Dagobert I and was convinced of its spurious nature. On the basis of a study of this and other Merovingian documents Papebroche wrote his famous dissertation entitled *Propylaeum Antiquarium circa veri ac falsi discrimen in vetustis membranis*, which attacked the genuineness of the fundamental charters of the great Benedictine Abbey of St. Denis. Unfortunately Papebroche was better acquainted with medieval narratives and chronicles than with charters.[17] The Benedictine Order everywhere, especially the Maurists, took alarm and were incensed, for they regarded Papebroche's work as an imputation of their integrity, their authority, their history, and an attack upon their property rights. Dom Mabillon of the community at St. Germain des Prés was delegated to frame a reply to Papebroche. He wisely decided not to write the usual "justification," but to keep the defense on a purely scholarly and scientific level of discussion by working out the general principles of historical criticism and the use of the auxiliary sciences of palaeography and diplomatics in which Papebroche was not well trained. In 1681 Mabillon's *De re diplomatica libri VI* was published, which founded the science of diplomatics and palaeography, and remains to this day a classic of its kind.[18]

These great Benedictine and Jesuit historical scholars of the seventeenth century were distinguished in an acrimonious age for their thorough intellectual honesty and scrupulous fidelity, combined with an independent spirit of historical criticism and an unsurpassed technical method. No finer example either of scholarly honor or of scholarly

[16] Excerpts translated in Patrick A. Collis, "The Preface of the *Acta Sanctorum*," *Catholic Historical Review*, VI (1920–21), 294–307, quotation from p. 307.
[17] On this subject see further Richard Rosenmund, *Die Fortschritte der Diplomatik seit Mabillon, vornehmlich in Deutschland-Oesterreich* (Munich and Leipzig, 1897), 9–13; Arthur Giry, *Manuel de diplomatique* (Paris, 1894), 60–62; F. W. Hall, *A Companion to Classical Texts* (Oxford, 1913), 110–13.
[18] Second ed., 1709; 3rd ed., Naples, 1789, in 2 v.

humility can be found than the letter which Papebroche wrote to Jean Mabillon after reading his famous treatise:

I avow to you that I have no other satisfaction in having written upon the subject than that of having given occasion for the writing of a treatise so masterly. It is true that I felt at first some pain in reading your book, where I saw myself refuted in so unanswerable a manner; but finally the utility and the beauty of so precious a work soon overcame my weakness, and, full of joy at seeing the truth in its clearest light, I invited my companion to come and share the admiration with which I felt myself filled. Therefore, have no hesitation, whenever occasion shall arise, in saying publicly that I have come over completely to your way of thinking. I beg for your affection. I am not a man of learning, but one who desires to learn.

The other experience which Papebroche had was less happy in its issue. The Carmelites clung tenaciously to the tradition that the Prophet Elijah had founded their Order! Papebroche distinguished between valid tradition and ignorant tradition. Father Sebastian, provincial of the Carmelites in Flanders, was the author of a polemical tract entitled *Exhibitio errorum* which violently attacked the critical historical method of the Bollandists and enumerated some eighty alleged errors of theirs. A long and bitter controversy ensued.[19] This brochure was published in 1693. Papebroche replied to it in his *Responsio ad exhibitionem errorum*, in two parts printed respectively in 1696 and 1697, in which he argued against the old traditional rule "that a source was to be venerated in proportion to its antiquity and the universality of its acceptance," and contended that sources were of value only by virtue of their genuineness and relation to facts.

The Carmelites stirred up a blaze in Italy and Spain, where the Inquisition was still active. The Inquisition in Toledo issued an injunction against the Bollandists, forbidding the reading or sale of the volumes of the *Acta* for March, April, and May under penalty of fines and excommunication. Rome followed suit by putting the *Propylaeum* to May on the Index. Papebroche appealed to Rome but the exoneration was not made until 1715, one year after the passing of the great scholar and critic, when a revocation of the earlier condemnation was granted by Pope Clement XI.[20]

The successors of the first Bollandists failed to maintain the high standard of excellence, but the work went on with undiminished industry. The first great blow to the work, which had continued through a century and a half of trouble, came with the suppression of the Order

---

[19] Aloys and Augustin de Backer, *Bibliothèque des écrivains de la Compagnie de Jésus* (new ed. by Carlos Sommervogel, Brussels and Paris, 1890–1932, 11 v.), I, 1655–64 list over forty such treatises.

[20] E. Babelon, "Une querelle scientifique entre les Jésuites et Bénédictins; origine de la diplomatique," *Le Contemporain*, I (1878), 297–320.

in 1773, but the then Bollandist Fathers, though no longer with the resources of their great organization behind them, pursued their tasks as best they could on their own resources until 1794, in which year the 53rd volume of the *Acta* was printed at Tongerloo. It contained the dates October 12 to October 15. Then came the invasion of Belgium by the French Revolutionary troops, and in that deluge everything was swept away. Much of the Bollandists' collection of paper and books was destroyed. Part was rescued, and found its way to various libraries in Holland and Belgium. It is to the credit of Napoleon I that he realized the value of the Bollandists' work and tried to get it continued, but the break of 1794 was complete, and it was not until 1837, that is to say forty-three years later, that the work was resumed. The Jesuits were now restored; the Belgian Government gave a subsidy; as much as possible of the old material was collected, and a fresh start was successfully made.

The first volume of the new series was printed about 1846. A new edition of the whole work so far as it had gone, that is to say, 61 volumes in folio, was printed in Paris between 1863 and 1875. This is the great edition as the libraries know it. Four additional volumes have since been issued; the fourth covers the days November 9–10, so that the completion of the whole work may be said to be in sight, except as the Church creates new saints.[21]

Recognizing the fact that their researches included materials and studies not suitable for the *Acta Sanctorum*, yet of value, the Bollandists in 1882 established a quarterly review *Analecta Bollandiana*, for publication of such matter. Beginning with the tenth volume of the *Analecta* in 1891 there has also been included a "Bulletin des publications hagiographiques," which studiously lists and reviews monographs, dissertations, etc., belonging to the field of hagiographical research, where and by whomsoever written. Thus by means of the *Analecta* with the included "Bulletin" one is able to keep fully abreast of current hagiographical activity. Particularly important are they for the newer Greek and Slavonic studies which have come to assume an important place. The Propylaeum to November was entitled "Synaxarium Ecclesiae Constantinopolitanae" and was devoted to the Greek and Eastern Churches in their bearing on the investigations of the hagiographer. There is also a Slavonic section in the work of the modern Bollandists.

We pass from the Jesuit Bollandists to the Benedictines of St. Maur. The history of Benedictine scholarship may be divided into three epochs: the growth, the decline, and the revival of superior learning. The first period was the epoch of the eighth to the thirteenth century inclusive;

---

[21] *Revue d'histoire ecclésiastique*, XVIII (1922), 379–81; and see the literature in n. 13 above.

the second extended from 1300 to 1600; the third was the seventeenth and eighteenth centuries.

On the continent the monasteries had escaped the dissolution visited upon those in England, though certainly their condition was as bad.[22] In the first quarter of the seventeenth century, however, a new monastic reform movement was initiated almost everywhere in Europe, but most of all in France. The reforms of Bursfeld in Germany, of Valladolid in Spain, of Monte Cassino in Italy, and of the Congregation of the Feuillants in France are examples of the new spirit. The movement was most successful in France.

The Congrégation de St. Maur, like the Society of Jesus, was a product of the Counter-Reformation. It began in the abbey of St. Vannes in Verdun, and before long reached such impressive dimensions that the French clergy in the States General of 1614 recommended the application of the same discipline to the monasteries of all France. In that time Verdun pertained to France, although ducal Lorraine was still a part of the German empire. This distinction, however, did not prevent many of the French abbeys from voluntarily adopting the reform. It was thought expedient, however, to establish a "congregation" independent of Lorraine, a measure which was approved by royal authority in 1618 and by Pope Gregory V in 1621. The Congregation was named in honor of St. Maur, a favorite disciple of St. Benedict who had founded the abbey of Glanfeuil on the Loire, called after him St. Maur sur-Loire, in the Merovingian age. In and near Paris the Congregation of St. Maur had three houses, the Blancs Manteaux, St. Germain des Prés, and St. Denis. By 1720 the Congregation comprised one hundred and eighty abbeys and priories, grouped in six provinces under the administration of a general who was appointed for life. But only the Paris group was distinguished for scholarship.[23]

[22] "The revenues of the monasteries were squandered in worldliness, and often in dissipation, by the titular abbots, who not only did not reside in, but very frequently were not even acquainted with the monastery. . . . It was their interest to get as much out of their abbacy as was possible. . . . In France this evil prevailed to a most enormous extent. The very prelates of the Council of Trent touched it with but a gentle hand." From a review of Émile Chavin, *Histoire de Dom Mabillon et de la congrégation de Saint-Maur* (Paris, 1843), in *DR*, XXI (1846), 218, entire review, 217–46.

[23] Most of the literature pertaining to the Benedictines of Saint-Maur has to do with Mabillon. The following are general references. Dom Edmond Martène, *Histoire de la congrégation de Saint-Maur*, new ed. by Dom G. Charvin (Ligugé, 1928–31, 5 v.: Archives de la France monastique, XXXI–XXXV); the work of E. Chavin cited in n. 22 above; Emmanuel de Broglie, *Mabillon et la société de l'abbaye de Saint-Germain des Prés à la fin du dix-septième siècle, 1664–1707* (Paris, 1888, 2 v.) [reviewed by Lord Acton in *EHR*, III (1888), 585–92, reprinted in his *Historical Essays and Studies* (London, 1908), 459–71, in which he has written that "the amiable weaknesses of biographers appear . . . in admiration of the monk, not of the scholar. The worth of the book consists in extracts from the archives of the abbey of St. Germain." See also A. Giry's notice in *Moyen Age*, 1888, pp. 161–71]; Gustave Lanson, *Hommes et livres, études morales et littéraires* (Paris, 1895), 25 ff. ("L'Erudition monastique aux

The initial purpose of the Maurists was the restoration of Benedictine scholarship, which had been the glory of that order in the Middle Ages. This endeavor was initiated by Dom Tarisse, who became general in 1630. The new historical research found its sources in the vast collections of documents possessed by the order throughout France. These "new" Benedictines were not mere antiquaries. First and last they were historians, who with the aid of the auxiliary sciences of palaeography, diplomatics, and chronology published many new documents and re-edited many old works. The movement encountered bitter opposition from the Trappists, who contended that piety, contemplation, prayer, and worship were the whole duty of monastic life. They were a modern offshoot of the Cistercians who never had been advocates of higher education or scholarship. This attack was answered by Dom Mabillon in his *Tractatus de studiis monasticis*, a masterly demonstration of the virtue of scholarship.[24]

In the seventeenth century alone one hundred and five writers may be distinguished amid this devoted circle of scholars. The first scholar-monk who attained eminence was Dom Luc D'Achery (1609–85), "the father of Maurist erudition," who immortalized himself by the *Spicilegium* (Paris, 1655–67), a collection of thirteen quarto volumes of original and unpublished medieval documents, which he meticulously edited although his health was so frail that for forty-five years he was unable to leave the infirmary of the abbey. In the latter years of the preparation of these immortal tomes D'Achery was assisted by a young member of the congregation named Jean Mabillon, destined to become not only the shining light of the Maurists, but, it may be said, the greatest historical scholar of the seventeenth century.

Jean Mabillon was born of peasant stock in 1632 in a village in Champagne.[25] After studying at the University of Rheims for the six year

XVII⁰ et XVIII⁰ siècles"); Alphonse Dantier, *Rapports sur la correspondance inédite des Bénédictins de Saint-Maur* (Paris, 1857), comprising 115 letters of D'Achery, Mabillon, Montfaucon, Durand, Durban, Martène, Massuet, and Bucelin, from 1663 to 1733; Antoine Valery, ed., *Correspondance inédite de Mabillon et de Montfaucon avec l'Italie* (Paris, 1846, 3 v.); a review of this, entitled "The French Benedictines," in *ER*, LXXXIX (1849), 1–47; A. Ettinger, "Correspondance des Bénédictins de Saint-Maur avec le Monte Cassin," a register of 133 letters, from 1671 to 1737, published in *Rivista storica benedettina*, January-February, 1913; Edmond Martène, *Voyage littéraire de deux religieux Bénédictins de la congrégation de Saint-Maur* (Paris, 1717–24, 2 v.), an account of a tour in search of material in France, Germany, Switzerland, and the Low Countries; Ph. Tanizey de Larroque, "Les Bénédictins de Saint-Maur à Saint-Germain des Prés," *RQH*, LXI (1897), 536–48; Joseph U. Bergkamp, *Dom Jean Mabillon and the Benedictine Historical School of Saint-Maur* (Washington, D.C., 1928); Sir James Stephen, *Essays in Ecclesiastical Biography* (London, 1850, 2 v.), I, 387–430.

24 This work was originally written in the French language, a fact significant of the popular appeal it was intended to make, and was translated into Latin by Joseph Porta and printed at Venice in three parts, 1729, 1730, 1732. This Latin version was widely circulated in Italy and Germany. The original French edition is a rare work and the Latin edition not common.

25 The literature on Mabillon is large. In addition to the more general works on the Maurists cited in n. 23 above, see FUETER, 387–89; the sketch by Mabillon's friend, Dom Thierry Rui-

course, he entered the diocesan seminary in 1650; in 1651 he received the tonsure and in 1652 the University granted him the degree of Master of Arts. He then entered the Abbey of St. Rémy at Rheims, a house of the reformed Maurist Congregation, but did not remain there long due to ill health which made it necessary that he move to the more rural houses of St. Maur. He undoubtedly had mental and emotional interests in the study of the past which were stimulated by this early travel and study in the ancient monasteries. Later, the Congregation of St. Maur, the intellectual life of his country, and finally, to some extent, the philosophical ideas of his age exerted an influence on his historical work.

We see indications of the working of the first of these influences, that of the monasteries where he lived, when at St. Remy Mabillon visited the old church famous for its connection with the consecration of the kings of France and the cemeteries filled with the remains of the first Christians of Gaul. At Nogent, whither he was sent in 1656, he studied the tombstones of the church of the monastery, at one time "unpaving almost the entire church in the hope of finding the tomb of Guibert, the most celebrated abbot of Nogent." After being at Corbie for a time, where he profited by the use of its fine library, he was moved to St. Denis in 1663. Here, in this sanctuary of the French church and by the graves of the French kings, his interest for Christian antiquity and history appeared in full force. At this time Mabillon assisted Dom Claude Chantelon in editing the works of St. Bernard, a labor which was completed by Mabillon at St. Germain des Prés after the death of Dom Chantelon.

At St. Germain Mabillon had the incalculable advantage of constant contact with the most distinguished historical scholars, not only in France but in Europe. Dom Butler in his article on Mabillon has charmingly described the life of these accomplished scholars. "Their tastes and studies were shared by a few members of other religious orders in Paris and by a few secular priests and laymen; and on Sunday afternoons a number of these learned men would attend vespers at the Abbey and then adjourn to a room in the monastery to exchange news and views with the monks on all matters relating to ecclesiastical or mediae-

nart, *Abrégé de la vie de Dom Jean Mabillon* (Paris, 1709); *Mélanges et documents publiés à l'occasion du 2ᵉ centenaire de la mort de Mabillon* (Ligugé and Paris, 1908: Archives de la France monastique, V), with articles by leading scholars and a bibliography by H. Stein, pp. xxxv–xlvii; the articles on Mabillon in the *Catholic Encyclopaedia*, IX, 479–81, and *La Grande Encyclopédie*, XXII, 853; SANDYS, II, 293–98; Rosenmund (n. 17), 1–21; Ph. Denis, "Dom Mabillon et sa méthode historique," *Revue Mabillon*, VI (1910–11), 1–64; Dom J. M. Besse, "Les correspondants cisterciens de Dom Luc d'Achery et de Dom Mabillon," *ibid.*, VIII (1912–13), 311–25; and other articles in this journal. There is a long bibliography in Bergkamp (n. 23), 116–19.

val learning, antiquities, and art. . . . There used to be seen Du Cange, Baluze, Cotelier, Menestrier, Renaudot, Fleury, Tillemont, Pagi—to name only a few." [26]

Mabillon's historical work, marked off rather carefully by the plans of the Maurist Order, covered the centuries from St. Benedict through St. Bernard, centuries "during which the Benedictine Order was the foremost association in Christendom." In his writings he made several types of contributions to the science of history; his work included historical accounts, contributions to the field of diplomatics, ecclesiastical, dogmatic and liturgical studies, and archeological work.

The first work of Mabillon, and one which showed his aptitude for historical research and his ability as a critic, appeared in 1667. It was *S. Bernardi Abbatis primi Clarevallensis opera omnia.* As has been mentioned, this work had been turned over to Mabillon in 1664 on the death of Dom Chantelon of St. Denis. In three years' time the edition appeared and was accepted as the work of a master. In this edition Mabillon arranged the works of St. Bernard according to subject matter and then subdivided these chronologically. The edition showed skill in handling unedited texts and the prefaces and commentaries gave evidence of knowledge of the history of the twelfth century.

After this work had been published Mabillon turned to the task for which he had been called to St. Germain des Prés, the arranging and editing of the *Acta* of the Benedictine saints, which had been collected for a general history of the Benedictine Order by D'Achery. The amassing of materials was continued. The first volume of the *Acta sanctorum ordinis s. Benedicti* appeared in 1668; the other eight volumes were published between this time and 1701. They cover the period between the life of St. Benedict and the end of the eleventh century. Although the preparation of this work was a joint labor, the prefaces were written by Mabillon himself, and were a revelation of critical and interpretative insight. In them he explained the chief events of each century (each tome of the *Acta* covers a hundred years of Benedictine history); he established the correct chronology of the popes and kings; he discussed points of interest about monasticism and the papacy; he cleared up such myths as that of Popess Joan and called attention to changes in religious customs. These prefaces were printed separately in a quarto volume of over six hundred pages (Rouen, 1732). Mabillon's *Acta* of the Benedictine saints differed from the plan of the *Acta Sanctorum* of the Bollandists, which arranged the lives after the saints' days of the year. The Benedictine *Acta Sanctorum* follows a chronological order, certainly a method better suited to historical study. Early historians of the order

[26] E. C. Butler, "Mabillon," *Downside Review*, XII (1893), 116–32, quotation on 119–20.

had claimed some eighty saints, but Mabillon would allow no more than twenty-five of these to have been Benedictines. Protest was made to the General Chapter and Mabillon was called upon to vindicate his historical method. He replied with a remarkable memoir, saying that he was quite willing not to write history at all, but if he wrote he must tell the truth; that the interests of history and real edification were the same. Never again was he challenged within his own congregation, though he had yet to encounter formidable criticism.

Preparations for the *Annals of the Benedictine Order* had been going on for fifty years, and for nine years Mabillon and Ruinart devoted all their time to the composition of the work. In 1703 the first volume appeared, a folio of some six hundred pages, and in the ensuing years three more volumes were published. The materials for two others were ready, and they were issued after Mabillon's death, carrying the history of the Order down to the middle of the twelfth century. This period was the limit of Mabillon's knowledge. The words of the Abbé de Longuerue, one of the scholars who used to frequent the Sunday afternoon meetings at St. Germain, are true: "Le Père Mabillon savoit fort bien le VII, le VIII, le IX, le X, et le XI siècles; mais il ne savoit rien ni en deça, ni au delà."

The *Annales ordinis s. Benedicti* is entirely an historical account. It is based on the *Acta* and other documents that Mabillon and his friends had gradually collected in further travels. The first volume was published after nearly ten years of preparation. It gives a history of the birth and development of the Benedictine Order from the end of the fifth century to the year 700. The second, third, and fourth volumes appeared between 1704 and 1707, the year of Mabillon's death. The unfinished work was carried on by several colleagues and successors.

In the interval between the *Acta Sanctorum O.S.B.* and the *Annales O.S.B.*, Mabillon had prepared his greatest work, the *De re diplomatica* (1681). The history of the origin of this work has already been related. In the preface, Mabillon told of the incentives which had led him to write this work: "the usefulness of the subject matter combined with its novelty, and the necessity of defence." Then he explained that "not alone ecclesiastical and civil history but particularly the conditions of private individuals and of ecclesiastics depend on documents of such sort." Perhaps this is a reference to the importance his Order attached to its archives. He laid it down as his aim to follow the middle course, neither to reject all documents nor accept all without discrimination, but to champion the facts of legitimate documents and to refute by certain information the falsity of forged documents. In other words, his was to be a positive criticism, to do what Bernheim says diplomatics should do, prove the honesty of sources as well as the falsity of some. None before him had shown that it was possible to prove beyond dispute that an early document was genuine; [27] this constructive work Mabillon did.

Mabillon had developed the rules and criteria for judging sources by comparing a great number of documents of the same time, place, and country. These documents he had examined palaeographically, and from them derived his rules. The documents themselves were used to gain the criteria for judging their authenticity. But in his presentation of these rules in *De re diplomatica* he presents his theses with very few concrete cases.

The first two books of the *De re diplomatica* state the principles of diplomatics, the tests by which charters can be known as true or false. In Book I, Mabillon clarifies and defines the different kinds of charters; then proves that ecclesiastical and royal charters were granted at a very early period (royal ones for the fifth century), therefore the great age of a document in itself is no cause for suspicion against it. He examined the five main materials generally used for documents; next he wrote of the ink, and the kind of writing. In Book II, Mabillon took up the language of the documents, showing that barbarity of language was one proof of antiquity. Here he was using the critical weapon of linguistic criticism forged by the humanists and used so ably by Valla. He discussed in detail the five characteristic parts of medieval charters, the seals, and particularly the systems of chronology. Thus in established and exact rules Mabillon stated what, for a particular time and place, was the correct form for a genuine document, [28] and presented in these two books the general principle of diplomatics.

The other books are devoted to proofs and illustrations of these principles and the manner in which they are to be applied. The third book discusses the charters which Papebroche had questioned or condemned as false, particularly those of the archives of St. Denis and other houses of the Benedictine Order. Book IV lists the residences, or "palatia," of the kings of France where charters were drawn up; the fifth book gives examples of old handwriting; the sixth is made up of more than 200 documents copied from the originals, with notes and arguments showing why they are considered authentic.

Thus was the new science of diplomatics established on a firm foundation. There were errors to be corrected, it is true, and much more is desired today in method and documents, but the foundations laid by Mabillon were true and have not been shaken. The critical principles of the *De re diplomatica* covered only a part of a very large field but they have been very fruitful.

[27] Acton, *Historical Essays* (n. 23), 461.   [28] Rosenmund (n. 17), 16–17.

While the Bollandists, though Jesuits, accepted the historical conclusions of Mabillon, other Jesuit scholars, notably Hardouin, carried
on the controversy over the genuineness of the Merovingian charters.[29]
The motive, one may suspect, was not wholly a zeal for critical accuracy
and the integrity of truth. For if the title-deeds to many Benedictine
monasteries of Merovingian foundation could be proved to be forgeries,
then the Jesuits stood a good chance to acquire possession of these ancient properties, especially as most of the Benedictine houses were de-
crepit. Mabillon's superlative critical abilities in conjunction with his
transcendent intellectual honesty kept him in almost constant conflict
with many other Catholic scholars. The Jansenists and the Molinists
attacked his edition of the *Opera* of St. Augustine.[30] This edition was
published from 1679 to 1700. The preface, written for the last volume,
Mabillon deliberately revised to make safe for publication, suppressing
his own views for those of Bossuet. This he felt to be necessary for
protection to his Order, for this edition of the works of Augustine had
involved the Maurists in points of faith and dogma still subject to the
violent contentions of Jansenists and Jesuits. The Benedictines, long
enemies of the Jesuits, and "always suspected of Jansenism," [31] had
been subject to attack by both groups since the first volume appeared.
So Mabillon took Bossuet's advice; he even let him revise the preface,
and tried to escape both the Jansenist and the Jesuit positions. Thuillier
says that Bossuet had forced Mabillon "to speak against his own
thoughts." [32] This is a clear abdication of Mabillon the historian on a
subject involving doctrine, and it indicates that he was not always his
own master. "He had to consider the credit of two hundred French
monasteries, the feelings and the interests of the studious body among
whom he lived. . . . And there were other ordeals, civil and ecclesiastical, to pass before honest manuscript could get into deceitful type.
Thuillier gives a clue when he says of Mabillon, 'que souvent il faut
deviner son sentiment, et qu'il ne l'insinue d'ordinaire que par un peut-
être, pourrait-on-dire.'" [33]

Mabillon's repudiation of the actuality of many popular but spurious

---

[29] *De veteribus regum Francorum diplomatibus et arte secernendi antiqua diplomata vera et falsa.
Disceptatio ad R. P. D. Jo. Mabillon* (Paris, 1703).

[30] The inside story of this famous controversy has been revealed by Richard C. Kukula,
"Die Mauriner Ausgabe des Augustinus," *Sitzungsberichte der k. Akademie der Wissenschaften*
(Vienna), CXXII (1890), no. 8, pp. 1–66, and CXXVII (1892), no. 5, pp. 1–48. The preface
to this great work, unlike everything else which Mabillon wrote, was definitely polemical and
controversial. This was due to the influence of Bossuet, who wanted Augustine's doctrines set
forth as "également opposée à Jansenius et à Molina."

[31] Giry (n. 17), 69.

[32] Thuillier, *Histoire de la nouvelle édition de Saint Augustin* (Paris, 1736), 31, quoted in
Bergkamp (end n. 23), 103.

[33] Acton, *Historical Essays* (n. 23), 469.

saints created a clamor of protests. In Rome Mabillon had studied the catacombs under the guidance of Fabretti, the inspector and the chief archaeologist of the city, and he had been interested in the excavating being done there by the Church, both from the religious and the archaeological point of view. He felt that not only was the archaeological basis for the saints a false one, but that there were many abuses among minor officials in charge of the work. After returning to France, Mabillon heard of other scandals in connection with relics and he decided that the only way to prevent these was by publicly denouncing them, and so in 1691 he wrote a treatise on the subject. He was afraid to publish it, but after showing it to several friends he felt that it might "leak out" and so gave it for publication in 1698 under the title *Eusebii Romani ad Theophilum Gallum epistola de cultu sanctorum ignotorum.* In this book Mabillon did not simply attack abuses which he knew existed, but he also stated rules which he had developed for distinguishing the relics of martyrs, rules which have been retained by modern archaeologists. In this letter he recalled the opinion given in the ninth century by Gregory IV to the archbishop of Mainz that he, the Pope, could at that time find no true relics of saints at Rome. Mabillon also showed that the principles used to determine the genuineness of the relics of martyrs which had been formulated by a decree of the Sacred Congregation of Rites in 1668 were incorrect. This was a delicate subject which Mabillon had treated with moderation, but it soon led to trouble. The opposition at Rome to the letter on the *Unknown Saints* grew and finally in 1701 it was brought before the Congregation of the Index. The Congregation of St. Maur had a "lobby" at Rome with a procuror-general in charge to defend its interests but the energetic and efficient Estiennot, procuror-general to 1699, had died suddenly and apparently the Maurist interests there were not very well defended, for the anti-Maurist group was able to push through this drastic action against the letter on the *Unknown Saints.* By 1704 Mabillon's friends were able, and just in time, to get Clement XI to protect Mabillon (Clement had before this promised to give his protection to the Maurists on condition that he be given a new edition of the works of St. Bernard) by bringing the case directly before the Pope for examination. As a result of this Mabillon was permitted to revise the letter for a second edition which was approved by the Congregation of the Index. In this edition the main changes are the omission of the statement of Gregory IV on the scarcity of relics in the ninth century and the omission of the disapproval of the decree of the Congregation of Rites of 1668. Mabillon, in the preface to this second edition, assumed the bearing of one who has been corrected and appeared to confess his error; however, he himself wrote, "Je l'ai donc retouchée sans l'affaiblir en rien, et l'ai augmentée de près de la moitié." Lord Acton accepts this statement of Mabillon's. He adds, "The historian who says that the finest moments in church history are the resistance of Luther and the submission of Fénelon, might find room for a third type in the example of Mabillon." [34]

Of interest in connection with Mabillon's work on the *Unknown Saints* is his letter on the Holy Tear of Vendôme, a relic of the Benedictines of Vendôme. In 1699 Jean Baptiste Thiers made an attack on this relic, supposed to be a tear shed by Christ at the tomb of Lazarus, which was put by an angel in a glass vial, and eventually reached Vendôme. In 1700 Mabillon defended the Benedictines who accepted this relic, even though the earliest mention of it is late in the twelfth century. Testimony, he says, is not necessary where we have prescription. Here he certainly compromised his principles as an historian. It would have been more like Mabillon to have stayed out of such a quarrel, but perhaps, considering the time when this defense was made, he found it necessary to publish his belief in this relic to offset the dangerous situation created by his letter on the *Unknown Saints*.

Already, even before the *De re diplomatica*, Mabillon had made several short trips outside of France in search of manuscripts. But his widest travels were made in 1683 and in 1685–86, the first to Germany, the second to Italy. The king defrayed the expenses of both journeys and he was commissioned to buy books and manuscripts for the royal library. These journeys were a sort of "progress." He was lionized by princes, cardinals, bishops, and abbots. But Mabillon kept his head amid all this pomp. His life-long friend and biographer, Father Ruinart, describes his mode of travelling, often on foot with a modest pack on his back. He entered Rome at five o'clock in the morning purposely to avoid the grand greeting which his friends had staged for him. Wherever possible he lodged in a religious house. The fruits of these two journeys were the *Musaeum Germanicum* and the *Musaeum Italicum*. An incident which occurred at Munich in 1683 sheds light on the simple life at St. Germain. When asked if the Bavarian ruler's palace was as grand as that at Versailles, Mabillon replied that he had never seen Versailles. Later, it may be said, he was introduced to Louis XIV by Bossuet and Le Tellier, the archbishop of Rheims.

It is almost dramatic to reflect that Descartes and Mabillon were contemporaries and natives of the same country, and that though one was a skeptic and the other an orthodox cleric, there was a subconscious nexus between the thought of the two men in their mutual search for truth, in their resolute determination to follow reason. There are ideas

[34] *Ibid.*, 467.

and even phrases scattered through Mabillon's many prefaces or found in his *Traité des études monastiques* which seem to be tinged with rationalism. In some ways Mabillon may be regarded as the clearer thinker of the two. Descartes' inclination to go to the extremes of logic sometimes terminated in un-reason. Mabillon, on the other hand, never permitted his mind to pass beyond the bounds of common sense; he kept a balanced and a perfectly poised mind, and always preserved his sense of proportion. He never sacrificed his passion for truth to make a point.

Yet for all his great abilities, Mabillon sometimes erred. He accepted without hesitation what he found in an authentic source, the genuineness of which could not easily be rejected on palaeographical, chronological, or geographical grounds. He fell short of the modern requirements of internal criticism. He had little conception of the principle of "authority" in use of a source other than the evidence of external criticism. He failed to perceive the importance of the source of a source. When Mabillon blundered as to facts, the gods nodded. One of his greatest errors is with regard to the date of the *Carmen satyricum* written by Adalberon of Laon, a curious source for the marriage of Robert the Pious of France and the Countess Bertha of Anjou, which Gregory V dissolved. Another is his belief that Alcuin was a monk instead of a canon regular.

Nevertheless, in spite of defects Mabillon, as Lord Acton has written, "belongs to the family of pioneers, and . . . is one of the best known names in the line of discoverers from Valla . . . to Morgan . . . [and] although disciplined and repressed by the strict reform of Saint Maur, he rose above all his brethren to be, as an historian, eminently solid and trustworthy, as a critic the first in the world." [35]

Mabillon died in 1707. His successor at St. Germain des Prés was Dom Ruinart, from whom we have a life of Mabillon, an edition of Gregory of Tours, and his most important work, the *Acta primorum martyrum sincera et selecta*. Ruinart died in 1709. [36]

What Mabillon did for the history of the Latin Church in the Middle Ages, that Montfaucon did for the history of the Greek Church. In his own field of scholarship he was as original and as great as Mabillon. Bernard de Montfaucon [37] was born in the department of the Aube in 1655 and died in 1741. He belonged to a noble family of Languedoc

---

[35] Acton, *Historical Essays* (n. 23), 460.
[36] Henri Jadart, *Dom Thierry Ruinart* (Paris, 1886).
[37] E. de Broglie, *La société de l'abbaye de Saint-Germain des Prés au dix-huitième siècle. Bernard de Montfaucon et les Bernardins, 1715–1750* (Paris, 1891, 2 v.), a better work than his life of Mabillon. See also the article by Louis Bréhier in the *Catholic Encyclopaedia*, X, 539–40; *La Grande Encyclopédie*, XXIV, 236; SANDYS, II, 385–89; and an essay in *ER*, LXXXIX (1849), 1–47, cp. XCIV (1851), 12–13.

and in 1673 at the age of eighteen entered the army, and served for two years in Germany. Among his papers preserved at the Bibliothèque Nationale is a short autobiography in which Montfaucon vivaciously relates how he came to be a scholar. As a boy in the paternal château at Roquetaillade he read all the books on which he could lay his hands, "surtout les historiens que je pus trouver." Among these was Amyot's sixteenth-century translation of Plutarch's *Lives*, which had fascinated Montaigne (*Essays*, bk. ii, 10) a century before it charmed Montfaucon. Another book was a French translation of Osorius' *Navigations and Conquests of the Portuguese in the East Indies*. He borrowed all the books he could and a fortunate accident supplied him with many others. A relative of the family who had lost his fortune came to live at the château, and brought a chest of books with him, which were stowed away in the garret. One day, in rummaging around, the curious lad discovered this chest and found that a rat had gnawed a corner of the box and he could see papers and books within. He pried the lid off and unveiled a rich collection of books, most of them of an historical and geographical nature. "Je lisais," he relates, "jusqu'à sept ou huit heures par jour les histoires de tous les pays, le livre des états et empires du monde, tous les histoires de France; les autres histoires en toutes langues, en italien et en espagnol." Disillusioned of the world as a result of his experience in the army, Montfaucon joined the Maurist house in Toulouse in 1675, and in 1687, for his learning, was transferred to St. Germain des Prés.

There Montfaucon began to edit those magnificent editions of the works of Athanasius (1698), Origen (1713), and St. John Chrysostom (1738), the last in thirteen folio volumes, which cost him twenty-three years of labor, and were not superseded until the nineteenth century. Meanwhile, during these years, Montfaucon—to use his own words— "having finished the edition of St. Athanasius and being taught by experience that there was no possibility of perfecting the Greek fathers without searching the libraries of Italy," in 1698 went to Italy. He was gone for three years. The fruit of that journey was not only a rich store of new manuscripts, but his own precious *Diarium Italicum*, a classic in the history of European scholarship and a coveted object of possession by many bibliophiles.[38] The results of this tour were embodied in two volumes of fragments of the Greek fathers in 1707.

[38] Paris, 1702. An English translation of this appeared in London in 1712, entitled *The Travels of the Learned Father Montfaucon from Paris through Italy*. "Containing I. An account of many antiquities . . . in France; II. The delights of Italy, viz. libraries, manuscripts, statues, paintings, monuments, tombs, inscriptions . . .; III. Collection of rarities, wonderful subterraneous passages and burial-places. . . ." The book was dedicated to Cosmo III, Grand Duke of Tuscany, whose kindness Montfaucon acknowledged with gratitude.

The greatest product of this Italian journey, however, was Montfaucon's *Palaeographia Graeca* (1708), which did for medieval Greek palaeography what Mabillon had done for medieval Latin palaeography. In the preparation of this monumental work Mabillon examined 11,630 manuscripts. His next labor was to compile the catalogue of the library of the Duc de Coislin, the prince-bishop of Metz, the whole of which was bequeathed to St. Germain and is now in the Bibliothèque Nationale. His next excursion was into the field of archaeology, into which Mabillon had not hitherto ventured.

Archaeology had been pursued more as a pastime or hobby in the Renaissance, but it did not become a scholarly science until the seventeenth century. In France it began with Nicholas Claude Fabre de Peiresc (1580–1637), the first to study monuments from the historical point of view, who was followed by Jacques Spon (1647–85). La Petite Académie, out of which sprang in 1701 the Académie des Inscriptions, was established in 1663.[39]

The discovery of the tomb of the Merovingian king Childeric in Belgium in 1635 had stimulated interest in medieval archaeology, and the great French minister Colbert had cherished the plan of having a great work prepared giving an account of all the ancient Roman monuments in France with illustrative plates. Montfaucon more than fulfilled Colbert's dream. His *L'Antiquité Expliquée*, "a vast treasury of classical antiquities," illustrated with 1120 large copper-plate engravings and containing thousands of smaller illustrations, in fifteen huge volumes, was published by subscription between 1719–24. In this great work Montfaucon "reproduces, methodically grouped, all the ancient monuments that might be of use in the study of the religion, domestic customs, material life, military institutions, and funeral rites of the ancients."[40] According to Sandys, "within two months the first edition of 1,800 copies, (or 18,000 volumes,) was sold off, and a new edition of 2,200 printed in the same year. . . . All the fifteen volumes were translated into English. The Russian nobleman, Prince Kourakin, had a complete set, sumptuously bound, and packed in a special case to accompany him on his travels in Italy."[41] As a supplement to this work, Montfaucon published *Les Monuments de la monarchie française*, in five volumes, between 1729 and 1733, but it is much inferior to his previous work.

Thus his prodigious labors continued. In 1739 Montfaucon endeared himself to all librarians and bibliophiles by producing in two

[39] For an account of the development of French archaeology in the seventeenth century see Salomon Reinach, "Esquisse d'une histoire de l'archéologie gauloise," *Revue Celtique*, XIX (1898), 101–17, and 292–307; and consult SANDYS, II, index.
[40] Bréhier, in the *Catholic Encyclopaedia* (n. 37).   [41] SANDYS, II, 387.

folio volumes his *Bibliotheca Bibliothecarum,* which included all the catalogues of Europe on libraries which he had collected over forty years.
In 1731 he was gathering materials for a projected work on French
archaeology, the second part of which was to deal with the churches of
France. In December of that year he read a paper on the subject before the Academy of Inscriptions; a foreign member who was presented
asked Montfaucon how old he was; he answered: "In thirteen more
years I shall be a hundred." Two days afterwards the last of the truly
great scholars of the Congrégation de St. Maur was dead. He was
buried in the same abbey-church which contains the ashes of Mabillon.

Another of the winning figures at St. Germain was Dom Félibien
(1666–1719), who spent his life in the composition of the *Histoire de
l'Abbaye royale de St. Denys* (1706). Although Colbert had taken an
interest in these scholar-monks of St. Germain, Louis XIV had not.
But a history of St. Denis interested him, for there were the tombs of
his ancestors, and it was out of a dislike at having to look down upon
this place, the sight of which affected him unpleasantly, from the palace
of St. Germain above the Seine, that the king built the palace at Versailles. Accordingly Dom Félibien received a summons to court, whither
no other brother had hitherto been save Mabillon.

Before the book was published [says the narrator] Dom Félibien, accompanied by
the prior of St. Denis, went to present it to the king and was introduced into the cabinet
of His Majesty by the Cardinal of Noailles. After the prior had paid his compliments
briefly, the author presented his book, begging the king to receive it with the same
kindness with which he had in former times received divers works which M. Félibien,
his father,[42] had composed for his service. The king read the whole of the title-page [and
made some comments upon the engraved frontispiece]. He ran through the first pages,
and coming upon the plan of the town of St. Denis, "There," said he, "is a town which
cost us a good deal in former times," referring to the civil wars of 1652. Again he turned
over the pages of the book for some time, and said: "There is a good book." Then,
closing it, he said to the prior of St. Denis: "Father, I thank you; pray to God for me
during my life and after my death." "Sire," answered the prior, "the whole kingdom is
too deeply interested in the preservation of your Majesty to fail in that." On going out
from the grand cabinet at Versailles, Dom Félibien and his prior went to present the work
to Messeigneurs the Dauphin, the Duke of Burgundy and the Duke of Berry, his brother,
who received it very favorably. After having made their present to the chancellor, they
went to St. Cyr to offer a copy to Madame de Maintenon. Some days afterward Dom
Félibien went with Dom Mabillon to [the palace of] St. Germain-en-Laye, where he presented his history to the young king of England, James III [the "Old Pretender"], who
received the present with evidences of joy and esteem. He presented it to the Duke of
Orleans, who promised to read it. Eight days after this memorable distribution the king,
seeing the Cardinal de Noailles, said to him: "Really, Monsieur le Cardinal, I did not
suppose that the history of St. Denis could be so varied and agreeable as it is. I have
found the reading of it extremely interesting. It must be that Father Félibien has had
good memoirs as materials, especially for what relates to my reign, for I find him very

[42] On whom see *La Grande Encyclopédie,* XVII, 128.

exact." These praises had no sooner proceeded from the mouth of the king than the new history became an object of interest to all the court, which occupied itself with it for several days. In consequence, the sale of the work was so rapid that in six weeks more than two hundred copies were disposed of.[43]

So much of the labor of the scholars at St. Germain was devoted to monastic literature that one might assume that all of their writings dealt with the monastic side of ecclesiastical history. This is not the case. Another of their achievements was the *Gallia Christiana*, in sixteen volumes (Paris, 1715–65).[44] The series was interrupted by the French Revolution and continued and completed by the Académie des Inscriptions in the nineteenth century. Ughelli's *Italia Sacra* had set the example for this work. It is the one instance in which Italian scholarship influenced that of France.

Other historical scholars there were in France of this time who were not of the fold of St. Germain des Prés, some of whom were as great as they. Port Royal was prevailingly given to philosophy and theology, but it had one historian of eminence. This was Le Nain de Tillemont (1637–98),[45] of whom Gibbon said that "his inimitable accuracy almost assumes the character of genius." At an early age he began to make those vast accumulations which culminated in his two monumental works: *Mémoires pour servir à l'histoire ecclésiastique des six premiers siècles*, which extend to 513 A.D., in sixteen volumes (1693–1712), and his equally learned *Histoire des empereurs et des autres princes qui ont régné durant les six premiers siècles de l'église*, in four volumes (1690–1738). From the age of fourteen Tillemont was interested in Roman imperial and early church history. He used to rise at four in the morning and work until nine at night, except for meals, and after he became a priest in 1676 to say the offices. With the exception of a visit to Holland in 1685, he never left France and hardly even his house at Tillemont where he resided after the dissolution of Port Royal in 1679. It has been said of him that "he studied for study's sake and had only the aim of truth." Gibbon alludes to Tillemont's *History of the Roman Emperors* as "so learned and exact a compilation" and to his "sure-footed" [46] erudition; and when writing of the religious disputes at Constantinople in 514 A.D. he adds in a note: "Here I must take leave

---

[43] This quotation is cited from Jameson (see n. 12 above), 23.

[44] Contents analyzed in Alfred Franklin, *Les sources de l'histoire de France* (Paris, 1877), 465–85; for an historical account of it see L. F. Guérin, "La *Gallia Christiana*," *RQH*, XI (1872), 199–212.

[45] There is an old life of Tillemont by Michel Tronchay, *Idée de la vie et de l'ésprit de M. L. de Tillemont* (Nancy, 1706). The best account of his life and works is to be found in a series of articles in *JS*, 1851, pp. 625–32, 1852, pp. 316–25 and 386–99, 1853, pp. 503–14 and 703–16, and 1854, pp. 47–57.

[46] GIBBON, III, 48 note.

forever of that incomparable guide—whose bigotry is over-balanced by the merits of erudition, diligence, veracity and scrupulous minuteness." [47] The late Thomas Hodgkin described the same work as "a perfect digest of all the authorities bearing on every fact in Roman imperial history." [48]

A far different sort of scholar was Étienne Baluze (1630–1718),[49] wit, bon vivant, and savant. He began his career as secretary and librarian to Pierre de Marca, the learned author of a *Histoire de Béarn* (1640), whom Mazarin made archbishop of Toulouse and who succeeded the notorious Cardinal de Retz as bishop of Paris in 1662, but died in the same year. In 1667, after some years as librarian to Le Tellier, Baluze became librarian to Colbert, a post which he retained until 1700, seventeen years after the death of the minister. His reputation and mastery of French legal antiquities also won him the chair of canon law at the Collège de France in 1670 which he held until 1713. Of his many works the most valuable is the *Capitularia regum Francorum* (2 v. folio, Paris, 1677; 2nd ed., 1780). The preface is a history of the capitularies which makes a landmark in the history of early medieval law. Begun in collaboration with Marca on the basis of a manuscript from the Spanish monastery of Ripoll, Baluze collated this manuscript with others which he found, one in the Vatican, one at St. Gall, another at Mont St. Michel, etc. To these texts he added the *Formulae* of Marculf, Pithou's *Glossary*, and Sirmond's *Notae*. His other most important work was a *History of the Avignonese Popes*.[50] Baluze was a friend of almost every historical scholar of the time, and a frequent visitor at St. Germain des Prés, where he collaborated with D'Achery and others. He left behind him three historical works of the first order, five collections of documents, eleven lesser books, and the *Miscellanea*, a manuscript collection of historical notes in seven volumes. La Monnoye wittily wrote of him:

> Qui mille auctores Baluzius edidit unus,
> Par ille auctorum millibus unus erat.

He was hated by pious Catholics for his rationalistic attitude to legends of the saints, and was an ardent advocate of Gallicanism and wrote several pamphlets in support of it.

Louis Thomassin (1619–95), an Oratorian, was professor of theology

---

[47] *Ibid.*, V, 132 note.   [48] *Italy and Her Invaders* (2nd ed., Oxford, 1892), I, 117.

[49] On Baluze see the dissertation of Charles Godard, *De Stephano Baluzio Tutelensi, libertatum ecclesiae gallicanae propugnatore* (Paris, 1901); *La Grande Encyclopédie*, V, 183–85; and Émile Bourgeois and Louis André, *Les sources de l'histoire de France: XVIIe siècle, 1610–1715* (Paris, 1913–34, 7 v.), II, 332–33.

[50] *Vitae Paparum Avenionensium, hoc est Historia pontificum romanorum qui in Gallia sederunt ab anno Christi MCCCV usque ad annum MCCCXCIV* (Paris, 1693, 2 v.; reprint Paris, 1914–27, 4 v.).

in the seminary of St. Magloire in Paris. In order to reconcile the doctrines of the Jansenists and the Molinists he composed a series of seventeen dissertations on church history and theology which raised the
wrath of the parlements and the clergy against him and his congregation. His capital work is the *Ancienne et nouvelle discipline de l'église
touchant les bénéfices et les bénéficiers* (1678–79, 3 v.), published in French,
of which he also made a Latin translation. He was an apologist of the
revocation of the Edict of Nantes.

Unlike any of the French scholars so far enumerated, in that he was
a layman and not of the clergy, and that his subject was unique, was
Charles Dufresne, seigneur Du Cange (1610–88).[51] The sciences of
palaeography, diplomatics, and medieval Latin philology were all born
of French scholarship of the seventeenth century. Du Cange was the
founder of the last, and like Mabillon, there is a modern historical
journal named in his honor—the *Bulletin Du Cange.*

Du Cange's early education was received from the Jesuits; later he
studied law at Orleans; in 1638 he abandoned the bar for historical
research and returned from Paris to Amiens, where he was born and
where his father was royal provost. In the same year he married a
daughter of Du Bois, a treasury official, and in 1647 purchased the office
from his father-in-law, which gave him an independent income. In
1668 he established himself in Paris where he died twenty years later.
During this time he made friends with every distinguished historian
there, notably with Mabillon and Baluze. Du Cange is best known
for his *Glossary of Medieval Latin* (*Glossarium ad scriptores mediae et infimae Latinitatis*) in three folio volumes (1678) [52] and a corresponding
Glossary of Medieval Greek in two volumes. Like Tillemont, Du Cange
habitually worked from twelve to sixteen hours a day, and for the Latin
glossary alone examined upwards of six thousand manuscripts besides
printed sources. His linguistic ability, his wide and varied knowledge,
his critical sense, his accuracy, are truly astonishing. He was far from
being merely "the lexicographer of the latest Latinity."

Du Cange enjoys the singular reputation of having contributed almost as much to Byzantine studies as to medieval Latin studies. It
may be said of him that he created Byzantine historical scholarship.
He had only two predecessors. The peril from the Osmanli Turks had

[51] SANDYS, II, 289–90; article in *Nouvelle biographie générale,* etc., ed. by Hoefer (Paris, 1862–77, 46 v.), XIV, 911–18; Léon Feugère, *Étude sur la vie et les ouvrages de Du Cange* (Paris, 1852); *La Grande Encyclopédie,* XIV, 1175; V. de Nors, "Du Cange et ses biographes," *RDM,* XIX (1853), 1237–51.

[52] Fourth ed. in six vols. (Paris, 1733–36); ed. by Charpentier in ten (1766); in six (Halle, 1772–84); ed. by G. A. L. Henschel in seven (Paris, 1840–50); latest ed. by L. Favre in ten (Niort, 1883–87). Material for future revisions is published by modern scholars in the *Bulletin Du Cange: Archivum Latinitatis Medii Aevi* (Paris, 1924 ff.).

first turned the mind of western scholars to the serious study of the history of the Byzantine Empire. In the previous century Hieronymous Wolf (1516–80), who had learned Greek from Melanchthon, and was for some years secretary and librarian of the rich merchant of Augsburg, Johann Jakob Fugger, and later from 1557 to his death in 1580 rector of the newly-founded gymnasium, had edited Suidas (1564) and published four volumes of Byzantine historians.[53] His pupil David Hoeschel (1556–1617) in 1601 published the *editio princeps* of Photius' *Bibliotheca*, and two years afterwards did the same for Constantine Porphyrogenitus' historic encyclopedia. The manuscripts which these two scholars used were part of a valuable collection from Corfu which the enlightened city council of Augsburg had purchased in Venice in 1544.[54] The impulse thus given endured down to the end of the seventeenth century.

In France under Louis XIV the motive of interest in Byzantine history was national pride. The remembrance of a once brilliant French domination in Greece and the Archipelago in the thirteenth and fourteenth centuries extended French interest to include the history of the Byzantine Empire. Cardinal Mazarin, regent of France during the minority of Louis XIV, possessor of the finest library in France, and not without scholarship, conceived the idea of a French edition of all the Byzantine historians. Louis XIV displayed an active interest in the revival of Byzantine studies, and the first great collection of Byzantine historical texts was begun under his auspices: the *Byzantinae Historiae Scriptores*.[55] In this great series Du Cange edited the texts of Anna Comnena, Zonaras, Cinnamus, and Villehardouin. In 1688, ten years after his Latin glossary, Du Cange gave to the world the *Glossarium ad scriptores mediae et infimae Graecitatis*.

The number of Du Cange's works would be incredible if the originals, all written in his own hand, were not still in evidence. His edition of the *Chronicon Paschale* was passing through the press when he died. Baluze published it, prefixed by a eulogy of Du Cange. Du Cange's manuscripts, and his extensive and valuable library, passed to his eldest son, Philippe Dufresne, who died unmarried four years after. François Dufresne, the second son, and two sisters, then received the succession and sold the library. The greater part of the manuscripts was purchased

---

[53] On Wolf see SANDYS, II, 268–69.   [54] *Ibid.*, II, 268, 272.

[55] In 39 volumes (or 47, or 23, or 27, according to arrangement), Paris, 1645–1711; best edition printed in Holland, 1672–74, 11 v., with good Latin translations from the Greek. Contents listed in August Potthast, *Bibliotheca historica medii aevi: Wegweiser durch die Geschichtswerke des europäischen Mittelalters* (2nd ed., enlarged and improved, Berlin, 1896, 2 v.), I, p. xlvi. Many of the texts from this collection were later reprinted in the Abbé Migne's *Patrologia Graeca*. Extracts translated into French by Louis Cousin in his *Histoire de Constantinople, depuis le règne de Justin jusqu'à la fin de l'empire* (Paris, 1672–74, 8 v.). About the same time, in Germany, Martin Hanke (Hankius) published a dissertation entitled *De Byzantinarum rerum scriptoribus graecis liber* (Leipzig, 1677).

by the Abbé Du Champs, who handed them over to a bookseller called Mariette, who re-sold part of them to Baron Hohendorf. The remaining part was acquired by D'Hozier, the genealogist. But the French Government, aware of the importance of all the writings of Du Cange, succeeded, after much trouble, in collecting the greater portion of these manuscripts, which are now preserved in the Bibliothèque Nationale.

The greatest of the historical scholars of France and the Catholic Netherlands in the seventeenth century have now been passed in review. Naturally there were many others, but they were less original and less able than those giants of erudition.

The Franciscans and Dominicans had hitherto not greatly contributed to historical scholarship. Even they, however, caught the infection in the Age of Erudition. Pierre Helyot (1660–1716), a Franciscan, labored for twenty-five years and left uncompleted a *Histoire des Ordres religieux et militaires*. He died while the fifth volume was in the press. The last three volumes were added by Bullot, of the same Order, who died in 1748. The entire work was published at Paris in 1714–19. It still remains unsuperseded. Soon after its appearance it was translated into Italian and German, and was last reprinted in 1829.

The bitter controversy between Louis XIV and Pope Innocent XI over the question of the "liberties" of the Gallican Church evoked some not unimportant historical works. The most prominent of such contributors was Louis Ellies Du Pin (1657–1719) a professor at the Collège de France, who in 1686 published a treatise on the ancient discipline of the Church, in Latin, which incurred the wrath of Bossuet. In the same year Du Pin published the first volume of his *Nouvelle bibliothèque de tous les auteurs ecclésiastiques, contenant l'histoire de leur vie; le catalogue, la critique, et la chronologie de leurs ouvrages*, etc., which when completed ran to nine volumes. For its time the work was a reliable and convenient account of the fathers of the Early Church and their writings. It was translated into English (1696–1706) as the successive volumes appeared, and was a staple work on the shelves of the more enlightened of the English clergy in the reign of Queen Anne.

Another minor historical scholar was Gabriel Daniel (1649–1728), a Jesuit whose best work is a *Histoire de la milice française depuis l'établissement de la monarchie française à la fin de la règne de Louis le Grand* (1721), but who was better known in his own time for a general *Histoire de France* (eds. 1713, 1755, 1758, 1760). The preface contained some "observations critiques" on the equally popular *Histoire de France* written by Mézeray, in which Père Daniel fell into the ancient trap of believing that the proper kind of history should be pragmatic.[56]

[56] See Bourgeois and André (n. 49), I, 312–13.

French Jesuit historical scholarship confined itself almost wholly to the history of the councils of the Medieval Church, as the Bollandists limited themselves to the lives of the saints. The initiator of these studies was Jacques Sirmond (1559–1651), who lived longer than any other scholar of the age. When a young man he had lived in Rome from 1590 to 1608, where he was a protégé of Cardinal Baronius, and later taught rhetoric at the University of Paris, where St. François de Sales was one of his pupils. So cautious and so critical was this learned Jesuit that he advised a young friend not to venture into print before he was fifty years old, and he himself was fifty when he published his first work. This was the *Concilia Generalia* in three volumes which was published in the years 1609–12.[57] This work was less important for what it was than for what it initiated. It was the beginning of that series of gigantic tomes containing the documentary history of the councils of the Medieval Church destined to be in the end the fine product of French and Italian historical scholarship. In 1629 Sirmond's three volumes pertaining to the ecclesiastical councils in France (*Concilia antiqua Galliae*) appeared. A few years later Sirmond was made confessor to Louis XIII and in this capacity fell under Richelieu's disfavor; he was suspected of being implicated in the conspiracy of Cinq Mars to do away with king and cardinal and to make Gaston of Orleans, the king's brother, regent of the kingdom. This ended Sirmond's career; he was lucky to have saved his head.

The conciliar history was renewed in 1644 under the supervision of Pères Labbé and Cossart, who edited twenty-three volumes. These were printed at the Royal Press, from which circumstance the series is known as the *Collectio regia*. In 1683 Baluze edited a single volume. The famous Hardouin continued the series with twelve more tomes (Paris, 1714–15). After that the fate of the *Concilia* was one of suspended animation for many years. The Parlement of Paris had long opposed the work on the ground that it was hostile to Gallican Liberties. The tension, not to say political enmity, between Louis XIV and the papacy, especially in the time of Innocent XI, estranged the king and the royal subsidy for printing the work was withdrawn. Under these adverse conditions the continuation of the *Concilia* was impracticable in France and the design was transferred to Italy. In Venice Nicolas Coleti continued the series for six years (1728–34), and when he passed away Mansi, archbishop of Lucca, carried on the labor to as near completion as the enormous series was brought in the Age of Erudition. Mansi

[57] On Sirmond see Backer, *Bibliothèque* (n. 19), VII, cols. 1236–61; J. P. Nicéron, *Mémoires pour servir à l'histoire des hommes illustres dans la république des lettres* (Paris, 1729–45, 43 v. in 44), XVII, 153–80.

died in 1769. Pope Clement XIV dissolved the Jesuit Order in 1773, but still the work was continued. The last pages of this grand series of tomes came off the press in Venice in 1798, just at the time when Napoleon extinguished the liberties of the Venetian Republic. Thirty-one volumes had been issued.[58]

It would be a mistake to infer that these prodigious historical researches, although for the most part the labor of Catholic scholars, interested only ecclesiastics and antiquarians. Many of these huge tomes were eagerly and critically read by the clergy of both camps in various countries, by civil officials, by the intelligent noblesse and bourgeoisie. Political thought in the sixteenth and seventeenth centuries was rich and various. The Reformation and Counter-Reformation, the growth of monarchy, gave birth to new and profound political theories. The new erudition was employed in systematic analysis of ancient, medieval, and modern forms of government, in explanation of the origin and nature of institutions. All sorts of questions were discussed—the nature of the state, "natural law," the nature and limits of sovereignty, political rights and social rights, class rights, individual rights, and property rights; the relations of Church and State; religious toleration and liberty; autocracy and democracy; absolute monarchy and limited monarchy. Every class in European society had interest in and need of the new historical scholarship, and sought evidence and argument in support of its contentions and interests. Hotman had led the long array of these polemists or politiques. He was a Silesian by descent, his grandfather having entered the service of France in the reign of Louis XI. In his *Franco-Gallia*, published as a Huguenot political tract in 1574, Hotman undertook to show that the fundamental laws of France provided for an elective monarchy subordinate to the states general of the realm. The Franks had delivered the Romanized Gauls from the Roman yoke, and fused into one people with them; the Franco-Gallic commonwealth was based on the sovereignty of the two races united into one nation. The king was, or should be, a limited monarch subject to deposition.[59]

[58] The authoritative account of the *Concilia* is Dom Henri Quentin's *Jean-Dominique Mansi et les grands collections conciliaires* (Paris, 1900). Paul Viollet, *Droit privé et sources: Histoire de droit civil français* (2nd ed., Paris, 1893), 35–40 contains a merciless criticism of Mansi's unscholarly work. The *Concilia* were not resumed until late in the last century. New edition and continuation, vols. 32–53, Paris, 1901 ff.; conspectus of the first forty-six volumes and an alphabetical index in vol. XXXVIa.

[59] One needs only to mention other classics of political theory which saw the light during the sixteenth and seventeenth centuries: the *Reveille-Matin* (1574); Jean Bodin's *La République* (1577); the *Vindiciae Gallicae* (1579) by Hubert Languet and Duplessis-Mornay; and Buchanan's *De jure regni* and Paruta's *Perfezione politica* in the same year; Sir Thomas Smith, *De republica Anglorum* (1584); Boucher, *De justa abdicatione* (1588); Hooker, *Ecclesiastical Polity* (1594); Mariana's *De rege* (1599); Althusius' *Politica* (1603); Suarez, *De legis ac Deo legislatore* (1617); Lebret, *La souveraineté du roy* (1632); Selden, *De jure naturali* (1640); Conring, *De*

That portion of the reading public known as the "general reader" class, of course, was not interested in the learned historical scholarship of the age. For it history was the story of the past—moving narrative and dramatic action—which adorned a tale and pointed a moral at the same time.

Mézeray (1610–83) was the most popular French historian of the time. The first volume of his *Histoire de France* appeared in 1643 and was soon twice reprinted (1646, 1651); when the whole work was completed in three big volumes, a second edition was required in 1685. Its popularity, indeed, survived the ancien régime, and the revolutionary and Napoleonic era; it was printed again as late as 1830. The serious merit of Mézeray's work—if any portion of it can be said to be serious, when it is not scholarly anywhere—does not begin until after 1300 when Mézeray could use sources in the French language; for he was an indifferent Latinist. He boasted to Du Cange that he "never read any of the monkish chronicles." [60] He believed in the ancient maxim that the style made the author. History was a branch of literature. He had a contempt for research, and regarded the use of annals and chronicles as sufficient. In this he followed Richelieu's dictum that "L'histoire doit être une simple narration," for the great cardinal distrusted deep and disinterested historical research, as well he might. Yet Mézeray seems to have acquired some respect for erudition in his later years. In 1667 he published an *Abrégé Chronologique* which shows a different method. In his former work Mézeray had looked back to the humanist historians of the past; in the latter he looked at his own present. He was a compiler, and his sources were chiefly at second-hand. Yet he formed a large collection of documents in manuscript, comprising twenty-nine folio volumes, which are now in the Bibliothèque Nationale. Politically Mézeray was very patriotic, and a number of the caustic pamphlets of that time are attributed to him. He succeeded Voiture in the French Academy in 1649, and became perpetual secretary in 1675.[61]

origine juris Germanici (1643); Rutherford, *Rex lex* (1644); Milton, *Tenure of Kings and Magistrates;* the *Eikon basilike* (1649); Hobbes, *Leviathan* (1651); Conring, *De finibus imperii Germanici* (1654); Harrington, *The Commonwealth of Oceana* (1656); Pufendorf, *De statu imperii Germanici* (1667); Spinoza, *Tractatus politicus* (1677); Filmer, *Patriarcha* (1680), which contended that kingship was a patriarchal institution established by God; and Locke's *Treatises on Civil Government* (1689).

For suggestive reading on the history of political theory in the sixteenth and seventeenth centuries see the *Cambridge Modern History*, III, ch. xxii; J. W. Allen, *A History of Political Thought in the Sixteenth Century* (London, 1928); G. P. Gooch, *English Democratic Ideas in the Seventeenth Century* (2nd ed., Cambridge, 1927); and F. J. C. Hearnshaw, ed., *The Social and Political Ideas of Some Great Thinkers of the Sixteenth and Seventeenth Centuries* (London, 1926), a series of masterly essays by various contributors.

[60] Mark Pattison, *Isaac Casaubon, 1559–1614* (2nd ed., Oxford, 1892), 449, n. 3.

[61] On Mézeray see Wilfred H. Evans, *L'historien Mézeray et la conception de l'histoire en France au XVIIe siècle* (Paris, 1930); C. A. Sainte-Beuve, *Causeries du Lundi* (3rd ed., Paris, 1885, 16 v.), VIII, 195–233.

This is a convenient point to notice the Jesuit Hardouin (1646–1729), whose extreme skepticism about the genuineness of historical documents marks him as a learned lunatic. For learned he undoubtedly was, a classicist, a chronologist, a numismatist. In 1690 he issued a famous tract, *Ad censuram scriptorum veterum prolegomena*, in which he contended that all the classics, both Greek and Latin, and most of the Church fathers, including St. Augustine and St. Jerome, were medieval forgeries. He maintained that the whole of ancient literature except Cicero, Pliny's *Natural History*, Vergil's *Georgics*, and Horace's *Epistles* and *Satires*, was concocted by a circle of wicked scholars in Italy between 1350 and 1480, and that all manuscripts professing to be earlier are forgeries. The publication of these startling theories was prevented by Hardouin's colleagues in his lifetime, but they circulated in manuscript. Hardouin, though obviously insane, was a most ingenious debater, and his extraordinary dissertation makes most excellent reading. He also attacked the actuality of all the church councils before the Council of Trent and maintained that the Vulgate was older than the Greek New Testament. The curious thing is that Hardouin founded a school of ultra-skeptics who pursue such fantastic studies even yet. Edwin Johnson's *The Rise of English Culture* (London, 1904) is an extended exposition of Hardouin's thesis, and most interesting to read. It is learned lunacy.

The stimulating intellectual atmosphere of the Age of Erudition was gradually diffused over Europe. But although the new scholarship was of Catholic initiation, the Catholic countries of Italy and Spain were inert to it until the eighteenth century. The scholars of the Protestant Netherlands contributed much to the advancement of classical philology and classical antiquities—one thinks of G. Vossius, Salmasius, Cluverius, Heinsius, Gronovius, Isaac Vossius—but little to the development of critical research in history. Next after France and Belgium, the first country which awakened to the new historical learning was Protestant England.

In a notable essay published in 1863 Mark Pattison wrote: "Learning, from Queen Elizabeth's day onwards, has always been a conspicuous mark of the Church [of England]. . . . In the Established Church there has prevailed all along a general respect for learning and learned men." [62] Pattison instanced classical philology as an example. He might as well have cited history.

English historical scholarship in the sixteenth century owed its encouragement almost entirely to one man: Matthew Parker (1504–75),

[62] "Learning in the Church of England," *National Review*, XVI (1863), 187–220, quotation on 189; reprinted in PATTISON, II, 263 ff.

archbishop of Canterbury, who began the salvaging of the manuscript treasures of England which had been scattered by the dissolution of the monasteries. He was one of England's greatest book collectors, and though no great historical scholar himself, made it possible for others after him to become historians. He made the first collection of Anglo-Saxon manuscripts and caused to be printed for the first time Asser's *Life of Alfred the Great.* He edited and published—at Frankfort, because he could not find competent proof-readers in England—the *Flores historiarum,* long attributed to Matthew of Westminster, who, we now know, is "an entirely imaginary person," and Matthew Paris' *Historia major.* Parker inspired Sir Thomas Bodley to make his great collection of books, and to found the Bodleian Library.[63]

As in France in the seventeenth century, so in England, one must sharply distinguish the learned historian and antiquary from literary and descriptive historians, whose waters ran smoothly but were not deep. Since there were no monks in England, these scholars were secular ecclesiastics or laymen. No group scholarship existed in England. Nothing similar to the Bollandists and the Maurists is to be found. It must be admitted that even the best of English Protestant historical scholarship in this century did not measure up to the quality of Belgian and French historical scholarship. The intellectual stimulus of the Counter-Reformation never got a foothold across the Channel.

Three historical scholars bridged the change from Tudor to Stuart England. The first was William Camden (1551–1623), whose *Britannia* (1586) is the first scholarly history of England.[64] The second was John Manwood (d. 1616), a barrister of Lincoln's Inn, gamekeeper of Waltham Forest, and justice of the New Forest. His *Treatise and Discourse of the Laws of the Forest* appeared in 1598 and is a black letter volume which Shakespeare may have read.[65] The third was Sir Henry Savile (1549–1622) who was even more learned in Greek and mathematics than in history. He became so indignant over the superficial and fantastic chronicles popular in England, like Holinshed, for example, that he was almost provoked into the writing of a history of England himself, and

[63] S. W. Kershaw, "Archbishop Parker, Collector and Author," *The Library,* new series, I (London, 1900), 379–83; E. C. Pearce, "Matthew Parker," *ibid.,* 4th series, VI (1925), 220–28.

[64] This eminent work ran through six editions during the reign of Elizabeth. The first English translation—there are three—was made by Philemon Holland (for Holland's work as a translator see SANDYS, II, 243). In 1603 Camden caused to be printed at Frankfort a collection of old chronicles entitled *Anglica, Normannica, Hibernica a veteribus scripta.* In 1605 his *Remains* were published. These were notes which Camden intended to use in a new edition of the *Britannia* and which were incorporated in the seventh (the best) edition in 1674. Finally in 1615 Camden published his *Annales rerum Anglicarum et Hibernicarum, regnante Elizabetha ad annum Salutis MDLXXXIX,* i.e., down to the defeat of the Spanish Armada, which had almost as much success as his *Britannia.* For a fuller account of Camden and for bibliography see volume I of this work.

[65] On Manwood see the article by E. Maunde Thompson in *DNB,* VIII (1886), 277–85.

might have done so but for Camden's *Britannia*. Instead, Savile tried to rescue the manuscripts of medieval English chroniclers "from dirt and dust" (*e situ squalore et pulvere*). His collection of *Scriptores post Bedam* was twice printed, first in London (1598) and afterwards at Frankfort (1601).

The labors of this great trio of English historical scholars were continued by two others—Sir Henry Spelman (1562–1641), and John Selden (1584–1654). Spelman was an English country gentleman of culture, an original member, with Camden and Sir Robert Cotton, of the Society of Antiquaries and founded a readership in Anglo-Saxon at Oxford.[66] In 1628 Spelman published a *Glossary of Law Terms;* in 1640 *The Councils, Laws and Constitutions of the English Church*. His most important work, *The History and Fate of Sacrilege*, was not published until 1698. The reason is not far to seek. The book is a sustained legal and moral argument against the dissolution of the monasteries. The temper of English public opinion when Spelman was writing the book was too anti-royalist to venture upon its publication. The book was composed between 1612 and 1634; Spelman entrusted the MS. before he died to a friend, Reverend Jeremy Stephens, himself the author of an unpublished manuscript in similar vein entitled: *The Design of the Cormorants upon the Church of England, Defeated in the Time of King Henry V, Effected in the Time of King Henry VIII*. Even during the Restoration, in 1663, an effort to have it published failed, because some of the highest persons of England in that time would have regarded it "as an unpardonable reflection upon their families," whose wealth and social position went back to the spoliation of the monasteries.[67] For this reason the book was suppressed for years.

John Selden was a graduate of Oxford and got his first training in historical work when employed by Sir Robert Cotton to transcribe and abridge some parliamentary records in the Tower. He enjoyed a lucrative practice in the law. In association with Camden in 1623 he published Eadmer's *Historia nova*. Selden, however, was more a publicist than an historian. The *Mare Clausum* (1632) is an historical and legal argument to prove England's claim to the sovereignty of the seas. As a member of Parliament Selden helped to draw up the Petition of Right

[66] The novelty also of Arabic studies was introduced at this time. Edward Pocock (1604–91) may be said to have founded Oriental studies in England. He was a fellow at Corpus Christi College, Oxford, and in 1630 became chaplain of the English factory at Aleppo. Six years later he was made professor of Arabic in Oxford. He published *Specimen historiae Arabum* (1649), the *Annals of Eutychius* in Arabic and Latin (1656), and edited the *History of Abulfaragius* (1663).

[67] A reprint of *The History and Fate of Sacrilege*, with an introduction by C. F. S. Warren, was published in London in 1846. It is a book worth possessing, for Spelman's work is the first inquiry made into the Dissolution. Protestant journals of that time ignored it, but the book was reviewed at length in *DR*, XXI (1846), 246–58.

in 1628 and was a representative of Oxford in the Long Parliament and a member of the committee which impeached Archbishop Laud, who was executed in January, 1645. In the next year he became master of Trinity College, Oxford, and withdrew from political life, and so escaped committing himself on either Charles I's execution or Cromwell's government. He was, according to Jusserand, "one of the few Englishmen who attained European fame before the eighteenth century." [68] Like many other thoughtful men of the time, he became a Parliamentarian only after some delay. While he was serving the Commonwealth he had time to act as co-editor (with Twysden) in publishing *Historiae Anglicanae scriptores decem* (1652). This is a critical study of the early chroniclers. [69]

Sir Robert Cotton (1571–1631) is important in this place, not for what he wrote, but for what he did in the promotion of historical studies in England in the reign of James I and Charles I as a collector of documents and other manuscripts. A contemporary described him as "the able understander and lover of antiquity." [70] In his study Bacon found most of the materials for his own *History of the Reign of Henry VII*. Cotton was a sympathizer with the Parliament in its struggle against the crown and a friend of Pym and Eliot. In his *Life of King Henry III* (1628) Cotton's political views were so obvious that there were those who thought his description of Henry III's conflict with Parliament and the barons in the thirteenth century was a derisive parallel to the conditions under James I. His library was confiscated by the king in 1631.

Spelman's work was suppressed. But Dugdale's (1605–86) *Monasticon Anglicanum* [71] was greeted with acclaim. Through Spelman Dugdale was introduced to Thomas, earl of Arundel, himself an antiquary and collector, and earl marshal of England, who gave him a lodging in

---

[68] J. J. Jusserand, *A Literary History of the English People* (New York, 1895–1909), III, 511.

[69] The Selden Society was named in recognition of the pioneer work of this scholar. Two of his best-known works are the *Analecton Anglo-Britannicon* (1607), and the *Summary of History of the Inhabitants of England: Jani Anglorum facies altera* (1610), a translation of the laws and customs of the Britons and Normans. Another learned work of Selden is *Titles of Honour* (1614), which deals in detail with such subjects as knighthood, knight-service, nobility, arms, and all degrees of dignity from an emperor down to a country gentleman. His account of foreign practices is even fuller than the English. See the article on Selden by Sir Edward Fry in *DNB*, LI (1897), 212–24.

[70] Arthur Wilson, *The History of Great Britain, Being the Life and Reign of King James the First* (London, 1653), 155.

[71] *Monasticon Anglicanum: sive, Pandectae Coenobiorum, Benedictinorum, Cluniacensium, Cisterciensium, Carthusianorum a primordiis ad eorum usque dissolutionem*, ed. by R. Dodsworth and Sir W. Dugdale, London, 1655–77, 3 v.; new ed. by J. Caley, etc., six volumes in eight, London, 1817–30. In 1722–23 John Stevens, Gent., issued two additional volumes dealing with things "not spoken of by Sir William Dugdale." In 1693 an epitome of the *Monasticon* was made by James Wright, with everything Englished. The preface mentions Dugdale and Shakespeare as "both Williams," but puts Dugdale first! It is an odd Shakespearean item.

the Herald's Office, which enabled him to examine manuscripts both for the *Monasticon* and his next work, *The Baronage of England*. The second has been praised as "the most ancient and valuable record next to Domesday Book of the history and descent of the greater portion of the landed property of England." Between these two ponderous works Dugdale wrote *The Antiquities of Warwickshire* (1656), which was dedicated to Sir Christopher Hatton. Dugdale was knighted in 1677 and died in 1686. His *Life*, written by himself, up to 1678, with his diary and letters and an index to his MS. collections, was edited by William Hamper and published in 1827. Modern research has diminished the halo long attached to Dugdale. He was a collector who mechanically compiled his voluminous materials, who had no critical ability and often failed to detect forgeries, and he even stooped to plagiarism.[72]

Three English ecclesiastics remain. William Cave (1637–1713) devoted a long life to church history and compiled the *Scriptorum ecclesiasticorum historia litteraria*. It reached no farther than the opening of the fourteenth century and was continued by the *Anglia Sacra* of Henry Wharton (1664–94).[73]

It is not without interest to observe that, with the exception of Cotton and Selden, these antiquarian historians of England in the seventeenth century were royalist sympathizers. Perhaps their veneration of tradition in a time of rapid and violent transition made them so. The Puritans were indifferent to history, except what they themselves were making. They were not interested in the past, but intensely interested in the present. Most of their historical writers were really political pamphleteers and there were no antiquaries among them.

The sole Puritan imbued with the historical spirit was John Rushworth. He was assistant clerk of the House of Commons and afterwards secretary of Lord Fairfax. His *Historical Collections of Private Passages of State, Weighty Matters of Law, Remarkable Proceedings in Five Parliaments* (London, 1859) was undertaken, he says, because of his conviction of "the impossibility for any man in after-ages to ground a true History, by relying on printed pamphlets of our days, which passed the press while it was without control." The *Collections* begin with the year 1618 and conclude in 1649.

The Restoration in 1660 introduced a new though brief appreciation of the care of archives. In the reign of Charles II, Prynne, who had

[72] David Douglas, "William Dugdale: the 'Grand Plagiary,'" *History*, n.s., XX (1935–36), 193–210.

[73] *Anglia Sacra, sive collectio historiarum . . . de archiepiscopis et episcopis Angliae . . . ad a. 1540* (London, 1691, 2 v. folio). For contents see T. D. Hardy, *Descriptive Catalogue of Materials Relating to the History of Great Britain and Ireland* (London, 1862–71, 3 v. in 4: Rolls series, no. 26), I, ii, 691–94.

been appointed Keeper of the Records, tells us how he tried to rescue the documents "which had for many years lain bound together in a confused chaos, under corroding, putrefying cobwebs, dust, and filth, in the darkest corner of Caesar's Chapel in the White Tower." He employed, he says, many soldiers and women to remove and cleanse them from their filthiness, who, soon growing weary of this tedious work, left them almost as foul as they found them. Prynne found "many rare, ancient, precious pearls and golden records." [74]

To the deep-seated veneration for tradition and antiquities the student of English history owes possession of Rymer's *Foedera*—impressive title.[75] Thomas Rymer was the son of a Cavalier Yorkshire gentleman, was educated at Cambridge, and called to the bar in 1673. After writing a play and spending fifteen years in unavailing literary work in different fields, for which he is now chiefly remembered by Macaulay's description of him as "the worst critic that ever lived," he succeeded another

[74] Yet when less than a century afterwards, reference had to be made to certain documents of the age of Charles I, nothing at all was known of them until a venerable clerk was discovered who had a dim recollection that he had heard in his youth of the existence of some old books in the room near the gateway of Whitehall, and suggested a search, which after many adventures with decayed staircases, locksmiths, flocks of pigeons, and accumulations of filth, proved eventually to be successful. Three quarters of a century later, in 1836, a committee of the House of Commons was appointed to investigate the present state of the records of the United Kingdom and produced a Blue Book of 946 pages, in which it is stated in evidence that some of the public muniments were: "in a state of inseparable adhesion to the stone walls; there were numerous fragments which had only just escaped entire consumption by vermin, and many were in the last stage of putrefaction. Decay and damp had rendered a large quantity so fragile, as hardly to admit of being touched; others, particularly those in the form of rolls, were so coagulated together, that they could not be uncoiled. Six or seven perfect skeletons of rats . . . were found imbedded, and bones of these vermin were generally distributed throughout the mass." Report quoted [by J. S. Brewer] in an article, "New Sources of English History," *QR*, CXXX (1871), 377–78.

[75] *Foedera, conventiones, litterae, et cujuscunque generis acta publica inter reges Angliae et alios quosvis imperatores, reges, pontifices, principes, vel communitates* [1101–1654], ed. by Thomas Rymer (London, 1704–35, 20 v., of which XVI–XX were edited by Robert Sanderson). For subsequent editions see Charles Gross, *The Sources and Literature of English History, from the Earliest Times to about 1485* (2nd rev. ed., London and New York, 1915), pp. 467–78, nos. 2097–99. On Rymer consult the article by Sidney Lee in *DNB*, L (1897), 65–68; and Sir Thomas Duffus Hardy, *Syllabus (in English) of the Documents Relating to England and Other Kingdoms Contained in 'Rymer's Foedera'* (London, 1869–85, 3 v.), I, pt. i, introduction, pp. lii–lviii. This *Syllabus* gives in English a condensed notice of each instrument in the several editions of the *Foedera*, arranged in chronological order. The third volume contains a complete index of names and places, with a catalogue of the volumes of transcripts collected for the Record edition of the *Foedera*. In 1869 the Record Office printed, for private distribution, Appendices A to E "to a report on the *Foedera* intended to have been submitted by C. Purton Cooper to the Late Commissioners of Public Records," in 3 volumes octavo (including accounts of MSS. in foreign archives relating to Great Britain, with facsimiles). In the British Museum there is preserved a folio volume of reports and papers relating to the Record edition (Add. MS. 24,699). Rymer left extensive materials for a new edition of the *Foedera*, bound in 59 volumes folio (!) and embracing the period from 1115 to 1698. This was the collection offered to the Earl of Oxford. It was purchased by the Treasury for £215 and is now in the British Museum (Add. MSS., nos. 4573 to 4630, and 18,911). A catalogue and index may be consulted in the XVIIth volume of Tonson's edition of the *Foedera*. The Public Record Office possesses a manuscript volume, compiled by Robert Lemon about 1800, containing instruments in the Patent Rolls omitted by Rymer. In the same place may be seen a volume of reports, orders, etc., on the *Foedera*, 1808–11.

bad poet, Shadwell, as historiographer-royal in 1672, Tate, the perverter of the Psalms, being made Poet Laureate on the same day. Rymer was commissioned to edit the national records, and from the publication of the first volume obloquy and poverty pursued him. He made an unfortunate error in the beginning by printing a spurious homage of Malcolm III to Edward the Confessor, to the wrath of the whole Scottish nation. Rymer transcribed and printed at his own cost and could not get his expenses reimbursed by the Treasury. No legal provision had been made for publication. The first hundred pounds paid were derived from the forfeiture of a Catholic priest. In 1697 he spent £210 and received from the Lords of the Treasury "£200 in lottery tickets of which I made £160." Up to August 1698 he had expended £1253 and had received only £500. Even when Queen Anne took his case up, the Treasury reduced his just claim of £600 to £200. To the day of his death he never received compensation for his labors as editor.

The historical erudition of England in the seventeenth century, both in quantity of production and critical nature, when compared with that of France in the same season, must be declared to be deficient. The restless and finally violent nature of the politics of the age undoubtedly was partly responsible for this defect. But the reason lies deeper than that. The break with Rome, the dissolution of the monasteries, the decay of higher education in the universities of Oxford and Cambridge, which lasted until the nineteenth century (Oxford Reform Act, 1854), these were the conditions which impaired historical studies in England. Too many English scholars labored in a controversial frame of mind in order to settle controversies. "The cause of their work and of its peculiar quality was a desire for a real and permanent solution of questions which the preceding age, that age of turmoil and ferment, of civil and religious struggle, had raised, but had not answered." [76] Selden, with a broader mind, made a genuine appeal to the past, and was more historically minded than all of them. A passage in the dedication of his *History of Tythes* shows the attitude of his mind:

The neglect or only vulgar regard of the fruitful and precious part of it [antiquity], which gives necessary light to the present in matter of state, law, history and the understanding of good authors, is but preferring that kind of ignorance which our short life alone allows us before the many ages of former experience and observation, which may so accumulate years to us as if we had lived even from the beginning of time.

One important work of Irish scholarship done at home and not abroad, as so much historical work done by Irish scholars in the seventeenth century was, deserves to be noticed. This is *The Annals of the Kingdom*

[76] Jameson (see n. 12 above), 28.

of Ireland by the Four Masters, compiled between 1632 and 1636 in a
lonely hut in the ruined Franciscan monastery at Donegal by Michael
O'Clery, Michael Conary, Cucogry O'Clery, and Ferfeasa O'Mulconry.[77]
An Irish scholar of another sort was Sir James Ware (1594–1666), an
antiquarian who published his *De scriptoribus Hiberniae* in 1639. He
was a friend of Selden and Cotton.

The Revolution in 1688 in England was something besides a political
change of vast significance and importance. It was a change in intellectual atmosphere as well. The Commonwealth period had been unkind
to scholarship. Even Milton ceased to be a scholar or a humanist then.
The Restoration, too, was indifferent to the advancement of scholarship. What little learning was manifested was mostly in natural science
(Boyle). But the fifty years—in the rough—which followed 1688 were
notable for a small number of historical students who enlightened the
knowledge if they did not enrich the imagination in tracking the past
of their country. England had antiquarians and scholars of historical
erudition, if she had not monks as France had.[78]

Passing only with mention the staunch Jacobite Thomas Carte (1686–
1754), author of a *Life of James Duke of Ormonde* (1736),[79] and John
Strype (1643–1737), compiler of *Annals of the Reformation in England*
(1709–31), and George Hickes (1642–1715) who must be regarded, together with Humphrey Wanley, as the founder of Anglo-Saxon philology
and history, we come to Thomas Hearne (1678–1735) who requires
larger notice, as the indefatigable editor of other scholars' works. Hearne
was graduated from Oxford in 1699 and immediately made assistant
keeper of the Bodleian, for already in his college days he had established
a reputation for his love and knowledge of books. In 1712 he was promoted to second-keeper, with the stipulation made by himself that he
should also be janitor so as to be able to obtain access to the library
at any time. He resigned in 1716 because unwilling to take the oaths
to the government. Like Carte, Hearne was a Jacobite. He spent the
rest of his life in preparing the works of old English scholars for the
press. He was a bibliographer and not an historian, but he deserves to

[77] *Annala Rioghachta Eireann: Annals of the Kingdom of Ireland by the Four Masters, from the
Earliest Period to the Year 1616,* Irish text with translation, ed. by John O'Donovan (Dublin,
1848–51, 7 v.). P. W. Joyce, *A Short History of Ireland from the Earliest Times to 1608* (London
and New York, 1893), 31, called O'Donovan's edition "the greatest and most important work
on Ireland ever issued by an Irish publisher." See also Eugene O'Curry, *Lectures on Manuscript Materials of Ancient Irish History* (Dublin, 1873), 140–61.

[78] See H. B. Walters, *The English Antiquaries of the Sixteenth, Seventeenth, and Eighteenth
Centuries* (London, 1934); and David C. Douglas, *English Scholars* (London, 1939), reviewed
in *LTLS,* 1939, p. 654. Robert Hunter wrote a *History of Great Britain* (1771–85, 5 v.), in
which the fourth chapter of each volume "comprehends the history of learning, of learned men
and of the seminaries of learning" in the period under discussion.

[79] On Carte see the article by E. S. Shuckburgh in *DNB,* IX (1887), 191–94; and *QR,* LXXIII
(1844), 546–49. There is much about him in Swift's *Letters.*

be remembered for so facilitating the studies of others. Gibbon, to whom Hearne's Jacobite sentiments were repugnant, after enumerating Parker, Savile, Camden, Spelman, Twysden, and Selden, wrote of him:

The last who has dug deep into the mine [of scholarly history] was Thomas Hearne. . . . His minute and obscure diligence, his voracious and undistinguishing appetite, and the coarse vulgarity of his style and taste, have exposed him to the ridicule of idle wits [this is in allusion to Pope's *Dunciad*]. Yet it cannot be denied that Thomas Hearne had gathered many gleanings of the harvest; and if his own prefaces are filled with crude and extraneous matter, his editions will be always recommended by their accuracy and use.

Six months after Hearne's death his fellow antiquary, Thomas Tanner (1674–1735), bishop of St. Asaph, died. Like many of his sort Tanner could collect but not interpret facts. When only twenty-one years of age he published the *Notitia Monastica*, which was again issued in a much enlarged edition in 1744 after his decease.[80] His enduring fame, however, rests upon the *Bibliotheca Britannico-Hibernica*, "a dictionary of writers containing much valuable historical material and in large part superseding the older work of Leland, Bale, Pits, Ware, Cave, and Nicholson." [81]

English medieval history has few more striking examples of scholarly accretion than that afforded by David Wilkins' (1685–1745) *Concilia Magna Britanniae et Hiberniae, 446–1717* (4 v., London, 1737). The first two volumes of this work had been compiled by Spelman a century before and left unfinished. They covered the medieval period when the deliberations of the councils were recorded in Latin. Wilkins continued this record in two additional volumes. The chief portion is in English, and in the precise orthography of the original records. Until superseded by Haddan and Stubbs (Oxford, 1869–78), the *Concilia* was among the most difficult works to procure.[82]

It has previously been observed that the period of the Commonwealth was indifferent to historical studies, and that except for Rushworth's *Collections*, what little was done was accomplished by scholars of royalist persuasion. The Restoration naturally was not eager to enhance the Cromwellian epoch, and the Age of Queen Anne was negligent of it. Amendment of this negligence was made in 1742 by Thomas Birch (1705–66) who published *Thurloe's State Papers*, in seven volumes, in that year. Thurloe had been Cromwell's secretary to the council of state, and in that capacity the Commonwealth's foreign secretary. His sources

---

[80] *Notitia Monastica: or, An Account of All the Abbies, Priories, and Houses of Friers Formerly England and Wales and also of All the Colleges and Hospitals Founded before A.D. 1560* (London, 1744); reprinted by J. Nasmith (Cambridge, 1787).

[81] Edited by David Wilkins, published at London in 1748. Cp. Gross (n. 75), no. 52; Hardy (n. 73), I, pt. i, pp. xxxvi–xlii; and William T. Davies' account of Tanner in *LTLS*, 1935, p. 856.

[82] On Wilkins see E. F Jacob, *Transactions of the Royal Historical Society*, 4th series, XV (1932), 91–131; and Hardy (n. 73), I, pt. ii, 754–62.

of information for events at home and abroad were so full and so accurate that through him it was said that "Cromwell carried the secrets of all the princes of Europe at his girdle." At the Restoration the Thurloe Papers were hidden until Birch gave them to the world.[83]

The greatest historical scholars of England in the Age of Erudition have been passed in review. But from Selden to Wilkins no one of them was the equal of Thomas Madox (1666–1727), the depth of whose researches and the quality of whose scholarship adorned the Age of Queen Anne. Madox' *The History and Antiquities of the Exchequer*, though published as long ago as 1711 (2nd ed., 1769) and partly super-seded by later works, has never been supplanted, and is still "the best authority on the subject." Madox, who was clerk of the lord treasurer's remembrance office, was the first British historian to delve into the pipe rolls and other public records. Before he wrote—and he was author of other works—the administrative history of England was a totally neglected subject. The "Prefatory Epistle," as Madox modestly called it, to this work, in addition to being a comprehensive survey of sources is even more remarkable as a dissertation on the nature and methods of historical criticism. It is regrettable that it is not better known. The whole deserves to be attentively read by every student of history.[84] A noble sentence in it is this: "In truth the writing of history is in some sort a religious act."

It is difficult in this day and generation, when there is an Oxford School of History and a Cambridge School of History of eminence, to understand the desolate condition of historical studies in England in the eighteenth century. Few of the real historical scholars of that age were at home in academic circles. Frederick William Maitland's account of the teaching of history at Oxford and Cambridge in the eighteenth century shows to what humiliating and grotesque depths it had fallen.

In 1724 George I founded for each university a professorship of modern history and modern languages. Cambridge welcomed the endowment in the hope that the professor of this chair would instruct his pupils sufficiently to enable them to supplant foreigners as tutors of noble youths going on the Grand Tour. At Oxford the conditions were even more backward.[85] Adam Smith was dismissed from Oxford—he was a Balliol man—without a degree in 1741 because he was surprised by the college authorities when reading Hume's new *Treatise of Human*

[83] See Sir Charles Harding Firth's account of Thurloe in *DNB*, LVI (1898), 341–44.

[84] The only account of Madox is that by Thompson Cooper in *DNB*, XXXV (1893), 305. After he was dead his widow gave ninety-four volumes of transcripts of documents which Madox had made to the British Museum, and they were added to the Sloane Collection.

[85] See Christopher Wordsworth, *Scholae Academicae. Studies at the English Universities in the Eighteenth Century* (Cambridge, 1877), 148–50.

Nature. The separation was a boon to Smith, for he could hear ampler thought in Glasgow University, then at its height, than he could hope to find in Oxford, then at the lowest point of its history. To go to five hundred eager-minded students at Glasgow and abandon a hundred odd drones and cads in Balliol was no loss.

The deficiency of historical spirit and indifference to archival research in England greatly disquieted Gibbon.[86] In his noble essay on history, entitled *An Address, &c.*, he deplored this intellectual inertness, and vainly tried to awaken British historical scholarship to a sense of its duty and its opportunity.

It is long, very long indeed [he wrote] since the success of our neighbours, and the knowledge of our resources, have disposed me to wish, that our Latin memorials of the Middle Age, the *Scriptores Rerum Anglicarum*, might be published in England, in a manner worthy of the subject and of the country. At a time when the Decline and Fall of the Roman Empire has intimately connected me with the first historians of France, I acknowledged (in a note) the value of the Benedictine Collection, and expressed my hope that such a national work would provoke our own emulation. My hope has failed, the provocation was not felt, the emulation was not kindled; and I have now seen, without an attempt or a design, near thirteen years, which might have sufficed for the execution. During the greatest part of that time I have been absent from England: yet I have sometimes found opportunities of introducing this favourite topic in conversation with our literary men, and our eminent booksellers. As long as I expatiated on the merits of an undertaking, so beneficial to history, and so honourable to the nation, I was heard with attention; a general wish seemed to prevail for its success: but no sooner did we seriously consult about the best means of promoting that success, and of reducing a pleasing theory into a real action, than we were stopped, at the first step, by an insuperable difficulty—the choice of an editor. . . . We knew not where to seek our English Muratori. . . .[87]

Gibbon's choice for editor of the contemplated collection was John Pinkerton. But the great plan came to naught, and was not realized until the series of *Chronicles and Memorials of Great Britain and Ireland during the Middle Ages* was instituted in 1858 under direction of the Master of the Rolls.[88]

We now return to the Continent.

Though today far behind every other country in western Europe in scientific bibliographical work, Spain three hundred years ago was in the

[86] In his Journal he wrote: "We live not in that age of industry when studies were valued in proportion to their extent and difficulty. Our men of letters are afraid to encounter two volumes in folio. . . . Latin is no longer the language even of learning." *Miscellaneous Works of Edward Gibbon, Esquire, with Memoirs of His Life and Writings, Composed by Himself*, ed. by John Lord Sheffield (London, 1796, 2 v.), II, 245–46.

[87] *Ibid.*, II, 713–14, the whole *Address*, 707–17.

[88] Perhaps David Dalrymple should divide honors with Gibbon in this endeavor to awaken interest in the British archives. The introduction to his *Memorials and Letters Relating to the History of Britain in the Reign of James II* (Glasgow, 1766) contributed something to English interest in the public archives.

forefront of this field. In 1597 Castillo de Bobadilla, a learned lawyer, published the two volumes of his *Politica para corregidores y señores de vassalos*, which is a mine of information on local administration in Spain in the reign of Philip II. It was reprinted in 1608, 1750, 1759, and again in 1775. The *Bibliotheca Hispana Vetus* and the *Bibliotheca Hispana Nova* of Nicolas Antonio (1617–84) have been declared to be "incomparably superior to any previous historical bibliography," and "still unsuperseded and indispensable." The former work is a literary history of Spain from Roman times to 1500. The latter deals with the works of Spanish writers from 1500 to 1684.[89] Among collections of sources we owe to three Jesuit scholars in the Spanish Netherlands the compilation of four folio volumes containing the works of famous Spanish historians of the Middle Ages and the sixteenth century: *Hispaniae illustratae, seu rerum urbiumque Hispaniae, Lusitaniae, Aethiopiae, et Indiae scriptores varii* (Frankfort, 1603–08). The first two volumes were edited by the learned Jesuit Andreas Schottus (1552–1629); the fourth by his brother Franciscus, and the third by Johann Pistorius. In the middle of the eighteenth century (1747) the first volume of a series which eventually extended to fifty-one volumes in 1879 appeared. This was *España Sagrada*, the Spanish counterpart of the French *Gallia Christiana*, and a mine of ecclesiastical information. All the minor monastic chronicles of Spain are found in it. The series was begun by Enrique Florez, an Augustinian, and continued by other scholars in the Order until the middle of the nineteenth century, when the Real Academia de la Historia took it up and completed its publication.[90]

In Germany, where the Thirty Years' War terminated in 1648, scholarship of every sort was impossible, if for nothing else than the destruction of so many of its libraries. In Catholic Germany, which had not been so wasted as the Protestant states, the Jesuits held sway, and they were more interested in theology than in historical studies like their Bollandist brethren in Belgium. Moreover, the Jesuits in Germany, unlike those in the Netherlands and in France, were deeply engaged in politics and ruled the courts at Vienna and Dresden. There were two Protestant historical scholars of eminence in Germany in the seventeenth century, and one Catholic. The Protestants were Herman Conring [91] and the great Leibniz. Conring (1606–81) founded the study of German law on an historical basis in his *De origine juris Germanici* (1643);

[89] Each was published in revised edition in two volumes, in Madrid, 1788.

[90] A table of contents for vols. I–XLVII is found in *El Bibliógrafo Español y Estranjero*, III (1859), 106–12, 115–17. For much additional information on Spanish historical sources see R. B. Merriman, *The Rise of the Spanish Empire* (New York, 1918–34, 4 v.), I, 42–50.

[91] Otto Stobbe, *Herman Conring, der Begründer der deutschen Rechtsgeschichte. Rede beim Abtritt des Rectorats der Universität Breslau* (Berlin, 1870). On the lack of a biography of Conring, cp. WOLF, 189, n. 1.

in the *De finibus Imperii Germanici* (1654) he discussed the relation of the Holy Roman Empire to the states comprehended within it. His most distinguished achievement, however, was in 1672 when he disproved the genuineness of the Charter of Lindau, one of the best pieces of historical criticism before Mabillon.[92]

Conring was a scholar of wide and varied interests. His services in the subjects of medicine, natural science, theology, philology, history, and law are still mentioned with respect. But above all his work opened new paths for jurisprudence and political science. He was the first, according to Roscher, who formed an adequate idea of political economy, or statistics, and of public administration. In teaching German public law he introduced a new method, based on history, and thus anticipated Savigny by a century and a half. His greatest achievement is the delineation of the development of German law down to the sixteenth century. His *De origine juris Germanici* first introduced the intelligent and systematic treatment of the Common Law of the country, which had been thrown into the background by the Civil Law, and defined the manner and extent of the reception of Roman jurisprudence. Conring's character, however, was not equal to his talents. "He belonged to that dangerous class of lawyers who in political questions are swayed not by their conviction of right, but by their party relations, and judge not by the standard of legality but by that of expediency." Even considerations of his own personal advantage, the hope of favor and reward from the powerful, often determined his advice and his whole political action. After he became a pensioner of the French court he repeatedly offered to write in favor of conferring the imperial crown on Louis XIV, and his legal advice supported the drastic policy initiated by the Chambers of Reunion.

Catholic German historical scholarship had one eminent contributor. This was the Benedictine historian Bernard Pez (1683–1735), an Austrian. He travelled widely, like his French contemporaries, in Austria, Bavaria, Belgium, and France, where he met Mabillon and Montfaucon. He was the author of many works, the greatest of which is his *Thesaurus anecdotorum novissimus* (Vienna, 1721–29, 7 v.). His less famous brother was Jerome Pez (1685–1762), a secular, who spent his long life as an archivist. He edited *Scriptores rerum Austriacarum veteres ac genuini* (Leipzig, 1721–25, 2 v.), and *Historia S. Leopoldi, Austriae marchionis* (Vienna, 1747).[93]

[92] G. Meyer von Knonau, "Das bellum diplomaticum Lindaviense," *HZ*, XXVI (1871), 75–130; Arthur Giry, *Manuel de diplomatique* (Paris, 1894), 60, n. 1; Harry Bresslau, *Handbuch der Urkundenlehre für Deutschland und Italien* (2nd ed., Leipzig, 1912–15, 2 v.), I, 20–22; BERNHEIM, 222.

[93] See *La Grande Encyclopédie*, XXVI, 564, with bibliography.

It is astonishing, however, to find an historical scholar in Hungary imbued with the spirit of erudition. This was Stephen Katona (1732–1811), the Hungarian Pertz. He was educated by the Jesuits and was a professor in the University of Tyrnau. When the Emperor Joseph II required the use of German in all teaching he resigned and became librarian of the archbishopric of Kalocsa. In later life he was abbot of Bodrog. He founded and edited the *Historia critica regum Hungariae* (884–1810), the publication of which took forty years (1778–1817). The whole set comprises forty-three volumes.[94]

Serious study of Danish history dates from the end of the seventeenth century. Then Clausen translated into Danish the work of Snorre Sturlason; Angrim Johnson went to Iceland to collect manuscripts; Ole Worm studied the ancient Danish monuments and laid the foundations of northern archaeology; Thomas Bartholin wrote a great work on Norse antiquities;[95] and the Sagas for the first time were subjected to critical study by Torfesen.[96] It was a customary practice of Torfesen to go to the palace to translate old Icelandic documents to King Frederick III, and King Christian IV followed the same course. In the eighteenth century Arne Magnussen, who had aided Bartholin, spent ten years in Iceland searching for documents, even among the peasantry, besides collecting antiquities and remains of all sorts. He and his collections were brought to Copenhagen in a Danish warship. But alas for all his endeavors. In 1728 a fearful fire in Copenhagen destroyed almost everything he had brought. What survived was given to the university.

Yet all was not lost. The spirit of scholarship survived. Denmark, too, was ready to enter into the Age of Erudition. Jacob Langebek (1710–75) was a poor theological student who learned Icelandic in order to have a broader foundation for the historical researches which he was resolved to make. He was twenty years of age when a place was made for him in the royal library. What Dom Bouquet and his colleagues and successors did for the historiography of medieval France, that single-handed Langebek did for medieval Danish history, in his *Scriptores rerum Danicarum medii aevi*. This collection includes all the annals and chronicles, all the charters and diplomata which Langebek could find pertaining to the history of Denmark from the eleventh century forward to the sixteenth century. In 1770 the first volume was completed, but Langebek could not afford to have it printed. A rich marriage provided the necessary means. Volumes I–II were published in

---

[94] Divided as follows: *Historia critica Hungariae ducum, 884–1000* (1778, 1 v.); *Historia critica regum Hungariae stirpis Arpadianae* (1779–82, 7 v.); *Historia . . . stirpis mixtae* (1788–93, 12 v.); *Historia . . . stirpis Austriacae* (1794–1817, 23 v.).

[95] *Antiquitatum danicarum*, etc. (Copenhagen, 1689).

[96] *Series dynastarum et regum Daniae* (1702); *Historia rerum norvegicarum* (1711, 4 v.).

1772–74. The fourth was almost finished when Langebek died. Peter Frederik Suhm,[97] a good scholar and a devoted friend, prepared and saw through the press volumes IV–VII, between 1776 and 1792. The eighth and ninth volumes did not see the light until 1834. Gibbon was right when he said that "little Denmark, whose scanty revenues might have apologized for neglect of historical studies, shamed English historical scholarship."

Italian historical scholarship had almost expired by the beginning of the seventeenth century. Scaliger expressed his contempt for it. The intellectual glory of Italy was science, of which Galileo was the genius. Only two scholars in Italy redeemed history, and one of these was an expatriated Irishman. The first was Ferdinando Ughelli (1595–1670), a Cistercian monk of Florence, whose *Italia Sacra* is a collection of documents classified according to bishoprics.[98] Luke Wadding (1588–1657) was an Irish Franciscan who lived most of his life in Rome. His *Annales Minorum seu trium ordinum a S. Francisco institutorum* (1208–1540) is the *magnum opus* of Franciscan historical scholarship in the Age of Erudition.[99] Wadding was an Irishman, born at Waterford in 1588, who was taken to Spain soon after the year of the Armada and received his education in the Irish College at Lisbon. He became a Cordelier in 1604. His early reputation for learning won him a professorship of theology in Salamanca. He accompanied Diego de Torres, bishop of Cartagena, himself a Cordelier, to Rome in the reign of Philip III, resided in Rome for the rest of his life as principal of the Irish College of St. Isidore, and died in 1657. In 1650 he caused to be reprinted the *Syllabus Fratrum Minorum*, a list of English Franciscans who had been put to death during the Tudor period, a pamphlet which had become very rare because most of the original impression had been sent to England and had been seized and destroyed by Queen Elizabeth.[100]

One may conveniently carry Italian scholarship over into the eighteenth century and dispose of the subject here, for there is little to be said though that little is important. The shadow of Baronius' incapacity lay heavily upon the land. The intellectual history of Italy in the Age

[97] Suhm was a very rich man, novelist, poet, critic, historian, book collector, patron of music and the arts, who left his library of over one hundred thousand works to the Danish Government.

[98] *Italia sacra sive de episcopis Italiae et insularum adiacentium, rebusque ab iis praeclare gestis*, etc. (Rome, 1644–62, 9 v. folio; 2nd ed. much enlarged *cura et studio Nicolai Coleti*, Venice, 1717–22, 10 v. folio). Fedele Savio's *Gli antichi vescovi d'Italia dalle origini al 1300 descritti per regioni: il Piemonte* (Turin, 1898) is the first part of a new edition of Ughelli.

[99] First published at Lyons, 1625–54, 8 v.; 2nd ed. with a syllabus, Rome, 1731–41, 16 v.; vols. XVII–XIX by J. de Luca, Rome, 1740 ff.; vol. XX by Micalesi, Rome, 1794; vols. XXI–XXVI by the Franciscans of Quaracchi, 1886 ff.

[100] See Gregory Cleary, *Father Luke Wadding and St. Isidore's College, Rome: Biographical and Historical Notes and Documents* (Rome, 1925).

of Erudition was a commixture of obscurantism, religious bigotry, dilettantism, and antiquarianism.[101] All Italy had only one historical scholar.

Ludovico Antonio Muratori (1672–1751) [102] was born near Modena and except for a few years spent all his life there. His interest was awakened in Roman antiquities by reading the works of Justus Lipsius and he was encouraged in the study by Bacchini, librarian to the Duke of Modena, and by Leibniz.[103] Though ordained as a priest he never went further in holy orders. For five years he was librarian of the famous Ambrosian Library in Milan—and thus a predecessor of Pope Pius XI in that capacity—but in 1700, when Bacchini died, he was recalled to Modena by the duke, whose pride had been hurt by Leibniz' strictures on the neglected condition of the archives. Here Muratori remained for the rest of his life.[104] His total output in their original editions amounted to forty-six volumes in folio and thirty-four in quarto. Muratori devoted fifteen years to the editing of the *Scriptores*. It is his greatest work.[105] It is a collection of the works of historians of Italy from the sixth to the fifteenth century, each work prefaced by a critical introduction and embellished with notes. This was supplemented by the *Antiquitates*, a collection of a vast number of documents relative to the political, institutional, military, economic, and social history of

[101] For an amazingly full survey which includes much information not worth knowing see Giulio Natali, *Il settecento* (Milan, 1929, 2 v.).

[102] There is as yet no exhaustive study on Muratori's life and work. The biography by his nephew, Gian Francesco Soli Muratori, *Vita del celebre Ludov. Ant. Muratori* (Venice, 1756) is largely a eulogy. His *Letters* with a *Life* prefixed, were published by Lazzari (Venice, 1783, 2 v.); and then more completely by M. Campori, ed., *Epistolario di L. A. Muratori* (Modena, 1901–22, 14 v.). See the chapter on Muratori in J. G. Robertson, *Studies in the Genesis of Romantic Theory in the Eighteenth Century* (Cambridge, 1923), ch. iii, pp. 60–95; the essay in GUILDAY, 212–39, with bibliography; FUETER, 395–97; J. P. Kirsch, "Muratori," *Catholic Encyclopaedia*, X, 641–42; Giulio Bertoni, in *Enciclopedia Italiana*, XXIV (1934), 50–52, with bibliography; Lacy Collison-Morley, *Modern Italian Literature* (London, 1911), 49–52; T. A. Trollope, "Muratori," *BQR*, LXXVII (1883), 368–400; G. Carducci, "*Rerum Italicarum scriptores* di L. A. Muratori," *La Nuova Antologia*, LXXXVII (1900), 3–19; and the *Life* written by Reina as preface to his edition of Muratori's *Annali d'Italia* in the *Scrittori Classici Italiani* (Milan, 1818).

[103] C. Cipolla, *Leibniz e Muratori* (Milan, 1893); A. W. Ward in *EHR*, VIII (1893), 788–91, review of *Corrispondenza tra L. A. Muratori e G. G. Leibniz*, ed. by Matteo Campori (Modena, 1892).

[104] Muratori's Latin and Italian works were published at Arezzo, 1767–80, in thirty-six volumes. They total altogether more than sixty-four titles, of which the most important are: *Anecdota ex Ambrosianae Bibliothecae Codicibus* (Milan, 1697, 1698; Padua, 1713, 2 v.); *Anecdota Graeca* (Padua, 1709, 3 v.); *Antichita Estensi* (Modena, 1717, 2 v. folio); *Antiquitates Italicae medii aevi* (Milan, 1738–42, 6 v. folio); *Annali d'Italia* (dated at Milan, but printed at Venice, 1744–49, 12 v.); and *Novus Thesaurus veterum inscriptionum* (Milan, 1739–42, 6 v.).

[105] *Rerum Italicarum scriptores ab anno aerae christianae 500 ad 1500* (Milan, 1723–51, 25 v. in 28), the first great attempt to gather into one collection all the medieval sources of one country. Chronological indices by J. Calligaris and others (Turin, 1885). A splendid new edition of the *Scriptores* was begun by G. Carducci and V. Fiorini (Città di Castello, 1900 ff.), and is being continued by the Istituto storico italiano. See the account in *ASI*, LXXXV (1927), 116–21, and reports of progress in the *Archivio Muratoriano* (Città di Castello, 1904 ff.).

medieval Italy, accompanied by many dissertations. In the preface
Muratori says:

I have treated first of the kings, dukes, marquises, counts, and other magistrates of the
Italian kingdom; after which I have investigated the various forms of the political government, and also the manners of the private citizens; the freedom and franchises of
some classes and the servitude of others; the laws, the judicial forms, the military system; the arts, sciences, and education; the progress of trade and industry; and other
matters of social and civil history.[106]

Gibbon described these volumes as "curious dissertations on the manners, government, religion, etc., of the Italians of the darker ages, with
a large supplement of charters, chronicles, etc." Later Muratori translated these essays into the Italian language. They are the basis of his
national reputation. The third volume of the *Antiquities* contains the
famous "Muratorian Fragment," one of the oldest sources of the early
history of the Church. From manuscripts Muratori passed to inscriptions in the *Novus thesaurus veterum inscriptionum*, the fourth volume
of which contains monuments of Christian epigraphy. In the last five
years of his life (1744–49) Muratori devoted himself to the composition
of the *Annali d'Italia* which appeared after his decease in eighteen
octavo volumes. Gibbon described this work as "a dry though accurate and useful abridgment of the history of Italy from the birth of
Christ to the middle of the eighteenth century." Muratori himself he
called "my guide and master in the history of Italy." [107]

Of all the historical scholars in France under the ancien régime, the
Benedictines of St. Germain, as a group, remained most loyal to the
great tradition of scholarship. Until the eighteenth century opened,
ecclesiastical scholarship had devoted itself almost wholly to the editing
and publication of documentary materials, and narrative history, as
annals and chronicles had been comparatively omitted. The labors initiated by Duchesne had not been followed up. Colbert not only took
an interest in the labors of these savant historians, but he sustained

---

[106] A new edition of the *Antiquitates* was published 1770–80, in 17 v.; chronological indices
by J. M. Battaglino and Joseph Calligaris (Turin, 1889–92).

[107] GIBBON, VII, 300 note, at the end of ch. lxx. Some years ago the heirs of Muratori,
who were living in Modena in extreme poverty, announced their intention to offer for sale
the valuable "Muratori archives" in the possession of the family. These consist of the manuscripts and prodigious collections used by that scholar in the preparation of his great work.
The Municipal Council of Modena, the Directors of the Biblioteca Estense, and a Deputazione
di Storia Patria thereupon applied to the Italian Government for aid to purchase the entire
collection, pointing out the danger of any dispersal of its contents and the loss to Italy by the
sale of the whole or any fragments of it to foreign libraries or collectors. Thanks to the instant
energy of the Italian Minister of Education any such catastrophe was averted. A grant of
45,000 lire was made to the city of Modena for the purchase of the archives, on condition that
they were placed in the Biblioteca Estense and made accessible to scholars. The city is to
repay the State in ten yearly instalments.

them with money.[108] In 1676 he convened the greatest scholars of the time to confer upon the completion of the project which André Duchesne had cherished.[109] But no progress was made and his death brought the scheme to a halt. Later on Le Tellier, the archbishop of Rheims, revived the plan and approached Mabillon. But Mabillon considered that the history of his own order had prior claim. Some time afterward, Chancellor D'Aguesseau, a lover of learning, enlisted the service of Père le Long, author of the *Bibliothèque de France*, in the undertaking, but his death soon interrupted the work. Then, upon the recommendation of Dom Denis de Sainte Marthe, superior of the Congregation of St. Maur, Dom Bouquet was assigned to the task.

In this wise the most widely circulated and the most familiar volumes of history which ever emanated from the precincts of St. Germain were begun. These were the *Rerum Gallicarum et Francicarum Scriptores*, or *Recueil des historiens des Gaules et de la France*, to 1328. Dom Bouquet himself edited the first eight volumes in the years from 1738 to 1752. Doms Haudigier, Poirier, Housseau, and Precieux produced volumes IX–XI; Doms Clement and Brial volumes XII and XIII between 1781 and 1786. The fourteenth volume was almost completed when the French Revolution broke out. Brial was expelled from his monastery, but was able to save his materials, and although in the popular fury against all clergy he was compelled to put off his frock, yet he quietly worked along during the storm. Finally, when the madness of the Terror was past, in 1796, under the Directory, the Institut de France resolved to resume the great work and the heroic Brial was called from his solitude to supervise the continuation of the *Recueil*.

"The last depository of the traditions of his order," this devoted and heroic scholar in 1805 was the connecting link between the ancien régime and the Napoleonic era. So highly was he regarded that when he became too old and infirm to attend the sittings of the Institute the unprecedented resolution was passed that he should always be considered as present at every séance. He died at the age of ninety-five in 1828, having alone and single-handed completed volumes XIV–XVIII (1806–22) and begun work on volume XIX, which was finished by Naudet and Daunou in 1833.[110]

---

[108] Cp. the tribute of Du Cange to Colbert in the preface of his *Historia byzantina* (Paris, 1680): "Opus numismatibus cum Regio ex Archeio, tum ex tuo praesertim expromptis adornavimus."

[109] Dom Martin Bouquet, ed., *Recueil des historiens des Gaules et de la France*, I, preface, pp. i–ii.

[110] A new impression of vols. I–XIX was supervised by Léopold Delisle (Paris, 1868–80); vols. XX–XXIII were published in 1893–94, with an index in the last; and vol. XXIV appeared in 1904. The contents of the first twenty-two volumes are analyzed in Franklin (n. 44), 82–94.

The *Recueil des historiens des Gaules et de la France* is the last monument of the Age of Erudition. It is almost unnecessary to add that careful collation of manuscripts was a constant practice in the preparation of these huge folios. Every volume abounds with examples of minute erudition—dissertations explanatory of institutions, laws, history, genealogy, etc., chronological abstracts, glossaries of technical words, historical and geographical indices, and synoptic tables connecting the statements of the different sources into one tabular narrative. Nevertheless, the *Recueil* has certain defects of method. Other great historical compilers before and after Dom Bouquet—such as Pithou, the Duchesnes, Bongars, Struvius, Leibniz, Muratori, and Langebek—all other compilers, in fact, had adopted the simple and natural plan of publishing the texts intact, as they were found, and assigning each author a place as nearly as possible in chronological order, according either to the century when he lived, or the period to which his work pertained. In this way the progress and continuity of historical writing were preserved. In spite of the fact that a great many medieval chronicles extend over centuries, in spite of the fact that they are often repetitious and prolix, this system was right and simple. Instead of adopting this method, Dom Bouquet and his successors followed the plan of combining all the sources of a given period within a single volume, dividing the narrations into sections cut according to periods. This practice has proved confusing to every scholar who has used the *Recueil*. Worse still, much matter was expunged. All material regarded as fabulous, irrelevant, or repetitious, or which had been related elsewhere was cast out—sometimes a whole book of some chronicle, sometimes a chapter, sometimes a line, sometimes a word—and the texts, after such castigation, cut up into larger or smaller divisions and arranged chronologically, with the result that the student frequently has to hunt through several successive volumes in pursuing a subject. The documents are thus deprived of their integrity, and a false idea of their nature conveyed. The matter for the reigns of Philip I, Louis VI, and Louis VII, which constitute a single period, is distributed through five huge folio volumes, XII, XIII, XIV, XV, and XVI. Volume XII contains excerpts from 124 different writers; XIII from 64; XIV from 180. Every writer of the period has suffered mutilation except Suger, the biographer of Louis VI, and one wonders how he escaped the general practice of anatomy of authors.[111]

[111] In the preface to the first volume (pp. viii–ix) Dom Bouquet explained the method. "Nous *coupons* nos Chroniques. . . . *On ne cherche dans les Chroniques que les faits;* et le plus souvent ces faits n'ont aucune connexion les uns avec les autres. D'ailleurs nous sommes souvent *obligés* de retrancher de ces Chroniques bien des choses qui nous sont étrangères . . .: si on peut en retrancher, on peut aussi les diviser." The italics are mine.

But there were many other historical works in the eighteenth century of the same fold. From Doms Martène and Durand, "whose names," it has been wittily said, "are associated together in a sort of antiquarian firm," we have the *Thesaurus novus anecdotorum* in nine folio volumes (1717) and the *Veterum scriptorum et monumentorum historicorum, dogmaticorum et moralium amplissima collectio* in nine more folio volumes (1724).

Dom Bouquet and his successors and Doms Martène and Durand were in line with the tradition of St. Germain. Nevertheless, even there, the beginning of the eighteenth century brought changes of policy and interest. A series of provincial histories of France was projected and partially executed. The outbreak of the Revolution in 1789 prevented completion of the design. These monographs were: Devic and Vaisette's *Histoire du Languedoc* (5 v., 1730–45), a model of its kind; Lobineau and Morice's *Histoire de Bretagne;* and Dom Plancher's *Histoire de Bourgogne.*[112]

Another intense interest of these St. Maurists in the eighteenth century was historical method and the auxiliary sciences. Mabillon had pointed the way in his *De re diplomatica.* To that treatise on palaeography and diplomatics was added in the eighteenth century a huge treatise on chronology—the *Art de vérifier les dates.* Its first form was in one volume, and Doms D'Antin, Durand, and Clemencet were the authors; later (1770) it was expanded into three volumes by Dom Clement, and a third edition was issued on the verge of the Revolution between 1783 and 1787. It is the least satisfactory and the most supplanted of all the productions of the Congrégation de St. Maur.

In 1710 the Assembly of the Clergy of France, some of whose more learned members knew Ughelli's *Italia Sacra*, or historical survey of the bishoprics of Italy, wished to emulate that example, and petitioned the monks of St. Germain to undertake a similar work in France. In 1715 volume I of the *Gallia Christiana* appeared—another great series which enhanced the glory of their scholarship. This initial volume was prefaced by a learned introduction dealing with the history of Christianity in Roman Gaul. Unfortunately, instead of beginning with the most important bishoprics, an alphabetical arrangement was followed, i.e., Albi, Arles, Avignon, Auch, etc. By the time volume V was completed, the progress of the project was arrested by the papal bull *Unigenitus,* because there was suspicion that some of the scholars at St. Germain

---

[112] The Bibliothèque Nationale possesses the manuscript accumulations made by the Maurists for completion of this project. There are 149 bound volumes of documents for Champagne, 25 for Normandy, 9 for Limousin, 279 for Picardy, 29 for Touraine, 191 for Languedoc, and 73 for Bourgogne; those for Guienne have all disappeared. Léopold Delisle, *Catalogue des actes de Philippe-Auguste* (Paris, 1856), pp. xxxviii–xl.

were tainted with Jansenism. The sixth volume appeared in 1741 (Paris) and thereafter the work was continued slowly until the French Revolution. The last volumes of the *Gallia Christiana* were completed by the Academy of Inscriptions in the second half of the nineteenth century. But even so, the history of some small bishoprics has not yet been written.[113]

De Quincey once complained that these great scholars of the Age of Erudition were "poor as thinkers," [114] to which Mark Pattison replied that "thinking was not their profession." [115] Their business was to collect and edit critically the sources of history. In every period of intellectual history there have always been some minds which are less interested in facts than in the meaning of the facts. It was so in France even in the seventeenth century, and by the eighteenth century the number of scholars of this nature who wished to supersede facts by interpretation and invention had greatly increased. Many of these students were of the opinion that conditions of the past might have lessons for the present. Such an one was the Comte de Boulainvilliers. In 1689 a movement was set on foot in France to restore the states-general. For this restoration conventions of nobles were to be summoned, and accordingly circular letters of inquiry were addressed to the intendants instructing them to transmit reports upon the ancient practices of the government in the provinces. The response was not great and nothing was done with the reports. In 1727, however, Boulainvilliers examined them. The result was his celebrated *Histoire de l'ancien gouvernement de la France*, a history not of wars and diplomacy, but of institutions. It set the vogue for institutional history in France, an interest which ever since has been one of the distinguishing characteristics of French historical scholarship. Boulainvilliers was of an old and eminent family of the noblesse. His solution of the evils of France was thoroughly aristocratic. The restoration lay in the hands of the nobles, just as the root of the decay of France was found in the reduction of the power and prestige of the nobles by Louis XI and his successors.

Almost at the same time the third estate found an advocate in the Abbé Dubos (1670–1742), in his *Histoire critique de l'éstablissement de la monarchie française* (1734). Dubos was the son of a tradesman of Beauvais and a burgess and *échevin* of the town. His intention was clear. He argued that the Frankish "conquest" was the result of a voluntary agreement between the provincials of Roman Gaul and the Franks, and that originally there was no nobility. Although his con-

[113] See Guerin, in *RQH*, XI, 199–212.
[114] *Works*, III, 168, quoted by Mark Pattison, *Isaac Casaubon* (2nd ed., Oxford, 1892), 448.
[115] *Ibid.*, 449.

clusion was all wrong, nevertheless Dubos discovered the important truth of the persistence of Roman institutions and the survival and continuance of Roman society under the Merovingians and Carolingians. He pointed out the path which was later broadened into a road by Guizot and Fustel de Coulanges.

Gabriel Bonnot de Mably (1709–85) [116] ranged more widely and more loosely over the fields of history. He was educated by the Jesuits, was a protégé of the Abbé Tencin, minister of state, became disgusted with court life, and being of liberal inclination, took up the study of history. He was a copious and popular author, writing upon Greek, Roman, medieval, and French institutions. He even wrote a History of the United States—in 1784! His fame as an historian of institutions was so widespread that he was consulted in the formation of the Polish constitution in 1771.

It would not be worth while to cite Dubos and Mably if it were not for the fact that they are examples of important changes in French historical scholarship. One of these is the new interest displayed in the history of institutions. The other is an uncritical disposition towards strained or eccentric interpretations, which shows that interpretation was in hard need of discipline. This weakness had manifested itself before. In the sixteenth century Adrian de Valois transformed the Merovingian kings into early Bourbons, and advocated the astonishing hypothesis that the Franks were romanized Gauls whose rule was a kindly domination. Mézeray pushed this fantastic idea further and contended that all the German tribes of the Age of the Migrations were Gauls except the Anglo-Saxons, and that the Lombards were really of Celtic blood. Leibniz in Germany and Freret in France protested against this "Celtic dream," but it flattered Louis XIV, and when Freret read an article before the Academy of Inscriptions contending that the original Franks themselves were Germans, the nucleus of whom probably were Caesar's Sicambri, the king was so offended that Freret was sent to the Bastille.

The awakened interest in the constitutional or rather institutional history of France was continued by Bréquigny in the remarkable prefaces to his great collection of the royal *ordonnances* of the French monarchy (1763–90). In one of these, the *Mémoire sur les communes*, Bréquigny anticipated Savigny's famous thesis of the survival of the Roman municipia and the continuity between them and the medieval towns. Bréquigny's historical interpretation was wrong but he had pointed out the true method of analysis, although unconscious of the application and value of this discovery.

[116] Ernest A. Whitfield, *Gabriel Bonnot de Mably* (London, 1930).

The many learned societies and academies, which had come into being in the sixteenth century and continued to increase in number in the seventeenth and eighteenth centuries, were more given to promote science than letters. But the Academy of Inscriptions was interested in epigraphy and other sources of history. It is to this learned society that students of late medieval history are indebted for the beginning, if not the conclusion, of the great series of *Ordonnances des rois de France de la troisième race (1328–1514)*, begun in 1725, interrupted by the Revolution, and completed in 1847, in twenty-three volumes, under the direction of Pardessus. The most important scholar who labored upon this work in the eighteenth century was Bréquigny (1714–94). Besides much other work, Bréquigny brought back from England transcripts of over 7000 documents which he found in London in the Tower, the Exchequer Office, and the British Museum. Almost all that he wrote apart from the introductions to various volumes of the *Ordonnances* is to be found in the proceedings of the Academy of Inscriptions. The list of his contributions is an imposing one. It has been said of him: "Sa prodigeuse activité lui permit de soutenir victorieusement le poids de travaux dont un seul eût suffiça l'immortaliser."

Looking backward, now that we have reached the terminus of the Age of Erudition, and attempting to appraise the value of the historical work done in it, we find that French scholarship, both in quantity and quality of production, was much superior to that of any other European country. Germany possessed three scholars of eminence, Italy two, Spain one; Belgium had in the Bollandists a small but select group of scholars. English historical scholarship may be said to have ranked next to that of France in number of writers of quality. But English historical scholarship lacked the broad and deep spirit that pervaded French scholarship. Its zest for research and its erudition were both much inferior. The archive spirit was lacking; where it was manifested it was liable to partake of mere antiquarianism.

CHAPTER XXXVIII

THE AGE OF REASON [1]

ASUBTLE change in the modes of thought and in the nature of intellectual interests is discernible to the historian of ideas as he passes from the seventeenth century into the eighteenth. By 1700 the philosophy of Descartes held sway in Europe. From the Age of Erudition thought passed into the Age of Reason. D'Alembert and Diderot and the *Encyclopédie* dominated the thinking of the time. Erudition, mere scholarship, yielded to interpretation, to speculation, to skepticism. [2] The full tide of the new thought may be said to have been in the years between the death of Louis XIV in 1715, and the

[1] FUETER, 415–83; SMITH, II, especially chs. i, vi, vii, but the whole book is very valuable and suggestive; Carl Becker, *The Heavenly City of the Eighteenth-Century Philosophers* (Yale Univ. Press, 1932); J. B. Bury, *The Idea of Progress. An Inquiry into Its Origin and Growth* (London, 1920), ch. vii; Harold Höffding, *History of Modern Philosophy*, tr. by B. E. Meyer (London and New York, 1900, 2 v.), II, Bk. VII; Moriz Ritter, *Die Entwicklung der Geschichtswissenschaft* (Munich and Berlin, 1919); the same, "Studien über die Entwickelung der Geschichtswissenschaft: Das 18. Jahrhundert," *HZ*, CXII (1914), 29–131; Ottokar Lorenz, *Die Geschichtswissenschaft in Hauptrichtungen und Aufgaben* (Berlin, 1886–91, 2 v.), II, 147–70; Ludwig Wachler, *Geschichte der historischen Forschung und Kunst seit der Wiederherstellung der litterärischen Cultur in Europa* (Göttingen, 1812–20, 2 v. in 5), II, 806 ff.; Ferdinand Brunetière, *Études sur le XVIIIᵉ siècle* (Paris, 1911); Emile Faguet, *Dix-huitième siècle, études littéraires* (7th ed., Paris, 1890); Ad. Franck, *Réformateurs et publicistes de l'Europe: dix-huitième siècle* (Paris, 1893); Albert Bayet and François Albert, eds., *Les écrivains politiques du XVIIIᵉ siècle: extraits avec une introduction et des notes* (2nd ed., Paris, 1917); Henri Sée, *L'Evolution de la pensée en France au XVIIIᵉ siècle* (Paris, 1925); D. Mornet, *La pensée française au XVIIIᵉ siècle* (Paris, 1926; English translation by L. M. Levin, New York, 1929); Marius Roustan, *Les philosophes et la société française au XVIIIᵉ siècle* (Lyons, 1906), tr. into English by F. Whyte as *The Pioneers of the French Revolution* (London, 1926); Alex. Vinet, *Histoire de la littérature française au XVIIIᵉ siècle* (Paris, 1853, 2 v.); Kingsley Martin, *French Liberal Thought in the Eighteenth Century* (London, 1929); Robert Flint, *The Philosophy of History in France and Germany* (Edinburgh and London, 1874); Leslie Stephen, *History of English Thought in the Eighteenth Century* (3rd ed., London, 1902, 2 v.); Wilhelm Hasbach, *Untersuchungen über Adam Smith und die Entwickelung der politischen Oekonomie* (Leipzig, 1891); for German historiography in the eighteenth century see SCHAUMKELL, and WEGELE, Bks. III–IV *passim;* Friedrich Meinecke, *Die Entstehung des Historismus* (Munich and Berlin, 1936, 2 v.); and BLACK, introduction. See also the lectures of Gustave Lanson, "Formation et développement de l'esprit philosophique au XVIIIᵉ siècle," *RCC*, XVII, pt. i (1908–09), 357–65, 499–508, 721–36, pt. ii (1909), 65–75, 211–18, 309–20, 713–20, and XVIII, pt. i (1909–10), 22–32, 106–15, 257–66, 534–44, 734–43, and pt. ii (1910), 241–50 [this last on "la critique historique"]. Other periodical literature: Louis Gottschalk, "Studies since 1720 of French Thought on the Period of the Enlightenment," *Journal of Modern History*, IV (1932), 242–60; Mark Pattison, "The Age of Reason," *Fortnightly Review,* XXVII (1877), 343–61; Gustav Buchholz, "Ursprung und Wesen der modernen Geschichtsauffassung," *Deutsche Zeitschrift für Geschichtswissenschaft*, VI (1889), ii, 17–37; Max Braubach, "Die kirchliche Aufklärung im katholischen Deutschland im Spiegel des 'Journal von und für Deutschland,' 1784–1792," *Historisches Jahrbuch*, LIV (1934), 1–63, 178–220.

[2] For some suggestive pages on this transition see the last of Lanson's lectures listed towards the end of the preceding note ("La critique historique au XVIIIᵉ siècle").

outbreak of the French Revolution in 1789. But the fount of this new
stream is to be found in the middle of the seventeenth century. This
new movement of thought was what is known as Rationalism; it appealed to reason against tradition and authority, dogma and faith.

The origin of Rationalism is to be found in the progress of physical
science and of mathematics in the seventeenth century. Galileo and
Newton revolutionized thought. Geometry became the queen of sciences. Exactness and demonstrability became the supreme criteria of
thought. The prophet of the new dispensation was the French philosopher and mathematician René Descartes who died in 1650, the author
of the famous *Discours sur la méthode pour bien conduire la raison* which
appeared in 1637, and whose *Geométrie* in the same year, by the adoption of the analytical method, inaugurated the period of modern mathematics. Descartes' brilliant deductive reasoning fascinated men's
minds, and it was not long before some writers appeared who sought
to apply Cartesian principles and methods to other fields of thought
than science. Fontenelle in the preface to his *Utilité des mathématiques*
contended that geometry was necessary even to the interpretation of
literature. The political scientists and the economists of the seventeenth
century were peculiarly influenced by Cartesianism. A relationship
was discovered between physics and government, and physics and political economy. The reason is obvious. Mechanics was then the only branch
of physics, and government and economics were considered to be largely
of a mechanistic nature. It was no mere accident that Hobbes invented
the term "balance of power," and took motion as his master-principle.
In his *Leviathan, or The Matter, Form and Power of a Commonwealth* he
described at length the conditions of political equilibrium, and then
considered how they are affected by Christianity. "His speculation on
this subject is perhaps the most famous part of the whole book. It
may be described in a few words as the earliest and one of the most
complete specimens of rationalism to be found in literature." [3] The
book was a study in the dynamics of government. "Such an inquiry
as Hobbes undertook would in these days be considered as essentially
historical . . . Philosophical history would hardly have been possible without the impulse given to historical inquiry by such theories
as those of Hobbes, Locke and Rousseau." [4] The phrase "balance of
trade" became a commonplace in seventeenth-century economic literature. The writers who stressed the "circulation of money" and the
"circulation of trade" perhaps were unaware that they owed the sug-

[3] Sir James Fitzjames Stephen, *Horae Sabbaticae: Reprint of Articles Contributed to the "Saturday Review"* (London, 1892, 3 v.), II, 32.
[4] *Ibid.*, II, 4–5.

gestion of the term to Harvey's discovery of the circulation of the blood in 1628.   Indeed, Hobbes described circulation of commerce as "the sanguification of the commonwealth." [5]

Descartes had a contempt for history, but admirers of his philosophy and his method sought to apply them to history, to political and social institutions, to economics. If the natural world was mechanically constituted and general laws could be applied to nature, then it followed that man, being a product of nature, was also ruled by "natural laws" capable of axiomatic formulation after the style of Euclid. [6] The eighteenth century was not historically minded. Its speculations concerning the origin of society, of language, of religion, are evidences of this, and in its blind attachment to imagined laws it ignored or denied or defied facts. [7] Thus it came to pass in the eighteenth century that "the infallibility of reason superseded the infallibility of dogma, and the Age of Reason resembled the thirteenth-century Age of Faith." [8]

But the Cartesian method was no more able to resolve what Bosanquet called "the doubtful record of successive events" than previous method and interpretation had accomplished for the understanding of history.   The boasted universal authority of human understanding, when represented by the best minds of the race, failed to enlarge the circle of truth in history. The errors of the rationalistic school of history in the eighteenth century were so many and so great that they dug the grave of the school before the century expired in the smoke and flame of the French Revolution. In the scheme of things visualized by the Cartesian philosophy there were no values except quantitative values, no room for the imponderabilia by which men really live—imagination, feeling, dream. Those qualitative values by which human life—as distinct from physical living—is measured did not exist for Descartes. Art, literature, poetry, and music were simply mechanical forms of human expression. Society from the state to the smallest family was but an agglomeration of human beings mechanically disposed and combined and mechanically regulated. Cartesianism had no perception of the organic nature of human society, and, therefore, was ignorant of the organic nature of historical development. To Cartesianism all values were quantitative and of fixed estimation and invariable operation under exactly determined laws. But qualitative values can never be fixed and

[5] On this subject see Jacob Viner, "English Theories of Foreign Trade before Adam Smith," *Journal of Political Economy*, XXXVIII (1930), 249–301, esp. 257–58, 285.
[6] For demonstration of this statement see Bertrand Russell, "The Revolt against Reason," *Atlantic Monthly*, CLV (1935), 222–32.
[7] Cp. the emphatic statement of James Ward, *The Realm of Ends* (Cambridge, 1911), 14–15.
[8] See the intriguing development of this thesis in Becker, *The Heavenly City of the Eighteenth-Century Philosophers* (start of n. 1).

always are variable—and they are of the nature of man. History is a genetic process of change and transformation and never a succession of fixed patterns.

The first writer to apply the principles of Cartesianism to historical subjects was Pierre Bayle (1647–1706).[9] Bayle was a Huguenot by birth and therefore traditionally of the opposition camp in the France of the reign of Louis XIV. He was not a great scholar but rather an intelligent and very versatile essayist. Before Voltaire, his *Dictionnaire historique et critique*,[10] published in five large folios in 1697, was the most popular book in France. In private libraries it was found oftener than any other work. Bayle's heaviest gunfire was directed against the Catholic interpretation of the Bible [11] and he may be said to have been a pioneer of the "higher criticism" of the Scriptures, but he ran almost the whole gamut of recorded knowledge with devastating effect. He was the incarnation of skepticism and nothing was sacred to his pen. Like Descartes before him, Bayle found refuge in the Netherlands, almost the only country in Europe where intellectual toleration and freedom of thought were to be found.

Next to biblical history, the history of most venerated tradition and authority, the foundations of which were regarded as fixed and immutable, was classical history. Classical literature was regarded as the production of men of a superior nature, as a revelation second only to Holy Writ. To question the accuracy or truthfulness of Greek and Roman historiography was irreverent, if not impious. Not until the latter part of the seventeenth century was the authenticity of earliest Roman history questioned by Perizonius (1615–1715), a Dutch scholar whose real name was Voorbroek; his acumen anticipated Niebuhr.[12] But the first destructive attack on the credibility of early Roman history was made by Levesque de Pouilly in 1722 in a memoir presented to the Academy of Inscriptions. Later, in 1738, Beaufort resumed the attack in his *Dissertation sur l'incertitude des cinq premiers siècles de l'histoire romaine*. The reduction of the whole regal period of Roman history to myth and legend was a sensation of the day.

The greatest exponent of the Cartesian interpretation of history was Louis de Secondat, baron de Montesquieu (1689–1755),[13] whose *Esprit*

[9] Howard Robinson, *Bayle the Skeptic* (New York, 1931); SMITH, II, consult index.

[10] An English translation appeared in 1734–38.

[11] It was typical of his reasoning that he denied miracles as a deduction of the geometrical conception of the universe.

[12] SANDYS, II, 330, 370.

[13] His famous *L'Esprit des lois* was first published in 1748 and soon translated into most European languages; within eighteen months twenty-two editions appeared. English translation by T. Nugent (Cincinnati, 1873, 2 v.; rev. by J. V. Prichard, London, 1914, 2 v.). Montesquieu's *Oeuvres complètes* [including his *Lettres persanes* and the *Considerations sur les causes de la*

des lois embodies every virtue and every defect of the application of rationalism to human institutions. It had greater influence upon political and historical thinking than any other book of the age, except possibly Adam Smith's *Wealth of Nations*.

Montesquieu was a lawyer and his profession tinctured his thought. His real purpose was to establish a science of society, which he believed rested upon deductions from collected facts. The aim of his famous book was to explain the origin and development of political institutions and the laws of government, which he could not do without going also into social and economic history. He had the Cartesian failing of much *à priori* reasoning and excessive analysis of his subjects, so that his findings frequently lack conclusiveness. The results of his studies are often too schematic. Montesquieu's analytic method, however, had the merit of introducing clarity and symmetry into the confused subject of institutions, for he assumed that political and social phenomena, like physical phenomena, were subject to general laws.

The general laws were, of course, taken for granted, but they led Montesquieu to a series of brilliant generalizations and acute analyses. "Many things govern men: climate, religion, laws, maxims of government, the examples of the past, customs, manners. . . ." [14] Climate, including the fertility of the soil, was to him the "first of all empires." But just as soil and climate mould men's character, so also does law "contribute to the formation of . . . a nation." [15]

Montesquieu distinguished three kinds of government, republican, monarchical, and despotic, and defined each form, without making a sharp distinction of degree between the various types of democracy

grandeur et de la décadence des Romains] have appeared in several editions, the best edited by Laboulaye (Paris, 1875–79, 7 v.).

On Montesquieu see FUETER, 475–78; A. Gazier in *La Grande Encyclopédie*, XXIV, 227–31, with bibliography; C. P. Ilbert, *Montesquieu* (Oxford, 1904: Romanes Lecture); A. Sorel, *Montesquieu*, tr. into English by G. Masson (London and New York, 1887); J. C. Collins, *Voltaire, Montesquieu and Rousseau in England* (London, 1908); Louis Vian, *Histoire de Montesquieu* (Paris, 1878); Cuvier, *Observations sur le livre de l'Esprit des lois* (1764); Joseph Dedieu, *Montesquieu et la tradition politique anglaise en France* (Paris, 1909); Michael Lipschutz, *Montesquieu als Geschichtsphilosoph* (Strassburg, 1927); W. A. Dunning, *History of Political Theories from Luther to Montesquieu* (New York and London, 1905), 391–434; Oliver Wendell Holmes, *Collected Legal Papers* (New York, 1920), 250–65; A. J. Grant, "Montesquieu," in F. J. C. Hearnshaw, ed., *The Social and Political Ideas of Some Great French Thinkers of the Age of Reason* (London, 1930), 114–35; J. C. Collins, "Montesquieu in England," *QR*, CXCVII (1903), 331–63; C. Dejob, "Montesquieu: Deux livres de l'*Esprit des lois*," *RCC*, VI, pt. i (1897–98), 506–12; Gustave Lanson, "L'influence de la philosophie cartésienne sur la littérature française," *Revue de métaphysique et de morale*, IV (1896), 517–50; C. A. Sainte-Beuve, *Causeries du lundi* (2nd ed., Paris, 1852–62, 15 v.), VII, 33–66.

[14] *De l'esprit des loix*, liv. XIX, ch. 4.

[15] *Ibid.*, liv. XIX, ch. 27. Laws, Montesquieu explained, should never be arbitrary, but should fit the spirit of a people; hence every type of government is good if it corresponds to the character of the nation. "When Solon was asked whether the laws he gave to the Athenians were the best, he replied: 'I gave them the best they could bear.' A beautiful phrase, which should be kept in mind by all law-givers." *Ibid.*, liv. XIX, ch. 21.

and oligarchy. In writing of republics, he drew heavily on antiquity, for there was nothing in contemporary Europe to approximate his curiously Utopian conception of republicanism. It must be pointed out in this connection that Montesquieu's knowledge of Rome was not profound and that he was uncritical and credulous, accepting fables for truths and generalizing from isolated data.[16] His favorite government was a constitutional monarchy, the kind that France had before Richelieu and Louis XIV changed it into that despotism which Montesquieu hated. After indicating his frame of thought, he proceeded to the "principles" of the three types of government. The ruling principle in a democracy, he explained, was "virtue," by which he meant, presumably, public spirit; the principle of an aristocracy was "moderation"; that of a monarchy "honor"; and that of a despotism "fear."[17] Montesquieu's importance lies in the stress which he put upon the institutions of society and his use of history. His references to historic events for proof of his theses are so frequent that contemporaries accused him of having a superstitious devotion to the "dark" past. "What the deuce," Helvétius exclaimed when reading his explanation of feudalism, "does he want to teach us by his treatise on feudal tenure? What new form of legislation can be derived from this chaos of barbarism that has been respected by brute force, but must be swept away by reason? He should have tried to derive some true maxims from the improved state of things that is at hand."[18] However, Montesquieu's institutional and comparative method of interpreting history broke new ground, especially in the hands of Voltaire.[19]

It was Montesquieu who first applied the comparative method to social institutions; who first considered physical conditions in connection with the laws of a country; who first perceived and illustrated how that natural order which the Physiocrats only considered in relation to the phenomena of wealth and its production, really extended over its political phenomena as well; who first set the example of viewing a great number of social facts all over the world in groups and classes; and who first definitely and systematically inquired into the causes of a set of complex historical events and institutions, as being both discoverable and intelligible. This was a marked advance upon both of

[16] In his *Considérations sur les causes de la grandeur des Romains et de leur décadence* (first published Amsterdam, 1734), Montesquieu traced the causes of the decline of Rome, including the destruction of liberty, corruption, and the splitting of the empire in two. Though an interesting attempt at discovering general laws, the work is thoroughly uncritical and unscholarly; cp. FUETER, 476.

[17] As Montesquieu conceived of three forms of government, so he distinguished three instrumentalities of government: the legislative, the executive, and the judicial. *De l'esprit des loix*, liv. XI, ch. 6.

[18] Quoted by Pasquale Villari, "Is History a Science?" in his *Studies, Historical and Critical*, tr. by Linda Villari (New York, 1907), 20.

[19] Gibbon, having read Voltaire's *Siècle de Louis XIV*, commented: "His method of treating every article in a distinct chapter I think vicious: as they are all connected in human affairs, and as they are often the cause of each other, why separate them in history?" *Miscellaneous Works of Edward Gibbon*, ed. by John Lord Sheffield (London, 1796, 2 v.), II, 69.

the ideas, by one or other of which men had previously been content to explain to them-selves the course of circumstances in the world; either the inscrutable decrees of non-human providence, or the fortuitous vagaries of an eyeless destiny.[20]

It is curious to observe, however, that although *The Spirit of Laws* was the triumph of the application of Cartesianism to history, Montes-quieu's excessive analytic method really proved to be illogical. His definitions are like geometrical axioms and postulates but his analysis is not as clear as that of his master. Gustav Lanson has pointed out [21] that *The Spirit of Laws* ought to have been divided into three parts instead of two. Part I should have been composed of Books I–XIII; Part II should have comprised Books XIV–XXVI; and Part III in-cluded Books XXVII–XXXI. The first thirteen books study things in themselves, without reference to conditions. Book XIV introduces the element of space, of which climate, geography, geology, flora, and fauna are concomitant forms which must be considered as conditioning the life of men on the earth; consideration of these subjects is continued through Book XXVI. With Book XXVII the time-factor in human institutions is introduced, and consideration of this theme continues to the end of the work. This last part is unique. It does not present new problems. It is a treatise on sociological pedagogy which few modern sociologists have discovered. It distinguishes natural law, political law, civil law, religious law, etc., and endeavors to formulate a science of law. Part III, Book XXIX, stands apart as a sort of manual for law-makers. It is out of place, however, for it ought logically to have con-cluded the whole work instead of being an introduction to the third part.

The rationalistic school of history introduced new methods of his-torical criticism and enlarged the content of history to include, at least as auxiliary sciences, the study of climate, geography, geology, and physical environment. Alert students of history became acutely con-scious of forces, conditions, events, and institutions which previous historians had either been unaware of or ignored. Science had broken down the narrow walls of theology and dogma and opened strange vistas into the past history of the race. The *philosophes* were no longer content with the traditional history upon which the minds of men had been fed. They raised new questions. How old was man? Was society an upgrowth out of savagery? Was there ever a Golden Age? What was the nature of primitive society? What was the best form of government, and how did the various distinctive forms of government originate and develop? And finally, what was the meaning of the whole human adven-ture, that is, the goal of man on earth?

[20] John Morley, *Biographical Studies* (London, 1923), 137.
[21] Lanson, *loc. cit.* (end n. 13), 541, note.

The break with tradition first manifested itself in the seventeenth century when the Rationalists definitely took the position that every epoch adds something to the given stock of knowledge, and therefore society, in its continuous ascent, becomes richer in wisdom and experience; in short, progress is a question of time. The increment of one generation is added to the sum of achievement of all previous generations. Progress means an accumulation of knowledge, and since man always adds his contributions to the past, it follows that there is never an old age or decline, but rather greater wisdom and ripeness. "Every science," Descartes wrote, "develops after a certain number of preceding sciences have developed, and only then; it has to await its turn to burst its shell." [22]

Natural science thus broadened man's outlook on the universe and, by means of the idea of progress, gave him a dynamic concept. History, or the record of man on earth, henceforth had a guiding idea which could be used in a twofold manner. On the one hand, the notion of progress enabled the *philosophes* not only to dispense with, but also to attack, the previous theological interpretation of the universe; instead of accepting God as the prime mover and ultimate explanation of causes, the intellectuals now adopted a secular, purely human, hypothesis. On the other hand, the concept of progress opened new vistas for the interpretation of society, laying emphasis on the development of the arts, manners, and science. In both cases the leader and spokesman was Voltaire. [23]

Montesquieu was almost a man of one book and wrote for the intellectual élite. Voltaire (1694–1778) was the author of many books and wrote for the intelligentsia of all Europe. [24] The most famous of Vol-

[22] Quoted in Bury, *The Idea of Progress* (n. 1), 110. On the subject of Bury's book cp. also SMITH, II, 226–36. Giambattista Vico is an exception to the general position of the Rationalists; instead of accepting the idea of progress he developed the notion of cycles. For Vico see the last pages of this chapter.

[23] There is a vast literature on Voltaire, but not much technical criticism of his historical works. See FUETER, 434–50; John Morley, *Voltaire* (2nd ed., rev., London, 1872); Gustave Lanson, *Voltaire* (Paris, 1906); Richard Mayr, *Voltaire Studien* (Vienna, 1879); Bury, *The Idea of Progress* (n. 1), 148–50 and *passim;* Martin, *French Liberal Thought* (n. 1), 282–84 and *passim;* Heinrich Morf, "Bossuet und Voltaire als Universal-historiker," in his *Aus Dichtung und Sprache der Romanen* (Strassburg, 1903), 300–11; F. Schevill, "Voltaire, Historian of Civilization and Exponent of Rationalism," in Rice, ed., *Methods in Social Science* (Chicago, 1931), 424–34; Émile Faguet, "La politique de Voltaire," *RCC,* X, pt. i (1901–02), 49–57; A. Geffroy, "Le *Charles XII* de Voltaire et le Charles XII de l'histoire," *RDM,* LXXXIV (1869), 360–90; P. Sakmann, "Die Probleme der historischen Methodik und der Geschichtsphilosophie bei Voltaire," *HZ,* XCVII (1906), 327 ff.; G. Lanson, "Voltaire," *La Grande Encyclopédie,* XXXI, 1117–29, with bibliography.

[24] Voltaire's collected works fill seventy volumes in the 1784–89 edition. See Georges Bengesco, *Voltaire. Bibliographie de ses oeuvres* (Paris, 1882–90, 4 v.). He wrote the following histories: *Histoire de Charles XII* (1731); *Siècle de Louis XIV* (1751); *Annales de l'empire depuis Charlemagne* (1753); *Essai sur les moeurs et l'esprit des nations* (1756); *L'histoire de la Russie sous Pierre le Grand* (1759–63); *L'histoire du Parlement de Paris* (1769).

taire's historical works are the *Essai sur les moeurs,* the *Siècle de Louis XIV,* and his *Histoire de Charles XII.* The first deals with the whole stream of culture history. The *Siècle,* probably Voltaire's most ambitious historical work, took twenty years to write. He began to collect materials in 1735, but did not complete it until 1756; the actual work of research and writing, however, took only twenty-seven months. His aim was to give a complete picture of the age, to include art and manners, war and diplomacy, science and crafts. For this purpose he not only consulted books and documents, but corresponded with various individuals of the last generations for illuminating personal details. The first draft was completed in 1739, but Voltaire spent years in polishing it. "One should," he wrote, "compose history as one does a tragedy." The work comprehended the whole course of the reign of Louis XIV, a "history of human stupidity," as Voltaire confessed. "The epoch of Louis XIII," the author wrote to a friend, "was still gross, that of Louis XIV admirable, and the present era [Louis XV] is only ridiculous." [25] Voltaire's *Charles XII,* dealing with the life of the famous Swedish warrior-king, has been subjected to a searching scrutiny on the part of a Finnish historian, who showed that Voltaire utilized the best primary sources of the period, mainly in French. He made a few errors in translation, especially from the German, a language which he understood but poorly, but he generally did not alter or invent facts. [26]

For sixty years this sparkling little Frenchman bestrode Europe like a Colossus, lashing fools with his sarcasm, pouring acid on bigots, fighting obscurantism with unmatched irony. His literary output was prodigious; his correspondence alone fills eighteen volumes. Poet and philosopher, essayist and dramatist, novelist and historian, Voltaire, though frequently superficial, was incapable of writing a dull page. He was read, imitated, flattered, hated, and talked about by intellectuals on two continents, from democrats like Jefferson to autocrats like Frederick the Great.

Voltaire made two remarkable contributions to historiography. He was the first scholar to survey history as a whole, correlating events in all the great centers of culture on earth and covering all the significant aspects of human life. Secondly, he conceived history as a record of human activity in all its manifestations: art, learning, science, manners, custom, food, technology, amusements, and daily life. And, what is equally important, his approach was always so fresh, so original, so sparkling that even the dull-witted were stimulated into reading the

[25] For an admirable account of the composition of the *Siècle,* see E. Bourgeois' introduction to the 5th ed. (Paris, 1906), pp. xxiv–xxxii.
[26] J. R. Danielson, *Voltaire, Kaale XII: nen historian kirjoittajana* (Helsingfors dissertation, 1878); cp. the review in *RH,* XI (1879), 54–55.

ironic master whose skepticism took nothing for granted and whose malicious irreverence was a perennial source of amusement.

In his article on "History," in Diderot's *Encyclopédie*, Voltaire gave a concise summary of his ideas. After dismissing the history of opinions as "no more than a collection of human errors" and ridiculing church history as a "succession of divine and miraculous operations by which it pleased God once to guide the Jewish nation," Voltaire proceeded to explain how history should be written.

One demands of modern historians more details, better ascertained facts, precise dates, more attention to customs, laws, mores, commerce, finance, agriculture, population. It is with history as it is with mathematics and physics. The scope has increased prodigiously. . . . In writing a history of a foreign country it is not necessary to cast it in the same mould as a history of your own country. If you write a history of France, you are not obliged to describe the course of the Seine and the Loire; but if you give to the public a history of the Portuguese conquests of Asia, a topography of the discovered country is necessary. . . . We have twenty histories of the Portuguese settlement in the Indies; but none makes known to us the various governments of those countries, their religions, antiquities. . . . The same applies practically to all the histories of foreign countries. If you have nothing more to say to us than that one barbarian succeeded another barbarian on the banks of the Oxus and the Iaxartes of what use are you to the public? . . . The art of writing history well is very rare. It requires a grave, pure, varied, agreeable style. There are laws for writing history as there are for all other arts of the spirit; many precepts, and few great artists.[27]

Admirable as Voltaire was as a stylist and humanist, his histories are vitiated by fatal defects. He was devoid of depth, though he boasted of being a philosopher. His interpretation lacks both philosophic and sociological insight. What he could not explain on obvious grounds he left to chance; there is no connecting link in his narrative. To account for complexities, he fell back on climate and "favorable circumstances."[28] In the second place, he conceived history as a means to an end, a school for statesmen. "There is no sovereign,". he wrote in the preface to his *Charles XII*, "who, in reading the life of this monarch, ought not to be cured of the folly of war."[29] History thus became a matter for moralists to choose facts for their sermons; what was disagreeable was ignored.[30] He had no conception of the continuity of history, and possessed an insensate hatred of medieval history.[31] Finally

[27] Voltaire, "Histoire," in Diderot's *Encyclopédie, ou Dictionnaire raisonné des sciences, des arts et des métiers* (Lausanne and Bern, 1778–82, 36 v.), XVII, 555–72.

[28] Abbé Basin [pseud.], *La philosophie de l'histoire* (Amsterdam, 1765), 11–15; cp. Benedetto Croce, *Theory and History of Historiography*, tr. by D. Ainslie (London, 1921), 257.

[29] *Oeuvres complètes* (Paris, 1878–85, 52 v.), XVI, 132. See the chapter on Voltaire in BLACK, 29–75.

[30] Cp. the sentence quoted in Black: "We ought to ignore the vulgar crowd of kings who would only serve to burden the memory."

[31] "Voltaire expressed a decided contempt for the 'learned lumber' of the antiquary, and in expressing it he showed himself unaware of the continuity of the past. He declared that

and inevitably, Voltaire was full of prejudices; a humanitarian, he hated war; a believer in reason, he loathed the clergy. He despised the whole "dark" past on the ground that men were then nothing but slaves of fanaticism. To him the Reformation was nothing more than the ridiculous spectacle of papists "who ate God for bread, the Lutherans bread and God, the Calvinists ate bread and did not eat God." [32] Plato was a "bad metaphysician," Dante a gloomy pessimist, Petrarch a monotonous sentimentalist, Spinoza a dry pedant. [33]

The philosophic trend of the age penetrated among ecclesiastical scholars, even if it did not prevail, as it did among secular historians. The chief example was the celebrated Abbé Fleury, author of a popular *Histoire ecclésiastique* (20 volumes, Paris, 1791) which was put on the papal Index, and an immense number of other works. In his *Discours sur l'histoire*, a bold and penetrating brochure, he wrote: "Un fait n'est ni plus certain ni même plus vraisemblable pour se trouver dans un grand nombre d'auteurs nouveaux qui se sont copiés les uns les autres. Quand tous les docteurs qui vivent aujourd'hui s'accorderaient à dire que la sainte Vierge a veçu soixante et quinze ans, cette opinion n'en serait ni plus vraie ni plus probable, puisqu'elle n'a aucun fondement dans l'antiquité, et que les faits ne se devinent point à force de raisonner." In another discourse Fleury energetically attacked the temporal power of the popes and the alleged Donation of Constantine. He vigorously condemned the Crusades in the sixth *Discours sur l'histoire ecclésiastique*. [34]

If the philosophers of the eighteenth century had done anything like justice to the past, Europe would have been spared much travail of soul, and a better understanding of the conditions and problems of society would have prevailed. [35] Yet could historical scholarship accomplish more when D'Alembert expressed the wish that all historical sources might be obliterated? In France the old order confronted the new with implacable antagonism so that the *ancien régime* had either to destroy criticism or itself be destroyed by criticism, and we know that the latter prevailed.

the early Middle Ages deserved as little study as the quarrels of wolves and bears. His *Essai sur les moeurs*, one of the most original works he wrote, exhibits most clearly this total absence of a belief in the continuity of history. . . . There is an elaborate contrast between the *misère du passé* and the *bonheur du présent;* and the moral of the story is that man is slowly winning a victory over the fanaticism and the brutality which soils the record of the race." Robert H. Murray, *Edmund Burke* (London, 1931), 77.

[32] Quoted in Croce (n. 28), 258.

[33] See G. G. Zerffi, "Voltaire in His Relation to the Study of General History, from a Philosophical Point of View," in *Transactions of the Royal Historical Society*, X (1882), 344–70.

[34] Quoted by Gustav Lanson, in *RCC*, XVI, pt. i (1907–08), 457–58.

[35] Cp. John Stuart Mill's almost bitter complaint in his *Dissertations and Discussions: Political, Philosophical and Historical* (New York, 1874–75, 5 v.), I, 347–48.

Next to France, English thought was most pervaded by Rationalism. The historian of ideas and of the way in which ideas are spread and transmuted will find no more interesting field of inquiry. In England there was the same tendency toward writing history didactically and rationally as in France. Intellectually the two countries were, in fact, closely linked. Both Montesquieu and Voltaire had visited England and studied English institutions and English thought, the former emphasizing the constitutional aspects and the latter the scientific (Newton) and rationalistic (Locke). "Mister Loke" had a profound influence on Voltaire and so had Bolingbroke (1678–1751), who was a friend of the exiled Frenchman.[36]

The parallelism between Bolingbroke, Voltaire, and Hume is best seen from their almost identical views on the uses of history. Voltaire conceived of history as a "witness and not a flatterer," its purpose being to cure people of folly. Hume, who primarily was a philosopher, thought that history should serve as a storehouse from which to draw facts for the verification of social science. "We must therefore," Hume wrote in the introduction to his *Treatise on Human Nature*, "glean up our experiments in this science from a cautious observation of human life, and take them as they appear in the common course of the world, by men's behavior in company, in affairs, and in their pleasures."

David Hume (1711–76) was the most popular and influential British historian of the eighteenth (and even early nineteenth) century.[37] The son of a Scotch laird, Hume was intended for the law, but, not being essentially a student, he abandoned that study for more congenial

[36] Adam Smith was also influenced by the French Physiocrats and by Hume. Though not an historian, one must mention him for his extraordinary significance as a student of society who, in his *Wealth of Nations* (1776), used the comparative method to establish a science of economics. Like Montesquieu, Smith constantly drew on history for his illustrations. It was said of him that he "explained the mechanism of society as Newton explained the solar system—by proving it." In 1764 Smith met Turgot at Paris and the two held long discussions. "Their opinions on the most essential points of political economy were the same; and they were both animated by the same zeal for the best interests of mankind." See W. W. Stephens, *The Life and Writings of Turgot* (London and New York, 1895), 60–62 for this and other influences of French thinkers on Smith. The recent work of W. R. Scott, *Adam Smith as Student and Professor* (Glasgow, 1937) minimizes the classical view of the connection between Hume and Smith. See also J. A. R. Marriott, "Adam Smith and Some Problems of To-day," *Fortnightly Review*, LXXXII (1904), 969–81.

[37] Macaulay, in 1828, called Hume the "ablest and most popular" historian; and Winston Churchill, almost three-quarters of a century later, said that Hume was his "boyhood's manual" (T. P. Peardon, *The Transition in English Historical Writing, 1760–1830*, Columbia University Press, 1933, pp. 19–23). See FUETER, 452–56; J. H. Burton, *Life and Correspondence of David Hume* (Edinburgh, 1846, 2 v.), cp. *NBR*, VII (1847), 539–59; the chapter in BLACK, 77–116; W. C. Abbott, *Adventures in Reputation* (Cambridge, Mass., 1935), 118–49; F. J. Teggart, *Theory of History* (New Haven, 1925), ch. xv; Lytton Strachey, *Portraits in Miniature* (London, 1931), 144 ff.; Sally Daiches, *Ueber das Verhältnis der Geschichtsschreibung D. Humes zu seiner praktischen Philosophie* (Leipzig, 1903); Julius Goldstein, *Die empiristische Geschichtsauffassung David Hume's* (Leipzig, 1903); Heinrich Göbel, *Das philosophische in Hume's Geschichte von England* (Marburg, 1897); and SCHAUMKELL, 14–18.

pursuits. "I found an insurmountable aversion to everything but the pursuits of philosophy and general learning; and while they fancied I was poring upon Voet and Vinnius, Cicero and Virgil were the authors I was secretly devouring." His was a critical youth, full of doubts and self-searching, not unmixed with hypochondria. "Having read many books of morality, such as Cicero, Seneca, and Plutarch, and being smit with their beautiful representations of virtue and philosophy, I undertook the improvement of my temper and will, along with my reason and understanding. I was continually fortifying myself with reflections against death, and poverty, and shame, and pain, and all other calamities of life." Hence he turned to "moral philosophy" and psychology. His first attempt to gain a hearing, the publication of the *Treatise of Human Nature* (London, 1739), fell on such deaf ears that the "author was hardly gratified even by abuse." His disappointment increased after he failed to obtain the chair of ethics at the University of Edinburgh. Unimpressive in appearance,[38] Hume was compelled to accept employment as a private secretary and came to have a bitter hatred of Englishmen who were neglecting his genius. This explains the political bias of his historical works. Their success in later years, however, brought him an appointment to the Undersecretaryship of State in 1766, and ten years later he retired on a pension.

Hume's *History of England from the Invasion of Julius Caesar to the Revolution of 1688* first began to appear in 1754,[39] three years after Voltaire's *Siècle de Louis XIV.* There are remarkable similarities between the two works; both are pragmatic, rational, anti-metaphysical. But Hume, a professional philosopher,[40] was more detached and skeptical than the ebullient Frenchman. Interested in causation, Hume applied his philosophy to history, working from effects to causes.[41] To

---

[38] Lord Charlemont, a contemporary, has left the following description of the famous philosopher-historian: "His face was broad and fat, his mouth wide, and without any other expression than that of imbecility. His eyes vacant and spiritless, and the corpulence of his whole person was far better fitted to communicate the idea of a turtle-eating alderman, than of a refined philosopher. His speech in English was rendered ridiculous by the broadest Scotch accent, and his French was, if possible, still more laughable; so that wisdom most certainly never disguised herself before in so uncouth a garb. Though near fifty years old, he was healthy and strong; but his health and strength . . . had only the appearance of rusticity." Burton (n. 37), I, 270-71.

[39] Hume, it should be explained, wrote his history backwards, as Laurence Sterne had written *Tristram Shandy.* The last part, two volumes covering the period from the accession of James I to the revolution of 1688, appeared first (Edinburgh and London, 1754-57). The middle section, two volumes dealing with the Tudors, was published in 1759. Two additional volumes (1761) covered the whole of English history from the landing of Caesar in Britain to the accession of Henry VII.

[40] Following Berkeley, Hume denied the reality of mind and matter; to him reality consisted of a succession of "impressions and ideas" (W. C. Dampier-Whetham, *A History of Science, and Its Relations with Philosophy and Religion*, New York, 1929, p. 206).

[41] Cp. the remark of Gibbon: "In every operation of the mind, there is a much higher de-

him history—apart from its value as a teacher of morals—was a record of the conscious mind; in other words, of ideas.[42] Rejecting materialist interpretations, Hume granted that climate and environment may affect the physical aspects of man, but not the "finer organs on which the operations of the mind and understanding depend." Hume, being bound by his philosophy, and convinced of the uniformity of human nature at all times and places, neglected underlying motivations and specific conditions.

Apart from his rigid application of philosophic ideas and his preconceived notions, Hume's chief weakness as an historian was his neglect of sources and his congenital aversion for hard work. Though he pretended to be impartial,[43] he chose only those facts which illustrated his particular point of view. "History is a collection of facts which are multiplying without end; and if they are to be made intelligible, they must, in some way, be abridged." Obviously, only the author was the final judge of what should be abridged, and Hume ignored all those facts which were favorable to his two pet aversions, Whigs and religion.[44] Added to his prejudice, was his laziness, which prevented him from doing rigorous research or checking facts.[45] These defects brought a storm of English criticism about his head—only forty-five copies of the *History of England* were sold in the first year—though his work was enthusiastically received on the continent.[46]

light in descending from the cause to the effect than in ascending from the effect to the cause" (BLACK, 77 f.).

[42] Voltaire once said: "Ideas have changed the world." The reason Hume chose to write about the seventeenth century rather than any other was that he thought it the "most curious, interesting and instructive part of our history." BLACK, *loc. cit.*

[43] "The first quality of an historian is to be impartial," quoted in Burton (n. 37), I, 409; "I may be liable to the reproach of ignorance, but I am certain to escape that of impartiality," *ibid.*, I, 381.

[44] Macaulay, a Whig, made a withering attack on Hume. "Hume is an accomplished advocate. Without positively asserting much more than he can prove, he gives prominence to all the circumstances which support his case; he glides lightly over those which are unfavourable to it; his own witnesses are applauded and encouraged; the statements which seem to throw discredit on them are controverted; the contradictions into which they fall are explained away; a clear and connected abstract of their evidence is given. Everything that is offered on the other side is scrutinized with the utmost severity; every suspicious circumstance is a ground for argument and invective; what cannot be denied is extenuated, or passed by without notice; concessions even are sometimes made: but this insidious candour only increases the effect of the vast masses of sophistry." Macaulay, "History," in his *Critical, Historical, and Miscellaneous Essays and Poems* (Boston, 1880, 2 v.), I, 301. For a more favorable view see J. S. Brewer, ed., *The Student's Hume. A History of England* (new ed., New York, 1880), preface.

[45] Hume's laziness is thus described by a friend of his: "Why, mon, David read a vast deal before he set about a piece of his book; but his usual seat was the sofa, and he often wrote with his legs up; and it would have been unco fashious to have moved across the room when any little doubt occurred." Hume wrote to Adam Smith, "Some push me to continue the *History*. . . . All the Marlborough papers are offered me. . . . I am become too wise either to want censure or praise."

[46] Hume's popularity was not ill-deserved; despite a Scottish style, he wrote history as literature, not as a compilation. Gibbon refers to Hume's "careless inimitable beauties," though

In spite of all the adverse criticisms which may be made of Hume's *History of England*, the work is a landmark in modern historiography. He is the first historian who attempted to make history something more a than chronicle of wars and royal genealogies. He anticipated Voltaire in his appreciation of the importance of social relations and the value of morals, literature, and art. But the greatest merit of Hume as an historian lies in the fact that he, first among all historical writers, perceived the nature and significance of *cause* in history, on which all historical change rests.[47]

Hume founded the Scottish school of history, and the Scottish school of philosophy as well. In history Robertson and Ferguson were his most important followers. William Robertson (1721–93)[48] was a Presbyterian clergyman so liberal that he vehemently acknowledged himself an admirer of Hume and Voltaire. In at least two respects Robertson was superior to both Voltaire and Hume. He was a conscientious scholar who carefully utilized all the available printed and archival sources. Secondly, he contributed a valuable method to historiography by relegating his notes and references to the end of each section, a technique conducive to straight and uninterrupted narrative without a sacrifice of scholarship.[49]

Robertson's masterpiece is the *History of Scotland* (London, 1759), which was enthusiastically received; it covers the period to 1603 and is based on the archives of Edinburgh and the British Museum. Robertson was a tireless collector of data, and he continued to incorporate new facts in later editions. His *History of the Emperor Charles V* (London, 1769) is not so massive; not only was the subject more alien, but there were immense difficulties in getting access to the Simancas (Spain) archives. Furthermore, Robertson knew no German, though he was familiar with French, Spanish, and Italian. His *History of America* (London, 1777), written with great verve and color, is the first authentic history of Spanish America.

Like Hume and Voltaire, Robertson was also didactic. Though he pretended "to relate real occurrences, and to explain their real causes and effects," [50] he despised persons and events which he considered

he points out that his language is full of "solecisms, Scotticisms, Gallicisms"; see *QR*, LXXIII (1844), 536 ff.

[47] Cp. the observations of Höffding, *History of Modern Philosophy* (n. 1), I, 428–30.

[48] On Robertson see FUETER, 456–58; BLACK, 117–41; Dugald Stewart's account of his life and writings prefixed to *The Works of William Robertson* (London, 1840, 8 v.), I, pp. lx–lxiii; Thomas Seccombe's article in *DNB*, XLVIII, 425–30; S. Austin Allibone, *Dictionary of English Literature and British and American Authors* (Philadelphia, 1874, 3 v.), II, 1824–32; Sir Archibald Alison, in *Blackwood's Magazine*, LVI (1844), 790–92; SCHAUMKELL, 18–20.

[49] Oliver Elton, *A Survey of English Literature, 1730–1780* (London, 1928, 2 v.), II, 278; and Peardon (n. 37), 23–29.

[50] *History of Scotland* (Edinburgh, 1842), bk. II, p. 180.

trivial; such matters, he held, should be "abandoned to the industry and credulity of the antiquary." History, he said, should teach wisdom and should concern itself with "dignified" matters. Thus speaking of Ignatius Loyola, the remarkable founder of the mighty Society of Jesus, the Scottish historian dismissed him as being beneath the notice of a serious scholar. "The wild adventures and visionary schemes, in which his [Loyola's] enthusiasm engaged him equal any thing recorded in the legends of the Romish saints; but are unworthy of notice in history." [51] This bias also led him, despite his relative detachment, to an exaggerated estimate of the "darkness" of the Middle Ages, although, unlike most contemporary historians, Robertson was keen enough to evaluate the medieval period as the seeding time of European civilization. [52]

It is necessary [he wrote in his introduction to *Charles V*] to mark the great steps by which they [European nations] advanced from the barbarism to refinement, and to point out those general principles and events which, by their uniform as well as extensive operation, conducted all of them to that degree of improvement in policy and in manners which they had attained at the period when Charles V began his reign. [53]

Sir James Mackintosh, a Scot like Robertson, wrote of him: "His merit consists in a certain even and well-supported tenour of good sense and elegance. There is a formality and demureness in his manner; his elegance has a primness, and his dignity a stiffness which reminds one of the politeness of an old maid of quality, standing on all her punctilios of propriety and prudery [but] . . . his singular power of interesting narrative prevails over every defect."

Robertson had a gift of style and pen portraiture. [54] His descriptions of character, though never ornate, are just and factual, frequently abounding in judicious reflections. Unfortunately he lacked insight into social movements and neglected to give an account of the rise of institutions and the development of economic forces. He was fully aware of the significance of what is now known as "cultural" history.

It is a cruel mortification, searching for what is instructive in the history of past times, to find that the exploits of conquerors who have desolated the earth, and the freaks of tyrants who have rendered nations unhappy, are recorded with minute and often disgusting accuracy, while the discovery of useful arts, and the progress of the most beneficial branches of commerce, are passed over in silence, and suffered to sink into oblivion. [55]

Adam Ferguson (1723–1816) [56] requires only passing notice. He was educated at St. Andrews, studied divinity, and for his knowledge of

---

[51] *The History of the Reign of the Emperor Charles V* (New York, 1848), bk. VI, p. 287.

[52] On Robertson's errors in his treatment of the Middle Ages see S. R. Maitland, *The Dark Ages* (5th ed., London, 1890), 9–122, 141–57.

[53] *Charles V*, p. 11. This introduction, entitled "View of the State of Europe," is a philosophic survey and analysis of the Middle Ages.

[54] See the review in *ER*, II (1803), 229–49.   [55] Robertson, *Works* (n. 48), VIII, 177.

[56] See the article on Ferguson by Francis Espinasse, *DNB*, XVIII, 337–40; John Small,

the Gaelic language was appointed to be chaplain to the Forty-Second Regiment. When this regiment was at the battle of Fontenoy, Ferguson went into action at the head of the column with a broadsword in his hand. In 1754 he resigned and resolved to devote himself to literature. On the resignation of Hume in 1757 he was made librarian and clerk to the Faculty of Advocates. Two years later he became professor of moral philosophy at Edinburgh and after publishing an *Essay on the History of Civil Society* began to collect materials for *A History of the Progress and Termination of the Roman Republic* which appeared in three volumes in 1783. Ferguson believed that "the history of that remarkable republic during the period of their greatness was a practical illustration of those ethical and political doctrines which were the object of his peculiar study."

In his ethical system Ferguson treats man throughout as a social being, and illustrates his doctrines by political examples. He believed in the progress of the human race. His speculations have been carefully criticized by Cousin, who says with reference to this theory: "We find in his method the wisdom and circumspection of the Scottish school, with something more masculine and decisive in the results. The principle of *perfection* is a new one, at once more rational and comprehensive than benevolence and sympathy, which in our view places Ferguson as a moralist above all his predecessors." By this principle Ferguson endeavors to reconcile all moral systems. With Hobbes and Hume he admits the power of self-interest or utility, and makes it enter into morals as the law of self-preservation. Hutcheson's theory of universal benevolence and Smith's idea of sympathy he combines under the law of society. But as these laws are the means rather than the end of human destiny, they are subordinate to a supreme end, and this supreme end is perfection. In the political part of his system Ferguson follows Montesquieu, and pleads the cause of well-regulated liberty and free government. In 1783 he resigned his chair and was succeeded by Dugald Stewart. In his old age he devoted himself to the study of Etruscan and early Roman antiquities and was elected a member of the Academy of Sciences of Berlin, of the Etruscan Society of Antiquaries at Cortona, and of the Arcadia at Rome.

The greatest *scriptor rerum gestarum* not merely of the eighteenth century, but of the English-speaking world, was Edward Gibbon (1737–94).[57] His *Decline and Fall of the Roman Empire* "is perhaps the sole

---

"Biographical Sketch of Adam Ferguson," *Transactions of the Royal Society of Edinburgh,* XXIII (1864), 599–665.

[57] The following account is reproduced from my article, "Edward Gibbon, 1737–1794," in celebration of the 200th anniversary of his birth, published in the *Pacific Historical Review,* VII (1938), 93–119. See also J. J. Saunders, "Gibbon and *The Decline and Fall*," *History,*

post-Renaissance history that takes permanent rank as a classic by reason not only of its form but of its substance." [58] Von Ranke's *Ecclesiastical and Political History of the Popes during the Sixteenth and Seventeenth Centuries* is the only other modern historical classic which approaches it, and, even then, allowance must be made for the great difference of scale between the two works. Ranke's period is limited to two hundred years. Gibbon's perspective extended over fourteen centuries. No historian before Gibbon had had such a concept of the continuity of history.

As with every great author—or for that matter every artist or statesman—any estimate of Gibbon must measure him in relation to the age in which he lived. Not even genius transcends the conditions of the time. The eighteenth century was eminently a philosophical and critical age. It had faith in reason when it had little faith in anything else. And who will blame over-much, considering that it was the age of Cartesianism, of Hume, of Diderot, of Kant? The New History saw its beginnings in Hume and Montesquieu, its climax in Gibbon.

Gibbon was born of good English stock, in circumstances of comfort, though not of great affluence. [59] As a child his health was frail. His

n.s., XXIII (1939), 346–55, with bibliography; *The Memoirs of the Life of Edward Gibbon*, ed. by G. B. Hill (London, 1900) [known in other editions as Gibbon's *Journal*]; D. M. Low, *Edward Gibbon, 1737–1794* (New York, 1937); the article of Leslie Stephen in *DNB*, XXI (1890), 250–56; FUETER, 458–60; WARD, X (1913), ch. xiii, and bibliography, pp. 560–64; the chapter in BLACK; Moriz Ritter, in *HZ*, CXII (1914), 118–31; "The Historian and The Gibbon," *LTLS*, 1937, pp. 297–98; my article "The Library of Gibbon the Historian," *Library Quarterly*, VII (1937), 343–53; and J. W. Swain, "Edward Gibbon and the Decline of Rome," *South Atlantic Quarterly*, XXXIX (1940), 77–93. For his writings see J. E. Norton, *A Bibliography of the Works of Edward Gibbon* (London, 1940).

[58] Oliver Elton, *Frederick York Powell* (Oxford, 1906, 2 v.), II, 24.

[59] The late Lord Acton, the distinguished British historian, was distantly related to the Gibbon family. Gibbon's grandfather (born 1666) was a prosperous cloth merchant who acquired a modest fortune clothing the army of King William III in Flanders. During his absence abroad his business at home was managed by his widowed mother, who soon afterwards married a widower of the name of Richard Acton, a goldsmith in Leadenhall Street. They united in marriage the children of their own first nuptials. Gibbon's grandfather married the daughter of Richard Acton and his sister married Sir Whitmore Acton of Aldenham. Gibbon the historian thus was connected with that ancient family of Shropshire baronets of Jacobite persuasion. For Edward Acton, whom Charles I created a baronet in 1644, followed Charles II into exile. The Acton family consisted at that time of seven brothers, all of very great stature, "one of whom, a pygmy of six feet two inches, confessed himself the last and least of the seven, adding that such men were not born since the Revolution." Gibbon's father was born in 1707 and after graduating at Emanuel College, Cambridge, was sent abroad. His journey through Besançon was marked by a singular result in the chain of human events. He fell seriously ill there and sent for a local physician and relative, a younger brother, who, after having studied medicine in Paris, had settled in Besançon to practice his profession. He married a lady of Besançon, became a Catholic, and was the father of three sons. The eldest of these was the Chevalier John Acton (1736–1811) who became famous as the chief minister of Ferdinand, king of Naples and Sicily during the Revolutionary and Napoleonic era, and with Admiral Nelson staged the bloody reaction in 1799. His two brothers lived in France and one of them called upon Gibbon when he was residing at Lausanne. He introduced himself as "Monsieur Acton, *mais pas le bon*." The *bon* (the Neapolitan minister) had lately succeeded to an estate in Shropshire and a baronetcy by inheritance from Sir Richard Acton,

mother died when he was very young, and he owed his bringing-up to the care of a stepmother who belied the invidious adage often applied to that relation. In his youth he was a voracious reader, mainly of classical and historical literature; his imagination was inflamed by the "barbaric splendor" of Oriental history, Persians, Moslems, and Byzantines. An indiscriminate reader, he was a poor student and not till later years did he, to quote his own words, "acquire the beauties of the Latin and the rudiments of the Greek tongue." The "barbarous" German tongue, one must explain, he never cared to learn. At the age of fifteen, in 1752, he matriculated at Magdalen College, Oxford, where, he has said, he arrived "with a stock of information which might have puzzled a doctor, and a degree of ignorance of which a schoolboy might be ashamed." Indifferent to university discipline (he was a gentleman commoner), Gibbon and the university developed a mutual dislike. After fourteen months he left the institution. "To the university of Oxford," he later wrote, "I acknowledge no obligation; and she will as cheerfully renounce me for a son as I am willing to disclaim her for a mother. I spent fourteen months at Magdalen College; they proved the fourteen months the most idle and unprofitable of my whole life." [60]

Gibbon was then sent abroad by his father to Lausanne where he was tutored by Pavilliard, a Calvinist minister. Under the influence of his excellent tutor who knew no English, the young man not only made French his "spontaneous" tongue, but, more important still, he studied the classics and French thought; he read Pascal, Montesquieu, as well as Giannone's *History of Naples*, and probably also the iconoclastic Voltaire who was then (1757) a neighbor of the twenty-year-old Gibbon. A few years later Gibbon visited Paris where he met the foremost *philosophes*—D'Alembert, Diderot, Raynal, Helvétius, and Holbach. "Had I been rich and independent, I should have prolonged and perhaps have fixed my residence at Paris," he wrote long afterward. Though he did not settle in the French capital, his mind was permanently affected by skeptical French thought.

Early in his youth Gibbon had contemplated writing some kind of history.[61] For several years he revolved in his mind various historical

the elder branch of the family. The late great British historian, Lord Acton, was a grandson of Chevalier John Acton, was born at Naples in 1834, and became a peer of England in 1869.

[60] Adam Smith expressed the same sentiment of condemnation of Oxford. "In the University of Oxford, the greater part of the public professors have, for these many years, given up altogether even the pretence of teaching." *The Wealth of Nations*, ed. by J. S. Nicholson (London, 1901), 319. University College has at last recognized the genius of Shelley, who once shocked the dons. But Magdalen College still refuses to honour the greatest man of letters whose name has graced her registers.

[61] "I know, by experience, that from my early youth I aspired to the character of an historian." *Miscellaneous Works of Edward Gibbon*, ed. by John Lord Sheffield (London, 1796, 2 v.), I, 106.

projects. A history of the expedition of Charles VIII in 1494 was abandoned "as too remote from us and rather an introduction to great events than great and important in itself"—accurate judgment but a singular conclusion, seeing that he finally settled upon a subject far more remote. He "successively chose and rejected the crusade of Richard the First, the barons' wars against John and Henry the Third, the history of Edward the Black Prince, the lives and comparisons of Henry V and the Emperor Titus, the life of Sir Philip Sidney, and that of the Marquis of Montrose." Then he contemplated a life of Sir Walter Raleigh, but concluded that although "the events of his life are interesting, his character is ambiguous and his actions obscure." The history of the liberty of the Swiss was one which he "would have preferred to all others"; he read Tschudi's *Chronicle* with diligence, but reluctantly abandoned the idea because so many of the sources were in German. He had gone so far in this project as to write an essay in French on the subject which was read before a society of foreigners in London. Fortunately for Gibbon, a friend showed the manuscript to Hume who gave him wholesome advice. "Why do you compose in French," he wrote, "and carry faggots into the woods, as Horace says with regard to Romans who wrote in Greek? . . . Let the French triumph in the present diffusion of their tongue. Our solid and increasing establishments in America promise a superior stability and duration to the English language." For a time Gibbon played with the thought of writing a history of Florence under the Medici: "a period of one hundred and fifty years which rises or descends from the dregs of the Florentine democracy to the title and dominion of Cosmo de Medici. . . . I might deduce a chain of revolutions . . . singular men and singular events— the Medici four times expelled and as often recalled . . . the character and fate of Savonarola . . . the revival of arts and letters . . . the fall of the republic." He thought that the history of Florence under the Medici, "a commonwealth, soft, opulent, and corrupt, which, by just degrees, is precipitated from the abuse to the loss of her liberty," contained an "instructive" lesson. He wrote: "On this splendid subject I shall probably fix."

But he did not yet know his own mind. Two years later he reached a decision with almost dramatic suddenness. He visited Rome in 1764 when he was twenty-seven years of age. To his classically-trained mind the view of the Eternal City was an unforgettable experience. Rome became the city of his soul. "My temper," he wrote retrospectively, "is not very susceptible of enthusiasm, and the enthusiasm which I do not feel I have ever scorned to affect. But at the distance of twenty-five years, I can neither forget nor express the strong emotions which

agitated my mind as I first approached the Eternal City. After a sleep-
less night I trod with a lofty step the ruins of the Forum; each memorable spot where Romulus stood, or Tully spoke, or Caesar fell, was at
once present to my eye; and several days of intoxication were lost or
enjoyed before I could descend to a cool and minute investigation."

"It was at Rome," he continues, "on the 15th day of October, 1764,
as I sat musing amid the ruins of the Capitol, while the bare-footed
fryars were singing vespers in the Temple of Jupiter,[62] that the idea of
writing the decline and fall of the city first started to my mind." Gibbon's memory slipped a cog when he penned this impressive sentence.
The church was S. Maria Aracoeli, but the structure is the Capitoline
Temple of Juno, not of Jupiter. The friars were Franciscans. The
monastery was pulled down in 1888.

His original design was to limit the subject to the decay of the city
of Rome. He did not then contemplate the decline and fall of the
Roman Empire. For four years he was "in a dark and doubtful perspective," and "contemplated [the subject] at an awful distance."
But the distance narrowed as his mind cleared and he grew more and
more conscious of his powers. "I began," he relates under the year
1768, "gradually to advance from the wish to the hope, from the hope
to the design, from the design to the execution of my historical work,
of whose limits and extent I had yet a very inadequate notion." He
had decided, however, by this time to write the history of the decline
and fall of the Roman Empire, and not merely that of the city of Rome—
a subject which was left for Gregorovius to deal with. "Insensibly,"
Gibbon goes on in this remarkable self-revelation of his mind, "I
plunged into the ocean of Augustan history, and in the descending
series I investigated, with my pen almost always in my hand, the original records, both Greek and Latin, from Dion Cassius to Ammianus
Marcellinus, from the reign of Trajan to the last age of the western
Caesars." Increasingly his mind became fascinated with this "tale of
a city which swelled into an empire."

He told no one his secret. Not even his dearly beloved stepmother
was informed until the first volume was nearly completed. In August,
1775, he wrote to her:

---

[62] Erected by Tarquinius Superbus, the last of the kings, and consecrated in 509 B.C. It
was burned in 83 B.C. during the civil war between Sulla and Marius, and again in 69 A.D.
in the triangular war of Vespasian, Otho, and Vitellius, and magnificently restored by Domitian.
In the early Middle Ages the temple and the hill on which it is situated were owned by the
monastery of S. Maria de Capitolio (Aracoeli), but in 1143 became civic property and the
meeting place of the municipal Senate, first mentioned in 1150. The hill originally was accessible only from the Forum, but in 1348 the lofty flight of 124 steps ascending from the Campus
Martius to the church of S. Maria in Aracoeli was constructed, the only public improvement
made in Rome during the exile of the popes at Avignon.

I am just at present engaged in a great historical work, no less than a History of the Decline and Fall of the Roman Empire, with the first volume of which I may very possibly oppress the public next winter. It would require some pages to give a more particular idea of it; but I shall only say in general that the subject is curious and never yet treated as it deserves, and that during some years it has been in my thoughts and under my pen.

As the work grew under his hand he became more and more convinced that he had "chosen an illustrious subject." The manuscript was not shown to any one. "Of such friends," he comments, "some will praise from politeness and some will criticise from vanity."

Boswell has recorded an interesting anecdote which illustrates Gibbon's remarkable reticence in regard to his work. One evening in the year 1775 Dr. Johnson, Boswell, Sir Joshua Reynolds, Gibbon, and some others were gathered in the library of Mr. Cambridge.

The common remark as to the utility of reading history being made: JOHNSON: "We must consider how very little history there is; I mean real authentick history. That certain kings reigned, and certain battles were fought, we can depend upon as true; but all the colouring, all the philosophy of history is conjecture." BOSWELL: "Then, Sir, you would reduce all history to no better than an almanack, a mere chronological series of remarkable events." Mr. Gibbon, who must at that time have been employed upon his *History*, of which he published the first volume in the following year, was present, but did not step forth in defence of that species of writing. He probably did not like to trust himself with Johnson.

There was no friendship between Gibbon and Dr. Johnson. One evening at a tavern, where the Literary Club was dining, when the talk turned upon bears, Johnson remarked: "We are told that the black bear is innocent; but I should not like to trust myself with him," whereupon Gibbon muttered under his breath: "I should not like to trust myself with *you*." The burly doctor was so base in his manners that he once jeered at Gibbon for his ugliness. And by the way, it may be added that the common phrase "Gibbon's sneer" is an invention of the sycophantic Boswell, who always barked as his master did.[63]

His father's death had left him possessed of independent means and he removed to London, where "no sooner was I settled in my house and library than I undertook the composition of the first volume of my

[63] The Literary Club was founded by Sir Joshua Reynolds in 1763. Gibbon was elected on March 4, 1774. Among its early members were Johnson, Boswell, Sheridan, Walpole, Goldsmith, Charles James Fox, Burke, Sir William Jones, and Bishop Percy. Adam Smith, who had come to London in 1774 in order to complete his *The Wealth of Nations*, was elected in January, 1775, and there he and Gibbon met for the first time, and became fast friends. In his *Decline and Fall*, chapter XXIV, note 15 (ed. Bury, I, 483), when speaking of the wheat supply of ancient Rome, Gibbon cites *The Wealth of Nations*, and adds: "I am proud to quote as the work of a sage and a friend." Boswell writing on April 28, 1776, immediately after *The Wealth of Nations* was published, to his friend Temple, said: "Smith, too, is now a member of our club. It has lost its select merit."

History. At the outset all was dark and doubtful; even the title of the work, the true era of the Decline and Fall of the Empire, the limits of the introduction, the division of the chapters and the order of the narrative; and I was often tempted to throw away the labour of seven years." Fortunately for Gibbon, who knew no German, J. J. Mascou's *Geschichte der Teutschen* (2 v., 1726), which covered the history of the ancient Germans from the earliest times to the accession of the Carolingian House, had been translated into English in 1737 by Thomas Lediard, "late secretary of His Majesty's envoy extraordinary in Lower Germany." This work, almost forgotten today, was one of the most substantial products of German historical scholarship written during the eighteenth century.[64]

Gibbon has given an illuminating account of the development of his style. "The style of an author," he says, "should be the image of his mind, but the choice and command of language is the fruit of exercise. Many experiments were made before I could hit the middle tone between a dull chronicle and a rhetorical declamation. Three times did I compose the first chapter, and twice the second and third before I was tolerably satisfied with their effect. In the remainder of the way I advanced with more equal and easy pace; but the fifteenth and sixteenth chapters have been reduced by three successive revisals from a large volume to their present size, and they might still be compressed without any loss of facts or sentiments." Hume, on the other hand, in his last journey to London told Gibbon that the narrative from the death of Commodus in 192 A.D. to the accession of Alexander Severus in 223 A.D. was too concise.

The first volume was written three times,[65] but he wrote the others with rapidity and with few changes in the text. He was influenced, he tells us, by "the perfect composition, the nervous language, the well-turned periods" of Robertson, and Hume's "calm philosophy" filled him with "a mixed sensation of delight and despair." But no historian ever owed less to another historian than Gibbon. His style is as original and individualistic as that of Thucydides.

Gibbon is equally interesting in what he tells us of his method. Locke's *Essay on Human Understanding* "led him into a deep and instructive train of reasoning"; from the *Provincial Letters* he "learned to manage the weapon of grave and temperate irony"; Montesquieu's

[64] Woldemar Goerlitz, *Die historische Forschungsmethode Johann Jacob Maskovs* (Leipzig, 1901). Gibbon got his knowledge of German law from two works by Heineccius on the history and the elements of medieval German law, which were written in Latin—*Elementa Juris Germanici*.

[65] Creighton was in error when he said "Gibbon wrote his first volume eight times." *Life and Letters of Mandell Creighton, by His Wife* [Louise Creighton] (London, 1904, 2 v.), I, 123.

"energy of style and boldness of hypothesis" fascinated him; in Giannone's *Civil History of Naples* he "observed with a critical eye the progress and abuse of sacerdotal power." He averaged a hundred pages a day in reading huge folios like those of Tillemont and Cluverius, and taking notes as he read. Sometimes he grew impatient over the copious erudition in some of these works. In his Journal he takes a fling at "one of those Dutch editions in which the text only peeps out amidst a heavy mass of commentary."

Gibbon had a wonderful dexterity in utilizing the researches of others. He had the power of forming a critical judgment as to the value of his authorities. "No man made greater use of the labors of others, or was less disposed to neglect any short cut to knowledge in the shape of abridgments, reviews, or translations which came in his way." [66] But he had utter contempt for compilations and scornfully said that "compilers multiply useless books, disgust serious readers and enrich none but booksellers."

There are two especially interesting passages descriptive of his method to be found, the one in his *Memoirs*, the other in the *Vindication*, which he published in reply to his critics after the appearance of the first volume of the *Decline and Fall*. The first gives us a peep into Gibbon's workshop:

The subsidiary rays of medals, and inscriptions of geography and chronology, were thrown on their proper objects; and I applied the collections of Tillemont, whose inimitable accuracy almost assumed the character of genius, to fix and arrange within my reach the loose and scattered atoms of historical information. Through the darkness of the middle ages I explored my way in the Annals and Antiquities of Italy of the learned Muratori and diligently compared them with the parallel or transverse lines of Sigonius and Maffei, Baronius and Pagi, till I almost grasped the ruins of Rome in the fourteenth century, without suspecting that this final chapter must be attained by the labour of six quartos and twenty years. Among the books which I purchased, the Theodocian Code, with the commentary of James Godefroy, must be gratefully remembered. I used it (and much I used it) as a work of history, rather than of jurisprudence; but in every light it may be considered as a full and capacious repository of the political state of the empire in the fourth and fifth centuries.

The second is of interest for Gibbon's reflections on the employment of authorities to supplement the information found in source material.

Besides the ideas which may be suggested by the study of the most learned and ingenious of the moderns, the historian may be endebted to them for the occasional communication of some passages of the ancients which might otherwise have escaped his knowledge or his memory. In the consideration of any extensive subject, none will pretend to have read all that has been written, or to recollect all that they have read. . . . It would surely be unreasonable to expect that the historian should peruse enormous volumes, with the uncertain hope of extracting a few interesting lines, or that he should sacrifice

[66] Sir James Stephen, *Horae Sabbaticae* (n. 3), II, 409.

whole days to the momentary amusement of his reason. . . . On these occasions . . . it is his duty, and it has been my invariable practice, to consult the original, to study with attention the words, the design, the spirit, the context, the situation of the passage to which I had been referred; and before I appropriated it to my own use, to justify my own declaration that "I have carefully examined all the original materials that could illustrate the subject which I have undertaken to treat." . . . In a very few instances, where I had not the opportunity of consulting the originals, I have adopted their testimony on the faith of modern guides of whose fidelity I was satisfied, but on these occasions, instead of decking myself with the borrowed plumes of Tillemont or Lardner, I have been most scrupulously exact in marking the extent of my reading, and the source of my information.

In 1776 through the influence of Lord Eliot, who had married his first cousin, Gibbon was returned at the general election for the borough of Leskeard. In Parliament he supported "with many a sincere and silent vote the rights, though not, perhaps, the interests, of the mother country." For "after a fleeting, illusive hope" that he might become a distinguished Parliamentary orator, "prudence condemned me," he confesses, "to acquiesce in the humble station of a mute." Gibbon was an assiduous attendant at Parliament. He admired Lord North's consummate mastery of debate, who wielded with equal dexterity "the arms of reason and of ridicule," when he was not indulging himself in a short slumber on the government bench between the attorney general and the solicitor-general, the "two pillars of the law and state," whilst he was upholden by the "majestic sense" of Lord Thurlow. Burke's "profuse and philosophic fancy" amused him, and Fox' "argumentative vehemence" commanded his admiration. "The eight sessions that I sat in Parliament," Gibbon proudly claims, "were a school of civil prudence, the first and most essential virtue of an historian." [67]

The first volume of the *Decline and Fall* was completed during the novelty and tumult of his first session, and was now ready for the press. The manuscript was offered to and rejected by Elmsly, neither the first nor the last publisher deficient of imagination. Thomas Cadell, a respectable bookseller, and William Strahan, an eminent printer, took the risk and thereby touched immortality. So moderate were the hopes of author and bookseller that an edition of only five hundred was projected until the number was doubled by the prophetic vision of Mr. Strahan, the printer. Gibbon awaited the publication with equanimity. "I was neither elated by the ambition of fame, nor depressed by the apprehension of contempt," he tells us. "My diligence and accuracy were attested by my own conscience. History is the most popular species of writing, since it can adapt itself to the highest or the lowest capacity. I had chosen an illustrious subject."

[67] *Miscellaneous Works* (n. 61), I, 146–47.

The first volume of the *Decline and Fall of the Roman Empire* appeared early in 1776, a year also made memorable by the death of Hume and the publication of Adam Smith's *Wealth of Nations*. When one reflects that only forty-five copies of Hume's *History of England* were sold in the first year, Gibbon's success was phenomenal. Like Byron later, when the first canto of *Childe Harold's Pilgrimage* appeared, he awoke to find himself famous. He has described his feelings with candor, yet modesty.

"I am at a loss how to describe the success of the work without betraying the vanity of the writer. The first impression was exhausted in a few days; a second and a third edition were scarcely adequate to the demand." Robertson wrote him a cordial letter, and one from Hume, who died a few months afterwards, "overpaid the labour of ten years." Adam Ferguson wrote in congratulation: "You have made a great addition to the classical literature of England, and have given us what Thucydides proposed leaving with his own countrymen, a 'possession in perpetuity.'"

The crossing of letters at this juncture is interesting. On April 1, 1776, in the letter which Hume wrote to Adam Smith congratulating him on *The Wealth of Nations*, he added: "I fancy you are acquainted with Mr. Gibbon. I like his performance extremely." And on that same day Gibbon wrote in reply to Ferguson's congratulatory letter: "What an excellent work is that with which our common friend Mr. Adam Smith has enriched the public."

Among Gibbon's most intimate friends he was alluded to as THE GIBBON. Yet only the discerning few perceived how great a book the first volume of the *Decline and Fall* really was. Edmund Burke reviewed Gibbon's and Smith's works, along with Watson's *History of Philip II* in the *Annual Register* for 1776. Gibbon and Smith were given two pages each, while Watson got sixteen! In 1788 Burke reviewed volumes II–VI; he praised his learning, condemned his spirit, and said that his style was execrable. Horace Walpole wrote himself down an ass in a letter dated February 18, 1776, which he wrote to the Reverend William Mason shortly after the first volume of the *Decline and Fall* appeared:

Lo, there is just appeared a classic work: a history, not majestic like Livy, nor compressed like Tacitus; not stamped with character like Clarendon; perhaps not so deep as Robertson's *Scotland*, but a thousand degrees above his *Charles V;* not pointed like Voltaire, but as accurate as he is inexact; modest as he is *tranchant* and sly as Montesquieu without being *recherché*. The style is smooth as a Flemish picture, and the muscles are concealed, . . . not exaggerated like Michael Angelo's to show the painter's skill in anatomy; nor composed of the limbs of clowns of different nations, like Dr. Johnson's heterogeneous monsters. This book is Mr. Gibbon's *History of the Decline and Fall of the Roman Empire.*[68]

The famous fifteenth and sixteenth chapters on the history of the Church under the Roman Empire gave rise to a storm of criticism. "I was startled," Gibbon has written, "at the first discharge of ecclesiastical ordnance." At first he endeavored to reply in polite but critical terms; but the violence of his opponents soon disgusted him and at last his "silence damped the ardour of the polemics." Of one of these adversaries, Travis, he caustically said that "the brutal insolence of his challenge can only be excused by the absence of learning, judgment and humanity, and to that excuse he has the fairest or foulest pretension." Among the "Oxford bigots" Porson was a shining exception, and his flagellation of Travis of Oxford was the acutest and most accurate piece of criticism since Bentley. Gibbon bitterly said that he presumed to attack, not his *faith*, but his *fidelity* as an historian. Priestley, a Unitarian minister by profession and a physicist by avocation, was particularly offensive, and Gibbon, though for the most part he ignored his attackers, broke silence with reference to him.

Milman, Gibbon's later editor, while condemning his "philosophical bigotry," justly praised "the inherent interest of the subject, the inexhaustible labour employed upon it, the immense condensation of matter, the luminous arrangement, the general accuracy," and candidly said that Gibbon's religious prejudice was no worse than the theological partialities of those ecclesiastical writers who hitherto had been in undisputed possession of this province of history. It may be added that Welsh patriots were incensed over Gibbon's statement that ancient Palestine was scarcely "superior to Wales either in fertility or extent."

The continuation of the *Decline and Fall* was interrupted by the outbreak of the American Revolution. At the request of the Lord Chancellor and of Lord Weymouth, the Secretary of State, Gibbon undertook the composition of a British vindication against the French manifesto. The *Mémoire Justicatif*, which he wrote in French, was delivered as a state paper to the courts of Europe. Beaumarchais, who believed that Lord Stormont, the former British ambassador in Paris, was the author, issued a reply in which he used such gross language that the Duc de Choiseul, although England and France were at war, compelled him to

[68] *Horace Walpole's England as His Letters Picture It*, ed. by A. B. Mason (London, 1930), 258. Lord Auckland has related an anecdote in his *Journal and Correspondence* (London, 1861–62, 4 v.), II, 280, which runs that the Duke of Cambridge, the king's brother, once met Gibbon in Reynolds' studio. "'So,'" says he, "'I suppose you are at the old trade again—scribble, scribble, scribble.'" But Lady Glenbervie [who was Lord North's daughter and whose husband was a brother-in-law of Lord Sheffield] says that it was King George III who said it. Cp. *The Glenbervie Journals*, ed. by Walter Sichel (London, 1910), I, 195, where the quoted passage runs: "'How do you do, Mr. Gibbon? Always scribble, scribble, I suppose.'"

retract one of his statements. As a reward for his service to his government Gibbon was appointed one of the Lords Commissioners of Trade and Plantations, and his private income was enlarged by the "clear addition of between seven and eight hundred pounds a-year." The appointment was in the nature of a sinecure. "It must be allowed," Gibbon admits, "that my duty was not intolerably severe and that I enjoyed many days and weeks of repose without being called from my library to the office."

Nearly five years elapsed before the appearance of the second and third volumes, which were published together in 1781.[69] Gibbon apologized for this—to him—"long delay" by explaining that in the interval he indulged his curiosity in natural science and took a course in anatomy under the celebrated Dr. Hunter and another in "chymestry" under Mr. Higgins. "The principles of these sciences," he records in his *Memoirs*, "and a taste for books of natural history contributed to multiply my ideas and images; and the anatomist and chymist may sometimes track me in their own snow." [70] Six months of Paris and pleasure must also be deducted from the account. After this vacation Gibbon returned to his task and sunk himself in the "mud of the Arian controversy." By now he felt himself to be master of his subject and his style, and while the measure of his daily portion was enlarged, he discovered less reason to cancel or correct.

As soon as Lord North's majority in the House of Commons was endangered, Gibbon resigned, and Burke's bill abolished the Lords of Trade. He abandoned what he called "my senatorial life" without regret. The second and third volumes, he noted with satisfaction, "insensibly rose in sale and reputation to a level with the first," though he thought that they were "more prolix and less entertaining than the first."

The fourth volume was continued with no interval between its predecessors and it. "My skill was improved by practice, my diligence perhaps was quickened by the loss of office." The fourth volume was finished, except for the last chapter, when Gibbon retired from London to Lausanne in 1783. London opinion unanimously condemned his

[69] The second volume was prefixed by Gibbon's portrait engraved by John Hall from the portrait by Reynolds, on which Lord North remarked: "Mr. Gibbon sells his purchasers a bargain in that volume." *Journal and Correspondence of William Lord Auckland* (n. 68), I, 12.

[70] When Gibbon was writing the history of the plague in the middle of the sixth century the famous Dr. Hunter called his attention to Thucydides' description of the plague in Athens in the fifth century B.C., and loaned him an elaborate commentary on this part of Thucydides, a quarto of six hundred pages by Fabius Paullinus Utinensis, an Italian physician (Venice, 1603). He was also indebted to Dr. Mead's short but famous treatise concerning *Pestilential Disorders* (7th ed., London, 1722). In this work Mead shrewdly accounted for the lighter mortality among monks and nuns by the two advantages which their houses had of isolation and abstinence.

voluntary banishment, but beyond doubt Gibbon was freer and happier in every way on the shore of Lake Leman than he had been on the banks of the Thames. He had taken his library with him and the fourth volume was soon terminated. He labored steadily but happily and closed his studies with the day, and commonly with the morning. He was now "straining for the goal," and in 1787 it was reached.[71] The last volume of the manuscript was sent to the printer without any intermediate transcript, so sure was Gibbon of the accuracy of his scholarship and the facility of his pen. Not a sheet of the entire manuscript from beginning to end was ever seen by any eyes except Gibbon's and those of the compositors before publication. He truly said, and with more pride than humility, that "the faults and the merits are exclusively my own."

Every lover of Gibbon knows the memorable words with which he described his emotions when he had completed the building of the noble bridge spanning the stream of history between ancient and modern times.

It was on the day, or rather night of the 27th of June, 1787, between the hours of eleven and twelve, that I wrote the last lines of the last page, in a summer-house in my garden. After laying down my pen, I took several turns in a *berceau*, or covered walk of acacias, which commands a prospect of the country, the lake and the mountains. The air was temperate, the sky was serene, the silver orb of the moon was reflected from the waters, and all nature was silent. I will not dissemble the first emotions of joy on the recovery of my freedom, and, perhaps, the establishment of my fame. But my pride was soon humbled, and a sober melancholy was spread over my mind by the idea that I had taken an everlasting leave of an old and agreeable companion, and that whatsoever might be the future fate of my *History*, the life of the historian must be short and precarious.

The day of publication of the sixth volume of the *Decline and Fall* was purposely delayed that it might coincide with Gibbon's fifty-first birthday (April 27, 1788), which was celebrated by "a cheerful literary dinner" among friends. Adam Smith wrote in congratulation: "It sets you at the very head of the whole literary tribe at present existing in Europe." As most of the previous purchasers were eager to complete their sets, the sale of the sixth quarto volume was rapid, and an octavo edition of the whole work at a cheaper price was soon put out.

French, German, and Italian translations of the *Decline and Fall*, or parts of it, soon appeared. Unusual interest is attached to the French version. When the first volume had been published in 1776 Louis XVI, who was a great reader and understood the English language well, at the suggestion of his former tutor who had taught him English, under-

---

[71] Vol. IV was begun March 1, 1782 and ended June 1784; vol. V was begun July 1784 and ended May 1, 1786; vol. VI was begun May 18, 1786 and ended June 27, 1787.

took to translate it, and did so until he reached the famous fifteenth chapter which so shocked him that he abandoned the design. Nevertheless the king read each succeeding volume as it appeared. A passage in the third volume of the first quarto edition (1781) gave him offense, and he took pains to have Gibbon informed of his resentment. The offending sentence was this prophecy: "A Julian or Semiramis may reign in the North, while Arcadius and Honorius again slumber on the thrones of the Bourbons." Louis XVI objected to being compared with the two degenerate sons of Theodosius the Great. Gibbon in the next edition altered the words "House of Bourbon" to "South," thus making the allusion ambiguous. In his *Memoirs* he wrote of this incident: "I shall neither disclaim the allusion nor examine the likeness; but the situation of the *late* king of France excludes all suspicion of flattery, and I am ready to declare that the concluding observations of my third volume were written before his accession to the throne."

Gibbon was not elated over the translations made of his great work, and complained of them that they "injure the character, while they propagate the name of the author." The first volume was "feebly though faithfully" translated into French by Le Clerc de Septchènes; after his death it was continued by Desmuniers and Cantwell, but the translation languished during the French Revolution, Desmuniers becoming a member of the National Assembly. A German translation was begun by Wenck, with valuable notes. Unfortunately he died soon after completing the first volume and the rest of the work was executed by an inferior hand. The Italian translation (3 v., 1779) was not made from the original, but from the French version. It could only have been of the first volume. Many years later an Italian translation was made of Dr. Smith's famous abridged form of the *Decline and Fall*.[72]

Gibbon was half-amused and half-nettled at the reproach of indecency which British moralists levelled at him, especially for matter in his three last volumes, since an equal degree of freedom in the first volume had passed without criticism. He justified himself by saying that he was painting the manners of the time; that the vices of Theodora formed an essential feature of the reign of Justinian.

My English text is chaste, and all licentious passages are left in the obscurity of a learned language, [he explained, and added:] Nevertheless the *History of the Decline and Fall* . . . may perhaps a hundred years hence still continue to be abused. . . . I have sometimes thought of writing a Dialogue of the Dead, in which Lucian, Erasmus and Voltaire should mutually acknowledge the danger of exposing an old superstition to the contempt of the blind and fanatic multitude.

[72] *Notes and Queries*, 5th ser., VI, 118. The famous forty-fourth chapter on Roman law was translated and used as a textbook in various universities on the Continent.

Viewing the *Decline and Fall* in perspective, Gibbon was justly proud of his achievement and so were his countrymen. "When I contemplate the common lot of mortality," he wrote in his *Memoirs*, "I must acknowledge that I have drawn a high prize in the lottery of life. . . . Twenty happy years have been animated by the labour of my History; and its success has given me a name, a rank, a character, in the world, to which I should not otherwise have been entitled." He calculated in 1788 that Nature would allow him fifteen more years to live, observing that "two causes, the abbreviation of time and the failure of hope, will always tinge with a browner shade the evening of life." But he lived only six of the span of years to which he had looked forward. He died in 1794 in his fifty-seventh year.

Gibbon's great work falls naturally into two parts which are sharply to be distinguished. Part I comprehends volumes I–IV, and extends from the second century to A.D. 641, the death of the Emperor Heraclius (chapter xlvii). The cornerstone of the Palladian structure is the age of the Antonine emperors. Who is there who does not remember his sonorous words in eulogy of that golden age? "If a man were called to fix the period in the history of the world during which the condition of the human race was most happy and prosperous, he would without hesitation name that which elapsed from the death of Domitian (96 A.D.) to the accession of Commodus (180 A.D.)."

The first four volumes accordingly cover approximately five hundred years. Volumes V–VI (chapters xlviii–lxxi) on the other hand suffice for a period almost ten centuries long. The disproportion is obvious. But the defect is more than one of difference in apportionment of space. It is mental. For all his genius Gibbon had the contempt of eighteenth-century scholarship for Byzantine history, which he characterized as "a uniform tale of weakness and misery." [73]

Gibbon followed the Abbé Mably, who advised the historian not to dwell too minutely on the decay of the Eastern Roman Empire to the detriment of his own reputation. Much of his research in the formation of these chapters must have been irksome to him, especially since his knowledge of the Byzantine Greek language was not as great as it should have been for such a task. Not one of the many important questions which modern Byzantine scholarship has illuminated was anticipated by Gibbon. Bury's severe but just verdict is that Gibbon's

---

[73] The introductory paragraphs of ch. xlviii sketch the plan of Gibbon's last two volumes and show how superficial was his understanding of Byzantine history (GIBBON, V, 169–71). "I should have abandoned without regret the Greek slaves and their servile historians," he wrote, "had I not reflected that the fate of the Byzantine monarchy is *passively* connected with the most splendid and important revolutions which have changed the state of the world." For criticism of Gibbon in this particular see Bury's introduction, *ibid.*, I, pp. xliv–lxi.

"history of the Empire from Heraclius to the last grand Comnenus of Trebizond is merely a sketch with certain episodes more fully treated." The most striking of these episodes are the Fourth Crusade in 1204 and the capture of Constantinople by the Turks in 1453.

Gibbon failed to perceive that Peter the Hermit was a charlatan and masquerader, and reduced the long and important history of the Crusades to a little more than one hundred pages, when he might well have devoted a volume to them. Yet that he felt the importance of the history of the Crusades is manifested in the last sentence of chapter lix, in which after relating the loss of Acre and the Holy Land in 1291, he concludes with the majestic words: ". . . and a mournful silence prevailed along the coast which had so long resounded with the WORLD'S DEBATE."

Nevertheless, in spite of the shortcomings of Gibbon's last two volumes, he must be given credit for the attempt to write Byzantine history at all. When Horace Walpole told him that "Constantinopolitan history was so disgusting that few would have patience to read it, however well written," Gibbon colored, "'all his round features squeezed themselves into sharp angles; he screwed up his button-mouth, and rapping his snuff-box said, 'It had never been put together before'. . ." [74]

In justice to Gibbon he must be judged by the first four volumes of his work. In these the accuracy and solidity of his scholarship, the massiveness of his structure are strikingly manifested. The vigilance with which he read his sources and the penetration of his thought are impressive to one who carefully follows him chapter after chapter. He was the first historian who perceived the significance of Justinian's closure of the school of Athens in 529 A.D. and the flight of Greek scientific studies to Persia, which was conquered in the next century by the Arabs, for the progress of Arabic science in the Middle Ages.[75]

It would be grossly unjust to complain of Gibbon that he did not perceive values in history which only the nineteenth and twentieth centuries have discovered. He failed to measure the influence of economic conditions and social forces, or to appreciate the importance of literature and art in history. His *Weltanschauung* was that of his age. It required the French Revolution, the Romantic movement, Kantian philosophy, and the Industrial Revolution to open new doors into the vault of past history. Gibbon was a genius but he was not a diviner. To him and to his generation "wars and the administration of public affairs are the principal subjects of history." The ideas of progress and of "natural law"—the great illusions of the eighteenth century—could

---

[74] Stephen Gwynn, *The Life of Horace Walpole* (London, 1932), p. 249.
[75] GIBBON, IV, 261–65.

not persuade him from the conviction that much of history is "little more than the register of the crimes, follies and misfortunes of mankind." [76] Gibbon's judgment and accuracy, except where he was hampered by deficient information, were little short of the marvellous. He was the first writer to grasp the idea of the continuity of history with largeness of vision and fulness of knowledge.

Next to France and England, but at long last, Italy was sensitive to the new thought. But in the nature of things intellectual freedom could exist only precariously in Italy. The peninsula was not only divided among foreign powers—the Spanish Bourbons controlled Naples and the south, and the Austrian Habsburgs possessed Milan and Lombardy—but was, with the possible exception of Tuscany under Leopold, completely under the sway of clericalism. In the absence of a vigorous national life there was little interest in or occupation with vital historiography.[77]

Pietro Giannone (1676–1748) was a celebrated Neapolitan lawyer whose deserved fame as an historian rests upon a single work, *Storia civile del regno de Napoli*, published at Naples in four volumes in 1723, the same year in which Muratori's *Scriptores* appeared. It was the fruit of twenty years of scholarship. The vigorous attack upon the political course of the papacy, combined with his skepticism, at once brought about the condemnation of the work and Giannone's excommunication. The author fled to Venice, where he remained for twelve years and, like Sarpi before him, continued to pour out pamphlets against the papacy's political conduct. He was marked by the Inquisition, and expelled from Venetian territory in 1735. For a time he found concealment in Modena—one wonders if Muratori knew of his presence there—and later fled to Geneva, although he still professed the Catholic faith. On a fatal Sunday he was treacherously induced to attend mass in a Catholic village situated on Savoyard territory and was seized by agents of the King of Sardinia and imprisoned at Turin for the rest of his life. The originality of Giannone lies in the fact that he was the first scholar to perceive the value of legal documents as *historical* sources. In this he anticipated Savigny by a century, as he also anticipated Montesquieu in his perception of the historical importance of institutions.[78]

[76] *Ibid.*, I, 77.

[77] Among Neapolitan scholars one must mention Gaetano Filangieri (d. 1788), the jurist who learned from Tenucci and influenced Beccaria; Alessio Mazzochi, the archaeologist; Serrafino Tansi, the chronicler; Placido Troyli, author of a history of Naples; for other, generally unimportant, writers, see C. Cesare, "Ueber die fortschreitende Entwicklung der geschichtlichen Studien im Königreiche Neapel von der zweiten Hälfte des 18. Jahrhunderts bis auf die Gegenwart," *HZ*, VI (1861), 293–348; the excellent article by Joseph Texte, "L'Italie et la critique française au XVIIIᵉ siècle," *RCC*, IV, pt. i (1895–96), 418–24; and Guido de Ruggiero, *Il pensiero politico meridionale nei secolo XVIII e XIX* (Bari, 1922).

[78] Giannone's work was republished at Milan when the Risorgimento was in its incipient

The second Italian historical scholar of distinction in the eighteenth century was Cesar Bonesana, Marquis di Beccaria (1735–93),[79] who, though not an historian, used the historical method in his famous treatise on penology, *Dei delitti e delle pene*,[80] "one of the little books that have moved the world," [81] a work of European reputation which did much for the extinction of legal barbarism. Beccaria was a Milanese noble, interested in mathematics and economics. Through his brother Alessandro, who was connected with the state prisons, Beccaria became interested in penology. His work was published in 1764 and had an instant success; within eighteen months it passed through six editions, was translated into French and English, was praised by Voltaire, and quoted by Blackstone. The little book had an influence on Jefferson in America, Catherine II in Russia, and Joseph II in Austria; thereby it laid the foundations of modern prison reforms.

In this *Essay on Crimes and Punishments*, Beccaria, after a judicious account of the principles underlying punishment, urged a humane and rational reform of judicial practice. Following Montesquieu and Voltaire, he advocated invariable and certain laws, open accusations, and the abolition of torture and capital punishment. What is important from the point of view of historiography is Beccaria's reliance on historic facts from which he drew his arguments.

If we look into history [he writes] we shall find that laws, which are, or ought to be, conventions between men in a state of freedom, have been, for the most part, the work of the passions of a few, or the consequences of a fortuitous or temporary necessity; not dictated by a cool examiner of human nature, who knew how to collect in one point the actions of a multitude, and had this only end in view, The Greatest Happiness of the Greatest Number.[82]

stage of revolt (*Opere*, 1823–24, 14 v. in 13, of which I–XI comprise the *Istoria*). English translation by James Ogilvie, *The Civil History of the Kingdom of Naples* (London, 1729–31, 2 v.); French version by Jean Bedevolle (La Haye, 1742). Giannone's autobiography was published by Fausto Nicolini in the *Archivio storico per le province napoletane*, XXIX (1904), 188–652. See also the life by L. Panzini included in the *Opere*; FUETER, 342–45; Nicolini's article in the *Enciclopedia Italiana*, XVI, 967–78; Giovanni Bonacci, *Saggio sulla Istoria civile del Giannone* (Florence, 1903), which is an attack on Giannone's originality; for a defense of the Neapolitan historian see Nicolini, *L'Istoria civile di Pietro Giannone ed i suoi critici recenti* (1907).

[79] Beccaria's *Opere*, ed. by P. Villari, were published at Florence in 1854; his lectures on political economy, delivered at the Palatine College of Milan, are to be found in *Scrittori Classici Italiani* (Milan, 1803–16, 50 v.), vols. XI and XII. See Coleman Phillipson, *Three Criminal Law Reformers; Beccaria, Bentham, Romilly* (London, 1923); Cesare Cantù, *Beccaria e il diritto penale* (Florence, 1862); A. Amati and others, *Cesare Beccaria e l'abolizione della pena di morte* (Milan, 1872); SMITH, II, 582–85; Lacy Collison-Morley, *Modern Italian Literature* (London, 1911), 46–48; A. Desjardins, "César Cantu et Beccaria," *ASMP*, CXXIV (1885), 218–37.

[80] Translated into English as *Essay on Crimes and Punishments* (London, 1768), from the French translation of Morellet (1766) inspired by Voltaire, who wrote an introduction for it.

[81] Murray, *Edmund Burke* (n. 31), 245.

[82] Quoted from the introduction.

But by far the most arresting Italian thinker of this period was Giambattista Vico (1668–1744),[83] the son of a petty Neapolitan bookseller. At the university, where the precocious youth entered at an early age, he devoted himself to scholastic philosophy, jurisprudence, history, and literature. His favorite authors were Plato and Tacitus, because "the former described the ideal man and the latter man as he really is." In 1697, at the age of twenty-nine Vico was appointed professor of rhetoric at Milan, and on a pitiable salary of 100 ducats annually he had to support a large family. Influenced by Bacon and Grotius, he spent the next quarter century studying and writing on jurisprudence; but despite his many publications, his application for the university chair of law (at a salary of 600 ducats) was rejected. Undiscouraged, the poor and obscure Vico pursued his profound researches. In 1725 he published the first edition of his famous *Principi di una Scienza Nuova*, and five years later the thoroughly revised *Seconda Scienza Nuova;* [84] these two works form the bases of Vico's renown.

One of the most striking of Vico's ideas is that of the group mind. Most of his contemporaries, as well as previous historians, had conceived of historical change as wrought either by the direct intervention of Providence, or by the genius of great legislators. Vico advanced the very modern conception of the collective mind as the creator of an ever-moving civilization. In the background of his thought is the fruitful conception of social evolution, together with the perception that every phase of culture is related to every other phase.

In short, Vico's achievement was the formulation of a philosophy of history, so much in advance of its time that it was not much prized until the era of Romanticism.[85]

Though an original thinker, Vico had little influence on his age; among the French *philosophes*, assuming that they knew about the Neapolitan, there is no trace of Vico's thought; he was neglected even in Italy.[86] The only eighteenth-century thinker who occupied himself

[83] On Vico see SMITH, II, 234–36; H. P. Adams, *The Life and Writings of Giambattista Vico* (London, 1935); Benedetto Croce, *La filosofia di Giambattista Vico* (2nd ed., Bari, 1922); Karl Werner, *Giambattista Vico als Philosoph und gelehrter Forscher* (Vienna, 1881); Giuseppe Ferrari, *Vico et l'Italie* (Paris, 1839); Gennaro Rocco, *Elogio storico di G. B. Vico* (Naples, 1844); Carlo Cantoni, *Giovanni-Battista Vico. Studii critici e comparativi* (Turin, 1867); Nicolò Tommaseo, *Vico ed il suo secolo* (Rome, 1873); Paolo Billeri, *S. Agostino e Giambattista Vico, ossia della teorica scientifica, della filosofia della storia* (Pisa, 1887); Collison-Morley (n. 79), 34–38; Ferrari, "Vico et son époque," *RDM*, July 1838, pp. 103–16; B. Dembinski, "Vico i jego metoda historyczna" [Vico and his historical method], in *Kwartalnik Historyczny*, VII (1893), 199–213.

[84] Both appeared in Naples. The 8th Italian edition in two volumes was published in 1826. German translation by Weber (Leipzig, 1822); French translations by Michelet, *Oeuvres choisies de Vico* (Paris, 1835, 2 v.), and by the Princess de Belgioioso (Paris, 1844). Michelet also published *Principes de la philosophie de l'histoire* (Paris 1827), a summary of Vico. Not only Michelet, but also Comte, Gambetta, and Fustel de Coulanges studied the writings of Vico. There are various editions of his complete *Opere;* the most recent is that edited by G. Gentile and F. Nicolini (Bari, 1911–14, 5 v.). See also Giudice, ed., *Scritti inediti di Vico* (Naples, 1896).   [85] SMITH, II, 235–36.

[86] See S. Jankelevitch, "La philosophie de Vico, d'après Benedetto Croce," *Revue de synthèse historique*, XXIII (1911), 312–18.

with Vico was Herder, who learned of him around 1797.[87] There were many reasons for this neglect of a profound mind. In the first place Vico's language was extremely obscure, clothed in abstruse theological forms; this was probably a deliberate device to escape the vengeance of the Inquisition and the fate of his compatriot Giannone. Secondly, Vico, being a believer in God, had rejected the dominant Cartesianism, and was therefore repugnant to the eighteenth-century Rationalists.

Unlike the *philosophes*, Vico was a psychologist and, in the deepest sense, a scientist. The question he asked was this: Why do we have a science of nature, but no science of history? He therefore set himself to solve two basic problems: "An ideal eternal history," and "Eternal principles of the nature of States and social relations (*cosa civile*)." This led him to posit two principles, that of uniformity and that of continuity. The former is based on the idea that the world "has been created by man himself, and human nature is everywhere the same." Human nature being the same, Vico concluded that it "does not change suddenly; it always retains a trace of a previous phase and former habits"; this is the principle of continuity.[88]

The notion of uniformity obviously makes possible a science of society, which is to be at the same time "history and philosophy of mankind." But the concept of continuity is more involved. It led Vico through devious routes and subtle probings to the well-known idea of historic cycles, since made popular by Spengler. Here Vico developed two useful concepts, *corso* and *ricorso*. *Corso* implies the general course of human history; it reaches its apex in monarchy, after which there comes the *ricorso*. But *ricorso*—coming from the Latin word *currere*, "to run"— does not mean a decline; like the English juridical word "recourse," it signifies a re-investigation, or new start. Thus to Vico, the period of antiquity is the *corso*, while the medieval age is the *ricorso*. These concepts were subtly tied up with the Christian religion; for the historical evolution, from the *corso* to the *ricorso*, is completed when the barbarous period, of violence in politics and imagination in science, is replaced by equity and truth. To translate this into simple historical terms, Vico implies that the real *ricorso* began with the establishment of Christianity, the true religion, in Europe, and this "permanently established" a real and just civilization, "a new order of humanity among nations." [89]

[87] Otto von Gemmingen, *Vico, Hamann und Herder* (Leipzig, 1918), 37–51.

[88] Otto Klemm, *G. B. Vico als Geschichtsphilosoph und Völkerpsycholog* (Leipzig, 1906), 13–43.

[89] Richard Peters, *Der Aufbau der Weltgeschichte bei Giambattista Vico* (Stuttgart and Berlin, 1929), 138–64. In his researches Vico also made a number of suggestive generalizations about Homeric society, early Roman civilization, linguistics, myths, legends, and religion; these may have influenced Wolf's famous Homeric theory; cp. Robert Flint, *Vico* (Edinburgh, 1884), 176–77.

Vico's philosophy is based, not on reason, which he rejected, but on the psychology of primitive ages, all of which, he affirmed, passed through three epochs, the divine (gods and myths), heroic (heroes and barbarism), and human (civilization); hence his deep studies in ancient history and literature. Affirming his belief in God as the source of all creation and wisdom,[90] Vico insisted that man can have true knowledge (*il certo*) only of the world which he himself had created, that is, human events (history) and social institutions (mental achievements). Man's knowledge is therefore necessarily limited to external things, but these, Vico was sure, lend themselves to thorough observation and hence to a science of society.[91]

The Rationalists, having broadened and refined the field of history, reaped a fine reward in the form of popular approval. No other age had such a voracious interest in historical literature as the eighteenth century. Everyone read and talked history. "History," Gibbon relates, "is the most popular species of writing." Both he and Voltaire were "best sellers" throughout Europe. "My book," Gibbon tells, "was on every table, and on almost every toilet." Hume and Robertson were equally popular. "I never leave off reading it," Catherine II of Russia said of Robertson's *Charles V*.[92]

One of the reasons for the popularity of history was that it was treated as literature. Another cause was that history was used as an arsenal of facts with which to bombard the *ancien régime* and bring about the desired reforms. For the eighteenth-century thinkers conceived history as the great teacher of human experience. Bolingbroke's "history is

[90] "God knows all things . . . but man, in endeavoring to know things, must have recourse to dividing them. Therefore, human science is a kind of anatomy of the works of nature. Thus, to illustrate this by examples, it has dissected man into body and soul, and soul into intellect and will; and it has selected, or, as it is termed, abstracted from the body figure and movement, and from these, as from all other things, it has drawn being and unity. Metaphysics considers being, Arithmetic the unit and its multiplication, Geometry figure and its dimensions, Mechanics motion from without, Physics motion from the centre, Medicine the body, Logic reason, and Moral Science the will." Vico, *Opere* (ed. 1852), II, 64, quoted in Flint, *op. cit.*, 88.

[91] "Seeing that human science is born of a defect of the mind—namely, of its extreme littleness—in consequence of which it is external to all things, contains nothing of what it desires to know, and so cannot produce the truth which it seeks to ascertain, those sciences are the most certain which expiate the defect in which they originate. . . . We may accordingly conclude that the criterion of truth, the rule by which we may certainly know it, is *to have made it*. Hence the clear and distinct idea of our mind not only cannot be the criterion of truth in general, but not even of that of the mind itself; *for while the mind apprehends itself, it does not make itself*, and because it does not make itself, it is ignorant of the form or mode in which it apprehends itself." *Opere*, II, 67, quoted in Flint, 89–90.

[92] See BLACK, introduction, 15. In this connection it is interesting to point out the *philosophes*' pre-occupation with style. Writers and scholars, especially in France, paid as much attention to form and expression as to content. Buffon, a natural scientist, is responsible for the dictum that "the style is the man himself." He insisted that only well-written books would pass on to posterity. Condillac said that "the whole beauty of style consists in two things: clarity and character" (SMITH, II, 301). Voltaire and Gibbon are the most brilliant examples of scholars who commanded a superb prose style.

philosophy teaching by example" is a famous dictum. Hume, in his *Treatise on Human Nature*, said that "we must glean up our experiments in this science from a cautious observation of human life, and take them as they appear in the common course of the world, by men's behavior in company, in affairs, and in their pleasures."

CHAPTER XXXIX

GERMANY AND THE AGE OF ENLIGHTENMENT[1]

THE promise and potency of German intellectual life in the fifteenth century—that brief era of the so-called German Renaissance—was destroyed by the Lutheran Reformation,[2] and the Reformation ultimately led to the Thirty Years' War, which nearly destroyed Germany.[3]

The first clear thinker in Germany after 1648 was the celebrated Gottfried Wilhelm Leibniz (1646–1716),[4] the liberator and restorer of

[1] In German, *Aufklärung*. See FUETER, 392–95 and Bk. IV; John Dewey, *German Philosophy and Politics* (New York, 1915), 44–132; J. F. Jameson, "The Development of Modern European Historiography," *Atlantic Monthly*, LXVI (1890), 322–33; K. Francke, *Social Forces in German Literature* (New York, 1896), chs. vii–viii; WEGELE, Bks. III–IV; WOLF, 198–210; BERNHEIM, 225–34 and *passim;* Ludwig Wachler, *Geschichte der historischen Forschung und Kunst seit der Wiederherstellung der litterärischen Cultur in Europa* (Göttingen, 1812–20, 2 v. in 5), II, 806 ff.; J. G. Hibben, *The Philosophy of the Enlightenment* (New York, 1910); Herman Hettner, *Geschichte der deutschen Literatur im 18. Jahrhundert*, ed. by E. A. Boucke (Brunswick, 1925–26, 3 v. in 4); G. M. Priest, *Anthology of the Classical Period of German Literature* (Princeton, 1934); Albert Köster, *Die deutsche Literatur der Aufklärungszeit* (Heidelberg, 1925); Alfred Heubaum, *Geschichte des deutschen Bildungswesens* (Berlin, 1905); Ernst Cassirer, *Die Philosophie der Aufklärung* (Tübingen, 1932); Elizabeth Heimpel-Michel, *Die Aufklärung, eine historischsystematische Untersuchung* (Langensalza, 1928); Karl Völker, *Die Kirchengeschichtschreibung der Aufklärung* (Tübingen, 1921); Lucien Lévy-Bruhl, *L'Allemagne depuis Leibniz. Essai sur le développement de la conscience nationale en Allemagne* (Paris, 1890); G. Zart, *Einfluss der englischen Philosophen seit Bacon auf die deutsche Philosophie des 18. Jahrhunderts* (Berlin, 1881); P. Berger, *William Blake: mysticisme et poésie* (Paris, 1936), ch. i; Konrad Bursian, *Geschichte der klassischen Philologie in Deutschland* (Munich, 1883, 2 v. in 1), 517–664; Albion W. Small, *The Cameralists, the Pioneers of German Social Polity* (Chicago, 1909); Wilhelm Dilthey, *Gesammelte Schriften* (Leipzig and Berlin, 1914–36, 12 v.), II–III; Ernst Troeltsch, *Gesammelte Schriften* (Tübingen, 1912–25, 4 v.), IV, 338–74; Immanuel Kant, "Was ist Aufklärung?" in his *Sämmtliche Werke*, ed. by G. Hartenstein (Leipzig, 1867–68, 8 v.), IV, 161–68. For manuals of the time see: J. G. Fessmaier, ed., *Grundriss der historischen Hilfswissenschaften* (Landshut, 1802); J. E. Fabri, *Encyklopädie der historischen Hauptwissenschaften und derer Hilfsdoktrinen* (Erlangen, 1808); Ch. J. Kraus, *Encyklopädische Ansichten [einiger Zweige] der Gelehrsamkeit* (Königsberg, 1809: vols. III–IV of his *Vermischte Schriften*).

[2] "Many a harvest," a Protestant theologian wrote, "seemed to be ripening. Then, suddenly . . . a storm burst and destroyed all prospects of a harvest." See F. M. Schiele, "Luther und das Luthertum in ihrer Bedeutung für die Geschichte der Schule und der Erziehung," *PJ*, CXXXII (1908), 381–95; and cp. the words of Leibniz: "Germany was scarcely beginning to breathe again, and peopled almost entirely by a generation under age—if war broke out afresh, there was reason to fear that this generation would be destroyed before it had reached maturity, and that a great part of the unhappy land would be all but turned into a desert." Quoted in A. W. Ward, *Collected Papers* (Cambridge, 1921, 5 v.), I, i, 338–39.

[3] For a brilliant account of the effects of the Thirty Years' War see Lévy-Bruhl, *L'Allemagne depuis Leibniz* (n. 1), ch. i.

[4] Leibniz' fame as an historian was negligible until Georg Heinrich Pertz in his preface to the *Annales imperii* (1846) for the first time gave the learned world an account of Leibniz as an historian—one hundred and thirty years after his death. For accounts in English see Ward (n. 2), I, i, ch. xiv; SMITH, II, index; E. H. Holthouse, "Leibniz as an Historian," *LTLS*, 1935,

intellectual Germany. Leibniz was the last of the polymaths, and the greatest all-round scholar of modern times, metaphysician, mathematician, scientist. Here we are interested in him only as an historical scholar of the Age of Erudition. His greater influence was on the German *Aufklärung*. After graduating at Leipzig where his father was professor of philosophy, he spent four years in Paris and met almost every French scholar of note. In 1673 he went to London and was a friend of Boyle, the great physicist. After a second sojourn in Paris in 1676 he settled in Hanover as librarian of the ducal library where he spent the rest of his life. He was commissioned by the duke to write the history of the House of Brunswick-Lüneburg. Accordingly, for three years Leibniz travelled far and wide, searching archives and collecting documents. "In this learned pilgrimage," Gibbon wrote of him, "he consulted the living and the dead, he explored the libraries, the archives, the monasteries, and even the tombs, and diligently collected or copied the books, the manuscripts, and the charters of every age." His historical studies were much delayed by philosophical and mathematical work, so that the first volume of the *Scriptores rerum Brunsvicensium* did not appear until 1701, and the third and last, in 1711. He left unfinished the *Origines Guelficae*, the five tomes of which were finished by Eccard and Scheid and published between 1750 and 1780. The hands of these several authors are apparent: the bold and original spirit of Leibniz, the crude erudition of Eccard, the annotations of Gruber, and the critical dissertations of Scheid. The marriage, in 1695, of the Prince of Modena with a Princess of Hanover had drawn Leibniz into the composition of this work. In his capacious mind the history of a province and a dynasty expanded into the annals of the Medieval Empire, especially the history of the great Guelf House of Bavaria and Saxony. In 1700 Leibniz made a second journey to Italy. He found the archives of Modena in a de-

746 (remarkable); and Gibbon's long memoir entitled "Antiquities of the House of Brunswick," in his *Miscellaneous Works*, ed. by John Lord Sheffield (London, 1796, 2 v.), II, 637–705, esp. 638–41. See also FUETER, 392–93; WOLF, 199 and the valuable bibliographical note; WEGELE, 618–61, and consult index; Leibniz' own autobiography as printed in his *Gesammelte Werke*, ed. by G. H. Pertz (1843–46), and Pertz' preface; Kuno Fischer, *Gottfried Wilhelm Leibniz, Leben, Werke und Lehre*, in his *Geschichte der neueren Philosophie*, III (4th ed., Heidelberg, 1902); Edmund Pfleiderer, *Gottfried Wilhelm Leibniz als Patriot, Staatsmann und Bildungsträger* (Leipzig, 1870); Francke (n. 1), 176–78; BIEDERMANN, II, i, 207–68; Zart (n. 1), 14–17; V. Basch, *Les doctrines politiques des philosophes classiques de l'Allemagne* (Paris, 1927), ch. iii; Cassirer (n. 1), 36–47 and *passim;* the same, *Leibniz' System in seinen wissenschaftlichen Grundlagen* (Marburg, 1902); SCHAUMKELL, 7–8; Marcel Drouin, "Leibniz historien," *RSH*, XXIII (1911), 148–64: Louis Davillé, "Le developpement de la méthode historique de Leibniz," *ibid.*, XXIII (1911), 257–68; this is a modification of Davillé's own book, *Leibniz historien* (Paris, 1909), cp. Fueter's review in *HZ*, CVIII (1911–12), 341–44; Erhard, "Leibniz als Geschichtsforscher und als Beförderer wissenschaftlicher Vereine," *Zeitschrift für vaterländische Geschichte und Altertumskunde*, X (1847), 235 ff.; Reumont, "Magliabechi, Muratori und Leibniz," in *Beiträge zur italienischen Geschichte* (Berlin, 1855), II, 215 ff.

plorable condition, with the result that the duke recalled Muratori from Milan to set his archives in order.

In an age when scholars were theological pedants priding themselves upon their Latinity, Leibniz urged both the teaching of science and the use of the native tongue.

> Our learned men [he wrote] have shown little desire to protect the German tongue, some because they really thought that wisdom could only be clothed in Latin and Greek; others because they feared the world would discover their ignorance, at present hidden under a mask of big words. Really learned people need not fear this, for the more their wisdom and science come among people, the more witnesses of their excellence they will have. . . . On account of the disregard of the mother tongue, learned people have concerned themselves with things of no use, and have written merely for the bookshelf; the nation has been kept from knowledge. A well-developed vernacular, like highly-polished glass, enhances the acuteness of the mind and gives the intellect transparent clearness.[5]

The great scientist likewise advocated a reform in the German school system, justly considering the German universities as "monkish" and obscurantist.

> The teaching of youth [Leibniz wrote] should be centered not so much upon poetry, logic and scholastic philosophy as upon *realia*, history, mathematics, geography, *vera physica;* instruction in *realia* should be pursued in collections of rarities, the study of man in anatomical theatres, chemistry in the apothecary's shop, botany in botanical, zoology in zoological gardens. The pupil should forever move in the *theatrum naturae et artis*, receiving knowledge and impressions.[6]

Inevitably Leibniz, who was a philosopher as well as a man of action, turned to history to support his views. As a young man he had read Livy, Herodotus, and Xenophon in his father's library. "Since my youth," he wrote, "my great aim has been to work for the glory of God by extending the sciences . . . although circumstances have obliged me to work . . . in history and political affairs."

Leibniz' historical researches were connected with his office as librarian and historiographer to the Guelf ducal House of Brunswick-Han-

---

[5] Quoted in Martha Ornstein, *The Role of the Scientific Societies in the Seventeenth Century* (New York, 1913), 213. When Christian Thomasius, professor of law at the University of Leipzig, in 1679 announced a lecture in the vernacular he was bitterly attacked and finally forced to flee. In 1690, when the University of Halle was founded, Thomasius gave the first university lecture in the German tongue, exclaiming: "We are not bound to Aristotle, we shall not be accused of *lèse majesté* even if we make fun of the king of philosophers, and philosopher of kings" (quoted *ibid.*, 272). Thomasius' great importance lies not only in his revolutionary introduction of German speech in the universities but also in the relentless war he waged on pedants, and in his editing the first German-language periodical of a literary nature. On Thomasius see Ludwig Gumplowicz, *Geschichte der Staatstheorien* (Innsbruck, 1926), 223–26; Biedermann, II, i, 346–80; R. Stintzing and E. Landsberg, *Geschichte der deutschen Rechtswissenschaft* (Munich, 1880–1910, 3 pts. in 6 v.), III, 45 ff.; Erik Wolf, *Grotius, Pufendorf, Thomasius. Drei Kapitel zur Gestaltungsgeschichte der Rechtswissenschaft* (Tübingen, 1927); on Halle see Wilhelm Schrader, *Geschichte der Friedrichs-Universität zu Halle* (Berlin, 1894, 2 v.).

[6] Quoted in Ornstein (n. 5), 212; cp. 210–14, 80–83, 262–63.

over. Ernest Augustus, remembering the glories of the great Welf House in the days of Henry the Lion, chafed under the reduced dimension and diminished importance to which the duchy of Brunswick had shrunk owing to the pernicious practice of partition. He was ambitious to restore primogeniture and to procure his elevation to an electorate, and for this reason employed Leibniz as historian and publicist. The designation of his patron as the ninth elector in 1692 and the succession of the House of Hanover to the throne of England in 1714 in the person of George I crowned Leibniz' labors as a publicist and propagandist.

Between these events, and indeed as an influential factor in promoting them, Leibniz' historical researches were pursued. His first book, his *Codex juris gentium diplomaticus* (1693) at once marked him as a successor to Grotius in the field of international law. A professional philosopher and scientist, Leibniz applied the scientific spirit to historical method and philosophical speculation to the meaning of history. To get at the truth of any matter, he thought it desirable to separate the historian (i.e., the witness) from his account (i.e., the rationalization); one must, he held, carefully study the psychology of the man who records events and then apply the same searching investigation to the sources. For, Leibniz believed, there was a grain of truth even in incredible accounts, such as legends and miracles. It is, therefore, the scholar's duty to search for these particles of truth; in brief, to separate the wheat from the chaff. From a technical viewpoint, these ideas were keen and suggestive, but they did not go far enough. Strangely enough for a philosopher, Leibniz was so occupied with textual criticism that he neglected the human element in history and paid little attention to social forces.

Another weakness of Leibniz as a social thinker was his tendency to schematize. Following the classificatory method of Bacon, he divided knowledge into three categories: "singular," or History; "observation," or Inductive Science; "universal and demonstrable," or Science. Certain necessary truths, Leibniz said, did not depend on experience; hence he called his attitude "the philosophy of history *à priori*." Since the "individual embraces the infinite," and the infinite is not subject to investigation, there was no reason for troubling one's self about human causes and effects, or of establishing "laws which govern historical phenomena."

Clearly, Leibniz was so thoroughly a scientist and philosopher that, in chaining history to a schema of the infinite, his "pre-established harmony," he unwittingly did away with history altogether. His seventeenth-century sophistication did not perceive that history could not be rigidly subjected to the methods of natural science. In a letter writ-

ten to Duke Ernst Augustus of Brunswick, in 1692, Leibniz makes
some remarkable statements about the nature of history.

> To judge history distinctly, one may compare it to the body of an animal, where the
> bones support everything, the nerves form the connection, the spirit which moves the
> machine, the humors which consist of nourishing juices, and finally the flesh which
> gives completion to the whole mass. The parts of history correspond thus: chronology
> to bones, genealogy to nerves, hidden motives to invisible spirits, useful examples to
> juices, and the detail of circumstances to the whole mass of flesh. I consider, accordingly,
> chronology or the knowledge of time as the basis or skeleton of the whole body, which
> forms the foundation and support of all the rest. The genealogy of illustrious persons
> corresponds, in my opinion, to the nerves and tendons of history, for since history records
> what has passed among men, it is necessary that it pay attention to the natural connec-
> tions among men, which consist of consanguinity. And since succession has always given
> power and authority, . . . it follows that histories of nations, of kingdoms and of princi-
> palities depend much on connections, changes and families, whence came wars, unions
> of many countries to form a great monarchy, and the pretensions of one prince on an-
> other. . . .
> Since history without truth is a body without life, it is necessary that one try to assert
> nothing without a basis of fact, and that gradually one purge history of fables, which
> have crept into it. . . . It is also necessary to admit that not all parts of history are
> equally susceptible to exactitude, for who could assure us of hidden motives reported
> in ancient history.[7]

Except for the last sentence, the whole letter is, to say the least,
incredibly naive. A comparison of history with animals or machines,
so typical of the age, is nothing but crude materialism. No wonder that
Leibniz' influence on history was small.

It would be an error, however, to underrate Leibniz' influence upon
the interpretation of history, for *that* was very great. Leibniz was
greatest in his metaphysics. Lessing, Kant, Wolf, Winckelmann, and
Herder may never have read his *Annales*, but they were imbued with
his philosophy. His fundamental ideas of the continuity of history, and
that change was a developmental principle and a genetic process in
human society, were destined to revolutionize the writing of history.

The first of the new philosophers who picked up the thread where
Leibniz dropped it, was Christian Wolff (b. 1679). As professor of philosophy and mathematics at Halle, Wolff came under the influence of
Leibniz. Nevertheless, Wolff did not accept all of Leibniz' rationalism,
insisting that all cognition must be based on experience. Leibniz admitted with some asperity that his pupil followed him only in mathematics
and physics, but not in philosophy. "Herr Wolff," Leibniz wrote to a
friend, "accepts some of my ideas, but since he is essentially occupied
with teaching mathematics, and since we did not have much exchange

---

[7] E. Bodemann, in *Zeitschrift des historischen Vereins für Niedersachsen*, 1885. The letter
was written in French and was intended as a preface to his history of the ducal house.

of ideas on philosophy, he can hardly know more about my views than what I have published." [8]

Wolff's philosophic system is contained in four works, on Logic (1712), Metaphysics, Ethics, and Social Science (*Gesellschaftslehre* and *Staatslehre*), the latter appearing in 1720–21. To Wolff, philosophy was the science of all possible things insofar as they are possible; what is possible is that which contains no inner contradiction. The importance of Wolff lies in his clear formulation of philosophic concepts and his emphasis on consciousness and experience; "for what is not known to us we can not experience." He had a deep influence on all subsequent German thinkers. [9] He was the real founder of the *Aufklärung*.

The first historian of New Germany in point of time was John Jacob Mascou (1689–1761), [10] professor at Leipzig, whose great service to historiography lies in his use of the German tongue and his emphasis— independently of Voltaire—on cultural and religious affairs. His best-known work is *The History of the Ancient Germans* (1726–37), to the period of the Merovingians. [11] By "Germans" Mascou meant all those tribes who by "language, stature, religion, and manners" were of "German extraction." He traced these "nations" through their various migrations to the new kingdoms which they founded in distant regions. His chief interest, he explained, was to get at the approximate truth concerning the lives, customs, wars, and politics of the ancient Germans. For this purpose he used, so far as possible, only contemporary authorities and remains. [12] Because of his use of sources and his impartiality, Mascou's history, though over two centuries old, is still readable today.

The low state of education in Germany in the first half of the eighteenth century had a depressing effect on the study of history. It is difficult in this day to imagine to what degradation it had sunk. As a spiritual force education seemed almost in danger of perishing. Even Latin and Greek were in disrepute. The New Testament was often the only Greek text to be studied. Thomasius, the first Rector of the Uni-

---

[8] Quoted in Moritz Kronenberg, *Geschichte des deutschen Idealismus* (Munich, 1909–12, 2 v.), I, 197.

[9] See Schrader (n. 5), I, 168–81; Zart (n. 1), 17–30; BIEDERMANN, II, i, 394–426. When, after being ousted from Halle by the Pietists, Frederick the Great reinstated Wolff in his position, Voltaire wrote: "Socrates is on the throne, and truth reigns." See Joseph Texte, "Les premiers vulgarisateurs de la littérature allemande en France," *RCC*, IV, pt. ii (1896), 133–41; Cassirer (n. 1), 160–77, 234–37, 306–07, 444–53.

[10] The Germans spell his name Maskow or Maskov. See FUETER, 394–95; Woldemar Görlitz, *Die historische Forschungsmethode Johann Jacob Maskovs* (Leipzig, 1901); Georg Voigt, "Johann Jacob Mascov," *HZ*, XV (1866), 327–58; R. Treitschke, in *Zeitschrift für Geschichtswissenschaft*, VIII (1847), 146–84.

[11] English translation by Thomas Lediard (London, 1737, 2 v.). A contemporary reviewer said of the German original that the work was so good that it was regrettable that it was not written in Latin; and such a Latin translation appeared in 1741.

[12] Cp. Lediard's translation (n. 11), I, p. vi.

versity of Halle, wrote: "I should think the Book of Wisdom, of Judith, or the Maccabees would be as good or better than that old fool . . . Homer and the other pagan poets and orators." [13] The first reliever of this darkness was Johann Matthias Gesner (1691–1761), rector of the Thomas Schule in Leipzig in 1730, where one of his colleagues was Johann Sebastian Bach. On the foundation of the University of Göttingen he became professor of rhetoric and librarian. Mr. Trevelyan has written of him:

> His fundamental principle was that the ancient authors were to be read for their content, for the wisdom of their thoughts and for the beauty of the form and expression which they gave to those thoughts, so that the pupil's mind and taste should be trained by a loving study of the greatest works of literature and philosophy. It was to be a training for life in the highest sense, a training of the mind and spirit to understand and judge the values of the world, so that in any circumstances the man should "have full knowledge of the right road. . . ." And it was to be something more than a training for life; for the gifted few it was to lead them to creative effort of their own, in literature, in philosophy and in art.[14]

The influence of the new universities upon the intellectual awakening in Germany is here to be observed. A list of such institutions may not be out of place. First in time and importance was the University of Göttingen, founded in 1737 and modelled after Halle (1694); it began with a meager appropriation of 16,000 thaler, but by 1763 Göttingen had a library of 200,000 volumes. The second great institution was the Berlin Academy of Science, founded by Frederick the Great in 1740. This Academy was not a university but a scientific institution after the pattern of the French Academy; in fact, its director (Maupertuis), many of its members, and the language of the publications were all French. In 1751 Göttingen followed Berlin in establishing a Society of Sciences which began to publish the famous *Göttingische Gelehrte Anzeigen*. These two model institutions were followed by many others: Erfurt (1756), Munich (1763), Mannheim (1766). The same period also saw the rise of a number of technical colleges: Brunswick (1745), Freiburg (1765), Clausthal (1775).[15] The new scientific and intellectual

---

[13] Cited in Humphrey Trevelyan, *The Popular Background to Goethe's Hellenism* (London, 1933), 6, cp. 26–34. The influence of Bayle's *Dictionary*, of which a German translation by Gottsched was published at Leipzig in 1741, was pernicious in the depression of classical studies (see *ibid.*, 63).

[14] Cp. Marshall Montgomery, *Friedrich Hölderlein and the Neo-Hellenic Movement* (London, 1923), 6.

[15] E. Conrad, "Learned Societies and Academies in Early Times," *Pedagogical Seminary*, XII (1905), 384 ff.; SMITH, II, 402–49; BIEDERMANN, II, ii, pt. 1, 660–84. On the Berlin Academy see Christian Bartholmess, *Histoire philosophique de l'Académie de Prusse depuis Leibniz jusqu'à Schelling, particulièrement sous Frédéric-Le-Grand* (Paris, 1850–51, 2 v.); and Adolf Harnack, *Geschichte der königlich preussischen Akademie der Wissenschaften zu Berlin* (Berlin, 1901, 3 v. in 4).

spirit which swept through Germany "did far more to transform the ideal of culture than all the princes and bureaucracies." [16]

The distinct characteristic of the German *Aufklärung* after Leibniz is its revolt against Rationalism and its reaction against such excessive scientific schematization as that of Leibniz, Descartes, and Bacon. The French Enlightenment—"of which Reason was God, Newton's *Principia* the Bible, and Voltaire the prophet" [17]—had exalted rationalism and utilitarianism. The German *Aufklärung* emphasized experience and intuition and subjective processes of thought which were held to possess eternal and universal values. While the French Rationalists were anti-historical and pragmatic, the German thinkers turned to the past, not for purposes of "learning by example," but of showing the continuity of human spirit and of social phenomena. In short, where the French discarded moral values and threw out God-in-history by the front door, the Germans (as will be seen in connection with Kant, Herder, and Hegel) brought Him in by the back door, though He had ceased to be a subject of Christian dogma in the transition.

Emancipation of German thought from bondage to French intellectualism was a long and slow process. Practically all the important German thinkers, figuratively speaking, went to school in France until the very end of the century. Before 1750 there was virtually no German literature and almost no independent German thought. Diderot was read, translated, and admired throughout Germany. "Diderot," Goethe wrote, "is Diderot, a unique person. He who disdains him or his writings is a fool." [18] Lessing was influenced not only by Diderot but also by Bayle. Wieland is full of Voltaire. As late as 1783 the Berlin Academy offered a prize on the subject of "What made French become a universal language," and the reward went to a Frenchman, Rivarol, for his book *Discours sur l'universalité de la langue française*, in which he propounded the thesis that the eighteenth century was *le monde français*. [19]

French culture dominated Germany essentially for political reasons. Germany was balkanized into more than three hundred principalities and there was, therefore, no vigorous political life and no unifying

[16] H. A. L. Fisher, *Studies in Napoleonic Statesmanship: Germany* (Oxford, 1903), 277.

[17] SMITH, II, 21.

[18] Karl Rosenkranz, *Diderot's Leben und Werke* (Leipzig, 1866, 2 v.), and the review of this by A. Béranger, "Diderot et l'Allemagne," *Bibliothèque universelle et revue suisse*, XXXII (1868), 192–212.

[19] Joseph Texte, "L'Hégémonie littéraire de la France au XVIIIᵉ siècle," *RCC*, IV, pt. i (1895–96), 319–29; J. J. Honegger, *Kritische Geschichte der französischen Kultureinflüsse in den letzten Jahrhunderten* (Berlin, 1875). In 1748 Melchior Grimm (b. 1723) went to Paris and joined the circle of Diderot, Rousseau, Helvétius, etc.; it was he who became the liaison man between French and Germans, though few French intellectuals knew or cared much about Germany.

national center.[20]   Throughout Germany the cultural level was as low as the contempt of the princes for learning was widespread.[21]

Distinguished Germans were, of course, aware of the deplorable condition of their country, although there was not much national feeling. "Don't try to form a nation," Lessing advised his countrymen; "be content to remain men." [22] Nevertheless, there was much critical thinking on the subject.   The following two quotations are illuminating:

> As to the Germans [Frederick the Great wrote to Voltaire] their defect is not a lack of mind.   Good sense has fallen to their share; and their character approaches that of the English.   The Germans are laborious and profound; when once they take hold of a subject, they lean heavily upon it.   Their books are tediously diffuse.   If they could be corrected of their heaviness and familiarised a little more with the graces I should not despair of my nation's producing great men.   But there is one difficulty which will always prevent our having good books in our language; and that is because the use of words is not fixed and, since Germany is divided among a vast number of sovereigns, there will never be any way of bringing these sovereigns to submit to the decisions of an Academy.
>
> There is no resource for our learned men except to write in foreign languages, and since it is very difficult to know them thoroughly, 'tis to be feared our literature will never make great progress.   And there is another difficulty as great as the first—the princes as a rule despise the learned . . .; they also take it upon themselves to scorn those who are worth a thousand times more than they are.[23]

It does not matter that the king of Prussia was wrong in his prognosis; he was right in his analysis.   Years later Goethe expressed himself in a similar spirit.

> All men of talent [the great poet said to Eckermann], all the good heads are scattered throughout Germany, separated one from the other by fifty, by one hundred leagues, and personal contact, personal exchange of views very rare. . . .   Now imagine a city like Paris, where the best heads of a great empire are united in one space, and by contact, conflicts, emulation of each day they instruct and elevate each other mutually.[24]

[20] "Not until we shall have a greater national interest," wrote Justus Möser, "will we . . . be able to express ourselves more fruitfully.   Until then history will remain at most an *Urkundenbuch* to teach morals and to preach an edifying sermon." *Sämmtliche Werke*, ed. by B. R. Abeken (Berlin, 1842–43, 10 v. in 5), IX, 156, from his article "Ueber die deutsche Sprache," 136–57.

[21] "The general level of character and intellect was low, and the scandals of courts and courtiers provoked disgust and indignation.   The most docile people in Europe watched with impotent despair the orgies of the last Elector of Bavaria, the capricious tyranny of Karl Eugen of Württemberg, the insanity of Duke Karl of Zweibrücken, and the Byzantine decadence of the ecclesiastical Electors on the Rhine.   On the eve of the Revolution the larger part of Germany was poor, ignorant, ill-governed and discontented." G. P. Gooch, "Germany and the French Revolution," *Transactions of the Royal Historical Society*, ser. 3, X (1916), 51–52.

[22] Texte (n. 19), 319.

[23] Frederick to Voltaire, July 6, 1737, in Richard Aldington, ed., *Letters of Voltaire and Frederick the Great*, selected and translated (New York, 1927), 77; cp. Richard Fester, ed., *Friedrich II der Grosse, Briefe und Schriften* (Leipzig, 1927, 2 v.), I, 291–92; Frederick the Great, *Dissertation sur la littérature allemande, les défauts qu'on peut lui réprocher, les causes de ces défauts et les moyens de les corriger* (Berlin, 1780).

[24] Translation from quotation in Texte (n. 9), 133.

"It is hardly an exaggeration to say that for almost a century the characteristic philosophy of Germany has been a philosophy of history. . . ." [25] Few of the men who shaped and formed the new historical spirit in Germany in the eighteenth century were professional historians. The greatest among them were Lessing, Winckelmann, Kant, and F. A. Wolf. The greatest historian was Justus Möser. In the sphere of historiography the practitioners were inferior to the theorists. Before the founding of the University of Berlin (1809), an event of incalculable significance in the history of German (and European) culture, Germany produced a Kant, but not a Gibbon. One of the reasons for the superiority of the philosophers of history over the writers of history was, as Justus Möser explained, the absence of a vigorous national life. In a period when the nation had no unity and no center, there was no stimulus for the writing of great history. Lacking the tangible, the Germans indulged in the speculative; where there was no visible reality to discipline one's thoughts, it was easy to soar in unrestrained absolutes. In the words of a well-known witticism, the English controlled the sea, the French the land, and the Germans the air. Broadly speaking, the originality of German historiography was in inverse proportion to the depth of its philosophy.

The most common type of historical writing in the first half of the eighteenth century was universal history, which usually treated one or more of the "four great monarchies" to the period of the migrations. In 1746 two Halle theologians published a *General World History* from materials taken out of an English *Universal History;* in the years following, these extracts were freely worked over by historians, including the well-known Schlözer. Such world histories were generally uncritical miscellanies of trivia. A few historians devoted themselves to Germanic history, but in a narrow and pedantic spirit. One need only mention, in passing, J. G. Eccard's *Historia Germaniae* (1737) and *De origine Germanorum* (1750); J. S. Pütter's works on the Germanic constitution (1786) and the Peace of Westphalia (1795). But a mere list of names and titles is of little significance. [26]

Gotthold Ephraim Lessing (1729–81) was the earliest German writer who possessed a clear and living apprehension of the characteristics of his age. [27] He had "the historic sense and a great capacity for appreci-

[25] Dewey, *German Philosophy and Politics* (n. 1), 92.
[26] SCHAUMKELL, 209–37; BIEDERMANN, II, ii, pt. 3, 702–06, and *passim;* WOLF, 152–53.
[27] James Sime, *Lessing* (2nd ed., London, 1890, 2 v.); Francke (n. 1), 265–99; BIEDERMANN II, ii, pt. 3, 748–801; Erich Schmidt, *Lessing: Geschichte seines Lebens und seiner Schriften* (1884–92, 2 v.); also *QR*, CXLVII (1879), 1–48 and CLXXIII (1891), 169–70; *FQR*, XXV (1840), 233–53; *BQR*, LXVIII (1878), 333–60; *LTLS*, 1929, pp. 49–50; and for a French view cp. Victor Cherbuliez, *RDM*, 1868: 1, 78–121, 981–1024.

ating the original intellectual contributions of earlier times," [28] with the ability to interpret his own period to his own people. "His discoveries have become commonplaces, his boundaries are landmarks" in the intellectual history of Germany. He was a very great critic, not only of literature but of the intellectual and moral life. He restored Aristotle—not the Aristotle of the medieval schoolmen, but of the Greeks. Of all the critics since Aristotle Lessing was most truly Aristotelian. He uncrowned Descartes by showing the extremes and abuse of thinking in the Rationalistic philosophy and reinstated Aristotle as a master of method. He had an intuitive aversion to Cartesian absolutes—"a feeling that truth is as much a quality of the minds that seek it as of the things wherein they find it." In his *Kleine Schriften* he wrote: "The manner in which one has come to a matter is as valuable, and even as instructive as the matter itself." Here was a new and refreshing view of method quite different from the abusive method of Cartesian logic. Truth to Lessing was not the Q.E.D. of a syllogism, but a verity. In his treatise on Berengar of Tours he wrote: "I know not whether it is a duty to sacrifice fortune and life for truth. The courage and decision necessary for this are not gifts with which we can endow ourselves. But I do know it is a duty to teach the truth, to teach it entire or not at all."

To Lessing history was a continuous process. He developed Leibniz' doctrine of continuity, and applied it to history. Everything human moved altogether. Because Rationalism was shallow, it was self-satisfied. The Enlightenment did not know how to study history because it had no sympathetic feeling for the past. The historical method was not yet born. He was aware that all approach to truth is an approximation, and that in one's power to hold various approximations together in a single act of apprehension lay the capacity for truth. In his *Laokoon* he expressed this creed of truth. "The ultimate object of the sciences is truth. Truth is necessary for the soul, and in the satisfaction of this essential need it is tyranny to employ even the slightest coercion (Der Endzweck der Wissenschaften ist Wahrheit. Wahrheit ist der Seele notwendig und es wird Tyrannei, ihr in Befriedigung dieses wesentlichen Bedürfnisses geringsten Zwang anzuthun)." This was noble teaching in a day when the speciousness and subterfuge of extreme Rationalism were glaring offenses of much current thought. Aristotle was Lessing's first master. His second was Leibniz, from whom he got the sense of the genetic and the organic in things which have life in them, from plants and animals, to men and the ideas in their brains.

If the advancement of truth be the first law of the historian, then

[28] Harold Höffding, *History of Modern Philosophy* (London, 1900, 2 v.), II, 19.

Lessing had the historical mind in all that he wrote. He revered classical culture and classical tradition. But his reverence was not idolatry and he deprecated "the tendency to exalt the remote merely because it is remote." [29] He held that "the name of the best historian is to be attributed to one who describes the history of his own times and of his own country." Yet even in subjects which seemed remote from his age Lessing discovered points of contact or of similarity with the living present.

Lessing died in 1782. In the same year Schiller published his first drama, and—what is of far greater significance—Kant issued the *Critique of Pure Reason*. It was another conjuncture of great books like that in 1776 when Gibbon published the first volume of the *Decline and Fall* and Adam Smith's *Wealth of Nations* saw the light.

What had been a flux of ideas with Leibniz and Wolf and Lessing became philosophic finality with Immanuel Kant (1724–1804). [30] He who is not a philosopher by profession approaches Kant with some trepidation; but the student of historiography cannot afford to neglect the Königsberg philosopher who dominated the intellectual universe of his time quite as much as his contemporaries Frederick the Great and later Napoleon overshadowed the political world. With this caution,

[29] From this sentence, in Sime's *Lessing* (n. 27), Tennyson was inspired to write: "The past will ever have a glory from its being far."

[30] The English literature on Kant is extensive. See H. St. Chamberlain, *Immanuel Kant*, tr. by Lord Redesdale (London and New York, 1914, 2 v.); Kuno Fischer, *A Critique of Kant*, tr. by W. S. Hough (London, 1888), ch. iii; Edward Caird, *A Critical Philosophy of Immanuel Kant* (2nd ed., Glasgow, 1909, 2 v.); A. D. Lindsay, *The Philosophy of Immanuel Kant* (London, 1919); John Watson, ed., *The Philosophy of Kant* (Glasgow, 1908); James Ward, *Immanuel Kant* (Oxford, 1923: British Academy annual philosophical lecture); Höffding (n. 28), Bk. VII; Reinhold Aris, *History of Political Thought in Germany from 1789 to 1815* (London, 1936), 65–105; Francke (n. 1), 328–31; W. C. Dampier-Whetham, *A History of Science, and Its Relations with Philosophy and Religion* (New York, 1929), 209–13; William Hastie, *Kant's Principles of Politics* (Edinburgh, 1891); A. C. McGiffert, *The Rise of Modern Religious Ideas* (New York, 1915); Josiah Royce, *Lectures on Modern Idealism* (Yale University Press, 1919); G. G. Zerffii, "Immanuel Kant in His Relation to Modern History," *Transactions of the Royal Historical Society*, IV (1876), 75–96; F. Adler, "A Critique of Kant's Ethics," in *Essays Philosophical and Psychological in Honor of William James* (New York, 1908); and *QR*, CLXXIII (1891), 167–68. Bertrand Russell, *An Outline of Philosophy* (London, 1927), 83 considers Kant—who "deluged the philosophic world with muddle and mystery"—"a mere misfortune."

In foreign languages, the best account is Karl Vorländer's *Immanuel Kant, der Mann und das Werk* (Leipzig, 1924, 2 v.), esp. vol. II, Bk. IV, ch. 4, "Kant as Politiker." See also Paul Menzer, *Kants Lehre von der Entwicklung in Natur und Geschichte* (Berlin, 1911); Konrad Dieterich, *Kant und Newton* (Tübingen, 1876), and his *Kant und Rousseau* (*ibid.*, 1878); A. Riehl, *Der philosophische Kriticismus und seine Bedeutung für die positive Wissenschaft* (Leipzig, 1876–79, 2 v.); Friedrich Paulsen, *Versuch einer Entwickelungsgeschichte der kantischen Erkenntnisstheorie* (Leipzig, 1875); Benno Erdmann, *Martin Knutzen und seine Zeit* (Leipzig, 1876); the same, *Kant's Kriticismus in der ersten und in der zweiten Auflage der Kritik der reinen Vernunft* (Leipzig, 1878); the same, *Immanuel Kant's Prolegomena* (Leipzig, 1878); Kronenberg (n. 8), II, 260–66; Gumplowicz (n. 5), 272–85; SCHAUMKELL, 166–79; BIEDERMANN, II, ii, pt. 3, 723–25, 865–925; A. Aulard, *La paix future d'après la révolution française et Kant* (Paris, 1915); Victor Basch, *Les doctrines politiques des philosophes classiques de l'Allemagne, Leibniz, Kant, Fichte, Hegel* (Paris, 1927), 60–71; Georges Dwelshauvers, "La philosophie de Kant," *RCC*, VI, pt. i (1897–98), 204–17, 459–68, 492–97, 612–21, 693–706, 763–65; D. Nolen, "Les maîtres de Kant," *Revue philosophique*, VII (1879), 481–503.

we will proceed to treat Kant as a thinker on social matters rather than as the author of the *Critique of Pure Reason*.

Kant had an uneventful life. Concerning his objective experiences, little can be said. He was born at Königsberg, lived at Königsberg, taught philosophy at Königsberg, died at Königsberg. He never travelled, never married, never did anything except think. His life was a long adventure in ideas.

Kant must be approached from the point of view of Kant's mind. All his adventures were concentrated in his thought. He was the son of intensely pious parents—his mother was of Scottish origin—and he was exposed to rigorous Pietism from his earliest youth. At the Frederician College where he studied, most of the hours were devoted to prayers, hymns, Bible, and more Bible. At the University of Königsberg, where Kant was registered in the faculty of theology, he quietly rebelled against the parental and tutorial clericalism and began to attend lectures on mathematics, science, and philosophy. The result of this silent intellectual conversion was a life-long interest in the natural sciences, a comprehensive acquaintance with Newton's *Principia*, and finally a doctoral dissertation on the "True Measure of Forces" (1755). Even at the university Kant displayed his extraordinary susceptibility to various streams of thought; from his professor Albert Schultz he imbibed the Wolffian combination of Deism and Pietism, and from Martin Knutzen he learned Leibniz' metaphysics and Newton's physics. Furthermore, Knutzen's colleague Rappolt taught young Kant the English language and literature, especially Pope and Addison (both of whom Kant quotes in his *Natural History of Heaven*, 1755). By the time Kant took his degree at the age of thirty-one, and was ready to teach mathematics and philosophy, his piety was already questionable. When the newly-created doctor applied for the chair of philosophy at Königsberg, Schultz interviewed him with some suspicion. "Do you fear God in your heart?" Schultz asked. Kant's answer is not known, but he did not get the chair until fifteen years later.

As a professor Kant lectured on philosophy, natural theology, anthropology, and geography. His life coincided with a number of revolutionary events, both in the sphere of politics and in the field of intellectual endeavor. He was the contemporary of Voltaire, Rousseau, Diderot, and the other French *philosophes;* he read the English thinkers, especially Locke and Hume; he followed the discoveries in science; he lived through the Frederician wars, the American Revolution, the French Revolution, and died just when Napoleon was transforming Europe. Kant stood above his time, participating in nothing, doing nothing; he simply permitted all the currents of thought to filter through his capacious and receptive mind, and after all these streams had converged, he produced the great synthesis.

Observe, for instance, the regular chronological sequence of his mental fermentation. Between 1740, the year when he became interested in philosophy, and 1760, he investigated the Leibniz-Wolff philosophy. From 1760 to 1770 he delved into the English skeptics, particularly Hume. In the following decade, 1770–80, he was silent—perhaps he was reading Rousseau and meditating. The fifth decade, 1780–90, saw the publication of his *Critique of Pure Reason* (1781), and the last period he devoted to the application of his system to the solution of the problems of universal history.[31]

Philosophically, Kant posited three fundamental problems which may be reduced to three question marks: "Who? What? Why? Who observes the phenomena? What is the essence of the phenomena? And Why do we see what we see? The *Critique of Pure Reason* solved the first problem. Here Kant investigated the perceptive faculties and demonstrated the subjective character of human knowledge. The world of the senses, Kant showed, originates in matter and form; matter is communicated to us by experience, and hence the mind is composed of sense impressions, without which it would be empty of content. We do not know the absolute truth, but we have demonstrable truths verified by experience. He owed this conception to Leibniz. But Kant contended that you must first ascertain the nature of knowledge before you can do any clear thinking. The second problem, the What, Kant analyzed in his *Critique of Practical Reason*, in which he formulated the doctrines of freedom and the moral order of the universe. Where, as Kant showed in his *Pure Reason*, the intellect is confined to the realm of the senses, the human will transcends those limitations and links itself with the eternal. True, the mind cannot demonstrate such assumptions as God, freedom, immortality; but the human will must make such assumptions as vital to its existence. The conscience experiences what the mind cannot prove, which does not mean that such absolute moral ideas do not exist. Man *feels* the moral law within himself, and this lifts him above himself. Concerning the Why of things, Kant confessed himself unable to give an answer; here the problem lies in the realms of cosmol-

[31] The following is a chronological list of Kant's major works: *Critique of Pure Reason* (1781); *Prolegoma of Any Possible Metaphysics* (1783); *Principles of a Metaphysic of Morals* (1785); *Metaphysical Introduction to the Natural Sciences* (1786); *Critique of Practical Reason* (1788); *Critique of Our Reasoning Faculty* (1790); *Religion within the Limits of Pure Reason* (1793).

Among the individual translations, consult: *Critique of Pure Reason*, tr. by M. Müller (New York, 1881); N. Kemp Smith, *A Commentary to Kant's 'Critique of Pure Reason'* (2nd ed., London, 1918); *Prolegomena to any Future Metaphysics*, tr. by P. Carus (Chicago, 1902); *Kant's Critique of Practical Reason and Other Works on the Theory of Ethics*, tr. by T. K. Abbot (6th ed., New York, 1909); *Kant's Kritik of Judgment*, tr. by J. H. Bernard (2nd ed., New York, 1914). There are a number of translations of the booklet on *Perpetual Peace*.

ogy, psychology, and theology. "We may reasonably say that the Kingdom of God is come on earth," he wrote, "as soon as ever the principle has taken root generally, and in the public mind, that the creeds of the churches have gradually to pass into the universal religion of reason. . . ." These works were written in 1793 when Kant was sixty-nine years of age. Nevertheless, though he was world-famous and hailed everywhere as the greatest philosopher, Kant was warned by the Prussian Government and compelled to speak no more of religion in his lectures.[32]

Not only were the implications of Kant's philosophic thought significant to the understanding of history, but his direct approach was fundamentally historical. Throughout his *Critiques* there runs the basic thread of historical development. The evolution of things in the objective world, Kant showed, coincides with their natural history, which to him was the "outer garb of inward forces, working in humanity according to a pre-arranged law, which law must be assumed to be as fixed as that by which the solar systems are brought into order and cohesion." In other words, the "outer garb" is an expression of the whole evolutionary process in nature, observed by man but not determined by him. "It is true philosophy," Kant wrote, "to trace the diverse forms of a thing through all its history." History, like philosophy, is a part of a continuous process through time, leading finally to civilization and freedom. Before Kant grasped this great idea that the understanding of history must repose on the perception of a distinct relationship between historical evidences and the pervasive influence of a developmental principle in events, history was but an "inorganic collection of facts . . . bound together by the classifications of *à priori* thinkers."[33]   Kant made inorganic history organic. "For Kant history was more than an enumeration of facts or an unmarshalled succession of events."

What was as significant was Kant's conception of causation, a problem which was first thrust upon his attention by Hume's philosophy. Cause implies priority in time, but since everything is relative, there must be a predicate to a cause. Kant thought of causation in phenomena, not as involving mysterious dynamic powers, but as equivalent to succession according to certain laws—in other words, the distinct relationship of phenomena is based upon a theory of evolution. This is the famous *werden*, i.e., "becoming," principle. Everything must develop in time and time is a creative force.

---

[32] Bernard Bosanquet, *Science and Philosophy and Other Essays* (London and New York, 1927), 350–51.

[33] Leslie Stephen, *History of English Thought in the Eighteenth Century* (London, 1876, 2 v.), I, 377.

Kant's principles not only had an immediate effect on philosophers such as Hegel and historians such as Ranke, but it revolutionized man's historical attitude. For Kant overturned the collective experience of mankind by his simple assumption that our notions do not regulate themselves according to things, but things appear according to our notions of things. It is not so much, he pointed out, the past which decides our attitude about the present as the present which decides as to the past; our concepts of the past change continually, depending upon the spiritual level of culture of the present. Hegel was subsequently able to take these ideas and subject them to his famous triad of thesis, antithesis, and synthesis, which, furthermore, led him to the glorification of the Absolute State.

Kant always believed in the individual as the embodiment of the moral idea. "The social value of man," Kant wrote in his *Idee zu einer allgemeinen Geschichte in weltbürgerlicher Absicht* (1784), "is the measure of culture." Culture to Kant meant the fulfilment of man's *idea* of freedom, an idea which impels him despite himself. The urge towards freedom is universal, working through the moral law, and ascending toward perfection by means of struggle. In the stage of barbarism, struggle (so necessary in the evolution of culture) is rude and harsh, but as man rises in the scale to achieve civil freedom, conflicts (Kant thought too optimistically, it would seem) become less destructive and involve less danger to man's freedom. Humanity can achieve its fullest capacities only under conditions of security, that is, as members of society; hence the need for public law to protect individuals. At this point Kant carried his ideas of freedom and man's inherent worth to their logical conclusion: the highest form of the State, he said, is a constitutional government. But even a constitutional State, the canny Scottish-Prussian concluded, does not guarantee security so long as nations persist in endangering freedom and existence by their barbarous warfare. Wherefor Kant urged—in the name of human needs and the moral law—the establishment of a sort of league of nations, a "Federation of Free Civilized and Constitutionally Governed Peoples."

Kant was the first German thinker to proclaim the principles of "liberty, equality, and property," which was the original form of the Revolutionary slogan, and "it was in his thought that the German middle classes became familiar with the idea of constitutional government." But his political influence has, in Dr. Aris' opinion, been strangely overrated. He was certainly in no way responsible for the French Revolution, and it is equally absurd to bracket him with Fichte and Hegel as an apostle of Pan-Germanism. He was, in fact, imbued with the cosmopolitan spirit of the Enlightenment, as is shown by his essay on "Perpetual Peace," which, for the rest, Wilhelm von Humboldt rightly described as "not very important."

Talleyrand once said of the French revolutionaries that they were "builders of theories for an imaginary world." The observation would have been as applicable to the German thinkers of the same period who first were interested in politics even when they were not radicals or revolutionists. The reason is evident. In a Germany split up into some three hundred states it was only for an imaginary world that their theories could be built. Moreover, living as they did under the rule of absolute sovereigns, they had no practical experience of politics, and the political ideas they evolved in their studies were apt to be vague and contradictory. Yet these ideas were destined to have important and lasting effects.

Thus we see how this remarkable little professor of philosophy was led from one inexorable train of thought to another. Starting as a Pietist, he became a disciple of Newton. He first abolished God and then adroitly brought him back in another form. A humble subject of Frederick the Great, he developed into an ardent pacifist and republican. And finally, when the nations of Europe were allying to destroy the French Revolution, Kant rose in defense of liberty by advocating a Pan-European league of republics!

Before analyzing Kant's social-political ideas and their effect on later thinkers, it may be illuminating to translate a passage from his little known *Ideas for a General History.*

The problem of establishing a complete civic constitution is dependent upon the problem of the relation between states regulated by laws, and can not be solved without the latter. . . . Nature had used the incompatibility of men, even the great communities and States, as a means of using the inevitable antagonisms for a condition of peace and security; that is, nature drives through wars, misery, destruction . . . to a league of nations, wherein each, even the smallest State, may expect security and law. . . . No matter how visionary such an idea may appear to be . . ., it is, nevertheless, an inevitable result of need which . . . forces the States to the same conclusion as that to which the barbarous man was once reluctantly forced, namely: to give up brutal freedom in order to seek peace and security in a lawful [gesetzmässig] constitution. All wars are, accordingly, so many attempts (though not in the design of man, but still in the design of nature to bring about new relations between States, to build anew through destruction, or at least dismemberment . . ., until finally—partly through the best possible arrangement of a civic constitution within the nation and partly through a general juridical agreement with other nations—a condition is established which resembles a common civic entity. . . .

We are cultured to a high degree by art and science. We are over-civilized [zivilisiert bis zum Ueberlästigen] to all manner of politeness and decency. But to consider ourselves as moral, much is still lacking. For the idea of morality belongs to culture; the use of this idea, however, which confines itself to love of honor and superficial decency, is only similar to morality, is merely civilization. Nothing of this sort [morality] can be expected, so long as States use all their forces for their vain and violent plans for expansion, and thereby incessantly block, as well as withdraw support from, the inner education of the way of thinking of their citizens; for morality requires a long inner elaboration of every common being for the training of citizens. But everything which is not based upon moral-good intentions, is nothing but mere pretence and glittering misery. Mankind will remain in this condition until it will have fought its way out of the chaos of its state-relationship in the manner which I have described.[34]

Kant wrote in a similar vein in his famous little treatise on Perpetual Peace. In this booklet, published during the reaction against the French Revolution, Kant contended that all European states must become republican and then form a federation of free governments to prevent war. When Louis XVI was executed, the gentle philosopher of Königsberg defended the rising terror at Paris on the ground that the French were preparing themselves for true liberty. "One must be free in order to learn how wisely to use one's powers. The first attempt will, of course, be imperfect, but experience will show the way; for God has created mankind for freedom."

As a lover of liberty, a thinker who considered inequality "monstrous," Kant differed from virtually every major German philosopher of his time. The difference is particularly noteworthy when one compares—as we shall in a subsequent chapter—the sage of Königsberg with Hegel, to whom the State was absolute, all-embracing, beyond good and evil. Unlike the other German thinkers, Kant put his chief emphasis on the individual, his freedom and his moral worth. "The man who is dependent," Kant observed with almost unwonted passion, "is no longer a man; he has lost this rank, he is nothing more than an appurtenance of another man."

Consequently Kant devoted much of his time to politics and to social studies. He had long outgrown his early attachment to Rousseau with his shallow sentimentalism; and finally achieved a synthesis which no French *philosophe* ever reached. The poised and mature wisdom of Kant is seen in the balance he achieved between the forces of nature and the urges of man. He did not, like Fichte and Hegel, swing to the extreme of reaction. Man—and not Force—always remained uppermost in Kant's thought. The human race, Kant was aware in his more pessimistic moments, had not yet achieved perfection; much still needed to be done, but he never lost hope.

In order to help to educate the human race towards a higher morality and betterment Kant wrote his philosophical works—this aspect of his career has been strangely neglected by professional philosophers who see only technical problems—and drew up an outline for a science of

---

[34] *Ideen zu einer allgemeinen Geschichte in weltbürgerlicher Absicht* (1784), par. 7.

anthropology, a subject on which he often lectured. Anthropology to him meant a closer acquaintance with human cultures, their growth and improvement. He was aware of all the limitations in the way of creating such a science: changes of places and circumstances, lack of adequate materials, the difficulties of getting at human motives. Still, the effort to *know* something about the human race was worth undertaking. As *Hilfsmittel* for such a study, Kant advised, the student should read books of travel, universal histories, biographies, even dramas and romances.

All advances in culture . . . have for their aim the utilization of acquired knowledge and skills for uses in the world; but the most important object of this . . . is man: for he is the final, ultimate aim of himself. To appreciate and recognize man according to his species as an earthling endowed with reason, deserves to be called a special *Weltkenntniss*, even though man is only one of the creatures on earth. Such a study of man, systematically constructed (Anthropology) can be approached either physiologically or pragmatically. The physiological study of man concerns itself with what nature makes him; the pragmatic approach deals with what man makes of himself, or what he can and should make of himself, as a volitional being.[35]

A clear understanding of the teaching of Kant's philosophy underlies an understanding of the modern interpretative historical method, and for the student of history perhaps most precious to be remembered is the great sentence: "The social value of man is the measure of culture," which deserves to rank with Aristotle's famous dictum: "Man is a social animal (*anthropos politikon zoon*)."

The largeness of view, the lambent "atmosphere" of German intellectualism by the second half of the eighteenth century, made the *Aufklärung* a movement of beauty and wonderment. It was fortunate in its founders; it was fortunate in its continuators, the greatest of whom are now to be considered. Lessing had once complained that "our clever writers are seldom scholars, and our scholars are seldom clever writers. The former will not read, will not turn up sources, will not collect materials—in short, will not work, while the latter will do nothing else but this. The former are deficient in materials, the latter in ability to give shape to their materials." It was a protest against mere amateurism in literature and excessive erudition.

But in Justus Möser (1720–94) [36] Lessing would have found a man

[35] Translated from the introduction to his *Anthropologie in pragmatischer Hinsicht abgefasst*, reprinted in *Sämmtliche Werke*, ed. by G. Hartenstein (Leipzig, 1867–68, 8 v.), VI, 431. Until Kant treated anthropology as a branch of philosophy it was restricted to anatomy and physiology.

[36] Möser's *Sämmtliche Werke* were edited by B. R. Abeken (Berlin, 1842–43, 10 v. in 5); the final tenth volume of this edition contains a life by Friedrich Nicolai. Review of the *Werke* by J. Grimm, in Schmidt's *Zeitschrift für Geschichtswissenschaft*, II (1844), 266–72; on Möser's literary works, especially his *Patriotische Phantasien* (1774–78), see Francke, *Social Forces*

after his own mind.[37] His whole life was spent in his native city of Osnabrück. He was not a university professor. He was not influenced by Montesquieu or Voltaire or Rousseau. His historical interest and his attitude of mind were formed by the tradition of the German cameralists.[38] After studying law at Jena and Göttingen Möser returned to his native city and became, in turn, state attorney, chief justice, privy councillor, and finally virtual prime minister to the infant Duke of York (the son of George III of England); in the latter capacity Möser had occasion to travel between Osnabrück and London for consultation about state affairs and thus to become familiar with English conditions.

It was not, however, Möser's activities as a statesman of a petty German principality which caused him to be remembered by posterity, but his celebrated work, *Osnabrückische Geschichte*, which first appeared in 1768. This *History of Osnabrück* is significant from many points of view. In the first place Möser put in the forefront of attention matters which go by the name of *Kulturgeschichte* rather than politics, and not only did he emphasize institutions, but—and in this he differed from Voltaire—he traced the underlying connection between economic organization and political institutions. Secondly, Möser wrote his history less from the point of view of a small territory than from the vantage point of a larger whole, that is, as an integral part of the German Reich. Finally, the statesman-author of Osnabrück, unlike the vast majority of his contemporaries, thought and wrote in terms of German nationalism and not of "particularist" territorialism.

These qualities make Möser a significant figure. As a responsible statesman, he was conservative and practical; there was in him nothing

(n. 1), 315–16. The best account of Möser in English is by my former student, W. J. Bossenbrook, "Justus Möser's Approach to History," in *Medieval and Historiographical Essays in Honor of James Westfall Thompson* (Chicago, 1938), 397–422. Karl Brandi, *Justus Möser. Gesellschaft und Staat* (1921); F. Kreyssig, *Justus Möser* (Berlin, 1857); P. Klassen, *Justus Möser* (Frankfort a. M., 1936: Studien zur Geschichte des Staats- und Nationalgedankens, II); Fritz Rinck, *Justus Mösers Geschichtsauffassung* (Göttingen, 1908); Ludwig Rupprecht, *Justus Mösers soziale und volkswirtschaftliche Anschauungen in ihrem Verhältnis zur Theorie und Praxis seines Zeitalters* (Stuttgart, 1892); WOLF, 205–07 and note; SCHAUMKELL, 30–39; Aris (n. 30), 222–34; BIEDERMANN, II, ii, pt. 3, 706–08; Hatzig, "Justus Möser als Staatsmann und Publizist," *Quellen und Darstellungen zur Geschichte Niedersachsens*, XXVII (1909); R. R. Ergang, "Möser and the Rise of National Thought in Germany," *Journal of Modern History*, V (1933), 172–96; J. Riehemann, in *Mittheilungen des Vereins für Geschichte von Osnabrück*, XXVI (1901); J. Kampffmeyer, "Möser als Geschichtsphilosoph," *Die Neue Zeit* (1899); Hoberg, "Mösers Geschichtsauffassung," *HZ*, CLVIII (1939), 492–503.

[37] Justus Möser must not be confused with Johann Jacob Moser (1701–85), the "father" of German international law. Moser, who was born at Stuttgart and became professor of law at Tübingen at the age of nineteen, devoted most of his life to *Staatsrecht*, on which subject he published a number of volumes. See August Schmid, *Das Leben J. J. Mosers* (Stuttgart, 1868); Hermann Schulze, *Johann Jakob Moser, der Vater des deutschen Staatsrechts* (Leipzig, 1869); and for bibliography WOLF, 214–15 and note. His work was continued and elaborated by his son Friedrich Karl Moser, author of *Der Herr und der Diener* (1759) and *Patriotisches Archiv* (1784–90, 12 v.); for bibliography on him see WOLF, 215 and note.

[38] On the cameralists see the work of Small (n. 1).

of Rousseauist sentimentalism. Möser was sharply opposed to the individualism and cosmopolitanism of the *Aufklärung*. He abstained from speculation and theorizing, insisting on realistic treatment of practical problems. With his experience as an administrator, Möser refused to accept either the practice of "enlightened despotism" or abstract political principles. He defended the small German States as corporate unities, as vital organisms rooted in the German body politic. The State, he said, was not a philosophical concept as the theorists would have it, but a capstone of such corporative associations—especially peasant *Genossenschaften*—based on private property. In describing the constitutional development of Germany, Möser brought into the picture all the factors, geographical, social, economic, which made up the totality. He conceived the whole process of development as a synthesis of the interactions between the various social-economic factors and their influence on the changing classes. These concepts had a deep influence on the later German historians, particularly Niebuhr, Ranke, and Nietzsche.

As a technical historian Möser must also be ranked high. He used primary sources—preferably documents—not merely for show or proof of pet theses but as an integral part of his structure and approach. Möser discounted narrative history and emphasized the economic and technological elements in society. To him, the peasant's common sense and experience were superior to bureaucratic interference. "The useful potatoes," he once remarked dryly, "spread more swiftly than the mulberry trees; and so long as the cultivation of flax brings the peasant good bread, he will not wish to grow silk in order to eat chestnuts." This kind of approach influenced his historical method. Möser really believed that the agrarian regime of his day was still "like that of the earliest times." [39] He was confirmed in this opinion by the discovery of a local peasant family which was still living on the "old farm," the farm in this instance being over six hundred years old. Möser thus introduced an important method of historical interpretation, that of inverse reasoning from present evidences back to the past. Möser believed in the free German village community—the *Mark*.

One of the ironies in the life of this realistic student of society was his unwitting influence on German Romanticism, that movement which Kant characterized as a "mental disease." Möser admired the Middle Ages, which he considered a period when "our nationality displayed the greatest feeling of honor and the greatest physical virtues and a national greatness of its own." The Romanticists who followed Möser

---

[39] *Osnabrückische Geschichte* (ed. 1780), I, 10.

had his admiration for the feudal age but not his critical sense in judging it. Möser, Herder said, was the "author of the first German history with a German head and heart." He was the first German historian who tried to penetrate into the meaning of events and to formulate them as principles.

Although no subject except theology had attracted more interest since the Italian Renaissance, the history of ancient Greece was still a museum of desiccated antiquities. Greek literature, Greek philology, Greek archaeology, Greek art were all dry-as-dust subjects.

A milestone not only in practical methodics but in what is much more, in the new genetic concept of the nature of history, was J. J. Winckelmann's *Geschichte der Kunst des Alterthums* (1764),[40] translated into English by G. H. Lodge. Johann Joachim Winckelmann was born in Prussia in 1717 and was murdered at Trieste in 1768, after having revolutionized man's conception of the art of antiquity; indeed, the present use of the term "art" derives from this remarkable German who spent the most fruitful (and happy) years of his life in Rome. Without Winckelmann the new renaissance in Germany would, perhaps, have been impossible.[41] "He was a man," says Justi, "who only had to open his eyes to see what no one had ever seen before, and to say what no one had said before." [42] It was finely said of him that "he made the Elgin Marbles live."

Winckelmann's ruling idea was that the art of any age is the product of the total culture of that age, that it can be understood only in relation to all other creative expressions of its age, and that, therefore, one must study all the social and economic influences of an epoch to comprehend its art. Thus Winckelmann became the true founder of *Altertumswissenschaft*, a science in which Germans were to excel for over a century.

In his great work, Winckelmann, for the first time, traced the develop-

---

[40] Winckelmann's *Sämmtliche Werke*, ed. by Fernow, Meyer, and Schulze, were published in 1808–20; his *Kleine Schriften und Briefe* were edited by Hermann Uhde-Bernays (Leipzig, 1925, 2 v.). See the excellent biography by Karl Justi, *Winckelmann und seine Zeitgenossen* (3rd ed., 1923, 3 v.); B. Valentin, *Winckelmann* (Berlin, 1932); Goethe, ed., *Winckelmann und sein Jahrhundert* (Tübingen, 1805), also tr. into English by George Kriehn as *Winckelmann and His Age* (1804); FUETER, 484–88; SCHAUMKELL, 39–46; Francke, *Social Forces* (n. 1), 271 ff.; WOLF, 207 and note; and the long review of Justi's biography in *QR*, CXXXVI (1874), 1–55.

[41] "Take away the life-work of Winckelmann from its place in the lives of Schiller and Goethe, and it is impossible to form an idea what those lives could have been" (Bosanquet, n. 32, 373). The influence of Winckelmann may be seen from the following inter-related works, all published in one generation: Baumgarten's *Aesthetica* (1750), which gave the name to this study; Winckelmann's *On the Imitation of Greek Art* (1755), and his *History of Ancient Art* (1764); Lessing's *Laocoon* (1766) and his *Education of the Human Race* (1780), the latter showing the evolutionist idea; Goethe's *Iphigenie* (1787), one of the finest classical plays; and Schiller's *Letters on Aesthetic Education* (1795). Goethe said of Winckelmann: "One learns nothing when one reads him, but one becomes something."

[42] Quoted in BIEDERMANN, II, ii, pt. 3, 687 note.

ment of art in relation to the whole culture of the Greeks. Specifically, he pointed out that Greek art was the expression of a harmonious evolutionary process; art, he said, was not merely a shadow-picture, a symbol, of the spiritual, but a unity of the subjective and objective states of man. Ideal beauty, Winckelmann taught, was superior to natural; for "the expression of a great soul [artist] goes far beyond nature; the artist must feel in himself the strength of the spirit which he impresses on his works." Such ideal beauty, or great art, was created only by the ancient Greeks and by a few artists of the Italian Renaissance. Among the Greeks, Winckelmann explained, the subjective and objective were balanced. Hence the Greeks were both practical and artistic.[43]

Winckelmann's life is a reflection of one of the finest social aspects of German culture in the eighteenth century. He and Kant, more than any other two thinkers, accomplished the miracle of making German culture significant for Europe. Certainly in charm of personality he was the most attractive scholar in Germany during the *Aufklärung.* "It is in his *Letters* far more than in any of his writings on ancient art that the complete man in his passionate humanity, something more precious and stimulating than the scholar, the antiquary and the writer, is revealed. . . . The richness of his humanity, his passion for the ennobling of man, for the establishment of a new ideal of balanced and self-determined life, as he saw it in ancient Greece and wished to transmit to others, has not been acknowledged hitherto."[44]

Winckelmann, whose style resembled classical Greek, so steeped was he in ancient Greek literature, and whose teaching embraced the total life of the ancient Greeks, climate, geography, race, religion, customs, politics, philosophy, literature, exerted an immediate and lasting influence on German scholarship. C. G. Heyne (1729–1812), who was professor of classics at Göttingen, in 1767 for the first time announced a course of lectures on archaeology, using that word in the wide sense in which Winckelmann employed it. He was "the first who with any decisiveness attempted . . . to read in the writings of the ancients, not their language alone, or even their detached opinions and records, but their spirit and character, their way of . . . life and thought."[45]

Heyne was a highly competent professional scholar whose authority was great, but he was not a genius. The creative criticism and interpretation which Winckelmann had inaugurated was carried on by Friedrich A. Wolf (1759–1824), to whom may be applied what the late Ba-

[43] Cp Kronenberg (n. 8), I, 312–16.
[44] From a review of Winckelmann's *Kleine Schriften*, ed. by Uhde-Bernays (n. 40), in *LTLS*, 1927, pp. 613–14.
[45] Thomas Carlyle, "Life of Heyne," in his *Critical and Miscellaneous Essays* (London, 1872, 6 v.), II, 81; the entire article 54–84. See also SANDYS, III, 36–44.

sil Gildersleeve said of *his* master, Welcker, whose pupil he was at Bonn in 1852: "The image of antiquity rose like an exhalation from his discourse." Wolf had begun as a pupil of Heyne but soon far outstripped his teacher. He taught at Halle from 1783 until 1807, when his health broke down.[46]

Varnhagen von Ense in his *Memoirs* relates the impression which Wolf made upon him. "He appeared as a king among the learned of Halle. His tall, comfortable (*behagliche*) figure, his dignified calmness, his energy that seemed to move the most multifarious details by a simple command, gave him the splendor of a dignity which he did not seem to require; for he never assumed any air of superiority, but rather, like the great Frederick, delighted to appear among men merely as a man. . . . He possessed all the common tolls and appendages of pedantry but he had thoroughly spiritualized even the barrenest of them (*alles hatte er durchgeistet*) while at the same time his immense knowledge communicated to others gave their loose and roving fancies a sure basis of historical fact on which to rest."

In English the word "philology" signifies linguistic science, or the study of the nature and development of a language. But Wolf used the word in the sense in which Winckelmann had used the word "art." To Wolf classical philology signified "all the knowledge of human nature manifested in antiquity." He held that Greek philology was the sum of all ancient Greek culture and that to understand philology one must know Greek life in all its aspects—climate, geography, natural resources, political, economic, and social institutions, religion, art, and literature. To Winckelmann art meant *Alterthumswissenschaft*, to Wolf *Alterthumswissenschaft* meant philology. At Halle Wolf gave at least fifty courses on classical authors and edited an immense number of texts. Both lectures and texts were illuminated by his deep knowledge of antiquity and his markedly interpretative imagination, which took cognizance of all the related sciences. In his *Seminarium* Wolf also contributed to historical method. One of his greatest pupils, Boeckh, was inspired to write his *Public Economy of Athens* by the way Greek antiquities were taught in Wolf's seminar and treated in his epoch-making *Prolegomena to Homer* (1795). The seminar method which Wolf devised was first

[46] For Wolf's letters see Siegfried Reiter, ed., *Friedrich August Wolf, ein Leben in Briefen* (Stuttgart, 1935, 3 v.), cp. Reiter's article in *Forschungen und Fortschritte*, XI (1935), 242–43; M. Bernays, ed., *Briefe an Friedrich August Wolf* (Berlin, 1868), 1–89. G. Bernhardy edited Wolf's *Kleine Schriften* (Halle, 1869). On Wolf see SANDYS, III, 51–60; PATTISON, I, 337–414; Bursian (n. 1), 517–48; Wilhelm Körte, *Leben und Studien F. A. Wolfs, des Philologen* (Essen, 1833, 2 pts.); Richard v. Volkmann, *Geschichte und Kritik der Wolfschen Prolegomena zu Homer* (Leipzig, 1874); J. F. Arnoldt, *F. A. Wolf in seinem Verhältnisse zum Schulwesen und zur Pädagogik dargestellt* (Brunswick, 1861–62, 2 v. in 1); BIEDERMANN, II, ii, pt. 3, 698–702; Schrader (n. 5), I, 434–62; Ch. Galusky, "Critiques et historiens de l'Allemagne: II. Wolf," *RDM*, 1848: 1, pp. 849–78.

applied to the study and criticism of historical documents by Ranke at the University of Berlin, itself an epoch-making event in the development of the study of history.

In the previous pages I have endeavored to trace the genesis and development of the intellectual changes which took place in Germany during the eighteenth century, insofar as these new attitudes of mind affected the study and writing of history. Except for Justus Möser, Germany in this period may not be said to have had any original and great historian. But the intellectual soil and the spiritual atmosphere of Germany were pregnant with life. It needed only the magic touch of Romanticism to convert Germany into a vast seminar for the study of history.

But before passing on into the Romantic movement and the nineteenth century something should be said of those honest and diligent historians whose lights were lower than those which were to blaze later on, yet who deserve to be noticed for their patient and careful scholarship. Göttingen University was the chief, almost the only, seat of historical studies.[47] The "Göttingen School of History" was the earliest institution of the kind, the founder of that form of academic tradition. Of these Göttingen scholars Mosheim, Gatterer, Schlözer, Spittler, Heeren, and Achenwall the statistician, merit remembrance.

John Lorenz Mosheim (1693-1755),[48] the church historian, was the co-founder and first chancellor of Göttingen University. Widely read and familiar with Cartesianism as well as the scientific achievements of the seventeenth century, Mosheim was, nevertheless, not altogether a child of the *Aufklärung*. He never, for example, challenged the old theological dogmas and was not quite skeptical of the devil and miracles. He approached church history, not so much as a speculative theologian, but as a practical man, a pragmatic historian. He was always fair, calm, detached, a bit pedantic, writing in the manner of a judge sum-

[47] On Göttingen see Emil F. Rössler, *Die Gründung der Universität Göttingen* (Göttingen, 1855); J. S. Pütter, *Versuch einer akademischen Gelehrtengeschichte der Georg-Augustus-Universität zu Göttingen* (Göttingen, 1765-1838, 4 v.), the first two volumes to 1788 by Pütter himself, the third from 1788 to 1820 by Saalfeld, and the fourth from 1820 to 1837 by Oesterley; G. Waitz, "Die Göttinger Historiker von Köhler bis Dahlmann," in *Göttinger Professoren. Ein Beitrag zur deutschen Cultur- und Literärgeschichte in acht Vorträgen* (Gotha, 1872), 231 ff.; *Memoiren des Ritters Karl Heinrich von Lang: Skizzen aus meinem Leben*, etc. (2nd ed., Munich, 1882, 2 v.), I, 236 ff.; SCHAUMKELL, 49-113; and see also WOLF, 202, n. 1, 208, n. 1.

[48] On Mosheim see FUETER, 333-36; Karl Heussi, *J. L. Mosheim* (Tübingen, 1906); F. C. Baur, *Die Epochen der kirchlichen Geschichtsschreibung* (Tübingen, 1852), 118 ff.; Karl Heussi, "Die Kirchengeschichtsschreibung Johann Lorenz von Mosheims," in the *Geschichtliche Untersuchungen*, ed. by Karl Lamprecht, I, Heft iv (1904); Bonwetsch's article in *Protestantische Realencyklopaedie*, XIII, 502-06 with a bibliography, and his address "Mosheim als Kirchenpolitiker," in the *Festschrift zur Feier des hundertfünfzigjährigen Bestehens der kgl. Gesellschaft der Wissenschaft zu Göttingen* (1901); and Wagemann's article in *Allgemeine deutsche Biographie*, XXII, 395 ff.

marizing a complex case, displaying no emotions when discussing the various theological conflicts, which to him were "mere verbal disputes." [49] As Gibbon acutely comments: "Less profound than Petavius, less independent than Le Clerc, less ingenious than Beausobre, the historian Mosheim is full, rational, correct, and moderate."

Mosheim published approximately eighty-five works on church history, the most famous of which are the *Commentarii de rebus Christianorum ante Constantinum Magnum* (1753) and the *Institutes of Ecclesiastical History*,[50] the latter intended as a textbook for his students; it has, therefore, all the shortcomings of such a work. It is too schematic, dry, factual, lacking all generalization.

My principal care [Mosheim writes in the preface] has been to relate events with fidelity and authority. For this purpose I have gone to the very sources of information—the best writers, that is, of all ages, and such as lived in, or near, the times which they treat of; consulting them with attention, and expressing in brief, clear, nervous language, what I found written by them. Those who write summaries of history, commonly do no more than abridge the more voluminous historians; and this method I myself before pursued to a considerable degree. This is a practice that has its advantages, and cannot be wholly condemned; but it is attended with this evil, that it perpetuates the mistakes, which are apt to abound in very large and voluminous works, by causing them to pass from a single book into numerous others. . . . I now perceived that writers pre-eminent for their diligence and fidelity are not always to be trusted. . . . I have, in general, made distinct reference to my authorities . . .; I had before me all the authors whom I quote, and I turned them over and read and compared them with each other, being resolved to follow solely their guidance.[51]

Mosheim was cautious in his statements, always careful to give exact and full references, preferably from the original sources. Nevertheless, he occasionally was capable of sweeping condemnations. In writing about the ecclesiastical corruptions in the tenth century, and relying on no less a Catholic authority than Baronius, Mosheim concluded as follows:

Nothing is more incontrovertible, than that the sacred order, both in the East and in the West, was composed principally of men who were illiterate, stupid, ignorant, of everything pertaining to religion, libidinous, superstitious, and flagitious. Nor can any-

[49] Mosheim's judicious attitude toward church squabbles aroused the mild ire of no less a scholar than Stubbs who complained of his "seemingly forced exclusion of any but the coldest and most dispassionate view of any subject whatever." What irritated the pious Stubbs most was Mosheim's treatment of the Protestants ("champions of the Truth") as "mere partisans blinded to the merits of their adversary's cause by obstinate attachment to their own prejudices." In short, what most historians nowadays consider a virtue, Stubbs regarded a fault. See Stubbs' preface to his edition of Mosheim's *Institutes of Ecclesiastical History*, tr. by James Murdock and H. Soames (London, 1863, 3 v.), I, pp. v–xi.

[50] In 2 vols., first published in 1737 and 1741, and republished in 1755. The first English translation from the original Latin, by A. Maclaine, appeared in 1764, followed by Dutch and French translations. German translations appeared in 1769, 1770, and 1780. For the English version edited and continued by Stubbs, see preceding note.

[51] *Institutes of Ecclesiastical History*, ed. Stubbs, I, pp. xiii–xvii.

one doubt, that those who wished to be regarded as the fathers and guardians of the universal church, were the principal causes of these evils. Nothing certainly can be thought of, so filthy, criminal, and wicked, as to be deemed incompatible with their characters by the supreme directors of religion and its rites; nor was any government ever so loaded with vices of every kind as that which passed for the most holy. . . .

That the history of the Roman bishops in this century is a history not of men, but of monsters, a history of the most atrocious villainies and crimes, is acknowledged by all the best writers; those not excepted even who plead for pontifical authority [i.e., Baronius].[52]

Four years after Mosheim's death, in 1759, Johann Christoph Gatterer (1727–99) [53] became professor of history at Göttingen. He was familiar with Voltaire's work and inclined to favor cultural history over purely political interpretation. But, at least as a practicing historian, he did not succeed in emancipating himself from the dominant stereotypes of his environment. Thus in his *Weltgeschichte* (1792), though he gave up the traditional schema of the "four monarchies," he still began his account with Adam, calling the first 1800 years of history the "Adam-Noah period." Fables, whether Graeco-Roman or Scriptural, he accepted with naive credulity and the center of his "world" history was still Europe.

Gatterer's service to historiography lies, not in the field of creative interpretation, but in his pedagogical methods. He justly emphasized the *Hilfswissenschaften* and trained his students in the related auxiliary disciplines, such as geography, chronology, diplomatics, palaeography, and numismatics. In this connection he founded the *Historisches Institut* (1764–66).

In 1759, the year when Gatterer was appointed professor at Göttingen, August Ludwig von Schlözer (1735–1809) [54] entered that university as a student of medicine. Exactly ten years later Schlözer, having spent some years in Russia where he studied that country's language and his-

---

[52] *Ibid.*, I, 593–94.

[53] On Gatterer see Hermann Wesendonck, *Die Begründung der neueren deutschen Geschichtsschreibung durch Gatterer und Schlözer* (Leipzig, 1876); Wegele, in *Allgemeine deutsche Biographie*, VIII, 413; WOLF, 208–09 and note; and FUETER, 464–66. Apart from his *Weltgeschichte* (1792), Gatterer wrote a *Handbuch der Universalhistorie* (1761), a *Weltgeschichte in ihrem ganzen Umfange* (1785–87), a *Historia genealogica dominorum Holzschuherorum* (1755), and a number of textbooks on diplomatics, genealogy, heraldry, and geography. For a bibliography of his works see Malchus in *Zeitgenossen*. [*Ein biographisches Magazin für die Geschichte unserer Zeit*, Leipzig], I (1816), 2 ff.

[54] For his correspondence see *August Ludwig Schlözers Briefwechsel, meist historischen und politischen Inhalts* (Göttingen, 1780–82, 10 v. in 5). F. Fürst, *August Ludwig Schlözer, ein deutscher Aufklärer im 18. Jahrhundert* (Heidelberg, 1928); Theodor Zermelo, *A. L. Schlözer, ein Publicist im alten Reich* (Berlin, 1875); J. M. Doring, *Leben A. L. v. Schlözers, nach seinen Briefen und anderen Mittheilungen dargestellt* (1836: Gallerie deutscher Historiker, II); Adolf Bock, *Schlözer, ein Beitrag zur Litteraturgeschichte des 18. Jahrhunderts* (Hanover, 1844); Wesendonck (n. 53); BIEDERMANN, II, ii, pt. 3, 714–16; for a bibliography see WOLF, 210 and note, and Christian v. Schlözer, *A. L. v. Schlözers öffentliches und Privatleben* (Leipzig, 1828, 2 v. in 1), II, 249 ff.

tory, became professor of history at Göttingen. Schlözer was perhaps the most thoroughgoing disciple of the historical school of Voltaire in Germany. Like his French model, he admired enlightened absolutism (having had close contact with Catherine the Great) and the powerful, materially prosperous State, though he lacked Voltaire's sensitive perceptions.

A list of Schlözer's works will throw light on his wide interests. He wrote *Neuverändertes Russland* (at the instigation of Catherine the Great) and *Geschichte von Russland* (1769). He was the author of an *Allgemeine nordische Geschichte* (1771), a *Summarische Geschichte von Nordafrika* (1775), *Kritischhistorische Nebenstunden* (dealing with Osmans and Mongols, 1797), and a *Weltgeschichte im Auszuge und Zusammenhange* (1792). One must also mention his *Essay on the History of Trade*, written in Swedish (1758), and his *Staatsanzeigen* (18 v., 1782–93) which made him famous as a publicist.

Schlözer's best-known work is his *Weltgeschichte*, probably the most ambitious attempt of its kind in Germany. He begins with an analysis of what he means by world history. It should embrace, he says, "all known periods, lands, and important events." Such an account becomes a "true history of mankind" only when "it teaches, by examples, man's origins, progress, improvement, decline, and thereby brings illuminating illustrations and proofs to psychology, political science, natural science, and other disciplines." A history of this kind, not being merely a list of "names and figures," becomes philosophy "always connecting effects and causes." Knowledge thus gathered would lead us to the conclusion that "men are always men, that under certain conditions they always act in the same way, that nothing new under the sun takes place, and thereby it ends with the high *nil admirari*." In short, Schlözer concluded this somewhat cavalier generalization, "To study World History means to think in terms of the connection between the most important changes of the earth and the human race, in order to have a fundamental appreciation of both today."

Unfortunately, Schlözer was both a shallow thinker and a poor scholar. His generalizations are facile and platitudinous, and his facts too meager to support a "world" thesis; furthermore, he lacked the gift of artistic presentation of his master Voltaire, expressing himself crudely and carelessly. Apart from his facility in languages, Schlözer's chief importance to historiography lies in his conception of the continuity of history, but even here Voltaire had preceded him.

Less erudite than Schlözer was his younger colleague at Göttingen, Ludwig Timotheus Spittler (1752–1810).[55] Though mainly a church

---

[55] On Spittler see FUETER, 467–71; Baur (n. 48), 162 ff.; G. J. Planck, *Spittler als Historiker* (Göttingen, 1811); N. Bonwetsch, in *Protestantische Realencyklopaedie*, XVIII, 677 ff.; David

historian, Spittler was a disciple of both Voltaire and Lessing; like Voltaire he was frankly pro-bourgeois, and like Lessing he was an outspoken liberal. His chief writings dealt with ecclesiastical history, which he treated in a secular spirit, and the history of small German states. A child of his time, Spittler was interested in the cultural history of mankind, tracing the relations between rulers and subjects, and depicting the development of the total culture. He is at his best when treating the seventeenth and eighteenth centuries, but when he deals with the Middle Ages he displays the prevalent contempt of the Enlightenment for the "dark" epoch in European civilization.[56]

German thought in the eighteenth century was only slightly tinctured by rationalism, except in the field of methodology.[57] Here again the methods of natural science had a profound influence. As the scientist exercised elaborate care in observation and classification of natural phenomena, so the scholar now began to refine his methods. John Martin Chladenius (*Allgemeine Geschichtswissenschaft*, Leipzig, 1752) was the first to make a clear distinction between actual events and the same events as modified by the personal equation of the observer and recorder. Chladenius, furthermore, laid down a number of tests for historical certainty, among which he listed: the reliability of authors, the notoriety of events, confirmation by witnesses and documents, agreement with existing conditions; he made a distinction between certainty and probability. Three decades later, the Frenchman G. B. Mably (*De la manière d'écrire l'histoire*, 1782) took up the same task and urged historians to emphasize the developments of events from their natural conditions. In England, Joseph Priestley (*Lectures on History and General Policy*, 1788) went beyond Chladenius in his discussion of historical sources, advising historians to broaden their knowledge of other subjects.

Göttingen University, it has been pointed out, excelled in history and

Strauss, "Ludwig Timotheus Spittler," in his *Gesammelte Schriften*, ed. by Zeller (Bonn, 1876–78, 12 v.), II, 83–117; for other bibliography see WOLF, 209 note.

[56] Spittler's *Sämmtliche Werke* were edited by K. Wächter (Stuttgart and Tübingen, 1827–37, 15 v.). His political writings include *Geschichte Wirtembergs unter der Regierung der Grafen und Herzöge* (1783); *Geschichte des Churfürstentums Hannover* (1786); and *Entwurf der Geschichte der europäischen Staaten* (Berlin, 1793). His ecclesiastical histories include: *Geschichte des Kanonischen Rechts bis auf die Zeiten des falschen Isidorus* (Halle, 1778), and *Grundriss der Geschichte der christlichen Kirche* (Göttingen, 1782), which was continued by his pupil, Gottlieb Jacob Planck (1751–1833). Planck differed from his master in that he wrote church history from the point of view of ideas rather than of persons; on him cp. FUETER, 471–72.

[57] The earliest manual dealing with the auxiliary sciences of history was that of Benjamin Hederich, *Anleitung zu den führnehmsten historischen Wissenschaften* (2nd ed., 1711; 8th enlarged ed., Berlin, 1782–83, 2 v.). Other popular manuals outlined the various *Hilfswissenschaften*, such as geography, chronology, genealogy, heraldry, numismatics, diplomatics, and even archaeology and statistics. In the latter half of the century the German universities, particularly Göttingen, became centers of specialized studies: church history (Mosheim, Walch, Spittler, Planck); philology (Heyne, Wolf); and statistics (founded by G. A. Achenwall).

classical scholarship, the last at least until Wolf went to Halle. Leipzig began to compete with Göttingen in history when Semler rose to eminence there. He stressed methodics in continuation of Chladenius and Gatterer, and particularly distinguished between the value and use of contemporary and second-hand evidence, between original and indirect sources.[58]

One Austrian scholar deserves notice, if only for one pregnant saying. Michael Ignaz Schmidt (1736–94), the director of the Vienna archives, wrote a *History of the Germans* in twenty-two volumes (1778 ff.), intended frankly for popular consumption. Unlike Mascou, Schmidt was altogether an imitator of Voltaire and Robertson, in treatment though not in interpretation. Like his French model, Schmidt had no nationalist passions; an admirer of the reforming Emperor Joseph II, he had an anticlerical bias. Otherwise, Schmidt was detached and impartial, particularly in his treatment of the Reformation. In his quiet fashion, he made critical use of the sources, intending to present a comprehensive picture of the total culture. Remarkably enough, it was Schmidt, and not Ranke, who made the famous statement about writing history *wie es eigentlich gewesen ist*. To quote Schmidt's own words: "My intention in this work is to show how Germany acquired her customs, enlightenment, laws, arts and sciences, especially her . . . constitutions of Church and State, in short, how the *things have come to be what they are*." [59]

In deference to his position, though not his scholarship, one should mention the King of Prussia. Frederick the Great, as is well known, devoted a considerable portion of his time to authorship. Most of his literary work was written under the direct influence of Voltaire, in fact, written to please Voltaire. Frederick composed some two dozen works on various subjects, some of which were histories. Among the latter are *Mémoires pour servir à l'histoire de la maison de Brandenbourg*, from 1415 to 1740 (1751); *Histoire de mon temps*, from 1740 to 1745, continued in *Histoire de la guerre de sept ans* (1763–64) and in *Mémoires depuis la paix de Hubertsbourg jusqu'à la fin du partage de la Pologne* (1788). Strictly speaking, the first of these works, the one dealing with the history of the House of Brandenburg, is historical in the objective sense; while the later *Histoires* and *Mémoires*, describing Frederick's own times, are semi-autobiographical and subjective.

Frederick's historical works are valuable only to the scholar who is

---

[58] Wilhelm Scherer, *History of German Literature*, tr. by Mrs. F. C. Conybeare (New York, 1901, 2 v.), II, 73.

[59] *Geschichte der Deutschen* (Ulm, 1785–1808, 22 v.), I, introduction. This work covered the period to 1660; it was continued by others. On Schmidt see FUETER, 466–67; and BIEDERMANN, II, ii, pt. 3, 708–10.

interested in Frederick, since they reveal the king's mind and attitude. As objective histories they fall far below Voltaire, their model, except in the treatment of technical problems, such as military administration, strategy, and tactics, matters on which the king was obviously an expert. The general approach is, as Fueter justly observed, that of a "statesman for statesmen." The king wrote, not as a scholar trying to weigh and balance complicated events, but as a leading actor seeing things from above, from the point of view of governments rather than of social forces.

Philosophically the King of Prussia was altogether Voltairean. History to him was didactic and utilitarian, teaching examples of "illustrious and virtuous men." To be useful, history should "preserve only the names of good princes," one of whom Frederick hoped to be.[60] Like the French *philosophes* (Frederick was a German only by birth and nothing else), the King of Prussia was a Rationalist, a Deist, a cosmopolitan. His knowledge of antiquity and the Middle Ages was scanty. Therefore he despised the past, especially the German past, about which he knew pitifully little. The ancient Germans were "greedy for booty," crude barbarians, the destroyers of Rome. The Middle Ages were "dark" and the Crusaders pious blunderers; strangely enough, the great King Frederick II knew little about his namesake, that other Frederick II of the House of Hohenstauffen, a truly enlightened and cultured man.[61]

A Swiss historian who also studied at Göttingen was Joseph Iselin (1728–82), who, in 1764, published *Philosophische Muthmassungen über die Geschichte der Menschheit* (it appeared in 1768 as *Geschichte der Menschheit*). Unlike Müller, Iselin was a dogmatic opponent of Rous-

---

[60] Frederick once expressed his conception of history in the following poem (*Oeuvres*, X, 65):

> La verité, tenant la plume de l'histoire,
> Embrassant tous les temps, présente à la mémoire
> Ces empires puissants que le ciel fit fleurir,
> Qu'on vit naitre, monter, s'abaisser et mourir.
> C'est là qu'on apprend l'art de régner sans puissance
> En pliant les esprits au gré de l'éloquence;
> Qu'on se connait soi-même, et que, maitre de soi,
> En domptant ses désirs on est son propre roi . . . (1748).

[61] Frederick's historical works are to be found in his *Oeuvres*, ed. by J. D. E. Preuss (1846–57, 31 v. in 14), I–VII; see also Hans Droysen, *Beiträge zu einer Bibliographie der prosaischen Schriften Friedrichs des Grossen* (Berliner Gymnasialprogramme, 1904–05, 2 pts.). For discussions see FUETER, 472–74; WOLF, 203–05 and notes; SCHAUMKELL, 22–30; S. K. Padover, "The Model Dictator," *American Mercury,* XXV (1935), 147–53; F. Schwill [Schevill], *Ueber das Verhältnis der Texte der 'Histoire de mon temps' Friedrichs des Grossen* (Freiburg, 1892); H. Disselnkötter, *Beiträge zur Kritik der 'Histoire de mon temps' Friedrichs des Grossen* (Leipzig, 1885: Historische Studien, XIV); Friedrich Meusel, "Friedrich der Grosse als historisch-politischer Schriftsteller," *PJ,* CXX (1905), 482–525; two articles by the same writer in *HZ,* XCVI (1906), 434–46, and XCVIII (1907), 560–69; Arnold Berney, "Ueber das geschichtliche Denken Friedrichs des Grossen," *ibid.,* CL (1934), 86–115; Leopold v. Ranke, *Sämmtliche Werke* (Leipzig, 1874–90, 54 v. in 27), LI–LII, 405–74; and see the literature listed in DAHLMANN-WAITZ, nos. 11823–26.

seau's theory of the state of nature. Men, Iselin tried to show with more theories than facts, are driven by instinct to seek happiness in association with other men, that is, in forming a State. The state of nature, far from being perfect, was in reality a stage of barbarism from which men gradually ascended toward morality and civilization. Following Montesquieu, Iselin paid attention to climate and environment as being determining factors in the development of civilization. The final aim of society, Iselin pointed out, was the spread of virtue and happiness, especially the improvement of the lot of the lower classes. Iselin concluded his treatise with a warm appeal to the rulers of Europe to bring about this state of perfection by wise and virtuous government.[62]

The foremost historian of the Göttingen school was Arnold Hermann Ludwig Heeren (1760–1842),[63] who was both a child of the *Aufklärung* and of post-Napoleonic Europe. He is best known in America because a number of distinguished American scholars, among them Bancroft, Motley, Ticknor, and Longfellow, studied under him in Göttingen.[64]

Heeren, already equipped with a knowledge of ancient languages, entered Göttingen in 1779, at the age of nineteen, and attended the lectures of Heyne, whose eldest daughter he married. Another great influence on Heeren was Spittler, from whom the young man learned historical methodology.

For each period [so Heeren describes Spittler's seminar method] the leading author was laid down as a basis, and excerpts were made in a chronological order. At the same time, other authors treating of the same subject were read, and the variations noted in parallel columns. I still believe that this is the best method for beginning the study.[65]

[62] Iselin's fellow-Swiss and contemporary, Wegelin, professor at the Ritterakademie in Berlin, likewise occupied himself with a philosophy of history, publishing in 1770 a book in which he traced the rise and decline of nations. See C. Schwarber, *Die schweizerische Geschichtsschreibung im 18. Jahrhundert und der nationale Gedanke* (Basel, 1927); BIEDERMANN, II, ii, pt. 3, 713–14; Rudolf Rocholl, *Die Philosophie der Geschichte. Darstellung und Kritik der Versuche zu einem Aufbau derselben* (Göttingen, 1878–93, 2 v.), I, 76–78.

[63] A biography of Heeren still remains to be written. His own *Autobiographische Nachrichten* can be found in the first volume of his *Historische Werke* (Göttingen, 1821–26, 15 v.), and prefixed to Heeren's *Manual of Ancient History*, tr. by George Bancroft (6th ed., London, 1854). See also FUETER, 478–83; SCHAUMKELL, 284–309; BIEDERMANN, II, ii, pt. 3, 712; William M. Sloane, "The Science of History in the Nineteenth Century," in *Congress of Arts and Science, Universal Exposition, St. Louis, 1904* (Boston, 1906), II, 28; A. W. Small, in *American Journal of Sociology*, XXIX (1923), 81–82; C. T. Perthes, *Friedrich Perthes' Leben* (Gotha, 8th ed., 1896, 3 v.), III, 22 ff.; and *Archiv für Kulturgeschichte*, XVII (1927), 286–97. For some reviews of Heeren see *NAR*, XVIII (1824), 390–406 and XXVIII (1829), 186–203; and *ER*, LIX (1834), 87–123.

[64] Heeren made an almost indelible impression on American historiography, and Bancroft translated a number of his works into English. For this influence of Heeren on American students see J. S. Bassett, *The Middle Group of American Historians* (New York, 1917), 178–79; M. A. DeWolfe Howe, *Life and Letters of George Bancroft* (New York, 1908, 2 v.), I, 209–10; Orie W. Long, *Literary Pioneers: Early American Explorers of European Culture* (Harvard Univ. Press, 1935); and W. M. Sloan, "George Bancroft," *Century Magazine*, XXXIII (1887), 473–87.

[65] Quoted in *NAR*, XXVIII (1829), 186–87.

After taking his Ph.D. degree, Heeren left the university to travel in Europe for two years. Upon his return to Göttingen in 1787, he was appointed professor of philosophy, lecturing on Roman antiquities and historians. The next twelve years he devoted to studying the sources of Asiatic and African history, the result of which was *Reflections on the Politics, Intercourse, and Commerce of the Chief Nations of Antiquity* (1796).[66] In 1799 Heeren saw his ardent hopes realized when his chair of philosophy was changed for that of history. Henceforth, for the next forty-three years until his death, he remained at Göttingen, honored by many governments,[67] and loved by pupils and friends, among whom were G. H. Pertz and Bismarck.

Heeren must be considered in a twofold capacity: as an historian of commerce and as a political historian. Apart from the book on ancient commerce already mentioned (dealing with the Persians, Phoenicians, Babylonians, Scythians, etc.), Heeren also published a *Handbuch der Geschichte der Staaten des Altertums* (1799).[68] His political works include a *Geschichte des europäischen Staatensystems und seiner Kolonien* (1809) from 1492 on; *Versuch einer Entwickelung der Folgen der Kreuzzüge* (1808); a history of British continental interests; a history of the development of the monarchical principle in modern Europe; and a number of lesser works. In 1829 Heeren, in collaboration with Ukert, inaugurated the famous series of historical works known as *Geschichte der europäischen Staaten*.[69]

Heeren's interest in commerce began when he was a schoolboy in the old Hanseatic city of Bremen, was stimulated by the struggle of the American colonies against Great Britain, and finally deepened by his reading of Montesquieu and Adam Smith. He manifested great acuteness in perceiving the relations between commerce and colonization, and the effect of both on politics, but his interest was greater in international trade than internal commerce. Heeren has thus described his approach to the problems presented by the commerce of antiquity:

---

[66] A part of this was first translated by George Bancroft under the title *Reflections on the Politics of Ancient Greece* (Boston, 1824). The entire work later appeared as *Historical Researches into the Politics, Intercourse, and Trade of the Principal Nations of Antiquity* (London, 1847–57, 4 v.).

[67] Heeren was chosen Aulic and Privy Councillor, was named a member of the French Académie des Inscriptions, and in 1819 appointed Rector of Göttingen. In 1834 William IV honored him with the knighthood of the Guelphic Order; three years later, on the fiftieth anniversary of his professorship, the French king conferred on him the ribbon of the Legion of Honor. The King of Sweden bestowed on him the Order of the North Star.

[68] With the full title: *mit besonderer Rücksicht auf ihre Verfassungen, ihren Handel und ihre Kolonien*. For Bancroft's translations of Heeren's works see Howe (n. 64), II, 180–81.

[69] For a discussion of the Heeren-Ukert series, which Perthes undertook to publish, see WOLF, 459–62. A complete bibliography is to be found in the *Verlagskatalog von Friedrich Andreas Perthes, 1796–1906* (1906).

In my lectures on ancient history, the chapter on Carthage always seemed to me the least satisfactory. . . . This led me to a closer examination of its character and history. . . . I soon became familiar with all that concerned this great trading and conquering republic, the first of antiquity; one new light after another broke in upon me; my horizon gradually extended; till at last the ancient world seemed spread out before me from a point of view from which I had never before regarded it. I now considered it with respect to the bearings and influence of ancient trade and intercourse, and, as closely connected therewith, the rise, formation, and constitution of the ancient states.[70]

Heeren does not trace the origins of ancient commerce; he contents himself with pointing out merely the difference between the past and the present. In antiquity, he points out, the lack of technological development (compass, etc.) bound man to his own spot; hence commerce was mostly by land. Modern commerce, on the other hand, benefiting from technological advances, is carried on by sea. Occidental techniques, Heeren explains, enabled European man to conquer a large part of the world and to spread his influence far and wide. This gave the Europeans a superiority over other (colored) peoples. "The new world at once became their prey . . .; more than a third part of Asia submitted to the Russian scepter; merchants on the Thames and the Zuyder Sea seized on the government of India; and if the Turks have thus far been successful in preserving the country which they have robbed from Europe, will it remain to them forever?" [71] As for the question of the reason why European (white) men were able to develop a superior technology, Heeren suggests that white color may have something to do with it—although he was too scholarly to be dogmatic on the point. "This, only, is intended: experience thus far seems to prove, that a greater facility in developing the powers of mind belongs to the nations of a clear color; but we will welcome the age, which shall contradict this experience, and exhibit cultivated nations of negroes." [72]

As a political historian Heeren's significance lies in his recognition of the material bases of States. Instead of studying ancient philosophers, that is, the theorizers (in Pareto's word, "derivatives"), Heeren went to the basic needs of men: their food, clothing, habitation. He wanted to know how men satisfied their material wants and in what respect these matters affected politics. Hence he may be regarded as the forerunner of Marx' "economic interpretation of history." Yet one must not consider Heeren a crude materialist; on the contrary, he insisted upon treating man as a moral being and history from a "philosophical point of view," as he said. To him, economic facts and figures served merely as illustrations of distinctive types of government. In his lec-

[70] Autobiographical sketch in his *Manual of Ancient History*, tr. by Bancroft (n. 63), pp. xvi–xvii.

[71] *Reflections on the Politics of Ancient Greece* (n. 66), 3.   [72] *Ibid.*, 4–6.

tures, he used to analyze four kinds of state-systems known to the West: a monarchy with a free constitution and a free administration—Britain; a monarchy with a free constitution but an arbitrary administration—France; a monarchy arbitrary in constitution and administration—Russia; a federal republic based on popular sovereignty—the United States. It was Heeren, in fact, who popularized the concept of a "state-system," and showed its inter-relationships. His words are still worth remembering:

> Whoever undertakes to write the history of any particular state-system (by which we mean the union of several contiguous states, resembling each other in their manners, religion, and degree of social improvement, and cemented together by reciprocity of interests), ought, above all things, to possess a right conception of its general character. In the system of European states, it is obvious this character must be sought for in its internal freedom, or in other words, the mutual independence of its members, however disproportionate they may otherwise be in regard to physical power.[73]

Among the bonds of union of a political system, Heeren acutely observed, was religion; in Egypt, for example, religion was not only a unifying force, but also a check on royal absolutism.

As a writer Heeren was lucid, sober, and direct. "I have aimed to be neither artificially refined nor carelessly negligent. . . . The end of my wishes and endeavors has been to write, not merely for the schools, but for the enlightened public." In this he succeeded, for he was one of the most widely-read historians of his time, although his influence on academic history (at least in Germany) was not great. "There is not a French historian," a French critic paid Heeren the supreme compliment, "superior to him in clearness of thought and method of composition."

One may not take leave of the Göttingen School without a brief discussion of Gottfried Achenwall (1719–72), who was professor at that university from 1748 until his death. Achenwall formulated and developed the science to which he was the first to apply the name *scientia statistica*, or statistics. His work, *Staatsverfassung der europäischen Reiche* (1749), was an early version of the *Statesman's Year Book*, containing relevant economic, political, and other "noteworthy matters regarding the state." The information thus included was dubbed *Staats-merkwürdigkeiten* (literally: state curiosities) by Achenwall's colleague Schlözer. This science, which the English statisticians, Petty and Graunt, called "political arithmetic" in the seventeenth century, came

---

[73] Cp. his autobiographical sketch (n. 70), p. xix. How this idea affected other historians can be seen from the following sentence with which Heeren's pupil, George Bancroft, begins the first volume of his *History of the United States:* "The United States of America constitute an essential portion of a great political system, embracing all the civilized nations of the earth."

to be widely used in the modern sense only after the publication of J. P. Süssmilch's *Die Göttliche Ordnung in den Veränderungen des menschlichen Geschlechts aus der Geburt, dem Tode, und der Fortpflanzung desselben erwiesen*, which was a systematic attempt at classifying "vital" and other statistical facts.[74]

[74] The word "statistics" is derived from the Latin *status*, or "state" in the political sense; hence statistics concern matters regarding the state. Perhaps the earliest work containing such facts is Francesco Sansovino's *Del governo et amministratione di diversi regni et republiche* (Venice, 1583). In 1660 Hermann Conring, "professor of medicine and politics" at Helmstädt University, lectured on subjects relating to statistical matters. See Robert Knoll, *Hermann Conring als Historiker* (Rostock dissertation, 1889).

CHAPTER XL

THE EMERGENCE OF ROMANTICISM [1]

IN THE sequence of phases in the development of modern historical scholarship three stages have so far been indicated. In two of these France excelled; in the third Germany was not only the outstanding but also the only exponent. Romanticism was the fourth movement in the general intellectual life of Europe. In his remarkable book *Die Entstehung des Historismus*, Friedrich Meinecke, the distinguished professor of history emeritus in the University of Berlin, has written:

> Romanticism . . . appears as originally a very nebulous thing which, moved by manifold dim impulses, discovers manifold human values apart from the classical norm. Yet in this seeking and groping, it suddenly discovers shape and form, meaning and coherence in hitherto unheeded creations of the past, and thus opens a road to Historicism.

Romanticism was destined, more than erudition, more than Rationalism, more than the *Aufklärung*, to become a general European intellectual movement in the nineteenth century. Although intimations of Romanticism are discoverable almost simultaneously in France, England, even in Italy and Spain, the new spirit was first really perceived, defined, and organized in Germany. Literature is subject to natural laws of evolution, as other phenomena of human nature, and has its epochs of power, transition, and decline.

The eighteenth century had a purely Rationalistic concept of history. Protest against this was bound to come, but this protest was not reactionary, but progressive. Romanticism was a reaction against the unhistorical reasoning, the formal logic of Rationalism. It was a protest of sentiment and imagination against pure intellectualism, of feeling against form, of individualism against the tyranny of system. It was a plea for sympathetic creative imagination, as against mere form and substance.

The Rationalists regarded the State as ordered reason; the Romanticists looked upon the State as a convenient civil institution. "It was the first principle of the Romantics to burn what their predecessors had worshipped." The battle was a new phase of the old conflict of ideas,

---

[1] For this chapter see Reinhold Aris, *History of Political Thought in Germany from 1789 to 1815* (London, 1936), ch. vi, with bibliography; FUETER, 478–79, 495–515, and beginning of bk. V; WEGELE, bk. V and *passim;* GOOCH, introduction; WOLF, 211–28, 232–35, with important bibliographical notes.

as between the Realists and Nominalists in the twelfth century, or that of the Ancients and the Moderns in the seventeenth century.[2]

In spite of his conservatism, intimations of Romanticism may be discerned as far back as Justus Möser. But the trumpeter of the dawn, the prophet of the coming movement, the "gate-keeper" of the nineteenth century, as someone has finely called him, was Johann Gottfried Herder (1744–1803).[3] He was philosopher, philologist, litterateur, anthropologist, social theorist, folklorist, preacher, and poet. Next to Kant, of whom he was a pupil, the greatest influence upon him was exerted by J. G. Hamann (1739–88), who was a native of Königsberg, where Herder knew him, and died at Münster. Justus Möser dubbed Hamann the "Magus im Norden," or Mage of the North. Hamann had a profound influence on the development of Romanticism independently of his influence through Herder. He was an original and a deep spirit and well versed in the sciences, theology, philology, Oriental literature, and art. He thought in images and symbols—hence his influence on Romanticism.[4]

From Kant, his master, Herder got the idea that the function of the

---

[2] Cp. V. F. Storr, *The Development of English Theology in the Nineteenth Century* (London, 1913), 126–27.

[3] ARIS (n. 1), 234–50; FUETER, 407–11; WOLF, 211–13 with bibliographical notes; BIEDERMANN, II, ii, pt. 3, 716–23, 801–46; Henry W. Nevinson, *Sketch of Herder and His Times* (London, 1884); Rudolf Haym, *Herder nach seinem Leben und seinen Werken* (Berlin, 1877–85, 2 v.); E. Kühnemann, *Herder* (3rd ed., Munich, 1927); Fr. M. Bruntsch, *Die Idee der Entwicklung bei Herder* (Leipzig, 1904); Theodor Genthe, *Der Kulturbegriff bei Herder* (Jena, 1902); G. E. Burckhardt, *Die Anfänge einer geschichtlichen Fundamentierung der Religionsphilosophie bei Herder* (Halle, 1908); Rudolf Stadelmann, *Der historische Sinn bei Herder* (Halle, 1928); Johannes Grundmann, *Die geographischen und völkerkundlichen Quellen und Anschauungen in Herders 'Ideen zur Geschichte der Menschheit'* (Berlin, 1900); Ernst Schaumkell, *Herder als Kulturhistoriker im Zusammenhang mit der allgemeinen geistigen Entwicklung dargestellt* (Ludwigslust, 1901); Theodor Litt, *Kant und Herder als Deuter der geistigen Welt* (Leipzig, 1930); Horst Stephan, *Herder in Bückeburg und seine Bedeutung für die Kirchengeschichte* (Tübingen, 1905); R. R. Ergang, *Herder and the Foundation of German Nationalism* (New York, 1931); Charles Joret, *Herder et la renaissance littéraire en Allemagne au XVIIIᵉ siècle* (Paris, 1875); H. Troucon, *La fortune intellectuelle de Herder en France* (Paris, 1918); Friedrich Bärenbach, *Herder als Vorgänger Darwin's und der modernen Naturphilosophie, Beiträge zur Geschichte der Entwickelungslehre im 18. Jahrhundert* (Berlin, 1877); R. Fester, *Rousseau und die deutsche Geschichtsphilosophie* (Stuttgart, 1890); Henri Sée, "La philosophie de l'histoire de Herder," *RSH*, XLVIII (1929), 21–36; Martin Schütze, "The Fundamental Ideas in Herder's Thought," *Modern Philology*, XVIII (1920–21), 65–78, 121–302; XIX (1921–22), 113–30, 361–82; XXI (1923–24), 29–48, 113–32; Otto Braun, in *Zeitschrift für philosophische Kritik*, CXLIV (1911), 165–81; CXLV (1912), 1–22, and "Herders Ideen zur Kulturphilosophie auf dem Höhepunkt seines Schaffens," *HZ*, CX (1912–13), 292–326; Gustav Buchholz, "Ursprung und Wesen der modernen Geschichtsauffassung," *Deutsche Zeitschrift für Geschichtswissenschaft*, 1889, pt. ii, 17–37; K. Bittner, "Herders Geschichtsphilosophie und die Slaven," *Veröffentlichungen*, etc. (German University, Prague), VI (1929), pt. 1. For Herder's complete works see below, n. 23.

[4] Hamann's collected writings in 8 volumes were published by Friedrich Roth (Berlin, 1821–43). For literature on him see C. H. Gildemeister, *Johann Georg Hamann's des Magus im Norden Leben und Schriften* (Gotha, 1863–75, 6 v.); Moritz Petri, *J. G. Hamanns Schriften und Briefe* (Hanover, 1872–74, 4 v.); Gustav Poel, *Johann Georg Hamann, der Magus im Norden* (Hamburg, 1874–76, 2 v.); Jacob Minor, *Johann Georg Hamann in seiner Bedeutung für die Sturm und Drangperiode* (Frankfort, 1881).

historian is to discover unity amid a vast number of diverse facts and to perceive a continuous developmental principle through all change.[5] Herder combined Kant's concept of genetic forces with Rousseau's individualism. He applied "genetic thinking" to all the expressions of human culture, poetry and art, language and religion. Despite the enthusiasm of his admirers for his originality, Herder was the direct descendant, the reaper as it were of the harvest sown by Rousseau, Winckelmann, and Kant. The reason for his fame was his prolific literary output, and the rhetorical brilliance of his style. He was author of no less than sixty volumes on almost every conceivable subject, generalizing boldly and brilliantly, not uncommonly with a disregard for facts.

Like Kant, Herder was an East Prussian, a child of poor parents, brought up in a Pietist atmosphere. Again like his older teacher, he was educated at Königsberg, and imbibed all the streams of thought of the age. As was usual with most Germans of his time, Herder was first influenced by the French. In 1769, at the age of twenty-five, he took a trip through France where he met many of the *philosophes*.

My time [he wrote from Paris] is divided here between the society of the learned, visits to libraries, picture galleries, and antiquities, the theatre and such public buildings as are interesting in conception and execution. Paris is the centre of taste and splendor, the arts and scientific institutions. As, however, taste is but the lowest apprehension of the beautiful, and splendor is but appearance, and often a substitute for it, France can never fully satisfy me, and I am already tired of it. Nevertheless, I would not, on many grounds, have forgone my acquaintance with it, or have wanted the experience and the ideas respecting its language, manners, morals, taste, arts, and sciences which I have acquired. I have studied books and men, dance and painting, music and the [French] public.[6]

At this time Herder began to jot down fragmentary ideas in a journal which became the basis of his famous *Ideen zur Philosophie der Geschichte der Menschheit*.[7] This work, containing Herder's fundamental thoughts on history, had a remarkable influence on his contemporaries.[8]

In early life [he once said of his *Ideen*] when the fountains of knowledge lay before me in all their morning splendor, the thought often occurred to me whether, as everything else in the world had its philosophy and regulative principles, that which so much

[5] Cp. Aris (n. 1), 239.
[6] Maria Caroline von Herder, *Erinnerungen aus dem Leben Gottfrieds von Herder* (Stuttgart and Tübingen, 1820, 2 v.), I, 142; see the review in *DR*, XIV (1843), 505–34.
[7] Riga and Leipzig, 1784–91, in 4 v., revised edition by Heinrich Düntzer, Berlin, 1879, in 4 pts.; English translation by T. Churchill, *Outlines of a Philosophy of the History of Man* (2nd ed., London, 1803, 2 v.).
[8] Burke's *Reflections on the Revolution in France* a few years afterwards inaugurated Romanticism in history in England.

concerns us, the history of mankind as a great and entire aggregate, had not also its philosophy and scientific laws. All things suggested this to me, metaphysics and morals, physics and natural history, but religion most of all.[9]

One must not expect to find a rigorous logical system in Herder's ideas on history; he was too poetic, too intuitive, to be a careful systematizer. Always swayed between reason and feeling, Herder flung out, as it were, a series of penetrating thoughts, rarely troubling himself about their logical connection. Hence one frequently finds, instead of facts and proofs, only images and poetical metaphors. His mind was highly original. Gemmingen has asserted that the connection between Vico and Herder is still to be traced.[10]

Herder, with limited means, undertook the gigantic task of conceiving all the living things on earth as a totality (he undoubtedly developed the idea of organic evolution half a century before Darwin),[11] continuously progressing upwards in an organic chain. "It is anatomically and physiologically true that there rules the analogy of a single organism throughout the whole living creation of our earth."[12]

On the basis of this organic evolution in nature, Herder built his history. In nature everything is organically connected, one condition leads to another, until it reaches man, the highest and last expression of the evolutionary chain.[13] Human reason, the summation of the experience of the race, undergoes the same evolution. "Herein lies the principle of the history of mankind, without which there would be no history."[14] Hence history is the "whole chain of the education of our race."[15]

Herder developed three stages in the growth of mankind: the poetical, the prosaic, and the philosophic. In the poetical age men sang and retained their historical memory through epics.

[9] *DR* (n. 6), 526.
[10] Otto Gemmingen, *Vico, Hamann und Herder; eine Studie zur Geschichte der Erneuerung des deutschen Geisteslebens im 18. Jahrhundert* (Leipzig, 1918), 37–51. Vico's ardent admirer, Benedetto Croce, however, claims Vico's primacy in forming Herder's ideas. Cp. his "Studii sulla storiografia: La nascita della storicismo," in *La Critica* [rivista di letteratura, storia et philosofia], XXXV (1937), 328–43. Croce even finds in Vico "anticipations of Max Müller's interpretation of mythology, Grimm's reconstruction of primitive culture by philology, Niebuhr's and Mommsen's conception of early Roman history, Wolf's theory of the Homeric epic, Savigny's school of jurisprudence, Fustel de Coulanges' conception of the Middle Ages, De·Sanctis' criticism of Dante, and Marx' idea of the class war. Such an exaggerated appreciation of Vico's merits reads into his seminal hints thoughts really unborn until they were more highly developed, and generally from other sources than Vico." SMITH, II, 236. However, G. J. Robertson, *Studies in the Genesis of the Romantic Theory in the Eighteenth Century* (Cambridge, 1923), 288, contends, that although the nexus cannot be proved, "the wonderful conception of Herder's *Ideen zu einer Geschichte der Philosophie der Menschheit* seems to me unthinkable without a knowledge of the *Scienza Nuova.*"
[11] See Schütze's article in *Modern Philology* (n. 3), 362–63.
[12] *Ideen zur Philosophie der Geschichte der Menschheit* (1784), I, 108.
[13] *Ibid.*, I, 335.　　　　　[14] *Ibid.*, II, 254.　　　　　[15] *Ibid.*, I, 255.

They sang in everyday life . . .; the language was sensuous and rich in bold images; it was still an expression of passion. . . . Since there were as yet no authors, the poets immortalized the most remarkable events through poetry; they taught through songs, and in the songs of that time were contained battles and victories, fables and maxims, laws and mythologies.

The prosaic stage represents a more mature period in human development.

The older the youth became, the more wisdom and political maturity entered his character, the more he becomes masculine and ceases to be a youth. His language in his masculine age is no longer poetry but beautiful prose.

Finally there is the age of ripeness and philosophical depth.

The ripe age [*hohe Alter*] knows, instead of beauty, only propriety. . . . The more the worldly-wise seeks to differentiate or reject synonyms, the more he is able to introduce proper instead of improper words—the more the language loses charm, but at the same time it also offends less. [16]

With all due respect for a rich mind, one is bound to conclude that much of this is verbiage. Herder's three stages are sheer poetry, uncontrolled by the evidences of antiquity, either from philology, archaeology, or anthropology.

The enormous difficulty of weighing the influence of a man like Herder lies in the fact that his original store of formal principles, of analytic terms of classification, is the smallest part of his historical contribution. His greatest service to the expansion of the modern mind is of a different character, difficult to analyze and state, and yet clearly discernible. Herder had the creative gift of exceptional flexibility, resource, and discernment in applying general formal conceptions, analytic generalizations like perfectibility and environment, to every new concrete condition which came under the notice of his indefatigable mind. He had more than any one of his contemporaries, the double gift of distinguishing in every field of reality both the specific and the general, the individual and the universal parts. It is this gift of clothing the few dominant generalizations of an age in the immeasurable richness of concrete individual experience, rather than the rationalistic opposite of stripping the latter to the monotonous poverty of the former, which is the living essence of modern humanism since Herder.

This gift was the source of Herder's genius. He saw the inexhaustible applicability of a few generalizations in the specific forms of individual life. And he taught this outlook to his contemporaries. Even at this day one cannot read his works without being enriched on every page by fresh illuminations, by new concrete revelations of general ideas. Herder reorganized the theories of art, literature, philosophy, religion and history within the double focus of individuality and environment. [17]

Among his many services to German culture, one may count his courageous stand for a national (*volkstümlich*) literature. [18] He never failed

[16] Moritz Kronenberg, *Geschichte des deutschen Idealismus* (Munich, 1909–12, 2 v.), I, 381–82, cp. 375–405.
[17] Martin Schütze's review of Henri Tronchon's *La fortune intellectuelle de Herder en France. La préparation* (Paris, 1920), in *Modern Philology*, XX (1922–23), 333, cp. 331–33.
[18] On this subject see Schütze's other article in *Modern Philology*, XIX (1921–22), 115–30.

to ridicule the classicists who were unoriginal imitators of the past. "Let us be idiomatic writers; let us be original; let us write for our own people in our own tongue. Let us leave to posterity whether we be classical or not." He deplored the interruption of Germany's national life in the Middle Ages, for which he blamed Charlemagne—"a man of misfortune, a child of the popes." [19]

Other nations [Herder wrote passionately] on the contrary have progressed with the ages, developing out of national productions on their native soil, and out of the remnants of the past on the foundation of popular belief and popular taste. Hence it is that their poetry and language became national. Whereas we poor Germans were destined never to remain true to ourselves. [20]

In Herder nationalism went hand in hand with the spirit of liberalism. Like Kant, he welcomed the French Revolution, and even flirted with democracy. Though a religious person, Herder was more of a pantheist than a Christian. He regarded the Bible as the most lofty literature in the world, but still an essentially human document. [21] To him, morality was "religion under whatever form it may show itself"; and it need not necessarily be Christian. In the same spirit Herder rejected the supernatural and the divine in history.

The God I look for in history must be the same as the God of nature; for man is but a tiny particle of the whole, and the history of mankind resembles that of the worm closely connected with the tissue it inhabits; therefore, the natural laws by which the Deity reveals itself must reign in man likewise. [22]

Like Lessing, whose work he immediately continued, he was a pioneer of the golden age of this literature. Lessing had given the first impetus to the formation of a national literature by exposing the folly of the current imitation of French writers. But in doing this he did not so much call his fellow-countrymen to develop freely their own national sentiments and ideas as send them back to classical example and principle. Herder on the contrary fought against all imitation, and bade German writers be true to themselves and their national antecedents. To him literature and art, together with language and national culture as a whole, were evolved by a natural process, and the intellectual and emotional life of every people must be correlated with peculiarities of physical temperament and of material environment. In this

[19] Charlemagne, Herder said, "despoiled Germany of her noble and pure originality. . . . Sword in one hand, cross in the other, he brought the worst debris of Roman science and imposed Latin, a monkish and vulgar dialect." Michel Bréal, "La tradition du latin en France," *RDM*, CV (1891), pt. iii, 564, the whole article 551–70.
[20] Quoted from K. Hillebrand, "Herder," *NAR*, CXVI (1873), 413, cp. 389–424.
[21] See his *Vom Geist der hebräischen Poesie* (1782–83, 2 v.), tr. into English by James Marsh under the title, *The Spirit of Hebrew Poetry* (Burlington, Vt., 1833, 2 v.).
[22] Quoted by Hillebrand (n. 20), 416.

way he became the originator of that genetic or historical method which has since been applied to all human ideas and institutions.

Herder was an evolutionist, but an evolutionist still under the influence of Rousseau. In tracing back the later acquisitions of civilization to impulses which are as old as the dawn of primitive culture, he did not, as the modern evolutionist does, lay stress on the superiority of the later to the earlier stages of human development, but stressed the simplicity and spontaneity of those early impulses which, since they are the oldest of the race, he regarded as the most real and precious. In this way Herder helped to found the historical school. Though not an historian, he possessed important historical concepts, and combined in himself most that was rich and fruitful in German thought of the *Aufklärung*. He had an immediate influence on his contemporaries. The Grimms' studies in folklore were derived from Herder's *Stimmen der Völker in Liedern* (1778–79, 2 v.); Karl Ritter built his scientific geography on Herder's evolutionary ideas; Savigny and Görres learned their politics from him; and finally Hegel and Ranke were Herderians in their "religion of becoming." In France Herder (whose *Ideen* were translated into French in 1825) was the inspiration of Quinet, Guizot, and Michelet. But these matters belong to subsequent chapters.[23]

In spite of its nebulous nature Romanticism exerted a powerful and beneficent influence on German historiography by its almost passionate appeal to the past, especially to the Middle Ages, as against the contemporary period; and by its teaching, first propounded by Justus Möser, that only that which has developed historically may claim to be useful, an argument which cut the ground from under the feet of the Rationalists. Herder, as has been said, was the intellectual father of the Romantic movement and stimulated the growth of nationalism in Germany, though he had no connection with the idea of a powerful and centralized state such as came to pass in Prussia after the fall of Napoleon. Herder, as Kant before him, conceived the state as a representative of organized and civilized humanity as a whole and not primarily as an absolute monarchy.

A brilliant but shallow contemporary of Herder, and the great popularizer of Romanticism, was the Swiss-born Johannes von Müller (1752–1809).[24] He was educated at Göttingen under Schlözer. Müller, like

---

[23] Space forbids the enumeration of all of Herder's works. His *Sämmtliche Werke* were edited by B. Suphan (Berlin, 1877–1913, 33 v.); an earlier edition was published in 60 v. (Stuttgart, 1827–30). For editions of Herder's works and letters see DAHLMANN-WAITZ, no. 12746.

[24] Autobiography in *Bildnisse und Selbstbiographien jetztlebender Berliner Gelehrten*, ed. by M. C. Löwe (3rd series, Berlin and Leipzig, 1806–07); Eduard Haug, ed., *Der Briefwechsel der Brüder Joh. Georg Müller und Joh. v. Müller, 1789–1809* (Frauenfeld, 1893); FUETER, 502–07;

his inspiration Rousseau, led a migratory life, his pen and brain at the service of many masters. At the age of twenty he became teacher of Greek at the Schaffhausen Gymnasium; two years later he served as tutor to a Geneva councillor's family. Switzerland was too small for his ambitions and in 1780 he went to see Frederick the Great. "I want to live and die with Prussia and for the Prussians, or not live at all." But the Prussian king, despising persons of Germanic origin, received him with contemptuous coldness. Müller then became librarian at Cassel and following that, served at Mainz; when the French took Mainz, Müller went to Vienna. From the Austrian capital the restless historian journeyed to Berlin once more, and in 1804 Frederick William III made him historiographer of Brandenburg. Two years later Napoleon destroyed Prussia and summoned the vain historian for an interview. Müller, who had considered the Corsican an Attila, now completely succumbed to the charm of the French Emperor. It took only an hour-and-a-half conversation with Napoleon to make Müller prostrate himself before the conqueror as a god-chosen being. "God," the historian exclaimed, "I now see, has given him the world, the empire." Napoleon, in turn, gave Müller the Secretaryship of State of the Kingdom of Westphalia. In 1809 Müller died at Cassel.

During these peregrinations Müller was busy at his histories. In 1780 he published the *Geschichten der Schweizer*, to 1388, which was the first volume of his great *Geschichten schweizerischer Eidgenossenschaft*, to 1489 (Leipzig, 1786–1808). His *Essais historiques* (1781), *Reisen der Päpste* (1782), and *Darstellung des Fürstenbundes* (1787), were minor works composed while on the lookout for a safe berth. All this while Müller was at work on an ambitious universal history, *Vierundzwanzig Bücher allgemeiner Geschichten, besonders der europäischen Menschheit*, which he began at Geneva in 1779 and which was not published until

BIEDERMANN, II, ii, pt. 3, 710–12; SCHAUMKELL, 254–76; Karl Henking, *Johannes von Müller*, 1752–1809 (Stuttgart, 1909–28, 2 v.) and cp. review by Eugen Guglia in *Euphorion* [Zeitschrift für Literaturgeschichte], XVII (1910), 396–404; A. H. L. Heeren, *Johannes von Müller der Historiker* (Leipzig, 1809), and "Etwas über die Seltenheit klassischer Geschichtschreiber, besonders in Deutschland," in his *Historische Werke* (Göttingen, 1821–26, 15 v.), VI, which deals with Gatterer, Spittler, Müller, etc.; Heinrich W. Thiersch, *Ueber Johannes von Müller den Geschichtsschreiber und seinen handschriftlichen Nachlass* (Augsburg, 1881); Paul Requadt, *Johannes von Müller und der Frühhistorismus* (Munich, 1929); Karl Schück, *Studien über Johannes von Müller* (Heidelberg, 1912); Arnold Jaggi, *Ueber Johannes von Müllers Geschichtsauffassung* (Bern, 1922); Heinrich Henel, *Die Entwicklung des geschichtlichen deutschen Prosastils bei Johannes von Müller* (Berlin, 1928; Historische Studien, CLXXIX); Paul Wernle, *Der schweizerische Protestantismus im XVIII. Jahrhundert* (Tübingen, 1923–25, 3 v.); Willy Andreas, "Johannes von Müller in Weimar (1804)," *HZ*, CXLV (1931), 69–89; Rudolph Stadelmann in *ESS*, XI (1935), 81–82; the same, "Grundformen der Mittelalterauffassung von Herder bis Ranke," *Deutsche Vierteljahrschrift für Literaturwissenschaft und Geistesgeschichte*, IX (1931), 45–88; Karl Post, *Johannes von Müllers philosophische Anschauungen* (Halle, 1905; Abhandlungen zur Philosophie und ihrer Geschichte, XXI); H. Ulmann, "Der Geschichtschreiber Johannes von Müller und Friedrich der Grosse," *PJ*, LVIII (1886), 150–60.

after his death (1811, by his brother J. G. Müller). It reaches to the year 1783.

Müller sought to awaken his Swiss countrymen to their former glories, by idealizing the virtues and achievements of medieval times. His story of the Swiss was a great epic of liberty, and inspired Schiller to write his drama *Wilhelm Tell*, as Schiller's drama later inspired Rossini.[25] Though a diligent collector, Müller was too impatient to sift his materials, and he perpetuated the old legends and traditions of the Swiss.

It is difficult to evaluate Müller as an historian. He was undoubtedly the most widely-read historian of his time, yet he was not essentially interested in historiography. Insensately ambitious, he wrote history for the sake of winning attention and acquiring power. Volatile, versatile, learned, imbued with generous principles, Müller, like his model Rousseau, was a literary artist. It is not sufficient, he said, for an historian to be merely critical and lucid; "he must possess a soul." The "soul" in Müller's instance was Rousseauist sentimentalism which, incidentally, had a vast appeal to his readers in and out of Germany. Hence, as one may expect, he was both careless as to facts and uncritical as to sources. No reader today would go to Müller for information on medieval Switzerland or feudal Europe. Yet the man is important for the history-reading public he created. Müller, one may assume, paved the way for the popularity of Niebuhr and Ranke in the next generation.[26]

The German Romantic school of history might have taken for its motto: "The past will ever have a glory from its being far." Unlike the Romantic school in France, which went to excess in sentiment and fantastic imagination, the German romantic historians tinged medieval history with a sunset glow. There was neither rhapsody nor poignancy in their treatment. The first to be noticed is Heinrich Luden (1780–1847), long professor at Jena and author of a *Geschichte des deutschen Volkes* in twelve volumes (Gotha, 1825–37), down to the year 1237. Luden idealized feudalism and the feudal epoch in medieval German history, and was popular in a time when German politics were in a critical condition in the years of stress after 1813, when the German people were inclined to listen to voices which praised the glamour of the past. Luden's history is full of information; copious notes give extracts from the sources. "The time of indifference to German history" declares

[25] As late as 1760 the public hangman burned the book of the rash individual who first dared to raise some doubts regarding the historicity of William Tell. This was the dissertation of Pastor Freudenberger, *Wilhelm Tell, eine dänische Fabel* (Bern, 1760), cp. Godefroid Kurth, "L'épopée et l'histoire," *RQH*, LIII (1893), 7 note.
[26] Müller's *Sämmtliche Werke* were edited by his brother, Johannes Georg Müller (1831–35, 40 v. in 20); the first edition, 1810–19, contained only 27 v. For a bibliography see **Georg von Wyss**, *Geschichte der Historiographie in der Schweiz* (Zurich, 1895), 305–17.

the preface, "is past. A generation ago the Middle Ages seemed to be a starless night. . . . Then the awful time of misfortune broke the bonds of indifference and prejudice. The need of self-respect sent us back to our fathers. . . . The delight in what we found has strengthened the desire for further search." [27]

Luden's chief pupil was Voigt,[28] to whom the master suggested the Life of Hildebrand. Voigt's *Hildebrand als Papst Gregorius VII und sein Zeitalter* (1815) was the first seriously critical work on that great pope. It was bitterly criticized in Protestant quarters. Voigt never continued along this line, however. He was called to Königsberg, where he found the immensely rich archives of the Teutonic Order and spent the rest of his life in writing his *History of Prussia*, to its union with Brandenburg in 1527, in nine volumes. Voigt's training like that of Luden, "to whom I owe everything that I am," was insufficient or defective and incapable of the high-power work inaugurated at Berlin by Ranke.

Gustav Adolf Harald Stenzel (1792–1854) [29] was an historian who devoted himself to national German history, independently of any school. His best-known work is the *Geschichte Deutschlands unter den fränkischen Kaisern* (1827–28, 2 v.), which was based on sources and won praise from no less a scholar than Giesebrecht. "I defy anyone," Stenzel wrote, "to show me a statement in my book which I cannot substantiate from the best authorities." On an equally high scholarly level is his five-volume *Geschichte Preussens* (1830–37). His work resembles Ranke—whom the three-year-older Stenzel imitated—in its detachment and lack of passion.

Stenzel's career and reputation have suffered both from his own querulous personality and his strained relations with Ranke. When Ranke was a student at Leipzig he met Stenzel, in whose house he first came in contact with historical sources.[30] Stenzel was, therefore, embittered when the younger man was called to a professorship in Berlin,

---

[27] Quoted in GOOCH, 72. See Luden's *Rückblicke in mein Leben* (1847); F. Herrmann, *Die Geschichtsauffassung Ludens im Lichte der gleichzeitigen geschichtsphilosophischen Strömungen* (1904), and review by G. v. Below in *HZ*, XCVI (1906), 494–95.

[28] GOOCH, 73 and n. 1.

[29] See *Gustav Adolf Harald Stenzels Leben* by his son K. G. W. Stenzel (Gotha, 1897); GOOCH, 74–75; WEGELE, 1023–25; Felix Rachfahl, "Gustav Adolf Harald Stenzel," in *Forschungen zur brandenburgischen und preussischen Geschichte*, XI (1898), 1–31; E. Gothein, "Gustav Adolf Stenzel und Leopold von Ranke," in *Beilage zur [Münchner] Allgemeinen Zeitung*, nos. 69–70 (March, 22–23, 1892); Markgraf, "Stenzels Wirksamkeit und Bedeutung für die schlesische Geschichtsschreibung," *Zeitschrift für Geschichte und Altertümer Schlesiens*, XXVI, 395 ff.

[30] "My memories go back to Stenzel, the tutor in the house of a preacher in the Nicolai church at Leipzig, but trained historian by profession. In his house I saw the first collection of *Scriptores* and there, under his direction, I began to read a portion of them." Ranke, "Die alten Schüler," in his *Sämmtliche Werke* (3rd ed., Leipzig, 1874–90, 54 v. in 27), LIII–LIV, 649–50.

while he himself had to be contented with a job in the Silesian archives at wretched pay. His correspondence with Ranke was petty, carping, complaining, appealing, until the famous professor of Berlin began to tire of his old friend. What annoyed the conservative Ranke most was Stenzel's constant criticism of the Prussian ministers. Finally when the position of Silesian historiographer fell open, Stenzel wrote to Ranke to intercede with minister Altenstein in his behalf; but he had the bad grace to add sarcastically: "He who like myself has ten children and earns, through truly magnificent kindness, a salary of 1200 thalers, can hardly compete." Ranke refused to answer and Stenzel continued to beg for a reply. Stenzel insisted he was not jealous of Ranke's fame; he hoped his old friend was not angry with him; he had always been honest with him—"though it is very natural that I do not agree with thee in all things." [31]

The so-called Heidelberg school, Schlosser, Gervinus, and Häusser, was composed of Romanticists. Though none of these men is now of much significance, their reputations among contemporaries were great enough to justify a brief discussion of their merits. Friedrich Christoph Schlosser (1776–1861),[32] professor of history at Heidelberg since 1817, belonged intellectually to the eighteenth century. Morally he was a Kantian, emotionally a Rousseauist, mentally an *Aufgeklärter*. His chief work was the *Geschichte des 18. Jahrhunderts*,[33] which, like his other writings, may be read with pleasure but hardly with profit. "In 1811 he began to write his *Weltgeschichte*. . . . It was largely through Schlosser that classical antiquity swam into the ken of the cultured middle classes of Germany." [34] Uncritical, unrealistic, judging matters from the point of view of a cut-and-dried pattern, Schlosser's writings, because of their facile generalizations and aesthetic treatment, had a wide popularity in Germany. No greater contrast could be imagined than that between the moralizing and impressionable Schlosser, and the detached and critical Ranke. There would hardly be any doubt as to where the intellectual mastery rested. So one is not surprised to find Georg Waitz, one of Ranke's greatest pupils who was then professor at Kiel, criticizing Schlosser and rejecting his philosophy.

---

[31] C. Varrentrapp, "Briefe an Ranke," *HZ*, CV (1910), 124–25.
[32] On Schlosser see G. Weber, *Friedrich Christoph Schlosser* (Leipzig, 1876); G. G. Gervinus, *Friedrich Christoph Schlosser, ein Nekrolog* (Leipzig, 1861); the same, *Briefe über den Nekrolog Friedrich Christoph Schlosser's* (1862); B. Erdmannsdörffer, *Schlosser* (Gedächtnisrede, Heidelberg, 1876); FUETER, 512–14; WEGELE, 1062–68; Ottokar Lorenz, *Die Geschichtswissenschaft in Hauptrichtungen und Aufgaben* (Berlin, 1886); anon., "Friedrich Christoph Schlosser," *PJ*, IX (1862), 373–433; "Zur Beurtheilung Friedrich Christoph Schlosser's," *HZ*, VIII (1862), 117–40; and review of his *Geschichte des Achtzehnten Jahrhunderts* in *FQR*, XXXI (1843), 24–57. For bibliography see WOLF, 232–33 notes.
[33] Acton, *Home and Foreign Review* (1863), 642–45.   [34] GOOCH, 106.

We North Germans [Waitz wrote] can be friendly to neither the Schlosser treatment nor the Schlosser books. This habit of seeing the dark side of all things and conditions, this almost deliberate disparagement of every great personality because it does not think and act like Schlosser, this total misjudgment of the characteristics of various times and lands—is very far from the ways of true history. The pitiless hatred of all that is evil and vulgar, the firmness of his convictions—these inspire the highest respect for the character of the man; but mere intentions do not make an accomplished historian, nor does great learning, which is so often praised in him but which is more of an industrious reading of sources than a truly careful and critical digest. . . . Schlosser has done little for German history directly, and I would have kept silent . . .; but his position in historical literature is too significant and his influence on the views on German history too influential for me to ignore him altogether.[35]

At Schlosser's death, his admiring pupil and colleague Georg Gottfried Gervinus (1805–71),[36] whom Waitz regarded as being as one-sided as his teacher, wrote an account of him in which he made some disparaging remarks about Ranke. The latter, according to Gervinus, was mainly a discoverer of documents, a seeker after methods, an optimist, a man "with the rare talent to see the best in everybody." The pro-Rankeans seized their pens to defend the master, and an acrimonious controversy filled the newspapers.[37]

Gervinus was born at Darmstadt, Germany, 1805 and died at Heidelberg in 1871. He became professor (extraordinary) at Heidelberg in 1835, and professor of history and literature at Göttingen in 1836; was one of the seven professors driven from that university in 1837 for protesting against the suspension of the constitution of Hanover; and became honorary professor at Heidelberg in 1841. His works include *Geschichte der poetischen Nationallitteratur der Deutschen* (five editions), *Geschichte der deutschen Dichtung* (1871–74), and *Geschichte des neunzehnten Jahrhunderts* (1856–66). Gervinus personates the average middle-class German from the smaller towns of the smaller states, crowded with indisputable information, skeptical and doctrinaire, more robust than elastic or alert, instructive but not persuasive, with a taste for broad paths and the judicious forcing of open locks.

Ludwig Häusser (1818–67)[38] was the third member of the Heidelberg group of liberals who were more or less in opposition to the Ranke

[35] G. Waitz, "Deutsche Historiker der Gegenwart," *Allgemeine Zeitschrift für Geschichte,* V (1846), 524–25, cp. 520–30.
[36] On Gervinus see Johannes Dörfel, *Gervinus als historischer Denker* (Gotha, 1903); GOOCH, 108–12; WEGELE, 1068–72; FUETER, 654–57; WOLF, 236 note; L. Ranke, "Georg Gottfried Gervinus," *HZ,* XXVII (1872), 134–46; G. Waitz in *Allgemeine Zeitschrift für Geschichte* (n. 35), 520–30.
[37] E. Guglia, *Leopold von Rankes Leben und Werke* (Leipzig, 1893), 320–22.
[38] See W. Wattenbach, *Ludwig Häusser, ein Vortrag* (Heidelberg, 1867); GOOCH, 131–33; FUETER, 675–77; WEGELE, 1072–74; WOLF, 236–37 note. The fullest bibliographies on Häusser are by Kluckhohn in *Allgemeine deutsche Biographie,* XI, 112, and E. Marcks in *Heidelberger Professoren aus dem 19. Jahrhundert* (Heidelberg, 1903, 2 v.), 286.

school. A political historian, he was an ardent Prussian patriot and his *Deutsche Geschichte* was, in the words of his eminent pupil Treitschke, "quite as much a political act as a scientific achievement." This work was popular enough to go through a number of editions and helped finally to destroy the credit of French radicalism among German intellectuals.[39]

The last and greatest historian of the German Romantic school was Friedrich Ludwig Georg von Raumer (1781–1873).[40] He was educated at Halle and Göttingen, principally in law and political economy. For ten years (1801–11) he was in the employ of the Prussian Government. These were the years when Hardenberg and Stein were energetically reforming the administration. At the age of twenty Raumer was made referendary in the Chamber of the Kurmark;[41] at twenty-one he was appointed assessor to Oberpresident von Bassewitz at Eichsfeld; at twenty-five he became director of the bureau of crown lands and when twenty-nine was made a counsellor of the government at Potsdam. From this post Hardenberg called him to Berlin in 1810, where he was employed in administration of the huge debt which Napoleon had imposed on Prussia after the French occupation of Berlin in 1807.

In 1803 while at Berlin he began to collect materials for his history of the Hohenstaufen. In spite of rapid promotion, Raumer soon perceived that he would have to resign from civil administration or else abandon history as a career. Three years before he had almost resolved, on the recommendation of Johannes von Müller, to become a professor in one of the universities in South Germany. In 1811 he took the step, and he himself drew up the cabinet order by which the king appointed him a professor at Breslau.[42] Here he remained until 1815 by which time he had become convinced that long researches in Italian archives were necessary for completion of his history of the Hohenstaufen. On the recommendation of Hardenberg the king gave him leave of absence and the means for travel; he was gone from the summer of 1816 to the

[39] The best-known of Häusser's works is *The Period of the Reformation, 1517–1648* (tr. by Mrs. G. Sturge, 1873). It was published posthumously (1868) by Wilhelm Oncken from Häusser's lecture-notes.

[40] There is no life of Von Raumer, but see his *Lebenserinnerungen und Briefwechsel* (Leipzig, 1861, 2 v. in 1). In the year after his death Ranke wrote a harsh criticism of him, "Eine Gedächtnisrede," *HZ*, XXXI (1874), 151–56; Giesebrecht followed suit but wrote in a gentler vein, "Nekrolog auf Friedrich von Raumer," *Sitzungsberichte der bayerischen Akademie* (1874), 179–87. Cp. GOOCH, 73, FUETER, 629–32; WEGELE, 1025–28. See reviews of his works in *NAR*, XLIII (1838), 445–58; *FM*, XIII (1836), 631–38; *ER*, LXIII, (1836), 198–224; *QR*, LI (1834), 304–42, LIV (1835), 78–108, LVI (1836), 530–83, LXII (1838), 452–75.

[41] The *Kammer* or Chamber was a financial board which had the management of the public domains and the quartering and provision of troops; it also exercised a superintendence over the police. The most important branch of knowledge required was economics, then called *Cameralwissenschaften,* from which such an official was known as a cameralist.

[42] Here he published a *Handbuch merkwürdiger Stellen aus den lateinischen Geschichtsschreibern des Mittelalters* (Breslau, 1813).

autumn of 1817. Two years later he was called to Berlin as professor of political science (*Staatswissenschaften*) and lectured on the ancient Orient and Greek history down to 281 B.C. But Niebuhr's lectures on early Roman history cast Raumer into the shade.

Raumer's treatise on the Prussian municipal system (*Ueber die Preussische Städteordnung*, Leipzig, 1828) opened a paper war out of which Raumer emerged triumphant. Stein, the creator of the system, warmly sustained him. This work was followed by one on the historical development of the ideas of law and government (*Ueber die geschichtliche Entwickelung der Begriffe von Recht, Staat und Politik*, Leipzig, 1826 and 1832) an examination of the theories from ancient times. Two visits to France resulted in his interesting *Briefe aus Paris und Frankreich*, where he was an eye-witness of the July Revolution in 1830, and *Briefe aus Paris zur Erläuterung der Geschichte des 16. und 17. Jahrhunderts*, the fruit of researches in the archives at Paris. A few years later there appeared Raumer's *Geschichte Europas seit dem Ende des 15. Jahrhunderts*. In the *Historisches Taschenbuch* for 1831 he published a long account of the downfall of Poland (*Polens Untergang*) which made a sensation. Raumer had become a person of suspicion to the increasingly reactionary Prussian Government; although he himself was a member of the High Board of Censorship (*Obercensurcollegium*), he resigned from it in a stinging protest against the practice of censorship.

Raumer's academic training was insufficient for a professional historian in this time when the historical school at Berlin represented standards and critical methods beyond those of the eighteenth century. Like Justus Möser before him Raumer was a bureaucratic liberal. He showed his liberalism in 1848 when he sat in the Frankfort Parliament. His cameralistic experience, while undoubtedly of value to him as an historian, nevertheless had deprived him of technical training as an historian. Stenzel said that "he was a remarkable success for a man without any proper training." In short, it may be said without injustice that Raumer was a brilliant amateur.[43] His style was brilliant and he wrote with almost French vivacity and clarity. Indeed, Fueter says that he manifestly imitated Voltaire's *Siècle de Louis XIV*.

Raumer was a voluminous writer; his fame rests on the *Geschichte der Hohenstaufen und ihrer Zeit*.[44] In preparation of this work he devoted years to exploring almost every important library, every collection of archives in Europe. Though a Protestant he passed the barrier at the

[43] When Von Raumer was nominated for membership in the Prussian Academy, Humboldt, Eichhorn, and Savigny opposed him and Ranke was elected (Humboldt's *Briefe*, nos. 23, 68). This episode partly explains Ranke's trenchant criticism of Raumer.

[44] Leipzig, 1823–25, 6 v.; 4th ed., 1871. The only notice in English of this work was in an article by Milman in *QR*, LI (1834), 304–42, a vapid and silly review in Milman's worst vein.

Vatican Library by adroitly replying when asked if he was of "our religion," that he was studying the history of the Hohenstaufen and was of the religion of that time. The breadth of Raumer's researches is shown in the "Verzeichniss der Quellen," manuscript and printed, appended to the sixth volume of his *Geschichte der Hohenstaufen*, which fills forty-five pages printed in double columns. A table of over a hundred pages shows the itineraries of the Hohenstaufen emperors through the evidence of documents and there are many topographical studies which Raumer made on the terrain. Raumer took a long start. The introduction is a survey of the history of medieval Germany and begins with a copious account of the Crusades. Conrad III, the first Hohenstaufen ruler, is not reached until page 321 (4th edition).

Though the body of the work is outdated today, Raumer's fifth and sixth volumes are still valuable to the medievalist. They are among the first substantial efforts to depict the *Kulturgeschichte* of Germany and Italy in the Middle Ages, and a mine of carefully selected and organized evidence. Finally in praise of Raumer it should be said that he was the founder in 1830 of the *Historisches Taschenbuch*, the first historical review in Germany, which continued to be published for the next sixty-two years (1830–92), and anticipated the *Historische Zeitschrift* (1859) by a generation.[45] To English readers, Raumer's most popular work was his *Letters from Paris*, already mentioned, a history of the sixteenth and seventeenth centuries illustrated by original documents in the form of reports of researches done in many European archives, which was translated into English in 1835 by Lord Francis Egerton.[46]

Raumer's Romanticism was too tempered by his long experience as a civil official to be passionate or lyrical, like Johannes von Müller or some of the French rhapsodists. But he had an intense and sympathetic imagination, whatever epoch he might be writing about. He once wrote in a letter: "There have been hours in which I have been Alexander the Great and Charles V and William of Orange and a Hohenstaufen emperor and a pope. This is a richer and more pregnant existence than can be understood by those who despise and condemn it." These last words are a gibe at the Berlin School of History.

[45] Von Sybel and Ranke loved Raumer the less for his insight in anticipating them in this particular.
[46] London, 1831, 2 v. See *QR*, LIV (1835), 78–108.

BOOK VII

THE FOUNDING OF MODERN GERMAN HISTORICAL SCHOLARSHIP

CHAPTER XLI

THE UNIVERSITY OF BERLIN: NIEBUHR AND RANKE [1]

"WHEN the time comes to sum up the intellectual life of the nineteenth century, it will probably be found that its principal feature was the study of history. The way to this study had been prepared by the skepticism of the preceding century, which had made a critical method possible; its interest was new-created by the growth of national life which the French Revolution and Napoleon fostered in their different ways in Europe. The opportunities for scientific work were enlarged when libraries were presently thrown more widely open, when unprinted documents were made accessible and the historical value of coins and similar 'bric-a-brac' became clearer." [2]

The new history which now began to be written especially in Germany was no longer content with mere erudition, but endeavored to ascertain the significance and continuity of events, to perceive and to understand the development of history.[3] This was the period of the Napoleonic wars when nationalism and romanticism were combined. This stimulated a new curiosity about the Middle Ages, an epoch which, under the influence of the Romantic movement, came to be regarded as both fruitful and glorious. The judicious Ranke later characterized Giesebrecht's praise of the medieval Germanic heroes as "at once too virile and too puerile." Croce regards this romantic cult of the Middle Ages as "nostalgic historiography." [4]

The romantic movement, however, was only one aspect of nineteenth-century historiography. Romanticism, especially in Germany,

---

[1] For general reading see GOOCH, chs. i–viii; FUETER, 574–605; WEGELE, Bk. V; WOLF, 211–43, with bibliographical notes, GUILLAND, 9–119; Georg v. Below, *Die deutsche Geschichtsschreibung von den Befreiungskriegen bis zu unsern Tagen* (2nd enlarged ed., Munich and Berlin, 1924), chs. i–iii; Friedrich Gundolf, *Anfänge deutscher Geschichtsschreibung* (Amsterdam, 1938); A. Horawitz, *Zur Entwickelungsgeschichte der deutschen Historiographie* (Vienna, 1865); Karl Biedermann, *Die deutsche Philosophie von Kant bis auf unsere Zeit* (Leipzig, 1842, 2 v.); Heinrich v. Sybel, "Ueber den Stand der neueren deutschen Geschichtschreibung," in his *Kleine historische Schriften* (Munich, 1863–81, 3 v.), II, 345–59; R. W. Seton-Watson, *The Historian as a Political Force in Central Europe* (London: School of Slavonic Studies, 1923), 20–27; Hermann Oncken, "The Study of History in the University of Berlin," [Chicago] *University Record*, X (1905), 113–18; and the articles of Giesebrecht, Waitz, Ranke, Pertz, and Droysen, "Zur Charakteristik der heutigen Geschichtschreibung in Deutschland,' *HZ*, I (1859), 1–42.

[2] F. Haverfield, "Roman History since Mommsen," *QR*, CCXVII (1912), 323.

[3] Cp. Eduard Zeller, *Geschichte der deutschen Philosophie seit Leibniz*, 824.

[4] Benedetto Croce, *Theory and History of Historiography*, tr. by D. Ainslie (London, 1921), ch. vi.

soon gave way to rigorous treatment of data. In Germany the sifting and publication of historical material was carried further than elsewhere in Europe. On the other hand, German scholars also went to an extreme in their special pleading. The Germans were not satisfied with merely constructing imposing historiographic foundations—in the form of such great source collections as the *Monumenta*—they also tended to subordinate all history to politics, especially Prussian politics; this was to some extent true even of the detached Ranke.

At perhaps no other period in Europe has there been so challenging a union of solid scholarship and bold interpretation as in nineteenth-century Germany.[5] The historian occupied himself with every problem of importance or interest to mankind. Hence innumerable schools of tendentious history developed. "Every historian who amounted to anything in our literature," says Sybel, "had his color; there were religious and atheistic historians, Protestant and Catholic, liberal and conservative; there were historians of all political parties, but there were no longer any objective, impartial, bloodless and nerveless historians."[6]

Politically, the influence of these German historians was decisive. "Without their aid," to quote Schmoller, "the Empire could never have been placed on its feet." The foremost historians were pro-Prussian. Many—Niebuhr, Droysen, Dahlmann, Mommsen, Sybel, Treitschke—were active in politics, and the Prussian government rewarded these scholars with honors and positions. This "alliance between history and politics" continued until 1914.

The great Renaissance of German scholarship began with the founding of the University of Berlin in 1810. Because the establishment of this institution was to prove epoch-making in European scholarship and science, its history should be traced in some detail. In 1806, it will be remembered, Napoleon destroyed the power of Prussia at Jena. The royal family fled to Memel, in East Prussia. Thither came two professors from the closed University of Halle and begged King Fred-

---

[5] Professor Charles Gross, the well-known American scholar, when a student in Germany wrote a letter to President Andrew D. White of Cornell, in which he compared the productiveness of two generations of German historians. Gross demonstrated that the older generation of scholars—Ranke, Droysen, Waitz, etc.—were, despite the far wider range of their work, sounder and more fruitful scholars than their more specialized successors. See G. L. Burr, "The Historical Work of Henry C. Lea," an address delivered at the University of Pennsylvania on May 28, 1925, quoted in E. S. Bradley, *Henry Charles Lea, a Biography* (Philadelphia, 1931).

[6] Sybel (n. 1), II, 349. Among the chief publishers of historical works was the well-known nationalist Friedrich Perthes, who opened his publishing business at Gotha in 1822. Perthes' first historical publications included the Heeren-Ukert series of histories, the *Geschichten der europäischen Staaten*. Apart from this series Perthes also published numerous histories of the small German states, like Rommel's *Hesse*, Sartorius' *Hanseatic League*, and Aschbach's *Emperor Sigismund*. See Clement T. Perthes, *Memoirs of Frederick Perthes, or Literary, Religious, and Political Life in Germany, from 1789 to 1843* (tr. from the German, 3rd ed., Edinburgh, 1856, 2 v.), II, 532–42.

erick William III to transfer that institution to Berlin. The exiled monarch, feeling the loss of Halle most bitterly, was favorably inclined. Humboldt, who was Prussian minister of education, said to King Frederick William, "The State must replace by intellectual force what it has lost in physical force." This saying fired the king so much that he used the very words in the famous proclamation of August 10, 1807, which called the University of Berlin into being. A month later, on September 4, Frederick William issued an order that all funds hitherto allocated to Halle should go to Berlin.

My dear Privy Councillor Beyme [the king wrote]. On account of the cession of the lands on the other side of the Elbe, the State loses the University of Halle, and with it the most important and accomplished educational institution. The filling in of this gap must be the first duty of the State during its re-organization. The Universities of Frankfort and Königsberg are not fitted, the first because of limited means . . . and the second because it is remote from the seat of the government. Berlin, on the other hand, unites in itself all that is required for an accomplished general educational institution together with the least expenses and the most useful effectiveness. I have, therefore, resolved to establish such an institution at Berlin in proper connection with the Academy of Sciences. . . . I authorize all the funds from the general and provincial treasuries for the University of Halle to be used as an additional supply.[7]

For the next two years there were long debates and arguments about the ways and means of establishing the new university. The distinguished Humboldt brothers were not in favor of an educational institution too close to the seat of the government; the pro-Berlin advocates won the argument by pointing out that "a constant contact between the heads of science and the chief officials" of the state would be "intellectually refreshing." Finally, on August 16, 1809, Frederick William issued an order assigning 150,000 thalers for the new university, which was housed in the palace of Prince Henry; the money was to cover the expenses for the university, the Academies of Science and Art, the libraries, botanical gardens, anatomical museum, etc.[8] Wilhelm von Humboldt, who was then chief of the Department of Religion and Education (*Cultusministerium*) in the Prussian government, undertook to invite the most eminent scholars and scientists in Germany to the new university. The following letter written by Humboldt to the king, May 9, 1810, throws an interesting light on educational conditions in Napoleonic Germany:

All universities have suffered; hardly one has more than 600 students; teachers and students are more ready than ever to come to a new seat of higher education. In the Kingdom of Westphalia [held by Napoleon's brother Jerome] they have generally come to the conclusion that the government will never understand the true German concept

[7] R. Köpke, *Die Gründung der königlichen Friedrich-Wilhelms-Universität zu Berlin* (Berlin, 1860), 163.
[8] Frederick William to von Altenstein, August 16, 1809, printed in Köpke (n. 7), 194–95.

of a University. . . . In Bavaria silly squabbles are destroying the hardly-established foundations. Austria and Saxony have shown that they have neither aptitude nor desire to utilize this period for their universities. Furthermore, in Göttingen, Kiel, and Heidelberg there has arisen discontent among the students for various reasons; Jena can not rise, since the Duke of Weimar has lost all interest in it; Halle's one faculty which still flourished was destroyed by the departure of Reil.

I would be acting against my duty if in such a moment I failed urgently to represent to Your Majesty what is to be done.

I can and must . . . prove factually that the hardly-founded institution has already won great confidence in Germany. No one who has been invited has as yet refused; Reil and Savigny have left very good positions and resisted all offers of their governments. A number of scholars, whom I do not find advisable to call at present, have told me that they would gladly come. . . . According to his last communication, Hugo most probably will come. . . . Kielmayer in Tübingen, from whom derive almost all good new physiological ideas, and who has for years refused calls to almost all great universities, recently to Halle, has expressed himself in favor of Berlin, without even being asked officially, and he will most probably come. Even now, the . . . university has in Willdenow, Klaproth, Karsten, Rudolphi, Reil, Hufeland, Fichte, Tralles, Eytelwein, Oltmanns, Erman, Wolf, Savigny, a number of men who must be considered the first in their fields, as no other university can show.

When the new university opened, Michaelmas 1810, it had 458 students [9] and a faculty which was unquestionably the most distinguished in all Europe. Wilhelm von Humboldt, himself a man of genius, brought together a group of the ablest professors he could find, in order to make Prussia the intellectual center of Germany. There were Fichte in philosophy; Schleiermacher, De Wette, Marheineke in theology; Savigny and Schmalz in jurisprudence; Friedländer, Kohlrausch, Hufeland, Reil in medicine; Tralles in mathematics; and in the historical sciences Wolf, Buttmann, Böckh, Heindorf, Spalding, Rühs, and Niebuhr. From its foundation the University of Berlin was an independent corporation. The man who reformed the educational system of Prussia and founded the university was suspicious of government control of education. [10] Wilhelm von Humboldt was the real founder of the University of Berlin, and he it was who "first pointed the way towards the application to historical studies of the comparative method."

The University of Berlin started with a group of first-rate historical scholars, particularly Niebuhr and Böckh. In the course of the next two or three decades there came others, notably Otfried Karl Müller and Leopold Ranke, who spread the reputation of Berlin as a great

[9] After the Napoleonic wars, the number of students at Berlin kept on increasing; in 1816 there were 519 students; in 1821, 724; in 1824, 920; in 1829, 1085.

[10] On the University of Berlin see Max Lenz, *Geschichte der königlichen Friedrich-Wilhelm Universität zu Berlin* (Halle, 1910–18, 4 v. in 5); J. R. Seeley, *Life and Times of Stein, or Germany and Prussia in the Napoleonic Age* (Cambridge, 1878, 3 v.), II, 430–35; Ernest Lavisse, *Études sur l'histoire de Prusse* (7th printing, Paris, 1916), 305–44 ("La fondation de l'Université de Berlin"); and H. W. Denis, "The Founding of the University of Berlin," *Educational Review*, XL (1910), 473–87.

center for historical studies. Finally Hegel, who joined the Berlin faculty in 1818, set the stamp of his philosophy on Prussia throughout the whole century.

The infant university boasted of one professor who was at the same time also a distinguished statesman. Barthold Georg Niebuhr (1776–1831) [11] was neither a professional historian nor a native Prussian. He was a Dane, son of Carsten Niebuhr, the famous traveller. At the age of eighteen Barthold Niebuhr knew eighteen European languages, as well as Hebrew, Persian, and Arabic. "My head," he wrote as a young student, "swims when I think what I have yet to learn—philosophy, mathematics, physics, chemistry, natural history, a complete knowledge of history, perfect acquaintance with German and French; the Roman law, as far as I can; and, at least to some extent, the constitutions of Europe, and the advanced study of antiquities." [12] The strangest thing was that Niebuhr actually mastered all these sciences—his memory was phenomenal—and most astonishing of all, also achieved distinction in the field of practical politics and administration. In 1806 Niebuhr left Copenhagen, where he was Secretary of the Board of Trade, for Berlin as a financial counsellor and henceforth he remained in Prussian service.

When, therefore, the University of Berlin opened, Niebuhr was not an academician, not an historian, and not a professional scholar. He was, of course, known for his limitless erudition and a friend, Spalding, suggested that he deliver a course of lectures at the new school. This was on August 31, 1810. On September 1, Niebuhr told his friend that he had made up his mind on what to lecture. The term began on September 29, and on that day Niebuhr began a sensational series of discourses on Roman history.

[11] The best biographical material is contained in *Lebensnachrichten über Barthold Georg Niebuhr, aus Briefen desselben und aus Erinnerungen einiger seiner nächsten Freunde*, ed. by D. Hensler (Hamburg, 1838–39, 3 v.), cp. review in *QR*, LXVI (1840), 515–64. See also, for his letters and other matter, DAHLMANN-WAITZ, no. 13445. A new edition of his *Briefe*, with additions, was ed. by Dietrich Gerhard and Wilhelm Norvin (1926–29, 2 v.), cp. the review by E. L. Woodward in *History*, XV (1930–31), 277–79. For reading see FUETER, 581–87; GOOCH, 14–24; WOLF, 219–20 and note; SANDYS, III, 77–82; GUILLAND, 41–68; Loebel, *The Life and Letters of B. G. Niebuhr* (tr. by S. Winkworth, London, 1852, 3 v.); Johannes Classen, *Barthold Georg Niebuhr. Eine Gedächtnisschrift* (Gotha, 1876); F. Eyssenhardt, *B. G. Niebuhr, ein biographischer Versuch* (Gotha, 1886); Heinrich v. Sybel, *Vorträge und Aufsätze* (Berlin, 1874), 23–36; Julius Hare, *A Vindication of Niebuhr's History of Rome* (Cambridge, 1829); Adolf Harnack, *Geschichte der königlich preussischen Akademie der Wissenschaften zu Berlin* (Berlin, 1901, 3 v. in 4), I, ii, 624–26, 670–72, and II, 379–409; H. Dreyhaus, "Niebuhr und Goethe," *PJ*, CXLII (1910), 433 ff.; J. Kärst, "Die Geschichte des Altertums im Zusammenhange der allgemeinen Entwicklung der modernen historischen Forschung," *Neue Jahrbücher für das klassische Altertum*, IX (1902), 32 ff.; E. Kornemann, "Niebuhr und der Aufbau der altrömischen Geschichte," *HZ*, CXLV (1932), 277–300.

[12] Francis Lieber, *Reminiscences of an Intercourse with Mr. Niebuhr the Historian, During a Residence with Him in Rome* (Philadelphia, 1835), 48. As a student at the University of Edinburgh, in 1798, Niebuhr studied mathematics, physical sciences, finance, politics, agriculture, topography; for recreation he had recourse to philology and history. See *NAR*, LXXVI (1853), 1–31.

I have determined to give a course of lectures on the History of Rome [he wrote to Madame Hensler, early in September, 1810]; I would never have undertaken to write the history of Rome, but to lecture on it is a somewhat less rash undertaking. I shall begin with the primitive state of Italy, and, as far as possible, represent the ancient races, not only from the narrow point of view of their subjugation, but also as they were in themselves, and as they had been in their earlier stages; then, in the Roman history, I shall give an account of the constitution and administration, of which I have a vivid picture before my mind's eye. I should like to bring this history down to the latest era, when the forms developed from the germs of antiquity became utterly extinct, and those of the middle ages took their place.[13]

Niebuhr's lectures on Roman history were attended not only by students but also by colleagues, statesmen, and officers; the lectures—delivered twice weekly—were an instant success. Here was something altogether new in ancient history.

He had written down his lecture verbatim, [to quote Savigny, Niebuhr's favorite student and later colleague,] and read it off before his hearers. This proceeding, which usually injures the liveliness of the impression, had, in his case, the most animated and powerful effect, such as in general only accompanies an extempore delivery. His hearers felt as if transported into ancient times, when the public reading of new books supplied the place of our printed books, and there was a less extended circulation, but they made a warmer and more personal impression.[14]

The lectures were published in the following year under the title of *Roman History,*[15] and were the most critical analysis of the subject which had yet appeared. Niebuhr, said the admiring Field Marshal von

---

[13] Loebell, *Life and Letters of Niebuhr* (n. 11), I, 306–07; cp. *NBR*, XVII (1852), 422–58.

[14] Quoted from *NBR*, XVII, 439. There is an interesting pen-portrait of Niebuhr in Lieber's *Reminiscences* (n. 12), 45–47: "Mr. Niebuhr was small in stature, and thin; his voice was of a very high pitch. He could not see well at a distance, and made sometimes strange mistakes. . . . He lived very frugally; wine and water was his usual beverage; he valued good wine, but did not drink it often. He frequently walked while walking up and down the room. . . . He disliked smoking very much and took snuff to such an excess, that he had finally to give it up. . . . His rare memory enabled him to study frequently without a pen; and I found him sometimes in a lying posture on a sofa, holding the work of an ancient writer over his head. . . . His memory . . . was almost inconceivable to others. He remembered almost every-thing he had read at any period of his life. . . . He said, 'Without a strong memory I never should have been able to write my History.'" Cp. the description of his pupil Thomas Arnold: "In person Niebuhr is short . . . his face is thin . . . his eyes remarkably lively." A. P. Stanley, *The Life and Correspondence of Thomas Arnold* (2nd ed., London, 1844, 2 v.), II, 384.

[15] The first two volumes of the *Römische Geschichte* appeared in 1811; the third volume came out posthumously in 1832. For Niebuhr's views see also *Vorträge über die römische Geschichte* (1846–48); *Römische Altertümer* (1858); *Geschichte des Zeitalters der Revolution* (1845); *Nach-gelassene Schriften nicht-philologischen Inhalts* (1842). An English translation of the first volume of the *Roman History* of Niebuhr, by Archdeacon Hare and Bishop Thirlwall, was published in 1828, the second volume in 1832; and the third volume was translated by Dr. William Smith and Dr. Leonard Schmitz (1840). It is worth observing that Hare and Thirl-wall were Cambridge men trained in the tradition of Porson. As the successive volumes came out they were eagerly reviewed by the leading English periodicals. See *QR*, LV (1835), 234–50; *BQR*, XIX (1854), 3–60; *ER*, LI (1830), 358–96; *NBR*, X (1848–49), 329–49, XXI (1854), 425–50, XXVIII (1858), 287–312; *FQR*, II (1828), 512–55, V (1830), 207–22, VIII (1831), 78–116, XI (1833), 406–35, XXXI (1843), 376–95; *DR*, VII (1839), 69–98; *FM*, LII (1855), 455–69; *NAR*, XVI (1823), 425–44, XLII (1836), 388–422, XLIII (1836), 120–32, and LXXIII (1851), 267–71.

Moltke, was like a surgeon whose "knife cut away the flesh of tradition and left naked the skeleton of truth." Though scientific criticism had been applied to tradition and legend by Wolf in his *Prolegomena* to Homer, Niebuhr seems to have been unaware of his distinguished predecessor's labors. In any case, Niebuhr was the first to do for history what Wolf had done for philology. This unprofessional historian had a religious passion for truth, to find which he thought was man's duty to God.[16]

Niebuhr was not merely a destructive critic, rejecting old legends and tradition; he reconstructed Roman history on a positive, factual basis. As he himself said, for years he contemplated the "confused and blended picture" until gradually there developed in his mind a substantial pattern. "The history of mistaken, misrepresented, and forgotten events, rises out of mists and darkness, and assumes substance and shape, as the scarcely visible aerial form of the nymph in the Slavonian tale takes the body of an earthly maiden beneath the yearning gaze of love." [17] He aimed to bring forth the kernels of historic truths hidden in the ancient Roman epics. On the social side, Niebuhr wove his story around the idealized free Roman peasant, as did Justus Möser for Germany. His peasant was not an idyllic creature, as in the case of Livy, but a flesh-and-blood producer of wealth and supporter of the state. Despite his political conservatism, Niebuhr had a liberal's dislike for aristocrats. "I hope," he once wrote to a friend, "that you will give me credit for the most decided hatred of despotism."

Niebuhr approached his history in the spirit of a dissecting physiologist. Where there were no historical facts, he utilized the poetical legends, which to him contained grains of truth. "To have formed these legends which so strongly influenced popular imagination, there must have been some truth at bottom." With his remarkable insight and unusual experience, he attempted to disentangle the true from the fictional. Where historic data did exist, Niebuhr proceeded in the manner of an exact scientist: he sifted the materials, then grouped them, and then formed conclusions strictly in accord with the facts at hand. "I dissect words," he said, "as the anatomist dissects bodies; I am trying to separate from foreign matters a skeleton of fossil bones collected too carelessly."

---

[16] "If we do not reveal the mistakes we discover," Niebuhr said to his students, ". . . if, when laying down the pen, we cannot, before God and our conscience, declare to ourselves that we have never tried to deceive ourselves or to deceive others . . ., we have made a wrong and irreligious use of study and literature." Quoted in GUILLAND, 48. For a discussion of Niebuhr's treatment of Roman legends see George Cornewall Lewis, *An Inquiry into the Credibility of Early Roman History* (London, 1855, 2 v.).

[17] *Lectures on the History of Rome from the First Punic War to the Death of Constantine*, tr. by L. Schmitz (London, 1844–53, 3 v.), II, 14. "He who calls back again into being what has vanished enjoys a bliss like that of creating." *Ibid.*, I, 5.

The *History of Rome*, which inaugurated modern historiography, might have become a classic had Niebuhr paid any attention to style. Unfortunately he lacked the literary gift. His stuff is rich and solid, but it has no unity, no color, no movement. The *History of Rome* is neither narrative nor essay, but a disconnected series of critical comments.

Niebuhr, one may summarize, wrote history as a statesman of wide experience. Practice in administration, finance, and diplomacy profoundly influenced his point of view and his approach. In fact, he went so far as to say that only a statesman could write the history of Rome.

The great misfortune [Niebuhr told Lieber] has been that, with one or two exceptions, those who have written on Roman history either had not the stuff for it, or they were no statesmen. Yet no one can write a history of this people without being a statesman, and a practical one too. . . . No wonder that so little has been done in Roman history; for a Roman historian ought to be a sound and well read philosopher and a practical statesman.[18]

Stein admired the *History of Rome* both for its learning and its ingenuity; but he had one objection: that with these high qualities Niebuhr did not write good German. Through his native language (Danish) English always peeped out. He had spoiled his German style by too exclusive an enthusiasm for English literature in his early years.

Niebuhr also made many contributions to archaeology and philology; he wrote archaeological essays, made translations, issued editions, and restored palimpsests. This work was done while Niebuhr was Prussian ambassador to Rome from 1815 to 1822. When he returned, as professor at Bonn, he organized a plan for the publication of a series of Byzantine historians, the *Corpus Scriptorum Historiae Byzantinae*, which, continued by the Berlin Academy, came to forty-eight volumes by 1855. In 1827 Niebuhr also founded the *Rheinisches Museum*, a journal devoted to classical history and archaeology.

Along with Niebuhr a number of other distinguished Berlin scholars made fruitful contributions to history and the related subjects. Among these the most prominent were Böckh, Müller, Eichhorn, and Savigny.

August Böckh (1785–1867),[19] whose training was in theology and philology, became a professor of classical literature at the University of

---

[18] Lieber, *Reminiscences* (n. 12), 67.

[19] On Böckh see GOOCH, 30–35; SANDYS, III, 95–101; Max Hoffmann, *August Böckh, Lebensbeschreibung und Auswahl aus seinen wissenschaftlichen Briefen* (Leipzig, 1901); *Briefwechsel zwischen August Böckh und Karl Otfried Müller* (Leipzig, 1883); K. J. Neumann, *Entwicklung und Aufgaben der alten Geschichte* (Strassburg, 1910), 45–46; R. H. Klausen, in *Lebensbilder berühmter Humanisten*, ed. S. F. Hoffmann (Leipzig, 1837), I, 29 ff.; E. Curtius, *Altertum und Gegenwart. Gesammelte Reden und Vorträge* (Berlin, 1886–92, 3 v. in 2), III, 115–55, II, 260–77; and "Economy of Athens," *NAR*, XXXII (1831), 344–67. For other literature see Basil Gildersleeve, *Oscillations and Mutations*, 2–7. Böckh's *Gesammelte kleine Schriften* were published in 1858–74, 7 v. in 4; his *Enzyklopädie und Methodologie der philologischen Wissenschaften* was edited by E. Bratuschek (Leipzig, 1877).

Berlin in 1811, the year of the publication of the first part of Niebuhr's *Roman History*. Under the stimulus of Niebuhr, he broke with the purely philological method and began to utilize inscriptions for historical data; in fact, Böckh may be regarded as the founder of epigraphy. In 1817 he published his remarkable *Staatshaushaltung der Athener*, which he dedicated to Niebuhr.[20] In this work Böckh traced in detail the finances and revenues of Athens, a subject in which he was the pioneer. One of the chief difficulties which Böckh faced was the problem of determining the approximate value of the coinage, weights, and measures of the ancients. Böckh established the relative values of those standards by weighing coins which have been preserved and comparing their gold content with the content of contemporary coins; generally, he concluded, the value of Athenian money was about three times that of European coins of his time.

A reviewer of his *History of the Athenian Navy* enthusiastically wrote:

> With him the violet-crowned city rises in all her ancient life, the deep lines of her philosophers, the rapt poetry of her bards, the fine policy of her institutes, the interior constitution of her republic, her orators, her generals, her courts, tribunals, navy, navy-boards, dock-yards, arsenals, stores, ships with their tackling and gear, all are presented to the view with such fidelity of vision that we are compelled to own that even modern Athens, with all the accurate description of Dr. Fiedler, is scarce clearer conveyed to the view by the distinguished and observant tourist, than the ancient city is delineated by Böckh.[21]

Böckh further applied his wide philological and chronological knowledge to editing the *Corpus Inscriptionum Graecarum* (the first two volumes, 1825–43), which was completed in 1877. His work was severely criticized by Hermann for his use of inscriptions at second-hand. Though not an interpretative historian, Böckh must be considered as a scholar who has enriched the historical sciences, and who prepared the ground for Mommsen. Some of the most eminent Hellenists in Germany were students of Böckh, who taught at Berlin for fifty-six years (1811–67); besides Müller, these students included Edward Meier, Trendelenburg, Droysen, Lepsius, and Otto Jahn. Furthermore, the students of that other great Hellenist, Gottfried Hermann, were among the "warmest admirers" of Böckh.

The most brilliant and versatile scholar to emerge from the Niebuhr-

---

[20] English translation as *The Public Economy of Athens* (London, 1828, 2 v.; 2nd ed., 1842). The second German edition, almost entirely rewritten and much enlarged, was issued in 1851; the second volume was made up of inscriptions referred to in the first, with a copious commentary. Among these Böckh included the tribute lists, or lists of states belonging to the Athenian Confederacy, with the amount of tribute paid by each set over against its name. From this revised German edition Anthony Lamb prepared another English translation, *The Public Economy of the Athenians* (Boston, 1857).

[21] *FQR*, XXVI (1841), 401, the entire review, 401–27.

Böckh school was Karl Müller (1797–1840),[22] who added Otfried to his name to distinguish him from many other Karl Müllers. Originally a philologist, Müller turned to history under the stimulus of Niebuhr. In 1816–17 he studied under Böckh at Berlin and became interested in Greece. His penetrating doctoral dissertation on Aegina, dedicated to Böckh, was the first detailed history of a Greek state, with emphasis on topography, race, religion, trade, art, government—in short, a comprehensive study of the total culture. "If he goes on with similar contributions," wrote the delighted Böckh, "we shall have a history of the Greeks of which till now there has been no conception." In 1819, the twenty-two-year-old Müller was appointed professor at Göttingen.

Though Müller died at the age of forty-three, he produced an astonishing number of works of primary importance. His studies included a *History and Antiquities of the Doric Race* (English translation, Oxford, 1850), an *Introduction to a Scientific System of Mythology* (English translation, London, 1844), a *History of Greek Literature* (English translation, Oxford, 1840), as well as histories of the Macedonians and Etruscans, and works on archaeology, art, and mythology. Intellectually, Müller belonged to the nationalist-Romantic movement, glorifying State and Nation, especially the Dorians, who to him were the pure Greeks. Müller's fundamental idea was the complete originality of Greek civilization, whose most striking quality was proportion. Among the Hellenes, Müller insisted, everything—religion, politics, war, education—was balanced, harmonious, and unified. This idea, it will be remembered, was developed first by Winckelmann and Wolf in the eighteenth century. On the technical side, Müller's contribution to Hellenic mythology followed the ideas developed by Herder. He studied local myths and legends, and traced their relations to other cults. This led him to the conclusion that the myth was a creation of the popular imagination, expressing a people's innermost thoughts. The same was true of Greek divinities, which, far from being the personifications of natural forces or of moral and intellectual qualities of men, were really created long before human reason conceived them in abstract. Müller proved, finally, that Greek religions

[22] See GOOCH, 35–41; FUETER, 587–89; SANDYS, III, 213–16; K. Hillebrand, "Étude sur Otfried Müller," in his French translation of Müller entitled *Histoire de la littérature grecque* (Paris, 1865, 2 v.), I, pp. xvii–ccclxxi, with a bibliography of his writings, cclxxiii–lxxx; J. W. Donaldson, "On the Life and Writings of K. C. Müller," in his English translation of Müller, *History of the Literature of Ancient Greece* (London, 1858, 3 v.), I, pp. xv–xxxi, and cp. the review in *FM*, LIX (1859), 357–77; Otto and Else Kern, eds., *Carl Otfried Müller, Lebensbild in Briefen* (Berlin, 1908), and see also DAHLMANN-WAITZ, nos. 15135, 15127; Lücke, *Erinnerungen an Karl Otfried Müller* (Göttingen, 1841); Karl Dilthey, *Otfried Müller, Rede zur Saecularfeier O. Müller's am 1. Dezember 1897* (Göttingen, 1898); P. R. Förster, *Otfried Müller: Rede*, etc. (Breslau, 1897); Curtius, *Altertum und Gegenwart* (n. 19), II, 247–60; W. Abeken, "C. O. Müller in Rom," *Zeitschrift für Geschichtswissenschaft*, II (1844), 114–26; Siegfried Reiter, *Göttingische Gelehrte Anzeigen*, CLXXII (1910), 324–62.

developed locally and particularly, and that later syncretism united individual cults into a complete system.

Müller was not only a sound scholar but also a fine artistic mind; unlike his masters, he had a brilliant style and great imagination. He planned to write the whole historic life of the Greek people in twelve volumes, but while he was pursuing his researches at Delphi he was struck by fever and died. His pupil Ernst Curtius said: "He fell a martyr in the land of his spirit, like a hero on his shield, in the fulfilment of his calling and in the preparation of greater, riper works."

The Berlin school likewise developed the science of legal history. Foremost among the scholars in this field were Karl Friedrich Eichhorn (1781–1854) [23] and Savigny. Eichhorn, who became professor at Berlin in the same year as Böckh (1811), was the author of a monumental *Deutsche Staats- und Rechtsgeschichte* (4 v., 1808–23). This solid history of German law and institutions was written in a national spirit, with an emphasis on law as an expression of the total folk culture. Here again one sees the influence of the fruitful ideas of Winckelmann and Wolf.

Friedrich Karl von Savigny (1779–1861) [24] did for Roman law what

[23] Karl Friedrich Eichhorn is not to be confused with his father Johann Gottfried Eichhorn (1752–1827), who was professor of Oriental languages at Jena and Göttingen, and whose chief work was an *Einleitung in das Alte Testament* (Leipzig, 1780–83).

On K. F. Eichhorn, see GOOCH, 42–47; FUETER, 525; WEGELE, 992–95; WOLF, 218–19 with bibliographical note; J. Fr. v. Schulte, *Karl Friedrich Eichhorn. Sein Leben und Wirken nach seinen Aufzeichnungen, Briefen, Mitteilungen von Angehörigen und Schriften* (Stuttgart, 1884); Hugo Lörsch, *Briefe von K. F. Eichhorn* (Bonn, 1881); Ferdinand Frensdorff, *Karl Friedrich Eichhorn* (Göttingen, 1881), an address, and his article on Eichhorn in *Allgemeine deutsche Biographie*, VI, 469–81; K. Jelusic, *Die historische Methode Karl Friedrich Eichhorns* (Leipzig, 1933); Albion W. Small, "Some Contributions to the History of Sociology: III. Eichhorn (1781–1854) and the Multiplicity of Factors," *American Journal of Sociology*, XXIX (1923), 42–57; A. L. Reyscher, "K. F. Eichhorn," *Zeitschrift für deutsches Recht*, XV (1855), 436 ff.; Brunner, "Karl Gustav Homeyer," *PJ*, XXXVI (1875), 26 characterizes Eichhorn and contrasts him with Homeyer. For general studies of the German jurists see the address of R. v. Stintzing, *Wendungen und Wandlungen der deutschen Rechtswissenschaft* (Bonn, 1879), delivered on the centenary of Savigny's birth; O. F. Gierke, *Die historische Rechtsschule und die Germanisten* (Berlin, 1903), which lists works on Eichhorn on p. 37; R. Stintzing and E. Landsberg, *Geschichte der deutschen Rechtswissenschaft* (Munich, 1880–1910, 3 pts. in 6 v.).

[24] For literature on Savigny and the historical school see WOLF, 221; GOOCH, 47–53; WEGELE, 988–92; Ernst Landsberg's article in *Allgemeine deutsche Biographie*, XXX, 425 ff.; Eduard Müller, *Friedrich Karl von Savigny* (Leipzig, 1906); James De Montmorency, *Great Jurists of the World* (1913); C. L. Arndt, *Rede zur Feier des Andenkens an F. K. von Savigny* (Vienna, 1861); Ludwig Enneccerus, *Friedrich Karl von Savigny und die Richtung der neueren Rechtswissenschaft* (Marburg, 1879); Freiherr von Canitz und Dallwitz, *Denkschriften* (Berlin, 1888, 2 v.), II, 174 ff.; John Austin, *Lectures on Jurisprudence* (3rd ed., rev. and ed. by Robert Campbell, London, 1869, 2 v.); Adolf Stölzel, *Brandenburg-Preussens Rechtsverwaltung und Rechtsverfassung* (Berlin, 1888, 2 v.), II, 526 ff., 731 ff.; Georg von Below, *Der deutsche Staat des Mittelalters* (Leipzig, 1914); Hugo Hälschner, *Geschichte des brandenburgisch-preussischen Strafrechts* (Bonn, 1855), 269–83; R. Ihering, "Friedrich Karl von Savigny," *Jahrbücher für die Dogmatik des heutigen römischen und deutschen Privatrechts*, V, 698–701; Rudorff, "Friedrich Karl von Savigny," *Zeitschrift für Rechtsgeschichte*, II (1863), 1 ff.; Bethmann-Hollweg, "Erinnerung an Friedrich Karl von Savigny als Rechtslehrer, Staatsmann und Christ," *Zeitschrift für Rechtsgeschichte*, VI (1867), 42 ff.; von Mohl, *Staatswissenschaft*, III, 55; *JS*, 1840,

Eichhorn had done for the Germanic. A professor at the University of Berlin since the opening day, Savigny became the leading spirit in historical jurisprudence in Germany. He had studied law at Marburg and history under Spittler at Göttingen, and later claimed that among the greatest influences in his life were Spittler in history and Goethe in literature. But Savigny can hardly be called an imaginative person.[25]

Savigny conceived that law was the expression of the whole life of a people, as Winckelmann had conceived of art and Wolf of literature. The German jurists and historians firmly believed in the doctrine of historical continuity; they believed in historical, not "natural" rights; facts were before theory. "This idea, applied to law by Savigny and to politics by Ranke and his disciples, was the strongest bulwark of that generation against the opposite dangers of reaction and revolution." [26]

Savigny's first important work was *Das Recht des Besitzes* (1803), which immediately won a European reputation; critics have since regarded it as the beginning of modern jurisprudence. By its rigid methodology and fruitful results, this work rendered obsolete most of the literature on the subject. Among other things, Savigny sought to solve the general problem of why possession, rightful or wrongful (as distinguished from property), should be protected. Savigny's second work, "On the Vocation of Our Age for Legislation and Jurisprudence" (*Vom Beruf unserer Zeit für Gesetzgebung und Rechtswissenschaft*, 1814), was an application of Winckelmann's ideas of Greek art to law: namely, that law is part of the national life and must be studied in relation to the total history of a people. This historical-genetic approach to jurisprudence was not without its political implications, since Savigny consciously strove to check the extension of the Code Napoleon to Germany. "I regard," Savigny wrote, "the law of each country as a member of its body, not as a garment merely which has been made to please the fancy, and can be taken off at pleasure and exchanged for another."

In 1815 appeared the first volume of his monumental *Geschichte des römischen Rechts im Mittelalter,*[27] which was originally intended to be a

---

pp. 41–52, 93–111, 152–65; M. Mignet, "Notice historique sur la vie et les travaux de M. de Savigny," *ASMP*, LXXI (1865), 121–56; *PJ*, IX (1862), 121–68; R. Pound in *Harvard Law Review*, June, 1911, 599–600.

[25] Cp. the description of W. W. Story, the Boston lawyer who visited Germany in the middle of the century: "Von Savigny, the celebrated jurist, I have seen repeatedly, and I can assure you that he is of all petrifactions the most remarkable I have seen. He is as dry as dust. Very courteous and affable and complimentary I found him, but living wholly in a book-world, and that book-world a law-book-world. He held up both his hands when he found out that I was an artist, and cried out, 'What, an artist and a lawyer? That is impossible!'" Story to Lowell, January 30, 1850, quoted in Henry James, *William Wetmore Story and His Friends* (Boston, 1903, 2 v.), I, 215–16.

[26] Carl Becker, in *Publications of the American Sociological Society*, VII (1912), 76.

[27] Heidelberg, 1815–31, 6 v.; 2nd ed., 1834–51, with a seventh volume containing additions and index.

literary history of Roman law from Irnerius to modern times, but was later changed to a philosophical treatment and continued only to the sixteenth century. From the viewpoint of historiography, Savigny's great history of Roman law is significant for its emphasis upon two ideas. In the first place, the work stressed the continuity in the history of Roman law from the earliest times to the foundation of modern states (sixteenth century); secondly, Savigny emphatically protested against the prevalent view that law was an arbitrary creation unconnected with the history of a nation. Savigny's general thesis was that the "Roman law was not destroyed even by such an upheaval as the barbarian invasion, but that the laws lived on in the customs and laws of the people, and spread in that form over Europe." He put such an emphasis upon the concept of *survival* or *continuity* that, as Professor Albion W. Small has said, "historical causation . . . thenceforth became an element which demanded a share of consideration in every social science problem." [28]

In 1815 Savigny founded, with Eichhorn and Göschen, the *Zeitschrift für geschichtliche Rechtswissenschaft*, which became the organ of the historical school of jurisprudence. The preface to the first number of the journal contained Savigny's exposition of the historical school:

Here is the general problem: What is the influence of the past on the present? What is the connection of that which is with that which will be?

And with regard to that some will tell you that each generation, free and independent in its sphere, lives happily and brilliantly, or unhappily and obscurely, in accordance with the measure of its ideas or its forces. In that system the study of the past is not absolutely disdained, since the past tells us what have been the results of their conduct for our ancestors. History is thus a kind of morality and politics in examples; but after all it is only one of those studies of the kind which may easily be dispensed with. . . .

If this is true, each age does not act arbitrarily and in an egoistic independence, but is entirely held to the past by common and indissoluble bonds. Each epoch then ought to admit certain previous elements, which are necessary and at the same time voluntary; necessary in the sense that they do not depend on the will and arbitrariness of the present; voluntary in the sense that they are not imposed by an outside will (such as that of the master in regard to his slaves), but that they are given by the very nature of the nation considered as a whole which subsists and maintains itself in the midst of its successive developments. The nation of today is only a member of this perpetual nation. It wills and acts in this body, and with this body, so that it can be said that whatever is imposed by the body is at the same time freely accomplished by the member.

Here, half a century before Darwin, we have the complete expression of continuity, or evolution, in social life, especially in its most sharply defined form; codified law. Again, however, one feels bound to empha-

[28] A. W. Small, "Some Contributions to the History of Sociology, II: The Thibaut-Savigny Controversy," *American Journal of Sociology*, XXVIII (1923), 733, the whole 711–34.

size that the general ideas of continuity and totality belonged to the eighteenth-century school of German thinkers. The scholars of the University of Berlin reaped the harvest, but the seeds had been sown by Kant and Winckelmann, Wolf, and Herder.

The German historians, especially those connected with Berlin, were intellectually encouraged and aided by the more enlightened statesmen, particularly von Humboldt and vom Stein. Stein's services in the organization of the *Monumenta*, soon to be discussed, are well known. Less known is the influence of Wilhelm von Humboldt on historical scholarship, although, as we have seen, he was instrumental in bringing together the faculty of the University of Berlin.

Carl Wilhelm von Humboldt (1767–1835) was the older brother of the more famous Alexander von Humboldt (1769–1859).[29] The two brothers showed remarkable versatility. Alexander became a celebrated explorer and natural scientist, while Wilhelm was not only one of the founders of comparative philology, but also a statesman of sufficient distinction to be praised by Talleyrand.

Wilhelm von Humboldt[30] studied antiquity under Heyne at Göttingen. Then, at the age of twenty-two, he visited Paris just at the time when the revolutionary crowd stormed the Bastille. Eager to witness what he regarded as an epoch-making event, Humboldt went to Versailles to attend the sittings of the National Assembly. He met Mirabeau and carried away a penetrating comment on politics uttered by the Frenchman: *Le difficile est de ne promulguer que des lois nécessaires, de rester à jamais fidèle à ce principe vraiment constitutionnel de la société, de se mettre en garde contre la fureur de gouverner, la plus funeste malade des gouvernements modernes.* Humboldt accepted these sentiments but when he became a servant of the autocratic and meddling Prussian government he found it impossible *de se mettre en garde contre la fureur de gouverner*, and finally had to resign.

Under the stimulus of the French Revolution, Humboldt composed a remarkable essay on politics, *Attempts to Set Limits to the Action of the State*, which deserves to be better known than it is. True enough,

---

[29] Alexander von Humboldt, author of the celebrated *Cosmos*, outlived his brother Wilhelm by a quarter of a century. In 1850 W. W. Story met Alexander at Berlin and described him thus: "First there is Von Humboldt, truly a noble old man [he was 81], full of knowledge, of a calm clear mind, of great capacity and of very equally-balanced powers. His knowledge is immense, even in respect to the most trifling subjects." James (n. 25), I, 215.

[30] See Gustav Schlesier, *Erinnerungen an Wilhelm von Humboldt* (Stuttgart, 1843–46, 2 pts. in 1 v.); Rudolf Haym, *Wilhelm von Humboldt, Lebensbild und Charakteristik* (Berlin, 1856); *Briefwechsel zwischen Schiller und Wilhelm von Humboldt* (Stuttgart, 3rd ed., 1900), cp. *QR*, CXXIV (1868), 505–24; *Letters of William von Humboldt to a Female Friend*, tr. by Catherine Couper (London, 1849, 2 v.); Eduard Spranger, "Wilhelm von Humboldt," *Forschungen und Fortschritte*, XI (1935), 121–23; and see DAHLMANN-WAITZ, nos. 13647, 12764. Humboldt's *Gesammelte Werke* were published at Berlin in 7 v., 1841–52.

the little work was not published until sixty years after its composition,[31] because the Prussian censorship refused its permission; but the essay is memorable for being one of the rare expressions of political libertarianism in German literature. Humboldt started out by asking: What is the object of government and what are its limits? He began with the Kantian assumption of human individualism and freedom. Since man's object is to develop himself, he needs not only freedom of action but also variety of scope. Hence the question, What can the state do to help man achieve these ends? Should the state educate, feed, govern, and protect its citizens? Should it provide for and regulate all social institutions? Not at all, Humboldt replied. The state's interference with man's activities tends to produce machine-like uniformity. What society needs is individual citizens, not slavish subjects. To produce strong and skilful citizens, the state should let men alone. Hence even public education, Humboldt wrote, is open to objection, since schools tend to become instruments of political compulsion. Nor should the state interfere with religion and public morals. A nation forced into moral action is a slavish mob without moral strength. What, then, are the limits of the state's activities? Humboldt concluded that the state has only two duties: to defend the nation from foreign enemies, and to secure the rights of the citizens at home. No wonder the Prussian autocracy refused permission to publish a book which was contrary to the whole spirit of Prussia.

After this attempt, Humboldt wrote no more theoretical works. Instead, he gave himself up to politics, hoping to moderate the bureaucratic meddling of the government; his authority was always on the side of moderation and liberalism. For sixteen years he occupied important political positions. From 1802 to 1808 he was Prussian minister to Rome. In the next two years he was chief of the Department of Public Worship, in which capacity he organized the University of Berlin.[32]

From 1810 to 1814 he was Prussian plenipotentiary to the various peace congresses, being, together with Hardenberg, one of the signers of the Treaties of Paris and of Vienna. In 1819 he was appointed one of the ministers of the interior, but was soon ousted by the reactionary party and retired to private life, devoting himself to philology.

---

[31] *Ideen zu einem Versuch, die Grenzen der Wirksamkeit des Staates zu bestimmen*, in his *Werke* (n. 30), VII, 1–188. It was soon translated into English by Joseph Coulthard, as *The Sphere and Duties of Government* (London, 1854), and later into French (1867).

[32] Interestingly enough, Humboldt, though himself hardly a professing Christian, urged the building of a chapel for the new university: "For that the university should have its own church, appears to me indispensably necessary, seeing that the youthful mind ought least of all to be left without religious influence at a time when it is especially open to receive it, and when, too, science is apt to form in him in a one-sided way the understanding alone." *Werke*, V, 321.

In 1821 the Berlin Academy of Sciences invited Humboldt to deliver a lecture. The retired statesman chose for his topic a subject of prime significance to historians: *Ueber die Aufgabe des Geschichtschreibers*, which expressed the subtlest ideas about historiography then dominant in Germany.

The office of the historian, Humboldt said, is, in the last analysis, the *Darstellung des Geschehenen*, the "description of what happened." Clearly, the essential point is the *happened*. Now a bare list of facts does not give us a history, does not tell us what really happened. Direct observation is incapable of giving us the whole picture (*ganze Gestalt*). If the historian should string together all the scattered facts he still would not have the full truth.

What, then, does the historian do to his materials? Humboldt compared the work of the historian to that of the poet and the artist. Like the poet, the historian must use his imagination, must put together isolated events in a logical unity, must present a living whole. "As philosophy strives after the first principles of things, and art after the ideal of beauty, so history strives to depict human destiny in its truth, living completeness and purity, apprehended by a mind so directed to its object that the views, feelings, and claims of personality are in it lost and dissolved." But more than that, the historian must have a dominating idea and a critical sense; he must recognize those forces in history on which causality is based (herein Humboldt is a pure Kantian). Ideas, Humboldt stressed this keypoint, are an *essential part of the happened;* hence when the historian gives expression to ideas in history he adds nothing arbitrary. In this the historian differs from the poet: where the latter strives to embody ideas by imitation of reality (since the poet does not deal with past experiences of mankind but with his personal expressions), the historian aims at a full knowledge of the truth of what has happened by means of ideas.

What Humboldt meant by ultimate ideas in history—*das seelende Prinzip*—was something transcending all sense experience. After the historian has exhausted his observations of such causes as climate, art, knowledge, law, government, and the like, there remains something that does not manifest itself to immediate cognition, something that gives these forces their start and direction. This something is in ideas lying outside the range of the finite, penetrating all parts, including the historian who does the recording. Thus the historian has three tasks: he must collect his materials; he must investigate the truth critically; he must enliven what is recognized as truth by means of ideas. Humboldt concluded: "The business of the historian in the last but simplest analysis is: the description of the effort of the idea to obtain existence in reality." [33]

Heinrich Friedrich Karl, Baron vom und zum Stein (1757–1831), was not an historian, yet his services to historiography were considerable. Stein, as is well known, was the Prussian (he himself was a Westphalian) reform minister from 1807 to 1808, in which year he was proscribed by Napoleon and exiled. After his activities in the Russo-Prussian alliance against Napoleon, Stein retired to private life. In 1819 he organized the *Gesellschaft für ältere deutsche Geschichtskunde,* a society whose purpose was to publish the great sources of medieval German history.

Stein had become interested in the subject when he tried to obtain information on German history for his daughter Theresa and discovered that practically no printed source material existed. What Muratori had done for Italy and the Maurist Fathers for France had never been done for Germany.

Since my retirement from public affairs [Stein wrote to the Bishop of Hildesheim], I have been animated by the wish to awaken the taste for German history, to facilitate the fundamental study of it, and so to contribute to keep alive a love for our common country and for the memory of our great ancestors. It was also my purpose to endeavour that the multitude of documents dispersed by the revolution of the year 1803 might be carefully collected and preserved from destruction; this however depends principally upon measures taken by the Governments and cannot be accomplished by the determination of individuals. But it is within the power of a society of private lovers of their country and its history to bring into existence a convenient collection of original authorities, and to collect a fund to pay the learned men who may devote their time and strength to the enterprise, and in this way to put the collection complete and cheap into the hands of the student of history.[34]

The purpose of the publication of German source materials was essentially patriotic. The French Revolution and the Napoleonic wars had stirred German nationalism. What Germans now needed was a pride

[33] Humboldt, "Ueber die Aufgabe des Geschichtschreibers," in his *Werke* (n. 30), I, 24, the entire essay, 1–25. Cp. Humboldt's letter to Goethe, March 18, 1822: "Was ich über die historische Wahrheit und die buchstäbliche Treue der Erzählung sage, wünsche ich vor allem Ihrer Prüfung zu empfehlen. Sie haben sich viel mit naturgeschichtlichen Erscheinungen beschäftigt, und es hat Ihnen vor allem daran gelegen, die Tatsachen rein und treu darzustellen. Sie wissen daher am besten, was es heisst, die Erscheinung rein aufzunehmen, und wie man es anzufangen hat, um aus den einzelnen Teilen derselben sie als Ganzes aufzunehmen. Ein Wort Schillers ist mir immer gegenwärtig geblieben und hat mir bei dieser Arbeit oft vorgeschwebt. Er sprach davon, dass man seine historischen Aufsätze zu dichterisch gefunden, und schloss: und doch muss der Geschichtschreiber ganz wie der Dichter verfahren. Wenn er den Stoff in sich aufgenommen hat, muss er ihn wieder ganz neu aus sich schaffen. Dies schien mir damals paradox und ich verstand es nicht recht. Der Bemühung, mir es nach und nach klar zu machen, dankt diese Abhandlung grossenteils ihr Entstehen." Cp. Eduard Spranger, "Wilhelm von Humboldts Rede 'Ueber die Aufgabe des Geschichtschreibers' und die Schellingsche Philosophie," *HZ,* C (1908), 541–63; Louis Erhardt, "Wilhelm von Humboldts Abhandlung 'Ueber die Aufgabe des Geschichtschreibers,'" *ibid.,* LV (1886), 385–424; H. Steinthal, ed., *Die sprachphilosophischen Werke Wilhelm von Humboldts* (Berlin, 1883–84).

[34] Seeley, *Life and Times of Stein* (n. 10), III, 441.

in their past, a knowledge of the glorious achievements of their ancestors in the Middle Ages, when Germany was a great power. Hence, after Stein finally succeeded in organizing the society for the publication of the sources (1819), the motto adopted was: *Sanctus amor patriae dat animum.*[35] Favorable replies, offering to collaborate, came from many scholars—Schlosser, Rühs, Wilken, Dahlmann, Voigt. But by far the most important letter, addressed to Büchler, the secretary of the *Gesellschaft*, came from an unknown young man, who made the following offer:

> I should like, if other considerations do not interfere, to edit a part of the Documents of the Carolingian period, particularly those of them which with the Collections of Laws and the Charters are the real foundation of the Carolingian History, and at the same time require to be investigated together, the Annales Nazariani, Tiliani, Petaviani, Fuldenses, Moissiacenses, Bertiniani, Mettenses, Eginhardi, and of the biographies those of Eginhard, Thegan, Nithard and the Lives of S. Boniface, S. Wala, Adalhard, in the Acta Sanctorum. If you should find it possible to entrust to me these, or—according to the number of collaborators and the length of time allowed for the accomplishment of the enterprise—few or more of the historians of that period, I should be able to send in at once an exact catalogue.[36]

The letter was signed by one Georg Heinrich Pertz. And it was Pertz who finally made the *Monumenta Germaniae Historica* [37] the greatest historical collection in the world. Pertz had just taken his doctor's degree at Göttingen under Heeren; his thesis was a history of the Mer-

---

[35] It strains one's imagination to learn that the Prussian aristocracy felt a secret contempt for Humboldt and Stein for being fond of professors, so wide was the gap between those who were *höflich* and the scholar-class. Prussian high society worshipped titles; it contemned university professors. Cp. Gustav Freytag's novel *Soll und Haben*, and *Life and Letters of Taine*, tr. by Mrs. R. L. Devonshire (London, 1902–08, 3 v.), II, 307.

[36] Seeley, *Life and Times of Stein* (n. 10), III, 444.

[37] Harry Bresslau, *Geschichte der Monumenta Germaniae Historica im Auftrage ihrer Zentraldirektion* (Hanover, 1921: *Neues Archiv*, vol. XLII); Wilhelm Wattenbach, *Deutschlands Geschichtsquellen im Mittelalter*, I (7th ed., Stuttgart and Berlin, 1904), 18–32; Gooch, 64–75; Wegele, 1013–18; W. T. M. Gamble, *The Monumenta Germaniae Historica: Its Inheritance in Source-Valuation and Criticism* (Washington, D. C., 1927), chs. xii–xiii; Paul Kehr, "Die Preussische Akademie und die Monumenta Germaniae und deren neue Satzung," *Sitzungsberichte der Preussischen Akademie der Wissenschaften*, XX (Berlin, 1935); the same, "Bericht über die Herausgabe der Monumenta Germaniae Historica," *ibid.*, XIX (1934); Oswald Redlich, "Goethe und die Monumenta Germaniae Historica," *Forschungen und Fortschritte*, VIII (1932), 80–81; Georg Waitz, "Ueber die Zukunft der Monumenta Germaniae Historica," *HZ*, XXX (1873), 1–13; the same, *Neues Archiv*, II; E. Dümmler, "Ueber die Entstehung der Monumenta Germaniae," *Im neuen Reich* (1876); Fedor Schneider, *Deutsche Literaturzeitung*, June 1923, pp. 258–71; and various review articles in *QR*, CLXXIII (1891), 159–79; *AHR*, XVI (1910–11), 426; *ER*, CIII, 104; *JS*, 1827, p. 753; and *RQH*, XIV (1873), 330, XLIV (1888), 243, XLVII (1890), 660, XLVIII (1890), 631.

To what extent this great series was encouraged by historical scholars of the time and countenanced by contemporary rulers may be seen in the list of subscribers at the beginning of vol. I, published in 1826. From this list it appears that, whereas the King of Prussia put his name down for twelve sets of the *Monumenta*, the King of Bavaria for six, and the Emperor of Austria for *one* only and that in the cheaper cloth binding—George IV, the King of England and of Hanover, tops the whole list with an almost extravagant subscription for twenty-four sets with the "fine" binding.

ovingian mayors of the palace. Upon receipt of the above letter, Stein engaged the young man (Pertz was born in 1795) to edit the Carolingian chronicles for the *Monumenta*. In November 1821, Pertz undertook a journey to Italy and Austria to collect manuscripts and documents in libraries and archives. For two years he was busy abroad, gathering precious materials. Then he received a letter from Stein, complaining of the incompetence of Dümge, the editor of the *Monumenta*, and concluding: "Providence seems to have chosen you to carry out this enterprise, which supplies a serious want of our historical literature and will give you a claim to the gratitude of all Germany."

In 1823 Pertz was appointed secretary of the Society and editor of its publication, the *Monumenta*, to which he devoted his whole life. He made frequent journeys of exploration to European libraries, publishing notes on the results of his findings in the *Archiv der Gesellschaft für deutsche Geschichtskunde* (1824–72), edited the *Gesammelte Werke* of Leibniz, and wrote a life of his patron: *Das Leben des Ministers Freiherrn vom Stein* (6 v.; Berlin, 1849–55).

The plan of the *Monumenta* group was to publish the important sources for Germany, Switzerland, and Austria, the time limit to be the fifteenth century (Stein proposed the end of the Hohenstauffen). It was agreed to consider only full documents; meager chronicles and fragmentary materials were to be published in a separate volume. In all matters relating to history after the sixth century, second-hand materials were to be excluded. All authors were to be published in their totality, rather than with a view to preserving chronological sequences. The editor at first estimated that the project would be covered in about eighteen volumes of one hundred sheets each, and Cotta, the Stuttgart publisher, estimated the total cost at 32,000 gulden (Stein immediately contributed 5,000 gulden). The work was to be divided into five sections: *Scriptores* (chroniclers), *Leges* (laws), *Diplomata* (state documents), *Epistolae* (letters), and *Antiquitates*.

The first two volumes of the *Scriptores*—the Annals of the Carolingian period, and the Chronicles and Biographies of the same period—appeared during Stein's lifetime (1826 and 1829). "Here," says Wattenbach, "the surest foundation for all further investigation was given." By 1874, the year when Pertz resigned and Georg Waitz became editor, twenty-four volumes (*Scriptores, Leges, Diplomata*) had appeared. In that year the Society which had hitherto been a private organization was dissolved and the work of publication was taken over by the Prussian Academy.

The *Monumenta Germaniae Historica* became the world's model for scientific history and scientific criticism; Germany's foremost historians

contributed to it, as will be seen later. It also served as an example
for other source collections, such as Philip Jaffé's *Bibliotheca Rerum
Germanicarum*, J. F. Böhmer's *Fontes Rerum Germanicarum*, and various
other *Fontes*, German and foreign, such as a *Fontes Rerum Austriacarum*,
a *Fontes Rerum Hungaricarum*, etc.

In 1825 Leopold Ranke (1795–1885) came to Berlin as professor of
history and inaugurated a new era in historiography. Ranke is undoubtedly the best-known historian since Gibbon—not excepting Macaulay—
and probably the foremost historian Germany has produced. The bibliography on Ranke is voluminous. Ranke and the Ranke method have
been debated, lauded, and criticized for half a century.[38]

Leopold Ranke came from a well-to-do middle class family, his father
being a lawyer; his childhood environment was one of strict, severe,

[38] For bibliography see Hans F. Helmolt, *Ranke-Bibliographie* (Leipzig, 1910); WOLF, 228–30
and note; William Price, "A Contribution toward a Bibliography of Leopold v. Ranke,"
Annual Report of the American Historical Association for 1896, I, 1265–74; DAHLMANN-WAITZ,
nos. 15163, 15500, and consult GOOCH, 76–102; GUILLAND, 68–119; FUETER, 589–615. The
literature on Ranke is too extensive to be given in detail here. Merely for convenience, the
following titles are grouped by language.
   In English, the best account is E. G. Bourne, "Leopold von Ranke," *Annual Report of the
American Historical Association for 1896*, vol. I, 67–81; Albion W. Small, "Some Contributions
to the History of Sociology, V: Ranke and Documentation," *American Journal of Sociology*,
XXIX (1923), 69–77; anon., "Leopold v. Ranke," *Athenaeum*, May 29, 1886, p. 715; Sophie
Weisse, "Leopold v. Ranke, Reminiscences of Berlin, 1884–86," *The Eclectic Magazine*, CVII
(1886), 522–28; Lord Acton, "German Schools of History," *EHR*, I (1886), 13–23.
   The chief literature is in German: the best source is Ranke's own *Zur eigenen Lebensge-
schichte*, dictated to his son, and ed. by Alfred Dove (Leipzig, 1890: *Sämmtliche Werke*, LIII–
LIV). Dove also wrote the authoritative article on Ranke in the *Allgemeine deutsche Biographie*,
XXVII (1888), 242–69, and *Rankes Leben im Umriss* (1898). Supplementary to Leopold's
own account is that of his brother (Friedrich) Heinrich Ranke, *Jugenderinnerungen mit Blicken
auf das spätere Leben* (Stuttgart, 1877, 2nd ed., 1886); Eugen Guglia, *Leopold von Rankes
Leben und Werke* (Leipzig, 1893); Ottokar Lorenz, *Leopold von Ranke* (Berlin, 1891); Emil
Michael, *Rankes Weltgeschichte*. *Eine kritische Studie* (Paderborn, 1890); Arthur Winckler,
Leopold von Ranke: Lichtstrahlen aus seinen Werken gesammelt und mit einem Lebensabriss
(Berlin, 1885), lists Ranke's noteworthy sayings; Theodor Töche, *Leopold von Ranke an seinem
90. Geburtstage* (Berlin, 1888); C. Rethwisch, *Ranke als Oberlehrer in Frankfurt a. O* (1891);
K. A. Martz, *Die Methodik der Geschichtswissenschaft nach Ranke* (1916); O. Diether, *Leopold
von Ranke als Politiker* (Leipzig, 1911); W. Nalbandian, *Leopold von Rankes Bildungsjahre
und Geschichtsauffassung* (Leipzig dissertation, 1901), excellent.
   Of periodical literature in German: Richard Fester, "Humboldts und Rankes Ideenlehre,"
Deutsche Zeitschrift für Geschichtswissenschaft, VI (1891), pt. ii, 235–56; C. Varrentrapp,
"Ranke's Historisch-politische Zeitschrift," *HZ*, XCIV (1907), 35–119, and E. Simon, *Ranke
und Hegel* (*Historische Zeitschrift*, 1928, Beiheft XV); R. Graf du Moulin-Eckart, "Ranke und
die Serben," *Deutsche Revue*, XXXIV (1909), pt. iii, 38–48; Theodor Wiedemann, "Sechzehn
Jahre in der Werkstatte Leopold von Ranke's," *ibid.*, XVI (1891), pt. iv, 164–79, 322–39,
XVII (1892), pt. i, 95–102, 208–20, 342–53, XVII (1892), pt. ii, 100–16, 232–40, 341–50, etc.;
A. v. Reumont in *Historisches Jahrbuch der Görresgesellschaft*, VII (1886), 608 ff.; W. Freytag,
"Ueber Rankes Geschichtsauffassung," *Archiv für systematische Philosophie*, N. F., VI, 129 ff.
and 311 ff.; B. Schmeidler, "Zur Entwicklung der Geschichtschreibung Rankes," *Schmoller's
Jahrbuch*, XXVII (1903), 465–510; J. Schmidt, "Leopold von Ranke," *Deutsche Rundschau*,
XLVII (1886), 218–36; J. Kaerst, "Die Geschichtsauffassung Rankes und Droysens in ihrer
nationalen Bedeutung," *Vierteljahrschrift für Sozial- und Wirtschaftsgeschichte*, XX (1927),
225–33; E. v. Noorden, "Ranke und Macaulay," *HZ*, XVII (1867), 87–138. Of the French
literature it is sufficient to cite, Rod. Reuss, "Leopold de Ranke," *RH*, XXXI (1886), 364–81;
RDM, March 1854, August 1886, and September 1887.

joyless Lutheranism, but dignified and scholarly. In 1814—soon after Napoleon's defeat at the Battle of the Nations—Ranke entered the University of Leipzig. Despite stirring and memorable historic events, young Ranke displayed no interest in history. His chief subjects were philology and theology, the latter confined largely to the Bible. He attended the philological lectures of Beck and Hermann,[39] and also listened to lectures in philosophy. Kant's *Critique of Pure Reason*, which young Ranke studied closely, left a deep impression; but the greatest influence was Fichte, for whose *Addresses to the German Nation* Ranke had a "boundless admiration." The young student also admired Goethe, then at the zenith of his fame, but did not imitate him, because, he said, "he really was too modern for me." Ranke also took up the study of Luther, mainly "in order to learn German from him."

All this time Ranke ignored history. He was repelled, he said, by "an endless number of barren notices." When Stenzel, the professor of history at Leipzig who later became jealous of Ranke, asked the young student whether he intended to devote himself to history, the reply was in the negative. Of historians, only Niebuhr made an impression on Ranke. Niebuhr's *Roman History* made the young man feel that "even in this recent period there can also be historians."

Nevertheless, intellectual curiosity and the desire for reliable information led young Ranke to history. In 1818, after he took his doctor's degree, he became professor of Latin and Greek classics at the gymnasium in Frankfort on-the-Oder. In this small Prussian town there was nothing to do but study. He taught Homer, Horace, Vergil, and the history of classical literature; soon he found that he needed a deeper knowledge of the past than was contained in the purely literary writers. How was he to get his information? Read textbooks? This his scholarly training resented. "How insipid is such literature," he wrote to his brother. Hence the young teacher began a systematic study of classic historians. Thucydides he already knew from his father's library. Now he carefully read—in the original Latin and Greek, of course—Herodotus, Xenophon, Livy, Dionysius of Halicarnassus, Appian, Dio Cassius, Sallust, Cicero, Caesar, Tacitus, etc. He took notes on his readings, and then compared his own findings with those of recent commentators. In Ottfried Müller he found "too much mythology." Only Niebuhr was satisfactory, though the acutely critical Ranke did

---

[39] Gottfried Hermann seems to have had some influence on Ranke. Hermann (1772–1848) was then professor of poetry, lecturing usually in Latin; his own teacher Reiz, so Hermann says, had taught him three principles: (1) never study more than one writer at a time; (2) never take any statements on trust; (3) always be able to give good reasons for holding any opinion. Cp. this with Ranke's own method as developed later in his seminar. On Hermann see SANDYS, III, 89–95.

not accept all his conclusions. "In his researches on the controversial aspects of the [Roman] constitution," Ranke says, "I could follow him no more than I could follow O. Müller in connection with the Greek."

Gradually the fascination of original historical researches led Ranke further afield. Ancient Rome gave way to medieval Germany. Ranke now began to trace this transition. When he came to the later Middle Ages he began to amuse himself by reading the romances of Sir Walter Scott "with vivid interest." But Ranke resented factual inaccuracy even in novels. Scott entertained him with his glowing portraiture, but annoyed him with his historical errors.

Among other things [Ranke relates] I was offended by his [Scott's] treatment of Charles the Bold and Louis XI in his *Quentin Durward*, which was in complete contradiction to the historical sources, even in details. I studied Commines and the contemporary reports which are attached to the recent editions of this author, and convinced myself that a Charles the Bold and a Louis XI, as portrayed by Scott, never existed. This the estimable and learned author knew himself; but I could not forgive him that in his story he presented outlines which were thoroughly unhistorical and which he gave in such a way as if he believed them. In making the comparison I convinced myself that the historical sources are more attractive and in any case more interesting than romantic fiction. I turned away from it [fiction] altogether and conceived the idea that in my works I would avoid all fabrication and fiction, and stick severely to facts.

This is a remarkable passage, a penetrating revelation of Ranke's mind and method. It shows his enormous respect for facts and wish for accuracy. Finally, we have a psychologically revealing sentence: that genuine history was more attractive and more interesting to him than fiction. The latter explains why Ranke took such keen joy in the study and writing of history, and how he could continue his vast output until the age of ninety-one.

But to return to his preparatory studies in the little town of Frankfort-on-the-Oder. The Romantic movement was then in full swing, and so was the Metternich reaction. But Ranke displayed an amazing detachment. His personal reactions against the times were rare. A conservative but moderate nature, Ranke disliked the violent measures taken by the contemporary governments against liberal movements and men; he once criticized the reactionary statesmen "who know no constitution but the will of the police, no fatherland but their sofa, no gains but cash money." He was also aware that environment influences ideas. "Historical studies," he said, "really developed as a reaction against the autocracy of the Napoleonic ideas." On another occasion he said, somewhat mystically, that "everybody lives under the influence of the stars which rule the world." On the whole, however, Ranke was not politically sensitive.

But he was—and this, though frequently neglected, should be emphasized—deeply romantic and genuinely religious. From his letters to his brother Heinrich, written during those seven years he spent at Frankfort, one gathers that, apart from his intensive studies, his chief recreation was walking in the evening and musing. On his walks he seeks the "nightingales and singing trees and those spirits which hover above the evening fragrance of the valley, ripple in the water, bloom in the flower, walk on the bare slopes of the hills." He thinks of the world-historic process with religious awe—"Those who conceive of antiquity superficially, flatly, sinfully, do so to their condemnation." He sees divine punishment in a shallow treatment of history; the historic spirit revenges itself. "Misery grows ever deeper, life more flat, thinking more numb. . . . The inner-living spirit revenges itself because it was despised." For, he muses as he walks under the moonlight, history is the proof of the divine being. "In all history God dwells, lives, is to be seen. Every deed demonstrates Him, every moment preaches His name, but mostly it appears to me, the continuity of history."

This religious feeling left a profound impression on his whole career. "All my attempts," he wrote when under the influence of Fichte, "should be devoted to the perception of the living God, the God of our nations and of the world." Together with this, went his moral duty to his work: all his actions are under a species of categorical imperative. "It seems to me that whatever I am and think, whatever I wish and desire, there is no will, at least no free will, but a must (*es ist ein Muss*)."

Ranke was at this time engaged on his first book which brought him a national reputation and a call to the University of Berlin. He wrote the *Geschichte der romanischen und germanischen Völker* (1824), as he told his brother, in order not "to lose and ruin" his life. "You will find therein unconcealed my opinions, part of my experience and my thoughts." He hoped to get away from the stagnating atmosphere of Frankfort and wrote the book to appeal to scholars, hoping, he wrote modestly in the preface, that no one would "expect a Tacitus and Herodotus in this first attempt."

The twenty-nine-year-old author was too modest. His book was so refreshingly original that, despite the customary jealousy always existing in the academic world (most virulently so in Germany), Ranke was widely hailed as a coming man. But what did the book contain? Its merit consisted of at least three novel contributions: the idea of the unity of the Romano-Germanic world, a penetrating criticism of historical sources, and the famous declaration that the author intended to show history *wie es eigentlich gewesen ist*.

Ranke rejected the conventionally accepted unities. What unities existed in Europe? Universal Christendom? No, said Ranke, because this would include Armenians, who are not Europeans. European unity? No, since this would also mean taking in Turks and Russians. Latin Christendom? Here the difficulty was that it would exclude Slavs, Letts, Magyars. What, then, was there left? Ranke's answer was that European civilization was a fusion of Roman with Germanic elements, that the "barbarians" had taken over many cultural elements of the declining empire and combined them with their own; in this way there developed on European soil the characteristic institutions known as State and Church, Empire and Papacy, the rise of which Ranke traced in bold strokes.[40]

As regards the criticism of historical sources, Ranke developed it in a famous appendix, *Zur Kritik neuerer Geschichtschreiber*, which inaugurated modern critical historiography. Ranke started with the question: What (printed) sources contain first-hand information? He then selected the "historical writers who appear to be at once the most celebrated," especially Machiavelli and Guicciardini, and submitted them to a devastating scrutiny.[41] Ranke levelled most of his heavy artillery against Guicciardini, with the result that he almost destroyed the Italian historian's reputation, showing that he had copied, invented, and misrepresented his materials. As an example of Ranke's critical method, the following passage on Guicciardini—"the foundation of all the later works on the beginning of modern history"—must be quoted:

In the case of the writers of original information whom we are accustomed to call the source-writers, and their work as sources, the first question is whether they were participants or whether they were merely contemporary. In the year 1492, from which Guicciardini makes his start, he was 10 years old. We may easily assume that for perhaps twenty more years, especially because he was devoting himself to the study and practice of legal science, his observations must have been inadequate. Even after he was sent to Spain he could have had only insufficient knowledge of Italian affairs, but later than this, while he was president of the Romagna, while he was commander in Reggio and Parma, while he was Luogotenente (lieutenant) of the Pope with the consolidated army, he took part in the transactions and observed much of importance.

The consequence is that his history falls into two portions. The one comprises the events in which he took part, the other those in which this was not the case. Obviously in case of the great mass which he tells, he was in part and often wholly dependent upon remote information. Before one uses his book, one must ask whether his information

[40] Ranke's thesis has been sharply criticized. Thus Ulrich von Wilamowitz-Möllendorff, in his *Reden und Vorträge* (Berlin, 1901), objected to Ranke's concept of the continuity of culture, insisting instead on "periodicity"; he also rejected the idea that European history began with the development of the Romano-Germanic peoples.

[41] The *Zur Kritik* is divided into five sections: (1) the general Italian historians of the period; (2) the particular Italian historians; (3) the Spaniards; (4) the Germans; and (5) the French. Each author was described as to his background, work, and antecedents. The whole was summarized in a section entitled: "What Remains to Be Done." The study was also published separately (Leipzig and Berlin, 1824), and is reprinted in Ranke's *Sämmtliche Werke*, XXXIII–XXXIV (2nd ed., 1874).

was original and when borrowed, in what way it was borrowed, and through what sort of investigation it was collected.

Obviously it must be presupposed that the last part, relating to a period in which the writer occupied places of high dignity . . . contains the most original, instructive and best sifted information. Precisely here, however, his work seems to be lacking in independence and dependent upon others.

There is in existence a work . . . by the so-called Capella, private secretary of the Milanese minister Marone. This book is at present forgotten. In the first eleven years, however, after it appeared, 1531–1542, it passed through eleven editions in Latin, and more than this, two German, one Spanish, and one Italian translation were made. It is the basis of many later books. Now I observe first that Guicciardini even in the case of the most important events in which he must have had a hand, mainly original reports, follows this Capella step by step. . . .

It is consequently certain that . . . Guicciardini . . . took the most of the information about his own time from a well-known book, part of which is false and part of which is very doubtful. . . . As a general proposition it must be observed that Galleazzio's book is either used or translated by Guicciardini from the 15th book on, or that it is at least chiefly in mind although always unnamed. . . . In view of these facts Guicciardini's historical work will scarcely be able to maintain its previous reputation. . . . It will be necessary to go over the sources of information which were accessible to him. . . .

Ranke then went on to analyze the political speeches which Guicciardini cited, and concluded that they were fiction:

We see that, of the speeches of Guicciardini, in all probability some were never made as he presents them, others were at least in different form, and it has yet to be proved that in a single case his report is entirely genuine. If we consider further that sometimes after speech and reply are elaborated, the real moving factors must be thought behind both . . . it is still more evident that they merely serve the discourse, the contemplation of a given subject from all sides, and confirm the possibility that they have practically nothing in common with historical monuments. Not merely the example of the ancients stimulated Guicciardini in this connection. The learned of that time had immersed themselves in the antique manner in such a degree that the same disposition on which Livy relied when he ventured to weave fanciful speeches into his *Decades* was taken by our author as a matter of course.

Under the heading "What Remains to Be Done," Ranke concluded as follows:

We repeat first what was said about the more general historians of this period, that is, everyone will recognize that their information was neither adequate nor authentic; that we are feeling around in the dark so long as we follow them wholly. We found only Jovius to be a genuinely rich source, but he is full of gaps, more eloquent than profound, and not everywhere unbiased.

Ranke thus proved that general histories were virtually useless as sources, and that to avoid such irresponsible data, the historian must use archives and documents.

Ranke's claim to write history as it actually took place will be analyzed later, in connection with his method and philosophy. At this point it is important to see what Ranke's contemporaries in the field of historiography said about the new book by the unknown young man. The chorus of approval was quite general, with one exception; this was Heinrich Leo, who made a virulent onslaught on Ranke's person, ideas, style, and method.[42] But almost all the others were impressed by Ranke as they were repelled by Leo's unrestrained attack.

It seems to me [so Niebuhr wrote to Ranke à propos of Leo's criticism] that there are people who imagine that it is with the priesthood of history as it was with the Aricinian Diana, where the aspiring candidate killed the incumbent in order to possess himself of his position. Such people know very well that they are *fugitivi* and *sevi neguam;* but you should not compare yourself and us with them. It can not but be pleasant for you to hear that Pertz thinks of you with esteem.[43]

Equally flattering was the attention paid by the veteran Heeren to the young historian. At the age of sixty-seven, the old professor who was an institution at Göttingen and who was one of the few remaining eighteenth-century rationalist historians, wrote a long letter to Ranke, discussing the work of the younger man. Ranke had, of course, sent copies of his book to all the eminent scholars in Germany, including Heeren; and here is Heeren's belated reply (March 27, 1827):

If I, my most honored Herr Doctor, tender you my thanks for your double gift somewhat belatedly, I beg you not to consider it as neglect. I received it a little late; but the main thing was: I wanted first to read your writings and I was prevented from doing so promptly by pressing business. The more sincere are my thanks, since you will not consider them as an empty compliment. Your smaller work attracted me first. Formerly, when I occupied myself with my history of the European State-systems, I often felt keenly the need for such a critical investigation, and since I myself carried on similar researches in the sources of older historians, you may easily believe how my interest was aroused by your work. Your critique of Guicciardini showed me immediately with what earnestness, but also with what success you have made this investigation. It was highly meritorious clearly to comprehend the sources of that author whose work has been regarded as the basis of this portion of history. And to what results have they not led! But also your larger work is not less deserving. In any case this is the beginning of modern history, and especially the Italian dealings penetrate so deeply in the history of general politics that one can not understand one without the other. In the case of Venice, I

---

[42] Heinrich Leo (1799–1878) was at this time professor of history at Berlin, but due to the controversy with Ranke he left for Halle, where he remained from 1828 to 1878. He was the author of a number of schematic histories of Italy. Mainly a narrative rather than a philosophical historian, Leo frequently contented himself with writing from second-hand information and in an uncritical spirit. His bitter feud with Ranke—in which the latter refused to answer—estranged Leo from many contemporaries who were *Rankeaner.* See on him GOOCH, 103–04; FUETER, 562–63; WEGELE, 1034–36; and Paul Krägelin, *Heinrich Leo* (Leipzig, 1908).

[43] This is the only letter between Niebuhr and Ranke that has been preserved. In July, 1829, after Ranke published his *Serbische Revolution,* Niebuhr wrote to the publisher Perthes: "Ich wünsche Ihnen grosses Glück zu Rankens Serbien, welches ich laut anpreise, wie Ihr Haus an den hier abgesetzten Exemplaren spüren wird. Es steht mir zu, zu sagen, dass dies kleine Buch, als Historie, das vortrefflichste ist, was wir in unserer Literatur besitzen. Ranke hat alles abgestreift, was früher in seiner Manier störte. Ich habe das Buch auch nach England und Frankreich empfohlen."

was sorry that you could not use the *Nobile Marini storia* [Sanudo?]. But this work is so rare in Germany, that it can not even be found in Vienna. . . . I hope that you will continue in these so meritorious researches.

Friedrich von Raumer, the well-known scholar and statesman, was more specifically critical than the cautious Heeren. Upon receiving the copy of the book which Ranke sent him, Raumer replied (January 2, 1825):

I should, properly speaking, pass no judgment before reading the whole; but I can already see with certainty that its learning, keenness, kindliness, noble sense are worthy of the highest praise. Also the language, insofar as you characterize personality, is correct, and I am not at all of the opinion that one should screw on a foreign beak and polish away all that is intrinsic. . . . Therefore I surmise that my honest opinion will publicly express the wish: that to your most admirable qualities you must add form. The best way to acquire it is constant reading of the great masters, the oldest Greeks, Davila, Hume and a few others, without any intention of imitation. I do not tell you this as if I doubted your respect for these masters; I merely repeat what J. Müller so often recommended to me. Tacitus, so he said, despite his unexcelled greatness, becomes dangerous to some; Livy is by some less respected than he deserves. . . . Your composition still has something restless, broken, the beginnings and transitions are often too similar, level; the great stream of history flows best quietly, in moderate measures. Still, *macte, virtute esto.* I have never before seen such learning and such sharpness of criticism in any one of your years, and because you can achieve everything, one must expect everything from you. . . .

The influential Raumer added a highly significant postscript to this appreciative letter: "Another thing: I have no doubt that after such an achievement the career of a university teacher will be open to you everywhere, and I gladly stand ready to help you with all my powers."

Ranke cleverly took care to send his book to Johannes Schulze, the chief counsel to Altenstein who was Prussian minister of education, expressing the hope of getting a better teaching position where he could use a good library. Schulze replied that he found such a wish "both just and natural." He would help, he said, to the best of his ability. "Perhaps there will soon be a favorable opportunity either here [Berlin] or in Halle or in Bonn; at least it does not seem improbable." Meanwhile Raumer approached Kamptz, the director of education in the ministry, and urged him to do something for Ranke. Kamptz was impressed by Ranke's work and offered to borrow books from Vienna for the young scholar "at ministerial cost"; he also promised him the use of the Berlin archives. As for a professorial position, there was a good chance:

I am eager to see you employed here as professor of history. Under the present financial conditions it is difficult, but possible and feasible. I hope that the answer of the ministry to your memorial will break the path; therefore, wait quietly for it and trust the ministry. In the meantime continue your admirable and thorough work and be persuaded that you live under a government which honors and exalts true merit.[44]

[44] This and the preceding letters are translated from C. Varrentrapp, "Briefe an Ranke von älteren und gleichalterigen deutschen und französischen Historikern," *HZ*, CV (1910), 105–31.

In May 1825, Ranke was appointed professor extraordinarius of history at the University of Berlin. His first course at Berlin was on the history of Western Europe and was relatively well attended, though his listeners kept on changing. He was glad, he informed his brother, that he had on the average thirty students, while the better-known von Raumer had an almost empty class room! According to all reports, Ranke was not an inspiring lecturer. Almost sixty years later, on the occasion of Ranke's death, his great pupil, von Sybel, thus described the master (with whom he had broken):

The first impression which Ranke's appearance made in the pulpit [*Katheder*] was a certain wonderment. The great head framed by dark curly hair set on the little figure, the incessant movement which followed the course of thought with hasty gestures, the lecturer himself, now standing still in search for the right expression, now again rushing forward in headlong rapidity and therefore often difficult for the ear to grasp, all this appeared curious yet not quite attractive. . . . Ranke spoke very freely, but had previously thoroughly worked out the subject in writing and thereby secured complete control of it for his oral presentation. . . . Lectures always were to him mainly a source of general education for youth, the preaching of the spiritual content in the concatenation of human fates; every semester he took up a large field of world history or some fifteen centuries of German life, knowing well that fruitful results were possible only in wide surveys.[45]

With his weak voice and insignificant figure, Ranke had none of the graces of the popular lecturer. W. W. Story, the American visitor to Berlin in 1850, describes him in extremely unflattering colors:

I have also been hearing Ranke, whose style is the acme of flippancy, without dignity, grace or intelligibility. He is a little round-faced man, with a baldish forehead, a high voice and thin hair; his head just appears above his desk, and he rolls himself round, looking up at the ceiling and jerking out with the extremest rapidity and nonchalance, and in a most equivocal tone, which one knows not whether to take as jest or earnest, little fragments of sentences. . . . Ranke seems . . . like a garden fountain which keeps spurting up little futile jets and then stopping.[46]

It was not to his lectures that Ranke owed his great success and worldwide influence, but to his genius as a teacher in the historical seminar which he inaugurated at Berlin. Out of this seminar came, directly and indirectly, over one hundred eminent scholars (and not alone historians:

[45] Heinrich v. Sybel, "Gedächtnisrede auf Leopold v. Ranke," in his *Vorträge und Abhandlungen* (Munich and Leipzig, 1897), 300-01, see 290-308 for the entire speech, which was delivered before the Berlin Academy of Sciences in 1886. Cp. the description of Ranke by his pupil Adolf Stern: "A small man, with sharp features, a large protruding forehead, beautiful, beaming eyes, smiles frequently playing on his lips. Reclining carelessly in his chair, he would let the forms of the past rise before him, coming as it were out of the twilight of antiquity, and obliged to give an account of themselves. Now and then bright flashes vibrated through obscure sentences, and pointed epigrams interrupted detailed descriptions."

[46] Story to Lowell, January 30, 1850, in James, *William Wetmore Story and His Friends* (n. 25), I, 213-14. Story adds: "Von Raumer I likewise have heard—dull, dry, hard in manner, and his lecture consisting of the dry bones of history."

Röscher, for instance) in the leading German universities, and they in turn created students in the Ranke tradition, supplying historians not only for Germany but also for America.[47]

The seminar was no original invention with Ranke. As far back as 1787 Wolf conducted a seminar in philology at Halle, not to mention Johann Christoph Gatterer who, in 1764, founded an *Historisches Institut* at Göttingen for the study of the historical *Hilfswissenschaften*. At Leipzig, where Ranke was a student, Beck had conducted a bi-weekly seminar in philology and Hermann one in Greek literature; Ranke, it must be stressed, had attended both these seminars. In his first semester at Berlin, Ranke offered a practice course in history, modelled after the philological seminars at Leipzig.[48] The aim of such a "laboratory" course was twofold: to bring able students into "vital relation" to the master, and to train teachers in history. Ranke's seminar, the model for all subsequent seminars, thus began the training of what proved to be the ablest historians in Germany. The first output of these students was the co-operative *Jahrbücher des deutschen Reiches unter dem sächsischen Hause*. To the first volume, that by Georg Waitz on Henry I (1837), Ranke contributed a preface explaining the genesis of the work and his own role in the project.

On the subjective and personal side [Ranke wrote in the preface] this undertaking began in the following way. A university professor very soon perceives that he has two classes of students, those who want to be well grounded in science either through their desire for general culture or on account of their future careers, and others who feel within themselves the impulse and call to take active part in the advancement of science. The lectures, I believe, may be suitably directed to both. It is certainly useful for the former to get some idea of the tools of the scholar and of original investigation, while the latter class must needs get a bird's-eye view of the whole field of their work, so that later they may not lose their bearings in the details of special investigation. . . . Yet the lectures are not enough. Especially for the latter and much less numerous class, is a closer introduction to the real work of the scholar, to personal activity, desirable. This need for many years has been met sometimes in the seminaries under public authority, and sometimes by personal encouragement in voluntary practice courses.

Since the beginning of my university teaching it has been a pleasure to me to conduct *historische Uebungen*. More than once I have had the good fortune to see young men of ability and zeal take part in them. Gradually works were produced which were not without scholarly significance; they threw light on difficult points in a new way, and, as they were additions to our knowledge, were not unworthy of being presented to the attention of the learned public.

[47] Waitz, for instance, one of Ranke's greatest students, conducted a brilliant seminar at Göttingen and proved himself "the most successful founder and leader of an historical school." Heinrich v. Sybel, "Georg Waitz," *HZ*, LVI (1886), 485, the whole 482–87.

[48] Wilken at Berlin also conducted a seminar in medieval history, but it was not popular. Ranke himself, according to Giesebrecht, "never spoke of a seminar, but his 'exercises' [*Uebungen*] became a model for all those seminars which we now have in our universities." Wilhelm Giesebrecht, *Gedächtnisrede auf Leopold v. Ranke* (Munich, 1887), 11.

Only those who intended to make history their profession were admitted to Ranke's seminar. The students were set to work on the Middle Ages, because here the most difficult and critical problems were to be found, and were allowed to choose their own topics. Ranke acted merely as a friendly, though severe, guide. He rarely theorized; his approach was consistently pragmatic. The principle which the master inculcated in his students was briefly this: Get at the truth of the matter and penetrate to the source. Every document, Ranke told his students, contains an element of the subjective; the historian's duty is to separate the objective from the subjective, to get, in other words, back to the essentials. The students were told always to remember three rules in their work: criticism, precision, penetration.

For training those who wished to make a profession of writing history [Sybel relates] he instituted special historical practice courses, in which, under his sure guidance, the pupil, without much theorizing, learned critical method through his own work. Ranke allowed him free choice of his subject, but was always ready from his inexhaustible store of knowledge to propose instructive problems. Errors arising from neglect of critical principles were judged unmercifully, yet in a friendly manner. For the rest, he suffered each mind to follow its own bent, mindful of that supreme rule of teaching that the work of the school is not the formation but the development of the native powers.[49]

In 1827 Ranke published his second work, *Fürsten und Völker von Südeuropa im sechzehnten und siebzehnten Jahrhundert*,[50] which was influenced, he admitted fifty years later, by the revolt of the Greeks against the Turks. This work was superior to the first mainly because here for the first time Ranke devoted much space to non-political matters, such as finances, economics, etc. The primary sources were in the Venetian archives. The young professor meanwhile had the benefit of social contact with many sophisticated men and women, especially women (Rahel von Varnhagen und Bettina von Arnim), of Berlin society, and they smoothed away some of his provincial stiffness. His style acquired a greater fluidity—this was also due, as Ranke himself said, to the influence of the lucidity of the Venetian Relations which he used—and his language acquired greater clarity. "Contact," Ranke relates, "with men and—I should not keep it silent—with women of worldly education, exercised a great influence on me." After he completed the work, the Prussian government sent him on a *Studienreise* abroad.

Henceforth Ranke's output was prodigious. He wrote histories of Germany, of England, of Prussia, of France, histories of wars, and biog-

---

[49] Heinrich v. Sybel, "Gedächtnisrede auf Leopold v. Ranke," *HZ*, LVI (1886), 474 note, the whole 463–87. On Ranke's seminar see also E. G. Bourne, "Ranke and the Beginning of the Seminar Method in Teaching History," *Educational Review*, XII (1896), 359–67; Georg Waitz, *Die historischen Uebungen zu Göttingen* (1867), 4–5.

[50] Translated by Mrs. A. Kerr as *A History of Servia, and the Servian Revolution* (London, 1847).

raphies of statesmen. His complete works, not including his *History of the World*, comprise fifty-four volumes.[51] The two most important works of Ranke are: *Die römischen Päpste, ihre Kirche und ihr Staat im 16. und 17. Jahrhundert* (1834–36) and *Deutsche Geschichte im Zeitalter der Reformation* (1839–47, 6 v.).

Ranke's *Popes* is certainly his best-known, and perhaps his best work. For its composition he ransacked the archives of Italy, especially those in Venice and Rome, as they had never been searched before. The Vatican, however, was closed to him. In partial compensation he found valuable material in the family archives of the Borghese, Doria, Barberini, and other old noble houses of Rome. Biography and literary portraiture were a characteristic of historiography during the Renaissance, and Ranke was so profoundly influenced by the sources which he read that he seems to have revived that lost art almost unconsciously. At any rate, his works abound in character-sketches. In writing about Caesar Borgia, he exclaims: "There is perfection even in depravity. Many of the sons and nephews of popes attempted similar things, but none ever approached Caesar's bad eminence. He was a virtuoso in crime." Ranke's critical acumen protected him against the danger in biographical history.

It is striking how history, when resting on the memory of men, always touches the bounds of mythology. The delineations of character become more sharp and vigorous; they approach in some respects to an ideal which the imagination can lay hold of; events are painted in a more marked and distinct manner; accessory circumstances and causes are forgotten and neglected. By such a process alone do the demands of the fancy appear capable of being satisfied. At a later period comes the scholar who wonders how such false notions could ever have been embraced, does his best to uproot errors and at last finds out that this task is not so easy. The reason may be convinced, but the imagination is not to be subdued.[52]

The sixteenth, seventeenth, and eighteenth centuries were the subject of Ranke's greatest works. Besides the *Popes* he wrote *A History of*

[51] Reprinted in *Sämmtliche Werke* (3rd ed., Leipzig, 1874–90, 54 v. in 27). The following works have been translated into English: *History of the Latin and Teutonic Nations, 1494–1514*, tr. by P. A. Ashworth (London, 1887), and again by S. R. Dennis (1909); *The Ottoman and Spanish Empires in the Sixteenth and Seventeenth Centuries* (London, 1843 and Philadelphia, 1845); *History of the Popes of Rome during the Sixteenth and Seventeenth Centuries*, tr. by Sarah Austin (London, 1840, 2 v.; 3rd ed., 1847 with slightly changed title); *A History of Servia and the Servian Revolution*, tr. by Mrs. Alex. Kerr (London, 1847), cp. H. Wuttke, "Serbien und Ranke," *Allgemeine Zeitschrift für Geschichte*, IX (1848), 228–49; *Ferdinand I and Maximilian II of Austria*, tr. by Lady Duff Gordon (London, 1853); *History of the Reformation in Germany*, tr. by Sarah Austin (London, 1845–47, 3 v.); *History of the Prussian Monarchy from Its Rise to the Present Time*, tr. by Prof. Demmler (London, 1847–48, vol. I); *Memoirs of the House of Brandenburg, and History of Prussia during the Seventeenth and Eighteenth Centuries* (London, 1849, 3 v.); *Civil Wars and Monarchy in France, in the Sixteenth and Seventeenth Centuries*, tr. by M. A. Garvey (London, 1852, 2 v., and New York, 1853, 1 v.); *A History of England, Principally in the Seventeenth Century* (Oxford, 1875, 6 v.).

[52] *History of the Popes*, tr. by Sarah Austin (Philadelphia, 1840, 2 v.), II, 328.

France Principally in the Sixteenth and Seventeenth Centuries, which gives the reader the impression of massiveness made by a great building, and *A History of England Principally in the Seventeenth Century,* which was a revelation to British historians. It required a German Lutheran historian to take the measure of Laud, and the literature of detraction with regard to Laud was almost equal to that of Cromwell. Carlyle's turgid praise was moderated by Ranke before Gardiner and Firth began to write. Yet even today no British historian's judgment of either Laud or Cromwell may be entirely trusted. Ranke's *England* is an extended commentary on the history of England in the seventeenth century rather than a history thereof. In the case of Cromwell Ranke admits that the Protector's authority was merely that of a tyrant "depending for its existence on the force of arms and his own personal character," he was "felt to be an oppressive burden," and "hated rather than loved." He condemns the Irish massacres and Cromwell's brutal description of them, and thinks his executions the result of "cold-blooded calculation and a violence which was deliberate." On the other hand Ranke is favorable or lenient in his judgment of Charles I.[53]

On his seventieth birthday, in 1865, Ranke was ennobled and given the right to prefix "von" to his name. He took as his motto: *Labor est voluptas.* In 1871 he retired from teaching and devoted the rest of his life to the writing of history. In 1884 when the American Historical Association was founded Ranke was elected the first and only honorary member. "We have meant this," wrote George Bancroft, who had been American minister to Berlin, "as a special homage to yourself as the greatest living historian."

He lived to be ninety-one and was incessantly busy. His secretary Georg Winter has left some illuminating records on Ranke at work in his old age.[54] Winter became Ranke's assistant in 1877—Ranke was then eighty-two—and the first thing the master said to the pipe-smoking young man was: "Can you not quit that habit? It is utterly impossible for me to endure the smell of tobacco." The old scholar displayed prodigious energy; he employed two assistants, whom he drove to exhaustion while he himself seemed tireless. He rose at nine and worked daily with one assistant from 9:30 A.M. to 2 P.M., and with another from 7 P.M. to 12 P.M. No recreations and no holidays were allowed, except Christmas (even then Ranke tried to persuade his assistants to work). Ranke's friends knew of his habits and never interrupted him.

[53] *A History of England* (n. 50), II, 550–53.
[54] Georg Winter, "Erinnerungen," *Nord und Süd,* August 1886; cp. J. H. W. Stuckenberg, "Ranke and His Method," *Andover Review,* VII (1887), 117–37.

In the afternoon in good weather he walked for a bit in the Tiergarten, accompanied by a servant. At 4 P.M. he dined, slept for one hour, and then worked until midnight, always attired in his dressing-gown. Only once did he go on a journey, at the invitation of Fieldmarshal Manteuffel to his estate at Topper. Ranke went there without any books. Upon returning, he drew out a manuscript and handed it to the surprised assistant with the words: "Here I have a biography of Frederick the Great, which I dictated at Topper." The biography was dictated without books or notes—from memory!

His method of work with his assistants was interesting. They brought documents from the archives and read them to him. Ranke would listen quietly and suddenly exclaim: "Omit that, it is not essential"; or, "Hold on! that is significant; we must make an exact copy." From these extracts he wrote his histories. He had no need to go out of his house for books, for his own library, filling five large rooms, comprised about 25,000 volumes; they were piled chaotically two and three deep on shelves and floor. Ranke objected to a systematic arrangement of his books on the ground that he would not be able to find what he wanted.

In his eighty-third year Ranke conceived the staggering plan of summarizing his vast knowledge of mankind by writing a *History of the World (Weltgeschichte)*. The first volume was published in 1880, and then one volume yearly, so that by the time of his death, in 1886, six volumes had come out and the seventh was ready for the press. He had reached the reign of Otto the Great (A.D. 962). "I have," the astonishing old man said, "made a compact with God. He must still give me five or six years for the work; then I will gladly go." In his ninety-first year he began to plan a new project: a philosophy of history; but he died before he got to it. And when he died, Germany and Europe mourned as if a national calamity had occurred.

Ranke's *History of the World*, being his last work, is as good an introduction to his philosophy and method as any of his writings. Psychologically, it is a phenomenon of great significance that Ranke's last work contained ideas which he expressed in his letters as a young man at Frankfort, more than sixty years before. One recalls how conscious the young Frankfort teacher was of the manifestations of God in history; here in his final work we see the same *Weltanschauung*. In universal history, Ranke wrote, the actors must be studied to discover the extent to which they express divine powers. The individual and the nation are agents in a world-movement. The mediating powers, connected with God, are what Ranke calls "ideas." It will be remembered that such, precisely, was also Wilhelm von Humboldt's thesis. Croce has justly criticized Ranke for his use of generalized concepts. In truth, Ranke was in the habit of playing with high-sounding and, in the last analysis, meaningless terms and phrases, which he rarely defined or elucidated. Thus Ranke speaks of "the objective ideas" and "the higher potencies," of "the powers born in the elements and holding them together," of "the general ideas that bear in themselves the life of the human race." The ideas are "the thoughts of God in the world"; "they are life-giving, are life itself, are moral energies." In the interaction of these ideas, their coming and going, "lies the great secret of history." [55]

Now, had Ranke done nothing else but use vague generalities, he would soon have been forgotten; but his contribution was far more important. Despite a semi-mystical leaning, Ranke was essentially pragmatic. "We find in general in Ranke," Croce observes with some disapproval, "an inevitable tendency to subside into the pragmatic method." It is Ranke's "pragmatic" method which is responsible for his fame. He had a thorough distrust of tradition, of hearsay, of gossip, of everything, in short, that could not be thoroughly substantiated.

> I came to the conclusion [Ranke said at the age of ninety] that in history everything must be avoided which deviates in essentials from trustworthy facts; I do not deny that I was confirmed in the considerations on the critical method which were regarded as characteristic of my works: namely, to cling to that which has been transmitted verbally, or what can be developed from it with some certainty. . . . Much has not been written down . . . but to adhere to the written facts, such essentially has been for me an immovable law. [56]

Ranke's distrust of what he could not see on paper, of what he could not check, was so great that he was led to neglect aspects and periods of history for which no documents existed. Thus he did not write on antiquity, or on economic history. He hated mystery and speculation. "He wanted only the light," his biographer Dove says of him. He looked only for the tenable. On the theory that history should be written only from materials preserved in writing, Ranke said that his fundamental principle was "to be content with that which is verbally transmitted or which can be developed with a degree of certainty from such verbal transmission." In his very first book he explained his approach: "To history has been attributed the function to judge the past, to instruct ourselves for the advantage of the future. Such a lofty function the present work does not attempt. It aims merely to show how it actually took place—*Es will bloss zeigen, wie es eigentlich*

[55] E. W. Dow, "Features of the New History, apropos of Lamprecht's 'Deutsche Geschichte,'" *AHR*, III (1897–98), 445. Cp. Croce (n. 4), 300.
[56] Constantin Rössler, "Leopold Ranke," *PJ*, LVIII (1886), 64–74.

gewesen ist." And Ranke added that to achieve this objective the "supreme law" must be "a rigorous presentation of the facts, however unconditional and unbeautiful they may be."

This point Ranke explained more fully in the afore-mentioned appendix, *Zur Kritik neuerer Geschichtsschreiber*, which was to be his "professional platform" for more than sixty years:

> One who for the first time confronts the multitudinous movements of modern history must have a feeling like that which one would have who confronted a great collection of antiquities in which genuine and spurious, beautiful and repulsive, important and insignificant, from many nations and periods, were heaped together without order. In either case the material confronted would speak in a thousand voices. It manifests the most diverse natures. It is clothed in all colors. Some of the specimens march solemnly back and forth. They aim to be demonstrative. They think they are exhibiting the ways of antiquity. Others attempt to derive from the past theorems for the future. Many want to defend or to attack. Not a few are zealous to develop the explanation of occurrences on deep grounds, from the basis of subjective conditions and emotions. Then there are some which have only the purpose of passing along what has happened. These are to be classed as the high witnesses who furnished reports. The persons participating in the action speak. Original sources, alleged and actual, are present in abundance. Before all, the question arises, "Which among many is a source of original knowledge? From which can we be truly instructed?" [57]

The best way to ascertain historical truth was to utilize source materials, particularly archival sources. Hence Ranke worked in the archives of Berlin, Vienna, Paris, Rome, and especially Venice, whence he brought forth a vast mass of hitherto unknown material. It was Ranke who was the first to use the marvelous reports of the Venetian ambassadors in Europe, especially for his *History of the Popes*. The Venetian *relazione* not merely threw new light on European politics, they also profoundly influenced Ranke's style. *Der Stoff*, he said of the lucid Venetian reports, *brachte die Form mit sich.*[58]

Having collected his materials and ascertained their relative value, Ranke proceeded to the task of composition. "History," he wrote, "is at the same time art and science. It has to fulfil all the demands of criticism and scholarship . . . but it should at the same time offer the same pleasure to educated spirits as any successful literary crea-

---

[57] When Gervinus insisted that science (*Wissenschaft*) should influence contemporary life, Ranke replied: "But to have an influence it must first of all be science . . . we can have a real effect on the present only when . . . we aim to rise to a free, objective science." Ranke, "Georg Gottfried Gervinus," *HZ*, XXVII (1872), 142–43 note. Cp. BERNHEIM, 16.

[58] In the Preface to his *History of the Popes* (n. 51), I, pp. ix–x, Ranke tells about his researches in Venice. "It was an almost universal custom among the great houses of Venice to have a cabinet of manuscripts attached to their library. . . . A few of these private collections are still remaining, and were accessible to me. . . . The library of St. Mark contains a valuable store of manuscripts which are indispensable to the domestic history of the city or republic. . . . The documents most appropriate . . . were the Reports of the ambassadors on their return from Rome. . . . I collected, in all, forty-eight Reports on Rome."

tion." [59] And Ranke was undoubtedly an artist. Though not a penetrating psychologist, he had an eye for the striking characteristic of
great individuals, and, most important of all, a genius for putting them in
their historic setting; in this he was perhaps influenced by Renaissance art, especially portraiture. Nor did Ranke, unlike most of his
Teutonic colleagues, burden his text with insignificant, trivial, repeti-
tive details; instead, he had the gift for the illuminating detail, for the
brilliant comment, for the swift and telling generalization. A few quotations will show Ranke's mastery over his multitudinous materials
and his gifts as a writer.

The introductory paragraph to Ranke's account of the French king
Henry III, reads:

As in antiquity Athens can not be thought of without Sparta, Rome without Carthage,
so in the sixteenth and seventeenth century France can neither be comprehended nor
understood without the counterpart of the Spanish monarchy.[60]

The following sentences introduce us to French politics in the fifteenth century:

In the Italian arsenals they call the great central beam, round which the smaller pieces
of wood are laid to form a mast, the Soul; in the Dutch dockyards it is named the King.
True kingship consists in the power which holds together the people and the Estates,
which maintains their equilibrium and supports them through the storm.[61]

But Ranke was even better as a portraitist. Here is his description
of Pope Paul IV (1476–1559):

Paul IV had already attained the age of seventy-nine, but his deep set eyes still
gleamed with all the fire of youth; he was extremely tall and thin, he walked quickly,
and appeared to be all nerve. His daily life was subject to no rule or order; he often
slept by day, and passed the night in study—and woe to the servant who entered his
room until he rang his bell. In everything he followed the impulses of the moment; but
these impulses sprang from a character formed by a long life and become a second nature.
He seemed conscious of no other duty, no other business, than the restoration of the
ancient faith in all its primitive might and authority.

From time to time characters like that of Paul re-appear on the theatre of the world.
Their conceptions of the world and of life are formed from a single point of view; their
individual bent of mind is so strong that their opinions are absolutely governed by it;
they are unwearied and eloquent speakers, and have always a certain earnestness and
freshness of conversation, in which they pour out an incessant stream of those sentiments
which seem to rule them by a sort of fatality. It is obvious that the influence of such men
must be enormous when they attain to a position where their actions depend solely and
absolutely on their opinions, and where power is combined with will.

[59] *Sämmtliche Werke* (n. 50), XII, 5. "Everything," Ranke said, "hangs together; critical
study of the genuine sources, impartial perception, objective presentation; the aim is to present the whole truth." *Ibid.*, XXI, 114.
[60] *Civil Wars and Monarchy in France, in the Sixteenth and Seventeenth Centuries,* tr. by
M. A. Garvey (New York, 1854), 305.
[61] *Ibid.*, 67.

What might not be expected from Paul IV, who had never known what it was to make a concession or a compromise, who had always acted on his opinions with the utmost vehemence, now that he had reached the summit of power? He was astonished at his own elevation, as he had never conciliated a cardinal by a single concession, and had never abstained from displaying the utmost severity. He thought himself chosen, not by the cardinals, but by God himself, by whom he was called for the execution of his purposes.[62]

Of the more romantic and dashing Henry IV, Ranke wrote:

By his life and habits Henry IV was a soldier. Outside of the great battles which have made him celebrated, he participated in two hundred combats. He distinguished himself among all military men by a joyous courage which he knew how to communicate to his captains and his army, and by the rapidity with which he could size up the movements, the power and even the look of enemies. Alexander of Parma compared him to the eagle who sees his prey from a distance and who pounces upon it with infallible swiftness. Others found in him a particular gift in always forming the order of battle in a manner most suitable for each position; in action he showed a gallantry which carried away all. The thing done, he did not wish to hear it mentioned again. When he was presented with the notched and blood-covered sword which he had worn at Ivry, he turned away his eyes with a sort of horror at the thought of what he had done through duty and necessity. At the death of Henry III, he was counselled to institute an order of vengeance . . . and rejected the idea: nothing was more repugnant to his character than revenge.[63]

Obviously Ranke was a great scholar and a brilliant writer. But since he made claims to "objective" and "impartial" truth, one must raise the question whether (1) he was justified and (2) whether such an aim is possible. In the first place, it must be emphasized that Ranke's mania for documentary sources—neglecting such materials as memoirs, for instance—*ipso facto* limited his scope. He wrote some fifty volumes of history on the basis of diplomatic and state documents. But is diplomatic and political history all there is to history? Of what significance is a report of an ambassador—or fifty reports of fifty ambassadors, for that matter—for an understanding of, say technological inventions? Or science? Or literature? Or the industrial revolution? Clearly, Ranke's documents gave him "history" of a kind, but hardly a *Weltgeschichte*, hardly sufficient data for generalizing about states, nations, religion, culture, or anything else, except of course treaties, wars, and dynasties.

But the chief criticism against Ranke and the Ranke school of "objective" and "scientific" history is its total unphilosophicalness. Far from being scientific, Ranke was profoundly biassed; we have seen that he observed God's handiwork in all history; he made no attempt at formulating a genuine philosophy or psychology. It sufficed him to see

---

[62] *History of the Popes* (n. 51), I, 177–78.
[63] *Französische Geschichte*, Bk. VII, ch. 6 (in *Sämmtliche Werke*, IX, 74).

God standing in history, according to Meinecke (*Die Idee der Staatsrä-son*), "like a holy hieroglyphic." Ranke was himself a product of his time, a loyal servant of the Prussian monarchy, a defender of Church and State; and what he wrote was a complete reflection of his notions, bias, and interests. "Persistently neglecting social and economic interests in history, successfully avoiding any historical writing that offended the most conservative interests in the Europe of his own time, Ranke may be correctly characterized as one of the most 'partial' historians produced by the nineteenth century." [64] The only difference between the detached and "impartial" Ranke and his frankly biassed colleagues and contemporaries (such as Droysen, Treitschke, Sybel) was that the latter were more outspoken in their prejudices, and had a clearer realization of their function.

To summarize: Ranke's great contribution to historiography lay in his whole-hearted devotion to history as a science *per se*, rather than a handmaiden of something else. Hence his efforts to develop a method which would lead to "objective" truth in history, his rejection of all that was unproven or unprovable, his refusal to enter mystical or speculative realms. Nevertheless, despite worldwide recognition, Ranke was not a "scientist" and was not "objective." His method, his sole use of diplomatic documents, his purely political approach—all these were but the shadow of history, not history, and certainly not "truth." Ranke misled a whole generation into believing that he was writing "objective" history, that he was at last approximating the truth. Actually, the most that can be said for his method is that it led to greater detachment, finer poise, and a broader outlook than had been customary before him, and this should be glory enough.

[64] Charles A. Beard, "That Noble Dream," *AHR*, XLI (1935), 78–87. In this Presidential Address before the American Historical Association, Professor Beard, following Karl Heussi's *Die Krisis des Historismus* (Tübingen, 1932), made a sharp attack on the Rankean method, and pointed out that Ranke's "so-called neutral or scientific history" was merely the expression of a German conservative who, tired of the "storm and stress of the French Revolution," wanted peace. "The ruling classes in Germany, with which he [Ranke] was affiliated, having secured a breathing spell in the settlement of 1815, wanted peace to consolidate their position." See Beard, "Written History as an Act of Faith," *AHR*, XXXIX (1934), 221–31. T. C. Smith in an article entitled "The Writing of American History in America from 1884 to 1934," *ibid.*, XL (1935), 439–49, took issue with Beard, and the latter replied in a stinging and penetrating critique of Ranke and the Ranke school of "impartial history." Uncomplimentary likewise is Benedetto Croce's comment that Ranke's ideas were slight and that he never defined the concepts he used. See Croce, *Theory and History of Historiography* (n. 4), 291–92. On the other hand, Friedrich Meinecke, the eminent German historian, considers Ranke a "great spiritual-historical phenomenon," cp. his article "Zur Beurteilung Rankes," *HZ*, CXI (1913), 582–99.

CHAPTER XLII

THE RANKE SCHOOL [1]

B Y THE middle of the nineteenth century Ranke's influence on German historiography was practically supreme. Out of the master's seminar in Berlin came, with few exceptions, most of the great historians of Germany. A list of Ranke's students reads like an historiographic *Who's Who*—to mention only the greatest there were Waitz, Giesebrecht, Köpke, Wilmans, Karl Nitzsch, Siegfried Hirsch, and Jaffé in medieval history; and Sybel, J. G. Droysen, Adolf Schmidt, Jacob Burckhardt, Rudolf Gneist, and Rudolf Delbrück in modern history. One may also mention economists like Roscher, jurists like Wilhelm Arnold, and men of affairs like the Swedish minister of education, Frederick Ferdinand Carlson. These by no means exhaust the list. Ranke practically dictated appointments in almost all the German universities. When Sybel retired from Marburg, Ranke proposed one of his students, Reinhold Pauli, and when Pauli was rejected, Ernst Herrmann, another Rankean, was accepted. Ranke, Sybel said, "dominates the history curriculum in virtually all Germany." [2]

But even more significant than the immediate students of Ranke were the students of Ranke's students. Sybel, Giesebrecht, and Waitz, to mention only three, conducted seminars which became as famous as those of the master, and produced hundreds of eminent scholars who in turn became the inspirers of other scholars. For example, Dietrich Schäfer, one of Waitz's students, fathered 124 doctors; and Harry Bresslau, a student of Droysen, Jaffé, and Köpke, had more than 100 doctors. Out of these seminars came the scholars who edited and con-

---

[1] GOOCH, ch. vii; FUETER, see index for individual names; WOLF, Einleitung and pp. 240–42 and notes; WEGELE, 1056–61; K. Brandi, "Mittlere und neue Geschichte," in *Aus fünfzig Jahren deutscher Wissenschaft*, ed. by Gustav Abb (Berlin, 1930), 174–91. Perhaps the best single work is Georg von Below, *Die deutsche Geschichtsschreibung von den Befreiungskriegen bis zu unseren Tagen* (2nd enlarged ed., Munich and Berlin, 1924). The book is reviewed by G. P. Gooch in *EHR*, XL (1906), 159, where he points out that in contrast with Fueter, who assessed the value of the work of great German historians, this book stresses *Geschichtsauffassung*. It is a study of the ideas and spiritual foundations of the great nineteenth-century historians. The first part deals with Ranke and his pupils; the second part stresses the development of economic and political history. It is a "shrewd, if often biased, elaboration of the differences between German and Western historiography and of the non-socialist fountainheads of economic history." Cp. the article on Below by Carl Brinkmann in *ESS*, VI, 543; and consult the *Allgemeine deutsche Biographie* for the individual names discussed in this chapter.

[2] Cp. C. Varrentrapp, "Briefe an Ranke von einigen seiner Schüler: Sybel, Carlson, Herrmann, Pauli und Noorden," *HZ*, CVII (1911), 44–69.

tributed to the *Monumenta*, the *Historische Zeitschrift*, the *Preussische Jahrbücher*, the *Allgemeine Deutsche Biographie*, the *Deutsche Städte Chroniken*, the publications of the Bavarian Historical Commission and various other source collections.[3]

Most of the students remained faithful to Ranke, and some, like Roscher, were worshipful. There were, however, a few exceptions, particularly Sybel, Droysen, and Duncker, who are treated in connection with the Prussian School. Ranke never quite forgave the brilliant Sybel his desertion and in his last comment on *Die alten Schüler*, the nonagenarian scholar studiously avoided all mention of his famous pupil. In this account, written not long before his death, Ranke gave concise opinions of his students. One spring day in 1884, Giesebrecht, who was himself an old man of seventy, came from Leipzig to Berlin to see his eighty-nine-year-old teacher. Ranke was much moved and, upon Giesebrecht's departure, he wrote as follows:

I recall the now grey, but once young, members who participated in the historical seminars on German history. I have just paged through a long series of Yearbooks of the German Empire. . . . What we had then begun quietly, the seeds we have planted, has now become a big tree, under which nestle the birds of heaven. . . .

I am still astonished at the talent and application of the young men who gathered around me. There were: Giesebrecht, who visited me today, Köpke, Wilmans; there also joined Waitz to whom I then said—for such was the impression he made on me—that he was destined to become the Muratori of German history. Giesebrecht was poetically inclined; even then he already knew how to write. Köpke was intellectual, with the gifts of a scholar. Dönniges was enterprising, full of practical intentions. In this circle the work throve. We came upon the *Chronicon Corbeiense*, whose spuriousness I first recognized without being able to prove it. The members of the seminar made the investigation which proved its falseness. Waitz was not present then; he had gone to Copenhagen, and, when he returned, was disinclined to accept our thesis but was finally convinced. Together with Hirsch, one of our most industrious members, he wrote a paper which convinced us all. Hirsch was the youngest of all, very well prepared and zealous. Then we joined together to work on the Yearbooks of the Saxon House. What influenced me to do it were the examples of von Raumer's *Hohenstaufen* and Stenzel's *Salian Emperors*. . . . We decided on partial publications, for which of course we could expect no publisher's remunerations. . . . Over these beginnings there reigned the blessing of heaven. The above-named men have made their way in the world; but still they—as many of them as are still alive—live in friendship with each other and with me. It is a species of family relationship in literature. May no breath of ill cloud this friendship.[4]

---

[3] In 1859 King Maximilian II of Bavaria, aided by Ranke, founded the Historical Commission. At the first meeting, at which Ranke presided, there were Jacob Grimm and Pertz, of whom Ranke said that no other nation possessed their like, and Waitz, Giesebrecht, and Sybel, whom the chairman proudly designated as his students—"men of the first rank." The Historical Commission published various important source collections, 160 volumes in the first 25 years; its most important achievement, however, was the *Allgemeine Deutsche Biographie* which includes 23,000 articles written by 1400 German scholars. See M. Ritter, "Ueber die Gründung, Leistungen und Aufgaben der historischen Kommission," *HZ*, CIII (1909), 274–301.
[4] Ranke, "Die alten Schüler," in *Sämmtliche Werke*, (3rd ed., Leipzig, 1874–90, 54 v. in 27), LIII–LIV, 649–50. Note the neglect of Sybel.

Essentially Ranke's main influence was on political historiography. Ranke himself was a political historian and his immediate students continued the tradition; only the third generation of Rankeans began to occupy itself with other than political history. There was, however, a difference between Ranke's political *Weltanschauung* and that of most of his students. Ranke treated the political states as vital parts of a larger whole; his students, particularly Sybel, were mainly *Machtpolitiker*, who had a precise political ideal, namely, their own state. This idealization of the state and its power was carried to a romantic excess by Dahlmann and to an almost pathological extreme by Treitschke, but neither of these historians was a Rankean.[5]

Though a conservative, a monarchist, and a Prussian in sympathies, Ranke himself kept aloof from the acrimonious political struggles which raged in the Germany of the 'forties, 'fifties, and 'sixties. Sometimes the revered master was criticized for his detachment; occasionally his students were attacked for their pedantry and "microscopism." The *Preussische Jahrbücher*, the leading pro-Hohenzollern journal which was edited by Rudolf Haym and Heinrich von Treitschke, carried an anonymous article (probably written by one of the editors) criticizing "Our Historians" for being remote from everyday problems.

A certain neglect of the great, driving, real forces all too easily results from a method which proudly claims to be objective but which, before it is executed, has become the opposite. The desire to find the motive forces of things exclusively in court and state actions, often prevents the great reading circles from learning about the value of national interests.

"The master himself," the article continued in its criticism of Ranke, "can not be altogether absolved from these reproaches." His detachment limits his influence. The little books of the patriotic Dahlmann, though not scholarly, "have had a greater influence than in all probability Ranke's works will have." But what was worse, these aloof historians tend to lose all perspective by becoming narrow specialists and antiquarians. "Too much in the small hurts science in the large." [6]

Such views were not shared by the vast majority of Ranke's admiring disciples, and to speak of Dahlmann's books as more influential is grotesque. In truth, the influence of Ranke on German historiography was deep and immense, and the personal filiation from the master possesses great interest. Before considering some of Ranke's best students—to take all of them up in detail would require a volume in itself—it may be helpful to glance at the following, much simplified chart:

[5] See G. v. Below, "Das gute Recht der politischen Historiker," *PJ*, CXCIII (1923), 283–303; and his *Die deutsche Geschichtsschreibung* (n. 1), chs. v–vi.
[6] "Unsere Historiker," *PJ*, VI (1860), 531–43.

LEOPOLD RANKE (1795–1886)

Arnold, Wilhelm (1826–83)
Bonnell, Heinrich (1829–70)
Burckhardt, Jacob (1818–97)
Carlson, Frederick Ferdinand (1811–87)
Cornelius, Karl Adolf (1819–1903)
Delbrück, Rudolf (1817–1903)
Dönniges, Franz Alexander (1814–72)
Dove, Alfred (1844–1916)
Dümmler, Ernst Ludwig (1830–1902)
Giesebrecht, Friedrich Wilhelm (1814–89)
Gneist, Rudolf (1816–95)
Herrmann, Ernst Adolf (1812–84)
Hirsch, Siegfried (1816–60)
Jaffé, Philipp (1819–70)
Kampschulte, Friedrich (1831–72)

Klempin, Karl (1816–74)
Köpke, Rudolf (1813–70)
Maximilian II (1811–64)
Mörner, Theodor (1817–74)
Nitzsch, Karl Wm. (1818–80)
Pauli, Reinhold (1823–82)
Roepell, Richard (1808–93)
Roscher, Wilhelm (1817–94)
Schmidt, Adolf Wm. (1812–87)
Simson, Bernhard (1840–1915)
Sybel, Heinrich (1817–95)
Waitz, Georg (1813–86)
Wattenbach, Wilhelm (1819–97)
Wilmans, Roger (1812–81)

WAITZ

Abel, Sigurd (1837–73)
Arndt, Wilhelm (1838–95)
Bernheim, Ernst (1850–1922)
Bezold, Friedrich (1848–1928)
Brode, Reinhold (b.1856)
Brunner, Heinrich (1840–1915)
Busson, Arnold (1844–92)
Cardauns, Hermann (1847–1925)
Creizenach, Wilhelm (1851–1919)
Damus, Rudolf (1849–1918)
Dehio, Georg (1850–1932)
Droysen, Gustav (1838–1908)
Ehrenfeuchter, Ernst (1846–82)
Ewald, Paul (1851–1888)
Frensdorff, Ferdinand (1833–1931)
Friedensburg, Ferdinand (1855–1930)
Grauert, Hermann (1850–1924)
Handelmann, Heinrich (1827–91)
Harnack, Otto (1857–1914)
Heller, Johannes (1851–76)
Hildebrand, Hans (1842–1913)
Höhlbaum, Konstantin (1849–1904)
Holder-Egger, Oswald (1851–1912)
Hüffer, Hermann (1830–1905)
Junghans, Wilhelm (1834–65)
Kaufmann, Georg Heinrich (1842–1930)
Kluckhohn, August (1832–93)
Koppmann, Karl (1839–1905)
Leser, Emanuel (1849–1914)
Liebermann, Felix (1851–1925)

Meyer von Knonau, Gerold (1843–1920)
Monod, Gabriel (1844–1912)
Pabst, Hermann (1842–70)
Pastor, Ludwig (1856–1928)
Perlbach, Max (1848–1921)
Pflugk-Harttung, Julius (1848–1919)
Posse, Otto (1847–1921)
Reuss, Rodolphe (1841–1924)
Rodenberg, Carl (1854–1927)
Ropp, Goswin v. der (1850–1919)
Sattler, Karl (1850–1907)
Schäfer, Dietrich (1845–1929)
Scheffer-Boichorst, Paul (1843–1901)
Schroeder, Richard (1838–1917)
Schum, Wilhelm (1846–92)
Schupfer, Francesco (1833–1925)
Steindorff, Ernst (1839–95)
Stern, Alfred (1846–1936)
Ulmann, Heinrich (1841–1931)
Usinger, Rudolf (1835–74)
Vischer, Wilhelm (1833–86)
Vogel, Wilhelm (1838–91)
Wartmann, Hermann (1835–1929)
Weiland, Ludwig (1841–95)
Wenck, Karl Robert (1854–1927)
Winkelmann, Eduard (1838–96)
Wittich, Karl (1840–1916)
Wohlwill, Adolf (1843–1916)
Zeumer, Karl (1849–1914)

SYBEL
|

Büdinger, Max (1828–1902)
Erdmannsdörfer, Bernhard (1833–1901)
Herbst, Friedrich (1825–82)
Holst, Hermann (1841–1904)
Kern, Theodor (1836–73)
Lenz, Max (1850–1930)
Maurenbrecher, Wilhelm (1838–1902)
Noorden, Karl (1833–83)
Varrentrapp, Eduard (1844–1911)
Voigt, Georg (1827–91)
Weech, Friedrich (1837–1905)
Zeller, Eduard (1814–1908)

GIESEBRECHT
|

Francke, Kuno (1855–1930)
Heigel, Karl Th. (1842–1915)
Oefele, Edmund (1843–1902)
Riezler, Sigmund (1843–1926)
Simonsfeld, Heinrich (1852–1913)

CORNELIUS
|

Druffel, August (1841–91)
Lossen, Max (1842–98)
Ritter, Moriz (1840–1923)
Stauffer, Albrecht (1860–1909)
Stieve, Felix (1845–98)

DELBRÜCK
|

Harnack, Adolf (1851–1930)
Lasson, Adolf (1832–1917)
Sommerfeld, Wilhelm (1868–1915)
Wolfstieg, August (1859–1922)

Ranke had more than thirty students who achieved high reputation as historians. Many of them—Jaffé, Köpke, Dümmler—became the chief contributors to the *Monumenta*. The *Monumenta*, in fact, was a sort of post-Ranke graduate school. Ranke himself used the early editions of the *Monumenta* in his seminars. "Without your great source collection," he wrote to Pertz, "it would never have been possible for me to attract a circle of young students for these studies." [7] A considerable number of these workers on the *Monumenta* left medieval for modern history, among them Hintze, Maurenbrecher, Noorden, Pauli, Bezold, Erdmannsdörffer, and A. Fournier. [8]

Most prominent for ability and productivity among Ranke's students were Wattenbach, Giesebrecht, Waitz, and Sybel. Wilhelm Wattenbach (1819–97) [9] came over to history from philology, having been a student of Otfried Müller at Göttingen. Upon Müller's death, Wattenbach went to Berlin and continued his philological studies under

---

[7] For a veritable mine of biographic materials, see Harry Bresslau's exhaustive *Geschichte der Monumenta Germaniae Historica*, which forms vol. XLII of the *Neues Archiv* (Hanover, 1921).

[8] *Ibid.*, 341.

[9] On Wattenbach see *ibid.*, 263–65 and index; Karl Zeumer, "Wilhelm Wattenbach," *HZ*, LXXX (1898), 75–85; S. Löwenfeld, "Wilhelm Wattenbach," *PJ*, LXIV (1889), 408–29; E. Dümmler, in *Abhandlungen der kgl. Akademie der Wissenschaften* (Berlin, 1898), 3–14, and in *NA*, XXIII, (1898), 569–78; Victor Bayer in *Biographisches Jahrbuch*, II (1898), 365–69; G. Seeliger in *Deutsche Zeitschrift für Geschichtswissenschaft*, N. F., II (1898), 205–11; and C. Paoli, in *ASI*, ser. 5, XX (1897), 437–44. For a Wattenbach bibliography see *Börsenblatt für den deutschen Buchhandel*, 1897, pp. 6871 ff.

Bopp, Lachmann, Jacob Grimm, and Böckh. It was Ranke who finally attracted him to history.

In 1843, at the age of twenty-four, Wattenbach joined the staff of the *Monumenta* and undertook a number of *Forschungsreisen*. Eight years later he began to lecture on diplomatics and palaeography at the University of Berlin. When, in 1876, Waitz took over the editorship of the *Monumenta*, Wattenbach was appointed director of the division *Epistolae* and editor of the *Neues Archiv*.

All this time he was at work on his comprehensive history of writing, which he never completed. Essentially interested in intellectual life, Wattenbach attempted to reconstruct the milieu under which books were produced in the past. His *Das Schriftwesen des Mittelalters* is still an indispensable source book. *Deutschlands Geschichtsquellen im Mittelalter*, a work of vast erudition, has not been superseded. His *Anleitung zur lateinischen Palaeographie* and *Anleitung zur griechischen Palaeographie* are standard works on these subjects.

Dietrich Schäfer, who in his turn became an inspirer of many historians, thus described Wattenbach:

> Wilhelm Wattenbach was a man of thorough, comprehensive knowledge, but of moderate teaching ability. In the summer semester of 1870 I attended, with great profit to myself, his lectures on the middle ages, which, alas, the war interrupted. Together with another student of law . . . I participated in his historical seminar, in which we read only the *Vita Bonifatii;* Jaffé's edition, which appeared in 1866, made it easier to read. I also attended one of Wattenbach's lectures on palaeography. The way in which Wattenbach traced the development of individual letters by means of the various types of writings, was unbearable to me." [10]

Wilhelm von Giesebrecht (1814–89) [11] was one of the earliest of Ranke's pupils and one of the few who heeded, or was able to heed, the master's exhortation that an attractive literary style was no disadvantage to an historian. Though a charming writer and thorough scholar, Giesebrecht never became the chief of a political party like Sybel or the founder of a school like Waitz. His remarkable achievement lies in one work, the *Geschichte der deutschen Kaiserzeit*. [12]

After leaving Ranke's seminar, Giesebrecht taught in the Joachims-

[10] Dietrich Schäfer, *Mein Leben* (Berlin and Leipzig, 1926), 68; see also K. Jagow, ed., *Dietrich Schäfer und sein Werk* (Berlin, 1925); and the *Festschrift* for Schäfer, *Forschungen und Versuche zur Geschichte des Mittelalters und der Neuzeit* (Jena, 1915).

[11] The best biography of Giesebrecht is by Sigmund Riezler, *Gedächtnisrede auf Wilhelm von Giesebrecht* (Munich, 1891), and see his article in *Beilage zur Allgemeinen* [Münchener] *Zeitung*, No. 15, January 18, 1890, pp. 1–3; FUETER, 610–12; WOLF, 240–41 and note; WEGELE, 1059; Sybel, "Giesebrecht und Döllinger," in his *Vorträge und Abhandlungen* (Munich and Leipzig, 1897), 320–25; E. Dümmler in *NA*, XV (1890), 611–12; H. Prutz in *Berliner National-zeitung*, January 5, 1890; E. Emerton, "Wilhelm von Giesebrecht," *The Nation* (1890), 89–90. Giesebrecht's writings are listed in the *Almanach der bayerischen Akademie* (1875, 1878, 1884).

[12] 5 v., 1855–88; vols. I–III, 5th ed., 1881–90; vol. IV, 2nd ed., 1877; vol. VI, ed. and continued by Bernhard Simson, 1895.

thal Gymnasium at Berlin, during which time he published his *Annales Altahenses*, a technical study so skillfully executed—Giesebrecht reconstructed the lost original text—that the Prussian minister Eichhorn gave him a stipend for study in Italy. The result of the Italian journey was a dissertation on Italian letters in the early Middle Ages—*De litterarum studiis apud Italos primis medii aevi saeculis* (1845). Afterwards he undertook, with characteristic Teutonic thoroughness, an investigation of the sources of the medieval German emperors. In 1855, he published the first volume of his *Kaiserzeit*, which attracted so much attention that the author was called to the chair of history at Königsberg.

Giesebrecht did not remain at Königsberg very long. Sybel, his fellow-Rankean, was not getting along well at the University of Munich, where his Hohenzollern partisanship annoyed King Maximilian II of Bavaria (another Ranke pupil). Sybel resigned, and the King of Bavaria asked Ranke to recommend another scholar in his place. Giesebrecht was recommended and invited, but, being a man of gentle nature, he declined on the ground that as a Protestant and a "foreigner" (i.e., non-Bavarian) he would not be happy in a devoutly Catholic community. Maximilian II, however, had read and admired the first volume of the *Kaiserzeit*, and in a personal interview he asked Giesebrecht to accept the appointment as a favor to him, the king. Unable to resist such mark of royal attention, Giesebrecht accepted the professorship of history at the University of Munich in 1862.[13]

Giesebrecht was so happy at Munich that he began to feel himself as a "citizen of a new fatherland." His opponents, mainly rabid pro-Prussians, attacked him for his Bavarian loyalty. Though born a Prussian subject and a Protestant, he often boasted, "Bin ich nicht ein guter Bayer geworden?"

His first lectures began in the summer of 1862; the hall was packed, for everybody flocked to hear the man who replaced the famous—notorious, to some—Sybel. A story-teller of great ability, his success as a lecturer was assured, and for the next twenty-two years Giesebrecht continued to lecture on all phases of universal history. His lectures on antiquity were received coolly; but the hall was filled when he "treated dramatically the history of the German middle ages." His lectures were only one aspect of his work. He was also active as secretary to the Historical Commission, member of the Bavarian Educational Council, and collaborator on the *Monumenta*. His student and colleague, K. T. Heigel, has described Giesebrecht's seminar for professional historians and philologists:

---

[13] On the whole subject of historiography at Munich see W. Goetz, "Die bairische Geschichtsforschung im 19. Jahrhundert," *HZ*, CXXXVIII (1928), 255–314.

Usually a famous or a notorious source was used as a text. Einhard's biography of Charlemagne or Bruno's pamphlet on the Saxon war, the universal chronicle of Otto of Freising or Benzo's panegyric on Henry IV, and once even Machiavelli's book on the Prince, were chosen. The members of the seminar had to be responsible not only for the translation, but also to be prepared for critical questions by the master, whereby not infrequently a lively debate occurred. Occasionally Giesebrecht submitted a knotty problem which he had himself come across in his work and explained his doubts and his conclusions; this gave the students the best opportunity to have a glimpse into the most intimate workshop of the experienced master and from this model to acquire the method of the critical use of sources. But those who told him of their intentions of becoming historians, he left in no doubt that the chief thing was not what can be learned, but that penetration and imagination were the innate gifts of the historical writer who must also have the necessary supplement in a many-sided education. Time and again Giesebrecht repeated Ranke's *Hauptgebote* for the historian: criticism, precision, penetration.

With such training in the study of sources there went hand in hand a minute historical problem which every student was given to solve. The teacher gave the theme, named the chief sources and the auxiliary materials (to those who were beginners), and then showed, either privately or in the presence of the whole seminar, where the completed paper failed, how this or that source should or should not have been used, and how others might have been substituted. Nor was the artistic presentation, the form, neglected; a sloppy style was mercilessly criticized, even though the paper was technically satisfactory. Altogether Giesebrecht judged the achievements of his students with great severity; his recognition was hard to get, and even then the praise came sparely. But he who was depressed by censure could at least console himself with the thought that all students were treated with severe impartiality, and, from the zeal with which he was constantly encouraged to new attempts and shown more suitable sources for his problem, the student had to acknowledge the teacher's sincere co-operation.

"*Tages Arbeit, Abends Gäste!*" From time to time Giesebrecht used to invite the participants in his seminar to his house for a festive banquet [*Schmaus*]. Here the Frau Professor was the ever solicitous hostess, whether toward the rich dandy "who just came to learn something too," or the poorest little student who had never before tasted any titbits or drinks; the host was actively engaged in not letting the entertainment flag. On such occasions he was nicely *aufgeknöpft* and related all possible adventures and merry tales from his career.[14]

Giesebrecht was a charming and lovable man, not too profound, not too philosophical. He held aloof from political controversies, tried not to make enemies, and avoided the aggressive dogmatism of his colleagues. He was not "a divine, a canonist, a politician, but a narrator of events."[15]

Nevertheless, Giesebrecht did not avoid trouble. His monumental *Geschichte der deutschen Kaiserzeit*, in five volumes, which took forty years to write, was begun as a sort of sermon on imperialism. The Berlin-born Giesebrecht wanted to show that Germany once had a glorious empire and, by implication, could have one again. He was not very particular about who should dominate the new empire, wherein he

[14] Karl Theodor Heigel, *Essays aus neuerer Geschichte* (Munich, 1892), 319–20.
[15] Lord Acton, "Wilhelm von Giesebrecht," *EHR*, V (1890), 309, the whole, 306–10.

differed from the pro-Hohenzollern historians like Sybel and Droysen. Before Giesebrecht was half finished, the German Empire he had hoped for was restored, and he doubted whether, now that his work was no longer necessary, he should continue. The *Kaiserzeit*, therefore, was a "panegyric of medieval German imperialism," and though based on rigorous criticism of the sources, it was written from a one-sided point of view which was bound to arouse criticism. Furthermore, Giesebrecht annoyed his pedantic colleagues by writing in a popular vein and in an artistic manner. When Giesebrecht was Ranke's student, the master asked him what he would like to be, and he replied: "a dramatist." "Nonsense," said Ranke, "you will be an historian." What Giesebrecht finally did was to write a great historical drama.

According to his own admission Giesebrecht had a political purpose. He wanted to arouse in the heart of young Germany the conviction of the need for German unity. After saying this in 1849–50, he repeated it in subsequent volumes. The Prussian victory over Austria at Sadowa in 1866 filled him with joy. But the mid-nineteenth century, it must be remembered, was aflame with nationalism. Poles and Bohemians, Danes and Magyars, who were asserting their own right to nationality, bitterly resented Giesebrecht's assumptions that they, being on the border of the medieval German empire, owed all their civilization to the Germans.[16] This was, and still is, a favorite claim of German chauvinists. But not all of the Germans themselves accepted Giesebrecht's thesis. The Prussian school—and the Prussians, it should be remembered, are northerners, largely of Slav descent—was angry because Giesebrecht attributed the splendid achievements of the medieval empire to central and south Germans (Franks, Swabians, Bavarians) and did not give sufficient recognition to the north Germans (Saxons). Giesebrecht's work was a laudation of the Hohenstaufen house.

But what aroused the keenest controversy in the German-speaking lands was the question of the value of the medieval German Empire. Giesebrecht had romantically glorified that period when the Germans dominated Europe. He wrote that the union of German kingship with the imperial crown had been beneficial to both Germany and Italy. Such an interpretation was contrary to the prevailing spirit of nationalism, particularly at a time when the nationalist elements in Germany were united under the Prussian banner and girded for a struggle against

---

[16] For a Slavic attack on Giesebrecht's glorification of the German race, German virtues, German loyalty, German honor, German thoroughness, and all the other virtues which, by implication, the other races around Germany did not possess, see Jan Lepař, *Ueber die Tendenz von Giesebrechts Geschichte der Deutschen Kaiserzeit* (Prague, 1868); for literature upon the influence of German feudalism on Poland, Bohemia, and Hungary, see G. v. Below, *Der deutsche Staat des Mittelalters* (Leipzig, 1914), I, 334, n. 2.

imperial, Catholic, non-national Austria. Sybel, now an outspoken Hohenzollern, took up the cudgels and in his address before the Bavarian Academy, "Ueber die neueren Darstellungen der deutschen Kaiserzeit" (1859), made a bitter attack upon Giesebrecht.

Sybel challenged this interpretation, declaring that . . . the event of 962 had diverted the national history of the German people out of its natural orbit, stimulated a false ambition in the minds of the German kings, and entailed the expenditure of an enormous amount of German blood and treasure beyond the Alps to no profitable use. Owing to this vicious tradition the German kings were drawn into the disastrous strife with the papacy, and the German nobles encouraged to rebellion against the crown, with the ultimate result that the Hohenstaufen lost the rule of Germany, and were not able to acquire Italy.[17]

Giesebrecht, a scholar of non-combative character, did not reply to Sybel's criticism. The counter-attack came from Vienna, where the Austrians resented Sybel's reflections on Habsburg prestige and Habsburg policies. In an address delivered at Innsbruck in 1861, *Das deutsche Kaiserreich in seinen universalen und nationalen Beziehungen,* Professor Julius Ficker of the University of Vienna came to Giesebrecht's rescue. Ficker justly accused Sybel of applying contemporary political concepts and conflicts to a period when nationalism was unknown, when the *Zeitgeist* was universalistic. The medieval empire, Ficker wrote, was "through and through a healthy state formation, based on real needs." It fell because Sicily destroyed it, not because it was unreal and artificial; without the empire, Germany would have collapsed sooner.

Owing to the strained relations between Prussia and Austria, the polemic assumed a political character. Sybel's counter-reply, *Die deutsche Nation und das Kaiserreich* (1861), stressed the idea that historical policies should be tested by their usefulness to present interests; the highly centralized medieval empire was bad (for modern Germany!) because it did not give youthful nations a chance to develop. Success, Sybel insisted, was the only criterion for judging historical relationships; Waitz, who summarized the controversy, wrote that such a generalization was "highly dubious." In another booklet, *Deutsches Königtum und Kaisertum* (1862), Ficker repeated his assertions and refuted those of his opponent. Finally Waitz, a scholar who possessed

[17] Quotation from my *Feudal Germany* (Chicago, 1928), 267, cp. 268, 288–89, 375. "It is easy to criticize the Holy Roman Empire; easy to charge the rulers of the Saxon, Salian, and Staufer houses with abandoning the substance for a shadow, in being jealous to preserve a chimerical power, in being tenacious of an illusory title, the effect of which was to mutilate the natural historical development of Italy, to divert the normal history of Germany out of its natural orbit, and to waste untold blood and treasure in fruitless wars with popes and Lombard cities" (*ibid.*, 376). Ranke in his *Weltgeschichte* (Leipzig, 1883–88, 9 v.), VIII, 246–47, speculates on what might have happened to Europe in the twelfth century if Frederick I had acquired Constantinople after the dethronement of the emperor Isaac Angelos, and regrets that he failed to do so. "Es war ein Moment, wie er nicht so leicht wieder kommen konnte."

almost as much poise as Ranke, concluded the acrimonious polemic by saying that neither side was altogether right nor altogether wrong. A great historic institution such as the Holy Roman Empire, Waitz observed justly, did not lend itself to monistic explanations, but had to be studied carefully as a totality.

I believe [Waitz wrote] . . . that Sybel has not proven the details of his chief thesis, namely, that the empire led to the unfavorable political development of Germany and to the misfortune of the German nation. One may agree with much that is said here. . . . But the manner in which it is stated has something harsh, some assertions are such that I must emphatically deny them; nay, the whole procedure of blaming the empire for everything unfavorable to the political life of the Germans seems to me to be most highly one-sided, and the opinion that in all its strivings there was only error and corruption is not only hopeless but also unjustified. Without going into greater detail, I wish to make no further comment on the considerations of both concerning the more recent history of Germany, the positions of Austria and Germany, the . . . formation of our future. I am here in the most emphatic opposition to Ficker. But I am firm in my opinion that these questions have nothing to do with any estimation of the old empire, and that one must strive always and everywhere that historiography should not be misled by the temper and wishes of the present.[18]

In one sense, the controversy was settled on the battlefield, when, four years after the Sybel-Ficker polemic, Prussia defeated Austria and definitely ousted her from Germany. But before that took place, a young Englishman, James Bryce, made a great reputation by writing a brilliant book on the disputed subject. Bryce's *Holy Roman Empire* (1864) was actually stimulated by the polemic, most probably by Waitz' assertion that the empire should be studied as an organic whole.[19] Bryce, it would seem, inclined to agree with Sybel, when he wrote: "But the real strength of the Teutonic kingdom was wasted in the pursuit of a glittering toy: once at least in his reign each Emperor

---

[18] G. Waitz, in a review of the works of Ficker and Sybel, *Göttingische Gelehrte Anzeigen*, 1862, pt. 1, 130–31, the whole article on pp. 121–31. On this controversy see Heinrich Hostenkamp, *Die mittelalterliche Kaiserpolitik in der deutschen Historiographie seit von Sybel und Ficker* (Berlin, 1934); FUETER, 673–74; GOOCH, 125–26; G. v. Below, *Der deutsche Staat des Mittelalters* (n. 16), I, 353–57, and also his *Die italienische Kaiserpolitik des deutschen Mittelalters mit besonderem Hinblick auf die Politik Friedrich Barbarossas* (Munich, 1927); J. Hartung, *Die Lehre von der Weltherrschaft im Mittelalter* (Halle, 1909); DAHLMANN-WAITZ, no. 7016; cp. Lepař (n. 16). For a recent critical study of the whole subject of the medieval empire see my *Feudal Germany* (n. 17), especially ch. viii, "Guelf and Ghibelline."

On Ficker, one of the chief representatives of the Austrian "documentary" school of history (together with Theodor von Sickel), see J. Jung, *Julius Ficker (1826–1902), ein Beitrag zur deutschen Gelehrtengeschichte* (Innsbruck, 1907).

[19] See my article, "Bryce's 'Holy Roman Empire,'" *Historical Outlook*, XIII (1922), 125–26. Bryce's brilliant essay was a remarkable production for one so young. But neither in its original form nor in its later expansion into a volume did it sufficiently recognize the debt which it owed to Döllinger's famous book, nor even to Gregorovius. "When these failed him Mr. Bryce sank in precision, and his later chapters betray rather the characteristics of the prize essay than of the ripe history. Admirable as his book is, it has become standard by virtue of its clear and striking presentment of large facts, not of scholarship or independent study." *CQR*, XLIII [1896], 80.

undertook a long and dangerous expedition, and dissipated in a costly and ever to be repeated strife the forces that might have achieved conquest elsewhere, or made him feared and obeyed at home." [20]

Unaffected by the controversy, Giesebrecht calmly continued to work on his *Kaiserzeit*. His critical researches were so meticulous and so minute and up-to-date that he never got beyond the reign of Barbarossa—after forty years of work! He not only exhaustively investigated the sources himself, but he also kept up with the researches of others, a vast undertaking, considering the mass of published monographs. According to Lord Acton, Giesebrecht acquired an almost "faultless knowledge of the sources, in print and manuscript," and the notes which he attached to his great history are the "most penetrating and instructive discussion of authorities to be found anywhere in modern literature." [21] These notes may, in fact, prove to be more lasting than the text.

The oldest and in many respects the foremost student of Ranke was Georg Waitz (1813–86).[22] Like so many other German historians (Niebuhr, Dahlmann, Wattenbach, Mommsen), Waitz was a Schleswig-Holsteiner, that is, he came from a border region where nationalist feeling ran high. Nevertheless, though Waitz participated in politics as a member of the Prussian party, in his historical work he preserved a large measure of poise and moderation.

He came to Berlin in his late 'teens determined to study law, and attended the lectures of Savigny, Homeyer, and Lachmann. Then he was attracted by Ranke and was definitely won over to history. In 1835 he completed the *Year Books of Henry I*, begun in Ranke's seminar, and after his graduation in the following year Ranke recommended

---

[20] *The Holy Roman Empire* (rev. ed., New York, 1904), 199.

[21] But Lord Acton (n. 15), who knew Giesebrecht personally, exaggerates when he says (p. 307) that to Giesebrecht "No fact was unwelcome, no proof traversed any favourite view; for he inherited no tradition, cultivated no prejudice, cherished no legend." It is true that Giesebrecht had no such well-formulated biases as Sybel or Treitschke, but he was likewise profoundly nationalistic and profoundly patriotic.

[22] See the short autobiography of Waitz attached to his *Deutsche Kaiser von Karl dem Grossen bis Maximilian* (Berlin, 1862); Eberhard Waitz, *Georg Waitz. Ein Lebens und Charakterbild* (Berlin, 1913); A. Kluckhohn, *Zur Erinnerung an Georg Waitz* (Hamburg, 1887); Sybel (n. 11), 308–14, reprinted from *HZ*, LVI (1886), 482–87; GOOCH, 117–22; FUETER, 608–10; WOLF, 3–4 and note; W. Wattenbach, "Gedächtnisrede auf Georg Waitz," *Abhandlungen der königlichen Akademie der Wissenschaften zu Berlin* (1886), 3–12; Herman Grauert, "Georg Waitz," *Historisches Jahrbuch*, VIII (1887), 48–100; W. v. Giesebrecht, "Worte der Erinnerung an König Ludwig II, Leopold von Ranke und Georg Waitz," *HZ*, LVIII (1887), 181–85; Ludwig Weiland, "Georg Waitz," *Abhandlungen der Gesellschaft der Wissenschaften zu Göttingen*, XXXIII (1886); J. Zeller, "Léopold Ranke et Georges Waitz," *ASMP*, CXXVII (1887), 430–61. For a bibliography of Waitz see E. Steindorff, *Bibliographische Uebersicht über Georg Waitz' Werke, Abhandlungen, Ausgaben, kleine kritische und publizistische Arbeiten* (Göttingen, 1886). This bibliography lists 743 items, 29 of which are books, 211 critical articles, 190 editorial works (including those in the *Monumenta Germaniae Historica*), 313 reviews, comments, etc. Waitz' *Gesammelte Abhandlungen* were edited by Karl Zeumer (Göttingen, 1896).

him to Pertz for the *Monumenta*. For six years Waitz worked under Pertz, and undertook a number of scientific journeys in search of manuscripts in Germany, France, and Denmark.

Waitz' discoveries while working for the *Monumenta* won him a considerable academic reputation. In 1841, at Merseburg, he discovered in a tenth-century codex the famous *Merseburger Zaubersprüche* which belonged to the pagan period of German history, and gave them to the philologist Jacob Grimm to publish. As a result of his discoveries, the twenty-nine-year-old Waitz was given the professorship of history at Kiel.

At this Schleswig university Waitz did two important things. He was the first to lecture on medieval German historiography, a subject which attracted many students. Although not a great lecturer in the way that Dahlmann was, Waitz was thorough and "uncommonly instructive." His lucidity and orderly presentation of his materials made him an outstanding academic figure. In the second place, while at Kiel he began to work on his monumental *Deutsche Verfassungsgeschichte*, being stimulated to do so by his resentment of Tacitus' misrepresentation of the early Germans.

Politics interrupted this phase of Waitz' career. He was his university's representative in the provincial diet. During the "revolution" of 1848 he represented Schleswig-Holstein in the Frankfort "parliament of professors." As a member of the Right Center party, his pro-German (i.e., pro-Hohenzollern) views made him obnoxious to the Danish government; hence, in 1849, he accepted a call to Göttingen where he remained for twenty-six years.

At Göttingen Waitz created what was undoubtedly the foremost medieval historical school in Germany. Though not eloquent like Droysen, or passionate like Treitschke, Waitz, a dry and uninspired speaker, yet attracted large crowds of students to his lecture room. His very detachment was an appeal, and his practical approach inspired confidence. But apart from his lectures, Waitz devoted much of his energies to his seminar which soon became even more celebrated than that of Ranke, who in his later years gave more and more time to his own work and paid less attention to students. To Waitz' seminar came students from all over Germany, from Austria, Switzerland, France, and Italy; and in his detached, meticulous manner Waitz trained these students as rigorously as possible.

In 1865 Gabriel Monod, a twenty-one-year-old Frenchman destined to introduce the German scientific method in his country, asked Hippolyte Taine whether it would be profitable for him to study history in Germany, and elicited a remarkable letter from the historian of the *ancien régime*.

I answer, yes, unhesitatingly [Taine replied]. Most of the great historical studies in our times have their source and their centre in Germany. This is indisputable for Sanskrit and Persian studies, for Biblical exegesis, and for Latin and Greek History and Philology. It is less true for Modern History; each nation, such as England and France, has its original historians. Nevertheless, even in that foreign province, in the history of Italy, of Provence, or Spain, Germans do as well as natives.

Their superiority in history is due to two causes. In the first place, they are philologists; they go straight to the texts; they read manuscripts and unpublished documents; they come to Paris, to Oxford, to Dublin, in order to compare different readings; they study at first hand. The defect of University education is that it imparts second-hand knowledge, through manuals, epitomes, lectures, and ready-made editions. . . . A writer, an historian, should stand face to face, and without an intermediary, with monuments before any rectification or restoration.

In the second place, they [the Germans] are philosophers. Almost all of them have attended, while at the University, or since then, one or two courses of lectures on Philosophy, so that they have acquired the habit of generalizing and of seeing objects in masses. Thence their ideas on the *ensemble* and development of a whole civilization. . . .

Such, Sir, is the best historical culture. . . . To make an effort to acquire it is a noble and a perilous undertaking.[23]

Monod took Taine's advice and went to Germany. "When one wanted to occupy oneself with the Middle Ages," Monod said later, "it was necessary to go to Göttingen to receive the scientific baptism," especially from Waitz who exercised "a sort of scientific kingship." The young Frenchman found the German scholar an admirable character. Waitz was, Monod relates, a man of great kindness, honesty, candor, completely devoid of vanity or malice; and he tells of a remarkable example of Waitz' great-heartedness. When the Franco-Prussian war broke out, Monod went to say farewell to his master. Waitz, far from showing any rancor or expressing any patriotic hostility, spoke his regrets at the disastrous consequences which he foresaw from the war, especially for France, and, taking Monod's hand, said in a moved voice: "May God bless your country."

There are many descriptions of Waitz' seminar at Göttingen.[24] Wattenbach says that Waitz always insisted on a thorough investigation of sources before making any kind of generalization; each student was free to choose his subject and his treatment, provided they were not arbitrary. According to Sybel, Waitz was over-conscientious. More critical than philosophical, Waitz was "highly suspicious of every résumé, every definition, every final word." What was not in the documents should not be stated! Monod writes that in his seminar Waitz emphasized three points: "Criticism of sources, criticism of origins,

[23] *Life and Letters of Taine*, tr. by Mrs. R. L. Devonshire (London, 1902–08, 3 v.), II, 264–65.

[24] For Waitz' own account of his seminar and his students see "Die historischen Uebungen zu Göttingen," reprinted in the *Göttingische Gelehrte Anzeigen*, 1867, pt. 1, 354–58; and *Die Jubelfeier der historischen Uebungen zu Göttingen* (1874); and cp. WOLF, 3 and note.

criticism of institutions." The following is Monod's lucid description of Waitz' seminar:

In the evening, in the study of the beautiful house which he occupied at Göttingen in front of the university, he assembled twice weekly eight or ten of his best students to expound the texts, give account of the critical work which he has given them to write, and to discuss it with them. For these discussions he prepared himself with the most attentive care, taking notes in a microscopic handwriting on small pieces of paper which he drew one by one from the pocket of his waistcoat; he listened to each student with friendly attention, then he examined each point with minute rigor which was also combined with the highest respect for the thought and work of others. He never yielded to the pleasure of criticizing without motive, but he excelled in showing all the difficulties of a question, all the arguments which could have been presented for and against each opinion, the caution with which conclusions should be made. One left these sessions not merely more instructed, not merely with more clarified ideas and a better ordered mind, but with greater love and respect for truth and science, with the perception of the price which they cost and the resolution to work for them.[25]

No wonder that his students loved him and remembered him with kindness. Just as Waitz generously acknowledged his debt to Ranke— he told his students to take Ranke as their "model and example"—so he himself hoped to live in his students. "My best works," Waitz told Monod, "they are my pupils; it is to them that I look forward most and in them that I believe I have succeeded best. My books will pass or be forgotten, but they, the students, will create other scholars who will write better books."

In 1876, when Pertz resigned from the directorship of the *Monumenta*, Waitz, strongly urged by Ranke, removed to Berlin to succeed him. It was he who attracted to the *Monumenta* such scholars as Mommsen, Dümmler, Giesebrecht, Wattenbach, and Sickel.[26]

Waitz' *magnum opus* is his *Deutsche Verfassungsgeschichte*, in eight volumes, 1844 to 1878, the first three of which were gratefully dedicated to Ranke—"a gift from one of the many who think of you with gratitude and love, you who taught us the methods of strict historical research and deep penetration into the life of all times and peoples." Monod calls the *Verfassungsgeschichte*, which reached only to the beginning of the twelfth century, "one of the historical monuments of our age." Actually, the work is too erudite, too scrupulous, too weighted with source-facts to be a great history. The data are there, and so is the critical treatment, but one will look in vain for any illuminating generalization, for any explanatory interpretation, for any flash of insight. Nevertheless, no student of early German institutions can afford to neglect Waitz.

[25] G. Monod, "Georges Waitz," *RH*, XXXI (1886), 382–90.
[26] For Waitz' connection with the *Monumenta* see Bresslau's *Geschichte der Monumenta* (n. 7), 219–35, 251–70, 366–68, 373–78, 420–23, 478–92, 502–07, 510–12, 519–34, 539–87, 602–04, 609–17, 618–25, 637–39, 663–68.

As Ranke lay dying—Ranke and Waitz died within two days of each other—he asked: "What is the faithful Waitz doing?" And *faithful* may serve as his epitaph.

Scheffer-Boichorst of the University of Berlin, a pupil of Waitz, initiated the study of the history of the Normans in Sicily,[27] and trained the accomplished scholars Karl Andreas Kehr,[28] a brother of Paul Kehr, a great authority on papal history, and Erich Caspar.[29]

Although not students of Ranke, this is the proper place to notice certain other important German historians who were his contemporaries. Johann Friedrich Böhmer (1795–1863) [30] was a native of Frankfort where he spent most of his life. He was educated at Heidelberg and Göttingen, and being possessed of ample means, spent several years in Italy. But "Old Frankfort," as he once said, "was my first love" and the picturesque city on the Main drew him into medieval history. In 1823 he met Stein and this meeting fixed his career. He was associated with Stein and Pertz from the founding of the *Monumenta* and was the first secretary and treasurer of the Society. In 1825 he was made city archivist and librarian of Frankfort. Like Mabillon, whom he greatly admired, Böhmer had a flair for documents and in 1831 began the great series of volumes which were his life-work, the *Regesta* or *Urkunden der römischen Könige und Kaiser von Konrad I bis Heinrich VII, 911– 1313* (Frankfort, 1831). Böhmer never wrote any narrative history, but his introductions to each reign of the German emperors are masterly examples of historical exposition. Two years later this was followed by the *Regesta diplomatica Karolorum*. Lord Acton thought that the introduction to the first collection was the finest piece of medieval history produced in Germany. Other less important collections of documents followed, the most important of which was the *Fontes rerum germanicarum* (3 v., 1843). Böhmer instituted the type of historical source collections known as *regesta*. He collected much more material than it was possible for him to edit; and in order that his collections might become useful after his death, he bequeathed funds for their publication and appointed certain scholars to supervise the work. Among these was Julius Ficker, professor at Innsbruck. It had always been Böhmer's wish to publish a complete collection of the imperial charters, and he had undertaken to do so for the *Monumenta Germaniae*. But the huge folio format of that series was distasteful to him, and having vainly tried to arrange that the charters should appear in a more convenient form, he withdrew

[27] Hermann Bloch, "Paul Scheffer-Boichorst," *HZ*, LXXXIX (1902), 54–71.
[28] *Die Urkunden der normannisch-sicilischen Könige* (Innsbruck, 1902).
[29] *Roger II und die Gründung der normannisch-sicilischen Monarchie* (Innsbruck, 1904).
[30] GOOCH, 68–71 has a sympathetic appreciation of Böhmer, with bibliography. See also Wattenbach's article in *Allgemeine deutsche Biographie*, III (1876), 76–78.

from the undertaking altogether. An edition containing all of Böhmer's documents being then out of the question, Ficker selected those which had not been published, and those which existed isolated and scattered in very rare works. To the transcripts left by Böhmer, Ficker added from his own rich store of documents, and from these combined sources produced the large volume of *Acta imperii selecta* which perpetuated the memory of Böhmer's scholarship. It contained 945 charters of German kings and emperors, from 928 to 1399 A.D. Böhmer's method had not been as acute as it should have, and in time other documents were discovered, so a revised and enlarged edition of the imperial *Regesta* was later undertaken. But he had an inspiring personality and deserves to be remembered along with Stein and Pertz.

The Austrian school of history had two centers: Innsbruck and Vienna. Both excelled in diplomatic studies. Ficker's [31] *Beiträge zur Urkundenlehre* (1877) was almost as epoch-making as Mabillon's *De re diplomatica*. After the Revolution of 1848 the liberal Count Thun, minister of education, invited Ficker to Vienna, and he died an Austrian subject though born a Catholic in Westphalia. The founding of the Historical Institute at Vienna in 1854 marked the inception of critical historical studies there.[32] It was modelled after the École des Chartes and owed its origin in a peculiar way to Theodor Sickel, the son of a Lutheran Saxon pastor, who was expelled from Berlin in 1849 on political grounds and went to Paris where he spent two years at the École des Chartes. In Vienna he met Ottokar Lorenz,[33] who was then a student at the Institute. He was invited to give a course of lectures on palaeography, since the École des Chartes was world-famous for the instruction in this subject, soon joined the staff, and in 1867 became director of the Institute.[34] Sickel's successor who carried on the labors which he initiated at the Institute was Michael Tangl.[35]

The Historical Institute at Vienna was one great organ of the Austrian school of history. The other was the Vienna Academy founded in 1847, whose historical studies for many years were dominated by Arneth, Director of the Austrian Archives, a great and liberal scholar.[36]

---

[31] A valuable biography was written by Jung, *Julius Ficker* (see n. 18). See also E. Mühl-bacher's necrologue in *Mittheilungen des oesterreichischen Instituts für Geschichtsforschung*, XXIV (1903), 167–78; and WOLF, 5, n. 2.

[32] Emil Ottenthal, *Das k. k. Institut für oesterreichische Geschichtsforschung, 1854–1904. Festschrift zur Feier des fünfzigjährigen Bestandes* (Vienna, 1904).

[33] Author of *Deutschlands Geschichtsquellen im Mittelalter von der Mitte des dreizehnten bis zum Ende des vierzehnten Jahrhunderts* (Berlin, 1870; 3rd rev. ed., 1886–87, 2 v.).

[34] See Sickel's *Denkwürdigkeiten aus der Werdezeit eines deutschen Geschichtsforschers*, ed. Wilhelm Erben (Munich, 1926), and Erben's earlier notice in *Historische Vierteljahrschrift*, XI (1908), 333–59. See also WOLF, 5 and n. 3.

[35] H. Krabbo, "Bibliographie der Schriften M. Tangls," *NA*, XLIV (1922), 147–50.

[36] On whom see GOOCH, 425–27.

German historical scholarship was gradually dove-tailed with Austrian historical scholarship, yet the stamp of French historical scholarship through the tradition of the École des Chartes always remained evident. The Austrian school excelled German scholarship in diplomatics and palaeography. Nor could even the suavity of Arneth smooth the differences between the two schools. The controversy between Giesebrecht and Ficker over the nature and significance of the Holy Roman Empire warmed into àn academic feud, was accentuated by the feeling between the North Protestant states and the South Catholic states, and aggravated again after the Prussian annexation of Hanover. After 1867 Onno Klopp, the Hanoverian historian, found refuge in Vienna, where he devoted his life to the defense of the Habsburgs and condemnation of the Hohenzollerns. His huge and misnamed *Fall of the House of Stuart* deals so copiously with England's relations with Central Europe that it really is a history of Germany in the seventeenth and eighteenth centuries.

Before concluding this chapter, it remains to mention that a noble endeavor was made in Germany by many distinguished historians to acquaint the cultured reading class with the results of German scholarship in sound popular works, minus the erudition and critical apparatus. The first of these, the *Allgemeine Staatengeschichte*, was started by the same impulses which created the *Monumenta Germaniae Historica* in 1819. The initiators were Heeren and Ukert; the series was continued by Giesebrecht, then by Lamprecht, and new additions occasionally appear.[37] In 1879 Wilhelm Oncken, professor in Berlin, began to edit a similar series, of which each volume was written by an acknowledged authority in the subject. Completed in forty-five volumes in 1893, it is generally known as the "Oncken series." Among the contributors were Dahn, Herzberg, Philippson, the younger Droysen, Brückner, and many others.

New times brought new interests. Even before the First World War German historical scholarship began to manifest a change of mind and interest. The old questions had lost their glow. A new orientation and a new interpretation ensued. This post-war school was irritated because medieval German history continued to be measured by "out-worn standards" and demanded a re-examination of the problems and evidence of the past.[38]

---

[37] WOLF, 459–62, has a good description of this series, with titles of the most important works. A complete list may be found in Victor Loewe, *Bücherkunde der deutschen Geschichte* (3rd ed., Altenburg, 1910), 109–11.

[38] On this transition see Schmeidler, in *HZ*, CXL (1929), 591–95, who flouts "yesterday's scholarship" (Die Wissenschaft von gestern).

CHAPTER XLIII

THE PRUSSIAN SCHOOL [1]

THE Prussian school of historians was a secession from the Ranke school. Dahlmann, Sybel, Duncker, Droysen, and Treitschke were its prophets. But as Kant's philosophy was innate in the *Aufklärung* and the Romantic movement, so Hegel's philosophy was the intellectual godfather of the Prussian School of History. In the opinion of Hegel's votaries his system contained the final and absolute truth. Hegel was the first philosopher who included the principles of all former systems and thereby rendered his own comprehensive of all, leaving no room for the independent growth of any new philosophy which could only proceed from and be a further development of his own. Moreover, Hegel had discovered the absolute method which makes the process of reason so rigorously certain as to ensure the accuracy of the result. The State was not only the highest expression of human reason —it was reason. The State could do no wrong because thinking and being are identical. What is true for thought is true for things. It was iron-clad logic formulated to forge an iron ring on the necks of the German people. [2]

Friedrich Christoph Dahlmann (1785–1860), who, like so many other eminent German scholars, came from that northern frontier region lying between the Reich and Denmark, is generally considered the "father" of the Prussian School of History. Except chronologically, the title of "father" cannot be granted to Dahlmann; it belongs more properly to Sybel. Nor can Dahlmann be regarded as a first-rate historian. He was, first and foremost, a passionate propagandist for German unity, an orator and a patriot, an inspirer of political action, and lastly a writer and teacher of history. The printed matter which he has left behind him is extremely meager.

Dahlmann's career is characteristic of a certain type of agitator. Born in Wismar, he studied philology at Copenhagen and at Halle, and took his degree at the age of twenty-five. When Napoleon invaded Germany, Dahlmann suddenly began to feel himself an ardent German. In fact, so impassioned was his hatred of the French that he walked across Germany to Aspern to join the Austrian forces.

---

[1] GOOCH, ch. viii; GUILLAND, introduction and chs. iii–iv.
[2] Amid the enormous mass of literature on Hegel's political philosophy I call the reader's attention to an article in the *Philosophical Review*, XLI, 261 ff.

Dahlmann belonged to a class of scholars which combined learning with politics. He could not endure the thought of yielding to violence and mere success, and teaching others that might made right. In 1812 he obtained a professorship at Kiel, where he was until 1829. He incurred the king's displeasure by a speech made on occasion of a commemoration of the battle of Waterloo. Later, as secretary of the permanent deputation of the Schleswig-Holstein nobility, he tried in vain to obtain a hearing for the duchies at the Bundestag. He has even been credited with the very creation of the Schleswig-Holstein Question. Niebuhr and Dahlmann split upon the July Revolution of 1830. The former deplored the weakness of governments in yielding to the revolutionary spirit and considered that Dahlmann had become a demagogue, although the two had formerly been in general agreement in politics as well as history. The great historian of ancient Rome accused Dahlmann of complicity with the French "bagauderie" and called him a revolutionist à la Lafayette. Dahlmann believed that revolution was better than reaction. When his idea was put to the test, and the revolution broke out at Göttingen, he proposed to put it down by force. He was a theoretical, not a practical revolutionist. His high idea of royalty and his admiration for the English constitution were combined with a thoroughly German dislike of France, and he held that the chief source of all French political troubles was the absence of monarchical institutions based on a landed nobility. Only a reckless violation of political right could have alienated Dahlmann from the royal cause, but the occasion was given by the revocation of the Hanoverian constitution of 1833 by King Ernst Augustus. Dahlmann and six famous colleagues—"the Göttingen seven"—the two Grimms, Gervinus, Ewald, Albrecht, and Weber entered a protest in consequence of which, by a royal rescript on December 12, 1837, they were dismissed and banished.[3] From 1837 to 1842 Dahlmann lived at Leipzig and Jena, studying history and writing most of his works. In 1842 he was made professor of history and politics at Bonn, where he remained until his death in 1860.

In the National Assembly at Frankfort (1848) Dahlmann was a member of the constitutional committee. He distinguished himself as an ardent champion of German unity under Prussian hegemony. Having failed in his aim, he returned to Bonn and devoted the last years of his life to writing political pamphlets and inspiring young students with passionate patriotism.

Politically Dahlmann was, in the discerning words of Fueter, a

[3] A. Springer, *Friedrich Christof Dahlmann* (Leipzig, 1870, 2 v.), reviewed in *NBR*, LII (1870), 568–69.

"Whig like Macaulay"; hence he favored a constitutional monarchy. From this point of view he wrote his *History of the English Revolution* (1844) and *History of the French Revolution* (1845), works which have only propaganda value. His constitutionalism is doctrinaire, unrealistic, and in a sense characteristically German; it does not, for example, strive to guarantee human freedom or independence, but to establish a powerful, centralized State. "I am always under the impression," he said, "that what we Germans need above all is power (*Macht*) rather than freedom, and I can not see any other way of acquiring power than by means of monarchy." [4]

Obviously Dahlmann need not be taken seriously as an historian, but as a teacher and inspirer he deserves first place. His influence on German youth was tremendous. A serious, imposing man, with a "Roman head of the period of the Republic," tight lips, feverishly-bright eyes, he seemed a prophet of nationalism to his hearers. His words were always direct, moral, dogmatic; he was incapable, according to the admiring Sybel, of half-judgments. To Dahlmann things were either black or white. *Es gab nur eine gute Sache und deren Freunde und Gegner.* "Whoever saw him, the powerful figure, the strong features, the bushy eyebrows, the faithful eye, knew that he stood in the presence of a man who, in his absolute submission to duty, was a source of unlimited independence and inexhaustible strength." The fact that the content of Dahlmann's lectures "was not what one may call rich," as Sybel ingenuously put it, was no detriment to the patriot's oratory. [5]

In 1830 Dahlmann published a survey of the principal sources and authorities of German history as a help to his own students at Göttingen. The work was soon widely adopted and in 1838 a second edition appeared. This edition contained a large amount of new matter. For the next thirty years no other edition was issued in spite of the progress made in historical scholarship. A third edition appeared in 1869, with 2800 titles. In 1875 Waitz published what was nominally a fourth edition, but actually a new work. The whole arrangement was more systematic and gained in clearness by a division into longer periods. Notwithstanding the exclusion of many works that had then become obsolete, there was a great increase in the number of titles cited. Where Dahlmann in 1838 had given some 700 titles, the fourth edition contains 3215 titles. Waitz gave careful attention to periodical literature.

[4] H. v. Treitschke, "F. C. Dahlmann," in his *Historische und Politische Aufsätze* (Leipzig, 1886, 4 v.), I, 432.

[5] Sybel, "Drei Bonner Historiker," *Vorträge und Aufsätze* (Berlin, 1874), 31–36. Sybel declares that Dahlmann's *History of Denmark* (1843 f.) "will remain forever an ornament and pride of German literature"—although it is merely a sound and critical achievement. See also FUETER, 674–75; WEGELE, 1030–32.

The ninth edition, edited by Hermann Haering and a host of collaborators, was issued in 1931. It contains 16,337 classified items, most of them including several titles combined together, and is beyond doubt the most complete national bibliography in existence.

Max Duncker (1811–86) [6] was a student of Ranke who was active in politics. He was not an outstanding historian. His best-known work is a *History of Antiquity* in nine volumes, the Greek part extending to the death of Pericles. The work has little merit apart from the fact that it is based on new material discovered by others. Despite his training in Ranke's seminar, Duncker was either unable or unwilling to use the sources critically; nor did he have the perception to see the organic connection between the various states of antiquity.

Duncker became professor at Berlin in 1859 (at the same time as his friend Droysen); two years later Bismarck appointed him Minister of State in charge of the press. In 1866 he became Prussian Civil Commissioner at Cassel, and in the following year Director of the Prussian archives, in which capacity he reorganized the provincial archives. In 1885, one year before his death, he was named historiographer of Brandenburg. Thus politics and administration detracted from Duncker's scientific career. [7]

In February 1867, on the occasion of Ranke's doctoral jubilee, Heinrich von Sybel (1817–95) [8] addressed the Prince of German historians (*historicorum Germaniae princeps*) in the flattering words of

[6] On Duncker see the biography by R. Haym, *Das Leben Max Dunckers* (Berlin, 1891), an essentially political life; Reinhold Brode, "Max Dunckers Anteil an der deutschen Geschichtschreibung," *Forschungen zur brandenburgischen und preussischen Geschichte*, VI (1893), 501–27; the same, "Max Duncker," in *Jahresberichte über die Fortschritte der klassischen Altertumswissenschaft*, XLIX, 147–74; Treitschke (n. 4), IV, 401 ff.; Constantin Rossler, "Das Leben Max Dunckers," *PJ*, LXVIII (1891), 404–25; W. Giesebrecht, in *Sitzungsberichte der bayrischen Akademie*, Ph.-hist. Klasse, I (1887), 294 ff.; S. Reinach, "Maximilien-Wolfgang Duncker," *RH*, XXXII (1886), 167–74; FUETER, 685; GOOCH, 133, 475; WEGELE, 1078; and the article and bibliography by Petersdorff in *Allgemeine deutsche Biographie*, XLVII, 171 ff.

[7] Duncker's *Geschichte des Altertums* first appeared in 1852–57; 5th ed., 1878–83, 7 v.; Neue Folge, 1884–86, 2 v. It was translated into English by Evelyn Abbot (London, 1877–82, 6 v.). He also wrote: *Aus der Zeit Friedrichs des Grossen und Friedrich Wilhelms III* (Leipzig, 1876); *Abhandlungen aus der neueren Geschichte* (Leipzig, 1887); *Abhandlungen aus der griechischen Geschichte* (Leipzig, 1887); *Die Krisis der Reformation* (Leipzig, 1845); *Feudalität und Aristokratie* (Berlin, 1858).

[8] For a bibliography and for notes on his life see Varrentrapp's biographical introduction to Sybel's *Vorträge und Abhandlungen* (Munich and Leipzig, 1897). See also FUETER, 668–77; WOLF, 240 and n. 1; WEGELE, 1059–61; GOOCH, 112–14, 124–25, 127–29, 140–47; GUILLAND, 171–253; A. Lübbe, *Friedrich Gentz und Heinrich von Sybel. Ein Beitrag zur Geschichte der neueren Historiographie* (Göttingen, 1913), in which the author points out that Sybel reached the same conclusions as regards the French Revolution as did Gentz about half a century earlier; F. Meinecke, "Heinrich von Sybel," *HZ*, LXXV (1895), 390–95; T. de Wyzewa, "La vie et l'oeuvre d'Henri de Sybel," *RDM*, CXXXII (1895), 217–27; *ER*, CXXVIII (1868), 289–323; A. Kluckhohn, "Heinrich von Sybel's *Geschichte der Begründung des neuen deutschen Reiches*," *Deutsche Rundschau*, LXI (1889), 451–61, LXII (1890), 127–40; Pflugk-Harttung, in *Westermanns Monats-Hefte*, June 1888; R. Reuss, in *RH*, LIX (1895), 450–56; *QR*, CXXIX, (1870), 454–84, CLXXI, 329 ff.; *AHR*, I (1895), 190.

a "faithful student." The man who thus acknowledged his debt to Ranke, in whose seminar he spent two years, was to be the most distinguished of Ranke's students who broke with the master. Sybel, more a *Politiker* than a scholar, became the foremost exponent of what is known as the "Prussian School" of history. He was born at Düsseldorf, the son of a free-thinking Prussian official. His early environment was characteristically Rhenish: liberal in politics, French in thought, upper-bourgeois in the way of life. It is astonishing how closely his environment resembled that of another Rhinelander, Karl Marx. If Sybel had not discovered Edmund Burke at a critical moment in his life, his career might have taken a different turn; he might, in fact, have gone the way of Marx. But Burke, he admitted, saved him from sinking "into the arid wilderness of abstract radicalism."

In 1841 Sybel had published a *History of the First Crusade*, one of the most critical products of Ranke's seminar. Three years later, in 1844, he became professor at Bonn. In 1845 he was called to Marburg and in 1856, at Ranke's recommendation, to Munich, where he was later replaced by Giesebrecht. From 1861 to 1875 he was again at Bonn. Then a grateful Prussian government appointed its most effective spokesman Director of the Archives. These years were full of political, scholarly, and journalistic activities, all subordinated to one aim: to rationalize and further the powerful Hohenzollern State. As Acton said of Sybel: "He became the first classic of imperialism, and helped to form that garrison of distinguished historians that prepared the Prussian supremacy together with their own, and now hold Berlin like a fortress." [9]

Even in the early years of his career Sybel displayed the qualities of a politician. He was cold—except where his patriotism was involved—calculating, disciplined. To him history was an instrument of politics. He criticized Ranke for his detachment, insisting that German historians must have a "national conscience." Politics, he said, was the "natural vocation (*Beruf*) of the scholar."

Sybel was only twenty-nine years old [relates his student Max Büdinger] when in April, 1847, I reported for his lectures. Pale and lean, he seemed to me to be much older; moreover, he was already *Ordinarius* [full professor] for three semesters, and therefore his somewhat older appearance was more desirable for the Hessian [this was at Marburg] student body. When I told him of my inclination to study history, he gave me a penetrating analysis of the difference between sources and auxiliary means (*Hilfsmitteln*). Marvelling and impressed, I listened to him as he stood there illuminated by the spring sun. He may have noticed my inner agitation, for suddenly he began to give me advice on how one should not devote himself uninterruptedly to historical studies;

[9] Lord Acton, "German Schools of History," in his *Historical Essays and Studies* (London, 1908), 378. This famous article is reprinted from *EHR*, I (1886), 7–42.

he had, under Ranke's direction, kept himself keen by cultivating music and chemistry. So I became his student and acquired an intimate acquaintance with his historical views during three semesters. For his part, he told my wife in the summer of 1874 that he had *rasieren gelernt* from me. The first lecture in the summer of 1847, before five and sometimes four students, was on German history from 1815 to 1830, given with a liberal tendency, but the opinions were actually conservative and especially Prussian. The lecture was followed by a conversation.[10]

This passage is significant, for it has been generally said that Sybel became a conservative pro-Hohenzollern only after the so-called Revolution of 1848. He represented Marburg in the *Vorparlament* at Frankfort, where he sharply opposed the establishment of a German republic. Sybel relates sarcastically how at a public meeting in Marburg he spoke "against equal, universal suffrage, and the sovereign people broke my windows, a pleasure which they repeated during every popular celebration."

The experiences of 1848 deepened Sybel's conservative inclinations and drove him still further to the Right. During his first years of disillusionment with politics he withdrew from active life and devoted himself to history, but no longer medieval history, a subject with which he broke as definitely as he did with his teacher Ranke. Instead, he resolved to devote himself to a work which would show his fellow-Germans the terrible dangers involved in radicalism and revolution. Sybel explained this attitude in a most revealing passage. "I devoted myself to scientific studies, but not to the Roman imperial period. The storm of the revolutionary years drove my historic researches into other directions, at the beginning of which I had of course no idea that I had started the chief work of my life. The radicals of 1848 had displayed various socialistic tendencies; it occurred to me, therefore, to write a pamphlet in which was to be shown what consequences such things (socialistic ideas) had in the great French Revolution."

This is a remarkable admission, particularly for a man trained in the Ranke school. Of course Sybel did not know, as he admits, that his "pamphlet" would run into five volumes and take a quarter of a century to write (1853–79). Nevertheless, herein we have a revelation of Sybel's mind. By means of the historic method, historic data, and historic prestige, he set out deliberately to discredit the French Revolution in order to prevent the spread of radicalism in Germany. In this work he was liberally helped by the authorities, for the conservative governments in Europe, especially Prussia, Austria, and France, gave him free access to their archives.[11]

---

[10] Quoted by Varrentrapp in his biographical introduction to Sybel's *Vorträge und Abhandlungen* (n. 8), 41.

[11] P. Bailleu, "Heinrich von Sybel," *Deutsche Rundschau*, LXXXV (1895), 58–76.

Sybel's *Geschichte der Revolutionszeit* is, indeed, a remarkable work, despite its *Tendenz*, though not "epoch making," as Ludwig Häusser would have it.[12] It is necessary to remember that intellectually Sybel had become anti-liberal and had espoused the Prussian ideas of discipline, order, moderation; hence any revolution was repugnant to his ideology. He was not, however, a reactionary like Treitschke or illiberal like Droysen. A keenly-intelligent and well-balanced mind, Sybel attempted to steer a course between Revolution and Reaction, hoping to teach his "State-less people" the wisdom of and need for a centralized, non-radical national state. The French Revolution was to serve as a model of how *not* to do things.

Consequently one is not surprised to see in Sybel's *History of the Revolutionary Period* an original emphasis. Instead of writing about Paris, or about French conflicts, or about the social implications of the Revolution, he built his great structure—and it is an imposing structure, based almost entirely on archival sources, critically sifted—around the European countries that were affected by the upheaval. To Sybel the great importance of the French Revolution lay in its effects on the rest of Europe, which, with keen insight, he treated as a unity. What mattered basically was, not what the Girondins said in the Convention, but how the events at Paris helped, say, to partition Poland, to aggrandize Russia, and to dissolve the ancient Holy Roman Empire. It must be admitted that such an approach was historical in the best sense and did much to widen the intellectual horizon of Germany.

Despite the immense range of his scholarship, Sybel interpreted revolutionary men and events with a lack of generosity; wherever possible, he diminished their importance. True, he admitted that the Revolution hastened the decline of feudalism—"A century would probably have passed over half Europe before the mouldering rubbish of feudalism could have been removed by peaceful means." But he always did that with bad grace. He sneered at the French revolutionary enthusiasm; he disparaged the heroism. Following Burke, Sybel contemptuously derided the revolutionary ideas and aims. The Rights of Man were to him "trivialities unworthy of an intelligent man." He criticized "those simpletons who imagine that a State is founded or a revolution accomplished by means of hopes and enthusiasm."

Nothing is more painful [he said], more tiresome, or more humiliating to read than these discussions in which they tried to decree by a majority of votes what the words "right" and "liberty" meant. . . . They destroyed with untiring zeal the last traces of tradition in order to build up the State according to the laws of nature.

[12] Reviewed in *Allgemeine Zeitung*, Sept. 24, 1853, pp. 4265–66, and Sept. 25, 1853, pp. 4281–83.

There was, of course, a deliberate purpose in writing so about an event which the civilized world has long regarded as of incalculable importance: Sybel strove to convince the German liberals that the French Revolution was a disastrous affair, to warn them against any imitation of the excitable French.

While working on the history of the French Revolution, Sybel was also busy with politics. Though pro-Hohenzollern, he opposed Bismarck in the Prussian Landtag; but the Prussian victory in 1866 over Austria—a country he hated bitterly—made him a sudden and enthusiastic follower of the chancellor. Sybel now became the leader of the so-called National Liberals and received full credit from Bismarck. The victory of 1870 moved him to tears. The glory was too much for this usually reserved man. "And how will one live in the future?" he exclaimed; "and where will one find another object for which to live?" Still, there was something left to live for. In 1874 he became a deputy in the Imperial parliament and as the Director of the Prussian Archives, he devoted much of his time to supervising the publication of many source collections.

Sybel's last years were devoted to another large history, *The Founding of the German Empire by William I,* based, as the title page says, "mainly on the Prussian *Staatsacten.*" The first five volumes appeared in 1889 and the last two in 1894, ending the story with Napoleon III. The work, written at the instigation of Bismarck, was, Sybel admits in the preface, frankly "Prussian and National Liberal." The hero of the political drama is Bismarck, though Emperor William I is also treated with reverence. The great chancellor does not live in these closely-packed pages. Unlike Ranke, Sybel did not have the painter's brush, possibly because he had so few sympathies. Sybel's portraiture, as Guilland has pointed out, is stilted, pedantic, and quite without life.[13]

Sybel was not a sparkling, colorful person. His qualities were those of a man of affairs. He stuck firmly to his convictions. Erich Marcks says quite justly that he "had neither the monumental greatness and the immortal, majestic wisdom of Ranke, nor Dahlmann's fury and power." Schmoller keenly observes that because Sybel was both historian and politician he was able to envisage vital problems and give practical solutions.[14] He had an instinct for what was significant. But

[13] See the characteristic examples of pedestrian prose given by GUILLAND, especially pp. 249–50.

[14] G. Schmoller, "Gedächtnisrede auf Heinrich von Sybel und Heinrich von Treitschke," *Forschungen zur brandenburgischen und preussischen Geschichte,* IX (1897), 357–94. "Ich gebe Sybel Recht, dass 1840–1880 die von ihm und den genannten Historikern vertretene Weltanschauung die wissenschaftlich und sittlich höchststehende, und darum kräftigste, berechtigste, siegreiche war. Und Sybels grosse Bedeutung liegt mit darin, dass er von diesem Standpunkt aus Geschichte schrieb und Welturteile abgab, dass er damit den Schritt von der bloss descrip-

Sybel, one is bound to observe, confused his convictions with his science. He was so profoundly convinced of the correctness of his scientific method that he believed that his doctrines were the consequences of his method. To Sybel, history was virtually as positive as a natural science. All that was necessary, he said, was to have the correct method and then "truth" would inevitably follow from it. *Die historische Wissenschaft ist fähig, zu völlig exacter Kenntniss vorzudringen.*[15] This is a conclusion too naive to be acceptable.

Finally one of Sybel's lasting contributions to historiography must be mentioned, the founding of the *Historische Zeitschrift*. This historical periodical had two German predecessors: Ranke's *Historisch-politische Zeitschrift* and Adolf Schmidt's *Zeitschrift für Geschichtswissenschaft* (1844–48). Ranke's journal did not last because it had few contributors and Schmidt's was killed by the uprising of 1848. The *Historische Zeitschrift* which Sybel established in 1859 was the result of a deep change that had come over Germany. The failure of 1848 had brought about a great deal of "soul-searching" among intellectuals; more and more historians came to be attracted to the national movement. Finally, largely as a result of Ranke's work, Germany possessed a sufficiently large number of professional historians to support a learned journal.

The *Historische Zeitschrift* was entirely the work of Ranke's pupils, though the old master himself kept aloof. Sybel hoped that the *Zeitschrift* would become a national organ for German historians, would affect German "life, public opinion and general education," and that, finally, it would enable history to play the same rôle in Germany "as did philosophy twenty years ago." In short, the *Historische Zeitschrift* was to become a vehicle for the will-to-power of Sybel and the other historians.

The *Zeitschrift* was to publish only materials which had some "connection with the life of the present." Meinecke relates that when in 1893 Sybel handed over the editorship to him, he (Meinecke) expressed doubts as to his competence in passing judgment on articles dealing with matters not within his knowledge. "I can not do that either," Sybel replied quietly. "If you test every essay to see whether it is completely lucid and thought out . . . you will as a rule reach the right decision." And, Meinecke concludes, "there really is no other way of doing it." Sybel himself, busy with other matters, left most of

tiven Wissenschaft zur kausal erklärenden, zu der die grossen Zusammenhänge aufhellenden in seiner Art vollzog."

[15] See his "Ueber die Gesetze des historischen Wissens," in his *Vorträge und Aufsätze* (n. 5), 1–20. "Die Wissenschaft aber kann nicht nach Neigung und Wünschen, sondern nur nach Wahrheit fragen [p. 20]."

the work on the periodical to a group of able young men—Kluckhohn, Varrentrapp, Maurenbrecher, etc.,[16] retaining only a final decision in critical matters. As is well known, the *Historische Zeitschrift* became perhaps the foremost historical journal in the Western world.[17]

In the last years of his life the course which historiography was taking brought disappointment to Sybel. Though he lived to see a powerful German State, he also witnessed a new phenomenon, the domination of materialist ideas. Philosophically an idealist, Sybel found materialism a most painful experience. He ridiculed "an historical science of a trade union character." The new radicalism hurt him as much as it did Treitschke. As an example of Sybel's pessimism, one may quote a letter which he wrote a few weeks before his death:

> I still agree with Treitschke: It is the strong personalities that make the times. The masses do nothing; they experience pressing needs in wide circles; whence educated men abstract the ideals of the future; the flood in this direction keeps growing, creates all kinds of useful detail or the reverse, and finally seems irresistible. But what happens . . . ends in failure. Until there appears the strong man who not only recognizes, like everybody else, the *Zeitströmung* but also seizes the right means to realize the ideals. Thus Bismarck as regards German unity. But when and where will social reform find its Bismarck? It seems to me that social reform is now in the same stage as was German unity before 1844: laudable striving, unclear exaggerations, false experiments.[18]

Among the non-Rankeans in the Prussian group, Johann Gustav Droysen (1808–84) [19] was the most challenging figure. Unlike Sybel the Rhinelander, Dahlmann the Holsteiner, and Treitschke the Saxon-Slav, Droysen was a Prussian subject by birth and parentage; his father had been a chaplain in the Hohenzollern army. In one other respect Droysen differed from his colleagues in the Prussian camp; he was more of a philosopher.

[16] The following were editors of the *Historische Zeitschrift* in Sybel's time: Konrad Varrentrapp, 1867–74; Max Lehmann, 1875–93; August Kluckhohn, 1859–61; Wilhelm Maurenbrecher, 1861–62; Theodor Bernhardi, 1862–66; K. Menzl, 1874–75; see F. Meinecke, "Geleitwort zum 100. Bande der *Historischen Zeitschrift*," *HZ*, C (1908), 1–10.

[17] The *Zeitschrift* was published at Munich by R. Oldenburg, a firm which still publishes it; see the necrologue by R. Oldenburg, "Heinrich von Sybel," *HZ*, LXXV (1895), 385–89.

[18] Sybel to Erich Marcks, 1895. Quoted in Marcks, *Männer und Zeiten* (Leipzig, 1911, 2 v.), I, 272–73 note.

[19] See the excellent biography by his son Gustav Droysen, *Johann Gustav Droysen* (Leipzig, 1910), cp. the review by Halvdan Koht in *AHR*, XVI (1910), 125–27; R. Hübner, ed., *Johann Gustav Droysen, Briefwechsel* (Stuttgart, 1929, 2 v.); F. Meinecke, "Johann Gustav Droysen, sein Briefwechsel und seine Geschichtschreibung," *HZ*, CXLI (1929), 249–87; Chr. D. Pflaum, *J. G. Droysen's Historik in ihrer Bedeutung für die moderne Geschichtswissenschaft* (Gotha, 1907); WOLF, 7–9; DAHLMANN-WAITZ, nos. 13778 and 13909; FUETER, 615–19; GOOCH, 134–40; GUILLAND, 215–18; SANDYS, 230–31; Acton (n. 9), 378–80; M. Duncker, "Johann Gustav Droysen," *PJ*, LIV (1884), 134–67; W. v. Giesebrecht, "Johann Gustav Droysen," *Sitzungsberichte der philosophisch-philologischen und historischen Classe der Akademie der Wissenschaften zu München*, XV (1886), 208–19; P. Frédéricq, "De l'enseignement supérieur de l'histoire," *Revue de l'instruction publique en Belgique*, XXV (1882); O. Hintze, "J. G. Droysen," in *Historische und politische Aufsätze* (Berlin, 1908), 4 v.), IV, 87–143, reprinted in *Allgemeine Deutsche Biographie*, vol. XLVIII; A. Dove, *Ausgewählte Schriften* (Leipzig, 1898).

Orphaned at the age of eight by the death of his father, young Droysen was educated by the generosity of friends and his own efforts. From the age of fourteen, while at the gymnasium at Stettin, he gave lessons to support himself. He was often undernourished; the fat which his poor mother sent him for his bread, he used to light the lamp. In 1826 he received his gymnasium certificate, giving him good grades in ancient languages, French, and mathematics, but a low record in history and Hebrew. The failure drove the desperate young man to the point of suicide, but, realizing his mother needed his support, he decided to continue with his career.

Penniless, Droysen went to Berlin, where he lived in the house of his father's friend Köpke, one of Ranke's pupils. The eighteen-year-old youth registered at the university in the faculties of philosophy and philology. Mainly a student of philology, Droysen took no courses with Ranke. In later years as colleagues at Berlin the two men were on indifferent terms. Among Droysen's teachers were Lange, Lachmann, and Bernhardi in philology; Ritter in the history of philosophy; Stuhr in mythology and the philosophy of history; Carl Ritter in ethnography and geography; Wilken in the Middle Ages; Gans in modern history; Bopp in Sanskrit. Every semester he attended the lectures of Böckh and Hegel, which helps to explain Droysen's familiarity with the Hegelian metaphysics. In 1829 he passed his examinations as *Oberlehrer* and joined the faculty of the Grauen Kloster gymnasium, where Giesebrecht was then a student.

While at the gymnasium, the young philologist worked on a history of Alexander the Great, to serve as a doctoral dissertation, and also lectured as a *Dozent* at the university, as usual without pay. Giesebrecht, who was six years younger, was then a student at Berlin and became one of the first hearers of Droysen. "I was attracted," Giesebrecht recalls, "by both the subject and by the young *Dozent*, whom I have known from the gymnasium, though I have never been his student. The fresh way in which he treated his material fascinated me so that in the following semesters I never missed his lectures."

Droysen's *Geschichte Alexanders des Grossen* (1833), and its sequel, *Geschichte der Nachfolger Alexanders* (1836),[20] although criticized on the ground that the author had no training in history, won him a professorship of history at Kiel with a salary of 1200 thalers. As was the case with Dahlmann, Waitz, and others, Kiel made an ardent patriot out of Droysen. In this frontier city he lost his interest in antiquity

---

[20] A third volume, *Geschichte der Bildung des hellenistischen Staatensystems*, appeared in 1843. The three books were united in a second edition under the title *Geschichte des Hellenismus* (Gotha, 1877–78, 6 v. in 3); French translation by A. Bouché-Leclerq (Paris, 1883–85, 3 v.).

and devoted himself to politics and modern history. At this outpost of German nationalism his enthusiasm for German unity was inflamed. No longer would he be a mere classicist, a mere academician, but a fiery man of action. "We are too sluggish, too haughty, too abstract," he wrote in 1845; "instead of filling sausages, which is now our essential merit as regards the students, we ought to kindle fires on the mountain tops of science for the guidance of the wayfaring folk in the dark valleys." This led him to teach modern instead of ancient history, in order to stimulate the students to patriotic action and to arouse in them fervor for national unity. The first literary fruit of his conversion was the publication of *Lectures on the Wars of Liberation* (1846). "Prussian patriot through and through," Giesebrecht comments, "he was convinced that there was no other salvation for Germany than union with Prussia."

As a leader of the Holstein nationalist movement, Droysen was elected to the Frankfort parliament. He was profoundly convinced that Germany's future lay with Prussia, the latter being, in the words of Lord Acton, the possessor of the "big battalions." Wherefore Droysen urged Germany's "incorporation" into Prussia, the latter to put her army, administration, and financial system at the disposal of the new empire. "The position left vacant by the Hohenstaufens belongs to the Hohenzollerns," he said.

In 1851 Droysen went to Jena, where he formed devoted pupils and attracted large audiences. He conducted seminars and lectured on modern history, from the Reformation to the French Revolution, on Prussian history, and the methodology of history. Though he had practically given up working in the classics, his seminar problems were connected with ancient Greek culture as well as with modern Prussian history. A considerable portion of his time, however, was devoted to his *magnum opus*, the *Geschichte der Preussischen Politik*, the first volume of which appeared in 1855 and the twelfth in 1886 (only to 1756). In 1859 Droysen joyfully and proudly accepted a call to the University of Berlin, where he remained to the end of his life. Like others among his colleagues, Mommsen for example, he was a prodigious worker and thought nothing of spending fifteen hours at his desk. He was Prussian to the core and a staunch supporter of the Prussian military system.[21]

The *History of Prussian Policy* is a remarkable achievement. It is based altogether on documents, especially those found in the Prussian archives, of which he became director after Dahlmann and before Sybel. From this point of view alone, the *Prussian Policy* is still indispensable.

[21] John W. Burgess, *Reminiscences of an American Scholar* (New York, 1923), 126–28.

Even in his youthful history of Alexander the Great, written before Droysen's full conversion to Prussianism, he had treated Macedonia as an ancient Prussia and Philip as a Bismarck.[22] Now, given such a subject as the rise of Prussia, Droysen applied all his erudition and eloquence and passion to showing the foreordained mission of Prussia for the regeneration of Germany.

The history of Prussia has a nature peculiar to itself. It is neither the history of a nation nor of a country. Neither is it the history of institutions which have grown from internal organic life. The Prussian state was a mere body of assorted military and administrative regulations. Nor again was Prussia the organic development out of an antecedent state of things, but rather a residuum out of the dissolution of the German Empire and the degradation of Poland. Out of these ruins modern Prussia was formed. Yet Droysen fantastically and chauvinistically derived the origin and progress of the Prussian monarchy from the internal necessity of German national development, the core of which he found in the Mark Brandenburg—a country originally Slavic and only Germanized in later times. He adroitly wove the history of Prussia into the web of an apparently national German history and often represented events as though the politics of Europe revolved around Berlin. The German Empire and the German people are regarded only as material for the aggrandizement of the House of Hohenzollern.

The absurdity of the arguments of the Prussian school is shown when we examine the historical facts. Prussia under Frederick William II, Frederick William III, and Frederick William IV knew nothing of her "German mission." She often went astray and stopped short in her policy. Much as the Hohenzollerns did for the Prussian state, they always in fact remained Hohenzollerns. This is why they sacrificed the left bank of the Rhine in 1795. This is why they dragged the heroes of the War of Liberation in 1813–14 before their tribunals and at Spandau and Köpnick furnished ocular demonstration to the youth of Germany that it was easier to die than to live for German freedom. And this also explains why Frederick William IV declined to accept the German imperial crown.

The French historian Taine, who greatly admired German scholar-

---

[22] "The Greeks by themselves," Droysen wrote, "were not able to realize their national unity: neither Athens, nor Sparta, nor Thebes was able to place itself at the head of the movement. They were continually in a state of rivalry. . . . The idea of the 'city state' dominated their minds. They did not consider the greatness of Greece. To them Greece was nothing. It was necessary for a barbarian to see this, to synthesize their civilization and spread it throughout the world." GUILLAND, 215 note; cp. J. R. Knipfing's paper read before the American Historical Association, 1919, "German Historians and Macedonian Imperialism," quoted by J. W. Swain, "What is History?" *Journal of Philosophy*, XX (1923), 314.

ship,[23] in a conversation with Karl Hillebrand in 1869 summed up the teaching of the Prussian school thus:

> We [the Germans say] renewed Europe, rescued the world from Roman decadence and ancient corruption by invasion, in the fourth and fifth centuries. . . . In the sixteenth century we originated Protestantism—a moral renovation. . . . Nations which are in the fullness of their growth . . . have shaken off the Roman yoke. . . . In Italy and Spain free-thought is smothered. . . . For the last sixty years all their books, all their historical, philological, ethnographical and philosophical researches have told them [the Germans] that they are the elect race.[24]

The work is written on an abstract plane, in impossibly turgid prose, and is devoid of personal portraiture, of anecdotes, of human color. Hegelian in his ideology,[25] Droysen emphasizes continuity and growth as a sort of divine and irresistible process. He is also a worthy disciple of his teacher Hegel in his total disregard of economic and social conditions—pure idealism must not be marred by mundane considerations.

Droysen expressed his more formal thoughts in a little booklet entitled *Grundriss der Historik*, which the English translator has called the "weightiest" book of its time,[26] but which a French critic uncharitably described as "a veritable Chinese head-racker written in German gibberish." [27] History, says Droysen, finds its full application in the upward and onward motion in nature; the science of history is the result of empirical perception, experience, and investigation; the essence of historical method is understanding by means of investigation. Man's nature speaks forth from its inner processes. "The combined influence of times, peoples, states, religions, etc., is only a sort of an expression of the absolute totality." The moral world, ceaselessly moved by many ends, is in a state of restless development, growing "on and on, as man eternalizes himself." The successive stages of this movement in the moral world is History; every advancing step gives us wider and deeper

---

[23] "They are superior to all from two points of view: (1) Erudition, . . . enormous reading, the exhausting of the subject. . . . (2) The philosophical spirit, panoramic views, general ideas; these are to be found even in the third- or fourth-rate men. . . . A German will not complete the expression of his thought until he has previously collected all his materials." *Life and Letters of Taine*, tr. by Mrs. R. L. Devonshire (London, 1902–08, 3 v.), II, 304–06.

[24] *Ibid.*, II, 299–300.

[25] To Hegel all history was a manifestation of a single force, whose works are just and whose latest achievement (i.e., Prussia) is best. The State is in the moral order what Nature is in the physical world. It is "a form of Reason or of Idea, realizing itself as Will. It is the Supreme Right, over against individuals, whose first duty is to be members of it." There is an immense literature on Hegel, but it lies beyond the limits of this work. See F. A. Lange, *History of Materialism and Criticism of Its Present Importance*, tr. by E. C. Thomas (Boston, 1881, 3 v.), II, 239–62; Acton (n. 9), 360–62; and especially Hegel's *Lectures on the Philosophy of History*, tr. by J. Sibree (London, 1857).

[26] Leipzig, 1867; English translation by E. B. Andrews as *Outline of the Principles of History* (Boston, 1893). The new German edition prepared by Rudolf Hübner (Berlin, 1937) has been much enlarged by the incorporation of other essays and studies of Droysen.

[27] GUILLAND, 216. The *Historik* is obscure, not to say unintelligible, to those unfamiliar with the jargon of Hegelian philosophy.

historical understanding. "The knowledge of History is History itself." Historical things have their truth in the moral forces, as natural things have theirs in the natural "laws," mechanical, physical, chemical, etc. Historical things are the perpetual actualization of these moral forces. To think historically means to see their truth in the realities resulting from that moral energy.

One may conclude with Droysen's Hegelian definitions of the State and of Freedom, two favorite words in German metaphysics.

The State assumes to be the sum, the united organism, of all the moral partnerships, their common home and harbor, and so far their end. . . . In the life of the State and of States, authority is thus the essential thing. . . . The law of authority is valid in the political world like that of gravity in the world of matter. . . . The State is not the sum of the individuals whom it comprehends, nor does it arise from their will, nor does it exist on account of their will.

The life pulse of historical movement is freedom. The word "freedom" has been understood differently at different times. Primarily it has only a negative meaning. The real meaning of freedom is unhindered participation in the life and work of each one of the moral spheres, not being disturbed or hampered in one of them by another, and not being excluded from any.

The youngest and best-known representative of the Prussian school was Heinrich von Treitschke (1834–96).[28] Unlike his admirer Droysen, Treitschke was not wholly a German in blood. By descent he was partly Saxon and partly Slav. "A tall, broad-shouldered figure," so writes an admiring friend, "dark hair and dark complexion, dark, pensive eyes, now dreamy, now vividly glistening—unmistakably Slav. With his black hair, the heavy mustache . . . and his vivid gesticulations, he could not conceal his Slav origin." [29] Treitschke's non-German origin must be emphasized, not merely because it is an ironic phenomenon that the most passionate champion of the Hohenzollerns should have been a "foreigner," but also because it placed him in opposition to his own background and family ties, which in turn resulted in a notorious lack of balance.

Treitschke was born in Dresden, the son of a Saxon general. Though

[28] The literature on Treitschke is considerable. See H. Eckerlin, *Heinrich von Treitschke* (Leipzig, 1898); M. A. Mügge, *Heinrich von Treitschke* (London and New York, 1915); T. Schiemann, *Heinrich von Treitschkes Lehr- und Wanderjahre, 1834–1866* (Munich, 1896); Adolf Hausrath, *Treitschke, His Doctrine of German Destiny and of International Relations Together with a Study of His Life and Work* (New York and London, 1914); W. Rittinghaus, *Die Kunst der Geschichtschreibung Heinrich von Treitschkes* (Leipzig, 1914); Ernst Leipprand, *Heinrich von Treitschke im deutschen Geistesleben des 19. Jahrhundert* (Stuttgart, 1935); O. Umfrid, *Anti-Treitschke* (Esslingen, 1907); GOOCH, 147–55; FUETER, 677–83; WOLF, 242 note; DAHLMANN-WAITZ, 14718–21, and 15510; GUILLAND, 254–325; H. v. Petersdorff in *Allgemeine deutsche Biographie*, LV, 263–326; P. Bailleu, "Heinrich von Treitschke," *Deutsche Rundschau*, LXXXIX (1896), 41–76, 237–71; K. A. v. Müller, "Treitschke als Journalist," *HZ*, CXXXV (1927), 382–412; and for bibliography, S. K. Padover, "Treitschke: Forerunner of Hitlerism," *Pacific Historical Review*, IV (1935), 161–70.

[29] Hausrath (n. 28), 7–8.

his early environment was "particularist" and anti-Prussian, Treitsch-ke evinced nationalist and unificatory sentiments in his teens. Having become deaf in childhood, the young man found an outlet for his militant emotions in martial verse. But he was not destined to become a poet, mainly because his first book of poetry was received with indifference. He attended the universities of Leipzig, Tübingen, Göttingen, and Bonn; in the last institution he came under the influence of Dahlmann. "He," Treitschke relates, "told me I must serve my fatherland; and as he gave me his hand with a piercing look, I gained courage and became conscious how much I had to do." Determined to become an historian, Treitschke went to Heidelberg, where Häusser inculcated in him patriotic sentiments similar to those of Dahlmann.

In 1858, the brilliant young poet-patriot became *Dozent* at the University of Leipzig and in the following year he published his *Gesellschaft-wissenschaft* (Leipzig, 1859). In this *Science of Society* Treitschke tried to show the inter-relation between politics (Prussian politics) and society, and to prove that "every effort of national life always tends towards reforms, at once political, social and religious." The book was at bottom a tract for German unification under Prussian hegemony, pretending to show "scientifically" the development of Prussian politics and the "sociological" inferiority of small states—"in little states monarchy has never been anything but a caricature."

From 1858 to 1863 Treitschke remained at Leipzig; in 1863 he went to Freiburg, where he stayed until 1866 when he was called to Kiel. In 1867 he became professor at Heidelberg; finally, he went to Berlin, where he taught from 1874 to his death in 1896. Between 1871 and 1888 he was a member of the Reichstag as a supporter of Bismarck. After Ranke's death in 1886 Treitschke was appointed Historiographer Royal of Prussia.

From the point of view of influence, Treitschke must be studied in a triple capacity: as a teacher, as a political agitator, and as an historian. As a lecturer and speaker he was worthy of Dahlmann. One of the greatest orators of his time, Treitschke swayed large audiences by his impassioned eloquence. Overcome by the rush of his rhetoric, Treitschke's listeners forgot to notice his raucous, hoarse, screaming voice—the voice of the deaf—and his bobbing head which trembled as "if affected by some nervous disease." What he preached, with all the conviction of an inspired prophet, was the pride and power of a united Germany and the degeneracy and inferiority of non-Germans.

One of Treitschke's listeners at Heidelberg was Dietrich Schäfer, who became professor of history at Berlin nine years after the great orator's death. Schäfer relates:

Treitschke lectured only on modern history. . . . In him the German youth saw the embodiment of its ideals; he was the inspired and inspiring prophet of German unity, his clear and firm political opinions being its infallible guide. His lectures were by far the most attended. The fact that practically every one of his sentences was a world judgment, this attracted more than it repelled. His candidness was refreshing. . . . I doubt whether since the days of Fichte any German professor made a greater impression on students than Heinrich von Treitschke.[30]

Treitschke's political ideas, which he disseminated in the form of lectures, speeches, and articles, were those of a special pleader and agitator, rather than an historian.[31] The best that can be said for them is that they made no pretense to being anything else than political ammunition. Sneering at objectivity as "bloodless," Treitschke frankly admitted that he was "a thousand times more of a patriot than a professor." Following Hegel, Treitschke preached the absolute superiority of the state. "The state is not an academy of arts or a bourse; it is power." He constantly emphasized the "stern and terrible" doctrine that the "state is a society united for offensive or defensive war." Outdoing the Hohenzollerns in realism and the Nazis in vehemence, Treitschke positively denied that the state rests on either the consent or the good-will of its subjects; "its laws must be observed, willingly or unwillingly." The state says to the subject: "It makes no difference to me what you think—you have got to obey."

Two consequences followed from this conception of the state; first, only a large and powerful government was worthy of respect; second, war was the greatest good of a strong state. Hence Treitschke's unrestrained hatred of the small German states and peoples. The emotional patriot poured venom and contempt on the hapless non-Prussians. To him they were "sub-Germans," "Philistines," "their rottenness stinking to heaven." In 1866 Treitschke wrote that Hanover, Hesse, and Saxony were "ripe and over-ripe for annihilation." Such ideas, expressed with tremendous force and propagated widely, did much to pave the way for Bismarck's work of unification.

As for war, Treitschke considered it the noblest activity of man. "War must be taken as part of the divinely appointed order." War, springing from "human sins and passions," had true "moral majesty."

We live in a warlike age; the oversentimental philanthropic fashion of judging things has passed into the background. . . . All the peacemakers in the world will never make

[30] Dietrich Schäfer, *Mein Leben* (Berlin and Leipzig, 1926), 63–64.
[31] Many of Treitschke's political articles and essays have been published in his *Historische und politische Aufsätze* (Leipzig, 1886–96, 4 v.); *Zehn Jahre deutscher Kämpfe* [1865–74] (Berlin, 1874), and his *Deutsche Kämpfe, neue Folge* (Leipzig, 1896). For his political speeches see *Reichstagsreden* (Leipzig, 1896). His lectures on politics have been published posthumously by M. Cornicelius, *Politik* (Berlin, 1898, 2 v.); an English translation, *Politics* by B. Dugdale and T. de Bille, appeared in 2 volumes in 1916. Other English selections are to be found in

the political powers all of one mind, and until they are, the sword will be the only arbiter. We have learned to perceive the moral majesty of war through the very processes which to the superficial observer seem brutal and inhuman. The greatness of war is just what at first sight seems to be its horror—that for the sake of their country men will overcome the natural feelings of humanity, that they will slaughter their fellow-men who have done them no injury, nay, whom they perhaps respect as chivalrous foes. Man will not only sacrifice his life, but the natural and justified instincts of his soul; his very self he must offer up for the sake of patriotism; here we have the sublimity of war. . . . He who knows history knows also that to banish war from the world would be to mutilate human nature.[32]

Treitschke's glorification of war, a sentiment which met with a warm response in imperial Germany, was not without ulterior motives. The spokesman of the Junker-dominated monarchy, Treitschke expressed the current opinions of the military about the need and desirability for armed conquest. The Germans, so this pre-Nazi doctrine ran, had given civilization to Europe. "Who was it," Treitschke asked, "who first showed the Scandinavian and the Muscovite the wide horizons of their own nationality? Copenhagen was as German as Novgorod." There was no Roman or Frenchman to ask Treitschke who gave civilization to the Germans. "The Germans," he wrote with an astonishing disregard for historic truth, "have carried out the greatest colonization which the world has known since Roman times." From this it followed that the Germans should dominate Europe once more. "Our age is an age of war, our age is an age of iron. . . . If the strong prevail over the weak . . . it is an indisputable law of life." By means of this right of *Macht*, Germany was to revive the naval glory of the old Hansa—this, incidentally, led to the naval rivalry with England and finally to the first World War—, should acquire Holland, and break the power of Britain. "We have settled accounts with Austria, France, and Russia; the reckoning with England is still to come."[33] It did— in 1914.

As an historian, Treitschke displayed all the virtues and shortcomings of an emotional patriot. His *Deutsche Geschichte im neunzehnten Jahrhundert*, extending to the year 1848,[34] is perhaps the most brilliant achievement in German literary scholarship. Despite its fierce bias and crude blatancies, the *History of Germany* is a masterpiece. It

Treitschke's *Germany, France, Russia and Islam* (London, 1915); in A. L. Gowans, tr., *Selections from Treitschke's Lectures on Politics* (London, 1914), and in Hausrath (n. 28), 137–332.

[32] Treitschke, *Politics* (n. 31), II, 395–96.

[33] Treitschke, *Deutsche Kämpfe, neue Folge* (n. 31), 349, 395. England knew of Treitschke's fierce hatred, which caused much ill-feeling on the eve of the first World War; see especially J. W. Headlam, "Heinrich von Treitschke," *EHR*, XII (1897), 727–47; cp. "The Political Philosophy of Treitschke," *QR*, CCXXVI (1916), 176–95.

[34] Leipzig, 1878–94, 5 v., totalling 3,733 pages; English translation by E. and C. Paul under title: *Treitschke's History of Germany in the Nineteenth Century* (London, 1915–19, 7 v.).

has every possible fault—unfairness, vehemence, one-sidedness, chauvinism, brutality, unrestrained passion—yet the narrative is gripping as an epic poem. Essentially a poet, Treitschke wrote his history as a combination of literature and scholarship; his style is more sparkling than that of any other German historian. The ideas are the same as those expressed in his *Politics,* but the structure is finer, more comprehensive, and the scholarship is thorough and exacting. The work, covering as it does every aspect of the national life, poetry and art, politics and science, throbs with life because the author possessed two qualities which no historian is supposed to have: he knew how to hate and he knew how to express his hatred in glowing words. "My blood, alas," he admitted, "is too hot for an historian."

It is quite true that, judged by ordinary canons of taste or science, Treitschke was right in confessing that he was not a scientific historian. But he was a splendid writer, who would have made his reputation either as a journalist or as a novelist. The following malicious pen-portrait of Emperor Francis II at the Congress of Vienna may serve as a characteristic example of Treitschke's ardent manner of writing; one should keep in mind that Treitschke hated both Catholics and Austrians:

Emperor Francis, the host of the assembly, played, not without ability, his part of honourable patriarch among the high nobility . . . the crafty reckoner knew well the advantages he gained by the position of host. How touching, to the serene highnesses who were his guests, seemed this unpretending figure in a shabby blue coat, with his good-natured petty bourgeois manners. . . . The mask of the frank, true-hearted, blunt Austrian, which he . . . assumed, now fitted him like a glove, because it was suited to his phlegmatic disposition and to his vulgar inclinations. No one could ever induce him to feel any sentiment of cordial benevolence; the changes of destiny of this gigantic time passed over his dull egoism without leaving a trace. He never commuted a death-sentence unless the offender himself begged for death; he himself supervised the maltreatment of political prisoners, himself determined the weight of the chains, and the number of the days of fasting, and knew no more enjoyable recreation than the reading of intercepted letters; he had already lost two wives, and was soon to bury the third, in order with invincible equanimity to marry the fourth. . . . Notwithstanding the evil expression in his cold, hard eyes, notwithstanding his close resemblance to Philip II of Spain to whom he was akin . . . in spirit, all the world believed in the child-like innocence of the heartless and suspicious despot. His political system was the simplest possible. . . . He wished at length to secure his own peace, wished at length to function as a diligent privy councillor, covering the margins of official documents with unmeaning observations, to play the fiddle in his leisure hours, cut out paper images, varnish bird-cages, and engage in other imperial dissipations. Stupid and dull-witted like the majority of his forefathers, completely incapable of even beginning to understand a new political thought, he regarded all the revolutionary and national ideas which were animating the new century as nothing more than wickedness and stupidity, as merely a punishable rebellion against the pious archducal house. With this poverty of spirit there was, however, associated a thorough-going peasant cunning. . . .[35]

[35] *History of Germany* (n. 34), II, 10–11.

As Fueter rightly observes, Treitschke's influence on German historiography was not great. Where he wielded enormous influence was on public opinion. In fact, his utterances were so widely accepted in Germany that he came to be regarded abroad as the official spokesman of the Reich, and one of Germany's foremost war-mongers. When the first World War broke out, more than a dozen hostile books on Treitschke appeared in London. Treitschke himself was the last great representative of the Prussian school of history. After him, as Max Lenz points out, German historians reverted to the old Ranke ideal of non-partisan historiography. In any case, German unity was achieved and there was no longer any need for vehement special pleading or impassioned polemics, until the rise of Nazism and Hitler.

BOOK VIII

*FRENCH AND ENGLISH HISTORIANS OF THE
NINETEENTH CENTURY*

CHAPTER XLIV

FRENCH HISTORIANS (1814–48) [1]

THE dominant idea of French historiography in the nineteenth century may be summarized in one word: Revolution. French historians were the inheritors of the ideas as well as the passions which had convulsed France between 1789 and 1815. To a nation that had been through the miseries and the glories of the First Republic and the First Empire, the Revolution was not merely a change in government, but a vital reality, an emotional experience which amounted to a transformation in the national psychology. In 1815 France was weary, exhausted, profoundly shaken, but not defeated; she was, at bottom, boundlessly proud of her almost epic achievements under the Consulate and the Empire, although it took years to stabilize the new traditions, and to achieve a balanced lucidity.

Whatever the Revolution may or may not have been, one thing it always was to Frenchmen: a great reality and not just a story which one reads in books. The country had not merely emerged changed in its most vital ideologies and basic institutions, but there were many active men who personally continued the great tradition, whether as poets like Hugo or historians like Michelet. It is a significant fact that as far down as the fourth quarter of the nineteenth century many men eminent in politics and literature personally remembered the Revolution or Napoleon. To take but three examples: Guizot was born two years before the French Revolution, and he lived until 1874, that is,

[1] For general accounts see GOOCH, chs. ix–xiii; FUETER, 551–67, 625–29, 632–39; HALPHEN, with bibliographical notes, 185–209; Gustave Lanson, *Manuel bibliographique de la littérature française moderne, 1500–1900* (rev. ed., Paris, 1921, 5 v.), IV; Louis Bourdeau, *L'Histoire et les historiens* (Paris, 1888); G. Monod, "Du progrès des études historiques en France depuis le XVIᵉ siècle," *RH*, I (1876), 5–34; C. Louandre, "Les études historiques en France depuis la guerre," *RDM*, XIX (1877), 428–56; Seignobos, "Histoire générale de l'Europe depuis 1814," *RCC*, II (1893), 40–43; Marcel Poëte, "Les sources de l'histoire de Paris et les historiens de Paris," *Revue bleue*, IV (1905), 693–95; G. Monod, "La chaire d'histoire au collège de France," *ibid.*, IV (1905), 801–06; *ER*, LXXIII (1841), 84–120; Carl Becker, "Some Aspects of the Influence of Social Problems and Ideas upon the Study and Writing of History," *Publications of the American Sociological Society*, VII (1913), 73–107.

On the historians of the French Revolution see H. M. Stephens, "Historiography of the French Revolution," *Annual Report of the American Historical Association*, X, 38 ff.; anon., "Historians of the First French Revolution," *BQR*, X (1849), 168–92; F. Harrison, "Historians of the French Revolution," *NAR*, CXXXVII; L. R. Gottschalk, "The French Revolution: Conspiracy or Circumstance," in *Persecution and Liberty, Essays in Honor of George Lincoln Burr* (New York, 1931), 445–72; "The Mendacity of History," in my *Byways in Bookland* (Berkeley, 1935), 147–52; H. Baudrillart, "Les historiens de la révolution française et de la révolution de février," *RDM*, IV (1850), 808–931.

after the establishment of the Third Republic. Michelet, who died in the same year as Guizot, was born one year before Bonaparte became First Consul. Lamartine was born in the second year of the Revolution and died just one year before the fall of Napoleon III. The longevity of French authors may have had something to do with it, but the living link was, nonetheless, of great importance in moulding French ideas and movements in the nineteenth century.

Under Napoleon France wrote little history; she was too busy making it. Nor did the Emperor encourage such a contemplative (and sometimes critical) intellectual luxury as historiography. He did not mind historians, so long as they devoted themselves to glorifying him. A practical statesman, the Emperor saw no reason for wasting time on the past, especially on his rivals the Bourbons. If historians wished to write, they should expose the weaknesses of the ancient French monarchy and church.[2] In other words, history should be written from an anti-Bourbon and anti-clerical point of view for the greater glory of Bonaparte. Few scholars cared for such a task.

After the fall of Napoleon there was a strong movement in the direction of Romanticism in literature and nationalism in historiography. Romanticism and nationalism, in fact, tended to fuse into one stream. One might almost say that literature became remotely historical and history vividly literary. Still shaken by the recent events, men sought escape in the distant and the unreal. The succession of dynasties, the rise and fall of kingdoms and republics, led to an investigation of the immediate past, and that, in turn, to the remote past. Literature and historiography marched hand in hand, each trying to explain, to justify, to understand, and—not least—to escape from, the present. The novelist-poet Victor Hugo wrote two semi-historical works. The poet Lamartine composed the history of the Girondins. Michelet always remained a poet at heart and a novelist in skill. Historical romances were the most popular literature in France.

Yet if Romanticism was the over-current, there were also under-currents —Royalist reactionism and Catholic reaction. The latter was of two kinds: there was an ecclesiastical-political reactionary school, and a Catholic romantic school, of which Chateaubriand was the leading representative. His *Génie du Christianisme* (1802) was the Bible of Romanticism.[3]

---

[2] *Correspondance de Napoléon Ier* (Paris, 1858–69, 32 v.), XVI, 575–77, April 12, 1808. Cp. the notes which Napoleon dictated in 1807 about the establishment of schools for history: "History and legislation should be placed in the first rank. . . . The second place should be held by the history of military art." See P. Frédéricq, "The Study of History in Germany and France," tr. from the French by Henrietta Leonard in *Johns Hopkins University Studies in Historical and Political Science*, Eighth Series, V–VI (1890), 59, n. 1. This is a valuable study.

[3] G. M. Brandes, *Die Hauptströmungen der Literatur des neunzehnten Jahrhunderts* (Leipzig,

The first emanations of Romanticism, we have seen, are to be found in Germany, and are to be primarily attributed to the influence of Herder. There are some who erroneously ascribe the introduction of Romanticism in France to Madame De Staël's *De l'Allemagne* (1810). France borrowed almost nothing from Germany in the literature of the Restoration. English literature, not German, was the popular foreign literature. Heine and Renan were the first to introduce German ideas into France.[4]

I believe [Augustin Thierry wrote in 1820] that the moment has come when the public is going to have a greater taste for history than for any other serious reading. Perhaps it is the order of civilization that after a period which has been strongly stirred by ideas there comes one moved by facts; perhaps we are tired of listening to slander of the past, as of an unknown person. . . . The reading of the romances of Walter Scott has turned many thoughts towards the Middle Ages from which not long ago one turned away with disdain; and if in our time there should be a revolution in the manner of reading and writing of history, these works [Scott's], frivolous in appearance, will have contributed to it in a singular way.[5]

Thierry, who was himself active in producing a taste for history, proved to be a prophet. The period of romance was succeeded by one of document-collecting, and the latter by historical interpretation. Under the stimulus of the historian-statesman Guizot, committees for the publication of historical documents were organized, and, with the financial aid of the government, they published thousands of documents in hundreds of volumes. The Paris and provincial archives were ransacked for "all the unedited and important documents of an historical character, such as manuscripts, charters, diplomas, chronicles, memoirs, correspondence, works even of philosophy, literature or art, provided that they disclosed some unknown aspect of the customs and the social state of any epoch in our history."[6] In connection with this movement toward documentary history the famous École des Chartes was founded in 1821, for the purpose of training palaeographers, bibliographers, and librarians. For years it was the only school of its kind in the world, and it produced some of the most brilliant technical scholars in the field, men like Quicherat, Lalanne, Bourquelot, and Himly. In the 1880's a Belgian scholar described it as "an institution without equal," a school which "furnishes the most solid, complete

1893–96, 6 v.), III. *Die Reaktion in Frankreich;* Harold Höffding, *History of Modern Philosophy* (London, 1900, 2 v.), II, 296–98.
    [4] *Life and Letters of H. Taine,* tr. by Mrs. R. L. Devonshire (London, 1902–08, 3 v.), III, 97. Cp. Taine's thoughtful exposition that there is a philosophy under all literature, in his *Histoire de la littérature anglaise* (Paris, 1911, 5 v.), I, 221–27.
    [5] Augustin Thierry, *Lettres sur l'histoire de France* (Paris, 1867), 59. Cp. HALPHEN, 19.
    [6] Xavier Charmes, *Le Comité des travaux historiques et scientifiques* (Paris, 1886, 3 v.), II, 14; see also *LQR,* LIX (1883), 401–30.

and truly scientific historical instruction to be found in Paris." [7] Other historical schools and institutions were organized later in the century— each with its own publications.

The man who set the fashion for the romantic type of history was Augustin Thierry (1795–1856),[8] a poor boy who was educated in the École Normale. A liberal and idealist, Thierry was for a time the secretary and "adopted son" of Saint Simon. Chateaubriand's *Les Martyrs* aroused his interest in history. The July Revolution, of which he was an ardent champion, further stimulated his historical zeal; but before that happened, he had already published two works which made him famous.

In his *Dix ans d'études historiques* (1834), Thierry relates his intellectual experiences from 1817 to 1827, a period when he wrote his histories of the English and the French people. His best-known work is the *Histoire de la conquête de l'Angleterre par les Normands*, which gave an impulse to the study of early English history; it was first published in 1825, and in the *Dix ans* Thierry tells how he came to write it. Eager to "win fame by picking history out of a parcel of monkish chronicles," Thierry roamed through libraries in search of knowledge.

> One day, when reading attentively some chapters in Hume, I was struck with a thought which appeared to me a ray of light, and closing the book, I cried, "All this dates from a Conquest; there is a conquest at the bottom!" Instantly I conceived the project of remaking the history of the English Revolutions by considering them from this new point of view.

While collecting materials for this purpose, his attention was attracted to French history as the background of the Norman adventure in 1066.

> I resolved . . . to build my *epopée*, to write the History of the Conquest of England by the Normans, by mounting up to its first causes, in order subsequently to descend to its latest consequences; to paint this grand event in the truest colors, and under the greatest number of aspects; and, as the theatre for such diversified scenes, to take not England only, but all the countries far and near, which had felt the influence of Norman settlements, or the repercussions of the Norman victory.

[7] Read Frédéricq's account in *Johns Hopkins University Studies* (n. 2), 58–66; cp. A. Giry, "Jules Quicherat," *RH*, XIX (1882), 241–64; F. le Play, "La vieille France, l'École des chartes et la Société d'économie sociale," *La Réforme sociale*, XXII (1891), 21–50.

[8] On Thierry see GOOCH, 169–73; FUETER, 558–62; Ernest Renan in his *Essais de morale et de critique* (Paris, 1864); Léon Aubineau, *Augustin Thierry et son système historique et ses erreurs* (2nd ed., Paris, 1879), an ultramontane critique; Arbois de Jubainville, *Deux manières d'écrire l'histoire; critique de Bossuet, d'Augustin Thierry et de Fustel de Coulanges* (Paris, 1896); Ferdinand Brunetière, "L'oeuvre d'Augustin Thierry," *RDM*, CXXXII (1895), 469–80; Camille Jullian, "Augustin Thierry et le mouvement historique sous la restauration," *RSH*, XIII (1906), 129–42. For some reviews see *FQR*, VI (1930), 283–321; *NAR*, LXXII (1851), 316–43; *QR*, LXXIV (1844), 284–91; *JS*, 1855, pp. 73–84, 366–79, 734–46, and 1856, pp. 337–47.

This was an ambitious project, magnificently conceived; and if carried out to its logical conclusion, the History of the Norman Conquest would have been a history of Europe in the central period of the Middle Ages. Such a work required long and patient and hard labor, and Thierry did not stint himself.

By dint of devouring long folio pages to extract a single phrase, and, in some cases, a single word, out of a thousand, my eyes acquired a faculty which astonished me, and for which I cannot account; that of reading, as it were, by intuition, and of falling almost immediately on the passage that ought to have an interest for me. . . . In the species of ecstasy which absorbed all my internal faculties, while my hand was turning over the leaves of the volume, or putting down notes, I had no consciousness of what passed around me. . . . The officials of the library and curious visitors came and went through the hall; I heard nothing, I saw nothing;—I saw only the apparitions called up in my soul by what I read. . . .

The work, whose success was instantaneous, was distinguished by three qualities. Admittedly influenced by Walter Scott ("My admiration for this great writer was profound"), Thierry wrote with all the verve and vividness of a novelist. A disciple of Saint Simon, he endowed his history with a passion for social justice. But Thierry inclined to see history too much as drama, as color, or as passion. His political theories and racial notions are highly dubious. Apart from the dramatic aspects of history, he saw in the historic process a struggle between the weak and the strong. This should not be confused with the "class struggle" concept of the Marxists. Where the more realistic Marxists, in a later period, saw all history as a conflict between impersonal forces, Thierry merely *personalized* this struggle and gave it an emotional tone. His work was essentially a party pamphlet in which the Anglo-Saxons represented the Third Estate in France and the Normans the French noblesse of the Restoration in 1814. Accordingly, Godwin and Harold were exalted as patriots and heroes, and William the Conqueror and his barons denounced as tyrants. Consider, for instance, the following passage from his *History of the Conquest*, in which Thierry expresses his sympathies with the conquered Anglo-Saxons:

Centuries after centuries passed away; yet, notwithstanding the predictions of the poets, the lands of the ancient Britons did not come back again to the hands of their descendants. If the foreign oppressor was vanquished, it was not by the nation justly entitled to this retributive victory. . . . The narrative of the reverses of the Anglo-Saxons, invaded and subjugated in their turn by a people from beyond the seas, will occupy the following pages. And here this race, hitherto victorious over all those that had preceded it in Britain, will excite a species of interest to which it had not previously given rise; for its cause will become the good cause, the cause of the suffering and oppressed. . . . In the presence of the old documents wherein these sufferings are described with a minuteness and a naiveté which seem actually to bring before us the men of remote ages, a sentiment of gentle pity awakens in our hearts, and blending with the impartiality of the historian, softens him, without in the least impairing his determination to be honest and just.[8a]

By and large, this was a remarkable work, unique in its emphasis on the history of the people, rather than the state. Thierry's faults—excessive dramatization, exaggerated coloring, emotionalism—are outweighed by his positive qualities. Here was a history vivid and lucid and full of feeling, a history brought home to the experience of the reader, and not merely a learned chronicle. It had an extraordinary success and a deep influence, especially on Michelet.[9]

Jules Michelet (1798–1874) [10] was a scholar, a poet, an historian, a

[8a] *History of the Conquest of England by the Normans* (London, 1885, Bohns Standard Library), I, 54.

[9] Augustin Thierry was also the author of *Récits des temps mérovingiens* (1840, 2 v.; 3rd ed., 1847); *Lettres sur l'histoire de France* (1827); *Essai sur l'histoire de la formation et des progrès du tiers état* (1853).

Not to be confused with Augustin Thierry is his brother Amédée Thierry (1797–1873), author of *Histoire des Gaulois* (1828–45, 3 v.); *Recits de l'histoire romaine au Ve siècle: La lutte contre les Barbares*, [and] *Les luttes religieuses* (1860; 2nd ed. in 6 v., 1880); *Nouveaux récits de l'histoire romaine aux IVe et Ve siècle. Trois ministres des fils de Théodose: Rufin—Eutrope—Stilican*. (Paris, 1865), which Mignet called "si curieux et si émouvant"; *Histoire d'Attila et de ses successeurs* (Paris, 1856, 2 v.), "aussi pittoresque que vraie." The *History of the Gauls*, which heads this list, covers a period of seventeen centuries; it is an attempt to create a unified story out of disconnected and fragmentary materials. Amédée Thierry admitted the difficulty. "C'était," he said, "essayer d'organiser un corps avec les lambeaux et d'y faire descendre une âme." Like his brother, he wrote vividly and well, and, again like his brother, he met with great success. Napoleon III, when still a prisoner, read his work with enthusiasm; on that occasion the future emperor made a significant comment: "I am going to read M. Amédée Thierry. There is serious and true history; what difference does it make if Tiberius was cruel and that Caligula had named his horse Consul, if they advanced the people in the great politics of the Caesars? Because the Tiber carries muddy waters, is it then less a stream which irrigates the eternal city?" When he became emperor, Napoleon, appreciating a historian who had shown the necessity of the Roman Empire, appointed Amédée Thierry Councillor of State in 1853 and Senator in 1860. See Mignet, "Notice historique sur la vie et les travaux de M. Amédée Thierry," *ASMP*, CVII (1877), 652–714; and *FQR*, X, (1832), 138–50.

Another member of the Walter Scott school was Prosper Brugière, Baron de Barante (1782–1866), a monarchist diplomat, whose *Histoire des ducs de Bourgogne* (13 v.; 1824 f.) was frankly a dramatic narrative, a glorified historical romance. His motto was *Historia scribitur ad narrandum, non ad probandum*. His other pseudo-historical works, especially on the French Revolution, were marred by a violent anti-republican prejudice. See Gooch, 173–75; Fueter, 557–58; Baron de Barante, *Souvenirs* (Paris, 1890–1901, 8 v.), III; Guizot, "M. de Barante, ses souvenirs de famille, sa vie et ses oeuvres," *RDM*, LXX (1867), 5–66; Sainte-Beuve, "Historiens modernes de la France. III. M. de Barante," *ibid.*, 1843, pt. 1, 917–35; Aulard, "M. de Barante, historien de la convention nationale," *Révolution française*, LXI (1911), 428–34, a review of Barante's *Histoire de la Convention Nationale*, 1851–53, 6 v.).

[10] See Michelet's *Oeuvres complètes* (Paris, 1893–98). The following are autobiographical works: *Ma jeunesse* (1884); *Mon journal*, from 1820 to 1823 (1888); *Un hiver en Italie* (1879); *Sur les chemins de l'Europe* (1893). Gabriel Monod has written most of the critical appreciations of Michelet, see *Jules Michelet, études sur sa vie et ses oeuvres* (Paris, 1905), reviewed in *EHR*, XXI (1906), 395–96; the same, *Les maîtres de l'histoire: Renan, Taine, Michelet* (Paris, 1903); and his articles, "Michelet, de 1843 à 1852," *RSH*, XVII (1908), 261–72, and "La place de Michelet dans l'histoire de son temps," *ASMP*, CLXXV (1911), 271–89. See also Fueter, 563–67; Gooch, 175–85; Halphen, 81–92, with a bibliography of his writings, 193–95; E. Chatelain, in *École pratique des hautes études, section des sciences historiques et philologiques. Annuaire*, 1912–13, 31 ff.; Mme. Quinet, *Cinquante ans d'amitié, Michelet-Quinet (1825–1875)* (2nd ed., Paris, 1903); Jean Brunhes, *Michelet* (Paris, 1898); Jules Simon, *Mignet, Michelet, Henri Martin* (Paris, 1890); Ernest Hamel, *M. Michelet historien* (Paris,

dramatic novelist, and a patriot. He vivified the past. *J'ai pris*, he said truthfully, *l'histoire pour la vie*. He not only took history for life, he lived himself into the past to an extent unexcelled before or since. His ideal of history was, literally, "resurrection."

Michelet was the son of a poor printer and his childhood was passed among a few great authors. Early in life he decided on the sacred calling of teaching. "I thought then, as Rousseau, that literature ought to be a thing reserved, the fine luxury of life, the inmost flower of the soul." His real profession was to teach. *L'enseignement*, said this child of French romanticism, *c'est le sacerdoce*. At the Collège Charlemagne which he attended he was not popular among his fellow-students, being small, sensitive, and shy "like an owl in the daylight." His brilliant school record brought him a teaching position at the Collège Sainte-Barbe, where he spent many happy years instructing the young. What was more important, he instructed himself. A voracious reader, he acquired a profound knowledge of literature, history, and science. One day he discovered Vico and his intellectual horizon widened to a clear perception of the interdependence of human thought. It was no accident that Michelet's first literary venture was an abridged edition of Vico's *Scienza Nuova* (1827), which won for the twenty-nine-year-old author a professorship at the École Normale.

In the same year Michelet published a remarkable little book, *Précis d'histoire moderne*, which had an appreciable influence in shaping French historical thought. Intended originally as a textbook for the students at Sainte-Barbe, the book was really no more than a *Précis*, and as such it became a manual for generations of teachers and students. The *Précis* was full of original ideas and novel interpretations. Michelet first developed the idea of a European equilibrium, not as a political theory but as a natural result of social evolution following the displacement of the feudal system by absolute monarchies. He also courted the resentment of patriots by not placing France at the head of the European powers in the early modern period; instead, he showed that the premier rôle was played by Italy, then by Germany, then by Spain,

1869); A. Ferey, *Jules Michelet et Hippolyte Taine* (Paris, 1910); Hippolyte Taine, *Essais de critique et d'histoire* (12th ed., Paris, 1913); Felix Rocquain, "Les travaux de Michelet aux archives nationales," in *Notes et fragments d'histoire* (Paris, 1906); Émile Gebhart's "Étude" of Michelet, prefixed to Michelet's *Précis de l'histoire de France au moyen âge* (Paris, 1898); Gustav Lanson, "La formation de la méthode historique de Michelet," *Revue d'histoire moderne et contemporaine*, VII (1905–06), 1–31; Ch. Langlois, "Michelet," *Questions d'histoire et d'enseignement*, n. s., 1906, pp. 33–95. For accounts and reviews in English see "Michelet as an Historian," *QR*, CXCIII (1901), 130–50, and LXXVI (1845), 299–354; *ER*, LXXIX (1844), 1–39 (a review of the first five volumes of his *Histoire de France*); *FQR*, XXV (1840), 420–46; *The Nation*, LXXXII (N. Y., 1906), 244–46; *BQR*, LXVI (1877), 369–94, and X (1849), 173–76; *LQR*, XLVI (1876), 425–51; and Gustave Lanson, "Historic Method of Jules Michelet," *International Quarterly*, XI (1905), 71–101.

and finally by France and England. His independence is likewise shown by a penetrating comment on the rôle of the Church. "Civil equality came to be established by the victory of the monarchy. The instruments of this revolution were the men of the Church and the legists. The Church, recruiting itself only by election in the midst of a universal hereditary system which gradually established itself in the Middle Ages, had raised the vanquished above the conquerors, the sons of bourgeois and even of serfs above the nobles. It is from them that the kings demanded ministers in their last struggle against the aristocracy." [11]

Another booklet, *An Introduction to Universal History,* published four years after the *Précis* (1831), shows a deepening of his historical outlook. Michelet now conceived history as a spiritual struggle, a conflict between the spirit and the flesh, a war between liberty and necessity. France was the apostle of liberty, the *peuple législateur* of the modern world. This actually was a turning point in Michelet's career. At last he found his mission; his lifework was to show the spirit and growth of the French people. France, he said, was the "center and the vital point of the world."

In the meantime Michelet was appointed chief of the Historical Department of the National Archives, and devoted much of his tireless energies to arranging and cataloguing the vast mass of scattered manuscripts. He was also busy lecturing at the École Normale, substituting for Guizot at the Sorbonne (1834 to 1836), filling the chair of history at the Collège de France (since 1837), and travelling throughout the country collecting materials. And all this time this *grand travailleur,* as his friends called him, was at work on his monumental *History of France.*

His ideas about history were taking definite shape. He intended to trace the intimate life of the people, to expose the national psychology. To that end he used ballads, coins, medallions, pictures, proverbs, architecture, and stained glass. To an historian of imagination all these historic remains were eloquent. The historian's task was to read meaning into these remains, contended Michelet; he must have the ability and the insight to reconstruct humanity as it had lived. Nor did he ignore the physical basis of civilization. He knew that climate, geography, food, the ways of making a living, determined man's behavior. These ideas, however, were implicit rather than stated. After all, he was a painter, a psychologist, a story teller, and not a formal scientist.

This is what France demands of us historians, not to make history . . . but to reestablish the chain of facts and ideas from which these results have issued. "I do not ask of

[11] See Monod's "Étude" of Michelet, prefixed to the *Précis de l'histoire moderne* (Paris, 1898), pp. i–xxxiv.

you," she says, "that you should make my creeds, and dictate my judgments; it is for you to receive them and conform yourself to them. The problem which I propose to you is to tell me how I came to act as I have acted, and to judge as I have judged."

In 1833 Michelet published the first volume of his *History of France* and by 1843 he had brought down his history to the close of the Middle Ages. At this point, when he was at work on the policy of Louis XI, his studies were interrupted by politics. Hitherto his work had absorbed him and though he was anti-clerical at heart, he took no open stand against the regime. But Louis Philippe had "sold out" to the Jesuits, and the latter in turn demanded from the king the control of education as the price of their support. The center of the battle was the Collège de France, founded by Francis I as an asylum of learning outside the clerical University of Paris; the Collège had remained more or less popular, lectures being open to the public. Now when the "Jesuit invasion" threatened the Collège the shy and retiring Professor Michelet faced a crisis. Should he, a liberal and republican, hide his head beneath a stack of manuscripts while the Church was making a drive against the secular mind? Or should he forget his books for a moment and enter the political arena in defense of the great French Revolutionary tradition? This crisis in Michelet's life has long been misunderstood; many critics have held that he became violently anticlerical and radical *after* his conflict with the Jesuits. In reality, as Gabriel Monod has shown conclusively, Michelet was hardly a Catholic even in his youth and his sympathy for the Revolution dated back to his student days. The first volume of his *History of France*, written more than a decade before his open break with the government, contains the following significant passage:

The middle ages could not suffice for the human species. . . . The temple had to widen . . ., humanity had to re-discover Christ himself. . . . The generalized ideal began to extend among the people. . . . It was necessary that the middle ages pass, that the traces of the completed middle ages vanish, that we see the death of all that we have loved, that which has suckled us when small, that which was our father and our mother, that which has sung to us tenderly in the cradle . . ., the condemned world was to go the way of the Roman world, the Greek world, the Oriental world. . . . Let us let Christianity undergo the universal law, to pass through the grave and re-enter in God, there to seek its purification.

If this passage means anything, it means that Michelet regarded Christianity as having come to an end with the end of the Middle Ages, that it was essentially a medieval religion, and that, consequently, it had no place in the modern world.

In 1843 Michelet, encouraged by his fellow-professors Edgar Quinet, the historian, and Adam Mickiewicz, the Polish poet, announced a

joint course of lectures with Quinet on "The Jesuits." Large crowds of
clericalists and liberals came to hear the famous professors. There were
some disturbances, although no violent interruptions. Some Catholic
students heckled the speaker; later the liberal students came in larger
numbers and intimidated the clericalists.[12] The result was that Michelet became a political figure, a center of conflict; free thinking students
considered him a hero, Catholics a devil. The clergy, in fact, placed a
partial interdict on his lectures. Having thus been drawn into the
maelstrom of Parisian politics at a time when the city was preparing
for another revolution, Michelet moved more and more to the Left.
He had hitherto been merely skeptical of the Church, or at most unsympathetic; he now became a bitter and outspoken enemy, and this
influenced his historical interpretation. So strong were his feelings,
that he refused to see anything good in the Church even in the Middle
Ages, which he called "a barren period—a thousand years during which
humanity made no progress." Fortunately for his reputation, this
change of mind came after he had completed the first six volumes of
his *History of France* which dealt with the Middle Ages—still regarded
as his best historical work.

Michelet's lectures on the Jesuits (*Les Jésuites*) were published in
1843; two years later he issued *Le Prêtre*, and in 1846 *Le Peuple*. These
three booklets may be considered as statements of faith. The first two
were obviously anticlerical; the third was a cogent expression of his
liberal creed. Though he knew no economics, he had an intimate
knowledge of and sympathy with workers. "Let me live," he said,
"with men of genius or with the poor." *Le Peuple* is a fine statement
of nineteenth-century French democracy. Michelet hoped to bring
about a union between the bourgeoisie and the small proprietors and
craftsmen on the basis of liberty and moderate property; such a programme would obviate absolute socialism on the one hand and Guizot's
torysme bourgeois on the other. "If it be true," Michelet wrote, "that
'Property is theft,' there are twenty-five million thieves in France who
have no intention of giving up their booty. The danger is quite the
other way. The mass of the people, whom you practically exclude
from citizenship, are becoming absorbed in selfish interests, and the
political life which animated the whole of France in the times of the
Revolution is almost extinct."

Le Peuple was published two years before the Revolution of 1848,
and the authorities, not without some justification, looked on Michelet
as one of those responsible for the uprising. After Napoleon III's coup
d'état Michelet refused to swear allegiance to the new government; in

[12] See Monod in *La revue de l'instruction publique*, 1909.

1851 he was, therefore, dispossessed of his chair at the Collège de France and lost his position at the archives. Paris was too expensive a city for an impecunious scholar, so Michelet moved out to the country near Nantes and devoted his time to a history of the French Revolution. Years later he returned to Paris; but again political events affected his life. During the Commune part of his house was burned. Despite his age and losses, he continued to work, this time on a history of the nineteenth century. When he reached the fourth volume, in 1873, he fell ill. He died early in February 1874.

Michelet's historical works should be treated under two separate heads; the history of France, especially during the Middle Ages, and the history of the French Revolution. The *History of France* fills seventeen volumes, but only the first six volumes deserve serious consideration. This portion, as has been said before, was written between 1833 and 1843, before Michelet's conversion to open anticlericalism. Here he traces, in intimate detail, the origins of France to the end of the feudal period. There is no obvious bias. Incidentally, Michelet went counter to the prevailing theory that France was made up mainly of Frankish and Roman elements, by insisting upon the importance of the Celtic stratum. "The foundation of the French people is the youthful, soft, and mobile race of the Gauls, clamorous, sensual and buoyant —prompt to learn, prompt to despise, greedy of new things." This race, he insisted, was characterized by a passion for equality—a dubious thesis. The story of the Middle Ages—based upon the lives of the people, not States—is grouped around certain central figures or chief events, so selected that approximately each half-century has one *tableau*. This gives the work great lucidity and easy readability. What is more, the narrative is based upon original sources.

As an example of Michelet's genius for generalization and vivid historical sense one may take his magnificent "Picture of France" in the Third Book of the first volume of his *History*. It serves as an introduction to the Middle Ages and gives a "roll-call" of the provinces and a bird's eye view of the country.

Let us view France in its whole. . . . Let us ascend one of the highest summits of the Vosges, or, if you choose, let us seat ourselves on the Jura—our back to the Alps. . . . We should distinguish an undulating line, extending from the wood-crowned hills of Luxembourg and of Ardennes to the balloon-shaped hills of the Vosges, and thence along the viny slopes of Burgundy to the volcanic crags of the Cevennes, and to the vast wall of the Pyrenees. This line marks the great water-shed. On its western side descend to the ocean the Seine, the Loire, and the Garonne; on the other, the Meuse flows to the north, the Saone and Rhone to the south. In the distance are two continental islands, as it were—Brittany, low and rugged, of quartz and granite only, a huge shoal placed at the angle of France to sustain the shock of the current of the strait; and Auvergne, green and rude, a vast extinct fire, with its forty volcanoes. . . .

Looking at France in its latitude, its zones are at once discriminated by their products. In the north are the low and rich plains of Belgium and of Flanders, with their fields of flax, hops, and of colewort, and the bitter northern vine. From Reims to the Moselle begins the region of the true vine and of wine; all spirit in Champagne, and good and warm in Burgundy, it grows heavier and duller in Languedoc, to awaken again at Bordeaux. The mulberry and the olive appear at Montauban; but these delicate children of the south are ever exposed to risk in the unequal climate of France. . . .

The latter part of Michelet's *Histoire de France*, from the Renaissance[13] to the Revolution, is considerably weaker than the first. Those volumes were written between 1855 and 1867, at a time when he had neither archival resources nor assistants and had to rely on style instead of facts. Brilliant essays, large canvasses, penetrating observations may make good literary criticism but not history. A declamatory argument, no matter how magnificently rhetorical, does not fill a factual gap. Identifying himself with his heroes, Michelet frequently lost himself in the stream of his narrative and tended to overuse emotion-laden words, such as the *grandeur, terror, irony* of history.

This, of course, was one of Michelet's characteristics. He had a deep emotional sympathy with his subjects; in fact, the stress of past events sometimes affected him physically. When he was writing about the Reign of Terror he fell ill from the strain and had to suspend work. He not only revived the past, he relived it himself. "Guizot calls history analysis; Thierry calls it narrative; I call it resurrection." "Others," he once said, "have been more learned, more judicious; as for me, I have loved more." It was this love, this sympathy with his theme, that earned him his great success and, one may add, what immortality he enjoys.

The volumes dealing with the *ancien régime* were, from a literary point of view, magnificent introductions to the Revolution. He seized upon the main events, the leading persons, the great minds, and painted them in intense colors. He had gotten through the "great, the sombre, the terrible fourteenth century" (by discarding Froissart, whom he accused of "putrescent irridescence"), and came to the no less terrible, albeit more brilliant, period of the Renaissance and pre-Revolutionary France. He viewed the history of his country in the large, from move-

[13] Michelet coined the word "Renaissance" in the modern usage of that term, and defined it as "the discovery of the world and of man." He used it to characterize an epoch. Vasari in his *Lives of the Painters* (1550) had used the word *rinascita*, but limited it wholly to Italian art. In the seventeenth century the French word *Renaissance* was applied also to the revival of literature; but Michelet was the first to extend the application of the word to the whole life of Europe in the fifteenth and sixteenth centuries. See Konrad Burdach, *Reformation, Renaissance, Humanismus* (Berlin and Leipzig, 1926).

ment to movement, rising and changing and reaching a dramatic climax. "Humanity," he paraphrased Vico, "creates itself."

When I re-entered, when I returned, re-examined my middle ages [he wrote in the preface to his *History of France* in 1869], that superb sea of follies, I was seized by a violent hilarity, and of the sixteenth and seventeenth centuries I made a terrible feast. Rabelais and Voltaire have laughed in their graves. The bloated gods, the rotten kings have appeared without disguise. . . . From the Medicis to Louis XIV a severe autopsy has characterized this government of cadavers.

But Michelet was capable of profound insight. Indifferent to state papers and diplomatic correspondence, he applied his intuitive intelligence not to politics; "a man without a scrap of true political judgment," a critic has said of him. He mocked at "our amiable and ingenious scholar, Ranke, who has taught us so much," for his preoccupation with diplomacy. Probably Ranke would have been incapable of writing a passage like the following, for such remarkable observations do not come from documents—they emanate from an illumination of the mind.

In this time of Spanish emphasis and heroes *à la* Corneille [Michelet wrote about Turenne] prose appeared in Turenne. It was seen that war was an affair of logic, mathematics, and reason, that it did not demand great heat, but, on the contrary, a cold good sense, firmness and patience; much of that special instinct of the sportsman and his dog which can perfectly be reconciled with mediocrity of character. Romances have invested Turenne with an air of philanthropy, making him a kind of philanthropist, a warlike Fenelon. There is nothing of all that. The reality is that the Thirty Years' War, having lost its furies and its heats, and having used up five or six generations of indifferent generals, without passions or ideas, finished by producing the technical man, or incarnate art, light, ice and calculus. No emotion remains. It is a quasi-pacific war, but none the less murderous.

Michelet's *History of the French Revolution* appeared between 1846 and 1853. He had interrupted his *History of France*, which he resumed in 1855, to plunge into the revolutionary period. In this instance, the word *plunge* is not merely a figure of speech, for that is precisely what Michelet did. He had so lived himself into the passions of the period that he actually spoke and thought like a revolutionist. He hated and loved and suffered with the men and women who destroyed the monarchy. Like the revolutionists, Michelet spoke of Marie Antoinette as a "foreigner," of Louis XVI as a "traitor," of the foreign counter-revolutionists as "barbarians." He orated with Danton, grumbled with the Paris crowd, trembled at the news of the invasion of 1792. This was a new way of writing history. "I have," he said of the revolutionists, "exhumed them for a second life."

None of these great actors of the Revolution [he wrote in 1868] has left me cold. Have I not lived with them? Have I not followed every one of them to the bottom of his thought, in his transformations, as a faithful companion? I have been one of them, an intimate in that strange world. It is good to breathe, to go, to come through those papers, those *dossiers*, those registers. They are not mute, and all that is not as dead as it seems. I have never touched anything there without something coming out, awakening: it is the soul.[14]

This was what Michelet called his "resurrection" of history. As far back as 1833 he explained his experience in resurrecting the past. He was at work among ancient manuscripts in the Archives Nationales when he felt those dead papers coming to life.

I did not delay in perceiving, in the apparent silence of those galleries, that there was a movement, a murmur which was not of the dead. Those papers, those parchments, left there for a long time demanded nothing better than to come back to life (*revenir au jour*). These papers were not papers but the lives of men, of provinces, of people. First, families and fiefs, blackened in the dust, implored against oblivion. The provinces rose in revolt, urging that centralization has wrongly believed them destroyed. The decrees of the kings claimed not to have been obliterated by the mass of modern laws. . . . All lived and spoke; they surrounded the author with an army of a hundred tongues which rudely silenced the great voice of the Revolution and the Empire.

Then Michelet, in his imagination, replied to those murmuring papers:

"Gently, gentlemen of the dead, let us proceed in order, if you please. All of you are right in history. The individual is fine as an individual, the general as a general. The fief is right, the monarchy even more, the Empire still more. *À vous* Godefroi! *À vous* Richelieu! *À vous* Bonaparte! The province should revive; the ancient diversity of France was characterized by stout geography. . . . Revives the monarchy, revives France! . . ."

And, in proportion as I breathed upon their dust, I saw them rise. They got out of the sepulchre, a hand, a head, as in the *Last Judgment* of Michelangelo or in the *Danse des morts*. This galvanic dance which they performed around me, I have tried to reproduce in this book.[15]

He wrote his history of the Revolution from the point of view of the people; not *about* the people but from *inside* the people, from the heart of the people with whom he identified himself. Take, for example, the following passage.

[14] *Histoire de la Révolution française* (Paris, 1868–69, 6 v.), I, 140.

[15] *Histoire de France* (Paris, 1879–81, 19 v.), II, 701, cp. 137–38. Similar emotional and subjective passages are to be found throughout his history of the Revolution. "It," he wrote of the French Revolution, "possesses a knowledge of which others are ignorant. It contains the secret of all bygone times. In it alone France was conscious of herself. . . . Here the inextinguishable spark, the profound mystery of life, is ever glowing within us. . . The Revolution lives in ourselves—in our souls; it has no outward monument. Living spirit of France, where shall I seize thee, but in myself?—at least agreed in this, to resuscitate, to awaken remote and departed ages. But thee they would have wished to bury. Yet why? Thou, thou alone dost live. . . ." *Historical View of the French Revolution* (Engl. trans., Bohn Standard Library, London, 1890), introduction.

With daylight, one idea dawned upon Paris, and all were illumined with the same ray of hope. A light broke upon every mind, and the same voice thrilled through every heart: "Go, and thou shalt take the Bastille!" That was impossible, unreasonable, preposterous. And yet everybody believed it. And the thing was done.

And the thing was done? A strange phrase for an historian. Here Michelet is an enthusiastic patriot, an emotional poet. He is in the stream of the Revolution, feeling and acting with the common people. This, he insisted, was the way the people thought. It mattered little what kings and nobles and the enemies of the Revolution thought. A conversation with the average Frenchman, Michelet wrote, would have sounded as follows:

> Who brought about the Revolution?
>> Voltaire and Rousseau.
> Who has lost the king?
>> The queen.
> Who began the Revolution?
>> Mirabeau.
> Who has been the enemy of the Revolution?
>> Pitt and Coburg.[16]
> Who has corrupted the Revolution?
>> Marat and Robespierre.

Rightly or wrongly—and Michelet would say rightly—this was what Frenchmen of the Revolutionary period believed. More than that, they still thought so in the middle of the nineteenth century. For the Revolutionary tradition persisted to the end of Michelet's days. When he began to write his history many of the actors of the Revolution were still alive. That is where Michelet got his "oral tradition."

When I say oral tradition, I mean the national tradition, that which remained generally scattered in the mouth of people, that which everybody said and repeated, the peasants, the townsfolk, the old men, the women, even the children, that which you may still hear if you enter of an evening into a village tavern, that which you may gather if, finding on the road a passerby at rest, you begin to converse with him about the rain, the season, then the high price of victuals, then the times of the Emperor, then the times of the Revolution. Note well his judgments. Now and then, in things, he errs; more often he does not know. In men, he very rarely deceives himself.

This may seem like a strange way of collecting historical data. In justice to Michelet, however, it must be said that he used manuscripts and printed materials copiously. One should remember that he was an archivist for twenty-two years. Of printed sources, he used the *Histoire parlementaire de la révolution française*, collected by Buchez and Roux

[16] It is a queer fact that Michelet had a deep dislike of England. "The middle ages," he once wrote, "only possessed one hypocrisy; we possess two: the hypocrisy of authority, the hypocrisy of liberty; in a word, the priest, the Englishman—the two forms of Tartuffe. The priest acts principally on women or the peasant; the Englishman on the bourgeois classes."

in forty volumes; the *Gazette nationale* or *Le Moniteur universel*, reprinted in 1840–45 in thirty-two volumes; Marat's *Ami du peuple*, and others. He does not seem to have used the valuable *Journal des débats*, or Thiers' history, which preceded his. By and large, according to the conclusion of Aulard, one of the great authorities on the French Revolution, Michelet's history is a "chef-d'oeuvre," a "monument of truth," an "exact and pure expression of genius." [17]

Closely connected with Michelet were Jules Quicherat (1814–82) and Edgar Quinet (1803–75). As a student of Michelet's, Quicherat acquired his ideas from his teacher, and his method in the École des Chartes, where he became the first professor of medieval archaeology. He edited for the first time the *Procès de condemnation et de réhabilitation de Jeanne d'Arc*, a monumental work in five volumes (1841–49), and was the author of a series of very remarkable articles on medieval French archaeology published in the *Revue archéologique*. "His knowledge of the monuments and antiquities of France was unrivalled." [18]

Edgar Quinet [19] was closer to Michelet, both intellectually and emotionally, than Quicherat. Having completed his studies at the lycée in Lyon, he went on a tour of Germany, England, and Greece. A gifted linguist, he read philosophic works in many European languages, and his first published work was a translation of Herder's *Ideas on the Philosophy of the History of Humanity*. This, Victor Cousin said, marked the "début of a great writer." It was in Cousin's house that Quinet met and formed his lifelong friendship with Michelet.

Like Michelet, Quinet was a voluminous writer and a lover of liberty; again like his friend, he was hostile to the Church. The two friends, it will be remembered, gave a joint course of lectures on (against) the Jesuits at the Collège de France. Together with the poet Mickiewicz, the three hoped to educate the youth of France in the ideas of democratic freedom. Severely attacked by the Church, Quinet published *Ultramontanisme* (1844), in which he accused Catholicism of having compromised Christianity. In the following year he issued *Christianisme et la révolution française*, a treatise on the incompatibility of

[17] See Aulard, "Michelet, historien de la révolution française," in *La révolution française*, LXXX (1928), 136–50, 193–213.

[18] GOOCH, 207; see also the preface to Quicherat's *Mélanges d'archéologie et d'histoire* (Paris, 1885–86, 2 v.). For literature on Quicherat see the account of him by his pupil Arthur Giry in *BEC*, XLIV (1882), 316–60, with a bibliography of his works, and Giry's article in *RH*, XIX (1882), 241–64.

[19] The best account of Quinet is Richard Heath's *Edgar Quinet, His Early Life and Writings* (London and Boston, 1881); see also GOOCH, 234–37; Charles L. Chassin, *Edgar Quinet, sa vie et son oeuvre* (Paris, 1859); Alphonse Peyrat, *La révolution et le livre de M. Quinet* (Paris, 1866); Eugene Spuller, *Figures disparues* (Paris, 1891–94, 3 v.), I, 17–32; Émile Faguet, *Politiques et moralistes du dix-neuvième siècle* (Paris, 1891–1900, 3 v.), II, 175–227; and Gabriel Monod, "Le centenaire de Quinet," *RH*, LXXXII (1903), 75–80.

Catholicism with modern ideas; he lamented the failure of the Reformation in France.

"France has made a political and social revolution before achieving a religious revolution." And so long as Catholicism remained dominant, Quinet held, there was no hope for liberalism, for the Church was the enemy of free thought, of progress, and of freedom. The French Revolution, though achieving much, had failed in destroying Roman Catholicism. What was equally important in the failure of the Revolution was the fact that the Reign of Terror and the Jacobins had stopped the development of free institutions by espousing absolutism.

In 1846 the government ousted Quinet from his professorship. Two years later, after the government fell, Quinet was re-instated in his chair at the Collège de France, but was again removed after Napoleon III's coup d'état. His most ambitious work was written in exile. In 1865 he published his *La Révolution*, a philosophic analysis of the causes which led to the comparative failure of the Revolution of 1789. The movement itself, he held, was admirable, leading as it did toward human emancipation. He pointed out that the main reason for the failure lay in the preceding centuries which had not succeeded in effecting a religious revolution. The Catholic environment was hostile to the growth of liberal institutions. Furthermore, the revolutionists themselves had defeated the movement by using violent means. This violence led to a new absolutism, that of Bonaparte. "Everything in your book," Michelet wrote to his friend, "is great, strong, magnanimous. It is a triumph for me too, as you and I are the same person."

The careers of Mignet and Thiers illustrate how, early in the nineteenth century, it was easy to make a national reputation by writing about the French Revolution. François Auguste Marie Mignet (1796–1884) [20] was born at Aix, in Provence, the son of a blacksmith who, in his day, had been an ardent *sans-culotte*. From his father the boy imbibed a love of liberty and democracy. In 1815 he entered the law faculty at Aix and there he formed an intimate friendship with another ambitious young man, Thiers. The excitement of the Restoration days turned the two friends away from law and toward history and politics. At the age of twenty-five Mignet wrote a book on the government of St. Louis which won the recognition of the Academy of Inscriptions. This decided him to go to Paris to seek his fortune. In 1821 he ar-

[20] For a bibliography of Mignet's works see Eugène de Rozière, *Bibliographie des oeuvres de M. François Mignet* (Paris, 1887). The best accounts are by Petit, *François Mignet* (Paris, 1889), and Jules Simon, *Mignet, Michelet, Henri Martin* (n. 10). See also the same, "Éloge de M. Mignet," *ASMP*, CXXIV (1885), 885–924; Gooch, 193–99; Halphen, 33–34; C. A. Sainte-Beuve, *Portraits contemporains* (Paris, 1876, 5 v.), V, 225–56; the same, "Mignet," *RDM*, 1846, pt. i, pp. 1090–1109; *QR*, XXXII (1844), 387–401; *FM*, LXXIV (1866), 489–500.

rived in the capital, where he was soon joined by Thiers. The two friends found employment as journalists, Mignet on the *Courrier français* and Thiers on the *Constitutionnel*. In a short time they made a reputation among the Opposition. Apart from journalism, Mignet also occupied himself with teaching. At the Athénée he gave a course on the period of the Reformation which was warmly received. "Everyone," Sainte-Beuve recalls, "felt himself gripped with a serious interest, dominated by the grave accent and the telling phrase." Years later Taine met Mignet and noted down his impressions:

There is in him a certain barrenness; he has evidently not lived among general ideas; he is not ready for them. Neither is he an artist; see his *History of Mary Stuart*, his *French Revolution*—it is icy-cold. He is capable of assimilating indigestible material, of setting out a clear exposition arranged in beautiful order. He has the French talent of perfect classification and aristocratic academical elegance. . . . It is clear that psychological history, like philosophical history, is a closed book to him.

He gets up at five every morning in order to work. He spends half an hour every evening with M. Thiers, who is his great friend. He goes out very seldom; one lady is said to have begged him for two years to dine at her house. . . . He was made for domestic life and ought to have been married. He has been very handsome and still has a very fine regular countenance. . . . He is rather stiff and measured—there is not enough devil about him.[21]

This psychological etching is memorable—and not untrue.

Mignet had a sound instinct for the needs of the time, and feeling the prevailing spirit of unrest against the reactionary monarchy of Charles X, he began to collect materials for a history of the French Revolution. The gathering of data took two years, the writing only four months. In 1824 there appeared his memorable *Histoire de la révolution française depuis 1789 jusqu'en 1814*. Like the work of Thierry and Thiers it undoubtedly helped to accelerate the Revolution of 1830, which, incidentally, Mignet warmly espoused. The new government rewarded him with a minor post as director of archives of the Foreign Office, a position which he held until 1848.

The success of the *History* was immediate; it was widely translated, at least six different editions of it appeared in Germany. The chief merit of the book is its lucidity; it is not strictly a work of scholarship but of logic. Mignet coolly estimated cause and effect, traced the logical connection between events. To him the Revolution was not a controversial subject but an historical event whose value should be determined calmly. The history has been criticized by Carlyle as too lifeless and by Sainte-Beuve as too deterministic. Both criticisms contain some truth; nevertheless, Mignet was not unaware of the fortuitous in history. As his friend Jules Simon said, he was accused of fatalism

[21] *Life and Letters of H. Taine* (n. 4), II, 186–87.

because he believed in logic. "His memory," Simon wrote about his friend, "was as sure as his judgment, and these two qualities made him redoubtable to men of imagination and of fantasy."

After his *Histoire de la révolution française* Mignet devoted himself mainly to the sixteenth and seventeenth centuries. In 1836–42 he published *Négociations relatives à la succession d'Espagne sous Louis XIV;* in 1851 appeared *Histoire de Marie Stuart;* in 1854 he issued *Charles Quint;* and in 1785, *Rivalité de François Ier et de Charles Quint.* He also ventured into dramatic history, writing *Antonio Perez et Philippe II*, which threw new light on the designs of Don Juan of Austria as well as the murder of Escovedo. Precise and orderly, Mignet's histories do not reveal too obviously the great erudition of their author. He rarely advanced any thesis without a sound factual basis (usually derived from authentic primary sources) and never failed to show the connection between the facts and the relation between events. His legal training always stood him in good stead.

The closing paragraph of the history of Mary Stuart may serve as a characteristic example of Mignet's manner.

The scaffold! Such was then the end of a life, which, commencing in expatriation, was chequered by reverses, filled with errors, unfortunate almost throughout its course. . . . Mary Stuart, a victim of the old feudalism and the new religious revolution of Scotland, carried with her to the grave the hopes of absolute power and of Catholicism. Her descendants, who succeeded to the throne of England sixteen years after her death, followed her in the dangerous course in which she had been preceded by so many of her ancestors. Her grandson Charles I, was, like her, beheaded for attempting to establish absolute monarchy, and her great-grandson, James II, for endeavoring, like her, to restore Catholicism, lost his throne and was driven into exile.[22]

In conclusion it should be added that Mignet's works, particularly his *Histoire de la révolution française*, made him a national figure. In 1836 he was received into the French Academy, and a few years later he was elected Perpetual Secretary of this institution, a position which he filled with wisdom and dignity for thirty-five years.

Louis Adolphe Thiers (1797–1877)[23] was in every essential respect

[22] François Mignet, *The History of Mary, Queen of Scots*, tr. by Andrew R. Scoble (6th ed., London, 1882), 465–66.

[23] See FUETER, 636–39; GOOCH, 199–205; HALPHEN, 34–36; Jules Simon, *Thiers, Guizot, Rémusat* (Paris, 1885); C. A. Sainte-Beuve, *Portraits contemporains* (n. 20), IV, 62–124; Paul de Rémusat, *A. Thiers* (Paris, 1889); Alexandre Laya, *Études historiques sur la vie privée, politique et littéraire de M. A. Thiers* (Paris, 1846, 2 v.); the same, *Histoire populaire de M. A. Thiers* (Paris, 1872); Nassau W. Senior, *Conversations with M. Thiers, M. Guizot, and Other Distinguished Persons during the Second Empire*, ed. by M. C. M. Simpson (London, 1878–80, 2 v.); W. de Fonvielle, *M. Thiers historien de la révolution française* (Paris, 1871); Pierre Lanfrey, *Études et portraits politiques* (new ed., Paris, 1880); Timon [pseud. of L. M. de la Haye, viscount de Cormenin], *Études sur les orateurs parlementaires* (8th ed., Paris, 1839, 2 v.); Jules Barni, *Napoléon Ier et son historien, M. Thiers* (Paris, 1869); Victor Chauffour-Kestner, *Sur l'Histoire du Consulat et de l'Empire de M. Thiers* (Paris, 1863); Comte de Martel, *Les*

different from his friend Mignet. Where Mignet had dignity, Thiers had picturesqueness. Mignet was a scholar interested in his subject; Thiers cared little about what he was writing so long as he had the exciting opportunity of chasing down interesting details. Thiers was first and foremost a politician—even in his history; secondarily he was an orator. Even when he was contemplating a history, so remarks the acute Sainte-Beuve, he was thinking of other things—a characteristic, incidentally, that was also true of Guizot, another politician-historian.

He had, of course, an exciting life. Born under the Directory, he died when the Third Republic was seven years old; in fact, he was the first president of that Republic. More than half his life was spent in active politics. Withal he was, if not a great, certainly a prolific historian who left his mark on French historiography. As Jules Simon of the French Academy said in his Éloge of Thiers:

I am going to speak to you of a man who has been a journalist, historian, chief of the opposition and chief of the government; who has made one revolution, healed the wounds of another, conquered a third; who has been celebrated at a time of life when one still seeks a career, and who, after having been calumniated, deserted, proscribed, found himself powerful and popular until his extreme old age.

When Thiers and Mignet came to Paris the opposition against the Bourbon government was in full swing; it was led by Manuel (a Provençal) in the chamber, by Béranger the poet, and by Lafitte the banker. The two young Provençals had letters of introduction to Manuel, who introduced them to Lafitte who, in turn, introduced them to the leading members of the opposition. Mignet, as we have seen, became a contributor to the *Courrier français*, one of the two liberal journals, and Thiers soon dominated the *Constitutionnel*, the other opposition paper. As a journalist, Thiers attracted national attention by his eloquent defense of liberal ideas.

Here [so a malicious contemporary described Thiers' appearance in Lafitte's drawing room] the littleness of his figure—the ordinary expression of his features, half hidden

historiens fantaisistes, M. Thiers (Paris, 1883); Ludwig Häusser, *Gesammelte Schriften* (Berlin, 1869–70, 2 v.), I, 352–586; M. Pellet, "Notes bibliographiques sur l'histoire de la révolution française de Thiers," *La révolution française*, XLVI (1904), 5–12; A. Aulard, "Thiers historien de la révolution française," *ibid.*, LXVI (1914), 492–520, and LXVII (1914), 5–29; L. Barthou, "Thiers historien de la révolution française," *ibid.*, LXXXII, (1929), 360–61; A. Rambaud, "M. Thiers, historien de la révolution française," *Revue politique et littéraire, revue bleue*, 2ᵉ sér., XIV (1878), 891–900; Sainte-Beuve, "M. Thiers," *RDM*, 1845, pt. 1, pp. 209–46; Lerminier, "Histoire du consulat et de l'empire de M. Thiers," *ibid.*, 1845, pt. 1, pp. 1096–1113. For some accounts and reviews in English see *QR*, LXIV (1839), 450–56; LXVII (1840–41), 481–500; LXXVI (1845), 299–354; CXLVI (1878), 443–84; *BQR*, X (1849), 168 ff.; *NAR*, LXXIV (1852), 280–300; *NBR*, XXXIII (1860), 133–64; *DR*, n. s., IV (1865), 141–70; *FM*, XXVII (1843), 289–302, XXXI (1845), 505–20; *ER*, CVII (1858), 358–96, CVIII (1858), 32–70, CXII (1860), 237–55, CXIV (1861), 486–512; and Lord Acton in *Home and Foreign Review*, 1863, pp. 244–48.

under a vast pair of spectacles—the singular cadence of his accents, which made a sort of psalmody of his conversation—the continual fidgety motion in which he indulged—a total want of the habits of society, remarkable even in the mixt cohort which encumbered the salons of M. Lafitte, all contributed to make Thiers a being apart, who attracted attention from the first. Once granted, M. Thiers knew well how to keep it; nothing appeared new to him, neither finance, nor war, nor administration; and he discussed all these matters in a manner sufficiently specious to seduce the bankers, the ancient functionaries of the empire, and the generals, all of whom he addressed without ceremony.[24]

The homely little man was, indeed, highly ambitious, and he did not have to wait long for his opportunity. During his first years in Paris the chief question he had to settle was: what career should he pursue—journalism, history, or politics? A frank careerist and opportunist, he finally decided upon all three professions. His first book, the *Histoire de la révolution française*, which brought him national renown, he candidly regarded as *"une arme de guerre"* against the régime. An astute man, Thiers knew that the French Revolution was still a "going concern" in France; it was possible, nay easy, to become famous and even rich—he was offered 500,000 francs to continue his history of the Revolution—by exploiting Liberty, Fraternity, Equality, and all the principles which Our Fathers fought and died for. Whether this was done as a journalist (agitator) or politician, mattered little.

Thiers succeeded immediately. The first volume of the *Histoire de la révolution française*, which appeared in 1823, bore two unknown names: Louis Adolphe Thiers and Felix Bodin; the story of the "collaboration" is somewhat shady, but soon Bodin disappeared into obscurity and Thiers continued on his triumphal journey. By the time the third volume came out, in 1824, the young Provençal was already a famous man. "This volume created quite a sensation in the capital. The boldness, not to say audacity, with which the young writer treated men and things equally· hated by the Restoration contributed to give the work a party value, independently of its literary merit." [25] In fact it soon became a textbook, a dramatic and vigorous manual of the recent past. "In a short time, it was in the hands of every intelligent Frenchman, and contributed not a little to discredit the administration of the Bourbons, and to prepare the public mind for the Revolution of 1830." Shortly after that Revolution the work had gone through three editions.

The *Histoire de la révolution française* filled ten volumes (1823–27), only the first two of which carried the name of Bodin.[26] To produce

[24] Quoted in *QR*, LXIV (1839), 451, cp. 450–54.
[25] *FQR*, XXXV (1845), 110, the whole article, 109–35.
[26] According to Sainte-Beuve: "The idea was Bodin's, who urged it upon Thiers and seeing him working so well at it, resigned his co-operation with a good grace." Bodin died in 1827.

ten volumes in four years, while being at the same time busy with politics and journalism, meant hasty preparation. Thiers had no time to use many sources or to familiarize himself with a large body of intricate details. This was particularly true of the first two volumes, which cover the first two years of the Revolution, perhaps the most difficult period for the historian to treat. As Jules Simon observed, these two years require three histories, that of the king and nobles, that of the bourgeoisie, and that of the people. Thiers had no time to deal with the burning problem of finances—one of the great contributory causes to the Revolution—nor with the military administration. But where Thiers failed in facts he made up in brilliance. "Never before," to quote Simon again, "has such light been cast on those terrible events." This was quite true, especially since Thiers was the first to treat of the Revolution as a whole—Mignet's book came out one year later—and had a genius for marshalling facts. "M. Thiers conducts one hundred thousand facts as a clever general conducts one hundred thousand men." But a hostile English critic pointed out that in all of Thiers' volumes there was not "one single page—hardly one line—of sincere and unadulterated truth." [27]

Thiers himself was conscious of the weakness of the first part of his history and, ambitious to be a true historian, he decided to make a thorough study of the records and to familiarize himself with political and military techniques. His ideals were always higher than his achievements. "I would believe myself dishonored," he once said to Jules Simon, "if I had written a single phrase of which I did not understand the meaning or foreseen all the applications." He began to study the sources and to interview various men of action. From Baron Louis he learned about finances, from Jomini military affairs, and from the officers at Vincennes military practice. So assiduous, in fact, was he in his pursuit of the technical problems of warfare that his friends twitted him about his military genius. Thiers retorted that Carnot had won battles from his cabinet. The result of all this application was soon apparent. Not only were the final volumes of the *Histoire de la révolution française* superior to the earlier ones, but also his *Histoire du Consulat et de l'Empire*, which is a continuation of the former, is a more solid and enduring work than his first effort.

The immediate effect of the completed *Histoire de la révolution française* was, in the words of Sainte-Beuve, that of a Marseillaise; from the point of view of Thiers' personal career, it was, recalling Bonaparte, "*sa campagne d'Italie.*" Now a prominent figure, Thiers, together with

[27] See the review of Thiers' *Histoire de la révolution* and the first four volumes of his *Histoire du consulat et de l'empire* in QR, LXXVI (1843), 521–83.

Mignet and Armand Carrel, founded the *National*, to protest against the reactionary conduct of the Polignac ministry. "Fussy, breathless, despotic, no one could have had to do with a more uncomfortable editor than Thiers." Although Carrel could bully Thiers, Mignet— "more devoted to keeping his hair in curlpapers, than to becoming First Consul"—could not.[28] Nevertheless, the three did yeoman service in overthrowing the government. One of Thiers' most famous editorials in this period was his "The King reigns, but does not govern," an eloquent statement of the idea of constitutional monarchy after the manner of England, which he always favored. Thiers had a hand in the events which led to the placing of Louis Philippe on the throne (1830). The chief question at this time was: "Shall we be governed by M. Thiers or by M. Guizot?" Under Louis Philippe France was governed alternately by both historians. In 1840 Thiers momentarily retired from politics and devoted a considerable portion of his time to history, that is, a continuation of his work on the French Revolution. The *Histoire du Consulat et de l'Empire* began with the end of the Directory (where the *Histoire de la révolution française* left off) and ended with the fall of Napoleon. The first volume appeared in 1843 and the twentieth in 1862.[29] In 1863 Thiers re-entered politics, and for the next seven years he was the spokesman for the small group of anti-Imperialists in the Chamber, contributing his full share to the events of 1870. When the Third Republic was declared after Sedan, the aged historian-politician became its first president. After his resignation in 1873 he continued his political activities in the Chamber until his death in 1877.

For two decades Thiers worked on his *Histoire du Consulat et de l'Empire*. Although a history of the Napoleonic period meant a history of Europe, Thiers did not utilize any foreign sources; his materials, like his point of view, remained consistently French. Nevertheless, in French affairs—he went through the papers in the Foreign Office—his preparations were thorough. He read books and studied manuscripts. He interviewed many survivors and visited the battlefields of Marengo, Ulm, Austerlitz, Jena, Wagram, etc. Eminent men permitted him to use their unpublished memoirs and family papers. Thus he read the memoirs, in manuscript form, of Jourdain, Macdonald, Davoust, Cambacérès, as well as the published autobiographies of Napoleon, Jomini, Thibaudeau. Thiers also utilized Napoleon's correspondence with his generals and officials. In Paris alone there were no less than 40,000 letters or orders signed by Napoleon; these were kept among his private

---

[28] *FQR*, XXX (1843), 319 ff.
[29] A twenty-first volume, containing the index, appeared in 1869.

papers until 1841, when they were transported to the Louvre. Such a mass of data required a skilled hand, and Thiers already possessed sufficient practice as an historian to master the details and enough experience as a statesman to penetrate into the essentials.

Fifteen years have elapsed [so Thiers began his work] since I traced the annals of our first Revolution. Those fifteen years have been passed amidst the storms of public life. I have seen the fall of an ancient throne, the erection of a new one. I have seen the French Revolution pursuing its invincible course. Although the scenes which I have witnessed have caused me but little surprise, I have not the vanity to suppose that I had nothing to learn from experience of men and affairs. I am confident, on the contrary, of having learnt much, and of being, consequently, more fit to understand and to relate the great things which our fathers did during those heroic times.

Thiers had once said to William Nassau Senior: "By birth I belong to the people; my family were humble merchants in Marseilles. . . . By education I am a Bonapartist." In truth, he belonged everywhere. In the 1820's he was a champion of the French Revolution and of liberalism; in the 1830's he was an official of Louis Philippe; in the 1840's and 1850's, while writing the *Histoire du Consulat et de l'Empire*, he was a Bonapartist, a defender of military autocracy; finally, in 1870, he became chief of the Republic. Thiers shows Bonaparte in his Consular days as the savior of France, and thus the historian becomes a brilliant panegyrist of the Corsican. Later there is a perceptible change; when Thiers traces Napoleon as emperor and despot and conqueror, he grows more and more critical. "No human being in the world's history," he writes, "has seemed to me to unite in himself qualities so mighty and so diverse, nor, after having meditated upon the end of his career, have I changed my opinion. But, on beginning his history, I thought, as I do now, at its close, that it was the abuse of those great qualities which caused his fall." And again: "Who could have foreseen that the sage of 1800 would be the madman of 1812? Yes, one could have foreseen it, remembering that omnipotence carries within itself an incurable malady. In this great career, where there is so much to teach soldiers, administrators and politicians, citizens must learn never to deliver their country to a single man."

Thiers' work has been severely criticized. He knew little of Germany, less of England. He ignored administration, dominant ideas, and public life. Foreign archives and printed sources were not within his ken. He made no use whatever of the published memoirs, diaries, despatches, and correspondence of such prominent Englishmen as Malmesbury, Fox, Castlereagh, or Wellington. Instead, he gleaned his information from the *Moniteur*, the official French journal which printed what Napoleon wanted it to print. No wonder that English criticism of

Thiers' history was merciless. "His misconception of our government is equal to his ignorance of our literature."

Another great fault of which Thiers has been accused was his lack of public morality. Consciously or not, he always seems to side with the victor—and this may explain his condemnation of the later Napoleon. Lamartine said that "Thiers is the accomplice of fortune; he only recognises the wrong when it is punished by failure." Lanfrey, the critic and historian of Napoleon, made a similar observation: "He has no appreciation of moral forces. *Tu ne réussis pas, donc tu as tort*—that is his whole philosophy." Across the Channel, the *Edinburgh Review* echoed those sentiments: "Thiers places what he terms *l'intelligence des faits* above every other historic quality." [30]

Thiers' own standards of history were high. In the well-known preface to volume XII he stated his case warmly.

> I entertain that respect for the mission of history, that the fear of alleging what is inexact fills me with a sort of confusion. I have then no peace, because I have not discovered the proof of the fixed object of my doubts: I search for it everywhere; I do not stop till I have found it. . . . In this case, compelled to pronounce as a juror, I speak according to my intimate belief, but always with an extreme fear of being in error, because I hold that there is nothing more to be condemned, since one assumes spontaneously the mission to speak truth to men on the great events of history, than to gloss it over by cowardice, to distort it by passion, to forge it by indolence, and to misstate, knowingly or not, to one's own age, and to ages to come.

This preface sets a difficult standard, and it cannot be said that Thiers always reached it. "History says not, I am fiction, but says, I am truth." Thiers meant to be as truthful as possible, and he often succeeded. What is equally important, his work has a high literary quality and a sustained interest. Even so discriminating a critic as Sainte-Beuve has praised Thiers for his narrative genius. Furthermore, Thiers' work was also a political document of the first importance, written by one of France's distinguished statesmen about the most stirring period in France's history; this alone would make the *Histoire du Consulat et de l'Empire* memorable, and this, likewise, explains the storm of criticism and applause which greeted Thiers' masterpiece.

The twenty-volume work, one must emphasize, was highly individualistic; it was no model for others to follow. Thiers never became the head of a school of history. His method was experimental; his psychology, that of Locke; his metaphysics, the existence of a creative God; his morals, those of the French Academy. In short, Thiers was a nineteenth-century French *savant*.

[30] See *ER*, CVII (1858), 358–96, and CVIII (1858), 32–70; these are reviews of the first 17 volumes of the *Histoire du Consulat et de l'Empire;* for a review of the 19th volume see *ibid.*, CXIV (1861), 486–512.

Such [one may conclude with Jules Simon] was M. Thiers, national historian and liberator of the land; great patriot, great liberal, great historian; celebrated in literature at the age of twenty-five, minister at thirty-one, dictator at seventy-five; participated all his life . . . in the greatest affairs of France and Europe; always ready to risk his popularity or life in a great cause; full, until his last breath, of curiosity and activity . . .; one of the most admired and injured men of his age.[31]

Throughout the first half of the nineteenth century the French Revolution remained a topic of perennial interest to historians, politicians, journalists—even to poets. More than two decades after Thiers and Mignet had written their histories, Alphonse Marie Louis Lamartine (1790–1869) [32] came out with his famous *Histoire des Girondins*. The work caused a sensation.

Lamartine, generally ranked with Hugo and de Musset among the foremost French poets of the period, was a Catholic by birth, a Romantic by temperament, and a poet by profession. He had served in the Napoleonic cavalry in 1814, but he was more interested in Byron than in Bonaparte, and went on a tour of the East where he remained several years. His *Méditations poétiques*, published in 1820, marked an epoch in the Romantic movement and went through thirty editions. Upon his return to France in 1833 the now famous poet entered the Chamber of Deputies where he displayed great gifts as an orator. The success of Thiers' history fired the poet with the ambition to become an historian also. And so in 1847 he published his *Histoire des Girondins* in eight volumes.

He had no equipment whatsoever for the task of the historian. His only qualities were a fertile imagination and a gift of narration. Except for its political effect, one would ignore Lamartine's history. But its success was sensational. "The publishers tell me there has never been such a success." It helped to undermine the Orleans monarchy, and Lamartine's reward in the provisional government of 1848 was a brief tenure of the ministry of foreign affairs.

The *Histoire des Girondins* is more than what the title implies; it covers the period of the Revolution from 1791 to the Thermidorian reaction.

As for the title of this book [the preface says] we have only adopted it for want of any other word to designate a narrative. This book has none of the pretensions of history, and must not assume its dignity. It is an intermediate work between history and

---

[31] Jules Simon, "Éloge de M. Thiers," *ASMP*, CXXI (1884), 837–78.

[32] Lamartine's *Histoire de la révolution of 1848* (Paris, 1849, 2 v.), is actually a species of autobiography; see *ER*, XCI (1850), 228–97. See also GOOCH, 227–28; Emile Deschanel, *Lamartine* (Paris, 1893, 2 v.); Alfred Nettement, *Les historiens de la révolution française. Études critiques sur les Girondins* (Paris, 1848); Edmond Biré, *La légende des Girondins* (Paris, 1881); *FM*, XXXVI (1847), 253–76; XLIV (1851), 355–74; *ER*, LXXXVII (1848), 1–46; and my *Byways in Bookland* (Berkeley, 1935), 149–50.

memoirs. Events occupy in it a subordinate place to men and ideas. It is full of personal details . . .

The preface at least is honest. As Dumas told Lamartine: "You have raised history to the level of the novel." A two-edged compliment! And as a novel the *Histoire des Girondins* must be considered. Possibly Lamartine was not consciously untruthful; but de Tocqueville insisted that he had never known a mind with "more contempt for the truth" than the author of the *Girondins*. In the poet's mind the boundary lines between fact and fiction were tenuous. He never gave proof for his statements; he never verified his assertions. Nevertheless, he claimed that he had authorities for his statements.

Although we have not encumbered the narrative with notes, with references and with *pièces justificatives*, there is not one of our statements which is not authorized either by authentic memoirs, or by unpublished memoirs, or by autograph correspondence, which the families of the principal personages have been pleased to confide in us . . .

The history is full of brilliant descriptions and vivid portraiture, but one is never sure that one is not reading an exciting novel. Individuals, notably Robespierre whom Lamartine idealized, stand out as living persons; events are submerged. The Revolution in general is glorified (as was the fashion then), and romantically exalted. Nowhere, however, can one trust Lamartine for a single statement. He does not seem to have known even the most common events. One critic filled no less than 113 pages with factual errors in Lamartine's history.[33]

Alexis de Tocqueville (1805–59)[34] was a much higher type of scholar in the field of the *ancien régime* than his predecessors. He came

[33] Nettement (n. 32). An amusing example: Lamartine tells that Marie Antoinette was one of the children whom her mother Maria Theresa had taken with her on the famous occasion when she appealed to the Hungarian barons for aid in 1741; actually Marie Antoinette was not born until fourteen years later.

[34] Tocqueville's works have been edited by G. de Beaumont, *Oeuvres complètes de Tocqueville* (Paris, 1860–65, 9 v.). A new edition is being prepared under the editorship of J. P. Mayer, who also wrote the most recent work on him, *Prophet of the Mass Age, A Study of Alexis de Tocqueville*, tr. by M. Bozman and C. Hahn (London, 1939), which shows "the compatibility of the democratic spirit with despotism," cp. the review in *LTLS*, December 16, 1939, p. 727. See also GOOCH, 231–34; HALPHEN, 95–96; Gustave de Beaumont, *Notice sur Alexis de Tocqueville* (Paris, 1897); F. A. Mignet, *Nouveaux élogues historiques* (Paris, 1877), and his article, "Notice historique sur la vie et les travaux de M. Alexis de Tocqueville," *ASMP*, LXXVII (1866), 351–82; Emile Faguet (n. 19), III, 65–114; Edmond Scherer, *Études critiques sur la littérature contemporaine* (Paris, 1876); R. P. Marcel, *Essai politique sur Alexis de Tocqueville* (Paris, 1910); Eugene d'Eichthal, *A. de Tocqueville et la démocratie libérale* (Paris, 1897); Louis de Lomenie, *Esquisses historiques et littéraires* (Paris, 1879), 397–439; James Bryce, *Predictions of Hamilton and De Tocqueville* (Johns Hopkins University Studies, 5th series, IX, 1887); Henry Reeve, *Royal and Republican France* (London, 1872, 2 v.), II, 79–190; F. X. v. Wegele, "Alexis von Tocqueville," *HZ*, XX (1868), 132–70; *ER*, XC (1849), 77–106, CIV (1856), 531–61, CXIII (1861), 427–60, CXXII (1865), 456–81; *FM*, LIV (1856), 363–74; *QR*, CII (1857), 6–32, CX (1861), 254–55, CLXII (1886), 518–43; *NBR*, XXXIV (1860–61), 330–49.

of an old Norman family. His father was an historian and a *philosophe*, the author of a *Histoire philosophique du règne de Louis XV*, and a prefect of Metz, Amiens, and Versailles under the Restoration. His mother was the grand-daughter of Malesherbes, that excellent Males-herbes, "Who loved justice, upheld the good right, sought liberty, practiced virtue, recommended the people with emotion to the king under the absolute monarchy, defended the king courageously before the triumphant republic, and . . . was immolated on the scaffold" (Mignet). Alexis de Tocqueville's background was, therefore, that of enlightened liberalism, although he always remained a constitutional monarchist.

He became a magistrate at Versailles at the age of twenty-two, but after four years he wearied of his position and received permission to go to the United States and examine the penal system. He spent two years in America, visiting eminent persons, meeting politicians, attending legislative sessions. Gradually this keenly observant young French aristocrat shifted his interests from politics to "the spirit and character of people, the influence of occupations and places, the nature, reach, and play of institutions." The result was one of the classics of political literature.

Democracy in America appeared in 1835 and made its author famous. It was immediately translated into most European languages and became a textbook of constitutional law in the United States. No less than sixteen editions had appeared by 1866.

I feel [the thirty-year-old De Tocqueville wrote to a friend] like a lady of the court of Napoleon whom the Emperor took it into his head to make a duchess. That evening, as she heard herself announced by her new title when she came to court, she forgot to whom it belonged, and ranged herself on one side to let the lady pass whose name had just been called. I assure you this is just my case. I ask myself if it be *I* that they are talking about? . . . I infer that the world must consist of a poor set of people, since a book of my making, the limits of which I know so well, has had the effect this appears to produce.

But modesty was only one of De Tocqueville's many virtues. His work—the first part was a history of American democracy, the second an analysis of democratic government—was a cool and not unsympathetic investigation of democracy in an age when the concept was still surcharged with revolutionary emotion; it was worthy of that other magistrate, Montesquieu. To so levelheaded a mind as Tocqueville democracy was not a fighting word, but merely a form of government which deserved sympathetic treatment. He felt that modern democracy tended toward absolutism unless counteracted by a love of freedom on the part of the citizens. He also stressed the paradox that the levelling process of democracy would destroy all ultimate resistance to despotism. Nevertheless, he saw that "a great democratic revolution is going on among us" and that democracy was bound to dominate the modern world.

My conclusions tend, in a word, to the progressive organization of democracy. I have sought, it is true, to establish what were the natural tendencies which gave to the spirit and institutions of man a democratic state. I have signalized the dangers which await a society on this path; but I have not claimed that one can fight against these tendencies.

Tocqueville's work was crowned by the French Academy and he himself entered into politics. In 1849 he became vice-president of the Assembly and for a short time Foreign Minister, but the coup d'état of 1851 destroyed his political career. Tocqueville, therefore, decided to withdraw from politics and devote himself to history. This gentlemanly, poised, and judicious scholar was not a political success at any time.

People [so he wrote to a friend] want to make me a party man, which I am not. They ascribe to me passions when I have only opinions—or rather but one passion, the love of freedom and of human dignity. All forms of government are in my eyes but means to satisfy this sacred and lawful passion of man. Democratic and aristocratic prejudices are alternately ascribed to me. . . . I came into the world at the end of a long revolution. . . . Aristocracy was already dead when I began to live, and democracy was not yet in existence. No instinct, therefore, impelled me blindly toward one or the other. I was an inhabitant of a country which had been for forty years trying everything and stopping definitely at nothing. I was not, therefore, easily addicted to political illusions. Belonging myself to the old aristocracy of my country, I had no natural hatred or jealousy of aristocracy. . . . The same may be said of the democratic element. No interest gave me a natural or necessary propensity to democracy; nor had democracy inflicted on me any personal injury. I had no particular motive to love it or to hate it.[35]

Tocqueville spent five years investigating the records of the ancien régime, especially the administration. "Probably no living Frenchman," an English critic said, "had acquired so accurate a knowledge of the state of France before the Revolution." [36] In 1856 he published the first volume of De l'ancien régime et de la révolution. "This work," he wrote (p. 377), "which I have undertaken should not remain there. My intention is, if time and energy will not be wanting, to follow through the vicissitudes of that long revolution of . . . the French . . . under the old regime." His basic thesis is that the Revolution was a logical product of the ancien régime, and hence its continuation. The Revolution, for example, had taken over the centralized administration from its predecessors. "As I advanced," Tocqueville tells about

[35] Gustave de Beaumont, ed., Oeuvres et correspondance inédites d'Alexis de Tocqueville (Paris, 1860, 2 v.), II, 270.
[36] ER, CXXII (1865), 457.

his researches, "I was surprised to find at every moment traits which meet us in France today." The ancien régime, by its bureaucratic administration, had already destroyed feudalism; it was not, Tocqueville pointed out, as oppressive as was generally thought. It was merely arbitrary. The better side of the ancien régime was to be found only if external political history, diplomacy, the corruption of the court were ignored. Its rehabilitation, begun by Tocqueville, was continued by Le Play, *La réforme sociale* (1864), Taine, *L'ancien régime* (1876), Sorel, *L'Europe et la révolution française* (1885), Babeau, *Le village sous l'ancien régime* (1878), *La vie rurale dans l'ancienne France* (1883), and others.

The Revolution hastened the process of destroying the feudal remnants, which were bound to go in any case. It "achieved suddenly, by a convulsive and painful effort, without transition, without precaution, without regard, that which would have been accomplished slowly by itself in the long run." The final effect of the Revolution—which like the ancient regime did not believe in liberty—was "to abolish those political institutions which have obtained . . . for several centuries among the majority of European peoples, and which have ordinarily been designated as feudal, in order to substitute a more uniform and more simple political order, which had equality of conditions for its basis." [37] Tocqueville did not live long enough to complete the second volume, which was to deal with the movements for reform. The *Ancien Régime* has remained a standard work and, by and large, unchallenged in its conclusions. "The work of De Tocqueville," Professor Becker has written, "especially if we include the *Democracy in America*, was perhaps the most important influence, of a literary character, in directing the attention of French historians to those aspects of history which the admirers of the [French] Revolution had neglected," [38] to which may be added Professor Woodward's statement that "Tocqueville took care to study in Europe and in the larger letters of America the democracy which he disliked. He came to the conclusion that the rule of mediocrity and ordinariness was destined to become world-wide." [39]

Another writer who turned his attention to the ancien régime was Henri Martin (1810–83). [40] A free-thinking republican and a notary

[37] Tocqueville, *L'ancien régime* (3rd ed., Paris, 1857), 30–31.
[38] Carl Becker in *Publications of the American Sociological Society* (n. 1), 83.
[39] E. L. Woodward, *Three Studies of European Conservatism* (London, 1929), 203.
[40] HALPHEN, 53, 94; GOOCH, 224–25; Gabriel Hanotaux, *Henri Martin, sa vie—ses oeuvres— son temps, 1810–1883* (Paris, 1885); Henri d'Arbois de Jubainville, *Quelques observations sur les six premiers volumes de l'Histoire de France de M. Henri Martin* (Troyes, 1857); Henri de l'Epinois, *Critiques et refutations. M. Henri Martin et son "Histoire de France"* (Paris, 1872); Jules Simon, "Notice historique sur la vie et les travaux de M. Henri Martin," *ASMP*, CXXXI (1889), 29–63.

by profession, Martin was more of a popularizer than a serious scholar. His *Histoire de France* is a compilation in nineteen volumes (1837–54); a revised edition, 1855–60, is only in sixteen volumes. This work includes the Middle Ages, but the volumes on the ancien régime are superior to those on the feudal period. The work had revolutionary sympathies. His thesis was the fundamental importance of the Gallic race in the history of France through the ages, down to the revolutionists of 1789.

Martin had a number of imitators. Bordier and Charton produced a French history in two volumes (1859–60); Trognon in five volumes (1863–65); Dareste in nine (1865–79); and Gouet in six (1864–69). A really good and popular survey of French history, however, did not come until Lavisse and Rambaud.

"God has granted me to work for three great things: education of the people, the foundation of a free government, and the maintenance of peace." In these words François Pierre Guillaume Guizot (1787–1874),[41] "the most philosophical of politicians and the most political of philosophers," gave expression to his peculiar achievements. Politician, journalist, historian, Guizot, unlike Thiers his contemporary and rival, always remained a moralist. He was a descendant of a Protestant family, a fact which influenced his whole life. His father was guillotined in 1794 and afterwards the family moved to Geneva, where young Guizot was brought up in a rigorously moral and intellectual at-

---

[41] See Guizot's *Mémoires pour servir à l'histoire de mon temps* (Paris, 1858–67, 8 v.); cp. *LQR*, XII (1859), 335–54, and XLIV (1875), 62–90; and the reviews in *PJ*, I (1858), 554–57, and VI (1860), 196–201; HALPHEN, 24–26; FUETER, 632–35; GOOCH, 186–92; Jules Simon, *Thiers, Guizot, Rémusat* (n. 23); the same, "Notice historique sur la vie et les travaux de M. Guizot," *ASMP*, CXX (1883), 863–905; Bardoux, "Guizot historien," *ibid.*, CXLII (1894), 505–42; Émile Faguet, *Politiques et moralistes* (n. 19), I, 307–71; Th. Deschères, *Biographie de M. Guizot* (Paris, 1842); A. Bardoux, *Guizot* (Paris, 1894); E. Pascallet, *M. Guizot* (Paris, 1842); Felix Drouin, *Notice biographique sur la vie et sur les travaux de M. Guizot* (Paris, 1841); Mme de Witt [née Guizot], *Monsieur Guizot dans sa famille et avec ses amis* (Paris, 1880), translated by Mrs. M. C. M. Simpson as *Monsieur Guizot in Private Life* (Boston, 1882); and Mme de Witt, *Lettres de M. Guizot à sa famille et à ses amis* (Paris, 1884); Hippolyte Taine, "M. Guizot: Histoire de la révolution d'Angleterre," in *Essais de critique et d'histoire* (6th ed., Paris, 1892), 23–47; Henri de l'Epinois, "M. Guizot, son rôle comme historien," *RQH*, XVII (1875), 439–505; Robert Flint, *Historical Philosophy in France and Germany* (Edinburgh and London, 1874), 219–41; John Stuart Mill, *Dissertations and Discussions* (New York, 1874–75, 5 v.), II, 297–362; the same, "Guizot's Essays and Lectures on History," *ER*, LXXXII (1845), 381–412; cp. *ibid.*, LXVII (1838), 357–83, and CVIII (1858), 408–36; *QR*, LXXXIV (1848), 127–42; *FM*, XLI (1850), 340–47, a scathing criticism of Guizot's *English Revolution* by Froude; *NAR*, LI (1840), 69–91, a laudatory review of Guizot's *Washington; Blackwood's Magazine*, LVI (1844), 786–804; *DR*, XXXVI (1854), 494–522; *BQR*, XIV (1851), 405–37 and LXV (1877), 165–95; *FQR*, XVI (1836), 407–37.

For a Guizot bibliography see T. D. Hardy, *Descriptive Catalogue of Materials Relating to the History of Great Britain and Ireland* (London, 1862–71, 3 v. in 4: Rolls series no. 26), I, pp. lxxii–lxxiii; C. H. Pouthas, *Essai critique sur les sources et la bibliographie de Guizot pendant la restauration* (Paris, 1923). In 1875 Guizot's library was sold and the Paris bookdealer Adolphe Labitte published a *Catalogue des livres composant la bibliothèque de feu M. Guizot* (1875). An analysis shows that 570 items are listed under belles-lettres, including works in English, German, Latin, and Italian; and over 2000 items were of an historical nature, including histories of civilization, of antiquity, of France, England, etc.

mosphere. As a student he displayed a rare aptitude for languages. In fact, the first published essay of the future premier of France was written in German. At the age of eighteen Guizot went to Paris to study law; he also observed political institutions and read thoughtful works. "Since I lived in Paris," he tells in his *Mémoires*, "German philosophy and literature have been my favorite studies." This *enthusiasme germanique* left an indelible mark upon his thought and style: Guizot is always heavier and more serious than his compatriots.

Until 1808 he showed no predilection for history. He was studying law and philosophy, hoping to become a professor. Then a change occurred. His first real contact with history came when, encouraged by Pauline de Meulan (whom he married in 1812), he undertook to edit and annotate Gibbon. He was impressed with Gibbon's vision of history, but he abominated Gibbon's incredulity and doubt. He began to develop a method. This plunge into history was followed by an attempt to publish, in collaboration with Pauline de Meulan, the *Annales de l'éducation*, a review for the study of methods of instruction and scholarship. For this journal he wrote reviews and criticisms and also a series of articles on the great educators, Rabelais, Montesquieu, and Kant.

In 1812 he was requested to write a historical brochure for Napoleon on the ransom of prisoners, a controversy which Napoleon was carrying on with England at the moment. This won him the attention of the government. In the spring of the same year he was named *professeur adjoint* of history at the University of Paris. Guizot's appointment was shared with Lacretelle. Soon, however, their functions were divided. Lacretelle assumed the teaching of ancient history, and Guizot undertook to teach modern history. Then it was that he began to develop his plan for a history of civilization and to prepare that broader approach to the study of the human race which has, since his time, become the peculiar attribute of the French school.

It was in Paris [he relates] in the year 1808 when I began to think about a new translation of Gibbon, with notes and corrections, that I became interested in historical inquiries. The history of the establishment of Christianity inspired me with a passionate interest. I read the fathers of the Church, and the great works of the German writers relating to that period. Never did any study more captivate my mind. It was by those researches, and by the philosophy of Kant, that I was led to the study of German literature. As to my investigations into the history of the ancient legislation of Europe, I undertook them when I was appointed in 1811 professor of modern history, at the Faculty of Letters in Paris, and with a special view to my lectures on the origin of the modern civilization of Europe. I then plunged into the original chronicles, charters, the civil and ecclesiastical laws of the barbarians and of the middle ages. The works of the modern historians, especially the Germans, helped me much, but, while studying them, I always consulted the original documents, and verified the accuracy of their statements. I thus learnt to entertain the greatest esteem for the German historians, but not to follow them implicitly.[42]

This translation of Gibbon, in thirteen volumes, appeared in 1812 (incidentally, the first French translation of Gibbon was begun by Louis XVI and his tutor Leclerc de Sept-Chenes, but it was never completed; Guizot incorporated some of those chapters). In the notes to his edition of Gibbon, Guizot characteristically criticized the English historian for his failure to appreciate moral forces.

A promising young man—he was associated with the mild liberals under Royer-Collard—Guizot became a member of the government of the Restoration, Louis XVIII showing his goodwill by appointing a Protestant bourgeois to office. In his capacity of secretary to the Minister of the Interior, who was a reactionary, Guizot "must have seen and done dirty work, such as the preparation of categories of exile and proscription." [43] In 1816 Guizot resigned his office and for fourteen years he held no other political position.

From 1830 to 1848 Guizot's political career spanned the reign of Louis Philippe; his life was part of the larger history of France. Minister of Public Instruction—during which time he did much for the school system and for historiography—ambassador to England, and finally (1840–48) Minister of Foreign Affairs, Guizot had an opportunity to give full expression to his various abilities. In a brilliant essay, Sainte-Beuve once analyzed Guizot's character and showed that of the five qualifications necessary for a statesman (which Guizot himself drew up), he had only two: character and eloquence. Fecundity of spirit and public passion were entirely lacking in Guizot: "he knew only how to resist with magnificent obstinacy, without varying the means, without finding resources or expedients." Ideas he understood: "*c'est son domaine.*" Passions he had none: "*il les traite de haut en bas ou les ignore.*" Sainte-Beuve, an expert judge, doubted whether Guizot was essentially a writer. He was, rather, an orator. "From speaking well he came to write almost equally well." Occasionally, however, the humorless Guizot would throw out some flashing remark or keenly etch a portrait.

Inflexible, rigorous, self-righteous, Guizot was not a popular figure. Renan said that he was a "stiff, lonely, tragic creature." An English writer sneered at him as "Aristides the Just, of whom at last France wearied." Thiers said: "He is a great orator, but a mere fool in states-

---

[42] Quoted in *QR*, XCIV (1853), 127, the whole article, 122–71.
[43] Karl Gutzkow, *Briefe aus Paris*, forming vol. XII of his *Gesammelte Werke* (Frankfurt am Main, 1845–46, 12 v.). Cp. *FQR*, XXX (1843), 316 ff.

manship." [44] But the shortcomings of his personality need not detract from his achievements in the field of historiography to which he made a twofold contribution. In the first place, as cabinet minister he not only reorganized the school system but also furthered historical studies. Secondly, as an historian he interpreted history from a bourgeois point of view. The law making education compulsory in all the 39,000 communes—and free to the poor—was the work of Guizot, who at the same time revived the history curriculum in the secondary schools. [45] Not only personal inclinations but also political motives moved him to further historical studies; a clear knowledge of French history, he believed, would educate his fellow-citizens. Hence he was instrumental in organizing the *Société de l'histoire de France*, which attracted the best scholars and published, at government cost, the most important "textes, mémoires, chroniques, lettres" of France. The *Société* continued its publications for years after Guizot's death; between 1835 and 1932 no less than 314 volumes were published. [46]

As an historian, Guizot is remembered for the following works: *Histoire de la révolution d'Angleterre*, to the death of Charles I; [47] *Cours d'histoire moderne* (1829–32, 6 v.), which was later divided into *Histoire générale de la civilisation en Europe*, *Histoire de la civilisation en France*, and *Histoire des origines du gouvernement répresentatif en Europe*. In 1840, when he was a member of the government, he also wrote *Vie, correspondance et les écrits de Washington* (1839–40, 6 v.), which was so well received in America that the author's portrait was hung in the Library of Congress.

Guizot, it must be stressed, wrote history as a deeply religious man and as a bourgeois. He once said to his wife, "I see God in the laws which regulate the progress of the human race as clearly, nay, much more clearly present than in the movements of the stars. . . . Human

---

[44] See Karl Hillebrand, "Guizot in Private Life," *CR*, XXXIX (1881), 478–90; and *LQR*, LXV (1885), 1–21.

[45] The following quotation, taken from a contemporary textbook, shows the kind of history that was taught in the French schools in the time of Louis Philippe: "France is not yet in possession of her natural frontiers; she does not yet possess the whole French region. . . . The French region includes in reality the territory of Nice and Savoy, Switzerland (i.e., the cantons of Geneva, Lausanne, Fribourg and Neufchatel), Rhenish Bavaria, the Prussian Rhinelands, the Grand-duchy of Luxembourg and Belgium. . . . Her natural frontiers are the Rhine from its mouth to its source; the Alps from the source of the Rhine on the Great St. Gotthard to the Col de Cadibonne."

[46] Among the earliest members of the *Société* were A. Thierry, Mignet, Fauriel, Cousin, Barante, Raynouard, Guérard. In 1866 Guizot succeeded Barante as president of the Society, and was in turn succeeded by Leopold Delisle.

[47] First published in 1826–27, 2 v. This was continued in his *Histoire de la république d'Angleterre et du protectorat d'Olivier Cromwell* (1854, 2 v.), the *Histoire du protectorat de Richard Cromwell et du rétablissement des Stuarts* (1856, 2 v.), and supplemented in his smaller works, *Monk ou la Chute de la République* (1850), *L'Amour dans le mariage* (1855). In 1856 Guizot published another book dealing with an English subject: *Sir Robert Peel*.

history has vast gaps, but no mysteries. There is much that I do not know, but nothing that I do not understand." This was not vulgar conceit, but religious conviction. The ideas he held were rigorous and dogmatic, because he believed them to be universal and timeless, emanating from God whose attribute, as seen through man, was virtue. "Science," he once said, "is undoubtedly fine . . ., but it would be a thousand times finer if it became a power . . . of virtue." As for his political convictions, he was frankly and completely a bourgeois by birth, education, and ideas. The fundamental element in French history, he believed, was the middle class. "Sometimes," he admitted "I have had the honor of carrying myself the standard of the middle classes, which was naturally my own." For this reason Guizot, as minister and historian, hated revolutionists and preached a conservative respect for law. One must recall that the first acts of his ministry were counter-revolutionary; in 1830 he suppressed a Paris workers' revolt, abolished the republican club, and crushed the popular parties; in 1831 he fought against the abolition of the hereditary peerage. Such was Guizot's "liberalism."

The bourgeois outlook in politics and history is the *juste milieu*, that is, the control of society (government) by the bourgeoisie, "which is the true mean between the rival absurdities of divine right and sovereignty of the mob." [48] Such an ideal Guizot read into his history. He believed in progress, a process which he tried to explain in his *History of Civilization in Europe*. So convinced was he of the reality of progress that he thanked God that he was infinitely better than his ancestors. [49] Ironically enough, this apostle of progress also preached contentment with the *status quo*, never seeing the absurd contradiction between progress and rigid conservatism.

Guizot's imagination thought of history in terms of long duration, in whole periods. He had followed the development of European society from the downfall of the Roman Empire, and analyzed its component elements in every age. "I have formed the habit," he said before the French Academy, in 1861, "of regarding diversity of composition as essential to the existence of our great European societies. I compared these constituent parts of the social order; I examined their rights and their relative importance; I gave each one its place and its function." Guizot took the "long view" of events of which he wrote. He knew that the history of the immediate past was of interest to few except those

[48] *Mémoires* (n. 41), I, 3.
[49] *History of Civilization* (New York, 1881, 4 v. in 2), I, 33; cp. Alexis de Tocqueville, *Democracy in America*, tr. by Henry Reeve (New York, 1889, 2 v.), II, 304: "No man upon earth can as yet affirm absolutely and generally that the new state of the world is better than its former one."

who had been actors in it. "Many years, perhaps even centuries, must pass away before the history of a recent age interests men's thoughts again."

Guizot was essentially a thinker about history rather than an historical narrator. He rarely treated of individuals or social movements; he saw only moral forces.[50] In each epoch this highly logical mind saw some dominant idea or expressions of Providence. The history of Europe from the earliest period is one long process leading up to the middle classes. The Roman Empire fell because the *curiales* were ruined.[51] From the confusions of feudalism with its wars the middle classes emerged into consciousness, dignity, and law.[52] "One cannot build a house with engines of war; one cannot found a régime of liberty with ignorant prejudices and bitter hate." The history of civilization is conditioned by the existence of the bourgeoisie. Constitutional and bourgeois government means "the dignity of power ennobled and sustained by the dignity of obedience."[53] Throughout the ages governments and kingdoms and empires have risen and fallen because they had no stability; only representative government has the elements of permanency. One-man rule is absolutism; aristocratic government means the rule of a minority; democracy spells chaos and confusion.[54] Guizot rejects the sovereignty of any class or of the majority. "Plurality," he quotes Pascal with approval, "which does not reduce itself to unity, is confusion. Unity which is not the result of plurality, is tyranny."[55] He concludes that the ideal government is the English, because it is a representative government run by able men, *capables*, as he calls them.[56]

Guizot's ideas of government and politics are best summarized in his reflections, scattered throughout his history. This on Napoleon may be regarded as typical:

Incomparably active and mighty genius, admirable by his horror of disorder, by his profound instinct of government, and by his energetic and efficacious rapidity in the reconstruction of the social framework. At the same time, genius without measure and without restraint, who would not accept from God or from men any limit to his desires

[50] "The moral world has, like the system of celestial bodies, its laws and activity." *History of the Origin of Representative Government in Europe*, tr. by Andrew R. Scoble (London, 1861), 11; cp. his *Essais sur l'histoire de France* (Paris, 1858), 73–76 and *passim* for other examples of determinism.

[51] *Essais sur l'histoire de France* (Paris, 1858), 1–44. Guizot never improved upon these essays.

[52] *Ibid.*, 312; cp. 299–314 and *passim*.   [53] *Representative Government* (n. 50), 21.

[54] "Le chaos se cache aujourd'hui sous un mot: démocratie." *De la Démocratie en France* (Paris and Brussels, 1849), 9.

[55] *Representative Government* (n. 50), 62.

[56] See his comments on Cromwell in *History of Oliver Cromwell and the English Commonwealth*, tr. by Andrew R. Scoble (Philadelphia, 1854, 2 v.).

and will, and thereby remained a revolutionist even while combating the revolution: superior in the discernment of the general conditions of society, but understanding only imperfectly—shall I say coarsely?—the moral wants of human nature. . . .[57]

The historian, Guizot explained, has a threefold task: to investigate facts, to study their relation to each other, and to reproduce their form and motion. He never lived up to his formula. Although he accumulated a large amount of documents, for which he had a passion, he did not make critical use of them, rarely taking pains to establish the authenticity of his data. But worst of all, he was constitutionally incapable of working inductively. The facts taught him nothing; rather, he taught the facts. He did not critically examine his data in order to reach a conclusion; his conclusion was reached before he began to investigate. He chose only those materials which fitted his thesis. "Guizot's history is far too logical to be true," said Sainte-Beuve.[58]

[57] Quoted in *LQR*, XII (1859), 347.
[58] *Nouveaux lundis* (Paris, 1867–84, 13 v.), I, 82–121.

CHAPTER XLV

FRENCH HISTORIANS (1848–1922) [1]

THE nineteenth century, it has been said, is the period of history-mindedness; one might add that it is also the age of dominant historians, particularly in France. Guizot and Thiers, professional historians, were the leading French statesmen for two generations. These men not merely wrote history; they used their high positions to stimulate its study. Guizot did much for historical scholarship, but he retired from politics in 1848 and his work was not completed. His real successor in historiographic statesmanship, if one may be permitted to coin a phrase, was Victor Duruy, whose work, in turn, was taken up and continued by Rambaud, Lavisse, and Monod. These men who functioned in the latter half of the nineteenth century and well into the twentieth, transformed and deepened historical studies, so that a line of division must be drawn between, roughly, the periods before and after 1870.

Victor Duruy (1811–94) [2] was born in Paris as the son of a worker in the Gobelin factory, and was sent to the Collège Rollin; thence he entered the École Normale. "Mine has been a singular destiny," he said years later on the occasion of his reception into the French Academy; "at college I entered at the foot and came out at the head; at the École Normale, the same; at the University I remained longer than any others on the lowest seat, and suddenly was sent to the highest. At sixty-two I had not yet been received at the Institute. And now I am a member of all three Academies."

Duruy's teachers at the École Normale were Michelet, Ampère, and Jouffroy, and from them he acquired a lifelong love for history, a subject in which he took first honors. After his graduation at the age of twenty-two he began to teach in the Collège Henri IV, where among his students were the two sons of King Louis Philippe. This, however, added nothing to Duruy's income. His pay was only about $320 a year (first-class professors received 6000 francs annually and juniors less than 3000) and, having a large family to support, the young professor was compelled

---

[1] See the literature cited at the head of the previous chapter, to which add GOOCH, ch. xii; and Louis Halphen in HISTOIRE ET HISTORIENS, I, 148–66.

[2] The best accounts are Ernest Lavisse, *Une ministre: Victor Duruy* (Paris, 1895), cp. *AHR*, I (1895), 142–49; A. Rambaud, "Victor Duruy (1811–1894)," *JS*, Sept. 1904, pp. 485–96; Broglie, "Victor Duruy," *RDM*, CXLV (1898), 524–61; HALPHEN, 145; GOOCH, 467.

to eke out a living from outside sources. There were three ways for an impecunious intellectual to supplement his income: he could give private lessons, he could do journalistic work, or he could write textbooks. Duruy chose the last course. The chief of the Hachette publishing house was then a fellow-alumnus and for him Duruy began to write a series—an astonishingly long series—of textbooks on geography, Roman history, Greek history, and ancient history. With incredible energy, Duruy produced no less than seventy-four such books, over sixty of which dealt with the classics. As Jules Simon said, "A large number of generations have been brought up on his books." And it must be added that Duruy's textbooks were not the usual type of hack stuff, but lucid works which embodied the latest findings; he always re-edited his books, deleting the old and inserting new materials, because he was always "*au courant* with the most recent discoveries."

One should also praise, in these small books, the excellence of the outline, always well organized, and presenting the facts in their chronological connection which is almost always a logical connection. He has no dissertations; opinions are rare; he does not speak his mind except when necessary; he gives it soberly, clearly, and almost always with good sense and fairness.[3]

While working on his textbooks, Duruy found time to write an excellent *Histoire des Romains* in two volumes (1843–44), which brought him a chair at the Lycée St. Louis. Busy with his books, which were already having a deep influence on French education, Duruy paid no attention to the political turmoil. He seems to have been oblivious to the Revolution of 1848. Later he said that, unlike most Frenchmen, he had not cried: *Vive la république! Vive la monarchie! Vive le roi! Vive l'empereur!* Nevertheless, politics affected his career. He could not publish the third and fourth volumes of his *Histoire des Romains* (completed in 1850) until 1872, after the fall of the Empire. In the meantime he added to his reputation as an historian by issuing the first edition—his books were always running into numerous editions—of his *Histoire des Grecs* and editing the *Collection d'histoire universelle*, for which series he wrote a *Histoire de France* in two volumes.

Duruy's political career began in a peculiar way. He had not favored Napoleon III, having voted No in the plebiscite of 1851. But that queer Bonaparte, like so many other people in France, had read Duruy (as if one could have escaped that flood of Duruy books!) and remembered him as a conscientious historian. One day, in 1859, Marshal Randon, seeing the *Histoire des Romains* on the Emperor's table, said: "There is a book whose author I know, and I would be very pleased to

---

[3] From the excellent account of Duruy by Jules Simon, "Notice historique sur la vie et les travaux de M. Victor Duruy," *ASMP*, CXLV (1896), 66–93.

see him here." "It is a good book," Napoleon III replied. "Since you know the author, send him to me." The next day Duruy came and the Emperor subjected him to a long interrogation. Napoleon asked the abashed scholar whether he was contented with his position. "Yes, sire, I am professor in a lycée in Paris; I am content." "But," the Emperor asked, "what is the best position to which you could aspire?" Duruy replied: "Inspector-general." "You shall be Inspector-general," exclaimed Napoleon, and added laughing, "I shall speak to the minister."

Nevertheless, it took two years before Duruy's appointment was made. The minister, Rouland, opposed Duruy, and Napoleon seems to have forgotten his promise. In 1861 when the government was in conflict with the papacy over the sovereignty of the Romagna, Rouland asked the encyclopaedic Duruy to write a pamphlet on the origin and nature of the papal claims. Duruy produced his *Papes, princes italiens* in a few days and published 10,000 copies under his own name, since the government could not afford to make it official. Duruy's reward came swiftly. Napoleon appointed him professor at the École Polytechnique, inspector of the Academy, and finally Minister of Public Instruction. In the eyes of the public, the last was the best appointment of Napoleon's reign.

Duruy did not disappoint the public, at least the more enlightened public. Having been a teacher for almost thirty years, he had an intimate knowledge of the French educational system, which, according to Lavisse, Duruy's disciple, consisted of a little writing, a little reading, some arithmetic, and much Bible. "Thousands of communes," to quote Lavisse, "were without schools for girls, and most, if not all, hamlets with no schools at all; there were no schools for adults; not a single village library; teachers were paid only starvation wages, some 5000 female instructors receiving less than $80 a year, some less than half that sum, and not any of them entitled to a retiring pension." Duruy decided to put an end to this system, although it was strongly supported by the Church and by the cabinet. For six years Duruy did heroic work in transforming France's educational system. Step by step he had to fight the clericals and the politicians. The cabinet refused to vote money; the Emperor authorized Duruy's budget. Napoleon III, indeed, warmly though fitfully supported his Minister of Public Instruction. "I do not," this strange monarch said, "share all of M. Duruy's ideas; but he is an intelligent man."

Duruy succeeded in establishing more than 6000 free communal schools; more than 2000 new school buildings were erected. The number of students increased to some 238,000. The curriculum was organized so that history took the first place; this led Duruy's enemies to the accusation that he was glorifying the Emperor in the courses on contemporary history. "In a country of universal suffrage," Napoleon III said, "everybody should know how to read." Duruy attempted to put this idea into effect by making primary education compulsory.

The influence of German historical methods on France was insignificant until after the Revolution of 1848, when moderate French liberals as Michelet and Quinet were disillusioned. Duruy aspired to introduce German methods of historical study. Having established a broad free school system in France, he hoped to found higher schools of learning for adults. "Without courses for adults," he wrote, "the primary school puts into the hands of the child an instrument which soon rusts." Hence came the École des Hautes Études (1868), which was epoch-making in the history of French education, especially in the field of the writing and teaching of history.

The end of advanced teaching [Duruy wrote to the Emperor in 1868] is not merely to rouse a love for study; it aims, above all things, to impart to the hearer methods of study and the science which those methods have created. In Germany such men as Böckh, Ritschl, Welcker, Ranke and Raumer gave, or give, to their lectures from eight to ten or twelve hours a week; but the lectures do not demand such [literary] preparation as our professors make. They are, rather, minute directions, carefully noted down by the students and used for reference. Thanks to the habits of study thus formed, Germany can always furnish for every branch of human knowledge several distinguished masters, each one surrounded by numerous disciples. France possesses, beside the eloquent professors who draw their daily hundreds of auditors, noted scholars whose worthy followers are as few as their competent critics; it is such chairs that sooner or later stand empty.[4]

This École des Hautes Études was to train teachers and scholars. Unable to overcome the ancient Faculties, with their entrenched medieval traditions, Duruy, on July 31, 1868, founded the École Pratique des Hautes Études to teach "methods" by means of practical "exercises" given by historians, philologists, and scholars. The Practical

---

[4] Quoted in Paul Frédéricq, "The Study of History in Germany and France," tr. from the French by Henrietta Leonard in *Johns Hopkins University Studies in Historical and Political Science*, Eighth Series, V–VI (1890), 75–76. Duruy had long had such a school in mind. Gabriel Monod relates: "I recall a conversation . . . with M. Duruy . . . when I came from Germany, during which he revealed to me the project of a School of Higher Studies. I said to him that we had too many special schools and that instead of creating a new one, he should rather reorganize the Faculties by changing the framework and letting enter a . . . new spirit. It is impossible, he said to me, one does not reform old bodies despite themselves and, moreover, I have no money; to reorganize the Faculties, much money should be needed; to create the School which I plan, a pen and a sheet of paper suffice. I should obtain money for it, where I could get none for the Faculties. To make the French understand an idea, it is necessary to find a name which strikes the mind. It will suffice to create a new school and put in men devoted to the idea. . . . The School of Higher Studies is a germ which I am depositing in the cracked walls of the old Sorbonne; in growing, it will crumble it [the Sorbonne]." Quoted by de Broglie, "Notice sur la vie et les oeuvres de M. Victor Duruy," *ASMP*, CXLIX (1898), 569–602, cp. 729–45.

School was divided into four departments: mathematics and physics, chemistry, biological sciences, and history and philology. Hoping ultimately to "crack the walls of the old Sorbonne"—a task in which he succeeded—Duruy appointed to the Practical School men absolutely independent of all university traditions. Some of them, like Monod and Michel Bréal, were trained in the German seminar method; others were ambitious young men eager to make a career. The chief object of the School was to train scholars to succeed their professors. None of the young professors—they were so young that they were sometimes taken for their students—had any reputation; all of them subsequently made reputations. In the historical sciences Duruy appointed Waddington (an Oxford Hellenist), Alfred Maury (an archivist), Gabriel Monod (a student of Waitz). The seminar and not the classroom was the vital cell; practical exercises and not lectures were the means of training.

As Duruy had foreseen, the success of the École Pratique revived even the old Sorbonne and stimulated fruitful—and scientific—historic studies in the Collège de France and the École des Chartes. The School started out with a handful of students and about half a dozen professors. In a little over a decade, according to Paul Frédéricq, who visited Paris early in the 'eighties, there were twenty-five professors giving more than fifty courses in various branches of history. The School produced some of the greatest scholars in France: Graux, Longnon, Hanotaux, Giry, Roy, etc. "It does not require an inspired prophet," Frédéricq wrote about a dozen years after France was defeated by Prussia in 1870–71, "to predict for France the rise of a brilliant school of historians, who, true to their national spirit of harmony, will be able to hold the balance steady between foundation and structure, between analytical study of detail and philosophical synthesis." [5]

After his retirement from office Duruy, whose services were given recognition by his appointment to all three French Academies, continued to work on his *Histoire des Romains*, the last three volumes (out of seven) of which appeared between 1879 and 1885, and his *Histoire des Grecs* (1887). These works are still standard French classics. Though not based upon original researches, these two histories of classical antiquity embody the best scholarship of Europe. They are, in the words of a French critic, "magisterial" in their dignity, lucidity, and exactness. Duruy also planned a history of France on the same scale, but he never

---

[5] Frédéricq (n. 4), 118, cp. 110–18. In December 1882, Duruy wrote to Jules Simon: "In the École Normale they take care to form the élite of our professors; in the École des Hautes Études, to prepare savants; in the Sorbonne, the task of making *licenciés*, doctors, even *agrégées* who nevertheless almost always lack the wide education of the École Normale." See Simon in *ASMP* (n. 3), 66 ff.

got beyond an *Introduction générale à l'histoire de France* in which he gave his ideas about history (p. 62):

History which narrates is an art. History which explains, classifies phenomena under laws, I want to say, facts under their cause, is a science. My ambition for the study to which I have consecrated my life is that it should reach this rank (science).

The profound change in French historiography which came with Duruy's reorganization of the educational system was climaxed by the founding of the *Revue Historique* in 1876. In objective and scope this *Revue*, founded by Duruy's younger followers, resembled the *Historische Zeitschrift*, organized seventeen years earlier by another politician-historian, von Sybel. Germany, in fact, was the model for France in historical studies.[6] "The Germans," Freeman remarked satirically after the Franco-Prussian War, "knocked some of their *Geist* into the Frenchmen's heads and so lost some of their own." [7]

Around the *Revue Historique* gathered the leading scholars of the new generation of the Third Republic. The guiding spirit was Gabriel Monod (1844–1912), who was educated in the École Normale (where his schoolmates were Lavisse, Gaffarel, Pingaud). After graduation he visited Italy and Germany. The latter impressed him deeply. A student of Jaffé in Berlin and of Waitz in Göttingen, Monod learned to admire the German seminar method and historical investigation. "Germany," he said later, "has made the strongest contribution to historic work in our century"—an assertion with which Hippolyte Taine heartily agreed. The country of Bismarck was "like a vast historical laboratory where all the efforts are concentrated and co-ordinated and where no effort is wasted." Ambitious to do the same for France, Monod joined Duruy's École Pratique as a professor at the age of twenty-four; his own seminar was in medieval history, specifically the Merovingian Annals on which he was a specialist. But he realized that the resources, both for work and publication, at the École Pratique were too limited.

[6] In 1864 Monod, an unknown young man, asked Taine whether a bright young man of "the best possible French education, will . . . do well to go to Germany to finish his education?" Taine's reply is interesting: "I answer, yes, unhesitatingly. Most of the great historical studies in our times have their source and their centre in Germany. . . . Their superiority in History is due to two causes. In the first place, they are philologists; they go straight to the texts; they read manuscripts and unpublished documents . . .; they study at first hand. . . . In the second place, they are philosophers. . . . Thence their ideas on the *ensemble* and development of a whole civilization. . . . Such, Sir, is the best historical culture, in my opinion. To make an effort to acquire it is a noble and perilous undertaking." Letter of August 30, 1864, in *Life and Letters of H. Taine*, tr. by Mrs. R. L. Devonshire (London, 1902–08, 3 v.), II, 263–65.

[7] *Life and Letters of Edward A. Freeman*, ed. by W. R. W. Stephens (London and New York, 1895, 2 v.), II, 437. "[After 1871 the French] were . . . so sulky and absurd that they broke off scientific intercourse, with the result of soon convincing themselves that they were thus only doing themselves harm." Wilamowitz-Möllendorff, *My Recollections, 1848–1914*, tr. by G. C. Richards (London, 1930), 149.

The École des Chartes, another place where history was taught, was highly specialized, training palaeographers and archivists; the École Normale, on the contrary, was too general. There was no place where scholarly yet general historians were trained. Hence Monod hoped to broaden the programme of the École Pratique so as to form historians who would be a mean between erudition and literature. For this purpose a scientific but well-written historical review was needed. Such was the genesis of the *Revue Historique*.

The first issue of the *Revue* appeared in January 1876, under the editorship of Monod and Gustave Fagniez.[8] Its *Avant-propos*, written by the editors, was a manifesto of the newer historical school.

Historical studies assume in our epoch an ever-increasing importance and it becomes more and more difficult, even for the scholars in the profession, to be *au courant* with all the discoveries, all the new researches which are produced daily in this vast domain. We believe that we are responding to the desires of a large part of the literary public by creating, under the title *Revue Historique*, a periodical intending to favor the publication of original works on various aspects of history and to furnish exact and complete accounts of the movement in historic studies in foreign countries as well as in France. . . .

We shall, then, issue neither a polemical work nor a work of vulgarization; but our *Revue* will not be a collection of pure erudition. It will not admit any but original and first-hand works which enrich the science either by researches which will be their base or by results which will be their conclusion; but despite all demand on our collaborators for strictly scientific procedure, where every affirmation should be accompanied by proof and reference to sources and citations, and severely excluding vague generalizations and oratorical display—we shall conserve in the *Revue Historique* that literary character to which French scholars as well as readers rightly attach so much value.

Our framework will not exclude any province of historical studies; nevertheless, our *Revue* will be principally devoted to European history from the death of Theodosius (395) to the fall of Napoleon I (1815). It is, in fact, for this period that our archives and libraries preserve most of the unexplored treasures; and we wish, as much as possible, to avoid all contemporary polemics.

Monod himself contributed the first article in the first issue of the journal. Anyone interested in the subject should read this "*Du progrès des études historiques en France depuis le XVIe siècle*," which is both a critical history and an outline for the future. He pointed out that all intellectual disciplines tended to acquire an historical character. "Our age is the age of history." Unfortunately, in France there was no regular development in the field of historical scholarship. The early—nineteenth-century—French historians were largely auto-didactics, who

---

[8] Gustave Fagniez (1842–1927) was co-editor of the *Revue Historique* from 1876–82. He had been a student at the Faculty of Law and the École des Chartes. Later he became editor of the bulletin *France*, in which he judged, firmly and keenly, recent historical publications; he also edited the collection on economic history: *Documents rélatifs à l'histoire de l'industrie et du commerce en France* (1898–1900, 2 v.). He was the author of *L'économie sociale de la France sous Henri IV, 1589–1610* (1897); *Études sur l'industrie et la classe industrielle à Paris au XIIIe au XIVe siècle* (1877); and *Le père Joseph et Richelieu, 1577–1638* (1894, 2 v.).

had neither masters nor pupils. They are—many were still alive when Monod wrote this—chiefly "littérateurs avant d'être des savants." They do not keep up with the latest findings in their fields; even when they revise their works they change nothing. *Sint ut sunt aut non sint.* What matters to them is form rather than facts. This is due to the absence of a scientific tradition as well as to the all-too-frequent presence of political or religious passions.

The most eminent of our historians [Monod wrote severely] have all let themselves be influenced strongly in their theories, in their appreciations, and even in their criticism of facts by contemporary passions. This is true of Thierry as well as of Guizot, of Michelet as well as of Thiers. The example and the memory of the eighteenth century, moreover, drove them to hasty generalizations, and they imagined that once the revolution was accomplished and above all the charter of 1830 proclaimed, the moment has come to write the general history of France in a definitive manner, or even, like E. Quinet, to trace, in a few pages, the Philosophy of History of France.[9]

But the greatest misfortune, Monod continued, from which French historiography suffered was the "antagonism between literature and scholarship." Littérateurs for a long time affected "a sort of contempt" for research; for them imagination and style took the place of everything. Scholars, on the other hand, have shown a disdain for literary form, an aversion for general ideas, "and they took refuge . . . in minutiae and factual details always without interest." The *Revue Historique* now hopes to correct these abuses. It will take no political or religious sides; it will permit diverging opinions, but not polemics. "History can be studied for itself, without any preoccupation with conclusions that can be drawn for or against such and such a faith." The *Revue* will be a forum for "positive science" and "free discussion," but will be confined to the "domain of facts." Monod concluded by paraphrasing La Popelinière: "It is thus that history, without proposing *any other aim than the benefit that can be drawn from truth,* works in a secret and sure manner towards the grandeur of the country at the same time as toward the progress of the human species." [10]

The first volume of the *Revue* carried fifty-three names as "collaborators." Among them were archivists and librarians, scholars and histo-

---

[9] Gabriel Monod, "Du progrès des sciences historiques depuis le XVIe siècle," *RH,* I (1876), 30, the whole important article 5–38. J. R. Green, *Stray Studies,* Second Series (New York and London, 1903), 175–82, was equally severe on Guizot, Michelet, and Thiers. See also Geffroy, Zeller, and Thiénot, *Rapports sur les études historiques* (Paris, 1867); and Green's review in *Saturday Review,* Oct. 17, 1868.

[10] *RH,* I, 36, paraphrasing La Popelinière, *Premier livre de l'idée de l'histoire accomplie,* 66. Monod wrote: "Nous ne prendrons donc aucun drapeau; nous ne professerons aucun credo dogmatique; nous ne nous enrôlerons sous les ordres d'aucun parti; ce qui ne veut pas dire que notre *Revue* sera une babel ou toutes les opinions viendront se manifester. Le point de vue strictement scientifique auquel nous nous plaçons suffira à donner à notre recueil l'unité de ton et de caractère."

rians, representing most of the academies and schools in France. They included Bordier, Bouché-Leclerc, Montpellier, Delisle, Dumont, Duruy, Fustel de Coulanges, Geffroy, Giry, Himly, Lavisse, Longnon, Maspero, Maury, Molinier, Morel-Fatio, Quicherat, Rambaud, Renan, Sorel, Taine, Tamizey de Larroque, and Viollet; no wonder the editors boasted that "les noms de nos collaborateurs diront mieux que toutes les paroles." [11]

Other distinguished historians sooner or later made their debut in the *Revue Historique:* Bourgeois, Hauser, Jullian, Langlois, Prou, Salomon and Theodore Reinach, Waddington. Monod remained editor for thirty-six years, from 1876 to 1912, and he not only published materials dealing with all periods of history, but also attracted foreign contributors. Upon Monod's death, in 1912, Charles Bémont, his oldest pupil at the École Normale, became editor. [12]

The *Revue Historique* was symptomatic of what was happening in the field of historical scholarship. In the generation following, more than a dozen other historical reviews were founded, [13] and dozens of learned societies were organized. [14] In consequence, history, with some remarkable exceptions, became more "scientific" but less synthetic. Sources,

[11] The first volume of the *Revue Historique* contained articles on the municipal régime in the Roman Empire (Duruy), the historians of the First Crusade (Thurot), Granvelle (Castan), Saint-Simon and Abbé Dubois (Chéruel), Custine's mission to Brunswick in 1792 (Sorel), Gregory VII (Giry), the second prince of Condé (Loiseleur), Revolutionary Committee of Agriculture and Commerce (Guiffrey), destruction of Magdeburg and Tilly (Reuss), fate of the Alexandrian Library (Chastel), Italian regions on the Peutinger map (Desjardins), and of course the leading article by Monod. In the first year the *Revue* was issued as a quarterly; from 1877 on it was bi-monthly.

[12] See M. C. Pfister, "Le cinquantenaire de la 'Revue historique,'" in Histoire et Histo-riens, I, vii–xvii.

[13] Among these reviews one may mention: *Revue d'histoire des religions* (1880); *Révolution française* (1881); *Moyen âge* (1888); *Revue d'histoire moderne et contemporaine* (1899–1914); *Revue des études anciennes* (1899); *Revue de synthèse historique* (founded, in 1900, by Henri Berr "pour approfondir et préciser la conception de l'histoire"); *Revue d'histoire de Lyon* (1902); *Annales révolutionnaires* (1908); *Revue d'histoire de l'église de France* (1910); *Revue de l'histoire des colonies françaises* (1912); *Revue des études Napoleonniennes* (1912, in 1926 the title was changed to *Napoleon: La revue du XIXᵉ siècle*); as well as a number of provincial historical reviews.

[14] This is not the place to enumerate all the learned societies, but a few should be listed: École française d'archéologie et d'histoire (Rome, 1876); Institut d'archéologie orientale du Caire (1880); École française d'extrême-orient (Hanoi, 1901); Institut de Florence (1908); École des hautes études hispaniques (Madrid, 1909); Institut de Saint-Petersbourg (1912); as well as Institutes at London (1913), Prague (1922), Sofia (1923), Warsaw (1923), and in Jugoslavia. In France there were: Société des études historiques (1872); Société asiatique; Société des antiquaries de France; Comité des travaux historiques et scientifiques; Société de l'histoire de France; Société d'histoire moderne (1901); Société de l'histoire de la révolution française (1888); Société de l'histoire de l'art français (1872, reorganized in 1906); Société des études Robespierristes (1907); Société d'histoire du droit (1913); Société d'histoire ecclesi-astique de la France (1914); Société d'histoire de la guerre (1919). See R. de Lasteyrie, E. Le-fevre-Pontalis, and A. Vidier, eds., *Bibliographie générale des travaux historiques et archéologiques publiés par les sociétés savantes de la France* (1886–1916, 6 v.), continued by Lasteyrie and Vidier, *Bibliographie annuelle des travaux*, etc. (1901–10, 3 v.); cp. Halphen in Histoire et Historiens, 148–66.

texts, *recueils*, monographs, *études* began to dominate the field. The plethora of materials ultimately necessitated some kind of selection and unity. By the turn of the century a reaction had set in once more, and, as will be seen, large co-operative syntheses were introduced.

As an example of the "scientific"—documentary—type of historian one may take Léopold Delisle (1826–1910). "It has long been an acknowledged fact," so wrote Fritz Milkau in his necrology of Delisle, "acknowledged by the consensus, not of France alone, but of the world, that the enormous progress of historical science during the latter half of the nineteenth century is due to no one else in so high a degree as it is to him." [15] That this statement is no exaggeration is shown by the remarkable *Bibliographie des travaux de M. Léopold Delisle* (1902), compiled by Paul Lacombe, which covers 549 pages and lists the astonishing total of 1900 numbers. It will be remembered that the bibliography of Mommsen, that champion of scholarly productivity, contains merely 1513 titles. The all-time prize for productivity of articles, but not of books, undoubtedly goes to Delisle.

Delisle was trained at the École des Chartes, but he supplemented his three-year course by voluntary work in the provincial archives of his native Normandy. Before 1852 he had made transcripts of most of the Norman charters previous to the conquest of Normandy by Philip Augustus. Although he wished to obtain a post as archivist in his beloved province, his teacher Benjamin Guérard would not permit him to leave Paris. Guérard appointed him assistant keeper of the department of manuscripts in the Bibliothèque Nationale, where he remained for the next half-century as assistant, keeper, and finally administrator general. It has been said of Delisle that he "found the Bibliothèque Nationale a mob of books and left it a library." In the course of his reorganization of the Bibliothèque, Delisle collected the materials which he embodied in his most famous work: *Cabinet des manuscrits de la Bibliothèque Impériale* (*Nationale*) (1868–81). The content of the publication is explained by the subtitle: "A study of the formation of this depot, comprising the elements of a history of calligraphy, miniatures, bookbinding, and the commerce of books in Paris before the invention of printing." Like his teacher Guérard, Delisle also made important contributions to medieval economic history; he published a number of chartularies, as well as *Études sur la condition de la classe agricole et l'état de l'agriculture en Normandie au moyen-âge* (1851), which won the Prix Gobert of the Institut. His writings, whether synthesis or monograph, are characterized by lucidity and perfect skill in

[15] Fritz Milkau, "Léopold Delisle. Ein Nekrolog," *Zentralblatt für Bibliothekswesen*, XXVII (1910), 385–401.

the presentation of facts. This rare type of librarian and scholar, with
his ". . . short, . . . sturdy figure, the studious stoop of the shoulders,
the bent head, and above all the clear intelligent eyes that looked
out from the broad face with the expression of frank honesty," [16]
achieved a world reputation not unlike that of Mommsen.

Consideration of Renan, Taine, and Fustel de Coulanges may be
found in other chapters of this book. But something should be said
here of Sorel and Aulard, Lavisse and Rambaud. Albert Sorel (1842–
1906) entered the French Foreign Office on the advice of Guizot in
1866, became professor of history at Paris in 1872 and at the military
school of St. Cyr in 1898. He is the author of one masterpiece, *L'Europe
et la Révolution française* (8 v., 1885–1904), "the best study of international complications" of the French Revolution.[17] The work com-
plements Taine's *Origines*, but its scholarship is of a much higher—or
shall we say, less controversial?—order. The originality of Sorel's history lies in its treatment of the Revolution outside of France; his scope
is European. Moreover, Sorel drew his materials from the archives of
France and Europe and, unlike Taine and Guizot, he permitted himself
to be guided by his data. An historian of the recent, "scientific"
school, Sorel wrote without any noticeable bias; he had no doctrinal
predispositions or metaphysical convictions like his friend Taine. He
viewed the Revolution, in the international sphere, as a continuation
of the foreign policy of the *ancien régime* (as Tocqueville, it will be
remembered, did in regard to the internal administration); hence the
conflict between the monarchical European powers and Revolutionary
France. The moment the revolutionists made efforts toward territorial aggrandizement, the European powers reacted in the same way
they did in the time of Louis XIV—with a military coalition against
France. "I consider" wrote Sorel, "that my work will not have been
useless if I can achieve this result: to show that the French Revolution,
which appeared to many as the subversion, and to others as the regeneration of the old European world, was the natural and necessary
result of the history of Europe." [18] Sorel soberly shows that the wars
of the Revolution were motivated neither by egalitarian philosophy on
the part of the Jacobins nor by counter-Revolution fanaticism on the

---

[16] E. Maunde Thompson, "Léopold Delisle," *EHR*, XXVI (1911), 76, the whole article, 76–
83; R. Lane Poole, in *Proceedings of the British Academy*, V (1905–06); the same, "A Great
French Scholar: Léopold Delisle," *QR*, CCXIV (1911), 473–90; GOOCH, 207–08; Ch. Bémont,
"Léopold Delisle," *CV* (1910), 84–91; Georges Perrot, "Notice sur la vie et les travaux de
Léopold-Victor Delisle," *BEC*, LXXIII, 5–72, also printed separately (Paris, 1912). Delisle
seemed to have only one weakness: he did not understand military history; cp. Charles Oman,
A History of the Art of War: the Middle Ages (Boston and New York, 1923, 2 v.), I, 384.
[17] Louis Gottschalk, *The Era of the French Revolution (1715–1815)*, (Boston and New York,
1929), 465.
[18] *L'Europe et la Révolution française*, p. 8.

part of the monarchs; in the one instance it was sheer territorial expansion, and in the other self-interest and self-defense. Europe was less interested in saving the French crown than in partitioning Poland. Russia and Prussia had both eyes on Poland and cared little what happened to Louis XVI; Austria had one eye on Poland and one on the Low Countries, and was happy to see France weakened by revolution. England, mainly concerned with her commerce and colonies, was regarded by the French, ever since the loss of the American colonies, as decadent and in decline; consequently the revolutionists, despite Mirabeau's plea to the contrary, played with the idea of destroying a country that was long regarded as the traditional enemy of France. The first part of the first volume contains an admirable sketch of the history of the European states in the last two centuries. Sorel shows that the period was virtually one of perpetual war; treaties were not binding; there was little international morality. In an earlier book, *The Eastern Question in the Eighteenth Century,*[19] Sorel had already shown how ruthless and unscrupulous were the three partitioners of Poland; and it was these three powers that later attacked the Revolution. Old Europe was drifting toward a violent upheaval, for it was morally bankrupt. There was a reform movement in practically every country in the eighteenth century, stimulated principally by the ideas of the French *philosophes* who had an international audience. But reform seemed unable to stem the inevitable revolutionary tide.[20]

Adolphe Aulard (1848–1928)[21] brings us down to very recent times. Like Sorel, he devoted himself mainly to the French Revolution, but, unlike Sorel, he was an ardent partisan. The Municipal Council of Paris, in 1886, founded for him the first chair of the history of the French Revolution; as such, Aulard became a sort of pontiff of Revolutionary studies. His hero was Danton, just as his opponent Mathiez' hero was Robespierre. In fact, from 1886 on down to our own day, the historiography of the French Revolution has been a battlefield between the champions of Danton and the defenders of Robespierre. Generally speaking, the Dantonists, following Aulard, were good bourgeois republicans; the Robespierrists, under the leadership of Mathiez, were more or less Marxist socialists. A good example is the socialist leader

[19] *La question d'Orient au XVIIIe siècle* (Paris, 1878); tr. by F. C. Bramwell (London, 1898).

[20] On Sorel see GOOCH, 246–49; FUETER, 740; Georges Picot, "Notice historique sur la vie et les travaux de M. Albert Sorel," *ASMP*, CLXVII (1907), 20–57; Gabriel Monod, "Albert Sorel," *RH*, XCII (1906), 91–99; for reviews of his works see *QR*, CCVII (1907), 534–58; *RQH*, XXXIX (1886), 680–82, and XLII (1887), 526–36.

[21] On Aulard see GOOCH, 250–52; Charles Bémont in *RH*, CLIX (1928), 214–15; Hintze in *HZ*, CXXXIX (1929), 448–49; A. Wahl, in *Historische Vierteljahrschrift*, V (1902), 416–20; Mathiez, "Aulard, historien et professeur," *Révolution française*, LV; Émile Faguet, *Discussions politiques* (Paris, 1909); and the appendix of Crane Brinton, *A Decade of Revolution, 1789–1799* (New York, 1934).

Jaurès who edited the *Histoire socialiste* (1901 ff.), the first volumes of which constituted a history of the Revolution from a socialist point of view.[22]

Controversy apart, Aulard performed invaluable services in further-ing the studies of the Revolution. "I am," he said, "a respectful and grateful son of the Revolution which has emancipated humanity and science." The subject, he decided, was worthy of the most intense cultivation. Together with his pupils, Aulard, in 1888, founded the Société de l'histoire de la révolution française and the monthly journal *La révolution française.* He also helped to organize the Commission municipale de recherches sur l'histoire de Paris pendant la révolution (1887) which published a series of studies on the history of Paris at municipal expense. These organizations issued a vast amount of im-portant materials on the Revolution. After twenty years of pains-taking and voluminous editorial work, Aulard published his chief work: *Political History of the French Revolution,* subtitled *Origins and Develop-ment of Democracy and the Republic.* As the title indicates, this is chiefly a political history; economics, diplomacy, war are neglected. Aulard's main purpose is to show the development of the democratic principles; his original contribution was to demonstrate the lateness of the republican idea in France.

I propose to show [he says in the preface] how the Declaration of Rights was put into operation between the years 1789 and 1804, in the institutions of the period: how they were interpreted in the speeches, by the press, in the policies of the various political parties and by the manifestations of public opinion. Two of these principles, that of the equality of rights and that of popular sovereignty were most frequently invoked during the elaboration of the new state policy. They are historically the essential principles of the Revolution—variously considered and differently applied as they were according to the times. The chief object of this book is the narration of the vicissitudes which these two principles underwent.

The work is divided into four sections: the Origins of Democracy and of the Republic (1789–92), the Democratic Republic (1792–95), the Bourgeois Republic (1795–99), and the Republic *plébiscitaire* (1799–1804). Aulard limited himself to the political history of France from the meeting of the States General in 1789 to the end of the Consu-late, omitting military events and even economic and social history. He began his labors in 1879 as a series of lectures at the Sorbonne, and year after year ploughed through the enormous mass of sources. Indeed, he boldly asserts: "Je ne pense pas avoir omis une source importante, ni avoir émis une seule assertion qui ne soit directement tirée des sources."

[22] See Margaret Pease, *Jean Jaurès, Socialist and Humanitarian* (New York, 1917); Gabriel Monod in *RH*, LXXVIII (1902), 354–64; Charles A. Beard in *Political Science Quarterly*, XXI; and *AHR*, XI (1905–06), 543.

The preparation for the Revolution lay in the "enlightenment" of the years preceding it. The first crisis occurred with the struggle between the king and the assembly, and was precipitated by the taking of the Bastille. Like Michelet, Aulard sees in the federations the spontaneous organization of France through her municipalities. A new administrative system was introduced by the Assembly which also transformed France into a limited monarchy. When the monarchy was overturned, a democratic republic, with universal suffrage, was established. Internal revolt and foreign invasion immediately necessitated a dictatorial government which, however, once the emergency had passed, gave way to a bourgeois republic. Soon there came a recrudescence of Terrorism and, to save herself from a renewal of the old horrors, France threw herself into the arms of Bonaparte. Such, briefly, are Aulard's "stages" of the political history of France during the Revolution. Despite his vast factual knowledge—and Aulard was probably the greatest authority on the period—he ignored many essentials. He admitted that it was "actually impossible in the life of one man to know all." Nevertheless, the Revolution cannot be understood without a full discussion of economic conditions, social forces, and, perhaps chiefly, the conflict between classes. One can find none of these things in Aulard, the self-confessed child and champion of the great Revolution.

Ernest Lavisse (1842–1922) and Alfred Rambaud (1842–1905) are two distinguished names connected with the best co-operative synthesis of French history. Lavisse was the continuator of the educational ideas of Duruy, whose private secretary he had been. He took his doctorate in Germany, and his thesis was on a German subject: *Étude sur l'une des origines de la monarchie prussienne, ou La Marche de Brandenbourg sous la dynastie Ascanienne* (1875); thereby he became one of the few French specialists on German history.[23] He taught at the École Normale and finally at the Sorbonne, whence he exerted a lasting influence on educational policies and historical method. Among his best students were Langlois and Seignobos. His constant emphasis was upon broad interpretation and universality of outlook. Although he lectured brilliantly on the Middle Ages, he despised those who devoted themselves merely to the "medieval waste lands" or to "minutiae fit for an entomologist." He ridiculed that type of student who abandoned the "highways for the footpaths, the footpaths for the blind alleys." He gave his students this advice: "If you have placed your magnifying glass on a speck of dust you must keep it there just long enough to

[23] Among Lavisse's other books dealing with German subjects were: *Études sur l'histoire de Prusse* (1879); *Essais sur l'Allemagne impériale* (1887); *La jeunesse du grand Frédéric* (1891); *Le grand Frédéric avant l'avènement* (1893)—the latter two are brilliant psychological studies.

make sure it is indeed a speck of dust, not one minute longer." Lavisse, moreover, had the character to practice what he preached. He always lived up to the significant words he once told his students: "We who live intellectually in the past should not forget that the majority of men live in the present and are concerned about the future." To him history was not an antiquarian pursuit but a living subject to be expounded to his fellow citizens who were not interested in erudition. Small wonder that he was famed as a teacher. A contemporary writes:

I heard M. Lavisse give several very striking lectures upon the France and Germany of the Middle Ages. In a few artistic, precise and sharply drawn lines he characterized Philip Augustus and St. Louis, continually citing passages from contemporary writers and documents. At another time he rapidly sketched the assembly roll of great men in France down to the thirteenth century, and warmly recommended this to his pupils as a subject for study, referring to the example of Germany. . . . He constantly referred, with precision, to passages of ancient chroniclers and to the best works of German historians. . . . At every step in his brilliant discourse M. Lavisse threw out original observations with moderation, accuracy and clearness, with a striking soundness which was often unexpectedly enhanced by a piquant word, an ironical reflection, a picturesque detail, or a sharp running fire, delivered with a resolute voice, vibrating with conviction and contagious animation. The pupils, numbering from twenty to fifty . . ., listened with almost passionate attention and eagerly devoured the master's words.[24]

Lavisse's first important achievement was his editorship of the *Histoire générale*, a co-operative work in ten volumes extending from the beginning of the Middle Ages to the end of the nineteenth century. The first volume appeared in 1894. His fellow-editor Alfred Rambaud was a specialist in Byzantine [25] and Russian history.

[24] Frédéricq (n. 4), 101–02. Cp. Othon Guerlac, "Ernest Lavisse, French Historian and Educator," *South Atlantic Quarterly*, XXII (1923), 23–42. "Coming from a little side office [at the Sorbonne], the lecturer would appear preceded by the traditional glass of water and three pieces of sugar on a tray. He was a man in the fifties, tall, vigorous, with a big head slightly inclined, a gray beard, sharp blue eyes, a strong, sonorous, well modulated voice. With his commanding stature, the rosette in his buttonhole, his somewhat abrupt delivery, he reminded one of a colonel in citizen's clothes more than of a professor. At the beginning of every year he would explain to his public two rules that were special to his course: the doors were closed after the beginning of every lecture so that no one could, in the midst of it, come in or go out. This was to discourage idle curiosity. . . . Likewise applause was discountenanced as foolish and insulting to the speaker." *Ibid.*, pp. 23–24.

[25] Rambaud wrote *L'Empire grec au Xe siècle: Constantin Porphyrogénète* (1870); *Études sur l'histoire byzantine* (1912), the latter being a collection of articles. Frédéricq (n. 4), 109–10, gives the following description of Rambaud as a lecturer: "M. Alfred Rambaud gave an excellent lecture upon France and Russia in the eighteenth century. . . . M. Rambaud drew a very graphic and amusing sketch. . . . A rare exception amongst French professors, M. Rambaud read rather indifferently, but he spoke with animation and faultless simplicity and depicted all the intrigues of palace and barracks with wonderful vigor. . . . I heard M. Rambaud describe some truly remarkable features of Catherine's administration; as when in 1766 she assembled at Moscow a sort of parliament, composed of more than 600 delegates from her immense states and constituting an ethnographical exhibition . . ., rather than a deliberative assembly. . . . In this connection M. Rambaud traced the origin of serfdom in Russia in the seventeenth century and described the heart-rending condition of Russian slaves a century after their subjection. But I cannot here analyze the lecture; it was admirable in its clearness, simplicity and originality."

In the preface to the initial volume of this great set the two editors gratefully paid homage to Victor Duruy, their master, who as far back as 1863 had declared that "l'histoire-bataille" is not everything. Voltaire's "les moeurs et l'ésprit des nations" were the true elements of history; "l'influence des idées sur la matière" was the chief purpose of historical research. There are magnificent sentences in this preface, as for instance: "De proche en proche la matière en ébullition se prend, se fige, se cristallise, s'organise. De ces poussières de peuples que le sabot d'un cheval hun, avar, magyar, arabe, suffisait pour faire lever en tourbillons, se condensent de vraies nations."

The *Histoire de France*, edited by Lavisse alone, fills eighteen volumes, and the *Histoire de France contemporaine*, nine volumes. The foremost scholars contributed to this collection, which at once became the most critical, comprehensive, and thorough account of French civilization, superseding all older summaries. Lavisse himself carefully planned the topics and always insisted upon not merely critical but also timely interpretation. He wanted his *History* to be of use to the general public. "It gives to men of the twentieth century a history written by men of the twentieth century. It keeps their interest because it satisfies their curiosity and tells them what they want to know and only what they want to know." [26]

The synthesis achieved by Lavisse and Rambaud set the style for other co-operative works. Henri Berr began to edit his *Évolution de l'humanité* in one hundred volumes, Gustav Glotz undertook to supervise a *Histoire générale* in fifty volumes, L. Halphen and Sagnac projected *Peuples et civilisations* in twenty volumes, Cavaignac started a *Histoire du monde* in twelve volumes. These works were on an international, or rather world, scale. In the field of national history Hanotaux edited a co-operative *Histoire de la nation française* (1920–29, 15 v.). Historical work in France has gone on apace. To quote Louis Halphen: "The time of the simple ferreters of libraries and denizens of archives has definitely passed." [27]

[26] See *RH*, CXL–CXLI (1922), 315–18; GOOCH, 219–20; HALPHEN, 174–75.

[27] HISTOIRE ET HISTORIENS, I, 166. There is no general bibliography of French history similar to Dahlmann-Waitz for Germany; but the nature and quantity of modern French historical writing can be ascertained from Gabriel Monod, *Bibliographie de l'histoire de France . . . jusqu'en 1789* (Paris, 1888); Pierre Caron, *Bibliographie des travaux publiés de 1866 à 1897 sur l'histoire de la France depuis 1789* (Paris, 1907–12, in 6 pts.); and the annual volumes of Pierre Caron and Henri Stein, *Répertoire bibliographique de l'histoire de France* (Paris, 1923 ff.).

CHAPTER XLVI

ENGLISH HISTORIANS OF THE EARLY NINETEENTH CENTURY [1]

ENGLISH historiography entered the nineteenth century with much of the traditions and philosophy of the preceding age. Hume, Robertson, and Gibbon had left a respectable legacy. But in 1800 national history was probably worse represented in England than in any other country of Europe save Spain. Prodigious ignorance prevailed regarding the earliest period of English history. The huge stores of source materials so happily preserved in the island were inaccessible; and historians exerted no efforts to master the material which was available. A deep prejudice against medieval history was universal. As late as the '40's the London *Times* editorially declared that the study of medieval history was "a foolish interference with the natural progress of civilization and prosperity." [2] The only period of English history which was passably well known was that from the sixteenth century onward.

History in England was still—and so it was to remain for long in the new century—considered a branch of *belles-lettres*. It was the occupation of the dilettante, of the gentleman of leisure, and occasionally of the dignified statesman or the ambitious literary worker. The two universities of Cambridge and Oxford, whose conservative doors were closed to the majority of England's talents, continued to cultivate the ancient classics, but instruction in history or modern languages was virtually nonexistent. The chairs for this subject were considered

[1] The *Dictionary of National Biography* has excellent sketches of English historians, with bibliographies. GOOCH, 282–401, has the fullest connected account anywhere; see also WARD, XIV, ch. ii [and, for writers on ancient and early ecclesiastical history, XII, ch. xiv]; A. J. Grant, *English Historians* (London, 1906), offers extracts, and pp. xxxix–lxxxvi of his introduction pertain to this century; *LTLS*, 1937, pp. 319–21, a precious survey; Charles Bémont in HISTOIRE ET HISTORIENS, I, 167–91; C. H. Herford, *The Age of Wordsworth* (London, 1901); Hugh Walker, *The Age of Tennyson* (London, 1900); the same, *The Literature of the Victorian Era* (Cambridge, 1921); John T. Merz, *History of European Thought in the Nineteenth Century* (Edinburgh and London, 1896–1914, 4 v.), I, introduction and ch. iii; Bishop Stubbs, *Seventeen Lectures on the Study of Medieval and Modern History* (Oxford, 1887), of which nos. i–iii are invaluable for information and suggestiveness; E. P. Cheyney, *International Monthly*, I (1900), 399–419; Stephen R. Dodds, "Some Modern Historians," *LQR*, CVIII (1907), 242–54; Ch. Petit-Dutaillis, "Histoire politique de l'Angleterre au moyen âge," *RSH*, VIII (1904), 358–80.

[2] Quoted in J. C. Thirlwall, Jr., *Connop Thirlwall, Historian and Theologian* (London and New York, 1936), 151. This equals Dr. Thomas Arnold's complacent remark in 1830 about England's "perfect social civilization." *Ibid.*, 95.

sinecures. Books came from churchmen or politicians, and not from professors.[3]

There was no pretense to "scientific objectivity." Each writer applied his straight-laced, aristocratic or moral standards, according to his party and religious persuasion. Nor did the national situation in the England of 1815, after the Napoleonic wars, augur well for sound historical writing.[4] A great foreign student has declared:

> The political background of the intellectual life of this period is . . . undoubtedly a dark one—dark with the terror produced in the middle classes by the excesses of the liberty movement in France, dark with the tyrannic lusts of proud Tories and the Church's oppressions, dark with the spilt blood of Irish Catholics and English artisans.[5]

Among the ruling classes no sympathy could be expected for the suffering lower masses, who were denied political expression. Tory writers like Mitford and Sir Archibald Alison maintained the blessings of the status quo, and the virtue of the principles on which England was being ruled, with a positiveness akin to that of the famous speech of the Duke of Wellington in 1830. The majority of the Whigs had a similar horror of universal franchise. Both parties were steeped in political and religious prejudice; and both were so convinced of the superiority of their "perfect social civilization" that they were incapable of forming a fair judgment upon the past.

In consequence, until near the middle of the century, English historical scholarship lagged shamefully behind that of the Continent, at least that of France and Germany. While the learned energy of these two countries had poured out immense historical collections carefully edited, England had only Rymer's *Foedera*. Before 1857, when the *Rolls Series* was inaugurated, there were only such volumes as those subsidized by the Camden Society; and the few editors of sources were hapless pioneers, whose financial returns were little better than their own inadequate preparation for the task.

Yet the first five decades of the nineteenth century were not a period

---

[3] "Yesterday's harvest at the Museum was a failure! I got nothing but dust." Frederick von Raumer, *England in 1835*, tr. by Sarah Austin and H. E. Lloyd (Philadelphia, 1836), 86.

"At the chapter-house, Westminster, . . . I found an immense number of old chronicles and rotuli or rolls of paper in the shape of large Swiss cheeses. . . . The greater part of these are still unexamined and unknown." *Loc. cit.* Raumer was in company with Sir Francis Palgrave.

"It is totally inexcusable that the study of history is neglected at Oxford, as in all the schools of Great Britain, in a manner without a parallel in the countries of Europe." *Ibid.*, 480.

[4] Sir Charles Oman, "Historical Perspectives," in *Studies in the Napoleonic Wars* (London, 1929), 21–22; the whole essay, 1–23.

[5] Georg Brandes, *Main Currents in Nineteenth Century Literature*, tr. by Diana White and Mary Morison (London, 1901–05, 6 v.), IV, 30. The whole chapter is a terrible indictment of British narrow-mindedness and intolerance.

without advancement.[6] There were various forces converging upon a better historiography. The Napoleonic wars had aroused the national spirit in Europe, and driven each nation to a new and eager study of its own past. For the first time even the lower classes, which had been unaffected by literature in the eighteenth century, took an interest in the subject. Romanticism added the flavor of a vivid imagination, and turned writers and readers back to the more remote centuries. The novels of Sir Walter Scott enthralled the public, old and young, and taught scholars the value of "local color."

In the twenty years between the death of Gibbon (1794) and the Congress of Vienna (1815) England produced no historical work of the first magnitude. But the return of peace brought a sudden change, and revealed a new historical temper. In 1818 the presses threw off Hallam's *Europe during the Middle Ages*, the terminal volumes of Mitford's *History of Greece*, and James Mill's *History of British India*. In 1819 came the start of Lingard's *History of England*. "To pass from Hume to Sharon Turner, from Robertson to Hallam and Lingard, is to enter a world in which the obscure beginnings and early growth of civilization have acquired a quite other value for the historian." [7]

In the first third of the nineteenth century, prior to the Reform Bill, there was still a group of writers who belonged to the generations of Hume and Robertson. William Mitford (1744–1827) [8] was a Tory squire, a member of Parliament, and a colonel of the Hampshire militia. The suggestion which led to his *History of Greece* is credited to his fellow officer, the great Gibbon himself. Though he is treated elsewhere among the historians of antiquity, Mitford is mentioned here because his five volumes (1784–1805) reflect the Tory prejudice of his day. He detested the Athenian democracy and eulogized all aristocratic movements. For his admiring Tory public he was the forerunner of Sir Archibald Alison thirty years later. A contemporary, William Coxe (1747–1828), devoted himself chiefly to biographical labors, such as the *Lives* of the Walpoles, of Marlborough and of Pelham, but his narrative was seldom raised above dullness. William Roscoe (1753–1831) [9] is only an interesting dilettante, self-educated, an attorney and a man of many hobbies. From copies friends made for him of manuscripts in Florence he wrote a

[6] T. Preston Peardon, *The Transition in English Historical Writing, 1760–1830* (New York and London, 1933), 183–310; Alfred W. Benn, *The History of English Rationalism in the Nineteenth Century* (London, and New York, 1906, 2 v.), I, 311–25, for the beginning of the fusion of German criticism and English romanticism about 1830; and Herford (n. 1), 1–34.
[7] Herford (n. 1), 40.
[8] See the memoir in the first volume of his *History of Greece* (ed. 1837); WARD, X, 361; Mahaffy's introduction to the English version of Victor Duruy, *History of Greece* (Boston, 1890, 4 v. in 8), I, i, 5–6; and Macaulay's hilarious review reprinted in his *Critical, Historical and Miscellaneous Essays and Poems* (Boston, 1880, 2 v.), I, 127–47.
[9] *ER*, VII (1806), 336–58.

Life of Lorenzo de' Medici (1793 f.) and then the *Life and Pontificate of Leo X*, which was put upon the papal Index though it was partial to the pontiff. Roscoe's work is anecdotal, artificial, and deficient in historical value, but his enthusiasms for Italian art and letters stimulated the interest of the English public.

English antiquarianism was represented by Sir Henry Ellis (1777–1869), for long years chief librarian of the British Museum (1827–56). After issuing a new edition of Brand's *Popular Antiquities* (1813), he was invited by the Commissioners of Public Records to write the introduction to *Domesday Book* (1816). For his *Original Letters Illustrative of English History* (first series 1824, second series 1827) he utilized manuscripts in the British Museum and the State Paper Office.

Gibbon had declared that the Anglo-Saxon epoch was "obscure to the most learned reader." In 1815 *Beowulf* was published, which the Dane Thorkelin had discovered, and hailed as the oldest extant epic of the Germanic peoples. The merit of opening up this new field to English readers goes to Sharon Turner (1768–1847).[10] He was apprenticed to an attorney in the Temple when fifteen, and upon his employer's decease six years later managed to continue the business. But his leisure hours were soon constantly applied to researches in the British Museum. While still a boy a translation of the "Death Song of Ragnar Lodbrok" had impelled him to take up the study of Icelandic and Anglo-Saxon, and revealed to him that philologists had paid little and historians almost no attention to the treasures these tongues could unlock. In 1799, after sixteen years of study, he published his *History of the Anglo-Saxons*.[11] Its preface deplored the long neglect of valuable sources. "The Anglo-Saxon manuscripts," wrote Turner, "lay still unexamined and neither their contents nor the important facts which the ancient writers and the records of other nations had preserved of the transactions and fortunes of our ancestors had ever been made a part of our general history." Turner was the first to look over those in the Cottonian library for historical purposes. His criticism led to an inquiry in Parliament (1800), and a commission was appointed "to methodize, regulate and digest the records."

Turner's work came as a revelation to the reading public. Based on solid and patient erudition, its judicious and authoritative note won approval. Southey hazarded the belief "that so much new information was probably never laid before the public in any one historical publica-

[10] *ER*, III (1804), 360–74; and the article of Thomas Seccombe in *DNB*, LVII, 356–57.

[11] *The History of the Anglo-Saxons from Their First Appearance above the Elbe to the Norman Conquest* (London, 1799–1805, 4 v.). The 7th edition in three volumes was revised by his son in 1852. This history was later incorporated as vols. I–III of his 12 vol. *History of England from the Earliest Period to the Death of Elizabeth* (London, 1820–39).

tion." [12] After speaking of the Britons and Romans, Turner described the life and customs of the Teutonic invaders before they left the mainland, and devoted much space to the religious, economic, and social features of the Anglo-Saxon kingdoms in England. Inferior to Hume in the narrative portions, he offered a far broader view of early life in the island.

Encouraged by his first success, Turner proceeded by successive stages to the times of Queen Elizabeth. [13] Overwork now forced him to give up his lawyer's practice and to retire to the country. Here he wrote his *Sacred History*, [14] which public indulgence and a devout orthodox tone carried to eight editions. Turner showed that he knew nothing of German criticism. [15]

The chief value of Turner's writings today is found in his notes. His artistic pretensions were least happy of all; his arrangement was neither orderly nor luminous, and digressions annoy the reader. Southey winced over some of his later volumes. When Turner emerged from the Saxon period he had little to offer which was new, and Lingard's work superseded these later portions. But in his proper domain he worked with enthusiasm and effectiveness, won the esteem of Hallam, Southey, Scott, and Tennyson, and had the satisfaction of stirring the English mind to a new consciousness of its ancestry. As a student of Anglo-Saxon materials, Turner held his own until Kemble and Thorpe appeared.

Henry Hallam's famous volume on the Middle Ages also illustrates the new interest taken in that period, though he was still primarily concerned with the fourteenth and fifteenth centuries. Hallam was born in 1777 and died in 1859. [16] His father was canon of Windsor, where Henry was born, and then Dean of Bristol. From Eton and

---

[12] *Life and Correspondence*, ed. by Robert Southey (New York, 1855), ch. xi, quoted in *DNB* (n. 10), 356.

[13] *The History of England from the Norman Conquest to 1509* (London, 1814–23, 3 v.). The 3rd edition (1830, 5 v.) was incorporated as vols. IV–VIII of *The History of England* (n. 11). *The History of the Reign of Henry the VIII, Comprising the Poetical History of the Commencement of the English Reformation* (1826, 2 v.: vols. IX–X of *The History of England*). This work was composed in answer to Lingard's version. *History of the Reigns of Edward the Sixth, Mary, and Elizabeth* (London, 1826–29, 2 v.: vols. XI–XII of *The History of England*.)

[14] *The Sacred History of the World, as Displayed in the Creation and Subsequent Events to the Deluge. Attempted to Be Philosophically Considered in a Series of Letters to a Son* (London, 1832–37, 3 v.; 8th ed., 1848).

[15] Milman's *History of the Jews* (London, 1829, 3 v.) pained his sensibilities, to which Milman, when informed, retorted that he would have placed a higher value on the other's opinion twenty years before. Turner was for years the legal adviser of John Murray, the publisher, and was instrumental in the founding of the *Quarterly Review*. He disliked the "smart severity" of the *Edinburgh Review*.

[16] Gooch, 283–84; the article in *DNB*; Mignet, "Notice historique sur la vie et les travaux de M. Hallam," *ASMP*, LIX (1862), 259–83; *ER*, XXX, 140–72; *JS*, 1821, pp. 734–44; *NAR*, XXIX (1829), 265–81, XLVI (1838), 248, L (1840), 43–75, XCII (1861), 163–77, XCIII (1862), 93 ff.

Christ Church, Oxford, Hallam went to the Inner Temple. A private income after 1812 made actual practice of the law unnecessary. He obtained an appointment as Commissioner of Stamps, which was virtually a sinecure. Though definitely committed to the Whig party, Hallam took no part in actual politics. He was interested in the abolition of the slave trade, but his aristocratic sympathies viewed the Reform Bill of 1832 with alarm as promoting a dangerous excess of democracy. Like many other English historians of the century, he began by writing for journals, in this case for the great organ of the Whigs, the *Edinburgh Review*. His fame is based upon three works, and was erected already by the first, *A View of the State of Europe during the Middle Ages*.[17] This consisted of nine chapters which are historical essays, surveying the chief circumstances which might interest a philosophical inquirer from the fifth to the fifteenth century. While decidedly uneven in value—Hallam was blind to most of the centuries preceding the twelfth—[18] the work laid special emphasis upon law and government, and the chapter on England was not excelled in this respect until the day of Stubbs.

Hallam's hatred of political and ecclesiastical tyranny manifested in the *Middle Ages* became even more evident nine years later in the *Constitutional History of England from the Accession of Henry VII to the Death of George II*.[19] By it Hallam became the first authoritative exponent of the Whig historical philosophy. When he wrote, the Whigs had been out of power for nearly seventy years. In a one-sided manner he sang the glories of 1688 and the happiness of England in limiting her sovereigns by law. For the crime of despotism he condemned Catholic and Protestant, high and low churchmen, and the Tories. His rod fell most heavily upon James I and Charles I; he regarded the first Stuarts as breakers of the law. His accuracy is usually less open to attack, for in this case Hallam erred in supposing that England already possessed at that period a definite and fixed constitution. The English lawyer peeps through; but if he wrote as a judge rather than as a mere recorder, it was as an impartial and fearless one. Hallam was a political philosopher, indulging in wise and melancholy reflections upon society and mankind, but he had no liking for philosophic systems or social theories. Southey accused him of "raking for buried slanders," but Macaulay's

---

[17] London, 1818, 2 v. A volume of supplementary notes appeared in 1848.

[18] Hallam wrote: "Many considerable portions of time, especially before the twelfth century, may justly be deemed so barren of events worthy of remembrance that a single sentence or paragraph is often enough to give the character of entire generations and of long dynasties of obscure kings."

[19] London, 1827, 3 v. Reviewed by Macaulay in *ER*, XLVIII (1828), 96–169, reprinted in his *Historical Essays* (London and New York, 1913), 1–83. For the Tories, Southey wrote a scathing criticism in *QR*, XXXVII (1828), 194–260.

verdict was that "on a general survey, we do not scruple to pronounce the *Constitutional History* the most impartial work that we have ever read." It became the textbook of English politics, and remained the leading guide for English constitutional history for many years.

The trilogy was closed a decade later by the encyclopaedic *Introduction to the Literature of Europe in the Fifteenth, Sixteenth and Seventeenth Centuries* (4 v., 1837). On a vast canvas Hallam projected the great writers on philosophy, theology, belles lettres, and science, but oddly enough omitted an adequate account of historiography.[20] The survey revealed its author's wide reading and vindicated his claim to learning.

Hallam led a studious and retired life.[21] He was a founder of the Statistical Society, and vice-president of the Society of Antiquaries. Freeman allowed that Hallam "was brought up in the teaching of the eighteenth century . . . (and) shows that teaching in its very best shape, accompanied by singular discretion, and by no small reading within his range," but he denied him the invaluable faculty of an historian, imagination. Hallam was a man who shunned controversy or the rough and tumble of politics. It was such scruples that moved him to terminate his *Constitutional History* before the accession of George III. He labored to be honest and accurate, and shied away from generalizations, the pitfalls of less conscientious workers. He kept to his path with a noble disdain for schools or traditional opinion, and though he could not deny his Whig coloring, he strove to be fair to Rome and her theological writers. Cromwell was for him a dictator to be compared with Napoleon, and Charles I's death, while his offense was grave, was illegal. He eschewed rhetoric and was commonly a severe and chaste writer, even verging on dryness. He was, says Vinogradoff, the English representative of the school which had Guizot for its brilliant continental representative.

Sharon Turner had given the impetus for the appointment of a Record Commission in 1800, but its members were busy officials or bishops neither fitted for the task nor supplied with the funds necessary to salvage the scattered archives and prepare them for publication.[22] In 1836, under pressure from Sir Harris Nicolas (1799–1848), the editor of *Nelson's Letters*, and other scholars, the government appointed a second Record Commission, and from its organization date

[20] See the review by Macaulay in *ER*, LXXII (1840), 194–226.

[21] His wife and eleven children all predeceased him. It was for the eldest, Arthur Henry Hallam, that Tennyson wrote his *In Memoriam;* and the poem's words: "Thy long, unlovely street," referred to their house in Wimpole Street.

[22] Gooch says that no one with historical qualifications joined the Commission before Mackintosh in 1825; that the few things printed were shamefully edited and funds squandered, e.g., in reprinting Rymer of whom various editions already existed. He quotes Maitland's words: "the scandalously bad elbowed the admirably good." GOOCH, 285.

the first substantial efforts to rescue valuable manuscripts. But the progress made was slow, and not until 1857 was the *Rolls Series* inaugurated.[23] With new attention turned to the original documents, there was hope for a better day.[24] The many volumes edited by J. A. Giles were rather pecuniary ventures of an antiquary than serviceable versions by a critical historian. More valuable were the contributions of Thorpe and Kemble. Benjamin Thorpe (1782–1870) had studied under the great Danish philologist Rask at Copenhagen, and published his teacher's *Anglo-Saxon Grammar* in English in 1830. He translated *Caedmon* (1832) and *Beowulf* (1855), as well as Lappenberg's *History of England under the Anglo-Saxon Kings* and Pauli's *Life of Alfred the Great*. From his own hands came a work on *Northern Mythology*, in three small volumes (London, 1851). He edited Caedmon's metrical paraphrase of parts of the Holy Scriptures, the Anglo-Saxon version of the story of Apollonius of Tyana (1834), *Analecta Anglo-Saxonica* (Oxford, 1834), and the *Codex Exoniensis* (1842). His reputation rested not least upon the *Diplomatarium Anglicum aevi Anglo-Saxonici* (1865), whose manner of composition led both Sir Thomas Duffus Hardy and Bishop Stubbs to consider Thorpe "a very dishonest old man." Hardy had been kind enough to allow him to see the transcripts from which (without even looking at the original charters) Thorpe compiled the *Diplomatarium*, and then Thorpe had the ingratitude to attack Hardy in the preface for inaccurate scholarship. There is evidence that he also pillaged the Anglo-Saxon documents which Henry Petrie had brought out in his *Monumenta historica Britannica*. Giles in his copying did the same sort of low thing.[25]

The years before Macaulay's death (1859) saw in turn the appearance of Thorpe's *Ancient Laws and Institutes of England* (1840), of Kemble's *Saxons in England* (1849), and a substantial portion of Palgrave's *History of Normandy and England* (1851–64).[26]

At this point the pioneers of the Anglo-Saxon period diverged along two lines: those who maintained the continued influence of Rome upon British life and institutions after the fifth century, and those who believed the Teutonic element was the strongest factor before the Norman Conquest. The first distinguished "Romanist" among English historians was Sir Francis Palgrave, who claimed to have arrived at his conclusions independently of Savigny in Germany or of his own coun-

---

[23] For the establishment of the *Rolls Series*, see *QR*, CLXII (1886), 295–98.
[24] For intimations of a "documentary school" in England in Thorpe, Kemble, etc., see *ER*, LXXXIX (1849), 154.
[25] Leslie Stephen, ed., *Letters of John Richard Green* (New York and London, 1901), 144.
[26] For early English scholars on Anglo-Saxon, see WARD, XII, 382. Edward Lye began the *Dictionary of Anglo-Saxon*, and Owen Manning finished it in 1876.

tryman Allen. Kemble was the first "Germanist" of note, and had the better of the argument.[27]

John Mitchell Kemble (1807–57) [28] came from an English family of actors famous for their Shakespeare repertory; for he was the son of Charles Kemble, and a nephew of John Philip Kemble and Mrs. Siddons. Perhaps he imbibed the love for philology from his father and uncle, but his actual early education was gotten from the lexicographer Richardson at Clapham. From putting on childish plays with his sister Fanny, young Kemble passed to the grammar school of Bury St. Edmunds, and thence to Trinity College at Cambridge, where he entered into friendship with Alfred Tennyson, Richard Trench, Charles Buller, and William Donne. The family expected much of his talents, but his excellent mind seemed averse to following dictation. He neglected the prescribed studies for reading, sports, and the pleasures of society, among which his fine appearance and unusual qualities as a singer and declaimer made him very popular. A reckless impudence during his examinations led to a temporary set-back, and he shifted to the Inner Temple to study law. But again he applied himself only to those portions of the subject which bore a definite relation to English history and antiquities. Then came the decisive event: with a friend he departed for Germany.

It is averred that all of Charles Kemble's children could speak German while still small. Whatever the reason for this training, John Kemble visited Heidelberg and Munich and found a strange fascination in Germanic philology. Yet he was still unsettled. He received his B.A. degree in England (1833) and seems to have thought of taking holy orders. Then followed a quixotic episode in which Kemble, together with Trench, the future archbishop of Dublin, took part in an expedition to Spain to foment rebellion against Ferdinand VII.[29] By a mere scratch they escaped with their lives. Upon his return from Gibraltar, Kemble, whose whole life was somewhat that of a rolling

[27] The Germanist school continued in Freeman and Green, and even Stubbs accepted many of its tenets. Later English students drew much from the German school led by Schmidt and Lappenberg, Waitz, Sohm, Brunner, Konrad Maurer, and Pauli.

[28] William Hunt, in *DNB*, XXX, 369–72; *FM*, LV (1857), 612–18; Reinhold Pauli has a charming memoir in the *Münchener Gelehrte Anzeigen*, 1858, pp. 370–83, Hefte 46 and 47; cp. also *The Athenaeum*, no. 1535 (March 28, 1857), 406, and no. 1536 (April 4, 1857), 439. Occasional references to Kemble occur in Maria Trench, *Letters and Memorials of R. C. Trench, Archbishop of Dublin* (London, 1888, 2 v.), and in Frances Kemble's *Records of a Girlhood* (2nd ed., New York, 1884), and its sequel volumes. See also W. R. Stephens, *Life and Letters of Edward A. Freeman* (London and New York, 1895, 2 v.), I, 114–16; and Vinogradoff, *Villainage in England; Essays in English Mediaeval History* (Oxford, 1892), 18–21.

[29] Kemble's diary of the expedition, covering 147 pages, and partly in the autograph of R. C. Trench, has never been published. It forms the bulk of vol. 14 in the Kemble Collection offered for sale by G. Michelmore and Company, London (pp. 160–64 of their Catalogue no. 24: "A Further Romance of Letters.").

stone, gave up the thought of a clerical career and came back to philology, studying under Jakob Grimm at Göttingen, and Andreas Schmeller at Munich. When he left Germany the second time it was with the determination to introduce into his own country the scientific study of Anglo-Saxon philology and history.

Kemble made his reputation by an edition of *Beowulf* (1833), and delivered on his own responsibility a series of lectures at Cambridge upon Anglo-Saxon language and literature in the style of his idol Grimm. But Cambridge did not see her way clear to forgive her truant son. Years of steady activity followed: from the stores of the British Museum Kemble hurried to university, cathedral, and monastic libraries to collect transcripts and pore over faded documents. He acquired a palaeographical skill that was the wonder and despair of others, and caused even Pauli to marvel. But such research, while it piled up knowledge, would not buy bread. He turned to literary tasks, like the editorship of the *British and Foreign Review* (1835–44). From 1840 till his death he obtained some income as the censor of stage plays.[30] In 1847 he was so reduced financially that he was forced to take a country house and advertise for pupils.

Between 1835 and 1848 there appeared the six volumes of Kemble's *Codex diplomaticus aevi Saxonici*, printed at the expense of the English Historical Society. It contained 1369 early English charters and documents, from 604 to 1061 A.D. Not all were new, for some had been printed before by Rymer or Hearne, and there were inaccuracies where Kemble had not collated the originals, or tried to establish an eclectic text. The bulk, however, was here published for the first time, and supplied with elaborate introductions. Upon this epochal collection Kemble based his own detailed study, *The Saxons in England* (1849), which had no equal until the appearance of the first volume of Stubbs' *Constitutional History* in 1874. It was Kemble's conviction that every institution of early English life, except the Church, was of pure Germanic origin. Despite such faults as diffuseness and the untenable theory of the *Mark*, the work provided a sound basis for his successors. It was unprecedented in two respects: the dependence upon many and new original sources, and the synoptic approach which studied Anglo-Saxon institutions in the light of other early Germanic evidence on the Continent.[31]

In his last years Kemble spent much time abroad, as his domestic

[30] He received this government appointment through his father's efforts. It was the last censorship to exist in England.

[31] Kemble was uniquely acquainted with German scholarship and Teutonic philology. He once wrote a work in German, *Ueber die Stammtafel der Westsachsen* (1836), and dedicated it to Jakob Grimm.

life was not happy. While in Hanover in 1854 he turned to prehistoric archaeology, and received a commission to rearrange and catalogue the collection in the Royal Museum, and to excavate for further finds. He plunged into the task with his characteristic ardor, even training himself to sketch his finds *in situ*. His excavations on the Lüneburg· Heath met with much success and public interest. In 1856 he was engaged on a comparative taphography [Greek τάφος = grave] of the North-European nations, which he hoped would end the dilettantism of antiquarian societies with respect to burial sites. He had been entrusted with arranging an archaeological exhibit at Manchester when death carried him away in his fiftieth year.

What Turner had begun, and Thorpe and Kemble furthered, was extended into the Norman period by Sir Francis Palgrave (1788–1861).[32] His Jewish father was a member of the London Stock Exchange, and provided his precocious son with excellent tutors. When the father's fortunes met with reverses, the son became a solicitor, was called to the bar in 1827, and for some years appeared in pedigree cases before the House of Lords. In the year of his marriage (1823) he became a Christian and adopted the maiden name of his wife's mother.

Palgrave's historical interests first found an outlet in articles in the *Quarterly Review* and the *Edinburgh Review* (1814–21); in 1818 he published a collection of Anglo-Norman chansons; but his real life's work was to be that of editor. He was first drawn to the publication of the public records in 1821, and the following year the Commission of Records approved a plan submitted by him. From 1827 to 1837 he was busy editing various volumes under their supervision: the *Parliamentary Writs of the Reigns of Edward I and II* (2 v., 1827–34), the *Rotuli Curiae Regis* (2 v., 1835), *Antient Kalendars and Inventories of His Majesty's Exchequer* (3 v., 1836), and *Documents and Records Illustrating the History of Scotland*.

In time Palgrave ventured into original composition. The duodecimo volume contributed to the Family Library as a *History of England* (1831) covered only the Anglo-Saxon period, and was never continued. It was shortly followed by the *Rise and Progress of the English Commonwealth* (2 v., quarto, 1832), which "boldly challenged the current view that it is necessary to begin with political events and to proceed to institutions." [33] Hallam praised the work for its "omnifarious reading" and its "fearless spirit." Freeman later commended

---

[32] Vinogradoff (n. 28), 11–16; Warwick Wroth, in *DNB*, XLIII, 107–08; *ER*, LV (1832), 305–37, XCV (1852), 153–79, CIX (1859), 486–513, CXXI (1865), 1–41; *NAR*, LXXXVI (1858), 301–29; T. F. Tout, *Scottish Historical Review*, XVII (1919–20), 52–55, XIX (1921–22), 60–61, 125; XX (1922–23), 61–62.

[33] GOOCH, 286–87.

Palgrave's "characteristic union of research, daring, and ingenuity." [34]
Palgrave's popularity was acquired by the elaborate *History of Normandy and England* (4 v., 1851–64, the last two posthumous). He
began with the aim to correct Thierry and to write the true history
of the Norman Conquest. His intimate knowledge marked him as the
man who promised most for the subject, but he wasted his energies on
the earlier history of the duchy of Normandy, and the history of the
Conquest remained unwritten. [35]

In 1832 Palgrave was knighted. When the Record Commission was
reorganized, he became Deputy Keeper of Her Majesty's Records
from 1838 to the time of his death. At the Rolls Office he consolidated
the materials scattered in fifty-six depositories; and the erection of the
first unit of the Public Record Office was due largely to his efforts. In
the pursuance of his duties he prepared twenty-two annual reports.
Such labors did not interrupt his private publications. *Merchant and
Friar* (1837) was an imaginary history of Marco Polo and Friar Bacon;
*Detached Thoughts on the Polity and Ecclesiastical History of the Middle
Ages* was printed for private circulation.

As editor, Palgrave set his successors new standards. His writings
are valued today for their source knowledge; his notes can still be
checked with profit. As a lawyer, he emphasized the importance of
legal institutions for understanding political history. Freeman declared
some of his theories more fascinating than true. He stressed the continuity of the Roman imperial tradition in the German kingdoms, and
saw the manifestation of Roman influence on all sides after 476 A.D.,
but thought that Germanic traditions led to the first constitutional
limitations upon an arbitrary kingship. Typical is Palgrave's assumption that the Britons were Germanic, and not Celts; hence he minimized
the revolutions wrought by each conquest. The Germanist school soon
assailed his doctrine of Roman survivals. Altogether, Palgrave offers
stores of curious research and information, but he was hardly qualified
to write history in a literary sense. His philosophical ideas are trivial,

[34] Edward A. Freeman, *The History of the Norman Conquest of England, Its Causes and Its
Results* (Oxford, 1867–79, 6 v.), I, 68 note, and V, 334.

[35] Palgrave scoffed at Thierry's notion that the Capetians were national leaders, descended
from the old Gallo-Romans, against the Teutonic invaders represented by the Carolingians.
"Now we cannot conceive," says a reviewer in *ER*, CIX (1859), 501, "two historians of equal
power more likely to fail in appreciating and understanding one another than Thierry and Sir
Francis Palgrave. Each sees half the causes of events, builds a theory . . . and remains blind
to the other half. Sir Francis can see nothing but the agency of individuals and of institutions.
. . . With the history of the nation he gives himself very little concern. Thierry . . . sees
nothing but the broad facts of race, conquest and language. Sir Francis hardly believes that
William the Conqueror was a foreign invader, because he called himself King of the English,
and did not formally abolish the old English laws; Thierry would have us believe that in the
wars of the seventeenth century an Anglo-Saxon people was trying to throw off the yoke of a
Norman king."

and his conjectures sometimes rash. His style is verbose and turgid; fantastic beauties alternate with fantastic absurdities. The prolixity was in part due to the habit of dictating to an amanuensis. He lacked the calm judgment of Hallam, but his original powers and his merits for medieval English history cannot be denied.

Hallam and Macaulay upheld the Whig honors; the Tory champion was Sir Archibald Alison (1792–1867),[36] who dealt with the modern period. Though born in Shropshire he made his studies at Edinburgh, and passed at the Scottish bar in 1814. A tour on the Continent resulted in his first book, *Travels in France during the Years 1814–15* (1815). While journeying through this land of recent upheaval, according to his own words, he "conceived the first idea" of writing a history of Europe since 1789, and "inhaled that ardent spirit, that deep enthusiasm," which preluded fifteen years of application. Meanwhile he became an advocate-deputy for Scotland (1822–30), and composed his *Principles of the Criminal Law of Scotland* (1832) and *Practice of the Criminal Law of Scotland* (1833). The repute of these works led Sir Robert Peel to entrust to him the office of sheriff of Lanarkshire, a high judicial appointment.

The leisure he was thus afforded enabled Alison to write the ten volumes of the *History of Europe from the Commencement of the French Revolution to the Restoration of the Bourbons* (1833–42). It ran to ten editions within a short time, appeared in several European languages, and even in Arabic and Hindustani.[37] Its popularity was due to the fact that it was the first sustained account of the French Revolution in English. The style was florid, and the author moralized with tedious affectation. As an obstinate Tory it was impossible for Alison to understand the period of which he wrote. With "gloomy presentiments," the conservative magistrate declared, he had long observed the "passion for innovation" which was seizing English public opinion and hypnotizing even the government. He was convinced the new democracy represented a worse danger than "aristocratic oppression." Having contended in *Blackwood's Magazine* against the proposed Reform Bill of 1832, Alison went to Paris the year after its passage to discover some demonstration of the thesis that popular convulsions lead to military despotism. He depicted the horrors in France, and was happy that a benign Providence had finally effected "the deliverance of mankind."

---

[36] See his *Some Account of My Life and Writings: an Autobiography*, edited by his daughter-in-law, Lady Alison (Edinburgh, 1883, 2 v.); *ER*, LXXVI (1842–43), 1–60; XCVII (1853), 135–270; CXI (1860), 119; *FM*, LIII (1856), 597–611; LX (1859), 211–26; LX (1859), 603–19; LXII (1860), 660–78; *NBR*, XXVII (1857), 275–324; *DR*, XXXIII (1852), 408–18; *Dublin University Magazine*, XXXVI, 631; *QR*, LXXIII (1843–44), 271 and 423.

[37] At the author's death, 108,000 volumes of the library edition and 439,000 of the popular edition had found purchasers!

When Alison offered the public a continuation of his work, entitled
History from the Restoration to the Accession of Napoleon III, 1815–52
(9 v., 1852–59), everyone knew what to expect. He splintered his
lance for the policies of Castlereagh and Wellington, and cast the evils
of the nation upon the act restricting paper currency, the Great Reform
Bill, and the abolition of the Corn Laws. Forgotten today, this Jere-
miah was for years the prophet of the men of Tory convictions.

The years from 1815 to 1860 saw works of some importance from
authors less renowned than those mentioned. Scott and Hazlitt wrote
the life of Napoleon, and Southey a history of the Peninsular War. The
last subject found a masterly historian in Sir Walter Francis Patrick
Napier (1785–1860),[38] an Irish gentleman and scholar, who fought in
the Peninsula and was in close relation to Wellington. To champion his
brother Charles, who also fought in Spain, Napier added two volumes
on the conquest and administration of Scinde.[39] At first much criticized,
especially for its author's democratic views, the *History of the War in
the Peninsula and in the South of France* (London, 1828–40) has maintained an enviable reputation for vivid writing and fairness, but it
scandalized the Tories by its admiration of Napoleon. Kinglake[40] performed almost as excellent a task in his account of the Crimean War.

Patrick Fraser Tytler (1791–1849) was a Tory, a Scottish lawyer, and
for years King's Counsel in Exchequer. His *History of Scotland*[41] was
begun, it is said, at the suggestion of Sir Walter Scott in 1826. Tytler
also wrote *Lives of Scottish Worthies*, and lives of James Crichton,
Wyclif, Raleigh, and Henry VIII.

English historians were early interested in India. Macaulay's two
essays are famous; though ostensibly devoted to Clive (1840) and to
Hastings (1841), they present in gorgeous panorama the history of the
Mogul empire and the rivalries and struggles which ended it. James
Mill (1773–1836) wrote a *History of British India* (1817–18) which was
a harsh criticism of the East India Company. He had never been in the
country, and knew none of its languages; but he considered this almost
a virtue. His sole test was that of utility: the history of India must be
studied so Englishmen might govern it. For Hindu civilization he had
only contempt.

[38] *ER*, LXXII (1840), 271–320, and CXXI (1865), 74–108; *QR*, LVI (1836), 131–219, 437–
89, LVII (1836), 492–542.
[39] *The Conquest of Scinde* (London, 1844–46); *History of General Sir Charles Napier's Administration of Scinde, and Campaign in the Cutchee Hills* (London, 1851).
[40] *QR*, CXIII (1863), 514–76.
[41] 1828–43, 9 v.; it covers the period from 1249 to the personal union of England and Scotland in 1603.

CHAPTER XLVII

MACAULAY, CARLYLE, AND FROUDE

T HIS chapter deals in turn with the three great literary historians of England, that is, men whose work is primarily literature, and as such admittedly of high quality and value, irrespective of their claim to historical accuracy. As in the case of Gibbon, their writings will probably continue to live even when they have been supplanted by works sounder in conception and detail.

Fortune and genius smiled on the cradle of Thomas Babington Macaulay (1800–59).[1] Literary fame came early, and then a long political experience and a style of matchless lucidity made him the chief exponent of Whig political philosophy and traditions. When a student at Cambridge (1818–22) the brilliant youth was turned from the Toryism of his family by Charles Austin, and after the Six Acts of 1819 he openly accepted the Whig doctrine. He read Plato's *Republic* with the eyes of a Whig and an Englishman, and the issue of 1832 ever remained the most important of his life. To please his father he read for the law, and was called to the bar in 1826. But the law was distasteful to him, and he never practiced. Already the characteristics of his genius had appeared:

The eagerness with which he devoured books of every sort; the marvelous memory which enabled him to recall for years whole pages and poems, read but once; the quick-

---

[1] The literature on Macaulay is immense; consult Johnston's bibliography in the Cambridge edition of his works. Of prime importance is the *Life and Letters* by his nephew, Sir George Otto Trevelyan (enlarged and complete edition, including his marginal notes, London, 1909, 2 v.). The best edition of the *History of England* is by Sir Charles Firth (1913); see also his *A Commentary on Macaulay's History of England* (1937), which was edited after his death by Godfrey Davies, of the Huntingdon Library, out of lectures which Firth was wont to deliver at Oxford before the First World War. Two of these had already appeared in periodicals, and if an approximate date is wanted, the reference to T. F. Henderson's edition of 1907 supplies one. Firth approved of Henderson's notes, but added that there was still room for an editor who would perform for Macaulay the same service which Bury had executed for Gibbon. Additional reading: GOOCH, 294–304; FUETER, 640–44; Mignet, "Notice historique sur la vie et les travaux de Lord Macaulay," *ASMP*, LXV (1863), 205–43; Leslie Stephen, *Hours in a Library*, 3rd series (London, 1879), ch. vii, 279–324; J. Cotter Morison, *Macaulay* (New York, 1882); Arthur Ponsonby, *English Diaries* (London, 1923), 389–93; Herbert Paul, *Men and Letters* (4th ed., London and New York, 1901); John Morley, *Critical Miscellanies* (London and New York, 1886–1908, 4 v.), I; Walter Bagehot, *Literary Studies* (London and New York, 1911, 2 v.), II; *BQR*, XXXI (1860), 285–328, XXIII (1856), 297–325, IX (1849), 1–41; *FM*, LIII (1856), 147–66, XXXIX (1849), 4–16; *NBR*, XXV (1856), 79–109; *DR*, XXVI (1849), 390–441; *ER*,XC (1849), 249–92; E. v. Noorden, "Ranke und Macaulay," *HZ*, XVII (1867), 87–138; George Macaulay Trevelyan, *England under Queen Anne* (London, New York, 1930, 3 v.), I, 178; W. R. Thayer, "Macaulay Fifty Years After," in *NAR* (1909), 735–52.

ness of perception by the aid of which he could at a glance extract the contents of a printed page; his love of novels and poetry; his volubility, his positiveness of assertion, and the astonishing amount of information he could pour out on matters of even trivial importance. . . .[2]

The articles which he published in Knight's *Quarterly Magazine* from his twenty-third year on attracted Jeffrey, editor of the great Whig *Edinburgh Review*, who was on the outlook for promising young talent. With the famous *Essay on Milton* (1825) Macaulay began his connection with this journal, and immediately his name became a household word in London society. For nearly twenty years he was chiefly an essayist, and nothing more polished and sparkling had ever appeared in English print than the thirty-six critical and historical studies he produced in this time. The four ballads published in 1842 as *The Lays of Ancient Rome* were equally popular.[3]

The *Essays* revealed the splendors and the flaws of Macaulay's genius. The flaws are like the flaws in a hard blue diamond; they only slightly diminish the beauty of the stone. Macaulay had little critical profundity, and admitted as much. His ostensible subject was merely a peg upon which he hung his reconstruction of the past. For the marvellous historical picture which each essay represents he drew upon an astounding reading in art, science, theology, history, literature, poetry, the drama, and even some philosophy. His prodigious memory supplied information, illustrations, and analogies in abundance. The portrait of the Puritan in the *Essay on Milton* and the tableau of the trial of Warren Hastings have become classic.

Macaulay's experience in Parliament and administration exceeded that of any other English historian. In the House of Commons, which he entered in 1830, he delivered prepared speeches rather than engaging in extempore debate. His literary style was readily converted into fluent oratory, and its extraordinary clearness was a powerful asset. His opponents were overborne by a myriad concrete examples for his points. He shared in the fight for the Reform Bill;[4] and was rewarded with an appointment to the Supreme Council of India which kept him

[2] John Bach McMaster, "Thomas Babington Macaulay," in Warner's *Library of the World's Best Literature*, XVI (1917), 9381.

[3] According to Trevelyan (n. 1), ch. ix, 18,000 copies of the *Lays* were sold in ten years in Great Britain, 40,000 in twenty years, and nearly 100,000 by 1875. The *Essays* were collected in a volume in 1843, after a Philadelphia printer had pirated them; and one publisher in the United Kingdom disposed of 120,000 copies in thirty years.

[4] In a letter to his friend Ellis he described the division of the Commons in 1831 when the Bill was carried by one vote: "You might have heard a pin drop as Duncannon read the numbers. Then, again, the shouts broke out, and many of us shed tears. And the jaw of Peel fell; and the face of Twiss was as the face of a damned soul; and Herries looked like Judas taking his necktie off for the last operation." Quoted in Hugh Walker, *Age of Tennyson* (London, 1904), 116.

out of England for four years (1834–38). On his return he sat in Parliament for Edinburgh, and in 1839 was Secretary at War.

Macaulay had now conceived the idea of writing his *History of England*. As the years slipped away, he begrudged more and more the time demanded by his political duties. Temporarily retired to private life by an election defeat in 1847, he brought out his first two volumes in the following year. Though he returned to his parliamentary seat again (1852), he abandoned political life permanently in 1856. A year before his third and fourth volumes had been published. His health was precarious, and he saw with regret that his project was on too vast a scale to be completed. In 1857 he was raised to the peerage, but died two years later, leaving his *History* a noble fragment and the fifth volume still unfinished.

No other history in English countries has ever approached Macaulay's *History* in popularity. It outdistanced even the novels and poems of Scott.[5] In his diary on October 25, 1850 the author wrote: "My birthday. I am fifty. Well, I have had a happy life. I do not know that anybody, whom I have seen close, has had a happier. . . . I wish the next ten years may be as happy as the last ten. But I rather wish it than hope it." [6] Macaulay's success was due to a style hitherto unknown, forceful, vivid, and marvellously coherent. In 1841 he had written: "I shall not be satisfied unless I produce something which shall for a few days supersede the last fashionable novel on the tables of young ladies." While this sentence has often been quoted, it cannot fairly be construed as proof of literary pandering. There is nothing tawdry about the popularity which the *History of England* won and steadily maintained. But his approach must be noted.

"Facts," said Macaulay, are "but the dross of history." In his twenty-eighth year he wrote an article on History for the *Edinburgh Review*, directed against the "nuda veritas" school of his day, which required that a scholar should relate the plain, unpolished truth. Macaulay held that history was a *moles indigesta*, a huge mass of data

---

[5] "Of 'Marmion' 2000 were sold in the first month; of the history 3000 copies were sold in ten days. Of the 'Lay of the Last Minstrel' 2250 copies were disposed of in course of the first year; but the publishers sold 13,000 copies of Macaulay in four months." Harper and Brothers wrote from the United States in 1849 of its phenomenal success over the Atlantic. "There have been three other editions [besides their cheap edition] published by different houses, and another is now in preparation; so there will be six different editions in the market. We have already sold 40,000 copies, and we presume that over 60,000 copies have been disposed of. Probably within three months of this time the sale will amount to 200,000 copies." Of the third and fourth volumes, a first printing of 25,000 was taken by the trade before a copy was bound. In the United States the sale exceeded any book ever printed, save the Bible and some school-texts; before 1875 140,000 copies had been taken in the United Kingdom. The royalties on sales in 1855 alone were $100,000, and the two volumes had been issued in November (26,500 copies sold in ten weeks). Cp. McMaster (n. 2), p. 9385.

[6] Trevelyan (n. 1), II, 286.

and phenomena that in themselves seemed hopelessly disarranged. He contended that the historian must use all his skill and powers of selection and presentation to weave these bits into a connected whole. "The perfect historian is he in whose work the character and spirit of an age is exhibited in miniature." Furthermore, he suggested that history must inevitably be written by advocates rather than judges.

The *History of England* is a picturesque reconstruction, a glowing piece of literary tapestry. Macaulay's mind spread over an enormous range of materials, and his memory was always at hand with parallels and illustrations. It was some advantage that he saw life as a rather simple affair, and had none of the horrifying doubts of the speculative philosopher. Lord Melbourne, when Macaulay had entered his ministry, once expressed a strong dislike towards him, complaining that "he is always so cocksure of everything." This cocksureness, and the confidence of Macaulay's staccato assertive sentences, convinced readers that here was a master of his subject. To modern critical readers, this very positiveness makes Macaulay suspect: his work is too plausible, the delineations always sharp-edged, and without any subtle graduation of values. But in his own time he was Sir Oracle to millions, the example of a rare good sense, providing positive opinions for the many who cannot form their own. He gave them pride in their generation.[7] He made history as charming as fiction. The burden of his song was English superiority, and this appealed to national patriotism. The Continent read him because he set forth the English blessings of freedom and constitutional government which the people of 1848 yearned to possess for themselves also.

What the general public perhaps could not detect was nevertheless still present beneath the glittering surface. Critics like Forster, Hepworth Dixon, and Paget exposed some of his errors.[8] But no subsequent editions carried any corrections. When faulty inferences tripped up his judgment, they were all too frequently connected with his partisanship. Throughout and always, Macaulay was the Whig historian. He probed into the dust-heap of the past for whatever might yield pleas for Whig party principles. He flayed the Tories without mercy before Alison tried to rise in their defense. William of Orange was his hero, and James II of course was cast in the villain's role. Macaulay had a zeal for "blacking chimneys." He was a master of adroit exaggeration and twisted his sources to comply with his prejudices. Sometimes his distortion amounts to gross misrepresentation, as when he calls Laud

---

[7] "The history of our country during the last hundred and sixty years is eminently the history of physical, of moral, and of intellectual improvement." *History of England*, ch. i.

[8] See the Tory review by Croker, in *QR*, LXXXIV (1848–49), 549–630.

"a ridiculous bigot," or balanced "the vices of his heart" against the "imbecility of his intellect." His treatment of Marlborough is a travesty of the truth; here the Whig historian became the dupe of the High-Tory vendetta against Marlborough and the tales of his avarice, meanness, and treachery which the genius of Swift had stamped so indelibly upon the national consciousness. Claverhouse and Penn fared little better at Macaulay's hands. He wrote with strong presuppositions, and sometimes when he missed the mark badly, it is charity to conclude that he was simply blind to whatever evidence told against his views. Samuel Rawson Gardiner's criticism of Macaulay has a finality about it that is almost crushing. "The way in which Macaulay and Forster regarded the past—that is to say, the constant avowed or unavowed comparison of it with the present—is altogether destructive of real historical knowledge." [9]

The famous third chapter on the condition of England in 1688 is often cited as proof that Macaulay liberalized the content of history, and based his work upon a wide knowledge of the life and literature of the people, as well as on the constitution, treaties, and military campaigns. Much of this celebrated chapter is full of over and under statements, or includes material that does not apply specifically to that year. However, the chapter is just the exception that proves the rule. Throughout the rest of his five volumes Macaulay wrote a political history, pure and simple, and revolved about the two foci of Whig and Tory.

A fault which is literary as well as historical is the *History's* lack of proportion. The scale of the work was unthinkable. If Macaulay had continued at that rate he would have required a hundred and fifty years of life to reach his own times. He was better suited to a theme covering a brief time than for dealing with an extended period. In contrast to Gibbon's majestic sweep over fifteen centuries, Macaulay devoted himself to less than two decades (1685–1702) of England's long history. He loved striking contrasts and was witty at the expense of historical truth. Ponsonby has cited two typical examples:

The Puritans hated bear-baiting; not because they thought it cruel to the bear, but because it amused the spectators.

And, at the end of a glowing description of the battle of Landen:

It is probable that among the 120,000 soldiers that were marshalled round Neerwinden, under all the standards of western Europe, the two feeblest in body were the hunchbacked dwarf who urged forward the fiery onset of France, and the asthmatic skeleton who covered the slow retreat of England. [10]

Macaulay was not above pretense to erudition, and his notes are some-

[9] *History of England*, preface (1884).   [10] Ponsonby (n. 1), 391.

times a parade of scholarship. He was writing on what he knew best; but on countries and periods other than his own he was darkly ignorant. In a curious blunder he confused George Neville and William Penn.[11]

Sir Charles Firth, in the preface to his illustrated edition of Macaulay (1913), wrote: "There is room for a critical study of Macaulay's *History*, and some need for one." [12] Such a study might ascertain how far Macaulay relied upon his own researches in domestic and foreign archives, and in how far he was indebted to the fifty volumes of notes and transcripts made by Sir James Mackintosh, and put at his disposal by the Mackintosh family. "I have never seen," he wrote in a footnote, "and I do not believe that there anywhere exists within the same compass, so noble a collection of extracts from public and private archives." [13]

It is not altogether fair to blame Macaulay because his *History* is "dated." The world was moving rapidly in his last years. Not long after his death a reaction set in. Cynical realism replaced romantic optimism. The material improvements and the political reforms hailed in the thirties and forties now revealed unsuspected drawbacks. There arose a scientific school searching for laws and interested in such new things as economics and sociology. Even in literary circles objectivity was being demanded. Matthew Arnold dubbed Macaulay an ill-disguised Philistine; and his stock with historical scholars continued to sink lower and lower. Leslie Stephen has said somewhere that in England the eighteenth century lasted on till 1830. Macaulay at bottom belonged to that eighteenth century, and he has nothing in com-

[11] *Life and Letters of H. Taine* (London, 1902–08, 3 v.), III, 261.
[12] *History of England*, Firth, ed., I, p. xviii.
[13] Firth's edition (n. 1), I, 381, n. 2. Mackintosh, whose *History of the Revolution of 1688* is but a noble fragment, after the fall of Napoleon in 1814 had, as his letters show, ploughed through the materials in the French Foreign Office so exhaustively, and taken such copious extracts that he excited the ire of the keeper and felt obliged to appeal to Talleyrand, then at the Congress of Vienna. Talleyrand's delicious reply deserves quoting: "Vous savez parfaitement bien, Monsieur, tout ce qu'il faut pour être un grand et utile historien: mais je vois que vous êtes peu au fait de ce que c'est qu'un Archiviste. Vous mettez vôtre gloire à repandre de l'instruction parmi les hommes; un Archiviste met tous ses soins à ne rien laisser connaitre des notions qu'il a pu recueiller. C'est un homme tout mystérieux; et vous—vous voulez dévoiler." Quoted from *Memoirs of the Life of the Right Honorable Sir James Mackintosh*, ed. by Robert James Mackintosh (London, 1835, 2 v.), II, 308 note. Under Oct. 29, 1814 Mackintosh wrote to a correspondent: "A glorious day at the depot. . . . The memory of King William vindicated about the negociations of the Marechal Boufflers with Lord Portland before the peace of Ryswick" (*ibid.*, II, 310). At home Mackintosh was no less assiduous. At Lord Hardwicke's house at Wimpole he examined the correspondence between Lord Chancellor Hardwicke and the Duke of Newcastle from 1737 to 1757, and the Stuart manuscripts at Carlton House (*ibid.*, II, 262). Among Mackintosh's volumes were extracts from the dispatches of Barillon and Bonrepaux, the French ambassadors in England, as well as from those of Citters, the Dutch ambassador and Ronquillo, the Spanish ambassador. Mackintosh and Dalrymple were the first to use these despatches, as students know.

mon with Carlyle, Froude, Newman, or Matthew Arnold, who represent the nineteenth. His *History* must be judged according to his lights.

Yet it is interesting and instructive to contrast Macaulay with Carlyle.[14] Macaulay was the favored child of fortune, who poured her gifts of fame and recognition in his lap; Carlyle through long years fought his way upward to lonely and scornful eminence. "Macaulay was an optimist, Carlyle was a pessimist." Macaulay looked at externals and was a man of the world; Carlyle searched the heart of a man and was a brooding philosopher. The one associated easily with his fellows; the other dreamed of super-men. Their style was as disparate as their natures: molten gold flowed from the pen of one, and rough granite blocks thundered from the hand of the other. Macaulay was the panegyrist of his own time, Carlyle was its merciless critic. The one accepted all the formulas of a political party, and believed in the value of parliamentary machinery; the other "accepted no formulas whatever," and thought little of only political reforms. "Macaulay was sunny, genial and agreeable"; Carlyle dyspeptic, irascible, "gey ill to deal wi'." The balance lies between them; one saw too much light, the other too much shadow, and the picture of each is wrong.

Macaulay has not been cast down from his high eminence, despite the change in historical fashion. He was a great literary artist, and an artist is the favored child of genius. Greece had but one Thucydides, Rome but one Tacitus, and England has had but one Macaulay. Since Darwin and Marx, to mention only two, it is no longer possible to write history as Macaulay and Michelet wrote it. But it is largely due to Macaulay's abiding influence that modern scientific English historiography stands closer to the lucid charm of the land that produced Renan's witching prose, than to the stolid ponderosity of the German professors.[15] Lord Acton felt an unconquerable repugnance towards Macaulay's faults, but admitted that he was "one of the greatest of all writers and masters."[16] On one occasion he informed the Trinity College Society at Cambridge:

I was once with two eminent men, the late Bishop of Oxford [William Stubbs] and the present Bishop of London [Mandell Creighton]. On another occasion I was with two far more eminent men, the two most learned men in the world. I need hardly tell you their names—they were Mommsen and Harnack. On each occasion the question arose: who was the greatest historian the world had ever produced. On each ocasion the name first mentioned, and on each occasion the name finally agreed upon, was that of Macaulay.[17]

[14] For this paragraph I am indebted to Walker (n. 4), 119–20.

[15] Freeman and James Ford Rhodes are only two of many workers who endeavored to form their style after that of Macaulay. His own grand-nephew, George Macaulay Trevelyan, regius professor at Cambridge, is a brilliant stylist as well as an impeccable historian.

[16] *Letters of Lord Acton to Mary Gladstone*, ed. with an introductory memoir by Herbert Paul (London, 1904), 168, cp. also 45.

[17] *LQR*, CVIII, 244.

Thomas Carlyle (1795–1881),[18] the grim philosopher of the mid-century, scorned conventional history as he did a good many other things, and called it nothing more or less than crystallized rumor. But this Cato of his age had an immense influence on at least the democratic reading of history. History was always the background of his thought, the court to which he appealed, the scroll on which were blazoned the eternal verities of God. Acton called him "the most detestable of historians," excepting only Carlyle's disciple Froude. Carlyle belongs properly to the post-Macaulayan period despite his early birth, to the years when optimism vanished; and to his dour temperament the times seemed badly out of joint. In the general content with material advance he saw only hypocritical smugness and threatening ethical bankruptcy. He understood no progress but moral progress, no prosperity except in the growth of better and nobler men and women. There was too much cant in politics, sham in religion, and rationalized greed in business. He could not comprehend the desire for, or trend towards, democracy. With Whiggism he was wholly impatient, and declared in his cutting way that its principles in regard to the working classes were simply "that the pigs be taught to die without squealing." The Electoral Bill of 1867 was "shooting Niagara." Society could only grow better when the wise ruled and the ignorant obeyed. With the years this creed matured into Carlyle's concept of the righteous dictator. He protested strenuously against the Utilitarian philosophy. "God's Laws are become a Greatest-Happiness Principle, a Parliamentary Expediency." Plato has been superseded by Bentham, who declares happiness to depend on circumstances instead of moral goodness and the mind within us. "I do not want cheaper cotton, swifter railways: I want . . . God, Freedom, Immortality." [19] Sentiments such as these fill his *Signs of the Times* (1829), *History* (1830), *Characteristics* (1831), *Chartism* (1839), and *Heroes and Hero Worship* (1844).

[18] See the biographical volumes by J. A. Froude, *Thomas Carlyle, a History of the First Forty Years of His Life, 1795–1835* (London, 1882, 2 v.), and *Thomas Carlyle, a History of His Life in London, 1834–1881* (London, 1884, 2 v.), and Froude's edition of Carlyle's *Reminiscences* (New York, 1881), and *Letters and Memorials of Jane Welsh Carlyle* (London, 1883, 3 v.). Other volumes of Carlyle's letters were edited by C. E. Norton and by Alexander Carlyle. GOOCH, 323–32 offers several references, to which add the excellent article in the *DNB*, IX, 110–27 by Leslie Stephen; FUETER, 567–71; *BQR*, X (1849), 1–45, LXXXI (1885), 143–59; G. M. Trevelyan, "Carlyle as an Historian," *Nineteenth Century*, XLVI (1899), 493–503; *LQR*, LXIV (1885), 1–25; *DR*, XXIX (1850), 169–206, XLVII (1860), 132–68, XCVI (1885), 63–90; *NBR*, XLV (1865), 79–126; *QR*, CLXI (1885), 142–71, LXVI (1840), 446–503, CV (1859), 275–304, CXVIII (1865), 225–54; *FM*, LVIII (1858), 631–49, LXIX (1864), 539–50; *HZ*, I (1859), 42–107; *ER*, CX (1859), 377–410; *CQR*, LVIII (1904), 395–421; *National Review*, VIII (1886–87), 588–604. For further mention, see also *Letters of Lord Acton to Mary Gladstone* (n. 16), index.

[19] The quotations are from *Past and Present* (London, 1843), 190; and "Signs of the Times," *ER*, XLIX (1829), 439–59.

Carlyle was the son of a Scottish peasant home, and his father hoped that he would enter the ministry. But he left Edinburgh University without a degree. His doubts caused him to give up the idea of entering the Church; he would not face the drudgery of teaching, and the study of law proved too dull. In turning to a literary career, it is significant that he had mastered German at a time when there was a demand for an English interpreter of that continental literature. He read Richter, Fichte, and Goethe, and the philosophy of Hegel reappeared in his "great man theory" of history. In need of money most of his life, much of Carlyle's writing was done to gain a living. Yet he was never a hack writer.

Carlyle was fundamentally a moralist. He was convinced that the march of time was to be seen in the advance of the selected great, and he shaded and colored his historical pictures so as to give these chosen few the light of heroes. His first great historical work, the *French Revolution* (1837), is a drama of human motives and passions. The study of the archives had not yet begun when Carlyle undertook to write on this subject, and his sources were limited. He did not understand the constitutional and economic problems of the Revolution, and failed to regard it as related to other eighteenth-century movements. He stopped with 1795 and said nothing of the consequences. Oddly, the book pleased both Radicals and Tories among his readers. To the first he demonstrated that the Revolution was necessary to overthrow a great imposture; the condemnation of the negative character of the Revolution appealed to the Conservative side. In a less earnest man the style would have offended the reader. Though his writing is uneven and he strains for effect, there are great passages. If hardly a chapter can withstand detailed criticism today, as a whole perhaps no truer picture of the French Revolution has been painted. The work has been described as a "rhapsodical sermon; a series of pictures seen in the flashes of a thunderstorm, and commented on by a Hebrew prophet." [20]

The *Letters and Speeches of Oliver Cromwell* drew the great Puritan figure forth from long obloquy. A reviewer has written of "Carlyle's disingenuous ingenuity," and declared: "So transformed are events as related by that literary magician, that the narrative would probably have puzzled and astonished Cromwell himself." [21] Carlyle was sometimes inclined to suppress evidence when it hampered his artistic intentions. But the *Letters* were edited with reasonable care, and the rehabilitation of Cromwell was a distinct service to English histori-

[20] A. J. Grant, *English Historians* (London, 1906), p. lxi.
[21] Quoted from the article in *CQR*, LVIII (1904), 395–421, which treats the method of Carlyle and of Gardiner in handling Cromwell. Cp. also Reginald Palgrave's "Carlyle, the 'Pious Editor' of Cromwell's Speeches," *National Review*, VIII (1886–87), 588–604.

ography. The criticism that might be made of *Cromwell* is the same that can be made of Carlyle's third great historical work, the *Life of Frederick the Great* (1858-65). Each is a vivid portrayal of a great man. Frederick is freed from the cloud that Macaulay's *Essay* had cast about his reputation; he is indeed the founder of Prussia's greatness, and Carlyle connects this with the justice of the German cause in 1870. But in neither work does he enter into the state policies or the constructive work of his heroes. Carlyle did not comprehend the problems they had to face, or the forces influencing their attempts at solutions. The military campaigns are very well handled. *Frederick* is the poorest of his three major works, as the *French Revolution* is the greatest.

James Anthony Froude (1818-94) [22] was the disciple and biographer of Carlyle. Froude's father, archdeacon of Totnes, gave his sons a good education, but did not burden his boys with theology. At Oriel College, Oxford, James Anthony like his brother Richard Hurrell came into contact with the fascinating personality of Newman. But Froude never was drawn wholeheartedly into the orbit of Tractarianism, and by the time of his graduation (1842) he had drifted away again. Carlyle's *French Revolution* first awakened his interest in history, and from Carlyle he passed to the Germans, Goethe, Lessing, Neander, and Schleiermacher. This touch of German theology alarmed the fellows of Exeter, who had chosen him Devon fellow. In 1844 Froude took deacon's orders, but he never went further towards a clerical career. Asked by Newman to collaborate in the *Lives of the English Saints*, he prepared the life of St. Neot, but a critical repugnance came over him at this excursion into the realm of medieval hagiography and miracles. A work of fiction, *Shadows of the Clouds* (1847), had pained his father; and *Nemesis of Faith* (1848), a novel, as Froude later described it, of "heterodoxy flavored with sentimentalism," made an uproar. Its subject was a student of Oriel who fell under the Oxford movement, and then came to ruin when his faith crumbled.

Froude resigned his fellowship at Exeter and became a private

[22] Herbert Paul, *Life of Froude* (2nd edition, New York, 1906); A. F. Pollard in *DNB*, supplement II, 247-51 with bibliography; Frederic Harrison, *Tennyson, Ruskin, Mill and Other Literary Estimates* (London, 1899), the same, "The Historical Method of J. A. Froude," *Nineteenth Century*, XLIV (1898), 373-85; Sir Leslie Stephen, *Studies of a Biographer* (London, 1898-1902, 4 v.), III; Algernon Cecil, *Six Oxford Thinkers* (London, 1909); *QR*, CXXVIII (1870), 506-44, CLXXXII (1895), 281-304; *BQR*, XXVII (1858), 289-339, LI (1870), 281-312; *CR*, XXXI (March 1878), 821-42, XXXII (April 1878), 116-39, 474-500, XXXIII (Sept. 1878), 213-41, and E. A. Freeman's article, "Last Words on Mr. Froude," XXXV (May 1879), 214-36; *ER*, CXIX (1864), 243-79, CXXIV (1866), 476-510 and CXXXI (1870), 1-39; *DR*, LXXXII (1878), 292-327, XLIV (1858), 445-85; *FM*, LVIII (1858), 359-78; Herbert A. Fisher, "Modern Historians and Their Methods," *Fortnightly Review*, LXII (1894), 803-16; Andrew Fish, "The Reputation of James Anthony Froude," *Pacific Historical Review*, I (1932), 179-92.

tutor. With Charles Kingsley [23] he cemented an intimate friendship and afterwards married Kingsley's wife's sister. In 1849 he was introduced to Carlyle, and later was a frequent visitor at the philosopher's house in Chelsea. Such was the admiration Froude nursed for this rough friend, that he elevated him to the unseen critic at his elbow. [24]

A score of Froude's years went into the writing of the *History of England from the Fall of Wolsey to the Defeat of the Spanish Armada.* [25] It sold extremely well, though for a time it had to contend for public favor with the last publications of Macaulay. [26] Froude also contributed to the *Westminster Review* and *Fraser's Magazine.* In 1860 he became editor of the latter, and carried this burden for fourteen years. *The English in Ireland in the Eighteenth Century* (1872–74, 3 v., new edition in 1881) sought to prove the folly of trying conciliation, and mirrors Carlyle's contempt for Gladstone and his Irish policy. It was bitterly criticized, but the best answer was given by the second volume of Lecky's *History of Ireland in the Eighteenth Century* (1878–90, 8 v.). Froude had no objection to the Irish as individuals, but rejected any notion of national existence.

Froude's ventures into politics were no happier than Freeman's, but they affected wider circles. In 1874, after the death of his second wife, he undertook, in the guise of a private visit, a reconnaissance tour through South Africa for his friend Lord Carnarvon, then Secretary of State for the Colonies, to sound out the prospects for colonial federation. Froude returned firmly persuaded that the past policy of England in South Africa had been both foolish and unjust, and recommended a hands-off policy. Asked by Lord Carnarvon to return once more, he executed his task in the most tactless manner, stirred up

[23] Cp. Stubbs' half-humorous, half-malicious "Hymn on Froude":

> Froude informs the Scottish youth
> That parsons do not care for truth—
> The Reverend Canon Kingsley cries
> History is a pack of lies.
>
> What cause for judgments so malign?
> A brief reflection solves the mystery.
> Froude believes Kingsley a divine,
> And Kingsley goes to Froude for history!

Leslie Stephen, ed., *Letters of John Richard Green* (New York and London, 1901), 315. Written when Froude was rector of St. Andrews, and Kingsley a Cambridge professor.

[24] "If I wrote anything, I fancied myself writing it to him, reflecting at each word on what he would think of it, as a check on affectations." Froude, *Thomas Carlyle, a History of His Life in London* (n. 18), II, 152.

[25] The first two volumes came out in 1856, followed by two each in 1858, 1860, 1863, 1866, and 1870. Froude at first projected the work to reach the death of Elizabeth, but decided with the ninth volume to stop with the Defeat of the Armada and avoid an anti-climax.

[26] The first two volumes reached their second edition in 1858, vols. 1–4, 7, and 8 went into the third in 1862–64; a cabinet edition of the whole was put on sale in 1870, and a cheaper form, in twelve volumes, 1881–2, 1893, etc.

excitement and ill feeling all round, and gave the final blow to Carnarvon's scheme.   On his return to England, Froude persisted in airing and defending his South African views, just as in 1878 he followed Carlyle's lead and opposed Lord Beaconsfield's policy in Eastern Europe.

When Carlyle died, in 1881, he left Froude as his sole surviving literary executor.   Froude has been harshly criticized for the manner in which he edited the *Reminiscences* (1881, 2 v.) and the *Letters and Memorials of Jane Welsh Carlyle* (1883, 3 v.). He defended his publication of even painful or intimate portions on the ground that Carlyle intended this as a posthumous penance towards his wife. Then Froude set to writing a mammoth biography of his hero. No one can say that *Thomas Carlyle, a History of the First Forty Years of His Life* (1882, 2 v., new edition, 1890) and *Thomas Carlyle, a History of His Life in London* (1884, 2 v., new edition, 1890) are marred by anything approaching adulation. Perhaps Froude had taken too well to heart Carlyle's own gibe at English biography: "How delicate, decent it is, bless its mealy mouth!" But few biographies are so readable, and Froude was right in reckoning it among the most permanent of his writings.

None of his later works reaches the importance of those mentioned thus far. His *Oceana, or England and Her Colonies* (1886) caused a wide stir. It was written after a visit to Australia and conversations with colonists abroad, and appeared at a time when English interest in the Empire was reviving. A volume on *Caesar* was a pale reflection of Mommsen. In two volumes Froude returned to the subject of his earlier successes, without any significant changes in his views or treatment: *The Divorce of Catherine of Aragon: the Story as Told by Imperial Ambassadors at the Court of Henry VIII* (1891, as supplement to his *History of England*) and *The Spanish Story of the Armada* (1892).

Whatever critics and foes might say, the years established Froude's title to a high position in English letters. When his strenuous opponent Freeman died in the regius chair at Oxford, in 1892, Froude had the satisfaction of receiving an invitation from Lord Salisbury to succeed him. He wrote to his friend Skelton:

> The temptation of going back to Oxford in a respectable way was too much for me. I must just do the best I can, and trust that I shall not be haunted by Freeman's ghost.[27]

His lectures were well attended, for he had polish and elocutionary powers. They were later published as *The Life and Letters of Erasmus* (1895), *English Seamen in the Sixteenth Century* (1895),[28] and *The Council of Trent* (1896).

[27] John Skelton, *The Table Talk of Shirley. Reminiscences of and Letters from Froude, Thackeray, Disraeli, Browning, Rossetti, Kingsley* (6th ed., Edinburgh and London, 1896), 216–17.
[28] This book inspired Kingsley's *Westward Ho!* and Tennyson's *Revenge*.

Since Freeman first launched his attacks in the *Saturday Review*, there has grown up a legend about Froude's "constitutional inaccuracy." [29] The influence of Freeman upon the new critical generation through his pretentious reviews was profound. It became fashionable to repeat the blunders of Froude. From an article by H. A. L. Fisher [30] the fateful judgment passed into Langlois and Seignobos' textbook of historical method; [31] and soon every beginner in historical study could talk of "Froudacity" and cite the famous description of Adelaide, the alleged errors of which have since then gone through a process of progressive reduction. Sir Francis Palgrave originated the malicious story that when working among the archives at Hatfield House, full of the Burghley papers, Froude examined the material found in only two of the ten presses there, and J. R. Green passed the word along to Freeman, writing: "Anthony looked a little into the two but never discovered the existence of the other eight!"—yet admitted that Palgrave's informant was the housekeeper. [31a]

Froude finally emerged from dignified silence and offered that an impartial committee should test any two or three hundred pages of his work by the transcripts of Spanish documents which he had made and deposited in the British Museum, provided the *Saturday Review* would publish the results. The offer was not taken up. Freeman, who never used manuscripts, ridiculed Froude for speaking of the *Ark Raleigh* instead of the *Ark Royal* when writing of the Armada. The original sources to which Froude went bear him out, but of course Freeman never saw them, and never would have apologized to Froude if he had known them. Freeman indulged in the most intemperate notations in the margins of his copies of Froude's works: "May I live to embowel James Anthony Froude. . . . Froude is certainly the vilest brute that ever wrote a book." [32]

There is no doubt that Froude was as inaccurate a worker as any great historian can afford to be and still retain some standing. He was unforgivably careless, not in only proofreading, but in copying from his sources, and the sanctity of inverted commas in quotations meant nothing to him. But it must be remembered that Froude, unlike Freeman, did the bulk of his work from almost illegible manuscript

[29] The growth of this legend is analyzed briefly in Curtis Howe Walker, "The 'True' Mr. Froude," *Texas Review*, VIII (1923), no. 4; and in greater detail in Herbert Paul's *Life of Froude* (n. 22), ch. v, 147–98.

[30] See above, n. 22.

[31] *Introduction aux études historiques* (Paris, 1899); English translation by G. G. Berry, *Introduction to the Study of History* (London, 1898), 125–26.

[31a] Stephen (n. 23), 239, letter dated 1869. It has been estimated by more competent historians than "Johnny" Green that the transcripts alone which Froude made from the Hatfield manuscripts must have required a month to copy. See Paul (n. 22), 156.

[32] Paul (n. 22), 160–61.

sources. He was the first Englishman to enter the rich depository at Simancas. It requires only a little consideration to realize the pains his twelve volumes must have cost him. They were projected on a large scale, with no previous works to follow. Nine-tenths of his sources were in manuscript, written in five different languages, and filled nine hundred volumes, in difficult handwritings. His troubles in decipherment he himself later described:

Often at the end of a page, . . . I have felt as after descending a precipice, and have wondered how I got down. I had to cut my way through a jungle, for no one had opened the road for me. I have been turned into rooms piled to the windowsill with bundles of dust-covered despatches, and told to make the best of it. Often I have found the sand glistening on the ink where it had been sprinkled when a page was turned. . . . There the letter had lain, never looked at again since it was read and put away.[33]

Of Froude's pains and his wish to tell the truth there seems to be no question. But his inaccuracy extended to another more dangerous fault, inseparably connected with his whole conception and method. This relates to the selection of his colors. Froude was a literary artist and not a scientific historian. He wrote with prejudice, or as an advocate. He pursued Mary Queen of Scots with hatred; but he vindicated Cranmer and the genius of Lord Burghley in the eyes of the world. His characters were by his literary magic individualized, and became human and plausible rather than the traditional saints and monsters. In the light of what Froude accomplished, it is regrettable that he was not always more accurate. His volumes remain the only, as they were the first, monumental treatment of English history in the sixteenth century. The greatest living authority on the age of Henry VIII has been singularly charitable:

It may be remarked that there is inadequate justification for the systematic detraction of Froude's *History* which has become the fashion. He held strong views, and he made some mistakes; but his mistakes were no greater than those of other historians, and there are not half-a-dozen histories in the English language which have been based on so exhaustive a survey of original materials.[34]

Like Carlyle, Froude's approach to history was largely moral. After his Oxford experiences he had come to believe in the English Reformation; he had detected the horror, as he thought it, of ecclesiasticism. Froude was convinced that the yoke of Rome would have meant a dimming of the light of freedom and civilization. Extraordinary times demanded extraordinary men and measures. He recognized these in Henry VIII, the monarch who with all his faults broke the shackles of Rome and ecclesiastical domination, and remained popular with an

[33] Quoted in Paul (n. 22), 192, cp. 169.
[34] A. F. Pollard, in the preface to his *Cranmer*, 1904.

approving people; in the cautious policies of Lord Burghley who really made Elizabeth great.   For the Queen herself he had contempt, and professed to read in the correspondence of Burghley and Walsingham proof of her incapacity.   Perhaps Froude was fighting a shadow of his student days, but he produced a great drama of the Reformation century.   As an Erastian, he was naturally obnoxious to the Tory and High Church party.   But for all its defects his *History* has the qualities of immortality.[35]

[35] "Pages and sentences in his history of Tudor England, in the 'Short Studies,' or in 'English Seamen' set forth power and endurance and suffering in eternal vibration, or hang on the air like chiming bells."   Quoted from "The Refashioning of History; a Line of Great Craftsmen," *LTLS*, 1937, pp. 319–21.

CHAPTER XLVIII

THE OXFORD AND CAMBRIDGE SCHOOLS OF HISTORY

IN GERMANY and France the universities have always taken the lead in historiography. Neither of the two English universities taught modern history at the opening of the nineteenth century.[1] Ancient history was a phase of the classics and part of a gentleman's education; it had maintained a hold in the curriculum, but was viewed as a branch of literature. The professorships of modern history founded in 1724 at Oxford and Cambridge go back to that Whig tradition in the time when Bishop Gibson persuaded Sir Robert Walpole to establish these chairs in both universities.[2] Instruction in modern languages languished along with history. English students were severed from a knowledge of contemporary progress in German scholarship by their inability to read German.

The evil was a greater one than an inadequate curriculum. It was one of general standards. In the first decades of the last century the universities were hardly entitled to the name of seats of higher learning. Attendance was low, and instruction was left in the hands of a few tutors of each college, who divided their attention between several subjects and hoped for appointment to church livings. The religious tests were not wholly removed until 1871; a non-conformist could not matriculate at Oxford or take the bachelor's degree at Cambridge.[3] Reforms were slow in coming.

Oxford early in the century had the pedantic Dr. Nares; Arnold's stay was altogether too brief. Goldwin Smith and Dr. Shirley, pro-

[1] See the long chapter on Oxford historians in Sir Charles Oman, *On the Writing of History* (London and New York, 1939); Thomas Humphrey Ward, ed., *The Reign of Queen Victoria; a Survey of Fifty Years of Progress* (London, 1887, 2 v.), II, 280–321; G. P. Gooch, "The Cambridge Chair of Modern History," *Studies in Modern History* (London and New York, 1921), 289–325; GOOCH, 340–58; William Stubbs, *Seventeen Lectures on the Study of Medieval and Modern History* (Oxford, 1887), 7–8; Friedrich von Raumer, *England in 1835*, tr. from the German by Sarah Austin and H. E. Lloyd (Philadelphia, 1836), 480; C. H. Firth, "Modern History in Oxford, 1724–1841," *EHR*, XXXII (1917), 1–21; Mary R. Stubbert, "The Cambridge School of History," *Annual Report of the American Historical Association for 1898* (Washington, D.C., 1899), 383–411; A. J. Grant, *English Historians* (London, 1909), pp. lxxv–lxxvii; "Modern History, and Other Matters at Cambridge," *FM*, XLV (1852), 170–82; Mandell Creighton, "The Oxford School of History," *CQR*, LIX, 92–126; Sykes, in *History* (1934).

[2] L. S. Wood, "The Inaugural Lectures of the Regius Professors of Modern History at Oxford and Cambridge since 1841," in *Historical Association Leaflets*, no. 80 (London, 1930). H. W. C. Davis in his inaugural spoke of "the inglorious annals of the chair up to 1841."

[3] Ward (n. 1), II, 289–92, 308.

fessor of ecclesiastical history, were men of learning, but as late as the 1870's conditions were still unsatisfactory. There was then a more substantial scholarship—more at Oxford than at Cambridge—but little teaching. Stubbs was at Trinity; Bryce at Oriel; Freeman and Anson, Dicey and Holland were at All Souls. But they gave only some thirty or forty lectures during the year, and no other form of instruction. "The instruction given by these scholars was more in the nature of a first reading to a public audience of the manuscript of a book soon to appear than in that of a leadership of students in research." [4] And what is one to think of the fact that Robert Louis Stevenson was seriously proposed as professor of history in the University of Edinburgh in the '80's?

American scholars got their start in history from the German school of the nineteenth century, but England got very little from France or Germany. It is significant that Lord Acton was trained on the Continent, and not in Oxford—which would not admit him because he was a Catholic. Save for Buckle, no Englishman showed any inclination to discuss the theory of history. The auxiliary sciences were not developed until later.

The change in English historiography may be said to have come in the years between 1859 and 1867. Macaulay died in 1859, the year in which Darwin's *Origin of Species* saw the light. Buckle died in 1862. In 1864 the fourth volume of Palgrave's *History of England and Normandy* was issued. In 1867—*annus mirabilis*—Stubbs was appointed to the regius professorship in Oxford. "To speak with the utmost respect of my predecessors," said Stubbs, "I do not find that they were men to whom the study of history, either English or Foreign, is in any way indebted." The systematic study of history in Oxford and Cambridge is of recent growth. [5] The result has been a singular ignorance of British history, and still more of European history, on the part of the average Englishman, which sometimes, one thinks, has been embarrassing in British diplomacy. Talleyrand's gibe that Castlereagh had abused "the Englishman's privilege of ignorance" was not without reason.

It has become the fashion to speak of "the Oxford School," and "the Cambridge School." M. Charles Bémont once said that properly speaking England never has developed any school of historians. [6] If there be one, it is the Cambridge School, and that is self-styled. The

[4] John W. Burgess, *Reminiscences of an American Scholar* (New York, 1923), 221.

[5] William Archbold, ed., *Essays on the Teaching of History* (Cambridge, 1902), introduction, by F. W. Maitland.

[6] Charles Bémont, "Angleterre. Publications relatives au moyen âge," *RH*, LVII (1895), 142–74.

most that the names signify is that the need for a more scientific and objective history was at last felt. In this sense the Oxford School began with Stubbs, and the Cambridge School with Seeley.

One thing united the Oxford group. Against Buckle's hypothesis of a scientific history which would make men mere automata, its members held for free will. History was not mathematical. Nor was it practical in the sense in which Seeley at Cambridge (1873) proclaimed its virtues for coaching diplomats and statesmen. History was to be studied for its own sake, and on the strength of all available materials. Barrows and dykes, place-names, manorial rolls and statutes were drafted to give testimony. The school was aided by the increasing flow of source publications. The *Chroniclers* and the *Calendar of State Papers* were begun under the Master of the Rolls in 1857 and 1862, respectively. The Historical Manuscripts Commission commenced in 1870, and the *Calendar of Patent Rolls* in 1901. Private societies like the Camden, the Surtees, and the Selden Society continued to subsidize volumes.

The greatest, the wisest, and the most learned of the regius professors of history at Oxford was William Stubbs (1825–1901).[7] G. W. Prothero said to the Royal Historical Society: "Perhaps no English historian that ever lived did more to advance the knowledge of English history and to set the study of it on a sound basis, than Dr. Stubbs." His powerful mind came from sturdy yeoman stock, and he once amused himself by tracing his pedigree back to certain crown tenants in the forest of Knaresborough in the fourteenth century. As a student at the Ripon grammar school he attracted the attention of Bishop Longley (later archbishop of Canterbury), and when his father died this benefactor obtained for him a servitorship at Christ Church (1844). Social restrictions made the young man's years at Oxford rather lonely ones, but he put in his time reading and impressed others by a remarkable memory. In the library of his college he pored over old manuscripts, having learned from his father, a solicitor, to decipher old charters and deeds, and developed the palaeographic skill which amazed experienced

[7] William H. Hutton, ed., *Letters of William Stubbs, Bishop of Oxford, 1825–1901* (London, 1904); also republished in abridged form as *William Stubbs, Bishop of Oxford*. Both volumes contain a bibliography of his writings; see also W. A. Shaw, *A Bibliography of the Historical Works of Creighton, Stubbs, S. R. Gardiner, and Lord Acton* (London, 1903); A. Hassall's preface to Stubbs' *Introduction to the Rolls Series* (London and New York, 1902); "William Stubbs, Churchman and Historian," *QR*, CCII (1905), 1–34, and reviews *ibid.*, CCXVI (1912), 1–28, CCXVII (1912), 413–36; F. W. Maitland, "William Stubbs, Bishop of Oxford," *EHR*, XVI (1901), 417–26; GOOCH, 340–46; FUETER, 610; *LQR*, XLVIII (1877), 265–99; *NAR*, CXIX (1874), 233–44 and CXXIII (1876), 161–65; *The Nation*, vol. 81 (Sept. 7, 1905), 201–03 and vol. 82 (June 28, 1906), 432–33; Gustave Masson, "Une nouvelle collection de documents rélatif à l'histoire écclesiastique de la Grande-Bretagne et de l'Irlande," *RQH*, VII (1869), 605–10, XI (1872), 521–25, and XX (1876), 201–06; R. H. Hodgkin, *A History of the Anglo-Saxons* (Oxford, 1935, 2 v.), I, 201–03; *CQR*, XXIV (1887), 398–418, LII (1901), 280–99, LIX (1904), 93–98, LXI (1905), 134–63; T. F. Tout, in *DNB*, Second Supplement, III, 444–51.

workers in later years. Trinity made him a fellow, in 1848 he was ordained deacon, and two years later priest.

The seventeen years Stubbs spent in the vicarage at Navestock
(1850–66) transformed him into the greatest medievalist in the England of his day. His first work, the *Registrum Sacrum Anglicanum*, required ten years and numberless visits to various libraries and sees.
Stubbs described it as "an attempt to exhibit the course of episcopal
succession in England . . . [and] a contribution to Ecclesiastical History in the departments of Biography and exact Chronology." [8]

Stubbs also took pupils to tutor. The most famous of these—though
not in history—was the poet Algernon Swinburne (1859), who remembered him with affection and admiration. Though burdened with
parochial duties, Stubbs found time to edit a translation of Mosheim's
Ecclesiastical History with a continuation of his own. In 1861 he
printed his first edition of a manuscript: *De inventione sanctae Crucis
nostrae in Monte Acuto et de ductione ejusdem apud Waltham*, to which
he added an admirable account of the foundation of Waltham abbey.
In 1862 Archbishop Longley appointed him to the librarianship of
Lambeth.

Stubbs' friendship with E. A. Freeman and J. R. Green was now
already of some years standing.[9] In 1858 he complained to Freeman
about the newly-founded *Rolls Series:* "I am sorry to see that the
philological side of things is to be kept so exclusively in view in these
publications. For, interesting and important as it is, it is not History—
but Tho[mas] Duffus Hardy tells me nothing but the Philological will
go down and the Books must be made to sell." [10] Stubbs' biographer
has said that his identification with the Rolls Series was "the most
important work of his life—the application to English medieval documents of the scientific methods of Continental scholars."

The Master of the Rolls required that each chronicle or document
be "treated in the same way as if the editor were engaged on an *Editio
Princeps.*" This meant the collation of manuscripts, the notation of
variants, and the investigation of origin, authenticity, possible corruption, recensions, and interpolations. Happily the restrictions upon
appended notes were gradually reduced. Among the list of excellent
editors were Macray, Luard, Brewer, and Shirley, but incomparably the
greatest was Stubbs. He began with the two volumes of the *Chronicles
and Memorials of Richard I* (1864–65). In all he edited and wrote mar-

---

[8] The story of its origin is recounted in the preface to the 2nd edition (Oxford, 1897), 41–42.

[9] In 1857 he wrote Freeman: "Have you seen Buckle on *Civilization*, Vol. I.? There are to
be ten. I do not believe in the Philosophy of History, and so do not believe in Buckle. I fear
you will make me out a heretic indeed after such a confession."

[10] Hutton, *Letters of William Stubbs* (n. 7), 44.

vellous introductions to nearly a score of volumes. He rescued Archbishop Dunstan from centuries of obloquy, performing a service comparable to what Brewer did for Cardinal Wolsey; and corrected a host of errors in regard to the reign of King Edgar. One of the finest critical studies Stubbs wrote was the analysis of the *Chronicle of Benedict of Peterborough.*[11]

In 1866 Goldwin Smith resigned the regius professorship at Oxford, and Stubbs hoped his friend Freeman would be appointed. "It would be painful to have Froude and worse still to have anybody else," he wrote. However, his own voice delivered the inaugural lecture on February 7, 1867, from which one may date the Oxford School. In a serious hour, ending even on a religious note, he presented himself to his audience, "not as a philosopher nor as a politician, but as a worker at history." To him history was "something worth knowing for itself and the truth's sake." [12] Recalling the recent progress made in the collection and publishing of sources, the new professor anticipated

the prospect of being instrumental . . . in the founding of an historical school in England, which should join with the other workers of Europe in a common task; which shall build, not upon Hallam and Palgrave and Kemble and Froude and Macaulay, but on the abundant, collected, and arranged materials on which those writers tried to build whilst they were scanty and scattered . . .[13]

As a teacher, Stubbs took great pains with his lectures, but their final printed form, since they were edited posthumously, hardly does him justice.[14] Among his pupils were J. Horace Round, T. F. Tout, C. H. Firth, and R. L. Poole. His audience at lectures was never large, and diminished with the years. The system of reading for examinations at Oxford drew capable students away, and a practical seminar after the German method was impossible. Stubbs hid his disappointment in further research and writing.[15]

The three volumes of the *Councils and Ecclesiastical Documents* which he edited together with A. W. Haddan appeared between 1869

[11] Cp. *ibid.*, 60–64.   [12] *Seventeen Lectures in Medieval and Modern History* (n. 1), 15, 27.
[13] Hutton (n. 7), 119. J. R. Green reviewed the inaugural lecture in the *Saturday Review*, XXIII (1867), 278–80, republished in part in his *Stray Studies*, 2nd series.
[14] From his academic lectures came the *Seventeen Lectures on the Study of Medieval and Modern History* (1887; 3rd enlarged ed., 1900); *Lectures on European History* (1904); *Lectures on Early English History* (1906); *Germany in the Early Middle Ages, 476–1250* (1908), and *Germany in the Later Middle Ages, 1200–1500* (1908).
[15] His pupil Tout introduced at Manchester a practical training in historical method, a system of real apprenticeship. He seems to have gotten this idea from Stubbs, for twice in his essays and lectures (*The Collected Papers of Thomas Frederick Tout*, Manchester Univ. Press, 1932–34, 3 v.) Tout mentions Stubbs' phrase "the historical teaching of history" (I, 139, III, 3). The latter passage reads: "The 'historical teaching of history,' as Stubbs once called that education of the historian which he dreamt of but despaired of as an impossibility in his own age and in his own university. This [continues Tout] is happily no longer the case, and the historian can now learn his trade in England in quite a satisfactory fashion."

and 1878. To the *Dictionary of Christian Biography* he contributed a long series of English saints, kings, and churchmen in Saxon times.[16] His life of Bede is a model of this sort. The volume of *Select Charters* (1870) illustrative of English constitutional history laid the foundation for almost all later investigations into constitutional origins by English scholars. It was the preparatory step to Stubbs' greatest work, the stupendous *Constitutional History of England*.[17] Nothing so massive had been attempted since Gibbon. No other English historical work has excelled it since. The original device of alternating annalistic with analytic chapters was a happy thought. Stubbs stressed the continuity of English history. The English Constitution was the result of Norman concentration of principally Anglo-Saxon institutions.[18] The treatment of the Angevin period is masterly. His first volume, however, from the Anglo-Saxon invasions to the Norman Conquest, is now obsolete. Of the field it covered, Maitland picturesquely said: "Many an investigator will leave his bones to bleach on that desert before it is accurately mapped." Stubbs' pronouncement on the Teutonic and free origin of the village was hotly disputed by the Romano-Celtic school, which proposed to find its origin in the *coloni* of a Roman villa.[19] His views on the origin of the hundred, the borough, and the frankpledge raised a long and lively controversy. The notion of self-governing assemblies, central or local, has been exploded. This revolutionary change of view is not due to a different interpretation of the sources, but to the use of new sources. Stubbs, Green, and Freeman relied upon Tacitus' *Germania*, the *Anglo-Saxon Chronicle*, and the *Laws*. The new school has used the literary sources as well, notably *Beowulf*, and avoided the dangerous analogy with Frankish and Lombard institutions as unsafe parallels.

A confirmed conservatism prevented Stubbs from making any revisions. His historical labors virtually ended with his departure from Oxford University in 1884. What the Church gained in the Bishop of Chester and Oxford, English historiography lost. The influence of his supreme example, however, was not lost. No other worker had so taken his readers behind the scenes and introduced them to the meticu-

[16] See the list in Hutton's bibliography (n. 7).

[17] Oxford, 1874–78, 3 v. Professor C. Petit-Dutaillis added notes and summaries of later scholarship to the French translation by G. Lefebvre (1907–27, 3 v); W. E. Rhodes published the notes in English as *Studies and Notes Supplementary to Stubbs' "Constitutional History"* (Manchester, 1908). For further comment see below, pp. 382–83.

[18] Paul Vinogradoff, *Villainage in England* (Oxford, 1892), 23–24.

[19] Cf. Charles H. Pearson, *History of England during the Early and Middle Ages* (London, 1867, 2 v.); Frederic Seebohm, *The English Village Community* (4th ed., London and New York, 1896); Fustel de Coulanges, *Histoire des institutions politiques de l'ancienne France* (Paris, 1888–1907, 6 v.), and *Recherches sur quelques problèmes d'histoire* (2nd ed., Paris, 1894). These titles are given in *CQR*, LIX (1904), 96, n. 1.

lous secrets of the historian's business: the search for manuscripts, the shredding of sources, the tentative reflection and the cautious rejection. Sympathetic and cheerful, possessed of an irrepressible humour, his greatness had no false dignity. "God forbid that we should speak contemptuously of any honest worker," he had said in his inaugural lecture; and it was his boast in later years that he had written only one review. He called himself "steeped in clerical and conservative principles," but rejoiced that he avoided "ecclesiastical prejudice or political bias" in his writing. He did not think it his task to make men Whigs or Tories at Oxford, but to make them good, wise, and sensible, whether Whig or Tory. Against history as a science, Stubbs admitted that generalizations whether broad or narrow are inexact. Despite his tolerance he had strangely conservative limits. "Great as Stubbs was, he wrote his *Constitutional History of England* in spectacles—the spectacles of Victorian Liberalism, which are all the more curious on his nose when one remembers that he was a natural Tory." [20]

Stubbs and Freeman were life-long friends and admirers of one another. An Oxford jingle ran:

> Each ladling largely from alternate tubs,
> Stubbs butters Freeman, Freeman butters Stubbs.

Edward Augustus Freeman (1823–92) [21] was a precocious lad who read Roman and English history before he was ten; at eleven he was well equipped in Latin and Greek, and had even taught himself some Hebrew. He attended various private schools under clergymen, and came under the influence of the High Church movement. He found similar sentiments among his fellow-students at Oxford, where he had a scholarship at Trinity (1841–45). The failure to win a prize with an essay on the Norman Conquest piqued him to a deeper study of this period. After his graduation he put aside the thought of entering holy orders, and retired with his bride to Gloucestershire to read ancient and modern history. His first serious work was a *History of Architecture* (1849), limited indeed to English ecclesiastical buildings; his second *An Essay on* [Gothic] *Window Tracery* (1855). These subjects were

[20] Ernest Barker, "Maitland as a Sociologist," *The Sociological Review*, XXIX (1937), 123, the whole, 121–35.

[21] W. R. W. Stephens, *Life and Letters of Edward A. Freeman* (London and New York, 1895, 2 v.), reviewed in *CQR*, LIX, 92–127. Stephens gives a complete list of his writings. See also William Hunt's article in *DNB*, supplement II, 247–51; ASHLEY, 432–39; FUETER, 612–15; GOOCH, 336–37, 346–52; James Bryce, "Edward Augustus Freeman," *EHR*, VII (1892), 497–509; Oliver Elton, *Frederick York Powell* (Oxford, 1906, 2 v.), II, 27–37; *ER*, CXXX (1869), 186–216; *QR*, CLXXV (1892), 1–37, and CLXXXII (1895), 281–309; Herbert Adams in *AHR*, I (1895), 149–53; *BQR*, LII (1870), 1–30; *LQR*, XXXIV (1870), 355–88, LIX (1882), 1–28, and XLVIII (1897), 1–28; *CQR*, XXIV (1887), 398–418; Henry Adams in *NAR*, CXVIII (1874), 176–81.

life-long hobbies of his, and linked up with his love for travel and ability in sketching. In 1855 began his association with the *Saturday Review*, which was to last for twenty-two years. Freeman's reviews did as much as any man's to earn this severe journal the nickname of the "Reviler."

Freeman continued to read avidly on Greek, Roman, and later history. In 1858 the coveted regius professorship in modern history at Oxford went to Goldwin Smith; in 1861 he missed the Camden professorship in ancient history, and the next year failed of the Chichele chair of modern history. But his reputation rose with the appearance of his *History of Federal Government* (1863),[22] and was established securely by the six volumes of the *History of the Norman Conquest of England* (1867–79).

The years prior to 1884, when Freeman succeeded Stubbs in the regius chair at Oxford, were filled with sound and fury. In one year he is said to have sent the *Saturday Review* ninety-six articles. There were a number of literary feuds, of which that with Froude was the most notorious,[23] some ventures into politics—that field which attracted Freeman so immensely[24]—visits to Dalmatia and strenuous efforts to relieve the harassed Christians suffering from the Turks (1876), and a lecture tour to the United States (1881). Meanwhile Freeman worked on his *Historical Geography, William Rufus,* and a *History of Sicily,* the last of which he began because "the oecumenical island, the meeting-place of the nations," illustrated so well his favorite theory of the unity of all history.

In 1884, when Stubbs was made bishop of Oxford, and the regius professorship was vacant, Gladstone offered the chair to Freeman— one thinks because both of them agreed on the Eastern Question. To Goldwin Smith Freeman wrote:

> It is something to succeed Arnold, you, and Stubbs—but I gnash my teeth that I have not had you and Stubbs to my colleagues, and not to predecessors. Years ago to fill one of the historical Chairs at Oxford was my alternative ambition with a seat in Parliament. . . . Now at last one has come when I am rather too old for the change.[25]

[22] Only the first volume was ever published. This was republished posthumously in a new form by J. B. Bury, as *The History of Federal Government in Greece and Italy* (London and New York, 1893).

[23] Froude was an intense Imperialist, and a Unionist. To Freeman he seemed to defend despotism, for Freeman was a Liberal in politics, an ardent Home Ruler, and a little Englander. In his later years Freeman became increasingly conservative, and J. R. Green chaffed him about "lying down with Froude."

[24] Politics was to him a moral question. He severed his connection with the *Saturday Review*, a personal sacrifice of much pleasure and an annual income amounting to £500, because it did not square with his views on the Eastern Question. Vinogradoff's judgment on this historian who declared politics the cream of history is interesting. Freeman's views, based upon a romantic racialism, struck the great Russian as infantile. "He is a great scholar, . . . but in politics a child of two." H. A. L. Fisher, ed., *The Collected Papers of Vinogradoff* (Oxford, 1928, 2 v.), I, 19.

[25] *Life and Letters* (n. 21), II, 278–79.

Freeman accepted the appointment because he thought that the honor was due him. But he had no heart for teaching and deliberately fixed the hour of his lectures at four o'clock—the sacred hour of tea and muffins in all England. An American student at Oxford who called upon him, and who had formerly met Freeman in Sicily, "heard him tell his parlormaid to run over to his lecture room across St. Giles and see if there were any auditors assembled. In this case, the Professor told me, he would be compelled to attend himself. The maid soon brought back the accustomed news that the lecture room was completely empty, and so we were enabled to have our tea in peace." [26] Such teaching did not benefit Oxford. Freeman died of smallpox in the summer of 1892 when on a visit to Spain with his wife and daughters.

Freeman's style was diffuse but always vigorous. He had an antipathy to words of Latin derivation and used Anglo-Saxon words when possible. In his zeal for clarity he avoided the use of pronouns and would repeat the antecedent noun instead time and again in the same paragraph. The late Basil Gildersleeve, the greatest of American Hellenists, in a review of Freeman's *History of Sicily* wrote: "With details of style and statement every one will have some quarrel. Quiet souls will resent the fife and drum movement that leaves one no rest from beginning to end, but when the march is over, one is better for the exercise even if a little fretted by the high pitch and the perpetual iteration." [27]

It is easy to fling stones at Freeman's blustering ways. He never wearied of preaching about what he thought were popular errors.[28] John Richard Green, his close friend, thought he clove too much to the factual; and Freeman's predilection for political and military items to the exclusion of other equally important factors in history is well known. "History is past politics, and politics is present history," was his maxim.

An odd characteristic in Freeman is his strange aversion to the employment of manuscript authorities.[29] He was ignorant of palaeography and had an insuperable repugnance to working with archival materials. Vinogradoff described him as a "well-to-do country gentleman who had never worked for a single day in a public library, never consulted a manuscript, but was content to rely upon the fine collection of books he had gathered around him." [30] When Döllinger proposed Freeman for membership in the Bavarian Academy, he apologized for

[26] L. P. Smith, "Oxford," *Atlantic Monthly*, CLXI (1938), 735, the whole article, 731–40.
[27] *American Journal of Philology*, XII (1891), 520–21.
[28] Thus, Charlemagne was not a Frenchman, Austria represents neither a nationality nor a language, the modern use of the word "empire" is unhistorical. Grant, *English Historians* (n. 1), p. lxvii.
[29] Bryce in *EHR* (n. 21).   [30] *Collected Papers of Vinogradoff* (n. 23), I, 16.

this defective method by saying that "nevertheless he mixes colors with his brains and is author of the profoundest work on the Middle Ages yet written in England." [31] Pauli wrote to Stubbs complaining of Freeman's ignorance of eastern Europe, the Hanseatic League, and the Slavs. [32]

Yet Freeman was not only an honest and forthright man, he was also one of England's greatest scholars. For learning and mental power he stood next to Bishop Stubbs in his generation. His range of knowledge was enormous, and his greatest single contribution was to break down the periodization of history and remove the wall between medieval and modern. Despite his staunch biassed English patriotism, he kept his race prejudices out of his books and gave a fair picture of persons he did not admire: Sulla, Nicias, Thomas Becket, and William the Conqueror. On the other hand Creighton considered Freeman's estimate of Godwin and Harold as amounting to a worship which was ridiculous. [33] It has been asserted that he allowed no imagination to enter into his work, and that he treated the life of a community as a map rather than a picture; [34] yet York Powell said that his historical portraits compared with those of Stubbs for life and vigor. In example and method, few English historians gave a greater and more wholesome impetus in the last century.

John Richard Green (1837–83) [35] was born in Oxford and remembered himself as a rather sickly child who loved books and read them on his way home from school, "knocking his head against the lamp posts." He was fond of exploring the streets of old Oxford, and later declared that every period of English history had left its traces there. His pennies were saved to persuade sextons of neighboring village churches to open the doors and let him rub brasses; and his later patron Freeman first carried little "Johnnie Green" around on his arm in Millard's library, "because I was so well up in mouldings." [36]

His grammar school experiences were less happy; he did not possess

[31] Lord Acton, "Doellinger's Historical Work," *EHR*, V (1890), 700–44.

[32] For Freeman's limitations as an historian, see his *Life and Letters* (n. 21), II, 467–69.

[33] Louise Creighton, *Life and Letters of Mandell Creighton* (London, 1904, 2 v.), I, 264.

[34] Stephen R. Dodds "Some Modern Historians," *LQR*, CVIII (1907), 242–54.

[35] Leslie Stephen, *Letters of John Richard Green* (New York and London, 1901), with bibliography of his writings, pp. 497–503, reviewed in *The Nation*, LXXIV (1902), 34–35; Mandell Creighton, in *DNB*, XIII, 46–49; the preface by Alice Stopford Green to the revised edition of *A Short History of the English People* (New York, 1916), and to *The Conquest of England* (New York, 1884), GOOCH, 352–58, FUETER, 665. See the revaluation of Green in *LTLS*, March 9, 1933, pp. 153–54. See also "John Richard Green," *CQR*, LIV (1902), 282–95, and reviews in *ibid.*, LX (1905), 443–47; *QR*, CXLI (1876), 285–323; CXCV (1902), 532–46; *NAR*, CXXI (1875), 216–24; *ER*, CXCV (1902), 429–55; *FM*, XCII (1875), 395–410 and 710–24; *LQR*, LXIII (1884–85), 137–56; *DR*, LXXVII (1875), 308–41, and XCII (1882), 158–82; Samuel Gardiner in *The Academy*, VI (1874), 601–02, XV (1879), 381 and XVIII (1880), 19.

[36] *Letters of John Richard Green* (n. 35), 10.

a good memory, and floggings were still the experience of boys forced to learn Latin from a grammar written in Latin. Green was reared in Tory and High Church surroundings, but a quiet independence carried him along his own paths. This was revealed to him with a shock when he was set to write a school essay on Charles I and concluded after his reading that the royal martyr had been on the wrong side. The essay won the prize, but the school authorities frowned upon such heretical views. The following year a private tutor put Gibbon into his hands, and the young boy read him from cover to cover. He entered Oxford in 1855 after winning an open fellowship for the Welsh Jesus College. Green made few friends, scorned the Welsh, and cared less for the curriculum. History was then classed with law, for which he had an aversion. He spent a year reading English literature from Pope to Macaulay and flouting the suggestions of his teachers. Then a chance visit to Stanley's lectures on the History of Dissent led to a change of heart; he repented of his wasteful ways and vowed to devote himself to history.

When he was graduated (1859) his uncle proposed the bar for a profession, but Green turned to the Church. His friend Stanley wished him to take a curacy in the West End of London, but he was influenced by the Christian Socialist movement of the time, and he chose to settle in the East End.[37] The years of labor there put a grievous strain upon his health, and he welcomed an appointment as the librarian of Lambeth in 1869.

Green's first historical writing was a series of papers for the *Oxford Chronicle* on "Oxford in the last century." He also projected a history of the archbishops of Canterbury to serve as a skeleton for a history of English civilization. His pastoral duties were heavy, but he snatched time for study at the British Museum, and often skipped a meal to apply the money on books. He never fingered the volumes of his *Acta Sanctorum* without a whimsical recollection of the sacrifices they had cost him. Oxford and London made him conscious of the neglected role of the towns in English national life, and he always believed his experiences in the crowded and unhappy streets of the metropolis gave him some of his best lessons on the effects of economic misery and on the thoughts of the common folk.

A paper upon Dunstan renewed his acquaintance with Freeman, who undertook to "blow Johnny Green's trumpet" and gave him opportunity to contribute to the *Saturday Review*. Many of the brilliant articles from Green's pen were written after a hard day, in the hours before or after midnight. When his physician warned Green that his

[37] For the years from 1861 to 1869 see *Letters of John Richard Green* (n. 35), 51–208; and Philip Gell, "John Richard Green," *Fortnightly Review*, XXXIX (1883), 734–47.

hold on life was precarious, he·determined to throw his past studies and notes together into a book that might serve as a summary if the worst occurred, or as an introduction to better work if he were spared. Thus, amid fits of illness and despondency, over a period of five years, the *Short History of the English People* (1874) was written. Friends were generous with their sympathy, but Green suffered endlessly from self-critical modesty. He was finally persuaded to let it pass into print, "with all its faults." Seldom has a work enjoyed so phenomenal a success. It has remained the acknowledged closest rival to Macaulay's work.

Green's book was deliberately different from all previous histories: it was a history of the people, instead of the kings, the Church, or the military exploits and political fortunes of successive monarchs. "I have devoted more space to Chaucer than to Cressy, to Caxton than to the petty strife of Yorkist and Lancastrian, to the Poor Law of Elizabeth than to her victory at Cadiz, to the Methodist revival than to the escape of the Young Pretender." Eschewing "drum and trumpet history," and coining a famous phrase thereby, he saved space for religious, social, and economic history, "for figures little heeded in common history— the figures of the missionary, the poet, the printer, the merchant or the philosopher." [38]

Green lived long enough to do a good deal of writing, but he never equalled his *Short History*. It was expanded to four volumes on a slightly different plan under the title *A History of the English People* (1877–80); and then he undertook to cover the whole of national life in a series of monographs. Only two of these were completed, the *Making of England* (1882), and the *Conquest of England* (1883). They were examples of critical insight combined with brilliant conjecture, and like Freeman's labors have been corrected and superseded, chiefly by W. H. Stevenson and R. H. Hodgkin. Few writers have studied English topography with greater care and a more intuitive imagination. Freeman learned how to read the historical significance of physical geography from him. Green also did much for the etymology of English place-names.

Green's fame rests upon one book, however. When he died at the age of forty-six, one writer said that had he lived he would have been the greatest historian since Gibbon; Bryce thought he might perhaps be put nearly equal to Macaulay; and Stubbs ventured to say, "there was no department of our national records which he had not studied and (I think I may say) mastered." The *Short History* sold 32,000 copies in the first year; by 1909 it had appeared in French, German, Italian,

[38] Preface to the first edition (London, 1874). See also his letter to Freeman in *Letters of John Richard Green* (n. 35), 364–65.

Russian, Japanese, and Chinese; and it is still the leading one-volume work among general readers. Such long popularity may puzzle the historical student who realizes it was only a sketch written with the now moribund enthusiasms of sixty years ago.[39]

Green was the last of the Whigs, and scorned to date his work by kings or conquests; he announced a chronicle of the People! Since Green wrote, the great debt England owes her kings has been set in a better light, and royalty's contributions to the constitution have been more justly appraised. He had an aversion for Edward I, pilloried Elizabeth's "shameless mendacity," and declared that George III "had a smaller mind than any other English king before him save James II." Gardiner criticized him for failing to perceive both sides of the Puritan Revolution, and Lecky corrected his account of England's role in the American Revolution. In writing of early England, Green was less cautious and more enthusiastic than Stubbs. He followed Kemble and became almost an out and out Germanist. No modern writer would dare to review in two pages the Celtic and Roman background, and then leap abruptly to Sleswick—the Home of the English Race. His glorification of the Anglo-Saxons led to a serious undervaluation of the Danish invasions, and especially of the contributions of the Norman Conquest. His worst error was the notion of an idyllic primitive democracy among the Old English, and the fallacy that popular representation has always been the essence of the English constitution's growth. "Green's story of English origins is based, in short, upon a legend. . . . The nineteenth century crowds in upon the sixth, and Simon de Montfort in the thirteenth speaks with the voice of Gladstone."[40]

The great authority on the seventeenth century of England was Samuel Rawson Gardiner (1829–1902),[41] who brought to his *History of England from 1603 to 1660* a single-minded devotion which lasted for forty years. Through his paternal grandmother the historian of the Puritan Revolution could claim descent from the marriage of Cromwell's daughter Bridget to Ireton. Gardiner was graduated from Christ Church in Oxford in 1851, but had to forfeit his fellowship for religious reasons. His parents were Irvingites, and he joined their church, wedding in 1856 the youngest daughter of its founder, Edward Irving. For thirty years Oxford ignored him. After his marriage he moved to London and began his life's task.

[39] See the article in *LTLS* (n. 35), 153–54. [40] *Ibid.*, 152.
[41] Charles H. Firth in *DNB*, supplement for 1901–11, pp. 75–78; GOOCH, 359–65; F. York Powell, "Samuel Rawson Gardiner," *EHR*, XVII (1902), 276–79; "Dr. S. R. Gardiner," *The Athenaeum*, March 1, 1902, pp. 272–73, and "Some Later Reminiscences of Dr. S. R. Gardiner," *ibid.*, March 8, 1902, 307–08. For a list of his writings see W. A. Shaw's *Bibliography* (n. 7); for reviews see *QR*, CXCV (1902), 547–66, and CXXXIX (1875), 3; *CQR*, LIX (1904–05), 113–18, and LVIII (1904), 395–421; *FM*, LXIX (1864), 419–34; *DR*, CXI (1892), 31–62.

The first two volumes of his *History*, covering the years from 1603 to 1616, were published in 1863, and aside from a hundred copies the edition went for waste paper. It was a stiff trial of Gardiner's courage. The next two volumes (1869), while they sold better, brought him not a cent of income. Undaunted he added volume to volume, and to maintain his family accepted a post as professor of history (1871–85) at King's College, London, where he succeeded to John S. Brewer's chair in 1877. Amid his major labors he also produced some excellent textbooks, of which *The Thirty Years War* (1874), *The First Two Stuarts and the Puritan Revolution, 1603–60* (1876), and the *Student's History of England* (1890–91, 3 v.) were the most important. Thus twenty-eight years passed until in 1883 a more appreciative public began to absorb a second edition of Gardiner's first ten volumes.[42]

In 1878 Christ Church elected Gardiner a fellow, and honors began to seek him out. Meanwhile he entered into the more involved portions of his subject: three volumes related the *History of the Great Civil War* (1886–91); and three more dealt with *The History of the Commonwealth and Protectorate* (1894–1903, 3 v. in 4). As if these sixteen volumes of his major work were not enough, Gardiner was a frequent contributor to the *English Historical Review*, and its editor for a decade (1891–1901). He edited twelve volumes for the Camden Society, two for the Navy Records Society, one for the Scottish Historical Society, and wrote articles for the *Dictionary of National Biography* and the *Encyclopaedia Britannica*. His one hope, however, was to finish his history to the end of the Commonwealth. When Froude died in 1894, Lord Rosebery tendered him the regius chair, but Gardiner preferred to conserve his remaining years for the history. He sorrowfully reduced his terminus to the end of the Protectorate, but did not live long enough to reach this point. His last words were the murmured regret: "I shall not live to see the end of Oliver."[43]

Gardiner was the first scientific English historian of the modern history of his country. He objected to Seeley's suggestion that history should be made the school of politics. "He who studies the society of the past will be of the greater service to the society of the present in proportion as he leaves it out of account," he said.[44] His method was

---

[42] Under the collective title: *A History of England from the Accession of James I, to the Outbreak of the Civil War, 1603–1642* (1884–86, 10 v.; new edition, 1894–96).

[43] His literary executor, Sir Charles H. Firth, undertook to add the necessary two volumes, *Last Years of the Protectorate, 1656–1658* (1909). Gardiner's own view on the last years of the great Puritan may be found in his *Life of Cromwell* (1899), and his Ford Lecture, *The Place of Cromwell in History* (1897).

[44] For Gardiner's view of history, see the preface to his tenth volume (1884); also reprinted in Grant (n. 1), 82–86. See also R. G. Usher, *Critical Study of the Historical Method of Samuel Rawson Gardiner* (St. Louis, 1915); for Firth's rebuttal of this, cp. n. 56 below.

to put himself in the position of a contemporary, and to study the development of events as they unfolded under his eyes. His method was thus strictly chronological; he insisted on reading history forwards and put all knowledge of later events out of his mind. He refused to read material even a twelvemonth beyond his point of investigation; if he were working at the year 1653 he would decline material for 1654 and say: "I am not ready for that yet." His thirst for manuscript materials was unquenchable. He worked in the archives of France, Spain, Italy, the Netherlands, and Sweden, and was master of the languages of Western Europe. At the Record Office he read through not only the originals of the State Papers Domestic—scorning the printed calendar— but also the uncalendared State Papers Foreign, whose bulk would dismay most workers. He went through a vast contemporary pamphlet literature, of which those 30,000 Thomason tracts which broke Carlyle's spirit were but a part. Whenever possible Gardiner tried to make his materials available to others. He gave the British Museum two volumes of transcripts he had made at Simancas. On holidays he would be off on his bicycle with maps to study the battlefields of the Civil War.

Gardiner admitted to his friends that the one great difficulty he felt was the right understanding of Cromwell's character and aims. The descendant of the Protector, the Liberal in political opinions, the man whom religious scruples had driven out of Christ Church, showed a startling appreciation of the cause of the Royalists and the Laudian party.

Before Gardiner, the revolution of the seventeenth century had gone through varied interpretations. In the eighteenth century, when religious issues were a matter of indifference, it was viewed solely from the political standpoint: as a question of parliamentary right. This was Hallam's conception. With the awakening of religious earnestness, the religious element in the movement was recognized; but the alignment in the revolution was still regarded as predominantly political and analogous to the party conditions of the nineteenth century. Such was the notion of Macaulay and of Guizot. Carlyle, Gardiner, and Masson unearthed hundreds of new documents, and discovered that the parties were formed during the conflict and had not previously existed, and that the issue of religious toleration was involved from the very beginning.

Gardiner held that the Puritan Revolution was the result of two conflicting theories of government: the monarchical and the constitutional. Both were represented in the English constitution of that time, and much could be said for each; the actual conflict was brought on by faults on either side. New problems confronted men then; they were confronted seriously, and often not without success and benefit to posterity.

> Gardiner found the story of the first Stewarts and Cromwell legend, and left it history. The reign of James I was untilled ground, the reign of Charles I a plot choked with warring weeds, the Commonwealth unexplored country till he came. James's policy and theories, Charles's character and aims, the position of Buckingham and Pym and Strafford, the foreign influences operating upon court, church, and people, the financial position from year to year (which Gardiner was the first to investigate), the varying fortunes of the war and the causes that determined the changes, the exact political meaning that the religious question assumed from year to year, the precise constitutional or unconstitutional attitude of the different parties and their ideals, the aims and achievements and incomplete enterprises of Cromwell, the Scottish difficulties (never dealt with so broadly and impartially before), the Irish *imbroglios* and the Settlement, even the military and naval history of the period . . . we know from evidence collected, marshalled, and weighed by Gardiner.[45]

The weakest point about Gardiner was his style. He wrote clearly, lucidly, and at times eloquently; but the art of presentation was not his. Freeman commented: "What strikes me in Gardiner is that I read him, not only with instruction, but with pleasure, but that I do not remember him as I do Macaulay."[46]　Lord Acton, no easy critic, said of Gardiner's volumes that they ranked with the very few in European literature "where the resources have been so employed that we can be content with the work done for us, and never wish it to be done over again."

Frederick York Powell (1850–1904)[47] wrote little, and that chiefly before he became professor, but he was a legend of omniscience when Lord Rosebery appointed him to succeed Froude at Oxford.[48]　His classes were always very small and for specialists, but his personal influence, his brilliant conversation, his services on committees and as a delegate of the Clarendon Press, gave a wholesome impulse to better historical labors at the university. Of Welsh and English descent, born in Woburn Place, Bloomsbury, in the shadow of the British Museum, he came from Rugby to Christ Church and took a first class in History and Law. Liddell obtained for him a law lectureship. In Oxford he was an unconventional, rebellious sort of person, and uncompromisingly frank. His catholic interests embraced art, anthropology, literature,

---

[45] Elton (n. 21), II, 43–44.　　　　　　　　　　　　[46] *Life and Letters* (n. 21), II, 393.

[47] Oliver Elton, *Frederick York Powell* (Oxford, 1906, 2 v.), of which the first contains his life and letters, and the second a bibliography of his writings and a collection of scattered papers. Reviews in *The Nation*, LXXXIV (April 4, 1907), 311–12; *The Athenaeum*, December 29, 1906, pp. 821–22; *CQR*, LXIV (1907), 239–41. See also *ibid.*, "The Oxford School of Historians," LIX (1904), 111–13.

[48] There is an amusing tale that Powell's secretary thought the flaming red missive of the prime minister was a tradesman's bill and put it behind the clock to spare his master until Lord Rosebery's secretary enquired for an answer.

numismatics, and the art of boxing. He called himself "a decent heathen Aryan" and never entered the cathedral at the time of service; his free views horrified some of his associates. York Powell's prejudices were as strong as his enthusiasms. He disliked highly educated women, Jews, and Americans. Lewis Carroll used to call his dinner guests "Powell's assassins." "I am tolerant," said Powell, "and I have a childlike ferocity." There was, however, an abundance of sweetness and light in him.

Early in love with Norse sagas, he entered into a deep friendship with the greatest Scandinavian authority on that subject, Gudbrand Vigfusson,[49] and a fruitful partnership resulted. The friendship lasted for a dozen years, and when Vigfusson died they had nearly completed their ambitious plan for introducing the English public to Icelandic literature. This consisted of a sketch-history of Icelandic literature in the Prolegomena to the *Sturlunga Saga*, an *Icelandic Prose Reader*, and the *Corpus Poeticum Boreale* (1883), the most valuable work of all. It was a complete collection, with commentary and translation, of the best Icelandic poetry. A fourth work, intended to be a complete library of northern prose, was begun in the *Origines Islandicae* (2 v.), not published until sixteen years after Vigfusson's death and a year after Powell's decease. In 1894 Powell wrote the introduction to Elton's translation of *Saxo Grammaticus*.

Of Powell's more purely historical writings, the chief are his *School History of England*, to the death of Henry VIII (1900, done together with T. F. Tout), and *Early England* (1876), which stopped at the Norman Conquest. Though only school texts, they contain broad and original ideas. Powell's contribution to a more scientific history lay elsewhere, however. He was one of the founders of the *English Historical Review* in 1886. As professor he urged the development of an advanced school of history at Oxford after the model of the École des Hautes Études and the École des Chartes. He aided in the founding of lectures for this purpose under the Royal Historical Society (1902), and in establishing the Lectureship in Diplomatic at Oxford (1896). He also emphasized the need of better care and method in gathering and preserving local records, and of historical bibliography in general. He admired France, but ridiculed German scholarship as pretentious. The study of literature and archaeology widens the understanding of history. "*Beowulf* gave us more English history than Asser's *Life of Alfred*." Economics, and even physiology, might be invaluable. "History is the necessary complement to biology and anthropology."

[49] Suggestions for materials for a needed life of Vigfusson are given by Professor Elton (n. 47) in an appendix, I, 454.

Sir Charles Harding Firth (1857–1935) [50] was the disciple and literary executor of Gardiner. In 1876 he was a Brackenbury scholar at Balliol and found himself among a group of young men who later distinguished themselves. [51] Firth early determined to become a specialist, and fixed upon the history of England in the seventeenth century. He adopted Gardiner as his ideal. After several critical studies upon the familiar sources, Firth turned to unused primary materials with the first volume of the *Clarke Papers* (1891). [52] The *Dictionary of National Biography* and the *English Historical Review* found him a valuable contributor. Firth was deeply interested in promoting the publication of the sources of his epoch and the calendaring of documentary materials, and submitted fifteen careful memoranda to the Royal Commission on the Public Records. In 1900 his *Oliver Cromwell* appeared; his Ford lectures of that year were upon *Cromwell's Army*. [53] His next task was to continue Gardiner; and *The Last Years of the Protectorate* (1909, 2 v.) brought the work to the death of Cromwell. A continuation to the Restoration was prevented by Firth's appointment to the regius chair at Oxford to succeed his friend York Powell. The requirements of the professorship as he conceived them were heavy; lecturing was not easy for him, and his advice was in much demand. [54] He developed a training school for historians at Oxford, and set the example in articles, reviews, and source editions. Like Lord Acton, Firth's knowledge exceeded what he printed. He was strongly drawn to naval and military history, and his last occupation, down to his seventy-eighth year, [55] was a regimental history of the parliamentary armies of the Civil War. He always deprecated any comparison of his work with Gardiner. [56]

Henry William Carless Davis (1874–1928) [57] left behind him the memory of a modest and learned scholar. At twelve he entered Weymouth College with an honor scholarship, and was a shy studious lad

---

[50] G. N. Clark, "Sir Charles Firth," *EHR*, LI (1936), 257–63. See his own *A Bibliography of the Writings of Sir Charles Firth* (Oxford, 1928).

[51] Professor Clark calls the roll: J. H. Round, R. L. Poole, Richard Lodge, T. F. Tout, Andrew Clark, Arnold Toynbee, F. C. Montague, Henry Morse Stephens, and W. J. Ashley.

[52] *The Life of Colonel Hutchinson* (1885); *The Life of the Duke of Newcastle* (1886); *Ludlow's Memoirs* (1894).

[53] Published in 1902. Professor Clark pronounces this the best single volume on military history in the English language.

[54] He was on the Royal Commission on Public Records (1910–19), on the admiralty committee on Nelson's tactics at Trafalgar (1913), and was president of the Royal Historical Society (1913 ff.).

[55] He resigned his chair in 1925.

[56] After the First World War Firth gave a course of lectures at Oxford on Gardiner, and refuted many of the charges made by Usher (n. 44) by a minute examination of Gardiner's writings and the sources he had used. He gave a similar course on Macaulay.

[57] F. M. Powicke, "H. W. C. Davis," *EHR*, XLIII (1928), 578–84; J. R. H. Weaver, *Henry William Carless Davis, 1874–1928; a Memoir* (London, 1933), together with a selection of his historical papers edited by Weaver and Austin Lane Poole.

who forced himself to play football. He obtained a scholarship at Balliol, and matriculated there in 1891. He read not only for History but also for the Classics, and amazed some of his companions by an essay on Alcaeus. A fellowship in All Souls fixed his permanent interest on history.

I can see him now [wrote a friend] in those days, nearly forty years ago, going off to Professor Earle's tiny class on Anglo-Saxon, to Dr. R. L. Poole (to master medieval diplomatic) in the sacred hours between 2 p.m. and 5 p.m., . . . and I can see him tackling the original sources for the life of Charlemagne—his first book—when, as he told me, he had not read the big secondary authorities first, for a framework.[58]

In 1897 Davis was appointed lecturer in history at New College, and in 1899 he passed to Balliol. By his thirtieth year he had written two books, lectured five years at Oxford, and one year at Bangor. His *Life of Charlemagne* (1900) was almost contemporaneous with Hodgkin's last two volumes which cover the same subject. In 1901 Putnams made him editor of the Heroes of the Nations series.

Davis' specialty was the sources for Anglo-Saxon and Norman history. In an article in the *English Historical Review* he defended the lament of the chroniclers of Stephen's reign against the contention of Richard Howlett and J. H. Round, who denied it was a time of anarchy.[59] Recent scholarship has supported Davis. In 1902 he was invited to write the second volume in the Oman series (Methuen), and produced his *England under the Normans and Angevins* (1905). The field of English feudalism was then a battle-ground: the "Old English" forces were almost worsted.[60] Davis contented himself with rewriting the narrative and the constitutional history from 1066 to 1272, incorporating the results gained by the last generation of research.[61] The book established his reputation as a medievalist.

In 1913 Davis revised Stubbs' *Select Charters* for the ninth edition, and in the same year saw the appearance of the first volume of the *Regesta regum Anglo-Normannorum*. He had planned a co-operative Calendar of Anglo-Norman royal charters, but the task had finally fallen upon his own shoulders. In 140 quarto pages Davis published an annotated hand-list of 487 charters, and an appendix exhibited the

[58] Weaver (n. 57), 15.
[59] The article, "The Anarchy of Stephen's Reign," *EHR*, XVIII (1903), 630–41, was reprinted in Weaver (n. 57), 81–96. Howlett and Round held that "the reign of Stephen was not one of anarchy tempered by efforts to govern, but rather of organised government which broke down for short periods in particular localities." *Ibid.*, 81.
[60] "Under the isolated but savage assaults of Horace Round the one-time commanding fortress of Freeman's learning had been reduced to little more than a picturesque ruin; and now the more scientific defensive system of Bishop Stubbs was showing unmistakable signs of giving way before the methodical advance of the followers of Maitland and Vinogradoff." *Ibid.*, 29–30.
[61] Cf. Powicke in *EHR* (n. 57), 579.

full text of 92 of these, most of them for the first time. The work survived the fury of a ten page review by Horace Round in the *English Historical Review*. Davis never published more, but the materials for the next two volumes were nearly ready when the First World War broke out.

The war proved a turning point in Davis' career. In autumn of 1914 his *Political Thought of Heinrich von Treitschke* analyzed the notorious lectures of the German historian. During the four years of the war, Davis was vice-chairman of a trade intelligence section of the Postal Censorship, a board whose duty it was to study the trade reports and the success of the blockade. The scholar from Oxford made a laconic and pithy writer of memoranda. He planned to write a history of the blockade in the war, but his duties consumed all his time and strength. In 1919 he was back at Oxford, but Oxford had changed; and in 1921 he was appointed to the chair of modern history at Manchester. His thoughts now turned to the political and social history of England since 1815. When chosen Ford lecturer he proposed to speak on "The Age of Earl Grey and Sir Robert Peel," and spent twelve months in the Rylands library studying rare tracts about the early Radicals, "digging," as he put it, "around the roots of modern Toryism." [62] When Sir Charles Firth resigned the Oxford regius chair it was given to Davis (1925). His premature death in 1928 was a shock to his friends and a loss to British historical scholarship. Professor Powicke, his successor in the regius professorship, in the tribute which he has written, concludes with these words: "He died in the height of his powers and reputation, as a man of his kind ought to die, at work. But he died more than twenty years too soon." And here we leave the Oxford line.

At Cambridge William Smythe held the regius professorship of history from 1807 to 1849, and died of old age. When Macaulay declined the post [63] the Prince Consort, as chancellor of the university, accepted Lord Russell's recommendation of Sir James Stephen, who had hoped for the Downing professorship of laws.[64] The argument advanced in his favor was that "experience in the practical business of life is a good

---

[62] *The Age of Grey and Peel*, a revision of the Ford lectures for 1926, was three-fourths done when Davis died; it was finished and seen through the press by G. M. Trevelyan (Oxford, 1929).

[63] G. O. Trevelyan, *Life and Letters of Lord Macaulay* (New York, 1880, 2 v. in 1), II, 261. In his diary he gave his reasons: "It would be strange if, having sacrificed for liberty a seat in the Cabinet and £2500 a year, I should now sacrifice liberty for a chair at Cambridge and £400 a year. Besides I never could do two things at once. If I lectured well my History must be given up; and to give up my History would be to give up much more than the emoluments of the Professorship."

[64] Leslie Stephen, *The Life of Sir James Fitzjames Stephen* (London and New York, 1895); G. P. Gooch, *Studies in Modern History* (London and New York, 1931), 307–10; *BQR*, XV (1852), 3–37; *FM*, XLV (1852), 170–82.

foundation for an historian. Xenophon, Tacitus, Davila, Guicciardini were all men engaged in political or military affairs." After leaving Cambridge Stephen had prepared for the bar, and then become the distinguished Under-Secretary in the Colonial Office (1834). His comprehensive knowledge and dominating personality earned him the names of Mr. Mother-Country Stephen, King Stephen, Mr. Over-Secretary Stephen. He had written for the *Edinburgh Review* and published a collection of these articles as *Essays in Ecclesiastical Biography* (1849). His inaugural lecture *On Certain So-called Philosophies of History* vindicated the theory of God in history. He felt himself superior to others "in that kind of historical knowledge which is derived from a long and intimate connection with the actual government of mankind." [65] Two volumes of lectures on the history of France and its internal development were his only other works. He held the chair from 1849 to 1859.

Charles Kingsley (1819–75),[66] who succeeded Stephen for a decade (1860–69), had even less training than his predecessor. Kingsley was a last resort, for Lord Palmerston had previously offered the post to Blakesley and Venables, both of whom declined it. Sir Arthur Helps was suggested but rejected. The Prince Consort finally appointed Kingsley. Though an attractive speaker Kingsley did not advance the standards of historical writing or study. He was a novelist and a preacher; his brother-in-law Max Mueller admitted: "History was but his text." *The Roman and the Teuton* was a glorification of God in history, and his second course, on the history of America, closed with the words:

If I have convinced you that well-doing and ill-doing are rewarded and punished in this world as well as in the world to come, I shall have done you more good than if I had crammed your mind with many dates and facts.[67]

Of his novels, Hodgkin judged *Westward Ho!* to be the most representative, setting forth as it did "his abhorrence of Jesuitism and the Inquisition, his admiration of the Elizabethan Age in our literature, *and* pre-eminently his love of North Devon." [68]

The origin of the Cambridge School is sometimes dated from Sir John R. Seeley (1834–95).[69] The successor to Kingsley had been pro-

[65] Gooch (n. 64), 308.
[66] *Charles Kingsley: Letters and Memoirs of His Life,* edited by his wife (London, 1876, 2 v.).
[67] Quoted in Gooch (n. 64), 311.
[68] Louise Creighton, *Life and Letters of Thomas Hodgkin* (London and New York, 1918), 270.
[69] See the Memoir by Prothero in Seeley's *Growth of British Policy* (Cambridge, 1895, 2 v.); Adolf Rein, *Sir John Robert Seeley. Eine Studie über den Historiker* (Langensalza, 1913), with bibliography; J. R. Tanner, "John Robert Seeley," *EHR*, X (1895), 507–14; H. A. L. Fisher, "Sir John Seeley," *Fortnightly Review*, LXVI (1896), 183–98; Mary R. W. Stubbert, "Cambridge School of History," *Annual Report of the American Historical Association for 1898* (Washington, D. C., 1899), 383–411.

fessor of Latin at University College, London, had published a critical edition of the first book of Livy, and won fame with *Ecce Homo*. In his inaugural the erstwhile student of the classics admitted that ancient history had little interest because it was too remote. The value and hence the interest of history lay in its application to contemporary politics. He proposed a school of statesmanship, "by giving due precedence in the teaching of history to the present over the past." Seeley roused dormant Cambridge in the years between 1869 and 1895. His *Life and Times of Stein* was a study in the development of Germany during the Napoleonic Age.[70] The *Expansion of England* (1883) is a classic in the history of British imperialism. It dealt with the conflict with France in the eighteenth century. The *Growth of British Policy* occupied his last ten years; in its unfinished form it covers the time from Elizabeth to William III.

Seeley was at Cambridge for a quarter of a century, but not always in an academic capacity. He sat in Parliament for a short time and was in one of Gladstone's ministries. As teacher he developed the practice of "conversation" classes, and endeavored to derive practical lessons from history and politics. When the historical tripos was established at Cambridge in 1873 he saw that political science might have a large place in it.

Lord Acton (1834–1902) [71] was the real founder of the Cambridge school of history. No modern historian has written less and left a greater reputation for learning. He was the son of an English baronet and a German mother, the Countess Marie Arco of Bavaria, whose house claimed to be one of the oldest ducal families of Germany. His mother's second marriage to the second Lord Granville [72] directed Acton's future towards England, but by temperament and education Acton was always more cosmopolitan than insular. Born in Naples, he passed in turn from a school in Paris to the Roman Catholic College at Oscott, then to Edinburgh, and at the age of fourteen came to the great Catholic church historian Döllinger at Munich, in whose home he spent six years. From Döllinger came in large degree Acton's serious application, the

[70] It was dedicated to Reinhold Pauli.
[71] His full name was Sir John Emerich Edward Dalberg, first Baron Acton of Aldenham and eighth baronet. See the article by J. Neville Figgis in *DNB*, supplement II (1901–11), 8–12; GOOCH, 379–93; ASHLEY, 440–44 (review of his inaugural); *Letters of Lord Acton to Mary Gladstone*, ed. with an introductory memoir by Herbert Paul (London, 1904), reviewed in *CR*, LXXXV (1904), 473–79; W. L. Blennerhassett, "Acton, 1834–1902," *DR*, CXCIV (1934), 169–88; R. L. Poole, "John Emerich, Lord Acton," *EHR*, XVII (1902), 692–99; *ER*, CXCVII (1903), 501–34, and CCV (1907), 273–98; *LQR*, CI (1904), 238 ff., and CXV (1911), 269 ff.; H. A. L. Fisher, "Lord Acton's Historical Work," *QR*, CCXV (1911), 166–88; *The Nation*, LXXVIII (1904), 252–53; *The Athenaeum*, June 28, 1902, pp. 817–18.
[72] Edmund Fitzmaurice, *The Life of [Lord] Granville* (London and New York, 1906, 2 v.), especially I, 32–33.

enormous erudition, the sense of critical method, and the intensity of his moral judgments. After visits to America in 1855, to Italy in 1857, and to Russia in 1858, where with his stepfather Lord Granville he attended the coronation of Czar Alexander II, Acton settled on the family estates at Aldenham in Shropshire. He sat in the House of Commons for several years (1859–65).

In 1858 Acton became part owner of the *Rambler*, a liberal Catholic monthly, which was converted to a quarterly in 1862 under the name of the *Home and Foreign Review*. Its purpose, as Acton wrote, was to "support the cause of religion by the discovery of truth. . . . A false religion fears the progress of all truth; a true religion seeks and recognizes truth wherever it can be found." [73] The journal fell under papal displeasure after two years, having reported the Munich congress at which Döllinger implored Catholics to replace the "medieval analytical method" by "the principles of historical development, and to encounter scientific errors with scientific weapons." The papal encyclical *Quanta cura* and the appended *Syllabus Errorum* (1864) condemned the effort "to make terms between the church and modern civilization."

Ultramontanism was to Acton a species of moral blindness, and he ultimately termed it the subtlest of all forms of Machiavellism. The papacy had been implicated in the Massacre of St. Bartholomew.[74] One is not surprised that Acton opposed the promulgation of the Catholic doctrine of papal infallibility at the Vatican Council of 1870. It was partly Acton's reports from Rome upon which Döllinger drew when he composed the famous *Letters of Quirinus*. Like his old teacher, however, Acton refused to leave his communion and died a devout Catholic. His objections, which have puzzled Protestants, related to the policy of the papal curia and never to doctrine.

The profundity of Acton's knowledge is well illustrated by the article on "German Schools of History" which he contributed to the first issue of the *English Historical Review* in 1886. In 1895 Lord Rosebery offered him the regius professorship of history in Cambridge to succeed Sir John Seeley. "He was the most commanding personality who has held the Chair of Modern History." [75] In his inaugural he reviewed the development of modern historical methods, but rejected his predecessor's notion of a school for diplomacy. "Ours is the domain that reaches further than affairs of State. It is our function to keep in view and to command

---

[73] *Letters* (n. 71), 34–35.
[74] Cp. his article, "The Massacre of St. Bartholomew," published anonymously in the *North British Review*, LI (1869–70), 30–70, which journal Acton helped Wetherell, editor of the Catholic *Chronicle*, to revise on liberal Catholic lines in 1868. The article is reprinted in Acton's *History of Freedom and Other Essays* (London, 1909), 101–49.
[75] Gooch, *Studies in Modern History* (n. 64), 315.

the movement of ideas, which are not the effect but the cause of public events."

The lectures he delivered in his sonorous and impressive voice to large audiences, not always appreciative of the superb mind before them, do Acton scant justice.[76] He was invited to edit a history of the modern world for the university press, and the brilliant outline of the *Cambridge Modern History* was his own. He did not live long enough, however, to write even the projected first chapter.

To Acton the science of history was only the art of collecting historical materials. He believed in the immanence of moral law. History was the record of man's moral progress. He once exhorted his students "to try others by the final maxim that governs your own lives, and to suffer no man and no cause to escape the undying penalty which history has the power to inflict on wrong." Facts were for him, he said, "not a burden on the memory, but an illumination of the soul."

Of his personal influence there can be no question. Herbert Paul has said: "To be in his company was like being in the best of historical libraries with the best of historical catalogues." But Acton remains the classic example of the inhibiting weight of erudition. For years he planned to write a *History of Liberty*. The subject as he conceived it would have required omniscient knowledge; not a line of that history was ever written. He left his enormous library to John Morley, who gave it to Cambridge University. The thousands of volumes had all been read and the margins annotated by the owner.

There were pigeon-holed desks and cabinets with literally thousands of compartments, in each of which were sorted little white slips with references to some particular topic, so drawn up (so far as I could see) that no one but the compiler could easily make out the drift of the section. I turned over one or two from curiosity—one was on early instances of a sympathetic feeling for animals, from Ulysses' old dog in Homer downward. Another seemed to be devoted to a collection of hard words about stepmothers in all national literatures, a third seemed to be about tribal totems.[77]

It is to be deeply regretted that with all his breadth of knowledge Lord Acton never presented the world with a work that would mirror the full powers of his mind.

[76] His lectures were published after his death and edited by J. N. Figgis and R. V. Lawrence: *Lectures on Modern History* (London, 1906); *The History of Freedom and Other Essays* (London, 1909); *Historical Essays and Studies* (London, 1907); *Lectures on the French Revolution* (London, 1910).

[77] Sir Charles Oman, *On the Writing of History* (London and New York, 1939), 209; cp. the review in *LTLS*, October 28, 1939, p. 621.

CHAPTER XLIX

GREAT ENGLISH AMATEUR HISTORIANS[1]

THE amateur historian has played a larger part in the historical literature of England than elsewhere, even than in the United States, where the tradition of Motley, Prescott, Parkman, Bancroft, and Lea is consecrate. On the Continent it is exceptional to find an historian without academic status. The amateur historical writer in England has a noble lineage—Kemble, Carlyle, Macaulay, Grote, Green, Lecky, Hodgkin, Seebohm, Wylie, Round, Symonds, Ramsey, and Kate Norgate were all amateur historians. This chapter deals with those after John Richard Green.

William Edward Hartpole Lecky (1838–1903) [2] was born in Dublin of a wealthy Scottish family which had emigrated to Ireland in the seventeenth century. His school days fell in the time of Daniel O'Connell, the Irish famine, the crowds of beggars, and the O'Brien rebellion. As a student of Trinity College he began to prepare for theology, but read widely. Geology was a hobby of his, and Sir Charles Lyell's discoveries stimulated much discussion, coming on the heels of the Oxford movement. Lecky's chief interest however was in Ireland. He knew passages from Irish orators by heart; but his loyalty was not blind. At the age of twenty-two he published anonymously a volume entitled *The Religious Tendencies of the Age*, an argument for toleration. It was not well received, and Lecky concluded that theology was not for him. His next work, *Leaders of Public Opinion* (1861), fell as flat.

An essay on *The Declining Sense of the Miraculous* (1863) was the nucleus of the famous *History of Rationalism* (1865, 2 v.). The latter was the first work to which Lecky signed his name, and an instant success. Lecky sought to demonstrate in detail that the progress of European culture was due to the recoil from the theological conception

---

[1] The word *amateur* as used in this chapter is to be understood in the primary sense of the word, i.e., one who pursues any form of study from natural love of the subject and not for gain. It is carefully to be distinguished from the secondary usage of the word which is one of disparagement, and signifies one who is deficient in knowledge of a subject, e.g., a "mere amateur."

[2] *A Memoir of the Right Hon. William Edward Hartpole Lecky*, by his wife (New York, 1909); Augustin Filon, "Les historiens anglais, II: W. E. H. Lecky," *RDM*, LXXXVI (1888), 56–90; reviews of his works: *CQR*, VII (1878–79), 93 ff., and XLIII (1896–97), 132–55; *BQR*, XLII (1865), 401–33; *FM*, LXXX (1869), 273–84; *DR*, LIX (1866), 51–79; *NBR*, L (1869), 381–405; *LQR*, L (1878), 302–36 and XXXIII (1869–70), 33–69; *ER*, CXXI (1865), 426–55, CLXXIII (1891), 1–30, and CXXX (1869), 36–56.

of history. The title misled many who expected the work to be associated with German higher criticism. Lecky could not read German. In some particulars the work reflects the influence of Comte, whom he admired for having tried "to look at history, not as a series of biographies or accidents or pictures, but as a great organic whole." [3] Buckle found in Lecky his most faithful disciple. Henry C. Lea of America wrote to Lecky commending him on his distinctive new contribution:

> We have had enough annalists to chronicle political intrigues and military achievements; but that which constitutes the inner life of a people, and from which are to be drawn the lessons of the past that will guide us in the future, has hitherto been too much neglected. Your richly stored pages show how much there is to be learned when apparently insignificant facts are brought together from the most varied sources and made to reflect light upon each other. [4]

Lecky spent the next four years in writing the *History of European Morals from Augustus to Charlemagne* (1869, 2 v.). He always said that this was his favorite book. At the age of thirty he was famous. He now turned to political history and threw himself into the *History of England in the Eighteenth Century* (1878–90, 8 v.). The excessive length of the portion devoted to Ireland was justified in the minds of many readers by the almost simultaneous appearance of Froude's *English in Ireland*, a work which irritated Lecky. "Since the history of a nation may be written in so many ways," he wrote, ". . . it has been my object to disengage from the great mass of facts those which relate to the permanent forces of the nation, or which indicate some of the more enduring forces of the national life."

The *History of England in the Eighteenth Century* is an unusual work; its structural formation is singular. The work is composed of two parts: a series of essays on English history from 1714 to 1793, and an account of Irish history from 1714 to 1801. Imbedded in the first is a history of the American Revolution and also a history of the French Revolution. Military events are almost ignored. Political ideas and institutions are given first attention, then economic and social subjects. No battle is described, indeed few are even mentioned. On the other hand, the volumes abound with information concerning the English aristocracy, the Church, the Dissenters, the decline of the doctrine of the divine right of kings, commerce and trade, finance and taxation, corruption and reform, art, literature and science, music, drama, medicine and sanitation. Lecky's treatment of Methodism, Chatham, Burke, and George III is especially to be noted.

When the last volume was finished (1890), Lecky was just over fifty, and "a little tired of history." A happy marriage and an established

---

[3] Cp. Gooch, 366.   [4] *Memoir* (n. 2), 52.

reputation allowed him to rest on his laurels. His later writings are either revisions or unimportant political pronouncements. *Democracy and Liberty* (1896, 2 v.) criticized democratic ideas and practice in a hostile spirit. But if Lecky ceased to write, he continued to be read. A recent commentator has pronounced his influence as broader, if not as lasting, as Seeley's.

The Irish Whig, whose spiritual forebears and heroes were Burke and Grattan, was not an original worker, and his view of Georgian England cannot today hold its own. But, till the age of Home Rule, he wrote with entire reasonableness and equity; his narrative architecture was simple and satisfying, his felicity and moral sympathy were wholesome, independent, and stirring.[5]

Thomas Hodgkin (1831–1913) [6] came from a prosperous middle class Quaker family. As Oxford and Cambridge were then still closed to Friends he was sent up to University College in London. Illness interrupted his studies, but when he obtained his degree in 1851 he hoped to follow his father in the legal profession. A physical breakdown turned him forever away from law, and led to a continental journey in search of health. It was decided that the life of a country banker would be the best for him to adopt, and Hodgkin set about learning the business in which he remained the rest of his life. But his literary loves would not be pushed aside. He continued to read theology, which had become a strong interest, and works of history. In 1859 he opened a bank in Newcastle in partnership with several other men, and two years later was able to marry.

In 1868 the Hodgkins made their first visit to Italy and found it one "continual feasting of the mind."

This time [he wrote] I have been—what I never was before—thoroughly bitten with the Italian Tarantula. I can understand now why Kings and Emperors in the Middle Ages flung away whole realms of dim transalpine regions to secure one bright duchy or county on the sunny side of the Great Wall.[7]

In 1870 he went to Rome. He was delighted with the remains of "Pagan Rome," but displeased with the modern city, and especially offended with the visible signs of "popery." The Oecumenical Council was then sitting at St. Peters. His letters reveal his thoughts:

The difficulty is, or seems to be at the first blush of it, not to remain Protestant, but to remain Christian. Everywhere the grand old Paganism shows itself so much nobler and better than the caricature of Christianity which is pasted over it. . . . Oh, those Vicars of Christ, how the earth groans and has groaned under them! [8]

[5] *LTLS*, 1937, p. 320.
[6] Louise Creighton, *Life and Letters of Thomas Hodgkin* (London and New York, 1918); and the account by T. F. Tout in *Proceedings of the British Academy*, 1914, pp. 503–07.
[7] *Life and Letters* (n. 6), 81.   [8] *Ibid.*, 83.

From his youth Hodgkin liked to write, and he found time for reviews and then public lecturing. Thus in 1869 he spoke on Savonarola at Liverpool. He was wholly engrossed in Italian history by that time, and another lecture foreshadowed the title of his future great work: "Italy, Her Invaders and Usurpers." For a time he dreamed of writing a continuation of Milman's *Latin Christianity* to fill the gap up to Ranke's *Popes*, or a survey of the History of Italy from Alaric to Garibaldi, such as the English public did not yet possess. By 1873 his reading had converged upon the fifth century. He now hoped to carry the history of Italy from Theodosius to modern times in nine volumes. He began to write at home, in the days and hours taken from his business.

I still try to paint not a cabinet picture but a panorama, but I feel how necessary it is even for this broad, seemingly-superficial style of painting that you should be thoroughly imbued with the spirit of the time. It seems to me that in order to reject details you must first be acquainted with them; to draw a good bold line you must be quite sure of your anatomy; the best way to avoid "scissors and paste" is to get the chief original authorities well into your mind, and then write from remembrance rather than from constant reference.[9]

He wrote rapidly and vividly, utilizing even scraps of time and leisure moments. A meeting with Creighton, who was vicar of Embleton in 1876, led to an enduring friendship; the vicar was amazed at Hodgkin's knowledge, and Hodgkin learned from Creighton:

He gave me all sorts of tips, but, more than all, he raised my standard of the way in which history ought to be written. I think I had been a little dazzled by Michelet, and thought that the main point was to make history picturesque, if necessary by a little use of one's imagination. He said, and the saying has been a watchword to me ever since, "I always like to keep very close to my authorities." [10]

As a check he thought of reading some authorities on the earlier history of Rome,

So I have stopped work, though it is rather tantalising to have to do so, and am going through Mommsen at a canter. It certainly is a noble history—I had never read it before—and stirs me like a good novel.[11]

When the first volume was ready for publication, Bryce introduced the author to the Delegates of the Clarendon Press. Bryce said it was a book "likely to make history popular by true and honest methods," and wrote his friend: "Your book interested me extremely. It seemed to me to have rare and uncommon merits in its vividness, its insight, its fire, its pictorialness, its moral force." Creighton reviewed it in the *Times*, and pointed out its contrast to Gibbon, who had mourned the

[9] *Ibid.*, 103, from a letter in 1875.
[10] *Ibid.*, 104, cp. the fine letter on the Creightons, 105; and *Life and Letters of Mandell Creighton*, by his wife (London, 1904, 2 v.), I, 195.
[11] *Life and Letters* (n. 6), 105–06.

decline of Rome and ignored the sturdier races about to take her place. There was general acknowledgment of Hodgkin's narrative and dramatic power, but R. W. Church and Creighton both found fault with his comparative neglect of the ecclesiastical history of his period.

As Hodgkin proceeded, he won new friends like Freeman and Ugo Balzani, and was willing to profit by their advice. The work he managed to do besides his regular banking duties is amazing; but he always found time for his "dear History." The third and fourth volumes, covering the period from 476 to 553, were well received. Hodgkin's account of Theoderic was the fullest yet written in English. Two additional volumes appeared in 1885. Creighton was pleased that his friend had now "filled in the ecclesiastical side. The chapters on S. Benedict and Vigilius are admirable." He hailed the topographical chapters, "the aqueducts especially," as a novel feature. Professor Gwatkin criticized the omissions concerning the Eastern Empire, particularly the lack of any clear picture of Justinian. Hodgkin's sympathies were evidently with such figures as Theoderic, Belisarius, and Totila. His extreme admiration for the Ostrogothic king made him a severe critic of Boethius. Balzani[12] lamented the excessive number of digressions, such as the long description of Rome and the chapter on the aqueducts. The progress of the main work was interrupted by an abridged translation of the *Letters of Cassiodorus*,[13] to which Hodgkin added, as an introduction, a monograph on Cassiodorus and the administrative system of the Gothic Kingdom which goes in scope beyond the material utilized in *Italy and Her Invaders* itself.

Lesser items from Hodgkin's pen appeared in the decade following, as articles in the *Encyclopaedia Britannica*, a series of lectures on the *Dynasty of Theodosius*,[14] a volume on *Theoderic the Goth* (Heroes of the Nations series) in 1891, and another on *Charles the Great* (for Macmillan's Foreign Statesmen) in 1897. The fifth and sixth volumes of *Italy and Her Invaders* were thus postponed nearly a decade. When they came out the chief criticism was still the old one: "Though Mr. Hodgkin does not avoid ecclesiastical affairs as he used to, he scarcely even yet allows them their full significance in secular history."[15] The seventh and

---

[12] Ugo Balzani in *Revista Storica Italiana*, III (1886), 773 ff. For Gwatkin's review see *EHR*, I (1886), 154–56.

[13] Dean Church wrote of it: "Cassiodorus in English is like unearthing a Blue Book of the Gothic Kingdom. There is a wonderful air of life in spite of his absurdities."

[14] In 1889 Hodgkin travelled in the East for three months, visiting Egypt, Palestine, Damascus, Smyrna, and Athens. St. Sophia in Constantinople he felt to be "one of the noblest temples ever reared by human hands!" Back in London he revised his first volume and lamented: "How one's standard of accuracy alters! I was satisfied to knock off the reign of Theodosius in one rather superficial chapter in 1877, and now I have to give him six chapters, which have cost me much labour." *Life and Letters* (n. 6), 157, 159.

[15] Gwatkin in *EHR*, X (1893), 781–82.

eighth volumes, dealing with the Frankish Empire and ending with the death of Charlemagne, appeared four years later. When he was nearing the end of the seventh in 1897, Hodgkin wrote to a friend:

> This volume will deal more with ecclesiastical matters than I like. It is difficult to say what one thinks about these rather covetous old gentlemen [the popes] without seeming to write a controversial Protestant tract, which is the last thing I desire to do, but I cannot help myself; the story, which certainly is not very creditable to the Popes of the eighth century, has to be told.[16]

He was invited to contribute the first volume to the *Political History of England* being edited by W. Hunt and R. L. Poole. Hodgkin hesitated about his qualifications for English history, but rapidly worked himself into his subject. "The story of Cerdic and Cealwin seemed to write itself, and I was always getting down to the bottom of the page." His intimate acquaintance with Northumbrian topography and ruins came to his aid. Hodgkin brought out more clearly than Green and Freeman the non-Saxon ingredients which entered into the making of England. As before, he chose in this book to stick close to his sources. He gave more attention to the political side of events than to the constitutional problems. A lady friend wrote to him: "You know no such things as dry bones, you make them live before they have time to get dry."

When elected to the British Academy, Hodgkin proposed to the secretary that something be done to import into English universities that valuable feature of German and French institutions, the practical seminar.

> One could not but feel that while most of our University curriculum is adapted only to the purpose of enabling a certain number of young men to pass a stiff examination, the method adopted in these "historical laboratories" was calculated to make real effective labourers in the field of historical research, and to do away with the reproach of "Amateurishness" which is so often brought, and sometimes not altogether unjustly, against some of us English workers.
>
> In listening to the admirable exposition of his method of teaching given by M. Gabriel Monod [at the Historical Congress in Rome, 1903], I was vividly reminded of the admirable monograph on Gregory of Tours, and some of the other historians of Merovingian France, which M. Monod presented to the world as the fruit of six months' labour *in conjunction with his pupils.*[17]

Hodgkin's last years were spent on Border History, though he never wrote any extended account of it as Creighton and he had planned.

John Addington Symonds (1840–93) [18] was an undergraduate at

---

[16] *Life and Letters* (n. 6), 197–98.   [17] *Ibid.*, 256.
[18] See Horatio F. Brown, *John Addington Symonds, a Biography Compiled from His Papers and Correspondence* (London, 1903); A. H. Miles, ed., *The Poets and Poetry of the Century* (London, 1892–97); and the fine article in *LTLS*, 1940, pp. 506, 507, 510.

Balliol and a fellow of Magdalen. Following his *Introduction to the Study of Dante* (1872) and the *Studies of the Greek Poets* (1873–76), he gave more than a decade to the famous *Renaissance in Italy* (1875–86). Reduced health forced him to spend the rest of his life in Switzerland. Aside from biographies of literary figures like Shelley (1878) and Michelangelo (1893) he composed verse and published translations, of which the best known is his vivid rendering of the *Autobiography of Benvenuto Cellini*. Symonds remains the most brilliant English interpreter of the Italian Renaissance, though many of his conceptions have been superseded. His longest work, *The Renaissance in Italy*,[19] is a series of picturesque and enthusiastic sketches, rather than a continuous treatment.

Sir James H. Ramsay (1832–1925) was the author of five works on the history of England from 55 B.C. to 1485 A.D., which are solid and useful, if not distinguished.[20]

I claim at any rate [he wrote in 1913] to have laid before the public a fully-referenced general history of England, from the earliest times to the accession of the House of Tudor. Till now a work of that description could only be found in a foreign tongue; [21] a *general* history, I say, because for internal affairs the Constitutional History of Bishop Stubbs stands alone. . . . The reader will stare if I inform him that it [the history] has been my standing occupation since the outbreak of the Franco-German War. My grown-up children do not remember the time when it was not in progress.[22]

All his volumes devote much space to military and fiscal history. The references to the sources are numerous and valuable.

John Horace Round (1854–1928)[23] was a private scholar who spent his life at Brighton. He had been a pupil of Stubbs at Oxford. His earliest writings have not all been identified; there was an anonymous *History of Colchester Castle* (1882) and many contributions to literary and historical journals. By the year just mentioned he was already criticizing Freeman, of whom he later said he belonged to a bygone school.[24] From 1885 on Round wrote articles for the first ten volumes of the *Dictionary of National Biography*. His first intimation of a scholarly future was probably the reading of three papers at the Domesday Book commemoration in 1886; they marked him as the leading authority on this unique source.

[19] Five parts in 7 vols., London, 1875–81, new edition, 1897–98: vol. I, *The Age of the Despots;* vol. II, *The Revival of Learning;* vol. III, *The Fine Arts;* vols. IV and V, *Italian Literature;* vols. VI and VII, *The Catholic Reaction.*

[20] *The Foundations of England, B.C. 55–A.D. 1154* (London, 1898, 2 v.); *The Angevin Empire, 1154–1216* (London, 1903); *The Dawn of the Constitution, 1216–1307* (London, 1908); *The Genesis of Lancaster, 1307–1399* (Oxford, 1913); and *Lancaster and York, 1399–1485* (Oxford, 1892, 2 v.).

[21] The allusion is to the earlier work of the German historians Lappenberg and Pauli.

[22] Preface to *The Genesis of Lancaster* (n. 20).

[23] James Tait, "John Horace Round," *EHR*, XLIII (1928), 572–77; *QR*, CLXXIV (1896), 122–38, review of his works; and "Mr. Round's 'Feudal England'" in ASHLEY, 83–86.

[24] See Round's article, "Historical Research," *Nineteenth Century*, XLIV (1898), 1004–14.

No scholar was sacred to Round's critical pen. In a paper on Charles I and Lord Clamorgan (printed in his *Studies in Peerage*, 1901) he attacked Gardiner, with whose conclusions he did not agree, for "neither critical nor exact" use of his sources. Before long Round had created a deserved reputation for his knowledge of genealogy, English peerage law and family history, in particular during the eleventh and twelfth centuries. He was a consultant of Cokayne, editor of the *Complete Peerage* (1887 ff.); and a charter member of the Pipe Roll Society, for which he prepared a model annotation for the sixty-nine original charters from 1095 to 1199 preserved in the Public Record Office, wrote the prefaces for the annual volumes from 1904 to 1915, and re-edited the *Rotuli de Dominabus*. From 1900 on he wrote or supervised the sections on Domesday Book in the *Victoria County Histories*. The sixty-odd articles and reviews he furnished for the *English Historical Review* embody many points of permanent value.

Round's earliest book came out in 1892, and in the same year he launched a ferocious criticism of Freeman's account of the invasion of William the Conqueror, which has been ironically called the "second battle of Hastings." His *Geoffrey de Mandeville, a Study of the Anarchy* is a valuable account of the reign of Stephen, but Liebermann was justified in calling it an incoherent book. Half the work is appendices, and Round interlarded his narration with charters cited in extenso! He had greater critical than constructive ability. But his *Geoffrey* ended the theory of Stephen's "fiscal earldoms"; it threw some new light on the early administration of London; it commenced the keen studies on castles which culminated in the rejection of G. T. Clark's theory of the pre-Norman origin of the moated mound; and it first distinguished the "third penny" of the county from that of the borough.[25]

On more than one occasion Round remarked that while the task of the last generation of scholars had been to interpret the "chroniclers," the task of the present [1895] was to supplement and correct that evidence by records of another nature. He felt that the *charters* were a neglected and invaluable class of evidence. Palgrave had used them occasionally, but being unprinted they were not easily available; Freeman, who employed only printed sources in his own library, ignored them entirely. Round endeavored to master these records as wholes, to determine their exact relations among each other, and to analyze their contents.[26] But he never again ventured to compose narrative histories, and some of his later volumes are merely collections

---

[25] Liebermann said these contributions "serve in the main to fill with concrete life the abstract theories of Bishop Stubbs."
[26] Cp. ASHLEY, 84.

of articles grouped together, such as the studies forming *Feudal England* (1895); *The Commune of London* (1895); *Peerage and Family History* (1901); *Peerage and Pedigree* (1910); and *The King's Sargeants and Officers of State.* Of the last Professor Tait has said that it contains those irrelevancies "which even while they distract are so full of instruction to Mr. Round's readers." For the governmental commission Round also edited the *Calendar of Documents Preserved in France Illustrative of the History of Great Britain and Ireland* (1899). "So piquant was his exposure of the 'genealogical mythology' of the heralds of the sixteenth and seventeenth century as reproduced in Burke, and of the pretensions of the Heralds' College and its modern defenders, that *Peerage and Family History* is said to have had a fashionable, if not a popular, success." [27] Its successor *Peerage and Pedigree* was his longest book, but too technical to encourage a repetition, though it brought him the appointment of honorary historical adviser to the Crown in pedigree cases.

Much has been said about the ferocious nature of Round's criticisms. He once defended it (1892):

If my criticism be deemed harsh, I may plead with Newman that in controversy I have ever felt from experience that no one would believe me to be in earnest if I spoke calmly.

It is true that some of his most objectionable offenses, in "full-toned pursuit of error," occurred when he had been irritated by the pontifical pretensions of Freeman and his school of admirers, and that in the end, Round was usually right. He claimed never to have printed a statement not verified three times.

The master of Lancastrian history was James Hamilton Wylie (1844–1914) [28] who wrote seven volumes on this period. A classical scholar, and an ex-schoolmaster, Wylie was for thirty-five years an inspector of schools, and found in the fifteenth century "the sole occupation of his leisure and the last thing in his thoughts when he died." Altogether he gave it more than forty years of lonely and difficult efforts. The first volume of a *History of England under Henry the Fourth* (1884) was preceded by twelve years of work, and fourteen more passed before the three sequel volumes were finished. In 1899 he was appointed Ford Lecturer at Oxford, and the result was his *Council of Constance to the Death of John Hus* (1900). Another interlude of fourteen years was broken by the first volume of another detailed work, on *Henry V* (1914). At his death shortly after the manuscript for a second volume

[27] Tait in *EHR* (n. 23).
[28] See *LTLS*, 1935, p. 71. It is lamentable that Wylie is not mentioned in any supplementary volume of the *Dictionary of National Biography.*

lay ready, and the family brought it out in 1919. The third volume necessary to complete the reign was supplied by the scrupulous care of the late Professor W. T. Waugh.

Wylie knew the charm England's greatest dramatist had thrown over Henry V:

No English reader [he wrote] can approach the new reign with his judgment quite unwarped. As he sits waiting for the opening, the curtain which is shortly to be lifted has been pictured for him by a magic hand, and with a resistless spell. His view is filled with visions of Falstaff rebuked, Gascoigne advanced, and the scapegrace King turned from his former self to mock the expectation of the world.

But Wylie's researches and his temperament dispelled most of that charm. His works are difficult reading, because of the peculiarities of his style, a chronological method of procedure, and a passion for facts that led into many digressions. When he came to Agincourt, he wove into his text not only an account of the excavations conducted by Sir John Woodford on the site in 1818, but even the later history of "that eccentric old gentleman in the Lake District, together with the story of his troubles with the parish sexton over tithes. 'Every year he allowed a certain cow to be seized . . . and bought it up again, until at length the animal had to be shot for her extreme old age.' It is characteristic of Wylie that even this sentence has a footnote." [29]

Among women historians of England Mrs. Alice Stopford Green, the widow of J. R. Green, clearly was inspired by her husband when she wrote *Town Life in the Fifteenth Century* (2 v., 1894). Miss Kate Norgate perhaps might be designated as Green's only "pupil," though Green never taught, for she herself called Green "her master" and was his and his wife's life-long friend. Green's viewpoint and influence is visible through all her works: *England under the Angevin Kings* (2 v., 1887), *John Lackland* (1902), *Richard the Lion Heart* (1924). [30]

This chapter may be concluded with a brief account of some of the notable English archivists since Palgrave, who, of course, were not amateurs, but experts in a scholarly and difficult profession. Sir Thomas Duffus Hardy (1804–78), John S. Brewer (1810–79), and James Gairdner (1828–1912) carried on the labor of Rymer and Sir Henry Ellis. Hardy was born in Jamaica and obtained a junior clerkship in the Record Office branch at the Tower of London in 1819, learning his profession as archivist under Henry Petrie. He prepared a number of series for the old Record Commission [31] and was made deputy keeper

---

[29] *LTLS, loc. cit.*

[30] Mary Bateson is noticed in a later chapter in connection with Maitland.

[31] The *Close Rolls*, 1204–27 (1833–44); the *Patent Rolls*, 1201–16, with an historical preface and an itinerary of King John (1835); the *Norman Rolls*, 1200–05 and 1417–18 (1835); the

at the new Record Office in 1861. In this responsible position he strove
to make England's historical records accessible to the public. Hardy
did much to bring about the appointment of the Historical Manuscripts Commission in 1869, and was one of its first members. Besides a
syllabus in English of the documents in Rymer's *Foedera,* he prepared
a valuable *Descriptive Catalogue of Materials Relating to the History of
Great Britain and Ireland,*[32] contributed various other volumes to the
Rolls Series, and drafted reports on the documents preserved at Venice
which had a bearing on English history. His comprehensive knowledge
never resulted in any great work upon any period of English history,
but as an archivist his services were great and fundamental.

John Brewer (1810–79)[33] was the son of a scholarly clergyman.
He entered Queen's College at Oxford, made a fine record in the classics,
edited Aristotle's *Ethics,* and subsequently took a deacon's orders.
After a chaplaincy in Bloomsbury, he found employment in the British
Museum. In 1839 he became lecturer in classical literature at King's
College (London), and then professor of English language and literature and lecturer in modern history. Before leaving Oxford he had
prepared for the Record Commission a catalogue of the manuscripts
in some of the colleges there. In 1856 the Master of the Rolls requested
Brewer to undertake a calendar of the state papers of Henry VIII.
Its preparation involved a constant circling from the Record Office to
the British Museum, and to Lambeth and other libraries. Brewer became a friend and adviser of Sir Thomas Hardy, and was appointed
reader at the Rolls. When Disraeli bestowed a crown living upon him
in 1877, he was able to resign his professorship, but continued as editor
of the *Calendar of State Papers of Henry VIII.* His excellent prefaces
to the various volumes were later reprinted by Gairdner as *The Reign
of Henry VIII.* In addition Brewer published the *Monumenta Fran-
ciscana,* and editions of Roger Bacon, Giraldus Cambrensis, Bacon's
Novum Organum, and Fuller's *Church History.* His greatest contribution as a writer was the full-length portrait he drew of Cardinal
Wolsey, setting the great churchman of Henry VIII in a new light.

The task which Brewer was unable to finish he passed on to his
assistant James Gairdner (1828–1912).[34] Gairdner had been privately

Fine Rolls of King John's reign (1835); the *Charter Rolls,* also of John's time, with a long descriptive introduction (1837); the *Liberate Rolls* of the same reign (1844); and the *Modus
tenendi Parliamentum* (1846). Besides these, he finished the first—and only—volume of the
Monumenta Historica Britanniae (1848), left by Petrie, and wrote the general introduction.

[32] Only the portion up to 1327 was ever published (London, 1862–71, 3 v. in 4: Rolls series,
no. 26).

[33] See the article by James Gairdner in *DNB,* VI, 294–95.

[34] See the article by R. H. Brodie in *DNB,* Supplement II, 206; WARD, XIV, 90–91; and
W. Hunt's preface to Gairdner's *Lollardy and the Reformation in England* (London, 1908–13,
4 v.).

educated, and entered the Public Record Office in 1846. He succeeded Palgrave in 1859 as assistant keeper of the public records and labored there until his retirement in 1893. Brewer had died when only nine volumes of the *Calendar of Henry VIII* were finished; Gairdner completed the series of twenty-one volumes, which summarize 100,000 documents.[35] His many other editions of works for the Rolls Series or the Camden Society cannot be listed here; the most famous was the edition of the *Paston Letters* (1872–75), to which he prefixed a long masterly introduction. After his retirement Gairdner still wrote a volume for the *History of the English Church* edited by Stephens and Hunt, for the years 1509–59, and then produced the four volumes of his *Lollardy and the Reformation in England*.

A great American historian who has devoted his life to the history of England characterized the nature of English historical scholarship in 1900 as follows:

It cannot be said to rank high. It cannot compare with that of Germany or France, possibly not with that of the United States. The number of books of serious historical value is relatively small. The amount of scholarly investigation into historical problems is not nearly so great as in the neighboring continental countries. The publication of source material in accessible form proceeds very slowly. It is, moreover, remarkable how little interest or attention is given in England to the methods of historical research, construction, or even teaching. England produces great historical works from time to time, because very able men have devoted themselves to history. Some good editing is done because there is a great wealth of material, and patient laborious workers are never entirely lacking. But the development of scientific methods of doing the work, training in historical work, coöperative work, any recognition that there is a trade of the historian which can and should be learned, is remarkably slight. The great energy and ability of the English race assert themselves in the writing of history as in other directions, but the slowness to adopt scientific improvements and the materialism which interests itself so much in results that it does not stop to perfect its processes show themselves here also.[36]

Happily, this picture is no longer wholly true.

[35] In the last eight volumes, Gairdner had the help of R. H. Brodie.
[36] E. P. Cheyney, in *International Monthly*, I (1900), 418–19.

CHAPTER L

GERMAN HISTORIANS OF ENGLAND

IT IS an anomaly of English historical scholarship that whole fields of English history have at times been dominated by foreign, and especially German, scholars. Ranke's great *History of England in the Seventeenth Century* anticipated S. R. Gardiner's monumental volumes in the same field and still holds the boards. The *Monumenta Germaniae Historica* carried its share of English materials. In 1904 F. W. Maitland warned his countrymen that the invasion by German scholars would soon convert large areas of English history into German "provinces." [1] The definitive edition of the Anglo-Saxon Laws was completed in 1916 during the War by a German; it was begun at the instance of the Bavarian Academy, printed at Halle at the cost of the Savigny Fund, and dedicated to the memory of Konrad von Maurer, himself a student of English antiquities. Nor may one omit the American Charles Gross, the Russian Vinogradoff, and several living French writers from this category of foreign scholars who have led in various portions of English history. This chapter, however, deals only with the Germans.

Johann Martin Lappenberg (1794–1865) [2] was equally important for the history of Northern Germany and Europe, of England, and of the Hanseatic League. He was a native of Hamburg, devoted to his city, and gave more than forty years to the care and publication of its archives. [3] His clergyman grandfather had written on the history of

---

[1] *The Collected Papers of Frederic William Maitland*, ed. by H. A. L. Fisher (Cambridge, 1911, 3 v.), III, 447–73, reprint of a review of Liebermann's *Die Gesetze der Angelsachsen* in *QR*, CC (1904), 139–57. It would be easy to multiply examples on special topics. By the middle of the nineteenth century, when the English legal system had come to interest many a German writer, the question of the jury, e.g., had attracted such jurists as Brunnel, Rogge, Phillips, Gunderman, Welcker, Mittermaier, and Gneist.

[2] Krause in *Allgemeine Deutsche Biographie*, XVII, 715–16; Elard Meyer, *Johann Martin Lappenberg, eine biographische Skizze, mit Benutzung von Briefen und Tagebüchern* (Hamburg, 1867); G. Waitz, "Zum Andenken an J. M. Lappenberg," in *Nachrichten von der k. Gesellschaft der Wissenschaften* (Göttingen), 1865, pp. 496–504; J. v. Döllinger, *Nekrolog* in *Sitzungsberichte der k. bayerischen Akademie der Wissenschaften* (Munich), 1866, vol. I, 408–12; Hans Schröder, *Lexikon der hamburgischen Schriftsteller bis zur Gegenwart* (Hamburg, 1851–83, 8 v.), IV, 356–72, an almost complete list of his many writings, with biographical material supplied by Lappenberg himself; H. Bresslau, "Geschichte der Monumenta Germaniae Historica," *NA*, XLII (1921), 167, and consult index.

[3] His friend Jakob Grimm once proposed the toast: "Ein halber Engländer, ein ganzer Deutscher, und ein eingefleischter Hamburger." Quoted by Krause in *Allgemeine deutsche Biographie* (n. 2).

the duchy of Bremen and aided in founding its historical society. Lappenberg's father was a Hamburg physician, with some official connections, a man of culture and wit, a friend of Heeren, Reimarus, Perthes, and Sieveking.[4] A sickly lad, Lappenberg's patriotism was stirred by the French occupation of Hamburg while he was still attending the Johanneum. His health forbade enlistment as a volunteer under Tettenborn; and so the young man bowed to his father's wishes and left for London and Edinburgh to study medicine and the natural sciences. When the Napoleonic blockade cut off his income from home, he turned to tutoring to support himself, and conceived a strong interest for the literature and history of his hosts. He met various Scottish and English celebrities, among them Dugald Stuart, Sir James Mackintosh, Wordsworth, and Sir Walter Scott. Ambitious for a political career, he applied in vain to Castlereagh. Next we find him matriculated at the recently founded University of Berlin for the study of jurisprudence and political science. From Berlin he transferred to Göttingen, and plunged into Roman and German law. Having obtained his degree in law (1817) he hastened back to Scotland, but his romance with a Scottish lady failed to materialize, and he returned to Hamburg to practice law. In 1819 his father died, and the Senate of the city sent him to Berlin in the capacity of minister-resident. His experience did not encourage his interest in politics. Throughout these earlier years his temperament was still romantic. He read widely in poetry and literature, knew the Arnims, Varnhagen, and Mendelssohn, and was especially influenced by Savigny. In 1823 he was appointed archivist of the Hamburg Senate, and his patriotic horizon was henceforth largely bounded by the confines of the little city-state.   •

Lappenberg had now determined upon the life of a scholar, and for this the rich Hamburg archives gave a splendid opportunity. His joy was to put them in order and make their treasures available to scholars. They were of particular value for the old archiepiscopal see of Hamburg-Bremen, and for relations with the rest of Northern Europe. To Pardessus he furnished materials for the *Lois maritimes*. When G. F. Sartorius of Göttingen died before completing his projected *Urkundenbuch* for the Hansa, Lappenberg augmented and edited it.[5] When in 1851 the old historic steelyard in London was sold and destroyed, Lappenberg began an historical essay which grew into a detailed treatment of the commercial relations between England and Germany in those centuries.[6] His studies showed that the nucleus of the Hansa is to be sought

---

[4] For the father's life and writings, see Schröder (n. 2), IV, 368–72.
[5] *Urkundliche Geschichte des Ursprungs der deutschen Hansa* (1830, 2 v. in 1).
[6] *Urkundliche Geschichte des Hansischen Stahlhofs zu London*, (1851).

in the relations of German merchants abroad. In his last years he returned again to the Hansa and wrote the programme for an edition of the *Hansa Recesse*,[7] of which he became the chief editor. Work was begun by Professor Junghans of Kiel, who had the manuscript for the older *Recesse* ready when he died. Lappenberg thought of taking up the task himself, but that proved impossible. The *Recesse* were completed by other hands.

His greatest single work was the *Geschichte von England*.[8] Through the intervention of F. Perthes (in 1829) Lappenberg was induced to furnish the history of England for the great series of Heeren and Ukert. His early love for that country, the location of Hamburg and its rich archives, the journeys which acquainted Lappenberg with the various north European countries, and the study of Anglo-Saxon, begun under the stimulus of Jakob Grimm, all made the task congenial. The two volumes which he completed were well received, not only in Germany but even in England; and through Benjamin Thorpe's translation its line of descent was continued in Stubbs and Freeman. The work was epochmaking in that it applied for the first time to English historical studies the critical philological method of the Berlin school. Döllinger regarded it as much superior to Lingard's work, and lauded especially the cultural and economic portions, in which he saw Lappenberg as a successor to Stenzel. The style was awkward and involved, but the research was masterly. As a trained jurist, Lappenberg was able to throw light on many Anglo-Saxon legal problems, and if his friend Sir Francis Palgrave occasionally differed with him, it must be remembered that Palgrave was unacquainted with Germanic legal institutions, whereas Lappenberg set the Anglo-Saxons in the frame of all Germanic antiquity. Particularly valuable were the literary and analytical studies upon the sources which terminated each volume, a feature so capably continued by Reinhold Pauli.

After Lappenberg had brought the *Geschichte von England* down to the time of the Plantagenets, friends and admirers hoped he would continue the work; but official duties and the preparation of a *Hamburger Urkundenbuch* turned his pen in other directions. When after a dozen years his sight began to fail, he reluctantly handed the continuation over to the son of a friend, young Reinhold Pauli.[9]

His archival duties made Lappenberg an excellent palaeographer.

[7] See the *Nachrichten* of the Historical Commission of Munich, appended to *HZ* (1859), II.

[8] Two volumes, 1834–37, from the earliest times to 1154. They were translated by Benjamin Thorpe, with additional notes and corrections, and published as *History of England under the Anglo-Saxon Kings* (London, 1845–81).

[9] Lappenberg gave him the notes and preparations he had already gathered, and had the satisfaction of seeing three more volumes appear, to 1509 (1853–58).

Lonesome as such a scholar may have felt in the busy mart of Hamburg, he found satisfaction in joining the editorial staff of the *Monumenta*. Niebuhr and Dahlmann won him as a collaborator, and Waitz later praised his loyalty, scholarship, and accuracy. His editions were models in their completeness, and many a critical essay found its way into the pages of Pertz' *Archiv*. His edition of Thietmar of Merseburg was the only critical one in its day (1839); Adam of Bremen appeared in 1846, and Helmold's *Chronicle of the Slavs* and Arnold of Lübeck's *Chronica Slavorum* were published posthumously.[10] Lappenberg also edited a number of local chronicles,[11] and was interested in a new edition of the Lübeck chronicles for the collection *Deutsche Städte-Chroniken*. In addition to these works of wider interest, a gathering stream of minor articles on all imaginable subjects connected with Hamburg's history flowed from his pen: juridical, economic, genealogical, topographical and literary studies.[12] Perhaps some of these subjects might have been left to lesser men,[13] but two works were notable. In 1842 he produced the *Hamburger Urkundenbuch*, which offers rich material for the history of the city down to 1300 A.D. and for the earlier period also on the bishopric. Three years later his *Hamburger Rechtsaltertümer* offered the texts and explanation of the older sources on city law (*Stadtrecht*). He was an enthusiastic promoter of the *Verein für hamburgische Geschichte* and its first president; its twenty-fifth anniversary was largely a festival in honor of its most distinguished member.

Much of Lappenberg's work was never finished, for he had many plans. The first disaster was the great Hamburg fire, which destroyed the manuscript of the second volume of his *Urkundenbuch* and all but one hundred copies of the first edition, and consumed the most valuable portions of his collections and many of his "*Vorarbeiten*." In 1848 he lost the sight of one eye and that of the other was much impaired, so that he turned more to the duties of editorship than of original writing.[14]

[10] The *Helmold* came out in 1869 as the most valuable portion of the twenty-first volume of the *Monumenta*. Among other editions, mention may be made of the *Annals* of Albert of Stade, the *Annales Hamburgenses*, the *Braunschweiger Reimchronik*, the *Chronicon Rastedense*, the *Holstein Chronik* of the Presbyter Bremensis, and the *Annales Mosellani*, which Lappenberg found in St. Petersburg.

[11] *Bremische Chroniken*, 1841, two volumes of the *Quellensammlung der Schleswig-Holstein-Lauenburgischen Gesellschaft für väterländische Geschichte* (1862, 1865), a collection of the older Hamburg chronicles (1861); and a new critical edition of Thraziger (1864).

[12] Schröder (n. 2), IV, 358–68 has a long list of his writings. Here under 59 general headings are arranged composite groups, like number 22 (his contributions to the *Monumenta*), 23 (articles in Pertz's Archiv, numbered from a to w), and 32 (his contributions to the *Zeitschrift des Vereins für hamburgische Geschichte*). The last alone runs to 73 items.

[13] Döllinger spoke of Praxiteles whittling at a school bench when he thought of Lappenberg's study of the early printing trade in Hamburg.

[14] Lappenberg's literary interests are illustrated by his editions of the *Reliquien des Fräulein S. K. von Klettenberg* (1849), Goethe's "schöne Seele"; Thomas Murner's *Till Eulenspiegel*

In reviewing the merits of Lappenberg, it must be remembered that he was the first German seriously to occupy himself with English history. He brought German thoroughness, the Ranke source-method, and the philological nicety of the Grimms to bear upon a field formerly at the mercy of conjecture and dilettante interest. No single writer did more for the Hansa or the history of North Germany. With his legal and historical knowledge, in a larger state he might have risen to distinguished appointment; but, as Döllinger has observed, like Böhmer who for forty years was merely librarian in Frankfort, Lappenberg served his city with all his great powers. He died before the regeneration of Germany in 1866–70.

Reinhold Pauli (1823–82),[15] the continuator of Lappenberg and an eminent historian in his own right, was the son of a strong-minded pastor in Berlin who was obliged to remove to Bremen because he refused to bow to the authorities in the *Agendenstreit*. On his mother's side, Pauli came from a merchant family of remote Huguenot extraction. He was reared in the old Hanseatic city of Bremen, his youth thus paralleling that of Lappenberg. After leaving the Friedrich-Wilhelm Gymnasium at Berlin, he commenced his studies at the university, concentrating on philology and history. He early made the acquaintance of Ranke, who impressed him tremendously. During a year spent at Bonn, his great attraction was Dahlmann. He took his degree with a dissertation in ancient history, and planned to become a teacher. But a position as tutor in the home of a Scottish lawyer in Glasgow turned his life into another course. Pauli already knew English and felt a powerful attraction for the literature and history of Britain. He threw himself upon this subject with such zeal that he felt it advisable to resign his position after a year; and then passed to Edinburgh, Oxford, Cambridge, and London in turn. For eight years he lived precariously, visiting libraries and poring over manuscripts. Then he was appointed private secretary to Freiherr von Bunsen, the Prussian ambassador in London. The social intercourse to which Bunsen's household introduced him expanded his mental horizon, and the income eased his poverty.

(1854), which was dedicated to his friends Savigny and Grimm; the low-German *Scherzgedichte des Lauremberg* (1861); and the German and Latin poems of Paul Fleming (1863–65, 2 v.). Posthumously there appeared the collected letters from and to Klopstock (1867).

[15] Alfred Stern, in *Allgemeine deutsche Biographie*, XXV, 268–73, and his *Necrolog* in *Allgemeine Zeitung*, Beilage, no. 283 (1882), pt. 4, pp. 4161–63; F. Frensdorff, "Rede auf Reinhold Pauli," *Abhandlungen der k. Gesellschaft der Wissenschaften* (Göttingen), XXIX, 1882; the same in *Deutsche Rundschau*, XXXIV (1883), 371–75; Otto Hartwig, "Zur Erinnerung an R. Pauli," in his edition of the *Aufsätze zur englischen Geschichte*, neue folge (Leipzig, 1883); L. Weiland, "Zum Andenken an R. Pauli," in *Hansische Geschichtsblätter* (1883); Giesebrecht, *Nekrolog* in *Sitzungsberichte der k. bayerischen Akademie der Wissenschaften*, phil.-hist. Klasse (1883), 97–103; PATTISON, I, 30–52; *NBR*, XXI (1854), 375–98.

In 1851 Pauli published his first solid study, dedicated to his patron: *König Aelfred und seine Stellung in der Geschichte Englands*. This monograph on King Alfred was projected at Oxford in November 1848, at a time when Pauli wished that his disturbed fatherland might find a hero such as Alfred. But the work is free of sentimentality, and remarkable for the manner in which the critical acumen of the maturing scholar separated the historical Alfred from the nimbus of legends which had gathered around him. The work was soon twice translated into English. In Germany Lappenberg, the old friend of Pauli's father, was pleased to such a degree that he entrusted to the young man the continuation of his *Geschichte von England*.

The three volumes of the *Geschichte von England* [16] are beyond question the greatest and solidest portion of Pauli's work. He was travelling paths often wholly uncharted, and endeavoring to apply the Rankean technique to a field in which the sources had not even been completely assembled or printed. Much time was consumed in preparing transcripts for his own use from the original manuscripts, and he passed through a thorough practical school of palaeography and diplomatics. The keeper of the Tower archives, Sir Thomas Duffus Hardy, was a helpful friend, but from Germany there came little aid from scholars or funds.

Not the least valuable portion of his history was the critical appendix on the sources which Pauli added to each of his volumes, following the practice begun by Lappenberg. He had thoughts of doing for English medieval chronicles what Wattenbach did for the German, and till the end of his life gathered materials for such a work, but it never appeared. He gave much attention to constitutional development and the external commercial relations of the island with the continent, and his edition of John Gower's *Confessio Amantis* [17] testifies that he was not blind to the early stirrings of English literature.

But after all, life in England was little better than exile to Pauli's sociable nature; and when his second volume of the *Geschichte von England* came out he determined to try for an academic career in Germany (1855). For a year he lectured as *Privat-dozent* at Bonn, and spent the winter of 1856–57 in the distinguished intellectual circle gathered by King Maximilian of Bavaria. Then Rostock called him as full professor. When this place became painful because of his wife's death he shifted to the larger field at Tübingen. His teaching duties were very exacting. He was a stimulating and fluent lecturer, but his

[16] They succeeded Lappenberg's two and carried the story from 1154 to 1509. Judged solely by the number of pages, Pauli wrote over two-thirds of the *Geschichte* himself.

[17] In three volumes, London, 1857.

studies became more shallow; besides, he was away from his English manuscripts. He could not resist writing, however, and a number of essays appeared as *Bilder aus Altengland* (Gotha, 1860, 2nd ed., 1876), translated into English as *Pictures of Old England*. For the fiftieth anniversary of the doctorate of his old teacher Ranke he prepared a study on Simon de Montfort, whom he considered the creator of the House of Commons.[18]

Pauli's one other larger work resulted when he undertook to write a history of modern England, covering the years from 1815 to 1852, for Salomon Kirzel's *Staatengeschichte der neueren Zeit* (Leipzig, 1864–75, 3 v.). Pauli was well aware of the difficulties presented by contemporary history; he compared it to handling glowing lava rather than stone that could be quarried and cut. He managed to produce a narrative without bias, though his sympathies were not concealed. He utilized unprinted sources like the reports and private papers of his former patron Baron von Bunsen, the Prussian ambassador, and the letters of Richard Cobden, whom he much admired. Incidentally, Pauli's interest in contemporary world happenings was irrepressible, and he had the habit of putting his opinions into print. In 1866 his outspoken Prussian sympathies led to a virtual dismissal from Württemberg; he went to Marburg (1867), and then to Göttingen as Waitz' colleague.

Pauli was a rapid worker and always had several projects in hand at once. The founding of the *Hansische Geschichtsverein* renewed interests of his boyhood years, and he became a valued contributor to its publications. Of major works, however, he produced no more. A projected history of Henry VIII never came to fruition, as the materials seemed overwhelming, and Pauli refused to write only a compilation from previous writers who had not themselves mastered the sources. Aside from studies for a history of the acquisition of the English crown by the House of Hanover, the labors of Pauli's last twenty years in Germany lacked integration. His chief task was to encourage others and to cement the bonds of friendship and scholarly intercourse between the two lands of his allegiance. He once said that his endeavor was "was England an echt germanischen Substanzen bewahrt hat, auf dem Boden der Urheimath wieder fruchtbar zu machen."

The least known but perhaps the greatest of all German students of English constitutional and legal history has been Felix Liebermann (1851–1925).[19] It was indeed fortunate from the viewpoint of scholar-

---

[18] English translation by Una M. Goodwin, *Simon de Montfort, Earl of Leicester, the Creator of the House of Commons* (London, 1876).

[19] T. F. Tout, "Felix Liebermann," *History*, X (1926), 311–19; H. W. C. Davis, "Felix Liebermann," *EHR*, XLI (1926), 91–97, based in part on information from R. L. Poole, H. G. Fiedler, and Sir Paul Vinogradoff. F. W. Maitland reviewed his *Gesetze der Angelsachsen* in

ship that a private fortune enabled him to devote his full time to re-search. When he completed the gymnasium, his father, a Berlin manu-facturer, wished him to pursue the commercial lines which had raised the family to ample means. Accordingly Liebermann spent four years, first in a bank at Berlin, and then in the employ of a German yarn-exporting house in Manchester. Thus he acquired the English language and became so enamoured of English history that a business career seemed repulsive. His elder brother Max had turned to painting; Felix went to the University of Göttingen. At this center, so friendly to English studies, he absorbed critical method from Waitz and further enthusiasm from Reinhold Pauli, whose greatest pupil he was to become. His dissertation marked out much of the course of Liebermann's future studies. It offered a critical introduction to the *Dialogus de Scaccario* which Stubbs had recently published in his *Select Charters*.[20] Some of the emendations the young scholar suggested were adopted by Stubbs in his next edition, and the biographical account of Richard Fitz-Nigel has stood till this day.

Instead of seeking the wider audience of a university chair Lieber-mann chose the ungrateful task of an editor, and was connected with the *Monumenta Germaniae* until 1888.[21] His critical introductions in volumes XXVII–XXVIII of the *Scriptores* are a penetrating study of the English chroniclers of the twelfth and thirteenth centuries. The *Un-gedruckte Anglo-Normannische Geschichtsquellen* (1879) was a welcome gift to scholarship; it had begun in collections he made for his own use in solving chronological problems. Occasionally he contributed essays to historical journals or *Festschriften*, and usually each left its mark.[22] Thus an article on Henry of Huntingdon[23] put to an end the view, still found in Freeman, that this chronicler had incorporated in his work fragments of folk-songs that might be safely used as historical evidence. Similar critical acumen was manifested in Liebermann's contribution to the *Festschrift* for W. Wattenbach,[24] representing "the best state-ment of the case against the Pseudo-Ingulf ever published." Palgrave had noted some absurdities in this work, but both he and Freeman believed there might still be a genuine core left. In this case Lieber-mann's superior critical method swept the board clean, and even nar-

---

QR, CC (1904), 139–57, reprinted in his *Collected Papers* (n. 1), III, 447–73; and H. W. C. Davis did likewise in *EHR*, XXVIII (1913), 417–30. There is a portrait in the *Festgabe für F. Liebermann* (Halle, 1921).

[20] *Einleitung in den Dialogus de Scaccario* (1875).

[21] He aided Pauli in the preparation of the English writers in vols. XIII and XXVII, and brought out vol. XXVIII alone (1888).

[22] Most of these studies are listed by Davis (n. 20).

[23] *Forschungen zur deutschen Geschichte*, XVIII (1878), 267–95.

[24] *Ostenglische Geschichtsquellen* (1892), originally written for vol. XXVIII of the *Scriptores* (n. 22).

rowed the time of the forgery down to the fourteenth century, and before 1360.

In 1883 Liebermann, with his competence already well established, determined to concentrate upon the *desideratum* suggested by Conrad Maurer. This great student of early Teutonic laws regarded early English institutions, like his own field of the Scandinavian institutions, as part of Germanic antiquity, and longed for a comparative study of all the old Germanic laws. The Munich Academy supported Liebermann's project of an adequate edition of the Anglo-Saxon laws,[25] and the Savigny Fund promised financial assistance. *Die Gesetze der Angel-Sachsen* is "one of the greatest triumphs of scholarship of our times." [26] Palgrave had collated twenty-three texts; but Liebermann utilized 180 texts, reduced them to order, and gave the most important texts side by side, all with such uncanny accuracy that later scholars have found the gleanings meager. The expert will find many cases of his ingenuity; e.g., in the first section of the laws of Ethelbert of Kent an important word was obliterated in the unique manuscript. Liebermann went back to the earliest transcribers, and found the lost word in a copy made in the sixteenth century. His critical analysis of the author, the date, the contents, and the prejudices of the writer makes his work enduring.

There is a case in Liebermann's labors which reminds one of Giesebrecht's famous reconstruction of the lost *Annales Altahenses* and the striking confirmation by the discovery of the manuscript of these annals by Oefele. On the basis of a fourteenth-century manuscript of the *Leges Anglorum*, Liebermann had argued that this work was originally written by a person of London, about 1210, who used the city archives, and he indicated certain passages as being later interpolations. In 1909 Professor Tout discovered the Rylands manuscript of the *Leges*, which demonstrably was written between 1204 and 1210, and contained the items Liebermann had ascribed to one compiler in the predicted order, minus the interpolated material.[27]

For a long time Liebermann went unnoticed in England, until his remarkable articles on the Pseudo-Ingulf, the *Instituta Cnuti* and similar subjects [28] attracted the attention of York Powell and Mait-

[25] For a review of what had been done previously, see Maitland's article (n. 1), or Liebermann's prefatory essay in his first volume.

[26] The verdict of T. F. Tout (n. 20), 313. Vol. I, which appeared in portions between 1898 and 1903, contains the texts with translations; vol. II (1906 and 1912, in two parts) contains a vocabulary and a remarkable glossary; and the last volume (1916) carried the introduction and summarized the editor's critical researches.

[27] F. Liebermann, "A Contemporary Manuscript of the 'Leges Anglorum Londoniis collectae' " *EHR*, XXVIII (1913), 733, the whole article, 732–45.

[28] The years from 1892 to 1903 were the most productive of his whole life, when he issued the *Instituta Cnuti* (1893), the *Consiliatio Cnuti* (1893), *Pseudo-Cnut de Foresta* (1894), the corona-

land.[29] Then recognition came rapidly. Cambridge gave him an honorary degree in 1896, and the Prussian government bestowed the honorary title of professor.

Besides his Anglo-Saxon laws, Liebermann's pen produced over a series of years mounting to half a century, forty larger studies and innumerable lesser articles. He ranged widely, from early law to philology, ecclesiastical history, and literary criticism.[30] His field was virtually old English *Kulturgeschichte*. He played an important role as mediator, and wrote reviews for German journals of many medieval works which appeared in the English press. His happy command of English also opened to him various English publications and collections. As a reviewer he drew upon his rich stores of knowledge, and was an appreciative and tactful critic.

Dealing all his life with critical problems, Liebermann preferred to write for scholars in his own compressed German, and rejected suggestions that he aim at the general public. The fact that he never lectured or conducted a seminar contributed to his obscurity; and cut him off, so to say, without direct academic issue. A self-made philologist, he attained the isolation of the great. The initiated valued him according to his scholarship, and in 1913 he was a prominent figure at the International Historical Congress at London. It was the tragedy of his life that the final volume on the Anglo-Saxon laws appeared at a time when Englishmen were fighting Germans; few copies reached England until the end of the war.[31]

Onno Klopp (1822–1904) [32] was a native of East Frisia, and became professor of history at Hanover. He possessed a fervent love for his adopted Hanoverian land, so that Prussia became the emblem of all that was evil. Klopp was the bitterest exponent of *gross-deutsch* historiography, an ardent political pamphleteer with Guelphic views. He blamed Frederick II for the dualism in Germany, and defended the Habsburgs. In later years he turned to ultramontanist views and

tion charter of Henry I (1894), the *Leges Anglorum* (1894), the *Leges Edwardi Confessoris* (1896), the *Textus Roffensis* (1898), the Dunsaete ordinance (1899), the *Leis Willelme* (1901), the *Leges Heinrici* (1901), and the *Rectitudines Singularum Personarum* (1902).

[29] Powell reviewed the attack on Pseudo-Ingulf in the Wattenbach *Festschrift*, and Maitland discovered Liebermann in the *Instituta Cnuti*.

[30] One of his last studies was on the historical value of G. B. Shaw's "Saint Joan" (*HZ*, 1925–26, pp. 20–40).

[31] The third volume was dedicated to Heinrich Brunner and F. W. Maitland, jointly, and the preface expressed a hope for peace and a renewal of friendly relations in the world of scholarship.

[32] His life and writings are detailed by Dr. Wiard Klopp in *Biographisches Jahrbuch und deutscher Nekrolog*, VIII (1905), 117–23. Cp. also by the same author *Onno Klopp, 1822–1903* (Osnabrück, 1907). His chief works are: *Geschichte Ostfrieslands* (Osnabrück and Hanover, 1854–58, 3 v.); *Der König Friedrich II von Preussen und die deutsche Nation* (Schaffhausen, Augsburg, 1866); *Tilly im dreissigjährigen Kriege* (Stuttgart, 1861, 2 v.); *Der Fall des Hauses Stuart* (Vienna, 1875–88, 14 v. in 7).

became a convert to Catholicism. His edition of the complete works of Leibniz came to an unhappy end with the eleventh volume, when he was exiled and the Hanoverian archives were closed to him. Klopp's longest work was ostensibly on an English topic, the *Fall of the House of Stuart*, though the center of gravity inclines to continental affairs in this work of thirteen volumes—surely an exhausting, if not exhaustive, treatment of a limited period.

Rudolf Gneist (1816–95) [33] was a German jurist who not only gave deep attention to English legal heritage, but believed in it enough to advocate some of its principles for his own country. He was the first legal historian of English constitutional and administrative institutions. The son of a judge in Berlin, Gneist studied under Savigny, and after obtaining his J. D. (1838) aspired to a position on the Bench. Several years spent abroad, in Italy, France, and England, preceded an appointment as professor extraordinarius of Roman law at Berlin. While Gneist carried on his academic career and writing, he also held various judgeships and took an active part in politics, sitting from 1858 to 1893 in the Prussian Landtag. His convictions allied him to the Left. In 1862 he launched a strong attack upon the budget for the reorganization of the Prussian army. His efforts were usually directed at the practical reformation or improvement of the legal code and the judicial procedure; thus his *Trial by Jury* (1849) resulted from impatience with the existing conditions. [34] Gneist's forceful and original mind was well able to combine enthusiasm for Prussian monarchy with admiration for another country's ways. In 1888 Frederick III ennobled Gneist and appointed him tutor in constitutional law to the crown prince.

Although he is a man of only one book, that work entitles Felix Makower, a Prussian barrister, to mention. His *Constitutional History and Constitution of the Church of England* [35] is a thorough, lucid, clearly organized and minute study of its subject, viewed objectively as only a foreigner and a lay historian can look at it. Its extensive footnotes indicate alike the author's erudition, and his modesty regarding his own opinions. Even if the text proper were truly inferior, the collection of references and data would make the work almost indispensable. The

[33] Otto Gierke, *Rudolph von Gneist, Gedächtnisrede* (Berlin, 1895); Karl Walcker, *Rudolf von Gneist*, Heft 1 of *Deutsche Denker und ihre Geistesschöpfungen* (Berlin, 1888); Eugen Schiffer, *Rudolf von Gneist* (Berlin, 1929).

[34] Some of his more important works are: *Adel und Ritterschaft in England* (1853); *Das heutige englische Verfassungs- und Verwaltungsrecht* (1857–60, 2 v.; 3rd ed. 1883–84); *Englische Verfassungsgeschichte* (1882), tr. by Philip Ashworth under title *History of the English Constitution* (London, 1886, 2 v.; 2nd ed., 1889).

[35] Translated from the German, London, 1895; reviewed by Alfred Plummer in *The Critical Review* (1896), 115–21.

book looks like a critical edition of some classical author: ten lines of text and thirty-five of footnotes and commentary. That the author should discuss the development of such offices as those of Archbishop, Bishop, and Archdeacon, or of such bodies as Convocations and Chapters, was imperative. Rural Deans and Rural Chapters also are subjects which we have a right to expect; and the same might be said of Curates and Churchwardens. But Parish Clerks, Sextons, Beadles, and Organists, Diocesan Synods and Conferences, Deaconesses' Institutions and Brotherhoods—all these Makower included and discussed. His work has not yet been superseded.

BOOK IX

HISTORIANS OF INSTITUTIONS

CHAPTER LI

FRENCH HISTORIANS OF INSTITUTIONS IN THE NINETEENTH CENTURY

IN 1895 J. H. Round, the English historian, said that while the task of the previous generation had been to interpret the chronicles, the task of his own generation was to supplement and to correct and enlarge the evidence of narrative sources by the critical utilization of charters and other documentary sources. Only occasional use of these could formerly be made, for few of them except in Germany were published until the last decades of the nineteenth century. Since charters and all other documents are emanations of government, church, or other institutions, documentary sources have to deal primarily with institutions.

A large interest was taken in the history of institutions by many German historians in the first half of the nineteenth century. They were pioneers in the field. There were several reasons for this unusual interest. In the first place the French Revolution had levelled or erased some of the oldest and greatest institutions in Europe. It was a profound political and social upheaval. Secondly, institutions are fundamental historical facts and the history of them penetrates to the roots of human society. Institutions are not the product of theory, but the fixation of experience in habit, custom, tradition, idea, interest, law, religion. They are revealing as the common habits and customs and ideas of a particular age. The great institutions of history are never enacted; they grow. They are among the most enduring things in history. If they fail, they become obsolete and survive only as archaic specimens of the past life of man. The study of institutions when they have reached that state is mere antiquarianism, historical palaeontology. Frequently only the word survives after spirit and structure have passed away.[1] The institutional historian, like the palaeontologist, is sometimes able to reconstruct a past institution out of the remnants which have survived, as so much of the civilization of the Ancient East has been reconstituted from the broken shards of ancient pottery.

---

[1] "By the slow and silent alchemy of time institutions change: but . . . the words which designate them remain permanent. We consequently tend to make the more or less unconscious assumption that the same word designated in past times what it designates now. Whereas what we have in fact to do with every name which we meet in ancient records is to treat it altogether independently of the accident that it has remained to our times." Edwin Hatch, *The Organization of the Early Christian Churches* (2nd ed., London, 1882), 15.

Hundreds of books and periodical articles upon institutional subjects were written in the nineteenth century, especially in "thorough" Germany. But one subject engrossed attention more than any other. This was the origin and formation of Feudalism.[2] There was a double problem in the subject—what was the particular institution which was, so to speak, the "germ-plasm" of feudalism, and next the question whether this fundamental nucleus was of Roman or of German origin. The controversy arose in Germany but soon spread to France and national feeling in each country aligned the German scholars, with two exceptions, in advocacy of the German origin or origins of feudalism, while French scholars to a man contended that feudalism as an institution was fundamentally of Roman origin. Reams of paper and floods of ink were spent by these two opposite schools, the "German School" and the "Roman School." While national prejudice sometimes distorted the evidence, in the heat of the controversy practically all the evidence of even remote bearing on the subject was critically scrutinized.

Before the question of the origin of feudalism was raised by members of the Berlin School the general opinion of the eighteenth century had prevailed that feudalism was of Roman origin. This was the contention of Abbé Dubos. Were not the French a "Romance" nation? Was not French feudalism in the Middle Ages *the* type of feudalism? Perreciot (1728–98) had made this doctrine consecrate, finding the germ of feudalism in the Roman *laeti*. Montesquieu alone had raised a dissentient voice and argued that the ancient German *comitatus* was the primordial germ of the feudal relation.

At first, even in Germany, the Roman School had things their own way. The great Savigny, author of *The History of Roman Law in the Middle Ages*, was pro-Roman, but he was not a slavish follower of French opinion. He was the first who stressed the importance of the Roman Colonate in the development of feudalism.[3] Eichhorn, from his studies in early German law, came to the conclusion that there must be a larger German ingredient in feudalism than hitherto suspected, but he did not expand the idea. The first who thoroughly studied the problem of the German element in feudalism was Waitz, who enlarged Montesquieu's suggestion with regard to the German *comitatus*, but

---

[2] The most recent account is in Alfons Dopsch, *Wirtschaftliche und soziale Grundlagen der europäischen Kulturentwicklung, aus der Zeit von Caesar bis auf Karl den Grossen* (2nd ed., Vienna, 1923–24, 2 v.), tr. into English by M. G. Beard and Nadine Marshall under the title, *The Economic and Social Foundations of European Civilization* (London, 1937). See especially chs. i and ix.

[3] *Journal pour la science historique de droit*, VI (1828), 273 ff. On the Colonate see M. I. Rostovtzeff, *Studien zur Geschichte des römischen Kolonates* (Leipzig, 1910); Fustel de Coulanges, *Recherches sur quelques problèmes d'histoire* (2nd ed., Paris, 1894), ch. i, "Le Colonat Romaine," pp. 3–186. See also the article "Kolonat" in Pauly-Wissowa's *Real-encyclopädie*.

did not carry the thought far enough. Waitz regarded the Merovingian state as a truly political form, but found in the *comitatus* a nascent element of feudalism and no more; whereas subsequent research has shown that the Merovingian government was at least of a semi-feudal nature. Moreover, Waitz failed to estimate the significance of the property element, i.e. land, in Merovingian feudalism.

A great stride forward in elucidation of the problem of the development of feudalism was made with the publication of three epoch-making works by Paul Roth of Munich: *Geschichte des Beneficialwesens* (1850), *Feudalität und Unterthanenverband* (1863), *Die Säkularisation des Kirchengutes durch die Söhne Karl Martells* (1874). Roth was an advocate of the predominance of Roman institutions in the formation of feudalism and contended that the origin of real property (land) was to be found in the feudal régime, although it remained for Fustel de Coulanges later to prove it. He asserted the Roman nature of the Merovingian state, with the exception of the antrustionate, which he admitted probably grew out of the *comitatus*. Crown-lands, he believed, were ceded allodially, as veritable property, none of them in fief, and public law, not private contract, was still the basis of social order in Merovingian times as under the Roman Empire. According to Roth's thesis, feudalism proper began with the secularization of ecclesiastical lands by Karl Martel, and the distribution of them as military benefices. Roth derived feudalism from three relations: (1) the antrustionate, (2) benefices, (3) the seigniorate or subjection of lesser freemen to greater freemen, the germ of later overlordship and underlordship (suzerainty and vassalage). Only the first relation existed in the Merovingian Age.[4]

In these same years Waitz enlarged his view and clarified his mind on the subject in *Ueber die Anfänge der Vassalität* (1856) and *Die Anfänge des Lehnswesens* (1865). Waitz held a position congruent partly with Roth, partly with the German School.[5]

In the meantime all French historians continued to be unimpressed by and even ignorant of the work of German scholarship on feudal origins, with the exception of Guizot. But Guizot spread his interest over too many fields of history, and besides was too engrossed in politics ever to be a thorough scholar. His study of the history of feudalism was confined to the academic year 1829–30 when he delivered his famous lectures on the *Histoire de la civilisation en France.*[6] In the second course and third lecture of this series Guizot severely criticized

[4] *Feudalität und Unterthanenverband* (Weimar, 1863), 205.
[5] For other literature on this subject see DAHLMANN-WAITZ, nos. 5578–5600.
[6] Paris, 1829–38, 5 v.; 6th ed., 1857, 4 v.; English translation by W. Hazlitt (New York, 1846).

the methods and prejudices of the German School without perceiving that he, too, was filled with prejudice. The two works by J. M. Lehuérou (1807–43) entitled: *Histoire des institutions mérovingiens et du gouvernement des Mérovingiens jusqu'à l'édit de 615* (1842) and *Histoire des institutions carolingiennes et du gouvernement des Carolingiens* (1843) continued the traditional teaching of Montesquieu and Dubos, and had no new interpretation; he was ignorant of what German scholars had written.

The only French historian before the 1870's who manifested originality, discovered new sources, and ploughed new ground in the history of feudalism was Benjamin Guérard (1797–1854). He was successively conservator of the department of manuscripts of the Bibliothèque Royale, director of the École des Chartes, and member of the Academy of Inscriptions. Guérard was the discoverer of the value of chartularies as historical sources and a pioneer editor of them. He belongs to the older generation of French historians, but his work on the Middle Ages was far more enduring than that of any of his contemporaries. He edited various chartularies of the great abbeys, and his *Polyptique de l'abbé Irminon* (2 v., 1844) has remained a classic; it covers the period 811 to 826 and its contents are explained by the subtitle: "Dénombrement des manses, des serfs et des revenus de l'abbaye de St. Germain de Prés sous le règne de Charlemagne." The introduction to the *Polyptique* is "one of the glories of French scholarship," being, together with Guizot's lectures, "the most important contribution to the study of early France produced in the first half of the nineteenth century." Guérard investigated the relations of classes, the methods of land tenure, and the conditions of institutions from the time of the German invasions. Rejecting the thesis that Gaul was civilized by the Frankish invaders, he showed that, on the contrary, the manor as well as the administration were Roman institutions. Other chartularies which Guérard published were those of St. Père de Chartres, St. Remi de Rheims, St. Bertin, and St. Victor de Marseille.[7]

Two schools of interpretation, Roman vs. German, thus stood over against one another, neither gaining nor losing until after 1870, when Fustel de Coulanges set himself to the task of demolishing the whole fabric of early medieval history created by the German School. Strange to say, so iconoclastic was Fustel's work, so novel his conclusions with reference to the nature of the barbarian invasions, that he even in-

---

[7] A new edition of the *Polyptique* was published by August Longnon (Paris, 1886–95, 2 v.). See J. H. Hessels, "Irminon's Polyptichum (811–26)," and "Polyptychum of the Abbey of St. Remi," in *Transactions of the Philological Society* (London), 1899–1902, pp. 471 ff. and 650 ff. On Guérard see GOOCH, 206–07; and *Notice sur M. Daunou par M. B. Guérard. Suivie d'une notice sur M. Guérard par M. N. de Wailly* (Paris, 1855).

curred the opposition of French historians to whom the names of Dubos and Montesquieu were sacred.

Numa Denys Fustel de Coulanges (1830–89),[8] like his contemporary Renan, came of a Breton family. He was born in Paris in the year of the July Revolution and the Barricades. After the early death of his father, a naval officer, the boy's education was supervised by a grandfather, and a friend of the family provided the funds to send him to the Lycée Charlemagne. At the age of twenty he entered the École Normale. Guizot's *La Civilisation en France* had won his heart for history, and the reticent youth took the opportunity afforded by an appointment as sub-librarian to spend most of his time in the seclusion of the library. Of his teachers, Chéruel gave him the habit of exactness and caution against preconceived ideas; Jules Simon taught him the habit of philosophic doubt which was to become so basic to Fustel's method.[9]

The Second Empire was not an auspicious time for higher education or expanding research. The political repercussions of the coup d'état of Louis Napoleon brought the saddest chapter in the history of the illustrious École Normale; teachers were dismissed, and the new director assigned to the school adopted a repressive attitude towards non-

[8] Paul Guiraud, *Fustel de Coulanges* (Paris, 1896), the work of his pupil and friend; the same, "L'oeuvre historique de Fustel de Coulanges," *RDM*, CXXIV (1896), 73–111. The centenary of Fustel's birth has called forth recent appreciations. J. M. Tourneur-Aumont, *Fustel de Coulanges, 1830–1889* (Paris, 1931), is the latest biography, by a pupil of Guiraud, who has also studied under Jullian and Monod; it contains a preface by Seignobos, Fustel's oldest living pupil. Camille Jullian, Fustel's literary executor and favorite pupil, has given extracts of his works in *Extraits des historiens français du XIXᵉ siècle* (Paris, 1897), and discussed his master in the excellent introduction, pp. lxxxviii–xciii, ci–cv, cxix–cxxiii. Accounts by Pfister, Bloch, Grenier, Peganiol, and Cavaignac in *L'Alsace française*, XIX (1930), 204–16; by Diehl, Jullian, Glotz, and Pfister, in *Revue internationale de l'enseignement*, LXXIV (1930), 178–203; a sympathetic account by Jules Simon, his former teacher, in *ASMP*, XVIII (1891), 33–72; A. Sorel, in his *Notes et Portraits* (Paris, 1909); A. Aulard, "Fustel de Coulanges, patriote, politique, philosophe," *Révolution française*, LXIX (1916), 385–89; Charles Bémont in *Encyclopaedia Britannica*, XI (1910), 374–75; C. V. Langlois in *La Grande Encyclopedie*, XVIII, 313–14; Langlois and Seignobos, *Introduction to the Study of History*, tr. from the French by G. G. Berry (London and New York, 1898), consult index; Marc Bloch in *ESS*, VI, 543; reviews of Fustel's books in *JS*, 1886, pp. 512–21, 595–603, 723–30, 1889, pp. 280–88, 329–37, 1890, pp. 69–83; Fournier in *RQH*, XL (1886), 183–97; Oliver Elton in *EHR*, I (1886), 427–44; H. A. L. Fisher in *ibid.*, V (1890), 1–6; E. R. Jenks, *ibid.*, XII (1897), 209–24; Gaston Dodu, in *Revue des études historiques*, C (1933), 41–66; Pierre Gaxotte, *Criterion*, VIII (1928), 258–69; Paul Vinogradoff, "Fustel de Coulanges, His Conclusions and Method," *Russkaia Mysl* (January, 1890), Book II, 83–103, cp. Vinogradoff's *Growth of the Manor* (New York and London, 1911), 86, 109–10 and note, and his *Villainage in England* (Oxford, 1892), 17–18, 321; P. Viollet in *Revue critique d'histoire et de littérature*, 1886, no. 32; Gustave Fagniez, in *La reforme sociale*, XLVI (1905), 669–86; *The Nation*, "Fustel as a Sociologist," LXXXI (1905), 93–94; G. T. Lapsley, "The Origin of Property in Land," *AHR*, VIII (1902–03), 427–28. Unfavorable accounts and reviews: C. M. Andrews, *Political Science Quarterly*, VI (1891), 734–36; Gabriel Monod, in *RH*, XLI (1889), 277–85; the same *Portraits et souvenirs* (1897); see also Barbey d'Aurevilly, *Les historiens* (Paris, 1888: La XIXᵉ siècle, 2. sér., Les oeuvres et les hommes); Paul Kehr in *HZ*, LXXI (1893), 144–51.

[9] "M. Jules Simon explained Descartes 'Discours sur la méthode' to me thirty years ago, and from that come all my works: for I have applied to history this Cartesian doubt which he introduced to my mind." Quoted by Paul Guiraud in his biography (n. 8), 8–9.

classical studies. Like the rest Fustel turned to the study of Latin and Greek, and drifted into the history of classical antiquity. His teachers did not consider him wholly responsive or docile; his comrades were struck by his original views. Already then Fustel saw things not as other men, and already then he had embraced with enthusiasm the inductive method, writing an essay in praise of Bacon. It was under similar influences that Taine received his training at the École Normale a few years after Fustel.

In 1853 Fustel de Coulanges was enrolled as a member of the recently established École française d'Athènes, then the only French school abroad. During a sojourn of two years in classic Greece he collected unpublished materials and wrote his first publication, a memoir on the island of Chios (1857).[10] In 1855 he was made instructor in history at the Lycée in Amiens, and during his short stay there he prepared the two theses for the doctorate at the École Normale. *Polybe* (1857) was a study of the Greek historian's account of the Roman conquest of Greece. It was praised for its erudition, clarity, and facile writing, and for the choice of proofs whereby Fustel sustained his thesis: that the Greek aristocracy had succumbed rather willingly to the rule of the Roman aristocracy. His Latin thesis on the cult of Vesta[11] showed the development of what was originally a domestic cult into the official cult of the city. Its central idea, the textual analysis, and the forceful exposition all heralded Fustel's coming masterpiece: *La Cité antique*.

After teaching at the Lycée St. Louis in Paris for two years, Fustel was called to the chair of medieval and modern history at the University of Strasbourg. His success in the ten years he was there (1860–70) was phenomenal. He found a faculty "aux trois quarts morte," and his vigorous and scholarly lectures elicited, as he himself testified, "un enthousiasme naif." He proposed to "embrasser l'histoire entière," and gathered around him more than a hundred students.

La Cité antique was written in six months in 1864, on the basis of a course of lectures given in 1862–63. In view of its instant and continuous success it seems odd that the author had to publish it at his own expense.[12] Its fundamental idea is that the beliefs of man are the determinants, and even the creators, of his institutions. In the preface to *La Cité antique* Coulanges wrote: "The past never completely dies for men. Man may forget it, but he keeps it with him always. For such as he himself is in each epoch he is the product and résumé of all anterior epochs. If he descends into his own soul, he can rediscover there

[10] Printed in *Archives des missions scientifiques*, I-er série, t. V.
[11] *Quid Vestae cultus in institutis veterum privatis publicisque valuerit* (1858).
[12] By 1890, the year after his death, it had reached the 13th edition; the English translation went to its twelfth. *The Ancient City*, translated by Willard Small (Boston, 1896).

these different epochs, and distinguish them according to the impress which each had made on him." Fraser's *The Golden Bough* is an extended commentary on this proposition. In antiquity Fustel found that religious beliefs were most powerful. Starting with the origins of the Greek and the Roman family, he discovered that the family group was built around the worship of deceased ancestors. Upon this cult of the dead was imposed a second religion: that of the forces of nature, which was better adapted to social progress. This formed a sort of common denominator to all families and presided at the rise of cities, replacing diversity by unity of belief. The city was still modelled after the family; it had its hearth, its god, and its cult. Its law and institutions drew their roots from religion.[13] In time men developed other interests and demanded new sanctions. A series of revolutions led to changes in government and in civil laws; the priest-king yielded to an oligarchy and that in turn to democracies. As the horizon of men widened, local deities were merged: "la fusion des divinités locales prepara insensiblement la fusion des cités." Thus a larger unity was presaged. Greek cosmopolitanism weakened the sense of patriotism, and Rome made the whole of the Mediterranean basin her own. The many cities yielded to one. With the advent of Christianity, however, a wedge was driven between religion and government, and with the ruin of the old religions, came the ruin of the old institutions. The new faith established a new society.

When it first appeared, *La Cité antique* possessed a bold novelty. One can discover traces of the influence of Montesquieu's *L'Esprit de lois* in it, or of Tocqueville,[14] or of the broad conception of history entertained by Michelet. Like Renan's *Vie de Jésus*, published in the previous year (1863), Fustel's book caught the tide of a strong interest in religious history.[15] Few, however, of his many readers realized the new method and intention of its author. For years Fustel was thought a Catholic and a clerical, because he gave such a prominent rôle to religion. Louis Ménard conceived a violent distaste for the work.[16] The

---

[13] "La religion, qui avait enfanté l'État, et l'État, qui entretenait la religion, se soutenaient l'un et l'autre et ne faisaient qu'un; ces deux puissances associées formaient une puissance humaine à laquelle l'âme et le corps étaient asservis." Quoted in Guiraud's biography (n. 8), 34–35.

[14] Jullian in his *Extraits* (n. 8), p. cii, points out the similarity of the beginning of *Démocratie en Amérique* with the title of Fustel's introduction: "De la necessité d'étudier les plus vieilles croyances des anciens pour connaître leur institutions."

[15] This interest in religious history came to France from Germany in the second quarter of the nineteenth century and increased towards 1848. Albert Broglie wrote *L'Église et l'Empire romain au IVe siècle* (Paris, 1860–66, 6 v.), orthodox authors contributed much, and there was another branch turning to ancient religions, among whom Louis Ménard was a prominent exponent of the beauties of the pagan cults. The double movement culminated on the one hand in Renan, on the other in Fustel. Cp. Jullian, *Extraits* (n. 8), pp. xc–xci.

[16] See the interesting brochure of Edouard Champion, *Les idées politiques et religieuses de Fustel de Coulanges d'après des documents inédits* (Paris, 1903). It deals chiefly with Fustel's

warm praise of the devout among his readers was a source of embarrassment to the author.[17]

In execution, arrangement, and style the book was a masterpiece and has become a classic of French historical literature. Two criticisms levelled against it, however, must be considered. The one is that Fustel wrote with *à priori* conceptions, with the *idées maîtresses* which he denounced so vehemently in his later years. This criticism was made by d'Arbois de Jubainville among others.[18] In justification of Fustel it must be said that in this earlier work he concealed the baggage of erudition. It was a work of synthesis, rather than one of detailed analysis which showed the reader the author's mental processes, his doubts, and slow advance of thought through a mass of sources. He said himself that in his researches one study led to another, and before he knew it, he had written some thirty essays, and his book was done. But the incisive clarity with which Fustel could present his final conclusions lent color to the notion of *à priori* history.

A second and perhaps more valid criticism is that *La Cité antique* assumes a concurrent phenomenon as a cause. If ancestor worship is encountered at the beginning of religion and was inseparable from family life, that does not prove that it was the causal principle in the family. If the beliefs of men change at the same time as the rest of their institutions, this does not prove that the former produced the change in the latter. Fustel went so far as to say it was the sole cause![19] But Fustel de Coulanges never pretended to exhaust the whole of history in any of his studies. "J'ai conçu mon sujet suivant de certaines limites; il suffit que, dans ces limites-là, je sois resté fidèle à la vérité."[20] One of his most authoritative interpreters, Camille Jullian, has said that if we seek in *La Cité antique* only the rapport between beliefs and social forms in antiquity, and the rôle of religion in the union of human groups and in the external life of men, perhaps not a line need be changed in Fustel's book.[21]

In the years spent at Strasbourg the rising scholar found few "compagnons d'étude et de pensée." Those who think of him as primarily a

correspondence with Ménard about *La Cité antique*, which that lover of pagan antiquity thought a Christian attack, and Fustel's private exposition of his aim and method in writing the book.

[17] See Fustel's own words in Guiraud (n. 8), 160 note; cp. 32.

[18] Henri d'Arbois de Jubainville, *Deux manières d'écrire l'histoire, critique de Bossuet, d'Augustine Thierry et de Fustel de Coulanges* (Paris, 1896). It contains a heated attack upon Fustel.

[19] "*Par cela seul* que la famille n'avait plus sa religion domestique, sa constitution et son droit furent transformés; *par cela seul* que l'État n'avait plus sa religion officielle, les règles du gouvernement des hommes furent changées pour toujours." Quoted in Jullian, *Extraits* (n. 8), p. ciii, n. 2.

[20] *Revue critique d'histoire et de littérature*, I (1866), 376, quoted in Tourneur-Aumont (n. 8), 28.

[21] Cp. Jullian, *Extraits* (n. 8), p. civ. For longer discussions of the book, see *ibid.*, pp. ci–cv; Guiraud, *Fustel de Coulanges* (n. 8), ch. iii, pp. 29–48.

medieval historian overlook the fact that his next great work, the *Institutions politiques de la France*, was projected for four volumes of which two would fall in the modern field. In 1870 he was called back to Paris to succeed Geffroy at the École Normale where he had entered as a student twenty years before.

The Franco-Prussian War was a turning point in Fustel's life. It directed his attention away from antiquity, and centered it once more on his native land. He turned his pen to the cause of the moment. In an open letter he protested against the religion of hate preached by the German pastors. In an article on Alsace he answered Mommsen, urging that such regions ought to have self-determination rather than be bandied about as any nation's private property. Patriotic fervor accounts for the tartness of his article on the German historians, published in 1872.[22] In view of all this it has frequently been said that the war made of Fustel a patriotic historian who hated Germany and her institutions, and this is used as a key to explain all his writings and attacks upon the Germanists following 1870. This has been proved to be a wrong opinion.[23]

It is easy to see how the legend was created. Nothing could have been more startling than the article in the *Revue des deux mondes* in 1872, entitled "L'invasion germanique au Ve siècle, son caractère et ses effets." [24] The article was a bold assertion that the much-discussed Germanic invasions in the fifth century had exerted no permanent influence on the history, religion, customs, government, or structure of society in France. Another surprising article on "La propriété foncière" in the Roman Empire and in Merovingian Gaul followed. Fustel was trying to find the origins of feudalism elsewhere than in Germany! The new thought grew, and filled with its luxuriance the whole of a brilliant volume issued in 1874: the first volume of his *Histoire des institutions politiques de l'ancienne France*.

Fustel's work was strongly subversive of the whole Germanist theory. The invasions, he declared, had been in part misunderstood, and in part misrepresented. They were not a conquest; they brought nothing new and changed nothing directly. Possibly they accelerated the development of feudalism; but feudalism would have come, even if there had been no invasions, as a result of the conditions in the Roman

[22] "La manière d'écrire l'histoire en France et en Allemagne," *RDM*, CI (1872), 241–51.

[23] Monod, one of the strongest and most persistent opponents of some of Fustel's views, has examined the cahiers of his lectures at Strasbourg and borne witness to the fact that the general tenor of Fustel's views on the early Germans were already on paper before the war, and changed only in points of detail in later years. *RH*, XLI (1889), 283. Simon proves the same conclusions to have appeared already in the lectures before the Empress. Cp. *ASMP*, XVIII (1894), 33–72. Simon points out that Dubos had published similar anti-Germanist sentiments earlier.

[24] *RDM*, XCIX (1872), 241, 268.

Empire itself. He rejected the conception of Thierry that the invasions were the triumph of one race over another, of Germans over Romanized Gauls. They were not a victory of conquerors who imposed new institutions of their own upon the vanquished, but either repeated acts of brigandage by warring bands, quickly forgotten, or a settlement of landless barbarians, not on their own terms, but as *coloni* of the Gallo-Roman proprietors of the soil. The personal allegiance so peculiar to feudalism was not first introduced by these invaders, for the Roman institution of clientage was steadily developing into this personal relation on its own account. Fustel de Coulanges further contended that the organization of the country districts and rural areas of Gaul *after* the invasions of the Germans still remained wholly Roman. The Romans remained either ignorant of, or only slightly acquainted with the German village community. The Germans found the Roman villa system everywhere and adopted it so completely that the German village ran into the Roman groove. The predominance everywhere, if not the supremacy of the villa over the village must be admitted. Monod has summarized the argument in a syllogism:

Gaul had never been oppressed or unhappy under Roman dominion;
The Germans possessed no original institution that they could transplant to the soil of the Empire;
The invasions had not the character of a conquest, but rather were a pacific settlement of Romanized Germans who regarded themselves as subjects of the Empire;
Therefore: the Frankish institutions could have been nothing but Roman institutions altered by barbarism and ignorance.[25]

It would be a mistake, though one which many have made, to conclude from this that Fustel regarded feudalism, whose discussion forms the core of this volume, as essentially Roman. He insisted that feudalism was neither Roman nor German, but that of all institutions it strikes its roots deepest in the soil of human nature. "Elle n'appartient ni à une époque, ni à une nation; elle appartient à la nature humaine." Fustel disliked to be called a Romanist, but he could not shake off the label. His own editor Jullian admits its truth in so far as he left little space for German traces after the invasions,[26] and in view of the persistence with which he harassed the Germanists. Today, when a saner balance has been struck between Romanist and Germanist, the position of Fustel is more justly appreciated.

It was Fustel's greatest grief that the reading public and his fellow-historians failed to appreciate the honesty and even the nature of his method. He complained that his critics never took the trouble to con-

[25] *RH* (n. 23), XLI, 282.
[26] Fustel excused this brevity of discussion by the paucity of texts.

sult the numerous references he gave at the bottom of every page. They contented themselves with denouncing his interpretation without going back to the texts themselves. After the storm of criticism against his first volume, Fustel felt obliged to abandon his plan to continue the work on the same scale down to recent times. He had announced a second volume, on the "régime féodal," for 1875, to be followed soon by a third on royalty limited by the estates-general, and a fourth on the absolute monarchy of France down to 1789. This great synthetic study of French political institutions had to be laid aside. Fustel had stated conclusions rather than elaborated his proofs; from all sides he was challenged to produce more evidence. To the task of enlarging the vestibule of his projected edifice Fustel gave the rest of his all-too-brief life. He turned to the analytic method and took the reader into his workshop. He did not spare him page after page of criticism and exposition of individual texts; he lugged all his *apparatus criticus* out into the open. Each chapter grew to the dimensions of a volume, each page bristled with references and was sown with the marks of erudition. It was not a vain parade of learning,[27] but a determined effort to hammer the truth into obstinate heads. It grew to be even more. He convinced himself that his generation needed a lesson in historical method. At any other time, he declared, "on n'avait traité les textes avec tant de legéreté." By example and by precept he set himself up as the teacher and critic of the historiography of his time.

The years took heavy toll of his strength. From 1870 to 1875 he lectured at the École Normale; in December of the latter year he entered the Sorbonne as assistant to Geffroy. His lectures were a matter of rigid discipline, for himself as for his students.[28] For years the Faculté des lettres of Paris had asked that a chair of medieval history be created for him, but the old reputation as a "clerical" from the time of *La Cité antique* prevented legislative action until 1878. Then in 1880 the director of the École Normale died, and Fustel was practically forced to accept the position. His genius was not suited to administrative labors; they interrupted his research and bore heavily on his health. After four years he resigned and returned to the Sorbonne.

The achievement of the last six years of his life (1883–1889) was tremendous. No one knew what it cost him to wring from his failing

---

[27] Camille Jullian, in editing the posthumous volume of *Les origines du régime féodal* (see below) said in his preface, p. vi, that he did not think he had to complete the bibliography. "M. Fustel de Coulanges avait lu tout ce qui se rapportait à son sujet, oeuvres modernes et textes anciens: il ne tenait pas à le montrer."

[28] "Vous venez chercher ici," he told his hearers, "non une distraction ou un pur plaisir d'esprit, mais un veritable enseignement. Il ne s'agit, dans cette maison, ni de leçons attrayantes, ni de beau langage. Un succès de parole serait pour nous un échec." Quoted by Langlois in *La Grande Encyclopédie*, XVIII, 314.

physical frame every atom of energy to sustain his flashing brain at its task. Fustel labored eight to ten hours a day, eliminated physical exercise, and weighed out his food in a meticulous diet. In 1889 he took to his bed, but still refused to stop writing. With reluctance he saw that death would soon remove his pen from his fingers, and entrusted his notes and manuscripts to his pupil Camille Jullian.

The larger and significant portion of Fustel de Coulanges' writings, save for numerous articles, was thus published posthumously. His *Histoire des institutions politiques de l'ancienne France* had grown from one volume (1874) to six octavo volumes of some five hundred pages each. Only the third and fourth were completed by the author himself, and published in 1888 and 1889. These were *La monarchie franque*, and *L'Alleu et le domaine rural pendant l'époque mérovingienne*. The other four were rapidly and piously edited by his literary executor from Fustel's manuscripts and notes. In the order of their appearance they were *Les origines du régime féodal: le bénéfice et le patronat* (1890), *La Gaule romaine* (1891), *L'invasion germanique et la fin de l'Empire* (1891), and *Les transformations de la royauté pendant l'époque carolingienne* (1892). In addition Jullian edited two other volumes of his teacher's collected studies: *Nouvelles recherches sur quelques problèmes d'histoire* (1891) [29] and *Questions historiques* (1893).

Fustel's mastery of the entire field of documentary evidence was complete. Nothing escaped him. He compelled a new evaluation of the Germanic invasions. He made it impossible to look upon them as a human torrent which swept everything of the old Gallo-Roman institutions away. He restored France once more to Roman civilization.[30]

No one could do more with texts than Fustel. Yet there is truth in Monod's charge that, "He loved difficult questions, but he reduced them to too simple terms; he saw their difficulty, but not their complexity." [31] He made history too logical. Flach said of Coulanges:

> He sticks to the letter. The institution is incarnated in a sacramental word. . . . If the word is not there, the institution is not.[32]

To this religion of texts Fustel remained faithful all his life. There was something of ascetic self-renunciation about the way in which he disciplined his mind under the great principle. "Le meilleur historien

[29] A first volume, *Recherches sur quelques problèmes d'histoire*, had been published by Fustel in 1885. All works appeared at Paris.

[30] Barbey d'Aurevilly, *Les historiens* (Paris, 1888: La XIXᵉ siècle, 2. sér., Les oeuvres et les hommes), 31: "Nous voilà degermanisés! Nous voilà rappelés à nos origines, qui sont essentiellement romaines."

[31] *RH* (n. 23), 284.

[32] *Les origines de l'ancienne France* (Paris, 1886–1904, 3 v.), II, 47: "Est-il absent des textes le village est absent des institutions."

est celui qui se tient le plus près des textes, qui n'écrit et même ne pense que d'après eux." He warned his students against the preliminary reading of secondary works. They would obtrude a cloud of preconceptions before their eyes; perhaps confirm them in error; at any rate obscure the new truth that the sources, objectively studied, might reveal. The first thing the historian must do, in approaching any epoch or problem, is to determine what means we have of knowing, i.e., what texts exist. Fustel was not afraid not to know, as when he found the materials on the ancient Germans insufficient for scientific pronouncement; he roundly scored scholars who took refuge in ingenious hypotheses rather than admit ignorance. Having determined what sources are available, the historian must settle down to patient and humble study. "Les textes ne sont pas toujours véridiques; mais l'histoire ne se fait qu'avec les textes, et il ne faut pas leur substituer ses opinions personnelles."

Analysis—as the chemist detects the elements in a strange mixture and notes their behavior and peculiarities—analysis of the sources was the historian's task. Every student of history knows Fustel's saying: "It requires years of analysis for a day of synthesis." Fustel gave many instructions as to how this intensive analysis was to be carried out. Documents should be read in their entirety rather than second-hand in fragments and without the context. The historian must assimilate the spirit of the age he studies. "He boasted of being the only man who had studied every Latin text from the sixth century B.C. to the tenth century of the Christian era." [33] Yet every document must be studied separately and by itself. Fustel criticized Monod for paralleling a chapter in Gregory of Tours with the Salic Laws, when not a word in Gregory's text hints at them. A historian must not read into a text things which are not there. Each word must be examined and scrutinized minutely, not only for its etymology but for its contemporary usage. "L'histoire d'un mot marque le cours des idées." [34] Fustel's own word-studies have been universally acknowledged as models. He caustically criticized great scholars both in France and Germany for what he thought were misinterpretations of words in the documents, e.g., Monod, Lavelleye, Maurer, and Lamprecht. On the other hand he gave due credit to the careful textual analysis of Guérard, Mabillon, Godefroy, Pardessus, Mommsen, and Waitz.

Fustel de Coulanges warned his students that "in order to search for some great truth one has almost always first of all to refute some great error." He counselled them continually not to bow before dogmatism,

---

[33] GOOCH, 211.
[34] *Histoire des institutions politiques de l'ancienne France* (Paris, 1888–1907, 6 v.), IV, 95.

or subject their thought to any individual, but "to see everything by themselves and to walk boldly alone." Fustel was a consuming fire when he chanced upon a writer who quoted his documents at second-hand. He had slight use for secondary works of any sort.

He abominated the philosophy of history. He believed that drawing analogies in history was a dangerous method. That favorite device of many historians, of comparing or contrasting some other age or problem with the present for the sake of vividness, or clarity, he regarded as almost criminal practice. As a student of Greek and Roman history, Fustel had observed how some modern writers treated Roman consuls as modern kings or princes, if the writer was a monarchist, or as revolutionary leaders, if he was a republican. It was absurd to compare ancient Gaul under Roman rule with modern Ireland under English domination, or Poland subjected to Russia! The most fruitful cause of error lies in patriotic influences. Fustel's withering comment was: history is a science, patriotism is a virtue; the two must not be confused. "For forty years I have fought prejudice, urging young historians to be independent, to read past ages through their own eyes rather than through ours." He once summed up his method in a preface:

In these researches, I shall follow the same method I have practiced for thirty-five years. It may be stated in these three rules: 1. study directly and only sources in the minutest detail; 2. only believe what they show; 3. resolutely separate from the history of the past modern ideas which might be read into it by a false method. No more in this new volume than in *La Cité antique* will I scruple to find myself in disagreement with some prevailing opinions provided I am in agreement with the sources. I am not ignorant of the hatreds to which this method exposes me. I irritate, without wishing to, all those whose systems my researches derange. I offend, without deliberate intent, all those whose traditional half-learning (demi-érudition) my work disconcerts. These are persons who will hardly pardon me. I expect from them, again, a mixture of violent attacks and sugared insinuations. But they have accustomed me to it so well for the last twenty-five years that I am no longer to be bothered. Besides, age and illness warn me to heed no longer the brambles beside the road and to keep my eyes fixed only upon science.[35]

The "day of synthesis" is the end and climax of historical research. Here too Fustel was a master; but this "last of the positivists" observed austere self-restraint. Occasionally his studies are highly condensed. A short chapter on the nature of the rural domain is a six page synthesis of extensive researches on villa and town names in Merovingian Gaul and the changes they underwent; these six pages have sixty-six citations.[36] The aim of history for Fustel was that of all sciences: to

---

[35] *Histoire des institutions* (n. 34), III, preface, p. ii.
[36] *Ibid.*, IV, 220–26.

understand.[37] The subject for the historian was "the facts, the usages, the ideas of each epoch." [38] These, and not persons, were the grist for an historian's mill. He did not rate highly Tacitus' ability for analyzing personalities.[39]

Waitz died in 1886 and Fustel de Coulanges in 1889. By the 1890's it may be said that the issue between French and German historians with regard to the origin of feudalism had been settled in favor of predominantly Roman origin. But the waters were soon troubled by a new contention.

In the last decade of the nineteenth century a group of scholars came forward contending that there was a Celtic factor in the formation of feudalism not yet recognized. As might be expected a French historian was the advocate of this doctrine—Jacques Flach. He contended that vassalage was a peculiarly Celtic contribution to feudalism, that the word *vassus* was a Celtic word and that the practice was descended from Old Celtic clientage which did not perish but passed into Gallo-Roman society and thence to the Franks.[40] Flach, however, did not stress feudalism as primarily of any racial origin. It sprang from the dissolution of Roman society and the formation of a Romano-German society in its roots; it proceeded from a general necessity of protection. Not until the Carolingian age did the new formation of society acquire the rigorous form of a political system and that, at that time, was too artificially devised and too personally imposed by Charlemagne to be permanent. *Natural*, spontaneous feudalism was formed slowly during and after the break-up of the Carolingian Empire. "Le régime seigneurial se présente au Xe siècle dans sa pureté native et il atteint au XIe son plein épanouissement."

Like Fustel de Coulanges, who died three years after Flach's first volume appeared, Flach relied chiefly upon documentary sources for evidence, although not so exclusively. His favorite documents were charters, which were a rich and less exploited mine of sources than other documents. He studied these province by province, almost do-

---

[37] "We do not believe we are obliged to find out if the institution [of colonization during the Roman Empire] was good or bad in itself. We are not asked for a moral judgment of the 'colonate.' . . . The historian wishes to understand, not to judge." *Recherches* (n. 3), 138.

[38] *Histoire des institutions* (n. 34), II, 480.

[39] "His [Tacitus] profundity of psychological observation is not precisely the most precious quality of an historian who, in the study of societies, should be less concerned with searching out the hidden depths of the human heart than with clearly perceiving social forms, usages, interests, and all the truths solely relative to changing humanity." *Ibid.*, II, 240.

[40] Flach preferred the expression *régime seigneurial* to that of *féodalité* or *régime féodal*. "Elle correspond mieux à un tableau d'ensemble de la société, car elle comprend à la fois et les rapports de suzerain à vassal et les rapports de seigneur à sujet, à tenancier ou à serf." *Les origines de l'ancienne France* (n. 32), I, introd. 7, note.

main by domain. Of all French historians Flach remains the master of
the use of chartularies.[41]

The most distinguished pupil of Fustel de Coulanges and his literary
executor was Camille Jullian (1859–1933), who made ancient Gaul his
special province and occupied the first chair of Antiquités Nationales
at the Collège de France for a quarter of a century.[42] Jullian had been
fired with a passion for antiquity during his own student years at the
École Normale, when he heard the lectures of Fustel and studied
Roman epigraphy under Ernest Desjardins at the Collège de France.
Before entering upon his own career he went to Berlin to hear the famous
Mommsen lecture. But strongest of all determining forces in Jullian's
experience was his stay at the École française in Rome.

For many years Jullian taught at the University of Bordeaux. In
1887 he began to contribute to the *Revue historique* the series of *Bulletins d'antiquités romaines* which was to run for more than twenty years,
and later alternated with *Bulletins d'antiquités nationales, gauloises et
gallo-romaines* (ending in 1908). About 1912 Jullian planned a great
Histoire romaine, as a counter-part to the *Histoire de la Gaule* he had
started to publish. The work was never really commenced.

. Fustel de Coulanges bequeathed the precious manuscripts of his last
years to his favorite pupil to publish. In the spring of 1890, less than
six months after Fustel's death, the first volume came forth, and by
1893 Jullian had seen through the press six volumes of his great teacher's
work. His own *Histoire de Bordeaux depuis les origines jusqu'en 1895*
was a model of French provincial history and inspired the *Histoire de
Nancy* of his friend Christian Pfister. In 1905 Jullian was called to the
Collège de France.

His name is above all else associated with his *Histoire de la Gaule*, in
eight volumes. Gaul has been justly termed his "patrimony." Other
writers before him had sketched the extension of Rome's power over
her northern provinces. Mommsen had seen only Rome and Caesar.
Jullian refused to take his stand on the Tiber and to watch Rome's
advance with the eyes of a Roman sympathizer.[43] Gaul had its own
historical justification apart from Rome. He followed the vicissitudes
of its people before the Romans came, their relations with the Greek
culture at Marseilles, and the struggle against the Roman yoke. Jullian's hero was Vercingetorix and not Caesar. It is interesting to note

[41] See his remarks *ibid.*, 3–14. Flach's subsequent volumes passed beyond the period of
origins of the feudal regime. His other works are considered below, pp. 379–81.

[42] The inaugural lecture of his successor, Albert Grenier, contains an eloquent tribute, cp.
RCC, XXXVII (1936), 2ᵉ série, 1–16. Maurice Toussaint, *Biographie de Camille Jullian* (Paris,
1935, Société d'édition, "Les Belles Lettres"), 66, and a bibliography of Jullian's writings in
RQH, CXXII (1935), 179–80.

[43] "Il prend son point de vue en Gaule même," says M. Grenier, "et non point de Rome."

that his teacher Fustel believed the Gauls accepted the Roman yoke willingly, whereas Jullian regarded them as heroes struggling for liberty. Of consuls, emperors, and conquerors, he says:

Cela c'est la façade consacrée de l'édifice, vaine et mensongère comme l'éloge d'un mort ou une harangue officielle. Elle nous cache la vie réelle des hommes et des peuples qui occupent cet édifice [IV, 453].

Throughout the whole work he stressed the importance of historical geography.

Paul Fabre (1859–1909) [44] was another ardent pupil of Fustel de Coulanges and married his daughter. Born at Saint-Étienne on the Loire, his presence at the École Normale, where he studied from 1879 to 1882, coincided with the years when Fustel served as director. The serious-minded student was captivated by the ideals of his teacher. A long sojourn in Rome as member of the École française (1882–86) determined the direction of his historical studies. He was drawn to ecclesiastical history and planned a study of the administration of the papal state in the thirteenth century, but Fustel advised him to begin earlier with the registers of Gregory the Great. The result of his researches was a brilliant monograph upon the history of the formation of the papal patrimony. This was followed by his most important work, a critical edition of the *Liber censuum* (1889 ff.). In 1895 he was appointed to the newly created chair of medieval history at Lille, but in 1899, at the age of forty, he died on the threshhold of new labors that would have enriched historical scholarship. He had broken new ground in papal history in the use of polyptychs and chartularies.

Achille Luchaire (1847–1909),[45] Fustel's successor at the Sorbonne, was perhaps the greatest French medievalist after the death of Giry. His approach to history was through philological studies upon the Basque and Gascon languages.[46] His major thesis, *Alain le Grand, sire d'Albret: l'administration royale et la féodalité du midi, 1440–1522* (Paris, 1877), was crowned by the French Academy as a striking contribution to the history of the Midi. Auguste Molinier, who reviewed the book, declared it was too short for the subject, and expressed the hope that

[44] See Georges Digard, "L'oeuvre historique de Paul Fabre," in the *Mélanges Paul Fabre* (Paris, 1902), pp. xi–xxx. This volume also has a frontispiece photograph, and a bibliography of Fabre's writings, pp. xxxii–xxxvi. For a longer biographical notice, see Aimé Puech and Georges Goyau in *Annuaire de l'Association amicale des anciens élèves de l'École Normale supérieure* (Paris, 1900), 120–35.

[45] Notice by his only American student, J. W. Thompson, in *The Nation*, LXXXVII (1908), 513–14. Funeral addresses in *ASMP*, CLXXI (1909), by A. de Foville, 589–92, and by Albert Croiset, 592–97. Imbart de la Tour, "Achilles Luchaire," in *RDM*, LII (1909), 876–901.

[46] Cp. his Latin thesis, *De lingua aquitanica* (Paris, 1877), reprinted in French with some additions as *Les origines linguistiques de l Aquitaine* (1877); also the *Étude sur les idiomes pyrénéens de la région française* (Paris, 1879), and his *Recueil de textes de l'ancien dialecte gascon* (Paris, 1881).

the author would continue to devote himself to the neglected field of the history of southwestern France. For a time, however, Luchaire, who was called to a professorship in the University of Bordeaux in 1879, continued in philology; he still had to find his métier.

In 1880 the Academy offered a prize of three thousand francs for the best study upon the progress of the royal power under the first six Capetian kings. Two years later Luchaire's memoir carried away the prize, and was published in revised form as *Histoire des institutions monarchiques de la France sous les premiers Capétiens, 987–1180* (2 v., 1883). This made Luchaire's reputation, and was followed by his *Études sur les actes de Louis VII* (Paris, 1885), which obtained the Prix Gobert of the Academy of Inscriptions, and *Louis VI le Gros; annales de sa vie et de son règne (1081–1137)* (Paris, 1890), prefaced by a valuable introduction. In 1890 appeared a volume of lectures he had delivered at the Sorbonne, *Les communes françaises à l'époque des Capétiens directs;* and in 1892 he brought out his *Manuel des institutions françaises, period des Capétiens directs*, an indispensable volume to every student of medieval institutions. To Lavisse's *Histoire de France* he contributed two volumes on the eleventh, twelfth, and early thirteenth centuries. The chapters devoted to Philip Augustus and the society of his time surpass anything ever written upon the subject. Luchaire's most popular work for the general reader was *La société française au temps de Philippe-Auguste*.[47] For years Luchaire had centered his researches upon the reign of this great French monarch, and no French scholar was better prepared for writing a detailed history of his reign.

But Luchaire abruptly changed from Capetian France to the history of Innocent III. The explanation is to be found in the fact that during the years he was writing on the early Capetians Professor Alexander Cartellieri of Heidelberg had begun to write his monumental history of the reign of Philip Augustus.[48] In the years 1902–07, Luchaire spent in Rome as much time as he could get from his university duties. In 1904 the first of his notable volumes upon Innocent III appeared. It was entitled *Innocent III: Rome et l'Italie;* and was followed in rapid succession by five other volumes with the sub-titles: *La croisade des Albigeois* (1905), *La Papauté et l'Empire* (1906), *La question d'Orient* (1907), *Les royautés vassales du Saint-Siège* (1908), and *Le concile de Latran et la reforme de l'église* (1908), the last containing a bibliography

    [47] 2nd ed., Paris, 1909. English translation by E. B. Krehbiel as: *Social France at the Time of Philip Augustus* (New York, 1912).
    [48] *Philipp II. August, König von Frankreich* (Leipzig and Paris, 1899–1921, 4 v. in 3). Luchaire reviewed the volumes as they appeared, cp. *RH*, LXXI (1899), 368–72, LXXII (1900), 181–88, 334–48, LXXIII (1900), 61–63, LXXVII (1901), 400–02, and XCIII (1907), 400–05.

for the six volumes. The volume on the Albigensian Crusade is undoubtedly his masterpiece. It is regrettable that Luchaire suppressed
his notes and references, though in the last volume he returned in part
to his old careful documentation, and analyzed or quoted many
sources.[49]

Paul Marie Viollet (1845–1914) [50] labored in the fields of the history
of French law and political institutions. He was a devout Roman
Catholic. After three years in the École des Chartes at Paris he graduated at the head of his class in 1862, with Gaston Paris holding the
second place. Viollet became archivist in his native Tours, and there
gathered the materials for his first publication, which illuminated an
obscure portion in the history of the Estates General. In 1866 he obtained a post in the Archives Nationales.

His first book, *Oeuvres chrétiennes des familles royales de France* (Paris,
1870), is a curious anthology ranging from the prayer of Clovis to the
testament of the unhappy daughter of Louis XVI. It is significant as
an expression of Viollet's philosophy of history. Behind ideas and the
slow and varying progress of society, Viollet posited a divine will; here,
as in his great *Histoire des institutions politiques et administratives de la
France* twenty years later, he summed his thought up in the old saying:
"l'homme s'agite et Dieu le mène."

In 1876 he was made librarian of the law library of the Faculté de
droit of Paris, and for thirty-six years, until his death, Viollet gave the
major part of his time to this work. But in spite of his duties he pursued his historical researches. For his masterly *Établissements de Saint
Louis* (4 v., 1881–86), he examined fifty-seven manuscripts, some of
which took him to Rome, Munich, and Stockholm. He proved that this
collection of medieval customs was not of an official nature, or issued
by the French king after which it is named, but was a compilation of
private law made by an Orleans lawyer.

In 1890 Viollet became professor of civil and canon law at the École de
Chartes, following his former teacher Adolphe Tardif, and in the same
year the first volume of his greatest work appeared, the *Histoire des*

---

[49] His texts had been studied most carefully, and some chapters had appeared first as
erudite memoirs in *RH* with the full armament of proofs and discussions: "Innocent III et le
peuple romain," LXXXI (1903), 225–57; "Innocent III et le quatrième concile de Latran,"
XCVII (1908), 225–63, and XCVIII (1908), 1–21. Other portions of his work, with detailed
notes can be found in *ASMP*, CLXI (1904), 490–514 and CLXV (1906), 513–28. In the
Bibliothèque de la Faculté des lettres of the University of Paris, fasc. 18 (1904), 1–83, Luchaire
published a critical study on "les Registres d'Innocent III et les 'Regesta' de Potthast."
When he began his second volume, he engaged with his students in the necessary task of a
new edition of the chronicle of Pierre des Vaux-de-Cernai, a fragment of which is printed in
the same *Bibliothèque*, fasc. 24 (1908), 1–75.

[50] Paul Fournier, in *Nouvelle revue historique de droit français et étranger*, XXXVIII (1914–15),
816–27; F. H. (comte) Delaborde, in *BEC*, LXXIX (1918), 147–75, of which pp. 171–75 contain a partial bibliography of Viollet's writings; Henry Lévy-Bruhl in *ESS*, XV, 267.

institutions (3 v., Paris, 1890–1903) previously mentioned. It covered the institutions of the three periods of the Gauls, the Gallo-Romans, and the Franks. Volumes II and III (1898 and 1903) completed the Middle Ages. A fourth volume under the separate title *Le roi et ses ministres pendant les trois derniers siècles de la monarchie* (1912) dealt with the workings of the French monarchy, with the conseils and the parlement and other organs in the state. Viollet held that in the last three centuries the French monarchy had experienced no new constitutional development.

Paul Fournier (1853–1935) [51] devoted a long life to canon law. Born in Calais, he came to Paris to study law (1871–74), and was licensed to practice. His thesis for the doctorate, *De collèges industriels dans l'Empire Romain*, augured a splendid future. Having a strong inclination for the history of institutions, he devoted four years to a course in the École des Chartes, which in these years when French scholarship was rising after the Franco-Prussian War was a "veritable nursery for the Institute." [52]

His thesis at the École des Chartes was printed the year after his graduation and remains a classic work on its subject. *Les officialités au moyen âge, étude sur l'organisation, la compétence et la procédure des tribunaux ecclésiastiques ordinaire en France de 1180 à 1328* (1880) showed a mastery of his method that the years were only to deepen. He was appointed to the chair of Roman law at Grenoble. In his thirty-three years at this university (from 1904 on he was *doyen*) he conceived a deep affection for the Dauphiné, and his interest in the south-east of France has left a permanent record in a volume entitled *Le royaume d'Arles et de Vienne, 1138–1378: étude sur la formation territoriale de la France dans l'Est et le Sud-Est* (1891). In 1914 he was named professor of Roman law at the University of Paris, and after the First World War a chair for the history of canon law was created there of which Fournier was the first incumbent.

Maassen of Germany had proposed to write a general history of the sources and works on canon law from the origins of the Church to the end of the Middle Ages. In his first and only volume (1870) he covered the first two of the three natural periods into which this history falls: the early period down to the collections of Dionysius Exiguus, and the second period which extends to the end of the eighth century. Another German, Friedrich von Schulte, covered an important section of Maassen's unfinished task in *Die Geschichte der Quellen und Literatur des*

---

[51] Roger Grand, "Paul Fournier," *BEC*, XCVII (1936), 228–32; and the notice on him by George La Piana, W. E. Lunt, and C. H. McIlwain, in the *Bulletin* of the Mediaeval Academy of America (1936).
[52] R. Grand, (n. 51), 228: "veritable pépinière de l'Institut."

canonischen Rechts von Gratian bis auf die Gegenwart (1875). But the two German scholars left untouched the keystone itself, that difficult period from the *False Decretals* to the time of Gratian's *Decretum*, when Europe witnessed the creation of hundreds of collections of canons, capitularies, and penitential books, and when the doctrine of papal supremacy expanded to universal jurisdiction in the church courts and became the chief starting-point in the new canon law.

Upon these sources, many of them still unexplored collections, extant only in the medieval manuscripts, Fournier threw himself with tireless energy. For twenty-five years he travelled over all Europe in his search of libraries, busy in the task of painstaking collation, criticism, and study of each group of manuscripts. A tremendous amount of palaeographical and critical labor was necessary to clear up their relations and to clarify the history of the transmission and use of each text.[53] Slowly but surely Fournier advanced through this land of confusion and made his results known. Between 1887 and 1927 he wrote forty-two learned articles and monographs. His achievement was summed up in the monumental *Histoire des collections canoniques en Occident depuis les Fausses Decretales jusqu'au Decret de Gratien* (2 v., 1931–32).[54]

Jacques Geoffroi Flach (1846–1919)[55] was a native of Strasbourg, where one of his ancestors had been professor of law at the university in the beginning of the seventeenth century. He too turned towards the legal profession, and after his classical and juristic studies (1854–63) in this same university was licensed to practice in 1866. Somewhat later he contributed to the *Revue historique de droit français* a valuable study on the history of a juridical theory.[56] His two theses for the doctorate were purely historical, which M. Bémont says was then a novelty.[57] This intimate connection between law and history was to be a

[53] A convinced Catholic, Fournier in the course of his travels made the acquaintance of Cardinal Ratti, then custodian of the Ambrosian library, and a lifelong friendship was begun which the Cardinal still remembered after his elevation as Pope Pius XI.

[54] Over three hundred items in his bibliography (prepared by Le Bras for the volume of *Mélanges* presented to Fournier by friends and pupils in 1929 when he retired from active teaching at the age of seventy-five) attest the breadth and erudition of this remarkable scholar. The Académie des inscriptions bestowed the Prix Gobert on his *Royaume d'Arles* in 1891 and later made him a member of their group (1901 corresponding member, 1914 titular member). He helped found the Société d'histoire du droit after the war, and was its president for fifteen years.

[55] Paul André, "Notice sur la vie et les travaux de M. Jacques Flach," *ASMP*, n.s., LXXXIII (1923), 173–200; Ch. Pfister, *ESS*, VI, 274; and reviews in *JS*, 1894, pp. 300–08 and 372–78, 1906, pp. 505; Charles Bémont in *RH*, CXXXIII (1920), 185–88; T. F. Tout in *EHR*, XX (1905), 141–43, and XXXV (1920), 587–90. Louis Halphen criticized the older man's work in *RH*, LXXV (1904), 271–85, to which Flach made a hot rejoinder, *ibid.*, LXXXVI (1904), 137–38.

[56] *De la Subrogation réelle*, issued in book form in 1870.

[57] *La "Bonorum possessio" sous les empereurs romains depuis le commencement du IIᵉ siècle jusqu'à Justinien exclusivement; Étude historique sur la durée et les effets de la minorité en droit romain et dans l'ancient droit français* (1870).

life-long distinction of Flach's writings. He was in Paris preparing for the agrégation de droit, when the news of his father's death obliged him to return to Strasbourg on the very eve of the Franco-Prussian War. When the disastrous siege of his city was over, he aided in the task of restoring the library and the museum and served on the Comité de secours.[58]   When Alsace passed into German hands, he gave up the thought of practice at home and shifted his life to Paris, to study at the École des Chartes and the École des Hautes Études. In the home of Gaston Paris he met celebrities like Taine, Sorel, Thurot, G. Monod. Flach was a very active member of the young Société de legislation comparée, and haunted the libraries of Paris in his studies of the history of law and of the high Middle Ages. Laboulaye, editor of the *Revue de droit français et étranger,* asked him to assist in his courses at the Collège de France (1879–80, 1882–83), and in 1884 Flach became his successor in the chair of comparative law. From 1877 on he also taught comparative civil law at the École des Sciences Politiques.

Flach began with studies on legal principles under the Roman emperors, and then, following Savigny, gave attention to the teaching of law in the Middle Ages and the Renaissance,[59] and to problems of old French law.[60]   He dealt repeatedly with the history and institutions of Ireland,[61] wrote on Austria-Hungary, the agrarian problem of Russia, and Chinese and Japanese problems. Sometimes his studies roamed far afield: he wrote a work on *Madame Krudenier et les origines de la Sainte-Alliance* (1889), another on *Mirabeau* (1891), on the primitive aborigines of America, Africa, and Oceanica,[62] on feminism, or even the Judaeo-Babylonian problem. He was interested in literary figures, and wrote a book on Alexander Pushkin.[63]   It was characteristic that he always acquired the language of a people before turning to its institutions. Thus he mastered Hungarian, Russian, and Assyrian, and

[58] He related its activity in *Strasbourg après le bombardement, 2 octobre 1870–30 septembre 1872* (1873).

[59] *Cujas: les Glossateurs et les Bartolistes* (1883).   Professor Bémont lists as other of his studies pertaining to Roman law: *La table de bronze d'Aljustrel, étude sur l'administration des mines au Ier siècle de notre ère* (1879); *Études critiques sur l'histoire du droit romain au moyen âge,* with unedited texts (1890); and *Le droit romain dans les chartes du IXe au XIe siècle,* in the *Mélanges Fitting* (Montpellier, 1908).

[60] *Axiomes du droit français par le sieur Catherinot,* with a notice on the life and the writings of the author by Ed. Laboulaye and a bibliographie raisonnée of Catherinot's works by J. Flach (1883); *Notes et documents sur l'origine des redevances et services coutumiers au XIe siècle* (1882).

[61] *Histoire du régime agraire de l'Irlande* (1883); *Jonathan Swift, son action politique en Irlande* (1886); *Le gouvernement local de l'Irlande* (1889); *Considérations sur l'histoire politique de l'Irlande* (1885).

[62] On primitive institutions, cp. his works *Les Institutions primitives; Le Lévirat et les origines de la famille* (1900); *La Poésie et le symbolisme dans l'histoire des institutions humaines* (1910).

[63] *Un grand poète russe: Alexandre Pouchkine* (1894).

when he began to write on the Code of Hammurabi was in a position to study the oldest legislation of the world directly from the cuneiform text.[64] A historical approach and the use of original sources marked Flach's treatment of social and legislative problems. His busy pen also produced various volumes on the history of political theories.[65]

In the medieval field, Flach wrote a volume, *L'Origine de l'habitation et des lieux habités en France* (1899), which dealt critically with the theories of August Meitzen in Germany and Arbois de Jubainville in France. His reputation as a great historian of medieval institutions reposes chiefly, however, on the four volumes of his greatest work, *Les Origines de l'ancienne France*, which appeared slowly and at long intervals.[66] Its pages were quarried exclusively from the sources: from published and unpublished charters, chartularies, chronicles, lives of saints, and even from the chansons de geste. Like Coulanges he contended that early medieval France owed no appreciable debt to Germanic influence, and that Gaul was not regenerated by the Germanic invasions. In the matter of the origin of feudalism, Flach stressed the survival and persistence of ancient Celtic practice and made more of personal than of property relations. Vassalage, he thought, was directly derived from Celtic clientage, and owed almost nothing to the German *comitatus*.

[64] *La propriété collective en Chaldée et la prétendue féodalité militaire du code de Hammourabi* (1907; cp. *RH*, XCV, 309); *Le Code de Hammourabi et la constitution originaire de la propriété dans l'ancienne Chaldée* (1907).

[65] *Platon et Montesquieu théoriciens politiques* (1908); *La Souveraineté du peuple et le suffrage politique de la femme* (1910); *Sully, homme de guerre et homme d'État* (1911); *Thomas Morus et l'île d'Utopie* (1912).

[66] *Le régime seigneurial* (1886); *Les origines communales, la féodalité et la chevalerie* (1893); *La Renaissance de l'État, la royauté et le principat* (1904); *Les Nationalités régionales. Leurs rapports avec la couronne de France* (1917). A fifth volume was in press in 1920.

CHAPTER LII

ENGLISH HISTORIANS OF INSTITUTIONS IN THE NINETEENTH CENTURY

ENGLISH institutional history was a fledgling until after the middle of the nineteenth century. The Germans and the French were far ahead. As late as 1904 a writer in the *Quarterly Review* deplored that English institutional history was so largely left to German scholarship. The British line may be said to have begun with Hallam's *Constitutional History of England from the Accession of Henry VII to the Death of George II* (3 v., 1827). But actually no promising start was made until Kemble published his *Saxons in England* (1849). Here was the first trustworthy account of the political and social institutions of the Anglo-Saxons. The brilliant and indefatigable student of the Anglo-Saxon charters had made his studies in Germany, notably under Jacob Grimm, and read German fluently. In almost every institution of early England, with the single exception of the Church, he found signs of Germanic origin. It was Kemble who imported into English historiography that touchstone of early German institutionalists, the *Mark*.[1] Against Kemble, Palgrave maintained the theory of the continuity of Roman influence upon British institutions after the Anglo-Saxon invasions, and was England's first great Romanist before the days of Seebohm. But the Romanist school failed to flourish, and the Germanist doctrines triumphed in the volumes of Freeman and the pages of John Richard Green. They and the lesser luminaries associated with them leaned heavily upon the German school.

The broadest view of the nature and importance of medieval institutions was held by Bishop Stubbs. "The history of institutions," he wrote in a preface which has become classic among historians, "cannot be mastered, can scarcely be approached without an effort. It affords little of the romantic incident or of the picturesque grouping which constitute the charm of history in general, and holds out small temptation to the mind that requires to be tempted to the study of truth. But

---

[1] The *Mark* theory, originated by Justus Möser, was developed by K. F. Eichhorn in his *Deutsche Staats- und Rechtsgeschichte* (1808), a work whose many editions became the standard history of German law. "His Mark theory was destined to become the cornerstone of the whole constitutional and legal history of that country" (Alfons Dopsch, *The Economic and Social Foundations of European Civilization*, London, 1937, p. 8. The whole first chapter of this book deals with the historiography of German institutional writers).

it has a deep value and an abiding interest to those who have the courage to work upon it. It presents, in every branch, a regularly developed series of causes and consequences, and abounds in examples of that continuity of life the realization of which is necessary to give the reader a personal hold on the past and a right judgment of the present. *For the roots of the present lie deep in the past, and nothing in the past is dead to the man who would learn how the present comes to be what it is."*

Stubbs' *Constitutional History of England* (3 v., 1874–78), which has been noticed elsewhere, virtually created a new discipline among English-speaking students on both sides of the Atlantic. So well did this English Waitz do his work that his three volumes, supplemented and corrected by English and French scholars in later years, still form the greatest book ever written upon English constitutional history. Stubbs had no theories to advance, no principle to demonstrate. He aimed solely at a correct understanding of the facts.[2] Stubbs opened to English workers an almost virgin field, indicated manuscript sources of unsuspected richness, and supplied the example of an austere method which left permanent traces upon later scholars.

The advance of English institutional history after Stubbs was along various lines: in Anglo-Saxon history, in the history of law, and again in problems of social and economic conditions. The great controversy in the last decades of the nineteenth century was still over the German-Roman issue. In the historical treatment of medieval society the distinction between feudalism and manorialism was not yet perceived. It was not until Arnold and Nitzsch in Germany, Fustel de Coulanges in France, and Maitland and Vinogradoff in England wrote that the subject began to be cleared up. Before them, a false analogy between fiefs and tenures prevailed; the manor was regarded as the lowest feudal unit, whereas it is now known that it was fundamentally an economic unit, and only incidentally of a political nature at all.

Understanding of the nature of early English institutions was greatly helped by the introduction of the comparative method by Sir Henry Maine (1822–88).[3] As Sir Frederick Pollock has said, Maine "did

[2] He deprecated popular demands for literary polish and finesse, referring to some "fireworks" of his as quite unworthy of remembrance. "The pleasant part of it," he wrote of his *History* in retrospect, "is but trifling, and the solid part, I fear, makes dull reading."

[3] Sir M. E. Grant Duff, *Sir Henry Maine; a Brief Memoir of His Life*, with some of his Indian speeches and minutes, selected and edited by W. Stokes (London, 1892); R. Dareste, "Notice sur la vie et les travaux de M. Sumner Maine," *ASMP*, CXXXI (1889), 598–611; William S. Holdsworth, *The Historians of Anglo-American Law* (New York, 1928); P. Vinogradoff, "The Teaching of Sir Henry Maine," *Law Quarterly Review*, XX (1904), 119–33, reprinted in his *Collected Papers* (Oxford, 1928, 2 v.), II, 173–89; William Graham, *English Political Philosophy from Hobbes to Maine* (London, 1899), 348–415; J. H. Landman, "Primitive Law, Evolution, and Sir Henry Maine," *Michigan Law Review*, XXVIII (1930), 404–25; Leslie Stephen in *DNB*, XXXV, 343–46; K. Smellie in *ESS*, X, 49–50; *Warner's Library of the World's Best Literature*, XVI (1917), 9605–16.

nothing less than create the natural history of law." In 1852 he was appointed first reader on Roman law and jurisprudence at the Inns of Court. His first book was *Ancient Law* (1861), in which he had a clear notion of the role of custom in the development of law. Sir Frederick Pollock later said of it: "The final solution will be found, whenever it is found, by working with the instruments which Maine has left us." [4] A great advance was his appreciation of the constant change in law, and his application of a kind of evolution, analogous to the great discovery Darwin had just published for the field of biology, to human institutions.

In 1861 Maine was offered the post of legal adviser of the Council of India, once held by Macaulay. After seven years he returned to England and was appointed to the Corpus professorship of Jurisprudence just established at Oxford (1869). The knowledge he had accumulated during his years in India appeared in his *Village Communities in the East and West* (1871), in which he drew an analogy between the living institutions of nineteenth-century India and those of Anglo-Saxon England. One of his statements in this work was that two kinds of knowledge were indispensable if historical and philosophical jurisprudence was to prosper in England: a knowledge of India, and a knowledge of Roman law. The former, because "it is the great repository of verifiable phenomena of ancient usage and ancient juridical thought; of Roman Law, because . . . it connects these ancient usages and this ancient juridical thought with the legal ideas of our own day." [5] He opened a new field with his thirteen lectures on the *Early History of Institutions* (1875). In some respects the book was a continuation of his *Ancient Law*. The comparative approach was still the same; but this time Maine devoted much space to the new materials for legal and social history which British scholars had found in the translations of the Brehon (ancient Irish) Laws, and to the sacred legal code of the Hindus. He threw a curious light upon the resemblances between primitive Aryan institutions and primitive Irish institutions. [6]

From Oxford Maine shifted to Cambridge when he was chosen Master of Trinity Hall (1877); his successor in the Corpus professorship at Oxford was Sir Frederick Pollock. *Dissertations on Early Law and Custom* (1883) was a revision of some of Maine's Oxford lectures and

---

[4] Quoted in Grant-Duff (n. 3), 2–21.   [5] *Ibid.*, 38–39.

[6] Comparing the Brehon mention of the Druids' with Caesar's account of them, he explains how Caesar, from his distant perspective, did not seize correctly all details of Celtic society and its many gradations, but made three general classes. "It had the imperfections of the view obtained by looking on the Gangetic plains from the slopes of the Himalayas. The impression made is not incorrect, but an immensity of detail is lost to the observer, and a surface varied by countless small elevations looks perfectly flat." Maine goes on to ascribe Caesar's fault to "mental distance," i.e., he was used to the Roman's legal idea of equality, much as (continues Maine) English administrators sent out to India often fail to understand Indian social conceptions because of their English background. Grant-Duff (n. 3), 44–46.

various published articles, in which the Sacred Books of the East, as translated under the supervision of Professor Max Mueller, provided the material for discussion.   But none of Maine's books achieved the sales of his *Popular Government* (1885), in which he desired to apply the historical method to the political institutions of man, as he had previously studied their private laws and institutions.   The work offended many readers who construed it as an attack upon democracy.[7] Maine's greatest gift to the world, however, remained his *Ancient Law*, which reads like literature as well as philosophy. Maine concerned himself chiefly with the origins of civilization, and valued the rich materials of legal history rather as a means than as an end. His historical and comparative method ended the sway of the Austinian school of positivist law. Sir Frederick Pollock, a decade after he succeeded Maine in the Oxford chair, said:

Maine . . . can no more become obsolete through the industry and ingenuity of modern scholars than Montesquieu could be made obsolete by the legislation of Napoleon. Facts will be corrected, the order and proportion of ideas will vary, new difficulties will call for new ways of solution, useful knowledge will serve its turn and be forgotten; but in all true genius, perhaps, there is a touch of Art; Maine's genius was not only touched with Art, but eminently artistic; and Art is immortal.[8]

The problem of the proportion of the ingredients—Roman, German, and Celtic—found in feudalism did not attract great attention until 1872–73. In the former year Maine's *Village Communities in East and West* appeared, in the latter year the first volume of Stubbs' *Constitutional History of England* came out, which embodied *in toto* the doctrines of Maurer and Waitz about the German Mark, its political nature, economy and social structure. When Denman Ross came to Oxford seven years later and ventured to disagree with Maurer and—what was heinous—with Stubbs, "he was promptly butchered to make an Oxford holiday." [9]   Assistance came to Denman Ross in 1883 when Sir Frederic Seebohm's *English Village Community* asserted that from the very beginning of English history many villages were "communities in serfdom under a manorial lordship" (preface, p. ix), and seemingly never had been free. Either the Angles and Saxons brought serfs over sea with them, or else the Roman servile villa-system had survived in

---

[7] In the preface he declared that just as he found legal studies blocked by baseless theories about a law and state of nature before any man-made laws, so he found his political investigations blocked by similarly foolish assumptions of political institutions not recorded by history, but eulogized by Rousseau and others, and these institutions of a far-off time they held to be of a highly popular character!

[8] Quoted in Grant-Duff (n. 3), 48.

[9] The quotation is from W. Ashley, "The History of English Serfdom," *Economic Review*, III (1893), 155, 153–73. Ross' work was *The Early History of Land Holding among the Germans* (Boston, 1883).

Britain with sufficient strength to contaminate the German free village communities. Either conclusion was anathema to English historians of the day.

But Frederic Seebohm (1833–1912) [10] started the reaction against the romantic Germanistic views which had persisted so long through the advocacy of Freeman and Green. Seebohm belonged to that unique group of English bankers and business men who have also been able to achieve an enviable reputation for research and literary brilliancy: George Grote, Sir John Lubbock (Lord Avebury), Walter Bagehot, and Thomas Hodgkin. Like the last-named, Seebohm was a Quaker and a man of deep religious convictions. His father was descended from Swedish ancestors. In his boyhood he observed the struggle of the handloom weavers of West Riding against the incoming machinery, and an interest in the economic conditions of the lower classes remained with him through life. The lectures of Sir Henry Maine first stirred his interest in history. He settled in the town of Hitchin, in northern Hertfordshire, as a local banker, and became a local magistrate.

His first notable book, *The Oxford Reformers* (1867), portrayed the influence of Colet, Erasmus, and More; and this was followed by *The Era of the Protestant Revolution* (1874). But Seebohm's fame as a scholar rests on *The English Village Community* (1883), into which went fifteen years of intense researches. It marked a milestone in the study of the economic history of medieval England, and though all that Seebohm advanced in this humble "essay" has not gone unchallenged, it was a master's contribution. In articles in the *Fortnightly Review*, 1865–70, he had traced the historical conditions behind England's population in the past, and his attention was drawn to the forms of economic organization which supported that population. In the countryside around Hitchin he could still find traces of the open-field system which had dominated English agriculture for more than a thousand years. His new volume carried this form of community farming, with its disadvantages of compulsion and strip intermixture, back to the manorial system. At this point he broke with the traditional views, and arguing from the known to the unknown pushed back into Anglo-Saxon and even Roman times. He concluded that manorialism had already existed in the *villa* of the Romans. Seebohm's work in England was simultaneous with that of Fustel de Coulanges in France and to much the same end, although his sources were different.

Seebohm found other problems in the subject of Celtic ingredients.

---

[10] See Reginald Hine, *Hitchin Worthies: Four Centuries of English Life* (London, 1932), 324–33; cp. review *LTLS*, 1932, p. 937; and the excellent centenary notice of Seebohm, *ibid.*, 1933, p. 824; Paul Vinogradoff in *DNB*, supplement III (1912–21), 488–90; see also the interesting appreciation of Seebohm in Vinogradoff's *Collected Papers* (n. 3), I, 272–76.

He investigated the scattered homesteads of Wales and other Celtic localities, and the vestiges of common tillage in the home countries of England. In Wales he met the phenomenon of co-aration practiced by the joint family. *The Tribal System in Wales* (1895) sought to get at the bottom of such peculiarities or anomalies in medieval organization.[11]

Tribal Customs in Anglo-Saxon Law (1902) is inferior to the last two works, but belongs to the trilogy. *Customary Acres* (1914) is a posthumous publication of Seebohm's unfinished studies on the continuity of land measurements and kindred topics. He worked until his last illness, "ploughing his headlands," it has been said, like the peasant sketched in his unfinished book, "nearing his end with laboured breath." In the words of Vinogradoff: "It was a beautiful end for a searcher after truth, symbolizing the eternal striving after the light, an end vouchsafed only to the best and purest among us."

Paul Vinogradoff (1854–1925)[12] was not an Englishman, but a Russian, trained in German seminars. His father had been principal of a school in Moscow. Vinogradoff entered the University of Moscow at sixteen, when it was flourishing; he attended Guerrier's seminar on the social and economic history of the Middle Ages, and won a gold medal with a brilliant thesis on landed property in the Merovingian period. A scholarship enabled him to spend a year at the University of Berlin, and to study in the seminars of Mommsen and Brunner (1875–76). To Mommsen he ascribed the chief scholarly inspiration of his life; from Brunner he received instruction in German law, and from Schäfer at Bonn he heard Greek history. The visit to Germany was only the first

[11] "Celtic custom was probably one reason why the West of England has always been, from very early times, a land of enclosed fields and small hamlets. But much must also be allowed for the nature of the soil. For even the Nordic invaders did not establish the open-field system and the large nucleated township in districts not suited to agriculture on the large scale—not for instance on the moors of the North, or in the fruit gardens of Kent, or in districts that remained largely woodland. But the Saxons did establish the open-field and the large nucleated township in most of the East and Midlands. The question is: had the Celts the open-field system and the nucleated village in those eastern cornlands, afterwards taken over by the Saxons? Seebohm thought that they had, and Vinogradoff that they had not. There is no certain evidence. 'Air photography' of areas in Wiltshire and Hampshire produces results said to be unfavourable to Seebohm's hypothesis, and to indicate Celtic methods of enclosure and agriculture which the Romans left unaltered but the Saxon conquerors superseded. See O. G. S. Crawford, *Air-Survey and Archaeology* (Southampton, 1928), 3–10." [This is G. M. Trevelyan's note at the end of the first chapter of his *History of England* (London and New York, 1926), 13–14.]

[12] H. A. L. Fisher, *Paul Vinogradoff, a Memoir* (Oxford, 1927); cp. also Fisher's memoir in Vinogradoff's *Collected Papers* (Oxford, 1928, 2 v.), I, 1–94; W. S. Holdsworth's obituary notice in the *British Academy Publications*, no. 401; the same, *The Historians of Anglo-American Law* (n. 3), 84–91; and his article, "Sir Paul Vinogradoff," *Slavonic Review*, IV (1926), 529–44; Bernard Pares, "The Public Man," *ibid.*, 544–51; A. Meyendorff, "Sir Paul Vinogradoff, a bibliographical appreciation," *ibid.*, V (1927), 156–69; Francis de Zulueta, "Sir Paul Vinogradoff, 1854–1925," *Law Quarterly Review*, XLII (1926), 202–11; F. M. Powicke in *EHR*, XLI (1926), 236 and 496, and reviews, *ibid.*, XLV (1930), 208–31, 177–207, 323–24; XXXIX (1924), 424–25; VII (1892), 444–65; *CQR*, XXXVIII (1894), 169–82; *AHR*, XI (1905–06), 361–65; XIV (1908–09), 102–04; XXVI (1920), 749–52.

of many journeys abroad which, in connection with Vinogradoff's masterly linguistic ability, made him a consummate cosmopolitan.[13]

In 1877 he began to teach at the University of Moscow. His first public paper, written in German on a medieval topic, dealt with the legal aspect of manumission. His first book (1881) was a treatise on the origins of the feudal system in Italy. Thus the legal aspect of his interests was early apparent. Two years later he came to England to work for fifteen months in the Public Record Office and the great British libraries. In 1884 this foreigner opened the eyes of British scholars to their neglected treasures. His famous letter to the *Athenaeum* (July 19, 1884) announced the discovery of Bracton's Note-Book; and in a chance meeting he gave the eager Maitland the first full insight into the matchless materials for legal history locked away in Britain's repositories: tons of plea rolls from which a vanished life and society could be restored.[14]

In 1884 Vinogradoff obtained the doctorate in history at Moscow and was advanced, first to extraordinary and then to full professor (1887) at the university. He was busy with a work on English land tenures and wrote for the *Vierteljahrschrift füer Sozial- und Wirtschafts- geschichte*. He wrote a school *Manual of Universal History*, drew up plans for the reorganization of the secondary school system, and became chairman of the educational committee in the Moscow Municipal Duma. He later manifested the same zest for teaching at Oxford. In Moscow the liberal views of Vinogradoff were doomed to collide with a reactionary government. He felt it impossible to continue teaching and resigned in 1901. In 1903 he succeeded Sir Frederick Pollock in the Corpus chair of Jurisprudence at Oxford, which he held until his death in 1925.

Vinogradoff's writings may be divided into two classes: those which deal with medieval English society and law, and those devoted more strictly to the theory of the law. Many readers are unaware that *Villainage in England* (1887) was first written and published in the Russian language, and not printed in English form until five years after (1892). Here was a new study on the social and legal aspects of the medieval English villein, which profited by Vinogradoff's acquaintance with the history of land systems in another country and another kind of village community. The first of the two essays comprising the book Maitland hailed enthusiastically as "by far the greatest thing done for

---

[13] He spoke twelve languages in middle life, and wrote in at least five. When he began the study of early English history, e.g., he felt it obligatory to master not only the history of Scandinavian institutions as well, but also Scandinavian tongues. It was on a prolonged stay in Norway that he met his future wife.

[14] H. A. L. Fisher, *Frederick William Maitland* (Cambridge, 1910), 24–25.

English legal history." It was a study on the legal aspects of villeinage. Its conclusions, which are generally accepted today, rejected the notion of an unbroken servile system of land tenure from the time of the Romans, espoused by such writers as Seebohm, and declared that the free village communities of early England were agrarian, and of German origin, instead of political, Roman-organized communities. Norman feudalism and the disorder following the Conquest changed the status of some of the free-holders. Seebohm objected to Vinogradoff's inferences but allowed that the picture of villeinage in the first two centuries after the Conquest was a high achievement.[15] His second essay treated the manor, the village community, and the open-field system. A very valuable portion of the book was the historiographical introduction, in which Vinogradoff assessed the contributions of previous writers. By bringing the English writers into the same list as the great continental workers stimulated by Savigny and Ihering, he gave a salutary jog to British insularity of mind and compelled some revision of their estimates of their own authorities.[16]

When Vinogradoff came to write his next book the great question of his earlier years had become a dead issue: how far can legislation affect the social advance of an agrarian community? The English villeins had ceased to have a living connection with his own Russia, throttled by a reactionary government. But writers like Maitland, Round, and Seebohm had continued to till the field. In the *Growth of the Manor* (1905) Vinogradoff took inventory of what had been done. Based upon his lectures it revealed his masterly power of harmonizing arguments and co-ordinating varied information. The book is full of "steady, broad-based generalizations" and its best feature is the clear description of the place which the manor occupied in the medieval state, a role comparable to that of the *civitas* in antiquity. Celtic influence was heavily stressed,[17] and English scholars were again warned that though the manor is strictly an English institution, they could not neglect to study the French *seigneurie* and the German *Grundherrschaft*.

English Society in the Eleventh Century (1908) presents two essays which are more elaborate and more original than the work just men-

---

[15] *EHR*, VII (1892), 444–65.

[16] Maitland put it almost quaintly: "All that you say about Stubbs and Seebohm and Maine is, I dare say, very true if you regard them as European, not merely English, phenomena and attribute to them a widespread significance—and doubtless it is very well that Englishmen should see this. . . . You are cosmopolitan and I doubt not that you are right. You are putting things in a new light—that is all—if 'the darkness comprehendeth it not,' that is the darkness's fault." Quoted in Fisher (n. 14), 50–51, and also by Holdsworth in *Slavonic Review* (n. 12), 532.

[17] "The history of Great Britain," he once declared, "rises on a rock-bed of Celtic institutions and customs." See preface, p. v. to the *Survey of the Honour of Denbigh, 1334*, ed. by Paul Vinogradoff and Frank Morgan (London, 1914).

tioned. In this book Vinogradoff returned to a fresh study of Domesday Book and other sources for the important eleventh century, which he called "the watershed in the development of English society." It is a difficult work to read, but experts find it valuable. Gathering up the various elements—Celtic, Saxon, Danish, and Norman—which went to form English society in this period, Vinogradoff produced a more detailed picture of eleventh-century society than any writer before him.

Many of Vinogradoff's shorter writings furnished valuable contributions to medieval social history. His various chapters in the *Cambridge Medieval History* sweep over a period from the fourth to the twelfth century and exemplify his sound knowledge of Roman law and the sources for early medieval history.[18] The *Survey of the Honour of Denbigh* (1914), which he edited for the British Academy with Mr. Frank Morgan, is important as the survey of a tract of land on the border between England and Wales, preserving much of importance on Welsh tribal law. The paper in the *Athenaeum* on Bracton's Note-Book has been mentioned, and his essay "The Text of Bracton" was a sequel to it.[19] Maitland said that Vinogradoff "had learned in a few weeks more about Bracton's text than any Englishman has known since Selden died." For the Year Books of the reign of Edward II he prepared careful editions, revealing his intimate acquaintance with complicated procedure. Professor Powicke has said that he used fourteenth-century legal terms as if he were a practicing lawyer of the time rather than an historical student living centuries after. On the other hand he was much less familiar with modern English law after that time and so failed to see, as Maitland could, the elements that became important in subsequent centuries. Few students can afford to neglect his little volume *Roman Law in Mediaeval Europe* (1909), "the only up-to-date authority in English," where he made continental researches available to English readers. Most famous of all his briefer writings, however, was the essay on *Folkland*,[20] in which he demolished the current theory, begun by Allen, that folkland meant *ager publicus*, and restored the seventeenth-century interpretation of Sir Henry Spelman, that it was land held by private persons according to the folk or customary law.

For many years after Maitland's death Vinogradoff acted as literary director of the Selden Society (1908–18). He superintended a series of *Records in Economic and Social History* for the British Academy. The task of editor was never quite agreeable to him, but he devoted

---

[18] *Cambridge Medieval History* (New York, 1911–36, 8 v.), I, ch. xix; II, ch. xx; III, ch. xviii. The last chapter is the important one in this collaborative work which describes feudalism and feudal theory in its heyday, 1000–1200 A.D.

[19] Published in *Law Quarterly Review*, I (1885), 189–200.

[20] *EHR*, VIII (1893), 1–17, reprinted in his *Collected Papers* (n. 12), I, 91–111.

sympathetic attention to the *Oxford Studies in Social and Legal History* (vols. I–IX, 1909–27). These were not restricted to the Middle Ages but were chiefly the work of his own students, and their quality is a testimony to the training in Vinogradoff's seminar at Oxford—an institution which the former pupil of Mommsen and Brunner introduced to the English university.

Vinogradoff's writings after the first decade of the twentieth century were juristic rather than historical, such as *Roman Law in Medieval Europe, Common Sense in Law,* and the article on comparative jurisprudence in the *Encyclopaedia Britannica.* The *Outlines of Historical Jurisprudence* never got beyond the first two volumes.[21] "His knowledge of the early history of England and English law was possessed by no continental historian or lawyer; and his knowledge of continental history and law was possessed by no English historian or lawyer." [22]

Frederick William Maitland (1850–1906) [23] was called by Vinogradoff the greatest historian of the law of England, and Lord Acton went even farther and termed him "the ablest historian in England" at a time when Stubbs, Gardiner, and Creighton were living. This charming Ariel of English historiography, who bore the weight of a tremendous erudition so lightly, and wove his gossamer prose about subjects ordinarily held dry and abstruse, was born in London, of intellectual parentage.[24] His mind was at first drawn to philosophy, and in Cambridge he fell under the influence of Henry Sidgwick. Family tradition, however, took him to Lincoln's Inn (1872), and in 1876 he was called to the bar. For eight years he was concerned with conveyancing, and always maintained that this training was valuable for one dealing with medieval

[21] 1920, 1922. See the reviews by Lord Bryce and Ernest Barker, *EHR*, XXXVI (1921), 237–39 and XXXIX (1924), 424–25, respectively.

[22] Holdsworth in *Slavonic Review* (n. 12), 530.

[23] See the bibliography appended to the article by B. Fossett Lock, in *DNB*, supplement for 1912–21, pp. 488–90; H. A. L. Fisher, *Frederick William Maitland* (Cambridge, 1910), and *The Collected Papers of Frederick William Maitland,* edited by the same (Cambridge, 1911); Arthur Smith, *Frederick William Maitland* (Oxford, 1908), with bibliography; Sir Frederick Pollock, "F. W. Maitland," *QR*, CCVI (1907), 401–19, and reviews in CCVIII (1908), 59–62, CCXVIII (1912), 413–36; P. Vinogradoff in *EHR*, XXII (1907), 280–88, cp. his *Collected Papers* (n. 12), I, 253–64, and 265–71; Charles Haskins, "Frederick William Maitland," *Proceedings of the American Academy of Arts and Sciences,* LI (1916), no. 14, pp. 504–05; Sir F. Pollock in *Proceedings of the British Academy* (1905–06), 455–60. There is a series of appreciations from many learned individuals in the *Law Quarterly Review,* XXIII (1907), 137–50. See also Edward Cheyney in *International Monthly,* I (1900), 400–05; *Political Science Quarterly,* XXII, 287; Ernest Barker, "Maitland as a Sociologist," *Sociological Review,* XXIX (1937), 121–35; T. F. Tout in *Scottish Historical Review,* VIII, 73–75, cp. IX, 81–84; an obituary of Maitland in *Manchester Guardian,* December 24, 1906; ASHLEY, 87–91; and reviews in *CQR,* LVI (1903), 118–42; *AHR,* XIV (1908–09), 338–39, III (1897–98), 130–33, I (1895–96), 112–20, IV (1898–99), 143–45; *EHR,* IX (1894), 755–58, XII (1897), 768–77, XIV (1899), 344–46, XV (1900), 293–302, XVII (1902), 358–61, XLV (1930), 177–207.

[24] His grandfather S. R. Maitland was the noted author of *The Dark Ages* (London, 1844); his mother's father had been a distinguished physicist and a fellow of the Royal Society at the age of twenty-three.

documents. But his interests turned from the practice of the law to its history and theory. He read Savigny's *Geschichte des römischen Rechts*, and even began a translation of it. The *Constitutional History* of Stubbs acquainted him with the prodigious amount of materials awaiting students in English archives. He acquired his own working knowledge of palaeography and diplomatics and conceived the ambition of doing for English law what Savigny had done for the Roman law on the Continent. Then occurred the decisive hour in his life, when on a Sunday tramp in 1884 he met Vinogradoff, who turned Maitland forever from the practice to the study of law. Maitland dedicated his first volume, the *Pleas for the Crown for the County of Gloucester* (1884) to Vinogradoff.

This work, and Maitland's record as a lawyer, obtained for him the election as Reader of English Law at Cambridge (1884). This readership was only a recent creation. In four years he was advanced to Downing professor of the laws of England (1888). Cambridge enjoyed his teaching for twenty-two years. His appointment afforded him much leisure for research and writing, and despite his precarious health (which always drove him southward in winter) he accomplished a prodigious amount before his premature death at fifty-six.[25]

Maitland's inaugural lecture, "Why the History of English Law is Not Written," set forth his own aims and appealed to fellow workers. He wanted to see a scientific and philosophical history from the time of origins, embracing all that related to the economic, political, constitutional, social, and religious life of the English nation.[26] Since no man could undertake the task single-handed, Maitland became the prime mover in the organization of the Selden Society (1887), the purpose of which was to publish the sources for English legal history. The introductions to his own eight volumes in this series illustrate his wide learning and his brilliant writing.

The year 1887 also saw the appearance of Maitland's *Bracton's Note-Book*. The letter of Vinogradoff in the *Athenaeum* had tentatively identified a manuscript in the British Museum with the materials the great medieval legist must have collected for his *De legibus et consuetudinibus Angliae*. Maitland edited this manuscript in three volumes, and con-

---

[25] Professor Haskins noted with regret: "It is, however, characteristic of the English university system that the duties of his professorship consisted of general lectures to undergraduates on the elements of law rather than of the training of scholars in his special field, so that he formed no school of disciples who could develop or continue his work." *Proceedings of the American Academy of Arts and Sciences* (n. 23), 904.

[26] His attitude toward legal history is illustrated by a quotation from Albert Sorel which he loved so well: "C'est toute la tragédie, toute la comédie humaine que met en scène sous nos yeux l'histoire de nos lois." Cp. F. W. Maitland, *Yearbooks of Edward II* (London, 1903), I, p. xx.

firmed his friend's brilliant hypothesis. In an introductory essay he explained how the thirteenth-century scholar probably worked, excerpting official plea rolls.

Bracton's Note-Book was the first of various works and editions that Maitland now launched in rapid succession, the most important of which are the *Yearbooks of Edward II* (as far as 1310), *Domesday Book and Beyond* (1897), *Township and Borough* (1898), and *Roman Canon Law in the Church of England* (1898).[27] Maitland's teaching has become part of the very texture of constitutional history.[28] His *History of English Law before the Time of Edward I* at once became an authoritative text for the period it covers. Maitland and Pollock hold that the law of Anglo-Saxon times was mainly Teutonic, and that whatever Roman influence is apparent came through the Franks after the Conquest. *Domesday Book and Beyond* is a masterpiece of inverse reasoning from the known to the unknown, in which Maitland contended that there was no homogeneous servile manorial system before the Norman Conquest, but that there were several types of land-holding, and many free peasants. The work consists of three essays; the first deals with conditions in *Domesday Book* itself, the second is on the state of England at the eve of the Norman Conquest, and the third deals with the meaning of the "hide," a question which appears purely technical but is actually of basic importance. Maitland showed that in the eleventh century the manor could not have had an areal meaning. "A manor is a house against which *geld* is charged," i.e., a unit of taxation, and not primarily a village or an agricultural whole, but the place where the tax upon certain land and its occupants was due in one lump sum. This definition concerned the old debated question as to whether the English people began in serfdom and rose to freedom, as Seebohm and Ashley claimed, or whether they were reduced from a previous condition of liberty, as Freeman, Green, and others held. According to Maitland, the term "manor" in *Domesday Book* did not suggest either serfdom or jurisdiction. The manor was created as a unit of taxation by the government; village and manor were not identical, and the lordless village was the normal thing.[29] Round rejected Maitland's definition of "manor," and it has not gained ground since.[30] In the quarrel of Romanist and Germanist, Maitland lined up as a "moderate Germanist."[31] If we are to conclude that England was full of Roman "villas," he wrote, we must equally infer from Bede's language that

[27] There is a full bibliography of his writings in A. L. Smith (n. 23).
[28] Cp. *LTLS*, 1937, p. 168.
[29] Cp. the analysis by E. P. Cheyney in *International Monthly*, I (1900), 401–03.
[30] J. H. Round, "The Domesday Manor," *EHR*, XV (1900), 302.
[31] James Tait, *ibid.*, XII (1897), 768–77.

she was full of Persian satraps. A reviewer declared that "it is not too much to say that for the first time Domesday as a whole stands revealed, not fully indeed, but in its most essential features." [32]

In his *Roman Canon Law in the Church of England* (1898) Maitland proved that supremacy of Roman canon law in England before the Reformation was virtually uncontested, and combatted the Anglican Church view, supported even by Bishop Stubbs, which held that papal canon law had been valid in England only when accepted by the English Church and when not contrary to English tradition. Maitland proved that English canonists had always regarded the papal decretals as binding and recognized no such discretionary power.

His translation of Gierke's *Political Theories of the Middle Ages* (1898) illustrates how Maitland's mind was never insular. He was much interested in the nature of corporate societies, and became the champion of Gierke's "realist" doctrine, which maintained that a corporation is not a fiction but a real person.

Maitland approached his profession as historian with reverence; as he once put it, "the writing of history is in some sort a religious act." [33] He began with the conviction that history would throw new light on law; he declared that "neither the social economy, nor yet the law of the Middle Ages can be profitably studied by itself." [34] He was without the lawyer's reverence for form and authority and never defended an ancient institution simply because it was old. He had, said Haskins, "the delicate sense of evidence, the flashing insight, the vivid imagination, and the human sympathy of the great historian. To him the history of law was the history, not of forms, but of ideas." [35] He frowned on the methods of the so-called school of comparative jurisprudence of Maine, but did not neglect the value of analogies; and he drew from the best of continental students of institutions. [36] As historian he was a master both of analysis and criticism, and of synthesis and construction. With all his qualifications he united an almost matchless style. [37]

British historiography has had its share of women scholars, and among these Mary Bateson (1865–1906) [38] takes high rank. This daughter of the master of St. John's College, Cambridge, owed her

---

[32] C. M. Andrews in *AHR*, III (1897–98), 130–33.

[33] Smith (n. 23), 15.   [34] Cp. *The Collected Papers of F. W. Maitland* (n. 23), I, 480–97.

[35] Charles Haskins (n. 23), 905.

[36] Vinogradoff instances Gierke on corporations, Keutgen's burg theory, Ficker and Heusler on early kingship. See *The Collected Papers of Paul Vinogradoff* (n. 12), I, 254–55, 262–63.

[37] For a concise sketch of developments in English legal history since Maitland, see Gaillard Lapsley's pages in *Maitland: Selected Essays*, edited by H. D. Hazeltine, G. Lapsley, and P. H. Winfield (Cambridge, 1936).

[38] R. L. Poole, "Mary Bateson," *EHR*, XXII (1907), 64–68; T. F. Tout, obituary in *Manchester Guardian*, December 3, 1906; and his article in *DNB*, supplement for 20th century (1901–11), 110–12.

inspiration to Creighton. Her first notable work was an article on "Rules for Monks and Secular Canons";[39] and Creighton hoped she would write a history of monasticism, but she turned instead to the subject of English towns. In 1891 she collaborated with Maitland in an edition of the borough charters of Cambridge, and calendared the municipal records of Leicester. Her most mature work was the *Borough Customs* (2 v., 1904–06), a permanent contribution to English legal history.

The "Manchester School" of history was created by the late Thomas Frederick Tout (1855–1929) and James Tait. Tout[40] was an Oxford man, and of all his teachers he probably owed the most to Stubbs. As chaplain of Balliol, Stubbs took a small number of students for private instruction, and Tout was among them. For nine years Tout taught at St. David's College in Wales. He delved into Welsh local history and acquired method and bibliography by writing many articles for Low and Pulling's *Dictionary of English History* and the *Celebrities of the Century*.[41] From 1886 on he was a prolific contributor to the *Dictionary of National Biography*.[42] In 1888 he published an excellent article on "The Welsh Shires" in *Y Cymmrodor*. His mind cherished the thought of doing a great history of the reign of Edward I, which was never realized.

When he was thirty-five, Tout was called to the chair of history at Manchester.[43] His predecessor, Sir A. W. Ward, who also taught English literature, had done much to promote the study of history there. Tout threw himself into the life of the college. He was a "healthy opportunist," and reminded his friends of "a kettle bubbling over a brisk fire."[44] The Manchester University Press was largely his own creation, and he took pride in the fact that nearly a third of the volumes in its historical series (fifty-five volumes by January 1930) were the product of his own students.

In his first dozen years at Manchester Tout wrote a great deal, but

[39] *EHR*, IX (1890), 690 ff.

[40] James Tait, "Thomas Frederick Tout," *EHR*, XLV (1930), 78–85; *The Collected Papers of Thomas Frederick Tout, with a Memoir and Bibliography* (Manchester, 1932–34, 3 v.). Vol. I, pp. 1–24 contains a reprint of F. M. Powicke's memoir in *Proceedings of the British Academy*, XV (1929), 491–518, and pp. 27–44 contains notes on his life. An obituary, "Professor Tout, a Great Medieval Historian," appeared in *LTLS*, 1929, p. 21; see also V. H. Galbraith in *DNB*, supplement for 20th century (1922–30), 845–48.

[41] Edited by L. C. Sanders (London, 1887). Tout contributed biographies of the historians Alison, Buckle, Freeman, Froude, Green, Grote, Guizot, Hallam, Lewis, Macaulay, and Stubbs.

[42] His articles in vols. III–XXIV (1885–90) would fill a volume in themselves. They were mostly on Welsh subjects. He continued to furnish copy down to 1910.

[43] Then Owens College, which became the Victoria University.

[44] For his larger significance for Manchester and education, which cannot be discussed here, see *The Collected Papers of T. F. Tout* (n. 40), I, 8–9, and 39–44.

these writings were chiefly contributions to the *Dictionary of National Biography* and the *Cambridge Modern History*. Aside from a short life of Edward I in Macmillan's *Twelve English Statesmen* series (1893), a volume which has been termed the most finished of his works, his pen produced chiefly textbooks in these early years. A number of articles in the *English Historical Review* showed his preparation for the volume he was invited to write in Hunt and Poole's *Political History of England* series, for the years 1216–1377. It was a substantial treatment.

The great work of Tout's life grew out of a review of Professor Eugene Deprez' book on English privy seals.[45] It suggested to him the intimate connection between English diplomatics and administrative studies. Tout had been struck by the "original importance of privy seal writs as exercising an authority parallel to and often almost in rivalry with the more formal instruments drawn up by the Chancellor."[46] The result was the six volumes of the *Chapters in the Administrative History of Mediaeval England: The Wardrobe, the Chamber and the Small Seals*.[47] Stubbs had merely mentioned the Wardrobe incidentally, and never once alluded to the Chamber. Tout discovered that the Wardrobe and the Chamber had often handled great sums of public moneys, or landed property, and taken an important position in the conflict between the Crown and the baronage. By 1913, in his Ford lectures,[48] he demonstrated that the permanent significance of the reign of the despised Edward II lay in the administrative reforms which arose from the conflict over the control of the household offices. Until 1327 these departments were independent of the Exchequer and the Chancery; after the crisis of 1340–41 a unified civil service began. Tout's merit is to have shown the constitutional importance of these household departments, and to have given "the most important single contribution after Stubbs and Maitland." [49]

[45] *EHR*, XXIII (1909), 556–59.   [46] His words in the original review, *loc. cit.*
[47] Vols. I–II, 1920; III–IV, 1928; V, after his death in 1930; VI, contains the index.
[48] Enlarged as *The Place of the Reign of Edward II in English History*.
[49] *LTLS*, 1937, p. 320.

CHAPTER LIII

INSTITUTIONAL HISTORIANS: THE PROBLEM OF TOWN ORIGINS

A S THE question of the origin and nature of feudalism absorbed most of the attention of institutional historians in the middle of the nineteenth century, so the question of the origin of the medieval towns, more than any other subject, engaged their interest in the latter part of the century. If anything, the historical literature on this subject is greater than that pertaining to feudalism, and certainly it has been one of more popular interest. The democratic spirit of the nineteenth century thought that it had struck a sympathetic chord in the history of the rise of the medieval towns.[1]

In France in 1820, when Romanticism was supreme, Augustin Thierry claimed that the real origin of the communal revolutions was to be found in "spontaneous insurrection."[2] In the France with memories of 1789 and aspirations of 1830 and 1848 this doctrine was immensely popular. It is obsolete today, for it has been shown conclusively that insurrection was the exception and not the rule in the history of the rise of the towns.[3]

Unlike the question of feudal origins which divided French and German historians into two contending camps, the question of the origin of the medieval towns proved to be so complex that scarcely any two writers agreed. The volume and variety of sources was almost infinite and national prejudices sometimes distorted interpretation or confused issues. For long years this antagonism estranged German and French scholars so that German writers were unaware of what French histo-

---

[1] For general literature on this subject see my *Economic and Social History of the Middle Ages, 300–1300* (New York, 1928), ch. 28, and bibliography, 848–50; F. Keutgen, "Medieval Commune," *Encyclopaedia Britannica* (11th ed.), VI, 784–91; W. J. Ashley, "The Beginnings of Town Life in the Middle Ages," *Quarterly Journal of Economics*, X (1896), 359–406; ASHLEY, 167–262; *Cambridge Medieval History* (New York, 1911–36, 8 v.), V, ch. 19 and bibliography, 903–08; H. Pirenne, "L'Origine des constitutions urbaines au moyen âge," *RH*, LIII (1893), 52–83, LVII (1895), 293–327; Georges Bougin, "Les origines urbaines," *RSH*, VII (1903), 302–27.

[2] *Lettres sur l'histoire de la France* (1827).

[3] It is amazing to find Stubbs, in his *Constitutional History of England* (Oxford, 1874–78, 3 v.), accepting the insurrectionary theory of Thierry and Guizot when Mignet before him was cautious about accepting it. Thierry's deficiencies as an historian have been critically stated by Giry's greatest pupil, Ferdinand Lot, in his tribute to Giry in *Annuaire de l'École Pratique des Hautes Études*, Section des sciences historiques et philologiques (1901), 22–23.

rians were doing, and French historians ignorant of German works on the same subject.[4] While today there is general agreement upon the origin and formation of the feudal régime, there still is wide diversity of opinion with regard to town origins.

When the nineteenth century opened there was universal agreement among historians that the medieval town was a direct descendant of the Roman *municipium*, however fragmentary the remains or however shattered the continuity. This was the opinion of Dubos in the eighteenth century, with whom Savigny in his *History of Roman Law in the Middle Ages*, and Raynouard in France, the historian of Provençal culture, agreed. All of these writers made a fundamental blunder in reasoning. They were deceived by a false analogy of terms. Because medieval town officials and organs of administration were frequently called *consules, curia, senatus*, etc., they inferred continuity of Roman municipia through the Middle Ages.

The first protest against the "Roman theory" came from Eichhorn, who was the earliest historian to call attention to the influence of domanial law (*Hofrecht*) in the formation of the burgher class.[5] This compromised the "Roman theory," though Eichhorn did not greatly develop his points. Over thirty years later Karl Hegel, son of the philosopher, demolished the whole edifice of the "Roman theory" in his *Geschichte der Städteverfassung von Italien* (1847). In this famous work Hegel took the ground that if the theory of the Roman origin of the medieval town were valid, the evidence for it would be greater in the history of the Italian towns than that of any other towns. But he found no evidence that any Italian town as a political corporation or as a corporate society could trace its lineage back to Roman times. All were strictly of medieval origin, even Rome.[6]

Into the vacuum created by the collapse of the "Roman theory" other and new theories rushed. Most of these new theories were of German authorship. In 1831 Wilda's *Gildenwesen im Mittelalter* argued that the ancient German *Schutzgilde* which survived across the centuries, was the nucleus of the medieval town. But there were many sorts of gilds in the Middle Ages. It was not long before almost every kind of gild found its advocate. The most popular and the most plau-

---

[4] Karl Hegel in writing his *Städte und Gilden der Germanischen Völker im Mittelalter* (Leipzig, 1891, 2 v. in 1) had no knowledge of Arthur Giry's *Étude sur les origines de la commune de St. Quentin* (St. Quentin, 1887), or Abel Le Franc's *Histoire de la ville de Noyen et de ses institutions jusqu'à la fin du XIIIᵉ siècle* (Paris, 1887), or Jules Flammermont's *Histoire des institutions de Senlis* (Paris, 1881).

[5] *Ueber den Ursprung der städtischen Verfassung* (1815–16, 2 v.).

[6] On Hegel see his *Leben und Erinnerungen* (1900); F. Frensdorff, "Karl Hegel und die Geschichte des deutschen Städtewesens," *Hansische Geschichtsblätter*, XXIX (1901), 141–60; WEGELE, 991, 1035, 1080; F. Keutgen in *EHR*, VIII (1893), 120–27.

sible of these "gild theories" was that which contended that early merchant gilds were the nuclei of the first medieval towns. Hegel, writing soon after Wilda, *en passant* proved that the "gild theory" was invalid for Italian towns, and in 1890 the American historian Charles Gross in *The Gild Merchant* proved that "the influence of the gild merchant manifested itself not in the origin, but in the development of the municipal constitution." The gilds emerged *after* the town had arisen. Worse still was the "industrial theory" which held that the nucleus of the first medieval towns was some form of an industrial gild. Here again it has been shown that the industrial gilds arose *after* the merchant gilds.

By far the most popular and most enduring theory of town origins, which most English historians accepted and even a few French historians adopted, was the "Mark theory" of G. L. von Maurer, elaborated in a famous work: *Einleitung zur Geschichte der Mark-, Hof-, Dorf- und Stadtverfassung* (1854). Maurer was the promoter of the theory of the "Mark" or free German village community with communal ownership of land.[7] The "Mark theory" was so much in harmony with the social idealism of Germany about 1848 that it had enthusiastic adherents. It was sustained as late as 1887 by von Below's *Zur Entstehung der deutschen Stadtverfassung*.

In the same year that Maurer's book appeared Wilhelm Arnold's *Verfassungsgeschichte der deutschen Freistädte* was published. This work represented a new departure, as Arnold limited himself to certain free cities of medieval Germany: Cologne, Mainz, Speyer, Worms, Strassburg, Basel, and Regensburg, all of them episcopal cities, and did not assume that what was true of them was necessarily true of other cities of Germany. Arnold originated the "immunity theory," i.e., the theory of the influence of the so-called "Ottonian privileges" as the seeds of town origin. In pursuance of his policy of playing the bishops against the great German nobles Otto I had showered market rights, toll rights, mintage rights, and immunities upon them. Arnold's demonstration was conclusive so far as these and many other episcopal cities were concerned. In 1872 Heusler's *Ursprung der deutschen Städteverfassung* demolished the "Mark theory" for all time and fortified Arnold's theory. But the immunity theory has not been widely accepted. The same statement may be made regarding the *Marktrecht* or market law theory advocated by S. Rietschel's *Markt und Stadt* (1897), which became popular among some German scholars, but was regarded with skepticism by others.[8] In France Huvelin introduced

---

[7] The inventor of the theory was Justus Möser, in the middle of the eighteenth century. Kemble had already applied the theory to Anglo-Saxon England in 1848.

[8] See literature cited in DAHLMANN-WAITZ, no. 2698.

the theory in his *Essai sur le droit des marchés et des foires*. Neither in Germany nor France has the market law theory stood the test of time.[9]

A variant form of the market law theory is the so-called "*Weichbild* theory" put forward by Rudolph Sohm, professor of law at Leipzig University in his *Die Entstehung des deutschen Städtewesen* (1890). Sohm argued that the market cross in the case of towns which arose on ecclesiastical lands, and the Roland, a statue of Charlemagne's paladin which stood in the market place in towns which arose on secular lands, were *weichbilder* or symbols of market peace and market law, out of which grew the town administration.

Even among German scholars the immunity theory and the market law theory have been received with skepticism. The first predicates too much.[10] In the market law theory it is to be remembered that the early medieval markets were annual or at most seasonal affairs and not permanent and continuous. Moreover, most markets were owned and controlled by private proprietary authority. It is not tenable that the market was the generative cause of towns. Mere increase of population, augmentation of the volume of trade and industry, will not solve the problem. One must find a legal principle to explain how private exemption or special jurisdiction could be converted into a jurisdictional entity composed of hitherto unfree peasants who suddenly were transformed into burghers.

In 1859 Wilhelm Nitzsch broke new ground. Abandoning the effort to find the origin of the medieval town in any legal sanction, he sought to show that many medieval towns, at least in Germany, emerged out of manorial communities. His *Ministerialität und Bürgerthum* contended that in towns which had arisen upon crown lands or feudal domains the nucleus of the later town government was to be found in the group of *ministeriales* or servile administrators of the manor for the lord thereof, who became the first officials of the town when it emerged. This theory, too, is more plausible than demonstrable.[11]

The "garrison theory" of town origins has found considerable acceptance. The *Burgwärde* or fortified and garrisoned places erected by Henry the Fowler (919–36) in Saxony as protection against the raids of the Hungarians; the Five Burgs (Leicester, Nottingham, Lincoln, Stamford, and Derby) similarly erected in England by Edward the Elder (901–25) to protect the Midlands from the ravages of the Danes;

---

[9] For the reasons see my *Economic and Social History* (n. 1), 768.

[10] Such a place was not always a locus of economic production. "Its inhabitants lived off the labor of peasants in surrounding estates; its court, its mint, its market were supported by outsiders." Carl Stephenson, "The Origin of the English Towns," *AHR*, XXXII (1926–27), 10–21.

[11] On the class of *ministeriales*, see my *Feudal Germany* (Chicago, 1929), 321–37.

the *castella* in France which Charles the Bald erected to protect the basin of the Seine from the invasions of the Norsemen, in which we find "watch and ward" instituted in a capitulary of 864, are pointed out as the nuclei of future towns. It is argued that settled life, commerce, and industry gradually developed in these protected communities and so towns arose. The weakness of the garrison theory is that it is too local and too military; the transition from military to civil rule is difficult to explain. In England the theory was propounded by Maitland. He thought that most boroughs antedating the Norman Conquest were established by the king for military reasons; he required the thegns to garrison them, and they erected buildings for their men. Under the royal peace traders collected at these boroughs. After the Norman Conquest castles were strewn over the land, and the garrison-towns lost their military significance, while their trading function remained.[12] Carl Stephenson has recently connected the garrison theory with the theories of municipal evolution devised by Pirenne.[13] At most the garrison theory will account for only a small number of towns.

Two recently deceased German historians are distinguished, not so much for original research, as for endeavor to synthesize the whole body of theories and facts with relation to town origins. These are von Below and Keutgen. Georg Anton Hugo von Below (1858–1927)[14] was born at Königsberg, Prussia, and his personal background was that of the native Prussian gentry. Constantly struggling for greater conceptual clarity, and a bitter polemist, Below covered a large field, opened up important problems, or indicated new directions for study. He had studied history at Bonn under F. von Bezold and M. Ritter, and economics under Th. von der Goltz and E. Nasse. His academic career began with a professorship at his native city of Königsberg (1889); in 1891 he was made professor in Münster, in 1897 he removed to Marburg, in 1901 to Tübingen, and for nearly twenty years he held a chair at Freiburg im Breisgau (1905–24).

[12] See F. W. Maitland's *Township and Borough* (Cambridge, 1898); and Mary Bateson, "The Creation of Boroughs," *EHR*, XVII (1902), 284–96. For the *Burgwärde* of Henry the Fowler and Otto the Great see my *Feudal Germany* (n. 11), 479–86, where much German material is cited.

[13] Stephenson, "The Anglo-Saxon Borough," *EHR*, XLV (1930), 181, the entire article, 177–207; cp. *AHR*, XLIII (1937–38), 96–99 for his review of James Tait, *The Medieval English Borough* (Manchester University Press, 1936), also reviewed by Miss Helen Cam in *EHR*, LII (1937), 303–06.

[14] Autobiographical sketch in *Die Geschichtswissenschaft der Gegenwart in Selbstdarstellungen*, ed. by S. Steinberg (Leipzig, 1925), vol. I; Carl Brinkmann, in *ESS*, II, 508–09; Hermann Aubin, "Georg von Below, als Sozial- und Wirtschaftshistoriker," *Vierteljahrschrift für Sozial- und Wirtschaftsgeschichte*, XXI (1928), 1–32. A list of his writings by L. Klaiber is included in each of the two Festschriften which were intended for Below but had to be brought out after his death as Gedenkschriften: *Aus Sozial- und Wirtschaftsgeschichte* (1928), and *Aus Politik und Geschichte* (1928).

The rise of medieval towns and their trade economy occupied much of his attention.[15] Below denied the manorial origin of the medieval town. Yet his own work cannot be regarded as final; he disregarded much that was valuable in the writings of other authorities whom he attacked, as Karl Bücher, Schmoller, Seeliger, and Sombart. In constitutional history Below founded, or helped to found, the modern German school. His chief work in the field of German constitutional history was *Der deutsche Staat des Mittelalters*, of which only the first volume was ever finished (1914, 2d ed., 1925).[16] He was a conservative in politics, a strong nationalist, and with advancing years grew more hostile to democracy and the republican government in Germany.

Friedrich Wilhelm Eduard Keutgen (1861–1936)[17] was born at Bremen, and died in Hamburg, at the age of seventy-five. As a youth, when put to the decision whether he would become a scholar or enter business, he felt he lacked the qualifications for the first, and left school to follow a commercial life. From 1879 to 1887 he lived in Manchester, as agent for a large German firm. He told his wife later of this period, however: "Ich jagte durch meine Arbeit, um abends zu den Büchern zu kommen." Finally he returned to school, and obtained his Ph.D. at Strassburg, habilitated at Jena in 1895, was named associate professor in 1900, and full professor in 1910 at the Kolonialinstitut which was opened in Hamburg in 1908. Here he was especially asked to give colonial history. When the University of Hamburg was organized in 1919, he passed into its faculty, and taught there till retired in 1933. He taught at Johns Hopkins University in 1904–05, but declined to stay.

Keutgen's method appeared in his *Untersuchungen über den Ursprung der deutschen Stadtverfassung* (1895), which examines a group of the most significant current problems of research in this field: the origin of the Stadtgericht, Marktrecht, städtisches Recht, and of the Rat. He shows all possible solutions, and then gives his own, with constant reference to the sources and the literature. His purpose, he stated, was

in den verschiedenen Theorien die Fehlerquellen entdecken, feststellen, was an jeder richtig ist, und zeigen, wie die einseitig verteidigten Faktoren sich ergänzend in der Entwickelung zusammengewirkt haben [p. 5].

Keutgen never left the first direction of his studies, but purposely expanded his work. Like Below, his best friend, he combated the doctrine that the gilds developed from the manor in his study on *Ämter*

---

[15] *Die Entstehung der deutschen Stadtgemeinde* (1889); *Der Ursprung der deutschen Stadtverfassung* (1892); *Das ältere deutsche Städtewesen und Bürgertum* (a popular presentation, 1898, 3rd ed., 1925); cp. also some of his studies in *Territorium und Stadt* (1900, 2d ed., 1923).

[16] Below's method is well sketched in a review by B. Schmeidler in *HZ*, CXL (1929), 386–92.

[17] Ludwig Beutin, "Friedrich Keutgen," *Vierteljahrschrift für Sozial- und Wirtschaftsgeschichte*, XXX (1937), 95–98; *EHR*, VIII (1893), 120–27.

und Zünfte (1903), but instead of presenting his own theory in a few sentences, he described the development of the gilds out of the various motives and conditions. Keutgen was one-sided in claiming the gilds can be explained solely from town law and economic life. His last article, "Ursprung und Wesen der deutschen Hanse," [18] dealt briefly with the Hansa, which he pictured as a league of merchants, and not of cities; to Keutgen the history of the later English and Dutch colonial companies offered related phenomena.

A once popular theory of town origins in France was that which contended that the Carolingian local civil administration survived, at least in the north, in a broken or mutilated form, and that out of the ancient *scabini* or *échevins*, the Frankish officials of township and hundred, sprang later the first town officials. This thesis has found startling confirmation in the case of Noyon east of Paris where the continuity of Carolingian local institutions seems to have been preserved; for as late as 1237 the electoral regulations preserved the identical formulas of the Carolingian capitularies. [19] This survival, however, seems almost unique.

The work of Arthur Giry (1848–99) [20] really falls into two parts, the one dealing with municipal institutions of medieval France, and the other with diplomatic studies. Giry was born at Trevoux (Ain), and passed away in his fifty-second year. His father and grandfather were employed in the government treasury branch of the *contributions indirects*, and came from Marseilles. On his mother's side he belonged to the family of Claude Roberjot, one of the French plenipotentiaries assassinated at the gates of Rastadt a century before. From the college at Chartres, to which city his father had been transferred, Giry came to Paris and entered the École de Chartes (November 1866), which was at that time cultivating in its students more of a taste for erudition which led to sterile dilettantism, than a vigorous scientific ambition. Sensing this defect, Giry enrolled the next year in the newly established École des Hautes Études (founded 1868), followed the courses in both institutions for a few years (till 1870), and then continued in the last-mentioned (1870–73). At the École des Chartes he was one of the three or four extremely rare pupils of the archaeologist Jules Quicherat;

[18] In *Hamburger geschichtliche Beiträge für Hans Nirrnheim* (1935).
[19] This has been shown in Abel Le Franc's *Histoire de la ville de Noyon* (n. 4). Le Franc was a pupil of Giry, the most considerable French historian of medieval towns in the past generation.
[20] Ferdinand Lot, *Annuaire (1901) de l'École Pratique des Hautes Études*, section historique et philologique (Paris, 1900), 20–47; Henri Omont, *BEC*, LXII (1901), 5–10, and a select bibliography of Giry's writings, 11–14; Louis Halphen in *ESS*, VI, 668–69; G. Monod, "Necrolog," *RH*, LXXII (1900), 103–07. There is an appreciation of the private man in the *Correspondance historique et archéologique*, of MM. Bournon and Mazerolle (1899), and in the same journal Henri Maistre published a full bibliography (1899, 1900) which includes Giry's two thousand articles in *La Grande Encyclopédie*.

but though this teacher impressed Giry, he never encouraged students to enter his field seriously, and would allow no thesis.[21] Thus perhaps the pure accident that Giry had been assigned to classify the archives of the town of Saint-Omer, led him to choose for a thesis subject at the École des Chartes a matter that proved surprisingly suggestive.

Taking up the collegiate chapter of Notre-Dame of Saint-Omer, he entered simultaneously into his two future fields. He thought of editing the chartulary of this church, and uncovered some forged Merovingian charters by which the canons had buttressed their claims. The excellent "Prolégomènes du cartulaire de Notre-Dame de Saint-Omer" with which he won the diploma of *archivist paléographe* (January 17, 1870) at the École des Chartes was never published,[22] but this acquaintance with the commune of Saint-Omer revealed to Giry that the whole history of municipal institutions in France was still a virgin field.

At the École des Hautes Études, where he continued his studies, Giry had become one of the first students of Gabriel Monod, and for four years he imbibed historical criticism from this teacher in reading narrative texts.[23] From Monod Giry received his first training in diplomatics, a subject which had fallen into oblivion in the country of Mabillon, but risen to new conquests across the Rhine. Monod learned it at Göttingen in the school of Waitz, and brought the discipline back into France. It may also be mentioned that in 1873–74 Giry took courses from Thevenin, who was another pupil of Waitz.

During the Franco-Prussian War Giry left his studies for a time to serve as captain in the second army of the Loire. After his discharge he resumed his place in the department of manuscripts of the Bibliothèque Nationale. In 1873 he was made archivist of the section of the secretariat of the Archives Nationales. By the next year he was able to present his completed *Histoire de la ville de Saint-Omer et de ses institutions jusqu'au* XIVe *siècle* at the École des Hautes Études. Even before the title of *élève diplomé* was conferred, Giry was asked, at Monod's suggestion, to substitute for a teacher absent on leave. His teaching was so satisfactory that a position was created for him; he was named *maître des conférénces d'histoire* in 1877, and in 1892 *directeur adjoint*. In 1878 Jules Quicherat also asked him to aid in the position of secretary of the École des Chartes, where Giry later followed the Comte de Mas Latrie in the chair of diplomatics (1885).

[21] "Cette influence sterilisante des hommes éminents est un des traits caracteristiques de l'érudition française; innombrables en sont les exemples dans toutes les branches de la science." F. Lot in *Annuaire* (n. 20), 22.

[22] He utilized his notes for an article: "Les Chatelains de Saint-Omer, 1042–1386," *BEC*, XXXV (1874), 325–55 and XXXVI (1875), 91–117.

[23] For Giry's own acknowledgments see *Études d'histoire du moyen âge dédiées à Gabriel Monod* (Paris, 1896), 107–08.

In his *conférences* at the École des Hautes Études he was asked to deal with the municipal history of medieval France. Half of his twenty-five years of teaching were given to this field, exclusively from 1874 to 1878, and much of his time from then on till 1886. Those who imagined that Augustin Thierry had settled the problems of municipal origins and development never realized that the brilliant writer had confused the subject more by his generalizations than he had prepared for any positive advance by the next generation. Only by patient research in dozens of local archives, and on the solid foundations of many monographs could a safe edifice of municipal history be reared. The theories of A. Thierry, without being wholly erroneous, were vague and ascribed too much importance to alleged types connected with either Roman or German influences, according to the region. It took some time to run such fallacies to earth. Giry's *Histoire de la ville de Saint-Omer* (1877) scandalized even liberal scholars when it denied to Louis VI the title "père des communes." But Giry was building soundly. Year after year he studied the manuscript sources of town after town in France with his students in model conferences, stressing the complexity of the subject, and assigning to them minute analyses of communal charters to establish their sources and filiations. His own vacations and small savings were spent on voyages of research from which he returned with fresh materials for new studies. After surveying the communes of the North and Belgium,[24] he turned to the west of France. The two volumes of his *Établissements de Rouen* [25] displayed the influence of the statutes of Rouen on all west and central France. It was acclaimed a magistral work, renewing a whole portion of French history. In 1885 he published a valuable source collection, *Documents sur les relations de la royauté avec les villes de 1180 à 1314;* and two years after an excellent "Étude sur les origines de la commune de Saint-Quentin" was printed as the introduction to the first volume of the *Archives anciennes de Saint-Quentin* (1887). It is to be regretted that not more of Giry's municipal researches were published, for after studying the west of France he spent five more years (1877–82) with his students upon the towns of the Midi, Languedoc, Provence, and the Centre, and then came back to the Nord again, completing his circle.[26] What heightens such regret is the fact that Giry conceived of his subject in a large way: his studies in the Midi embraced, on the testimony of his

[24] Gand, Cambrai, Amiens, Saint-Omer, Senlis, etc.

[25] Published in 1883 and 1885 as vols. LV and LIX of the *Bibliothèque de l'École des Hautes Études.* The full title continues: ". . . études sur l'histoire des institutions municipales de Rouen, Falaise, Pont-Audemer, Verneuil, la Rochelle, Saintes, Oleron, Bayonne, Tours, Niort, Cognac, Saint-Jean-d'Angély, Angoulême, Poitiers, . . ." etc.

[26] In 1885–86 he gave his students a connected review of the progress to date in French municipal history.

pupil, Ferdinand Lot, almost the whole of its social life.[27] If Giry never wrote all that he might have written, his numerous students were fired to write books of their own, many of which were begun in those fruitful *conférences*.[28]

In 1885, when Giry was made professor at the École des Chartes, he was recognized as the authority and the moving spirit in municipal history in France. Yet two years later he turned his back, as he thought "for a time," upon this field and plunged his students into diplomatics. The studies of town charters had long ago called his attention to this important technique, and since in 1878 Giry had devoted one of his conferences to it annually, at the École des Hautes Études. From 1887 on almost all his courses in both schools were given to it. The excellent *Manuel de diplomatique* (1893) still remains without a peer; it won the author the *grand prix Gobert* when it appeared (1893) and three years later a seat in the Academy of Inscriptions. It rested upon much independent labor, for the German specialists Sickel, Ficker, Muehlbacher, and others were of no help in the special problems of the late Carolingian and the Capetian rulers, when chanceries were disorganized and forms not observed. Delisle's study covered only the reign of Philip Augustus, and Quicherat, the only man capable of covering the previous centuries, had embraced too immense a field to find time for more than indicating *desiderata*. The École des Chartes had failed of its original purpose. After Monod, it was Giry who created the renaissance of diplomatics in France.

As the revision of Böhmer's *Regesta* directed by E. Muehlbacher in Germany had omitted the diplomata of the French Carolingians after 840, Giry had conceived the notion of filling this gap as early as 1880. The work of collating manuscripts and hunting up hundreds of archives and depositories was shared by willing students, but still the brunt fell upon their teacher. Giry often sighed wistfully when he thought of the rich subventions of the workers on the German *Monumenta:* he had neither funds nor assistants. For twelve years he stinted himself on his salaries and loyal pupils helped at the risk of slipping up in their examinations. It is eloquent testimony to Giry's power as an inspiring teacher that in 1888 some eight of his students proposed to share the toil-

[27] He instances: the condition of men and of lands, the justice of the bishops, the peace and the truce of God, the *salvetates* of the XIth and XIIth centuries, the relations of the cities on the Mediterranean shore among each other, and with the Italian towns, the curious office of the *podestat*.

[28] Thus Jules Flammermont, *Histoire des institutions de Senlis* (Paris, 1881); Maurice Prou, *Les Coutumes de Lorris et leur propogation aux XIIe et XIIIe siècles* (Paris, 1884); Abel le Franc, *Histoire de la ville de Noyon* (n. 4); L. H. Labande, *Histoire de Beauvais et de ses institutions communales jusqu'au commencement du XVe siècle* (Paris, 1892), etc. If some studies begun under Giry's tutelage were never published, Lot suggests this happened "probablement sous l'influence de ce dilettantisme qui sterilise les trois quarts des 'chartistes.' "

some task of preparing the *Regesta;* and at the same time each undertook to prepare the annals of one reign, similar to the German *Jahrbücher.*[29] Giry was to finish the diplomata of Charles the Bald and prepare the annals of his reign. In the collection of materials, Giry prescribed the topographical approach, taking each of the ancient ecclesiastical provinces of France in succession, rather than the chronological. Many advantages ensued from this method, e.g., the diplomata issued by all the several kings to one and the same abbey were thus brought together and valuable information elicited by comparison, so that forgeries were detected and developments in the chanceries could be followed. Indeed, no other method would have satisfied the peculiar conditions of the French diplomata.

It is no reflection on Giry that the books of his students progressed faster than his. The Annals of Charles the Bald were never finished.[30] In 1895 the chief editor saw his responsibilities increase when, to prevent the *Monumenta* from including all the diplomata of the Carolingians, even in France, it became necessary to replace the projected *Regesta*, which would have been only a calendar of the documents, with a full critical edition of all the diplomata of the rulers of France, Acquitaine, and Provence-Burgundy. The much higher cost of such an undertaking made it necessary to put the work under the aegis of the Academy of Inscriptions, which had already once resolved to publish the diplomata of the French Carolingians. Giry's students were somewhat displeased that the glory should go to an organization only financially interested when the burden of the work had long been borne by them at the École des Hautes Études. Each year Giry hoped to see the end of his task approach, but his aversion to haste and his resolution to unravel the history of each abbey and bishopric by adducing not only the charters but also all narrative sources, made his progress slow, though sure. When he died the great edition was only half done, and since it was still topographically incomplete, his Annals were not written either. They would have been valuable as precipitating his studies on what he considered the skeleton source of the reign of Charles the Bald, the *Annals of St. Bertin.*[31]

[29] Lavisse at the Faculté des lettres had often praised this series, and advised his students to emulate the Germans, but with the set-up of requirements for the examinations the students knew better than to waste their time on such labors. An exception is Petit-Dutaillis, *Étude sur la vie et la règne de Louis VII, 1187–1226* (Paris, 1894).

[30] But of his students, dealing with briefer reigns, we have: F. Lot, *Les derniers Carolingiens, Lothaire, Louis V, Charles de Lorraine, 954–991* (1891); Edouard Favre, *Éudes, comte de Paris et roi de France, 882–898* (1893), begun under the inspiration of Monod, Giry's colleague; Auguste Eckel, *Charles le Simple* (1899); Philip Lauer, *Règne de Louis IV d'Outre-mer* (1900); René Poupardin, *Royaume de Provence sous les Carolingiens, 855–933* (1901); Christian Pfister, *Études sur le règne de Robert le Pieux* (Paris, 1885), came similarly from the conferences of Monod.

[31] The Académie des Inscriptions carried on the edition under the supervision of d'Arbois de Jubainville; Giry's share, or the unfinished part relating to Charles the Bald, was entrusted to one of his favorite pupils, Maurice Prou, who followed him in the chair of diplomatics.

It should be clear that Giry's labors in the last twelve years of his life are not adequately reflected in anything he left written, but enough has been said to show that they can hardly be called sterile. Besides his teaching, he felt the need of sound popularization of historical knowledge. For many years (1872–79) he wrote an annual series of critical articles on historical works that appeared in the journal *La République française.* He took over the task of historical editor in *La Grande Encyclopédie,* and himself wrote more than two thousand articles for it (1886–99).[32] Two chapters in Lavisse and Rambaud's *Histoire générale du IVe siècle à nos jours* (1893–1901) came from his hand.[33]

The late Professor Otto von Gierke spent a long life in writing a great book, *Das deutsche Genossenschaftsrecht,*[34] to prove the wide diffusion of the "principle of association" in medieval society, and some historians have sought to find the origin of the medieval town in this principle. But to most medievalists the principle seems too intangible to be so applied, whatever other application may be made of it.

A theory which seems to answer to more established facts than any other theory must be not far from truth. Such a one is the latest and now current "mercatorial theory" which the late Professor Henri Pirenne of Ghent sustained in many writings. Primarily an economic-social historian, Pirenne sought in the history of medieval commerce for evidence and found the nucleus of many a town in the mercantile colony (*negotiatores, mercatores*) which sprang up near some castle and for sake of protection dwelt in a walled compound called a *burg,* the inhabitants of which by the end of the eleventh century had come to be called *burgenses,* to whom the local lord in course of time granted certain rights of person, property, and community government which distinguished them from the servile population roundabout from which they had sprung. The new burg in course of time became *the* burg. Pirenne's mercatorial theory is especially applicable to the towns of Flanders, the lower Rhinelands, and northeastern France, but need by no means be limited to these regions, for some Westphalian, Lombard, and Tuscan cities seem to fit into the scheme.[35]

---

[32] He was one of the founders and chief directors of the *Collection de textes pour servir à l'étude et à l'enseignement de l'histoire* published by the Société historique (1886 ff.), and was concerned in the *Mémoires et documents* published by the Société de l'École des Chartes.

[33] Vol. II, chs. viii, pp. 411–78, and ix, pp. 480–537.

[34] 1868–1913, 4 v. Part of vol. III was translated by F. W. Maitland under the title *Political Theories in the Middle Ages* (Cambridge, 1927).

[35] Cp. F. Powicke's article "Henri Pirenne," *EHR,* LI (1926), 78–89. Pirenne's mercatorial theory and other contributions are best epitomized in his *Les anciennes démocraties des Pays-Bas* (Paris, 1910), published in English by J. V. Saunders as *Belgian Democracy, Its Early History* (London and New York, 1915); see also Pirenne's articles in *RH* (n. 1), and his Princeton lectures, published by the University Press in an English translation by Frank Halsey, as *Medieval Cities, Their Origins and the Revival of Trade* (1939), improved French version *Les villes du moyen âge: essai d'histoire économique et sociale* (Brussels, 1927).

What I have written elsewhere may be repeated here: "We can discern the chief factors in the origin of the towns, but are unable to determine the relative weight and importance of each one of them, or even their relation to each other. But beyond doubt no single germ and no single explanation is sufficient for all cases. The weakness of much historical scholarship hitherto has been that each writer has emphasized his own theory too exclusively, and sometimes national prejudice has warped judgment. According to the way in which these new institutions were formed, various systems have been proposed; each author attaches them to a preceding different institution, but all are [more or less] conjectures established upon generalization from certain cases. What is true for Germany may not apply in equal degree to Flanders and France and Italy. Local conditions, geographical and historical, must always be given due weight. The elements of town life in medieval Europe differed greatly, both in degree and in kind. . . . In the face of so many divergent theories it would seem that this wide difference of opinion represents a real variation in the history of different towns. It is vain to seek to derive the towns from this or that principle of either Roman or German law. The medieval town was the product of economic and social forces." [36]

[36] Quoted from my *Economic and Social History* (n. 1), 771.

CHAPTER LIV

HISTORIANS OF ECONOMIC AND SOCIAL HISTORY [1]

ECONOMIC history presents a vast and confusing field of study. The confusion has been aggravated by abstract philosophy and partisan politics. As a battleground for the discontented historian and the perplexed economist, neither of whom is willing (or able) to delimit his science or define his objective, economic history has become an enormous receptacle for scattered materials and disjointed theories. To this day the economic historian has been unable to make up his mind whether he is an economist or an historian. He insists that he is neither, that he is both, that he is something else. But nobody knows exactly what he is, least of all the economic historian himself who emphatically does not wish to be considered an historian and is just as emphatically not an economist.

One of the reasons for this confusion is that economic history was born and brought to maturity in Germany; it was, in fact, a direct outcome of specific German social-economic conditions. In the hothouse atmosphere of German philosophic abstraction and violent politics,

[1] Max Weber, *Wirthschaftsgeschichte.* ed. by S. Hellmann and M. Palyi (Munich and Leipzig, 1923), 17–18, 19–20 n., 174 and *passim* [also in English translation by Frank Knight, as *General Economic History*, London, 1927]; Felix Flügel, ed., *Select Bibliography of Economic and Social History and Contemporary Economic and Social Problems* (in mimeograph, Berkeley, 1933, lists only periodical articles); W. Roscher, *Geschichte der National-Oekonomik in Deutschland* (Munich, 1874), chs. xxix–xxxv and notes; G. Cohn, *A History of Political Economy* (March, 1894, *Supplement* to the *Annals of the American Academy of Political and Social Science*), especially chs. v–viii; Georg v. Below, *Probleme der Wirtschaftsgeschichte, eine Einführung in das Studium der Wirtschaftsgeschichte* (Tübingen, 1920); the same, *Die deutsche Geschichtschreibung von den Befreiungskriegen bis zu unsern Tagen* (Munich and Berlin, 1924), 161–94 and notes; E. Salin, *Geschichte der Volkswirtschaftslehre* (2nd ed. Berlin, 1929); Hutcheson M. Posnett, *The Historical Method in Ethics, Jurisprudence and Political Economy* (London, 1882); Ernst Troeltsch, *Der Historismus und seine Probleme* (Tübingen, 1922: Vol. III of his *Gesammelte Schriften*); Georg Brodnitz, "Die Zukunft der Wirtschaftsgeschichte," *Jahrbücher für Nationalökonomie und Statistik,* XCV (1910), 145–61; Bernhard Pfister, "Bemerkungen zu dem Thema: Theorie und Geschichte," *ibid.,* CXXXI (1929), 481–512; and reviews in *ibid.,* XL (1883), 170, and LIV (1890), 75–95; W. Hasbach, "Die klassische Nationalökonomie und ihre Gegner," *Schmollers Jahrbuch,* XX (1896), 857–79; E. Salin, "Zur Methode und Aufgabe der Wirtschaftsgeschichte," *ibid.,* XLV (1921), 483–505; Werner Sombart, "Probleme der Wirtschaftsgeschichte," *ibid.,* XLIV (1920), 1021–39; the same, "Economic Theory and Economic History," *Economic History Review,* II (1929), 1–19; E. M. Burns, "Does Institutionalism Complement or Compete with 'Orthodox Economics'?" *American Economic Review,* XXI (1931), 80–87; W. H. Hamilton, "The Institutional Approach to Economic Theory," *ibid.,* IX (1919), supplement, 309–18; Paul T. Homan, "The Institutional School," *ESS,* V, 387–92; H. E. Barrault, "L'idée d'évolution dans la science économique," *Revue d'histoire économique et sociale,* X (1922), 38–83; XI (1923), 305–82; XV (1927), 137–76; H. St.-Marc, "Étude sur l'enseignement de l'économie politique dans les universités des pays de langue allemande," *Revue d'économie politique,* VI (1892), 217–49, 423–70.

economic history developed as an intellectual hybrid on the one hand
and a political weapon on the other. In the fast-developing German
Reich economic history was utilized by various interested parties as a
tool to buttress factional demands and to rationalize the *status quo*.
Gustav Schmoller, one of the two founders of economic history, wrote
somewhat boastfully that this *Wissenschaft* was a German invention.

Perhaps only in the days of Luther or possibly in those of the Saxon and Staufen emperors did one have so much reason for pride in being a German as in the half-century
from 1838–1888; never before had German science obtained such esteem as in our days.
And among the disciplines which soared most especially in Germany, those of the social
sciences (*vom Staate und von der Volkswirthschaft*) deserve an honorable place. . . .

Beginning with Friedrich List, German political economy sought to throw off the
fetters of English theory. Today our technicians and natural scientists, our historians
and philologists, our economists and social scientists are as much at the head of the
world's scientific movements as our statesmen and generals are indisputably recognized
as foremost.[2]

The German scholar J. E. C. Conrad, speaking at the St. Louis Congress of Arts and Sciences in 1904, explained that the purpose of economic history was "not only to investigate and describe the actual processes of economic life in different periods, but must especially follow
their development with a view to explaining causal relations."[3] The
peculiar thing about this definition is, that is precisely what historians
have been saying about their craft since Voltaire and Justus Möser.
Sir William J. Ashley, who introduced economic history into the United
States and England, admitted that it was like any other history, but it
differed in one respect: its emphasis on economics. "It (economic
history) asks what has been the material basis of social existence."[4]
W. S. Holdsworth, the eminent English scholar in legal history, sees an
intimate connection between legal and economic history. "That connection is so very close that I do not think that either the legal or the
economic historian can do justice to his subject without extensive bor-
rowings from the other's learning."[5] Professor Gras of Harvard would
"safely and profitably divorce our economic history from general

[2] Gustav Schmoller, *Zur Litteraturgeschichte der Staats- und Sozialwissenschaften* (Leipzig,
1888), preface in the form of a dedicatory letter to Roscher, pp. vii–viii.

[3] Johannes Conrad, "Economic History in Relation to Kindred Sciences," *Congress of Arts
and Sciences, Universal Exposition, St. Louis, 1904* (Boston, 1906), II, 202, the whole article,
199–214.

[4] W. J. Ashley, "On the Study of Economic History," *Quarterly Journal of Economics*, VII
(1893), 115–36; reprinted in his *Surveys, Historic and Economic* (London and New York, 1900),
1–21. "It may be granted that, as things are now, economic history belongs equally to the
departments of history and economics. There is no reason in the nature of things why the
'pure historian' . . . should not investigate both the history of religion and the history of law.
But, as a matter of fact, the work of research in these two fields has usually been carried on
by . . . theologians and lawyers in the narrow sense."

[5] W. S. Holdsworth, "A Neglected Aspect of the Relations between Economic and Legal
History," *Economic History Review*, I (1927), 123, the whole article, 114–23.

history." "Economic history is the study of economic phenomena in their time, genetic and causal sequences." [6] Ever since the time of Niebuhr and Ranke historical scholars have accepted the basic idea that historic phenomena should be treated "in their time, genetic and causal sequences." Another economic historian pretends to see in economic history the "essential nature of economic progress." He would also separate economic from general history because the former "is life, and living men make it according to the ways they think and act." [7]

It is customary to begin the history of economic history either with the French Utopian Socialists or with Karl Marx. [8] Such an approach is unsatisfactory in a work on historiography, mainly because the various types of Socialists were more interested in political action than in *Wissenschaft.* [9] Nor may one begin with the economic theorists, although they undoubtedly had a great influence on the historians. Of these economists, Adam Smith was one of the few who paid attention to history; the others employed logic.

Long before the German school of economic history there were historians with an economic slant. It would be a vain display of erudition to trace a materialistic interpretation of history back to the Greeks. Plato, as a brilliant passage in his *Critias* shows, was keenly aware of the material basis of civilization. [10] So was Aristotle in his *Politics*, and, to come closer to our own times, so were Bodin, Harrington, Voltaire, Heeren, and especially Justus Möser. [11] It is also easy to compile a list of early works dealing with some aspect of economic history. In this connection one may mention K. D. Hüllmann, *Deutsche Finanzgeschichte des Mittelalters* (Berlin, 1805); Wilhelm E. Wilda, *Das Gildenwesen im Mittelalter* (Halle, 1831); Edward Baines, *History of the Cotton Manu-*

---

[6] N. B. S. Gras, "The Rise and Development of Economic History," *ibid.*, I (1927), 30, the whole article, 12–34.

[7] W. T. Jackman, "The Importance of Economic History," in *Facts and Factors in Economic History. Articles by Former Students of Edwin Francis Gay* (Cambridge, Mass., 1932), 3–17.

[8] "But it is to the clearer formulation from the pen of Karl Marx that we must look for real scientific influence. At least since the publication of the first volume of *Capital* (1867), the idea has been in the air that economic history is important because it is the key to other kinds of history." Gras (n. 30), 21–22.

[9] Among these early Socialists one may mention Claude Henri Saint-Simon (1760–1825), Barthélemy Enfantin, *le Père* (1796–1865), Charles Fourier (1772–1837), and Pierre Proudhon (1809–65).

[10] "In consequence of the successive violent deluges which have occurred within the past 9,000 years," so Plato describes the geographic basis of Attica, "there has been a constant movement of soil away from the high altitudes; and, owing to the shelving relief of the coast, this soil . . . has been perpetually deposited in the deep sea . . .; what remains of her substance is like the skeleton of a body emaciated by disease. . . . All the rich, soft soil has moulted away, leaving a country of skin and bones." Plato, *Critias*, quoted in A. J. Toynbee, *Greek Historical Thought from Homer to the Age of Heraclius* (London and New York, 1924), 169.

[11] James Harrington, *The Commonwealth of Oceana* (London, 1656); A. H. L. Heeren, *Ideen über die Politik, den Verkehr, und den Handel der vornehmsten Völker der alten Welt* (Göttingen, 1793–96, 3 v.); Justus Möser, *Osnabrückische Geschichte* (Berlin, 1768). On Heeren and Möser see above, ch. XXXIX, pp. 127–30 and 114–17 respectively.

factures in Great Britain (London, 1835); Thomas Tooke, *A History of Prices* (London, 1838–57, 6 v.); James Bischoff, *A Comprehensive History of the Woollen and Worsted Manufactures* (London, 1842, 2 v.).[12] But these were isolated studies, neither connected with any school nor based upon any general theory.

The German school of economic history properly begins with Wilhelm Roscher (1817–94).[13] It is a significant fact that Roscher was trained as an historian, especially under Ranke. He had also studied under Heeren and Gervinus. In a revealing letter to Ranke, Roscher asked his revered teacher for the honor of dedicating his first book, on Thucydides,[14] to him, and explained his own educational experiences.

In you I admire not merely the foremost living historian, but also, together with Niebuhr, the foremost historian of our people, altogether one of the few contemporaries who has successfully contended with the great ones of antiquity. . . .

At the outset of my literary activities, I would consider such a dedication as a shibboleth, in that I do not wish to belong either to the "thorough" quibblers who do not see the forest for the trees, or to the "intellectual" philosophers who, from their scaffolding, have too weak an eye to distinguish things on the plain earth. Added to this is that you are my teacher, precisely the one teacher to whom emphatically I am most indebted.

My first teacher was the old Heeren; his *Ideen* [15] was the first modern history which filled me with love even as a Gymnasium student. You will agree with me that no one was more suitable to acquaint young minds with the ancients. All my life I shall also have this in common with Heeren, that I shall prefer to work in ancient history as well as the more recent centuries of modern history.

My second teacher was Gervinus. I am in no way blind to the weaknesses of this man.

[12] Gras (n. 30), 14–17, has given a short list of even earlier economic histories. Among them are John Wheeler, *A Treatise of Commerce* (1601); Isaac de Laffémas, *L'histoire du commerce de France* (Paris, 1606); Johannis de Werdenhagen, *De Rebuspublicis Hanseaticis Tractatus* (Frankfort, 1629, 4 v.); John Evelyn, *Navigation and Commerce, Their Original and Progress* (London, 1674); Daniel Defoe, *A General History of Trade* (London, 1713); Pierre Daniel Huet, *Histoire du commerce et de la navigation des anciens* (Paris, 1716), and his *Mémoires sur le commerce des Hollandais dans tous les états et empires du monde* (Amsterdam, 1717); John Smith, *Chronicon Rusticum-Commerciale; or Memoirs of Wool* (London, 1747, 2 v.); Adam Anderson, *An Historical and Chronological Deduction of the Origin of Commerce* (London, 1764, 2 v.); Timothy Cunningham, *The History of Our Customs, Aids, Subsidies, National Debts and Taxes, from William the Conqueror to the Present Year 1761* (London, 1761, 4 v.); Sir John Sinclair, *History of the Public Revenue of the British Empire* (London, 1784, 3 pts.).

[13] The best English account on Roscher and his school is William B. Cherin, *The German Historical School of Economics* (manuscript dissertation in the University of California library, Berkeley, 1933); see also W. Cunningham, "Why Had Roscher So Little Influence in England?" *Annals of the American Academy of Political Science*, V (1894), 317–34; Carl Arnd, *Das System W. Roscher's gegenüber den unwandelbaren Naturgesetzen der Volkswirtschaft* (Frankfort, 1862); Hugo Eisenhart, *Geschichte der Nationalökonomik* (Jena, 1891); L. Brentano, "Wilhelm Roscher," *Nationalzeitung*, June 12, 1894, no. 352. W. Neurath, *Wilhelm Roscher und die historische-ethische Nationalökonomie* (Vienna, 1894); C. Roscher's introduction to Wilhelm Roscher's *Geistliche Gedanken eines Nationalökonomen* (Dresden, 1895), i–xxix; M. Brasch, *Roscher und die sozialwissenschaftlichen Strömungen der Gegenwart* (Leipzig, 1895); A. v. Miaskowski, "Wilhelm Roscher," *Deutsche Rundschau*, LXXXIV (1895), 214–38; A. Schaeffle, "Wilhelm Roscher," Harden's *Zukunft*, VIII (1894), 25 ff.

[14] Roscher, *Ueber das Leben, Werk und Zeitalter des Thukydides* (1842).

[15] The reference is to Heeren's, *Ideen über die Politik, den Verkehr, und den Handel der vornehmsten Völker der alten Welt* (Göttingen, 1793–96, 3 v.).

Had I not later come into your school, he might have become injurious to me in some respects; but just as there are few people who are more charming, so also are there few teachers so stimulating, who can evoke so many ideas. He had induced me to study equally the various aspects of historical development, namely political and literary history. To him I owe the method of penetrating into history by means of continuous analogies. It is a dangerous thing, analogy; this I in no way fail to appreciate. Who would approve that Gervinus, Schlosser, and others, frequently enough let the reader touch analogies instead of the thing itself? Today they compare Turkey with the German Empire of the fifteenth century and tomorrow with the Napoleonic monarchy, today they compare Petrarch with Hutten and tomorrow with Lessing. But a knife which can not wound is also of no use to the surgeon. In my opinion, everybody unconsciously makes use of analogy. I have formed two principles for the use of this tool. First, never to consider it as an aim in itself but only as a means. . . . Then to compare only corresponding stages: the middle ages of the Greeks with the middle ages of modern nations, contemporary Turkey with the last period of the ancient Persian empire, etc. These principles, I believe, are correct, even though it is frequently difficult to remain true to them in practice.

Finally I came to your school; and I hardly know whether I owe more to your lectures, your seminar, or your writings, whether I received from you more spur or curb. But everything of yours that I have either heard or read has left a spur in my soul. Even though I came too late to participate in your *Jahrbücher*, you may be sure that none of your students is attached to you with greater love and reverence, is more eager, not to imitate, but to emulate you and joyfully to consider himself his life long as your student. Would to God that I may succeed in not bringing dishonor to this name! [16]

Roscher then described his academic activities as a *dozent* at Göttingen. His lectures, he explains, include "politics, economics, statistics, history of the ancient historians and history of political theories." He also lectured on political history and had full audiences; soon he hopes, so he writes, to teach ancient history, for since the time of Schlözer it was the custom in Göttingen to combine history with politics. "To me politics is the study of the laws of the development of the state, and political economy the study of the laws of the development of economics." He hoped to "find" these laws, he informed Ranke, by comparing the histories of nations, "by grouping the uniform and defining the dissimilar."

More significantly, Roscher confided that he was planning a book on economics, hoping that it would be "regarded as historical." Here we have the first intimation of his lifelong work: to combine history with economics and connect them by means of "laws." "In Germany, so far as I know, this tendency in economics was first expressed by List, not without spirit, but often inconsistently, even with charlatanry,

---

[16] Roscher to Ranke, February 27, 1842, quoted from "Wilhelm Roscher an Leopold Ranke," *PJ*, CXXXIII (1908), 383–85. Though Roscher did not mention it in his letter, Otfried Müller and Dahlmann were also his teachers at Göttingen; at Berlin he also attended the courses of Böckh, the economic historian of ancient Greece, and Karl Ritter, the geographer. Undoubtedly Böckh and Ritter left a deep impression on Roscher, for he certainly learned no economics either from Gervinus or from Ranke.

and only in connection with one point, the tariff system." So the ambitious Roscher tells his great teacher that he is going to be the pioneer in economic history.

One year later, in 1843, Roscher published his *Grundriss zu Vorlesungen über die Staatswirthschaft nach geschichtlicher Methode*. This work, according to Ashley, the foremost English advocate of economic history, "sounded the first clear note of the new movement in academic circles." Roscher's *Grundriss* served both as a manifesto and a programme.[17]

Roscher remained surprisingly faithful to this programme. For the next half century he continued to publish and lecture on history and political economy, and he never thought it necessary to alter his ideas. One year after the publication of the *Grundriss* he became a full professor; four years later he accepted a call to Leipzig, where he remained, the honored father of the historical school of economics, until his death in 1894, when his school was generally in discredit.

It must be stressed that despite his obeisances to history and his reverence for Ranke, Roscher was not really an historian and hardly an economist. To history, according to the friendly account of Karl Bücher, Roscher was unsympathetic (*innerlich fremd*). Another critic says that Roscher was a *Geschichtsphilosoph* rather than an historian. His thinking was not always consistent, but his learning was always evident. A well-equipped linguist, he was at home in many fields of history, especially antiquity, on which he relied heavily for his illustrations and analogies. He was one of the few German scholars who could express himself in lucid prose. Hence his books, particularly his textbooks, appealed to a large public, just as his lectures attracted numerous hearers.

Roscher's ideas are most fully applied in his *magnum opus*, the four-volume work entitled *System der Volkswirthschaft*. The content of each volume may be gathered from its individual title: Volume I, *The Fundamentals of Political Economy* (1854); II, *Political Economy of Agriculture and the Related Primitive Production* (1859); III, *Political Economy of Commerce and Industry* (1881); IV, *System of the Science of Finance* (1886). The object of the whole system of political economy was to discover the basic laws which govern economic life. Economics he defined as the "study of the laws of development of political economy." The method by which he would discover these laws of development, he called "historic-physiological." Historic because he used materials

---

[17] See "Roscher's Programme of 1843," in ASHLEY, 21–37, reprinted from *Quarterly Journal of Economics*, IX (1895), 99–105, and Karl Bücher, "Wilhelm Roscher," *PJ*, LXXVII (1894), 104–23.

from history and connected the present state of economics with its immediate past; physiological, because he held the thesis that every nation, like any living organism, passes through definite stages of development, from childhood through youth to maturity and old age.

Roscher's object was not only scientific; it was also political. He was, in one sense, a continuator of Friedrich List (1798–1846), the brilliant German economist and politician who had challenged the free trade doctrine of Adam Smith and the English school. List had spent over five years in the United States, from 1824 to 1830, and as editor, business promoter, and manufacturer in America, he had become profoundly imbued with the ideas of the "American System." [18] List brought these ideas back to Germany, where he became the champion of protection, pointing out logically enough that free trade may have been applicable to a manufacturing country like England but was of no help to an industrially immature country like Germany. Adam Smith and Ricardo had underrated nationalism; List stimulated it, for obvious reasons.[19] Roscher tended in the same direction as List, although not in the same polemical spirit.

Unlike later economic historians, Roscher constantly stressed the idea that human culture was an indivisible whole; that the economic development—like the intellectual, religious, political, and ethical—was simply one wave in the whole stream of *Völkergeschichte*. Roscher may have gotten this concept from Winckelmann and Herder, but it was nevertheless a great service to emphasize it again.

> Roscher [to quote Schmoller's fine and discerning tribute to a man whom he considered his teacher] has the polyhistorical trait in common with the older Göttingen culture-historians; from Rau and the older generation he had taken over the deep respect for Adam Smith, Ricardo and Malthus. He is a fine, aristocratic, reserved, scholarly nature, crashing in nowhere but wanting to reconstruct slowly. He wanted to remain a dogmatical political economist as much as to deepen historically the concepts of the old school. He stands midway between two scientific epochs; he concludes the older period and opens the new. He did more than all others to raise political economy to the level of a scholarly and systematic specialty and historical causal investigation.[20]

Closely connected with Roscher and the historical school of economics are Bruno Hildebrand (1812–78) and Karl Gustav Knies (1821–98). Since neither of these men was an historian they will not be treated here in any detail. Hildebrand, who was professor at Marburg, published his *Nationalökonomie der Gegenwart und Zukunft* in 1848, in which he

[18] W. Notz, "Friedrich List in America," *Weltwirtschaftliches Archiv,* XXI (1925), 199–265. In 1840 List published his principal work, *Das nationale System der politischen Oekonomie;* note that this book came out only two years before Roscher's *Grundriss.*

[19] Alfred Marshall, *Principles of Economics* (London, 1916), 767–68.

[20] Gustav Schmoller, "Wilhelm Roscher," in his *Zur Litteraturgeschichte der Staats- und Sozialwissenschaften* (Leipzig, 1888), 147–71, quotation on 170.

argued in favor of an historical treatment of economics, but substituted psychological (ethical) laws for Roscher's economic-materialistic laws, on the assumption that man was an ethical being. Knies, the author of *Politische Oekonomie vom Standpunkte der geschichtlichen Methode* (1853),[21] accepted Hildebrand's ethical-psychological interpretation. "The life of a nation," he wrote, "follows a continually evolving path which excludes the supposition that the course of life of later peoples is entirely identical with that of antecedent ones." He admitted that he was less interested in history than in transforming the concepts of economics. As such he sought to discover the psychological aspects of economic life and traced the connections between economics, history, geography, philosophy, and law. Like Roscher, Knies accepted the idea that the life of a nation was organic and that the various types of national expression, including the economic, were interdependent. Hence economics can be studied only as part of social life in general.[22]

A large group of later economic historians followed Roscher, Hildebrand, and Knies. The most distinguished of these was Gustav Schmoller (1838–1917),[23] who did more for this subject than any other man since Roscher. He was professor of political science at Halle, then professor at the reorganized University of Strassburg (1872), and finally professor at Berlin (1882). In 1887 he was appointed Historiographer of Brandenburg. Schmoller considered himself a student of Roscher and, indeed, theoretically he improved little on his master. Like Roscher, Schmoller believed in descriptive economic history based upon historical facts and data; his method, too, that of collecting historical sources, was historical. But unlike Roscher, Schmoller actually wrote excellent economic histories, some of them, such as the study of the Strassburg weavers' gild, serving as models. Apart from his own writings, Schmoller was one of Germany's most distinguished promoters of the

---

[21] In the second edition the title was changed to *Die politische Oekonomie vom geschichtlichen Standpunkte* (Brunswick, 1883).

[22] See Schmoller (n. 20), 204–10; Eugène Schwiedland, "L'historisme économique allemand," *Journal des économistes*, 4th ser., XXXI (1885), 17–36; M. Hueter, *Die Methodologie der Wirtschaftswissenschaft bei Roscher und Knies* (Jena, 1928); C. Jaffé, *Roscher, Hildebrand und Knies als Begründer der älteren historischen Schule deutscher Volkswirte* (Berne diss., 1916); M. Weber, "Roscher und Knies und die logischen Probleme der historischen Nationalökonomie," *Schmollers Jahrbuch*, N. F., XXVII (1903), 1181–1221, and N. F., XXIX (1905), 1323–84; Robert Wilbrandt, "Das Ende der historisch-ethischen Schule," *Weltwirtschaftliches Archiv*, XXIV (1926), 73–108, 228–74.

[23] For review articles on Schmoller see: Georg v. Below, in *Vierteljahrschrift für Social- und Wirtschaftsgeschichte*, V (1907), 481–524; K. Diehl, in *Jahrbücher für Nationalökonomie und Statistik*, LXXXIV (1905), 233–37; W. Hasbach, *ibid.*, LXXVIII (1902), 387–403; E. C. K. Gonner, *Economic Journal*, XVI (1906), 261–66; K. T. v. Inama-Sternegg, *Zeitschrift für Volkswirtschaft, Sozialpolitik und Verwaltung*, XV (1906), 462–75, cp. his *Neue Probleme des modernen Kulturlebens* (Leipzig, 1908), 100–28; Thorstan Veblen, "Gustav Schmoller's Economics," *Quarterly Journal of Economics*, XVI (1901–02), 69–93. For bibliography see J. Conrad and others, eds., *Handwörterbuch der Staatswissenschaften* (Jena, 1909–11, 8 v.).

study of social science, being the founder of the *Verein für Sozialpolitik*, the editor of a series of historical investigations: *Staats-und Sozialwissenschaftliche Forschungen*, and finally editor of the important annual, *Jahrbuch für Gesetzgebung, Verwaltung und Volkswirtschaft im deutschen Reiche* (since 1881), generally referred to as *Schmoller's Jahrbuch*.

As for Schmoller's ideas, he was at one with the other advanced German scholars and thinkers in recognizing the close connection between the economic and all other social expressions in the life of a nation; but he differed from, say, Roscher, in his strong emphasis on the rôle of the State in the promotion of economic activities. In one sense, Schmoller was a member of the "Prussian School" of history; where, for example, Treitschke stressed the political superiority of the state, Schmoller emphasized the economic. Schmoller underrated individual action in the development of economic institutions. "The idea that economic life has ever been a process mainly dependent on individual action . . . is mistaken." For individual initiative (as was the case in the United States), Schmoller substituted political organization. To him, political organization, or the State, exercised the "most penetrating influence upon the various forms of economic organization that have made their appearance in history." [24]

The whole German historical school of economics, and particularly Schmoller, was sharply attacked by Carl Menger of the University of Vienna. The polemic was characteristically acrimonious.[25] But it lies beyond the scope of this work, since the quarrel was essentially concerned with the meaning and aim of economics. Briefly, the economist

[24] Schmoller's works include: *Zur Geschichte der nationalökonomischen Ansichten in Deutschland während der Reformationsperiode* (1861); *Zur Geschichte der deutschen Kleingewerbe im 19. Jahrhundert* (Halle, 1870); *Ueber einige Grundfragen des Rechts und der Volkswirtschaft: Ein offenes Sendschreiben an Herrn Professor Dr. Heinrich von Treitschke* (Leipzig, 1874–75); *Die Strassburger Tucherund Weberzunft, . . . Ein Beitrag zur Geschichte der deutschen Weberei und des deutschen Gewerberechts vom XIII bis XVII Jahrhundert* (Strassburg, 1879); *Studien über die wirtschaftliche Politik Friedrich des Grossen* (1884); *Zur Sozial- und Gewerbepolitik der Gegenwart: Reden und Aufsätze* (Leipzig, 1890); *Ueber einige Grundfragen der Socialpolitik und der Volkswirtschaftslehre* (Leipzig, 1898); *Grundriss der allgemeinen Volkswirtschaftslehre* (Leipzig, 1901–04, 2 v.).

[25] The following passage may serve as an example of the spirit of the conflict: "Mag der Methodiker Schmoller in Hinkunft noch so löwenhaft im Spree-sande einherschreiten, die Mähne schütteln, die Pranke heben, erkenntnisstheoretisch gähnen; nur Kinder und Thoren werden fürderhin seine methodologischen Gebärden noch ernst nehmen. Durch den weiten Riss in seiner gelehrten Maske wird aber mancher Wissbegierige, leider vielleicht auch mancher Neugierige blicken und die wahre Gestalt dieses Erkenntnisstheoretikers mit Heiterkeit und Genugthuung betrachten." Menger, *Die Irrthümer des Historismus in der deutschen National-ökonomie* (Vienna, 1884), 86–87; see also Menger, *Untersuchungen über die Methode der Socialwissenschaften und der politischen Oekonomie insbesondere* (1883). For criticisms of the historical school see also G. v. Below, "Zur Würdigung der historischen Schule der National-ökonomie," *Zeitschrift für Sozialwissenschaft*, VII (1904), 145–85, 221–37, 304–29, 367–91, 451–66, 654–59, 710–16, 787–804; F. Lifschitz, *Die historische Schule der Wirtschaftswissenschaft* (Bern, 1914); Bernhard Pfister, *Die Entwicklung zum Idealtypus: eine methodologische Untersuchung über das Verhältniss von Theorie und Geschichte bei Menger, Schmoller, und Max Weber* (Tübingen, 1928); R. Schüller, *Die Wirtschaftspolitik der historischen Schule* (Berlin, 1899).

Menger criticized the "historical school" for having brought in "foreign," i.e., historical, concepts into economics and having caused much confusion. The reform of political economy, Menger pointed out, will not come from historians, or mathematicians, or physiologists, but must come from within, "from us specialists, who are in the service of this science." Menger was bitter because historians had invaded the field of economics and imposed "their language and habits, their terminology and method." He had, he said, no quarrel with the historians as such, but they should mind their own business. Each science had its own method and objective; the goal of economics was not that of history.

But quarrels over method apart—these were carried on mainly by economists—economic history as a specific discipline continued to gain in depth, width, and prestige all over Europe and America. In 1876 Karl Theodor von Inama-Sternegg (1843–1908), the distinguished Austrian economic historian, said that the historical treatment of economic problems was already so generally accepted that it was by then a "banal idea." It is virtually impossible to discuss all the German economic historians after Roscher. In general, they accepted Roscher's method as well as his fruitful idea of the inter-relation between the economic and all other social phenomena. Inama-Sternegg, the author of a remarkable *Deutsche Wirtschaftsgeschichte* (1879–1901, 3 v.), treated German economic history from an evolutionary standpoint, on the assumption that the present was an outgrowth of the past. In a programme for the study of German economic history, Inama-Sternegg suggested a "rigorous critique" of historical sources—including laws, statutes, registers, decrees, account-books, and even *belles lettres*—and their genetic treatment. His aim was a "living connection between economic life and all other branches of human social and cultural life in the past as well as in the present." [26]

Between the years 1900 and 1927 no less than 340 works on economic history were published in German.[27] It is necessary to notice at

[26] Inama-Sternegg, "Ueber die Quellen der deutschen Wirtschaftsgeschichte," *Sitzungsberichte der k. Akademie der Wissenschaften*, phil.-hist. cl., LXXIV (Vienna, 1876), 135–210; see also H. Rauchberg in *Zeitschrift für Volkswirtschaft, Sozialpolitik und Verwaltung*, XVIII (1909), 1–28; E. Mischler in *Schmoller's Jahrbuch*, XXXII (1909), 1129–59; and for bibliography, the same in *Biographisches Jahrbuch und deutscher Nekrolog*, XIII (1910), 116–24; cp. ASHLEY, 111–14.

[27] Georg Brodnitz, "Recent Work in German Economic History, 1900–1927," *Economic History Review*, I (1928), 322–45; valuable survey chapters by a score of scholars in *Die Entwicklung der deutschen Volkswirtschaftslehre im neunzehnten Jahrhundert. Gustav Schmoller zur siebenzigsten Wiederkehr seines Geburtstages* (Leipzig, 1908, 2 v.); Karl Bräuer, "Kritische Studien zur litteratur und Quellenkunde der Wirtschaftsgeschichte," in *Volkswirtschaftliche und wirtschaftsgeschichtliche Abhandlungen Wilhelm Stieda als Festgruss zur 60. Wiederkehr seines Geburtstages dargebracht* (Leipzig, 1912), 88 ff.; Armin Tille, "Quellen zur städtischen Wirtschaftsgeschichte," *Deutsche Geschichtsblätter*, IX (1908); Georg Caro, "Zur Quellenkunde der deutschen Wirtschaftsgeschichte," *ibid.*, XI (1910).

least two other German economic historians, Nitzsch and Lamprecht, the one for his inherent significance, the other for his ambitious attempt and even more ambitious claims.

Karl Wilhelm Nitzsch (1818–80) [28] was, like Roscher, a student of Ranke (from 1839 to 1842). A reading of Niebuhr, who was next to Ranke the greatest influence in his life, [29] led him to Roman history; and his first published work was *The Gracchi and Their Forerunners* (1847), an economic interpretation of this Roman political revolution. It is significant that this work appeared at about the same time as the Marx-Engels' *Communist Manifesto* which presaged the now famous materialistic interpretation of history.

About half of Nitzsch's professorial career was spent at Kiel (where his father was professor of philology); and though he had married a Danish girl, his sympathies were pro-German. The political conflict centering about Schleswig-Holstein stimulated Nitzsch—as it had Dahlmann a few decades earlier—to a study of the history of the duchies. In this connection he wrote *Der holsteinische Adel im zwölften Jahrhundert* (1854). His medieval studies were enriched by a new interest in legal and constitutional problems and led to the publication of his remarkable *Ministerialität und Bürgertum im 11. und 12. Jahrhundert* (1859), a study of the relation between the bourgeoisie and the functionaries (*Ministerialität*). His highly original thesis was that the free bourgeoisie was an outgrowth of the functionary class and that the city constitutions were derived from the *Hofrecht* of these *ministeriales*. This hypothesis was later attacked, especially by Georg von Below.

In 1862 Nitzsch was called to Königsberg, where he remained for ten years. Thence he went to the University of Berlin. All this time he was working on both Roman history and medieval German history. Though he grew more and more conservative, becoming a champion of the Prussian State and army (which he compared to the Roman), he

[28] On Nitzsch see ASHLEY, 242–48, reprinted from the *Economic Journal*, III (1893), 686–90; Herbert Merzdorf, *Karl Wilhelm Nitzsch, die methodischen Grundlagen seiner Geschichtschreibung* (Leipzig, 1913), cp. the review by Below in *HZ*, CXIII (1914), 559–66; G. Matthäi's introduction to Nitzsch's *Geschichte des deutschen Volkes* (2nd ed., Leipzig, 1892, 3 v.), I, pp. v–xii; J. Jastrow, "K. W. Nitzsch und die deutsche Wirtschaftsgeschichte," *Schmoller's Jahrbuch*, VIII (1884), 873–97, and his article in *Allgemeine deutsche Biographie*, XXIII (1886), 730–42; Richard Rosenmund, in *PJ*, XLVIII (1881), 321–45, 425–48, and XLIX (1882), 262–89, 337–54; G. Waitz, "K. W. Nitzsch," in *Jahresberichte über die Fortschritte der klassischen Altertumswissenschaft* (1880); for Nitzsch's letters see *Archiv für Kulturgeschichte*, VIII (1910), 305–66 and X (1912), 49–110. Of reviews, cp. *HZ*, II (1859), 443–57, LVI (1890), 215–24, and several pages on Nitzsch in Neumann's review of Burckhardt's *Griechische Geschichte* in LXXXV (1900); and *PJ*, LXIV, 337–54.

[29] The article on Nitzsch in *ESS*, XI, 384, makes the point that at Berlin he studied under Ranke and Niebuhr; since Nitzsch was born in 1818 and Niebuhr had left Berlin in 1816 and died in 1831, when Nitzsch was only thirteen years old, the statement in the Encyclopaedia is somewhat misleading.

remained a staunch believer in economic interpretation, insisting, like Karl Marx, that economic conditions influenced political developments. Unfortunately he died before he could complete his two great works, which were edited by others. His student Georg Matthäi published the *Geschichte des deutschen Volkes bis zum Augsburger Religionsfrieden* (1883–85, 3 v.), and G. Thouret issued the *Geschichte der römischen Republik* (1884–85, 2 v.). Nitzsch's reputation rests on these two post-humous works.

The central thesis in Nitzsch's work is the dominance of economic elements in the life of a nation. He was at one with Roscher, Knies, Hildebrand, Inama-Sternegg, and the eighteenth-century *Aufklärung* in stressing the inter-connection between the various aspects of national life and their organic, evolutionary development. If he selected the economic forces as being the preponderant elements it was due to his conviction—typically Marxist, be it said, though Nitzsch would not have considered himself as such—that the key to history lay in the rise and organization of economic classes and interests. In short, since the historian has to select a central thesis, even if only as a means of exposition, in order to give both unity and intelligibility to his work, he might as well take what is basic—and economic conditions and movements are undoubtedly basic.

Nitzsch's emphasis on the economic aspects of history cost him his popularity in Germany; he never received the credit he deserved—he was not elected to the exclusive Prussian Academy until one year before his death, in 1879—and he left no school. His interpretation was a reaction to both liberalism and idealism. He challenged both Mommsen and Ranke, the former because of his lack of concreteness and the latter because of his exclusive occupation with politics and diplomacy. Nor was he able to accept the conclusions of the political economists. Nitzsch was, in short, an isolated thinker, guided only by his own vigorously independent mind and the inspiring spirit of Niebuhr.

Ancient history [he wrote, apropos of his determination to tell the truth as he saw it at all costs] is the kernel and central point of all humanistic studies, and these will only withstand the inroads of materialism, if a presentation of the same is attained which will abstain from a collection of dry facts or a well-meaning pathos, and will on the contrary show antiquity moved to its very depths by the same economic problems which even today, in part unsolved, occupy every honest man.

Nitzsch attempted, though not always successfully, to balance his economic factors with the influence of leading personalities. Writing of the interpretation of history, he asked:

Is its duty the exact development of the universal ideas with which the human spirit seeks to make itself more and more familiar? Or shall it attempt to keep in mind the independence of a particular act and a particular personality? Shall it . . . permit the individual to recognize that he carries within himself an unlimited power and freedom of will and that at all times the free act of self-conscious characters and not a hidden spiritual power of fate has conditioned the event? [30]

He decided in favor of the free individual.

Nitzsch likewise rejected nationality—or as one would call it today, "racism"—as an explanation of historical phenomena. Not nations as such, but their social and economic conditions at a given stage of development influence their culture. He protested against the universal tendency of treating legal and constitutional history as primary forces, as things apart, rather than as results of social-economic factors.[31] Constitutional and economic history have an intimate connection, Nitzsch argued, whether in the Roman republic or in medieval German history.

On almost every page which Nitzsch wrote there are fruitful and stimulating ideas. He possessed that gift which makes an historian great, namely, the divination of relations; he had an intuitive sense for perceiving what had not been perceived before and for seeing in a flash the connections between material cause and social effect. It was Nitzsch who first saw what no one had seen before him, that the location of the Saxon crown lands in the time of Henry I predicated an inevitable German expansion to the Slavic East (*Drang nach Osten*)—a stroke of brilliant historical interpretation. There are many other examples of his penetration.

Since Nitzsch's ideas were basically in conflict with the dominant German ideological interpretation of history and were contrary to national pride, he died without having left much influence on German historiography. Nitzsch has been virtually relegated to oblivion. Nevertheless his ideas did not altogether die. Many of his fruitful notions were taken over—often without acknowledgment—by Karl Lamprecht (1856–1915), the most disputed figure in recent historiography. "If," to quote an ironic French comment, "the value of an historian were measured by the noise which his name makes in the world, Lamprecht would be one of the great ones." [32]

---

[30] Karl W. Nitzsch, *Die Gracchen und ihre nächsten Vorgänger* (Berlin, 1847), 8.
[31] See his *Geschichte des deutschen Volkes* (n. 28), I, 36–39 and *passim*.
[32] An excellent summary on Lamprecht is to be found in J. Goldfriedrich, *Die historische Ideenlehre in Deutschland* (Berlin, 1902), 431–56; also in BERNHEIM, 711–18, with bibliography; GOOCH, 588–93; Hans F. Helmolt's introduction to *Porträtgalerie aus Lamprechts Deutsche Geschichte* (Leipzig, 1910); E. W. Dow, "Features of the New History: Apropos of Lamprecht's 'Deutsche Geschichte,'" *AHR*, III (1897–98), 431–48; Antoine Guilland, "Karl Lamprecht," *RH*, CXXI (1916), 83–108; G. des Marez, "Conception sociale et économique de l'histoire du droit," *RCC*, X (1902), pt. ii, 603–22; W. Goetz, "Geschichte und Kulturgeschichte," *Archiv für Kulturgeschichte*, VIII (1910), 4–19; A. B. Show, "The New Culture-History in Germany," *History Teacher's Magazine*, IV (1913), 215–21. At Lamprecht's death in 1915 there appeared

That Lamprecht was one of the great ones is open to doubt. But his ambitious efforts deserve a careful estimate. He was educated at Göttingen, Munich, and Leipzig, and took his degree in the last university in medieval economic history. After holding professorships in history at Bonn (1885) and Marburg (1890), he went to Leipzig (1891), where he remained to the end of his life. While at Bonn he published his *Deutsches Wirtschaftsleben im Mittelalter* (1886, 3 v.), a solid work on the economic life on the valley of the Mosel and the middle Rhine, which took six years to write. It contains a vast amount of data and is full of statistical tables on mills, parishes, vineyards, rents, etc. There are sections on medieval law, agriculture, trade unions, land-cultivation, manorial organization, social classes, administration, and all the ramifications of a complicated social-economic system.[33] Lamprecht's later histories have been attacked and his conclusions disputed, but this early work still stands as a model.

Until about 1890 Lamprecht's career was as normal and meritorious as that of any other German professor. His work, though solid, was more or less in the conventional pattern and his academic career quite regular. Then, in 1891, there appeared the first volume of his *Deutsche Geschichte* and it immediately created a furore in academic circles and in the press. Henceforth, for the next quarter-century, Lamprecht was at war with all his colleagues in the field of history.[34]

In the immediate background of the Lamprecht controversy were two pamphlets. In 1888 Dietrich Schäfer published a booklet, *Das eigentliche Arbeitsgebiet der Geschichte*, in which he argued, in the tradition of the political school, that the "proper sphere of history" was politics and nothing else. His "History is not a feeding trough" has become a famous phrase. The aim of historiography, so Schäfer insisted, was the history of the state; psychology, law, economics, etc.,

a number of obituaries. Among them may be listed: Georg Küntzel, "Lamprechts Stellung in der Geschichtswissenschaft," *Frankfurter Zeitung*, May 13, 1915; P. Schweizer, "Karl Lamprecht," *Neue Züricher Zeitung*, May 22, 1915: M. Muret, "Karl Lamprecht," *Mercure de France*, May 1, 1915; Carl Brinkmann, "Karl Lamprecht und die Geschichtswissenschaft," *Neue Rundschau*, XXVI (1915), pt. ii, 969–74; H. Barge, "Karl Lamprecht," *Die Hilfe*, May 20, 1915; E. Spranger, "Karl Lamprechts Geschichtsauffassung," *Vossische Zeitung*, June 6, 1915; F. Lifschitz, "Karl Lamprecht," *Wissen und Leben*, August 15, 1915; Van Outhorrn, "Karl Lamprecht," *De Gids*, no. 10, 1915. For some criticisms of Lamprecht see Felix Rachfahl, "Deutsche Geschichte vom wirthschaftlichen Standpunkt," *PJ*, LXXIV (1896), 542–55; M. Lenz, "Lamprecht's *Deutsche Geschichte*," *HZ*, LXXVII (1896), 385–447; O. Hintze, "Ueber individualistische und kollektivistische Geschichtsauffassung," *ibid.*, LXXVIII (1897), 60–67; Georg v. Below, "Kulturgeschichte und kulturgeschichtlicher Unterricht," *ibid.*, CVI (1910), 96–105; cp. the same in *ibid.*, LXXXI (1898), 269 ff.; H. Finke, *Genetische und klerikale Geschichtsauffassung*, (Münster, 1897); Bernheim, "Geschichtsunterricht und Geschichtswissenschaft," *Neue Bahnen*, X (1899), 275 ff.; Ashley in *Political Science Quarterly*, December 1894.

[33] See the review by Adolf Bruder in *Historisches Jahrbuch*, VIII (1887), 502–19.

[34] Henri Pirenne, "Un polémique historique en Allemagne," *RH*, LXIV (1897), 50–57.

were merely *Hilfswissenschaften* to history. The historian should occupy himself with individuals as being an expression of moral forces.
Such a narrow, reactionary interpretation, running counter as it did to
the most advanced thought in the social sciences, caused a great stir.
Niebuhr was dead, Nitzsch was dead, Ranke was dead, so the task of
replying to Schäfer fell to Eberhard Gothein, one of the younger historians interested in *Kulturgeschichte.* In his *Die Aufgaben der Kulturgeschichte* (1889), Gothein, who had written a book on Loyola and
the Counter-Reformation, pointed out that political history was only
one aspect of the history of civilization, that the state may be the most
important expression in the life of a nation, but was not the exclusive
achievement of a people. There were other aspects of human life which
required treatment and deserved attention—economic movements,
law, politics, art, religion—and, therefore, it was the historian's task
to write about these phases, to regard them as an organic whole, and
to abstract from these complex social facts some underlying and unifying ideas.

The Schäfer-Gothein polemic helped to clear the air by bringing the
conflict between political history and culture history to a focus. Neither
side convinced the other. Lamprecht, a man of prodigious vanity,[35] was
emphatically on the side of *Kulturgeschichte.* In a short time this ambitious man was to exclaim: "I am the man of progress who has accomplished a revolution in history."

The first volume of his *Deutsche Geschichte* was the first shot in this
"revolution." It was issued without preface or explanation in order
that it might make its own reputation. Other volumes continued to
appear for the next quarter-century, so that by 1913 there were twelve
volumes in fourteen parts, covering German history to the year 1870,
and an *Ergänzungswerk* in two volumes, treating the period since 1870.
Between 1891 and 1895, six volumes had appeared; they proved so
popular that three editions were exhausted.

While the popular acclaim was great, the critical offensive was immediate, sharp, and uncompromising. To a considerable extent, one
was the cause of the other. The reader cannot, indeed, escape the
impression that Lamprecht's professorial colleagues were jealous of
his success. Max Lenz, in a devastating review of the fifth volume,
said that when laymen praised a book it was time for scholars to protest; because, Lenz wrote, "there is danger that the work might be
snatched up by our teachers and disseminated." [36] Lamprecht, who
was of a vigorously combative nature and replied to his critic in kind,

---

[35] For examples of Lamprecht's vanity see Brinkmann in *Neue Rundschau* (n. 32).
[36] Quoted from his article in *HZ* (n. 32), 385–47.

never succeeded in attracting either a single prominent champion to his cause or a single distinguished adherent to his school.

What, then, were these "revolutionary" ideas which caused so much controversy? In the first place, Lamprecht made a sweeping attack on the older historic school, the *alte Richtung*, as represented by Ranke, whom he accused of being mere collectors of facts, particularly political facts, without penetrating into the deeper causes and without seeking either coherence or unity. These Rankeans had persistently ignored social psychology and the underlying causes of social progress. They had treated history as the expression of "mystic-transcendental spiritual forces" which animated leading individuals; they had considered history as the life of persons and not the "generic life of mankind." If Ranke himself was guilty of such superficial thinking, his followers, the *Jungrankianer*, were even worse.[37]

Rejecting this *alte Richtung*, Lamprecht substituted his own philosophy, the *neue Richtung*. This *Richtung* would treat the mass and not man as an individual; instead of writing the history of eminent persons, it would write about the collective work of humanity. The individual, Lamprecht held, did not determine society, but society conditioned the individual. The historian, like the social scientist, must consider society—the human totality—as the basic element in his work and must keep in mind that the individual was merely a contingent and ephemeral phenomenon dependent upon the larger group.

In the second place, the scientific-social historian of the *neue Richtung* must adopt a method different from the Rankeans. Where Ranke and the political historians had asked, "How did it happen?" (*Wie ist es eigentlich gewesen?*), Lamprecht and the new school wished to know "How did it become?" (*Wie ist es eigentlich geworden?*). The Ranke question implied a narrative; Lamprecht's query required a genetic treatment of society as a whole in order to determine its psychic consciousness, or, as modern sociologists would say, its behavior patterns. Although the Rankeans resented the attack on their master and made a weak defense to the effect that Ranke too had been interested in the *Werdegang* of past events, Lamprecht's acute criticism had struck home.

The object of Lamprecht's *kulturgeschichtliche Methode* was to establish a science of history, based upon sociological laws. "History,"

[37] Among these *Jungrankianer* was Friedrich Meinecke who had criticized Lamprecht. See Lamprecht's reply, "Zum Unterschiede der älteren und jüngeren Richtungen der Geschichtswissenschaft," *HZ*, LXXVII (1896), 257–61, and Meinecke's answer *ibid.*, 262–66, in which he stated that Lamprecht had misunderstood Ranke's *Ideenlehre*; Meinecke also accused his opponent of being a "materialist," because he interpreted "German unity, at bottom, as an economic process."

so reads the first sentence in his *What is History?* "is primarily a socio-psychological science." [38] Lamprecht discerned six different periods in the *Geistesleben* of the German nation. These stages were a diapason which characterized every civilization, and resembled Comte's *solidarité* (though Lamprecht denied having taken his concept from the Frenchman). The first epoch, which Lamprecht labelled *Symbolism*, covered the primitive period up to the tenth century. The second stage was what he called *Typism*, a word used to describe the early Middle Ages. The third phase was *Conventionalism*, covering the era from the thirteenth to the fifteenth centuries. *Individualism*, from the sixteenth to the first half of the eighteenth centuries, was the fourth stage. *Subjectivism*, the period of Romanticism and the Industrial Revolution, was the fifth epoch. And finally came the period of *Reizbarkeit*, or nervous tension, which describes the most recent era.

With every stage, Lamprecht claimed, the *Geistesleben*, the spiritual life of the nation, becomes more intense and the passions more balanced. And, what was most significant in his interpretation, these periods of growth in the realm of the mind corresponded exactly with the material development. Thus, paralleling Nitzsch, he found that his first stage, that of Symbolism, corresponded with the era of *occupatorische Wirtschaft*, fishing and hunting. Typism and Conventionalism, Lamprecht's second and third stages, were parallel to a collective and private property economy in land—*Naturalwirthschaft*, while Individualism and Subjectivism corresponded to a money economy—*Geldwirthschaft*.

The universal principle which Lamprecht claimed to have found in the history of civilization was that with the intensification of socio-psychological consciousness there came a constantly increasing differentiation among individuals in society, and that this led to *seelische Freiheit*. In short, the purpose of history, if history had a purpose, was the purely Hegelian concept of the "freedom of the spirit," stated in psychological, rather than metaphysical, terms.

Enough has been said to show the boldness of Lamprecht's interpretation. But whether his system is valid remains open to doubt. His method is highly dubious. Ashley has pointed out that Lamprecht operated "with far too few economic conceptions" and that his simple contrast between *Naturalwirthschaft* and *Geldwirthschaft*—taken bodily from Nitzsch—was insufficient for the treatment of a complex economy. From the point of view of history, even graver faults must be pointed out. Lamprecht was so obsessed by his presuppositions that he blithely ignored large sections of historical evidences and distorted other data

[38] Karl Lamprecht, *What is History? Five Lectures on the Modern Science of History*, tr. by E. A. Andrews (New York and London, 1905), 3.

to prove his theses.[39]   He imposed generalizations upon insufficient materials; his method was generally that of the giant Procrustes—if the sleeper was too tall for the bed he cut off his limbs, and if the bed was too long for the sleeper he stretched his limbs. Lamprecht rarely took the trouble to prove his facile generalizations or to show any organic causality. Ashley has stated this criticism with succinctness, not unmixed with irony. Lamprecht had written that the fifteenth-century bureaucracy in Germany was the outcome of the new money economy.

Before I accept or deny this proposition [Ashley wrote] I should like to see it proved (1) that there was a "bureaucracy" in the fifteenth century, (2) that there was a *Geldwirthschaft*, and, when this preliminary task is completed, (3) that the bureaucracy was actually supported by the *Geldwirthschaft*, and (4) that in all the other countries that had a bureaucracy there was a *Geldwirthschaft*, and in every country where there was a *Geldwirthschaft* there was a bureaucracy.[40]

Perhaps the chief criticism that the historian may level at Lamprecht is that in his attempt to make a science of history he had betrayed history and had ceased to be an historian. His method, on his own admission, was that of sociology and his aim that of a psychologist. "History in itself is nothing," he insisted, "but applied psychology. Hence we must look to theoretical psychology to give us the clew to its true interpretations." [41] Now if history is psychology, why call it history and why use historical materials? And if we must go to psychology to give us true history, why not stay in the realm of psychology? For, clearly, if history is psychology, then it is not history; so why take all this trouble? Or would psychologists agree with Lamprecht that the way to acquire a knowledge of psychology is to go to history? One doubts whether psychologists would have any use for Lamprecht's method or his materials. "The important milestones in the development of historiography," he boasted, "are Voltaire, Bernheim, and I." But he actually did not know enough social science to be a milestone. He borrowed his ideas extensively and, with his craving for publicity, filled the press with his pretensions. Of him one may say what Stendhal had said about certain German scholars: "To them truth is not that what is but what, according to their system, it should be."

Historians have generally rejected Lamprecht, but he believed himself to be a creative genius, a revolutionary innovator, an inspiring prophet —in short a Man with a Mission. When after two decades of bitter polemics he still found himself with but few converts or defenders—even

---

[39] For specific examples of Lamprecht's omissions and distortions see Lenz' criticism in *HZ* (n. 32).

[40] ASHLEY, 28, the whole article, 22–30.   [41] *What is History?* (n. 38), 29.

his fellow professors at Leipzig persisted in the *alte Richtung*—he undertook to create a school of his own. With the financial assistance of sympathetic friends, he formally opened, in May, 1909, the Royal Saxon Institute for Cultural and Universal History. The Institute, though affiliated with the University of Leipzig, was independent, having its own instructors, funds, equipment, and a library of some 30,000 volumes (Lamprecht started the library with 4,000 volumes which he contributed as a nucleus). A dozen teachers, all trained by Lamprecht and expressing his own ideas, gave courses in the philosophy of history, genealogy, bibliography, ethnology, economic and social history, child study, court ceremonial, comparative law, *Kulturgeschichte* of Germany and of China. Lamprecht himself taught cultural history and historical method. The Institute published monographs— about forty altogether—under the general title *Lamprecht's Beiträge zur Kultur- und Universal-Geschichte*. Steinhausen, one of Lamprecht's students, edited a periodical for the history of culture: *Archiv für Kulturgeschichte*. But the world of German scholarship remained skeptical, although Lamprecht received some attention abroad.[42]

A parallel movement took place in England, but without the embittered polemics of Germany. Despite the fact that German theories were to some extent carried over into England, especially in the 1880's, the country in which the Industrial Revolution [43] had developed most fully did not succumb to continental abstractions. English economic historians remained characteristically English. The constitutional and legal historians of England left their deep traces also on economic history. Bishop Stubbs carried more weight with his country's economic historians than did Professors Roscher or Schmoller. Furthermore, the country of Darwin was more hospitable to an evolutionary and functional interpretation of society than was the home of Hegel. This is not implying that German thinkers had no evolutionary standpoint; but the difference between Germany and England was a matter of interpretation. Where the Germans tended to generalization, theories, and schemata, the English were factual and concrete, and little inclined to abstractions.

It is also necessary to remember that in England there was no such

[42] Lamprecht himself defended his views in various pamphlets. Among them are his *Alte und neue Richtungen in der Geschichtswissenschaft* (1896); *Was ist Kulturgeschichte?* (1896); *Zwei Zeitschriften* (1897); *Die historische Methode des Herrn von Below* (1899); *Die kulturhistorische Methode* (1900); *Historische Methode und historisch-akademischer Unterrıcht* (1910). There is a vast bibliography on the Lamprecht controversy, for, as Guilland said, he "entendait à merveille l'art de la réclame." For a bibliography see M. Muret, *La littérature allemande d'aujourd'hui* (Paris, 1909), 373–93.

[43] The phrase "Industrial Revolution" was first used by Arnold Toynbee in his lectures in 1881–82, and he made it popular; Marx used the phrase once for the cotton industry in 1735; see A. Hutt, *This Final Crisis* (London, 1935).

sharp class distinction as in Germany. In the latter country, the professors were a carefully selected élite, generally appointed by a bureaucratic-paternalistic government; hence German scholars had little, if
any, touch with their fellow citizens. The problems of the "man in the
street" were not the problems of the secluded savant. Consequently
the German professor was at greater liberty to create theories and evolve
generalizations. In England, on the other hand, there was a closer
contact between the intellectuals and the people. English professors
were not servants of a bureaucratic state like their German colleagues.
Furthermore, English scholars were generally bourgeois, that is, they
belonged to the commercial middle class—the dominant and most
numerous class in the nation—and were interested in its problems.
Thus we find English scholars reacting to such crises as those of 1866
and 1873, which brought economic problems to their attention. Hence
one is not surprised to see English economic thinkers stressing the individual rather than the institution, considering man more important
than wealth. In Germany, as we have seen, scholars like Schmoller and
Lamprecht had thrown out the individual in favor of the state or of
society, while a solitary protesting voice like that of Nitzsch was unable
to restore man to his proper place in the social-economic system. Both
Weltanschauungen had their advantages and disadvantages. The Germans, roughly speaking, were philosophical and scientific, and the
English were ethical and moral.[44]

The first important work in the field of English economic history
was that of James Edwin Thorold Rogers (1825–90),[45] the pioneer
in the field of English rural history. His *A History of Agriculture and
Prices in England*, in seven volumes, was written over a period of
forty-two years and was "compiled entirely from original and contemporaneous records." [46] Despite inevitable faults, this work ranks
as a monumental achievement, especially when compared to other
works in the field of economics. A few comparisons may be illuminating.
Smith's *Wealth of Nations*, for example, took only twelve years to write;
Eden wrote his *State of the Poor* when he was but thirty-two years old;

[44] As an example of English moral-humanitarian attitude, one may cite the following passage
from Thomas Ruggles, *The History of the Poor* (London, 1797), 68: "The dignity of history
very seldom stoops to record the distresses or comforts of the bulk of the people; the business of
the historian is with wars and revolutions, treaties and the infringement of them, the intrigues
of party, and the excesses of the higher orders of the state; but rarely does he condescend to
relate the short and simple annals of the poor."

[45] On Rogers see Ashley, *An Introduction to English Economic History and Theory* (4th ed.,
London and New York, 1906–09, 2 v.), I, 5, 68, 185, and II, 264–65; see also Gustav Cohn, *A
History of Political Economy*, tr. by Joseph A. Hill (Philadelphia, 1894), 127–28. For some reviews see *BQR*, XLVI (1867), 125–42; *The Nation*, LXXVI (1903), 195–96.

[46] The full title reads: *A History of Agriculture and Prices in England, from the Year after the
Oxford Parliament (1259) to the Commencement of the Continental War (1793). Compiled entirely
from Original and Contemporaneous Records* (Oxford, 1866–1902, 7 v. in 8).

Macpherson's *Annals* occupied fifteen years of his life. But Thorold Rogers projected his work in 1860, published the first two volumes in 1866, and the last one, edited by his son, appeared posthumously in 1902. The *History* begins with the year 1259 and ends in 1793, the period of the Continental War—a span of almost five and a half centuries.

Rogers did not begin his professional career either as an economist or as an historian. He was trained as a classical scholar and became a clergyman, a career which he abandoned for academic work and practical politics. He was appointed professor of political economy at London and Oxford, was elected to Parliament, and became an ardent free trader and follower of Gladstone; in short, Thorold Rogers was an English liberal of the mid-Victorian era, and this, incidentally, colored his historical interpretations, especially his hatred of the tyranny of landlords.

In the preface to the second volume, Rogers tells how he came to write his *History*. He had attended the meeting of the International Statistical Congress in 1860 and his attention was called to the need for a study of ancient values and the determination of the relation between the price of labor and food. Rogers then searched the Bodleian Library for evidence, but found little; he then obtained permission to study the account books of the older colleges and found, he tells, "a vast store of the most valuable documents." This led him farther back than he had originally intended—he had planned to confine himself to the sixteenth century. "I have thus become," he admits, "an antiquary by accident."

His original purpose was, it must be stressed, to write history and not economics. The early volumes were distinctly historical, revealing, in the words of Rogers, "the bygone life of the English people." In the introductory chapter of the first volume he wrote: "It is my purpose, in the work before me, to attempt a history of agriculture in England, and to supply a record of prices, especially of corn and labor, from the time at which the earliest consecutive annals begin, down to the close of the eighteenth century." But after six years of research his data had become so enormous that he had to seek for some principles to explain them. His materials forced him to find "maxims of political economy"and "bases for economical inductions."

Some of the problems of political economy, therefore, I venture on stating, can be discerned and determined with greater ease from the facts which I am able to bring before my readers, fragmentary as they sometimes are, than they could be out of the wider information of our own time. Thus, for instance, the laws which govern prices will, I think, be seen more clearly in these medieval records than they could be in a modern Price Current.

Consequently Rogers became more and more dogmatic about his own achievements and his own ability to formulate economic truth. Although his authority as an economic theorist has been undermined—or perhaps never accepted—as an economic historian, especially in the field of medieval prices, he is still pre-eminent. His method, too, had much to recommend it. Instead of only stating prices as given in the original documents, he converted them into terms of purchasing power.[47]

Of the younger generation of English economic historians, Cunningham and Ashley are the most prominent. William Cunningham (1849–1919),[48] like Thorold Rogers, was a churchman, educated at Edinburgh, Cambridge, and Tübingen. In 1878 he began to teach economic history at Cambridge. Apparently his stay at Tübingen had a deeper influence on him than his studies in England, for he was more or less a follower of the German economic school. Although a voluminous writer, he made few, if any, original contributions either to the theory or the practice of economic history. Nevertheless, his *Growth of English Industry and Commerce* (1882),[49] which he used as a textbook, helped to popularize economic history.[50]

William James Ashley (1860–1927) [51] was perhaps more important as a teacher than as a scholar. Ashley, more than any other single person, was responsible for the introduction of German economic thought in the English-speaking world. He had taken first prize in history at Balliol and then went to Heidelberg where he met Knies. In 1885 he returned to Oxford to teach history as Fellow of Lincoln College; in the following year he read Schmoller and was deeply influenced. Finding no opening for economic history in Britain, Ashley went as professor of political economy to the University of Toronto in 1888. Here he wrote his *An Introduction to English Economic History and Theory*, which is a "landmark in the study of economic and social development of English-speaking countries." This compact and suggestive work, together with his foundation of a school of political science at Toronto, got Ashley an

---

[47] Rogers summarized the first four volumes of his *History of Agriculture and Prices* in a book entitled *Six Centuries of Work and Wages* (London and New York, 1884; 8th ed., London, 1906); see also his *The Industrial and Commercial History of England* (London and New York, 1892).

[48] See W. R. Scott, "William Cunningham," *Proceedings of the British Academy*, IX (1920), 465–74; H. S. Foxwell and L. C. A. Knowles, in *Economic Journal*, XXIX (1919), 382–93.

[49] This work was constantly revised and enlarged; the fifth edition, that of 1910–12, was in 2 v., that of 1925–29 was in 3 v.

[50] Cunningham also wrote *Western Civilization in Its Economic Aspects* (Cambridge, 1898–1900, 2 v.). His *The Progress of Capitalism in England* (Cambridge, 1925), 136–42 contains a list of his writings. He was the author of more than 100 articles and monographs, compiled with the help of research assistants.

[51] On Ashley see J. H. Clapham, in *Economic Journal*, XXXVII (1927), 678–83; W. R. Scott, "Memoir, Sir William Ashley," *Economic History Review*, I (1928), 319–21; O. Weinberger, "William Ashley," *Jahrbücher für Nationalökonomie und Statistik*, 3rd ser., LXXII (1927), 630–38.

invitation to Harvard, where, in 1892, he occupied the first chair of economic history in any country. In 1901 he returned to England as professor of commerce at the University of Birmingham, and there organized the first school of commerce in Britain.

Though Ashley was active until 1925, the year of his retirement, his literary output is not great. The chief reason for this paucity was the fact that he was essentially a man of action, serving on various government commissions and being one of the most prominent exponents of a tariff policy. His influence, nevertheless, was considerable, particularly in his successful endeavors to bring English scholars in touch with the German school of economic historians. Though he did not altogether accept the conclusions of the German school—he conceived of economic history as a discipline embracing historical criticism and economic theory—he was sensitive to the work of the Germans, especially Schmoller. In fact, it was to Schmoller that he dedicated his collection of critical essays, *Surveys, Historic and Economic* (1900), in these characteristic words:

> Yet I feel that for a dozen years I have received more stimulus and encouragement from your writings than from those of any other; encouragement in the effort, which academic and popular opinion renders so difficult, to be an economist without ceasing to be an historian.

That is the best summary of Ashley's aims: "to be an economist without ceasing to be an historian." [52]

Ashley's *Introduction* [53] closes the most important decade in English economic history. Many books appeared later, but they were almost "all built upon, or merely added to" the preceding work of writers like those mentioned.

The most important British economic historian of the first quarter of the present century was George Unwin (1870–1935).[54] He was a Welshman by birth, an Oxford man by education, and studied in Germany under Adolf Wagner and Gustav Schmoller. In 1904 he produced his first book, *Industrial Organization*. His researches were "of fundamental importance, but he was primarily a social philosopher." He believed that economic history contained the best answer to the problems of the growth of society. His basic faith was the principle of voluntary association. He believed that in the Middle Ages the gilds were a dynamic

[52] Ashley was also the author of *James and Philip van Artevelde* (London, 1883); *The Early History of the English Woollen Industry* (Baltimore, 1887); *The Progress of the German Working Classes in the Last Quarter of a Century* (London and New York, 1904).

[53] The fourth edition, in 2 v., appeared in 1914–23.

[54] *Studies in Economic History: the Collected Papers of George Unwin*, ed. with an introductory memoir by R. H. Tawney (London, 1927), contains a list of his published works, pp. 465–71; G. W. Daniels' *George Unwin: A Memorial Lecture* (Manchester University Lectures, XXIV, 1926).

force in society; but when they got rich they became identified with vested interests and ceased to be a constructive influence. Unwin opposed the meddling of government with economic organization, and criticized works which connected the social and economic progress of a nation with the "judicious alliance of economic interests and political power in pursuit of a consistent and strongly directed national policy." He was gratified when he and his students proved to Cunningham that there was no consistent policy under Edward III as Cunningham had said.[55] Unwin viewed English history as a "series of opportunist expedients, usually inspired by sectional interests." He contended these expedients had not been the cause of progress, but rather had been obstructions to it. This "authoritarian view of progress," constructed from a study of statutes, state papers, and other official documents, he claimed should be abandoned. Unwin proposed to work from local records, sources revealing the lives of individuals and of families, business firms, and other economic organizations, as the groups in which society carries on its work. *The Gilds and Companies of London* (1908), his second work, clarified his first book. The two together, plus an essay on "Some Economic Factors in General History," [56] contain the kernel of his teachings.

In the summer of 1908 Unwin was appointed lecturer in economic history at the University of Edinburgh. Two years later he was called to the chair of economic history at the University of Manchester. Here he taught for over fourteen years, and the novelty of his teaching at first bewildered his students. He cited works and documents they had never heard of, and his lectures did not help systematic note-taking. He lectured chiefly on the sixteenth and early seventeenth centuries. His work on the Arkwrights, considering his scrappy sources, is a marvel of industry and shrewd discovery of clues. But it is only a fragment of what he hoped to do.

The English-speaking world has seen an extraordinary increase in the interest and productivity which, in 1900, according to Ashley, "academic and popular opinion renders so difficult." Today economic history is taught in most universities.[57] Outside of Germany, England, and America, however, economic history has not flourished to any great

[55] *Finance and Trade under Edward III* (University of Manchester Publications, XXXII, 1918).

[56] Published shortly before his death in *The New Past and Other Essays on the Development of Civilisation*, ed. by E. H. Carter (Oxford, 1925).

[57] In 1933 the late Professor Flügel of the Department of Economics in the University of California compiled a *Select Bibliography of Economic and Social History* (mimeographed) to December, 1932, which lists only periodical articles in English journals. It contains no less than 335 writers, each being the author of a number of articles, ranging from one to ten. If we estimate only an average of four articles per author, we have the astonishing total of 1,340 articles.

extent. Although the movement influenced French economic thought, "it did not result in the founding of a French school of economic historians." [58] The same comment may be made about Italy,[59] Spain, and Russia, although in the latter country economic history has developed under the influence of Marxism.[60]

Among the older more-or-less economic French historians, two, Blanqui and Louis Blanc, should be mentioned. Adolphe Blanqui (1798–1854) [61] was the disciple of the economist Jean Baptiste Say, who obtained for him the chair of history and economics at the School of Commerce. In 1833 Blanqui succeeded Say as professor in the Conservatory of Arts and Trades. Blanqui founded the *Journal des économistes*, was a member of the Chamber of Deputies, and became a reporter of financial and agricultural conditions for the Academy of Moral and Political Sciences. He was a champion of free trade and an advocate of the study of economic history. In the latter connection he wrote a

[58] Charles Gide and Charles Rist, *A History of Economic Doctrines from the Time of the Physiocrats to the Present Day* (London, 1917), 388.

[59] In Italy the best-known economic historian is Giuseppe Salvioli (1857–1928), the author of *Il capitalismo antico* (Storia dell' economia romana) (Bari, 1929), tr. into French by Alfred Bonnet under the title *Le capitalisme dans le monde antique; études sur l'histoire de l'économie romaine* (Paris, 1906), in which he denied the existence of true capitalism in classic antiquity. His *Stato e popolazione d'Italia prima e dopo le invasioni* (1890) contains the thesis of the continuity of Roman economic institutions in medieval Italy. See G. Brindisi, *Giuseppe Salvioli* (Naples, 1928).

[60] In Russia there was considerable activity in the field of economic history, especially in the last decades of the nineteenth century, when the country was being rapidly industrialized. This led to a keen interest in Marxism and European economic problems; the model of the former was Germany, and of the latter England. "English economic history and theory and the history of the Labour movement in England became the dominant subjects in the university courses of political economy and modern history." It is significant that in 1900–01 Lenin translated Webb's *Industrial Democracy* into Russian.

Of the three great Russian historians in this period, Kluchevsky, Kovalevsky, and Vinogradoff, only the first worked exclusively in Russian history; the other two devoted themselves to non-Russian problems. Maxime Kovalevsky, though he was personally acquainted with Marx, was more of a sociologist than an historian and stood closer to Comte. Kovalevsky was the author of two works on medieval English administration—*The Justices of Labourers in England in the Fourteenth Century and the Justices of the Peace* (1876); and *A History of Police and Administration in the English Shires from the Earliest Times until the Death of Edward I* (1877). His most important work is *The Economic Development of Europe before the Beginnings of Capitalism* (in Russian, 1898 ff.), German translation as Kowalewsky, *Die ökonomische Entwicklung Europas bis zum Beginn der kapitalistischen Wirtschaftsform* (Berlin, 1901–14, 7 v.).

Vinogradoff belongs properly to England, and has been treated in that connection. His Russian students also occupied themselves with English economic history. Demetrius Petrushevsky, professor of medieval history in Moscow, wrote [in Russian] *Wat Tyler's Rebellion* (1897–1901, 2 v.); *Labour Legislation under Edward III* (1889); *Essays on the History of the English State and Society in the Middle Ages* (1903–1909); and *Magna Carta* (1915–1918). In political matters Petrushevsky followed Stubbs and in economic problems Dopsch. Another disciple of Vinogradoff, Alexander Savine (d. 1923), professor of history in Moscow, likewise worked in English history.

On these and other Russian economic historians see E. A. Kosminsky, "Russian Work on English Economic History," *Economic History Review*, I (1928), 208–33. On Kluchevsky see *Slavonic Review*, XIII (1935), 320–29.

[61] He is not to be confused with his younger brother Louis Auguste Blanqui, the radical. To distinguish him from his brother, Adolphe Blanqui is usually referred to as Blanqui *ainé*.

Résumé de l'histoire du commerce et de l'industrie (1826); *Notice sur M. Huskisson et sur sa réforme économique* (1840); *Des classes ouvrières en France, pendant l'année 1848* (1849, 2 v. in 1); and finally a tribute to his master: *Notice sur la vie et les travaux de M. J. B. Say* (1841). His once-celebrated *Histoire de l'économie politique en Europe depuis les anciens jusqu'à nos jours* (1837) is now out of date.[62]

Louis Blanc (1812–82) is mainly known as a revolutionist. His first book, *Organisation du travail* (1840), was a protest against the sufferings of the working classes as a result of the Industrial Revolution; he insisted upon the obligation of society to provide the means of livelihood to every member. This book became one of the most potent forces in the Revolution of 1848. After the overthrow of Louis Philippe, Blanc became a member of the provisional government, but was forced to flee to London when the Second Empire was established. In London, where he lived for more than twenty years, Blanc wrote his two histories: *History of the Revolution of 1848* and *History of the French Revolution*.

In the second half of the nineteenth century we find few French economic historians. The Vicomte d'Avenel was the author of a *Histoire économique de la propriété, des salaires, des dénrees et de tous les prix en général depuis l'an 1200 jusqu'en l'an 1800* (2 vols., 1894). He ransacked the archives and used a multitude of documentary sources; his tables of prices of food, of rents, and of revenues are severe and precise in method, giving in each case a statement of the source, the quantity as found in the original, and the value in money of the time.[63] He is the French counterpart to Thorold Rogers of England.

Pierre Émile Levasseur (1828–1911) [64] was the best-known economic historian of France, professor of geography, history, and statistics at the Collège de France. His masterpiece is his *Histoire des classes ouvrières en France*, first published in 1859 and a pioneer work in the history of the working classes.[65] Paul Guiraud,[66] a student of Fustel de Coulanges, devoted his life to the economic history of antiquity, especially Greece. He published a *Histoire de la propriété foncière en Grèce*

[62] The English translation by E. J. Leonard, *History of Political Economy in Europe* (New York, 1880), contains a biographic sketch of Blanqui, pp. ix–xii.
[63] See the criticism in *EHR*, XI (1896), 123–29, and d'Avenel's reply, *ibid.*, 609–11.
[64] On Levasseur see A. Liesse, "Notice sur la vie et les travaux de M. Émile Levasseur," *ASMP*, CLXXXI (1914), 337–61; M. Marion, "Faits économiques et sociaux," *Revue Bleue*, LI, pt. 1, 1913, pp. 146–50; Yves Guyot, "M. E. Levasseur," *Journal des économistes*, série 6, XXXI (1911), 123–24, 177–97; Georges Espinas, in *Vierteljahrschrift für Social- und Wirthschaftsgeschichte*, I (1903), 146–57.
[65] The first two volumes were entitled *Histoire des classes ouvrières en France depuis la conquête de Jules César jusqu'à la révolution* (1859, new ed., 1900–01, 2 v.); in 1867 there appeared a continuation: *Histoire des classes ouvrières en France depuis 1789 jusqu'à nos jours*, new ed., 1903–04. Levasseur also wrote *Histoire du commerce de la France* (Paris, 1911–12, 2 v.)
[66] On Guiraud see P. Boissonnade, "M. Guiraud et l'histoire économique de l'antiquité," *RSH*, XII (1906), 67–71.

jusqu'à la conquête romaine (1893); *La main d'oeuvre industrielle dans l'ancienne Grèce;* and finally, *Études économiques sur l'antiquité* (1905). His viewpoint is stated succinctly in this last book: "The system of property, the state of commerce and industry, the distribution of wealth, the organization of work, the systems of taxation, these are questions as worthy of interest as the recital of battles and political institutions." [67]

Henri Sée, one of the leading contemporary French economic historians recently deceased, regretted that "there is no general survey of French economic history." In recent times much work has been done on special industries, regional histories, and the period of the French Revolution. The *Commission pour la recherche et la publication des documents relatifs à la vie économique de la révolution* was founded in 1903, and has since published a number of books, especially *cahiers*. The Commission publishes a *Bulletin d'histoire économique de la révolution.* An annual bibliographical bulletin of economic and legal history is published as a supplement to the *Revue historique de droit français et étranger.* For the period of the First World War there is C. Bloch's *Bibliographie méthodique de l'histoire économique et sociale de la France pendant la guerre mondiale* (Paris, 1926).[68]

The last of the great economic historians who have passed away was the Belgian scholar Henri Pirenne (1862–1935).[69] His native Verviers had been for centuries a seat of the linen industry, and there is no question that his early surroundings affected the alert and active boy. His university studies began at Liège, where he was a pupil of Paul Frédéricq, and more particularly of Godefroid Kurth in that "cours practique d'histoire," established after the German example, of which Pirenne later said that here, for the first time in Belgium, historical criticism was taught. To this instruction he added impressions received from Arthur Giry in Paris (1883–84) and from various masters in Germany: W. Arndt in Leipzig, G. Schmoller and H. Bresslau at Berlin.

---

[67] *Études économiques*, 26.

[68] Henri Sée, "Recent Work in French Economic History (1905–1925)," *Economic History Review*, I (1927), 137–53.

[69] Henri Hausser, in *Revue d'histoire moderne*, nouvelle série, no. 20, Nov.-Dec. (1935), 409–14; F. M. Powicke, in *EHR*, LI (1936), 79–89; H. Laurent, in *Moyen âge*, VI (1935), 241–51; Van der Essen, in *Revue d'histoire ecclésiastique*, XXXII (1936), 89–98; Henri Gregoire, in *Byzantion*, X (1935), 813–17; R. Holtzmann, in *HZ*, CLIII (1935–36), 451–52, cp. also *ibid.*, CXLVI (1932), 581; G. L. Van Roosbroeck, in *Romanic Review*, XXVI (1935), 368–75; Marc Bloch in *RH*, CLXXVI (1935), 671–78; F. Quicke, in *Revue belge de philologie et d'histoire*, XIV (1935), 1665–79; P. Bonenfant, *Revue de l'université de Bruxelles*, XLI (1936), 209–13. *La Flambeau* (November, 1935) carries the funeral orations by Paul Hymans for the Belgian Government, and by Joseph Bidez in the name of the Union Académique Internationale. The bibliography of his writings which F. L. Ganshof and G. G. Dept prepared for the first volume of the *Mélanges d'histoire* presented on the occasion of his fortieth anniversary as a teacher in Ghent (Brussels, 1927) includes only the works prior to August, 1926.

Another German influence upon him was Lamprecht. Though he never studied under the idol of Leipzig, it was this admired friend who suggested the composition of a Belgian history for Heeren-Ukert's *Staatengeschichte*, which grew into Pirenne's *magnum opus*.[70] His closest friend in England in later years was Vinogradoff. A man of broad interests and independence of mind, Pirenne was an adherent of no particular school.

Throughout life he was a teacher, whether when the young doctor was put in charge of a cours de paléographie et diplomatique at Liège, or during the long and honorable years at the University of Ghent (1886–1930). As teacher he left his deep impress upon the study of social and municipal institutions of the Middle Ages.

Pirenne's *Histoire de Belgique* has become a national classic. During the First World War the third edition of the second volume, on the period of the great Burgundian dukes, was completely exhausted. A steady stream of articles in the decade 1890–1900 preceded the appearance of the first volume:[71] studies in municipal origins, text editions such as the work of Galbert of Bruges or a volume of unedited sources for *Le soulèvement de la Flandre maritime de 1323–1328*. It was in connection with this first volume that some of Pirenne's most suggestive work was done, or the way paved for future studies by himself and his disciples upon the rise of medieval towns, a subject already treated elsewhere.

In 1889, before he was thirty, he had written his first book, on Dinant and its kettle-industry. In 1906 and 1909 appeared the two volumes of *Collections de documents relatifs à l'histoire de l'industrie drapière en Flandre*. On these and similar materials he built his panorama of the great industrial development of the Low Countries, "in the course of which capitalism captured the countryside, the big towns lost their leadership, and the system of estates took their place as the expression of a national consciousness." [72] Here Cloth ruled, as later King Cotton was to dominate the American South in the nineteenth century. After the War, in 1926, in collaboration with Alfred Espinas he published another volume of documents on the Flemish draperies. He preserved much of the invaluable records of Ypres for posterity. When Hausser last visited him, the seventy-three-year-old scholar, restive in his illness, spoke eloquently of his hopes of attacking the publication of the archives of the collieries (houillères) of Liège—the oldest, as he said with pride, of Western Europe and comparable to those of the English mines (charbonnages).

[70] *Histoire de Belgique* (Brussels, 1900–32, 7 v.); German translation of the first four volumes by F. Arnheim, Gotha, 1899–1913.
[71] In 1893 Pirenne published the first edition of his *Bibliographie de l'histoire de Belgique* (3rd ed. with the collaboration of Henri Nowé and Henri Obreen, Brussels, 1931).
[72] Cp. his *Histoire de Belgique* (n. 69), 258 ff.

Professor Hausser has called Pirenne the greatest French-writing historian since the First World War. His historical interpretation sometimes was bold, but backed by great knowledge. Pirenne's ingenious thesis of the influence of the Arabic domination in the western Mediterranean as the true beginning of the medieval epoch engaged his interest in the last years of his life.[73] He argued that there was no great lapse as generally supposed between Roman and Merovingian times; the Mediterranean was still open to trade and cultural contacts. The break came, in his opinion, with the advance of the Saracens; and medieval trade and communications began a fresh start under the Carolingians. "En somme, on peut dire que, sans Mahomet, Charlemagne n'aurait jamais existe." [74] The thesis has met with varied reception; [75] Pirenne himself offered evidence on the trade in papyrus and in gold, on the education of the merchant classes, and left at his death a more elaborate work recently published by his family.[76]

To summarize the achievements of economic history, one may remark that the German historical school of economics did not result in what its exponents had hoped for: a real science of economics. This discipline has since taken a different course from that laid down by Roscher. As for economic historians proper, they have undoubtedly made some fruitful contributions. Like the historical school of economics and the culture-historians of the type of Lamprecht, the students of economic history have also widened and enriched the field of historiography. This was done not only by the publication of special studies and monographs on economic subjects, but also by an emphasis on the importance of economic institutions and forces in general culture, warning the general historian against his tendency to confine himself to politics and diplomacy, and to ignore the wider implications of his work.

[73] The theory was first sketched in a *Histoire générale de l'Europe* which Pirenne wrote largely from memory during his captivity at Kreuzburg in 1917. It was publicly announced in an article in 1922 entitled *Mahomet et Charlemagne, Un contraste économique: Merovingiens et Carolingiens*, and defended in a brilliant ten-minute speech at the Historical Congress of Oslo (1928). The *Histoire générale* was published after Pirenne's death by his son (8th ed., Brussels, 1936); and translated by Bernard Miall as *A History of Europe from the Invasions to the XVI Century* (New York, 1939).

[74] Quoted in *RH*, n. s. IV, 413.

[75] It was approved by Ferdinand Lot. For a criticism see Norman H. Baynes, "M. Pirenne and the Unity of the Mediterranean World," *Journal of Roman Studies*, XIX, 1929, pt. ii, 230–33.

[76] *Mahomet et Charlemagne* (Brussels and Paris, 1937), tr. by Bernard Miall as *Mohammed and Charlemagne* (New York, 1939).

CHAPTER LV

THE POSITIVIST SCHOOL OF HISTORIANS: THE INFLUENCE OF NINETEENTH–CENTURY SCIENCE ON THE WRITING OF HISTORY [1]

A FAMILIAR phenomenon in the history of ideas is the application of the concepts of one field of thought to another and quite different field of thought. A striking example of this transference is the influence of science upon the interpretation of history. Since the time of the Greeks, the pioneer age in the development of science, the two great ages in the progress of science have been the seventeenth and the nineteenth centuries.

As the history of the Great Renewal of science may be said to have climaxed with Harvey's demonstration of the circulation of the blood (1628) which both closed and opened an era, so the history of science in the seventeenth century may be said to extend from that date to the appearance of Boerhave's first great work in 1708, which ushered in the history of science in the eighteenth century. Leibniz died in 1716 and Newton in 1727, but their work was over before 1708. Within the eighty years between 1628 and 1708, the advancement of science was relatively greater than in any other epoch of modern times.

No period in the whole history of science—unless it be that of the ancient Greeks—was so original and progressive as the seventeenth century. Professor Alfred North Whitehead has expressed the opinion that "a brief, and sufficiently accurate, description of the intellectual life of the European races [since 1700] . . . is that they have been living upon the accumulated capital of ideas provided for them by the genius of the seventeenth century." [2]

The progress of science in the seventeenth century is the glory of that epoch, and far transcends any other form of progress made. The distinguished historian Leopold von Ranke has admirably described the nature of the change in the intellectual tendency of this age. He writes:

---

[1] F. S. Marvin, "Science and History," CR, CXIII (1918), 325–33; James H. Robinson, "The Relation of History to the Newer Sciences of Man," Journal of Philosophy, Psychology and Scientific Methods, VIII (1911), 141–57; J. T. Shotwell, "The Interpretation of History," AHR, XVIII (1913), 692–709; Alvin H. Hansen, "The Technological Interpretation of History," Quarterly Journal of Economics, XXXVI (1921), 69–93; H. Magnus, Die Werte der Geschichte für die moderne induktive Naturbetrachtung und Medizin (Breslau, 1904); J. B. Bury, "Darwinism and History," in Evolution of Modern Thought (1911), 246–63.

[2] Alfred North Whitehead, Science and the Modern World (New York, 1939), 57–58.

This change . . . is connected with the inevitable progress of scientific discovery. For, though all science had formerly been drawn directly from the ancients, this was now no longer possible. On the one hand, the materials had enormously accumulated. . . . On the other hand, a deep and searching spirit of investigation had arisen. . . . Those who began their inquiries under the conduct of the ancients, emancipated themselves from their authority; discoveries were made beyond the limits which they had prescribed, and these again opened the way to further researches. The study of nature especially was pursued with equal ardor and independence of mind. . . . Inquiries were more and more extended and active, and science was no longer limited to the regions explored by antiquity. It followed . . . that as the antique was no longer studied with the same veneration and confidence with reference to matter, it could no longer have the same influence with reference to form, which it had hitherto exercised. Works of erudition began to be valued mainly in proportion to the accumulation of materials. . . . Be the cause what it may—whether it be a change founded in the nature of the human mind—this much is manifest, that all productions . . . are pervaded by a new spirit. . . . Antiquity was deserted.[3]

There is a more intimate relation between history and science than is usually supposed. For all history and all science, in the last analysis, is idea. The history of science is an important kind of historiography. Unfortunately many writers, both political historians and historians of literature, have looked upon the history of science as something alien to the general intellectual development of a people or an epoch. Sir Leslie Stephen could write his *History of English Thought in the Eighteenth Century*, and not mention any British scientist. The true humanist and the true scientist ought to look upon *every phase* of intellectual development as having its place within the entirety of knowledge, and strive to bring these subjects into organic relation to one another. Humanism and science should not be ignorant of each other, or of what each really signifies. Philosophy should be made aware of science and science of philosophy, and literature should be common to both.

Unfortunately in every age thought has been inclined to flow along parallel lines. Thus, to change the figure, there has been too little intellectual cross-fertilization, and each body of knowledge has inclined to be self-contained and self-sufficient.

Yet there has been a saving remnant of thinkers in every age who have imagination enough to surmount the barriers of convention and prejudice. The earliest historian who embraced science in the categories of his mind was Paolo Sarpi, the Venetian historian. "Every branch of mathematics and natural science had been explored by him with the enthusiasm of a pioneer. He made experiments in chemistry, mechanics, mineralogy, metallurgy, vegetable and animal physiology. His practical studies in anatomy were carried on by the aid of vivisec-

---

[3] *History of the Popes of Rome during the Sixteenth and Seventeenth Centuries*, tr. by Sarah Austin (Philadelphia, 1841, 2 v.), I, 287–90.

tion. Following independent paths he worked out some of Gilbert's discoveries in magnetism, and of Da Porta's in optics, demonstrated the valves of the veins, and the function of the uvea in vision, divined the use of the telescope and the thermometer. When he turned his attention to astronomy, he at once declared the futility of judicial astrology; and while recognising the validity of Galileo's system, predicted that this truth would involve its promulgator in serious difficulties with the Roman Inquisition." [4] Harvey published his work on the circulation of the blood in 1619, the very year of the publication of Sarpi's *History of the Council of Trent*, and admitted that he had been aided in this discovery by the work of his master Fabricius and by Servetus, Caesalpinus, and Sarpi.

The premier sciences of the seventeenth century were mechanics, physics, and mathematics; it is to these sciences that we are to look for the earliest important influence of science upon the interpretation of history, including economics, political science, and the study of society, subjects which then were not differentiated from history as now. In history the familiar concept of the "balance of power" emerged out of the great struggle between France and the double house of Habsburg, in which France, Spain, Austria, England, Prussia, and the Netherlands all participated. Hobbes in *Leviathan* formulated the principles of government in terms of the mechanics of the seventeenth century, and "reached his position by gathering up the revolutionary scientific thought of his time and relating it to the life and human nature he saw around him. Hobbes took motion as his master-principle." [5]

Since, however, the values of mathematics and physics are wholly of a quantitative nature, economics and the science of society in that age were most influenced by science. Edward Misselden is credited with introducing the term "balance of trade" in 1623, the date of his pamphlet entitled *The Circle of Commerce, or the Balance of Trade*, although the phrase "balance" as a term in bookkeeping had reached England from Italy about 1600. Barrington derived his doctrine of the "balance of property" from the idea of equilibrium in mechanics. The phrases "circulation of trade" and "circulation of money" owed their usage to Harvey's discovery of the circulation of the blood. Thus Hobbes wrote in 1651:

[4] SYMONDS, VII, 89. Sarpi was either too modest or too afraid to publish the results of his researches, and they are now lost to the world. The memory of them survives in the notes of Foscarini and Griselini who examined the manuscripts before they were accidentally destroyed by fire in 1769. *Ibid.*, p. 93. For other reading on Sarpi as a scientist see an article in *Scottish Review*, XXX (1897), 251–82; Alexander Robertson, *Fra Paolo Sarpi, the Greatest of the Venetians* (London, 1894), 40–67; Arabella G. Campbell, *The Life of Fra Paolo Sarpi* (1869), 46–49, 64–65. For Sarpi as an historian see vol. I, 541–46.

[5] Cp. also G. N. Clark, *The Seventeenth Century* (Oxford, 1931), 219–23.

By the means of which measures [i.e., the reduction, by "concoction" of all commodities which are not immediately consumed, to money] all commodities, moveable
and immoveable, are made to accompany a man, to all places of his resort, within and
without the place of his ordinary residence; and the same passeth from man to man,
within the commonwealth; and goes round about, nourishing (as it passeth) every part
thereof; in so much as this concoction is as it were the sanguification of the commonwealth; for natural blood is in like manner made of the fruits of the earth; and circulating, nourisheth by the way, every member of the body of man.[6]

Locke is commonly credited with having coined the phrase "the
quantity theory of money," but the term is found long before he wrote.[7]
The original statement of the principle goes back to Copernicus who
died in 1543. "Although these theories had little in them that was truly
scientific," yet, as Professor Clark has said, "they stood for more than
a mere borrowing of the scientist's vocabulary. Beneath them lay a
serious, if misguided attempt to explain by weighing and measuring,
by adding and subtracting."[8]

This new interpretation of history was more than the application of a
new method, it was the introduction of a new mind. Medieval philosophy and medieval theology had held that thought was authoritative.
Copernicus, Galileo, Newton, and the whole galaxy of eighteenth-century men of science triumphantly asserted that *facts* were authoritative, not opinions. It took the historians a long time before they realized
the import of this truth. Partisanship, political or religious prejudice,
hero-worship, ambition, national sentiment, pride of race or nation,
induced historians to misrepresent or to conceal the evidence which
they had in hand. They did not have that reverence for facts which
the scientist possessed. When the evidence failed them, some historians
were even not above assuming their "facts." And when they did not
sin in this way they were frequently disposed to sin by indulging in
theoretical speculation or omitting important evidence because it would
upset their preconceived idea. This was an evil of historical thought
in the eighteenth century under the influence of Cartesian analytics
and dialectics. Rationalism dehumanized history, made man an abstraction, and history schematic. The effect of Cartesian analysis upon
history was to make historians classify men and events into categories
and so produce an artificial pattern far from an accurate presentation.

As the seventeenth century had been dominated by mathematics and
physics, so the eighteenth century was dominated by the science of

---

[6] Thomas Hobbes, *Leviathan* (Everyman's Library ed.), 133.
[7] For these examples see Jacob Viner, "English Theories of Foreign Trade before Adam
Smith," *Journal of Political Economy*, XXXVIII, 257, 285, 288. Cp. E. A. J. Johnson, *Predecessors of Adam Smith;* and the stimulating and suggestive book of G. N. Clark, *Science and
Social Welfare in the Age of Newton* (Oxford, 1937).
[8] Clark, *op. cit.*

chemistry, next to which the most progress was made in natural history.[9]

But Cartesianism still held sway over the minds of historians in the eighteenth century. It was the Age of Reason of which Montesquieu and Gibbon are outstanding examples. Gibbon records in his *Autobiography* that in the five years' interval between the appearance of the first and second volume of the *Decline and Fall of the Roman Empire*, he indulged his curiosity in natural science and attended the lectures of the celebrated Dr. Hunter in anatomy and those of Mr. Higgins on "chymestry." "The principles of these sciences," he says, "and a taste for books of natural history contributed to multiply my ideas and images, and the anatomist and chymist may sometimes track me in their snow." I shall have to take Gibbon's word for this influence of science upon him, for I have not been able to detect it.

When science passed over into the nineteenth century, Bentham had revived the old seventeenth-century quantum theory of value which had been ignored in the eighteenth century. His problem was the relation of wealth to happiness. He laid down the principle as axiomatic that "the effect of wealth in the production of happiness goes on diminishing as the quantity by which the wealth of one man exceeds that of another goes on increasing; in other words, the quantity of happiness produced by a particle of wealth (each particle being of the same magnitude) will be less and less at each particle; the second will produce less than the third, the third less than the second, and so on." [10]

At the opposite pole to the philosophy of Utilitarianism was Romanticism. In the early part of the nineteenth century Romanticism's response to science was absurd in its extravagance, and brought science into bad odor with many thinking men. How may one take seriously such a fantastic interpretation of the relation between history and science as this propounded by the Polish economist Cieszowski in his *Prologemena zur Historiographie* (Berlin, 1838): "Light is the type of ancient Persia, Mechanism of China, Dynamic Electricity of Athens, Static Electricity of Sparta, Macedon in the time of Alexander the Great was Electro-Magnetic. The expansive energy and power of Rome is symbolized by Heat."

A curious adverse current which science encountered in the early nineteenth century, which might have been serious if the days of Galileo had not been long past, was Catholic reaction. The University of Rome had

[9] In 1738 Daniel Bernouilli asserted that gases were composed of molecules; in 1754 Black discovered carbonic acid gas; in 1766 Cavendish discovered hydrogen; in 1774 Priestley discovered oxygen; in 1779 Ingenhousz proved the power of plants to purify or poison the air; Lavoisier's epoch-making *Traité élémentaire de Chimie* was published in 1789.
[10] Wilbur M. Urban, *Valuation, Its Nature and Laws* (London and New York, 1909), 157.

once counted among its faculty great names, such as Pomponio Leto (who used to lecture before daybreak), Lorenzo Valla, Eustachio, Cesalpino, Copernicus, Lancici, and Malpighi. But in 1816 the papacy, alarmed over the advancement of science, established a chair of "Sacred Physics" divided into six sections, as many as the days of the Creation.[11]

The first serious influence of science in the nineteenth century upon historical interpretation, I think, may be said to have been in giving historians a deepened sense of the importance of origins. "In science the chief triumphs have been won by tracing things to their beginnings; in physical structure to atoms and molecules, in animal life to nerve cells, protoplasm, or whatever is simplest and most primitive. Exactly the same effort is made in modern history; and nothing is more distinctive of it, in contrast with the comparatively superficial historical school of the eighteenth century, than the determination to trace the starting-point and original meaning of institutions. Ages which had been previously left to legend and myth have been patiently investigated."[12] Thus Palgrave's *Rise and Progress of the English Commonwealth* (1832) "boldly challenged the current view that it is necessary to begin with political events and [then] to proceed to institutions."[13]

The first historical scholar who took cognizance of the importance of the history of science was Leopold von Ranke in his *History of the Popes*, which appeared in 1839.[14] In 1858 he presented a remarkable memoir to the Historical Commission of the Bavarian Academy urging the necessity of a great History of German Science to be written by a group of scholars, each of them a recognized authority in the particular science which he would treat.[15] In the following year Ranke developed this idea further, in a second address to the Bavarian Academy entitled *Entwurf zu einer Geschichte der Wissenschaft in Deutschland.*[16]

But long before Ranke's appeal for a history of science, Scientia had been taken captive by ardent social philosophers who abused the methods of science and brought it into disrepute with most historians. It is to be said by way of defense of historical scholars that the perpetrators of this rape were not themselves historians but sociologists, if I may anticipate the use of this word which was coined by August Comte, although Comte did not create the idea of sociology. That goes back to the radicals and dreamers of the ancien régime and the French

---

[11] See Nicola Spano, *L'Università di Roma* (Rome, 1935).
[12] Hugh Walker, *The Age of Tennyson* (London, 1900), 110–11.
[13] GOOCH, 286–87.   [14] *History of the Popes* (n. 3), I, 287–96.
[15] Printed in *HZ*, I (1859), 28–35, and reprinted in Ranke's *Sämmtliche Werke* (3rd ed., Leipzig, 1874–90, 54 v. in 27), LI–LII, 485–91.
[16] This is printed, so far as I know, only in *HZ*, II (1859), 54–61. The *Sämmtliche Werke* (n. 15), LI–LII, 492–500 contain his address at the opening session of the Bavarian Academy in 1859, but not the *Entwurf*.

Revolution, and immediately to Saint-Simon (1760–1825) and Fourier (1772–1837), who contended that "political phenomena are as capable of being grouped under laws as other phenomena. . . . The true destination of philosophy and science must be social, and the true object of the thinker must be the interpretation and reorganization of society by means of the application of the methods of the positive sciences to the study of society."

Fourier planted, Saint-Simon watered, but Comte gave the increase. Comte's purpose was the study and understanding of what he called "social physics"—the very term is significant. The aim of the Positive philosophy was to emancipate social phenomena from the inhibitions imposed by theology and metaphysics and to introduce into the study of society *the same scientific observation of the laws which prevail in physics, chemistry, and physiology*. When the Positive method, he said, had been extended to the study of society as it has been to chemistry, and the other physical sciences, these social facts would be resolved.

In 1822 Comte published his *Plan* for the reorganization of society. This is the charter of the Positive Philosophy. Comte's plan for the reorganization of historical studies was "an abandonment in political philosophy of the region of metaphysical idealities in order to assume the ground of observed realities (notice the stress laid on observation) by a systematic subordination direct and continuous, of imagination to observation." In this way Comte thought that it would be possible to discover "determined laws" which governed human society as the world of nature is ruled by physical laws. In regard to history Comte said: "The prevailing tendency to specialization in study would reduce history to a mere accumulation of unconnected delineations, in which all idea of the true filiation of events would be lost amid the mass of confused descriptions. If the historical comparisons of the different periods of civilization are to have any scientific character, they must be referred to the general social evolution."

As history constituted the raw material of the understanding of society, Comte in 1832 importuned Guizot, then prime minister of Louis Philippe, to establish a chair of history in the Collège de France, and for this he deserves to be remembered. The faith of Comte and his disciples in the Positive Philosophy—though at bottom it was a method, and not a philosophy—was boundless. They believed that an understanding of the "laws" of society would enable the state not only to control the direction of history, but to predict the course of history. "The aim of the Positivists in short, was to discover a set of working hypotheses or laws for the interpretation of history, as Newton and others had done for science. Their problem was: 'What is the ultimate explanation of history, or, more modestly, what are the forces which determine human events, and according to what laws do they act?'"[17]

One of the most influential of Comte's ideas borrowed from science and applied to history and the social sciences (so-called) was Comte's new application of the word *milieu*. This word was first employed by Lamarck in his *Philosophie zoölogique*. Comte borrowed the word and extended its application from zoology to human society, and not always even then to physical environment. For "environment" in the minds of some historians and many sociologists became a very flexible word. Taine and Quetelet were almost hypnotized by the word *milieu*. In the second half of the nineteenth century this vague word was as flexible as the word *environment* is today, and perhaps in final analysis it means the same thing.

There is no doubt about Comte's immense influence, even if one hesitates to accept Émile Faguet's opinion that he was "the most powerful sower of ideas and intellectual stimulator that our country has seen; the greatest thinker that France has had since Descartes." [18]

Henry Thomas Buckle (1821–62) in England and Hippolyte A. Taine (1828–92) in France were the two greatest advocates of the application of Comte's ideas to the interpretation of history. Buckle's *History of Civilization in England, France, Spain, and Scotland* [19] in two volumes is only the introduction to a unique work projected for fifteen tomes. Buckle despised the mere compilation of facts and data which biographers and historical writers seemed to cultivate, and spoke boldly of a "science of history" on the basis of a much broader induction.[20] Capable critics regarded his work as a magnificent attempt to show deductively the effects of material causes on human civilization. Though Buckle's account was incomplete, it was full of much suggestion, which has never been denied; and apart from his conclusions, the stimulating effect upon the young men of his generation ought not to be forgotten. If he did not write great history himself—an open question—he was surely the cause of its being written by others.[21]

---

[17] George Burton Adams, "History and the Philosophy of History," *AHR*, XIV (1909), 229, cp., 221–36.

[18] Émile Faguet, "Auguste Comte, I, Ses idées générales et sa méthode," *RDM*, CXXX (1895), 296–319. Carlyle declared that Comte was "the ghastliest algebraic factor that ever was taken for a man." *A Memoir of the Right Hon. William Edward Hartpole Lecky* (New York, 1909), 63 and note.

[19] This was the title of the edition in 3 v., 1866, and is more appropriate than the briefer form *History of Civilization in England* first used. A German version was printed in 1860, and a French in 1865; there have also been several Russian editions.

[20] See the first chapter of his history, and the extract quoted in Arthur J. Grant, *English Historians* (London, 1906), 55–64.

[21] John M. Robertson, *Buckle and His Critics, A Study in Sociology* (London, 1895), is a good corrective of the misconceptions current about Buckle. For further information on Buckle see: *Miscellaneous and Posthumous Works of H. Thomas Buckle*, ed. with a biographical notice by

There was a great difference between Buckle and Taine. Buckle was a brilliant amateur and self-trained. Taine was a gifted scholar, historian, litterateur, philosopher, psychologist, zoologist and one of the few men in France—along with Renan—who kept abreast of the progress of German thought along almost all lines. "German writers," he said, "are to us what England was to France in the time of Voltaire." [22]

Taine [23] received the doctorate in 1853 and for a short time taught in a provincial lycée, but soon resigned and henceforth lived by his pen. Literary critic, historian, philosopher, and psychologist, Taine was a practical worker in physiology and zoology also. In his first work, *Essai sur Tite Live*, he set forth the formula to which he steadily adhered and never renounced. "A soul," he wrote, "whether of an individual or of a nation, is like a plant. It is a matter for science to study. From the moment that one knows the power which actuates it, one can, without discomposing its works, reconstruct it by pure reasoning." History is "psychological anatomy" and psychology itself is primarily a mechanical expression. In this latter statement it will be seen that Taine anticipated by half a century the modern advocates of Behaviorism. To discover the faculties and functions of the soul of a nation, i.e., to write history, there are no means so sure as the physical and biological sciences. The education, habit, ideas, ways of thought, aesthetics, philosophy of a people are primarily based upon climate, race, and milieu.

Taine was a rebel against the popular eclecticism of his day represented by Victor Cousin which nauseated him, and a rebel also against the current Romanticism. Cousin and Victor Hugo were his pet aver-

Helen Taylor (London, 1872, 3 v.), of which the second and third contain his common-place books; Alfred H. Huth, *The Life and Writings of Henry Thomas Buckle* (New York, 1880); the article on Buckle in *DNB*, VII, 208–11; GOOCH, 585; J. Hutchison Stirling, "Mr. Buckle and the Aufklärung," *Journal of Speculative Philosophy*, IX (1875), 337–400; Louis Étienne, "Le positivisme dans l'histoire.—L'historien anglais Henri Thomas Buckle," *RDM*, LXXIV (1868), 375–408; R. Usinger, "Thomas Buckle," *HZ*, XIX (1868), 24–37. Droysen's criticism of Buckle, which appeared originally in *HZ*, IX (1863), 1–22, was translated by E. B. Andrews, and included with his translation of the *Grundriss der Historik* in *Outline of the Principles of History* (Boston, 1893). For further reviews of Buckle's *History of Civilization* see: PATTISON, II, 396 ff.; *NAR*, LXXXVII, 388–423, XCIII, 519–59, CXV, 65–103; *ER*, CVII (1858), 465–512; *NBR*, XLVII (1867), 359–403; *QR*, CIV (1858), 38–74; *LQR*, XII (1859), 1–54, and XVII (1862), 301–25, and *MacMillan's Magazine*, July, August, and September, 1861.

[22] *Life and Letters of H. Taine*, tr. by Mrs. R. L. Devonshire (London, 1902–08, 3 v.), I, 186, written in 1852.

[23] In addition to his *Life and Letters* (n. 22), see Gustave Lanson in *La Grande Encyclopédie*, XXV, 817–18; André Chevrillon, *Taine, formation de sa pensée* (Paris, 1932); Albert Léon Guérard, *French Prophets of Yesterday; a Study of Religious Thought under the Second Empire* (New York and London, 1913); Crane Brinton, *A Decade of Revolution, 1789–1799* (New York, 1934), 293–94; A. Albert-Petit, "Deux conceptions de l'histoire de la Révolution—Taine et M. Aulard," *RDM*, LIX (1910), 77–97; Robert H. Fife, "The Renaissance in a Changing World," *Germanic Review*, IX (1934), pt. ii, 73–95; Émile Faguet, *Revue de Paris*, IV (1899), 297–328, 627–53; Hilaire Belloc, "Ten Pages of Taine," *International Quarterly*, XII (1905–06), 255–72 [exposes Taine's untrustworthy writing].

sions. There was a sort of scientific asceticism in Taine. In 1855 he wrote: "Let us therefore separate science from poetry and from practical morality. . . . Science must not accommodate herself to our tastes, but our tastes to her dogmas. She is a queen, not a servant. . . . Let her remain in solitude; let her pursue truth alone; dominion will come to her later, or it will never come, it matters not. She is miles above practical and active life . . . and has nothing more to do or to claim, as soon as she has found truth." [24]

Taine has an analytic, not a descriptive mind. His highest praise of Beethoven's symphonies is that "they are as beautiful as a syllogism." Pascal and Descartes had led him to philosophic determinism. This philosophy, with its ideas of a world of general laws, led Taine to science itself, and his determinism and positivism were to him confirmed by chemistry and physics and biology.

The influence of physiology and natural history upon him was enormous. In order to understand psychology he studied medicine and pathology. The best exposition of his ideas with reference to history is to be found in the introduction to his *Histoire de la littérature anglaise* (1863), where he analyzes at great length the soil, climate, food products, etc., of England and claims that only by understanding these conditions can one understand the English nature and spirit. "Aujourd'hui, l'histoire comme la zoölogie a trouvé son anatomie." [25] In the preface to *L'Ancien régime* (1876) he wrote: "The historian may be permitted the privilege of the naturalist: I have observed my subject as one might observe the metamorphosis of an insect."

Taine's letters are very luminous, and no apology is necessary for copious quotation from them:

History is not a science similar to Geometry, but to Physiology and Geology. Just as there are fixed but not numerically measurable relations between the organs and the functions of a living body, likewise are there precise but not numerically measurable relations between the groups of facts which comprise social and moral life. I expressly said so in my Preface, distinguishing exact science from inexact science, that is, those branches of science which belong to the mathematical group and those which group themselves around History, both operating on quantities, but the first on measurable quantities, and the second on unmeasurable quantities. The question therefore reduces itself to this: is it possible to establish precise but unmeasurable relations between moral groups, i.e. Religion, Philosophy, the social state, etc., of a century or of a nation? Those precise, general and necessary relations are what I, after Montesquieu, call *laws;* it is also the name given to them in Zoology or Botany. My Preface [to the *Histoire de la littérature anglaise*] sets out the system of these Historical Laws, the general connexion of great events, the causes of these connexions, the classification of these causes, and, in

[24] Guérard, *Prophets of Yesterday* (n. 23), 214.
[25] *Histoire de la littérature anglaise* (12th ed., Paris, 1905, 5 v.), I, introduction, p. xiii. English translation by H. Van Laun, *History of English Literature* (rev. ed., New York, 1900, 3 v.).

short, the conditions of human transformation and development. . . . You quote as an example my parallel between Shakespeare's psychological conception and that of our French classics, and you say that those are not laws; they are types, and I have done what zoologists do when, taking fishes and mammals, for instance, they extract from the whole class and its innumerable species an ideal type, an abstract form common to all, persisting in all, whose different features are connected afterwards, to show how the unique type, combined with special circumstances, must produce the species. That is a scientific construction similar to mine; I do not, any more than they, claim to guess at a living being without having seen and dissected it; but, like them, I endeavour to indicate the general types on which living beings are built, and my method of construction or reconstruction has the same range, together with the same limits. . . . I adhere to my idea because I believe it to be true and capable—if it should, later on, fall into good hands—of producing good fruit. It has been lying on the ground since Montesquieu's time, and I have picked it up, that is all [II, 250–52].[26]

My system, if that name can be inflicted on it, is but a law; that is, a general fact observed a great many times in several centuries, nations, or individuals. According to all the rules of scientific induction, it may be applied to other cases not yet observed. It is not a supposition, an invention, or a gratuitous hypothesis. All my ambition is to claim for this method a place in the sunshine. . . . I admire painters; I have not enough talent to become one. I am but an anatomist, and I merely contend that a scalpel should be tolerated by the side of the paint-brush [II, 135].

You, who know my ideas so well, are aware that, on the whole, I am an idealist. Properly speaking, facts do not exist, they only seem to our mind to do so; in reality nothing exists but abstracts, universals, general things which appear to us in the guise of particular things. It is Spinoza's own doctrine. . . . [II, 215–16].

But on another occasion Taine the idealist wrote:

The universe is a mechanically constituted organism and history is nothing but a problem of mechanics applied to psychology.

In a letter to Ernest Havet (April 29, 1864) Taine affirms that there are in history theorems analogous to those in geometry, and talks about "'formulas,' 'curves,' and 'mechanics.'" He sharply declares that history is a science analogous to physiology and zoology. Just as there are fixed relations, although not quantitatively measurable, between the organs and the functions of the human body, so there are precise relations, although not susceptible of numerical evaluation, between groups of facts in economic and social life, even between religion and philosophy and social conditions. These precise relations, these general and necessary relations he calls "laws," and adds: "C'est aussi le nom qu'on leur a donné en zoölogie et en botanique."

Taine's historical thinking along the lines of natural science can be illustrated by other examples:

I am born to analyze and classify [II, 68]. . . . It is by actual observation that it (the type) can be isolated [II, 326]. . . . The typical fact of each order: Industry, Family,

[26] This and subsequent references in the text refer to pages in *Life and Letters* (n. 22).

State, Art, Religion, Philosophy . . . must not be sought for in History or in the masses, but in the unequal molecule which is the acting individual [II, 326]. . . . My physiological studies are teaching me History [II, 83]. . . . I love History because it shows me the birth and progress of Justice, and I find it all the more beautiful in that I see in it the ultimate development of Nature [II, 102].

Finally, two curious quotations:

Like the organized molecules of nature, each individual develops under the influence of his milieu and responds to the thrust of the propitious moment.[27]

To say that vice and virtue are products, as vitriol and sugar are products, is not to say that they are chemical products like vitriol and sugar. They are moral products created by the union of moral elements, and just as it is necessary to know the chemical matters of which vitriol and sugar are composed in order to make it or unmake it, so it is useful, in order to give man a hatred of falsehood, to seek the psychological elements which by their combination produce veracity. Applied to present day matters, such as for instance the analysis of the revolutionary or the clerical spirit, similar study would doubtless prove illuminating.[28]

Scientifically Taine was a physiologist, philosophically a Hegelian. Facts only seem to exist, but in reality there are only abstracts, universals. "The more I study the things of the mind the more mathematical I find them. In them, as in mathematics, it is a question of quantities; they must be treated with precision. I have never had more satisfaction than in proving this in the realms of art, politics and history." [29]

Taine's *History of English Literature* is the best exposition of his ruling ideas. The real title of the work should have been: History of the English Nation and of English Civilization as Exhibited in Its Literature. The book is actually a philosophy of history; a philosophic history of the English people and its civilization judged through the medium of its literature, which is regarded as a composite historical document. His *L'Ancien régime* is the best exposition of his method. In this work he anatomizes and dissects the ancien régime in all its elements in order to study its mechanism and the working of all its parts, and he mounts each discovery as a specimen as an entomologist mounts insects. The book is an extraordinary assemblage of discrete documents. It is a combination of assorted facts, few of which are of great importance. The weight is in the mass of evidence. The notes fill from one-third to one-half of every page. In short the *L'Ancien régime* is a formidable compilation fashioned with extraordinary mechanical art, and the Old Regime is represented as a terrible machine in which all the parts fitted together.

[27] *Essais de critique et d'histoire* (12th ed., Paris, 1913), p. xxxii.
[28] *Life and Letters* (n. 22), III, 100–01.
[29] *Ibid.*, III, 239. A. Chevrillon, *Taine: formation de sa pensée* (Paris, 1905), 132 quotes from a note on Aristotle's *Analytics* which Taine wrote when a student at the École Normale: "L'homme est un théorème qui marche, une civilisation est une définition qui se développe."

Taine was convinced that the soul of a people was primarily formed by the influence of the physical geography, climate, and resources of a country. When he went to England in 1871 and met Grote and Freeman he was filled with contempt for them. Of Grote, then 75 years of age, he wrote: "the type of the 'gentleman,'—but he understands history only according to the English treatment, from the political point of view alone. He has written a history of Greece without having visited the country; the influences of locality and climate do not appeal to him as significant" [III, 48]. He used Freeman as a fearful example of the narrowness of English historical writing. "In all I hear or read," he wrote, "I never come across any true delicacy of literary feeling, never the gift, the art of really understanding the souls and passions that animated past humanity. It is all just erudition, very solid, but little more: take Mr. Freeman, for instance, who is re-writing Augustine Thierry's history of the Norman Conquest" [III, 59].

If English scholars made a bad impression on Taine, British impression of him was one of repugnance. Creighton said: "Taine ought to promulgate a new beatitude—Blessed are the cocksure." [30] York Powell described him as "an austere and narrow doctrinaire, wedded to method and believing that out of a classification of facts truth must necessarily spring. A man honest and hardworking, but painfully stiff, and with his historic eyesight strictly limited by the blinkers of his unyielding maxims and his unbending method." [31]

Taine was especially eager to get information about Tennyson, and meeting Sir Francis Palgrave, who was a friend of the poet, he asked: "Was he not in early youth rich, luxurious, fond of pleasure, self-indulgent? I see it in his early poems—his riot, his adoration of physical beauty, his delight in jewels, in the abandonment of all to pleasure, in wine and——." "Stop, stop," cried Palgrave. "As a young man Tennyson was poor. His habits were as they still are, simple and reserved. He has never known luxury in your sense; and if his early poems are luxurious in tone, if they are full of beautiful women and pearls and gold, it is because he is a poet and gifted with a poet's imagination." Yet when Taine's book came out, Tennyson was portrayed as a young voluptuary, a rich profligate. The anecdote is an index to Taine's character. He construed evidence according to his own purposes and asserted what he wished in his own mind in defiance of evidence.

"Historians repudiate Taine's philosophy and criticize his scholarship; but they have adopted the fundamental idea, which all his works

[30] Louise Creighton, *Life and Letters of Mandell Creighton* (London, 1904, 2 v.), I, 99.
[31] Oliver Elton, *Frederick York Powell* (Oxford, 1906, 2 v.), II, 79–80.

enforce, that history is concerned, not merely with political history, but with the whole social life of nations." [32]

It was natural that Taine should have introduced Burckhardt's *Renaissance* to French readers. There was a great affinity between them. Taine saw in Burckhardt a convert to his ideas. Both were in search of "types." To Taine the primary factor in the formation of "types" was *milieu*—race and physical environment; to Burckhardt the formative factor was *Kultur*—state and religion. But Burckhardt's methodology was totally without Taine's "scientific" bias.

Jacob Burckhardt (1818-97),[33] the author of *The Culture of the Renaissance in Italy* (1860), which Acton pronounced "the most penetrating and subtle treatise on the history of civilization that exists in literature," acquired his training under Ranke, but really belongs to the positivist school. Master and student went their separate and opposite ways. Ranke was essentially interested in politics; Burckhardt devoted his life to art. Ranke was a scientific student of society, especially in politics; Burckhardt was an ardent aesthete. Personally the two famous men never were close; the aesthetic Burckhardt, for one, distrusted his teacher's calm detachment. Nevertheless, from a technical point of view, Ranke's influence on Burckhardt was abiding.

Burckhardt was a descendant of an old Swiss family; his father was a preacher and he himself studied theology, a study which he rejected before he was twenty. Then he went to Berlin where he attended the classes of Droysen, Böckh, Grimm, but mainly Ranke and his seminar. In 1843 he took his degree under Ranke, and two years later he became professor of history and of the history of art at the University of Basel, a position which he held with great distinction for almost fifty years. So wide was his fame, in fact, that in 1872 he was offered the chair of history at Berlin as Ranke's successor; but, being a vigorously independent Swiss and disliking Prussian servility, he refused the flatter-

---

[32] Carl Becker, "Some Aspects of the Influence of Social Problems and Ideas upon the Study and Writing of History," *Publications of the American Sociological Society*, VII (1913), 83, the whole article, 73-107.

[33] Autobiographic details are to be found in Burckhardt's *Erinnerungen aus Rubens* (Basel, 1898). For bibliography see Walther Rehm, *Jacob Burckhardt* (Frauenfeld, 1930), 289-93. By far the best study of Burckhardt's mind is K. Joël's article, "Jakob Burckhardt als Geschichtsphilosoph," *Festschrift zur Feier des 450 jährigen Bestehens der Universität Basel* (Basel, 1910); see also GOOCH, 580-84; FUETER, 748-51; H. Trog, in *Biographisches Jahrbuch und Deutscher Nekrolog*, II (1898), 54-75; the same, *Jacob Burckhardt. Eine biographische Skizze* (Basel, 1898); R. H. Fife, *Germanic Review*, IX, 1934, pt. ii, 78-79; Eberhard Gothein, "Jakob Burckhardt," *PJ*, XC (1897), 1-33; Carl Neumann, "Griechische Kulturgeschichte in der Auffassung Jakob Burckhardt's," *HZ*, LXXXV (1900), 385-452; *ibid.*, XCVII (1906), 557 ff., CXLII (1930), 457 ff.; Carl Neumann, "Jakob Burckharts politisches Vermächtnis," *Deutsche Rundschau*, CXXXIII (1907), 37-54, 252-64, which forms a chapter in Neumann's *Jacob Burckhardt* (Munich, 1927); the same, "Jacob Burckhardt. Ein Essay," *Deutsche Rundschau*, XCIV (1898), 374-400.

ing offer. Burckhardt was a life-long friend of Nietzsche, and his literary executor together with Overbeck, professor of philosophy in Basel.

In Burckhardt's pages the historical, political, moral, intellectual, economic, and social aspects of the Renaissance are all treated. "The men and women of it look out at us from the canvases of the time, whose remains rest beneath the sculptured tombs, whose piety or whose pride raised the churches, whose love of learning gathered the libraries, whose patronage of art formed the galleries, who erected the stately palaces and laid out the beautiful gardens. The subject is presented first from a political point of view—the state as a work of art, especially expressed in the despotism or enlightened tyranny of the age. New notions of administration, political economy, finance, the conduct of foreign affairs were gradually developed. War became a science. The Papacy as a government was behind the other Italian states in practicing these ideas. In Burckhardt's opinion the Reformation alone prevented the fall of the temporal power of the popes three hundred years before it actually fell. He thought, too, that under so many stimulating conditions Italy would have bloomed without the impulse given by the rediscovery of antiquity."

Burckhardt must be studied as a personality before he can be understood as an historian, for his historical works are complete personal expressions. In one sense, indeed, he was hardly an historian, since he *personalized* his records and readings, and had little interest in politics or state relationships. Where he excelled was in the same sphere that the artist excels, namely, in treating of the individual and his soul. His splendid *Culture of the Renaissance*—a subject perfectly fitted for a mind like Burckhardt's—has been justly criticized for its failure to explain origins, its omission of all material foundations, its confusion of different generations of authors.

One has said almost everything important about Burckhardt when one has used two key words: *personality* and *culture*. All the thought, the learning, the interests, the labors of this Swiss aesthete revolved about those two concepts. He was not a philosopher or even a thinker; he said to Nietzsche, "I have never had a philosophic mind, and even the history of philosophy is unknown to me." "I have never in my life thought philosophically." To Nietzsche he also wrote these revealing words: "Into the temple of true thought I have, as you know, never penetrated, but have always taken pleasure in the court and halls of Peribolos, where reigns the plastic in the widest sense of the word." Consequently, Burckhardt also had an aversion for any philosophy of history, because, he said, it "proceeded chronologically," and treated of events and cultures as contraries rather than as similarities. He himself, he admitted, was interested in the "repeated, constant, typical."

Burckhardt was most attracted to subjects and periods in which personality held sway, such as classic Greece, the Italian Renaissance, the French ancien régime. His lectures on these subjects, delivered with marvelous irony and based upon inexhaustible knowledge, were works of art. Himself an artist of first rank, he identified himself with his subjects and he was undoubtedly the foremost art critic in Europe. His conversations, especially when surrounded by eager young students and stimulated by red wine (the personal habits of this bachelor were peculiar),[34] were famous. Of his oratory, Professor Ludwig Cohn of Göttingen said: "There are only two incomparably great orators (among historians): Roepell in Breslau and Jacob Burckhardt in Basel."

This emphasis upon personality pervades all of Burckhardt's works. Paradoxically enough, it led to keen pessimism, particularly as Burckhardt was a close reader of Schopenhauer. His pessimism was largely the result of his deliberate isolation from the great European mass movements of his time, which were nationalistic, patriotic, centralistic. Burckhardt, a proud and free citizen of Basel, detested all that was compulsory, uniform, non-individualistic. He favored small, free, independent communities; hence his contempt of and dislike for Bismarck's Germany. It is noteworthy that Burckhardt impressed these individualistic, aristocratic, anti-state ideas on the sensitive Nietzsche, who, in his turn, became a "good European" and a hater of nationalism.

From these feelings and convictions sprang Burckhardt's interest in and devotion to culture. He may be considered as the founder of *Kulturgeschichte*. To him culture was the value, the positive sense of history. It meant freedom, not arbitrary, external freedom, but the inner, spiritual evolution: "the sum total of those developments of the spirit which take place spontaneously and do not claim any universal or compulsory validity."

"It was chiefly to the French historian Michelet that he owed the suggestion which led him to draw his great synthesis of political life and theory, literature, religious thought, scholarship, social life, morality and superstition, between Dante and Michelangelo. . . . Although much separates him from Taine, nevertheless there are many points common to the method of both Burckhardt and Taine. . . . Both he and Taine looked upon history as the interworking of certain stable elements (in Taine, the race; in Burckhardt, state and religion) with

[34] See the personal recollections of H. Gelzer, "Jakob Burckhardt als Mensch und Lehrer," *Zeitschrift für Kulturgeschichte*, VII (1900), 1–51.

elements of time and place (for Taine, the milieu; for Burckhardt, 'Kultur'). . . . Taine gave high praise to Burckhardt's work, for in reality it illustrates Taine's theories without Taine's conscious methodology. Like Taine, Burckhardt sought the 'typical' in history and he had the same conviction as Taine that the type which he selected was a faithful representative of its epoch." [35]

Another German historian influenced by science was Heinrich von Sybel, the author of the *French Revolution* and of *The Founding of the German Empire*. Perhaps because he was both an historian and a politician, he had an intuitive understanding of problems which sometimes elude the mere historian.[36] Sybel confused his convictions with his science. He was so profoundly convinced of the accuracy of his method that he believed that his doctrines were the consequences of his method. To Sybel history was virtually as positive as a natural science. All that was necessary, he said, was to have the right method and the truth would unerringly proceed from it. "Die historische Wissenschaft ist fähig, zu völlig exacter Kenntniss vorzudringen." [37]

Renan and Fustel de Coulanges, contemporaries of Taine, were no less positivist than he, but their method was less obvious. Each had perfect confidence in his own critical ability to extract the truth about men and events from the historical sources under his hand. Renan's method was so subtle, the blend of subjective thinking with objective reality so elusive, the transition from analysis to synthesis so adroit that the reader's mind is often more seduced than convinced, though he does not know it. Yet the reader is never in doubt that Renan's purpose is to reveal the close relation between religious belief and intellectual development, and the influence of both upon social conditions. Renan held that the history of ancient Judaea, Greece, and Rome exemplified a law of history according to which nations and civilizations are

[35] R. H. Fife, in *Germanic Review* (n. 33), 78–79. Only three of Burckhardt's works were published during his lifetime: *Die Zeit Constantins des Grossen* (Leipzig, 1853, 4th ed., 1924); *Die Kultur der Renaissance in Italien* (Leipzig, 1860, 2 v., 12th ed., edited by L. Geiger, Leipzig, 1919, 2 v.); and *Geschichte der Renaissance in Italien* (1867, 7th ed., Stuttgart, 1924). The other works were published from Burckhardt's lectures by J. Oeri. Among them are *Griechische Kulturgeschichte* (2nd ed., Berlin and Stuttgart, 1898–1902, 4 v.); *Weltgeschichtliche Betrachtungen* (Stuttgart and Berlin, 1905, 4th ed., 1921); *Beiträge zur Kunstgeschichte von Italien* (1898, 2nd ed., 1911). A complete edition of his works, *Jacob Burckhardt-Gesamtausgabe*, ed. by Hans Trog, Emil Dürr, and others was published at Stuttgart, 1929–34, in 14 v.

[36] "Ich gebe Sybel Recht dass 1840–80 die von ihm und den genannten Historikern vertretene Weltanschauung die wissenschaftlich und sittlich höchststehende, und darum kräftigste, berechtigste, siegreiche war. Und Sybels grosse Bedeutung liegt darin, dass er von diesem Standpunkt aus Geschichte schrieb und Welturteile abgab, dass er damit den Schritt von der bloss descriptiven Wissenschaft zur kausal erklärenden, zu der die grossen Zusammenhänge aufhellenden in seiner Art vollzog." Gustav Schmoller, "Gedächtnisrede auf Heinrich von Sybel und Heinrich von Treitschke," *Forschungen zur brandenburgischen und preussischen Geschichte*, IX (1897), 357–94.

[37] Cp. his address, "Ueber die Gesetze des historischen Wissens," in his *Vorträge und Aufsätze* (Berlin, 1874), 1–20.

weakened and exhausted by the services which they render to civilization and humanity; they finally die that a new culture may be born out
of the humus. But if this be true, then the "survival of the fittest" is
not a law of history, however it may be in the biological world. Or is it
that human stock is like fruit trees, in which the best kind tend to grow
barren after several generations?

Fustel de Coulanges believed too that history was as pure a science
as mathematics, if only the forms of mathematical demonstration and
the principles of logic were applied to the interpretation of the sources
of history. Strictly speaking, Fustel held that it was not for him to
interpret but to reveal. If rightly used the documents of history would
speak for themselves. He once reproved some students who applauded
him, saying: "It is not I who speak, but History which speaks through
me."

Since Darwin, no historian can afford to ignore the factor of evolution in historical development. This concept has given the historian an
idea of the time-factor, or duration, in history of far greater dimension
and significance than he had before. In especial it has given the historian a new understanding of the growth of institutions, a perception
that the roots of the present are deep in the past, and a reverence for
tradition. Practically every historian admits today the *evolutionary*
nature of the growth of human institutions. "It was the peculiar ability
of Darwin," writes E. G. Conklin, "to see nature in four dimensions—
length, breadth, depth, and duration." The tendency of "segregation"
or the tendency of similar materials to collect together in groups, which
the scientist recognizes everywhere today in the biological world, and
the counter-condition of "isolation" have potently influenced the thinking of students of the social sciences in the matter of the formation of
racial and other social groups. The principle of geographical isolation,
for example, is a very important one to the historian and the economic-
social historian.[38]

Let us take another example. "The idea of regarding the religions
of the world not dogmatically but historically—in other words, not as
systems of truth or falsehood to be demonstrated or refuted, but as
phenomena of consciousness to be studied like any other aspect of
human nature—is one which seems hardly to have suggested itself
before the nineteenth century."[39]

But history can be written—indeed sometimes has to be written—
in terms of decline and decay instead of in terms of evolution and de-

[38] Herbert W. Conn, *The Methods of Evolution* (New York and London, 1900), 282, thinks
this idea of isolation of such importance as "to deserve to rank with natural selection in the
origin of species."

[39] Sir James G. Frazer, *The Gorgon's Head* (London, 1927), 281–82.

velopment. For each age is an age that is dying in order that a new age may have birth. There is no incompatibility between organic growth and organic degradation. Witness the great works inspired by the decline of the Roman Empire, as Seeck's *Geschichte des Untergangs der antiken Welt*, and Rostovtzeff's *Social and Economic History of the Roman Empire*, or—more remotely—Oswald Spengler's *Decline of the West*.

Professor Julian Huxley, as Havelock Ellis has pointed out, has set forth "the place of biology as the bridge between inorganic science and humanist studies if we are to have a coherent outlook on the world and a just integration of scientific method in human affairs. The historian is enormously indebted to the biologist for the suggestive idea of the organic nature of society in which he sees every individual as a cell in the body politic and body social. It has given the historian a new insight, a new interpretation, a new understanding of history, both present and past. For as human nature is the same in every age, history has learned to understand the past by the present and the present by the past.

The bacteriologist and the germ-theory have helped the historian by analogy to understand institutional and social lesions, the decadence of an age, the decay of a civilization. So far has this reasoning gone that the phrase "diseases of society" is a commonplace. No one can read a modern work upon the decline of the Roman Empire without coming in contact with this biological-bacteriological interpretation of history. Otto Seeck, for example, Mommsen's most brilliant successor, in his *Geschichte des Untergangs der antiken Welt* says that Roman civilization "rotted down" and that out of the muck heap of a decayed civilization sprang "spores," new organisms, which eventually blossomed and bloomed into a new culture, a new civilization. The modern historian who writes that "the normal group which formed, as it were, the constitutive cell of medieval society is the manor," or who talks of "the molecular nature of society," or "social fermentation," is drawing an analogy from science to illustrate history; he is not writing history. "What seems to be a corroboration may really be a confusion. . . ." An analogy is one thing, an identity is quite another thing. If in any contrast the differences exceed the number or importance of the likenesses, then the analogy ceases to exist.[40]

Walter Bagehot's *Physics and Politics* published in 1873 was among the most impressive works which endeavored to interpret history in terms of science. The title, however, suggests only half the purpose.

---

[40] O. F. v. Gierke, *Natural Law and the Theory of Society, 1500 to 1800*, tr. by Ernest Barker (Cambridge, 1934, 2 v.), I, pp. xxix–xxx.

The full title reads: *Physics and Politics, or Thoughts on the Application of the Principles of Natural Selection and Inheritance to Political Society.* Evidently "physics" stands for the inorganic as well as the organic sciences, and "politics" for all the social sciences.

From the time of Darwin and Pasteur until recently zoology and bacteriology have been the most influential sciences in the interpretation of history. Of late, however, the famous Second Law of Thermo-dynamics has stirred a few historians. Most of them, however, have refused to draw historical inferences from experimental knowledge of the economy of heat, in spite of the fact that the late Wilhelm Ostwald exulted in the thought that "natural science has at last been able to seize from its conservative guardians the world of values, hitherto conceived as the exclusive possession of the *Geisteswissenschaften*." [41] For Ostwald, Physics englobes History. Energetics must be extended to life and mind. "The entire world of ends and values rises from the law of the dissipation (of energy) as its deepest source."

Historians have weakly left the refutation of the application of the Second Law of Thermo-dynamics to philosophers, as William James, who contended that it was irrelevant to history except as it set a terminus to history, on the ground that history has to do with values, and physics deals with quanta. [42]

But Henry Adams in dismay declared that this law left social studies "gasping for breath." He was unduly alarmed. Adams failed to see— or else would not admit—that history fundamentally deals with qualitative, not quantitative values. And these are not merely differences of degree—they are differences in kind. So far as I can perceive, the only bearing which the Second Law of Thermo-dynamics has upon history is that it prophesies the inevitable extinction of the human race as a part of the extinguishment of the earth itself. But history is the story of mankind, not a chapter in geology. The Second Law of Thermo-dynamics is not itself an historical principle, in spite of the fact that there are those who gravely believe that with it "a historical element has been introduced from physics."

There is no true relation between the method of history and the method of science, and real comparison falls to the ground. We can make analogies, but we cannot establish identities.

The preoccupation of natural science is with the *quantitative*. The primary interest of the scientist is to describe *metrically*, i.e., in terms of measurement, the processes of nature, from which proceeds the in-

[41] Wilhelm Ostwald, *Der energetische Imperativ* (Leipzig, 1912); also his autobiography in *Die deutsche Philosophie der Gegenwart in Selbstdarstellungen* (Leipzig, 1932).

[42] *Letters of William James*, ed. by his son Henry James (Boston, 1926, 2 v. in 1), II, 345, letter to Henry Adams.

clination of the scientific mind to *classification*. The historian, on the other hand, is not interested in quantitative matters, except incidentally. His primary interest is in *qualities*—in ideas, purposes, emotions. He is interested in *facts*, not in things. And here it may be remarked that the word "fact" is singularly appropriate for the data used by the historian. For it means *factum est*, i.e., something *made* or *done*, but *not made or done by nature, but by man*.

There is a kinship between history, philosophy, and religion in that each of these subjects puts "the emphasis upon individual things, unique things, incalculable and spontaneous things, qualitative entities having no exact counterpart anywhere in the universe." [43]

Science is interested in the metrical aspects of the world and neglects the individuality in it, while history, on the other hand, neglects the former and is interested in the latter. Science always has a leaning towards the *mechanical* and the deterministic, for these are concepts in the scientific frame of mind. Science may begin with qualitative ideas, such as "heat expands" and "cold contracts." But the higher stages of sciences are largely efforts to formulate processes in purely quantitative terms.

On the other hand, the historian is primarily interested in qualitative matters, in the *how* and the *why* of events. Merely quantitative values are of slight importance to an historian. Napoleon had practically the same number of men at Waterloo as Wellington had. The quantity makes no matter. The *why* and *how* Napoleon lost Waterloo is not explicable in quantitative terms.

History and science in general have this interest in common: each is interested in the relation of the particular to the general, and in the long run it is the general which has value.

> For science the particular visible object is unimportant, or important only as an example of a general law . . . or as a member of a species. . . . The particular member of a species has no importance, unless it has some individual peculiarities which make it different from its species, in which case it may be important as one of the new species. But in no case has it any importance in itself. It has importance either as being an example of a species in which the characteristics of the species may be known and demonstrated; or as a link in a chain of causation, and it is the *chain*, not the link which is important.[44]

Similarly, history is not interested in any single event or in any individual man, but in the *relations* of men and of events. The scientist and the historian are at one also in that each makes the order and relation of the phenomena intelligible, in that each derives processes and

[43] Joseph Needham, "Religion and the Scientific Mind," *Criterion*, X (1931), 249, the whole article, 233–63.
[44] *Collected Essays of W. P. Ker*, ed. by Charles Whibley (London, 1925, 2 v.), 246–47.

results genetically, in spite of the fact that scientific phenomena and historical phenomena are very different sorts of evidence. The close relation of evolution to life—or at least genetic process—and the fact that history deals with the life of the past makes for the use of evolution in an interpretative capacity by the historian.

The positivist scholars deceived themselves. The influence of science in the nineteenth century has sometimes been stimulating to the imagination of the historians. But it has also been prejudicial, and has not infrequently had a cramping effect comparable to the influence of theology and metaphysics in previous centuries.[45] On the other hand, "All modern thought and science is historical in method. Whatever is studied is considered not only as it is now observed to be, but in the light of the process by which it has come to be. Natural History, until recently, was the classification of existing species: now it is quite equally concerned with the origins of species. Geology is not only a study of the crust of the earth, but an examination of the question how that crust has been formed. . . . This use of the historical method is the main distinguishing characteristic of our own modern thought as compared with the thought of all former ages; and it coheres closely with the notion of Evolution as a general term for a process whereby things not only are, but come to be, and indeed have their being in the process of coming to be."[46]

[45] "The intellectual formulas borrowed from natural science, which have cramped and distorted the operations of history as thought, have taken two forms: physical and biological. The first of these rests upon . . . the assumption of causation: everything that happens in the world of human affairs is determined by antecedent occurrences, and events of history are the illustrations or data of laws to be discovered, laws such as are found in hydraulics. . . . Historians have been arranging events in neat little chains of causation which explain, to their satisfaction, why succeeding events happen; and they have attributed any shortcomings in result to the inadequacy of their known data, not to the falsity of the assumption on which they have been operating. . . . Growing rightly suspicious of this procedure in physico-historiography, a number of historians, still bent on servitude to natural science, turned from physics to biology. . . . The achievements of Darwinism were impressive. . . . Perhaps the biological analogy of the organism could be applied. . . . So under the biological analogy, history was conceived as a succession of cultural organisms rising, growing, competing and declining." Charles A. Beard, *AHR*, XXXIX (1934), 222–23.
[46] William Temple, *Nature, Man and God* (London, 1935), 101.

BOOK X

THE ANCIENT ORIENT, CLASSICAL ANTIQUITY, AND BYZANTINE STUDIES

CHAPTER LVI

THE RECOVERY OF THE ANCIENT ORIENT [1]

NOWHERE does the widening of men's minds with the progress of the suns become so apparent as in the new perspective the Nineteenth Century brought to Ancient Oriental History. In the first chapter it has been related how the trilingual inscription on the Rosetta Stone furnished the key for the decipherment of the Egyptian hieroglyphs. But it required many years before the ancient Egyptian language was wholly mastered. The founder of Egyptology was the French scholar Champollion.

Jean François Champollion (1790–1832) [2] was educated by his brother, who was twelve years his senior, [3] and at an early age began to study Hebrew, Arabic, and Coptic. When sixteen he presented a paper at the Academy of Grenoble on ancient Egyptian place-names, and contended that Coptic was the ancient language of Egypt. He came to Paris, hoping that Coptic would prove the clue to the hieroglyphics that had taken his fancy. His first success in decipherment, with the aid of the Rosetta stone, came in 1821, and two years later he was able to expound the elementary principles of Egyptian writing in a series of memoirs before the Institute. [4] King Charles X commissioned him to

[1] There is a good summary of the story of the explorations and excavations in the *Cambridge Ancient History*, I (1923), ch. iii, by Professor R. A. Stewart Macalister, with a bibliography, 625–29; for popular accounts see R. Magoffin and E. Davis, *Magic Spades; the Romance of Archaeology* (New York, 1929), and H. V. Hilprecht, *Explorations in Bible Lands during the Nineteenth Century* (Philadelphia, 1903). The literature on recent excavations is copious.

[2] His biography has been written with thoroughness and devotion by Hermine Hartleben, *Champollion, sein Leben und sein Werk* (Berlin, 1906, 2 v.); see also *Lettres de Champollion le Jeune*, collected and annotated by Hermine Hartleben (Paris, 1909, 2 v.); Aimé Champollion-Figéac, *Les deux Champollion, leur vie et leurs oeuvres* (Grenoble, 1887); Alexandre Moret, *Le Nil et la civilisation égyptienne* (Paris, 1926, vol. VII of the *L'Évolution de l'humanité* series), tr. into English by M. R. Dobie.

[3] Jacques Joseph, usually surnamed Champollion-Figéac (1778–1867) to distinguish him from his more famous brother le Jeune. He was librarian, then professor of Greek literature, and successively secretary and dean of the faculty of letters in the Lycée of Grenoble. Then he became archaeologist and keeper of manuscripts at the Bibliothèque Nationale; professor of palaeography at the École des Chartes and in 1849 librarian of the palace at Fontainebleau. He had been an active writer and friend of letters while at Grenoble; Napoleon Bonaparte directed him to draw up an account of the famous passage from Elba to Grenoble. Besides various works on local history there, and on palaeography, he collaborated in editing his deceased brother's manuscripts, and (though he never studied the hieroglyphics himself) composed various volumes on Egyptian and oriental history. For *Égypte ancienne* (1839) and *L'écriture démotique égyptienne* (1843) he utilized his brother's notes and collections. His son Aimé (1812–94) served as his assistant at the Bibliothèque Nationale, and wrote a history of the family (see previous note).

[4] They were published in the following year at state expense. The story, together with an

study Egyptian antiquities further in Italy and in 1824 Champollion visited in turn the museums of Turin, Leghorn, Rome, and Naples. He was appointed director of the Egyptian exhibit in the Louvre, and further commissioned to undertake an expedition to Egypt at the king's expense. This journey was made in co-operation with Ippolito Rosellini, professor at Pisa, who had received a similar commission from the grand-duke of Tuscany. After a year Champollion returned to France to fill a chair of Egyptian antiquities created for him in the Collège de France (1831), but died untimely the following year. His report on the expedition was issued posthumously. Champollion with rare intuition had been the first to prove that all three scripts represented on ancient Egyptian monuments—the hieroglyphic, the hieratic, and the demotic— were basically the same language; and that the hieroglyphic consisted of about nine-tenths of phonetic characters and one-tenth symbols or ideograms. Once the phonetic basis of the writing was established, transliteration showed the relation of ancient Egyptian to Coptic. Young as he was when he died, Champollion had founded the science of Egyptology.[5]

The leadership in the new science now passed from France to Germany, and fell into the hands of Karl Richard Lepsius (1810–84).[6] The influence of Otfried Müller, the Greek scholar, moved him to choose archaeology as his life's work; but Bunsen and Alexander von Humboldt were responsible for turning him to Egypt. The son of a Saxon official, Lepsius passed with highest honors from the gymnasium of his native Naumburg to the universities of Leipzig, Göttingen, and Berlin, and pursued linguistic and archaeological studies. Böckh directed his dissertation (1833). A year after Champollion's death Lepsius came to Paris and was introduced to celebrities like Silvestre de Sacy, the great Arabist. The Duc de Luynes employed him to collect Greek and Roman material for a work on the weapons of the ancients. Then Bunsen, Prussian ambassador at Rome and general secretary of the Archaeologi-

account of his predecessors, is given in detail in the biography by Hermine Hartleben (n. 2), I, ch. vii, 345–500.

[5] Writings of Champollion (those marked with an asterisk are indispensable to students of the hieroglyphics): *L'Égypte sous les Pharaohs* (1814, 2 v.); **Sur écriture hiératique* (1821); **Sur l'écriture démotique; Précis du système hiéroglyphique des anciens Égyptiens* (1824); **Panthéon égyptien, ou collection des personnages mythologiques de l'ancienne Égypte* (incomplete); *Monuments de l'Égypte et de la Nubie considérés par rapport à l'histoire, la religion,* etc.; *Grammaire égyptienne* (1836); *Dictionnaire égyptienne* (1841), both posthumous; *Analyse méthodique du texte démotique de Rosette; Aperçu des résultats historiques de la découverte de l'alphabet hiéroglyphique* (1827); *Mémoires sur les signes employés par les Égyptiens dans leur trois systèmes graphiques à la notation des principales divisions du temps. Lettres écrites d'Égypte et de Nubie* (1833); *Notices manuscrits* (1844 ff.), descriptive of his results in Egypt.

[6] His pupil Georg Ebers has written a grateful biography, *Richard Lepsius*, tr. by Zoe Dana Underhill (New York, 1887); see also Ebers' sketch in *Deutsche Rundschau*, XLI (1884), 184– 201.

cal Institute, invited Lepsius to come to Italy to study the Umbrian, Oscan, and Etruscan inscriptions there, and then to proceed with the unsolved mysteries of Egypt.

Lepsius' first fruits in the field of Egyptology were a lucid summary of Champollion's discoveries, and a revision of his phonetic alphabet. But his most important contributions were made in connection with chronology, numbers, metrology, and the Egyptian religion. He introduced method and critical analysis into a field where scholars still followed their unrestrained imagination and jumped impatiently from one half-solved problem to another. Lepsius ended this unbridled phantasy and prepared a solid foundation on which later generations could build, by scientifically mapping the field.

He began to form complete and ordered collections of the materials. In four years of study, including a visit in 1838 to the collections in England and at Leyden, Lepsius assembled the monumental material, and sorted and revised it into groups according to provenience and probable period of origin.

Most confused of all was the field of Egyptian religion. No one before him had thought of bringing order into this chaos of divinities, or tried to form a pantheon. As always, Lepsius eschewed hasty generalizations or conjectures. He put the whole problem on an historical basis, and sought relations. Researches at Turin led him to the significant conclusion that the numerous religious texts on papyri, sarcophagi, amulets, and mummy wrappings all came from one large work, which he aptly christened the "Book of the Dead." This work Lepsius recognized as the essential source for the religious views of the ancient Egyptians and their belief in immortality. It is characteristic of his careful approach that in the 1830's he did not yet dare to attempt a continuous translation of these texts. Two careful collations of the great manuscript of Turin led to the publication of the text and seventy-nine plates in 1842.[7] His division of the chapters in the *Book of the Dead* has remained substantially unchanged. After his return from Egypt Lepsius was enabled to round out his studies of the Egyptian pantheon, and to prove, by historical method, the connections of the leading deities and to demonstrate how local or temporal causes led to the injection of other divinities.[8]

---

[7] The hieroglyphics of this edition were so excellently cut by the two Weidenbach brothers, that they equalled the beauty of the Egyptian originals, and became the prototype of the type-faces they cut for the Berlin Academy (1884), which have been universally adopted the world over.

[8] See his conclusions in the *Abhandlungen der Königlichen Akademie der Wissenschaften zu Berlin*, phil.-hist. Classe (1851), 157–214, (1856), 231–34, 259–320. In the later volume occurs the statement: "Es wird . . . in allen antiquarischen Untersuchungen stets der sicherste Weg bleiben, mit einer chronologischen Scheidung des Materials zu beginnen, ehe zu systematischen Darstellungen weiter geschritten wird" (p. 224).

Lepsius was appointed to a professorship in Berlin (1842). He was barely thirty when Humboldt and Bunsen persuaded King Frederick William IV of Prussia to entrust him with the leadership of an expedition to Egypt, in imitation of the French and the Italians. The expedition of Champollion in 1828 had been in the main a voyage of discovery. Lepsius now resolved to fill the gaps, to allot a certain length of time to the study of each monument, and to bring historical order into his finds so that serious study of Egyptian art, history, and civilization might begin. He began at Memphis, with its pyramids, which Champollion had almost wholly neglected,[9] and made the first examinations of private tombs in the necropolis. These were systematically photographed, plotted, and squeezes made of the inscriptions. He visited the Fayum, the tombs of Upper Egypt with materials bearing on the end of the Old and beginning of the Middle Empire, and the ruins at El-Amarna. Finally Lepsius sailed up the Nile to Khartum, in the heart of Africa, and opened up modern knowledge of the old Ethiopian civilization. Five months were given to Thebes, and a side-excursion visited for the first time the old copper mines in the Sinaitic peninsula. The entire expedition took three years, and a special ship was dispatched to bring back the inscriptions, plans, and monuments which Muhamed Ali presented to the Prussian king.

For forty years Lepsius taught at Berlin. His first task was to edit the findings of the expedition in twelve gigantic volumes, the *Denkmäler aus Aegypten und Aethiopien* (1859), with a thousand plates.[10] Contrary to the volumes of Napoleon's commission, which had followed a geographical arrangement, or to Rosellini's topical order, Lepsius adopted the more scientific chronological arrangement, separating the documents and materials of one age from those of another, and furthering the comprehensive study of single epochs in their unity.

The problems of editorship led directly to the composition of his *Chronologie der Aegypter* (1859) which discussed the methodology of all ancient chronological studies, and is devoted chiefly to a critical analysis of the sources. His next important volume, *Das Königsbuch der alten Aegypter* (1859) presented all the names anywhere listed of all the rulers of Egypt, with the dates and references, and often detailed proof. Egyptian chronology was thus put upon a relatively secure footing.

Lepsius next turned to studies in ancient weights and measures, not

---

[9] Lepsius advanced the theory that the pyramids were not built at one time, but begun by each ruler at his ascension to the throne, and increased by successive layers or casings until the Pharaoh's death, so that the size of the pyramid was an index to the length of reign. Hilprecht (n. 1), 632.

[10] Georg Ebers says of them: "Die *Denkmäler* sind das grosse Haupt- und Fundamentalbuch für das Studium der Aegyptologie und werden es in aller Zukunft bleiben."

only in Egypt, but in Assyria and Babylonia as well. A second visit to Egypt in 1866 resulted in the happy find of the table of Canopus, in the ruins of Tanis. This was a second Rosetta stone; its trilingual inscription proved beyond a doubt the correctness of Champollion's method, and provided hints for the Egyptian calendar.

Fully half a hundred learned societies elected him to membership. Lepsius was the true father of German Egyptology; all its great masters save Brugsch sat at his feet.

The success of Lepsius' Prussian expedition was exceeded by that of the French excavator, François-Auguste-Ferdinand Mariette (1821–81),[11] who was the virtual master of Egyptian excavations for thirty years, from 1850–80. His father was only a town clerk in Boulogne, and having finished his college course under some difficulties, Mariette began as a secondary school teacher. Interest in the strange writings on an Egyptian sarcophagus in the museum of Boulogne led him to acquire the difficult language by his own efforts from Champollion's grammar and to publish a little catalogue on the Egyptian section of the local museum. Continuing his studies at the Bibliothèque Nationale (1849) he won the patronage of Charles Lenormant, who procured him a position as restorer of the papyri in the Louvre, and then a mission to Egypt for Coptic and other oriental manuscripts. Mariette was determined to seize the opportunity to search for ruins. He abandoned his first mission, and his brave fight against the unfriendly authorities and financial weakness was crowned by the discovery of the Serapeum, the burial-place of the sacred Apis bulls in Memphis. Sixty-four of these were uncovered; the inscriptions were priceless because they ranged from the time of the Eighteenth Dynasty down to Cleopatra, and provided an almost complete list of the kings in this period. Near the great Sphinx of Gizeh Mariette uncovered a magnificent temple. He returned to the Louvre with some seven thousand specimens and monuments. Saïd Pasha of Egypt himself became interested; a museum was established at Cairo and in 1857 Mariette was asked to return as its director, and given authority to excavate anywhere in Egypt that he pleased. His eagerness outstripped his wisdom. In the following twenty years, work was carried on in no less than thirty-seven places. It proved beyond one man's power to superintend all these locations, so that the rude hands of the workmen often spoiled priceless specimens, for want of supervision; and Mariette could not possibly publish or even record his findings in a full and satisfactory manner. Breasted has said of him that he jeopardized the findings of every excavation.

[11] A list of his chief works will be found in *La Grande Encyclopédie*, XXIII, 115–16. See the "Notice biographique" of G. Maspero in *Auguste Mariette. Oeuvres diverses* (Paris, 1904).

Fifty years after there was still no comprehensive work on the Serapeum, and many finds were not published at all. But in those earlier decades even scholars did not observe the scrupulous care of the modern archaeologist.[12]

Over twenty places were excavated in the Delta, including Sais and Bubastis. At Tanis (the Biblical Zoan), in the temple, Mariette unearthed the sphinxes; at Memphis he uncovered more than three hundred mastabas. At Abydos he laid bare the temple of Seti I of the Nineteenth Dynasty, and found the "List of Kings";[13] in the surrounding country he found 15,000 monuments and 800 tombstones, mostly of the Middle Empire. The temple of Hathor at Dendera, that of Horus at Edfu, and the oldest portions of the temple at Karnak were among his more noted excavations. In 1867 he brought back to the International Exposition the famous wooden statue of the "Village Chief" (Sheikh el-Beled), the image of Queen Amneritis cut from a block of alabaster, and the jewels of Queen Aah-Hotep. But the world's acclaim could not dispel the gathering clouds over Mariette's spirit. In 1865 the cholera swept away his wife and two children; the financial distress of the Egyptian Government hampered him; and the War of 1870 seemed to complete the disaster. Patriotic motives moved him to stay, for he feared the field might be lost to France. His last years were a struggle against declining health and harassing problems, and after a final visit to France in 1880 he returned to die at his post. His body was taken to Gizeh a decade later and rests there at the doors of the new museum, guarded in its granite coffin by the sphinxes "which were, at the Serapeum, witnesses of his first labors."

Heinrich Brugsch (1827–94)[14] was no great discoverer or lucky excavator like the men already mentioned, but he built solidly in the fields of Egyptian lexicography, geography, and history. He was born in Berlin; and when but a youth undertook the study of the demotic script which scholars had generally ignored in their fascination for the hieroglyphs. In 1848 when twenty-one years old he published a Latin memoir on the elements of demotic grammar. Its flaws drew the unsparing criticism of Lepsius; but E. de Rougé encouraged the young student and corrected his method. The King of Prussia aided him in

---

[12] Mariette's chief concern was to procure fine specimens for his Museum. He clung to his privileges as excavator in a most jealous manner, and would not allow even his greatest friend, the German scholar Heinrich Brugsch, to dig for himself. Hilprecht (n. 1), 639.

[13] This was a relief representing Seti I with his son Rameses II offering incense to seventy-six of his ancestors on their royal thrones, all accompanied by their names and titles. *Ibid.*, 637.

[14] For the man see his autobiographical *Mein Leben und mein Wandern* (Berlin, 1894). For the scholar, cp. the account by G. Maspero in *Actes du Dixième Congrès International des Orientalistes, session de Genève, 1894*, quatrième partie (Leyden, 1897), 95–102, tr. into English in the *Annual Report of the Smithsonian Institution* (1896), 667–72. For a list of his works see *La Grande Encylopédie*, VIII, 219–20.

making a journey to Egypt, where Brugsch met Mariette and studied demotic inscriptions on the spot in the Serapeum.[15] Extending his visits to the Saïd and Thebes, he assembled the material for his *Grammaire démotique* (1855), and finally unlocked the secrets of this writing to scholarship.

Next Brugsch turned to Egyptian history and geography. When he began there existed on the first only the account of Champollion-Figéac; and the geography was equally poorly represented. Brugsch brought back from Egypt new lists of names on the monuments, catalogues of native Pharaohs before the Ptolemies, of cities, and of peoples they had vanquished. His geographical studies were summed up in his *Geographische Inschriften altägyptischer Denkmäler* (1857–60, 3 v.), and in his monumental *Dictionnaire géographique de l'ancienne Égypte* (1879–80). In 1860 appeared his *Histoire d'Égypte*, written in French, and including the discoveries of Rougé and Mariette. Another French edition came out in 1875; the German edition of 1879, carrying the account of dynasty after dynasty down to the Macedonian conquest, crowned Brugsch's reputation. In 1896 Maspero declared that it "is today the classical work on the subject." [16]

Brugsch's great *Hieroglyphisch-demotisches Wörterbuch* in seven volumes (1867–82) comprised the studies of thirty years; it "has rendered and still renders a greater service than any other work of any other Egyptologist." Brugsch also investigated the Egyptian calendar, astronomy, and religion. His later years were marred by bitterness, scorn for the new generation of workers, and the uncertainty of no regular appointment.[17] "Three men," Maspero has said, "have contributed more than all others to make Egyptology what it is. Champollion founded it; E. de Rougé has created for it a method; Brugsch forged the tools which for a long time have served and will continue to serve the science." [18]

George Moritz Ebers (1837–98),[19] scholar and novelist, popularized

---

[15] Maspero says that the study of demotic is very exacting because the letters are so minute and curious that even photographs will not suffice, and only constant access to originals enables continual progress, a circumstance which discourages many workers. *Annual Report of the Smithsonian Institution* (n. 14), 669.

[16] *Ibid.*, p. 670. *Geschichte Aegyptens unter den Pharaonen* (Leipzig, 1877), translated by H. D. Seymour and Philip Smith as *A History of Egypt under the Pharaohs* (2d ed., London, 1881, 2 v.).

[17] He was Prussian consul at Cairo 1864–68, professor at Göttingen 1868–70, called in 1870 to direct the school of Egyptology created by the viceroy at Cairo, but after 1886 lived in Berlin.

[18] *Annual Report* (n. 14), 672.

[19] *Die Geschichte meines Lebens* (Stuttgart, 1893), tr. by Mary Safford as *The Story of My Life, from Childhood to Manhood* (New York, 1893); R. Gosche, *G. Ebers, der Forscher und Dichter* (2nd ed., Leipzig, 1887). Many of his *Gesammelte Werke* (Stuttgart, 1893–97, 32 v. in 21) have been translated into English. Among his scholarly works are: *Aegypten und die Bücher Moses*

Egyptology in Germany in a somewhat different way than Maspero advanced it in France. He was born in Berlin some two weeks after his father's death, and reared by his Dutch mother. Fanny Ebers had known Baron von Humboldt, Rauch, and Schleiermacher, and played cards with Hegel. In his charming autobiography Ebers has related his youthful reminiscences of the Berlin of Frederick William IV. For a time the Ebers lived in the same house as the famous Grimm brothers. To remove George from the capital in 1848, his mother sent him to the boys' school of Keilhau, founded by Froebel. Those who are not aware that Froebel did more than propose a kindergarten should read the eloquent pages in which Ebers pays tribute to Keilhau, where love of nature, sturdiness of body, and serious study were inculcated. At the University of Göttingen Unger's course on the history of art made a deep impression upon the young student. For several days this teacher discussed the art of the Egyptians, and mentioned Champollion's story. It attracted Ebers' interest, and he returned to his lodgings with Champollion's grammar. Then weeks of illness fettered him to his bed, and he seemed doomed to remain an invalid, but his interest in Egyptology did not die. At the intervention of Jacob Grimm, the great Lepsius called upon Ebers, and with great sacrifice and kindness continued for many semesters to give his invalid student private lessons. Later Ebers heard the lectures of Gerhard, Droysen, and August Böckh at Berlin, and made the acquaintance of Brugsch. The debt he owed to Lepsius he repaid in a warm biography.

While convalescing and pursuing his Egyptological studies at home, Ebers began to write a historical romance. Lepsius frowned when his student first produced the manuscript, but after reading it, he was warm in his praise. Published in 1863 as *An Egyptian Princess* it found an indulgent public, and ran to eleven editions in a score of years. Its author felt, however, that such writing was inferior to the scholarly tasks set by his science, and settled down to serious philological work. In 1865 he began to lecture as *Dozent* in Jena; in 1869–70 he was able to make a journey to Egypt and Nubia and was called to a chair at Leipzig. Ebers went to Egypt again in 1872, to make several finds, the chief of which was a medical papyrus of the second century B.C. which he found at Thebes and edited in 1874 ("Papyrus Ebers"). Until poor health forced his resignation in 1889, he was a respected teacher at Leipzig. Aside from a number of scholarly works, he prepared a guidebook, *Cicerone durch das alte und neue Aegypten* (Stuttgart,

(1868); *Aegypten in Bild und Wort* (1879–80, 2 v.); and his biography of his old teacher *Richard Lepsius* (1885). His greatest successes were his novels, the chief of which were: *Urada* (1877, 3 v.); *Homo Sum* (1878); *Die Schwestern* (1879); *Der Kaiser* (1881, 2), a picture of Egypt in the days of Hadrian; *Serapis* (1885), *Die Nilbraut* (1887, 3 v.); *Kleopatra* (9th ed., 1894).

1886, 2 v.). In 1876 he issued his second historical novel, *Uarda*, which was finally followed by fourteen others. None ever equalled the vogue of the first, but Ebers' thorough acquaintance with contemporary archaeological research and his gift for romantic and skilful presentation always earned him a wide popularity. The series of novels covered various ages of antiquity, from early Egypt to the time of Christianity's triumph. Aside from popularizing Egyptology for his countrymen, Ebers' historical romances had the merit of drawing attention to many sides of Egyptian life beside the strictly political. In effect, he taught cultural history. He was the counterpart of Felix Dahn and Gustav Freytag.[20]

The parents of Gaston Camille Charles Maspero (1846–1916) [21] were of Lombard origin. As a student in the Lycée Louis-le-Grand (1853–65) the fourteen-year-old lad was fascinated by the hieroglyphic inscription he found in Duruy's *Histoire ancienne*. He pursued the study of the language on the sly besides his classical studies, and astonished Mariette in 1867 by translating two inscriptions just brought back from the East. After such proof of his singular powers, he travelled to South America to assist a scholar of Montevideo who hoped to establish the relation of the ancient Peruvian tongue Khechua to Sanskrit. On his return Maspero read before the Academy of Inscriptions a paper on *Un enquête judiciaire à Thebes au temps de la XXᵉ dynastie*, and obtained a position as tutor in Egyptian language and archaeology in the École des Hautes Études (1869). After grammatical studies, he prepared his theses for the doctorate;[22] and in 1874 he followed Rougé in Champollion's famous chair at the Collège de France, at the unusual age of twenty-eight.

In the subsequent year Maspero laid down the lines for his future labors in the first synthetic treatment of the peoples of the ancient East: *Histoire des peuples de l'Orient*. It proved immensely popular; the eleventh edition appeared in 1912, and translations were made into English, German, Spanish, Russian, and Hungarian. Studies in mythology and religion, in navigation, art, economic life, and popular literature enabled him to present a more comprehensive picture in his three-volume *Histoire ancienne des peuples de l'Orient classique*, down to Alexander (Paris, revised 1894–99).

[20] Ebers never published a history, but he did prepare a large manuscript on the history of the ancient East before he thought of converting it into a novel. *Story of My Life*, 374 ff.

[21] Henri Cordier, *Bibliographie des oeuvres de Gaston Maspero* (Paris, 1922); Edouard Naville, "Sir Gaston Maspero, K. C. M. G.," *Journal of Egyptian Archaeology*, III (1916), 227–34; Maurice Croiset, "Un grand égyptologue français; Gaston Maspero," *RDM*, 6th series, XXXIV (1916), 757–77; René Cagnat, "Notice sur la vie et les travaux de M. Gaston Maspero," *ASMP* (1917), 445–82; J. H. Breasted, "Gaston Maspero," *The Nation*, CIII (August 29, 1916), 176–77.

[22] *De Charchemis oppidi situ et historia antiquissima;* and *Du genre épistolaire chez les anciens Égyptiens*, 1873.

In 1880 he was entrusted with an archaeological mission which resulted in the establishment of the Institut Français de l'Archéologie Orientale at Cairo. Soon after his arrival, Mariette's position as director general of Egyptian remains and monuments for the Egyptian Government fell vacant, and Maspero accepted the position. For the next five years he labored under many difficulties, both financial and political (in the disturbances of 1882 he was once given up as lost), but accomplished most creditable results. The Institute was thrown open to scholars and students of every nationality and race who were moved to serious efforts in Egyptian, Arabic, Assyrian or Sanskrit; and their labors fill many ponderous volumes. Maspero made fortunate changes in the methods of his predecessor Mariette. He took measures to insure the preservation of the ruins all over Egypt against the thieving Arabs and the careless hand of the tourist. A system of caretakers and guards was installed over Karnak, Abydos, Edfu, and Philae. His happiest find was in the pyramids of Saqqarah, which Mariette had persistently ignored. Maspero not only found that they went back to the Fifth and Sixth Dynasty, but collected from their interiors over 4,000 lines of the oldest Egyptian literary remains known, of incomparable value for the study of religion and the development of the Egyptian language. He also conducted excavations at the temple of Luxor, Thebes, and the Sphinx of Gizeh, and discovered a great cache of royal mummies at Deir el-Bahri (1881).

Failing health drove Maspero back to Paris (1886–99), where he resumed his teaching at the Collège de France and at the École des Hautes Études. He continued to produce a series of works so beautifully illustrated and fascinatingly written that Egyptology became almost a popular interest.[23] At the end of the century he returned to Cairo as director-general of the department of antiquities. In the thirteen years of his absence, the various collections in Egyptian depositories had swelled tremendously. He supervised the removal of them from Gizeh to new quarters at Kasr en-Nil (1902) and directed the making of a vast catalogue. Repairs at Karnak led to the most remarkable discoveries in later years.[24]

[23] "I have been trying for about fifteen years to bring a science supposed to be only comprehensible to experts within the reach of ordinary men, and it would be gratifying to find that I have not wasted my time, and that through my efforts, some portion of the general public has become interested in it." G. Maspero, *New Light on Ancient Egypt*, tr. by Elizabeth Lee (New York, 1909), author's note.

[24] His works are as follows: *Histoire ancienne des peuples de l'Orient classique* (4th ed., Paris, 1895–99, 3 v.). This is the more mature statement of the following work, and covers the whole near East down to the time of Alexander the Great. *Histoire ancienne des peuples de l'Orient* (1875; 11th ed., 1912). It was translated into various other languages. *Études de mythologie et d'archéologie égyptiennes* (1893–1913, 8 v.); *L'Archéologie égyptienne* (1887, new ed., 1907). This work, which popularized its subject, was translated into German in 1889, and several editions

No recent scholar has done more to systematize Egyptian philology and to reduce it to scientific order than Adolf Erman (1854–1937).[25] Throughout life Erman was a sturdy rationalist, a scholar with a rare practical sense and humor. He was largely self-taught. In 1885 he appeared as extraordinary professor, and in 1892 he was promoted to full professor and Director of the Egyptian Museum in Berlin, a position he held for thirty years, until his retirement in 1923, in the same year as Eduard Meyer. Erman has justly been styled the father of modern Egyptology. Though his hand was felt in many a field, it was upon the linguistic domain that his intellect ranged with a master's sweep. In this connection a reviewer of Erman's autobiography has said:

Those of us who can remember the conditions ruling in Egyptian philology at the time when Erman's work was beginning to take effect—the grammars without form and void, the dictionaries built upon inadequate and confused materials—must bless the day when there arose a scholar determined to revise, redigest and reconstruct the mass empirically and unmethodically got together by his predecessors; whose purpose it was in short to treat the language of the hieroglyphics exactly as scholars had long been treating other languages, as one subject, like all the rest, to constant change and divisible into recognizable epochs.[26]

The giant work for which all Egyptologists will hold him immortal is of course his *Wörterbuch der aegyptischen Sprache* (1926 ff.), edited with H. Grapow at the request of the German Academies. But Erman was more than a philologist; his various works struck out new paths and always were built on a sound historical foundation. "He succeeded in interpreting for us the daily life, the religion, and the literature of Egypt, at once with a vividness and a convincing reasonableness such as none before him had achieved." [27] Though written for the public his *Aegypten und aegyptisches Leben* (tr. as *Life in Egypt*) in its original

---

appeared in English, such as that by A. S. Johns (London, 1914), from the 6th French ed. *Les inscriptions des pyramides de Saqqarah* (Paris, 1894). The last is perhaps his greatest work from the point of historical-philological scholarship. *Les Momies royales de Deir el-Bahari* (1889); *Les contes populaires de l'Égypte ancienne* (1882, 4th ed., 1911, tr. into English by A. S. Johns, London, 1915); *Causeries d'Égypte* (1907), tr. by Elizabeth Lee as *New Light on Ancient Egypt* (1908); *Essais sur l'art égyptien* (Paris, 1912, tr. into English by E. Lee, London, 1913). His larger *Histoire ancienne* was translated into English by M. L. McClure with a separate title for each volume: *The Dawn of Civilization* (1894), *The Struggle of the Nations* (1896), and *The Passing of the Empires* (1900). Maspero also founded the *Recueil des travaux rélatifs à la philologie et à l'archéologie égyptiennes et assyriennes*, and directed the Bibliothèque égyptienne, comprising studies by French Egyptologists.

[25] See his interesting autobiography, *Mein Werden und mein Wirken* (Leipzig, 1929); for an obituary see *Forschungen und Fortschritte* (1937). Among his works, those of a philological nature are: *Die Pluralbildung des Aegyptischen* (1878); *Neuägyptische Grammatik* (1880); *Sprache des Papyrus Westcar* (1889); *Aegyptische Grammatik* (1894, 4th ed., 1928). More of an historical nature are: *Aegypten und ägyptisches Leben im Altertum*, revised by H. Ranke (1923); *Die ägyptische Religion* (2nd ed., 1905). Literary studies and editions: *Märchen des Papyrus Westcar* (1890, 2 v.); *Gespräche eines Lebensmüden mit seiner Seele* (1896); *Zaubersprüche für Mutter und Kind* (1901); *Die Literatur der Aegypter* (1923); *Aus dem Papyrus der königlichen Museen* (1899); *Die Hieroglyphen* (1912).

[26] *LTLS*, February 6, 1930, p. 94.   [27] *Ibid.*

edition has not yet been surpassed for scholarly breadth, vigor, and interest by any similar work, not even by the revision which Erman entrusted to Hermann Ranke.

In the case of Assyria and Babylonia, as with ancient Egypt, the feeble historical memory of their former splendor was dominated until the last century by the Biblical account. Travellers recorded their emotions at the imposing ruins of Nineveh and Babylon, and identified the spectacular mound of Borsippa as the Tower of Babel. But stone was rare in the structures of Mesopotamia, and most of its ancient cities had sunk into unattractive earth mounds, whose outward appearance gave no clue to the fascinating secrets within.[28]

The first complete copy of an inscription found above-ground at Persepolis was given to the world in 1711 by the Chevalier Chardin.[29] A half century later Carsten Niebuhr, father of the famous historian, took extensive copies at the same location and recognized that they represented three types of cuneiform writing, each more complex than the other; but he did not realize that the texts were actually in three languages: Persian, neo-Elamitic, and Babylonian. While European scholars pored over Niebuhr's plates, a young Englishman, Claudius James Rich (1787–1820), for thirteen years a resident of the East India Company in Baghdad, devoted his leisure time to visiting and surveying the mounds accessible to him. He died at the age of thirty-four and collected only casual bits of antiquity; but Rich was the first to give European readers some knowledge of the extent and location of these mystifying hills.

The decipherment of the cuneiform writings was incomparably more difficult than the solution of the Egyptian hieroglyphics. The first successful move was scored by G. F. Grotefend (1775–1853), a professor of classics at the Lyceum of Hanover. By marvelously bold combinations he identified in 1802 the three royal names of Darius, Hystaspes, and Xerxes in Niebuhr's texts, and found the correct values for eleven characters of the simplest, or Persian, script.[30]   Next the

---

[28] *Cambridge Ancient History* (n. 1), I, ch. iii and bibliography, pp. 625–29; Robert W. Rogers, *A History of Babylonia and Assyria* (6th ed., rev., New York, 1915, 2 v.); Hilprecht (n. 1), 1–577; Morris Jastrow, *The Civilization of Babylonia and Assyria* (Philadelphia and London, 1915), chs. i–ii, with excellent bibliographical footnotes; Charles Fossey, *Manuel d'assyriologie* (Paris, 1904–26), I; C. J. Gadd, *The Stones of Assyria*, and *The History and Monuments of Ur* (London, 1929); L. W. King and H. R. Hall, *Egypt and Western Asia in the Light of Recent Discoveries* (London, 1907). In addition to numerous general treatments that exist, almost every expedition and society has published volumes on local sites and finds, often profusely illustrated.

[29] *Voyages de Monsieur le Chevalier Chardin, en Perse et autres lieux de l'Orient* (Amsterdam, 1711, 3 v.).

[30] For Grotefend and his method, see Rogers (n. 28), I, 61–79, and Jastrow (n. 28), 69–79. His extraordinary discovery did not wholly meet with the approval of the Göttingen Academy to which he presented his dissertation, and it was not printed in full from his manuscript until 1893.

Danish scholar Rask demonstrated the relation of Zend, as Old Persian was then called, to some of the Persepolitan texts, and added two letters to Grotefend's alphabet. Eugene Bournouf, Saint-Martin, and Christian Lassen all contributed several new letters. Thus the first labors were shared by several nations, but the final demonstration came from an Englishman working in Persia itself.

Sir Henry Creswicke Rawlinson (1810–95) [31] was in many respects the most remarkable of all these early decipherers. Distinguished as a soldier and diplomat in India and Persia, he was not an academic scholar and never held a chair. At seventeen he had sailed for India to seek his fortune as a young military cadet in the pay of the East India Company. His rapid progress in Indian tongues, especially modern Persian, marked him for advancement, and between 1833 and 1839 he was engaged in Persia in drilling the troops of the Shah.

In 1835 at Mount Elwand Rawlinson saw his first cuneiform inscription, and started to copy the accessible portions of the texts on the impressive Behistun Rock. [32] Without any knowledge of the progress that had been made in Europe, Rawlinson gathered a list of the signs in his copies, and searched for proper names. He hit upon the same method as Grotefend, and by one of the strangest coincidences in history, the first three names he read were Darius, Xerxes, and Hystaspes. Thus the key to Old Persian cuneiform was found twice. Not until the end of 1836, when Rawlinson had distinguished 18 of the 42 letters, did he learn of Grotefend's discovery a generation before. Two years later Rawlinson communicated to the Royal Asiatic Society of London and the Asiatic Society of Paris his translation of the first two paragraphs of the Persian portion of the Behistun inscriptions. He now began to correspond with scholars like Bournouf and Lassen but continued to outstrip them. [33] After the Afghan War (1839–42), when appointed political agent at Baghdad, Rawlinson succeeded at great risk of life and limb in completing his copies of the Persian inscription at Behistun, and by 1844 he had produced a careful literal translation of two hundred long lines. The copy for his published two volumes of

[31] George Rawlinson, *Memoir of Major-General Sir Henry Creswicke Rawlinson* (London, 1898); Rogers (n. 28), 80–92; Jastrow (n. 28), 82–85. For a list of his works and further bibliography see the article by Stanley Lane-Poole in *DNB*, XLVII, 328–31.

[32] In 516 B.C. Darius Hystaspes had a trilingual account of his glories and triumphs sculptured upon the sheer face of a rock jutting upward 1700 feet above the surrounding plain, at Behistun, near Baghdad. The inscription, placed 300 feet above ground, offered a text of 400 lines, in Old Persian, neo-Susan, and Babylonian, with many geographical and proper names. Standard edition by L. W. King and R. C. Thompson, *The Sculptures and Inscription of Darius the Great, on the Rock of Behistun in Persia* (London, 1907).

[33] The superlative merits of Rawlinson as a decipherer become clearer when one realizes that of Grotefend's 30 characters only 8 were correct, and of Saint-Martin's 27 only 10. Rawlinson's method is described fully in his brother's *Memoir* (n. 28), ch. xx.

text, translation, and analysis [34] was prepared in a Baghdad apartment when the outside temperature ran between 90 and 120 degrees Fahrenheit, and his study rarely under 90.

By this time Rawlinson was a famous man in Europe. He now turned from Persian to the vastly more difficult problem of the third unknown writing, today known as Babylonian. In 1846 he met Layard, who had begun excavations at Nimrud the year before,[35] and learned that Layard's finds bore what was substantially the same language as the third texts of Behistun. Back to the high rock he went and with the aid of ladders, ropes, and assistants, obtained paper squeezes of the remaining texts. In 1849 he took up the study of Arabic and Hebrew, two Semitic languages that were to prove invaluable to him, and returned to England to recruit his health after 22 years in the East. Queen Victoria received him for an evening, the Prince Consort was an interested patron, publishers proposed contracts for books, but most of Rawlinson's time was given to papers and addresses intended to publish his results and establish his priority in the reading of Babylonian as well as Persian.[36]

When he returned to India in 1852, the trustees of the British Museum gave him a commission to excavate and collect oriental antiquities for them as successor to their former agent Layard (1845–51). Even before Layard the French consular agent at Mosul, Paul Botta, had begun to dig in the mounds for their secrets. He failed at Kuyunjik, but a native suggested Khorsabad, and there he uncovered the sculptures of the palace of Sargon. Layard opened the mound of Birs Nimrud (Biblical Calah) and discovered the palaces of Ashur-nasir-pal, Sargon, and Shalmaneser, with their huge winged bulls. At Kuyunjik (1849–50) he found the palace of Sennacherib, and the first of the great tablet libraries. His native assistant, Hormuzd Rassam, then laid bare the palace of Ashur-bani-pal, with its famous library (1853). The European public was becoming wildly excited over these finds,

[34] *The Persian Cuneiform Inscription at Behistun*, which appeared as the whole of vol. X (1846–47) and the first part of vol. XI (1849) of the *Journal of the Royal Asiatic Society*.

[35] Of Sir Henry Layard, Canon Rawlinson has written:

"Layard was a man excellently fitted for the work of an explorer and excavator, strong, robust, determined, able to exert a powerful influence over Orientals, and calculated to compel obedience from them; active, energetic, and inured to hardship by his previous travels in wild regions. He was also familiar with Arabic and Turkish, and clever at catching up dialects. But he was not a scholar, or a man of any great culture, or of any wide reading. Probably no better pioneer could have been found for the rough work then needed in the East." Rawlinson, *Memoir* (n. 31), 151–52.

[36] In 1851 the *Journal of the Royal Asiatic Society* carried his memoir ("On the Inscription of Assyria and Babylonia," in vol. L, pp. 401–83), comprising the text of the Babylonian version at Behistun, an interlined transliteration, and a Latin translation of 112 long lines, with other similar but briefer texts, also a list of 246 characters with their phonetic or syllabic values, etc. Cp. Canon Rawlinson's *Memoir* (n. 31), 327–28.

and when Rawlinson arrived, there was some jealousy on the part of the French excavators. In 1853 Rawlinson unearthed a clay cylinder with the annals of the first Tiglath-Pileser. This text was used four years later in a striking vindication of the new science of decipherment, when it was independently rendered by Edward Hincks, Julius Oppert, Fox Talbot, and Rawlinson, and their versions were found to be in substantial agreement. At Kuyunjik it was Rawlinson who first determined the nature and varied contents of the clay libraries. Through his efforts the Assyrian Excavation Society was organized and carried on work independently of the British Museum.

The last forty years of his life Rawlinson spent mostly in London (1855–95). He continued to pore over inscriptions, and joined in editing the *Cuneiform Inscriptions of Western Asia* (1861–70). Of strictly historical works, he wrote only an *Outline of the History of Assyria*,[37] a sketch written, as he said, "in great haste, amid torrents of rain, in a little tent upon the mound of Nineveh, without any aids beyond a pocket Bible, a notebook of inscriptions, and a tolerably retentive memory." Rawlinson's chief merit is to have copied with scientific accuracy the first long historical inscription, and offered the key to the sources for the history of the Oriental East. He himself was impatient, and as Oppert has said, rather an explorer or discoverer than a scholar. His labors were refined and supplemented by the subtle and brilliant intellects of Hincks and Oppert.

It can hardly be questioned that save for Henry Rawlinson's superior opportunities in the East, he would have been anticipated by the uncanny powers of Hincks, as indeed he was in many important particulars.[38] Hincks first discovered that the third writing was syllabic and ideographic;[39] by adopting Hincks' suggestion of syllabism Rawlinson was enabled to solve the riddle. The lists of signs which both prepared showed the staggering fact that in this third writing a symbol could be *polyphonic*, that is, express more than one syllable. Then the French scholar Oppert[40] found in the British Museum the "syllabaries" or dictionaries which the Babylonians themselves had prepared. It developed that the difficulty of deciding what reading to give to a symbol had been met in part by linking syllables with similar letters (e.g., lib-bi, dan-nin).

[37] It appeared in the *Journal* of the Asiatic Society, and was also translated into German.

[38] For Edward Hincks, who deserves a future biographer, see the sketch, with complete bibliography compiled by Dr. Cyrus Adler, in the *Journal of the American Oriental Society*, vols. XIII–XIV; also Rogers (n. 28), vol. I, where a portrait is included.

[39] "On the Third Persepolitan Writing, etc.," in *Transactions of the Royal Irish Academy*, XXI, pt. ii (1847), 249–56.

[40] For Oppert, see W. Muss-Arnolt, "The Works of Jules Oppert," *Beiträge zur Assyriologie*, II (1894), 523–56.

For long years this third writing had borne no name, until in 1818 Botta realized it was represented on his finds at Khorsabad. As it was found most plentifully in the north, it was finally denominated "Assyrian," though historically it came from the southern or Babylonian civilization. Not until the syllables could be read in the "fifties" did scholars realize that it was a Semitic tongue, whose cousins Hebrew and Arabic had been known to Europe for centuries. But the development of wonders did not cease there, and the sequel illustrates how history can become imbedded in a language.

As in the days of Champollion, there were many skeptics. Savants like Renan of France and Alfred Gutschmid in Germany questioned the correctness of the results.[41] How could one be sure of a translation if each of several hundred symbols might indicate various different syllables? Here the brilliancy of Hincks opened up new historical vistas, and one may say with justice that he "discovered the Sumerians." He set forth the proof that the contents of the writing were in grammar and vocabulary Semitic, but that the mechanics of the script were obviously not designed for a Semitic tongue. Hence, he suggested, it was borrowed writing that originally belonged to a non-Semitic people.[42] Its inventors used it for ideographic meanings, and the Babylonians added syllabic or phonetic values in their own tongue.

A long controversy ensued as to the source and manner of this cultural borrowing. After various rival proposals, Oppert's suggestion of the name Sumer (Shinar, in *Genesis* 11,2 and 14,1) was adopted for the original language, for which actual texts were unearthed at Shirpurla (Lagash) by De Sarzec. Yet the capable Joseph Halévy questioned the existence of such a shadowy race as the Sumerians, unknown to previous history, and poured scorn and contempt on the mystery-mongers in his *Revue Semitique*. According to his view, the Mesopotamian culture was purely of Semitic origin.[43] As time went on, however, the progress of the excavations plainly showed that the early population of the Euphrates valley was mixed in character, for the monuments depicted a Turanian race by the side of the Semites, with a different physiognomy and dress than their neighbors. This view of a mixed population was definitely vindicated by Eduard Meyer in his *Sumerier und Semiten in Babylonien* (Berlin, 1906). The question of priority

---

[41] Renan's criticism of Oppert's *Expédition scientifique en Mesopotamie*, in *JS*, 1859, pp. 165–86, 244–60, 360–68; Gutschmid in *Neue Beiträge zur Geschichte des alten Orients* (Leipzig, 1876).

[42] "On the Language and the Mode of Writing of the Ancient Assyrians," in the *Transactions* of the twentieth meeting of the British Association for the Advancement of Science, p. 140 ff.

[43] See the summary of his views in his *Précis d'allographie assyro-babylonienne* (Paris, 1912).

and relationship between these two racial layers, however, has not yet been made entirely clear.[44]

The principles for Assyro-Babylonian decipherment had been securely laid by the time Oppert offered his analysis in 1859. Thereafter the slow and careful labor of publishing and editing the texts as they were found began. For a time France and England were in the lead, but after the establishment of the German Empire the Germans made brilliant contributions, and in the "eighties" Americans entered the field. In France Jules Oppert easily topped all rivals. The first German Orientalist to delve into Assyriology was Eberhard Shrader. His work *Die Assyrisch-Babylonischen Keilinschriften* (1872) settled the doubts of all save Gutschmid,[45] and were particularly interesting for the light he threw on the Old Testament. When Berlin determined to establish a chair for the subject in 1875, Schrader was invited to occupy it. Active until 1908, he introduced into Assyriology the method and philological care which Lepsius and Brugsch had given to Egyptology. The chief of his enthusiastic students was Friedrich Delitzsch, who in turn was the teacher of more modern Assyriologists than any other man of the nineteenth century. The son of the Biblical scholar Franz Delitzsch, he began at Leipzig and Breslau, and after 1906 taught at Berlin. His grammatical and lexicographical studies have become the vade mecum of every student.[46] Besides training specialists, Delitzsch performed a great service for his science by his popular writings. His lectures on *Babel und Bibel* provoked world-wide attention. He led in the organization of the Deutsche Orientgesellschaft, in which William II took such an interest. While the great philologist wrote no strictly historical work himself, his studies have disseminated the knowledge of Assyrian and Babylonian civilization. On a broad front the work of these pioneers is being continued; and already the day of specialization has arrived, and scholars devote themselves exclusively to religious texts, to business contracts, to literary fragments, and the like.

The excavations proceeded faster than they could be assimilated by European scholars. Layard's find of the library of Ashurbanipal (B.C. 668–626), the greatest of Assyrian rulers, comprising thirty thou-

---

[44] A summary of the controversy from 1874 to 1898 is given by F. H. Weissbach, *Die Sumerische Frage* (Leipzig, 1898).

[45] On Schrader's controversy with Gutschmid, see GOOCH, 508–09. See also F. Rühl's sketch in Gutschmid's *Kleine Schriften* (Leipzig, 1889–94, 5 v.), V.

[46] Delitzsch wrote the first chrestomathy, *Assyrische Lesestücke* (1876, 5th ed., 1912), the first substantial grammar, *Assyrische Grammatik* (1889, 2nd ed., 1906, English translation in 1889), and the first important Assyrian dictionary, *Assyrisches Handwörterbuch* (Leipzig, 1896). James H. Breasted's account of the great Assyrian dictionary now in progress at the University of Chicago will give some idea of the progress in lexicography during recent decades, see *The Oriental Institute* (Chicago, 1933), 387–400.

sand tablets, has not yet been fully studied.[47] It will remain the chief source for Babylonian literature, containing as it does copies made in the south from originals which have been lost. Layard's accomplishments in his second expedition of two years were enormous, but modern scientific methods had not yet been developed, and expeditions wandered from mound to mound, looking for lucky "strikes," instead of conducting systematic and complete studies at one location.[48]

The north-land led in interest, with Ashur, Calah, and Nineveh opened by 1854. In that year the first effort was made in the south of Babylonia, by Loftus, at Erech. Taylor, the British Consul at Basrah, was the first to excavate Ur in 1853–54, at a period when sculptures and other such museum pieces were held to be the first essentials of a successful expedition. Southern Babylonia has never been a satisfactory hunting-ground from this point of view, and its brick temples and palaces, built in a land almost without stone, could not compete with the more northern sites where an easily worked marble was close to the sculptor's hand. Yet Taylor secured a class of antiquities which was shortly to come into great favor, the cuneiform clay cylinders of Nabonidus; and these settled the identification of the name of the ancient city once and for all, with all its Biblical tradition. No further excavations were carried on there until the last year of the First World War. Rawlinson exploded the myth of the "Tower of Babel," which turned out to be a tower-temple of Nebuchadrezzar. Its name, "Babel," signifies "Gate of God," and has no connection with the Hebrew root *balal*, "to confound." But the most tremendous thrill in Babylonian discoveries came in England itself. On December 3, 1872 George Smith, hitherto an unnoticed assistant at the British Museum who had served his apprenticeship under Rawlinson, began a paper before the Society of Biblical Archaeology with the words: "A short time back I discovered among the Assyrian tablets in the British Museum an account of the Flood." In the popular excitement that swept England, the *Daily Telegraph* undertook to finance an expedition to send Smith to Assyria to hunt for additional tablets. While he collected valuable items, he found nothing to equal his first discovery, and in 1876 he died prematurely at Aleppo, on his way to Nineveh for a third attempt. Between 1878 and 1882, Hormuzd Rassam continued operations, shifting from

[47] A general account of the library of Ashurbanipal will be found in the introduction of Carl Bezold's *Catalogue of the Cuneiform Tablets in the Kouyunjik Collection of the British Museum* (London, 1889–99, 5 v.).

[48] Layard has written the story of his life in *Early Adventures in Persia, Susiana and Babylonia* (2nd ed., London, 1894, 2 v.). See also his *Nineveh and Its Remains* (New York, 1849, 2 v.).

mound to mound, and making notable finds at Abu Habba (60,000 tablets in temple archives) and at Birs Nimrud.[49]

After Rassam a new epoch begins, that of the truly scientific archaeological excavations when each site is carefully opened and completely exhausted. De Sarzec, French consul at Basrah, labored at the mound of Telloh, and discovered an unknown art. He had found Shirpurla or Lagash, an early Sumerian city; besides various statues of its great king Gudea, he found numerous inscriptions in old Sumerian and 30,000 tablets. In 1889 the University of Pennsylvania sent Dr. Peters to Niffer (ancient Nippur), and his work was continued by Haynes and Hilprecht. Before long the University of Chicago had also taken in hand praiseworthy projects. The most systematic and thorough of all was the last comer, the Deutsche Orientgesellschaft (organized in 1900). It worked at various places in Egypt and Palestine, as well as at Ashur, Babylon, and Warka (Erech or Uruk), and its methods were brought to the peak of perfection by Robert Koldewey and Walter Andrae. It provided current reports every two or three months in its *Mitteilungen*, and by the outbreak of the First World War had published eighteen solid volumes of texts and studies.

It was no easy task to weave the new and confusing materials revealed by excavators and philologists into the woof of ancient history, and those who first attempted it often had not been able to master the new languages themselves. Max W. Duncker (1811–86) prepared the first extensive German account.[50] Lenormant and Maspero wrote for Frenchmen. Their counterpart across the Channel was Canon Rawlinson.

While not as widely famous as his older brother, George Rawlinson (1812–1902) [51] from the point of view of historiography has definite deserts. His record as a student at Oxford was exceptionally brilliant. In 1840 he became a fellow of Exeter College, and in 1842 he was ordained priest. In 1859 he was chosen Bampton lecturer, and strove to justify the historicity of Scriptures with reference to the recent discoveries.[52] In the year before, he had begun to bring out what has re-

[49] Rassam's account covers a long period, beginning with his master Layard and running down to the latest epoch, under the title *Asshur and the Land of Nimrod* (New York, 1897).

[50] *Geschichte des Altertums* (Berlin, 1852–57, 4 v.; 5th ed., 1878–83, 7 v.). English translation by Evelyn Abbott, *The History of Antiquity* (London, 1877–82, 6 v.). Cp. Salomon Reinach, "Maximilien-Wolfgang Duncker," *RH*, XXXII (1886), 167–74.

[51] See the article by Ronald Bayne in *DNB*, Supplement for 1901–11, 165–67; preface by William F. McDowell, with a portrait, prefixed to Rawlinson's *Ancient History* (New York, 1900; reprint in the World's Great Classics); notice in *LTLS*, October 7, 1902, p. 4, and the *Athenaeum*, no. 3911 (1902), pt. ii, 486; and the account in *Men and Women of the Time, a Dictionary of Contemporaries* (13th rev. ed., London, 1891).

[52] *The Historical Evidences of the Truth of the Scripture Records, Stated Anew, with Special Reference to the Doubts and Discoveries of Modern Times* (1860), 8 lectures delivered from the Oxford University pulpit. There was an American reissue.

mained his most permanent achievement. The new light from the
Ancient East naturally called for constant comparison with the story
of Herodotus, the Greek "Father of History." Rawlinson undertook,
in co-operation with Sir J. G. Wilkinson and his own brother Henry, to
prepare a new accurate translation of Herodotus, with annotations that
should incorporate the most recent and complete information afforded
by the cuneiform and hieroglyphic discoveries. The substance of the
oriental notes Henry was to supply. It is true that these novel features
of the edition lost value with succeeding decades, but it would not be
difficult for a modern editor to recast them. The Greek portions are
accurate and authentic, and the translation itself is a model in dignity
and beauty.[53] It was dedicated to Gladstone.

In 1861 the Camden professorship of Ancient History at Oxford was
tendered him. This post, which he maintained until 1889,[54] afforded
him time for his writing. Rawlinson possessed a marvellous industry,
and an interesting and facile pen. His famous *Five Monarchies* was
intended to give a continuous history of the Ancient East down to the
beginning of the Ottoman Empire. The five monarchies were Chaldaea,
Assyria, Babylonia, Media, and Persia. The volumes constituted an
admirable survey, integrating a wealth of old and new information on
the geography, history, religions, customs, arts, and building of these
lands. Copious illustrations and half-tones supplemented the interest
of the account. The series was subsequently completed by the *Sixth
Great Oriental Monarchy* (Parthia) in 1873 and the *Seventh Great Oriental
Monarchy* (Sassanid Persia) in 1876. Today Rawlinson's inability to
read the cuneiform and hieroglyphic languages would disqualify him
for the writing of an authoritative history, but it was not so in the early
sixties; and his classic equipment at least was excellent. Thirty years
later his volumes still drew the approval of an expert like Maspero.

The *Manual of Ancient History* (1869) was modelled frankly after the
German work of Heeren, then antiquated. It added to Heeren the
labor of three fruitful generations, and the curious reader will be interested to turn to the first pages where Rawlinson gives his bibliography of other works then extant.[55] Rawlinson's volumes on Egypt (1881),
Phoenicia (1889), and Parthia (1893), of which the last two were pre-

---

[53] *The History of Herodotus, a New Version, Employing the Historical and Ethnographical
Evidence Brought by the Cuneiform and Hieroglyphical Discoveries* (1858–60, 4 v.). There are
numerous reprints. Rawlinson also wrote the article on Herodotus in the 9th ed. of the *Encyclopaedia Britannica*, XI (1880), 756–59.

[54] In 1872 his friend Gladstone prompted the Government to appoint him canon in Canterbury.

[55] Charles K. Adams, when he compiled his *Manual of Historical Literature* (New York,
1882), said of this work: "As a guide to a student in the thorough study of Ancient History,
Rawlinson's *Manual* has no equal in our language."

pared for the *Story of the Nations* series, fell short of his other work, though the *History of Parthia* still towers alone in that field. Nothing as comprehensive as Rawlinson's *Five Monarchies* has yet appeared in English from the hands of one man.

By the end of the nineteenth century the mass of archaeological material which had been accumulated concerning the history of Antiquity—the Ancient Orient, Greece, and Rome—had become so great, and so much preliminary study had been made of it by scholars, that it seemed time to make a synthesis. Fortunately a scholar of remarkable competence was found in Eduard Meyer (1855–1930),[56] a scholar in the tradition of Ranke and Mommsen, and long professor at the University of Berlin. A giant beside the industrious Rawlinson, he began when the new materials still appeared manageable by a single exceptional intellect, and contrived for decades to keep step with the increasing volume of publications and discoveries.

Meyer early determined to make history his life's work. He was attracted to antiquity by the classics and cartographical studies in Strabo. From the very beginning, however, he made it his goal to conceive and treat history as a whole, as *Weltgeschichte*. Having acquired a thorough foundation in the classics and Hebrew and Arabic, he came to Bonn at seventeen (1872), and plunged into oriental philology. After a semester at Bonn he went to Leipzig, then the center of oriental studies in Germany. Ebers taught him Egyptian. But none of his teachers, no matter how thorough, was a strong historian; Eduard Meyer was in a large measure self-taught. After obtaining his degree he was tutor in the home of the English consul-general at Constantinople. Amid historic surroundings he began his *Geschichte Troas* which he finished in England when his charges returned there. At the age of twenty-four he began to lecture at Leipzig, became assistant professor five years later (1884) and then full professor at Breslau (1885). Chairs in ancient history were still rare. After a few years at Halle, he came to Berlin (1902).

Meyer's phenomenal powers were devoted particularly to the history of the Ancient Orient, which he placed upon entirely new foundations. The entire written remains of antiquity were open to him in their original tongues as to no other scholar. Though he excluded India purposely from the old Orient, he realized the strength of its influence and possessed a working knowledge of Sanskrit. He was particularly well

[56] Eduard Meyer, "Selbstbiographie mit Schriftverzeichnis," in the *Almanach der Wiener Akademie der Wissenschaften*, LXXXII (1932), 207–15; Walter Otto, "Eduard Meyer und sein Werk," *Zeitschrift der deutschen Morgenländischen Gesellschaft*, Neue Folge, X (1931), 1–24; also the same writer's two articles, "Dem Historiker Eduard Meyer, zu seinem 70. Geburtstag," and "Dem grossen Historiker zum Gedächtnis: das Werk Eduard Meyers," in *Münchener Nachrichten* (1925), no. 21, and (1930), nos. 247 and 248; Victor Ehrenberg, "Eduard Meyer," in *HZ*, CXLIII (1931), 501–11; M. Rostovtzeff in *ESS*, X, pp. 402–03; GOOCH, 483–84.

versed in Egyptology, though oddly enough he did not visit that country until his seventy-first year. His work on Egypt was the first detailed study that deserves the name of a history of Egypt. It is thoroughly integrated in Meyer's best manner, and contrasts most strongly with the performance of Brugsch or the monstrosity of Dümichen which Meyer had been asked to continue, though he has been criticized for assuming that the Hyksos ruled over a world empire from Crete to Mesopotamia. The finest of his contributions was doubtless the correction of Egyptian chronology from the old high figures of Petrie's school to more conservative numbers. He was particularly proud of the date 4241 B.C. (the institution of the Egyptian Sothic calendar), which he regarded as the oldest determinable date in history.[57]

In Babylonian-Assyrian and Hittite problems Meyer was not so fortunate. His contribution was rather that of inspiration than of important advances. On the Hittites his pupil Forrer led him astray, and in the field of Assyriology he did not have friends as among the Egyptologists to guide and assist him. In the difficult Sumerian question, Meyer advocated the priority of the Semitic civilization. This was hardly happy. Recent discoveries indicate that the problem is even more involved than had been suspected, and that in addition to the Sumerian and the Semites, there may be a third and very old people involved in the Mesopotamian cultural problem.

In Grecian history Meyer towered to his full height again. Here the obstacles were the heroic figures of Grote and Ernst Curtius, standing for political liberalism and classical aestheticism respectively. In contrast to Grote, Meyer held that Athens possessed no strong government, but was in a permanent state of anarchy, and that Pericles was an inferior statesman because he was an idealist. Meyer's sense of sober reality rejected the vagaries of Curtius' sentiment; he brought forward the material, economic, political, and social features of Greek life. The dominance of the historical scene by democratic Athens was ended when he gave justice to Sparta and especially to the monarchy of Macedonia. Meyer put forth Philip against Demosthenes. In his reconstruction, he may have gone too far in importing modern terms like "capitalism" into an older society (he once said one could not picture the Athenians modern enough); this was one of the things he had in common with Mommsen. Meyer demonstrated rare power in his treatment of relatively unknown Greek dialects. Hellenism in Asia

---

[57] For the best discussions of Egyptian chronology see James H. Breasted, *Ancient Records of Egypt, Historical Documents from the Earliest Times to the Persian Conquest* (Chicago, 1906–07, 5 v.), I, 25–72, and Eduard Meyer, "Aegyptische Chronologie," in the *Abhandlungen der k. preussischen Akademie der Wissenschaften*, phil.-hist. Classe (1904), 3–212. Breasted was a pupil of Meyer.

at the time of the Seleucids intrigued him. But the contempt of a classical scholar for Persia, imbibed from Herodotus, never deceived him; he early emphasized the world-historical position of the Persians and especially of Darius I. If Meyer's picture of Greek history is among the most authoritative we have, it is because he always viewed it in its relation to the rest of the Mediterranean world.

His Roman studies were much inferior. For this he may be forgiven; even the great Mommsen a generation before felt the time for a synthesis on the Empire had not come. In *Caesars Monarchie und das Principat des Pompejus* (1918; 3rd ed., 1922) Meyer inclined to give Pompey excessive credit for anticipating the creation of the Augustan Empire, and he thought correspondingly less of the revolution effected by Octavian.

Two fields of history attracted some of his most fruitful efforts: economic history and the story of religions. Rodbertus and Buecher had oversimplified ancient economies as *Hauswirthschaft*, and denied or neglected the evidence for the existence of *Stadtwirthschaft* and the use of currency. One realizes immediately what revolutionary changes in this picture Meyer could draw from the commercial tablets of Mesopotamia and the universal-historian's appreciation of the intercourse between the great empires of Egypt and the East. Interest in religious problems dated back to his doctoral thesis on the god Set-Typhon of Egypt (1875). He pursued the origins of Judaism and of Islam, and leaped into the nineteenth century to study that of the Mormons. He had contended, against Wellhausen and other higher critics, that the royal decrees of Darius I and Artaxerxes I in the Old Testament book of Ezra were genuine, and significant as showing the assistance the Persian government lent to the great Jewish religious reforms. His study of the Aramaic papyri found at Elephantine (dealing with a Jewish community of the fifth century B.C.) indicated that at that period the old Jewish national religion had not yet been supplanted by the strict Priestly Code. Those who follow Meyer will therefore conclude that Judaism as it developed in Palestine after the Exile must be viewed as a creation first made possible, and influenced, by the religious policy of the Persian kings. Towards the Jewish scriptures his stand was that of an advanced Protestant critic. He considered the Exodus from Egypt to be a pure legend, and without historical foundation. Palestine, before the recent excavations in Syria, seemed to him to afford the best promise of information on the connections between the great civilizations of Egypt and Mesopotamia. Finally he attempted what no secular historian had ventured to do: to write a work on the origins of Christianity. The movement is presented on a masterful background-sketch of Judaism in the preceding centuries. The work is marked by a cool and sober tone; his sketch of Jesus is rationalistic.

Though Meyer's achievements in single fields were ample for any ambitious specialist, they were but preliminary studies or subsidiary to his great *Geschichte des Altertums*. Its first volume was issued in 1884, and the fifth came out nearly two decades later, in 1902. Even so it remained unfinished, a torso which lacked a comprehensive treatment of the Roman Empire. Its basic idea is the "unity of antiquity," which is elaborated with unexcelled fullness. Meyer not only treated the histories of individual nations of antiquity as parts of a larger whole, in their perspective and true proportion, but also brought into his frame the movements of culture and religion. The war disturbed his mental equilibrium, but the chief fault was the necessity of revising the history, a task which occupied the hardworking author to his end. His difficulties may be seen when he began to revise volume I in 1908, and looked back on the changes twenty-five years had wrought.[58]   In 1885 Egyptian history still began with the Fourth Dynasty; the existence of the Sumerians was still an academic question; no one thought as yet of separating the older Babylonian culture of the second and third millenniums from the much later one of Assyria and Chaldaea. Sir Arthur Evans did not uncover the old Cretan civilization until after 1900, and then threw new light on the Aegean. Even in Jewish history progress was difficult, and the Old Testament literature could only gradually be "controlled"; the Elephantine papyrus find was made in 1911. Meyer was constantly obliged to revise his views with the current excavations. It speaks for his honesty and love of science that he preferred the toilsome task of rewriting page after page, rather than finishing the work and leaving the corrections to others.

No one man will ever again undertake to equal the *Geschichte des Altertums*. Specialists will have to collaborate in the future, as in the noted Cambridge series. But the need of a universal history, and of a synoptic vision of antiquity such as Meyer advocated, will remain.

His history is not of those, like Mommsen and Ranke, that will live by the charm of its style. Meyer wrote ordinarily, not to say badly. His was a clear, sober German such as the scientist uses to report his observations; not a medium for literary creation or imaginative reconstruction. He attached no importance to such writing. Yet the *Geschichte* has something of the author's own appearance and character. It is towering, strong, rough, and lapidarian.[59]

[58] See his preface to this volume.
[59] "Das ist kein wohlgefügtes Gebäude mit Pfeilern und Säulen, mit Giebeln und Türmen, sondern ein kyklopisches Mauerwerk, riesig, ungefügt und ungefüge, von grandiosem Willen und souveränem Geist getürmt und gestaltet." Victor Ehrenberg, "Eduard Meyer," *HZ*, CXLIII (1930–31), 502, cp. 501–11.

History was to Meyer a scientific discipline rather than an art. In the first volume of the revised edition of the *Geschichte des Altertums* he offered an extended discussion of history and methodology: his term "Anthropology" was rather unfortunate and twisted out of its accepted sense. He accepted Aristotle's thesis that the state is older than man. While political history was his chief ingredient, he did not overlook other sides. His weakness was the assumption that an historian needed no more than a command of the sources, the method and the literature. But something more than truth is necessary, and Meyer fell short on certain spiritual qualifications. He was a rationalist, and brushed aside what he did not understand. Another great historian has summarized his theory of history: "He conceived of history as a result of interaction between free will and accident; no historical laws exist; History is individual and never repeats itself; furthermore its presentation is always subjective and therefore never final. History moves in cycles, of which ancient history forms one; modern history repeats, *mutatis mutandis*, the various periods of ancient history." [60] Unlike the specialists, he found much to praise in Oswald Spengler, whose work he compared with Herder's *Ideen zur Philosophie der Geschichte der Menschheit*, and Spengler in turn called him the greatest German historian since Ranke.

[60] Rostovtzeff in *ESS* (n. 56).

CHAPTER LVII

MODERN HISTORIANS OF GREECE AND ROME

NIEBUHR and Böckh at the University of Berlin had founded the critical history of ancient Rome and Greece. The new critical spirit soon reached England which in the post-Napoleonic period was intellectually closer to German thought than any other country. It found the British reader still relying on Mitford's *History of Greece*, the first volume of which had been published in 1784. The completion of the later volumes coincided with the French Revolution, when Mitford became a handbook for Tory statesmen. Liberalism and democracy, whether in ancient Greece or in Great Britain, were equally despised. Macaulay leaped to fame by his review of the fourth volume.[1] He began by giving Mitford his due, praising him for his trustworthiness, his use of contemporary sources, and his revelation of the "state of parties in Greece." But, Macaulay continued, Mitford's hatred of democracy vitiated his learning, warped his judgment, and led him to unwarranted conclusions. Take, for instance, the question of the Macedonian government under Philip. Mitford admired it because it was supreme and avoided being despotic; the king was controlled by constitutional checks not unlike the British. "Thus far," Mitford concluded a bit rashly, "our information is positive and clear." To which Macaulay replied, justly enough, that "there is, in truth, little positive, and no clear information, to be gleaned on this subject from the ancient writers." Mitford's statement was based on "presumptions almost irresistible," and Macaulay proved that Macedon was not a limited monarchy but an absolute despotism. "In one word, Mr. Mitford *philippizes*." "Mitford," Freeman wrote, "was a bad scholar."[2]

The one good effect of Mitford's *Greece* was that it inspired Henry F. Clinton (1781–1852), a member of parliament and a student of the classics, to undertake a systematic study of ancient chronology. His *Fasti Hellenici, a Civil and Literary Chronology of Greece* (1824–34, 4 v.), contains many facts, but the serious student would rather not consult the work, for it is boundlessly credulous. To Clinton the Old Testament was an "authentic narrative written . . . under the guid-

---

[1] *ER*, XII (1808), 478–517.
[2] E. A. Freeman, *Historical Essays*, 2nd series (London, 1873), 110.

ance of inspiration"; and as regards Greek history and genealogy, Clinton acknowledged as real all those persons—Cadmus, Danaus, Hercules—"whom there is no reason for rejecting." An epitome of his *Fasti Hellenici* was published in 1851 and one of his *Fasti Romani* in 1853.[3]

With Connop Thirlwall (1797–1875),[4] the bishop of St. David's, critical historiography of antiquity may be said to begin in England. Thirlwall was a remarkable scholar, having learned Latin at three, Greek at four, and published a collection of sermons and poems at twelve. At Charterhouse his schoolfellows were Grote, the historian, and Hare, his later collaborator in the translation of Niebuhr. After finishing his studies at Cambridge in 1818, Thirlwall went on a continental tour, and at Rome met the Prussian scholar-diplomat Bunsen. Upon his return to England he studied law, but gave it up for the church. The legal profession probably lost a great jurist, but the church won a splendid orator, and a sound scholar. "Before he uttered ten sentences," Mill said of him, "I set him down as the best speaker I had ever heard, and I have never since heard any one whom I placed above him."

In 1828 Thirlwall and his friend Julius Hare published their translation of Niebuhr's *History of Rome*, which was severely criticized in the *Quarterly Review* (XXXIX, January, 1829, p. 8 ff.), a criticism now remembered only as having called forth a reply which is now remembered as "Hare's bark and Thirlwall's bite." The two friends also issued the *Philological Museum*, a review whose aim was "to revive the taste of the English public for philology in the highest sense"; but it expired with the sixth number. These activities must be stressed, for they show Thirlwall's interest in the achievements of continental, especially German, scholarship. Thirlwall, indeed, was one of the earliest scholars in England to possess a competent knowledge of German. In the field of philology he was familiar with the German works of Wolf, Hermann, and Karl Otfried Müller. With such equipment his own productions were bound to be on a high level of scholarship.

The publisher of Lardner's *Cabinet Cyclopaedia* invited Thirlwall to write a history of Greece. He complied and published the first volume

[3] C. J. F. Clinton, *The Literary Remains of H. F. Clinton* (1854); GOOCH, 309–10.

[4] J. C. Thirlwall, Jr., a collateral descendant, contributes much new matter from unpublished family papers in his biography, *Connop Thirlwall, Historian and Theologian* (London, 1936), cp. the review in *LTLS*, June 20, 1936, p. 510; J. J. Stewart Perowne, ed., *Remains, Literary and Theological of Connop Thirlwall, Late Lord Bishop of St. David's* (1877); J. W. Clark, *Old Friends at Cambridge and Elsewhere* (1900); GOOCH, 310–12; SANDYS, III, 437; "Thirlwall," *The Nation*, XXVI (1878), 155–56; reviews in *ER*, LXII (1835–36), 83–108, and CXLIII (1876), 281–316; E. A. Freeman, *Historical Essays*, Second Series (London, 1873), 106–206, *passim*.

of the *History of Greece* in 1835 and the eighth in 1847; but when Grote's volumes began to appear, Thirlwall gave up continuing his own work.[5] As an historian Thirlwall was conspicuously fair, poised, and judicious. His scholarship was impeccable and his knowledge of the sources and the authorities quite unexcelled. Except for Socrates, this chilly writer had no heroes. He wrote history as if it were a judicial decision, without warmth or enthusiasm, but with grave dignity and "more or less conscious irony."

Thirlwall excelled in his treatment of the Macedonian period and in tracing the gradual spread of Roman domination over the Greek world. Of the skill which Rome displayed in winding the toils of her diplomacy around her conquests he said that in such arts the Roman Senate surpassed every cabinet, ancient and modern. It was to them more than to the pilum and the sword that Rome owed the reduction of Macedonia into a province subject to a city of which Philip and Demosthenes may have barely heard the name.

Thomas Arnold (1795–1842),[6] of Rugby fame, "the prince of schoolmasters," had met Niebuhr personally and was impressed to the point of emulation. When he began his *History of Rome*—a "splendid fragment"—he admitted that though he was not fit to be Niebuhr's continuator, he had "at least the qualification of unbounded veneration for what he has done." Three volumes of Arnold's *History* appeared between 1838 and his death in 1842; the work did not reach beyond the end of the Second Punic War. Freeman heard Arnold's opening lecture and has borne witness to the tremendous impression which the lecturer made upon his auditors. Arnold had a perception of the unity of history—which Freeman ever afterwards stressed—and believed that history conveyed a moral lesson. His teaching was didactic. Arnold was an intense hater of Caesar and Caesarism, and a warm Victorian moralist. "The history of Greece and Rome is not an idle inquiry about remote ages and forgotten institutions," he wrote in his preface to Thucydides, "but a living picture of things present, fitted not so much for the curiosity of the scholar, as the instruction of the statesman and the citizen."

Up to about the middle of the nineteenth century Niebuhr's influence in matters of Roman history was dominant not only in Germany but also in England. Niebuhr had been an advance on the older historiog-

---

[5] Grote and Thirlwall, as mentioned, had been school-fellows, but although they occasionally met in London after their university days, Thirlwall knew so little of Grote's life that he was astonished when he learned the other was writing a history of Greece.

[6] The best account of Arnold is by A. P. Stanley, *The Life and Correspondence of Thomas Arnold* (London, 1844, 2 v.); cp. review in *QR*, LXXIV (1844), 467–508; *ER*, LXXI (1845), 190–234; GOOCH, 319–20; and "Arnold's Lectures on Modern History," *FM*, XXXIII (1846), 596–605.

raphy; he had displayed admirable skepticism concerning the legendary period of Roman history, but he had not been skeptical enough. Later scholars, in fact, accused him, not without justice, of erecting his foundations on untenable premises.

In 1855 George Cornewall Lewis (1806–63) [7] published an *Inquiry into the Credibility of the Early Roman History* (2 v.) which once and for all destroyed the older assumptions and undermined Niebuhr's prestige. Henceforth no student of Roman history could do his work without taking Lewis' destructive critique into consideration. Niebuhr had overthrown one historical creed and set up another. His "ballad theory" was as much a figment of imagination as early Roman history was. He had advanced the hypothesis (which was accepted by Arnold and Macaulay) of the existence of early ballads and epic lays. This would sound reasonable, except that, as Lewis pointed out, no such ballads were known to the Romans of the historical age. The only sources that seem to have existed were oral statement and family tradition; such may have been the "substratum of notation" which Fabius used for his history. "Some assistance," Lewis writes, "may have been derived from popular songs, and still more from family memoirs; but there is nothing to make it probable that private families began to record the deeds of their distinguished members before any chronicler had arisen for the events which interested the commonwealth as a whole." The whole so-called kingly period of Roman history is known to us from oral details, uncontrolled by ascertainable fact. Lewis, after a minute analysis of all possible sources, concludes bluntly:

All the historical labour bestowed upon the early centuries will, in general, be wasted. The history of this period, viewed as a series of picturesque narratives, will be read to the greatest advantage in the original writers, and will be deteriorated by reproduction in a modern dress. If we regard a historical painting merely as a work of art, the accounts of the ancients can only suffer from being retouched by the pencil of the modern restorer. On the other hand, all attempts to reduce them to a purely historical form, by conjectural omissions, additions, alterations, and transpositions, must be nugatory. . . . Those who are disposed to labour in the field of Roman history will find a worthier reward for their toils, if they employ themselves upon the time subsequent to the Italian expedition of Pyrrhus.[8]

George Grote (1794–1871) [9] was a banker who wrote the greatest

[7] On Lewis and his work see George Grote in *ER*, CIV (1856), 1–24, reprinted in *The Minor Works of George Grote*, ed. by Alexander Bain (London, 1873), 207–36; *QR*, XCVIII (1856), 321–52.

[8] *Inquiry into the Credibility of the Early Roman History* (London, 1855, 2 v.), II, 556.

[9] The best account is Mrs. Grote's *The Personal Life of George Grote, Compiled from Family Documents, Private Memoranda and Original Letters* (2nd ed., 1873). See also Alexander Bain, ed., *The Minor Works of George Grote, with Critical Remarks on His Intellectual Character, Writings, and Speeches* (London, 1873); FUETER, 645–47; GOOCH, 312–18; Robert von Pöhlmann, *Aus Alterthum und Gegenwart* (Munich, 1895); Theodor Gomperz, *Essays und Erin-*

English history of Greece. He displayed the same skepticism toward Greek legend and myth as did Lewis his friend toward earliest Roman history. But what distinguishes Grote is not so much his skepticism as his re-interpretation of ancient Greek civilization.

In the ingenious biography of her husband, Mrs. Grote has given some interesting details about the life of the historian-politician. When she was collecting notes for his biography, he exclaimed: "My life, why, there is absolutely nothing to tell." "Not in the way of adventures, I grant," she replied, "but there is something nevertheless. Your life is the history of a mind." And that it undoubtedly was.

Grote was brought up in a rigorously Calvinist home. On his father's side he was of Dutch, or Low German descent, his ancestors having settled in England in 1710; the family was in the banking business since 1766 ("Grote, Prescott, & Company"). George Grote's mother, the severely pious daughter of a clergyman, taught her son Latin before the age of six. At the age of ten Grote went to Charterhouse where Thirlwall and other men of future eminence were his schoolmates. Six years later he was taken into his father's bank. Busy in the bank during the day, Grote devoted his mornings and nights to reading and studying, especially the classics—Aristotle was a lifelong favorite—history, political economy, and metaphysics. He also learned German, French, and Italian. A characteristic entry into his diary, December, 1822, reads: "Rose at 6:00; employed all my reading-time upon Diodorus; got through 80 pages, taking notes. A few articles in the *Dictionnaire Philosophique* filled up odd moments."

"You are always studying the ancient authors," Mrs. Grote told her husband in 1823; "here is a fine subject for you." And so, twenty-three years before the publication of the first volume, Grote began to collect materials for his history of Greece. In the meantime he kept himself occupied with political and intellectual matters. He had met David Ricardo the economist, James Mill (father of John Stuart Mill), the radical author of *An Analysis of the Human Mind*, and Jeremy Bentham, the moralist. All these men, particularly Mill, had a profound influence on Grote. "He found himself inoculated as it were with Mill's conclusions—his hatred of aristocracy and of the Established Church," Mrs. Grote comments disapprovingly. Grote, in fact, remained a radical all his life. Inspired by Mill with an "enthusiasm for

nerungen (Stuttgart, 1905), 184–95. See also the following reviews, many of them excellent critical essays: *QR*, LXXVIII (1846), 113–44, LXXXVI (1850), 384–415, LXXXVIII (1851), 41–69, XCIX (1856), 60–105, CXXXV (1873), 98–137; *LQR*, VII (1856–57), 51–71, XLII (1874), 393–416; *NAR*, LXXVIII (1854), 150–73; *BQR*, XIII (1851), 289–331; *ER*, LXXXIV (1846), 343–77, XCI (1849–50), 118–52, XCIV (1851), 204–28, XCVIII (1853), 425–47, CXXXVIII (1873), 218–45; *NBR*, XXV (1856), 141–72; *The Nation*, XIX (1874), 91–92.

humanity," Grote visited Paris on the eve of the revolution of 1830 and contributed £500 to help the revolutionists. In this same year Grote's father died and left him an estate worth over £40,000. Free to devote all his time to politics and history, Grote helped to found the University of London, wrote a book on the extension of the franchise, and was elected to Parliament where he remained for over eight years. But always there was a Tauchnitz copy of Plato in his pocket.

In 1841 Grote retired from Parliament and visited Rome where he studied antiquities. It is significant that he did not think it worth while to visit Greece—an extraordinary omission, in view of his projected history. Upon his return to England in 1842 Grote began to revise his notes and re-read the authorities, especially Niebuhr, in preparation for the first two volumes of the *History of Greece* which treated the legendary period. The myth, indeed, had been Grote's favorite subject for years. As far back as 1823 he had written:

> I am at present engaged in the fabulous ages of Greece, which I find will be required to be illustrated by bringing together a large mass of analogical matter from other early histories, in order to show the entire uncertainty and worthlessness of tales to which early associations have so long familiarized all classical minds. I am quite amazed to discover the extraordinary greediness and facility with which men assert, believe, re-assert, and are believed.

Though Böckh had pointed out the way, Grote did not use inscriptions, and was inclined to undervalue them.

The first two volumes of the *History* were published early in 1846 and had an immediate success. Having worked leisurely for more than two decades, Grote did not expect any popularity. "I suppose," he said to his wife, "I shall have to print it at my own expense." The reception of the work, even in the Tory universities, was such that it moved the cool scholar. "From all sides," to quote Mrs. Grote again, "congratulation and eulogy flowed in upon the author, insomuch that he himself now began to feel something like confidence in the success of his long-cherished work." For once "gratified self-love" pierced through that "imperturbable veil of modesty." Dean Milman reviewed the two volumes in the *Quarterly Review* and John Stuart Mill in the *Edinburgh Review*. Both were highly laudatory, Mill commenting that "there is hardly an important fact in Greek history which was perfectly understood before he re-examined it." Mitford was taken off the shelves.

The next ten volumes appeared in the course of ten years and the colossal work was completed in 1856.[10] Grote closed his work with the

---

[10] Vols. III–IV, to the battle of Marathon, were published in 1847; V–VI, to the Peloponnesian War, in 1849; VII–VIII, to the end of the war, in 1850; IX–X in 1852, XI in 1853, and XII in 1856.

period of Alexander the Great, "whence," he wrote, "dates not only the extinction of Grecian political freedom and self-action, but also the decay of productive genius, and the debasement of that consummate literary and rhetorical excellence which the 4th century B.C. had seen exhibited in Plato and Demosthenes." Farther than that this champion of democracy would not go, although in 1865, after nine years of work, he published his *Plato and the Other Companions of Sokrates* in three volumes, which, he said, was "intended as a sequel and supplement to his *History of Greece.*"

Grote's *History* is distinguished for two basic characteristics: the treatment of the legendary period and the emphasis (vindication, some would call it) of Athenian democracy. He did not accept Greek mythology as historical proof, but gave the early legends in full, because a mere summary meant narratives with their "life-blood sucked out of them."

I describe the earlier times by themselves, as conceived by the faith and feeling of the first Greeks, and known only through their legends, without presuming to measure how much or how little of historical matter these legends may contain. If the reader blame me for not assisting him to determine this—if he ask me why I do not undraw the curtain and disclose the picture—I reply, in the words of the painter Zeuxis, when the same question was addressed to him on exhibiting his masterpiece of imitative art—"The curtain is the picture." That curtain conceals nothing behind, and cannot by any ingenuity be withdrawn. I undertake only to show it as it stands—not to efface, still less to re-paint it.[11]

Grote rejected Greek mythology as accurate history, but accepted it as a reflection of the Greek mind, as a product of the imagination which was interwoven with the general culture. The myth, he pointed out, had to be studied as a work of art and was, therefore, not subject to the ordinary canons of historical truth.

We are not warranted in applying to the mythical world the rules either of historical credibility or chronological sequence. Its personages are gods, heroes, and men, in constant juxtaposition and reciprocal sympathy; men too, of whom we know a large proportion to be fictitious, and of whom we can never ascertain how many have been real. . . . The myths were originally produced in an age which had no records, no philosophy, no criticism, no canon of belief, and scarcely any tincture either of astronomy or geography.

For this reason he began the real history of Greece with the First Olympiad, 776 B.C., the period when historical records become somewhat more trustworthy.

I begin the real history of Greece with the first recorded Olympiad, or 776 B.C. To such as are accustomed to the habits once universal, and still not uncommon, in investi-

11 *History of Greece,* I, 294. In connection with the myth Grote also made one of his rare puns: "It is the record of a past that never was present."

gating the ancient world, I may appear to be striking off one thousand years from the scroll of history; but to those whose canon of evidence is derived from Mr. Hallam, M. Sismondi, or any other eminent historian of modern events, I am well-assured that I shall appear lax and credulous rather than exigent or sceptical. For the truth is, that historical records, properly so called, do not begin until long after this date.[12]

The most significant part of Grote's *History* is his treatment of Athenian democracy. Grote wrote his history of ancient Greece from the point of view of a nineteenth-century Victorian English liberal, an ardent believer in constitutional government and a zealous champion of universal suffrage. Indeed, he was so little interested in anything else that, as we have seen, he did not take the trouble to visit Greece to familiarize himself with its geography, climate, and monuments.

Grote's work may have been one of the "glories" of English historiography, but that of his contemporary, Charles Merivale (1808–93), was not. Merivale was an English divine and he wrote Roman history as a smug moralist and an advocate of Caesarism. His *History of the Romans under the Empire* (1850–62) was to fill the gap left open by Niebuhr and Arnold; it began with Julius Caesar and ended with Marcus Aurelius, at a point where Gibbon had started his *Decline and Fall*. Merivale is forgotten today, not so much because of his naïve admiration of a powerful imperialist government but because he depended altogether on literary sources. The work of Mommsen and his associates made Merivale useless.

Other Englishmen who worked in Roman history were George Long (1800–79), J. H. Parker (1806–84), Robert Burn (1829–1904), J. H. Middleton (1846–96), and Henry Pelham (1846–1907). The list of the more recent scholars, especially those influenced by Mommsen, is too long to mention. Pelham, professor of ancient history at Oxford, did much to introduce German scholarship in the field of antiquity into England. "While he lectured much, he wrote little." But his small *Outlines of Roman History* (1890), based on the most recent discoveries, has been called "the most useful, as it is also the most able, sketch of the subject that has yet been published." [13] He helped to organize the British School at Rome (1901) out of which grew the Society for the Promotion of Roman Studies (1910). The excavations of Schliemann, Evans, and others resulted in much new light in ancient history. A re-evaluation of the subject in the light of modern scholarship may be found in *The Cambridge Ancient History* where bibliographies are also given.[14]

[12] For the two quotations see *ibid.*, I, 402 and preface, p. vii.
[13] F. Haverfield, "Henry Pelham," *The Athenaeum*, No. 4138 (1907), 197; J. E. Sandys, *A Companion to Latin Studies* (Cambridge, 1910), 868.
[14] G. B. Grundy, "The Cambridge Ancient History," *QR*, CCLVIII (1932), 341–62.

Niebuhr, through Thirlwall and Arnold, had stirred the stagnant waters of British classical scholarship. But by the middle of the century German scholarship in ancient Greek and Roman history had forged far beyond the line marked by Niebuhr, Böckh, and Müller. Britain was behind the times, while French classical scholars were in total ignorance of what was being accomplished across the Rhine.

It is necessary at this point to return to Germany. The most distinguished historian of Greece since Böckh and Müller was Ernst Curtius (1814–96),[15] a direct intellectual descendant of Müller. Like so many other eminent German scholars, including Niebuhr and Mommsen, Curtius was a Holsteiner. He was born in Lübeck of an old patrician family, the son of the city syndic. In 1834 Curtius went to Bonn to study philology and there he came in intimate contact with Christian August Brandis (1790–1867), who had been Niebuhr's secretary of legation at Rome. Since 1822 Brandis had been professor of philosophy at Bonn and had written histories of Greek and Roman philosophy.[16] Following the German custom of studying at various universities Curtius left Bonn for Göttingen to work under Otfried Müller, who had then a European reputation as an Hellenist.

> It is an unspeakable advantage [Curtius wrote] to have a long course of daily attendance on Müller's lectures, for as a teacher he is without a rival. The clearness of his explanations, the vivacity and charm of his delivery, the fulness and soundness of his learning, fascinates one every day more and more, and continually gives one fresh enthusiasm for that department of knowledge to which he by his exceptional mental endowments has given an altogether new life.

That department of knowledge was the Greek past, especially archaeology, which young Curtius eagerly learned from his teacher. Another thing that Curtius imbibed from Müller was the notion of the organic unity of antiquity, which Müller had learned from Herder who, in turn, had gotten it from Winckelmann. It is necessary to emphasize again and again that the idea of cultural totality and social

---

[15] Curtius' biography was written by his son Friedrich Curtius, *Ernst Curtius. Ein Lebensbild in Briefen* (Berlin, 1903); see also FUETER, 621–24; GOOCH, 475–78; SANDYS, III, 228–29; R. Kekule von Stradonitz, *Ernst Curtius* (Berlin, 1896); Konrad J. Plath, *Ernst Curtius und die Erforschung des deutschen Altertums* (Berlin, 1897); H. Gelzer, "Wanderungen und Gespräche mit Ernst Curtius," in *Ausgewählte kleine Schriften* (Leipzig, 1907); Charlotte Broicher, *Erinnerungen an Ernst Curtius* (Berlin, 1897); A. Michaelis, "Ernst Curtius," *Allgemeine Zeitung* (1896), nos. 182–84; T. Hodgkin, "Ernst Curtius," *Proceedings of the British Academy* (1905–06), 31–34; Freeman (n. 2), 148–60; James Hadley, *Essays, Philological and Critical* (New York, 1873), 1–36; Robert P. Keep, "Ernst Curtius, Müller, and Mommsen," *International Review*, II (1875), 745–62; A. W. Ward, *ER*, CXCIX (1904), 403–31; *NAR*, LXXXVII (1858), 481–507; *PJ*, I (1858), 337–65. For criticisms of Curtius' theories see E. Babelon, "L'histoire grecque de M. Curtius et les récentes découvertes archéologiques sur la Grèce," *RQH*, XXXIV (1883), 596–608; Arthur Milchhöfer, *Die Anfänge der Kunst in Griechenland* (Leipzig, 1883).

[16] See E. Curtius, "Zum Gedächtnis von Chr. A. Brandis und A. Böckh," *Nachrichten von der Königlichen Gesellschaft der Wissenschaften zu Göttingen*, phil.-hist. Klasse, 1867, pp. 552–73; SANDYS, III, 173.

evolution had been widely accepted and propagated in Germany since the eighteenth century.

From Göttingen Curtius went to Berlin in pursuit of Greek art and archaeology. In Berlin he attended the classes of Böckh, Otfried Müller's much-admired teacher. But most of all Curtius studied the rich collections in the museums. "Berlin," he said, "is a highly favored spot for an archaeological student, and especially its collection of vases is beyond price."

Four years of study under such masters as Brandis, Müller, and Böckh gave Curtius a rich equipment, but his most significant experience was still ahead of him. At the termination of the Greek struggle for independence from the Turks and the establishment of the Greek kingdom under Prince Otto of Bavaria, the newly-elected king invited Professor Brandis to accompany him to Greece as his confidential advisor, and Brandis in turn asked his former student Curtius to join him as tutor of his children. Curtius and the Brandis family left Germany in the autumn of 1837 and for six weeks travelled in a large wagon to the Adriatic. It was, according to all accounts, an exhilarating journey.

For about two years Curtius lived in Brandis' house in Piraeus, and here he not only met many visiting Hellenic scholars but also undertook a number of voyages of exploration in a land rich with historic remains; at the same time he learned modern Greek and made himself familiar with Pausanias and Strabo. One of his extensive tours was taken in the company of the geographer Carl Ritter, and another with his teacher Müller in 1840. Müller came to copy inscriptions and to excavate temples. The forty-three-year-old Göttingen professor worked too strenuously in the hot July days and Curtius, who was familiar with the Greek climate, urged his teacher to take care of himself. "No siesta for me," Müller replied. "My brain is as strong as iron: I need not cover my head for fear of sun-stroke. All this spring the weather has been cold and damp. Your sun of Attica is not half so terrible as he is described." But while they were digging at Delphi Müller caught fever and was hastily taken to Athens, where he died on August 1, a victim of his eager thirst for knowledge.

Müller's mantle now fell on Curtius. From Athens Curtius went to Halle, by way of Rome, took his degree in 1841, and began to teach at the Joachimsthal Gymnasium at Berlin. His first public appearance took place two years later when the university's Lecture Union for the popularization of science invited him to speak on the Acropolis before a select audience. The young teacher, not yet thirty, had stage fright. "Next Saturday, at 10 minutes past 5," he confided to his brother, "I shall be unhappy standing on the platform, opposite the royal family of Prussia, in a brilliant assemblage of 950 persons. My heart will thump a bit, but let us hope that all will go well."

Not only was the royal family there but also the brains of Berlin, including Humboldt, Böckh, and Carl Ritter. Curtius was a great success. He stood on the platform seemingly unmoved, "his usual wild disorder of hair now combed into exceptional neatness, and his neck-cloth and gloves of dazzling whiteness." In his enthusiasm for his subject he forgot his audience and gave a graphic description of the Parthenon, bringing to life the activities of Athens in the height of her glory. When he got through the applause was spontaneous and unrestrained.

The success of my lecture [he wrote] has surpassed my expectation. I have set all Berlin on fire for the Acropolis, and I am only blamed for one thing, that in my final reverence I did not bow deeply enough towards the royal box. People thought they saw in this the stiff-necked republican of Lübeck.

The lecture brought Curtius an appointment as tutor to Prince Frederick William of Prussia (afterwards Frederick III), a position which he held for six years and which was not altogether a blessing. Not only did tutoring leave Curtius little time for his own work, but living in the palace at Potsdam made a decided royalist out of the "stiff-necked republican of Lübeck." In 1850, when the prince matriculated, Curtius settled at Berlin where he delivered lectures as a *Dozent* at the university. Although his income was paltry, he was now free to work. In 1851–52 he published his *Peloponnesus* in two volumes, a vivid description of Greece. He also edited the third volume of the *Corpus Inscriptionum Graecorum* which won him membership in the Prussian Academy. Among his smaller works in this period were *Road-making among the Greeks* (1855), and *The Ionians before the Ionian Migration*, which demolished the Greek tradition that the Ionians had been emigrants from Greece, showing, instead, that they had originated in Asia Minor. At last, in 1856, when Curtius was forty-two years old and probably the greatest living authority on Greek topography and art, he was given Otfried Müller's chair at Göttingen, where he remained for twelve years. He made two more scientific trips to Greece, carrying out archaeological excavations south of Athens and at the prehistoric city of Cranea. In 1869 he was called to the University of Berlin as professor and director of the Royal Museum.

While at Göttingen Curtius, like his colleague Waitz, not only wrote his greatest history but also trained a school of historians. At Berlin he continued his teaching activities, infusing into his lectures "a contagious enthusiasm and a perfume of antiquity." [17] This "perfume of

[17] The phrase is that of Paul Frédéricq, who gives an interesting description of Curtius in his "The Study of History in Germany and France," tr. from the French by Henrietta Leonard in

antiquity" is the special quality of his *Geschichte Griechenlands.* "The new note which Ernst Curtius introduced into the study of Greek history," Bury has said, "is that which might be described as *geographical vividness.*" The work of course contained much more than mere vividness. It was published by Weidmann, the same firm that issued Mommsen's *Roman History*, and was therefore intended for popular consumption. Consequently Curtius, like Mommsen, stated theories and drew conclusions without citing authorities. An artist like Burckhardt, Curtius aimed to present a graphic but correct picture of Greek life, and having a profound knowledge of the topography, art, and archaeology, he succeeded in his task. This "poetic" history, as Paul Frédéricq called it, was an immediate success, going into six editions and many translations, including English.[18]

In one essential respect Curtius' history was in contrast to that of Grote, and that was in the treatment of the mythical period. Mommsen had rejected the myths in Roman history and Grote did not accept Greek myths as historical evidence; but Curtius held that much history could be derived from legend because, far from being the fabrication of a single individual, it was the memory of a whole people.

Remembering the ideas of his master Otfried Müller, Curtius treated the Hellenic world as a "Greek unity," embracing all the manifestations of its culture, religion and priesthood, gymnastics and agriculture, road building and colonization, art and poetry, architecture and philosophy. Here Curtius is both a reliable and a delightful guide, depicting the Hellenic past with a warm grace that sprang from intimacy with its subject. It is for that reason that the Swiss Burckhardt, who disliked Germans, had a high admiration for Curtius, in whom he saw a fellow-artist.

The chief criticisms came from experts in philology and political historians. There can be no doubt that Curtius failed in the subject where Grote, for example, was at his best, namely the treatment of politics. The German scholar had neither a love for nor interest in political matters. An enthusiastic lover of beauty, especially Hellenic beauty, Curtius was comparatively cold to diplomatic events and political institutions; for that same reason he did not show much concern for such "hard necessities" as economics. A man who was inspired by the curve of a vase or the line of a column could not wax warm over

Johns Hopkins University Studies in Historical and Political Science, 8th Ser., V–VI (1890), 12–13; cp. also the pen-portrait by Keep in *International Review* (n. 15), 760.

[18] The *Griechische Geschichte* first appeared in 1857–67, in three volumes; the 6th rev. ed. in 1887–89, also in three volumes. The English translation was prepared by A. W. Ward (New York, 1867, 5 v.); of this the last four volumes were revised from later German editions by W. A. Packard (New York, 1871–73). The French translation by A. Bouché-Leclercq, *Histoire grecque* (Paris, 1880–83), was made from the 5th German edition.

the subject of voting or slavery. As Fueter remarks, "He was too much of a poet to be an historian." One may be emotionally inclined to sympathize with Curtius' viewpoint but one must, nevertheless, conclude that his inferior treatment of politics and his neglect of economics mar his total picture of Greek civilization.

Curtius' greatest achievements were in the spheres of geography and archaeology rather than in history. The excavation of Olympia was entirely due to him, and Wilamowitz-Möllendorff pronounced his *Peloponnesus* "one of the few books written in the 'fifties' which had not been superseded." "His lectures were finished orations," the late Professor John W. Burgess has written, but the classic eloquence and elegance of Curtius were not as convincing as the more objective method of Mommsen.[19] The greatest of all American Hellenists, Basil L. Gildersleeve, described Curtius' literary style as "elegant patrician which he filed over and over in successive editions."

The increasing number of inscriptions and archaeological data, particularly after Schliemann had unearthed the Mycenean cities, led to fresh attempts at interpretation of Greek civilization. Adolf Holm (1830–1900), who was professor of ancient history at Palermo, Naples, and Freiburg wrote a four-volume *Griechische Geschichte* (1886–94) in which he gave a balanced account of Greece; the work, based to a considerable extent upon numismatics and written in a rather pedestrian style, stated the known facts, without indulging in theories. On the other hand, Georg Busolt (1850–1920), professor at Kiel and Göttingen, compiled detailed and scholarly notes and published them under the title *Griechische Geschichte* (1884 f.); though of great importance to the scholar, this work is more of a collection of carefully worked out monographs than a history. "My history is written rather for learning than for reading, and it makes no pretence to compare in attractiveness with Curtius or Duncker."

Karl Julius Beloch (1854–1929)[20] was a more individual nature. Ever since his gymnasium days he was interested in Greek, history, geography, and especially statistics. He disliked Curtius, but Mommsen had a great effect upon him. "Outside of statistics by Kolb and the *Iliad*, no book had so great an influence on my intellectual development as Mommsen's *Roman History*." Bronchial trouble prevented Beloch from studying in Germany; he went to Italy and there he remained virtually all his life, having been given the professorship of ancient history at Rome in 1879. Greek history and social statistics

---

[19] John W. Burgess, *Reminiscences of an American Scholar* (New York, 1923), 123.
[20] See the autobiographical sketch in S. Steinberg, ed., *Die Geschichtswissenschaft der Gegenwart in Selbstdarstellungen* (Leipzig, 1925–26, 2 v.), II, 1–27; Gooch, 481–82.

were his favorite occupations. In 1884 he published *Attische Politik seit Perikles*, and in 1886 *Die Bevölkerung der Griechisch-Römischen Welt*. The problem of population in antiquity had long been an "arena of a confused dilettantism," because "statisticians generally understand nothing about antiquity, philologists nothing about statistics." Neither Böckh nor Mommsen had added anything to our knowledge of population in antiquity. Beloch, therefore, undertook to discover some reliable population data. In his own words:

It was necessary to create a secure foundation for areal-statistics on the basis of plane-metrical surveys, which had hitherto not existed. Population data are worthless unless we know to what surface area they refer. . . . Then all the statistical materials which have been preserved from antiquity had to be collected and critically sifted. . . . Finally, all these data had to be collated and brought into a closed system with respect to the economic conditions.

For years Beloch had been planning a comprehensive history of Greece from the earliest period to the time when Greece and Rome began to merge. He made six trips to Greece and spent seven years on the first volume. When he reached the third volume he was too weary of the work to continue: "das Altertum hatte ich für den Augenblick satt." He devoted his later years to a work on early Rome, and to a history of the population of Europe which was never finished.

Beloch's history differs from other German histories of Greece in being unconventional and liberal. A resident in Italy, Beloch was frankly a believer in democracy and reason. "I saw," he comments on Germany, "how Bismarck crushed under heel the rights of the people, and I have not forgotten it to this day. I have always considered freedom as the highest good and have remained a republican all my life." No German living in Germany could have written those words. He held that all progress depended upon knowledge and that the latter derived from freedom. Beloch thus characterized his new interpretation of Greek history:

Not much was to be done in the fifth century B.C.; but the history of the fourth century was thoroughly transformed; the battle of Chaeroneia, instead of being the end of Greek history, became its apex. Economic history, which had never been treated before, now received its proper place. In the history of the mind, next to literature and art, science now entered into the foreground, for after all it was the highest creation of the Greeks. My judgments of Pericles, Socrates, Plato, Demosthenes wounded many in their most tender feelings.

The work was widely criticized by pedants and authorities, but, Beloch concludes triumphantly, it was bought and read, "and Curtius was henceforth no longer published." [21]

[21] Autobiography, *loc. cit.* (n. 20), 16.

The study of Roman history was transformed by Theodor Mommsen (1817–1903),[22] one of the marvels of German scholarship. "A poet who was also a lawyer, a critic who was also a creator, emotional, excitable, and imaginative, and yet able to face unlimited drudgery and to work out whole multitudes of minute and tedious statistics, he combined qualities which have perhaps never been united before in any one man. Hence his work is unique." [23] Mommsen's published works include 1,513 different titles, over 1,000 of them independent works and original articles in diverse fields. These thousands of pages were written in longhand, without the aid of a secretary or stenographer. No wonder that one contemporary scholar remarked that it would take him 400 years to copy by hand what Mommsen had published.

The originality and diversity of Mommsen's work are equally astonishing. He was master in at least six different fields. No scholar excelled him in epigraphy, numismatics, history, law, archaeology, and early Italian philology; to each of these disciplines he made permanent contributions. A British scholar has said that in quantity and quality Mommsen's achievement was "the most wonderful life's work done in the nineteenth century."

[22] The bibliography on Mommsen is extensive. For a list of biographies see L. M. Hartmann, *Theodor Mommsen. Eine biographische Skizze* (Gotha, 1908). In English the following may be mentioned: Freeman (n. 2), contains a review of his *Roman History;* Gooch, 454–65; Guilland, 120–70, reprinted from *Revue Bleue,* XXXVI, 1899, pt. ii, 417–25; W. Warde Fowler, "Theodor Mommsen: His Life and Work," in *Roman Essays and Interpretations* (Oxford, 1920); W. P. Allen, "Theodor Mommsen," *NAR,* CXI (1870), 445–65; F. Haverfield, "Theodor Mommsen," *Athenaeum,* November, 1903, 615–16; F. W. Kelsey, "Theodore Mommsen," *Classical Journal,* XIV (1918–19), 224–36; K. Schurz, "A Tribute to Mommsen," *Massachusetts Historical Society,* 2nd ser., XVIII (1904); Sidney Whitman, "About Theodor Mommsen," *CR,* LXXXIV (1903), 865–72; J. B. Carter in *Atlantic Monthly,* March, 1904, 373–78; F. B. Copley, "Theodor Mommsen, a Near View," *The Critic,* XLIV (1904), 64–70; J. S. Mann, "Mommsen and Our Severance from Germany," *Fortnightly Review,* LXXX (1903), 1002–17; E. Ettore Pais, "On Roman History," *Annual Report of the American Historical Association,* 1904, pp. 81–88; E. Reich, "Theodor Mommsen," *Report of the Smithsonian Institute,* 1903; *Scribner's Magazine,* XLV (1909), 132 ff.; *The Bookman,* XVIII (1903–04), 346–48; Harry T. Peck, "Theodor Mommsen and Guglielmo Ferrero," *ibid.,* XXVIII (1908–09), 436–42; *The Dial,* XXXV (1903), 339–40; B. L. Gildersleeve, *American Journal of Philology,* VI (1885), 483–86; *The Nation,* XLV, 412 ff., LXXVII, 377 ff.; *Outlook,* LXXV (1903), 631–32; *ER,* CXV (1862), 440–77; *NAR,* CXXI (1875), 433–42; *EHR,* XVI (1901), 219–91; and F. Haverfield, "Roman History since Mommsen, *QR,* CCXVII (1912), 323–45.

For German and French studies of Mommsen see: Fueter, 549–56; C. Bardt, *Theodor Mommsen* (Berlin, 1903); Hirschfeld, "Gedächtnisrede auf Theodor Mommsen," *Abhandlungen der Preussischen Akademie der Wissenschaften,* 1904, pp. 1–38; F. Jonas, "Zum achtzigsten Geburtstage Theodor Mommsen's," *Deutsche Rundschau,* XCIII (1897), 399–416; W. Weber, *Theodor Mommsen. Zum Gedächtnis seines 25. Todestages* (Stuttgart, 1929); T. Gomperz, *Essays und Erinnerung* (1905), 133 ff.; Maurice Lair, "Mommsen, homme politique," *Annales des sciences politiques,* XXV (1910), 640–69; H. Blümner, "Theodor Mommsen," *Neue Züriche Zeitung,* Nov. 4 and 6, 1903; A. Dove, "Zur Erinnerung an Theodor Mommsen," Beilage zu *Allgemeine Zeitung,* February 2 and 3, 1904, nos. 26 and 27; O. Gradenwitz, "Theodor Mommsen," *Zeitschrift der Savignystiftung für Rechtsgeschichte,* rom. Abt., XXV (1904), 1–31; A. Harnack, *Rede bei der Begräbnisfeier Theodor Mommsen's* (Leipzig, 1903); Karl J. Neumann in *HZ,* XCII, 193–238; *Historische Vierteljahrschrift,* VII (1904), 313–42.

[23] F. Haverfield, "Roman History since Mommsen," *QR,* CCXVII (1912), 324.

Like many other German scholars, Mommsen was born in the province of Schleswig. He was the son of a poor pastor whose annual income was about 600 marks. The weekly schedule of the school which he attended shows the severe mental discipline which either made or broke German students. Two hours were devoted to theology, three to Cicero, two to Horace, two to Tacitus, two to Latin exercises, three to Thucydides, two to Sophocles, one to Greek language, and two hours each to English, French, and Danish; in the more "modern" studies, three hours were given to history and one hour each to philosophy, rhetoric, physics, and German literature.

In 1838, at the age of twenty-one, Mommsen registered in the law faculty at the University of Kiel. His favorite teacher was Otto Jahn who had studied antiquity and inscriptions at Berlin under Böckh. Jahn, only four years older than his student, taught Mommsen all he knew. In 1843, Mommsen took his degree in public law, and was given a travelling fellowship by the Danish government. He went to Italy, where he spent three years collecting Latin inscriptions in Naples. During the period of his residence abroad (1844–47) he published no less than ninety articles.

His publications brought him a professorship at Leipzig in 1848. But the revolutionary period moved him to participate in politics on the liberal side, and he lost his position. In 1852 he was called to Zürich, where he began to write his famous *Römische Geschichte*. From Zürich Mommsen was called to Breslau, where he finished it (first edition in 3 v., 1854–56). In 1858 he settled permanently in Berlin.

In 1852 Mommsen had published a volume of Latin inscriptions he had collected during his stay in Italy. The Prussian Academy now undertook the publication of all extant Latin inscriptions, and appointed Mommsen editor and director. It was a colossal task which Mommsen thought would take no less than twenty years to achieve. The work of collecting, editing, organizing, and publishing the famous *Corpus Inscriptionum Latinarum* occupied Mommsen for the rest of his life. In the absence of adequate written records the collection of inscriptions was a prime necessity if ancient history was ever to be known.[24] Searchers were sent out to southern and central Europe, England, North

[24] In the case of Greece, Böckh and his collaborators had collected some 9,000 inscriptions. Systematic excavations and the establishment of the kingdom of Greece facilitated a further collection, so that in the late nineteenth century some 30,000 Greek inscriptions had been published. See C. T. Newton, *Essays on Art and Archaeology* (London, 1880), 95–209. For the work of Schliemann and his excavations in Greece, see *ER*, CXXXIX (1874), 405–44; Emil Ludwig, *Schliemann, the Story of a Gold-seeker*, tr. from the German by D. F. Tait (Boston, 1931); E. Egger in *JS*, 1871, 157–83, 226–40; *August Böckh's gesammelte kleine Schriften* (1858–74, 7 v. in 4); and Adolf Kirchoff, *Studien zur Geschichte des griechischen Alphabets* (Gütersloh, 1887).

Africa, Asia Minor, Syria, and Egypt, to discover and to decipher every material trace which the Romans had left. Mommsen made it a condition that every staff-member should, if possible, see the stone—or the original manuscript of a preserved copy if the inscription was gone—for himself, the reason being that there were too many published inscriptions which were forgeries. In the *Corpus* these false inscriptions were printed by themselves so that no scholar need confuse them in the future. The main work was done in Italy, where some 36,000 inscriptions were collected, most of them edited by Mommsen himself. The thinnest volume of the *Corpus* contains the inscriptions found in Britain, about 1,500. The total came to 15 volumes, in 41 parts, containing the stupendous total of 130,000 inscriptions. But Mommsen was not only the general editor, but also prepared 14 out of the 41 parts, over 8,000 folio pages, "a life-work in itself." Camille Jullian said that the *Corpus* was "the greatest service ever rendered by any scholar to the knowledge of the past." [25]

Though a work of his earlier years, Mommsen is known to most persons as the author of the *Römische Geschichte*. In a letter to Gustav Freytag he explained how he came to write it.

Do you know how I came to write the *Roman History?* In my youth I was thinking of all kinds of other things, a treatise on Roman criminal law, an edition of Roman legal sources, or in any case a compendium of the pandects, but thought of nothing so little as writing history. Then I was stricken by the well known children's disease of young professors, to deliver a boring lecture on anything before the cultured of Leipzig, and since I was then at work on the agrarian laws . . . I gave a political talk on the Gracchi. . . . In the audience there were K. Reimer and Hirzel, and two days later they came to me and asked if I would not write a Roman history for their collection. Now this came as a great surprise, for such a possibility had never entered my mind, but then you know what confusion reigned in those days, everybody venturing in everything; and when a professor was teased with the question: Wouldn't you like to become minister of public instruction? he usually promised. So I, too, promised, but I did so because those two men impressed me, and I thought to myself: if they have confidence in you, then you can also have confidence in yourself.[26]

This account is significant because it shows Mommsen's propensity to rush into print. Camille Jullian pointed out that if Mommsen had not had an "incredible desire" to publish something every few weeks, he would have become another Ranke.[27] As it was, his strictly historiographic output was limited. In any case, he always preferred law to history. "The son of Clio or the son of Themis?" Boecking asked.

The *Römische Geschichte* was an instant success and was hailed as the best history of Rome in existence, although scholars criticized it for its

[25] Quoted in GOOCH, 459.
[26] Published in the *National Zeitung* (Berlin), November 17, 1903.
[27] Camille Jullian, "Mommsen," *RH*, LXXXIV (1904), 113–23.

lack of references and footnotes. Since the work was intended for popular consumption—"its aim is to bring a more vivid knowledge of classical antiquity to wider circles"—it omitted all discussion of difficult problems or controverted points, as the credibility of early sources and myths which had troubled Niebuhr and George Cornewall Lewis. It was in these earliest portions that Mommsen was least valuable. He had never heard of the Ice Age or of Totemism.

Mommsen traced the stages of Rome's rise to world dominion, denying that there was any deliberate plan to create an empire. "Their distant conquests," he wrote of Rome's gradual expansion, "were in some cases almost forced upon them, and they often drifted into foreign wars as much through the result of circumstances as from any deliberate intent." Mommsen greatly admired the way the Romans exerted their authority internally and abroad. Even where harshness and brutality were involved he refused to condemn. To him, no less than to Treitschke, the victory of the "noble over the common" was "necessary." Although he did not glorify force as crudely as his colleagues of the Prussian School, he still held that historical movements could not be judged by moral standards. "Any revolution," he said, "or any usurpation is justified before the bar of history by exclusive ability to govern." [28]

Mommsen's third volume stopped with the end of the Roman Republic and the battle of Thapsus (46 B.C.). The fourth volume, to deal with Caesar's dictatorship and death, and the imperial period, was never written, though at times Mommsen thought of continuing it. [29] In partial compensation he wrote a fifth volume (1885) on the history of the provinces from Caesar to Diocletian. But if he did not cover the period of the Empire in narrative form, he wrought a revolution in the study of the Roman government of these centuries by his epochal *Römisches Staatsrecht*, volumes teeming with information, which "trace the basic lines on which a history of the Imperial civilization must be built up." [30] Haverfield declared the *Staatsrecht* "perhaps the most remarkable piece of constitutional writing in all historical literature." [31] His revision of the view of the Roman constitution in this work was mostly based on known sources, but in the field of Roman administration many facts had been wanting—Marquardt's *Italien und die*

---

[28] For examples of his ethico-political ideas see *Römische Geschichte* (Berlin, 1903–07, 3 v.), I, 8, 812; II, 93, 450; III, 93, and *passim*.

[29] He was dissuaded in part by his son-in-law Wilamowitz-Möllendorff, who writes in *My Recollections, 1848–1914* (tr. from the German by G. C. Richards [London, 1930]), 217 note: "Anyone who can judge properly of the structure of the third volume and its artistically effective close, must admit that the three volumes are a whole, to which nothing can be tacked on."

[30] *Ibid.*, 219.

[31] F. Haverfield, "Theodor Mommsen," *EHR*, XIX (1904), 80–89.

Provinzen (1851) had appeared prior to the *Corpus*—which Mommsen now derived from the inscriptions.

In the latter years of his life, "with almost fabulous speed," Mommsen also edited for the *Monumenta Germaniae* various historical and legal sources of the early Middle Ages, including Cassiodorus' *Variae*, Jordanes' *History of the Goths*, and Paul the Deacon's *History of the Lombards*.[32]

Mommsen's "Caesarism" has been much misunderstood or distorted. If he were living today he would have condemned the totalitarian Germany of the present. This is what he wrote of the great Julius:

> The history of Caesar and Roman Imperialism . . . is in truth a more bitter censure of modern autocracy than could be written by the hand of man. According to the same law of nature in virtue of which the smallest organism infinitely surpasses the most artistic machine, every constitution, however defective, which gives play to the free self-determination of a majority of citizens infinitely surpasses the most brilliant and humane absolutism; for the former is capable of development and therefore living, the latter is what it is, and therefore dead.[33]

In politics Mommsen stood midway between Sybel and Bismarck, detesting absolute monarchy but admiring superior aristocratic ability. He hated Junkers, whether Roman or Prussian, but also despised democracy. "Tyranny is everywhere the result of universal suffrage." Only a democratic aristocracy had the right to rule—"by virtue of the highest of all rights . . . the right of the superior." [34] Mommsen took an active part in the politics of his time. In 1861 he entered the Prussian parliament. In 1881 he was elected to the Reichstag where he allied himself with the Radical party of Bamberger which had seceded from the National Liberal Party when Bismarck introduced Protection. In his rectorial address of 1874 he deplored the drift towards materialism of the new imperial Germany and prophesied the decay of higher culture and humanistic studies. He strongly opposed the anti-Semitic movement instigated by Stöcker and Treitschke and was filled with rage

---

[32] It is impossible to enumerate all of Mommsen's important works; see the bibliography collected by K. Zangemeister, *Theodor Mommsen als Schriftsteller* (2nd ed., enlarged by E. Jacobs, Berlin, 1905). A partial list follows: *De collegiis et sodaliciis Romanorum* (1843); *Inscriptiones regni Neapolitani Latinae* (1852); *Inscriptiones confoederationis Helveticae Latinae* (1854); *Corpus inscriptionum Latinarum* (1863–1936, 16 v. in 47); *Die römische Chronologie bis auf Cäsar* (1858; 2nd ed., 1859); *Römische Forschungen* (1864–79, 2 v.); *Römische Geschichte* (1854–56, 3 v.; many reprints and translations, vol. V, 1885); *Römisches Staatsrecht* (1871–75, 2 v.; 3rd ed., 1887–88, with a third volume); *Römisches Strafrecht* (1899). Mommsen also edited several volumes of the *Auctores antiquissimi* for the *Monumenta Germaniae Historica*. The *Römische Geschichte* was translated into English by W. P. Dickson as *The History of Rome* (New York, 1871, 4 v.; reprinted in Everyman's Library), and Dickson also translated the supplementary fifth volume as *The Provinces of the Roman Empire from Caesar to Diocletian* (New York, 1887, 2 v.).

[33] *The History of Rome*, Bk. V, ch. xi (Everyman's Library edition, vol. IV, 439–40).

[34] W. P. Allen, "Theodore Mommsen," *NAR* (1870), 451; for other selections see the whole article, 445–62.

when Traube, whose contributions to medieval palaeography are epoch-making, was driven from Greifswald by a Jew-baiting policy imported from Berlin, and found refuge in Munich.[35] He had independent opinions which he expressed vigorously either in the Prussian parliament, of which he was a Liberal member, or in the press, to which he was a much-too-frequent contributor. In the heat of his convictions he did not hesitate to call even Bismarck's protection policy a "swindle" or to make violent attacks on Britain for her Boer policy. Mommsen "could easily be made to utter oracles on politics." [36]

Before he had reached middle age Mommsen was already a famous, almost a legendary figure. Probably no other scholar in the world was so widely known. Hundreds of anecdotes were current about him.[37] Many acquaintances have left descriptions of Mommsen, portraying his eccentricities, his inexhaustible energy, his total absorption in his work. It was the favorite talk of Berlin that every morning he would enter the tram on his way to the university, always occupy the same seat, and immediately begin to read. Well-known to his fellow-passengers, they would make room for him and never interrupt him. Arrived at the University station, the conductor would inform the professor who would then hurry out to be on time for his eight o'clock morning lecture. "This man," the admiring Germans would murmur proudly, "wastes no time."

The following description is from the pen of one who knew him:

Mommsen is in figure extremely slender. His face is thin and sharp; his eyes, though light blue, are piercing; his iron-gray hair is like a mass of fine wires. Though quick and active in his movements, he is not graceful, nor, while intellectually on all occasions in the highest degree self-possessed, is he free from that physical helplessness which often marks the scholar outside of his study. His daily lecture is delivered summer and winter at 8 A.M. Many who have studied at Berlin, will retain a vivid impression of the crowd of steaming, half-dressed students of every nationality who, loudly talking, or confusedly scrambling to their places, fill the largest auditorium of the university shortly after that hour. At 8:15 a side door opens, and Mommsen's slender figure glides to the desk; and almost before his shrill child's voice has enunciated the opening words "Meine Herren," the hum and noise subside into utter silence, broken only by the lecturer's voice, who reads with great rapidity and in a conversational tone to the end of the hour. These lectures, if current report is to be accepted, are prepared on the morning on which they are delivered, and are always fresh, for even if the title of the course be not new, so con-

[35] Wilamowitz-Möllendorff (n. 29), 231 note.   [36] Ibid., 296.
[37] Mommsen had a very large family. A visitor seeing from his study window a dozen or more children in boisterous play in the court yard of the apartment house in which he lived, and remarking to him that the neighbor's children must sometimes be an annoyance to him, he replied, "Ach, Gott, sie sind alle meine."
He once was asked why, in his opinion, the Kaiser was so bent on building a mighty fleet, "Because he dreams of a German Trafalgar," was the reply. "At whose expense?" he was asked. "Either England or America," said Mommsen. "Preferably America, because he has no grandmother buried there."

stant is Mommsen's research, that the point of view from which he regards even important questions is often changed. . . . His numerous researches in the various departments of Roman antiquity employ a number of young philologists, the élite of his own
scholars, who, though each engaged upon his peculiar specialty, and animated at once by
devoted attachment to their teacher and by an honest pride in their own powers, half-
despairingly declare that Mommsen excels each of them in their own field, and that he
can throw off in a few hours' labor that which would cost them days.[38]

A poor lecturer, with a thin squeaking voice, Mommsen always held
the attention of his students from beginning to end. He read his lecture
from notes but from time to time he swept the class with his ice-blue
eyes. Monday evenings his seminar students met in his house and read
their reports. Mommsen criticized them severely but fairly; few students ever dared interrupt or challenge him. He was always at the
service of his students after their graduation, giving them help, advice,
and the benefit of his knowledge.[39]

Mommsen's contemporaries did not always accept his leadership.
Albert Schwegler (1819–57), Karl Peter (1808–93), and Wilhelm Ihne
(1821–1902) wrote histories of Rome in the spirit of Niebuhr. Perhaps because Mommsen himself had so thoroughly gleaned the field
of the history of the Roman Republic, certainly because of the wealth of
inscriptional material now brought together, the younger scholars
turned towards the Empire rather than the Republic.[40]

Ludwig Friedländer (1824–1909), a student of Mommsen and Riehl,
devoted himself to *Kulturgeschichte*. His *Darstellungen aus der Sittengeschichte Roms* [41] contains the most comprehensive account of social
conditions and behavior under the empire. Hermann Schiller (1839–
1902) wrote the political history of the empire, but Dessau's *Geschichte
der römischen Kaiserzeit* is a better work, for he had grown grey in study
of the *Corpus*. Demaszweski's *Geschichte der römischen Kaiser* is a series
of personal studies. The greatest of all Mommsen's students was Otto
Seeck (1850–1921) who edited the *Notitia dignitatum* and *Symmachus'*

[38] Robert P. Keep, "Ernst Curtius, Müller, and Mommsen," *International Review*, II (1875),
759–60, the whole article, 745–62.
[39] For a description and appreciation of Mommsen by one of his eminent students see
O. Seeck, "Zur Charakteristik Mommsens," *Deutsche Rundschau*, CXVIII (1904), 75–108.
[40] See F. Haverfield, "Roman History since Mommsen," *QR*, CCXVII (1912), 323–45;
GOOCH, 465–74; SANDYS, III, 233–35, Wilhelm Kroll, ed., *Die Altertumswissenschaft im letzten
Vierteljahrhundert* (Leipzig, 1905). See also *The Year's Work in Classical Studies*, which begins
in 1906.
[41] Originally in three volumes (1862–71); the 10th ed. (1921–23) is in four. English translation from the 7th ed. by L. A. Magnus and others, *Life and Manners under the Early Empire* (London, 1908–13, 4 v.). See also Arthur Ludwich, "Ludwig Friedländer," *Jahresbericht
über die Fortschritte der klassischen Altertumswissenschaft*, CLIII (1911), 1–24; H. Passy,
"Rapport sur un ouvrage intitulé: Moeurs romaines . . . par L. Friedlaender," *ASMP*,
LXXV (1866), 355–66, who says of the author: "Rechercheur indéfatigable, érudit ingénieux
et sagace, doué au plus haut degré du sens critique, ne hasardant aucune assertion avant d'avoir
recueilli à l'appui des preuves irrécusables. . . ."

Letters and wrote the profoundest study of the decline of the Roman Empire—in six volumes—yet penned: *Geschichte des Untergangs der antiken Welt* (Berlin, 1895–1920).

As in the first part of the nineteenth century British students of Greek and Roman history were the first to appreciate the work of Böckh and Niebuhr, so they were also the first in the latter part of the nineteenth century to learn from Mommsen. The work of Francis Haverfield (1860–1919),[42] Henry Pelham (1846–1907),[43] H. J. Greenidge (1865–1906),[44] T. Rice Holmes (b. 1855),[45] James Leigh Strachan-Davidson,[46] and William Warde Fowler (1847–1921),[47] was in Mommsen's method and spirit. To this list of English writers on Roman subjects one may add the late Samuel Dill, who was a professor of Greek in Belfast University, but whose published works deal with Roman history. Dill was the author of *Roman Society in the Last Century of the Western Empire* (1898), *Roman Society from Nero to Marcus Aurelius* (1904), and *Roman Society in Gaul in the Merovingian Age* (1926).

French scholars, before the 1860's, while interested in classical literature, were indifferent to classical history. The best work on history in the classical period produced under the Second Empire was the *Histoire des Romains* by Victor Duruy, the scholarly minister of Napoleon III. The first two volumes had been published in 1843–44. The third and fourth on Caesar and the Roman Empire were held back until after the fall of the emperor, for Duruy looked askance on the imperialistic pretensions of that supple mountebank.[48] The dawn of a new day broke with the appearance in 1858 of Fustel de Coulanges' *Polybe, ou la Grèce conquise*, prophetic of the future greatness of the author. In 1858 also the *Revue germanique* was established, "to follow the intellectual movement in Germany," said the prospectus, "particularly the historical and philological sciences." Mommsen's works began to be translated into French in the time of the Second Empire, but the *Staatsrecht* and *Strafrecht*, and Marquardt's *Römische Verwaltung* were not translated into French until the 1890's.[49] A translation of Friedländer's

---

[42] *The Romanization of Roman Britain; The Roman Occupation of Britain.*

[43] *Outlines of Roman History* (various editions); *Essays.* A notable essay is that on "The Imperial Domains and the Colonate."

[44] *A Handbook of Greek Constitutional History* (London and New York, 1896); *History of Rome during the Later Republic and the Early Principate* (New York, 1905).

[45] *Caesar's Conquest of Gaul; an Historical Narrative* (London and New York, 1899); *The Roman Republic and the Founder of the Empire* (Oxford, 1923, 3 v.), etc.

[46] *Problems of the Roman Criminal Law* (Oxford, 1912, 2 v.).

[47] *The City-State of the Greeks and Romans* (London, 1893).

[48] Ernest Lavisse, *Un ministre: Victor Duruy* (Paris, 1895); Jules Simon, "Notice sur la vie et les travaux de M. Duruy," *ASMP*, CXLV (1896), 66–93. Also see above, pp. 264–69.

[49] The *Roman History* in two different versions as follows: *Histoire romaine*, tr. by C. A. Alexandre, vols. I–VIII (Paris, 1863–74, 8 v.), with Mommsen's 5th volume on the provinces as a continuation, vols. IX–XI (Paris, 1887–89, 3 v.), tr. by R. Cognat and J. Toutain; and

Römische Sittengeschichte in four volumes was completed between 1865 and 1873. In 1866 Belot's *Histoire des chevaliers romains depuis des rois jusqu'au temps des Graques* was published, the preface to which declared that it would have been impossible to write the book without the works of Mommsen, Schwegler, Peter, Henzen, Marquardt, Drumann, and other less celebrated German scholars. The laxness of French scholarship of this time is illustrated by the fact that although the French archaeological expedition to Asia Minor under Perrot discovered at Ancyra the famous inscription recording the Testament of Augustus (*Monumentum Ancyranum*) which Busbecq had seen in the sixteenth century, no French scholar was competent to edit it, and Mommsen had the honor of publishing the most celebrated inscription of Roman history.

French classical scholarship in the late nineteenth century was fortunate in having writers who combined scientific method and criticism with a translucent literary style. Renan was one of these in the field of the ancient Orient and another was Gaston Boissier (1823–1908) [50] in Roman history and literature. Boissier was a native of Provence, that part of France which preserves the most and the noblest monuments of ancient Roman genius. The ancient Latin spirit, it would seem, fired Boissier's imagination almost from birth. He began to teach Roman history and literature in Paris in 1863 and died full of years and honors in 1908. Boissier united Roman history, Roman archaeology and Roman literature most happily together. *Ciceron et ses amis*, a study of Roman society in the first century B.C., appeared in 1865 and established his reputation. His *La fin du paganisme* (1891, 2 v.) is the most searching, the most profound, and the most sympathetic study of the decline of the Roman religion in any language. [51]

It is perhaps charitable to explain the apathy of Italian scholarship towards ancient Roman history by saying that Italy, especially from 1859 forward, was too intensely occupied in developing her own present history to give time and thought to her past. A noble exception was Count Bartolommeo Borghesi (1781–1860), a celebrated epigraphist. [52]

Histoire romaine, tr. by de Guerle (new ed., Paris, 1882, 7 v.). Mommsen's work on Roman coinage was translated as *Histoire de la monnaie romaine*, by le duc de Blacas (Paris, 1865–75, 4 v.). The Mommsen-Marquardt series including Mommsen's *Staatsrecht* and *Strafrecht* and Marquardt's *Verwaltung* were translated from the German as *Manuel des antiquités romaines* (Paris, 1887–1907, 19 v.).

[50] See a sympathetic account of Boissier by E. K. Rand in *The Nation*, LXXXVI (1908), 550–51.

[51] Other works of Boissier: *La religion romaine d'Auguste aux Antonins* (1874, 2 v.); *L'opposition sous les Césars: Tacite* (1903); *La conjuration de Catilina* (1905); and three *Promenades archéologiques: Rome et Pompéi* (1880), *L'Afrique romaine* (1895), and *Horace et Virgile* (1886).

[52] He had studied under Marini, whose work on the *Fratres Arvales* (1795) laid the foundations of modern epigraphy; it contained a thousand unknown inscriptions.

He had begun with the ambition to follow Muratori, but found that the palaeography of medieval documents was too trying on his eyesight. In 1819 he published a new work on the *fasti* of the magistrates of ancient Rome which re-established the chronology of ancient Roman history. Thereafter for years Borghesi's communications might be found in the proceedings of every learned society. He projected a vast work comprehending all the Latin inscriptions of the ancient Roman world but death frustrated the plan. Borghesi spent his life at San Marino, for he was not in sympathy with the drift of Italian politics. Most of his writings were written in French. He found a patron in the Emperor Napoleon III, himself an amateur antiquarian, who had initiated archaeological studies of remains of Caesar's campaigns in Gaul, and caused Borghesi's complete works to be printed by the Imprimerie impériale, in ten volumes. The last volume contains a long account of Borghesi's labors. It was not published until 1897. Italy has yet to produce a Mommsen.[53]

[53] The best Italian historian of classical antiquity is Gaetano de Sanctis, author of *Storia dei Romani* (Turin, 1907–23, 4 v. in 5). The fourth volume extends to the battle of Pydna.

CHAPTER LVIII

THE PROGRESS OF BYZANTINE STUDIES[1]

IN THE confusion concerning the ideal nomenclature for that empire whose capital from the fourth to the fifteenth Christian century was Constantinople, scholars have seen fit, as Krumbacher knew they would, to follow the lead of his *Byzantinische Zeitschrift*. The controversy regarding its title, however, has been only one of a score of mishaps that this field of history, so long despised and ignored, has to chronicle.

The prime historical reason for the long neglect of Byzantine history was theological prejudice. After reaping a bounteous harvest from its Hellenic neighbors in the first centuries of Christianity, the Latin West set out dourly upon paths of its own. The Greeks, while they were allowed some pretension to culture, were viewed as schismatics. Gregory the Great (590–604), who spent many years in Constantinople, never deigned to learn the Greek language. It was not love for these sneering Easterners that induced the Crusaders to mount horse and mortgage castle and land for armor and victuals. The looting of the great city on the Bosphorus in 1204 was rendered possible by this lack of true fellowship between two worlds each professing the same religion. The Byzantines who treasured the heritage of their fading civilization repaid the contempt and hatred of the Franks (French) with the same coin. "I would rather," said the Greek archon Notaras near the fateful middle of the fifteenth century, "I would rather see the turban of Murad over the gate of St. Sophia, than the hat of a cardinal of Rome."

[1] A good beginning for any student of Byzantine bibliography is Charles Diehl's essay, "Les études d'histoire byzantine en 1901," *RSH*, III (1901), 177–225; it suggests the wealth of the field, and the difficulty of encompassing its scattered literature. See also the same author, "Les études byzantines en France," *Byzantinische Zeitschrift*, IX (1900), 1–13; J. B. Bury's introduction to his edition of GIBBON, I, pp. liii–lxiii; F. Krumbacher, "Vorwort," *Byzantinische Zeitschrift*, I (1892), 1–12, also reprinted in his *Populare Aufsätze* (Leipzig, 1909); the same, *Geschichte der byzantinischen Litteratur* (Munich, 1891; 2nd ed., 1897, with a critical appendix on works to 1896); A. A. Vasiliev, *History of the Byzantine Empire*, tr. from the Russian by Mrs. S. Ragozin (Madison, 1928–29, 2 v.), I, 13–54, 213–16; Louis Brehier, "Le développement des études d'histoire byzantine du XVIIᵉ au XXᵉ siècle," *Revue d'Auvergne* (1901); the same, "Empire byzantin," in HISTOIRE ET HISTORIENS, II, 655–78; V. Vasilievsky, *A Survey of Works on Byzantine History* (St. Petersburg, 1890, in Russian); K. Dietrich, "Die byzantinische Zeitschrift und die byzantinischen Studien in Deutschland," *Internationale Monatschrift*, VI (1912), 345–76; for works published in Slavic lands see the *Vizantijsky Vremennik; Blackwell's Byzantine Hand List: a Catalogue of Byzantine Authors and Books on Byzantine Literature, History, Religion, Art, Archaeology*, etc. (Oxford, 1937). Mention should also be made of the *Byzantinische neugriechische Jahrbücher*, the *Revue de l'Orient latin* (Paris, 1893 ff.), and the *Archiv für slavische Philologie* (founded by Jagic at Berlin, 1876 ff.).

The humanists of the Renaissance, with their aversion to the medieval epoch, found nothing to entice their interest in the contemporary annals from the East; and while reformers in the sixteenth century talked about returning to the pristine condition of the Church, none really sought it in its original habitat or Hellenistic environment. If then we exempt the school of workers in Byzantine jurisprudence, dominated by Jacques Cujas (1590),[2] there was down to the seventeenth century no true interest in Byzantine history in Europe.

The birth of modern Byzantine historiography may be placed in the year 1648, when from the royal press of Louis XIV there issued the first volume of the first collection of Byzantine historians. Out of the faithful labors of the editor Labbé (Labbaeus), and Fabrot, the genius of Du Cange, and the munificence of Louis XIV, there resulted over a space of three-score years thirty-four folio volumes of the *Byzantinae historiae scriptores varii*, more familiarly cited as "the Byzantine of the Louvre." Of individual scholars, none did more than the erudite and indefatigable Du Cange, who left a *Histoire de l'empire de Constantinople sous les empéreurs français*, and put scholars into even deeper obligation by the instrument he provided in his *Glossarium mediae et infimae graecitalis*. This counterpart to his Latin glossary appeared when the author was seventy. Not to be forgotten also is Montfaucon, important for Greek palaeography and epigraphy.

But after these promising beginnings something worse than neglect ensued. The eighteenth century turned a blast of withering scorn upon the Byzantine Empire. An empire exemplifying "a thousand years of decadence" was just the thing for the deadly thrusts of Voltaire or the solemn and judicial sentences of Gibbon. Its history "contains nothing but declamations and miracles; it is the disgrace of the human mind" (Voltaire);[3] "is nothing but a tissue of revolts, seditions and perfidies" (Montesquieu);[4] "presents a disgusting picture of imbecility; wretched, nay insane passions stifle the growth of all that is noble" (Hegel).[5] The term "Bas-empire" had a most convenient double entendre. Nor did the first great scholars of the nineteenth century escape the myopia of their illustrious predecessors. Savigny in his *History of Roman Law* gave no attention to the continued existence and development of Roman

---

[2] Jean Mortreuil, *Histoire du droit byzantin* (Paris, 1843–46, 3 v.), I, preface, 17–18. Of casual editors of Byzantine works in the sixteenth and early seventeenth century, Vasiliev (n. 1), I, 13, mentions Hieronymus Wolf in Germany, Meursius in Holland, and two Greeks, Alemannus and Allatius, in Italy.

[3] *Le pyrrhonisme de l'histoire*, ch. xv, quoted in Vasiliev (n. 1), I, 16.

[4] *Considérations sur les causes de la grandeur des Romans et de leur décadence*, ch. xxi, quoted *ibid.*

[5] *Lectures on the Philosophy of History*, tr. from the German by J. Sibree (London, 1890), 353, quoted in full in *ibid.*, I, 17.

law in the Eastern Empire; Guizot did not find Byzantine culture worth mentioning in a history of civilization in Europe; and Lecky declared the "universal verdict of history" upon the Byzantine Empire to be "that it constitutes, with scarcely an exception, the most thoroughly base and despicable form that civilization has yet assumed." [6] Gibbon had mordantly summarized his *magnum opus* with the words: "I have described the triumph of barbarism and religion."

Yet active hostility was perhaps something better than complete oblivion. If the whole truth is not seen, half of it may still become apparent. Montesquieu, in his *Considérations sur les causes de la grandeur des Romains et de leur décadence* (1734), cited above, devoted the four final chapters to the Byzantine Empire, thereby recognizing it as a continuation of Roman history. It is true that he spent an entire chapter in elucidating the miracle of its preservation as far as 1453, in view of its great defects; yet to read Montesquieu is not wholly without profit, and Sorel has called it "a masterly account and a model interpretation." [7] The perception of historic continuity is a well-known merit of Gibbon's work. Its adequacy for a history of the Eastern Empire, however, is marred by a double defect. Gibbon did not possess a command of Greek comparable to his facility in Latin. For his more detailed and valuable accounts down to the year 518 he had the guidance of Tillemont, [8] but after this point the loss of such a guide becomes painfully evident. Secondly, Gibbon exercised all too constantly what Freeman termed his "matchless faculty of sarcasm and depreciation." Without incurring the charge of falsifying or historical carelessness, he managed always to turn the worst side outward. The mere mechanical allotment of space testified to his contempt: after having spent page after page upon the Antonines, he finished off the rulers from Heraclius down to Isaac Angelus in a single chapter. Still, if Gibbon's color be wrong and whole portions of Byzantine history were still obscure terrain in his day, the hand of a genius had touched the subject and helped to ensure it life. [9] For most of the nineteenth century, English-speaking readers derived their knowledge of Byzantium from his pages.

If others, particularly in France, cultivated Byzantine studies with less of an animus than the eighteenth-century thinkers mentioned, their talents were of an inferior order. Le Quien's *Oriens Christianus* (1740) was not without its good points; but when Lebeau undertook a very

---

[6] William Lecky, *History of European Morals from Augustus to Charlemagne* (New York and London, 1910, 2 v.), II, 13.

[7] Albert Sorel, *Montesquieu* (2nd ed., Paris, 1889), 64, quoted in Vasiliev (n. 1), I, 18.

[8] Le Nain de Tillemont, *Histoire des empereurs et des autres princes* (Brussels, 1690–1738, 6 v.).

[9] For criticism of Gibbon see Freeman, *Essays, Historical and Critical*, 3rd ser. (London, 1879), 234–35, and Vasiliev (n. 1), I, 18–23.

detailed treatment he "noya cette histoire sous le flot d'ennui qui s'échappe des trente volumes où il prétendit la raconter." [10] His *Histoire du Bas-Empire* was carried on by a continuator, but its twenty-seven volumes (1756–86) are defunct today. Lebeau had small Greek himself, and made uncritical use of Latin translations. Some interest attaches to a reissue at Paris (1824–36, 24 v.) by two Orientalists, Saint Martin, a specialist in Armenian, and Brosset, a specialist in Georgian history. Their additions from oriental sources, notably Armenian, were something of an innovation. The nine-volume *Histoire du Bas-Empire* of J. C. Royou was only a journalistic effort to replace the "unreadable" Lebeau; it lacks all scholarly merits. [11] In the field of Byzantine history the record of the eighteenth century was a sorry one of incompetency, ignorance, or arrant prejudice.

Slowly the nineteenth century inaugurated the revival. Romanticism and nationalism both played their part, as will appear. Schlosser's volume in 1812 on the Iconoclastic Emperors was a brave but isolated venture. [12] The definite turn of the tide can be traced to three influences: the travel literature written by gentlemen scholars on the Near East, the war for Greek independence and Phil-hellenism, and the controversy raised by Fallmerayer's racial theories.

Napoleon's expedition to Egypt and Syria in 1798 had drawn the eyes of the world towards the Levant. The works on travel in Greece and Asia Minor which are listed in the French, German, and particularly English book catalogues of the first half of the nineteenth century found an indulgent public. Written by men trained in the classics, and sometimes with a modicum of training in archaeology or numismatics, they could also interest serious scholars. It was to Colonel William Martin Leake, "Model Traveller," as William Miller calls him, that Finlay later dedicated the fourth volume of his *History of Greece*. [13] After a government mission to Greece in 1799, Leake returned again to study contemporary conditions there, to identify sites and to collect coins and inscriptions of value for Byzantine times as well as classical antiquity. The English public could also rely upon such works as Edward Giffard's *A Short Visit to the Ionian Islands, Athens, and the*

[10] Quoted from Charles Diehl in *Byzantinische Zeitschrift* (n. 1), 1–13.

[11] *Histoire du Bas-Empire depuis Constantin jusqu'à la prise de Constantinople en 1453* (Paris, 1803, 4 v.).

[12] Friedrich Christoph Schlosser, *Geschichte der bilderstürmenden Kaiser des oströmischen Reichs* (Frankfurt, 1812).

[13] ". . . whose long and laborious exertions in clearing the ancient history of Greece from obscurity, and the modern from misrepresentation, have merited the applause of Britain and the gratitude of Greece." On Leake's travels, cp. *ER*, XXIV (1814–15, 353–69). He was the author of *Researches in Greece* (1814), *Travels in the Morea* (1830), *Travels in Northern Greece* (1835), *Numismatica Hellenica* (1854), and other works; all figure prominently in Finlay's footnotes.

Morea,[14] and William Mure's *Journal of a Tour in Greece and the Ionian Islands*,[15] and Christopher Wordsworth's *Athens and Attica: Journal of a Residence There*.[16]

Travel literature was increased in volume, but eclipsed in interest by the Greek war for independence. The cause of this little nation submerged under the barbarism of the Turks awakened all over Europe the fervor of a War of Liberation. Today, when the classics are less honored in educational systems, it is difficult to realize the enthusiasm for the land of Homer and Plato in the early nineteenth century. Men reminded themselves that the Morea was the home of the Lacedaemonians who died at Thermopylae under Leonidas. Fallmerayer as a lieutenant in the Bavarian army against Napoleon had exhorted his comrades about the camp fires at night to bravery and self-sacrifice by citing the examples of the Romans from his classical texts. The interest of Lord Byron (d. 1824) and Hobhouse in the Greek struggle is a matter of common knowledge. Geneva had its Eynard, Germany its Wilhelm Müller, and America its Dr. Howe. The whole philhellenic movement raised the question of the continuity of Greek history, and stimulated interest in the history of the Greeks in the Middle Ages. Niebuhr and Bekker in 1828 began publication of a corpus of Byzantine historians (known as the Bonn edition) which dragged on until 1897 and is "the most lamentably feeble production ever given to the world by German scholars of great reputation." [17] The year 1828 also saw the appearance of Böckh's *Corpus Inscriptionum Graecarum*, the first collection of epigraphic sources of value for the Byzantine period.

Yet it may be questioned whether even the universal atmosphere of sympathy and emotionalism which swept Europe during the Greek war of liberation in the third decade of the last century would have produced the spate of literature on Byzantium which the subsequent years witnessed, if it had not been for Fallmerayer's heresy. Jakob Philipp Fallmerayer (1791–1861) [18] began life as a poor peasant's son at Tschötsch, in the Tyrol, south of the Old Rhaetian episcopal seat of Brixen. As a choir boy in the cathedral school there he acquired a sound foundation in Greek, but felt his surroundings stifling, and fled during the Tyrolese revolt of 1809 to the more liberal air of Bavarian Salzburg.

---

[14] London, 1837, reviewed in *QR*, LIX (1837), 217–40.

[15] Edinburgh, 1842, reviewed *ibid.*, LXX (1842), 129–50.

[16] London, 1836, reviewed *ibid.*, LXIV (1839), 64–83.

[17] Bury's introduction to Gibbon, I, p. xlix; cp. review of Niebuhr's *Corpus Scriptorum* in *FQR*, X (1832), 102–21.

[18] See his own *Studien und Erinnerungen aus meinem Leben;* the sketch by George M. Thomas, editor of his *Gesammelte Werke* (Leipzig, 1861, 3 v.); and the charming essay in Ludwig Steub, *Herbsttage in Tirol* (Munich, 1867), 40–84. Fallmerayer's *Gesammelte Werke* were reviewed in *NAR*, XCIX (1864), 281–87.

For two years he followed theology and the Semitic languages, supporting himself as a private tutor. Then he shifted to Landshut, where the University of Bavaria was located before it was removed to Munich, and after a brief fling at law, finally found his métier in history and philology. The Napoleonic Wars of 1813 called the young student, like hundreds of his fellows, to join the colors. While on garrison duty at Lindau (on Lake Constance) after the second peace of Paris, he devoted his leisure to Modern Greek, Turkish, and Persian. Receiving his discharge from the army in 1818, he became instructor at the gymnasium at Augsburg, and soon advanced to the lectureship of history at the Lyceum of Landshut. To obtain a gold prize medal offered by the University of Copenhagen, he produced the *Geschichte des Kaisertums von Trapezunt* (Munich, 1827).[19] It rested upon diligent and independent researches in Greek and Oriental manuscripts at Vienna and in the library of Cardinal Bessarion in Venice. Although the greatness of the Empire of Trebizond had filled the songs of medieval Europe, the story of three centuries (1204–1426) had been lost, and Gibbon himself had given up all hopes for the recovery of its history. By discovering the chronicle of Michael Panaretos and drafting Turkish and Persian manuscripts into service, Fallmerayer was able to cast a brilliant light upon this forgotten period. Europe had a right to expect much of this coming scholar.

Between 1831 and 1847 Fallmerayer travelled much in the East.[20] After the revolution of 1848 he was invited to a chair of history in Munich, and made delegate to the Frankfort Congress. His independent views spoiled his chances with either side, and after following the rump-parliament to Stuttgart he lost his position and had to flee to Switzerland until the amnesty of 1850. After 1849 he lived in comparative retirement. Four years before had appeared the work that made him famous in German literature. The *Fragmente aus dem Orient* [21] were the precipitation of his travels, and their exquisite style caused their author to pass generally under the appellation of "the Fragmentist." Here the poet spoke in the idyllic descriptions of Eastern scenery. In the German public's mind, they were the epitome of that travel literature already referred to.[22]

[19] For the historians of Trebizond, see GIBBON, VI, 421 note.

[20] In 1831–34 he visited Egypt, Palestine, Syria, Cyprus, Rhodes, Constantinople, Greece, and Naples. He was in the company of Count Ostermann Tolstoi of Russia, a staunch patron of his. In 1836 he went to southern France and Italy; in 1840 (after spending most of the preceding four years with the Count at Geneva) he visited Constantinople, Trebizond, Athos, Macedonia, Thessaly, and Greece, and after another stay at Munich he was back in Palestine, Syria, and Asia Minor in 1847.

[21] Stuttgart, 1845, 2 v.; 2nd ed. in 1 v., with introduction by G. M. Thomas, 1877.

[22] "The stillness of the palm groves and the murmur of the streams, the fragrant air and the gorgeous sunset, the mystery of ruins and the luxury of life, all the sadness and all the splendor

Fifteen years before Fallmerayer had given Europe its first rude shock. Picture the horror of the curious Phil-hellene in 1830, who considered the Greek kingdom now at last established, and read at the very start of the preface of the *Geschichte der Halbinsel Morea:*

> Das Geschlecht der Hellenen ist in Europa ausgerottet. . . . Eine zweifache Erd-schichte, aus Trümmern und Moder zweier neuen und verschiedenen Menschenrassen aufgehäuft, decket die Gräber dieses alten Volkes. . . . Denn auch nicht ein Tropfen ächten und ungemischten Hellenenblutes fliesset in den Adern der christlichen Bevölkerung des heutigen Griechenlands.[23]

Fallmerayer's startling thesis was that the old Hellenic stock had been completely displaced by successive invasions of Slavs and Albanians. The modern Greeks were a mongrel nation. A later treatise maintained that from the sixth to the tenth century Athens lay waste and empty and without a history.[24] Philanthropic souls felt they were being made a laughing-stock; the newly-risen Greek nation mentioned Fallmerayer's name with loathing and vindictive hatred; diplomats resented the rise of an historical theory which would justify Russia's pretensions toward Constantinople. But in the face of the hue and cry the Bavarian teacher stood at bay, and the controversy [25] led to ethnographic studies which opened the eyes of European scholars to the importance of the Slav factor in the Byzantine Middle Ages. The sweeping generalizations of Fallmerayer were quite untenable, but Europe was soon disappointed that the revived Greek race failed to produce geniuses comparable to those of antiquity.[26] Zinkeisen was the first opponent to see the light and establish the right method: a systematic reading of the Byzantine historians. Hopf, another critic, reduced Fallmerayer's thesis to the more reasonable statement that there is a large admixture of Slavonic blood in the veins of the modern Greek.[27]

of the East,—are nowhere rendered more vividly than in the *Fragments*. . . . Well might Abd-ül-Medschid, in silent reproach of Germany, decorate him with the brilliant order of Nischan-Iftichan." *NAR* (n. 18), 286.

[23] Stuttgart and Tübingen, 1830–36, 2 v. in 1. Vol. I, preface, pp. iii–iv.

[24] *Welchen Einfluss hatte die Besetzung Griechenlands durch die Slawen auf das Schicksal der Stadt Athen und der Landschaft Attika?* (1835); cp. also "Das Albanesische Element in Griechenland," *Abhandlungen der historischen Klasse der kgl. bayerischen Akademie* (Munich), VIII, pt. ii (1857), 417–87, pt. iii (1860), 650–736, and IX, pt. i (1862), 1–110.

[25] Summarized in Gustav Hertzberg, *Geschichte Griechenlands*, 1, 121–29; and Vasiliev (n. 1), I, 213–16.

[26] "All came expecting to find the Peloponnesus filled with Plutarch's men, and all returned thinking the inhabitants of Newgate more moral," said Sir Charles Napier.

[27] It may put Fallmerayer's labors and writings in a clearer light if he is considered as something of a Slavophobe. The heroic Hellenes whom Europe cheered were to him but a confused horde of Slavs masking the grim and insidious advance of Russia. To weaken the Ottoman Empire was to subvert Germany. "Destroy Constantinople, and dam up the Bosphorus," he cried to the statesmen of Europe long before the Crimean War, "or the Cossacks will be upon you." From the fifth to the thirteenth century, and again in the nineteenth, the stream of Slavic desires has moved southward. "No longer content with the birch-juice of the north, Gog craves the oranges of the South. The grapes of Kerasant taste sweeter to him than the

Fallmerayer is a case of those scholars who do otherwise than they intend. His contentions do not have the support of modern scholars; his very boldness and obstinacy have led to his discredit, and even originality has been denied him; but the history of Byzantium and of the Balkan nations owes him much. Since his day the Byzantine Empire has become a chapter in the history of nations, and no one has cultivated it more avidly than the Slavs.[28]

The outstanding works of the second third of the nineteenth century were either treatises on Graeco-Roman law, or general histories of Byzantium. Harking back to the traditions of the sixteenth-century French school of Cujas, and contemning Savigny's neglect, Heimbach produced a six-volume edition of the *Basilica* (1835–50), and Mortreuil wrote a *Histoire du droit byzantin* (1843). At Heidelberg Karl Eduard Zachariae von Lingenthal lectured on Graeco-Roman law,[29] and his solid researches culminated in the *Geschichte des Griechisch-Römischen Rechts* (1856–64) and the great collection of the *Jus Graeco-Romanum* (1866–84).

Meanwhile in England the mantle of Gibbon had fallen upon George Finlay (1799–1875).[30] Two men could hardly be further apart in life and temperament. Born of Scotch parents at Faversham in Kent, Finlay studied for the law at Glasgow, and then crossed the Channel to Göttingen. But the serious young student of Roman jurisprudence became enthralled with the fascinating question of Greek independence. "I conversed much with everybody I met who had visited Greece, read all the works of modern travellers, and associated a great deal with the only Greek who was then studying at Göttingen." In 1823 he transferred his studies to Greek soil, met Lord Byron and Sir Charles Napier, and for two months spent nearly every evening discussing Greek affairs with the former. Quitting the peninsula for reasons of health after a stay of more than a year, he came to Edinburgh University and took his examinations for the Scottish bar. But life at home was dull, and the voice of Hellas could not be resisted. In 1827 Finlay took part in the attempt of Lord Cochrane and Sir Richard Church to relieve Athens.

whortle-berries of Smolensk." If Russia with its allied neighbors, one in blood and kin, possesses Constantinople and the Illyrian triangle, he warned, it will be master of the Old World. Europe's future lies at the Bosphorus! *NAR* (n. 1), 286–87.

[28] The Russian Byzantinists are conveniently summarized in Vasiliev (n. 1), I, 42–52.

[29] H. Mounier, "Charles-Edouard Zachariae von Lingenthal," in *Nouvelle revue historique du droit*, 1895, p. 678.

[30] His illuminating autobiography is printed in H. F. Tozer's edition of Finlay's *History of Greece, from Its Conquest by the Romans to the Present Time* (Oxford, 1877, 7 v.), I, pp. xxix–xliv; Vasiliev (n. 1), 24–28; see also the article in *DNB*, XIX, 30–31; Freeman (n. 9), 231–77, 310–78; GIBBON, I, introd., pp. liv–lv; William Miller, "The Journals of Finlay and Jarvis," *EHR*, XLI (1926), 514–25; *ER*, CXLVIII (1878), 232–62; *NBR*, XXII (1854–55), 343–75; *FM*, XXX (1844), 450–65.

With Greek independence attained, he determined to settle down in his adopted land, and aid in its economic recovery. He purchased an estate, but his hopes of introducing more efficient agricultural methods merely brought him to bankruptcy in a very short time. Unembittered by his experience, Finlay turned to cultivate the fields of Greek history and to excavate the treasures of her past. The series of volumes which began in 1843 with *Greece under the Romans* and which his editor Tozer later combined in seven volumes under a comprehensive title [31] cover two millenniums of the life of the Greek nation "in Roman subjection, Byzantine servitude, and Turkish slavery." Finlay declared that "two thousand years of suffering have not obliterated the national character, nor extinguished the national ambition." A keen observer who in all cases departed from his contemporary surroundings, Finlay traced back link by link the chain of political, social, ecclesiastical, and especially economic conditions which explain the Attic peasant of today, and of all intervening ages since the peasant of Alexander the Great. He was more concerned with internal history than with external events. He brought a great mass of new knowledge, and illuminated his material with fresh reflections. Freeman, writing shortly after the mid-century (1855), hailed it as the greatest work in English historiography since Gibbon. The whole bespeaks original study and a keen awareness of the subject, and abounds in modern analogies; but Finlay wrote when no monographs existed to guide or control him. Gregorovius pointed out that it was written without the use of any archival material; and by the end of the century Diehl dismissed the work as superficial. Yet Gibbon and Finlay remain the only Englishmen who have treated the entire eleven centuries of the Eastern Empire. The author who had begun to write the history of the Greek Revolution finally took up Byzantine history because without it he could not make the story of modern Greece intelligible. As Greece, and not Constantinople, forms the center of his picture, the work is not wholly homogeneous. [32]

Meanwhile French interest in the Balkans and Greece had increased. A host of books on the subject poured from the press, [33] the most notable of which was Edgar Quinet's *La Grèce moderne et de ses rapports avec l'antiquité* (1830). In 1828 Charles X sent out a geographical and archaeological expedition to Greece; later Louis Philippe, urged by Guizot, his minister, sent Texier to Asia Minor; and in 1842 Le Bas

---

[31] *A History of Greece from Its Conquest by the Romans to the Present Time, B. C. 146 to A. D. 1864* (Oxford, 1877). The portion from 146 B.C. to 1453 A.D. has also been translated into German.

[32] For his own summary of his division of Greek history after 146 B.C. into six periods, see Tozer's edition (n. 31), I, xvii–xix.

[33] For a list of them see Louis Halphen, "La Renaissance de l'histoire ancienne en France," *RH*, CXVI (1914), 47–60.

bróught back a great collection of ancient Greek inscriptions.[34] Finally, in 1846 the École française at Athens was established, though in the first years it pursued archaeology and art more than history.

While Finlay was writing her history, Hellas might also lay claim to the filial labors of a native professor at the University of Athens. Papparigopoulos (1815–1891)[35] followed briefer studies by a history of his people whose five volumes occupied him for thirty years.[36] The work is significant for being composed in the modern Greek vernacular. Nearly four of the volumes pertain to the Byzantine period. A strongly nationalistic tone carries his narrative, and he asserted that the Hellenic reforms of the eighth century (his favorite epoch was that of the Iconoclastic emperors) were from a social viewpoint broader and more systematic than those essayed later in the West. Indeed they failed because they were too advanced for their time and led to a reaction. He went so far as to claim that Byzantine Hellenism was the inspiration and ancestor of modern Hellenism, and assumed some national spirit to have existed through all the centuries. For foreign readers he summarized his results in a French volume, the *Histoire de la civilisation hellénique*, and presented a similar résumé in Greek to his own nation.[37] Lack of an index or documentation makes it difficult to consult or verify his work. Vasiliev allows him merit for having brought out the importance and the complexity of the Iconoclastic movement.

More substantial than either of these two works was one of German authorship. Unfortunately the history of Carl Hopf (1832–73)[38] never became accessible to the general public, but was "buried," as Gregorovius put it, "in the catacombs of the encyclopedia of Ersch and Gruber."[39] This form of publication also precluded the addition of any table of contents or index. Hopf was one of the tireless scholars of his century, a native of Westphalia, where his father was a secondary school teacher and especially interested in Homer. From his youth Hopf manifested a remarkable memory and a gift for languages. He made his studies at Bonn, became assistant there, and was drawn to the period of Greek history under the Frankish domination after 1204.

---

[34] Halphen, *loc. cit.*, 53 and notes. For a full account of this subject, see René Canat, *La renaissance de la Grèce antique, 1820–50* (Paris, 1911), chs. ii–iii.

[35] Vasiliev (n. 1), I, 28–29.

[36] *Historia tou Hellenikou ethnous* (Athens, 1860–77, 5 v.; several other editions, the last by Karolides, Athens, 1925, 6 v.), reviewed in *RH*, VII (1878), 133–34, and IX (1879), 246–50.

[37] The French volume appeared in Paris, 1878. The work in Greek was entitled *The Most Instructive Results of the History of the Greek People* (Athens, 1899).

[38] Bibliography in *Byzantinische Zeitchrift*, IV (1895), 240.

[39] *Geschichte Griechenlands vom Beginne des Mittelalters bis auf die neuere Zeit*, (1867–68), in volumes LXXXV and LXXXVI of the *Allgemeine Encyklopädie der Wissenschaften und Künste*. Quotation from Ferdinand Gregorovius, *Geschichte der Stadt Athen im Mittelalter* (3rd ed., Stuttgart, 1889, 2 v.), I, p. xix.

In 1853–54 he made his first journey to Italy. Diligent labors in private archives led to the publication of various documents and monographs on the history of individual Frankish kingdoms in Greece itself and on the Aegean islands. Advanced to a professorship at Greifswald, and later made librarian and professor at Königsberg, Hopf continued his researches in the later Middle Ages. On a second journey (1861–63) to Genoa, Naples, Palermo, Malta, Corfu, Zante, Scyros, Naxos, and Greece, he collected an enormous number of manuscripts; but death cut him off in his prime before he was able to edit them. The chief study which he left behind was largely a political history, written with an extraordinary fidelity to detail, based upon archival matter and often upon his own collected manuscripts. It centers upon the Frankish period, and was the first thorough account of the external history of this period, not only in the chief centers, but also throughout the small islands. As not all of his manuscripts have yet been published, the work on occasion takes the place of a primary source.

Hopf's work was a revelation, and contained a scholarly polemic against the theories of Fallmerayer upon the question of the Slavs in Greece. But it lacked the benefit of a final revision, and its execrable style masked the real achievements. Luckily Gustav Hertzberg [40] popularized Hopf's researches in his *Geschichte Griechenlands* (1876–78) and the *Geschichte der Byzantiner und des osmanischen Reiches* (1883), the first of which Diehl, in 1901, called the best manual on the subject. Gregorovius himself turned Hopf's pages to good account, and he has remained a quarry for many lesser writers. His manuscripts are preserved in the Berlin national library.

While dealing with Hopf, it is proper to mention Gregorovius' contribution. Famous for his history of Rome in the Middle Ages, the great scholar was led to study another center of culture. His *Geschichte der Stadt Athen im Mittelalter* (Stuttgart, 1889) declared that Hopf was the basis for all future investigations; but his own brilliant study utilized new-found materials and added the cultural phases which Hopf generally neglected. The story of the famous city was carried down to the nineteenth century, with the empire as a background.

French scholarship could point to a few contributions in the first six decades of the century, but they were chiefly the works of scat-

---

[40] Hertzberg was first a student of Greek and Roman antiquity, then became interested in the Middle Ages. He was no original writer himself. The *Geschichte Griechenlands seit dem Absterben des antiken Lebens bis zur Gegenwart* comprised 4 volumes (Gotha, 1875–79). Of the other work, *Geschichte der Byzantiner und des osmanischen Reiches bis gegen Ende des sechszehnten Jahrhunderts* (Berlin, 1883), a Russian translation was published at Moscow (1896), by P. V. Bezobrazov, which added summaries of the recent work done by Russian scholars, particularly on internal affairs, and supplemented Hertzberg on court ceremonial, industry and peasant life, serfdom and taxation.

tered philologists, or of students of jurisprudence already mentioned. Buchon [41] was the first after Du Cange to resume the treatment of the Latin Empire and the Frankish states in Hellas. No scholar may forget, however, the *Patrologia Graeca* of the Abbé Migne (165 volumes, Greek and Latin, 1857–66) which with all its faults remains the most complete collection of Byzantine texts. But any widespread interest in Byzantium did not appear in France, until the years 1868 to 1870. In the former year the École Pratique des Hautes Études was established; in the latter year Rambaud published his *Constantin Porphyrogénète*. It inaugurated a new period, when the rash composition of general histories was replaced by careful monographs, and Rambaud thus initiated the scientific handling of Byzantine history. [42] In the study of a single ruler he combined a critical examination of the historians and literature of his era, a lucid exposition of the status of the provinces and vassal states, a sketch of the neighbors of the Empire, and a new concept of Byzantine history. Many regretted that Rambaud did not make Byzantium the field of his life work, but let himself be drawn away first to Russia, and then to French civilization. He returned to his earlier field only in a few essays, and the sketch in the *Histoire générale* which he edited together with Lavisse. Nonetheless, his first great work helped to stimulate French scholars into an energy which threatened the leadership in Byzantine studies formerly held by Germany and England.

For the last thirty years of the nineteenth century the tide of enthusiasm continued to rise. Historian after historian marvelled at the injustice or blindness of their predecessors. These apologists for Byzantine civilization wrote with almost the fervor of the Romanticists who had restored the Middle Ages of the West. [43] Bikelas [44] wrote from the point of view of a Greek in whose brain the ideas of the Greek insurrection were still vibrating. Frederic Harrison, Rambaud, and Diehl alleged that the bulk of the odium cast upon the Byzantine Empire was due to the Latin Church. No empire, it was asserted, could face incredible dangers and difficulties for eleven centuries without manifesting weaknesses or yielding to vices; but the strange vitality of the Byzantine

[41] Jean-A. C. Buchon, *Recherches et matériaux pour servir à une histoire de la domination française aux XIIIᵉ, XIVᵉ, et XVᵉ siècles dans les provinces, démembrées de l'Empire grec* (Paris, 1840, 2 pts., 1 v.); *Histoire des conquêtes et de l'établissement des Français dans les États de l'ancienne Grèce* (Paris, 1846).

[42] Alfred Rambaud, *L'empire grec au dixième siècle: Constantin Porphyrogénète* (Paris, 1870). In Germany he was anticipated by Hergenröther's magnificent work, *Photius, Patriarch von Constantinopel, sein Leben, seine Schriften, und das griechische Schisma* (Regensburg, 1867–69, 3 v.).

[43] Freeman (n. 9), 234–40, discusses sanely and comprehensively the causes for the long neglect of Byzantine history.

[44] Demetrios Bikelas, *Les Grecs au moyen âge*, tr. from Greek into French by Émile Legrand (Paris, 1878), 129.

civilization was lauded.[45]   They stressed the merits of the Eastern Empire as a bulwark for the kingdoms of the West against the Arabs, Turks, and Slavs, and its contributions to medieval civilization. Schlumberger finally wrote, with the poetic diction of the French savant, of "la belle et palpitante histoire de Byzance." [46]

The nationalistic spirit which surged upward impetuously among the Slavic nations led them to investigate their past history, and for materials they were obliged to search Byzantine chroniclers. Every step in the research of these historians was a corresponding revelation for the student of Byzantium itself. In addition to Paparrigopoulos' work upon the Greeks, already mentioned, prominent examples of such indirectly useful works may be found in Jireček's *Geschichte der Bulgaren* (1876), or Xenopol's *Histoire des Romains* (1896). Western writers themselves were subdividing the Empire; thus Fallmerayer's *Morea* was a predecessor of Gregorovius' *Geschichte der Stadt Athen*, and of Diehl's *L'Afrique byzantine* (1896). For Italy, there was Hodgkin's *Italy and Her Invaders*, Diehl's *Études sur l'administration byzantine dans l'exarchat de Ravenne* (1888), and Hartmann's *Untersuchungen zur Geschichte der byzantinischen Verwaltung in Italien* (1889). Brooks [47] and Vasiliev [48] began to open a new field in Arab-Byzantine relations. By the early nineties, there could be no doubt of it: Byzantine history was an established discipline all by itself, a subject which no scholar need be ashamed of, and one which employed as acute and delicate tools as any other field of history. But labors on the prodigious front of such a medieval civilization were still largely scattered or separated by national boundaries; and there was no organization or division of labor.

The internationalization of Byzantine history, if one may employ the term, was largely the work of one man and one organ: Karl Krumbacher's *Byzantinische Zeitschrift*. The year 1892 which saw its establishment was a landmark. The new journal became a clearing-house for recent researches, an indispensable bibliographical tool in a difficult field,[49] and set new and broad standards for work in Byzantine civilization. Krumbacher (1856–1909) [50] could never have begun his review so

[45] Rambaud (n. 42), quoting from Manasses, writes p. viii: "L'empire, cette vieille femme, apparaît comme une jeune fille, parée d'or et de pierres precieuses."

[46] *L'Épopée byzantine*, II, p. vi.

[47] E. W. Brooks, "Byzantines and Arabs in the Time of the Early Abbasids, 750–813," *EHR*, XV (1900), 728–47, and other articles by the same author *ibid.*, XVI (1901), 84–92; "The Arabs in Asia Minor (641–750), from Arabic Sources," *Journal of Hellenic Studies*, XVIII (1898), 182–208; and *ibid.*, XIX (1899), 19 ff.

[48] *Byzance et les Arabes au temps de la dynastie amorienne* (St. Petersburg, 1900).

[49] For some notion of the difficulties of keeping abreast with modern Byzantine researches, see the article of Diehl in *RSH* (n. 1), 177–225.

[50] See preface to *Byzantinische Zeitschrift*, XIX (1900), pp. iii–vi, with portrait, and the complete list of his writings *ibid.*, 700–08; see also Karl Dietrich, in *Biographisches Jahrbuch und deutscher Nekrolog*, XIV (1912), 136–42; the same, "Zum Gedächtnis an Karl Krum-

successfully, however, if it had not been that his *Geschichte der byzantinischen Litteratur* published the year before (1891) had put him at once at the head of the German Byzantinists. He was a native of Kuernach, in Bavaria, and then professor of medieval and modern Greek at Munich (1897–1909). Reading a history of the Greek war for independence as a boy determined his future; he became an ardent Philhellene. His studies were made in Munich and Leipzig, and he began to teach at the former place in 1891. The Bavarian government established a special chair for this founder of medieval and modern Greek philology, and his seminar became the world center for these studies. But his spirit swept far beyond the confines of mere philology. The *Geschichte der byzantinischen Litteratur* was virtually an encyclopedia of Byzantine culture. Bury said of the second edition that it was "a work whose reputation is now so thoroughly established that it would be an impertinence to praise it." Its bibliographies still form the greatest single tool of any Byzantinist.[51]

Krumbacher appreciated that Byzantine studies labored under the double burden of dilettantism and the lack of any organ of co-ordination. The famous charter essay in the first issue of his *Zeitschrift* set forth the aims and indicated the scope of the science of *Byzantinistik* which herein declared its right to a separate and individual existence. No longer should it be a mere auxiliary study, or a contemptible appendix to classical philology and history. Here was a "grand, articulate, pregnant history," to be studied primarily for its own sake. In turn, it might be expected to throw light on classical and Romance philology, on the Slavic tongues, theology, the legend and story literature of the Occident, innumerable fields of history, geography, ethnography, art, Roman and Turkish law, and medicine. A journal as Krumbacher planned it would be possible only with the co-operation of many lands; it would publish articles in any of the chief European languages.[52] To preserve the needed unity of a civilization, it welcomed essays upon social, economic, intellectual, and aesthetic problems as well as political and ecclesiastical history. Almost the entire gamut of human activity might find shelter in its pages, provided it pertained to Byzantium.

bacher," *Neue Jahrbücher für das klassische Altertum*, XIII (1910), 279–95; A. Vasiliev in *ESS*, VIII, 605; Hermann A. Buk, *Karl Krumbacher zur zehnten Wiederkehr seines Todestages* (Trier, 1919); A. Heisenberg, in the *Allgäuer* [Krumbacher's native canton] *Geschichtsfreund*, N. F., XXIV (1925); Kuhn-Marc, "Nekrolog auf Karl Krumbacher," *Sitzungsberichte der k. bayerischen Akademie der Wissenschaften*, phil.-hist. Klasse, 1910.

[51] See Bury's two reviews in *Classical Review*, V (1891), 318–20, and XI (1897), 207–12. The second edition in 1897 included chapters on theological and hagiographical literature by A. Ehrhard, and a sketch of the history of the Empire by Gelzer which Bury called "a miracle of able exposition." At the end of the work are nearly a hundred pages of an elaborate classified bibliography.

[52] Its first volume included contributions in German, English, French, Italian, and modern Greek.

From its opening number the new periodical sustained a uniformly high quality,[53] until its exhausted but zealous editor laid down his pen forever at the age of fifty-four. He had guided its policies for eighteen years. Modestly he felt his responsibility. From the beginning Krumbacher foresaw that it would be the rallying point of a young and eager host of scholars, and that he would have to be the captain of their fortunes. He also appreciated the pedagogical role his journal must play, and allotted large space (and what proportion of his own time!) to critical reviews of all work published. Seldom has a great organizer seen more clearly or planned more wisely and courageously.

The example of the *Byzantinische Zeitschrift* led to a Slavic counterpart. In 1894 the *Vizantijsky Vremennik* was founded at St. Petersburg under the direction of Vasilievskij and Regel. The good seed that these and later journals scattered over Europe brought gladdening results. In the last decade of the nineteenth century, the École des Hautes Études undertook to offer a course in Byzantine and modern Greek philology, and another on "Christianisme byzantin." The Russian Archaeological Institute established at Constantinople devoted most of its attention to the Byzantine Middle Ages. The French School at Athens, which since the days when Coulanges wrote on the island of Chios had maintained a tradition of interest in the Eastern Empire through the labors of such men as Diehl and Bayet, began work on a corpus of Byzantine inscriptions. Bavaria, we have seen, established a chair at Munich for Krumbacher in 1893. The universities of St. Petersburg, Leyden, Budapest, and Odessa began to give similar courses in philology, and in 1898 Leipzig added Byzantine art. The University of Paris had the distinction of establishing the first chair in Byzantine history (1898), which Charles Diehl has honorably occupied for more than a quarter century.

At the turn of the century, when Diehl paused to review the progress that had been made,[54] Byzantine studies had "arrived." They had won the grudging welcome of Western medieval scholars and classicists. They had captured even the more popular field of the theater and the novel (Sardou, Jean Lombard, Paul Adam). When in 1868–70 Leger, Drapeyron, and Rambaud laid their doctoral theses before the Sorbonne on *Cyrille et Méthode*, *Heraclius*, and *Constantin Porphyrogénète*, they made only a passing impression. Ten years brought a complete volte-face. The progress of the nineties could be read in the first ten volumes

---

[53] The first volume is a roll-call of famous names: Carl de Boor, Heinrich Gelzer, J. B. Bury, Josef Strzygowski, Charles Diehl, G. N. Hatzidakis, V. Jagic, Edwin Patzig, Spyr. P. Lambros, Th. Noeldeke, Carl Neumann, L. Duchesne, etc.

[54] In *RSH* (n. 1).

of the *Byzantinische Zeitschrift*, or the doubled size of Krumbacher's *Literatturgeschichte* in its second edition (1897).

As we pass into the twentieth century, the great scholars in France were Gustav Schlumberger,[55] Rambaud, and Charles Diehl. Krumbacher was until his death in 1909 the arbiter in Germany. Russia had Vasiliev and F. Uspenskij.[56] England had produced one of her greatest scholars in John Bagnell Bury (1861–1927).[57]

To be strictly correct, Bury was born in Ireland. His father was a clergyman who early introduced his son to the classics. There is a story that he began Latin at four and was well grounded in Greek grammar at ten. From Foyle College, Londonderry, he went to Trinity College, Dublin. He seemed to be destined for a brilliant career as a classical scholar. In 1880 he spent six months at Göttingen, studying Sanskrit under Benfey, as well as Syriac and Hebrew. He took many prizes, but none testified more eloquently to his abilities than the fact that Professor Mahaffy chose this undergraduate student of twenty to collaborate in an edition of the *Hippolytus* of Euripides. In 1885 Bury obtained a fellowship at Trinity. The same year he acquired a knowledge of Russian. He possessed an uncanny ability to pick up a language in weeks where other scholars required months; eventually he could read most Slavic savants in their own medium.

Bury approached Byzantine studies through classical antiquity. For some time he busied himself composing notes on his Greek and Latin readings, and edited the Nemean and the Isthmian Odes of Pindar, whom he admired as expressive of the characteristic Greek spirit. Before long his wide active interests swept him into the Byzantine chroniclers. In 1885 he knew little of the Byzantine Empire. Four years later, at the age of twenty-seven, he had produced one of the most profound and solid works of the century: *A History of the Later Roman Empire, from Arcadius to Irene, 395–800 A.D.*, which won the warm approbation of Freeman.[58] In 1893, when Bury was only thirty-two years of age, he was appointed professor of modern history at Dublin, and five years later he was elevated to the regius

[55] See *Byzantinische Zeitschrift*, XXIX (1929), 159.
[56] See the notice on Uspenskij in *Byzantinische Zeitschrift*, XXVIII (1928), 479–80. For Russian scholars let reference be made again to Vasiliev (n. 1), I, 42–52.
[57] *A Bibliography of the Works of J. B. Bury*, together with a memoir by Norman H. Baynes (Cambridge, 1929); the memoir of R. H. Murray, prefixed to his edition of Bury's *History of the Papacy in the Nineteenth Century, 1864–1878* (London, 1930), on p. lxi of which will be found a valuable list of notices in the various journals after his death; G. P. Gooch, "The Cambridge Chair of Modern History," in his *Studies in Modern History* (London and New York, 1931), 319–23.
[58] London, 1889, 2 v. It may be remarked that few writers influenced Bury as much as Freeman. Bury later edited Freeman's *Historical Geography* and his study on the Greek federations.

professorship of Greek, so that he held two Trinity chairs simultaneously. He resigned them both in 1902 to become regius professor of modern history at Cambridge.

Many readers of history know Bury only as the erudite editor of Gibbon's monumental history, which he provided with an introduction and numerous notes (1896–1900). No scholar today quotes any edition of Gibbon save Bury's.[59] Even disregarding his Byzantine historical writings, Bury would have left his mark as a classical Greek scholar. The *Life of St. Patrick and His Place in History* (1905) is a sample of his sound and critical method. Few hagiographers have so cut to the core of nebulous matter surrounded by sentiment and hallowed tradition. But most of his writings have been devoted to the Greek East. He continued his former two volumes twenty-three years later by what should be called the third, *A History of the Eastern Roman Empire from the Fall of Irene to the Accession of Basil I, 802–867 A.D.* (London, 1912). After another dozen years, the first work appeared in an enlarged and rewritten edition, the *History of the Later Roman Empire from 395–565 A.D.* (1923).

Bury contended for the existence of a continuous Roman Empire, and was very careful to defend his nomenclature. He declined to employ the terms "Byzantine" or "Greek," as the Roman emperors continued from Augustus down to Constantine XI in 1453. Only after the coronation of Charlemagne, he believed, is it proper to speak of a Western and an Eastern Empire. Like Gibbon, Bury held that no empire fell in 476; and Charlemagne's coronation in Rome in 800 was only a new offshoot of a still living trunk.[60]

Bury possessed the equipment of the philologist, but he was also a profound philosopher. His attitude was that of a rationalist; he declared that Christianity and similar religions demanded a faith that reason could not justify. "There is nothing for it but to trust the light of our reason. Its candle power may be low, but it is the only light we have."[61] Yet he had a profound faith in progress, which he believed to be a constant, though slow, evolution upwards. In that struggle he believed the historian could find a useful part.

In his volumes on Byzantine history, Bury did not try to write a

[59] There is a certain anomaly in Bury having been the editor of this revised edition of Gibbon. For he condemned the Middle Ages as roundly as the historians of the eighteenth century, describing the epoch as "a millennium in which reason was enchained, thought was enslaved, and knowledge made no progress."—*History of Freedom of Thought* (London, 1913), p. 52. One is constrained to think that his passion for Greek, not for Greek history, led him into the medieval history of Greece and the Balkans.

[60] Cp. the introduction of Bury's first edition, pp. v–viii (omitted in the second). Bury once hazarded the surmise that it was really the ambitious Irene who suggested the coronation of Charlemagne prior to her matrimonial hopes.

[61] Quoted from the article by Norman Baynes in *ESS*, III, 79.

Kulturgeschichte, but he did give unusual space to internal history. Administrative institutions, literature, social life, geography, and topographical discussions fill his pages. His wife wrote an excellent chapter on Byzantine art in one of the volumes. As a classical scholar, he neither scorned the productions of Byzantine writers, nor gave them extravagant praise. He has said that the scholars of Byzantium did not make over to posterity a legacy of one single original work of genius. Bury weighed separately the literary and the historical value of a source. Procopius, "the most excellent Greek historian since Polybius," was a man of intellect, but a despicable character. Like Ranke he decided adversely in the question of Procopius' direct authorship for the *Secret History;* but modern writers have tended to follow Dahn's view that it is genuine.

Bury's life coincided closely, as Miller has pointed out, with the revival of Byzantine studies. He took over the torch from Finlay, but was more objective than either of his two great English predecessors, Gibbon and Finlay. His perspective was a long one, and the Byzantinist wrote one of the finest manuals on Ancient Greece (1900) and planned the magnificent structure of the *Cambridge Ancient* and the *Cambridge Medieval History.* Oddly enough, though he read everything, Bury was himself hardly known in Greece (among any but scholars) or his works translated there. Despite his many travels in the lands of his interest, he had no concern for a closer acquaintance with the modern Greeks, such as Finlay possessed, or the warm sense of kinship which filled Paparrigopoulos or Bikelas. He possessed little that could have made him a blind Phil-hellene.

Krumbacher once remarked how in the division of labor national psychology might be observed.[62] In the critical treatment of texts the Germans took the lead. The Louvre and the Bonn Byzantine collections proved unequal to the demands of modern scholars. In 1870 the famous Teubner house began to add Byzantine writers to their series of ancient classics, and Dindorf and Reiffenscheid furnished excellent texts. De Boor,[63] a pupil of Mommsen, gave the classic example of a critical edition in his version of the *Chronicle* of Theophano (1883–85). Gelzer began a series for the University of Jena: *Scriptores sacri et*

---

[62] "Die Deutschen wie Tafel, Hopf, F. Hirsch, De Boor, Gelzer, Karl Neumann, Seger u.a. haben sich die kritische Zubereitung des Quellenmaterials und sonstige philologische Kleinarbeit ausgesucht, die Russen und Franzosen wie Vasiljevskij, Uspenskij, Kondakov, Rambaud, Diehl, Schlumberger widmen sich vornehmlich der innern Geschichte, dem Verwaltungs- und Finanzwesen und der Kunstgeschichte, die Englaender (Gibbon, Finlay, Bury) beschraenken sich fast ausschliesslich auf die zusammenfassende, durch philosophischen, staatsmaennischen Geist belebte Darstellung der Hauptmomente." *Byzantinische Zeitschrift,* I (1892), 8.

[63] Nekrolog in *Byzantinische Zeitschrift,* XXIV (1923), 495–96.

profani. Bury superintended a series of Greek and Oriental texts for
Methuen in England, but many of these were printed as *inedita*. A
prime difficulty with Byzantine materials, however, has been the frequent plagiarism of one author from another, so that strict editing is
necessary to indicate all valueless multiplication of testimony. Regel
began the *Fontes rerum byzantinarum* in Russia (1811), and the tireless
Papadopoulos-Kerameus [64] started a *Fontes historiae Trapezuntii* (1897).
The task of editing has been lightened by the publication of the catalogues of many great European depositories of manuscripts.[65] There
were occasional happy finds, as when Hirschfeld came upon the life of
the patriarch Euthymios in a "couvent perdu du lac d'Egherdir en
Pisidie" (1874). To date the chronicles have received far more attention than the memoirs and state documents. For the Munich Academy,
which took up the long-orphaned project of a corpus, Franz Doelger
began the *Regesten der Kaiserurkunden* (Vol. I, covering 565-1025 A.D.,
in 1924). Egyptian papyri offer many suggestions, and scholars have
not neglected the editing of Slavic and Oriental sources.[66]

Cardinal Pitra earned merit for his work on the canonist Demetrios
Chomatianos, and Nicole's edition of the *Livre du Préfet* (1893) threw
light on the excessive regulation of trade and commerce in the ninth
century. A most promising field is being uncovered in the popular
literature, whose relation is to classic Greek as the Romance languages
are to Latin. Pitra's contribution on the Byzantine religious poetry
(the melodes) is described elsewhere in this volume. Textual analysis
has attracted many German scholars since Hirsch began his *Byzantinische Studien* in 1876 on the writings of the ninth and tenth centuries.
In the auxiliary disciplines, Jean Psichari [67] deserves to be singled out
in philology, and Gustave Schlumberger has provided a most excellent
Sigillographie de l'Empire byzantin (1884).

General works and syntheses still wait the future, while the old works
of Hertzberg and others are quite outmoded. Gelzer, Jorga, and Diehl
have written excellent summaries. Bury never covered much more
than four centuries. The only deep scholar who has brought all of Byzantine history between the covers of one work is Vasiliev.[68] Good
monographs and studies are legion, and cannot be considered here.
Diehl has preempted the age of Justinian, and his countryman Schlumberger has dealt capably with the Macedonian emperors. Meanwhile

---

[64] *Ibid.*, XXI (1912), 678.

[65] E.g.: Omont's, for the Greek MSS. of French libraries, 1886–98, 4 v.; that of the Bollandists
and Franchi de Cavalieri on the hagiographical Greek MSS. of the Vatican; of S. Lambros on
the Greek MSS. of Mount Athos, 1895, 1900, 2 v.

[66] The first volume of the *Byzantinische Zeitschrift* brought an article on a Syrian chronicle.

[67] Necrology *ibid.*, XXXI (1931), 240.   [68] *History of the Byzantine Empire* (n. 1).

international co-operation has reknit the bonds severed by the Great War. The first congress of Byzantine studies exclusively was held in 1924 at Bucharest under the auspices of the Rumanian government. From the Historical Congress of 1923 at Brussels came the special section for Byzantine Studies, and the creation of the journal *Byzantion*. Such a book as Pirenne's posthumous *Mahomet et Charlemagne* suggests additional reasons for associating Byzantine history closer than ever with the origins and course of Western European history.[69]

[69] See *Byzantion*, X (1935), 815–17.

BOOK XI

*CHURCH HISTORIANS OF THE NINETEENTH
CENTURY*

CHAPTER LIX

CATHOLIC HISTORIANS [1]

T HE Catholic Church had shown alarm over the spread of rationalism in the eighteenth century. But the position of the Papacy was peculiarly difficult. Between 1767 and 1773 the Jesuit order almost everywhere, even in Catholic countries, was abolished. "Illuminism" bored within the hierarchy. In Germany there was a movement similar to Gallicanism among the archbishops.[2] Then came the French Revolution and the Napoleonic era, years of trial and humiliation for the Catholic Church.

In the first half of the nineteenth century, however, the history of the Church was profoundly tinged with romanticism. This culminated in France and Germany in Ultramontanism, which led to a new increase in the power of the Church and a greater appreciation of it among believers. A Protestant analogue of Ultramontanism was the Oxford movement in England. Together with the renewed rise of the Church went a revival of historical studies.

The new Catholic historiography in Germany began with Johann Adam Möhler (1796–1838).[3] He had studied for the priesthood under the Catholic faculty at Tübingen, and was called there in 1822 to replace certain insufficient teachers. Since he had never specialized in

---

[1] Karl Werner, *Geschichte der katholischen Theologie seit dem Trienter Konzil* (2nd ed., Munich and Leipzig, 1889); Martin Grabmann, *Die Geschichte der katholischen Theologie seit dem Ausgang der Väterzeit* (Freiburg i. Br., 1933); Heinrich Brück, *Geschichte der katholischen Kirche in Deutschland im neunzehnten Jahrhundert* (Mainz, 1902–08, 4 v. in 5); Carl Mirbt, *Der Ultramontanismus im 19. Jahrhundert* (Leipzig, 1902). E. L. Woodward, *Three Studies in European Conservatism* (London, 1929), has several fine chapters on the Papacy and Ultramontanism, the loss of temporal power, and the Vatican council of 1870.

[2] "Febronianism" derived its name from a treatise which the Trier professor and episcopal adviser Johann Nicholas von Hontheim published in 1763 under the pseudonym of Justinus Febronius, *De statu ecclesiae et legitima potestate Romani pontificis*. In effect it demanded for Germany the same privileges as France possessed in the Gallican liberties, and in the Emser Punctation of 1786 the archbishops of Cologne and Mainz demanded that the Pope surrender to the episcopate all the rights wrongfully drawn from the pseudo-Isidorean Decretals. Only the preference of the German bishops for the rule of the Pope rather than that of the archbishops prevented a strong movement toward a national Catholic Church. See F. K. Nielsen, *The History of the Papacy in the Nineteenth Century* (tr. by A. J. Mason), I, ch. v.

[3] Balthasar Wörner, *Johann Adam Möhler, ein Lebensbild*, ed. by P. B. Gams (Regensburg, 1886); J. Friedrich, *Johann Adam Möhler, der Symboliker, ein Beitrag zu seinem Leben und seiner Lehre* (Munich, 1894); GUILDAY, 240–76; F. Vigener, *Drei Gestalten aus dem modernen Katholizismus: Möhler, Diepenbrock, Döllinger* (*Historische Zeitschrift*, 1926, Beiheft 7); A. v. Schmid, "Der geistige Entwicklungsgang J. A. Möhlers," *Historisches Jahrbuch*, XVIII (1897), 322–56, 572–99; Bihlmeyer, "Möhler als Kirchenhistoriker," *Theologische Quartalschrift*, C (1919), 134–98; and *DR*, XVI (1844), 93–122.

church history, he was given a year's leave of absence, and divided his time between Berlin, Göttingen, and Vienna. At Göttingen Möhler listened to Planck, and at Berlin he was deeply impressed with Neander's idealism. Neander moved him, he said, to try to catch the spirit of the Church Fathers rather than their ideas.

Möhler returned to take up his duties at Tübingen in 1823 at the end of a decade of great changes. With the triumph of political reaction in Europe the Jesuits had been restored, and the Church had recovered many of its old privileges. In southern Germany a romantic neo-Catholicism arose. The triumvirate that guided it were Möhler at Tübingen, Döllinger at Munich, and Joseph von Görres, its publicist.

Möhler began the movement with *Die Einheit der Kirche* (1825),[4] the pioneer Catholic work on the history of dogma in Germany. Few read it without sharing the deep feeling of the author as he stressed the mission of the Church in promoting the common spiritual life of men. The book was an invitation and a challenge to young Catholics.[5]

While Möhler was writing his next monograph, on Athanasius, he was struck by the analogy between the liberal and rationalistic currents of the fourth century and those of his own contemporary Germany. This led to his famous *Symbolik* (1832), a review of the various non-Catholic churches, based upon a study of their creeds. The book created a furore and was translated into English, French, and Italian. Though Möhler felt his purpose had been irenic, the Protestant world took it as an attack, and his own colleague at Tübingen, F. C. Baur, countered with a sharp answer. Möhler was glad when Döllinger obtained for him an appointment at Munich.[6] There Möhler continued his preparations for his projected church history, but his health gave way, and much he planned was interrupted by his death in 1838 in his fortieth year.

It is difficult to judge Möhler as an historian, because such works as his *Kirchengeschichte* or *Patrologie* were published posthumously from notes taken by his students. Still there is a vividness and freshness about them, and the narrative sometimes attains brilliancy. Möhler's mental attitude may be understood from his famous saying:

[4] Other writings of his: *Athanasius der Grosse und die Kirche seiner Zeit, besonders im Kampfe mit dem Arianismus* (1827; 2nd rev. ed., Mainz, 1844); *Symbolik* (1832; 5th ed., Mainz, 1835); *Geschichte des Mönchtums in der Zeit seiner Entstehung und ersten Ausbildung*. Though the last was but a sketch, it was happier than his *Versuch über den Ursprung des Gnostizismus* (in the Festschriften for Planck, 1831). Möhler's well-known *Kirchengeschichte* (ed. by P. B. Gams, Regensburg, 1867–70, 4 v.) and *Patrologie* (ed. by F. X. Reithmayr, Regensburg, 1840) were only lecture notes edited by his students.

[5] GOOCH, 549 quotes Döllinger's remark to Friedrich in later years: "It fascinated us young men. We felt that Möhler had discovered a fresh, living Christianity. The ideal of a Church purified from its abuses became our goal, and the revival of theological science would bring with it the reform of the Church."

[6] Lord Acton has described their association and contrasted their characters, in *EHR*, V (1890), 700–44, reprinted in his *History of Freedom and Other Essays* (London, 1907).

He who truly lives in the Church will also live in the first age of the Church and understand it; and he who does not live in the present Church will not live in the old and will not understand it, for they are the same.[7]

He believed that only a Catholic was competent to write the history of Catholicism, but the integrity of the man speaks in his indignant words on the conditions in the Church at the time of the Reformation.[8] Möhler did not believe that history should be a mere catalogue of facts; he demanded an organic development and was the first Catholic writer to adopt the Hegelian principles in history, substituting for the impersonal Idea the Catholic God.

Johann Joseph Ignaz von Döllinger (1799–1890) [9] was the greatest of Catholic historians in the middle of the last century. Unfortunately, like his greatest disciple Lord Acton, his powers exceeded anything he ever left in writing. He entered the University of Würzburg at the age of sixteen, with the ambition of studying history, philology, philosophy, plus the natural sciences (!); but in 1818 he turned to theology, and finished at the seminary in Bamberg.

When Döllinger was called to Munich in 1826, Catholic theology lay supine, and the field of ecclesiastical history was most fallow of all. In view of Döllinger's great gifts this worked for an unfortunate handicap. He was fated to begin his career, as Lord Acton has pointed out, instructed by no powerful mind and guided by no surer hand than that of his own experience. His years of schooling had antedated the great rise of German historiography.

He had begun when Niebuhr was lecturing at Bonn and Hegel at Berlin; before Tischendorf unfolded his first manuscript; before Baur discovered the Tübingen hypothesis in the congregation of Corinth; before Rothe had planned his treatise on the primitive church, or Ranke had begun to pluck the plums for his modern popes. Guizot had not founded the *École des Chartes*, and the school of method was not yet opened at Berlin. The application of instruments of precision was just beginning, and what Prynne calls the heroic study of records had hardly molested the ancient reign of lives and chronicles. None had worked harder at his science and at himself than Döllinger; and the change around him was not greater than the change within. . . . He lamented that he had lost ten years in getting his bearings, and in learning, unaided, the most difficult craft in the world. Those years of apprenticeship without a master were the time spent

---

[7] From his first work, quoted by GOOCH, 549.

[8] See the long quotation in Acton, *History of Freedom* (n. 6), 378–79.

[9] J. Friedrich, *Ignaz von Döllinger, sein Leben auf Grund seines schriftlichen Nachlasses* (Munich, 1899–1901, 3 v.); Luise von Kobell, *Ignaz von Döllinger, Erinnerungen* (Munich, 1891), tr. into English as *Conversations of Dr. Döllinger* (London, 1892); Emil Michael, *Ignaz von Döllinger, eine Charakteristik* (Innsbruck, 1894); Heinrich von Sybel, *Vorträge und Abhandlungen* (Berlin, 1897); Vigener, *Drei Gestalten aus dem modernen Katholizismus* (see n. 3 above); and two important essays on his teacher by Lord Acton in *EHR*, V (1890), 700–44 and the *Rambler*, IV (1861), 145–75, reprinted in his *History of Freedom* (n. 6), 301–74, 375–435; *QR*, CLXXII (1891), 33–64; *ER*, CLXXV (1892), 48–83; and *DR*, XXV (1848), 204–36, LII (1862–63), 467–503, LV (1864), 200–17, and LVI (1865), 214–26.

on his *Kirchengeschichte*. The want of training remained. He could impart knowledge better than the art of learning. Thousands of his pupils have acquired a connected view of religion passing through the ages, and gathered . . . some notion of the meaning of history; but nobody ever learnt from him the mechanism by which it is written.[10]

Döllinger managed to keep abreast of the new generations, but always just abreast. When asked to prepare another edition of his *Church History* in 1865, he declared hardly a sentence was fit to stand. This *Lehrbuch der Kirchengeschichte* (1833–38), incomplete, with four volumes up to the Reformation, was his first major work, and written in a strong Catholic spirit. It was translated into English, French, and Italian. By his slashing attacks upon the Protestant heroes in *Die Reformation* (3 v., 1846–48) [11] and *Luther* (1851), Döllinger fell heir to Möhler's role as the chief defender of Catholicism in Germany.

The *Reformation* has interesting anticipations of the later famous thesis of Janssen. Döllinger argued that the Reformation was nothing new, that it did not usher in a new era, but that it was only the culmination of previous reform movements beginning with Cluny. He reduced the Lutheran Reformation to the adoption and propagation of the single principle of justification by faith. Upon this, in Döllinger's eyes, the entire Reformation logically hinged. Since it was evident by 1846 that Lutheranism had often repudiated this doctrine of its founder, the Catholic historian thought the way was open for a return to a united fold, and he was among the first to welcome the Tractarians of England.

This first period in his career, one of uncritical enthusiasm, ended in 1864 with the Papal *Syllabus of Errors*, which condemned some of Döllinger's own writings. He had offended the Ultramontanists, led by Hergenröther, by a series of lectures delivered at the Odeum in Munich (1860), in which, in the light of events in Italy, he had considered the possibility that the Catholic Church might lose its historical position as a temporal power. The second period in Döllinger's life was one of suspicion, when he endeavored to persuade the Church of the truth of historical tradition and contended strenuously against the adoption of the doctrine of papal infallibility at the Vatican Council

---

[10] Acton, *History of Freedom* (n. 6), 392–93.

[11] *Die Reformation, ihre innere Entwicklung und ihre Wirkungen.* Other writings: *Die Lehre von der Eucharistie in den drei ersten Jahrhunderten* (Mainz, 1826), his dissertation; *Heidenthum und Judenthum: Vorhalle zur Geschichte des Christenthums* (1857), tr. by Nicholas Darnell as *The Gentile and the Jew in the Courts of the Temple of Christ, an Introduction to the History of Christianity* (London, 1862; 2nd ed., 1906, 2 v.); *Die Papstfabeln des Mittelalters* (1863, 2nd ed., Stuttgart, 1890), tr. by Alfred Plummer as *Fables Respecting the Popes in the Middle Ages* (1872); *Kirche und Kirchen* (1860), his Odeum lectures; *Der Pabst und das Konzil*, under the pseudonym of "Janus" (1869; 2nd ed. as *Das Pabsttum*, 1891), which was immediately translated into English as *Letters of Janus: The Pope and the Council* (1870); and *Das erste Zeitalter* (1866), tr. into English by H. N. Oxenham as *The First Age of Christianity and the Church* (4th ed., London, 1906).

of 1870. Then, according to his biographer Friedrich, came the third period of complete disillusionment, after his excommunication (1871), when "The scales fell from my eyes," and he beheld what he deemed the true nature of the Catholic hierarchy. Döllinger refused to join in the secession of the *Altkatholiken* following the Vatican Council, but to his deathbed he maintained what he conceived to be the truth of history. Aside from this fateful controversy in his life, his historical knowledge and judgment were widely respected. When he died even Hergenröther said: "Ubi bene, nemo melius."

Karl Joseph von Hefele (1809–93) [11a] had studied at Tübingen and was called there to fill the vacancy left by Möhler's departure for Munich. In the classroom he was noted for his simple and beautiful diction and his grasp of detail without losing sight of the salient points of his subject. Hefele was probably the first Catholic theologian to lecture on Christian archaeology, and he had a feeling for ecclesiastical art. For thirty-two years he taught at Tübingen, and his lectures influenced the later manuals of Knoepfler at Munich (1895) and of his successor F. Funk at Tübingen. Hefele's own fame as a scholar outside of the university was established by a biography of Ximenes (1844). His masterpiece, however, was the great *Conciliengeschichte* in seven volumes.[12] Its wide sweep touches on many a field: the history of dogma, canon law, political questions, liturgics, and ecclesiastical discipline. Materials for it had accumulated in Hefele's hands since as student he first undertook to write a prize essay on Nicholas of Cusa.

The reputation of the *Conciliengeschichte* brought Hefele a summons to Rome in 1868, to act as consultor for the coming Vatican Council. The next year he was appointed bishop of Rothenburg, and the pressure of duties in this see, which he held for twenty-four years, virtually ended his writing. At the Vatican Council, which the bishop attended, he took a stout stand against papal infallibility, sharing the historical doubts of Döllinger. The Council adjourned without the reconsidera-

[11a] Funk in *Theologische Quartalschrift*, LXXVI (1894), reprinted in *Allgemeine deutsche Biographie*, L (1905), 109–15; J. B. Sägmüller in *Catholic Encyclopedia*, VII, 191–92; the article in the *Protestantische Realenzyklopaedie*, ed. Hauck; Granderath-Kirsch, *Geschichte des vatikanischen Konzils* (Freiburg, 1903–06, 3 v.); III, 31, 163, 174, 559, and index.

[12] First edition, 1855–74. Of the second, Hefele himself got out only the first five volumes (Freiburg, 1874–79); Knoepfler edited the rest (1886–90). Hefele's volumes went only as far as the fifteenth century, and Hergenröther later provided two additional volumes (1887, 1890) to carry the material up to the Council of Trent. The first edition of the *History of the Councils* was translated into French by Goschler and Delarc (Paris, 1869–78, 12 v.), and the Benedictine H. Leclercq provided a similar translation of the improved second German edition (*Histoire des conciles*, Paris, 1907–13, 5 v. in 10).

Other writings of Hefele: *Geschichte der Einführung des Christentums im südwestlichen Deutschland* (1837); *Patrum Apostolicorum Opera* (1839; 4th ed., 1855); *Das Sendschreiben des Apostels Barnabas* (1840); *Der Kardinal Ximenes und die kirchlichen Zustände Spaniens am Ende des 15. und Anfange des 16. Jahrhunderts* (1844; 2nd ed., 1851), also translated into French and English; *Chrysostomuspostille* (1845); and *S. Bonaventurae Breviloquium* (1845; 1861).

tion Hefele had hoped for, and reluctantly he published its decrees in his diocese in 1871.

The stoutest champion of the Ultramontanists before and after the Council was Joseph Hergenröther (1824–90),[12a] the pride of Würzburg. He had studied at the University there and then spent four impressionable years in Rome before the revolutions of 1848. Döllinger was among his examiners when Hergenröther took his degree at Munich (1850), and he induced the young man to begin there as *privat-dozent*. One wonders what their future relations might have been if Hergenröther had remained at Munich. In 1852 he accepted a chair at Würzburg, and joined Denzinger, Hettinger, and Hähnlein in giving that faculty a reputation for active Catholicism.

Hergenröther, aside from much writing for Catholic journals, delved deeper into patristics. After twelve years of occupation with Photius he published a great monograph on the patriarch of Constantinople which was one of the finest pieces of historical writing of the century. It was doubly significant as just preceding a sudden rise of Byzantine studies in Europe. Hergenröther's thesis was that not Rome, but Photius, had been responsible for the Greek schism.[13]

With the appearance of Döllinger's *Kirche und Kirchentum* (the Odeum lectures) in 1860, Hergenröther's Ultramontanism came to the fore. He soothed the feelings of timid Catholics by an essay on the *Syllabus of Errors* (1864). He was invited, with his colleague Hettinger, to be consultor (1868) in the preparations for the Vatican Council, and was committed heart and soul to the projected program. When *Janus* appeared in the autumn of 1869, he rushed into the breach with *Anti-Janus;* and during the sessions he answered Döllinger's "Letters of Quirinus" in the *Allgemeine Zeitung* (based on reports sent by Acton and Friedrich from Rome) by a series of articles in the *Historische-politische Blätter*. Such weapons, however, seemed rather unsatisfactory, and Hergenröther, after the Council was over, sat down to produce an armory of texts and quotations for the Vatican party. To the Ultramontane groups his two works [14] appeared the ultimate in historical answers, a thesaurus of triumphant arguments.

[12a] Lauchert in *Allgemeine deutsche Biographie*, L (1905), 228–31; J. P. Kirsch in the *Catholic Encyclopaedia*, VII, 262–64; GUILDAY, 289–320; *DR*, LXXXI (1877), 308–39; *RQH*, XXI (1877), 271.

[13] *Photius, Patriarch von Constantinopel, sein Leben, seine Schriften, und das griechische Schisma* (Regensburg, 1867–69, 3 v.). He had previously published an edition of Photius' *Liber de Spiritu Sancti mystagogia* (Regensburg, 1857); and later he issued a fourth volume to his monograph containing sources never before printed: *Monumenta graeca ad Photium ejusque historiam pertinentia*.

[14] *Das unfehlbare Lehramt des Papstes* (Passau, 1871); *Katholische Kirche und christlicher Staat in ihrer geschichtlichen Entwickelung und in Beziehung auf die Gegenwart* (1872). The latter also appeared in Italian (Pavia, 1877), and English (London, 1876; Baltimore, 1889).

Hergenröther's plan to write an exhaustive history of the Church in the eighteenth century never progressed beyond preparatory sketches. But his manual of Church history passed through several editions; its last editor, J. P. Kirsch, has declared that for fifty years it furnished the marrow of historical knowledge and spirit to Catholic students. Hergenröther began the organization of the second edition of the *Kirchenlexikon*, but Pope Leo XIII needed him in Rome. He was appointed a cardinal deacon in 1879, then placed in charge of the Vatican Archives as their first Prefect, in which capacity he befriended Pastor on his first appearance in Rome, and arranged for the opening of the archives to European scholars at the pope's command in 1883. He found time to begin the *Regesta* of Leo X, and provided two excellent volumes to supplement Hefele's *History of the Councils*. Hergenröther represents the triumphant grasp of Ultramontanism upon historiography as a tool in its own defense.

Friedrich Emmanuel von Hurter (1787–1865) was originally a Protestant pastor at Schaffhausen, his native village in Switzerland. He received his training at Göttingen, abjured Protestantism in Rome (1844), and went to Vienna the following year as historiographer of the Empire.[15] Another recruit from the ranks of Protestant theologians was August Friedrich Gfrörer (1803–61), whose works speak of diligent research (he was librarian in the royal library at Stuttgart after 1830), but tend to exceed the sober judgment of a critical historian. Like Hurter's writings, they cover varied subjects and are not confined to church history.[16]

Aside from the great exceptions of Janssen and Pastor, the accomplishments of Catholic historians in German-speaking countries has not been comparable to those of the Protestant writers since that climax of Ultramontanism in the seventies.[17] The secession of the *Altkatholiken* had its deleterious effects.

Johannes Janssen (1829–91)[18] appeared in an age of ugly controversy,

---

[15] *Geschichte Papst Innocenz III und seiner Zeitgenossen* (1834–43, 4 v.; also in French translation); *Denkwürdigkeiten aus dem letzten Decennium des 18. Jahrhunderts* (1840); *Zur Geschichte Wallensteins* (1855); *Wallenstein's vier letzte Lebensjahre* (1862); *Geschichte Ferdinands II, und seiner Eltern* (incomplete, in 11 vols., 1850–64); and the useful *Nomenclator litterarius theologiae catholicae* (3rd edition, Innsbruck, 1903–10, 4 v.), which does for the theological literature of the Middle Ages what Potthast did for its historical literature.

[16] *Geschichte der ost- und westfränkischen Karolinger vom Tode Ludwigs des Frommen bis zum Ende Conrads I* [840–918] (Freiburg, 1848, 2 v.), a landmark in the study of the Pseudo-Isidorean Decretals and virtually a biography of archbishop Hincmar of Rheims; *Papst Gregorius VII und sein Zeitalter* (Schaffhausen, 1859–64, 7 v. and index), the first extended work on the great pope.

[17] Professor Albert Eberhard has attempted to supply the reasons, in the section "Katholische Theologie," of *Aus fünfzig Jahren deutscher Wissenschaft: Festgabe an Dr. Schmidt-Ott*, ed. by Gustav Abb (1930).

[18] The standard biography is by Ludwig Pastor, *Johannes Janssen, 1829–1891, Ein Lebensbild* (Freiburg, 1892). Pastor has also edited his *Briefe* (Freiburg, 1920, 2 v.). There is an essay

but there was something of the romanticist about him that belongs in the age of Möhler. Though he was feeble of body and often despairing of life, the wings of his imagination soared. Perhaps the historic genius of his birthplace touched the boy, for Xanten on the lower Rhine had been a Roman camp, and the legendary birthplace of the dragon-slayer Siegfried. Poor health and an over-hesitant conscience led him to leave the seminary at Münster, and he went to Louvain (1850) to study French and English. In the quaint streets of the Belgian town the voices of the past again spoke to him, and he decided to devote his life to history. At Bonn he presented his dissertation on the twelfth-century churchman Wibald of Stablo and Corvey, and became acquainted with Dahlmann, the German patriot, with Wattenbach, and Ritter, founder of modern comparative geography.

Having rounded out his preparation with a scholarship at Berlin, Janssen delivered his first lecture at the Academy of Münster (1854), but left almost immediately for Frankfort-am-Main for a position in a Catholic gymnasium. The reason why he deserted a university career for undergraduate teaching was probably his desire to be near J. F. Böhmer. This master of diplomatics, a full thirty years his senior, was for Janssen the oracle that he later presented to his own pupil Pastor. From Böhmer he received the axioms of historical writing, and it was Böhmer who led his thought to doing the *Geschichte des deutschen Volkes*. "I lived in Böhmer," he wrote on the other's passing, "and his death means for me the conclusion of one period of my life."

After working on the twelfth and thirteenth centuries under Böhmer's tutelage, and completing various writings,[19] Janssen's mind centered upon one great project. He would write the history of the German people in all its aspects before the Reformation, and cover not merely military and political history, but their literature and art as well, and especially the state of their spiritual life. The Frankfort libraries were crammed with manuscript treasures, and his notes accumulated at an alarming rate. He began his work with the blessings of religion,[20] and as he continued it the desire for peace of mind led him to resume his theological studies and to enter holy orders (1860). Thenceforth Janssen regarded the *Geschichte* as his special religious mission.

in GUILDAY, 321–53, with a bibliography. For a slaughtering review, see Hans Delbrück, "Historische Methode," *PJ*, LIII (1884), 529–50.

[19] He finished the second volume of his friend H. C. Scholten's work on St. Louis (1855); wrote a series of articles on the Rebellion of the Netherlands, and another on the medieval sources for the history of Cologne; prepared a volume of critically-edited chronicles for "Munsterland," his native region (1856); wrote *Frankreichs Rheingelüste* (1861); and in 1864 published his critical essay on Schiller as an historian.

[20] "On September 8, 1857 as I returned from St. Leonard's church, I made up my mind to begin the History with the close of the Middle Ages. That day I formed my plans under the patronage of the Blessed Mother of God, whose help and intercession I had invoked."

But for a little the *History of the German People* would have missed its uniqueness and chief merit. Lack of space had dictated many omissions, and Janssen was minded to exclude what is today known as cultural history. It is due to August Reichensperger's advice that this which was marked for rejection became the headstone of the corner. The first volume appeared in 1876, at a time hardly calculated to help its reception. The *Kulturkampf* had stirred all Germany. But the incredible wealth of material, and the ingenious manner in which Janssen had woven pungent extracts and telling phrases from the sources into his text, won a grudging respect from the Protestant world.

As volume followed volume, and the frail author continued with researches that would have killed another man, the work assumed its fuller outlines, and a storm of criticism and abuse came from the Protestant camp. The Protestants had always pictured the Reformation as a purification, a necessary upheaval after a sordid Church had sunk to unbelievable depths towards the close of the Middle Ages. The Schism, the Babylonian Captivity, the new financial expedients, indulgences and pilgrimages, the morals of the Renaissance popes—it was a well-known story. But Janssen was reversing the entire plot! He was showing how steadily morals rose and the material prosperity of the nation increased as the Middle Ages drew to a close. Then, subtly adding stone to stone, he suggested that the Reformation threw all into chaos, and that national decay set in, long before the ruinous march of Swede and Czech, of Frenchman and German Lutheran scarred the face of their beautiful land. This reversal of light into shadow stunned the Protestants, and in their anger they only ran their heads against the solid structure of Janssen's researches.[21]

Only time and detailed studies could settle the controversies. The *Geschichte* drew so wide a furrow and touched so many topics that only several generations of further study could draw safe conclusions. It was psychologically natural, and no reflection on his honesty, that Janssen should be struck by hopeful signs in the centuries vilified by Lutheran and Reformed scholars, and that he should detect grave rifts in the lute between the Diet of Augsburg and the Defenestration of Prague. Janssen opened new fields and furnished many corrections. Such extremes as proved untenable in his work have been admitted by his literary executor Pastor, who completed the work and revised several later editions.

[21] At the appearance of the fourth volume (covering 1555–80), a non-Catholic reviewer wrote: "Many a man has tried his luck with the previous volumes, but without much success. It is not likely that anybody will feel the impulse of breaking his teeth with the present one." Quoted in GUILDAY, 345. Janssen himself prepared two lengthy answers, *An meine Kritiker*, and *Ein zweites Wort an meine Kritiker*.

Heinrich Suso Denifle (1844–1905) [22] was one of the learned orna-
ments of the Dominican Order. He entered its portals at Graz in Austria at the age of seventeen, having received his earlier training at the
hands of his father, a Tyrolese schoolmaster at Imst, and at the seminary of Brixen. The new brother took the name of the medieval mystic
Heinrich Suso. He underwent a thorough course of study, and dreamed
of composing a great commentary on St. Thomas Aquinas from a
historico-literary viewpoint, beginning with the sources of the *Summa*
itself. His first major contribution, however, was in the field of medieval
mysticism. *Das geistliche Leben: eine Blumenlese aus den deutschen
Mystikern* (1873) is a marvelous anthology of several thousand passages
culled from the medieval mystics.

For ten years Denifle served as professor in the Houses of Study in
Hungary and Austria, and then in 1880 he entered the path which was
to make him a world-famous palaeographer. He was entrusted with
making a survey of all manuscripts available in Europe for the critical
edition of St. Thomas which Pope Leo XIII wished to forward. After
three years spent in visiting the libraries of all important European
countries, Denifle was made sub-archivist of the Vatican archives at
the recommendation of Cardinal Hergenröther. These famous archives
had been opened to the world only a few months before. The value of
their materials for cultural history Denifle illustrated in 1885 by the
publication of a stout volume entitled *Die Entstehung der Univer-
sitäten des Mittelalters bis 1400*. It demolished the old pretentious
Latin history of the University of Paris by Du Boulay (Paris,
1665–73, 6 v. folio), revealed scores of forgotten medieval universities which Denifle had rediscovered in the Papal Registers,
and revolutionized the study of medieval higher education. It is to be
regretted that Denifle never completed the other four volumes which
were to follow.

Since the University of Paris, most famous of all in the Middle Ages,
had recently decided to publish the sources for its early history, Denifle
was asked to undertake the editorship, and given the librarian of the
Sorbonne, Émile Chatelain, as his assistant. The results splendidly
justified the confidence: in the amazingly brief time of ten years Denifle
issued the definitive four folio volumes of the *Chartularium universitatis
Parisiensis* (Paris, 1889–97), and two supplementary volumes containing longer documents, the *Auctarium Chartularii* (1894–97). Virtually
all the important libraries of Europe were laid under tribute for this
work. In the introduction of the second volume of the *Chartularium*

[22] Martin Grabmann, *P. Heinrich Denifle, O. P. Eine Würdigung seiner Forschungsarbeit*
(Mainz, 1905). There is an essay in GUILDAY, 354–72, with a brief bibliography.

Denifle remarked that he had looked through 200,000 letters in the Papal Registers, and employed 8,000 of them for the notes to that volume. The documents in the *Chartularium* are a mine for the historian of the intellectual life of the Middle Ages, for they cast light not only upon the external organization of the university, and the succession of teachers, but also upon the rise of scholasticism, the history of science, and the relations of the religious orders to the university. The work is rich in by-products, as in information on the Schism or on the trial of Joan of Arc. It is a monument by a master palaeographer.[23]

Together with Ehrle, who succeeded Cardinal Hergenröther as Prefect of the Vatican Archives, Denifle founded the *Archiv für Literatur- und Kirchengeschichte des Mittelalters* (1885), and many an article from his pen found its way into the first six volumes. Some of these were on the mendicant orders. His interest in ecclesiastical history led in a curious manner to another important work. As Denifle tells the story, he had read page for page through some three hundred volumes of registers of petitions in the Vatican in his researches for the *Chartularium*, when the thought occurred to him that here was splendid material for a history of the disastrous effects of the Hundred Years' War upon the French churches. Hereupon he began again at the beginning and re-read the three hundred volumes, though he still had several hundred to finish for the *Chartularium*. Thus *La désolation des églises, monastères, hôpitaux en France pendant la guerre de cent ans* (1897–99, 2 v.) is really a source collection of over a thousand documents from 123 dioceses, presenting a graphic picture of decay and tribulation. A sequel volume on the fourteenth century and the military side of the Hundred Years' War followed in 1899.

Upon the decline of the Church in the fifteenth century followed the chaos of the sixteenth century, and thus Denifle was led to the problem of Luther. As was his inveterate habit, he sought out the original manuscript literature rather than printed editions, and found fault even with the critical Weimar edition of Luther's works. Denifle adopted a unique plan of approach: he resolved to study Luther backward, year by year, from his mature position, and to concentrate upon his inner life and psychology. The first volume of *Luther und Luthertum* (1903) was sold out in four weeks. It fell like a bomb into the Protestant camp. The most august of Lutheran scholars turned in surprise upon what

[23] When Leo XIII celebrated the golden anniversary of his ordination to the priesthood, the personnel of the Vatican Archives presented him with a sumptuous monograph prepared by Denifle, the *Specimina Palaeographica Regestorum Pontificum ab Innocentio III ad Urbanum V* (1888), containing a history of the script of the Papal chancery for two centuries, with facsimiles.

they considered the venomous tongue of this Dominican; Kolde, Walther, Seeberg, and even Harnack started to the rescue.[24]

Denifle did to the great idol of North Germany what Janssen had done to the Protestant idea of the Reformation. He demonstrated that Luther's life had been anything but pure and monkish; that his fears over his sins were due either to ignorance of the commonest doctrines of the Church, or to a very bad conscience. He took Luther at his word when he said he felt himself to be a very bad man. Luther thus became a pathological case: a man driven by sin and vice to rebel against authority and celibacy, a character who after the break from Rome fortified himself by lies and misrepresentations. In brief, Luther was the final horrible example of that decadence which Denifle had already traced down from the fourteenth century.

Protestants had once been used to having their opponents discover the lineaments of the evil one in their leader. But calumnies had been laughed off, and a little wall of legend had grown up around Luther and his contemporaries. The sting in Denifle's work was that here was a serious scholar who refused to be laughed out of court, and presented facts, with citation to volume, page, and line.[25] Happily, the historical problem of Luther proved to be greater and more worthwhile than the question whether he was a wine-bibber or had misquoted a passage of St. Augustine. But Denifle's work drove Protestant scholars to re-check their research, and led to some revision of the national hero.

The greatest light of modern Catholic scholarship was Ludwig von Pastor (1854–1928),[26] who narrowly missed being raised a Lutheran. His Protestant father, a merchant of Aachen, died when the boy was four years old, and the mother in moving the family to Frankfort

[24] Denifle was unmoved by their criticisms; the second edition in 1904 remained virtually unchanged. See his retort, *Luther in rationalistischer und christlicher Beleuchtung: Prinzipielle Auseinandersetzung mit A. Harnack und R. Seeberg.* Part II of his work on Luther appeared in 1905, and Father Albert Weiss issued the remaining portions in 1906 and 1908 from Denifle's manuscripts.

[25] Denifle's acquaintance with the mystics enabled him to show that Luther had not always understood or quoted them correctly. He showed that Luther's knowledge of Catholic dogma was deficient, and that he knew little about the scholastics he was so ready to denounce. He discovered inconsistencies and changes in Luther's views, and asserted Luther could not be trusted to tell or to remember the truth about himself at an earlier time, e.g., in the story of the journey to Rome. Above all, Denifle criticized the Protestant historians of dogma, and said that no one understood Luther less than his biographers and the Protestant theologians.

[26] See his own autobiography in Siegfrid Steinberg, ed., *Die Geschichtswissenschaft der Gegenwart in Selbstdarstellungen* (Leipzig, 1926, 2 v.); and cp. *HZ*, CXLVI (1932), 510–15, and the attack on its "concealments" by W. Goetz, *ibid.*, CXLV, 550–63; GUILDAY, 373–415, with a bibliography; Emilio Re, in *La Nuova Antologia*, CCCXL (1928), 96–102; L. Johnston, "Historians of the Mediaeval Papacy," *Catholic University Bulletin*, IX, 347–68; *EHR*, XXV, 571; G. L. Burr in *AHR*, I (1895–96), 526–29; XII (1906–07), 361–62; XIII (1907–08), 635–36; XV (1909–10), 847–49; XIX (1913–14), 168; XXVII (1921–22), 112–15; XXX (1924–25), 134–36; XXXI (1925–26), 852; XXXIII (1927–28), 181–82; XXXIV (1928–29), 113–14; *DR*, CXI (1892), 1–30; *Historische Vierteljahrschrift*, I (1898), 126–42; X (1907), 437–42; XI (1908), 565–69; *CQR*, XXXV (1892), 342–66.

determined to raise them in the Catholic fold. Some of the most famous Catholic celebrities of the time visited their household; Pastor has written the lives of two of them: August Reichensperger, leader of the Center Party, and the kindly and hard-working Johannes Janssen, who uncovered the boy's gift for history. A set of Ranke's *Popes* which the historian presented to his young friend was one of the two works to which Pastor has ascribed the dawn of an interest in Rome and the Papacy.[27] Following Janssen's advice and example, young Pastor went first to Louvain and then studied at Bonn. At Berlin he heard the lectures of Georg Waitz and Karl Nitzsch, and was introduced to Ranke; but the atmosphere of North Germany was uncongenial, and he only regained his ease at Vienna (1877). Janssen introduced him to Onno Klopp, who counselled Pastor to stay in Austria, as the *Kulturkampf* in Germany would close his avenues of promotion there. For three semesters Pastor lived in his house, and Klopp's influence upon him must be assessed as important.[28] The years of preparation came to an end at Graz in Styria, where Pastor presented his dissertation, and was free to commence his ambitious project: a Catholic history of the Popes.

The years of Pastor's youth had been years of grave struggle for the German Catholics and for the papacy. But Ultramontanism had triumphed, and the thunders of the *Kulturkampf* merely consolidated their ranks. The alarms of the early seventies were succeeded by a new confidence, and it was in this moment of returning hopes that the idea of the *History of the Popes* was born. "It was the daughter of the Germany of the Catholic Center, of the Rome of Leo XIII." [29]

Only in exceptional cases had access to the Vatican archives been granted to scholars. But here also the new era was important. The Papacy had learned the value of popular opinion. Open discussion in European parliaments was bringing state secrets into the light of day. With the disappearance of the Papal States many jealously-guarded documents had lost their legal significance. The new pontiff Leo XIII was inclined to take a broader view. Thus by a singularly fortunate conjunction in 1879 the man and the materials for a new history of the papacy were brought together, and Pastor enjoyed a privilege denied to Ranke and Creighton, to Voigt and Gregorovius. His first volume in 1886 was the first fruits of the new policy. Even before it appeared Leo XIII had decided on a momentous step. By the papal *breve* "Saepenumero desiderantes" of August 18, 1883, the Vatican Archives were unlocked to all scholars without reserve, and the Holy Father him-

[27] The other was J. Fichard's *Italia*, published in Frankfort, 1811–15.
[28] On his relations to Pastor, see *HZ*, CXLV (1931), 550 ff. and the answer of Pastor's son, *ibid.*, CXLVI (1932), 510–15.
[29] Emilio Re (n. 26), 97.

self, resorting to Cicero, laid down the canons of good historiography.[30]

The *History of the Popes*, in fifteen volumes, was the work of fifty years of great labor. But Pastor had other duties; for twenty years he was professor at Innsbruck (1881–1901), until an appointment to the directorship of the Austrian Historical Institute at Rome freed him from teaching. His literary output is amazing.[31] Of his six biographies, the greatest is the picture he drew of his teacher Janssen. Much labor went into the completion and revision of the first fourteen editions of Janssen's *Geschichte des deutschen Volkes*. There were editorial services on the *Historisches Jahrbuch* and the *Historische-politische Blätter*. But amid all these chips of his workshop, Pastor's one thought was of his *History of the Popes*, the work which he styled "die grosse Liebe meines Lebens." He had planned it for six volumes, but it grew under his hands. At the moment of his death, volume XIII was being released from the press, and the manuscript for the two final volumes XIV and XV lay ready. In his labors he was aided constantly by his faithful wife, who assisted in the copying of the manuscript and relieved him from correspondence and financial duties. Physically Pastor was small but robust, very nearsighted from constant poring over documents, and subject to occasional breakdowns from his prodigious application. He possessed great powers of concentration, and could resume a sentence immediately after a visitor left.[32]

Two notes are characteristic of the *History of the Popes*. It purports to be modern scientific history, based on archival materials and a conscientious pursuit of the monographic literature, accurately documented, with a straining after honest objectivity. Its very caution sometimes blunts the style. Pastor lacked that happy immediacy by which the historian simultaneously presents the reader with the facts and his judgment upon them. The work is thoroughly conservative; there are

---

[30] "Enitendum magnopere, ut omnia ementita et falsa, adeundis rerum fontibus, refutentur; et illud in primis scribentium observetur animo, 'primam esse historiae legem, ne quid falsi dicere audeat: deinde ne quid veri non audeat; ne qua suspicio gratiae sit in scribendo, ne qua simultatis.' . . . Est autem in scholarum usum confectio commentariorum necessaria, qui salva veritate et nullo adolescentium periculo ipsam artem historicam illustrare et augere queant." The full text is given in *Archiv für katholisches Kirchenrecht*, L, 428 ff.; see also *DR*, XCIII (1883), 413–19, 417.

[31] Pastor's widow presented Pope Pius XI with a cabinet containing her husband's bust, his medals and all his works, diaries, and papers. There were forty-six volumes of his own writings, about two hundred separate essays and articles, and twenty-two volumes of Janssen and other writers which Pastor had edited. In addition to these printed works, he composed during his years at the University of Innsbruck fourteen series of lectures, from the beginning of the Middle Ages to 1880, with particular wealth on the nineteenth century. Cp. Goetz, *HZ*, CXLV (1931), 550 ff.

[32] Pastor relied not only upon the papal archives, but searched many other repositories of manuscripts, the archives of the Colonna, Ricci, and Gaetani families in Rome, and collections in Germany, France, and other countries. For volumes V–VI alone he visited 80 libraries, and examined over 600 printed books, besides using hundreds of documents.

no sensational new discoveries. Solidly buttressed on fact and a true erudition, the substance of the work may be regarded as permanent.

The other note is one of loving apology for the Church of which Pastor always realized himself a devoted son. Like Möhler he was convinced that only a Catholic could write a true history of the Papacy and grasp its spiritual significance in history. Ranke had stressed the political side. In assuming the spiritual definition of the Papacy, Pastor also set up a moral criterion, and it must be allowed that on individual popes like Alexander VI he passes as harsh a judgment as Protestant writers do. Yet the institution throughout retains its sanctity: "Petri dignitas etiam in indigno haerede non deficit." [33]

Pastor was at his best in describing the hierarchy, and ecclesiastical institutions or general tendencies, but lacked the power to portray an individual in a few vivid strokes, as Ranke could. The vehicle of his expression is a dignified but rather sober German. Vladimir Zabughin once congratulated him on his early volumes. Pastor's laconic reply was: "Viel Arbeit." [34] He interests the student of historiography because of his thorough exploration of the papal archives, but he represents no advance in historical method and contributed no new idea to the interpretation of history. Walter Goetz has written that Pastor does not even represent the steady advance of modern Catholic historiography towards greater objectivity, but still headed as its greatest exponent the "curialistic" direction. In other words, he consciously allowed the *Popes* to become the "official publication" of the Holy See.[35] The great work which came to an end in 1928 was still the child of 1870.

It was pointed out in the beginning of this chapter that after 1815 Catholicism was characterized by reaction everywhere. In France this reaction was even more deeply tinged with romanticism and sentimental emotionalism than in Germany. As early as 1802, Chateaubriand's *Génie du Christianisme* sustained Catholicism as an emotional and aesthetic influence. His *Les martyrs* (1809) sentimentalized the history of early Christianity. In 1824 Lamennais (1782-1854) [36] at-

[33] This is prefixed as the motto of vol. III, which deals with Popes Alexander VI and Julius II. Of the painful revelations which he was obliged to make, Pastor said: "I have said all, but said it like a son constrained to unveil the faults of a very dear mother."

[34] Related by Emilio Re (n. 26), 102.

[35] *HZ*, CXLV (1931), 550 ff., where Goetz also gives references to some Catholic critics who have been equally severe. They have accused Pastor of writing under the influence of the Jesuits, and of accepting what the Congregations and the Curia said for historic truth. It is conceivable that Pastor tended to overvalue his Vatican findings: an illuminating example is his controversy with Schnitzer over Savonarola.

[36] The best account is Charles Boutard, *Lammenais: Sa vie et ses doctrines* (Paris, 1905-13, 3 v.). There is a fine chapter on Lamennais and his relations with Pope Gregory XVI in Woodward (n. 1).

tacked Gallicanism and advocated the new theocracy and the political supremacy of the Papacy. In 1830 he founded the famous journal *L'Avenir*, in association with Montalembert, Lacordaire, and Rohrbacher. This periodical became the prototype of a powerful Ultramontane press, whose most virulent editor after the fifties was Veuillot of *L'Univers*.

The Comte de Montalembert (1810–70) [37] raised the romantic cry: "Nous sommes les fils des croisés et jamais nous ne reculerons devant les fils de Voltaire." As peer of France he employed his hereditary seat in the Chamber to plead the cause of the liberties of the Church. He was an intimate friend of Lacordaire, and a contributor to *L'Avenir*, but he also did some historical writing. His youthful romantic *Du catholicisme et du vandalisme dans l'art* (1829) was among the first works that restored medieval architecture and sculpture to honor. The *Vie de sainte-Elisabeth de Hongrie* (1834) was wholly uncritical; despite its literary qualities it is mostly pious legend, poetically told. None of his works compare with the profusion of picturesque detail represented by his *Monks of the West*. [38] It was a life-long interest, and planned on such a scale that although the first volume appeared ten years before his death, it was never completed. Though often mentioned, it is a romantic effusion and of no scholarly value.

Antoine-Frederic Ozanam (1813–53) [39] was the greatest historical scholar of the French neo-Catholic movement. Deeply religious, he was frequently assailed by doubts and despair in his student days until Abbé Noirot, his teacher in philosophy, showed him the way to light. In 1832 he came to Paris to study law, and became the moving spirit of a circle which met regularly at the home of Bailly, owner of the journal *L'Univers*. In 1833, at the age of twenty-two, Ozanam founded the charitable society of Saint Vincent de Paul. [40] After practicing law in Lyon, he was called to the Sorbonne, and in 1844 succeeded Fauriel

---

[37] Sainte-Beuve, *Causeries du lundi* (1853–58, 10 v.), I; Léon Gautier, *Portraits littéraires* (Paris, 1868), *NBR*, XLVIII (1868), 163–95, XXXV (1861), 31–60; *ER*, CXIV (1861), 318–47, CXXVII (1868), 397–432; *BQR*, XLVIII (1868), 201–40, XVIII (1853), 170–87; *DR*, LXXII (1868), 1–44, CXXVI (1900), 102–20, XLIX (1861), 434–57; *FM*, LXXXVII (1873), 180–89, and LIII (1856), 563–83; *QR*, XCVIII (1856), 534–72, CXXXIV (1873), 415–56.

[38] *Les moines d'Occident depuis saint Benoit jusqu'à saint Bernard* (Paris, 1860–67, 4 v.; first complete revised ed., 1863–78, 7 v.), tr. into English (1861–79, 7 v.). His complete works were published at Paris, 1860–68, 9 v.

[39] Mme. E. Humbert, *Frédéric Ozanam, d'après sa correspondance, étude biographique* (Paris, 1880); C. A. Ozanam (a brother), *Vie de Frédéric Ozanam* (3rd ed., Paris, 1889); Kathleen O'Meara, *F. Ozanam . . . His Life and Works* (London, 1879), reviewed in *DR*, LXXX (1877), 304–24; see also *ibid.*, CLIV (1914), 33–50; H. H. Brann, in *Catholic World*, LXXVIII (1903), 299–309; W. P. Kitchin, "The Centenary of F. Ozanam," *ibid.*, XCVII (1913), 758–68; *American Catholic Quarterly*, XXXVIII, 151–74.

[40] Its membership rose rapidly; in a year it counted a hundred, and at its founder's death twenty years later nearly 2,000 members. The society proved a most efficient weapon in the dissemination of Ultramontane thought.

in the chair of foreign literatures. His literary and historical efforts were all elaborations of his one conviction: the superiority of Catholicism as a foundation for social organization of men.[41] He confessed to have tried to prove the contrary of Gibbon's thesis, viz., that the Church succeeded, where the Caesars had failed, in giving a higher life and civilization to the barbarians. Only fragments remain of his projected great history of early medieval civilization. Ozanam was a capable scholar, but as has been said, "trop poète pour tenir compte de la realité des faits et trop dogmatique pour les comprendre." Yet he was a beautiful personality, his knowledge of the Catholic Middle Ages was deep and intimate, and his special strength lay in an appreciation of their literary and cultural side.

No historian can speak without a warm sense of gratitude of the Abbé Jacques-Paul Migne (1800–75),[42] publisher of the *Patrologia*. As a young priest in the diocese of Orleans he resigned after a conflict with his bishop and came to Paris, where he founded a religious journal which later became *L'Univers*, the great Ultramontanist organ. After three years he sold out, and with the most meager funds established the Imprimerie Catholique in the suburb Petit-Montrouge of Paris. John Bigelow, the American minister in France, visited the Abbé's plant in 1859 in the full flush of its activity and has left a vivid account.

It was one of the largest book manufactories in the world. Its outside was plain, save for a sign in large letters. The printing room measured 150 by 160 feet, and its walls were lined with stereotype plates. Migne was "a remarkably fine looking man, and withal, as I had reason to expect, an intellectual man." As a result of his occupation he "talked Latin with greater facility than any other language," including his French mother-tongue. What amazed the American more, however, was that this huge establishment had been built upon a shoestring, entirely on Migne's credit with the clergy.

All publications of the house, the visitor was told, were devoted to theology, and for economy all were printed in quarto. Every work or collection was as complete as possible, designed to extend to the very

---

[41] His chief writings were: *Deux chanceliers d'Angleterre, Bacon de Verulam et Saint Thomas de Canterbury* (Paris, 1836); *Dante et la philosophie catholique au XIIIe siècle* (Paris, 1839, 2nd ed. enlarged, 1845); *Études germaniques* (1847–49, 2 v.); *Documents inédits pour servir à l'histoire d'Italie depuis le VIIIe siècle jusqu'au XIIe* (1850), a valuable and rare collection; *Les poètes franciscains en Italie au XIIIe siècle* (Paris, 1852).

[42] John Bigelow, *Retrospections of an Active Life* (London and New York, 1910–13, 5 v.), IV, 1–6; Pierre de Labriolle, *History and Literature of Latin Christianity*, tr. from the French by Herbert Wilson (London and New York, 1924), 33–36; cp. also *Bulletin d'ancienne littérature et d'archéologie chrétiennes*, III (1910), 203 ff.; H. von Hurter, *Nomenclator literarius recentioris theologiae catholicae*, V (Innsbruck, 1911), col. 1605 ff.; the article on Migne by J. P. Kirsch in the *Catholic Encyclopaedia*, X, 290–91; *QR*, CXIII, 378; Matthew Arnold, *Essays in Criticism* has a chapter on pagan and medieval religious sentiment.

boundaries of its field. Twenty years before Migne had printed the twenty-five-volume set of the *Cours complet de Théologie* entirely on subscription. Then the *Cours complet d'Écriture Sainte* had provided the funds for expansion. Next had followed two collections of sacred orators,[43] and various complete editions of a long list of famous churchmen and theologians. But the Abbé's pride was his *Cours complet de Patrologie*. The 217 volumes of the Latin series, from Tertullian to Innocent III, covered practically all that was written between the fourth and the twelfth centuries: a total of 3,000 authors in crowded columns. Yet this stupendous collection sold for about five francs or $1 a volume if ordered entire. Single volumes came to six francs. Bigelow felt bound to admire the four volumes of indices for this series, "the most complete apparatus for consultation perhaps that was ever prepared for any publication." [44] The Greek series, of which sixty volumes in the bilingual edition (with Latin translations) were ready at Bigelow's time, sold for eight or nine francs a volume, and finally comprehended, as scholars know, a total of 166 volumes. In brief, the Latin series comprises 297,567 pages, and the Greek 235,724 pages, making the staggering total of 533,291 pages, all stereotyped! [45]

Bigelow learned from the Abbé that he had "over a thousand scholars" engaged in the search for manuscripts, and the preparation of copy. Migne frequently advertised for works known to exist: in 1859 there was a standing offer of twenty francs for information as to the whereabouts of a letter of St. Francis "On the power of the demons." Typographical accuracy was attained by first preparing the copy word for word down to the final page. Then it was read in type according to this copy, and reread after corrections had been made. Three addi-

---

[43] *Collection Integrale et Universelle des Orateurs Sacres* (102 volumes in two series, 1844–66). The first series was a complete printing of the great pulpit orators of the Church, of the first and second magnitude, in 67 volumes quarto, selling in Bigelow's day for the equivalent of $67! The second series was a selected printing of most of the stars of second magnitude, arranged chronologically to show the rise, decline, and revival of preaching in France. This came to 33 volumes, or about $33, and Bigelow thought it a bargain—for it included the best preachers since 1789, the outstanding diocesan addresses of bishops and archbishops of France, Savoy and Belgium, sermons of the twenty-three greatest living French divines, and an anthology of all the great pulpit masters in history.

[44] Of the 231 separate and complete indices on all subjects, "alphabetical, chronological, statistical, synthetical, analytical, analogical," etc., two are of great value: (1) a table giving references to all that each Father had written on any one subject, and (2) a table of references to all comments each author had made on any verse of Scripture. According to the preface in vol. CCXVIII, the 231 tables employed 50 men for ten years after the collection was finished, which is estimated as the work of one man for 1800 years, allowing 15 days for each book, or 231 tables for each of 50,000 volumes.

[45] The *Patrologia Graeca* were published either in Greek-and-Latin or in the Latin translation alone. The former includes 166 volumes, 1857–66; the Latin translation came to 81 volumes, 1856–61. No index to the Greek series was prepared, but a Greek, D. Scholarius, added a list of authors and subjects (Athens, 1879), and began a complete table of contents (Athens, 1883). The *Patrologia*, both Greek and Latin series, are fully analyzed in the Catalogues of the British Museum.

tional readings checked the corrections and possible omissions. There was another revision before the stereotype plates were prepared, and another before the actual printing, "so that the proof-reading and corrections cost as much as the composition."

For almost a decade after his impressed American visitor left, Migne's great work went on.[46] Then in 1868 disaster befell: a great fire destroyed the Montrouge establishment, including the remnant stock of many volumes and the valuable stereotype plates of the *Patrologia*. The loss was estimated at over six million francs! Migne's heroic efforts to retrieve his fortunes were thwarted by the Franco-Prussian War and the hostility of the archbishop of Paris, who scented commercialism and finally suspended Migne from his priestly office. He died in 1875 without recovering prosperity, and the business, the remaining stock of printed volumes, and the copyrights were acquired by Garnier Frères.

For the historian, Migne's claim to fame is based solely on the *Patrologia*. His intention was to base it upon the latest critical texts and to supply the necessary introductions and commentaries. But original research was hardly compatible with the scale of the enterprise, and usually only reprints were offered. The selection was not always fortunate; inferior editions were followed, and sometimes variant readings and notes are completely lacking. The supervision of the series in its first years was under the care of the learned Benedictine J. B. Pitra.[47] Migne's great service was to bring together a widely scattered literature, often available only in manuscript or out-of-print editions centuries old. Typographically also it was an achievement, though in the volumes re-issued after the fire misprints sprinkle the pages with disturbing frequency. For critical work on a single text, later editions must always be consulted. But the vast scope of the collection makes it unique, and for availability it will hardly ever be surpassed.

Jean-Baptiste-François Pitra (1812–89),[48] archaeologist, theologian, historian, and cardinal librarian of the Vatican, was another of those gifts that the Benedictine Order has made to scholarship. He studied at Autun, was ordained in 1836 and for the next five years taught rhetoric and history in the seminary there. In 1842 he entered the

---

[46] Besides the printing-shop, there were ateliers for religious objects such as pictures, statuary, and organs.

[47] Cp. Dom Cabrol, *Histoire de cardinal Pitra* (Paris, 1893), 108.

[48] The work of Dom Cabrol cited in the previous note, also translated into German by Buehler in *Studien und Mitteilungen aus dem Benediktiner- und Cistercienser-Orden*, XXVIII–XXX (Brunn, 1907–09); A. Battandier, *Le cardinal Jean Baptiste Pitra, évêque de Porto, bibliothécaire de la Sainte Église romaine* (Paris, 1893 and 1896); Dom Cabrol, "Le cardinal Pitra. Ses travaux et ses decouvertes," *Science catholique*, 1889, also translated in *The Lamp* (1899); *DR*, XCVIII (1866), 340–58; Michael Ott in *Catholic Encyclopaedia*, XII (1911), 119–20; a valuable essay in *CQR*, VI (1878), 533 ff.; and *Bibiiographie des Bénédictines de la Congrégation de France* (Paris, 1906), 120–31.

Benedictine order at the Abbey of Solesmes, then under the direction of Dom Gueranger, famous for his hymnological studies. In the next year Pitra became prior of St. Germain in Paris, and his subsequent career reminds one of Montfaucon before him. While he was prior he prepared the list of authors to be included in Migne's *Patrologia;* but the dissolution of the priory, due to financial difficulties, drove Pitra from Paris and dissolved the partnership after the first four volumes had appeared (1845). Pitra's travels through France and adjacent countries in the next years brought him into contact with many unpublished manuscripts bearing on the early centuries of the Church, and he rapidly won a reputation with his writings.[49] The French Government desired him to resume the *Gallia Christiana*, that great undertaking whose publication had lapsed before the Revolution. In 1852 Pitra published the first volume of his *Spicilegium Solesmense*, which work, followed by two later series, provided scholars with a remarkable collection of rare fragments and unpublished manuscripts from all the famous libraries of Europe.[50]

In 1858 Pope Pius IX sent Pitra to visit the libraries of Russia, and to collect materials on Greek canon law. The writings on this subject and on Greek hymnology which resulted from the seven months he spent in St. Petersburg and elsewhere form Pitra's greatest contribution to scholarship. The discovery of a Greek manuscript with metrical markings in red ink enabled him to establish the laws of Byzantine hymnology. He proved that what was formerly thought to be merely a rhetorical prose, and could not be forced into the schemes of classical quantitative meter, was really verse written on a strictly syllabic basis.[51] The Pope instructed him to supervise a new edition of the liturgical books of the Greek Rite, prepared by the Propaganda. In 1863 Pitra

---

[49] *Histoire de Saint Léger, évêque d'Autun et martyr, et de l'église des Francs au VIIe siècle* (Paris, 1846), ostensibly on a legend of the seventh century, is virtually a monograph on Merovingian times: *La Hollande Catholique. Études sur la collection des actes des saints* par les RR. PP. Jesuites Bollandistes (Paris, 1850).

[50] *Spicilegium Solesmense* (1852–60, 5 v.), followed by the *Analecta sacra spicilegio Solesmensi parata* (1876–91, 8 v.) and the *Analecta novissima, Spicilegium solesmensis altera continuatio* (1885–88, 2 v.). The first volume of the Spicilegium contains unedited fragments of Greek, Oriental, and Latin writers before the fifth century; the second and third volumes offer much material on the Christian Creeds; the fourth volume is devoted to the ecclesiastical writers of the African and Byzantine Churches, etc. Pitra's *Analecta Sacra* contains some important contributions to ante-Nicene literature; but what an able reviewer, Loofs, wrote is true: "Much, in spite of the title, is not new; and of the new, the more interesting is uncertain, and the comparatively certain is without interest" (*Theologische Literaturzeitung*, 1884, p. 455).

[51] "It is interesting," observes a reviewer, "that by far the greater part of the Byzantine hymns were composed about the ninth century and by the men who so nobly opposed the last of the Byzantine heresies, that of the Iconoclasts. The syllabic system of verse-meter has a very significant connection with dogma. It was a measure so rigorous and precise that not a word or a syllable could be taken away or added to it, without its being noticed by the simplest of the faithful. And the truth is that there never was again a popular heresy." *DR*, XCVIII (1886), 345.

was made cardinal, and in 1869 librarian of the Vatican, in which capacity he supervised the preparation of a catalogue of its manuscript treasures during the pontificate of Leo XIII.[52]

Ernest Renan (1823–92),[53] one of the most exquisite of French prose writers, was born in Treguier in Brittany. When he was five his father died and his sister Henriette, then seventeen, undertook to run the household. Dupanloup, later the famous bishop of Orleans, procured for the bright lad a scholarship in the college of St. Nicolas du Chardonnet, which offered instruction to sons of the best families; and after St. Nicolas came a stay at Issy, which prepared students for St. Sulpice at Paris. Thus Renan seemed launched on his studies for the priesthood. But he never took orders and instead resolved to live the life of a scholar. While tutoring in a boys' school, Renan studied Semitic philology, and in 1847 was given the Prix Volney for a history of the Semitic languages. Four years later the government recognized his talents and sent him on a scientific mission to Italy.

A work on *Averroes et l'averroisme* (1852) brought him the doctorate and some recognition as a thinker. His translations of Job and of the Song of Songs showed that he was qualified for the chair of Hebrew and Chaldaic languages in the Collège de France, and the Emperor would have given it to him; but the Catholic party and the Empress were hostile to a turncoat seminarist with heretical tendencies, so Napoleon sent him to study the archaeology of Phoenicia (1860–61). The inscriptions Renan collected on this expedition formed the basis for the future *Corpus inscriptionum semiticarum*, and there was no reason to withhold the coveted professorship any longer.

Taine has described the scene at Renan's opening lecture.[54] Renan entered the lecture-room amid a thunder of cheers and jeers. For twenty minutes he could not say a word, but attempted by gestures to obtain silence. He spoke on what civilization owed to the Semites. There were some bold passages on Christianity and the Pope; Jesus was referred to as "an incomparable man." His lectures were finally

[52] A brief list of Pitra's writings is given in the *Catholic Encyclopaedia*. Besides those already mentioned, the chief are: *Hymnographie de l'Église grecque* (1867); *Des canons et des collections canoniques de l'Église grecque* (Paris, 1858); *Juris ecclesiastici Graecorum historia et monumenta* (Rome, 1864–68, 2 v.); *Trinodion katanacticon* (Rome, 1879).

[53] Francis Espinasse, *Life of Ernest Renan* (London, 1895); E. Grant Duff, *Ernest Renan, In Memoriam* (London, 1893); *Selected Essays of James Darmesteter*, tr. from the French by H. B. Jastrow (Boston and New York, 1895); Gabriel Monod, *Les maîtres de l'histoire* (1894); Sainte-Beuve, *Nouveaux Lundis* (Paris, 1867–84, 13 v.), II, 382–421, VI, 1–23; *ER*, CXIX (1864), 574–604, CXXXI (1870), 470–502, CXL (1874), 485–515; *DR*, LIV (1864), 386–419; *QR*, CCIII (1905), 360–64; *NBR*, XL (1864), 184–209; XLVIII (1863), 63–85; *Fortnightly Review*, V (1866), 513–36, XXVIII (1877), 485–509, XXXIII (1880), 625–43, the last by G. Saintsbury. This is only a fraction of a large literature.

[54] *Life and Letters of H. Taine*, tr. by Mrs. R. L. Devonshire (London, 1902–08, 3 v.), II, 190–91.

suspended as a disturbance of the peace. He refused a substitute position as librarian, and turned to his pen for a living.

In 1863 Renan published his *Vie de Jésus*, which he had begun in Syria at his sister's suggestion.[55] Started with no scholarly resources save the New Testament and Josephus, it revealed deep intimacy with the Bible and the Orient alike. Admittedly not a scholarly work, it was something more: the poetic gift of Renan caught the intangible Oriental atmosphere as no writer before or since. Romantic biography rather than a work of edification, it treated Jesus as a man and not a god. The book was denounced thunderously by the clergy, but read with delight by the public.

The *Life of Jesus* was the first in a series of volumes which Renan entitled *Histoire des origines du Christianisme*,[56] and which together present a picture of the first two Christian centuries. The final volume on Marcus Aurelius and his age is one of the finest syntheses of Roman and classical civilization ever written.

The Franco-Prussian War was a shock to Renan, for he and Taine had been admirers of German scholarship. Henceforth many of his writings were of a literary or philological nature. But at the age of sixty the great scholar, on finishing his *Origines*, undertook to write a three-volume *Histoire du peuple d'Israel* (1887–94). He lived to complete it, drawing on the studies of a lifetime, and the materials now available in the early volumes of the great collection he had himself suggested, the *Corpus inscriptionum semiticarum* published by the Academy of Inscriptions (1881 ff.). His *History of Israel* is a rationalization of the Old Testament, explaining its origin by the environment and the racial characteristics of the Jews.

Renan was the most perfect type of French savant, combining learning with a literary style of the highest order. He was a consummate literary artist. Taine liked to say that what he admired most in the writings of Renan was that "one could not see how it was done." He possessed a remarkable power of analysis and synthesis, but was perhaps greater in the latter than the former; he happily employed what he called "le art de divination et de conjecture." "He has impressions, a word which expresses the whole thing," said Taine, " (he is) a poetical Kant with no formula . . . a skeptic who where his skepticism makes a hole, stops up the hole with mysticism . . . for everything else, he is a pure Positivist. He believes in natural laws only, and absolutely

---

[55] See the dedicatory letter to her spirit at its beginning. Henriette had died before their re-imbarcation for France.

[56] Paris, 1863–83, 8 v. The others were: *Les Apôtres* (1866); *Saint Paul* (1869); *L'Antechrist* (1878); *Les Évangiles et la seconde génération chrétienne* (1877); *L'Église chrétienne* (1879); *Marc Aurèle et la fin du monde antique* (1882).

denies all supernatural intervention." [57] For the time in which Renan wrote his views on the New Testament were extremely radical, but today he would be regarded as a moderate or even conservative "higher critic." He questioned the genuineness of only Paul's letters to Ephesians, Titus, and Timothy.

The greatest church historian of France in recent years, Louis Duchesne (1845–1922),[58] was like Renan of Breton birth. His bishop, who observed him at the seminary, marked him for a teaching career, and sent him for two additional years to the French seminary at Rome (1867); and in his youth Duchesne was a stout Ultramontanist. His further education, however, forecast a somewhat different career; for he learned textual criticism at the École des Chartes in Paris, and in 1872 was appointed to the recently established École de Rome, where the great archaeologist de Rossi became his close friend.[59] His doctoral thesis was his famous *Étude sur le Liber Pontificalis*, the text of which he afterwards edited.

A state position was offered him, but Duchesne chose to remain in the service of the church. Yet he was spiritually out of place as teacher in the conservative Institut catholique at Paris. His researches in French hagiography raised a storm of protest, beginning with an article in 1885 which exploded the claims of the see of Sens to an apostolic foundation. His *Fastes épiscopaux de l'ancienne Gaule* (1894–99, 2 v.) disposed of the cherished legends of the saints of the Midi and Provence. Duchesne's friend, the rector of the Institut, twice tried to lay the storm by giving him leaves of absence from his teaching duties, which Duchesne used for finishing his great edition of the *Liber Pontificalis* (1886–82, 2 v.). In 1895 Duchesne found relief in the École de Rome, maintained by the French government, where he was beyond the reach of the hierarchy.

From the critical editing of texts, Duchesne turned to constructive historical composition.[60] As the first volume of his *Histoire ancienne de l'Église* (Paris, 1906–10, 3 v.) appeared, there was no critic who could think of its equal. It at once commanded respect for its "vast

[57] *Life and Letters of H. Taine* (n. 54), 203–04.

[58] Claude d'Habloville, *Monsignor Duchesne* (Paris, 1911); Ch. Guignebert, "Mgr. Duchesne," *RH*, CXLI (1922), 307–14; Batiffol," Louis Duchesne, His Life and Work," *Journal of Theological Studies*, XXIV, 253 ff.; *QR*, CCXXI (1914), 15–26; *DR*, CXLIV (1909), 132–43; obituary in *Catholic Historical Review*, II (1922), 214–16.

[59] They collaborated in an edition of the Hieronymian Martyrology for the *Acta Sanctorum*. De Rossi conceived such a respect for Duchesne's judgment that he later said: "I write nothing without asking myself what Duchesne thinks of it."

[60] His *Origines du culte chrétien* (1889) was a successful attempt to popularize the liturgical researches of the nineteenth century. It was translated into English from the 3rd French edition by M. L. McClure, as *Christian Worship: its Origin and Evolution. A Study of the Latin Liturgy up to the Time of Charlemagne* (London, 1903).

learning, the sureness of selection which picks one fact of twenty, the illuminating summaries, the impartial justice, the witty epigrams." When a surer terrain was reached in the third volume, however, adverse criticism manifested itself. This was the time when modernism was a burning issue in the Church, and the work was put upon the Index. It is told that a friend asked him when he would finish the fourth volume of his *History*. The answer was: "Je n'ose pas." [61]

[61] A supplementary volume, *L'église au VIe siècle* (Paris, 1926) was edited after Duchesne's death from his nearly completed manuscript by Dom H. Quentin. The earlier volumes have been translated into English as *Early History of the Christian Church* (New York, 1904–24, 3 v.).

CHAPTER LX

PROTESTANT HISTORIANS

THE new awakening of Protestant ecclesiastical history in the nineteenth century began in Germany and was due to the influence of three movements. The first was religious in nature and arose from a vigorous reaction to Rationalism. To the frigid orthodoxy, or the indifferent intellectualism of the eighteenth century, Pietism opposed a strong current of emotion. The second influence was Romanticism. This new appreciation of the past, especially of the Middle Ages, also implied greater sympathy for, and a new understanding of, the history of the church. Finally, German philosophy, particularly Kant, Schelling, Fichte, and Hegel, profoundly influenced the new theological thought.

The revival of Protestant historiography may be said to begin with Gottlieb Jakob Planck (1751–1833),[1] professor at Göttingen and teacher of Neander. He lectured and wrote on church history, theological method, and the history of dogma.[2] Doctrines, he declared, must be based upon a critical exegesis, freedom of research was essential, and tolerance must be accorded to others. Planck's *Lehrbegriff* was epochal as the first attempt at a non-partisan account of the Reformation, and a treatment of the rise of Lutheranism as a system of theology. He made large and critical use of the original sources, and was much fairer to his subject than his friend Spittler.

The call to impartiality was seconded by Johann Karl Ludwig Gieseler (1793–1854).[3] Gieseler was educated at Halle, interrupted a tutorship to carry arms against Napoleon in 1813, and rose after those exciting years to a chair of theology, first at Bonn (1819), and later at

---

[1] For all the historians mentioned in this chapter see the excellent articles in the *Realencyklopädie für protestantische Theologie und Kirche*, 3rd ed. edited by Albert Hauck (Leipzig, 1896–1913, 24 v.). On Planck see also F. Chr. Bauer, *Die Epochen der kirchlichen Geschichtsschreibung* (Tübingen, 1852); Karl Aner, *Die Theologie der Lessingszeit* (Halle, 1929); *Allgemeine deutsche Biographie*, XXVI, 224–27.

[2] *Geschichte der Entstehung, der Veränderungen und der Bildung unseres protestantischen Lehrbegriffs* (Leipzig, 1781–1800, 6 v.); *Geschichte der Entstehung und Ausbildung der christlich-kirchlichen Gesellschaftsverfassung* (Hanover, 1803–09, 5 v.); *Geschichte des Christentums in der Periode seiner ersten Einführung in die Welt durch Jesum und die Apostel* (1818, 2 v.).

[3] There is a biographical sketch of Gieseler, by his continuator and literary executor E. R. Redepenning, in the fifth volume of his *Lehrbuch der Kirchengeschichte* (see next note); see Herzog's article in the *Protestantische Realencyklopädie:* and the article by Wagenmann in *Allgemeine deutsche Biographie*, IX (1879), 163–66.

Göttingen (1831). His large manual of church history [4] struck a new note. It was composed on the principle of letting the sources speak for themselves. A succinct text outlines the chief divisions, and the very full notes present the evidence. Under Gieseler's skillful hands the work became a veritable mosaic of source-extracts. The method goes back indeed to Tillemont and Mosheim. Gieseler's merit lay in introducing his generation to the raw materials of history, but he was so self-effacing that Döllinger called him the most leathern and unimaginative of historians.

The man who really gave life and spirit to German Protestant historiography was August Neander (1789–1850) [5] at Berlin. Born a Jew, he originally bore the name of David Mendel, and through his mother was distantly related to the philosopher Mendelssohn. At the Hamburg gymnasium the precocious lad became absorbed in Plato's idealism. Schleiermacher's *Reden* induced him to accept Christian baptism (1806), at which time he adopted the name of August Neander. He went to Halle to study law, but turned to theology. When war-time conditions necessitated a removal to Göttingen, Neander attached himself to Planck, and resolved to devote his life to church history. After a brief and not very happy experience in the practical ministry, he took his degree at Heidelberg. The publication of his monograph on the Emperor Julian focused national attention upon his talents; [6] and he was invited to join Schleiermacher, Marheinecke, and De Wette at the newly-founded University of Berlin as the youngest member of Germany's most celebrated theological faculty.

Neander was the guide of Germany's youth for thirty-eight years. Never robust, he was frequently ill, and practically blind in the last three years of his life. Yet he toiled unceasingly, and his great learning, wide sympathies, and lovable personality endeared him to his students.

[4] *Lehrbuch der Kirchengeschichte* (Darmstadt and Bonn, 1824–57, 5 v.; repeated editions, with a sixth supplementary volume by Redepenning). English translation by F. Cunningham (Philadelphia, 1836, 3 v.), and by S. Davidson (Edinburgh, 1848–56, 5 v.), later revised by H. B. Smith and Mary A. Robinson (New York, 1857–81).

[5] Adolf von Harnack, "Rede auf August Neander" (1889), reprinted in his *Reden und Aufsätze* (2nd ed., Giessen, 1906, 2 v.), I; K. F. Schneider, *August Neander* (Schleswig, 1894); J. L. Jacobi, *Erinnerungen an August Neander* (Halle, 1882); A. Wiegand, *August Neanders Leben* (1889); Philip Schaff, *Saint Augustine, Melanchton, Neander. Three Biographies* (New York, 1886); *NBR*, XIV (1850–51), 421–49; J. H. Stuckenberg, *Lutheran Quarterly*, X, 220; K. R. Hagenbach, "Neander's Services as a Church Historian,' *Bibliotheca Sacra*, VIII (1851), 822–57; *NAR*, LXXX (1855), 199–208.

[6] His chief works: *Ueber den Kayser Julianus und sein Zeitalter* (Leipzig, 1812; English translation by G. V. Cox, New York, 1850); *Der heilige Bernhard und sein Zeitalter* (Berlin, 1813; English by M. Wrench, London, 1843); *Der heilige Chrysostomus und die Kirche besonders. des Orients in dessen Zeitalter* (1821–22; English by J. C. Stapleton, London, 1838); *Allgemeine Geschichte der christlichen Religion und Kirche* (Hamburg, 1826–52, 6 v.; English translation by J. Torrey, London, 1850–52, 8 v.); *Die Geschichte der Pflanzung und Leitung der christlichen Kirche durch die Apostel* (1832–33, 2 v.; English by J. E. Ryland, New York, Philadelphia, 1844).

He was scholar, romanticist, and pietist in one, but the last was always the dominant note. Neander recognized that history must not only state events, but explain their causes. The force which unified all history for him was the Christian life. Christ was, as it were, the Platonic Idea realizing itself over and over again in a procession of human biographies. In so interpreting history, Neander lost sight of the Church as an institution. He is at his best in the monographs on individual churchmen, but lacked appreciation of the great tides of impersonal forces that sweep across centuries. Neander invested ecclesiastical history with a new spirit after the sterile treatment of the rationalists. His influence was tremendous.[7]

Karl August von Hase (1800–90),[8] who outlived Neander for forty years, was a mind more acute, but his talent for biography was of the same order. Instead of constantly idealizing, he strove for exact and true characterization. His textbook of church history may be mentioned because it revealed a master's skill in compression, and contained novel sections, e.g., on comparative religions or on the relations of the fine arts to Christianity. At the end of a busy life Hase undertook a detailed treatment of ecclesiastical history on the basis of his lectures, but lived to complete only four volumes.[9]

A real advance in critical method came with the rise of the Tübingen school in the thirties, headed by F. C. Baur. Baur and his followers made the first attempt to write the origins of Christianity on strictly historical lines. Ranke was setting the ecclesiastical writers an example of objective history in his *History of the Popes* (1834–36), later followed by the *History of the Reformation Period* (1839–47). It was with the method of Ranke, founded upon a critical examination of the sources (based in turn upon the philological method of Wolf and Niebuhr) that the Tübingen group intended to attack their subject. Though they were theologians, they proposed to interpret history just as the secular writers did.[10]

[7] In Germany Heinrich E. F. Guericke (1803–78) epitomized his volumes, and Karl R. Hagenbach (1801–74), his pupil and a professor at Basel, popularized him for the general reader. Through the numerous textbooks and lucid manuals of Johann Heinrich Kurtz (1809–90) the seed passed into the gymnasia and lower seminaries. The diligent Philip Schaff represents an American off-shoot. These, with Nieder, Gieseler, and Karl Hase, are sometimes denominated the "evangelical or pietistic" historians.

[8] Richard Bürkner, *Karl von Hase, ein deutscher Professor* (Leipzig, 1900); see also his own *Ideale und Irrtümer* (1872; 5th ed., 1894), and the *Annalen meines Lebens* (Leipzig, 1891); Frédéric Lichtenberger, *History of German Theology in the Nineteenth Century* (Edinburgh, 1889).

[9] *Lehrbuch der Kirchengeschichte* (1834, 12th ed., 1900); *Kirchengeschichte auf Grundlage akademischer Vorlesungen* (3 parts in 4 vols., parts 2–3 edited by Krüger, 1891–97; part 1 in 3rd ed., 1901), the first volume of which was published in 1885, when Hase was 85 years old. Other works· *Franz von Assisi, ein Heiligenbild* (Leipzig, 1856; new ed., 1892); *Die Jungfrau von Orléans* (Leipzig, 1851).

[10] Critics may not agree as to the exact relation of David Friedrich Strauss (1808–74) to the Tübingen group. Baur had been a favorite teacher with this acute and passionate mind,

Ferdinand Christian Baur (1792–1860),[11] the son of a Württemberg pastor, was a solid and somewhat reserved student of philosophy and theology who manifested no alarming signs during his years at the seminary of Blaubeuren and the University of Tübingen (1809–14). Fichte and Schelling were then at the height of their success, but Baur quietly attended the lectures of Bengel, whose theological learning and piety made the older Tübingen school so renowned. He returned as instructor to Blaubeuren, and became interested in the relations of early Christianity with contemporary pagan and Jewish thought. His first important publication, *Symbolik und Mythologie* (3 v., Stuttgart, 1824–25), had more than a touch of Schleiermacher, and contained the significant phrase: "Without philosophy, history seems to me to be deaf and dumb." His reward was a call to the reorganized faculty of Tübingen, where Bengel had passed away. Baur's ability to attract and inspire students soon left him without a rival.

Further studies, especially in Manichaeism and Gnosticism, led him away from Schleiermacher and closer to Hegel. By applying the notion of development to dogma, after the antithetical process of the Hegelian dialectic, Baur became the father of the modern history of dogma (*Dogmengeschichte*). This was an important step in ecclesiastical historiography. The old un-historical concept of dogma thought of it as a doctrinal pronouncement imbedded full-grown, though perhaps only in implicit form, in the Christian scriptures. Baur led the way in the recognition that dogmas are ideas which are only assembled, developed, and grafted upon each other in a long historical process; and that they mirror the thoughts and fortunes of the factions in the Church at any given century. Baur's writings on the history of various dogmas re-

but Strauss' *Leben Jesu*, published in 1835, antedated most of his master's own studies in New Testament literature. At any rate, the work which cost Strauss his coveted academic career and made his name anathema in Germany, though it rested upon specious philosophical assumptions, served a valuable purpose. Strauss' task was purely destructive. He revealed the fatal weaknesses of the traditional orthodox and rationalistic exegesis and raised the question of the nature of the biblical sources. On Strauss see the lives by Adolf Hausrath, *David Friedrich Strauss und Theologie seiner Zeit* (Heidelberg, 1876–78, 2 v.); and Samuel Eck, *David Friedrich Strauss* (Stuttgart, 1899); G. Krüger, *American Journal of Theology*, IV, 514–35; "Strauss and the Mystic Theory," *NAR*, XCI (1860), 130–48; E. Zeller, "Strauss und Renan," *HZ*, XII (1864), 70–133; and "Die Tübinger historische Schule," *ibid.*, IV (1860), 90–173; "David Friedrich Strauss," *BQR*, LX (1874), 41–68; *ER*, LXXXVIII (1848), 94–104, and CXXXVIII (1873), 536–69; "New Testament Criticism," *QR*, CXCVII (1897), 270–307.

[11] F. Ch. Baur, *Die Tübinger Schule und ihre Stellung zur Gegenwart* (Tübingen, 1859); R. P. Dunn, "The Tübingen Historical School," *Bibliotheca Sacra*, XIX (1862), 75–105; PATTISON, II, 230–37; also published in the *Westminster Review*, XXI (1862), 169–200; Richard Fester, *Die Säkularisation der Historie* (Berlin and Leipzig, 1908); *DR*, series 4, XXIV, 46; Zeller, "F. C. Baur," and "Die Tübinger historische Schule," in *Vorträge und Abhandlungen*, vol. I (1875).

vealed strong powers of analysis and the ability to track ideas and intellectual movements across the centuries.[12]

Consistency drove Baur, when he came to the writings of the New Testament, to apply the same critical method he had used on other historical sources.[13] According to his own story the preparation of his lectures on the Epistles of Paul to the Corinthians first opened to him new vistas for historico-critical study. Commencing with the factions in the Corinthian congregation, he discovered rifts, divergent tendencies, and controversial matter in much of the New Testament, and it occurred to him that these quarrels might serve to date the literature and reflect back on its contents and purpose. He assumed a division in the early Church between the Jewish followers of Peter and those who upheld the Gentile freedom proclaimed by Paul. Baur reasoned that (in accordance with the Hegelian formula of thesis, antithesis, synthesis) the opposition between these two groups must have been strongest in apostolic days, that only time and the urge of self-preservation could have brought about compromise and unity. This conciliation, he argued, did not take place until after several generations. As each book of the New Testament was meant for contemporaries, writings which are early must reveal such party spirit, or *Tendenz*. Conversely, any book which appears to be conciliatory, or is silent on the matters of dispute, must *ipso facto* be of a later origin. *Ephesians*, which stresses the united church, must be post-apostolic, and cannot be ascribed to Paul himself!

The work of dissecting and classifying the Epistles was slowly but carefully done. Baur had begun in 1836 with *Romans;* in his monograph on Paul in 1845 he believed he could announce that the apostle had composed only the four great letters (*Galatians, I and II Corinthians*, and *Romans* save for the last two chapters). *Acts* was definitely declared to be post-apostolic. In due time the Gospels themselves passed into the same crucible, though Baur took ten deliberate years to lead his followers to that point. In 1844 he moved his battery up

[12] Chief of these writings were his study on the Atonement (1838), and works on the doctrines of the Trinity and of the Incarnation (1841, 1843).

[13] Baur always appeared to resent the imputation that he had gotten his impetus from his former pupil Strauss. He maintained that he had travelled independent lines, and that Strauss' method was quite inferior. Strauss himself compared his task to the storming of the citadel, Baur's to the slow siegework by which, inch by inch, the territory is won and the enemy obliged to retreat. "From the point of view of the orthodox believers there was little to choose between the systems of Strauss and Baur. Both denied supernaturalism; both left the Person of Christ in obscurity; both removed from Christian theology much of the basis of historical fact on which it rested. Both translated religion into terms of thought, and confused the faith of simple souls with speculative theories. But they effected this salutary result. They set criticism on a surer path, put new life into theology, and taught apologists the value of doubt." V. F. Storr, *Development of English Theology* (London and New York, 1913), 214.

on the Fourth Gospel, and in 1847 opened fire on them all. When the first barrage ceased, and the smoke rolled away, it appeared the damage was less than expected. Yet the landscape had a different air and meaning. The traditional order of composition of the Gospels remained, but the intervals of time between them had been lengthened, and over against the earlier Synoptics (Matthew, Mark, and Luke) the Gospel of John was assigned to the Gnostic period of the second century, because of its obvious conciliatory motive.

To this point Baur had carried on the work almost single-handed, but now he received the strong support of his pupils, who included Koestlin, Zeller (Baur's son-in-law), Schwegler, Weizsäcker, Hilgenfeld, and for a time Ritschl. Schwegler in particular produced some penetrating studies of the Christian literature of the first three centuries. The triumph of the Tübingen group was dampened somewhat by the hostility of reactionary governments after 1848, which held liberalism even in theology suspect.[14] But Baur moved on to the constructive task that still awaited him: to write the genetic development of the early Christian Church from the sifted documents. His merits are hardly diminished by the unsuccessful solutions he offered in the last years of his life. Their great weakness is the burden of Hegelian philosophy. What proved a suggestive idea in the first stages was a treacherous guide thereafter, as the Catholic scholar Döllinger so well saw. Thus it happened that the Tübingen school as a "criticism of tendency" passed away with the death of its founder (1860).

Nevertheless, it must be granted that the Tübingen group applied their basic ideas with rare constancy and care. The Hegelian idea of development brought about a much larger appreciation of the religious factors already in existence before Christianity; comparative religions arose as a new and fascinating study. The critical note was maintained, to the very destruction of Baur's proudest discoveries; the opposition of Paulinism and Petrinism was softened down; literary and philological analyses, and lexical and metric studies replaced the hunt for phrases revealing a "Tendenz." But the principle that all historical documents are subject to the same criteria remained established and unshaken. Even conservative scholars followed the lead. Tischendorf and Gregory, Oscar von Gebhardt and Bernhard Weiss, Nestle and Von Soden (as well as Westcott and Hort in England) applied the finest methods of lower textual criticism as developed by philology to the reconstruction of entire families of New Testament manuscripts. Theodor Zahn devoted the prodigious powers of his mind and the

---

[14] Märklin turned to a secular calling; Zeller had to leave theology and accepted a chair of philosophy at Marburg (1849).

research of a long life to the study of the historical formation of the canon, and to commentaries built upon the earliest Christian writers. Investigation of the biblical writings has gone far since the day when Buxtdorf insisted that even the Massoretic punctuation of the Hebrew Old Testament was "inspired by the Holy Ghost," and Bengel dared not publish a critical text of the Greek New Testament.

In the seventies of the last century a new influence made headway which originated in the person of Albrecht Benjamin Ritschl (1822–89).[15] While a student at Bonn and Halle he had pained his father, a conservative bishop of Pomerania, by the way in which he veered towards a critical and speculative position. He was much interested in Hegelianism, and after taking his doctorate (1843) he joined the Tübingen circle around Baur. But Ritschl's mind was independent in its operations, and after several works in the Tübingen manner he began to question his own theses.[16] By 1857 he had broken definitely with Baur and his group and presumed vigorously to upset their hypotheses. Passing to a professorship at Göttingen, he broadened his studies in the history of dogma, especially on Justification and Reconciliation, these specifically Protestant doctrines. After the turn of the seventies in the growing and throbbing German Empire Ritschl was a well-known figure on the theological horizon. He refused calls to Strassburg and Berlin. His importance for German theology is that he retained the critical method, but directed it into new channels. The Tübingen influence was asserted by many to be purely destructive. Ritschl eschewed philosophy, and built his Protestant system upon a few but powerful ideas. He himself claimed to carry on Luther and Schleiermacher.

What is called the Ritschlian school was never a closely knit group; all tendencies were represented. Ritschlianism bowed neither to philosophy nor the fiat of orthodoxy, but sought to establish a tenable position between religion and modern science. It gave great support to the *religionsgeschichtliche Schule*. All theories of a special divine inspiration of the Scriptures were rejected, and the ethical and experiential nature of religion was stressed. In contrast to the eighteenth-century conception of Christianity purely as a system of doctrines, a

---

[15] O. R. Ritschl (a son), *Albrecht Ritschls Leben* (Freiburg, 1892–96, 2 v.); J. H. Stuckenberg in *American Journal of Theology*, II, 268; Gustav Ecke, *Die theologische Schule Albrecht Ritschls und die evangelische Kirche der Gegenwart* (Berlin, 1897); Robert Mackintosh, *Albrecht Ritschl and His School* (London, 1915).

[16] Ritschl's writings of an historical nature: *Das Evangelium Marcions und das kanonische Evangelium des Lukas* (Tübingen, 1846); *Die Entstehung der altkatholischen Kirche* (Bonn, 1850); *Die christliche Lehre von der Rechtfertigung und Versöhnung* (3 v., Bonn, 1870–74; English translation, 1872 and 1900), his masterpiece; *Geschichte des Pietismus* (3 v., Bonn, 1880–86).

Weltanschauung which men could put on or off as something external, these historians at the end of the nineteenth century came to look upon Christianity as the organic religious life of a great human community, embracing many movements, but never ceasing to readapt its materials to changing needs and different circumstances. Religion thus escaped the straight-jacket of fixed creed and final formula. In such an atmosphere Julius Wellhausen rewrote the story of the Jewish religion, and Old Testament scholars applied Baur's methods to the analysis of the Pentateuch. The extremists applied the notion of evolution to Christianity itself, and professed to see in it a syncretistic formation from other religions (e.g., the Greek mystery religions), which in turn was likely to be changed or superseded. Troeltsch emphasized the social duties of the church. The rise of socialism and the *Kulturkampf* brought these historical problems and questions home to the churches of Germany.

In 1876 the *Zeitschrift für Kirchengeschichte* was founded and long edited by Hermann Reuter (1817–89),[17] who was professor at Breslau, Greifswald, and Göttingen (1876 ff.) and died shortly after Ritschl. After the passing of the great church historians of the first half of the nineteenth century, Reuter was one of the leading Protestant scholars. For decades he excelled his fellows in the severity of his method, which alone raised him above all the other pupils of Neander. Reuter felt that church historians had neglected the political side of the Church, its place and influence in world affairs, and he was not minded to maintain the restricted boundaries Neander had set for the discipline. His *History of Alexander III* recaptured, after a long interval, the respect of secular historians for ecclesiastical writers; Ranke said of the book that one did not notice at all that a church historian had written it.[18]

The last and greatest light of Protestant Germany was Adolf von Harnack (1851–1930),[19] a Ritschlian. The quality of his historical

[17] See the notice of Reuter by Theodor Brieger, his pupil, in the *Zeitschrift f. Kirchengeschichte*, II (1890), 434–447; and the article by Theodor Kolde in the *Protestantische Realenzyklopädie* (3rd ed., 1905), vol. XVI.

[18] *Geschichte Alexanders des Dritten und der Kirche seiner Zeit* (1845, 1 v.; 2nd ed., 1860–64, 3 v.). He also wrote *Geschichte der religiösen Aufklärung im Mittelalter* (Berlin, 1875–77, 2 v.); *Augustinische Studien* (Gotha, 1887).

[19] *Adolf von Harnack*, by his daughter Agnes von Zahn-Harnack (Berlin, 1936); E. Schmidt and E. Seeberg, *Adolf von Harnack* (in *Sammlung gemeinverständlicher Vorträge und Schriften aus dem Gebiet der Theologie und Religionsgeschichte*, Heft 150, 1930); Felix E. Hirsch, "The Scholar as Librarian, to the Memory of Adolf von Harnack," *The Library Quarterly*, IX (1939), 299–320, with valuable bibliography; F. B. Clogg, "Adolph von Harnack," *LQR*, CLIV, 241–46; Thomas Nicol, "Harnack among the Apologists," *ibid.*, CVII (1907), 23–29; *American Journal of Archaeology*, series 2, XXXV (1937), 65; *DR*, series 4, XV, 1; *QR*, CCXX, 62. Lists of Harnack's earlier works may be found in the *Protestantische Realenzyklopädie*; cp. also J. L. Neve in *Lutheran Church Quarterly*, III, 351–55; Friedrich Smend, ed., *Adolf von Harnack, Verzeichnis seiner Schriften* (Leipzig, 1927). His chief historical works are: *Lehrbuch der Dogmengeschichte* (Freiburg, 1886–90, 3 v.; 6th ed., 1922; English tr. by Neil Buchanan

workmanship was second to that of no secular German historian of his day. He was indeed the peer of the greatest of them, and that fact spells the revolution which the nineteenth century brought in Protestant historiography. Harnack has described his four grandparents as "a middle-class East Prussian, a Westphalian peasant's son, a Livonian bourgeois, and a Livonian noblewoman." Born in Dorpat, he was educated at the local university and among his Balt kinsfolk; and he retained throughout his life social sympathies of the widest order. He spoke Russian like a second mother tongue.

Harnack's own powers, and the circumstance that Hans Delbrück, the Imperial tutor and adviser, was his brother-in-law, early brought the young man into the circle of great minds like Mommsen (whose daughter he afterwards married), Dilthey, and Wilamowitz-Möllendorff. He began his academic career as *privat-dozent* in church history at Leipzig (1874), and soon established a national reputation by his sound textual work in a collection of the early Christian Fathers (in collaboration with von Gebhardt and Theodor Zahn). In a triumphal procession he moved from one university to another: Giessen (1879), Marburg (1886), and finally ended at Berlin (1888). Before the outbreak of the First World War he was one of the most famous scholars in imperial Germany, took a great interest in public affairs, and influenced the educational program of the nation. In the unhappy years of the post-war Republic Harnack was a rallying-point for German scholarship and staunchly aided in the revival of research and publication.[20]

The output of Harnack's pen is equally astounding for its quantity and its uniformly high quality. He has no less than 1,800 titles of books and articles to his credit, an achievement which invites comparison with Mommsen and Leopold Delisle. Any detailed discussion is impossible. A scholar above reproach, a high authority on the ante-Nicene period of Christian history, Harnack also possessed a popular and fluent style. He and his fellows sought to establish, on the basis of a critical study of history, a reconciliation between ecclesiastical Christianity and modern culture. Harnack's method was the same as that

as *History of Dogma*, London, 1895–1900, 7 v.); *Geschichte der altchristlichen Litteratur bis Eusebius* (Leipzig, 1893–1904, 2 v. in 4); *Die Mission und Ausbreitung des Christentums in den ersten drei Jahrhunderten* (Leipzig, 1902; 4th ed., 1924; English by James Moffat under the title: *The Expansion of Christianity in the First Three Centuries* (London and New York, 1904–05, 2 v., new ed., 1908).

[20] For any adequate conception of Harnack's place in public life, the reader must turn to his daughter's biography. In 1900 he prepared the official history of the Berlin Academy of Science; from 1905 to 1921 he was general-director of the Preussische Staatsbibliothek at Berlin; and from 1910 he was president of the Kaiser-Wilhelm-Gesellschaft zur Förderung der Wissenschaften which was founded at his suggestion on the centenary of the Berlin University. In 1929 this association erected a "Harnack-Haus" in his honor as an accommodation for foreign savants coming to work in Berlin.

of the secular historian, and naturally his results did not please the orthodox theologians. In his *Lehrbuch der Dogmengeschichte* (1886 ff.) he explained the early Christian doctrines as Hellenistic conceptions imposed upon the original Gospel; they originated from apologetic endeavors to place Christian tradition into the framework of Greek philosophy. No one has studied these earlier centuries with greater acumen and penetration. Harnack's greatest historical work is the *Expansion of Christianity* (1902). Its critics objected to the notion of a gradual Hellenization of a Jewish religion, but it must be granted that the author reached behind the screen of haphazard events to those intangible but powerful threads which compose the woof of cultural history. Wherever one reads him, in Harnack Protestant historiography has attained objectivity,[21] perfected its method, and accepted the requirements of scientific work. Harnack exemplifies his own contention that church history and secular history are one.[22]

The early Church, however, was not the only field where Protestants labored. Ranke and von Sybel had caught the Reformation within the coil of German national achievements. With the establishment of the Empire, the study of Germany's great hero of the sixteenth century was pushed feverishly on. Several valuable editions of Luther's writings and letters were begun, but they have virtually all been superseded by the critical Weimar edition, which is still in progress. Julius Theodor Koestlin (1826–1902),[23] a former student and disciple of Baur, set a new fashion in his Luther-biography, which was accepted for more than a generation as a standard work. Judicious, based on painstaking source-work, with the customary devout gratitude for the Reformer's existence, it tried to present Luther as a gradual psychological development, and traced the course of his life as his mind was molded by experiences at home, in the monastery, the university, and Rome, and in the pulpit. It attempted to answer the problem why the devout

[21] His freedom over against the historic creeds was manifested in the famous "Apostolikum-Streit" of 1892, when a certain Christoph Schrempf refused to employ the Apostolic Creed in his pastorate for critical reasons. Harnack's students asked his opinion, and although he advised moderation, he took a rather critical view of this creed. Subsequently he published *Das Apostolische Glaubensbekenntnis* (1893), and gave his fuller personal beliefs in *Das Wesen des Christentums* (1900), which was translated into several languages, and sold in the 70th thousand in Germany in 1925.

[22] "Relation between Ecclesiastical and General History," *CR*, LXXXVI (1904), 846–59.

[23] Koestlin was born at Stuttgart, studied at Tübingen (1844–48), and then at Berlin. He began as lecturer in the seminary at Tübingen, and his first work was inspired by a visit to Scotland in 1849. He spent five years at Göttingen, ten at Breslau, and a quarter of a century at Halle as professor of the New Testament (1870–96). Chief works: *Martin Luther, sein Leben und seine Schriften* (Eberfeld, 1875, 2 v.; English translation, New York, 1883, 1 v.); *Luthers Theologie in ihrer geschichtlichen Entwicklung* (Stuttgart, 1863, 2 v. in 1; English translation by C. E. Hay, Philadelphia, 1897, 2 v.); *Die schottische Kirche, ihr inneres Leben und ihr Verhältnis zum Staat* (Hamburg, Gotha, and Jena, 1852).

monk came to turn against the Church for which he first professed obedience. Koestlin's labors have been most ably continued by men like Buchwald, Kawerau, Kolde, and Böhmer; and no small influence has been brought to bear on the revision of the old Luther-tradition by the Catholic works of Janssen and Denifle.

In comparison with the Lutherans, the Reformed scholars of Germany have accomplished little, even if the products of Holland, France, and Belgium are thrown in for good measure.[24] Richard Rothe's lectures on church history deserve passing mention.[25] The Reformed historian most widely circulated in English-speaking countries has probably been Merle d'Aubigné (1794–1872), the uncritical and zealous historian of the Reformation. Of Huguenot descent, D'Aubigné conceived the ambition to write his works in 1817, when visiting Germany during the Reformation tercentenary; and was for a time a student of Neander at Berlin. But D'Aubigné is an example of what a church historian should avoid.[26] The one German Reformed scholar who deserves some praise is Johann Jakob Herzog (1805–82), who studied under Schleiermacher and Neander, and taught at Basel, Lausanne, Halle, and Erlangen. He did much for the study of the Waldensians and revolutionized some views about them; but his great service to German theology was the care and labor he devoted to the *Protestant-ische Realenzyklopädie*. The third edition of this capstone of Protestant scholarship was brought out by Albert Hauck (1845–1918), who also wrote a truly model history of the German church up to the Reformation, the like of which no other country can show.[27]

In England the Catholic John Lingard (1771–1851)[28] properly did

[24] J. F. Thym, *Historische Entwicklung der Schicksale der christlichen Kirche* (Berlin, 1800–01, 2 v.); G. Muncher, *Lehrbuch der christlichen Kirchengeschichte* (Marburg, 1804); Fr. Schleiermacher, *Geschichte der christlichen Kirche* (ed. by Bonnell, Berlin, 1840); Petrus Hofstede de Groot, *Institutiones historiae ecclesiae* (Groningen, 1835); H. J. Royaards, *Compendium historiae ecclesiae christianae* (Leipzig, 1840); W. J. Matter, *Histoire du christianisme et de la société chrétienne* (Strassburg, 1829, 4 v.; Paris, 1838); Edmund de Pressense, *Histoire des trois premiers siècles de l'église chrétienne* (Paris, 1858–77, 6 v.); Joh. H. Ebrard, *Handbuch der christlichen Kirchen- und Dogmengeschichte* (Erlangen, 1865–67, 4 v.); C. R. Hagenbach, *Kirchengeschichte von der ältesten Zeit bis zum 19. Jahrhundert* (Leipzig, 1869–72, 7 v.); the same, *Lehrbuch der Dogmengeschichte* (1847, 2 v.).

[25] F. W. Nippold, *Richard Rothe. Ein christliches Lebensbild auf Grund der Briefe Rothe's* (Wittenberg, 1873–74, 2 v.); Adolf Hausrath, *Richard Rothe und seine Freunde* (Berlin, 1902–06, 2 v.); *BQR*, LVIII (1875), 305–35.

[26] He wrote: *Histoire de la Réformation du seizième siècle* (1835–53; new ed., 1861–62, 5 v.; tr. into German by Martin Runkel, New York, 1852, 4 v., and into English by H. White, New York, 1843–53, 5 v.); *Histoire de la Réformation en Europe au temps de Calvin* (Paris, 1863–78, 8 v.; tr. into English, New York, 1873–76, 6 v., and into German, 1863–66, 4 v.). The *Encyclopaedia Britannica* (9th ed.) estimates that 200,000 copies were sold in the British Isles, and twice that number in the United States.

[27] *Kirchengeschichte Deutschlands* (Leipzig, 1887–1920, 5 v. in 6; vols. I–IV in 3rd and 4th editions).

[28] The standard life is by Martin Haile and Edwin Bonney, *Life and Letters of John Lingard*

not write church history at all. He wrote the secular history of England from the Catholic point of view. Lingard was the son of a converted carpenter and of a mother descended from stout-hearted Catholic recusants. When eleven years of age he was sent to Douai to be educated for the priesthood. The French Revolution destroyed the school at Douai, and its scattered members reassembled at Crook Hall in England, later to move to Ushaw College, the first new Catholic seminary in England, in which Lingard became a teacher.

The *Antiquities of the Anglo-Saxon Church* appeared in 1806. It was the prologue, so to say, of Lingard's great *History of England*. In 1811 he left Ushaw College, and was a priest in the village of Hornby for the next forty years. From this rural place he carried on his researches by letter and the aid of friendly copyists abroad. In 1817 he made a trip to Rome and obtained access to the Vatican Archives. The first volume of his *History* appeared in 1819 from the press of a Protestant publisher. Within fifteen days 500 copies were sold. Lingard described his purpose in a letter to a friend:

> Through the work I make it a rule to tell the truth, whether it made for us or against us; to avoid all appearance of controversy, that I might not repel protestant readers; and yet to furnish every necessary proof in our favour in the notes; so that if you compare my narrative with Hume's, for example, you will find that, with the aid of the notes, it is a complete refutation of him without appearing to be so. This I thought preferable. In my account of the Reformation I must say much to shock protestant prejudices; and my only chance of being read by them depends upon my having the reputation of a temperate writer. The good to be done is by writing a book which Protestants will read. . . .[29]

The Catholic Bishop Milner was the first to attack the work, and declared: "It's a bad book; only calculated to confirm Protestants in their errors." The eighth and final volume was finished in 1831. Lingard's account of the Tudor period aroused Protestant resentment, as it appeared in the years immediately preceding the Catholic Act of 1829. Still he went a long way towards realizing his goal, by constantly suppressing any arrogant statement, skilfully turning the blackguard side of men like Cranmer outwards, and always disarming, if not winning over, the reader by his open appeal to authentic documents. He wrote with candor and an effortless grace; his narrative does not possess a great sweep, but it constantly moves along, and there are no wearisome soliloquies on human nature as in his predecessors. Lingard's *History* was, until John Richard Green, the best general history of England.

(London, 1911). See also *ER*, XXV (1815), 346–54, XLII (1825), 1–31, LV (1831), 1–43; *DR*, XII (1842), 295–362, XL (1856), 1–66, XLI (1856), 1–27; *NAR*, XXIX (1829), 265–81.
  [29] Haile and Bonney (n. 28), 166.

The Oxford Movement was the English analogue of French Ultramontanism. It was a revolt against liberalism, and a species of religious sentimentalism. Tory conservatism and Anglicanism were alarmed over the question of disestablishment. Though the Oxford Movement promoted historical study, it was unhistorically-minded. The historical vision of its supporters was neither tolerant nor comprehensive. They revived patristics, but were the foes of intelligent critical study. Professor Gwatkin of Oxford has gone so far as to lay on their shoulders the blame for England's failure to produce any great achievement in the field of church history.

Henry Hart Milman (1791–1868) [30] did not belong to the Oxford group. He was a popular English liberal-minded historian who ended his life as Dean of St. Paul's, a social lion, and one of the foremost churchmen of England. He almost forfeited his chances of a career because an early work of his offended British conservatism. In 1827 a critic had harshly reviewed an English translation of Niebuhr's *Roman History* because Niebuhr's rough treatment of the "legends" in early Roman history was leading other spirits to apply similar treatment to the Christian Scriptures. Milman should therefore not have been surprised at the reception of his little three-volume work on the *History of the Jews* (1830). His aim had been to bring the life of the Hebrews, as he said, within "the sphere of fact, rather than of pulpit convention." Critics insisted he had invested the tents of Abraham with the disreputable air of Bedouin felt tents; the patriarchs were called "sheiks," and the Israelites lowered from the dignity of the "Chosen People" to the status of a wandering desert tribe. He had rationalized various miracles and declared the chronology of the Old Testament untrustworthy.

Milman's next work was an edition of Gibbon (1838), but Gibbon himself was not in good odor with the theologians, and the work did not help his popularity. It is just to say, however, that his notes show an immense erudition. His *History of Christianity under the Empire* (1840) met with a universal conspiracy of silence, though Newman later declared in his *Apologia* that when he read it he sensed it was a "sort of earnest" of the approaching battle with Rationalism. Yet the historical method was to triumph, despite all attempts of the Oxford Movement to set the hands of the clock back. In 1849 Milman became

---

[30] Arthur Milman, *Henry Hart Milman* (London, 1900); Richard Garnett in *DNB*, XXXVIII, 1–4; William Lecky, *Historical and Political Essays* (London and New York, 1908), reviewed in *NBR*, LIII (1870–71), 603–04; see also "Dean Milman," *ibid.*, L (1869), 99–122; "Dean Milman and St. Paul's," *QR*, CXXVI (1869), 218–47, and the review *ibid.*, XCV (1854), 38–70; *ER*, CVII (1858), 51–87, CXCI (1900), 510–27, CXIX (1864), 137–67; *NAR*, XXXII (1831), 234–65, C (1865), 581–85; *FN*, XXI (1840), 633–47; L (1854), 430–39.

Dean of St. Paul's, and in 1863, when a new generation had arisen, he could reissue his *History of the Jews;* now Englishmen accepted the notion that biblical peoples must be interpreted in the light of other evidence available on their civilization.

Milman's masterpiece is his *History of Latin Christianity in the Middle Ages,*[31] a sort of by-product of his studies on Gibbon. Based upon the sources, which he sometimes fumbled most inexcusably, it preserved the parallel lines of Latin, Greek, and Teutonic Christianity. Macaulay, his friend, acknowledged that the substance was good, though he confessed that concerning the style his judgment would be quite otherwise. There was a refined quality of Christian Romanticism in Milman.

Historical scholarship must always regret the transfer of Mandell Creighton (1843–1901)[32] to the bishopric of London, for history would have been richer had he been able to continue his *History of the Papacy from the Great Schism to the Eve of the Reformation.* For nine years he was fellow and tutor of Merton in Oxford, an equal period he spent in a quiet country vicarage where the first two volumes of his masterpiece were written; for six years he was Dixie professor of ecclesiastical history at Cambridge. A quarter of a century claimed him for one of England's most brilliant scholars. To these accomplishments he added eleven years of administrative duties as bishop, the last four in the most trying of English sees.

As a tutor at Merton he lectured on ecclesiastical, Italian, and Byzantine history. But he found small time for the creative leisure he required, and was glad to leave Oxford for the beautiful church and the historic parsonage of Embleton where he began his famous work. He was put to some difficulty by the lack of an accessible library, and in the end was forced to purchase most of his books. To be a rural dean under Bishop Lightfoot was no sinecure, and again Creighton welcomed a change to Cambridge. The only other historian there in 1885 was Sir John Seeley, whose conception of history was that it provided a valuable preparation for future statesmen. Creighton strove in all possible ways to stir the students out of their sluggishness.[33] He was

---

[31] London, 1854–55, 6 v.; latest edition, 1883–1905, 9 v.

[32] Louise Creighton, *Life and Letters of Mandell Creighton* (London, 1904, 2 v.); G. W. Prothero in *DNB*, Supplement II, 82–88; *ER*, CCI (1905), 109–39; *CQR*, XXVI (1888), 338–406, and Claude Jenkins, "Bishop Creighton's View of History," *ibid.*, CIX (1929–30), 193–238; "Mandell Creighton," CXCIII (1901), 584–622, and *ibid.*, CCII (1905), 458–84; *LQR*, CIII, 45; *The Athenaeum*, January 2, 1904; *The Nation*, LXXX (1905), 35–36.

[33] He tried to interest all the students, but would single out the most promising, encourage them to write books, and insist that they at least select the subject. He refused to be solemn and hidebound by professorial tradition. Once he admonished a student accompanying him on his beloved hikes: "Never say there is nothing to see in a place; always trespass until you are turned out; talk to the natives."

one of the founders, and the first editor, of the *English Historical Review* (1886). The idea of such a journal had been circulating for twenty years, but it took the better part of a year to get out the first issue, and the help of men like Lord Acton was gratefully appreciated.

Creighton was a prolific and rapid writer, but all that he wrote pales into insignificance before the masterly structure of the *History of the Papacy*. Creighton did not possess the advantages which Ranke and his later rival Pastor had; he saw no archival sources. A history written in a Northumberland vicarage from a few books and printed sources cannot compare with the results of a half-century of study amid the treasures of the Vatican. But Creighton's work will live by virtues of its own. He was free from religious or other prejudices. He did not wish to prove anything or to sustain any pet theories. "I do not aspire to write a history of the Reformation," he said, "but merely of the Papacy as a factor in European affairs." Creighton believed in the sincerity of the reforming councils, and thought that the conciliar action was genuine, while Lord Acton, who reviewed him in the *English Historical Review*, felt that Gerson and all the rest were fishing in the troubled waters for their own profit. Acton praised Creighton's learning in his ponderous fashion—"the Northumbrian vicarage in which Bulaeus and Traversari are as familiar as Burnet must be a rare and enviable spot"—but disagreed with his interpretation of history.

The work lacks formal judgments, and it is well known that Acton's strictures fell along this line. He believed that Creighton was slighting the duty of an historian in not pointing out that the Papacy became a despotic power crushing toleration and liberty. Creighton understood Acton to demand "that history should be primarily a branch of the moral sciences," and answered that the very worth and secret of history lay in its aloof and incorruptible impartiality.[34] The Cardinal who reviewed the *History of the Papacy* in the *Dublin Review* wrote that it was "marked by research of original documents, by accuracy in dealing with ecclesiastical matters, and by a calm judicial discernment." York Powell said of the author: "There was always something of the Renaissance about Mandell Creighton. He would have been at his ease in a cardinal's hat."[35]

Creighton's avowed object in his *History* was "to bring together materials for a judgment of the change which came over Europe in the

[34] Letter to Acton: "The inflexible integrity of the moral code is to me the secret of the authority, the dignity, the utility of history. If we may debase the currency for the sake of genius or success or reputation, we may debase it for the sake of a man's influence, of his religion, of his party, of the good cause which prospers by his credit and suffers by his disgrace."

[35] Oliver Elton, ed., *Frederick York Powell; a Life and a Selection from His Letters and Occasional Writings* (Oxford, 1906, 2 v.), II, 51.

sixteenth century, to which the name of 'the Reformation' is loosely given." His penetrating and independent mind did not allow him to accept the party-cries of that time at face value, however. He felt that men must not be thought of as always being swayed by great movements of emotion or thought. It only appears so because the men who make history were clever enough to find a formula in which "the chance of saving sixpence, of gaining sixpence, or of escaping being robbed of sixpence," can be called a decent motive. "If the Pope would have left off pillaging Germany, 'justification by faith only' would have created only a languid interest." He answered Professor Kolde's criticisms by a clear exposition of his approach to the Reformation:

> My point of view is that it was a misfortune for Christendom that the Reformation took the form of a breach of the unity of the Church. . . . I do not think that any breech was inevitable. The question is, Whose fault was it? I have investigated this question as I would investigate any political secession. I have regarded it as a question of Governmental wisdom and justice. I have tried to show that the Papacy behaved towards Luther foolishly and unjustly at first. Luther made no demands which the Church ought not to have been able to supply according to its own principles. The Curia was responsible for driving Luther to revolt.[36]

Thus Creighton deserted the theological arena, where Döllinger and the German Lutherans had maneuvered, for a wholly neutral study which suggested many of the more recent economic and political versions of the Reformation. He moved with perfect sang-froid. Even in the case of Alexander VI he preserved fairness to the uttermost and enumerated the few good things that could be said of him. His treatment of Savonarola is thought to be classic. Bishop Gore put his finger on the real merit of Creighton's work, when he professed his "great gratitude for the 'spirit of judgment' found there."

[36] Letter to Kolde. Some years before Creighton had written of the Reformation that it was "primarily a demand for a redress of the grievances inherent in the absolutism of the Papal administration over the Church. There was no discontent with the doctrines. If the Papacy could have put its administration into better order there would have been no Reformation, but the new learning would have modified men's attitude towards dogma without causing a breach of the unity of the Church."

CHAPTER LXI

BIBLICAL AND JEWISH HISTORY

THE history of Israel and later Judaism ran a course all its own in the last century. Alone of all Eastern peoples of antiquity the Jews had survived as a people and had maintained a written tradition. The Old Testament offered a record of their life and letters, characterized by a remarkable breadth and variety, and unified by a religious purpose. In this story Christian Europe expected no change, but only confirmation and amplification from the excavations begun after the mid-century. Though the public could be readily touched for funds, these excavations were generally disappointing. No sensational finds were made, and the monuments of other lands threw little direct light on the Jewish Scriptures. Not a line was found bearing on the existence of Abraham and the patriachs. Yet the story of the Jewish race bore quite different contours as the twentieth century dawned. The revolution here was wrought, not by the spade of the archaeologist, but by the acumen of the "higher critic"; not by the opening of new sources, but by a more scientific working of the old ones.[1]

Biblical criticism is not new.[2] The *Song of Songs* and *Ezekiel* had passed into the Jewish canon only with difficulty, and *Esther* was long suspect because it did not contain the sacred name Yahweh. Celsus in the second century of the Christian era attacked *Genesis*, and Trypho in the time of Justin Martyr anticipated the views of Gesenius on *Isaiah*. In the third century, Porphyry called *Daniel* in question, and the Clementine Homily disputed the Mosaic authorship of the Pentateuch. In the fourth century Jerome took a non-committal attitude on the composition of the Mosaic writings. In 1520 Luther's friend Carlstadt (Andreas Bodenstein) detected differences in style within single books

[1] For a brief account of the progress of German scholarship, see *Aus fünfzig Jahren deutscher Wissenschaft* [Festgabe an Dr. Schmidt-Ott], ed. by Gustav Abb (Berlin, 1930), 50–52 (Old Testament), and 250–61 (Semitology). The literature on "Higher Criticism" can be easily run down from the bibliographies in the standard introductions to the Old Testament by S. R. Driver, H. Strack, E. König, etc. For the excavations consult H. V. Hilprecht, *Explorations in Bible Lands during the Nineteenth Century* (Philadelphia, 1903), 579–622; S. R. Driver, *Modern Research as Illustrating the Bible: The Schweich Lectures for 1908* (London, 1909); F. J. Bliss, *The Development of Palestine Exploration, being the Ely Lectures for 1903* (London, 1906). See also vol. I, 13, n. 22.

[2] For a rapid review of Old Testament criticism from the second century of the Christian era to the end of the eighteenth, with interesting quotations from various authors, see Edward McQueen Gray, *Old Testament Criticism, Its Rise and Progress* (New York and London, 1923).

ascribed to one author; and Luther and Calvin both excluded the Apocrypha from the canon. Hobbes in his *Leviathan* (1651) appeared as the first English literary critic of the Bible. On the Continent Baruch Spinoza, the Jewish philosopher and pantheist, declared: "in the Pentateuch we have merely notes and collations to be examined at leisure; materials for history rather than the digested history itself." [3]

After Richard Simon (1678) made the repetitions, or doublets, and variety of style an argument against Mosaic authorship of the first books of the Old Testament, criticism stood still in the first fifty years of the eighteenth century. Then in 1753 a little duodecimo work on *Genesis* entitled the learned physician Jean Astruc [4] to be regarded as the Father of Modern Criticism. He printed the book of *Genesis* in four parallel columns, and was the first to separate the "Jahvist" and the "Elohist." A devout believer, Astruc feared that his deductions might be misapplied against religion. He did *not* deny the Mosaic authorship, but suggested that Moses employed various ancient records, dividing them into portions which he incorporated in their entirety. This view Astruc based (1) on the repetitions in *Genesis*, (2) on the alternate use of the names for God (Elohim, Adonai-Jehovah), and (3) on items misplaced out of chronological order. At the present day hardly a biblical scholar of note questions the main contention of Astruc, that *Genesis* consists of a separate E and a J stratum.

There were other forerunners, but the next important light was Johann Gottfried Eichhorn (1752–1827). [5] His three-volume *Introduction to the Old Testament* appeared in 1780–83, and simultaneously with its last portions his friend Herder brought out the famous *Spirit of Hebrew Poetry* (1782–83). Eichhorn, a remarkable and prolific writer, who held a professorial chair at the age of twenty-two, and for 52 years taught Oriental languages at Jena and Göttingen, was the great polyhistor of his day. He has over forty books on history, literature, and science to his credit. Accepted as omniscient, he was really more superficial than his contemporaries realized. Still his merits were many. He strove for historic reality, approaching the Bible as an oriental book, and regarding its contents from the point of view of people of its time. Thus he explained many a miraculous passage by reference to natural

---

[3] In his *Tractatus Theologico-Politicus* (1670), quoted by Gray.

[4] Astruc was of Jewish origin, over twenty years consulting physician to Louis XIV of France, a famous medical authority and writer of textbooks, and professor at the Collège de France. The work mentioned appeared in his seventieth year. See Gray (n. 2), 130.

[5] T. K. Cheyne, *Founders of Old Testament Criticism* (London, 1893); S. I. Curtiss, "Sketches of Pentateuch Criticism," *Bibliotheca Sacra*, XLI (1884), 1–23, 661–97, a fine account of the early critics; Alexandre Westphal, *Les sources du Pentateuque* (Paris, 1888); for biblical criticism in England before 1860, see V. F. Storr, *The Development of English Theology in the Nineteenth Century* (London, 1913, only one volume published).

laws and the superstitions of another day. He was less concerned with
the theological value of the sacred writings than with the light they
cast on antiquity, while his romantic friend Herder popularized their
poetic beauty and brilliant imagery. But while Herder held the Old
Testament to be an epic without a peer, Eichhorn thought that it was
hardly history. Eichhorn's work went through five editions (5th, 1824,
in 5 v.) and became the standard text in many Protestant theological
faculties. He argued that Moses or an author like him wrote the Pentateuch, but employed various documents or sources. His divisions were
much the same as Astruc's. Though jealous scholars scorned his literary manner of presentation, Eichhorn's views found wide acclaim in a
time of general intellectual stirrings.

In 1794 Carl David Ilgen succeeded Eichhorn at Jena, and four years
later he published a book which divided the Elohist in *Genesis* into two
sources (first and second Elohist). While he did not continue his Old
Testament studies, and was too anxious to prove his points, the step
was epoch-making, for one of the two sources was later identified as the
Priestly Code. In 1806 De Wette fixed the date of the first actual publication of *Deuteronomy*, on the basis of *II Kings* XXII, 23. His opinion
that the entire Pentateuch is the result of a gradual development is
the heart and core of the accepted critical view today. Here was a
finished canon, with a minutely elaborated cult and code: clearly this
religion had not sprung into final existence all at once. It was the task
of the nineteenth century to explain its origin, to discover the history
of the *growth* of the Jewish religion.

Staehelin, Hupfeld, and Graf each forged an important link, and
then came Heinrich Ewald (1803–75).[6] Like the great Hebrew lexicographer Wilhelm Gesenius, Ewald was a pupil of Eichhorn.[7] The
tragedy of his life was that of a great genius separated from his colleagues by personal faults and an irritability amounting to intolerance.
Ewald came from a linenweaver's family of Göttingen, attended the
local university and spent most of his life there. Thus he never quite
shook off a certain provincialism of mind. At nineteen he was teacher
in Wolfenbüttel, with access to the Arabic manuscripts of the library
with which Lessing had been associated. Ewald's mind possessed
much of the broad sweep of Eichhorn, through whose influence he was
accepted as tutor in the theological faculty (1824). He had determined

[6] Wellhausen has written the best qualified study of his teacher, in the *Festschrift zur Feier des hundertfünfzigjährigen Bestehens der kgl. Gesellschaft der Wissenschaften zu Göttingen* (1901); see also Cheyne (n. 5), 66–118.

[7] As Wellhausen was his own. Other pupils of Ewald: as diverse as Hitzig, Schrader, Nöldeke, and Dillmann. It is interesting to note in passing that the first Hebrew student of Gesenius was the church historian August Neander.

upon the East as his life's work while still in the gymnasium, and hurdled the difficulties of one oriental language after another. Competing with Gesenius for their deceased teacher's chair, he issued a *Hebrew Grammar* (1827) characterized by rare lucidity and logic. Arabic was a favorite study of his; but he also turned to other than Semitic tongues, and lectured on Sanskrit, Persian, Turkish, Armenian, and Coptic. In Biblical scholarship Ewald ranged over both Old and New Testaments.

His *magnum opus* was the *Geschichte des Volkes Israel*,[8] to which Ewald by 1859 had given more than three decades of thought and revision. Numerous exegetical studies had paved the way for it, and he utilized the processes of criticism as far as it had been developed up to that day, not least by his own efforts. Ewald took a rather equivocal position over against miracles. Devising his own nomenclature, he dissected the Pentateuch into the Book of Covenants, the Book of Origins, three prophetical narrators, and finally the Deuteronomist. The dominant note of Ewald's history, however, was something nearly the opposite of critical. Perhaps the neatest characterization was that by Karl Hase, who called him a prophet with backward gaze and the oriental gift of tongues.[9] Ewald set out to write the story of the spiritual life of Israel with almost a religious urge. He relied much on intuition, and felt the poetic literature and the Psalms were the best approach to the eloquent heart of a great people, before one studied its prophets. Israel's mission in history was to bring forth the one true religion for mankind. This mission ran its course between the exodus from Egypt and the coming of Christ, which time he divided into three great periods. Moses and the theocracy characterized the age of the Hebrews; David and the monarchy led the Israelites; Ezra and the developed priesthood dominated the Jews. The work offers a multitude of details, and while not always easy reading, sometimes rises to inspiring intensity. It was a synthetic effort of great brilliancy, but it closed rather than opened an epoch.

Like the prophets of old, Ewald could brook no views but his own. He resented the contempt of Schleiermacher, Hegel, and F. C. Baur for the Old Testament, and the critic within him turned apologist. In Ewald's eyes, Baur and his Tübingen school were destructive revolutionaries, and the foundations of faith were likely to be ruined by those wise in their own conceits. This explains Ewald's later works on the

---

[8] First edition, 1843–52; third edition, 1864–68, 8 v. It was translated into English by Russell Martineau and J. E. Carpenter as *History of Israel* (London, 1867–74, 5 v.).

[9] "Nach Gesenius hat Ewald die Geschichte des alttestamentlichen Volkes aufgerollt, er ein rückschauender Prophet mit der orientalischen Zungengabe, kühn und zu Opfern bewährt für die Freiheit, nur durch seine sittliche Entrüstung gegen jede abweichende Meinung leicht verstört." Hase, *Kirchengeschichte*, 582, quoted by Cheyne (n. 5), 118.

New Testament. He would hardly have approved the views subsequently developed by his own pupil Wellhausen.

The greatest tribute to Ewald's scholarship was the enormous extension of his influence. Through Dean Stanley the substance of his *History* was disseminated in England,[10] where Milman had already scandalized readers in the "thirties" by his frank treatment of the Jews as an oriental and not the "chosen" people. In England, as on the Continent, the study of Jewish history revived, and began to burst into full flower at the same time that Assyria and Egypt afforded new knowledge to supplement the old. Ewald had been obliged to rely almost wholly on Biblical materials. The power of his name is evinced not least in the fact that for nearly a generation criticism forged ahead in only a select circle, and in the face of public disapproval.

New forces, however, could not be forever denied, and chief of these was the evolutionary hypothesis. Herder had conceived of literature as folklore, and extended this to the Hebrew literature; Hegel emphasized the continuity of ideas. Religion came to be recognized as the creation of a people and not of a single writer or a small group of men. In 1835, the same year that David Strauss' *Leben Jesu* laid down new foundations for the Tübingen school to follow, Wilhelm Vatke (1806–82)[11] released his *Die Religion des Alten Testamentes*. It failed to make the stir of the *Leben Jesu*, though it was equally lashed by criticism, and disappeared from view until the late "sixties." For this Vatke's manner of writing was partly to blame. Reuss, who came to develop similar theories, later explained why he had failed to read it. "The table of contents, with its Hegelian formula, of itself terrified me." Pondering the mental development of a people, Vatke concluded that a people could not rise all at once, and that a slow rise was more logical than an elevated beginning and then a dark decline, as was supposedly presented in Israel by the time of the Judges. He balked at recognizing the advanced religious level and the elaborate cult of the Pentateuch as possibly contemporary with the great leader Moses. If the Pentateuch came from his hand, why should the prophets afterwards object to temple worship and zealous sacrifices? The answer obviously was that Moses never really managed to raise his people as a whole above the polytheism of their neighbors, that the prophets preceded the priests, and that the Law (Torah) ascribed to Moses

---

[10] A. P. Stanley, *Lectures on the History of the Jewish Church* (New York, 1870–77, 3 v.); cp. H. H. Milman, *Essays on the Question of Church and State* (1870).

[11] Heinrich Benecke, *Wilhelm Vatke in seinem Leben und seinen Schriften* (Bonn, 1883); Cheyne (n. 5), 131–42. For Hegel's importance in this connection, see Otto Pfleiderer, *The Development of Theology in Germany since Kant and Its Progress in Great Britain since 1825* (London and New York, 1890), 71 ff., and for Vatke, 252–56.

actually arose in a much later period. The detailed evidence for this view was provided by Vatke's successors: Reuss, Graf, Kayser, and Duhm,[12] and given convincing form by Kuenen and Wellhausen.

While the Tübingen school was revaluating the early Christian documents in Germany, their spirit and method were being applied in Leyden by Scholten to the New, and by Abraham Kuenen (1828–91)[13] to the Old Testament. Kuenen was of an independent mind, but possessed a rare love of truth, sobriety of judgment, and beauty of character. The son of an apothecary at Haarlem, he would have been obliged to discontinue his studies in his fifteenth year when his father died, save for the generosity of friends. At the University of Leyden (1846–51) he studied Semitic languages under the Orientalist Juynboll, and Scholten made him a theologian. After presenting for his doctorate (1851) an edition of part of the Arabic version of the Samaritan Penta-teuch, the promising student was made fellow and then extraordinary professor of Theology (1853). Two years later he was promoted to a full chair, and married the daughter of W. Muurling, one of the founders of the Groeningen school, which marked the first departure from strict Calvinism. His life was quite uneventful, and passed for the most part in Leyden. In 1882 Kuenen went to England to deliver the Hibbert lectures,[14] and the following year he presided at the international Oriental Congress that met at Leyden.

In his inaugural lecture, while rejecting the extremes of certain Biblical critics, Kuenen had said: "The abuse of a thing should not prevent us from using it." He refused to bind Scriptural study by dogma. His volume on the *Religion of Israel*[15] omitted the divine factor. Furthermore, it adopted the Grafian hypothesis, and stated frankly its author's view: that "not only is the priestly legislation chronologically later than the preaching of the prophets, but the priestly historiography is later than the prophetic." Kuenen proceeded to reveal the tenuous

---

[12] For these and others, see Cheyne (n. 5), and the bibliographies of the standard Old Testament introductions; also *Eduard Reuss' Briefwechsel mit seinem Schüler und Freunde Karl Heinrich Graf*, ed. by K. Budde and H. J. Holtzmann (Giessen, 1904).

[13] K. Budde edited a German translation of Kuenen's collected works. A complete list of his writings will be found in *Gesammelte Abhandlungen Kuenens*, also tr. by Budde (Freiburg, 1894), 501–11. For a list of reviews see E. C. Richardson, *An Alphabetical Subject Index and Index Encyclopaedia to Periodical Articles on Religion, 1890–99* (New York, 1907). For his life: P. H. Wicksteed, his English translator, in the *Jewish Quarterly Review*, V (1892), 571–605; C. P. Tiele, "Levensbericht van Abraham Kuenen," in the Year Book of the Amsterdam Academy of Sciences, 1892; Albert Reville, in *Mannen van beteekenis in onze dagen*, XXI (Haarlem, 1890). Critical estimates: C. H. Toy in the *New World*, I (1892), 64–88; Cheyne (n. 5), 185–94; Montefiore in *Jewish Quarterly Review* (1890), 311–21.

[14] *National Religions and Universal Religions* (London and Edinburgh, 1882). It was translated into German by Budde (1883), and there are also Dutch and French translations.

[15] *De Godsdienst tot den ondergang van den Joodschen staat* (1869–70, 2 v.); English translation by Alfred H. May as *The Religion of Israel to the Fall of the Jewish State* (London, 1882–83, 3 v.).

nature of early legendary evidence in any history, and laid stress on inverse reasoning from more recent developments in the life of a people as the basis for sounder conclusions.

To Kuenen the Jewish religion was but one among many religions, albeit of a more elevated nature. A work on the Hebrew prophets [16] developed his views further. He considered them merely a phenomenon in the natural evolution of a nation's religious consciousness, and polemized against those who would base dogma upon the fulfilment of prophecies. Yet he held that the prophets had a claim to posterity's reverence.

Kuenen's greatest work in the field of higher criticism was the *Inquiry* [17] on the Hexateuch and its sources. It had first appeared in the early sixties; the writings of Bishop Colenso and of K. H. Graf, among others, moved him to advance his position in a later revision halted by his death. The *Inquiry* was a careful elaboration of the views characterizing the school of Ewald, with much that was original. Wellhausen in Germany and his followers have all paid tribute to the penetration of the Dutch scholar. Wellhausen himself regarded Kuenen's criticisms as the only valid ones he received on his own *Composition des Hexateuchs*, and welcomed them as leading to his final emancipation "from some relics of the old leaven of a mechanical separation of sources."

Kuenen pointed the way for future inquiry. Having found a new order in the stages of Jewish religion, he utilized a method similar to Baur's, though he came by it independently. Since Kuenen's day the modern practice of beginning a study of primitive Christianity with Paul and not the Jesus of the Gospels is paralleled in the study of the Old Testament by taking the prophets of the eighth pre-Christian century in advance of the professedly earlier historical books. Kuenen realized that higher criticism must entrench itself also in the field of archaeological research in order to check its conclusions. Like Reuss, he labored and died in the quiet conviction that truth would win out and our knowledge continue to expand. His nobility and honesty make his life a fine defense, if one were needed, for the consequences of a critical stand on biblical matters.

The boldest conception of ancient Jewish history has come from the fertile mind of Julius Wellhausen (1844–1918).[18] He came from the

[16] *De Profeten en de profetie onder Israel* (Leipzig, 1865, 2 v.), tr. into English by Adam Milroy as *Prophets and Prophecy in Israel* (London, 1877).

[17] *Historisch-Kritisch Onderzoek naar het onstaand en de versameling van de Boeken des Ouden Verbonds* (Leyden, 1861–65, 3 v.); 2nd ed., much modified (1885–93), of which P. H. Wicksteed rendered a portion into English as *An Historico-Critical Inquiry into the Origin and Composition of the Hexateuch* (London, Oxford, 1886), and T. Weber and C. T. Muller prepared German translations (Leipzig, 1885–94, 3 v. in 2).

[18] Ernst Sellin, "Julius Wellhausen," *Deutsches Biographisches Jahrbuch*, Ueberleitungsband,

home of a Protestant pastor in Hameln. While studying theology at
Göttingen he was captivated by the aged Ewald's lectures and his
Geschichte des Volkes Israel. After his first theological examination
(1865) and two years spent as a private tutor, he returned to the university and studied oriental philology under Ewald's direction. Long
before his thirtieth year he was installed as full professor at Greifswald.
The first of his brilliant studies on the Hexateuch appeared in 1876, when
he was thirty-two. But the opinions which Wellhausen expressed raised
him many enemies, and after a decade he resigned his theological chair, [19]
to start once more at the bottom of the academic ladder with an assist-
ant-professorship in Semitic languages at Halle (1882). He regained
his former status of full professor at Marburg (1885), where among
stimulating colleagues and admiring students he entered upon the happiest period of his life. In 1892 he was invited to Göttingen to take the
Old Testament chair of the great Lagarde. The last fifteen years of his
life were seriously clouded by a growing deafness that became complete
and made his childless old days bitter and lonely. He died in the last
year of the First World War, before Germany's final collapse.

Wellhausen devoted himself successively to three great fields, and in
two at least he proved himself a master. His last studies in New Testament criticism, especially on the Gospels, lacked his first bold originality,
and have failed to maintain themselves in the eyes of scholars. But for
Jewish and for Arabic history and religion the work of Wellhausen has
been epoch-making.

The uninformed who hear an occasional pronouncement that the
views of Wellhausen are outmoded believe this the knell of the passing
of higher criticism, which has succeeded in "disintegrating the disinte-
grators." Such a view is a misconception. The thesis of Wellhausen
and the critical view of the Hexateuch are not synonymous, nor need
the latter fall if the first be denied. Scholars may accept the source-
analysis of higher criticism, without agreeing on the subsequent historical reconstruction on the basis of these sources. Actually, Wellhausen
worked at both tasks, making one serve the other.

As the greatest disciple of Ewald, he equalled his master's largeness
of view and power of construction, but differed from him *toto caelo* in

II (1917–20), 341–44; Eduard Schwartz, *Rede auf Julius Wellhausen* (Berlin, 1919); C. H.
Becker, "Julius Wellhausen," *Der Islam,* IX (1918), 95–99; H. Willrich, "Zur Erinnerung an
Julius Wellhausen," *Deutsche Rundschau,* CLXXV (1918), 407–12; W. R. Smith in *The
Academy,* XV (1879), 429–31, reprinted in his *Lectures and Essays* (London, 1912), 601–07.
A long list of his chief works is given in Schaff-Herzog, and a complete bibliography by Rahlfs
in the *Festschrift: Studien zur semitischen Philologie und Religionsgeschichte, Julius Wellhausen
zum 70. Geburtstag* (Giessen, 1914), 353–68.

[19] Sellin says this was because he felt his views precluded any prospects of a call to some
other theological faculty; the writer in Schaff-Herzog ascribes it to religious scruples.

his conception of the course of Israel's religious development. Wellhausen accepted the hypothesis of Graf: that the Priestly Codex (and related portions of the historical books outside the Pentateuch) was the youngest of the sources. He contended that the Mosaic law was in its final form post-exilic, the creation of "Judaism," by which he meant the sect which survived the annihilation of the majority of the Israelites by the great empires of the East. Graf's theory had enjoyed little favor prior to the appearance of Wellhausen's first volume of the *Geschichte Israels* (1878), better known by the title of the reissue as *Prolegomena zur Geschichte Israels*. Now Wellhausen, with brilliant discernment and a captivating style rare in German scholarly circles, won many of the new generation over to Graf's view.

Wellhausen's writings revolutionized the history of ancient Israel. "The Old Testament does not furnish a history of Israel, though it supplies the materials." He was right in stressing the importance of the dating of the Mosaic law. Against the traditional opinion that it was common racial property before the Twelve Tribes entered the Holy Land, Wellhausen believed it was not assembled until Israel was captive in foreign bondage and subject to foreign powers. The Law was both cause and effect in the recreation of the race after the Babylonian exile. Unless this fact is appreciated, Wellhausen warned his readers, "one will above all fail to understand the great work accomplished by the prophets in destroying Old Israel, and preparing the way first for Judaism, and then for the Gospel." Far from resting his case only on literary arguments as his predecessors had done, Wellhausen traced the development of religious forms and practices. He offered a study of the religious cult of the Hebrews, their ceremonials and holy places, and an analysis of the historical books of the Old Testament. The reconstruction of Israelitish history which a subsequent volume was to develop was never written, but fortunately the world possesses a sketch prepared for the ninth edition of the *Encyclopaedia Britannica.*[20] Whatever corrections may be made in details or even in the main thesis, the *Prolegomena* will remain a classic for beauty of utterance, profundity of vision, and boldness of outlines.

The significance of Wellhausen was that he was an historian rather than merely a higher critic. He could dissect and analyze sources in brilliant—and sometimes specious—fashion, as he demonstrated in *Die Komposition des Hexateuchs und der historischen Bücher des Alten Testaments* (1885; 3rd ed., 1889). But his chief interest was in the history

[20] See the article "Israel," vol. XIII, 396–432. It was reprinted in enlarged form in 1884 as the first number of his *Skizzen und Vorarbeiten* (Berlin, 1884–92, 5 v.), under the title *Abriss der Geschichte Israels und Judas*. In 1894 there appeared the still more complete *Israelitische und jüdische Geschichte* (7th ed., 1914).

behind these sources, in the story of the religious development of the Jews, rather than the import of Old Testament criticism for Christian dogma. Critics of his books contended that Wellhausen offered little that was new, and merely set up wild assertions which he buttressed by constant use of the words "gloss" and "interpolation." His friends and followers have admitted that he sometimes tended to overstress an argument and to exceed tenable positions. Some capital has been made of his limited linguistic equipment. He taught Hebrew, Aramaic, Syriac, and Arabic at Marburg; but his knowledge of Assyrian and Babylonian literature was largely second-hand, and he never devoted much study to the archaeological research of his generation. The whole of the *Prolegomena* devoted only six pages to stylistic and linguistic arguments. He was most unfortunate in dissecting *Judges* and *Samuel*. *Genesis* was written by a priest after the Captivity, incorporating ancient materials. Naturally this demanded some ingenious argumentation to prove why *Genesis* failed to contain allusions to a time after the Exile. A not unfair example of his wealth of illustration and cumulative argument is the introduction of the use of incense as evidence of "increased luxury"; hence its lack of mention in certain writings mark them as dating from the time of poverty after the Exile. More valid perhaps than all these points is the criticism that like Baur and the Hegelians, he wrote "conceptual" history, and forced the texts and facts to fit the Procrustean bed of his own stages in Jewish history.[21]

From Wellhausen stems the *religionsgeschichtliche Schule* in Germany. In his way, he unleashed as powerful forces in the field of theology as Ritschl did in the "seventies" in German Protestant dogmatics. But Wellhausen was properly neither philologist nor theologian; he was a creator and vivifier of great historial hypotheses. In this respect he presents interesting parallels and contrasts with his teacher Ewald and his French contemporary Renan. Something of Wellhausen's views has gone into the making of every considerable modern Old Testament scholar. In the thirty years before Wellhausen's death (1888–1918) one may distinguish two currents or schools: those who accept him unconditionally—as Reuss, Stade, Smith, Cornill, and Steuernagel—and a group which is less skeptical of Jewish tradition and refuses to accept his critical results in so far as they emerge solely from his religio-historical system—as Riehm, Driver, Strack, Koenig, and Baudissin. Meanwhile a new discipline has arisen: the history of Israelitic literature, considered in the setting of the ancient Orient, with repre-

---

[21] For a hostile review of Wellhausen, see *ER*, CLXXVI (1892), 58–80. For a sympathetic account of him as a man, see Wilamowitz-Möllendorff, *My Recollections, 1848–1914*, tr. from the German by G. C. Richards (London, 1930), 225–28.

sentatives like Gunkel, Winckler, Zimmern, Jeremias, Kittel, and Sellin.

As Arabist, following his removal to Halle (1882), Wellhausen spent over a score of years opening the sources for the history of Arabia prior to and after Mohammed, and produced the first critical history of Islam.[22] He began by a translation of Vakidi, a work he excerpted from a London manuscript, affording the oldest and least legendary account of Mohammed in Medina. Occupation with the poetic literature of the Hudhailites, sprung from the same soil as the Islamic religion, prepared him to write a study of pre-Islamic paganism. After further researches into Mohammed's organization at Medina, and of the religious-political parties in old Islam, he ventured to issue his masterpiece in this field: *Das arabische Reich und sein Sturz* (1902). The slashing imagination, the genial reconstruction, and the historical logic of the great historian of religion here appear at their best. His presentation of the Khalifate of the Ommayads, and of the beginnings of their ruin by the Abbasids vindicate Wellhausen's right to the title of a great historian. It is to be regretted that it was his last work on Arabia.

England has had a long line of Old Testament critical scholars, from the days of Bishop Lowth and the recalcitrant Catholic Geddes, to Colenso, Davidson, and Driver. They are all characteristic figures; Bishop Colenso with his polygamist Zulus and their disconcerting questions is only a little more colorful. The keenest of them all was W. Robertson Smith (1846–94),[23] who wrote the preface to the English translation of Wellhausen's *Prolegomena*. Smith and his brother received an excellent training under their father, a Scotch minister of unusual qualities, and "brilliant" is a weak word for their record at the University of Aberdeen. The natural sciences and mathematics exerted a very strong attraction upon William. In 1870 he was strongly recommended for the chair of oriental languages in the Free Church College at Aberdeen, his teacher A. B. Davidson lauding especially his "great advancement in Sacred Criticism." The new appointee paid a visit to Göttingen, where he formed a lifelong friendship with Paul de Lagarde. After five years of teaching at Aberdeen, his article on the Bible in the ninth edition of the *Encyclopaedia Britannica* caused offense. Smith had to defend himself against formal charges of heresy. It was a battle for the liberty of criticism and led to great excitement even in

[22] *Muhammed in Medina. Das ist Vakidis Kitab al Maghazi, in verkürzter deutscher Wiedergabe* (1882); "Lieder der Hudhailiten," in Arabic and German in his *Skizzen und Vorarbeiten* (1884), Heft I; "Reste arabischen Heidentums," *ibid.*, Heft III (1887). Other studies in Heft 4 and 6, and "Die religös-politische Oppositions-Parteien im alten Islam," in *Abhandlungen der kgl. Gesellschaften zu Göttingen*, phil.-hist. Klasse, neue Folge, V (1901–04), no. 2, 99 pp.; *Das arabische Reich und sein Sturz* (1902).

[23] J. S. Black and G. W. Chrystal, *The Life of William Robertson Smith* (London, 1912). The same edited his *Lectures and Essays*, including his scientific papers.

foreign circles. Franz Delitzsch wished him well, and Nestle from Tübingen mournfully noted that the times had changed little in the past two hundred years. Smith was acquitted on the heresy charge, but he lost his chair and carried his case before the Scotch public in two series of lectures published as *The Old Testament in the Jewish Church* (New York, 1881) and *The Prophets of Israel* (2nd ed., London, 1919). In 1883 Cambridge called him to be Wright's colleague in Arabic, for which he had recommendations from Nöldeke, Wellhausen, Socin, Lagarde, and Kuenen, though the last questioned whether a testimonial from "a notorious freethinker" would aid his friend's cause. Smith continued writing for the *Britannica*. The greatest and most original of his several volumes was *The Religion of the Semites* (1889). It was a brave venture into the field of comparative religions, though its eleven essays on Israel's primitive religion were but a fragment of the projected whole. Hitherto the Old Testament had been considered unique. Smith now offered a "systematic comparison of the religion of the Hebrews as a whole, with beliefs and ritual practices of the other Semitic peoples." The work laid down the prime importance of the study of ritual, the social order, and the blood tie in primitive religions. Further labors were interrupted by the author's premature death from tuberculosis. Few of Robertson Smith's bitter opponents realized that this alleged destroyer of faith remained throughout his life "a convinced believer in the divine inspiration of the Old Testament." [24]

France, the land of Simon and Astruc, failed to keep step with Germany and England in biblical criticism proper, but surely one of the greatest of histories of the Jews has come from the hands of Ernest Renan (1823–92).[25] The *Histoire du peuple d'Israel* (1888–94, 5 v.) was a work of his old age, but the brush of the artist had not lost its colorful magic. The professor of Hebrew, Chaldaic, and Syriac in the Collège de France brought the knowledge of a lifetime of study; but it was with the touch of the poet, of the master of psychology, that he wrote, and not as a laborious critic. He wasted no time on discussions of the *Vier-Quellenhypothese*, or the respective idiosyncrasies of P and J. Specialists are likely to agree with W. Robertson Smith [26] that M. Renan was too eclectic, and let "divination" control the use of critical results. The period before David rests largely on "epical tradition," but Abraham and the patriarchs are solely legendary. The author's burden is

[24] *Life of Smith* (n. 23), 537–38; see the final chapter for a general estimate of Robertson Smith as scholar and man.
[25] For a sketch of his life and work, see the chapter on Catholic Church Historians, pp. 555–56 and n. 53; GOOCH, 527–30; FUETER, 744–48.
[26] Review of Renan's first volume, reprinted in Smith's *Lectures and Essays* (n. 20), 608–22. Cp. also A. Kuenen, "Drei Wege, Ein Ziel," in his *Gesammelte Abhandlungen* (n. 13).

therefore an imaginative reconstruction of the way things may have been. "Comme pour la *Vie de Jésus* je réclame pour le présent volume, consacré à des temps forts obscurs, un jeu de l'indulgence qu'on a coutume d'accorder aux voyants, et dont les voyants ont besoin." David, the first historical character, was distasteful to the aesthetic spirit of Renan; "the brigand of Adullam and Ziklag" was equally unjust, cruel, superstitious, and irreligious. Renan's pictures of the prophets are sharply etched by comparisons with modern personages; more than one suggests the lineaments of a Jesuit, a Puritan, an intolerant theologian. Yet they proclaimed the beauty of holiness, and provided for the moral regeneration of their race. On the post-exilic period, which Robertson Smith at first feared Renan was likely to overlook altogether despite its great importance for the diffusion of the Law, he offered little more than somber criticism. When the five volumes were finished and joined with his *Origines du Christianisme*, Renan had written the most extended account of the Jewish race from its origins to the development of early Christianity. But the series was literature rather than history.

Schürer has given a detailed picture of Jewish life in the time of Christ and the first centuries of our era. The story of the race since then has naturally been most cultivated by its own members. Perhaps the broadest sweep, from the beginnings to the third quarter of the nineteenth century, has been attempted by Heinrich Graetz (1817–91).[27] But his *History of the Jews* is full of prejudice, and glaring inaccuracies of scholarship. He was ignorant of the immense progress made in biblical studies of either the Old or the New Testament. What can be thought of a writer with any pretensions to history who began his work with the words: "It was on a sunny spring day that some pastoral tribes passed across the Jordan"? Or a writer on ancient Hebrew history who omits any mention of the works of Jost, Bleek, Graf, Nöldeke, Schrader, Reusch, Delitzsch, Kuenen, Wellhausen, and Stade? Graetz' wise and good men in history are almost constantly Jews, his weak and foolish men as constantly Christians. St. Louis of France is said to have "acquired his reputation for piety from the simplicity of his heart and the narrowness of his head"; St. Ambrose of Milan is described as "a violent official, ignorant of all theology, whom a reputation for violence in the church had raised to the rank of bishop." Hirsch, to whom Graetz dedicated an earlier work on Gnosticism, said of him: "What does Graetz know? What can he know?" Geiger

---

[27] *Geschichte der Juden von den ältesten Zeiten bis auf die Gegenwart* (Leipzig, 1863–76, 11 v.; 3rd ed., 1879 ff.). There is a memoir of 86 pages by Dr. Philipp Bloch in the sixth (index) volume of the English version, *History of the Jews* (London and Philadelphia, 1891–98).

condemned him as ignorant of philology, comparative religion, the anthropology of the ancient peoples of the Orient, and even of history.[28]

Systematic exploration in Palestine did not begin until the sixties of the last century. Centuries before Burckhardt found the rock-city of Petra (1809), and before Costigan tried to sail along the shores of the Dead Sea (1835), pilgrims had satisfied pious sentiment by describing the spots pointed out in Jerusalem and its environs. Such traditional identifications, however, rested upon well-known principles of human psychology. In the three centuries prior to Constantine the eschatological expectations of the Christian movement had induced a neglect of historical knowledge. The location of many a site was forgotten, and a new Jerusalem had arisen on the debris of the old. Few modern visitors realize that the city of Christ lies in places fully 100 feet underground, that walls have disappeared, valleys have filled up, and that vital landmarks can be recovered only by the spade of the excavator.[29]

The beginning of scientific geographical study of Palestine is due mainly to two men, Robinson and Tobler. Edward Robinson of New York, a Congregationalist minister and professor of theology, based the three volumes of his *Biblical Researches* (1841) on a visit made in 1838. In contrast to credulous travellers who took their guides' word on faith, he proposed to accept only Biblical testimony (i.e., contemporary evidence) for the identification of places. Interested in getting off the beaten path, he took with him a skilled linguist who knew the country, and in 1838 and again in 1852 they traversed the land, measured distances, buildings and angles, prepared sketches, and drew up minute topographical descriptions. They were the first to crawl through the famous Siloam conduit. But Robinson's work was eclipsed by Titus Tobler, a Swiss doctor, who, stimulated by a vacation visit to Palestine, sat down to master the pilgrim travel literature of all centuries. Wisely confining himself to Judaea, he recorded his second journey (1845), when he spent twenty weeks in Jerusalem, in seven volumes. His work remains the starting point and the mine of reference for the historical geography of the Holy Land. Tobler was the first to investigate the ancient Jewish tombs about Jerusalem, and to prepare a correct map of the city giving the streets their native names. The "Hakluyt" of Palestine, he did not live to realize his hope of publishing critical edi-

---

[28] See the review of Graetz' work in *CQR*, XXXV (1892), 68–97; and *Jewish Quarterly Review*, IV, no. xiv. The best one-volume history of the Jews in any language is M. Margolis and A. Marx, *History of the Jewish People* (Philadelphia, 1927).

[29] On this problem of identifying the "holy places," cp. Benzinger in Hilprecht (n. 1), 579–622, and the volumes of Titus Tobler on Jerusalem, Golgotha, Nazareth, etc.

tions of all travel narratives from the third to the fifteenth centuries; but Tobler remains unsurpassed in knowledge of the Palestine of the medieval and early modern times.

The efforts of these men and others like Guérin and Van der Velde showed that the Holy Land was still truly unexplored. Realizing that the task lay beyond the casual efforts of individuals, interested spirits in England founded the Palestine Exploration Fund (1865). Within three years, it could send Captain Wilson into the field on the strength of a treasury of £8,000. While it hoped to serve Biblical knowledge, it was not a religious organization. The great work the society took in hand was the much-needed geographical survey which should provide reliable maps, locate the often abrupt topographical changes, note the exact latitude of hills and ravines, cities and villages, valleys, roads, springs, and significant ruins. Expeditions under Captain Conder and Lieutenant Kitchener (later British Commander-in-Chief) in 1872–75 and 1877–78 resulted in a detailed map of Palestine west of the Jordan, bearing 10,000 names and accompanied by four volumes of memoirs. Of the 600 places mentioned in the Bible over half could now be tentatively identified. Studies on flora and fauna and some observations on ruins were provided for. The Fund also worked on the regions east of the Jordan, but this task was more accurately and fully performed by the German Palestine Society (founded in 1878), whose scholars mapped this unknown country, interesting geologically as well as historically. A very great advance over all previous efforts was made possible by a photographic army survey undertaken during the First World War.

Research and excavation in Jerusalem itself has been conducted under the greatest of difficulties and has required extreme patience. Because of public fanaticism the government withheld permission for the first half of the century; and only accidental finds during the repair or digging of wells, or the excavation of foundations for new houses, could be utilized. Dr. Schick spent over fifty years in the city, waiting for these casual opportunities to sketch and observe. With the last third of the century the Turkish government became more generous. Warren led all other excavators by nearly a score of years (1867–70), and traced the former course of the valley between Mounts Zion and Moriah, where debris lay 42–65 feet high. Lying in the course of armies from the south (Egypt) or the north (Syria and Mesopotamia), Jerusalem has been levelled and rebuilt on its own ruins perhaps more often than any other noted city of antiquity. The presence of the modern dwellings and the unwillingness of the Turkish government to grant a *firman* (license) for a period of more than two or three years rendered most attacks sporadic and incomplete. Important has been the search for the course of the various city walls.[30]

From Jerusalem the archaeologists advanced to other sites: Bliss dug at Tell el-Hesy, Jerusalem, and Gath; Macalister at Gezer; and Mackenzie and Newton at Beth-Shemesh (for the Palestine Exploration Fund); Schumacher attacked Megiddo; and Sellin operated at Taanach and Jericho; Samaria has been attempted with American funds; and since the First World War Garstang has assailed Ashkelon and Jericho.

The results of these various expeditions has been very different from those conducted into Egypt and Mesopotamia. In contrast to the startling finds at Thebes and Kouyunjik, the harvest has been pitifully barren. It is plain that the Jews, whatever their genius in other ways, had no native art and small talent for building. The epigraphic material is extremely limited, and the two great finds bearing on Palestinian political history (the stele of King Mesha and the Tell-el-Amarna letters) have come from without its own immediate borders. Aside from the Siloam tunnel inscription,[31] a few Samarian ostraca, cuneiform clay tablets and some unimportant seals, no cases of pre-exilic Hebrew writing has been uncovered. Of later texts, most are in the Greek of the Hellenistic period, like the minatory stele of Herod's temple.

Thus little light is shed upon the early history of the Jews by records of their own aside from the Old Testament, and the powerful brilliance of the Nile and Mesopotamian valleys has almost thrown their little land into the shadows. Professor Friedrich Delitzsch, in delivering a popular lecture on Assyriological research, set out to demonstrate the value of this science for elucidating ancient Israel, and seemed to end by deriving all that had been formerly placed to the credit of the Jews from their mightier eastern neighbors. The conflict provoked by his *Babel und Bibel* (1900) convulsed German circles for several years, and great scholars arrayed themselves on either side. Conservative minds revolted at placing the origin of the Jewish and Christian religion, and particularly the stories of Creation, of the Deluge, and the Fall, in polytheistic Babylon. From the battle emerged a wider and saner understanding of the interactions of ancient cultures, and the field was cleared for the judicious combinations of Eduard Meyer, who turned the discovery of the Elephantine Aramaic papyri to the vindication of the Book of Ezra. Driver's *Schweich Lectures* (1909) show clearly that

---

[30] A summary list of the various sites and expeditions down to 1922 is given in Professor Macalister's account in the *Cambridge Ancient History*, I (1923), 112–14.

[31] It relates how workmen cut through the rock from either side in building an underground channel for a water supply flowing into the pool of Siloam, within the city of Jerusalem, against the time of a siege. Executed in the time of King Hezekiah, it presents a noted feat of engineering (583 yards), but the inscription is little more than an impromptu record made by the workmen themselves on completing their novel task. Cp. Hilprecht (n. 1), 613–15.

the higher critic has now combined his textual studies with archaeological research which may prove the touchstone to his results. Egyptian and Mesopotamian studies have compelled new studies in the social, literary, and religious background of Israel of which Wellhausen never dreamed.[32]

[32] See the excellent survey by Hugo Gressmann, "Die Aufgaben der alttestamentlichen Forschung," *Zeitschrift für die alttestamentliche Wissenschaft*, XLII (1924), 1–33, when he became editor of this journal; and a similar article by Rudolf Kittel, *ibid.*, XXXIX (1921), 84 ff. Readers of this chapter should also be reminded of George Adam Smith, *The Historical Geography of the Holy Land* (25th rev. ed., London and New York, 1932), a most remarkable book, and a classic illustration of the relation between a land and its history.

BOOK XII

THE MINOR COUNTRIES OF EUROPE

CHAPTER LXII

THE NORTHERN COUNTRIES

BELGIUM [1] did not commence its national existence in 1830 with any remarkable scholars. Baron Étienne-Constantin de Gerlache (1785–1871),[2] a liberal Catholic who had studied law at Paris, took an active part in the political and educational questions of his country, and as president of the Belgian Congress had proposed the choice of Leopold of Saxe-Coburg as king in 1831. After holding high judicial office for some decades, he devoted his last years exclusively to historical studies. They had begun with a *Histoire des Pays-Bas* (3 v.) in 1839; and continued with a *Histoire de Liège* (1843) and an *Essai sur les grandes époques de l'histoire nationale* (1859). Alphonse Guillaume Wauters (1817–98)[3] was the archivist of his native Brussels, and professor of national history at the Musée de l'Industrie, where he delivered public lectures for thirty years (1861–92). Self-taught like most of his generation, he became a model in documentation. An industrious pioneer in many obscure corners of Belgian history, he has left among other works a history of Brussels (*Histoire de la ville de Bruxelles*, 1843, 3 v.), a work on *Duc Jean Ier et le Brabant de 1267 à 1295* (1862); and spent much time on the collection of documents and charters.[4]

When the University of Brussels was founded in 1835, Jean Jacques Altmeyer (1804–77) of Luxemburg began a long career as instructor in history and classical antiquities. After writing a number of less important volumes, he spent the last twenty years of his life on a great history of the Netherlands in the sixteenth century. The manuscript, purchased by the Belgian government at his death, still rests in the royal library of Brussels, and only portions have been printed.[5]

It was perhaps natural that Belgian historians inclined to the six-

[1] Henri Pirenne, *Bibliographie de l'histoire de Belgique* (3rd ed., Brussels, 1931); the same, in HISTOIRE ET HISTORIENS, I, 51–71; Charles Potvin, *Histoire des lettres en Belgique*, IV. *Cinquante ans de liberté* (Brussels, 1881); *Biographie nationale de Belgique* (Brussels, 1866–1928, 27 v. in 24); *Bibliographie de Belgique, bulletin mensuel des publications belges ou rélativs à la Belgique* (Brussels, 1876 ff.). Cp. *La Grande Encyclopédie*, VI, 17.

[2] See the bibliography in *La Grande Encyclopédie*, XVIII, 843.

[3] Henri Pirenne, "Notice biographique d'Alphonse Wauters," in *Annuaire de l'Académie royale de Belgique* (1902).

[4] E.g., his *Table chronologique des chartes et diplomes imprimés concernant l'histoire de la Belgique* (Brussels, 1866–74, 4 v.).

[5] *Les Précurseurs de la Réforme aux Pays-Bas* (Brussels, 1886, 2 v.).

teenth century. This was the chosen field of Louis Prosper Gachard (1800–85). Born a Frenchman, he was appointed royal custodian of the Belgian archives in 1831 and spent a quarter-century in gathering and arranging his treasures. His zealous labors were varied by journeys of exploration to foreign archives, and most of his writings rest upon documents. Drawn particularly to the Spanish side of his favorite century, he edited the correspondence of William the Silent, of Philip II on Netherlandish affairs, and of the duchess of Parma. While chiefly an editor and collector, he has a study of Don Carlos, a national history of the early eighteenth century, and volumes of essays to his credit.

The popular but not very critical Baron Joseph Kervyn de Lettenhove (1817–91) dabbled with Froissart and Jacques van Artevelde, wrote a history of Flanders and *Les Huguenots et les Gueux*. He had a violent Catholic bias. Fruin, the great Dutch historian, declared it was a pity that Kervyn had not published the many documents which his industry ferreted out in European archives without adding his own commentaries. Henne did better by Charles V and his reign in the Netherlands; and Van Praet covered the rulers from Charles V to the French Revolution in various excellent studies. The most prolific pen in the nineteenth century belonged to Théodore Juste (1818–88), curator of the royal military museum and instructor in history at the École militaire and the École de guerre. He devoted two volumes to the Revolution of 1830 (1872), and five to the times of Philip II (1855), but his *magnum opus* is the biographical series *Gallerie des fondateurs de la monarchie belge* in twenty-seven volumes (1862–84), for which he utilized the private papers of King Leopold, Stockmar, Van de Weyer, and other Belgian statesmen. His execution is occasionally good, but on the whole uneven, and he often loses himself in endless detail. But Juste gave his contemporary Belgium the taste for historical reading.[6]

The last decade of the nineteenth century saw the infiltration of German scientific ideals. Vanderkindere represented the new methods at Brussels, and Godefroid Kurth (1847–72) at Liége began the first practical seminar in Belgium. Kurth began his professorship in 1872, and in 1907 was made director of the Institut historique belge at Rome. A sympathetic teacher, a Catholic with ultramontane convictions, and a gifted, eloquent writer, his influence upon Belgian historical instruction was not small. He was a writer of unusually fine and delicate distinction, and his *Histoire poétique des Mérovingiens* is a classic.[7] Kurth's greatest pupil—and greater than his master—was the late Henri Pirenne,

---

[6] P. Henrard, *Biographie de Théodore Juste* (Brussels, 1890).

[7] Paris, 1893. During 1899–1900 Kurth edited the journal *Deutsch Belgien* for the German-speaking Belgians.

who has already been considered in the chapter on Economic Historians.[8]

Paul Frédéricq of the University of Ghent was author of a *History of the Inquisition in the Low Countries* and an authority on the splendid Burgundian period and the transition to Spanish rule. He was a scholar of wide outlook and unusual command of the international relations of Europe in the sixteenth century. Pirenne wrote the third volume of his *Histoire de Belgique* under the inspiration of Frédéricq's teaching.[9]

In the Netherlands [10] in the beginning of the nineteenth century there were two opposing schools of historians, neither of them competent. One was ultra-monarchical and systematically maligned the character of all Dutch statesmen who had opposed the Stadtholderate. The other was of a more moderate view and took the ground that much was yet to be ascertained regarding both sides of the conflict. Out of the conflict historical criticism was born in the Netherlands and the door thrown open to deeper documentary studies, biographies, and monographs.

Hooft, Wagenaar, and Bilderdijk were the three chief Dutch historians up to the middle of the century. The ungrateful task of bibliography was assumed by Visscher of Utrecht. Kluit began work on the Dutch constitution, and Vreede studied the history of Dutch diplomacy. Van Hoevell's work on Surinam played a role in the abolition of slavery; it was "neither romance nor history, but an inquest." Naturally the Dutch over-seas empire attracted its share of scholars.

The first prominent Dutch historian was Wilhelm Groen van Prinsterer (1801–76),[11] who had been a pupil of Bilderdijk, and was a graduate of the University of Leyden. At the age of twenty-six he became private secretary to King William I. After six years of this intimate contact with royalty he turned wholly to historical studies, and began to edit with great care the *Archives ou Correspondance inédite de la Maison d'Orange-Nassau* (Leyden, 1835–64, 15 v.). A zealous politician, he posed for long years as leader of the ultra-Calvinists against

[8] For further information on Kurth see Pirenne's *Notice sur Godefroid Kurth* (Brussels, 1923); the same, "Discours prononcé à la manifestation en l'honneur de G. Kurth," in the [Mélanges] *À Godefroid Kurth*, etc. (Liége, 1899), and his obituary notice of Kurth in *Annuaire de l'Academie royale de Belgique* (1924), 193–261.

[9] Powicke, *EHR*, LI (1936), 80.

[10] P. J. Blok, *Geschichtschreibung in Holland* (Heidelberg, 1924); the same in HISTOIRE ET HISTORIENS, I, 266–86; Samuel de Wind, *Bibliotheek der Nederlandsche Geschiedschrijvers* (Middleburg, 1835); Lepp, *Bibliotheek der Nederlandsche Kerkgeschiedschrijvers* (Leyden, 1886); *Bibliographie de Belgique, bulletin mensuel des publications belges ou rélatives à la Belgique* (Brussels, 1876 ff.); Alphonse Esquiros, "La Néerlande et la vie Hollandaise, IX: L'histoire et les historiens de la Hollande," *RDM*, X (1857), 275–315.

[11] H. T. Colenbrander in *Annual Report of the American Historical Association for 1909* (Washington, D. C., 1911), 245–56; James Mackay, *Religious Thought in Holland during the Nineteenth Century* (London and New York, 1911), ch. i; GOOCH, 447–48; Cohen Stuart, *Bibliographical Notice on G. Groen van Prinsterer* (Utrecht, 1876).

the liberal Thorbecke. His last book, *Maurice de Nassau et Barnevelt* (1875), was composed in answer to Motley's work, and defended the Prince over against the Commoner.

The giant after the mid-century was Robert Jakobus Fruin (1823–99),[12] born in Rotterdam of English ancestors, and a student of classical philology at Leyden until the works of Heeren, Otfried Müller, and Niebuhr diverted him into history. He began with Egyptology, but turned to the history of the Netherlands. Those who call him "the Ranke of Holland" point to his brilliant *Tien jaren uit den tachtigjarigen oorlog, 1588–1598 (A Decade out of the Eighty Years' War).*[13] A quiet little man in black, who spent most of his life in his study, Fruin cast his influence over a wide circle, and made it felt also among the general reading Dutch public by his popular articles in *De Gids*. For ten years (1865–75) he was one of the editors of this journal. His detailed knowledge of history was extensive,[14] but most of his writing is monographic or scattered in lectures and essays. His inaugural address as professor was on "de onpartijdigheid van den geschiedschrijver (the impartiality of the historian)." He took history in a broad sense, touching all sides of life, and once said Ranke's works were unsatisfactory in that they dealt only with political history. Politically he was allied with the Liberals, and opposed the conservative theories of Groen van Prinsterer. He abhorred the notion of historical laws, and considered the quest for purpose all-important.

During the last forty years of the nineteenth century various tercentenaries of important events in the struggle for Dutch independence gave the incentive for studies on the Sea Beggars, the Pacification of Ghent, William the Silent, and kindred topics. There were occasional sharp clashes between writers of opposing religious denominations.

The chief historians and archivists of Holland have been the pupils of Fruin. They followed their master, without losing their independence. The greatest was Petrus Johannes Blok (1855–1929)[15] who inherited his teacher's chair at Leyden in 1894, and filled it honorably for thirty-five years. He had taught a decade before that at Groningen. Blok sought to overcome the faults of Fruin's school, which employed

---

[12] Petrus Blok, *Verspreide Studien* (Groningen, 1903); S. Muller Fz. in *De Gids*, June, 1894, 353–62, and April, 1899; F. Rachfahl in *HZ*, XCVIII (1907), 507–43; Ruth Putnam, "Robert Fruin, 1823–1899—A Memorial Sketch," in *Annual Report of the American Historical Association for 1899* (Washington, D. C., 1900), I, 516–26; GOOCH, 448; Koppel S. Pinson, "Robert Jacobus Fruin (1823–99)," *ESS*, VI, 507.

[13] Published in 1856; 8th ed., 1924.

[14] "Inderdaad ben ik overtuigd, dat de geheele loop der wereldgeschiedenis van Manetho tot Gijsbert Karel van Hogendorp (den jongsten historischen persoon, over wien hij, zoover ik weet, geschreven heeft) hem niet slechts in groote trekken, maar in bijzonderheden duidelijk voor den geest staat." S. Muller Fz. in *De Gids*, June, 1894, p. 354.

[15] See the article on Blok in *ESS;* GOOCH, 448; WOLF, 687–88.

only Dutch sources, and began to draw upon the diplomatic stores in Germany, England, France, Italy, Spain, and the Scandinavian and Baltic countries. His *Relazioni Veneziane* (1909) demonstrated what might be done in this direction. Five years before he had succeeded in establishing an *Istituto storico neerlandese* at Rome which among other things connected the thread of Italian and Dutch art and delved into ancient and medieval archaeology. His great ambition was to write a comprehensive national history for his people. This work of love and labor [16] has been compared to Green's *History of the English People*, though it hardly approaches that classic in literary beauty. It is both a patriotic and a scholarly work, noteworthy for the care with which the economic strands have been woven into the narrative of Dutch expansion and Dutch greatness. Blok also wrote a *History of Leyden*.[17]

J. von Arz ushered in the historiography of Switzerland [18] in the nineteenth century with his monumental *Geschichten des Kantons St. Gallen* (1810–13), largely a documentary history, and a salutary reproach to Johannes von Müller's romantic composition. But Swiss history was first effectively submitted to the acid test of modern criticism in the writings of Joseph Eutych Kopp (1793–1866).[19] He was born at Beromünster and died at Lucerne in the same canton. After teaching in Hofwil and Zursach, he was professor at the Lyceum of Lucerne for nearly half a century (1819–65). The *Urkunden zur Geschichte der eidgenössischen Bünde* (vol. I at Lucerne, 1832; vol. II at Vienna, 1851) swung open the portals of a new era in Swiss historiography. He established that the version which Tschudi and Müller offered of the origin of the Swiss confederacy (including the tales of the *Rütlibund*, of Tell and the *Vögte*) could not be confirmed by any contemporary sources. Kopp's most important contribution was constructive, in the form of an extensive history of the confederacy.[20] He collaborated in the edition of the *Amtliche Sammlung der älteren eidgenössischen Abschiede, 1291–1420* (1839). To round out his picture, be it

---

[16] *Geschiedenis van het Nederlandsche volk* (Groningen, 1892–1908, 8 v.; 3rd ed., 1924–26, 4 v.). It has been translated into German by O. G. Houtrouw (Gotha, 1901–12); and into English by O. A. Bierstadt and R. Putnam under the title, *History of the People of the Netherlands* (New York and London, 1898–1912, 5 v.).

[17] *Geschiedenis eener Hollandsche stad* ('s-Gravenhage, 1882–84, 2 pts., 2nd ed., 1910–18, 4 v.).

[18] G. von Wyss, *Geschichte der Historiographie in der Schweiz* (Zurich, 1895); A. Guilland and E. Gagliardi in HISTOIRE ET HISTORIENS, I, 396–412, see especially the works cited on p. 397 and note 1; *HZ*, XXIV (1870), 43–93 and XXXIV (1875), 144–80; *RSH* (1901), 233–35; *RDM* (1834), pt. 1, 599–600; (1844), pt. ii, 565–610; (1856), pt. 1, 223–24; (1870), pt. 1, 214–40; *RH*, I (1876), 585–86; V (1877), 383–93; and XXIV (1884), 143–64.

[19] Alois Luetolf, *Joseph Eutych Kopp als Professor, Dichter, Staatsman und Historiker dargestellt* (Lucerne, 1868, with supplements); GOOCH, 445–46.

[20] *Geschichte der eidgenössischen Bünde* (1845–82, 5 v.). It was continued by A. Busson, A. Luetolf, and F. Rohrer.

said that he was forty years professor of classical philology. But the grace of style wholly fled from his writings; they are a vast confused mosaic.

Karl Dändliker (1849–1910), professor at the University of Zürich, wrote on the history of his canton, but also produced a *Geschichte der Schweiz* which he quarried from Kopp's pages.[21] Similarly Johannes Dierauer (1842–1920), professor of history at the chief school of the canton of St. Gall, and city librarian there, wrote a five-volume general history which has run to three editions and been rendered into French, and contributed studies centering around St. Gall.[22] A much-read historian in the first half-century was Johann Heinrich Daniel Zschokke (1771–1848), a German born at Magdeburg and trained at the University of Frankfort-on-the-Oder. Emigrating from Prussia he achieved a distinguished position in Swiss letters by his short stories, *Bilder aus der Schweiz*. His various historical efforts were intended for popular consumption, but deserve no critical attention.[23]

With the coming of the second half of the century the principles which Kopp had announced in his first little volume of *Urkunden* obtained more general acceptance, and the great need was now for a critical publication of all available sources. Private historical societies, as the Allgemeine Geschichtsforschende Gesellschaft founded at Baden in 1840, individual cantonal and municipal governments, and the federal archives furnished the opportunities and funds for the task. The documents upon the Swiss recesses threw light on the history of the confederacy; Kopp brought out the first volume. For reliable evaluation it was essential to analyze the old chronicles and determine what elements had a right to be cited as contemporary evidence. G. von Wyss, G. Scherrer, and G. Meyer von Knonau, who died at a great age in 1926 and was the last surviving student of Ranke, were the only distinguished editors. The first-mentioned added a chartulary to his excellent *Geschichte der Abtei von Zürich*. Wartmann collected the charters of St. Gall, and Knonau was the authority on its literary sources. For a while it seemed as if source-publication was the only talent the Swiss possessed, and the plentitude of new materials threatened to overwhelm anyone who tried to cover it single-handedly. L. Vulliemin near his eightieth year undertook to acquaint the public with the progress made in Swiss history in the two little volumes of his *Histoire de*

---

[21] See Gottfried Guggenbühl, *Karl Dändliker, Lebensbild* (Zürich, 1912). The three-volume history appeared in 1884–87; 3rd ed., 1900–04.

[22] A list of his publications will be found in the *Anzeiger für schweizerische Geschichte und Alterthumskunde*, 1920.

[23] Selected works in 40 v., 1824–28, in 35 v., 1851–54. His *Selbstschau* is autobiographical, and there are lives by Muench and by Emil Zschokke.

la Confederation suisse (1875–76). The articles in the journals of historical societies threshed out many a local issue. J. J. Blumer and A. P. de Segesser turned to the field of *Rechtsgeschichte*, recalling the tradition of Johann Kaspar Bluntschli (1808–81). The writers of the French Cantons have dealt with external affairs to the west, and de Mandrot covered the war with Burgundy, declaring of the Swiss and Louis XI: "dans la main de ce genie patient et positif ils furent un instrument habilement manié." Oehlmann produced a classic study of the Alpine Passes in the Middle Ages,[24] and Planta has done well by the local history of Rhaetia. The finest case of Swiss erudition on foreign subjects are the conscientious volumes of Meyer von Knonau for the *Jahrbücher*.[25] The late Eduard Fueter has left us his *Geschichte der modernen Historiographie*.[26] For the last fifty years the critical principles of historical science have been fully accepted in Switzerland, and little remains of the monument Müller once erected to their ancestors.

Jean Charles Leonard de Sismondi (1773–1841)[27] was born in Geneva and spent most of his life there, but he wrote on Italian and French and not Swiss history. His father was a French pastor whose ancestors had emigrated from France after the revocation of the Edict of Nantes. The family possessed some property, gave Jean a good education, and started him off as a banking clerk in Lyons. When the French Revolution broke out, the family fled to England for eighteen months. In 1794 Sismondi returned to France, and was imprisoned for a time. When released he bought a farm near Lucca, but now the Austrian po-

---

[24] E. Oehlmann, "Die Alpenpässe im Mittelalter," *Jahrbuch für schweizerische Geschichte*, III (1878), 165–289, and IV (1879), 165–324.

[25] *Jahrbücher des Deutschen Reiches unter Heinrich IV und Heinrich V* (Leipzig, 1890–1909, 7 v.).

[26] Munich and Berlin, 1911; tr. into French by Émile Jeanmaire, under the title *Histoire de l'historiographie moderne* (Paris, 1914).

[27] The family name was Simonde. In 1801 the author noticed that the arms of his house were identical with those of an Italian family whose forbears had been Ghibellines living in Pisa. Dante referred to the name in the *Inferno*. Some of the family had fled to France in 1524, and Sismondi decided to assume the connection and changed his name accordingly. *Fragments du Journal et de la Correspondance de J. C. L. Simonde de Sismondi*, with biographical introduction by J. J. C. Chenevière (Geneva, 1857). See also *Lettres inédites de J. C. L. de Sismonde* [and others] published with an introduction by Saint-Rene Taillandier (Paris, 1863) and *Lettres inédites écrite à sa mère pendant les cent jours*, ed. by Gabriel Monod (Paris, 1877). His journal and correspondence have also been edited by Mlle. Mongolfier (1863) and by Villari. See also GOOCH, 165–68; Louis de Loménie, *Galerie des contemporains illustres* (Paris, 1842), VII; F. A. Mignet, *Portraits et Notices historiques et littéraires* (Paris, 1877, 2 v.), II, 75–76; the same, "Life and Opinions of Sismondi," *NAR*, LXVI (1848), 32–72; the same, "Notice biographique et critique sur Simonde de Sismondi," *ASMP*, VII (1845), 379–403, and Alph. Courtois, "Notice sur la vie et les travaux économiques de Sismondi," *ibid.*, CXXXIX (1893), 835–64; Sainte-Beuve, *Lundis* (Paris, 1863), VI, 24–81; *FQR*, XXX (1843), 258–61; *ER*, XXV (1815), 31–63; reviews by Daunou in *JS*, 1821, pp. 486–94, 552–62; 1823, pp. 409–16; 1824, pp. 77–84; 1825, pp. 707–17; 1829, pp. 755–61; 1831, pp. 679–86; 1833, pp. 350–60.

lice threw him into prison. After his liberation in 1800 he removed to
Geneva, where the rest of his life was spent.

Sismondi's first writings were on economic subjects, but his formal
reputation began with the publication of the *Histoire des républiques
italiennes du moyen âge* (1807–18). The Institut de France refused
to crown these sixteen volumes, but the author won many literary
friends, among them Madame de Stael. The work dealt with the revolutions of all the Italian states from 1100 to 1530 A.D. The chief difficulty of such a subject was the political disunity of Italy during these
four centuries, but Sismondi skilfully unfolded his story without en-
tangling or losing its threads. He prefaced it by a survey from 476 to
1100, and added an epilogue for the centuries after 1530. His thesis
as propounded in the introduction was that government is one of the
most potent factors in shaping a people. Laws are more important than
climate or race in affecting virtues and vices, energy and talents. He
held no brief for any governmental system, but considered liberty essential. Hence he preferred a federation to a monarchy,[28] and declared
that the greatness of the republics varied with the freedom each possessed. The fifteenth century was the time of their greatest independence and culture. Perhaps he had too jaundiced a view of the rule of
Cosmo and Lorenzo de Medici, and overestimated the value that medieval men placed upon the modern concept of liberty. He was equally
hard upon the French kings from Charles VIII to Francis I. To the
popes he denied all administrative talent. The masterpiece of Sismondi
was not based upon archival materials and as an historical treatment
it has grave faults. Sismondi applied an inflexible moral standard (liberty vs. despotism) instead of interpreting each age by its own needs.
The Protestant and the republican peep out in every judgment of Catholicism and royalty. In view of his interest in economics it is odd that
Sismondi never probed for the economic and social causes of the political struggles which he chronicled.

The year 1813 witnessed his first introduction to the salons of Paris.
A liberal in his earlier years, and almost an Anglomaniac, he was sorry
to see the Empire go, and defended Napoleon by publishing, during
the Hundred Days, his *Examen de la Constitution française*. The Corsican offered him the brevet of a chevalier of the Legion of Honor, but
he refused the recognition, though he counted the interview with Napoleon as the greatest moment of his life. When his history was completed in 1818, he travelled to London,[29] then declined a chair at the

---

[28] Of the Etruscans he said: "Honneur aux peuples qui savent préférer le plus noble des
biens, la liberté, au pouvoir et à la gloire." *Histoires des républiques italiennes du moyen âge*
(Paris, 1840, 8 v.), I, 3.

[29] In 1819 Sismondi married a sister-in-law of Sir James MacKintosh.

Collège de France and at the Sorbonne, to return to Geneva and begin a still vaster work, a *Histoire des Français*. In his remaining twenty-three years of life he wrote 29 volumes! [30] It was the first detailed and complete history of France ever written, and reflects alike its author's industry and his admiration of the French nation. No more than in his work on the Italian republics was he impartial; he unfolded the Catholic sins in the Wars of Religion, but sought to veil the faults of the Huguenots. In these later years he was almost reactionary and mistook indignation for penetrating justice. A man of common sense, he was not over acute and lacked the gift of grasping things in the large. His style was clear and sober, lacking color and movement; and like many industrious but mediocre writers, he mistook application for genius. Sainte-Aulaire wrote cuttingly to Barante: "Sismondi interests me as much as it is possible to be interested when one is bored." [31] Sainte-Beuve with "benevolent sarcasm" dubbed Sismondi "the Rollin of French History." The praise and the blame are both fair.

A singular characteristic of the historians of the three countries of Scandinavia—Denmark, Sweden, Norway,[32]—is that one and all of them have written about their own country and their own people, and of no other kind of history, whereas English, German, and French historians have found subjects in the ancient Orient, in the classical period, in medieval and in modern history, and the history of every country and people of the globe has been written by them. No such single-mindedness of purpose, no such concentration upon a single area of territory is to be found anywhere else. There is no important history of Greece or Rome, or of the Reformation or of the French Revolution by a Danish or Swedish or Norwegian writer. No Northern historian has ever by his own research enlarged the history of any other country than his own.

The outstanding name in Danish historiography in the nineteenth century is that of C. F. Allen, author of a *History of Denmark* [33] unexcelled in the language. More original because limited to a period and the product of prolonged research is his *De tre nordiske rigers historie, 1497–1536* [*History of the Three Northern Kingdoms*] (Copenhagen, 1864–

---

[30] Volume I appeared in 1821; vol. XXIX, bringing the story to the death of Louis XV, was published posthumously in 1842. Amédée Renée completed the work with two more volumes, 1844.

[31] Baron de Barante, *Souvenirs* (Paris, 1890–1901, 8 v.), III, quoted in GOOCH, 168.

[32] Johannes Steenstrup, *Historieskrivninger i Denmark i det 19de Aarhundrede, 1801–63* (Copenhagen, 1889). In a number of the volumes of *RQH*, XXVII–XLVIII, will be found a "courrier du Nord" by E. Beauvois, which provides a complete survey of all important historical contributions in the years concerned pertaining to the history of Denmark, Sweden, and Norway.

[33] French translation from the seventh Danish edition by E. Beauvois (Copenhagen, 1878). The bibliography is the best available.

72, 5 v.). In the sphere of church history are A. D. Joergensen, *Den Nordiske Kirkes Grundlaeggelse og første Udvikling* (Copenhagen, 1874–78, 2 v.); and L. Helweg, *Den Danske Kirkes Historie til Reformationen* (2nd ed., Copenhagen, 1869–70, 2 v.), and his *Den Danske Kirkes Historie efter Reformationen* (2nd ed., Copenhagen, 1882, 2 v.). An excellent monograph is C. Paludan-Müller's *De første konger af den Oldenborgske slaegt* [*The First Kings of Oldenburg*] (Copenhagen, 1874).

J. J. Worsae (1821–85) was a pioneer in the history of the Norsemen. In 1851 there appeared his *Account of the Danes and Norwegians in England, Scotland and Ireland* (London, 1852), followed twelve years later by *Den danske erobring af England og Normandiet* [*The Danish Conquest of England and Normandy*]. Of similar subject but of wider scope and more scholarly is the four-volume *Normannerne* by Johannes Steenstrup (Copenhagen, 1876–82).[34]

The "father of Swedish history" was Erik Geijer (1785–1847),[35] professor at Upsala University, whose *History of Sweden*, written for the Heeren-Ukert series, was left unfinished at the time of his death. He had reached the reign of Charles XII and Carlson completed the fifth and sixth volumes. Geijer also prepared an edition of the chronicles of Swedish history.[36] In 1843–45 he published the papers of Gustavus III. In the later years of his life Geijer lectured on humanism and social and religious subjects. He was a man of talent, being also a poet and a composer of music. His translation of *Macbeth* holds the Swedish stage. His autobiography (*Minnen*) is full of charm.

Anders Fryxell (1795–1881) was the son of the scholarly librarian and antiquary of the Royal Library in Stockholm. Like Freytag in Germany he was the author of a long series (46 volumes) of *Bilder* of Swedish history from pagan times to the reign of Gustavus III (1772), which are still popular and have gone through over twenty editions. Fryxell also edited four volumes of state papers from the archives of foreign affairs (1836–43). His lenient judgment of the Catholic Church and of the rôle of the aristocracy in the history of Sweden were set forth in many articles and brochures, and involved him in a controversy with Geijer.[37]

The third member of this trio of Swedish historians found in the first half of the nineteenth century was Anders Magnus Strinnholm (1786–1862). He was not a teacher nor a university professor, but was sub-

---

[34] For contents of this work see Charles Gross, *The Sources and Literature of English History, from the Earliest Times to about 1485* (2nd rev. ed., London and New York, 1915), p. 303, no. 1535, and for a masterly review of it Karl v. Amira, "Die Anfänge des normannischen Rechts," *HZ*, XXXIX (1878), 241–68.

[35] Jørgen Nielsen, *Erik Gustav Geijer* (Odense, 1902).

[36] *Scriptores rerum suecicarum medii aevi* (Upsala, 1828).

[37] S. A. Hedin, *Fryxell mot Geijer* (1861).

ventioned by the government in 1828 and for thirty-four years unremittingly pursued his historical researches. Among his works are: *History of the Swedish People under the Kings of the House of Vasa* (3 v., 1819–23), which stops with the year 1544; *Life of Magnus Stenbock* (2 v., 1821); and his *opus magnum: History of the Swedish People from the Earliest Times to the Present*, which, however, is actually a history of Sweden during the Middle Ages, for it does not extend beyond the revolution in 1319 (5 v., 1834–54).

Norwegian historical studies in the nineteenth century are not easily differentiated from the history of Denmark and Sweden. The first Norwegian historian of eminence was Peter Andreas Munch (1810–63), professor of history in the University of Christiana from 1841 until his death. His most important work is a *History of the Norwegian People to the Union of Calmar in 1397 (Det Norske Folks Historie)* (8 v., 1851–64), which had been preceded in 1838 by a *History of Norway, Sweden and Denmark*—the order of enumeration of these countries is interesting. Munch also edited *The Ancient Laws of Norway to 1397* (3 v., 1846–49), and the *Codex diplomatarius monasterii Sancti Michaelis* (1845). He died in Rome still in pursuit of his researches.

Contemporary with Munch was Jakob Rudolf Keyser (1803–64), who founded the museum of antiquities in the University of Christiana. Among his works are: *History of Norway to 1687, History of the Norwegian Church before the Reformation*, and a series of studies on the origin and religion of the Norsemen: *Om Nordmoendenes Herkomst*. Sophus Bugge (1833–1907) opened new fields of research in Norse linguistic, myths, and saga literature.

Norwegian history was founded by Munch and Keyser. "They had written great works on the earlier periods of Norwegian history," it has been pointed out, "but a systematic exposition of the national development of the Norwegian people was still lacking. All the older historians had regarded the history of Norway as consisting of two parts . . .; the earlier period up to the time of the Kalmar union [1397], and the modern period after 1814. The period of union with Denmark was regarded as an era of dependence and national stagnation, about which they preferred to keep silent." [38] Precisely this neglected gap in the history of Norway J. E. Sars strove to fill in his most prominent work: *Udsigt over den Norske Historie*. His findings proved the truth of what Henrik Wergeland had pointed out earlier in his *Norges Konstitutionis Historie*. Sars "showed that the Norwegian people in early times did not consist only of *bønder* under a patriarchal rule, but that an aristocracy had been developed, more powerful than that of Sweden and Den-

[38] Knut Gjerset, *History of the Norwegian People* (New York, 1915, 2 v.), II, 551–52.

mark. When Harald Haarfagre united all Norway under his rule, the
herser, or chieftains, lost their former power, but the struggle between
the kings and the aristocracy continued until the chieftain class was
destroyed. When the old royal line died out, Norway entered the union
with Denmark without a warlike aristocracy strong enough to be the
leaders of the people. Norwegian society had become democratic at a
time when Sweden and Denmark were ruled by a strong warlike aristocracy. This explains the inferior position of Norway during the period of union." [39] Sars' second important work was a *Political History
of Norway, 1815–1885*, strongly patriotic in tone.

Just after the turn of the century J. E. Sars, Alex. Bugge, E. Hertzberg, O. A. Johnsen, Y. Nielsen, and A. Tarabger each contributed a
volume to a co-operative *History of Norway*. [40]

[39] Gjerset (n. 38), II, 552.
[40] *Norges Histoire, Fremstillet for det Norske Folk* (Christiana, 1909–17, 6 v. in 13 pts.).

CHAPTER LXIII

THE SOUTHERN COUNTRIES

THE idea of Italian independence and unity had existed for centuries before the *Risorgimento*, but it did not become a matter of practical politics until the time of the French Revolution. Despite the community of Dante's language and the religion of Rome, there was prior to 1792 no trace of real national feeling, or of hostility to the Austrians who held Lombardy, and to the native despots over the rest of Italy. The political education of the people of the peninsula still remained to be achieved. In this work the historical writers performed yeoman service.[1]

During the French regime (1796–1815) new ideas were grafted into the Italian mind. History passed from the hands of the religious orders to soldiers, politicians, and men of letters who loved their country and cherished its progress. They differed in their proposals as to ways and means. Troya, Capponi, Cantù, and Tosti put their hope in the old Guelfic idea of a confederation of the Italian states under the papal headship. For those who were strongly anti-papal, other devices seemed more attractive. Colletta was anti-Bourbon, Amari both anti-

[1] The standard work is Benedetto Croce, *Storia della storiografia italiana di cominciamenti del sec. XIX ai nostri giorni* (Bari, 1921, 2 v. in 1), also printed as a series of articles in *La Critica* in volumes XIII–XVIII (1915–20). See also Croce's articles on contemporary writers, *ibid.*; Georges Bourgin in HISTOIRE ET HISTORIENS, I, 219–32; Pasquale Villari, *Studies, Historical and Critical*, tr. by Linda Villari (New York, 1907); N. Tommaseo, "Sopra gli studi storici e le pubblicazioni dei monumenti che debbono sussidiarli," *Archivio storico italiano*, ser. 2, I (1855), pt. 1, pp. 97–111; M. Tabarrini, "Degli studi storici in Italia e del più fruttuoso loro indirizzo," *ibid.*, ser. 2, IV (1856), pt. 2, pp. 101–16; and consult the reviews, *ibid.*; A. Bartoli, "Degli studi storici in Italia nel secolo scorso e nel presente," in *La famiglia e la scuola*, January, 1861; Francèsco Lanzani, *Del carattere e degli intendimenti della istoriografia italiana nel secolo XIX* (Padua, 1878), a brief but useful sketch, mainly on the period of national awakening and the attainment of unification; A. Cosci, "Gli studi storici in Italia dopo il 1859," *Rivista Europea* (1878); G. Romano, "Gli studi storici in Italia allo stato presente," *Rivista filosofia*, II (1900), 319; and by the same author, "Gli studi di storia medioevale negli ultimi cinquant' anni," *Atti della Soc. Ital. per il progresso della scienze*, 1911 (Rome, 1912), 631–44; J. J. Ampère, "L'histoire de l'Italie et ses historiens," *RDM*, 1856, pt. 5, 45–81; G. Libri, "Des publications historiques en Italie," *ibid.*, 1841, pt. 3, 876–94; Louis Etienne, "Les historiens modernes de la Republique Florentine," *ibid.*, 1867, pt. 1, 135–66; Greene, "Italian Historians," *NAR*, XLVIII (1839), 325–51; G. W. Greene, *Historical Studies* (New York and London, 1850), 130–52; Lacy Collison-Morley, *Modern Italian Literature* (London, 1911), ch. xiii. For historians dealing with medieval Italy, consult Pietro Egidi, *La storia medioevale* (Rome, 1922), and C. W. Previté-Orton, "Recent Work in Italian Medieval History," *Cambridge Historical Journal*, I (1923), 10–22; Carlo Cesare, "Ueber die fortschreitende Entwiklung der geschichtlichen Studien im Königreich Neapel von der zweiten Hälfte des 18. Jahrhunderts bis auf die Gegenwart," tr. by A. Beer in *HZ*, VI, 293–348; J. C. L. Simonde de Sismondi, "Political Conditions of Italian States," *ER*, LV (1832), 362–97.

Bourbon and anti-clerical, and Ferrari was revolutionary in sentiment. Most of the historians took an active part in the *Risorgimento,* tasted the bitterness of prison or exile; and their political experiences left traces upon their works.   Such a writer as Villari, on the other hand, represents the generation after 1861, when the Italian kingdom had been formed; thereafter the historians are more dispassionate and scholarly.   For the first two-thirds of the century most of Italian historiography served a political purpose.

Vincenzo Cuoco (1770–1823), a Neapolitan who had served in the French armies, provided the prologue to the nineteenth century in his *Saggio storico sulla rivoluzione di Napoli* (1801). His political novel *Platone in Italia* (1804) hearkened back to the days of a mythical golden age in Italy before the Romans. Cuoco proclaimed to his fellow-Italians the blessings of equality and unity; he called upon France either to liberate his country entirely, or not to trust her at all. With Cuoco the influence of Vico returns strongly.

Contemporary with Cuoco was Giuseppe Micali, born at Leghorn. In 1796–99 he was in Paris and was an eye-witness of the fall of the Directory. He made topographical and antiquarian researches, the results of which were published in two large works, *Storia degli antichi popoli Italiani* (1822, 3 v.) and *Monumenti per sirvire all' storia degli antichi popoli Italiani* (1832), which Niebuhr adversely criticized. He was also author of *The Commerce of the Maritime Republics of Italy.*

Although Florence had produced the greatest school of historians during the Italian Renaissance—one thinks of Villani, Poggio, Machiavelli, Guicciardini—there was no general history of Tuscany before Lorenzo Pignotti, grand ducal historiographer and professor in Pisa University, who began as far back as 1793 to trace out the first lines of his work and gave his countrymen a *History of Tuscany from the Time of the Etruscans,* published after his death in 1812. This is a pleasant and not uninforming work—the best portion is the long essay on Tuscan literature and the arts which concludes the fourth volume— but perhaps would not merit mention if it were not for the fact that the English translation of it [2] first awakened the interest of the British reading public in Florence's history and culture.

The first true historian of Italy in the new age was Carlo Giuseppe Guglielmo Botta (1766–1837).[3] Like his ancestors for five generations, he studied medicine, and obtained his degree at Turin when twenty.

[2] By John Browning (London, 1826, 4 v.).
[3] Paolo Pavesio, *Carlo Botta e le sue opere storiche con appendice di lettere inedite* (Florence, 1874); *NAR*, XLVIII, 325 and L, 30; Emilio Tipaldo, *Biografia degli Italiani illustri del secolo XVIII* (Venice, 1834–35, 10 v.), VIII, 424–48; François Perrens, *Histoire de la littérature italienne* (1867).

His republican manifestations during the flurry of 1792 brought him two years in prison, and even a taste of torture. Allowed to go into exile at Grenoble, he returned to Italy as army doctor in Napoleon's army. From 1798 to 1814 he played a role in the government of Piedmont, but his views on Italian independence caused Napoleon to frown upon his advancement. Rector of the University of Rouen for a brief season during the Hundred Days, Botta was retired from political life after Waterloo, and gave himself wholly to writing. A conversation in the home of Manzoni's mother at Paris in 1804 had already moved him to write the *Storia della guerra dell' independenze degli Stati Uniti d'America* (1809). Its four volumes were written in three years, after the Italian manner of the sixteenth century; the whole was more a literary effort than the result of any adequate knowledge of the materials. It was well received in French and English versions, as the first acceptable treatment of the subject; but the Italian edition, after halting sales, was finally disposed of as waste paper to pay the cost of his wife's illness. Botta's fame among his countrymen rests upon the *Storia d'Italia dal 1789 al 1814.*[4] It deals with matters of which he could speak with first hand information, and is carried by a patriotic tone throughout. Botta had wearied of the excesses of the Revolution, and lamented that the boundless egotism of Bonaparte had been the cause of all of Italy's recent woes. Though he had become a naturalized French citizen in the meantime, there can be no doubt of his anti-French feeling. Even the style is purged carefully of all Gallicisms. While he occasionally rises to eloquence, Botta strove too much to imitate the classical Roman and Florentine historians to attain simple ease.[5] Admirers pressed him to continue Guicciardini's famous history. The ten volumes in which he performed this task are a worthless compilation vitiated by haste. Poverty drove Botta to write in four years what would tax the resources of a scholar's lifetime. Despite the careless ease with which he strode over details, he was immensely popular with his generation, and was received with distinct favor by Charles Albert when he returned to Piedmont in 1831. His son Paul Emile Botta (1805–70) was the famous Assyrian archaeologist and excavator of the mound of Khorsabad (1843).

Pietro Colletta (1775–1831),[6] a Neapolitan politician and general,

---

[4] Paris, 1824, four volumes in quarto. There were numerous re-issues, and a French translation by Th. Licquet (1824, 5 v.).

[5] "The obsolete Tuscanisms, for which Zanella considers a dictionary necessary, gave rise to the remark, even in his own day, that his histories were written for his ancestors rather than for posterity." Collison-Morley (n. 1), 293.

[6] Gino Capponi, "Notizia intorno alla vita di Pietro Colletta," in the preface to *Storia del reame di Napoli dal 1734 sino al 1825* (3rd ed., Florence, 1856, 2 v.); G. Bigoni, in *ASI*, ser.

produced only one work, the *Storia del reame di Napoli, 1734–1825*, which was edited after his death by Gino Capponi (1834). After rising to high honors under Joseph Bonaparte and Murat, Colletta was employed by the restored Bourbon government to suppress the rising of 1820 in Palermo. The method of his negotiations made him suspect to the Carbonari and the reactionary government alike, so that he was exiled for two years to Moravia. Allowed to return to Florence, he devoted his life to his history and the acquisition of a vigorous and characteristic style molded in imitation of Tacitus. Judgments on his work, which was published in Geneva and smuggled into Italy to enjoy a wide circulation, varied from warm approval to passionate attacks upon his rancor and distorted presentation. His experiences were hardly calculated to make him an impartial writer.[7] As an exile he had no access to Neapolitan sources and relied upon his memory; hence there are gaps and numerous inaccuracies. His conception of history as a classic artistic composition [8] led him to color or rearrange facts and to labor at artificial contrasts. He criticized severely the rule of the hated Bourbons and condemned the Carbonari whom he had formerly praised to the skies to win their support. Colletta appreciated the value of civilization, and by turning to industry, agriculture, and the effect of legislation on social conditions, he gave a broader picture than his predecessors.

Romanticism brushed away the empty phrases of rhetoric and returned to the treasures of Muratori. From the grievances of the present, Italian scholars ranged back to the achievements and struggles of the medieval period. In 1839 Charles Albert appointed the first royal historical commission, and the official publication of documents, chronicles, and records was inaugurated. This antedated the Rolls Series of England by nearly twenty years. In 1842 Vieusseux established the *Archivio storico italiano*, and Naples and other provinces soon provided humbler counterparts. The *Archivio* was begun as a means of publication for works and documents that were rare or unedited, especially for the Middle Ages, but in 1855 its character was changed to that of a historical review with wider interests.[9] Printed documents

5, XXXIX (1907), 489–94; Luchaire, *Essai sur l'évolution intellectuelle de l'Italie, 1815–1830* (1906), 198–214.

[7] He called his work ". . . compagna nell' esilio, consolatrice delle . . . pene, promettitrice (lusinghiera forse) di fama. . . . Ella empiva gli ozii nuovi a un' anima operosa; ella nei mali, che mi venivano dalla prepotenza, suggeriva i lamenti e le vendette." Quoted by Bigoni (n. 6), 490.

[8] His own view of history was that it is: "un dramma della specie umana, che per azioni vere, mena allo scoprimento d'una catastrofe: dimostra la virtu e i falli degli attori: premia e punice in eterno." Quoted by Bigoni (n. 6), 492.

[9] The next great journal was the *Rivista storica italiana*, founded in 1884 by Rinaudo, Villari, and others.

and source criticism made a new kind of history possible. Benedetto Croce has referred to the Romantic School as the "nostalgic" historians, but the term seems somewhat harsh and ignores their real accomplishments.

Allessandro Manzoni (1785–1873), the author of the greatest Italian historical novel (*I promessi sposi*), had made serious studies in Lombard history. But no one more than Sismondi, who wrote in Switzerland but came of a Tuscan family, aroused interest in the medieval history of Italy, and won for Italians the sympathy of liberals everywhere. Sismondi declared that the enmity of Guelfs and Ghibellines had proved fatal to the cause of Italian liberty. Now arose a neo-Guelfic school of historians who combined the Catholic revival with patriotic fervor. Dismissing the *ignis fatuus* of unity, they proposed a federated Italy under Rome's leadership. Over against the rising tide of anti-clericalism, they represented the work of the Papacy throughout the Middle Ages as one of benevolence and progress; the Papacy was the preserver of the Latin genius against the Germanic hordes and the moral regenerator of Europe. The writers next taken up all belonged to this direction.

Count Gino Capponi (1792–1876) [10] was one of the most attractive figures of the century. He came from an old Florentine family, loyal subjects of the grand dukes. Capponi was a moderate liberal, and in favor of a Guelfic federation under the leadership of the Pope. The failure of the efforts of 1821 led him to despair of liberation through revolution, and he devoted himself to the patronage of Italian arts and letters. In 1820 he founded the *Antologia*, a literary journal modeled after the *Edinburgh Review*. Herein he was aided by the Swiss Vieusseux, and later became one of the strongest supporters of Vieusseux's *Archivio*. Capponi wrote a work entitled *La storia della republica di Firenze* (1875, 2 v.), which reaped excessive praise at home and abroad. In theory he wished to be democratic and just, but his temperament turned against proletarian uprisings like the Ciompi. His views, as a reviewer has said, were always those of a man "a little behind his times; too much governed by the past to dare greatly; too large-minded to favour reaction." [11] When he began his work a quarter-century before it appeared (he was over eighty when he finished writing), no critical study existed on the sources of medieval Tuscany. Scholarship has since undermined portions of his earlier sections. He was uncritical in borrowing whole pages from Villani.

[10] Alfred v. Reumont, *Gino Capponi, ein Zeit- und Lebensbild* (Gotha, 1880); W. J. Stillman, "Gino Capponi," *The Nation*, XXXII (1881), 321–22; *ER*, CXLIII (1876), 474–510; *NAR*, CXXI (1876), 450–56.

[11] *ER* (n. 10), 479. A cabinet which he formed at the request of Grand Duke Leopold II in 1848 proved too moderate for the liberals.

Cesare Cantù (1804–95),[12] a Lombard, was the chief disciple of Manzoni in history, and one of the most prolific of nineteenth-century historians. For a time he was a prisoner of the Austrian government, and spent many years in exile prior to the establishment of the Italian Kingdom. His list of writings includes poetry, essays, and stories, but his *magnum opus* was a *Storia universale* in thirty-five volumes (1838–46, numerous reprints). Scholars may look for little accuracy and less originality in a work of such compass, but it was widely known and long a popular book of reference for Italians. His *Storia degli Italiani* (1849–50, 6 v.) was the first complete history of their country. He divided it into three great periods: the "età pagana" from the origins of Rome to the fall of the Western Empire, the "età cattolica" ending with Savonarola and the discovery of the New World, and the "età politica" of modern times. This was the age of the balance of power and of diplomacy, when the pagan element of force returned. His constant comparisons of the nineteenth century with the "età cattolica" show a rather blind preference for the latter, and indulgence for the Church as the protector of civilization and the classics. The work is meritorious in dealing not solely with politics, but covering social and economic conditions, literature and religion as well. But in general Cantù's work is superficial, written with an eye to the public, and an occasional spurt of venom. His clerical bias is exemplified in *Gli eretici d'Italia*, which surveys the precursors of the Reformation era, and supports the thesis that the splendors of Italy were contemporaneous with the great periods of papal supremacy before the Reformation. The decadence of the last two centuries was not due to Catholicism, but to the undermining influence of heretics and rationalists who vitiated sound morals and religion. Cantù was one of the few liberals who were sympathetic to Maximilian's promises of reform in 1857, and so was branded a traitor. He founded the Lombard Historical Society, and was supervisor of the Lombard archives. His most accurate book is *L'Abate Parini e la Lombardia nel secolo passato* (1854). For students of literature he has left his *Reminiscences of Manzoni* (1882).[13]

Carlo Troya (1785–1858) [14] of Naples was led into medieval history by the *Divine Comedy*. His *Del Veltro allegorico di Dante* has the merit of being among the first works to use this literary masterpiece as an historical source and interpreting it in connection with Dante's own life and times. He read the conflict of Guelf and Ghibelline as the clash of two natures, the Latin and the Northern. In seeking to explain

[12] Marco Tabarrini, *Studi di critica storica* (Florence, 1876).
[13] The best edition is that revised by Stampa, Manzoni's stepson.
[14] Necrology in *ASI*, ser. 2, VII (1858), 185–89; Marc Monnier, *L'Italie, est-elle la terre des morts?* (Paris, 1860), ch. xi; Majocchi, *Troya* (1876).

their origin, his studies carried him back to the time of the Goths and then to the Lombards. From the remarkable archives of Monte Cassino and other Italian monasteries, he collected materials for a history of the Lombards.[15] His *Storia d'Italia nel medio evo* (Naples, 1839–59, and Florence, 1847–49), was preceded by twenty-five books of material on the origins and nature of the barbarian invaders of Italy, and of their governments and customs before they entered the peninsula.[16] He did not aim to produce a work of art (of which his literary powers were scarcely capable), but to compile from his country's archives a work that would give the causes of Rome's decay and show the nature and conduct of her barbarian masters. The *Storia* itself was never finished. Covering the time from Odoacer to Alboin, it ends where Troya intended to begin. The work is significant for contesting the view traditional since Machiavelli, Giannone, and Muratori, and supported by Savigny, that the Italians had retained their rights of citizenship under the Lombards, and that the Roman law had persisted in general use. While admitting that in private affairs they were allowed to retain their law, Troya insisted that the Italians were completely disfranchised and lost the right to carry arms. He believed the revival of Roman law was due to a memory the Lombard lands retained, and to its incessant employment in Rome, Naples, Amalfi, Venice, and other parts untouched by the Lombard domination.

Luigi Tosti (1811–97),[17] abbot of Monte Cassino, was born at Naples, and entered the monastery at the age of eight. Ten years later he had already begun his *Storia della badia di Monte Cassino* (1841–43). It is a valuable work because of the many unedited documents which it employed. He appeared in it as a neo-Guelf, dreaming of a federated Italy under the Pope. In the medieval empire he saw only a despotic force aimed at destroying the city-republics, which he regarded as the most perfect form of civil government. Unity, then or now, to him meant despotism. His *Storia di Bonifazio ottavo e dei suoi tempi* declared that this unfortunate pontiff had consistently been a good Italian patriot. Philip IV was responsible for the decline of the Holy See, and its consequent inability to lead Italy. Tosti's hatred of the empire and of foreigners generally was applied with monkish severity to the entire range of Italian history. Just before the outbreak of 1848 Tosti laid his *History of the Lombard League* at the feet of the Pope,

---

[15] *Codice diplomatico longobardo dal DLXVIII al DCCLXXIV* (1852–54, 4 pts.), forming vol. IV of his *Storia d'Italia nel medio evo*.

[16] *Apparato preliminare alla storia dal medio evo* (1829 f.).

[17] *The Roman Journals of Ferdinand Gregorovius, 1852–1874*, ed. by Friedrich Althaus and tr. from the 2nd German ed. by Mrs. G. W. Hamilton (London, 1907), 67–68; Ernest Renan, *Essais de morale et de critique* (Paris, 1859), 205–41.

asking him to follow his medieval predecessor.[18]   The pope's actual behavior during and after the revolution destroyed his faith in the papacy.   The first blow of the reaction fell upon Monte Cassino, which under Tosti had become the center of intellectual and liberal life in southern Italy.   The monastery was occupied by soldiers, the printing press was closed, and Tosti forced to leave.

In view of its influence, especially among clerical circles, another Guelf work must be mentioned.   Vincenzo Gioberti, a Piedmontese priest, composed a work on the *Moral and Civil Supremacy of the Italians* (1843) which condemned their modern political and moral degradation, and is supposed to have contributed towards the election in 1846 of a reforming pope in the person of Pius IX.

Cesare Balbo (1789–1853) [19] was another of the statesmen of Italy who turned to literary production as a means of national education. Of good birth, and a native of Turin, he entered the employ of the Napoleonic government from 1808 to 1814; but after the fall of Bonaparte he devoted himself, like his father who was minister of the interior, to the cause of Italy.   Allowed to return from exile after the revolution of 1821, he found politics closed to him, and from the composition of historical dramas and novels developed into one of the most popular of Italian scholars.   His two-volume *Storia d'Italia* (1830) had for a thesis the idea that independence from all foreign interference was essential to Italian happiness.   Balbo did not look for true Italian unity, but his warm desire was for a confederation of states under the Papal headship. He too represents the Guelfic idea in historiography.   His *Vita di Dante* (1839) was written because "Dante is a great part of the history of Italy," and played its share in promoting the Dante revival of the nineteenth century.   His *Sommario della storia d'Italia* (1846), written in forty days for the *Enciclopedia popolare*, proved a popular and influential outline, and passed through many reprints.   Balbo's chief demand was for external freedom, but he did not believe in revolution, and his political influence was thrown behind moderation, so that he opposed democracy as much as the existing despotism.   His writings, couched in a forceful and compact style, owe much of their dignity and weakness to his theocratic conception of Christianity.

If the Catholic-liberal writers, who espoused the leadership of the Church in a re-made Italy, attracted a wide public, other voices spoke no less vehemently on the other side.   The anti-clerical group which followed Giuseppe Mazzini drew much of its inspiration from the French

[18] "I lay these chapters at your feet as a sacred thing.   Give us back the standard of Alexander III.   The hour has struck, humanity awaits you."

[19] A. Reumont in *Zeitgenossen. Ein biographisches Magazin für die Geschichte unserer Zeit*, I (1862); a review of the *Delle Speranze d'Italia* in the *NAR*, LXVI (1848), 1–32.

Revolution. These writers declared for a closer political unity, rather than federation, under a republican system, and demanded the abolition of the temporal power of the papacy. Niccolini, in his historical novels *John of Procida* and *Arnold of Brescia*, assailed the papacy as the perpetual enemy of Italian unity, because it had so frequently called in foreigners to suppress native movements. D'Azeglio expressed a similar hostility in his *Fieramosca* and *Niccoli di Lepi*. True historical scholars in this camp were few, but time was to tell against neo-Guelfic hopes.

The greatest of the South Italian historians stood on a higher vantage point. Michele Amari (1806–89) [20] was born at Palermo in Sicily. Employed in the Bourbon civil service, yet a member of the Carbonari, he later took part in the revolution of 1821. Amari became famous by a work on the Sicilian Vespers, which ran to eight editions in his life-time, and was translated into various languages. [21] By implication the work preached revolution in the superheated atmosphere of Europe, and purported to show how a nation by courageous conduct could rid itself of foreign oppressors. The Bourbon government forced the author to flee to Paris, and the Pope condemned the book. Aside from its contemporary appeal, it was a study of real historical merit. Amari demolished the old legendary interpretation of the Vespers as a conspiracy of nobles led by Giovanni di Procida, and ended its episodic character. He contended it was only the beginning and not the end of a revolution. The tumult was prepared by social and political conditions, and the insolent Angevin rule. Its importance must be sought in the reform of the political constitution and the moral and social forces it created. Its effects extended horizontally over other kingdoms and vertically down through Sicilian and even Italian history, as "una gran tradizione." [22]

In the eighteenth century, the discovery of Pompeii had revived interest in the ancient and medieval period of Italian history, and in this revival the history of the Arab domination in Sicily shared. A chair of Arabic language and literature had been established at the University of Palermo, and Sicilian scholars turned their attention both to manuscript works and to inscriptions. Notable among their

[20] Gustave Dugat, *Histoire des orientalistes de l'Europe du XIIᵉ au XIXᵉ siècle* (Paris, 1868–70, 2 v.), I, ch. iii; Oreste Tommasini, *Scritti di storia e critica* (Rome, 1891); A. Vannucci in *ASI*, ser. 2, III (1856), pt. 2, pp. 131–70; Allessandro d'Ancona, *Carteggio di Michele Amari raccolto e postillato* (Turin, 1896, 2 v.) and "the sumptuous volumes," *Centenario della nascita di Amari* (Palermo, 1910, 2 v.); Hartwig, Derenbourg, *Opuscules d'un Arabisant, 1868–1905* (Paris, 1905); and reviews in *QR*, CXLI (1876), 211–23; *NAR*, CXLI, 211 ff.; *FM*, XLVIII (1853), 679–88.

[21] *La guerre del Vespro Siciliano, o un periodo delle istorie siciliane del XIII secolo* (1841). The English version is by Lord Ellesmere.

[22] See his preface, pp. x–xiii (edition of 1849, two volumes; the preface is the same as the Paris edition of 1843; this edition is fully annotated).

productions were Rosario di Gregorio's *Rerum arabicarum quae ad his-toriam siculam spectant, ampla collectio* (1790), and Martorana's *Notize storiche dei Saraceni siciliani* (1833). Now came a greater scholar. During his years at Paris, Amari turned to the treasures of her libraries in Oriental manuscripts, and plunged into Arabic, modern Greek, and palaeography. After collecting fragments, geographical descriptions, and Arabic prose and poetry composed in Sicily (a hunt that sent him over all Europe), he issued the first volume of the *Storia dei Musulmani di Sicilia* (1853). The last volume of this set appeared a score of years later. He proposed to write the story of the two conquests of his native island, by the Arabs and by the Normans, and to portray the conse-quences as they extended down to modern times. The first volume depicted conditions before the Arabs, the origin of the Moslem empire, and their culture in Africa. The next three volumes dealt with their rule, the fifth with the Norman conquest, and the sixth with conditions until the middle of the thirteenth century, when Italian civilization changed its seat from Sicily to the mainland of Southern Italy. The work is the recognized authority on the subject, throwing light into many dark corners, demonstrating the brilliant civilization of the Arabs and their happy rule after the Byzantine exploitation, and giving space to the various sides of life and institutions.

In 1859 Amari returned to Italy as professor of Arabic at Pisa. He was made a senator and twice was minister of education. Amari wrote with an eye on Italian nationality. Liberty he called a plant native to South Italy and Sicily, preserved by the Lombards, Greeks, and Sara-cens till the tenth century. The Norman rulers were respected because their government preserved the balance between the crown and the people. But Charles of Anjou for sixteen years exploited and oppressed, and so the Vespers restored the beloved constitution of their ancestors.[23] Never was there a more thoroughly national contest. Thus one Italian writer found the Golden Age in Sicily.

The disappointments of 1848 and 1849 fell heavily upon the ardent patriots, and most so upon the neo-Guelfs. Tosti hoped for another pope; but many writers followed Gioberti, who discarded his former ideal of a federation under Rome's aegis and announced his new hope in a close unity effected by the house of Savoy.[24] Thus Italian sentiment was gradually united around one formula for the cherished establish-ment of national independence. With some writers, however, pessimism

---

[23] The mistrust of the Bourbon government may be pardoned, when they read: "The history of this period places before the eyes of the present oppressors of Italy a terrible example of the energy displayed in defence of their most sacred rights, by the ancestors of the people whom they now trample upon." *NAR*, LXIV, 510.

[24] In his *Del rinnovamento civile d'Italia* (1851).

remained. Luigi Carlo Farini (1812–66) composed the first portion of his *Storia dello stato Romano dal anno 1815 al 1850* in exile at Turin (1850, 2nd volume in 1859). As an official of the government and member of the Sardinian parliament, and as editor of a political journal (*Il Piemonte*), he was a strong supporter of Cavour. In 1859 he negotiated the annexation of Modena to Piedmont. He held office in Cavour's cabinet, and for some months (December 1862–March 1863) headed a cabinet himself till overwork brought on his death. The first volume of his history had the distinction of being translated into English by no less a person than Mr. Gladstone.[25]

Giuseppe Ferrari (1812–76) was less active in politics than most of the other Italian writers, and much of his life was passed in France. He best represents the inclination towards despair in the decade between 1849 and 1859. In his works revolution and reaction become a perpetual cycle which the historian views with fatalistic resignation.[26] According to the *Histoire des revolutions d'Italie, ou Guelfes et Gibelins* (Paris, 1858, 4 v.) the Pope and the Emperor were the two principles about which Italian history revolved. The grandeur of the nation lay in the absence of the Emperor and the military weakness of the Pope, in the liberty they represented, and the ability of Italians to make or unmake them, because of their elective nature. In sum, Italy's greatness was that she never permitted a strong national monarchy to arise! Such a government Ferrari considered synonymous with passivity and servile obedience, and in 1859 he returned to Italy to oppose Cavour and to fight for federalism. But neither did he accept the Guelfic formula, for Italy was neither a church nor a convent. The medieval republics which Sismondi and Mazzini so admired had never been able to federate, and the princes had done no better. After studying the 7,200 revolutions Ferrari professed to find in Italian local history from Roman days to 1530, he concluded these were only one long conflict between two recurrent parties, with the victories alternating between them. One represented democratic ideas and institutions, but it was blind and opposed to intellectual liberty and individual freedom. The other represented only a legal liberty, was insolent and tyrannical and was not concerned about the interests of the people. Whether they were called Guelf or Ghibelline, or some other name, it mattered little: it was always the same story, and would probably continue so. But after all these oscillations had not been without their value. Ferrari seemed to believe

[25] Farini's political correspondence was published as *Lettres sur les affaires d'Italie* (Paris, 1860). His *Storia dello stato Romano* appeared in a French translation in 1862. See Ettori Parri, *Luigi Carlo Farini: Commemorazione* (Rome, 1878).

[26] Ferrari has given a clear summary of his views in the preface of his work, and Renna (n. 17) has criticized them with equal clarity, pp. 243–68.

revolutions were not such bad things after all, since all the fruits of
Italian genius had been produced during Italy's disorderly history. To
which Renan has rightly answered that such a regime of revolutions as
Ferrari proposes, affords solely the liberty that is in civil war, and that
he failed to appreciate the other alternative of a limited type of government.

Little historical writing was done during the ten years after Novara,
but Parma (1854) and Genoa (1856) began to publish the sources for
their histories. When Victor Emmanuel was proclaimed King of Italy
in Turin, the task of the patriotic writers was not yet over. "Italy is
made. Let us now make Italians." Villari uncovered in Machiavelli
the unsuspected lineaments of a national hero. Francesco Lanzani
pointed to morals in his *History of the Italian Communes down to 1313*,
and Ettore Pais in his *History of Rome* proved himself the most nationalistic of all nineteenth-century Italian historians. Everywhere local
societies and journals took up the task of recovering the national story
from oblivion. In 1890 the Institute of Italian History began the *Fonti
della storia d'Italia* series, now numbering more than fifty volumes.

The most eminent of the post-unification writers was Pasquale Villari
(1827-1932),[27] who is perhaps as well known to English readers as any
other of his countrymen. This prolific writer was born in Naples, was implicated in the anti-Bourbon riots of 1848, and found a new home in
Florence. His *Storia di Girolamo Savonarola e de suoi tempi* initiated a
veritable Savonarola cult. It rested upon a decade of study of the
archival sources, but its sympathetic and highly laudatory picture is
now acknowledged to be overdrawn. Its monastic subject is presented
as a compound of many virtues, and contending against the most evil
machinations. It is a picture solely of whites and blacks. Villari has
done best when treating his hero as an isolated psychological study,
and least well in fitting him into the broader historical background. He
failed to modify his work in the face of later historical evidence, as
A. Gherardi's *Nuovi Documenti*. The life of the friar as a figure in secular
history still waits for an historian. Equally interesting is Villari's *Niccolo
Machiavelli e i suoi tempi*. For this he used ten volumes of unedited
manuscripts of Guicciardini, the diplomatic materials of most of the
Italian provinces, and many hundreds of official letters composed by
the busy secretary of Florence. He hoped to present a new picture of
this maligned figure, by showing him in relation to his time. Villari
contended that Machiavelli recognized the difference between public

---

[27] Francesco Baldasseroni, *Pasquale Villari, profilo biografico e bibliografia degli scritti*
(Florence, 1907); Croce (n. 1), II, 160 ff.; E. Armstrong, "Recent Criticism upon the 'Life of
Savonarola,'" *EHR*, IV (1889), 441–59.

and private morality, and attempted to formulate this scientifically; but that he failed to consider how they were connected. Machiavelli's passionate desire to see his country unified (*Il Principe*) is allowed not only to exculpate, but even to exalt him. It is an excellent biography, but the defense of Machiavelli is largely a case of "tu quoque" over against his many accusers from the sixteenth to the present century. L. A. Burd admits that as a study of Machiavelli's life and works it is superior to other attempts, but "the history of Machiavellism remains to be written." [28]

After a series of essays published under the title *I primi due secoli della storia di Firenze* (1893), Villari turned to more popular composition, for he declared that the history of his country should be not only a pedagogical discipline, but an instrument of national education, and serve to mould the moral and political character of Italians. [29] He began a series of simple narrative histories with Balzani and Orsi, composing *Le invasioni barbariche in Italia*, and *Medieval Italy*. His keynote is both patriotic and didactic; he inclines to moralizing and preaching. Italy's degradation was due to the poison of the Renaissance; emancipated reason corrupted moral character. Religion is a necessary element in civilization, and the only real progress, even for the masses, is moral and spiritual. His *Studies, Historical and Critical* are amateurishly metaphysical.

Spanish historical scholarship reached its highest point in the seventeenth century when the Spanish monarchy was still living on the heights to which Charles V and Philip II had raised it, and when Spanish literature, and art too, were at their climax. After that time, historical scholarship gradually declined along with the general decadence of Spain in everything.

The study of history in Spain in the nineteenth century was more distinguished by the publication of general collections of sources [30] than

---

[28] *EHR*, XI (1896), 366–69.

[29] See his *Barbarian Invasions of Italy* (New York, 1902, 2 v.), I, p. vi.

[30] Among the most important of these sources are: Proceedings of the *Cortes de los antiguos reinos de Léon y de Castilla 1020 à 1559*, published for the Real Academia de la historia (Madrid, 1861–1903, 5 v.); *Actas de las Cortes de Castilla 1563–1620* (Madrid, 1877–1912, 35 v.); *Cortes del antiguo principado de Cataluña*, to 1458 (22 v.); *Colección de documentos inéditos relativos al descubrimiento, conquista y organización de las antiguas posesiones españolas de Ultramar* (Madrid, 1885–1932, 25 v.); *Colección de documentos de las antiguas posesiones españoles de America y Oceania* (Madrid, 1864–84, 42 v.); *Colección de documentos inéditos para la história de España* (Madrid, 1842–95, 112 v.); *Memorial Histórico Español: colección de documentos, opusculas y antiguedades* (Madrid, 1851–1912, 45 v. in 36). Among collections of narrative sources Cayetano Rosell y Lopez has edited *Historiadores de sucesos particulares* (Madrid, 1858–63, 2 v.) and *Cronicas de los Reyes de Castilla* (Madrid, 1875–78, 3 v.), extending from Alfonso X to Ferdinand and Isabella; Menendez y Pelayo has edited the *Primera Cronica General*, two volumes of historians of the Indies and four chronicles of the Great Captain (Madrid, 1905–12). The energetic and very competent Spanish historian Ballesteros y Beretta of the University of Madrid, who received his historical training in Vienna, early in this century organized

by the writing of individual histories. First to be mentioned is Modesto Lafuente's *Historia general de España* (30 v., Madrid, 1850–67) a huge work to which Spaniards point with pride. But, alas, Lafuente cannot bear criticism. The pioneer historian of Spain in the nineteenth century was the French Protestant Eugène Rosseeuw Saint-Hilaire who devoted a lifetime to a *History of Spain* (Paris, 1837–79) in fourteen volumes. Lafuente's biographer boasts that his assiduity was so great that he wrote twice as many volumes as his French rival. He did not add—if he knew—that Lafuente shamelessly borrowed from Saint-Hilaire's briefer but better work.[31]

In the last decade of the past century the Real Academia de la Historia initiated a *Historia general de España* under the direction of Antonio Canovas del Castillo, a collaborative work similar to Lavisse and Rambaud's *Histoire générale,* which had recently appeared. Eighteen volumes were published and then the assassination of Canovas in 1897 stopped the work. The first genuinely scholarly history of Spain is Rafael Altamira's *Historia de España y de la civilización española,*[32] which "marks an epoch in the study of Spanish history. By reducing the narrative portions to the smallest possible compass the author leaves a chance to devote the greater part of his book to social, constitutional, economic and cultural history." [33]   The work terminates in 1808. The only other Spanish historian deserving of mention with Altamira is Ballesteros y Beretta, author of a *Historia de España y su influencia en la historia universal* (Barcelona, 1918–29, 5 v.), which is a history of Spain in the New World as well as the Old, or rather of Spanish influence and civilization. The accuracy, the references at the end of each chapter, and the indices of these five volumes are evidences that Ballesteros was trained in the Austrian school of historical scholarship.[34]

Justice requires the inclusion of one other Spanish scholar, Menendez y Pelayo (1856–1912). He was the author of a *Historia de los heterodoxes españoles* (Madrid, 1880–81, 3 v.) which exhibits as substantial learning

the Centro de Estudios Historicos, answering to the German Monumenta Commission, for the publication of sources of Spanish history in four parts: (1) Chronicles (2) Literary sources (3) Laws (4) Liturgical Texts. Two volumes in the first series appeared in 1918 and 1921. Ballesteros has also a valuable *Bibliografía de la historia de España* (Gerona, 1921). For an account of recent work in Spanish history see R. Konetzke, "Spanischer Literaturbericht," *HZ,* CXXXVI (1927), 155–67.

[31] For examples of this plagiarism see R. B. Merriman, *The Rise of the Spanish Empire in the Old World and the New* (New York, 1918–34, 4 v.), I, 45.

[32] Barcelona, 1900–11, 4 v.; 3rd ed., 1913–30, 5 v. in 6. Volume IV contains a valuable bibliography.

[33] Merriman (n. 31), I, 46.

[34] Ballesteros has also translated into Spanish in abridged form Bernheim's *Lehrbuch der historischen Methode.* Spanish students of history were reluctant to go to any German university. The Habsburg tradition drew them to Vienna instead.

and is as painful reading as Henry C. Lea's *History of the Inquisition.*

This short account may be concluded by merely recapitulating the authors and titles of sundry works in one or another field of Spanish history. In constitutional history there was Colmeiro, *De la constitución y del gobierno de los reinos de Léon y Castilla* (Madrid, 1885); and his *Derecho administrativo español* (4th ed., 1876–80, 3 v.). Colmeiro is also author of a *Historia de la economia politica en España* (1863, 2 v.). In legal history one may name: J. M. Antequera, *Historia de la legislación española* (4th ed., 1849); A. Marichalar and C. Manrique, *Historia de la legislación y recitaciones del derecho civil de España* (1861–76, 9 v.); E. de Hinojosa, *Historia general del derecho español* (1887); *Estudios sobre la historia de derecho español* (1903); and the remarkable *El poder civil en España* of Danvila y Collado, in six volumes (1885–87), the introduction to the first volume of which contains a long and important survey of the history of Spain during the Middle Ages.

It must be admitted that, with the exception of Altamira and Ballesteros, modern Spanish historical scholarship was far behind that of the other countries in Western Europe. Careless and uncritical publication of sources and shameless neglect of archives almost everywhere except at Simancas, Seville, and Barcelona characterized modern historical scholarship. For an understanding of the history of Spain in any period, whether ancient, medieval, or modern, one must go to German, French, and English works,[35] nor should the names of the American authors Prescott, Ticknor, and Lea be omitted.

We come next to the historians of Portugal.[36] After the Peninsular War, national feeling was almost extinct, and it appeared a universally accepted conclusion, both among the Miguelites and the followers of Queen Maria, that Portugal would eventually unite with Spain. That Portugal is independent today, and a spirit of nationalism still throbs in the hearts of her citizens, may be put largely to the credit of three men: the poets João Baptista Almeida-Garrett and Antonio Feliciano de Castilho, and the historian Alexandra Herculano de Carvalho e Araujo.

In the eighteenth century Portuguese literature had fallen captive to classical French models, but here also the Romantic movement follow-

[35] To verify this statement it is only necessary to examine the bibliographies appended to the chapters dealing with the history of Spain in the successive volumes of the *Cambridge Medieval* and the *Cambridge Modern History.*

[36] See the article by Marcel Bataillon in HISTOIRE ET HISTORIENS, I, pp. 304–19; Rudolf Baxmann, "Ueber den gegenwärtigen Stand der Geschichtschreibung in Portugal," *HZ*, IX (1863), 105–26; Theophilo Braga, *Curso de historia da litteratura Portugueza* (Lisbon, 1885); I. F. da Silva, *Dicionario Bibliografico Portuguez* (Lisbon, 9 v., continued by others to 22 v.); T. W. H. Tolbort, "Authorities for the History of the Portuguese in India," *Journal of the Asiatic Society of Bengal*, XLII (1873), pt. i, 193–208; H. M. Stephens, "Modern Historians and Small Nationalities," *CR*, LII (1887), 106–21; *La Grande Encyclopédie*, XXVII, 394–97.

ing upon the French Revolution turned up new subsoil. Almeida-
Garrett set about creating a fashion in folk-songs, medieval literature,
and Camoẽs. The French influence is quite obvious in the case of Herculano (1810–77). A native of Lisbon, he came to Paris for his education, and returned home a revolutionary. The rise of Dom Miguel
obliged him to go to England, where he learned to read the novels of
Walter Scott in the original. Coming again to Paris he entered the
group of Romantics headed by Guizot, Cousin, Villemain, Lamartine,
and Victor Hugo. Returning to Portugal in 1834 he edited a political
journal for some years, but the constant civil wars caused him to despair of parliamentary government, and he turned to the composition
of historical poems and novels.[37] Thereupon he began to collect the
notes he had gathered for literary purposes in the Lisbon archives in a
Historia de Portugal. With the appearance of the first volume (1845)
the first scientific historian of Portugal had made his debut.[38] The popularity of the work, which ran to three editions, owed much to his power
of sympathetic recreation of the past. A school of ardent young disciples arose, and the nation was gradually recalled from party feuds and
civil wars to a sense of unity, and ceased to talk of annexation to Spain.
This was, however, a gradual and so to say subterranean process. The
immediate reaction of the clerical and conservative party was acrid.
Herculano's rough handling of some of the beloved Portuguese legends
aroused a wave of hostility. Portugal was not yet ready for "debunk-
ing." Touched to the quick by this national ingratitude, he dropped
the *Historia* and composed a work on the origin and establishment of
the Inquisition in Portugal (1854–55). Its severe indictment of the
Church for the degradation of Portugal in the seventeenth century gave
an impetus to his friend Castillo's scheme for secular education, but
proved most unpalatable in many quarters. It mattered not that the
author had based his book upon a mass of sources; there was a storm of
protest. Herculano decided to return to historical novels. Thus tradi-
tionalism cost Portugal nearly twenty years (1859–77) of the work
of a true genius. Herculano was not iconoclastic, but his acquaintance
with French and German writers had taught him critical acumen and
patience with minutiae coupled with veracity. His romantic background had taught him that men of all times are human, so he made
them neither gods nor fiends, and discounted legendary stories without

---

[37] Herculano's two poetical volumes *Voz do Propheta* (1836) and *Harpa do Crente* (1838)
show the influence of Lamartine, and his command over the Portuguese language. His historical novel *O Monasticon* (*Eurico o Presbytero*) (1843) similarly is reminiscent of Scott.
Heine translated it into German.

[38] The second volume (1850) brought the account to the year 1279; there were four volumes in all.

eliminating the legitimately picturesque. He wrote no more histories, but edited a number of valuable chronicles and initiated the *Monumenta Portugalliae Historica*, printed at government expense.

While Herculano's countrymen still had much to learn, an enthusiastic following during the next generation did much to end the reign of obscurantism and bigotry. His disciple Rebello da Silva produced a *Historia de Portugal nos seculos XVII–XVIII* (1860–71, 5 v.), and like many others, continued to nurture the historical novel. Important for the nationalist movement were the mournful *Dissonancias* (1890) of the poet Thomas Ribeiro (b. 1831) on the decadence of his country. Theophilo Braga defended positivism in history. To Oliveira Martins one authority feels we may apply Camille Jullian's word on Taine: "Il marchait insensiblement à l'histoire." He died early in life. Since then Portugal has failed to produce a scholar of importance. The chief difficulty is still the disordered condition of the archives and the lack of guides. Instruction at the universities has likewise been inadequate, and many of the workers are self-taught. The writer of Portugal's first great comprehensive history has yet to appear.

CHAPTER LXIV

EASTERN EUROPE AND THE BALKANS [1]

BY REASON of its size and the importance of its history, Russia should lead all Slavic countries. The bane of Russian historiography under the old Czaristic regime was obscurantism, general illiteracy, and a vicious censorship. Of late foreign interest has increased; but the country which has most cultivated Russian history is Germany.[2] Here as in the case of all Slavic and Eastern countries, the language difficulty has been the great deterrent.

When Peter the Great initiated his far-reaching reforms in Russia he drew most heavily on Germany for administrators. Among these foreigners came Theophilus Siegfried Bayer, whose *Origines Russicae* published in 1726 in the "Acta Petropolitana" founded historical studies in Russia. He was succeeded under the Empress Anne by Gerhard Friedrich Müller, who in the years 1732–65 compiled a great series of ten volumes, partly sources and in part narration of Russian history, known as *Sammlung russischer Geschichte*, a title which abundantly illustrates the influence of German scholarship in early Russian historiography. Müller's mantle fell on August Ludwig Schlözer, whom Catherine the Great appointed a professor of history in the Imperial Academy. His chief work, his edition of the *Chronicle of Nestor*, with German notes, was not printed until 1802–09 (5 parts). Long before, in 1769, Schlözer had returned to Göttingen, having incurred the displeasure of Lomonosov, the all-powerful mentor and favorite of the Empress.

By this time a reaction had begun in court circles against German domination of learning in Russia. Its pioneer was Vasilii Kirillovich Trediakovski who had studied in Paris and in 1773 published a work to prove that the Varangians, the traditional founders of the Russian state in the ninth century, were not Swedes, as had been contended by

---

[1] A. G. Mazour, "Modern Russian Historiography," *Journal of Modern History*, IX (1937), 169–202; the same, *An Outline of Modern Russian Historiography* (Berkeley, 1939); S. R. Tompkins, "The Varangians in Russian History," in *Medieval and Historiographical Essays in Honor of James Westfall Thompson* (Chicago, 1938), 465–90, an article to which I am greatly endebted; V. S. Ikonnikov, *Sketch of Russian Historiography* (1896, in Russian); P. Miliukov, *Principal Currents in Russian Historical Thought* (St. Petersburg, 1913, in Russian); A. Starchevskii, *Survey of the Literature of Russian History up to Karamzin* (St. Petersburg, 1845, in Russian).

[2] E.g., the *Deutsche Gesellschaft zum Studium Osteuropas*, founded October 16, 1913, to further, from a non-political angle, the knowledge of East-European history, economics, and culture within Germany. Its organ is *Ost-Europa*.

Bayer, Müller, and Schlözer, but Slavs. This new interpretation was supported by Boltin (1735–92), in his *On the Origin of Russia*.

A few years later Russia's first man of letters appeared in the person of Nikolay Mikhaylovich Karamzin (1765–1826). He was poet, novelist, essayist, and historian in one. Of Tartar extraction, the child of a Russian army officer and born near Simbirsk, he studied at Moscow and then at St. Petersburg. As a youth he derived his idealism from Masonic friends, but he was soon stripped of any illusions, and grew more conservative with the years. At the age of twenty-four he made a journey through Western Europe (1789), and the *Letters of a Russian Traveller* made his reputation. By this work and his novels and stories he introduced into Russia a brief reign of sentimentalism which was the reaction from the pseudo-classicism of the eighteenth century. After some years as editor of literary journals, Karamzin went into seclusion to compose his *History of the Russian Empire*. In 1803 the Czar made him official historiographer, and paid him a yearly salary. Then Alexander I invited him to Tver, where he read to the Czar his first eight volumes. This happy patronage was continued at St. Petersburg (1816 ff.). Failing health halted Karamzin at the eleventh volume, when he had reached 1613 and the accession of the Romanoff dynasty. The Czar ordered a frigate to take his historiographer to warmer climes but failed to prolong his life.

Karamzin is important, first of all, for his reform of the Russian literary language before the advent of Pushkin. He endeavored to copy the fluidity of French writers. His newly-coined expressions proved superior to the old Slavonic idioms and the clumsy syntax of Lomonosov. In this new medium he produced the first important history of Russia.[3]

Karamzin was a diligent collector, and the notes to his volumes are mines of curious information. Some of them will always remain valuable because the extracts came from sources which are now unknown or lost. As was to be expected from an official history it was an apology for czardom and autocracy. The work has been styled the "Epic of Despotism." Romanticism threw a cloak over the crude and harsh native manners of the early periods. Ivan the Terrible and his grandfather Ivan III emerge from Karamzin's vivid pages as the pillars of Russia's greatness. The author devoted himself to personalities rather

---

[3] *Istoriya gosudarstva rossiyskago* [History of the Russian Empire] (first 8 v., St. Petersburg, 1818; first complete edition, 1818–29, 12 v., the last completed by Bludow). The best reprint is the fifth, which contains a valuable guide by P. M. Stroyev (1842–43, 12 v. in 3). There is a German translation, *Geschichte des Russischen Reiches* (Riga, 1820–33, 11 v.); a French by St. Thomas and Jauffret, *Histoire de l'Empire de Russie* (Paris, 1819–26, 11 v.); and even one in modern Greek.

than to impersonal circumstances and conditions. His heroes and villains, however, are frequently merely personified virtues and vices. There is little that is original and nothing constructive about the whole; he hardly swerved from the path that Müller and Schlözer had hewn. But Karamzin's gift for vivid portrayal and bold character delineation made the work extremely popular, and it expressed the views of the conservatives in the days of Nicholas I.

With the exception of the forgotten work of Nicholas Polevoy, twenty-five years passed until Karamzin found a successor. "The work of the eighteenth century . . . could not continue to hold the field in face of the growing skepticism about the testimony of the chronicles." [4] The first strong voice of protest was that of P. M. Stroyev, in his *On the Untrustworthiness of Old Russian History* (1834). This critical work led to the beginning, in 1846, of the publication of the *Complete Collection of Russian Chronicles* by the Imperial Russian Archaeographical Commission.

The time was ripe for the emergence of a really trained and accomplished historian. This was Sergey Mikhaylovich Solovyev (1820–79), who was born at Moscow, visited Paris as a tutor of a Russian family, and settled again at Moscow to lecture and write at the university for thirty years (1847–77), during the last seven of which he was also rector. In 1851 he began an immense *History of Russia* which he carried into the twenty-ninth volume to 1774 by the time of his death. A scholar who did not meddle in politics or public questions, he gained a leisure and an impartial judgment that caused his writings to eclipse all that went before and many that came after. Too huge to be read through by the general public or even the student, his *History* serves as a quarry to which hundreds have resorted. In contrast to Karamzin's narrative of the Russian court, Solovyev conceived of history as embracing the whole of the life of the Russian people. The reforms of Alexander II were bringing Russia within the attention of the Western nations. When the Slavophils objected that Russia was selling her Slavic heritage, Solovyev contended that segregation was neither possible nor natural.

Nikolay Ivanovich Kostomarov (1817–85) lacked the complacency of Karamzin and the judicial calm of Solovyev. It is not without significance that he came from the Ukraine and had studied at Kharkov. His first thesis for the doctorate (on the union of the churches in Western Russia) was burned at the complaint of the archbishop of Kharkov. Four years later, as professor at Kiev, he combined with Ukrainian friends to form a secret society which proposed to work for

---

[4] Tompkins (n. 1), 475.

social and liberal reforms and a federation of independent Slavic states under the headship of the Czar. The sentence of banishment to Saratov by the government of Nicholas I also prohibited him from lecturing or writing. Alexander II allowed him to return to a chair of Russian history at St. Petersburg (1859–62) where he was much beloved, but two years later the permission to teach was revoked, and he spent the long rest of his life in writing. It has been said that he did for Russian history what Thierry did for France. There is little question about his literary abilities. Ignoring the state, he laid stress upon the life of the people and the past of the provinces, especially during the earlier times when Novgorod, Pskov, and the Ukraine were still independent. Local history owes much to him, but it was hardly fair to accuse him of separatism. Much of his renown may be traced to the *History of Russia in Biographies* (1872 ff.). Kostomarov opposed the Muscovite aristocracy as a degeneration of the original Slavic institutions among the pure Russians, produced by the influence of the Tartar horde; and claimed to find these primitive forms best preserved in his own Ukraine.

The universities continued to prepare the majority of Russian historians, and various lines of descent are noticeable. When A. Rambaud wrote his *Histoire de la Russie* (1877), the three great masters were Solovyev, Kostomarov, and Bestuzhev-Ryumin (1829–97). Solovyev, who had dealt with administration and politics, was followed at Moscow by his student V. Klyuchevsky (1879–1911), who developed social and economic history. For many years the notes of Klyuchevsky's lectures were rewritten and lithographed by his students, and widely circulated. His students, among them Milyukov, have retained the economic basis, and turned to agrarian history and state finance; some accepted the materialistic interpretation of Marx even before the First World War.

From Kostomarov stems, by one remove, the greatest historian of the Ukraine, Mikhail Hrushevsky (1866–1934).[5] His nine-volume history, written in Ukrainian, is a monument of erudition, a veritable encyclopedia of the researches of whole generations of Ukrainian, Russian, German, and Polish scholars. With this work Hrushevsky, who presided over the parliament which declared the Ukraine independent (for a time) in 1917, has given his people the scientific basis for its national ideology.

Bestuzhev-Ryumin, whose notions of history coincided with Solovyev's, began what was for a score of years the most critical history of Russia, and included an essay on Russian historiography (1872–75, 2 v.). Towards the end of the century the number of significant schol-

[5] See the accounts in *Ost-Europa*, January, 1935, pp. 212–16.

ars rapidly increased, and selection is difficult and unjust.   Kovalev-
sky wrote on economic subjects; Pipin and Spasovich on the history of
Slavonic literatures; V. Vasilievsky (d. 1899) on Byzantine history; and
J. Zabelin (d. 1908) on ethnography and the history of customs.

In religion and culture, Old Russia was a child of Constantinople;
but until the rise of Byzantine studies in the course of the nineteenth
century medieval Greek sources were as closed to Russian scholars as
to Western students.   In 1872 the Byzantine chronicle of Michael Atta-
liota,[6] covering the years 1034–79, was published by the Greek scholar
Sathas; and four years later Sathas edited Psellos' more important history for the years 1043–75.[7]   These two works introduced Russian historians to Byzantine sources as an additional body of material for the
study of Russian origins.   In this work V. Vasilievsky was a pioneer
(1881); and the Greek sources later drew him into the study of Armenian and Syrian chronicles.[8]

The discovery of the value of Arabic sources for Russian history came
in the early part of the nineteenth century, when the Russian Government purchased a collection of about five hundred Arabic manuscripts
first explored by a German scholar named Fraehn, who had studied
in Leyden and Paris.   Fraehn's book, *Ibn-Foszlans und anderer Araber
Berichte über die Russen älterer Zeit* (1823), established the important
fact that the Moslems of the ninth and tenth centuries were well informed about Russian affairs.   Thus another fruitful field of study was
opened.

This is perhaps the place to say something about the theory of history which sometimes goes under the name of Marxism.   This theory
sprang from the Industrial Revolution and the political revolutions of
the nineteenth century.   Though Karl Marx must have taken much
from Roscher, and particularly Nitzsch, his philosophy is based altogether on Hegel, whose famous dialectic Marx applied to explain social-economic (i.e., "materialist") forces.   Since the literature on Marxism would fill a good-sized library and a bibliography on this literature
a large volume, it is not possible to do anything more to this subject
than give a bare summary, especially since the Marxists have been prolific in theory but barren in practice.

Briefly stated, the materialist interpretation of history is based upon
two general assumptions: (1) the class struggle, which supplies the *modus operandi* in history; and (2) the economic (or material) basis of all
social phenomena, historic movements, and human relationships.   As

---

[6] On this see Krumbacher, *Geschichte der byzantinischen Litteratur*, pp. 269–74.
[7] For literature see Potthast, *Bibliotheca historica medii aevi*, II, 944.
[8] His *Works* were printed at St. Petersburg in 1908.

Friedrich Engels, who was even more responsible for ·the materialist theory of history than Marx, said bluntly: before human beings can develop political institutions, ideas, art, and religion, they "must first eat, drink, dwell, and clothe themselves." [9] The Marxists have also taken over the idea of evolution from Darwin and applied it to social phenomena. Perhaps the best statement of the Marxist theory is that of Lenin who obviously spoke with authority:

> The materialist conception of history, or strictly speaking, the application of material-ism to the sphere of social phenomena, has removed two of the main defects of the theory of history as hitherto understood. History has, at best, up to now, considered the ideal motives of the historical activity of human beings, without examining into the cause of these motives, without discovering the objective law behind the development of the system of social relations, without seeking the root of these relations in the degree of development of material production. Secondly, the theories applied up to now have over-looked precisely the activity of the great masses of the population, while historical materialism has for the first time made it possible for us to examine, with the precision of natural science, the social conditions influencing the life of the masses, and the changes taking place in these conditions. [10]

It is not necessary to go into greater detail in criticizing the Marx-ist philosophy than to say that it is even more insufficient as an explana-tion of historic phenomena than the more complex system of Lamprecht. The Marxists' claim to being scientific may be dismissed as propaganda; their insistence upon the universality of their explanation may be taken as an expression of wish-fulfillment. [11] In any case, they have as yet written so little history that it is not possible to test their theories. "In the field of history," to quote Charles A. Beard, "Marx and his fol-lowers undoubtedly have helped to turn the attention of historians from purely political and diplomatic affairs to the more permanent and fun-damental forces in the development and conflict of nations, but in this sphere the Socialists have not been so productive. Apart from some disconnected studies, they have written little history." [12] Jaurès, the distinguished French Socialist who edited a comprehensive history of France, simply threw out Marxism when it came to applying it to prac-tical historiography. "The almost infinite complication of human life,"

[9] F. Engels in *Züricher Sozialdemokrat*, March 22, 1883; quoted by Franz Mehring, *Die Lessing Legende* (Stuttgart, 1892), 434.

[10] Lenin, "Materialist Conception of History," *Labour Monthly*, IV (1923), 265.

[11] For a philosophic criticism of Marxism see Oliver de Selincourt, "Some Aspects of the Materialist Conception of History," *Journal of Philosophical Studies*, II (1927), 190–204; see also M. Eastman, "Against the Marxian Dialectic," *The New Republic*, LXXVIII (1934), 35–39.

[12] Beard, "Socialist History of France," *Political Science Quarterly*, XXXI, 111 ff.; on Soviet historiography see S. R. Tompkins, "Trends in Communist Historical Thought," *Slavonic Review*, XIII (1935), 294–319; S. K. Padover, "Kautsky and the Materialist Inter-pretation of History," in *Medieval and Historiographical Essays in Honor of James Westfall Thompson* (Chicago, 1938), 439–64.

Jaurès admitted, "does not allow itself to be reduced brutally, mechanically, to an economic formula." [13] It remains to see what the Russians will do.

The Bohemian [14] nation could point to a fair proportion of historical writers from Cosmas of Prague to Paul Skala ze Zore (1583–1640); but evil days came upon the land of Huss after the Battle of the White Mountain. Nowhere in Europe was the Counter-Reformation put through so determinedly and brutally. The Czech language was proscribed in schools and universities, and descended more and more to the level of a peasant jargon. John Amos Komensky (1592–1670), better known as Comenius, wrote his Latin works in exile. Bohemian nobles were educated and married at German Vienna. The Austrian imperial policy of stamping out Czech nationality obliterated the memory of a stirring and honorable past. Only the Jesuit Balbinus strove, with caution, to keep a flicker of national spirit alive.

There were traces of a revival among German-writing authors in the late eighteenth century: Bienenberg, Publicka, and Pelzel. Joseph II himself unwittingly furthered the beginnings. He failed to realize the importance which a people attach to their national tongue, and tolerated the return of Bohemian as a written language. When he later announced his intention to Germanize all his lands, the reaction was forthcoming. At Prague a chair for Czech literature and language was created for the historian Pelzel (1793).[15] The great initial impulse towards the revival of Czech as a literary language came from the Jesuit Joseph Dobrovsky (1753–1824), the father of Slavic philology, whom the Bohemian Academy commissioned in 1792 to visit Stockholm, Abo, St. Petersburg, and other northern libraries in search of manuscripts scattered by the Thirty Years War. Romanticism caused the hearts of a new generation of litterati to rejoice over real or spurious finds of an-

---

[13] Quoted by Beard (n. 12), 112 note. The most complete statement of the Marxist philosophy of history is Karl Kautsky's *Die materialistische Geschichtsauffassung* (Berlin, 1927, 2 v.). For an authoritative life of Marx, see Franz Mehring, *Karl Marx* tr. from the German by Edward Fitzgerald (New York, 1935). The works of Marx and Engels have been published by D. Rjazanov, *Historisch-kritische Gesamtausgabe* (Frankfort, 1927–32, 4 v., to be 10); see also F. Mehring, *Aus dem literarischen Nachlass von Karl Marx, Friedrich Engels und Ferdinand Lassalle* (Stuttgart, 1902, 4 v.). For excellent English summaries of Marxism see Edward Seligman, *The Economic Interpretation of History* (London and New York, 1934); M. M. Bober, *Karl Marx's Interpretation of History* (Cambridge, Mass., 1927); F. J. C. Hearnshaw, *A Survey of Socialism* (London, 1928). A sharp and often bitter and unfair criticism of Marxism is the book by W. Sombart, *Der proletarische Sozialismus* (Jena, 1924, 2 v.).

[14] Frantisek Palacky, *Würdigung der alten böhmischen Geschichtschreiber* (Prague, 1830); Count Lützow, *Lectures on the Historians of Bohemia* [Ilchester Lectures for 1904] (London, 1905), reviewed in *EHR*, XXI (1906), 197; J. Sušta in HISTOIRE ET HISTORIENS, I, 413–37; Jaroslav Vlček, *Geschichte der böhmischen Litteratur* (Prague, 1897–99, 2 v. in 3); I. Goll, "Bohème," *RH*, VI (1878), 429–43; H. Morse Stephens, "Modern Historians and Small Nationalities," *CR*, LII (1887), 106–21. The reader of Czech may consult the various histories of literature by Jungmann, Sabina, Sembera, and Tieftrunk.

[15] *QR*, LXIX, 350.

cient Czech epics and folk-literature. Joseph Jungmann (1773–1847) enriched the modern Czech repertory by translations from European classics (Milton, Goethe, Schiller), prepared a great Czech dictionary (5 v., 1835–39), and began two periodicals.

In the years 1836–37 there appeared almost simultaneously Kollar's study on the literary and linguistic relations of the Slavic peoples, the *Slavonic Antiquities* of Šafarik, and the first volume of Palacky's *History of Bohemia*.

Jan Kollar (1793–1852) was more a poet than a scholar. As a student of theology at Jena he had attended the Wartburg festival in 1817. His *Slavy dcera* (1824) is a collection of over six hundred sonnets glorifying Slavism and complaining of the encroachment of the Germans. His *Ueber die literarische Wechselseitigkeit zwischen den Staemmen und Mundarten der slawischen Nation* (in Czech and German, 1837) created a sensation and was the start of romantic, cultural Pan-Slavism.

Paul Joseph Šafarik (1795–1861) had also imbibed the ideas current at Jena when he attended the university there (1817 f.), and translated the *Clouds* of Aristophanes and Schiller's *Maria Stuart* into the language of his people. While teaching in Novi Sad (1819–33) he collected Serbian literature and antiquities, and wrote a pioneer *Geschichte der slawischen Sprache und Literatur nach allen Mundarten* (1826). His famous *Slavonic Antiquities* [16] accused German scholars of writing detailed volumes on some obscure Indian tribe, but in their ignorance circulating a prodigious mass of misinformation about their Slavic neighbors. He proposed to write an exhaustive and critical work on the political history, the religion, customs, literature, and arts of the Slavs from Herodotus to the introduction of Christianity in the tenth century. In opposition to the general view that the Slavs entered Europe at a comparatively late date, Šafarik claimed they were indigenous in their seats since at least the fifth century B.C. While this view is today considered untenable, Šafarik's public within and without Bohemia received this announcement of the hoary antiquity of their race with delight. It was a conviction with Palacky himself. Šafarik's philological studies and his Slavic ethnography (*Slowansky narodopis*, Prague, 1842; 3rd ed., 1849) gave a great impetus to Pan-Slavism.

The rebirth of Bohemian nationalism, however, must be placed to the credit of the fiery Frantisek Palacky (1798–1876).[17] His family had

[16] *Slovanské starožitnosti*, vol. I, 1836–37, vol. II posthumous; 2nd ed., 1862–64, 3 v. It has been translated into German by Masig v. Aehrenfeld as *Slawische Alterthümer* (Leipzig, 1843–44, 2 v.); and into Polish and Russian.

[17] Autobiography in Czech (1885; 2nd ed., 1920), and his letters and memoirs, also in Czech, edited by Nováček (1908–11); J. Pekař, *Frantisek Palacký* (Prague, 1912); Lützow (n. 14), 88–105; the same, *A History of Bohemian Literature* (New York, 1900); Louis Leger, *Nouvelles études slaves, histoire et littérature* (Paris, 1880–86, 2 v.); J. Goll, *Vybrané Spisy* [Selected

once belonged to the Moravian Brethren, and under Joseph II it embraced "Augsburg" religious views. His father was a village schoolmaster, and Palacky grew up among Bohemian peasants. At Pressburg he began his classical studies, with the first intention of preparing for the Protestant ministry, but devoted his outside time to literature and living languages. Jungmann's *Essay on the Bohemian Language* first awakened in him, as it did in his young friend Šafarik, a fervid national sentiment. In 1817 Palacky translated Ossian, then so popular in Europe, into Czech, and the following year he collaborated with Šafarik in a work on the principles of Czech poetry. In later life he was to emphasize with pride that during all his adolescent years he had been free from German influence and German training. For a time he was tutor to wealthy families; but in 1823 the young man, already known for his contributions to various Czech journals, was warmly received at Prague by Jungmann, Presl, Hanka, and others. Dobrovsky introduced him to the Count of Sternberg, and from these relations came the journal of the Bohemian Museum (*Casopis ceskeho Musea*) which Palacky edited from 1825 to 1838.

In 1827 the Bohemian estates invited Palacky to continue the Latin history which Publicka had begun.[18] He proposed a new work and was appointed historiographer of Bohemia (1829), though Vienna did not acquiesce in this title until 1839. Assured of funds, he visited the chief European archives to begin his plan for a great history of his country, infused with life and written from the rich manuscript stores of the private archives of the nobility, to replace the meatless skeletons of Pelzel and Publicka. The first five volumes of the *Geschichte Böhmens* appeared 1836–67 in both German and Czech, but it was continued in Czech and printed at the expense of the estates.[19] It was a work which touched the heart-strings of the Bohemian people, and has become a national monument. Written with philological and critical acumen, it rested throughout on sources, and breathed a spirited patriotism. The manuscript had to meet the bitter scrutiny of the Viennese authorities,

Essays] (Prague, 1928); T. G. Masaryk, *Palacky's Idee des böhmischen Volkes* (Prague, 1898); Matthias Murko, *Deutsche Einflüsse auf die Anfänger der böhmischen Romantik* (Graz, 1897); M. Gavrilovitch in *La Grande Encyclopédie*, XXV, 817–18; Emanuel Radl in *ESS*, XI, 534–35, with bibliography; the Czech encyclopedia, *Slovník Náučný;* "Austria and Germany," *QR*, LXXXIV (1848–49), 186–222; A. H. Wratislaw, "How History Is Sometimes Written," *FM*, XCII (1875), 219–70; Saint-René Taillandier, "L'histoire et l'historien de la Bohème, Franz Palacký," *RDM* (1855), pt. ii, 360–97; Pypin and Spasowiz, *Geschichte der slawischen Literaturen*, tr. from the Russian by Traugott Pech (Leipzig, 1880–83, 2 v.), vol. II; or the French translation by Ernest Denis as, *Histoire des littératures slaves*, and the following articles in *HZ:* Josef Pfitzner, "Heinrich Luden und Frantisek Palacky," CXLI (1929), 54–96; F. Palacky, "Die altböhmischen Handschriften und ihre Kritik," II (1859), 87–111; and reviews of Palacky's works, V (1861), 398–475, and XX (1868), 203–07.

[18] Prague, 1776–1808, 6 v.

[19] *Dějiny Národu Českého*, rewritten in Czech, 1848–76, 6th ed., 1904.

and even Metternich was asked to pass upon it. The third volume, dealing with Huss, cost Palacky many a bitter hour, for the Catholic censor insisted it must be made palatable to Catholics, and dictated the insertion of the words "obstinacy, inflexible self-will, and dogmatical positiveness (*Hartnäckigkeit, unbiegsamer Eigensinn, und Rechthaberei*)" in the description of Huss.[20] Perhaps these difficulties, as much as failing health, moved Palacky to end his work when he reached the accession of the Habsburgs in 1526.

Palacky was a tireless and rapid worker, leaving in print and manuscript enough to fill fifty ordinary volumes. Dr. Kalcusek declared that when Palacky visited Rome and the Vatican in 1837, he read through 45,000 documents in ten weeks, and copied 400 of them with his own hand! While his writing possessed no extraordinary literary qualities, there was a certain vigor about it. He was perfectly willing to sacrifice on the altar of criticism the patriarch "Czechus" and many similar legends. On the other hand, his five volumes are a forceful presentation of the claim of the Bohemian nation to be a great people, and a proud rejection of the odium of racial inferiority which, Palacky felt, German writers had been laying at their door for ages. Giesebrecht in his *Kaiserzeit* had lauded the medieval German Empire for bringing civilization to its Eastern neighbors. Such an obligation Palacky regarded as synonymous with intellectual servitude. It was his aim to rouse the Czech nation from the dead, to have them recollect their former self-sufficiency. When invited to join the *Vorparlament* at Frankfort in 1849, he declined, declaring in a famous letter that as a Czech he had no interest in German affairs. Instead he worked for Czech autonomy within the Austrian Empire, and entered himself into the temporary ministry of Pillersdorf. He was bitterly disappointed over the reactionary stand of Vienna, but returned to his former task of organizing scientific societies and establishing national journals. "Father" Palacky, as Bohemians called their great writer, was a follower of Herder and Rousseau, and had the Romanticist's belief in the natural democracy of man. He distinguished between a nation and a state; the latter was merely artificial and accidental (not even essential), while the former was a kinship group with a common but individual culture. Palacky believed in his nation, and at his call it was miraculously reborn.

He found worthy followers. Confining himself to a narrower field, Vaclav Vladivoj Tomek (1818–1905) equalled his master in scientific achievements and surpassed him in accuracy. Tomek was professor of

---

[20] The story of Palacky's struggles with the censorship has been told in his semi-autobiographical *Zur böhmischen Geschichtsschreibung* (1871), and again by Wratislaw in *FM* (n. 17).

Austrian history at Prague from 1850 to 1888. When the university was divided in 1882 he became the first rector of the new Czech institution. In 1885 his former political career was climaxed by an invitation to sit in the Chamber of Lords. Tomek's monumental history of the city of Prague, which remains unfinished after twelve volumes, is in reality a history of the kingdom of which Prague formed the capital.[21] It depicts the life at court, the customs and vicissitudes of the people, and the relations of the social classes. The third volume covering the years 1378–1419 on the basis of sources never used before, portrayed the moral decadence of the clergy and afforded a new and original picture of the beginnings of the Hussite movement. Tomek himself was a Catholic. He has also written an epochal work on the historical topography of Prague,[22] a biography of Zizka (1880), and two volumes of memoirs under the title *Pameti z meho zivota* (1904–05).

Tomek of Prague, and later Rezek continued the work of Palacky, but it is generally believed that his mantle fell upon the great student of the Thirty Years War. Yet Antonin Gindely (1829–92)[23] represents a notable exception to most of the historians in this chapter. Though he was Palacky's successor as archivist of Bohemia, and taught for years in the University of Prague, Gindely was free of nationalistic bias. Actually he was a German, educated in German schools, and preferring to go with the German portion of the university when it divided in 1882. The ancestors of his father had moved in the eighteenth century from Swabia to Hungary. His mother was Czech. Born in Prague, and reared in the German schools on the "Kleinseite," Gindely began his university studies in theology (1848–49), then shifted to law (1850), and finally hesitated between history and mathematics. Eventually he became assistant-master in the *Realschule* of Prague. By this time he had made the acquaintance of the historian Constantine Hoefler at the university, and of Baron Helfert in the ministry of public instruction, whose patronage later was to prove of great value. After publishing an essay on the Bohemian Brethren and a monograph on Comenius, he was given a subvention to travel and study abroad, and visited Herrnhut (where the bulk of the archives of the Brotherhood remain), Berlin, and Holland. Then came his *History of the Bohemian Brethren to the*

---

[21] *Dĕjepis mĕsta Prahy* (Prague, 1853–1901). The first volume also appeared in German, *Geschichte der Stadt Prag* (1856).

[22] In five parts, 1859–61 and 1865–75 (in Czech).

[23] See A. W. Ward, "Anton Gindeley," *EHR*, VIII (1893), 500–14. His chief works are: *Ueber des Johann Amos Comenius Leben* (Vienna, 1851); *Geschichte der Böhmischen Brüder* (Prague, 1857–82, 2 v.); *Rudolf II und seine Zeit, 1600–1612* (Prague, 1862–65, 2 v.); *Geschichte des dreissigjährigen Krieges* (Leipzig, 1869–80, 4 v.); *Waldstein* [sic] *während seines ersten Generalats* (Leipzig, 1886, 2 v. in 1); *Geschichte der Gegenreformation in Böhmen* (Leipzig, 1894). He has edited: *Monumenta historiae bohemica* (1864–90, 5 v.); *Die böhmischen Landtagsverhandlungen vom Jahre 1526 an bis auf die Neuzeit* (Prague, 1877–92, vols. I–VII).

Year 1609 (2 v., 1857), followed by some of the sources in the nine-teenth volume of the *Fontes rerum Austriacarum*. Gindely was still thinking of devoting himself to Bohemia's history, which Palacky had dropped with the end of the house of Jagello. Palacky had proven the value of archives, rather than depending on the meager grist of chroni-cles and memoirs, so in 1859 Gindely spent a year in the treasures of Munich, and shared the noon-day walks of Döllinger. Then began the journey which was to fix both his future subject and method. Travelling over Brussels and Paris, he arrived in December of 1860 at Simancas. Here he stumbled upon virgin soil indeed. In the eighteen years these archives had been open only eight persons had visited them, and only two of these had been Spaniards! [24] With feverish joy he worked in this chill and damp old monastery, and the stack of his notes on the years after 1600 grew at a surprising rate. [25] Viewing with contempt the documentation even of Ranke, he eventually planned to devote from twelve to fifteen years to assembling his materials. [26] Among the mines from which the magnificent torso on the Thirty Years War was quarried were the private archives of Bohemian nobles, Dresden, and especially Bernburg, where he found the complete chancery records of Christian of Anhalt, the master mind of the Protestant Union.

But these plans only matured gradually. In 1862 he received an appointment at the University of Prague, and was also made director of the Bohemian archives which Palacky had initiated. His *History of the Bohemian Brethren* had been virtually a work on Bohemia and Mora-via in the century of the Reformation. He now superintended the pub-lication of the proceedings of the Bohemian Diet. His two volumes on *Rudolf II und seine Zeit* (1862 and 1865) already gave inklings of new things. Here was shown how under a weak and almost imbecile emperor independent forces began to swing in the direction of the movement directed by Christian of Anhalt. In 1869 appeared the first volume of his *History of the Thirty Years War*, and many Czechs began to complain that their historiographer was neglecting Bohemia and its archives to win renown elsewhere. The desertion became more obvious as he proceeded, but European scholarship began to take notice. Volumes II and III were published in 1879, but Gindely had cast his work on too great a scale, and could add only a fourth volume (1880). If his masterpiece remained

[24] Ward in *EHR* (n. 23), 506. On the Simancas archives see G. Constant in *RH*, XCVI (1908), 50–68.

[25] When nearing 1619 he wrote: "When I now . . . bestow a general glance upon all that I have collected, whereof one half is wholly new, while the other half teaches me how to under-stand after a wholly different fashion what is already known, I often feel intoxicated with joy." Quoted by Ward (n. 23), 508.

[26] See his own account, "Beiträge zur Geschichte des dreissigjährigen Krieges," *Sitzungs-berichte der k. Akademie der Wissenschaften* (Vienna), XXXI (1859), i, 3–64.

unfinished, we are still fortunate to have from his hand a three-volume compend for the entire Thirty Years War written for a popular series edited by Baron von Helfert (1882), a mere byproduct which many English-speaking readers take for his large work. Despite serious illness, the author picked his way through the mazes of his subject. *Waldstein während seines ersten Generalats* (1886, 2 v.) was not favorable to that enigmatic figure; now Gindely was accused of Czechish prejudices! Two years before his death he presented the Academy of Budapest with his *History of Bethlan Gabor* (1890), and posthumously there appeared the *Geschichte der Gegenreformation in Böhmen* (1894), which pictured the horror and desolation that followed the Battle of the White Mountain.[27] Undeterred by criticism or the love of praise, Gindely gave his life to the revelation of historical truth, and set Bohemia in its proper relation to the history of Germany and Europe in the momentous first half of the seventeenth century.

The historical labors of the last quarter of the century continued to advance and to emancipate themselves from patriotic leanings. Vincent Brandl, first archivist for Moravian sources, supplemented his excellent editions with a Glossarium after the style of Ducange.[28] J. Emler has likewise edited important sources and provided a guide through the peculiarities of the Bohemian chronology.[29] Jaromir Hanel has touched upon the influence of German law in Bohemia and Moravia, and J. Jirecek has performed a useful service in his history of Bohemian literature.[30] Antoine Rezek (d. 1909) is noted for his works on the time of Ferdinand I. The chief representative of the best in the modern Bohemian School is Jaroslav Goll.

The foremost recent Czech historian, Josef Pekař, died in Prague on January 23, 1937 at the age of sixty-seven. He had been a professor at the University of Prague since 1905 and was editor of the *Český Casopis Historický*, the principal Czech historical journal. Several of his many books are outstanding contributions to historical scholarship, notably *Valdštejn* (1933–34), a monumental work dealing with the four critical years of Wallenstein's life, and *Žižka a jeho doba* (4 v., 1927–33), which treats of the Hussite wars. Concerning himself chiefly with the critical periods of Czech history, he had a deep influence on Czechoslovak national life, and he trained a whole generation of Czech historical scholars. The results of his learning were presented in a masterly prose style.

[27] He is said to have written an entire volume on Richelieu, which still awaits publication.
[28] *Glossarium illustrans bohemica-moravicae historiae fontes* (Brünn, 1876).
[29] *Rukovět chronologie křeštannké, zvláště české* [Manual of Christian Chronology] (Prague, 1876).
[30] *Rukovět k dějinám literatury české* (Prague, 1875–76, 2 v.). It goes to the end of the eighteenth century and is really an alphabetical dictionary composed on the basis of sources, with information on editions and manuscripts. Some of the articles are almost monographs.

Poland [31] began the nineteenth century, not as a dead, but as a divided nation. Like all Gaul, it was divided into three parts. Historical labors were perhaps the most scholarly in Austrian Galicia, and least happy under the weight of Russian censorship. There was much dilettantism, literary swaggering, and patriotic pyrotechnics. The work of the one great genius of the first half century was vitiated because he wrote in exile, away from his sources. Joachim Lelewel (1786–1861) [32] came from German ancestry (the family name was originally "von Loelhoeffel"), studied at Warsaw and then at Vilna, where he was the pupil of the philologist Groddeck, and then was schoolteacher in Volhynia. In 1814 he accepted an appointment to teach history at Vilna. At Warsaw he was director of the public library and taught bibliography in the university. Returned again to Vilna (1821–24), his popularity with the students caused the Russian authorities to mistrust him. His republican sentiments were carried through all Lithuania and impelled the youth to form patriotic and secret societies. When removed from his chair he returned to Warsaw to labor on his historical compositions. Nicholas I considered him a most dangerous man. But though Lelewel briefly shared in the revolutionary government of Poland as minister of public instruction (1830), he fled to Paris before the Russian armies, and there organized the committees of the Polish emigrants. The French government obliged him to quit the city, and General Lafayette offered him hospitality. When finally asked to leave France altogether (1833), he went to Brussels, where he lived an almost anchoritic existence, tormented by poverty, and continued his writing. He continued to correspond with Lafayette, Mazzini, and Engels, and has been mentioned as one of the signatories of the *Communist Manifesto*. A tireless student, painstakingly accurate (he would trust no one but himself to engrave the fifty plates for his *Géographie du moyen âge*, Brussels, 1850–52),

[31] W. J. Rose, "Polish Historical Writing," *Journal of Modern History*, II (1930), 569–85; B. Dembinski, O. Halecki, and M. Handelsmann, *L'historiographie polonaise du XIXe siècle et du XXe siècle* (Warsaw International Historical Congress, 1933); Marcel Handelsman, "La methodologie de l'histoire dans la science polonaise, XVIe–XIXe siècles," *RSH*, XXXIV (1922), 73–99; the same, "Les études d'histoire polonaise et les tendances actuelles de la pensée historique en Pologne," *ibid.*, XXXIX (1925), 65–93; the same, in HISTOIRE ET HISTORIENS, I, 287–303; "Uebersicht der geschichtlichen Literatur der letzten Jahre," *HZ*, XVIII (1867), 359–410; Alexander Brückner, *Geschichte der polnischen Litteratur [Die Litteraturen des Ostens*, Band I] (Leipzig, 1901). For the seventeenth and eighteenth centuries consult K. Waliszewski, "Historyografia Polska przed Krytyka Rossyjska," *Kwartalnik Historyczny*, II (1888), 555–70; Ludwik Finkel, *Bibliografia historyi Polskiej* (Cracow, 1891–1906, 7 pts. in 3 v.).

[32] Autobiographical: his *Experiences* while prosecuting researches on Polish matters [in Polish] (1878–79, 2 v.); Marcel Handelsman in *ESS*, IX, 406, gives a long bibliography and a partial list of Lelewel's works; complete bibliography in S. Krezeminski, *Wiek XIX. Sto lat mysli polskicj* [Nineteenth Century: One Hundred Years of Polish Thought] (Warsaw, 1908), IV, 1–41; Brückner (n. 31), 296, 443; W. R. Morfill, *Poland* (New York, 1893), ch. xiii; Heinrich Nitschmann, *Geschichte der polnischen Literatur* (Leipzig, 1882).

Lelewel cut a broad swath. He produced two books on bibliography. He became an authority on numismatics; he translated the *Edda;* he ranged back in point of time to Pytheas and the Arabians (*Géographie des Arabes*, 1851), but chiefly he devoted himself to monographs and studies on his own country.[33] He employed both Polish and French as a vehicle, and a curiously garbled collection of styles which makes him both easy and difficult to read, according to his subject. Though wholly rational in his treatment, he resembled the Romantics in centering his studies around the development of the Nation as something that had existed in earliest times, and he glorified the happy and free institutions of early Poland in the manner so common among writers of his time.

Lelewel had been a scholar of Catonian simplicity and moral strictness, to whom detailed research was a matter of conscience. Moreover, with him Polish historiography had almost approached a genetic treatment of its subject. After his passing there was a temporary retrogression to which the only significant exceptions were August Bielowski and Karl Szajnocha (1818–68). The latter was poet and dramatist as well as historian, but paid for his patriotic utterances with three years in an Austrian prison. His greatest work, on *Jadwiga and Jagiello* (1855–56, 2nd ed., 4 v., 1864), has been compared by an historian of Slavic literature to Macaulay's *History of England* and Thierry's *Norman Conquest*. One of his works is devoted to the thesis that the Polish nobility originated like the Russians from the Varangians. Szujski (1835–82) died prematurely, and Heinrich Schmidt (whom the Austrian government once sentenced to death) for all his labors only perpetuated the school of Andreas Moraczewski, which with myopic vision sought the reason for Poland's ruin in the eighteenth century alone.[34]

An important change in Polish historiography followed upon the political debacle of 1863, and the subsequent grant of autonomy to Galician Poland. The new generation proposed to replace patriotic exhortations and rhetoric by the new scientific history. The Polonization of Galicia made this region the rallying-point for all the rest, and thus the students from the seminars of the German-Austrians Sickel, Ficker, etc. could

---

[33] These have been collected in *Polska, dzieje i rzeczy jej* (Poznan, 1846–68, 20 v.).

[34] It was customary for this group, and indeed most Polish historians, to premise that the form of government of a people is their national idea, and cannot be changed without violating the genius of the race. Pouncing upon this "key" they subjectively tortured their materials and extracted manifestations of this national idea *ad libitum*. The national idea of Poland was supposed to be the rule of the people (*Volksherrschaft*), and as monarchy is opposed to popular rule, all kings and high officials were distorted, and monarchists are *ipso facto* disloyal. In general, the Constitution was considered an almost sacrosanct and ideal institution, which the Polish people were unable to appreciate, and so they lost their wonderful government. Writers laid the blame upon the magnates, the king, or the lesser nobles, according to their prejudice. Schmidt and Lelewel both held, contrary to their contemporaries, that the kings, and not the nobility and the diets, had brought Poland to fall.

put through their principles. Bobrzynski's *Compendium of Polish History* (1879) directed students into the channels of institutions and Polish law. Xavier Liske opened the first historical seminar at Lwow. Instead of confining efforts to the seventeenth and eighteenth centuries alone, the curtain was rolled back on medieval and even ancient Poland. Askenazy was the first to treat contemporary history and living subjects. Korzon and Smolenski threw their influence behind critical historiography, and Estreicher and Finkel attacked the problem of bibliography. The advance was on all fronts, but source publications and analytical studies far exceeded other types of work in quantity. Scholars of Lwow and Cracow co-operated in the *Monumenta Poloniae Historica* (1864–93, 6 v.); Zakrzewski proved a great editor, and Stanislas Krzyzanowski trained a generation in palaeography and diplomatics at Cracow. The restoration of Poland after the First World War saw a recrudescence of nationalism. In 1924 there were 650 students working in the historical seminars at Warsaw.

Hungary [35] did not possess a professional school of historians until classical studies and the example of the rest of Europe had invaded her. A strong nationalism and the demand for autonomy inclined to affect her historiography adversely. Matthias Bél (1684–1749) in the eighteenth century had written various works on Hungarian history in Latin. The first significant modern historian was Ignaz Aurelius Fessler (1756–1839).[36] He was born of German parents at Zurany, and wrote in German. He began a checkered career as a Capuchin, and made himself odious by relating to Joseph II the abuses in the monasteries, thus bringing about an investigation. He forfeited his professorship at Lemberg when his drama *Sidney* (1788) attacked the English Roman Catholics, and had to leave the country, turning to Lutheranism. Eight years later (1796) he was commissioned with Fichte to reform the statutes of the Freemason lodge at Berlin. He failed to maintain himself in a chair in St. Petersburg offered by Alexander I (1809) and finally ended as Lutheran clergyman and superintendent of the congregations in the Russian capital. His numerous volumes gave the Magyar race in Hungary their first general history.[37]

[35] Articles by J. Kont in *RSH*: "Histoire Générale: Hongrie," II (1901), 167–200; "Langue et littérature hongroises," IV (1902), 205–35; "Littérature hongroise; Époque moderne—de 1772 à nos jours," IV (1902), 346–67; T. Barath, "L'histoire en Hongrie, 1867–1935," *RH*, CLXXVII (1936), 84–144, 595–644, 25–74; Alexander Flegler, "Beiträge zur Würdigung der ungarischen Geschichtschreibung," *HZ*, XVII (1867), 318–95; *DR*, CXXIX (1901), 352–53; Frigyes Riedl, *Hungarian Literature* (London, 1905); Nitschmann (n. 32); Brückner (n. 31).

[36] Autobiographical: *Rückblicke auf seine siebzigjährige Pilgerschaft* (Breslau, 1824, 2nd ed., Leipzig, 1851); Janos Koszo, *I. A. Fessler* (Budapest, 1915).

[37] *Die Geschichten der Ungarn und ihrer Landsassen* (Leipzig, 1815–25, 10 v.); *Mathias Corvinus* (Breslau, 1793–94, 2 v.); *Die drey grossen Könige der Ungarn aus dem Arpadischen Stamme* (Breslau, 1808).

Also in German were the poems and histories of Johann, Graf Mailath von Szekhely (1786–1855), who was first in the employ of the government, then turned to writing, came to live in Munich, and finally committed suicide because of poverty. Besides his *Magyarischen Sagen, Märchen und Erzählungen* (1825, 2nd ed., 1837, 2 v.) he composed various histories which improved upon Fessler, and whose literary qualities gained a wider public.[38] But the man who did most for the diffusion of historical studies was Bishop Mihaly Horvath (1809–78),[39] minister of public instruction during the revolution. A Catholic priest of simple birth, he long was in intimate contact with the peasants and lower classes, then tutor to aristocratic families. In 1844 he became professor of Hungarian language and literature at Vienna (Theresianum). As member of Kossuth's revolutionary cabinet, he was sentenced to death after his flight and remained an exile for eighteen years (1849–67), until amnestied, when he returned to play an active role in politics and church. For ten years after his return he was president of the newly-founded Hungarian historical society. In many respects he is entitled to be called the father of Hungarian historiography. He rejected patriotic rhapsodizing and the old feudal sentiment "Extra Hungariam non est vita"; he had a full appreciation of the demands of critical history writing, and of Hungary's vital connection with European history. Furthermore he wrote in Hungarian. In a vigorous style he traced with conviction but with the endeavor to be impartial, the social and economic phases of his nation's life, and replaced old aristocratic ideals with a modern breath of liberalism and democratic outlook.[40] Horvath shows the influence of Guizot. He was not content to catalogue his facts, but was always preaching liberalism and nationalism. His writings appealed to the Hungarian spirit and were a veritable arsenal during the struggle with Austrian absolutism. The first impartial historian to arise in Hungary was Francis Salamon. In 1875 the study of sources was still in its infancy, and the critical spirit was still lacking. Against the German historians Budinger, Dümmler, and others, patriotic spirits insisted in defending the authenticity of the earliest sources of Hun-

---

[38] *Geschichte der Magyaren* (1828–31, 5 v.); *Geschichte des österreichischen Kaiserstaates* (1834–50, 5 v.); *Religionswirren in Ungarn* (1845, 2 v.).

[39] Oscar Jázsi in *ESS*, VII, 461–62, with bibliography.

[40] *Magyar történelmi okmánytár* (Budapest, 1857–59, 4 v.), is a collection of all documents he could find in the Brussels archives, during his exile, bearing upon the history of his land. *Huszönotév magyarország történetéböl 1823 tól 1848 ig* (Geneva, 1865, 3rd ed., Budapest, 1885), tr. into German by Joseph Növelli as *25 Jahre aus der Geschichte Ungarns, von 1823–48* (Leipzig, 1867, 2 v.); *Magyarország függetlenségi harezának története* [*History of the Struggle for Hungarian Independence*] (Geneva, 1865, 3rd ed., 1898, 2 v.). He also wrote a *History of Trade and Commerce in Hungary* (1840–42, 2 v.); *History of the Hungarians* (1842–46, 4 v.; a German version, 1851–55, 2 v.); *History of Hungary* (1860–63, 6 v.; 2nd ed., 1871–73, 8 v.). His collected minor writings appeared in 1868, 4 v.

garian history.[41] Salamon, a brilliant mathematician and soldier in the revolution, finally drifted to Budapest as a journalist, and joined the party of Deák. As historian he was wholly self-taught; but a happy genius threw him into a minute study of the sources, and his style, molded by reading the classics, was distinctive and among the best of Hungarian writers. Among his other merits is that of going beyond institutions and the upper classes; he introduced the people into Hungarian history.

The millennium of the conquest of Hungary by the Magyars (set at 906 A.D.) brought a feverish activity. Jules Pauler, devoted to minute questions in early Hungarian history, followed a somewhat eclectic criticism. Koloman Thaly eulogized the prince Rakoczi beyond all critical balance. Bishop William Fraknoi (b. 1843), something of a prodigy and an important editor, applied himself to the glories of Mathias Corvinus, the high era of Hungarian existence, and the subsequent decadence down to the battle of Mohacs (1526), and to the influence of Italy upon Hungarian humanism. The finest exponent of scientific historical writing, however, has been the modest Heinrich Marczali (b. 1856) professor at Budapest (1895–1924), who was proud to call himself the pupil of Waitz, Wattenbach, and Gabriel Monod. With him Hungary fell heir to the best traditions of Germany and France.

When we come to Greece and the Balkan countries, it must be acknowledged that progress in these lands has for varied reasons been limited, and that the status of historical studies is still unsatisfactory. Their checkered history in the nineteenth century in itself tended to impair historical writing. Nationalism and bitter partisanships have prejudiced education and culture. The synoptic view we now have of Byzantine history, e.g., could never have arisen within the borders of any of its heirs of today.

With the fall of Constantinople, Greek science and letters went into an eclipse which lasted for centuries.[42] The gap between the popular speech and the literary tongue continued to widen. Late in the eighteenth century a renaissance began, when modern ideas and models began to be introduced from Western Europe, and the Phanariot movement seized wide classes. In the "twenties" of the nineteenth century Greek thoughts and writings revolved about the struggle for the libera-

[41] Marczali calls the Anonymous Notary of King Bela (XIIIth century) the Shibboleth of Hungarian historiography.

[42] William Miller, "Modern Greek Historians of Modern Greece," *History*, X (1925), 110–23; Ed. Driault and Michel L'Héritier, in HISTOIRE ET HISTORIENS, I, 192–208; Albert Thumb, "Die neugriechische Literatur," in *Die Osteuropaeischen Literaturen (Die Kultur der Gegenwart*, Teil I, Abteilung IX), 1908, pp. 246–64, deals with belles-lettres and the conflict over the language, but gives barely a hint on history or science.

tion from Turkish rule. New Greece gloried in its remote past or dwelt upon its present, and ignored the inglorious Middle Ages. Thus Greek historiography long offended against the cardinal rule of continuity. History as a scientific account had no place in the vogue of war memoirs and reminiscences. Spyridon Trikoupis (1788–1873) in relating the story of the Greek *War of Independence* (1853, 4 v.), wrote of the things he had himself helped to form. He showed a surprising lack of bias, and gave to his work the value of a contemporary treatment. He was grateful to England for her assistance, and stands opposed to John Philemon (1798–1874), whose six-volume history of the Greek War [43] reveals a friend of Russia.

In the poor and weak new state after 1830 writers sought solace by cultivating the patrimony of the classical past, Fallmerayer notwithstanding. They asserted the continuity of the Hellenic race and civilization. Upon this thesis their greatest light, Constantine Paparrhigopoulos (1815–91), wrote his *History of the Greek People.*[44] Believing that a national history, such as Greece still lacked, could be written only by a member of the race, he sought to provide his compatriots with a knowledge of the past and a torch for the future. To an excellent survey of Greek classical civilization around the Aegean and the shores of the Mediterranean, he added an enthusiastic sketch of the Byzantine period during which for a thousand years Greek civilization was preserved. Paulos Karolides (b. 1849) continued the history of Paparrhigopoulos, and wrote another *History of the War of Greek Independence* (Athens, 1892–93, 3 v.). One of the chief effects of this Hellenic thesis of continuity was the encouragement of local ancient history, which provided material for local pride and national propaganda. Even each little island found an historian.

Greek education from the lowest grades upward has assigned a large place to history, but it has rather been as a milieu within which to train young citizens in the tradition and temperament of the race. Even mythology was not excluded. History, as MM. Driault and L'Héritier have said, "s'enseigne en Grèce un peu comme une religion." [45] The majority of historical writers have not been professors, but amateurs. Writers, politicians, and private persons have taken a hand in composing works in which the critical scholar will miss evidences of specialization, rigorous method, and a care for chronology. Sometimes the motive is a political party bias, and sometimes it is a general cultural interest. Demetrios Bikelas (1835–1908), a Greek business man

---

[43] Athens, 1859–61, 4 v., unfinished; it extends to 1821.
[44] For further data, see above, ch. LVIII, n. 36.
[45] HISTOIRE ET HISTORIENS, I, 192.

with a penchant for letters, is a convenient example. His *Les Grecs au moyen âge* [46] is a series of lectures which friends at Marseilles induced him to give when he stopped there on a journey from London to Athens.

The best historian of Greece in the last century was Constantine Sathas (1841–1914), who studied at Paris and spent much of his life at work in the Venetian and Parisian archives. He was the first modern Greek Byzantinist, and a powerful influence in the promotion of Byzantine studies. His chief works are: *Bibliotheca graeca medii aevi* (Venice, 1872–94, 7 v.) and *Documents inédits relatifs à l'histoire de la Grèce au moyen âge* (Paris, 1888–94, 10 v.).[47] Professor Sp. Lambros was chiefly a popularizer. Constantine Rados of the University of Athens studied the maritime history of Greece and wrote an excellent monograph on the battle of Salamis. Greek historiography on the whole has been too much given to literature and not enough science. Save for the War of Independence, the modern period has been grossly neglected, and for general histories reliance must still be put upon foreign translations.

The latest Greek historian to be mentioned is the late André M. Andreades (1876–1935). He studied in Paris, receiving the doctorate in jurisprudence in 1899 and the doctorate in economic science in 1901,[48] and taught in the University of Athens. He was a productive writer on economic and financial matters dealing with ancient Greek, Byzantine, and modern history, and his articles appeared in almost every prominent European periodical devoted to economic history, for he wrote readily in French and English.[49]

Rumania [50] obtained its independence in 1878. Down to 1882 the native language was proscribed, and the upper classes instructed only in the alien tongue of their rulers, i.e., either Slavonic or (under the Phanariots) Greek. The great mass of peasants were left to steep in their ignorance. Again the creation of a national literature rallied a people. Of those writers who strove to make Rumanian a literary language, the first place belongs to Georg Schinkai of Transylvania. In order to revive his people by means of history, he compiled their annals from the first to the eighteenth century (86–1739 A.D.). But the Hungarian government prevented publication, and the censor gave as his terse opinion: "opus igne, auctor patibulo dignus." His friend Peter Major was more pliable or more fortunate; his history on the origins of the Rumanians in Dacia was printed at Bucharest in 1813. Schinkai's

---

[46] See above, ch. LVIII, n. 44.

[47] On Sathas see L. Brehier, *RH*, CXVI (1914), 447.

[48] His thesis was: *Histoire de la Banque d'Angleterre* (Paris, 1904); English translation 1909, by Christabel Meredith.

[49] See A. J. Sbarounes, *André M. Andréadès, fondateur de la science des finances en Grèce* (Paris, 1936), bibliography pp. 267–89.

[50] N. Iorga in HISTOIRE ET HISTORIENS, I, 320–40.

work appeared forty years later, and then outside Hungarian lands. George Asaky, a teacher, introduced the first instruction in national history by a ruse into the Greek academy at Jassy (1813). Commissioned to teach surveying, he got permission to start a class in Rumanian on the pretext that surveying ought to be taught in that language, as questions would have to be constantly asked of the peasants. Into his lectures he injected passages on Rumanian history. The princes of Moldavia and Wallachia encouraged its study, and when the Rumanian Academy was founded, a section was devoted to history.

When Rumania entered the family of independent nations, materials were still scarce or wholly unpublished. Within the last fifty years, her scholars have learned how to gather and edit sources, and imbibed scientific principles from abroad. The statesman Michel Kogalniceanu had studied at Berlin, and there published a juvenile history of his race. Papiu Ilarian gathered the rare materials for his three volumes of documents in the Royal Library of the Prussian capital. From Bessarabia came the Bogdan Petriceicu Hasdeu (1836), with a knowledge of ancient Slavonic and modern Slav tongues. His *Archiva istorica a Romaniei* is a mine of information on the formation and etymology of the Rumanian language. His *Etymologicum Magnum Romania* was printed at Bucharest in 1887. Employing a copious documentation, he gave to Rumanian history a romantic fascination and touched unsuspected possibilities in sources. Bishop Mechisedec, trained at Kiev in Russia, collected inscriptions from the religious buildings of Moldavia. Gregory G. Tocilescu was a pupil of Hasdeu, and then continued his studies at Prague. His manual for Rumanian schools passed through many editions, and he initiated archaeological studies. Alexander Demetrios Xenopol, professor at the University of Jassy, was perhaps the most remarkable of Rumanian historians. His *History of the Rumanians*, in five volumes, was intended to relate the fortunes of the race regardless of boundaries and provincial lines. He had studied law at Berlin in the days of Ranke, written a thesis there on Roman institutions, and devoted some time to Buckle whom he much admired. Xenopol was a careful workman and had literary talent. His philosophic leanings took form in *Les lois fondamentales de l'histoire*.[51] As his popular history rested upon the untrustworthy monographs of others, and he did not try to use archive sources, there still remained room for improvement. This need Professor Nicola Jorga of Bucharest (1871–1941) tried to meet. He was the leading representative among Rumanian authors and very prolific. It is significant for the dependence of Rumanian historiography that Jorga also went to Paris and Leipzig for his training.

[51] In Rumanian, French, and Spanish versions.

Bulgaria,[52] like its neighbor Rumania, also first obtained independence at the Congress of Berlin (1878); and its scientific societies and the University at Sofia date from after that change. The chief impetus to recent historiography comes from the Academy of Sciences, founded in 1911. But there were historians of influence for a century and a half before that. Bulgarian scholars date the "renaissance" of their nationalism from the *History of the Slavs and Bulgars* of the monk-priest Paisij in 1762. As the struggle with the Turks grew more acute, the historians aided in founding journals and writing articles for national propaganda. The over one hundred volumes of the *Periodicesko Spisanie* (*Revue périodique*), begun in 1870 and continued by the Academy, preserve many an important contribution to national history, whether it be on ancient Thrace, the period of Byzantine rule, or Turkish sources; but chiefly on the modern era. The greatest force in molding racial consciousness among the Southern Slavs was Constantine Joseph Jireček (1854–1918). A Bohemian born at Vienna, he took his degree at Prague, and then travelled among the Bulgarian people and studied their language and history. In 1876 he published his famous *History of the Bulgarian Nation.*[53] For a brief time he was minister of public instruction in the Bulgarian government (1880–82) and director of the new National Library of Sofia. As professor at the Czech university in Prague and then at Vienna, he continued to write in Czech, German, Serbian, and Bulgarian on literary, philological, and historical subjects.[54]

The historian of the Bulgarian Middle Ages and the founder of the contemporary school of historiography was Vasil Nikolov Zlatarski (1866–1935).[55] As professor of history at the University of Sofia he trained most of his colleagues and wrote prolifically during the forty years of his career. Most of his work appeared in periodicals. He left uncompleted the fourth volume of his *Geschichte der Bulgaren*, projected for five volumes from 679 to the Turkish Conquest. The third volume (1934) carried the work to 1187. Zlatarski was in the tradition of Drinov and Jireček. Of recent years Bulgarian scholarship has become aware of the problems of archaeology in a land where Sassanid, Byzantine, and Turkish art mingled and mixed.

Modern Yugoslavia comprises the kingdom of the Serbs, the Croa-

[52] Gaston Cahen in HISTOIRE ET HISTORIENS, I, 72–85.

[53] Prague, where a German edition appeared the same year; a Russian edition followed at Odessa in 1882.

[54] See the article by L. Leger in *La Grande Encyclopédie*. Ledger has analyzed a part of his *Travels in Bulgaria* (Czech, 1888) in his own *Russes et slaves, études politique et littéraires* (Paris, 1890).

[55] Jaroslav Bidlo, in *Ročenka Slovanského Ústavu*, VIII (1935), 136–53; and Josef Páta, *ibid.*, 154–56.

tians, and the Slovenes.[56] Prior to 1918 the members of this agglomer-
ated state lived under seven different governments. Such political mor-
cellation may account for the late awakening of modern historiography.
In Croatia it began in the fourth decade of the nineteenth century. In
Serbia it was a score of years later. Thus two chief centers arose,
Zagreb and Belgrade, with secondary points among the racial fragments
in the dispersion among neighboring governments.

In Croatia historical studies arose when the Magyars of Hungary
claimed that Croatian autonomy was a cowardly advantage taken during the time of the Turkish invasions. Documents were sought to refute
this accusation and to demonstrate that autonomy was a legal right of
"association" since the first connection of the two countries. J. Chmel
was the first compiler of such *ad hoc* collections (1846), followed by the
similar projects of Sulek and Ivan Kukuljevic Sakcinski. The last
named found a valuable collaborator in the canon Dr. Franjo Rački
(1828–94),[57] the father of Croatian history. Kukuljevic, himself once
given to patriotic effusions in verse, furthered the history of Croatian
literature and art in his *Arkiv za Povestnicu Jugoslavensku* (Archive for
South-Slavonic History) (1851 ff.), and prepared the ground for the
Jugoslav Academy (1867). Seven years later the Croatian university
was opened at Zagreb. Both enterprises found a generous Maecenas in
Bishop Strossmayer of Djakovo, the famous speaker for the opposition
at the Vatican Council. For the next twenty years Rački produced
studies and monographs ranging from Croatian origins and the labors
of Cyrill and Methodius to the modern era. The first generation of
Croatian historians were not professionals. Kukuljevic was an officer
whom patriotism drew into politics, Rački was a priest, and Chmel and
Sulek were not even Croats. They were succeeded by the professors at
Zagreb, of whom Sisic has undertaken an extended history (vol. I,
1917) to follow his earlier resume. Of contributors from without, one
may mention Ignaz Vatroslaff Jagic (b. 1835), a Croat who was professor first at Berlin and then at St. Petersburg. His monument is the
Archiv für slawische Philologie (1875 ff.). Constantine Jireček produced
studies on Dalmatia and Ragusa, and then a *Geschichte der Serben bis
1373* (1909).

---

[56] E. Haumant, in HISTOIRE ET HISTORIENS, I, 455–68; Leger, "Les publications historiques
chez les Slaves méridionaux," *RH*, II (1876), 223–34; Cyprian Robert in *RDM*, 1846, pt. i,
pp. 365–75; 1852, pt. iv, pp. 1117–47; 1853, pt. ii, 1159–4200; 1854, pt. ii, pp. 140–69; William
Miller in *EHR*, XXXII (1917), 589–90, a review of H. W. Temperley's *History of Serbia;*
Gesemann, *Die Serbo-kroatische Literatur* (Potsdam, 1930); Pypin and Spasowiz (n. 17).

[57] His work, the foundation of Croatian history, is entitled: *Documenta historiae Chroaticae
periodum antiqua illustrantia, 548–1100* (Zagreb, 1877). He wrote many political pamphlets
and was a fluent writer in Latin, Croatian, Italian, and Hungarian. See the thèse de doctorat
of V. Zagorski, *François Rački et la renaissance scientifique et politique de la Croatie* (Paris,
1909).

Serbian historiography has been traced back to the bitter manuscript of Count George Brankovic, who was held captive for twenty-two years at Vienna and Eger (1689–1711) by the Austrian government. For many years the fruit that grew from a nation's resentment was unlovely and without the flavor of veracity. Once Serbian independence was achieved, the legendary past paled before the stirring tale of the heroic present. Memoirs were late in coming, but the philologist Vuk Stefanovic Karadzic wrote his various works on the basis of an acquaintance with most of the leaders in the revolt. From his papers Ranke wrote *Die serbische Revolution aus serbischen Papieren und Mittheilungen* (1829). The unpopular pioneer in critical history was Hilarion Ruvarac, a Serb living in Hungary. With its legends discredited and a paucity of documents, Serbia could not very well look back, like the Croatians, to a "thousand-year old Constitution." Instead of editing sources, the Serbs have undertaken to write original studies on ethnography, on the times of the revolt of Karageorge, and particularly on the claims against their neighbors, of which the most famous is the Serbo-Bulgarian quarrel. The historiography of the Slovene lands is almost nil, and has as yet produced no notable historian.

INDEX